AF904495

Computational Thinking and Problem Solving

Computational Thinking and Problem Solving

Dr. Punit G Bajpai

ARCLER
PRESS

www.arclerpress.com

Computational Thinking and Problem Solving

Dr. Punit G Bajpai

Arcler Press
4164 Lakeshore Road
Burlington, ON L7L 1A4
Canada
www.arclerpress.com
Email: orders@arclereducation.com

© 2026 Arcler Press

ISBN: 978-1-77956-966-0 (Hardcover)

This book contains information obtained from highly regarded resources. Reprinted material sources are indicated and copyright remains with the original owners. Copyright for images and other graphics remains with the original owners as indicated. A wide variety of references are listed. Reasonable efforts have been made to publish reliable data. Authors or Editors or Publishers are not responsible for the accuracy of the information in the published chapters or consequences of their use. The publisher assumes no responsibility for any damage or grievance to the persons or property arising out of the use of any materials, instructions, methods or thoughts in the book. The authors or editors and the publisher have attempted to trace the copyright holders of all material reproduced in this publication and apologize to copyright holders if permission has not been obtained. If any copyright holder has not been acknowledged, please write to us so we may rectify.

Notice: Registered trademark of products or corporate names are used only for explanation and identification without intent of infringement.

Arcler Press publishes wide variety of books and eBooks. For more information about Arcler Press and its products, visit our website at www.arclerpress.com

ABOUT THE AUTHOR

Dr. Punit Bajpai is an experienced academician with 29 years of total experience, including 25 years in teaching and 4 years in industry. Currently serving as Assistant Professor and Head of the Department of Computer Science, with additional responsibility as IQAC Coordinator at MGM's College of Computer Science & IT, Kamothe, Navi Mumbai (affiliated to University of Mumbai, NAAC B++, Cycle 1, 2024). Expertise in Computer Science education and academic administration. Education • Ph.D. (Computer Science) Shri JJT University, Rajasthan (2020) • M.Sc. (Computer Science) GJ University of Science and Technology, Hisar, Haryana (2007) • B.Sc. (Mathematics, Physics, Chemistry) Agra University, Uttar Pradesh (1984) • Diploma in Computer Technology (Polytechnic) MSBTE, Maharashtra, Pravara Nagar (1989) • X & XII UP Board, Allahabad, Uttar Pradesh (1985) Professional Experience MGM's College of Computer Science & IT, Kamothe, Navi Mumbai Assistant Professor & HOD, Computer Science (April 2008 – Present) • IQAC Coordination: Apart from coordination with other criteria team owners, handled Criterion 6, Developed POs, COs and formulated Attainment calculation, Designed HR Policies for the institute. • Subjects taught: C Programming, Data Structure, Operating System, Soft Skills, Computer Networks, Combinational Circuits, Cyber Forensics, Cyber Law & IPR, Project Management Hiltron CALC Center Manager (Aug 2002 – Mar 2008) Senior Faculty (Mar 1999 – Aug 2002) Vision Computers (MCED) Senior Faculty (Dec 1994 – Oct 1998) Usha Rectifier Corporation Customer Support Executive (Jan 1993 – Dec 1994) MGM's College of Engineering & Technology Systems Programmer (Jan 1992 – Dec 1992) Research & Publications • Designing and Implementing Parallelism in Solution Techniques of Transport Model, Vol-11, Centum, Special Issue, 2231-1475 (2019) • Green Computing: New horizon of efficient energy and E-waste minimization, Centum, Vol-10, Issue 2, 2017, ISSN 2231-1475 (2017) • Cloud Computing: The technology, Models and, Implementation, Centum, Vol-9, Issue 1, 2016, ISSN 2231-1475 (2016) • Green Computing: To initiate for improvement of Environment and Ecology, EBSCO, Nov. 2013 • Cloud Computing, EBSCO, Feb 2013 Professional Development & Participation • Participated in seminars and FDPs on topics including Green

Technology, Research Management, ICT-enabled teaching, E-content development, Digital Learning, Innovation, IPR, NEP, and more (2015–2024) • Attended workshops and training on examination committee roles, NEP preparedness, concept mapping, and youth festivals Key Skills • Computer Science Education • Academic Administration: Served as In-Charge Principal from 2016 to 2019. • Curriculum Development: VAC such as Basic / Advance Excel, Cyber Security & IT infrastructure, IPR, Recent Trends in Computation. • IQAC Coordination • Project Management: Guided final year students for their Projects

TABLE OF CONTENTS

LIST OF FIGURES

PREFACE

Computational thinking is a disciplined way of thinking about problems as systems that can be comprehended, deconstructed, and refined. It encourages us to make objectives explicit, inputs and outputs clear, and solutions in terms of well-defined steps that one—and a computer—can take. The habits behind it—abstraction, pattern recognition, algorithmic design, and evaluation—inject order into reasoning. They help a student plan a science project, a manager prioritize options under constraint, an engineer design a robust process, or a data analyst convert messy data into good insight. In short, computational thinking converts uncertainty into a sequence of tractable decisions.

Problem solving is the vehicle through which these habits pay off. It begins with careful problem framing: what is known, what is unknown, what assumptions are permissible, and what counts as success. From there, we model the situation, propose stepwise methods, test those methods with examples, and refine our approach in response to failures. The cycle is practical and humane—it values clarity over cleverness and improvement over perfection. Running this loop over and over again, students master pseudocode, flowcharts, debugging practices, and empirical mindsets. They also learn to estimate effort, analyze alternatives, and build solutions explainable, testable, and maintainable. *Computational Thinking and Problem Solving* seeks to instill these habits repeatedly and noticeably.

The book moves from ideas to execution, from charts to working code, and from individual tricks to integrated strategies. Explanations are supplemented with step-by-step figures, short proofs of correctness where necessary, and annotated excerpts that illustrate how to apply logic into programs. Theory and practice are balanced in each chapter, so readers can see not only what to do but also why a technique works and when to apply it. Chapter 1 introduces computational thinking's foundations—decomposition, pattern recognition, abstraction, and algorithm design—and illustrates how they reinforce one another when solving real-world tasks. Students learn simple, mundane scenarios (from organizing a daily schedule to verifying a computation) to see how precise definitions and procedures lead to better outcomes. Chapter 1 also introduces pseudocode as a platform-independent way to write logic before tackling any programming language.

Chapter 2 Centers on the creativity of problem solving. It lays down definitions for problem statements, specifications, constraints, and success criteria; distinguishes assumptions from fact; and models problems in terms of input, output, and state. The reader learns to design test cases before writing code, estimate time and space costs in relative terms, and choose between brute force, heuristics, and refinement. Timeless problem-solving devices—working backward, invariants, and proof by contradiction—are introduced slowly and used throughout the book.

Chapter 3 discusses algorithms and flowcharts as two notations of procedure. Convention and standard notation are reminded, with examples involving solutions to which the worked solutions begin in prose description, proceed to flowchart, and conclude with readable pseudocode. Traceability is the central issue: the reader practices simulating execution by means of a table of variable states, considering termination and correctness, and comparing two designs each of which does something useful.

Chapter 4 establishes programming fundamentals. It establishes variables, data types, expressions, assignment, I/O, and program structure. Students learn the scope and lifetime, naming conventions and documentation practices, and how to identify a script, a function, and a module. The chapter demonstrates how pseudocode is translated into code and displays typical pitfalls like uninitialized values, integer division surprises, and off-by-one indexing.

Chapter 5 constructs control structures—sequence, selection, and iteration—with readability and reliability as objectives. Conditional logic is presented with decision tables and readable nested patterns. Loops are specified with invariants and guard conditions such that termination and forward progress are easy to justify. Helpful topics include short-circuit evaluation, sentinel values, fencepost errors, and how to unroll nested loops with compound constructs.

Chapter 6 proceeds with functions and modularity programming. Students learn how to construct clean interfaces, split parameters from arguments, and select value-returning versus procedure-style procedures. The chapter explains cohesion and coupling in simple language, illustrates information hiding using modules, and illustrates recursion along with guidelines on when it enhances clarity or performance. Documenting contracts methods (preconditions, postconditions, and side effects) lay the foundation for systematic testing.

Chapter 7 covers arrays and strings as basic data containers. Topics covered are indexing, traversal patterns, searching over sequences, fixed-size versus dynamic arrays, and simple memory models to ease understanding. For strings, immutability, character encodings, substring operations, and common operations like tokenization, validation, and formatting are covered. Efficiency and safety are thread-insensitive concerns: bounds checking, copying overhead, and avoiding unnecessary conversions.

Chapter 8 surveys search and sort algorithms and explains why they are essential to real programs. Linear and binary search are contrasted on cost and precondition. Sorting algorithms—selection, bubble, insertion, merge, and quick—are presented with visual traces, invariants, and stability problems. Readers gain experience choosing a method appropriate to data size, partially ordered inputs, or memory limitations, and learn how to use library routine calls responsibly, with an eye to correctness and efficiency.

Chapter 9 employs problem solving using data structures. Chapter 9 covers stacks, queues, linked lists, hash tables, trees, and simple graph representations, always linking selection of structure to the needs of the problem. The chapter presents operations (insert, delete, search, traverse) as well as amortized and worst-case thinking at the appropriate level for novices. Examples demonstrate how other structures make otherwise cumbersome code and how to measure the value of a better choice.

Chapter 10 focuses on error handling and debugging as professional habits. Students learn to replicate failures, narrow down causes using binary search in code, understand stack traces, and program instruments with assertions and logs. The chapter identifies syntax, runtime, and logical errors; covers unit tests and test-driven habits; and discusses exceptions, graceful recovery, and friendly failure messages. The aim is confidence: failures will happen, and there are predictable ways to locate and repair them.

This book is written for undergraduate computing and engineering students, scientific and quantitative first-time students needing a thorough introduction to algorithmic thinking, and self-students seeking an ordered path from idea to code.

It also helps teachers who value clean explanations, formal notation, and examples that promote hands-on practice. Low prerequisites are assumed: knowledge of high-school algebra and a willingness to write and tinker with little programs. Employed in an introductory programming class, a methods seminar, or independent study, the book attempts to cultivate practical judgment—thinking clearly about problems, explicitly stating solutions, and sharpening them with evidence and testing.

CHAPTER 1

INTRODUCTION TO COMPUTATIONAL THINKING

Contents

DEFINITION OF COMPUTATIONAL THINKING

Computational thinking is increasingly viewed as a fundamental skill that transcends traditional computer science. It is an approach to problem solving that allows individuals to solve challenging problems systematically and methodically. Computational thinking is all about a set of mental processes that include decomposition, pattern recognition, abstraction, and algorithm design. By breaking down a problem into smaller, manageable pieces through decomposition, the individual is able to handle each piece more effectively, thus better understanding the complete problem. This is not only enhancing one's analysis skills but also equipping the learners with the ability to apply them across disciplines, from mathematics to arts, thereby promoting interdisciplinary learning and critical thinking. Computational thinking has developed through technological advancements and the acknowledgment of its applicability in modern-day education. Computational thinking has gained prominence within school curricula over recent years, focusing on its necessity to equip learners for a digital age. Park City Math Institute stresses the consensus among instructors that data science teaching requires a systematic curriculum, which inherently demands computational thinking abilities (Agarwal et al., 2017).

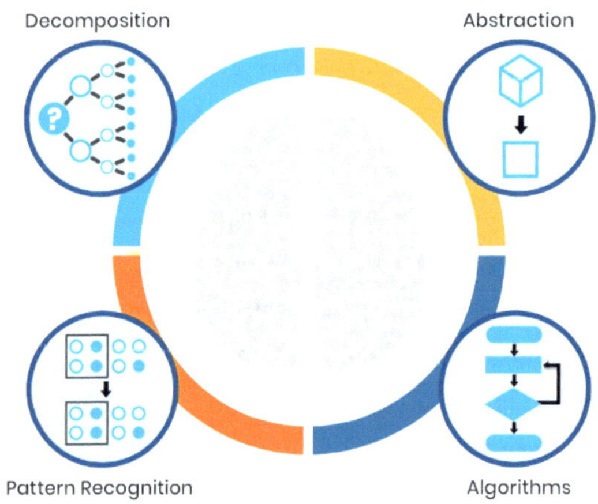

Figure 1.1. *Computational thinking.*

Source: *https://www.digitaled.in/blogs/wp-content/uploads/2022/12/computational-thinking.png.*

This integration is to create a next generation of problem solvers with the competencies necessary to manage the complexities of life in contemporary times. Hence, computational thinking is not merely a thought experiment but also a necessary skillset for success in all professional disciplines. Moreover, the principles of computational thinking complementarily intersect other disciplines to enhance teaching and learning processes. As introduced within tectonic discussions related to architecture and structural integration, interdisciplinarity is a significant part in augmenting pedagogical frameworks (Oxman et al., 2010). Through adopting computational thinking strategies, educators can create an engaged learning environment in which learners concentrate diligently on content, building creativity and innovation. Eventually, employing computational thinking as a primary aspect of education can lead to more effective problem-solving methods and adequately informed decision-making processes. In this, computational thinking serves as a bridge connecting theoretical hypotheses and practical application, preparing learners to thrive in an integrated world (Figure 1.1).

Explanation of the term

The term computational thinking describes a fundamental problem-solving methodology that breaks down complex problems into easy-to-handle components. This methodology is at the center not only within the boundaries of computer science but across most areas like mathematics, engineering, and social sciences. Computational thinking, in its core, requires individuals to think algorithmically, recognize patterns, and build models which can be applied towards the solution of abstract and real-world problems. A study of the subtleties of computational thinking encompasses more than demonstrating that it is not merely the application of algorithms, but includes conceptual thinking as well. For instance, good problem solvers tend to blend formal mathematical argument with conceptual understanding, demonstrating that computational thinking takes as much sense as skill (Elby et al., 2012). Also, the integration of computational thinking within learning spaces points toward a shift in paradigm for the manner in which we learn and gain knowledge. This framework emphasizes the importance of gaining not just traditional content but also thinking processes and approaches utilized in computational thinking. Such kinds of learning contexts facilitate student engagement in practices leading to algorithmic thinking that paves the way for the application of these skills on a large scale. Computational thinking is particularly valuable in a technology- and data-driven world where knowledge of complex systems is necessary. By including computational thinking as part of learning, technical skills are developed, of course, but also critical thinking and problem-solving skills that are invaluable both in the educational environment and in the workforce. The applications of computational thinking also extend to cognizance in discussions regarding pedagogy and cognitive science. Specifically, the interplay between formal mathematical thought and conceptual thought provides rich ground for comprehension of how an individual approaches and solves problems. The analysis of case studies, such as the cases of Alex and Pat students, indicates that good problem solvers use a mix of mathematical procedures with concepts, and this calls for pedagogical focus on combining this mix of categories of reasoning (Elby et al., 2012). In addition, emerging cognitive science theories such as the 4E cognition perspective emphasize the interconnectedness of embodied, embedded, enactive, and extended cognition in explaining computational thinking. This comprehensive approach lends credence to a totalist view of human cognition, suggesting that computational thinking is not only a natural ability but cognitive practices that can be learned and mastered within various environments.

Historical Context and Evolution

The historical context to computational thinking is one of dense intellectual paradigm development. Widely grounded in mathematics and logic, the origins of computational thinking began firmly taking shape in the mid-20th century with the advent of digital computing. Gradual development was spearheaded by individuals such as Alan Turing, who developed visions of machines able to perform algorithmic procedures, laying the foundation for problem-solving in a different manner. This transition from theoretical model to application was a significant milestone; the binary opposition between human cognition and machine logic started to break down. Throughout the subsequent decades, increased complexity of algorithms and programming languages pushed computation toward a paradigmatic model, which made it possible to create computational thinking as a foundational model of cognition for most disciplines, from computer science to the humanities. As computational thinking emerged, it became intertwined with structural and architectural design advancements, which reflected deep shifts in designing physical and virtual systems practice. Tectonics, or the relationship between structure and form, best encapsulates this merging. As researched, tectonics evolved through the dynamism of changing relations between architectural aesthetics and engineering ideas, highlighting how digital media and morphogenetic processes are generative in contemporary design practices (Oxman et al., 2010). This complementarity highlights computational thinking not just as a method but also as a means of reinvigorating disciplines outside of traditional computing. The history of the development of these ideas demonstrates that computation thinking extends past technological realization, embellishing various disciplines with more robust problem-solving methods and groundbreaking design methods. In considering the profound significance of computational thinking, one must consider it in terms of its cognitive foundations and its philosophical roots. The study of such notions as meaning, belief, and understanding reveals the intricate interplay between computational processes and the human psyche. Theory presumes that a robust theory of communication grounded in evolutionary concepts is able to harmonize the diverse cognitive phenomena and provide a common ground to comprehend the way we handle information in computational environments (Gelepithis et al., 2009). This historical evolution emphasizes that computational thinking is not merely an abstract paradigm; it is deeply rooted in the principles of logical reasoning, providing critical insights into the nature of human cognition and its interaction with technology. Consequently, the historical trajectory of computational thinking encapsulates not only technological advancements but also a fundamental shift in our approach to understanding intelligence itself.

Importance in Modern Education

The integration of computational thinking in modern education is imperative as it serves as the basis for problem-solving skills acquisition. With technology undergoing rapid development, understanding computational concepts not only enhances the technical abilities of students but also boosts their intellectual abilities. Research indicates that school leavers lack the computational ability needed to thrive in the work environment mainly due to the fact that computation gets insufficient curriculum attention. Curricula that effectively incorporate computational skills into their programs prepare the students to meet industry demands and handle complex systems. Through creating a curriculum that highlights such skills, instructors can prepare students to effectively transition from the classroom into working environments so that they can apply analytical thinking and good judgment in circumstances with plenty of data (Caballero et al., 2015). Besides, modern education must recognize the transformative role of information in building knowledge societies. Information is an intellectual development and technological innovation source resource, just like oil drove industrial development. Computational thinking in the modern-day context, where collaboration and interdisciplinarity are standard, enables efficient engagement across diverse fields. The ability to synthesize and contextualize information from diverse perspectives and disciplines becomes increasingly important in solving intricately complex problems. Collaboration across disciplines enriches the learning experiences of students and provides a culture of creativity and innovation. Through the efforts of teachers to instill these conventions, the students are better prepared to solve real-world problems that require a multi-perspective understanding of disciplines (Almér et al., 2016). Lastly, emphasis in schools on computational thinking is a pioneering step toward a larger understanding of learning and the utilization of knowledge. By structuring curricula around the attainment of computational skills, schools do not merely prepare students for specific career positions but also create versatile lifelong learners capable of adjusting to a continuously evolving technologically advanced world. This approach emphasizes the importance of adaptability, creativity, and problem-solving capabilities—skills that are highly relevant in an increasingly automated and information-driven world. The future will only increase the importance of computational thinking, making it even more important for education systems to keep up with technology developments to enable students to possess the skills they need to excel in their own endeavors (Caballero et al., 2015) (Figure 1.2).

Figure 1.2. *Importance in modern education development.*

Source: https://lh7-rt.googleusercontent.com/docsz/AD_4nXdWKVCw9UhCiHGwpIW0McWCJBO_DVegROY2NcO6IfpaUYEDPs-30BoytNFsMqS_GMh8M_XK4QbPXW4Xpa_mTDG-WEfw_HW1n90rzr_svdbJJ-ONMNC-89fqrJUF2nSI3GTi7JSmTy?key=jDRNYrrcK7YRxfkcpVMIrw.

1.1. KEY COMPONENTS OF COMPUTATIONAL THINKING

The concept of computational thinking (CT) has emerged as a cornerstone paradigm for comprehending and addressing complex problems in the age of computers. In essence, CT is concerned with problem-solving skills that integrate computational practices with systematic strategies. This involves well-defining problems, constructing solutions via algorithms, and implementing such solutions on various programming environments. The value of teaching CT is not only to encourage programming skills but also to develop critical thinking along with analytical ones. As emphasized in recent discussions, traditional programming pedagogy falls short when it addresses formal problem-solving methodology, with CT providing the necessary unification of the two domains—enabling a crucial gap in today's pedagogy (Michaelson et al., 2015). Moreover, another critical feature of CT is the ability for abstraction and the fragmentation of problems into manageable pieces. Through abstraction, individuals can focus on the inherent features of a problem and ignore irrelevant details and make the process of solving the problem more effective.

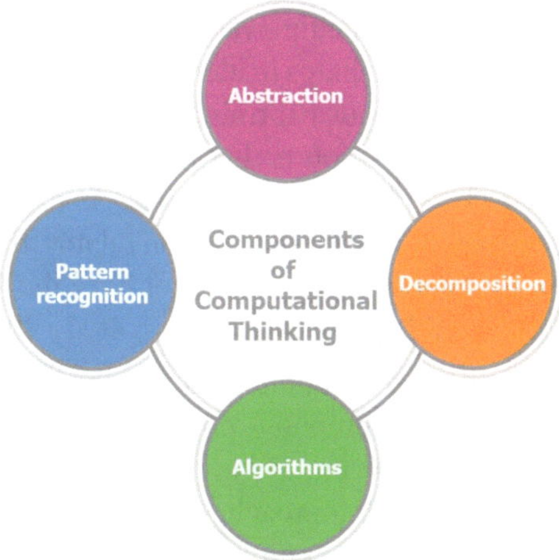

Figure 1.3. *Key components of computational thinking.*

Source: https://leighlancasterconsulting.com.au/wp-content/uploads/CT-process-image-v3.jpg.

Fragmentation of problems into smaller, manageable pieces allows for easier comprehension and facilitates monitoring trends in different fields. Through cultivating this skill, students are more likely to deal with challenging problems, applying their knowledge in various fields. In effect, CT fosters a cycle of exploration of problems, where one returns and enhances methods, which aligns with modern paradigms of education that value flexibility and creative problem-solving (Almér et al., 2016). Finally, the collaborative nature of computational thinking cannot be overstated. As information continues to grow as a motive power of societal progress, collaborative work across disciplines is now imperative. CT offers an architecture for unleashing shared knowledge so that individuals from different disciplines can contribute to information processing, knowledge creation, and solution development. Such convergence is most significant in our multimensional, technology-saturated world, where problems are multimensional in complexity and require diverse perspectives and collaborative methods. By embracing the values of CTs, education systems can prepare students not just to excel in a technology-driven society but also to manage the social and ethical dimensions of technology, enabling learners to thrive in a globalized world (Michaelson et al., 2015) (Figure 1.3).

1.1.1. Decomposition

The decomposition process is vital in computational thinking since it serves as a basic foundation in solving problems and coding. Breaking down complex problems into smaller, easier-to-grasp pieces enables individuals to address each piece systematically without being overwhelmed. Decomposition not only simplifies comprehension but also helps in identifying interdependencies among the problem's various elements, thus forming effective solutions. Among the greatest advantages of decomposition is that it aligns with how human beings think and learn as well as how they solve problems. As has been emphasized in programming pedagogy, how problem description relates to systematic solution is central, but most traditional pedagogy does not have this crucial step of task decomposition into manageable parts (Michaelson et al., 2015).

Furthermore, the method incorporated as Computational Thinking (CT) emphasizes decomposition in computer programming. CT emphasizes the relationship between problem-solving and computer programming and ensures that repetitive and systems-based approaches to problem-solving can actually gain from decomposition. By restructuring complex problems, students are better able to apply core methods that trace their beginnings back to CT, thus fully bridging the gap between theoretical understanding and practical implementation.

While in the past programming involved a focus on writing code, contemporary models of learning have begun to promote more integral approaches, such as evaluating the role of information structure alongside problem-solving method (Michaelson et al., 2015). This has the recognition that professional-level programming is not only about technical skills but also a better understanding of how various components react to one another with a problem.

The shift from traditional computational metaphors to a finer appreciation of the interactions between different components indicates the dynamic nature of computational thinking. By embracing the concept of a community of interacting objects rather than a sequential step-by-step approach, one can create a culture in which decomposition becomes a group effort. This approach taps into cognition and makes it easy to tap into diversity of thought when solving a problem, something crucial to develop in making innovative solutions. Using this multi-directional thinking leads to the acceptance of complexity rather than rejecting it, and this spurs critical thinking and creativity. Hence, the cultivation of decomposition abilities not only enhances the quality of programming outputs but also prepares one to manage the increasingly sophisticated environments of information systems and technology.

1.1.2. Pattern Recognition

Pattern recognition is a key component of the paradigm of computational thinking as it serves to span the gap between abstract concepts and practical applications. Pattern recognition is a term used to describe the process of recognizing, decomposing, and understanding recurring patterns in data sets, a process that is essential to the solving of problems in most cases, especially mathematics and computer science. As students engage in the identification of pattern exercises, they not only become more analytical but also learn to predict potential outcomes and develop systematic solutions to complex problems. The ability is exemplified best in the classroom, where students are most likely to be given the task of identifying patterns in numbers, thus laying the groundwork for more intricate mathematical concepts and developing an algorithmic approach to thinking. Research highlights gender difference in developing pattern recognition skills among students as significant, and it may affect their computational thinking process.

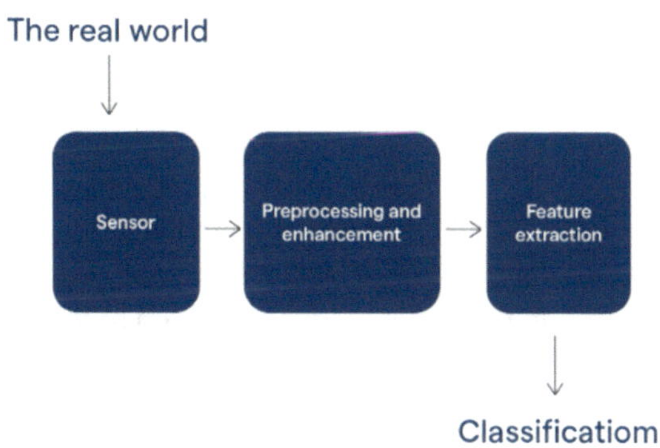

Figure 1.4. *Pattern recognition stands.*

Source: https://cdn.botpenguin.com/assets/website/Pattern_Recognition_5138cb6e29.png.

For instance, one study on junior high school students identified varying problem-solving styles among boys and girls. The male student would create structural models, such as rows and columns, in order to recognize patterns effectively, while the female student employed a subtle approach by isolating important information and grouping similar characteristics. These results show that the differences must be taken into consideration by teachers when implementing methodologies to instruct so that all students can cope with computational thinking processes, particularly pattern recognition, which is fundamental for future mathematical education and logical thinking. The study of pattern recognition in educational research also underscores its use in stimulating the creative problem-solving capacity of students. One of the studies conducted among high school students revealed that students with better creative thinking skills employed principles of computational thinking effectively, particularly decomposition and abstraction. Such students easily recognized patterns and structured solutions in a systematic manner, thereby proving the interconnectedness of different elements of computational thinking. Students with poor creative skills struggled to grasp fundamental concepts and clung to memorized formulas rather than understanding underlying patterns. This highlights the significance of specific teaching practices that promote students' recognition of patterns within mathematical settings, ultimately boosting overall problem-solving capacity and reaffirming the value of computational thinking within the learning process (Antoro et al., 2025) (Figure 1.4).

1.1.3. Abstraction

Abstraction plays a crucial role in the realm of computational thinking, serving as a foundational element that enables individuals to simplify complex problems into manageable parts. By fostering the ability to identify essential features and relationships while ignoring extraneous details, abstraction allows learners to focus on the core of a problem rather than getting lost in complexity. This is particularly pertinent when addressing mathematical challenges, where recognizing patterns and structuring solutions is vital. For instance, students engaged in problem-solving often leverage abstraction to move beyond specific instances of problems, thereby developing general strategies applicable across various contexts. In educational settings, teaching students how to effectively utilize abstraction can enhance their creative problem-solving abilities, as evidenced by research highlighting the importance of computational thinking in improving students mathematical skills and logical reasoning (Antoro et al., 2025). Moreover, abstraction is integral to the process of programming, bridging the gap between theoretical concepts and practical applications. In the landscape of programming education, the ability to abstract is vital for understanding and manipulating software. Students must often grapple with the relationship between problem-solving and coding and should be equipped to break down problems into abstracted components that can be coded efficiently. This interplay between abstraction and programming underscores the need for pedagogies that intertwine these elements. Unfortunately, traditional approaches have often overlooked the nuances of teaching problem-solving in programming, leading to a disconnect. By integrating abstraction more thoroughly into programming pedagogy, educators can foster a deeper understanding of how systematic problem-solving can streamline coding practices and enhance computational skills (Michaelson et al., 2015). Lastly, the implementation of abstraction within computational thinking frameworks can catalyze broader creative processes in various disciplines. It instills a mindset that encourages learners to view challenges through a lens that emphasizes critical thinking and innovation. When students engage in abstraction, they develop the ability to generalize solutions and apply learned principles across different scenarios, thereby enriching their educational experiences. This is especially relevant in interdisciplinary applications, where researchers and practitioners can benefit from abstracting core concepts to address complex societal issues. As computational thinking continues to gain prominence in curricula, emphasizing abstraction not only equips students with essential problem-solving tools but also cultivates a culture of creativity and innovation. Ultimately, such skills are indispensable in a world increasingly driven by technology and data, highlighting the transformative power of adept abstraction in shaping future thinkers and innovators (Antoro et al., 2025).

1.2. APPLICATIONS OF COMPUTATIONAL THINKING

Computational thinking has applications outside the central computing field, with important applications in other fields of study such as education, medicine, and environmental science., Within education, computational thinking equips students with problem-solving skills to handle complex systems and solve complicated problems. Through abstraction and focus on algorithms, educators can design curricula that utilize these principles, facilitating innovative pedagogical practices adaptable to the needs of an interactive world. The practice of data analysis, modeling case scenarios, and developing simulations results in thorough comprehension of concepts by students. These methods of teaching, increasingly popular today, are a testament to the growing realization of the importance of training computational thinking ability in equipping students to meet the challenges of the future (Adams et al., 2015). Also, computational thinking applied to the health sector cannot be exaggerated. In this rapidly evolving field, the application of computational methods is revolutionizing patient care and clinical research. Computational methods such as data mining and predictive modeling enable clinicians to sort through vast amounts of data in an effort to identify patterns, improve diagnosis, and tailor treatments to individual patients' unique features. Moreover, the fusion of computational thinking with interdisciplinary collaboration facilitates innovation that optimizes health outcomes. With the increased dependence on technology and data-based decision-making in healthcare, the ability to apply computational thinking provides significant advantages in managing complicated health issues and optimizing available resources. Such value for change proves the pivotal role of computational thinking in the provision of efficiency and effectiveness in the healthcare sector (Adams et al., 2015). Computational thinking also enhances the comprehension of ecological processes and enables sustainable practices in environmental science.

With the help of computational models, scientists are now capable of simulating environmental changes, assessing the impact of human activities, and forecasting future ecological conditions. These models not only assist in learning complex interactions within an ecosystem but also assist in decision-making processes for resource planning and conservation efforts. Incorporation of computational thinking in environmental research promotes interdisciplinary research efforts by scientists from different fields, thereby promoting a holistic approach towards understanding critical global issues. Such collaborative efforts illustrate how computational thinking serves as a foundational skill that transcends disciplinary boundaries, ultimately driving progress toward sustainable solutions for our planet (Almér et al., 2016).

1.2.1. Problem-Solving in Computer Science

Problem-solving is the backbone of effective programming and algorithm design in computer science. It includes the detection of complex problems and their breaking down into vulnerable segments, a capability that computer scientists need. Once problems are defined, professionals rely on systematic practices to develop solutions, illustrating the interdependence between problem-solving and programming.

The historical lack of a pedagogical model unifying problem-solving pedagogy has only highlighted the call for complementary methods. A clear connection between theoretical assumptions and applied environments provides students with the ability to explore the recursive nature of problem-solving, fostering greater insight and creativity within solution creation. This foundation is crucial as technology progresses, setting the success of computer science studies in a more technological era, in which expertise in how to solve intricate problems is of utmost importance. Recognizing that problem-solving in computer science involves more than memorizing techniques is the basis required for creating effective learning techniques. Traditional approaches failed to take into consideration the creative and multi-dimensional nature found in problem-solving exercises. Moreover, the emphasis tended to be on programming itself rather than the most important skill of knowing how to identify and characterize problems. Computational Thinking (CT) has emerged as a promising alternative, striving to blend problem-solving into programming education.

Figure 1.5. *Problem-solving in computer science.*

*Source: https://miro.medium.com/v2/resize:fit:1024/1*xmLNnPwcGpk4_zi3c_Wa5g.jpeg.*

Emphasizing the computational nature of problems, CT encourages students to engage in processive rather than algorithmic uses. This shift is a reaction to the limitations of conventional programming pedagogy and an introduction of more integrated problem-solving concepts as an active discussion between theory and practice, particularly when faced with complicated computational spaces. Ultimately, computer science education in the future lies in successful convergence of problem-solving and programming through means like Computational Thinking. The Data Science undergraduate program Guidelines emphasize that building such integration is essential to provide the students with the problem-solving they will be facing in the field. With well-structured frameworks for solving problems, teachers can enhance the learning process as well as create flexibility in the use of solutions. Moreover, awareness of the iterative and dialectical aspect of problem solving allows the building of resilience by the students in their solutions. As computer science continues to become more involved in various facets of society, problem-solving skills that are resilient will be needed to ensure future professionals possess the capacity to innovate and be able to adequately resolve emerging problems in a technologically-dominated world (Michaelson et al., 2015; Agarwal et al., 2017) (Figure 1.5).

1.2.2. Use in Various Academic Disciplines

Computational thinking as applied throughout the curriculum reflects the growing demand for cross-disciplinary strategies in the face of complex challenges. Computational thinking as a mental strategy addresses the solution of problems through capabilities shared by computer science, thus facilitating experts in various fields to decompose problems into manageable sub-components. Such an approach is particularly useful for the sciences, in which high-level data analysis and modeling require as much technical competence as analytical acumen. By fostering a language of computation, educators can train an algorithmic way of thinking among students, thus allowing students in such disparate disciplines as biology, engineering, and social sciences to exploit computational abstractions within their respective research endeavors. The use of computational techniques enables more subtle investigations of data, driving innovation and enabling more detailed comprehension of complicated systems. In the humanities, the potential of computational thinking is realized in the analysis and interpretation of large text corpora, or "digital humanities.." Researchers apply computation to perform text mining, sentiment analysis, and cultural analytics that bring forth patterns and insights that are not observable with qualitative analysis in isolation. This complementarity between humanities and computation opens up rich soil for new interpretation and inter-disciplinary understanding, emphasizing the way in which computational competency can enhance traditional research techniques. These practices of integration reflect a fundamental shift in academic research where the merging of multiple disciplines produces extensive knowledge. Such a shift in integration constantly suggests that computational thinking is bound to be an intrinsic part of reshaping the production of knowledge in the humanities. Furthermore, the demand for a multi-disciplinary orientation towards computational thinking meets the challenges posed by modern technological advancements. As data grow more elaborate, they demand multidimensional insights from various knowledge fields. Based on subsequent research, for example, in the presentation of the importance of information in the knowledge society, interdisciplinary collaboration also generates a climate that is favorable to innovation (Almér et al., 2016). In such an environment, computational thinking not only imparts the necessary skills to students but also enhances their abilities further to work with ethical, aesthetic, and sustainability dimensions of technology-based initiatives. The creation of transdisciplinary teams offers possibilities for rich discussions and mutual understanding among experts of different disciplines, further embedding computational thinking in academe and giving students a platform to approach the significant global issues of our times collectively (Figure 1.6).

Figure 1.6. *Use in various academic disciplines.*

Source: https://prepwithharshita.com/wp-content/uploads/2023/12/Professional-5-Steps-Women-Career-Tips-Graph.png.

1.2.3. Real-World Applications in Industry

In the modern-day industry, computational thinking is most applicable, influencing as much as manufacturing to information technology. It builds problem-solving skill required to design sound processes and systems. For instance, organizations currently employ data science to analyze massive volumes of data, identify patterns, and make sound decisions. These rigorous analytical abilities rest on a mathematics, statistics, and computer science foundation, as emphasized by the standards created during the PCMI 2016 Summer Undergraduate Faculty Program (Agarwal et al., 2017). Such courses are meant to equip students with the computational knowledge to thrive in developing working cultures, with an emphasis on the growing demand for data-savvy professionals across industries. In addition, cross-disciplinary methodologies stress the importance of computational thinking in industrial use. Information is a key asset within the knowledge economy, just as oil is in industrial society, propelling innovation and progress (Almér et al., 2016). This methodology stresses cross-disciplinary collaboration that leads to transdisciplinary projects for the future advancement of technology. Professions are increasingly being required to navigate complex problems that need to be solved using a mix of technical proficiency and creative thinking. As companies embrace the interconnection of different theoretical bases, they create employees whose problem-solving is promoted by collaboration, hence improved productivity and creativity. Last but not least, design ideology with focus on human-centeredness is central to designing successful industrial products from computational thinking. With technology artifacts getting more complex in the present era, user experience is crucial in effective product development. Emphasis on usability, good looks, and sustainability aligns with the needs of the contemporary marketplace that consider ethical aspects alongside environmental issues (Almér et al., 2016). Companies can design innovative solutions that engage people while addressing broader societal challenges using computational thinking principles. This integrated approach not only enhances the quality of products and services but also ensures that industry practices reflect a tendency towards ethical and sustainable growth in an ever-changing global world (Figure 1.7).

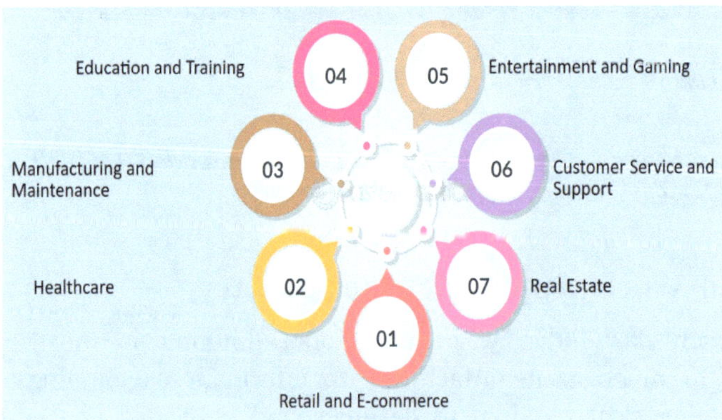

Figure 1.7. *Real-world applications in industry.*

Source: https://fastercapital.co/i/Augmented-Reality--Enhancing-Real-World-Experiences-with-AAI--Applications-of-AR-and-AI-in-Various-Industries.webp.

1.3. COMPUTATIONAL THINKING IN EDUCATION

The integration of computational thinking into learning is a significant pedagogical transformation, emphasizing problem-solving and critical thinking across the curriculum. With technology-prevalent classrooms, educators have more pressure to equip students with the skills to master complex problems. Computational thinking enables students to solve problems in a structured manner by breaking them down into manageable pieces, finding patterns, and developing algorithms. This approach not only prepares students for computer science professions but also reinforces their science, math, and everyday decision-making abilities. Furthermore, as new curriculum standards are adopted by schools, the application of computational thinking has been a top issue to stimulate creativity and analytical aptitudes required to thrive in an increasingly digital world.

Figure 1.8. *Computational thinking in education.*

Source: https://www.gettingsmart.com/wp-content/uploads/2018/05/Digital-Learning-K12-Students.jpg.

An appropriate method for developing computational thinking in school teaching is observable through interventions using programming languages, that is, Scratch. It has been observed through studies that computer programming among students enhances their self-efficacy in computational ability, which finally leads to better performance in STEM-related tasks. Programs at the middle school level demonstrate that while students are actually engaged in coding operations, their confidence and problem-solving skill improve significantly. By integrating such interventions, instructors can create an engaging learning environment that not only develops technical skills but also fosters cooperation and creativity. Such programming activities assist in wedding theoretical understanding with real implementation, allowing learners to gain skills that are greatly needed in today's employment market in the 21st century (Bean et al., 2016). It also cannot be overemphasized that the training of future instructors in computational thinking matters. As noted in pilot studies conducted during preliminary teacher training programs, preparing educators to embrace computational thinking while creating a well-rounded education system is crucial. According to such studies, empowering teachers with necessary skills and experience to develop computational thinking within their classrooms is essential. By involving teacher candidates in programming and multimedia projects, teacher training programs can effectively promote the incorporation of computational thinking into their future teaching practices. Ultimately, equipping future teachers with computational abilities not only serves their professional development but also enables them to transfer the same abilities to students, thereby building a more technologically advanced society (Ramos et al., 2013) (Figure 1.8).

1.3.1. Integration into K-12 Curricula

Application of computational thinking in K-12 education is quickly being recognized as a major driver for preparing students for challenges in a digital world. Such a pedagogical model encourages students to pursue problem-solving approaches and analytical thinking that cross subject silos. Through the incorporation of computational thinking ideas into disciplines like mathematics, science, and even the humanities, students are prepared to approach problems with a holistic view. Integration of these abilities in everyday learning is essential, as it prepares learners to navigate and make sense of the complicated systems that define contemporary life. As schools refresh curricula to include computational thinking, setting standards that guide teachers on optimal practices can enhance learning outcomes significantly, providing a framework for enhanced interdisciplinary teaching and learning practices. Moreover, recent evidence shows that computational thinking is not only a foundation skill of computer science but also enriches a variety of learning experiences throughout the curriculum. To illustrate, the National Research Council's next-generation science standards framework emphasizes computational thinking as a key practice of the learning process. An experiment with 9th-grade students in physics illustrated the potential of using computational models to understand complex physical systems. Those students who engaged in constructing and dissecting these models demonstrated more integrated knowledge of physics and computer science. This enhances how computational thinking can be applied to augment learning, as students are forced to visualize relationships and apply rational thinking to overcome harder problems, as seen through their ability to successfully execute programming assignments and reflective essays under testing conditions (Aiken et al., 2012). The integration effort is also supported by cooperation between instructors from various schools, as through initiatives like the Park City Math Institute. Instructors from various departments convene to craft guidelines for constructing curricula to make data science and computational thinking fit. These guidelines serve as a model for schools in coordinating their K-12 programs in an orderly fashion. Through highlighting collective resources and collective effort, schools are able to innovate and develop their curricula to fit the changing social needs and job market. With computational thinking being more embedded in K-12 educational settings, there is a necessity for education frameworks that are responsive and flexible, preparing students for skill requirements of future challenges (Agarwal et al., 2017) (Figure 1.9).

Figure 1.9. *Integration of computational thinking into K-12 curricula.*

Source: https://static.wixstatic.com/media/8e9d83_46e25411ec1f47029cdf60dc9b7007e3~mv2_d_4032_3024_s_4_2.jpg/v1/fill/w_767,h_575,al_c,q_85,usm_0.66_1.00_0.01,enc_auto/8e9d83_46e25411ec1f47029cdf60dc9b7007e3~mv2_d_4032_3024_s_4_2.jpg.

1.3.2. Role in Higher Education

The application of computational thinking in the post-secondary setting is increasingly considered to be crucial to preparing students to thrive in a technologically driven society. This education requires students to engage analytical and problem-solving abilities that traverse disciplinary boundaries. Through integrating computational thinking into curricula, not only does an institution expand students' abilities to address challenging problems, but it also equips them with skills for future professional life in areas ranging from science and engineering to the humanities. The shift toward integrating this method into academic programs appears in the recommendations that Park City Math Institute (PCMI) has made in terms of designing structured Data Science majors at universities. These standards emphasize the computer science, mathematics, and statistics that students need to master in order to succeed in a data-rich world, demonstrating the wide range of the role computational thinking plays in contemporary higher education (Agarwal et al., 2017). Further, the embrace of novel pedagogical approaches grounded in computational thinking makes possible new pedagogical modalities for teaching and assessment to promote students' engagement. As institutions strive to keep pace with the fast-paced evolution of technology and learning needs, they are invited to explore new methods of assessment prioritizing innovative problem-solving and critical thinking skills. Briefings from collective reviews like those published by the Institute of Educational Technology indicate the adoption of cutting-edge education practices.

Figure 1.10. *Role in higher education.*

Source: https://cdn.kqed.org/wp-content/uploads/sites/23/2011/10/Kids-computers.jpg.

These accounts emphasize 10 prospective innovations for changing learning models, proposing that universities need to convert the manner in which they educate to enable their graduates to meet the demands of the digital age (Adams et al., 2015). Such groundbreaking approaches can optimize the learning process, building a generation of learners skilled at solving complex problems. Overall, the integration of computational thinking in higher education is a driver of curricular and pedagogical change that will ultimately benefit students and faculty. By the ongoing revision and enhancement of programs to integrate computational thinking, institutions of higher education are helping to build a more flexible, adaptable, and critical-thinking workforce to address global challenges. This emphasis not only enriches individual learning experiences but also connects educational success with evolving labor market demands. By fostering a culture where computational thinking can flourish, tertiary education becomes a source of great innovation, allowing students to become more than just passive observers in their own fields and in society as a whole. As can be seen from the current debates and standards arising from programs such as the PCMI, there is no doubt that computational thinking is at the center of pedagogical transformation, leading to the manner in which knowledge is developed, examined, and utilized in the 21st century (Agarwal et al., 2017) (Figure 1.10).

1.3.3. Teaching Strategies and Methodologies

Teaching strategies and approaches are also crucial in order to facilitate effective transfer of computational thinking skills among learners. Heterogeneous learning environments must be provided to accommodate varying learning styles and interests, which would significantly enhance the learning process. A flexible learning environment facilitates diverse teaching approaches, including blended, online, and face-to-face learning (Gibbings et al., 2007). For instance, the integration of asynchronous online material, such as taped lectures and interactive quizzes, serves to supplement the learning process. By creating self-learning opportunities, the students can access course work at their own pace, thus gaining a better grasp of underlying principles in computational thinking. Measurement of the success of these disparate methodologies also demonstrates heightened student engagement and academic performance. Offering chances for joint learning is also a critical approach in the realm of computational thinking. By adopting cooperative learning frameworks, instructors can encourage learners to work together in groups and share information and knowledge that improves their understanding of complex concepts. Development of virtual networks, as researched in inter-disciplinary subject areas like Economics and Business, illustrates how these collaborative efforts can transcend geographical boundaries and generate beneficial interactions between peer learners (Brândao et al., 2005). Joint problem-solving activities challenging students allow them to appreciate the social nature of learning and appreciate multiple styles of problem-solving. While students persevere through the intricacy of computing issues within group settings, they not only become more technically proficient but also develop essential soft skills such as collaboration and communication. Furthermore, formative assessments are an essential aspect of assessing student knowledge and refining instruction. These assessments, which may include quizzes, peer review, and project reflection, provide constructive criticism that can help shape instruction and identify areas of needed improvement. When embedded judiciously in the curriculum, these assessments can boost learning outcomes by enabling teachers to make adjustments in teaching relying on real-time students' performance metrics. Furthermore, according to studies that analyzed online learning methods, learners are more likely to be engaged with their learning experience when formative assessments are integrated in the curriculum (Gibbings et al., 2007). This sense of belongingness and engagement assists in the attainment of greater academic accomplishment and motivation and, in return, fosters a more vibrant learning culture better suited to learning computational thinking (Figure 1.11).

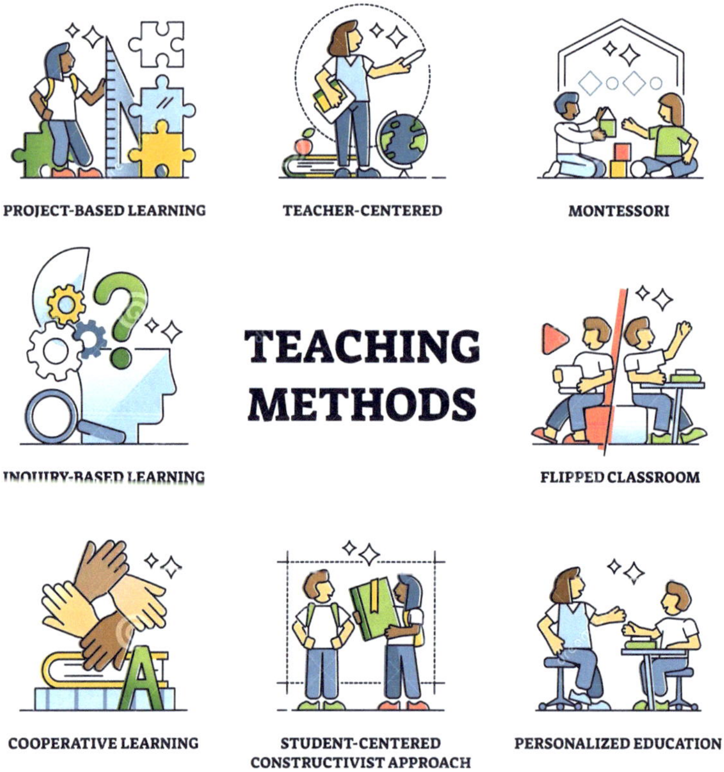

Figure 1.11. *Teaching strategies and methodologies thinking skills to students.*

Source: https://thumbs.dreamstime.com/z/teaching-methods-as-school-education-approach-types-outline-collection-set-labeled-examples-learning-strategy-techniques-232106696.jpg.

1.4. TOOLS AND RESOURCES FOR COMPUTATIONAL THINKING

Under computational thinking, there are numerous tools and resources through which one can learn and implement related capabilities. These tools make use of technology to provide an interactive learning experience beyond conventional teaching methods. Examples include coding platforms such as Scratch and Code.org, which utilize friendly user interfaces for students to create programs through the manipulation of visual blocks. This interactive approach not only demystifies programming concepts but also encourages problem-solving through iterative design. Further, the application of educational games creates enthusiasm and simultaneously instills logical and algorithmic thinking. Through these applications, instructors are able to adopt a practice-oriented approach that sharpens the students' understanding of computational concepts in an engaging environment. Therefore, the shared access to these resources fosters an inclusive learning space for diverse students, ultimately symbolizing the essence of computational thinking. Apart from those specific coding locations, cross-disciplinary tools comprising arts and digital technologies are also vital in the pedagogy of computational thinking. A well-documented example is the use of visual mapping software, whereby students can develop concept maps that reflect their understanding of abstract ideas. This is following Knowledge Cartography guidelines, where students are directly engaged in producing the map to depersonalize their thinking process and enhance their understanding of complex subjects. The learning of such interactive maps increases the understanding not only of computer concepts but also of connections between various concepts. Moreover, through such interdisciplinary practices, teachers can enable improved creative and critical thinking so that the necessary skills for dealing with an increasingly complex digital world are learnt by students. Finally, these tools bring to the fore the importance of aligning teaching practices with the demands of contemporary learning processes. Furthermore, the use of responsible research and innovation (RRI) principles in computational thinking can even increase students' engagement along with maintaining ethical considerations in their work. The RRI model, as identified by existing literature, is aimed at promoting skills and values for responsible participation in an open debate of science and technology. By employing RRI-oriented methods, educationists are able to craft activities in terms of collaboration and inclusiveness, thereby allowing a diverse perspective and ethical debate to flourish in learning environments. For instance, digital media and arts-based methods can support the development of the student's inquiry skills as well as the potential for a broader examination of the societal implications surrounding technology. However, current evaluation of these methods indicates that while participation and critical thinking are supported well, matters of gender equality and ethics integration may require greater attention. Hence, ongoing research in this area is important to optimize the impact of learning processes and foster ethical professionals in the field of computational thinking (Torruella et al., 2020; N/A, 2008) (Figure 1.12).

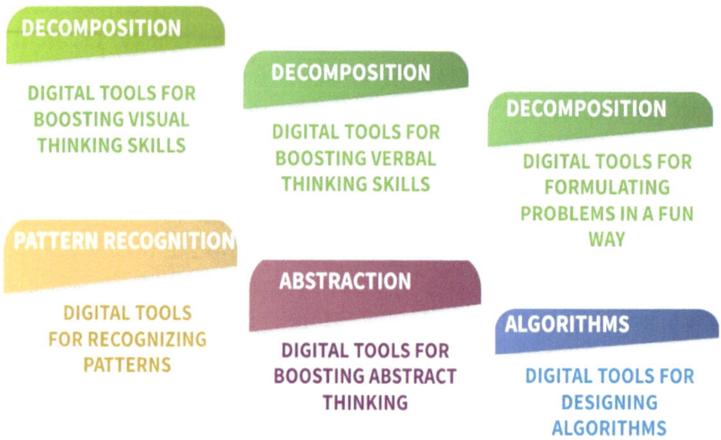

Figure 1.12. *Tools and resources for computational thinking.*

Source: https://thumbnails.genially.com/5712a75b1561e807349ce37c/screen-shots/c06e1340-7422-4249-8f9f-b2d0c1a67cbc.jpg.

1.4.1. Software and Programming Languages

The merging of software and programming languages is imperative in the domain of computational thinking. Because computers have entered every sector of life in the 21st century, the role of software translates into the central component that not only enables it to function but also fuels innovation in numerous other areas (Michaelson et al., 2015). Programming languages are the tools through which this software is constructed, allowing for the translation of problem-solving sequences of detailed steps into code that machines can execute. While there are numerous programming languages available today to accommodate diverse technical needs, the basic principles of computational thinking remain constant. This process encourages individuals to systematically think through problems and apply solutions utilizing systematic coding methods, emphasizing the importance of acquiring programming skills in addition to a strong realization of the computational problem-solving milieu. The methods of teaching programming languages have become better with the passage of time, yet there are some challenges that they still face. Traditional methods sometimes emphasize memorization over learning a better grasp of programming principles and their application. This lacuna demands improved pedagogies to meet the current gap between computational thinking as a theory and real-life programming practice (Michaelson et al., 2015). Current trends have sought to integrate problem-solving skills alongside programming studies, advocating for pedagogies that support creativity and critical thinking. This shift recognizes that effective programming is not merely a function of syntax but also one of establishing a logical framework for knowledge to be studied and use in problem-solving in multidisciplinary environments. Through the recognition of the inter-relation between problem-solving and programming, the students can more effectively prepare themselves for real-world software development issues. The emergence of inter-disciplinary fields, such as Data Science, also showcases the importance of having a solid foundation in programming languages and software. Institutions now have a greater likelihood of creating academic offerings that provide students with end-to-end education in computational modeling, machine learning, and data analysis. Such offerings tend to necessitate an even understanding of statistical methods as well as programming proficiency, acknowledging the necessary integration of software development with higher-level computational ideas. With educational institutions re-examining their curricula, the integration of programming languages with advanced models of analysis marks a further progression of the abilities necessary to be successful within a technology-driven world. Not only does this process educate talented programmers but also problem solvers with the ability to analyze enormous data landscapes, ensuring usefulness within a perpetually changing job market (Figure 1.13).

Figure 1.13. *Software and programming languages.*

Source: https://cdn.hackr.io/uploads/posts/attachments/1677927034t0ScViNfXE.png.

1.4.2. Online Platforms and Courses

The advent of online platforms and courses has fundamentally altered the landscape of education, particularly in fields that require computational thinking. With the exponential growth of the internet and advancements in technology, learners can now access vast resources from anywhere in the world. These platforms do not merely replicate traditional educational experiences; rather, they enhance them by offering interactive, user-centered interfaces that facilitate learning. For example, the convergence of the internet and vast data sources has led to what is termed the Second Machine Age, a concept explored by Brynjolfsson and McAfee. This age reflects an era where digital accessibility is unbounded, allowing learners to explore computational concepts through multiple lenses and experiences, thereby enriching their understanding (Delic et al., 2017). Moreover, online platforms like Massive Open Online Courses (MOOCs) exemplify this shift by providing flexible learning environments that empower individuals to engage with content at their convenience. The diverse range of courses available on these platforms covers various aspects of computational thinking, from programming fundamentals to complex algorithm design. While MOOCs have democratized education, they have also introduced challenges related to accessibility, particularly in STEM disciplines. Accessibility issues can create barriers for disabled learners, limiting their ability to fully engage with mathematical content. This highlights the ongoing need for continuous improvement in web accessibility to ensure that all learners can benefit from these modern educational resources (Amado-Salvatierra et al., 2017). As the demand for computational skills in the workforce continues to rise, the role of online platforms in fostering these competencies cannot be overstated. Educational institutions are increasingly recognizing the importance of integrating computational thinking into their curricula, leveraging the flexibility and breadth of online courses to meet diverse learner needs. These platforms not only provide essential skills pertinent to modern careers but also cultivate a culture of innovation and lifelong learning among individuals. In this rapidly evolving educational ecosystem, the integration of advanced online learning experiences becomes crucial for preparing learners to navigate the complexities of a data-driven world while fostering their ability to think critically, solve problems, and approach tasks systematically. As such, online courses have become vital in bridging the gap between foundational knowledge and real-world application in computational thinking.

1.4.3. Community Resources and Workshops

Local resources and community workshops are vital for computational thinking development due to their provision of accessible learning opportunities and collaborative spaces. The resources involve participants by familiarizing them with complex concepts and making them more accessible through the immediacy of hands-on experience. Workshops have a tendency of incorporating local teachers, professionals, and technology enthusiasts who guide learners through real-world applications of computational thinking concepts in practice. This co-creation approach not only develops individual expertise but also builds a support network in which shared experience and wisdom contribute to collective awareness. By tapping into local resources, these workshops provide space for engagement among participants, bridging knowledge gaps, and a culture of continuous learning. These initiatives are central to making technology and computational literacy available for all and enabling people to become more effective problem solvers in an increasingly digitalized world. The key to the success of community resources lies in the ability to adapt the learning material and approaches to accommodate various needs. Programs that are put in place to accommodate varying ages and levels of skills ensure that everyone in the community has the opportunity to participate, thereby fostering inclusivity. For example, workshops may be devised to introduce coding information to children through engaging games or teach adults how to use data analysis tools relevant in their professions.

Additionally, the workshops typically identify critical skills, such as collaboration, innovative thinking, and critical thinking, that constitute the foundation of computational thinking. By providing a formal yet flexible learning environment, community resources allow individuals to gain new concepts and technologies without restraint. Through these procedures, individuals are not only gaining technical skills but are also learning an innovation attitude, which is emerging as an increasing concern in contemporary knowledge society. In addition, the impact of community workshops extends beyond the formation of skills for an individual; they have a tendency to trigger larger cultural shifts towards embracing technology and innovation. These gatherings prompt the feeling that technology is not an apparatus but part of modern-day life, which can improve problem-solving in all areas. By blending concepts from different fields, such as design thinking and information processing, workshops can create a transdisciplinary culture, thus reflecting the complexities of actual challenges. As defined in existing studies, the convergence of multiple competencies fosters innovative solutions towards social, ecological, and ethical dimensions in design and technology (Parisi et al., 2018; Almér et al., 2016). Highlighting such intersections allows community workshops to remain relevant and effective because they equip participants not only to understand computational thinking but to apply it judiciously in various settings and, ultimately, make the world a wiser and more capable place.

1.5. CHALLENGES IN APPLYING COMPUTATIONAL THINKING

Its implementation in schools is marred by numerous challenges that must be surmounted if it is to successfully be integrated. A significant challenge is the huge variation in teachers' awareness of computational thinking concepts. The majority of teachers, particularly from non-mathematics and science, technology, engineering, and mathematics subjects might not possess the needed skills or training to enable them to effectively educate these concepts. This thus presents a knowledge gap that could discourage student participation and comprehension. Moreover, teachers themselves will not be able to implement computational thinking in the classroom if not taught adequately, and students will miss out on opportunities to develop higher-order problem-solving and analytical thinking skills. This issue can be overcome by a shared commitment among schools to provide comprehensive professional development and support to teachers at all levels (Copeland et al., 2010). Another top challenge involves the curriculum itself; the majority of existing programs do not reflect the values of computational thinking. Most existing educational paradigms lean towards memorization and not higher cognitive capacity, thus preventing the ability of students to think computationally. Moreover, curriculum constraints may limit the intensity and breadth of computational thinking training, potentially excluding provision of an integrated learning experience that adequately prepares learners for the issues of the digital age. Even as seen with attempts at formulating guidelines for undergraduate Data Science degree programs, cautious re-design of curricula is called for to facilitate a holistic awareness of computational ideas. These transformations must be supplemented with apparent goals and interdisciplinary frameworks that facilitate computational thinking integration across different academic domains (Agarwal et al., 2017). Finally, socio-cultural challenges are also fundamental in the challenges of computational thinking integration. Student populations with diverse cultures can experience varying levels of access to technology and resources, which translates to disparity in the opportunities to learn computational thinking. Moreover, instructional strategies may fail to cater to the diverse learning styles and backgrounds of learners, thus excluding those who most require such competencies. These disparities have to be tackled through an inclusive curriculum design and pedagogical design that allows all learners to interact positively with computational thinking. By recognizing and proactively working to overcome such socio-cultural barriers, teachers are able to produce a more balanced learning environment that can allow all students to succeed in a technology-oriented society (Figure 1.14).

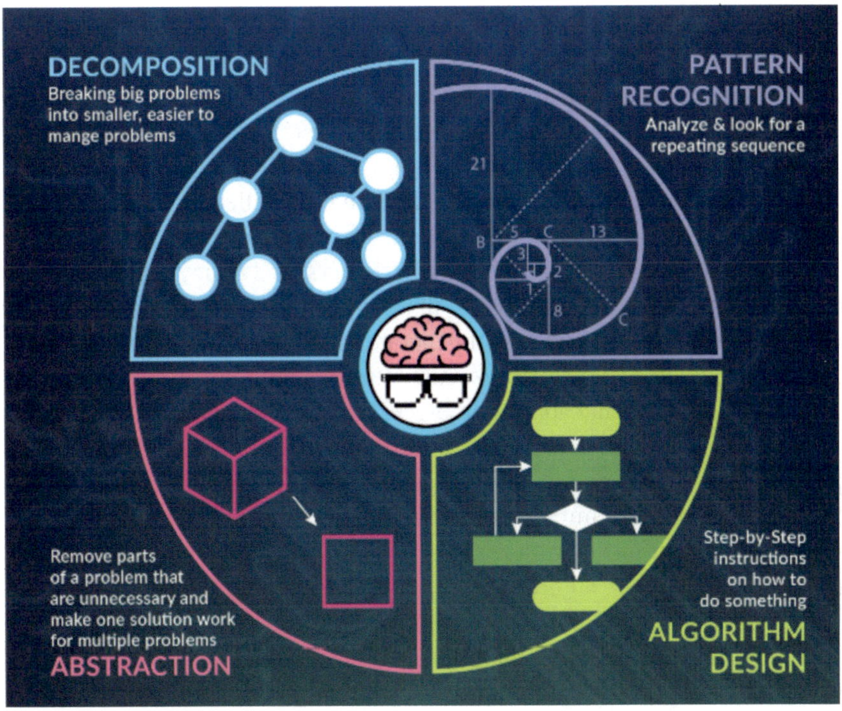

Figure 1.14. *Challenges in implementing computational thinking.*

Source: https://steamacademy.edu.vn/wp-content/uploads/2018/12/ComputationalThinkingProductLogo.png.

1.5.1. Resistance from Educators

Teacher resistance is the biggest obstacle to proper adoption of computational thinking (CT) in K-12 classrooms. Despite its established utility in the enhancement of analytical and problem-solving skills, teachers are reluctant to integrate CT into their curriculum. This resistance is typically caused by lack of familiarity with computational tools and methods and a sense of inadequacy in presenting such ideas to students efficiently. This is in line with the conclusions of previous research, which has shown that implementation of new teaching methods is regularly resisted because educators are resistant to change and resentful of the perceived pressures on their established frameworks and pedagogies (Phelps et al., 2004). If teachers do not have adequate professional development and mentoring, they can struggle to integrate CT into their classrooms, thus undermining the wider educational goals of creating a digitally literate, innovative student body. In addition, the organization of the education system often hinders the application of CT. Limits in curricula, testing demands, and emphasis on memorization may smother creativity and innovation in teaching approaches. Teachers may resist including computational thinking because they may feel that pedagogical reform is incompatible with these long-standing systems of education. Achieving consensus on the value and significance of CT in a rigorous curriculum is a challenging goal, especially with administrators who themselves are reluctant to change. The competing agendas of stakeholders—administrators, teachers, and policymakers—are also detrimental. Reform efforts therefore that do not take into consideration these institutional and cultural forces will generate much resistance, more cementing educators' reluctance to adopt computational thinking (Benétreau-Dupin et al., 2014). Lastly, educators' perceived technical complexity itself can be a barrier to adoption by teachers. Teachers worry that implementing CT will require undergoing wholesale shifts in practice or that they lack the technical proficiency to properly implement it. Technical complexity can get educators jumpy, and most prefer sticking with what is familiar rather than taking a risk at new. In addition to this, without any specific framework outlining CT and how it should be implemented, teachers may struggle to relate it to their students' contexts. Thus, encouraging an improved understanding of computational thinking and articulating its ability to take learning outcomes to another level is extremely critical. Strategies need to be taken to demonstrate how CT aligns with existing learning goals and pupil competencies, and hence reduce anxiety among educators and encourage a more open attitude toward integrating these essential skills in their classrooms (Phelps et al., 2004).

1.5.2. Accessibility and Equity Issues

In computational thinking, the ability to deal with accessibility and equity matters is critical in ensuring inclusive learning spaces. Integration of disability awareness into the curricula of learning institutions is a reaction to heightened focus on various learning needs in higher education. As highlighted by attempts to enhance disability awareness, it is necessary for institutions to equip both staff and students with knowledge to work with and value different abilities. This acknowledgment needs to transcend adherence to accessibility guidelines per se; rather, it must be transformationally oriented, reflecting inclusive practices and embedding subtle routines within pedagogical design. Such endeavors benefit not only equity but also the learning experience of all, promoting an environment for holistic growth and continued interest in computational thinking (Clay et al., 2013). Also, the technologies employed in computational thinking education present their own accessibility barriers when not implemented cautiously. While advanced computer algebra systems like

MuPad can ease mathematics teaching, their symbolic interface may discourage those without pre-exposure or those with specific disabilities. Being sensitive to the wide variety of exposure students have to such technologies is important in determining how usable they are. Studies that have examined students attitude towards such tools have noted that exposure isn't always enough to guarantee success; hence, teachers must take a proactive approach to ensure equitable access to such learning technologies. By facilitating the careful incorporation of such systems, teachers can eliminate accessibility concerns while promoting equity, enabling all students to engage meaningfully with computational concepts (Ewart et al., 2019). Finally, building a fair approach in computational thinking necessitates that schools follow uniform review and adjustment of teaching procedures. Schools ought to review uniformly the effect of varied approaches on learning participation and academic achievement. All this is done by gathering data from pupils and teachers with the aim of making practices changes based on evidence-based findings. In addition to workshops and shared learning spaces, embedding these facilities also helps prototype inclusive practices effectively, where staff members share strategies and challenges in making learning accessible. By establishing a culture of continuous development and reflection, institutions not only cultivate equity in the classroom but engage more generally with discourses about the benefits of inclusive education in computational thinking that are more embedded in wider societal missions of diversity and inclusion (Clay et al., 2013).

1.5.3. Misconceptions About Computational Thinking

The concept of computational thinking is generally prone to various misconceptions that impact its effective implementation in the learning environment. The general misconception is that computational thinking is equivalent to programming or computer science. While programming is clearly a valuable skill, computational thinking encompasses a much broader perspective of problem-solving strategies of relevance to a wide range of subjects. According to recent studies in education, there is a need for creating awareness that computational thinking involves thinking through logic, having the ability to recognize patterns, and the ability to deconstruct complicated problems into simpler parts (Adams et al., 2015). This awareness would help teachers incorporate computational thinking into their coursework without restricting it to coding itself, ultimately forming a more comprehensive approach to cultivating critical thinking among students. Another common myth is regarding the complexity of computational thinking and specifically in young children. Computational thinking is assumed by many parents and teachers to be too complex for primary learners, which can be used as a barrier for its use in primary school. Nonetheless, studies suggest that the concepts of computational thinking can be learned in ways that are recognizable to younger audiences, employing appropriate examples and problem-solving situations accessible to their daily lives. For example, kids can learn about algorithms and sequence through straightforward games and hands-on activities. This double focus on simplicity and usability contradicts the myth that computational thinking is only suited for bright students and reaffirms its significance and application from a very young age (Maclellan et al., 2001). Finally, there is a misconception that computational thinking is relevant to technology or STEM courses alone. This narrow definition overlooks the interdisciplinary nature of computational thinking and how it is being used across many disciplines, from arts and humanities to social sciences. By pointing out such flexibility, teachers can entice students with diverse backgrounds to come to computational thinking as a useful tool in their own areas of study. As seen in recent education reports, incorporating computational thinking in other subjects not only expands learning but also prepares students to thrive in a more globalized world where analysis and problem-solving skills are necessary everywhere (Adams et al., 2015). Thus, shattering this myth is instrumental in nurturing a generation of students who possess the intellectual skills that will enable them to thrive in all walks of life.

1.6. FUTURE OF COMPUTATIONAL THINKING

The future of computational thinking is poised to reshape not only academic coursework but also the fabric of society. With teachers increasingly cognizant of the need for computational literacy, coursework is being redesigned to incorporate problem-solving and analytical critical thinking grounded in computational methodologies. This trend is particularly evident in the realm of data science, where institutions of higher learning are endeavoring to establish standards for undergraduate students based on the complexities of the discipline. The Park City Math Institutes program is one manifestation of this change in that it aims to bring together mathematical, statistical, and computational ideas within a coherent framework of education. These developments promise that computational thinking soon will be an elementary proficiency by which students can function not merely across technological platforms, but the ethical, social, and economic risks associated with computation development. Concurrently, the emergence of neurocognitive informatics brings forth new paradigms beyond the standard computational approaches. This field explores the interaction between artificial systems and human thought with a goal to create processes and algorithms that mimic or complement human patterns of thinking. By focusing on how humans represent, process, and manage information, researchers seek to crack hard problems that currently lie outside the ability of computers. The importance of duplicating human information processing capabilities in machines underlines the possibilities of creating more flexible and more natural interfaces. This coming together of theoretical models and pragmatic application will not only enhance computational thinking but also propel the innovation of artificial intelligence, which in turn will find application in a variety of industries, from medicine to education. In the coming times, using computational thinking as a multidisciplinary approach will increasingly become streamlined from interdisciplinary approaches that draw both on technological developments and human mental processes. As witnessed through collaborative efforts towards establishing data science initiatives, identification of computational thinking as a cross-disciplinary skill will be crucial towards preparing a workforce capable of addressing future challenges. This confluence of disciplines experiences a broader vision of education in which disciplinary boundaries are scorned and knowledge is being exchanged across disciplines. As computational thinking evolves further, both as a critical ability and as a force behind interdisciplinary innovation, its role in shaping society's response to complicated problems in an increasingly fast-moving digital world will be priceless (Figure 1.15).

Figure 1.15. *Future of computational thinking.*

Source: https://d3sujgifhk94se.cloudfront.net/wp-content/uploads/2023/10/29152222/computational-thinking.jpg.

1.6.1. Trends in Technology and Education

The intersection of technology and education is increasingly shaping modern pedagogy, and as such, a revolutionary change has been witnessed in how computational thinking is integrated into curricula. One prevailing trend is embracing innovative digital tools that build an interactive learning space, focusing on student engagement. Platforms that embed artificial intelligence, for instance, are able to provide personalized learning experiences, adapting content to varied learner needs. This tailoring not only benefits improved individual learning outcomes but also fosters critical thinking abilities that are imperative in effective problem-solving. The development of blended learning architectures combining face-to-face classroom instruction with internet-based learning is another evolution worthy of mention. This mixed-methods approach welcomes learners to be invested participants in their own learning process, building an interiorized motivation to confront difficult concepts and gain computational thinking capabilities relevant in a computer-centric world (Sandford et al., 2009). Moreover, incorporating coding and programming into the curriculum is a testament to growing recognition of computational thinking as a core ability. Schools are increasingly making coding a part of their curriculum, beginning at the level of elementary education, which represents a forward-looking response to what the 21st-century workforce requires. This introduction of computer science principles early on not only de-mystifies what computing is all about, but also prepares students for future advancements in technology. Strives to bridge the digital divide to ensure equitable access to such resources, hence empowering all learners to thrive in an increasingly digital world. Furthermore, partnerships between schools and technology companies offer exposure to up-to-date equipment and facilities, enhancing educators' ability to introduce computational thinking into students' lives with depth (Berry et al., 2011). With the ever-changing educational environment, data-driven decision-making becomes increasingly important. Educational technologies are now able to collect and analyze large amounts of data regarding students' performance, thereby giving teachers information on areas that need improvement. The data-driven approach enables the use of instruction methods that are tailored to address learners' different needs. Furthermore, the integration of analytics can lead to the identification of successful pedagogies that can be replicated and scaled across various learning environments. When these trends are embraced by stakeholder groups, the support for a culture of feedback and continuous improvement will play a critical role in enhancing learning outcomes and ensuring all students possess the computational thinking skills necessary to thrive in an age of accelerating technological change (Sandford et al., 2009).

1.6.2. Potential Impact on Workforce Skills

The rapidity of technological change demands a highly skilled labor force, particularly those associated with computational thinking. As industries adopt automation and artificial intelligence more than ever, traditional skills become obsolete, demanding a paradigm shift in education. Computational thinking develops problem-solving skills and logical thinking, which are crucial when handling complex technology environments. Research has indicated that there is massive potential to integrate such skills into school curricula, implying that individuals who learn computational thinking are in a better position to adapt to evolving needs within the workplace. The scope of this implication is huge; interventions by education that enhance such skills have the potential to close existing gaps in work readiness, eventually leading to a better-skilled workforce. Therefore, computer-based thinking education must be prioritized highly to provide future generations with the ability to succeed professionally in a technology-driven economy (Chowdhury et al., 2024). Moreover, incorporating computational thinking into educational curricula can facilitate broader understanding of technologys application in various disciplines. With growing needs for graduates who are familiar with coding, software development, and data analysis, the education system must adapt by providing suitable content across the curriculum. For instance, bringing computational thinking ideas into other than typical computer science classes can turn students into more analytical minds and problem-solvers, which contributes to innovation. The recent UK education system reform, where computer science is made a required subject, is a case in point (Brown et al., 2014). By integrating these skills at an early stage of the curriculum, students are not just prepared for postsecondary education, but also for future employment opportunities in a technology-oriented society. Thus, computational thinking equips students with efficient skills that can be utilized for different job positions and sectors. Closing the skills gap in the workforce also involves the necessity to acknowledge the importance of continuous professional learning among current employees. As workspaces emphasize more on digital transformation, there is a requirement for lifelong learning in maintaining workforce longevity. Organizations can benefit from the presence of a culture of continuous learning with an emphasis on the importance of computational thinking and other related skills. This makes workers competitive and capable of working with new tools and technology. Moreover, companies that put investment in training and upgrading employees will have increased innovation and productivity, thereby general economic development. According to the study, educational and workplace practices for developing computational thinking can significantly minimize skill gaps and empower individuals to deal with the challenges brought about by a rapidly evolving technology environment (Chowdhury et al., 2024). Creating mechanisms for skill development in the workplace is important to group and individual accomplishment.

1.6.3. Predictions for the Evolution of Computational Thinking

The evolution of computational thinking is projected to be hand-in-hand with tremendous advances in technology, in the form of artificial intelligence, potentially reshaping human-to-machine interaction to its very core. Transhumanism theory is at the epicenter of such predictions as it imagines a world where the distinction between human and artificial intelligence is blurred more and more every day. As Iuga et al. (2016) indicates, this paradigm foretells a revolutionary new direction away from the notion of human improvement through technology towards a place where there is not only intelligent machinery but also self-improving systems. Therefore, with the changing landscape of computational thinking, it would certainly have to be incorporated with these next-generation technologies, which would lead teachers to rethink traditional teaching pedagogies for imparting this learning. Therefore, human beings will need to acquire skills that merge human consciousness with machine learning and, in the process, redefine computational literacy in a more mechanized world. The integration of computational thinking into learning models is predicted to undergo its very core transformation, driven by digital media and interactive ecosystems. With tools such as spreadsheets redefining mathematical problem-solving, it is clear that such new mediums hold special affordances for learning. The knowledge one gains from studying the implications of spreadsheet environments indicates how they are capable of influencing students' conceptualization and inquiry pathways, towards more enriching learning experiences (Calder et al., 2010). This kind of shift means that the learning practices of the future will emphasize the necessity of leveraging digital technologies not only as tools but as an integral component of learning. In this manner, computational thinking will be shaped from a set of skills to a leading attitude that fosters creativity, critical thinking, and flexibility in students. Besides, as computational thinking keeps evolving, emphasis will increasingly be put on interconnectedness and collaboration, reflecting the increasing problem-solving complexity in the context of a digital world. The emphasis on teams can lead to breakthroughs in pedagogical and practical methods of teaching and implementing computational thinking across fields. It is based on projections that creating a collective environment for problem-solving will enable students to utilize diverse perspectives and experience in order to enhance their computational skills (Iuga et al., 2016). Also, the development of online collaborative systems will further enhance this debate as students interact with others worldwide, exchanging ideas and solutions. For this purpose, educators must lead students not only through learning computational thinking skills but also through building a sense of collaboration that will prepare them for a world in which answers must be generated from the community.

SUMMARY

Conclusion of essay on Introduction to Computational Thinking is a significant afterthought regarding the concepts and approaches under discussion. The discussion highlights that computational thinking not only pertains to computer science but also crosses disciplines in enhancing problem-solving abilities. It acknowledges the growing significance of Computational Thinking in today's education industry, which it supports crucial skills needed in dealing with intricate problems. With increasing technology, instructors are challenged to incorporate these concepts into their courses, thus developing a more integrated and multidisciplinary education that prepares students for real applications. Moreover, the dissemination of Interactive, Connected, and Smart (ICS) material, as emphasized in current design research, shows how emerging technology influences much of what it touches, including computational thinking. The challenge and opportunity that these materials pose necessitate realignment of existing paradigms in education to equip students effectively for the future challenges. Embracing the dynamic nature of these resources enables teachers to better impart the potential to innovate and adapt in changing environments, and it becomes increasingly important in this regard to consider computational thinking as a way to achieve this (Parisi et al., 2018). Briefly, the overlap between computational thinking and interdisciplinary learning highlights flexibility in the face of ongoing technological progress. By synthesizing ancient disciplines with computer science principles, instructors can produce a generation of thinkers that is capable of solving complex problems creatively as well as pragmatically. This discussion in theoretical debates for information theory continues to enhance the discourse, with suggestions that fields of study like library and information studies can lead significantly in the development of computational thinking. Such an alignment of knowledge domains could one day change how knowledge is thought about and communicated in the digital economy era, a tremendous paradigm leap (Bawden et al., 2020). The introduction of computation thinking into educational curricula is a paradigm shift regarding how students learn to solve difficult problem-solving and logical reasoning. This foundational approach emphasizes conceptual frameworks rather than merely learning about programming. Computation thinking at its core is all about decomposing problems into manageable pieces, allowing students to analyze and solve problems step-by-step. Adherents theorize that this strategy goes beyond traditional computer science education, enabling students from diverse academic backgrounds to acquire important reasoning, which can be applied in most scenarios, therefore prepared for the technology-driven future. This process is also equated with prescriptions from some educators suggesting the integration of computational thinking across subjects as a means of enhancing general learning (Agarwal et al., 2017). Moreover, the relevance of computational thinking extends beyond contexts of learning and on into practical implementation, whereby individuals employ computational concepts in addressing real-world issues. Through mechanisms such as abstraction and algorithmic thought, students can craft sound solutions—skills ever more crucial in a world where technology and data dominate. Such a bridge between computation thinking and application in reality signifies its significance not only in the sciences, technology, engineering, and math (STEM) fields but more so in the social sciences, humanities, and arts. As the diverse disciplines embrace the significance of data literacy and reasoning aptitudes, the principles of computational thinking can fuel innovative inquiry and enhanced problem-solving capacity, indicating an even broader educational movement towards interdisciplinarity (Gelepithis et al., 2009). Finally, the development of guidelines for data science undergraduate curricula, as discussed in recent workshops like the Park City Math Institutes 2016 summer program, reflects a tendency to position computational thinkings position in institutions. Educators from various institutions came together and created a systematic model with the goal of harmonizing data science courses so that they highlight the applicability of mathematics, statistics, and computer science towards building an integrated comprehension of data. With the focus on systemic computational thinking, the guidelines invite education reforms in accordance with industrial and social demands. This is a step ahead in anticipation that not only heightens students' preparedness but also paves the way for educational innovations in the future, ultimately showing the importance of adopting computational thinking into education curricula profoundly (Agarwal et al., 2017).

REFERENCES

1. Adams, A., Alozie, N., Ferguson, R., FitzGerald, E., et al. (2015). Innovating pedagogy 2015: Open University Innovation Report 4. https://core.ac.uk/download/42536671.pdf (accessed on 9th September 2025).
2. Agarwal, M., Averett, M., Baumer, B., Bray, A., et al. (2017). Curriculum guidelines for undergraduate programs in data science. https://core.ac.uk/download/287356701.pdf (accessed on 9th September 2025).
3. Aiken, J. M., Burk, J. B., Caballero, M. D., Douglas, R., et al. (2012). Understanding student computational thinking with computational modeling. http://arxiv.org/abs/1207.1764 (accessed on 9th September 2025).
4. Almér, A., Dodig-Crnkovic, G., Holstein, T., Kade, A., et al. (2016). Trans disciplinarity seen through information, communication, computation, (inter-)action and cognition. http://arxiv.org/abs/1604.04711 (accessed on 9th September 2025).
5. Amado-Salvatierra, H. R., Breslow, L., De Waard, I., Herman, R. L., Iniesto, F., McCulloch, R., et al. (2017). Raising awareness of the accessibility challenges in mathematics MOOCs. https://core.ac.uk/download/131316835.pdf (accessed on 9th September 2025).
6. Antoro, B., & Wahyuni, D. (2025). Eksplorasi pola berpikir kreatif siswa dalam pemecahan masalah matematika berbasis computational thinking. https://core.ac.uk/download/660286020.pdf (accessed on 9th September 2025).
7. Bawden, D., Dixon, D., Floridi, L., Furner, J., et al. (2020). Information and design: Book symposium on Luciano Floridi's *the Logic of Information*. https://core.ac.uk/download/233029849.pdf (accessed on 9th September 2025).
8. Bean, N. H., Feldhausen, R., & Weese, J. L. (2016). The impact of STEM experiences on student self-efficacy in computational thinking. https://core.ac.uk/download/77980044.pdf (accessed on 9th September 2025).
9. Benétreau-Dupin, Y., & Garik, P. (2014). Report on a Boston University Conference December 7–8, 2012 on 'How can the history and philosophy of science contribute to contemporary U.S. science teaching?.' https://core.ac.uk/download/33752903.pdf (accessed on 9th September 2025).
10. Berrens Torruella, K., Heras López, M., & Ruiz Mallen, I. (2020). Responsible research and innovation in science education: Insights from evaluating the impact of using digital media and arts-based methods on RRI values. https://core.ac.uk/download/322837097.pdf (accessed on 9th September 2025).

11. Berry, D. (2011). The computational turn: Thinking about the digital humanities. https://core.ac.uk/download/30608773.pdf (accessed on 9th September 2025).

12. Brândao, E., Díez de Castro, E. C., García Ordaz, M., Luna Huertas, M., et al. (2005). A learning experience in the fields of economics and business: Creation of student-managed inter-university virtual networks. https://core.ac.uk/download/186617453.pdf (accessed on 9th September 2025).

13. Brown, N. C. C., Crick, T., Humphreys, S., Sentance, S., et al. (2014). Restart: The resurgence of computer science in UK schools. https://core.ac.uk/download/30704035.pdf (accessed on 9th September 2025).

14. Caballero, M. D. (2015). Computation across the curriculum: What skills are needed? http://arxiv.org/abs/1507.00533 (accessed on 9th September 2025).

15. Calder, N. S. (2010). Affordances of spreadsheets in mathematical investigation: Potentialities for learning. https://core.ac.uk/download/29197557.pdf (accessed on 9th September 2025).

16. Chowdhury, S., Doddanavar, I. A., & Muhamad, M. Q. B. (2024). Determining youths' computational thinking skills using confirmatory factor analysis. https://core.ac.uk/download/613185795.pdf (accessed on 9th September 2025).

17. Clay, L., Hale, L., Janssen, J., Rutherford, R., et al. (2013). Exploring the integration of disability awareness into tertiary teaching and learning activities. https://core.ac.uk/download/9637015.pdf (accessed on 9th September 2025).

18. Copeland, M. K. (2010). Benefits, limitations and best practices of online coursework…Should accounting programs jump on board? https://core.ac.uk/download/81665642.pdf (accessed on 9th September 2025).

19. Deane, G., Dewhurst, J., & Kersten, L. (2017). Resolving two tensions in 4E cognition using wide computationalism. https://core.ac.uk/download/223236434.pdf (accessed on 9th September 2025).

20. Delic, K. A., Denning, P., Johnson, J., Sousa-Rodrigues, D., et al. (2017). Big data, digitization, and social change (Ubiquity Symposium). https://core.ac.uk/download/223197519.pdf (accessed on 9th September 2025).

21. Duch, W. (2009). Neurocognitive informatics manifesto. https://core.ac.uk/download/pdf/87330.pdf (accessed on 9th September 2025).

22. Elby, A., Gupta, A., Hull, M. M., Kuo, E., et al. (2012). How students blend conceptual and formal mathematical reasoning in solving physics problems. http://arxiv.org/abs/1102.3453 (accessed on 9th September 2025).

23. Ewart, P., Khanna, J., & Louie, K. (2019). A double-edged sword: Use of computer algebra systems in first-year engineering mathematics and mechanics courses. https://core.ac.uk/download/322841915.pdf (accessed on 9th September 2025).
24. Gelepithis, P. A. M. (2009). Outline of a new approach to the nature of mind. https://core.ac.uk/download/pdf/87224.pdf (accessed on 9th September 2025).
25. Gibbings, P., & Young, F. R. (2007). Learning flexibility: The environment and a case study. https://core.ac.uk/download/11036936.pdf (accessed on 9th September 2025).
26. Iuga, I. (2016). Transhumanism between human enhancement and technological innovation. https://core.ac.uk/download/131210269.pdf (accessed on 9th September 2025).
27. Maclellan, E. (2001). What counts as numeracy? https://core.ac.uk/download/9019809.pdf (accessed on 9th September 2025).
28. Masriyah, D., & Sekar, L. S. (2020). Proses berpikir komputasi siswa SMP dalam memecahkan masalah pola bilangan ditinjau dari perbedaan jenis kelamin. https://core.ac.uk/download/482198830.pdf (accessed on 9th September 2025).
29. Michaelson, G. (2015). Teaching programming with computational and informational thinking. https://core.ac.uk/download/29822230.pdf (accessed on 9th September 2025).
30. N/A. (2008). *Knowledge Cartography: Software Tools and Mapping Techniques*. https://core.ac.uk/download/1723.pdf (accessed on 9th September 2025).
31. Oxman, R. (2010). Digital tectonics as a morphogenetic process. http://hdl.handle.net/10251/6959 (accessed on 9th September 2025).
32. Parisi, S., Petrelli, D., Rognoli, V., Spallazzo, D., et al. (2018). ICS materials. Towards a re-interpretation of material qualities through interactive, connected, and smart materials. https://core.ac.uk/download/161527657.pdf (accessed on 9th September 2025).
33. Phelps, C. L. (2004). Advances in Teaching & Learning Day Abstracts 2005. https://core.ac.uk/download/46714715.pdf (accessed on 9th September 2025).
34. Ramos, J. (2013). Exploring computational thinking in initial teacher training: A preliminary study and reflection on practice. https://core.ac.uk/download/62460523.pdf (accessed on 9th September 2025).

35. Sandford, R. (2009). Robots, drugs, reality and education: How the future will change how we think. https://core.ac.uk/download/4151800.pdf (accessed on 9th September 2025).

36. Stein, L. A. (1999). Challenging the computational metaphor: Implications for how we think. https://core.ac.uk/download/pdf/84443.pdf (accessed on 9th September 2025)

CHAPTER 2

FUNDAMENTALS OF PROBLEM SOLVING

Contents

INTRODUCTION

The discipline of problem-solving is the foundation of all other areas of study, including science, mathematics, and philosophy. Problem-solving is all about an orderly procedure of identifying, analyzing, and resolving problems. The procedure begins with the identification of a problem, typically with complexity and uncertainty, to be approached through a systematic solution. Understanding of the fundamentals of problem-solving is essential to being capable of thinking critically and to being capable of navigating the doubt that pervades a lot of areas. As knowledge evolves, the principles of effective problem-solving remain, integrating theory and practice in true situations. Creativity and adaptability form the hub of problem-solving discussion. Modern issues are apt to require creative solutions that more traditional approaches may not offer, inviting thinking outside the box and flexibility in strategy. This can be observed in educational systems making use of interactive media, such as video games, as a learning tool. This can be illustrated in tasks concerning the N-puzzle game, such as how interactive problem-solving can inform basic concepts in artificial intelligence and enhance learning through firsthand experience (Markov et al., 2006). This kind of project identifies the significance of creativity as a fundamental component of the problem-solving model to allow students to try out alternative approaches and solutions. Moreover, the worth of diverse opinions guarantees complete practice in problem-solving. Exposing oneself to different opinions allows one to comprehend problems and suggested solutions more profoundly, as shown in discussions of the historic and technological methods of sketching. The debate in the realm of manual technical drawing in the wake of computer-aided design supremacy says a lot about this, evoking information on skills accountable for proficiency and creativeness in various settings. Evidence indicates that students enjoy traditional methods because of the particular problem-solving skills they acquire, such as visualization and accuracy (McLaren et al., 2007). These findings suggest that the integration of multiple approaches, both conventional and contemporary, can enhance learning and prepare people more adequately for complex challenges, in confirmation of the n-dimensional nature of effective problem-solving (Figure 2.1).

Figure 2.1. *Fundamentals of problem solving.*

Source: https://www.oneeducation.org.uk/wp-content/uploads/2020/07/Creativity-and-Problem-Solving-Skills-1.jpg.

Definition of Problem Solving

In cognitive operations, problem solving is the process through which one acquires the ability to determine solutions to obstacles or challenges. The applicability of this definition is underscored by its applicability across all fields of life, from academia to business administration. The essence of problem-solving is that it is methodical in its usage, where the identification of the problem first, then the discovery of possible solutions, and lastly the implementation of the most probable one takes place. It is through such a methodical approach that not only is critical thinking fostered but that theoretical knowledge is applied to practical problems as well. Without the systematic process, individuals will resort to ad-hoc solutions that may yield second-best solutions, demonstrating the need for a good understanding of problem solving. In technical environments, problem solving may be associated with some structures and tools that guide towards resolution in complex situations. For example, under fields like artificial intelligence (AI), the scope of definition is enlarged to encompass the creation of algorithms that simulate and analyze solution planning. The article in Markov et al. (2006) illustrates how machine learning can act as a background story in attempting to understand basic principles in AI while linking theoretical to practical understanding perfectly. By transposing the problem-solving concepts into interactive environments, like in the case of the N-puzzle game, learners are exposed to an experiential learning experience that roots them in the principles of searching and thinking algorithmically. These approaches highlight the intrinsic connection between problem solving and applicability, revealing the larger picture of a solid problem-solving framework. Furthermore, problem-solving complexity often includes issues of fairness and effectiveness, particularly in structured systems like computer networks. The study of the resource allocation issues addressed in Low et al. (2006) illustrates well how problem-solving transcends solution-finding to encompass a richer sense of users' needs and QoS requirements. Along these lines, problem-solving must take into account different utility functions between users and therefore prioritize equitable resource allocation as well as optimal outcomes. The proposed distributed flow control algorithm shows the necessity for adaptive problem-solving mechanisms that accommodate different priorities in a system. This multi-dimensional approach to problem-solving reaffirms its central role in not only finding solutions, but also ensuring that they are equitable and consonant with the specific needs of the situation at hand.

Importance of Problem-Solving in All Areas

In talking about the significance of problem-solving in a number of disciplines, it is then possible to recognize its vital function in stimulating innovation and effectiveness. In the hospitality industry, for instance, the adaptation to shifting enrollment trends in academic courses demonstrates the relevance of critical thinking and solution-seeking strategies. With dwindling student enrollment, stakeholders must consider underlying causes and respond to mobilize student engagement. This can include revising curricula to incorporate skills that enhance technical and soft skills essential to leadership roles. Central to this is the understanding that problem solving is synonymous with more than mere rapid technical resolutions, requiring an in-depth examination of pedagogical practices to define pathways for student success and career development, directly influencing the future stability and success of the industry (Wong et al., 2015). Similarly, in the built environment, the areas of risk management and liability exemplify that good problem-solving is critical to professional practice. Legal studies, as peripheral to some traditional curricula, are now increasingly critical to equip future professionals with the capacity to handle difficult situations.

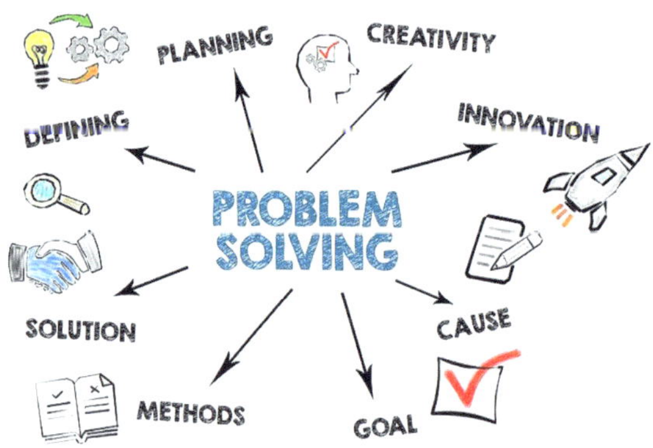

Figure 2.2. *Importance of problem solving in various fields.*

Source: https://www.workitdaily.com/media-library/problem-solving-concept-technique.jpg?id=32029977&width=1200&height=800&quality=85&coordinates=0%2C18%2C0%2C18.

Practical simulations with decision-making and risk topics allow for the convergence of law principles with real application and ensure that legal education becomes more relevant and practical. Such a strategy, apart from educating students to handle legal issues in their workplaces, instills in them a culture of anticipatory problem-solving where emerging professionals are able to anticipate and solve problems before they happen (Anderson et al., 2009). Finally, problem-solving is a value that transcends any single field; it creates a foundation for interdisciplinary collaboration and synergy. As the job market becomes increasingly dynamic, the ability to solve intricate problems is a prerequisite skill for professionals across industries. Organizations are increasingly valuing individuals who have the capability to combine knowledge and skills across various domains in order to innovate and problem-solve. Through instilling the culture of lifelong learning and growth, education schemes can impart the competency to navigate the complexities within their discipline. Focusing on enabling the development of problem-solving skills among students not only enhances employability but also fosters well-rounded next-generation leaders who can drive change in their area of expertise (Wong et al., 2015; Anderson et al., 2009) (Figure 2.2).

2.1. TYPES OF PROBLEMS

Understanding the various categories of problems is the foundation of effective problem-solving. Problems can be generally categorized as well-structured, ill-structured, and dynamic types. Well-structured problems are problems with defined objectives and boundaries, enabling solutions within terms defined by systematic methods. These types of problems mostly exist in technical fields such as engineering or mathematics, where established procedures can be applied. Conversely, ill-structured problems are not well-defined in terms of their solution path and may change significantly with context or stakeholder views. These types of problems tend to appear in social sciences or strategic planning, wherein multiple variables and human elements need to be addressed. Lastly, dynamic problems change over time, which may be unpredictable at times, necessitating ongoing evaluation and adaptation of strategies. It is such understanding that helps individuals in approaching problems appropriately, based on the specific nature of the problem at hand. One way in which these kinds of problems are utilized can be demonstrated through the understanding gained from classical hand technical drawing methods and its usability in contemporary education. As detailed in McLaren et al. (2007), traditional draftsmanship techniques have much to contribute to the encouragement of problem-solving, visualization, and precision, demonstrating the advantages of formalized problems. Students performing manual drafting not only acquire the technical skills but also acquire artistic and critical thinking skills. This discussion identifies that despite a computer age dominated by CAD technologies, the underlying principles of problem-solving continue to be based on hand-on techniques. These approaches encourage individual accuracy and discipline, leading to versatile skills that can be utilized across numerous fields beyond technical drawing. Secondly, the intersection of gaming and problem-solving demonstrates the potential of virtual worlds in solving ill-structured and dynamic problems. With computer games, it is possible to engage in action learning, as discussed in Gallagher et al. (2012), offering a safe environment in which to experiment with real-life issues. Players will replay realistic scenarios, which allow them to come up with solutions in a simulated setting. This kind of setup encourages collaboration and interaction, which are necessary for the resolution of problems without straightforward solutions. The ability to model realistic problems within a game enables players to test and observe different strategies and then see the outcomes without real-world implications. This new solution to learning and problem-solving has the potential to bridge education and business practice gaps, ultimately leading to the overall skillset needed to tackle today's complex issues (Figure 2.3).

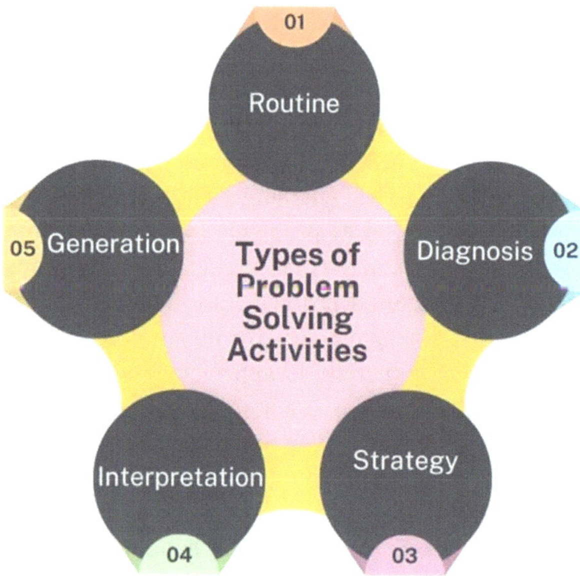

Figure 2.3. *Types of problems – solving.*

Source: https://b1879915.smushcdn.com/1879915/wp-content/uploads/2022/05/types-of-problem-solving-activities.jpg?lossy=2&strip=1&webp=1.

2.1.1. Well-Defined Problems

Definition of well-specified problems is the core in the field of problem-solving, particularly through providing a self-evident and structured framework that leads individuals to solving problems. Well-specified problems all share specific features, including well-specified goals, specifiable obstacles, and a limited number of solutions. All these aspects decrease considerably the cognitive burden on the problem solvers so that they can utilize systematic approaches rather than relying on intuitive approaches. As an illustration, mathematical problems will be designed in such a way so that there exists a consistent sequence from the problem to the solution through rational deduction. Badly defined problems, on the other hand, may lead to confusion and puzzlement and are harder to tackle without the right methodology or understanding of the task at hand. Application of well-defined problems extends to other artificial intelligence and to others like educational environments where organized learning and skill acquisition are crucial. Well-defined problems in artificial intelligence can be described by taking the N-puzzle game as an example of organized problem where a finite number of moves equals a specific solution. This game, in addition to involving students in deductive reasoning, also emphasizes the connection between problem-solving techniques and algorithmic steps, as noted in recent research into AI curricula (Markov et al., 2006). Such educational instruments serve to reinforce the argument of valuing well-structured problems, offering students a place where they can use concepts systematically acquired in order to achieve desired outcomes efficiently. Also, understanding gained through well-formulated problems can significantly improve problem-solving techniques in numerous disciplines. Research on extended second order cones, for example, has helped clarify approaches to solving advanced mathematical issues such as mixed complementarity problems and variational inequalities (Ferreira et al., 2018). Through establishing elaborate conditions and projection formulas, researchers assist in attaining deeper understanding of how to tackle such mathematical problems. The introduction of well-defined problems into advanced studies not only enables theoretical research but also enhances practical application, ultimately instituting a more robust system for overcoming simple and complex problems in diverse scholarly as well as working contexts.

2.1.2. Ill-Defined Problems

Ill-defined problems are a common occurrence in many fields, including engineering, management, and social sciences. Unlike well-defined problems, which possess exact parameters and solutions, ill-defined problems are characterized by ambiguity and uncertainty. This ambiguity tends to stem from partially missing or conflicting information, thereby complicating decision-making processes significantly. For instance, the software development lifecycle has several ill-defined phases in which goals can shift, hence making it difficult to establish a linear process from conception to deployment. As indicated in Johannes et al. (2025), even with improved methodologies in the last fifteen years, coping with the ill-defined aspect of software development is still vital in an attempt to mitigate the risks of cost overrun and project delay. Therefore, understanding the ill-defined character of problems is paramount to the evolution of innovative solutions and to the promotion of effective problem-solving projects. Solving ill-defined problems requires an efficient framework that allows for flexible thinking and flexibility. Problem solvers must use innovative methods that transcend traditional ways of solving problems, primarily through iterative processes and collaboration. This versatility is particularly critical in fields like software development, where problem-solving has to occur in the midst of evolving technologies and end-user needs. The artificial intelligence techniques discussed in Johannes et al. (2025) indicate just how vital it is that one is able to identify and address problems early in software development. Such planning ahead not only enhances the quality of the final product but also streamlines processes by addressing potential landmines before they explode. Therefore, an adaptive problem-solving culture enables people and teams to address ill-defined problems more creatively and with greater confidence. A further important tool in the solution of ill-defined problems is the application of systematic processes for the estimation and analysis of necessary variables. Ill-defined problems can actually be solved successfully, for example, in engineering by modeling and parameter estimation techniques, as demonstrated in research into Stereolithography (SLA) surface finishes. In, there is a systematic approach to obtaining optimal process parameters by least squares minimization and thereby converting an ill-posed problem into a well-posed one. This solution not only enhances the surface quality but also demonstrates the potential of engineering disciplines evolving systematic methodology that may guide problem-solving endeavors. Through the use of systematic strategies, specialists are able to decompose intricate issues into manageable pieces, which in turn enable them to develop innovative solutions that answer the poly-centric aspect of ill-defined problems.

2.1.3. Complex Problems

Challenging issues are complex in form, resulting from numerous variables that interact with each other and create difficulties in finding a suitable solution. Such issues are hard to solve because they contain uncertainty and variability in their nature. An example is an issue such as climate change, which has environmental, economic, and social components, and policymakers find it hard to devise complementary interventions. The multilateral character of such problems necessitates a robust analytical framework capable of withstanding various orientations and fields of expertise. Most notably, interdisciplinary approaches are becoming better appreciated as central to solving such complex challenges, considering that they draw upon various skill sets and pools of experience in order to create new solutions. Such interaction in solving problems can ensure a more sophisticated appreciation of underlying issues, ultimately translating into more viable long-term agendas for a solution. Most importantly, however, is the role of education in equipping individuals with the capacity to solve complex problems. Old pedagogy is rather focused on rote memorization and linear thinking, which might not be sufficient in the case of interrelated problems. In contrast, new pedagogical models encourage learning by doing, which encourages students to tackle real-life problems constructively. For instance, in a manual technical drawing study, it is illustrated how learning traditional skills can assist in enhancing problem-solving skills, visualization, and personal discipline (McLaren et al., 2007). Through the provision of hands-on exercises that stimulate critical thinking, schools are able to ensure people are adequately prepared to handle the complexity and interdependence of problems. Lastly, the creation of flexible problem solvers within learning environments is essential for responding to the requirements of our rapidly changing world. Furthermore, utilization of technology for problem-solving capability significantly enhances the resolution of complex problems. Advanced analysis software and artificial intelligence are capable of navigating massive data sets to pull out patterns and linkages that may not be visible to the naked human eye. Consider, for example, the experiments involving games like the N-puzzle to learn basic AI principles through practical experience. Besides providing an understanding of the basics of machine learning and AI, they demonstrate the ways in which problem-solving strategies are employed to simplify complex situations (Markov et al., 2006). As the student works with these technologies, they learn a toolkit of methods and techniques that can be used in a variety of settings. This adaptability is helpful in managing the uncertainty of complicated problems, so that future generations can better confront such challenges (Figure 2.4).

Figure 2.4. *Complex problems.*

Source: https://prolearn.mit.edu/sites/default/files/images/MITPE-SolvingComplexProblems-website-banner-1600x800.jpg.

2.2. PROBLEM-SOLVING PROCESS

Problem-solving is an orderly process through which people and organizations attempt to surpass problems and arrive at workable solutions. It begins with the identification of the problem, an action that decides the remainder of the solution course. Problems are usually ill-defined or messy and require the work involved in breaking down underlying causes. For instance, instructors might use Problem-Based Learning (PBL) techniques, engaging the learners in real-life problem-solving scenarios, which enhances critical thinking and collaboration. In these cases, students not only learn how to identify problems but also develop action plans that can lead to tangible solutions. This active learning approach focuses on the identification of problems as a bridge to the construction of meaning in interventions, which serves as a building block for future analytical thinking and innovative brainstorming in resolving the problem (Albert et al., 2023). Following the identification step is the effort to search for possible solutions, which requires analytical thinking and creativity. This stage is usually marked by brainstorming sessions where solutions are proposed and tried out for their practicability and efficacy. For situations such as the creation of Early Warning Systems (EWS) to predict financial crises, for instance, experts have to browse through many potential indicators in order to construct quality models that can provide useful information. Such systems benefit from a multinomial logit model approach, allowing for having an advanced understanding of different economic situations beyond dichotomous decisions. Keeping in mind numerous potential outcomes and thoroughly examining relevant information, problem solvers manage to get more precise solutions and eliminate risks associated with sudden crises in order to optimize the robustness of their solutions (Fratzscher et al., 2025). Lastly, the implementation of chosen solutions marks the end of the problem-solving process. This step is inherently connected to successful coordination and communication, since the solutions must be implemented in such a way that the stakeholders are taken aboard. Additionally, real-time feedback and adjustment measures need to be in place to track results and make adjustments so that the solutions are brought in line with the desired ends. Where interventions are applied, such as in educational interventions with PBL, ongoing feedback loops must be employed to adjust and refine the learning process. Lastly, good problem-solving is not just about coming to a solution but also continued improvement and adaptability so that individuals and organizations may prosper in spite of adversity. The recursive nature of the process emphasizes the need to view problem-solving as a reflective and dynamic practice, not as a linear one, which sets the stage for future learning and development (Figure 2.5).

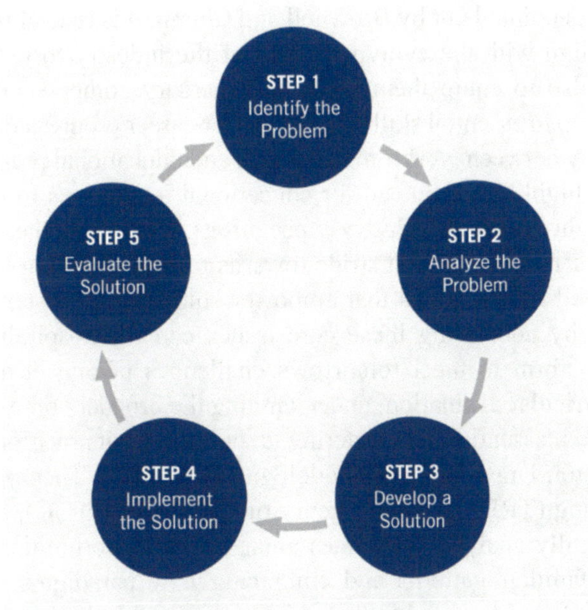

Figure 2.5. *Problem-solving process.*

Source: https://broadcast.lds.org/elearning/development/psd/DI/deseret-industries-6/development/img/inline/PD60002541_Problem_Solving.png.

2.2.1. Identifying the Problem

Effective problem identification is a crucial first step in the problem-solving process, particularly in complex fields such as hospitality management. As enrollment in hospitality educational programs declines, stakeholders must delve into the underlying causes of this trend. Various factors contribute to the diminishing interest in formal education; notably, potential students often perceive that a degree is unnecessary for entry-level positions. This perception, coupled with the rise of self-directed learning through technology, suggests that many individuals are opting to bypass traditional pathways in favor of immediate employment opportunities. However, such decisions often lead to long-term consequences, as these individuals may find themselves lacking the requisite skills for advancement within their careers. Therefore, recognizing these dynamics is essential in addressing the foundational issues behind declining enrollment and ensuring the effective development of future leaders in the hospitality sector (Wong et al., 2015). Understanding the problem requires a thorough analysis of both the internal and external factors affecting educational frameworks. As pointed out by Brownell and Chung, it is crucial for hospitality curricula to align with the evolving needs of the industry to not only attract students but also to equip them with the necessary competencies for future success. The gap in essential skill sets can hinder career progression, illustrating a clear disparity between workforce demands and educational preparation. This misalignment highlights the need for educational institutions to reassess their programs in light of current industry expectations. Identifying these educational shortcomings serves as the first stride towards reform, enabling institutions to develop targeted interventions that empower students and foster professional growth. Only by addressing these core issues can the hospitality education landscape transform to meet tomorrows challenges (Wong et al., 2015). In addition to curricular evaluation, understanding the broader context of problem identification is essential for fostering a culture of innovation within the hospitality sector. Drawing on methodologies such as the Theory of Inventive Problem Solving (TRIZ) and the Theory of Constraints (TOC), organizations can systematically analyze challenges and identify opportunities for growth. By breaking familiar patterns and embracing new paradigms, stakeholders can uncover actionable insights that drive meaningful change. For instance, understanding the disconnect between educational initiatives and industry demands presents a unique opportunity to innovate curricula that emphasize practical, competency-based learning. This approach not only prepares students for immediate entry into the workforce but also cultivates their leadership capabilities, ultimately contributing to the industrys long-term resilience. Thus, a comprehensive understanding of the problem landscape is paramount to devising effective solutions that lead to sustained progress (Figure 2.6).

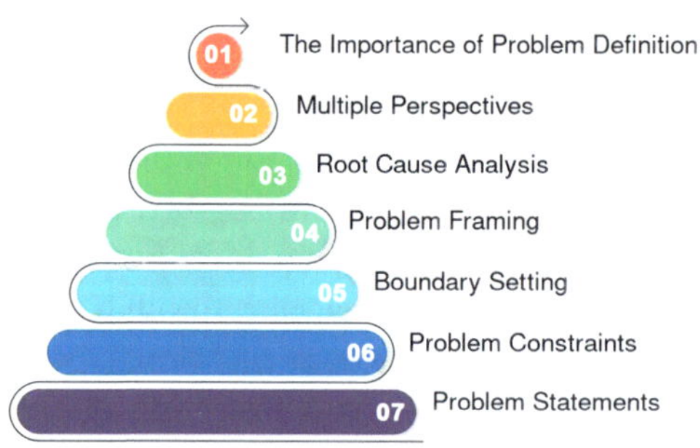

Figure 2.6. *Identifying the problem.*

Source: https://fastercapital.co/i/Problem-solving-and-Innovation--How-to-Solve-Complex-and-Wicked-Problems-with-Innovation--Identifying-and-Defining-the-Problem.webp.

2.2.2. Generating Potential Solutions

Generating potential solutions is a critical aspect of problem-solving that requires creativity and analytical mind. It typically involves brainstorming and collaboration that fosters innovation among the team members. Creating a safe culture where individuals feel comfortable sharing ideas without fear of rejection is one way of accomplishing it.

Techniques such as mind mapping or the nominal group technique may facilitate such an environment, allowing participants to debate freely several alternative avenues before assessing the viability of each. Using virtual worlds, such as are available in online gaming forums, problem-solvers can experiment with new methods under minimal-stakes environments. As indicated in the application of action learning through gaming, this activity does not only offer a platform for attempting new solutions but also provides an arena where individuals can reflect on their experience in groups and gain insights that they may use to resolve actual problems (Gallagher et al., 2012). When developing solutions, it is critical to consider the evolving nature of the problem because problems tend to evolve over time. Hence, adaptive means are essential to cope with changing situations. One of the new approaches is employing Digital Ecosystems which mimic the self-organization properties of biological networks. These ecosystems facilitate the continuous migration of knowledge and resources so that solutions do not remain stagnant. Employing this methodology, agents in a decentralized network work in concert with each other to find and refine solutions that are beneficial to global aspirations as well as local constraints. This two-stage optimization process is an example of how advanced computational approaches can aid problem-solving tasks by drawing on collective knowledge and robustness and generating more robust solutions (Briscoe et al., 2011).

In addition, the evaluation of solutions at hand should be as rigorous as their design. Once alternatives have been established, it is necessary to prioritize them and evaluate them against defined criteria such as feasibility, impact, and resources availability. Engaging stakeholders in this process of assessment can bring several views and create a sense of ownership in the final decision. This aligns with action inquiry approach, whereby reflection is itself an integral part of the learning cycle. Through firmly weighing the pros and cons of each potential solution and facilitating participative debate, teams can manage complexity and uncertainty effectively. The circular method of this analysis provides in-depth information, leading to highly educated conclusions that address the core issues behind the root problems and promote innovative thinking essential to problem-solving basics (Gallagher et al., 2012) (Figure 2.7).

Figure 2.7. *Generating potential solutions.*

Source: https://fastercapital.co/i/Problem-solving--How-to-Solve-Problems-and-Overcome-Obstacles--Generating-Possible-Solutions.webp.

2.2.3. Evaluating and Selecting Solutions

The evaluation and choice process of solutions in the context of problem-solving are essential to ensuring that the adopted action significantly addresses the identified problem. This is the phase that follows generating a myriad of possible solutions, which requires a structured evaluation against criteria predetermined beforehand. Evaluation criteria may include feasibility, cost, probable impact, and whether they support long-term goals.

Besides, engaging stakeholders in this exercise can potentially enhance the validity of the assessment by introducing varied views into the equation, which might offer insights that a single view would not have access to. Therefore, this process can lead to an equitable process of decision-making that not only considers the technical benefits of a solution but also emotional and social aspects of the implications involved in its implementation. To facilitate them in making a good decision, problem solvers generally use various decision-making tools and techniques to make the evaluation process easy. Cost-benefit analysis, decision matrices, and SWOT analysis help an individual systematically weigh the strengths and weaknesses of alternatives.

For instance, making use of a decision matrix allows for comparison of a number of options against various criteria, thus providing a visual representation that can simplify the most viable directions. These tools are best utilized when combined with clearly outlined project objectives and stakeholders' requirements since they ground the decision-making process in quantifiable information and not subjective opinions. Therefore, the application of such methods forms an objective procedure for bargaining solution difficulties, having ended up with more robust outcomes. Additionally, the implementation of selected solutions needs to consist of an official appraisal cycle to assess how efficiently they perform in resolving the issue. The feedback loop is a part of the whole problem-solving process, allowing for improvement and enhancement based on actual performance. In order to offer effective evaluation, there must be quantifiable goals that align with the original goals. Performance metrics and outcome assessments can provide tangible numbers, which can enable decision-makers to identify whether the solution is meeting its intended goals. Following this, the kind of systems like the Intelligent Tutoring System Builder (ITSB) allow for assessment via embedded performance analyses, which can aid teachers and developers in informing their approaches through learner outcomes and engagement metrics (Naser et al., 2016). This continuous assessment refines problem-solving, with solutions adapting as conditions shift and new problems emerge.

2.3. CRITICAL THINKING IN PROBLEM SOLVING

Critical thinking is the basis of effective problem solving, enabling a person to analyze complex problems and arrive at fully informed conclusions. Critical thinking is implemented through a series of intellectual processes that include evaluating information, identifying biases, and checking out alternative perspectives. Such a framework of analysis is greatly required in areas where rapid decision making is critical, for example, in engineering or business disciplines.

For instance, when faced with technical problems, those with good critical thinking are able to deconstruct the issue into segments, thus making it simpler to take a more structured approach towards solution derivation. Through the application of critical thinking, problem solvers not only get to decide on possible solutions but also anticipate possible flaws, thus coming up with a more comprehensive and well-thought-out solution to the issues at hand. The value of this skill is recognized throughout professional fields, where the ability to critically assess information is linked to the key to effective results and effective decision making. In schools, the establishment of critical thinking skills is increasingly becoming accepted as key to creating able problem-solving skills in students.

Traditional teaching methods of rote memorization often prove ineffective in preparing students for real-world problems beyond the classroom, where creativity is demanded by generating innovative solutions. Empirical research has proved that problem-based learning experiences can sharpen the critical thinking abilities of students, allowing them to address problems creatively as well as systematically. Furthermore, as research in technical drawing teaching indicates, the value of practical learning exercises extends beyond that of being just technically competent to encompass essential competencies such as visualization and coordination that are essential to problem-solving (McLaren et al., 2007). Effective for this reason, there is the need for teachers to prioritize adding critical thinking exercises to the curriculum to prepare students to deal with the complexity of modern-day professional settings. Furthermore, the downward trend in hospitality education program enrollments signals an immediate requirement for curriculum that not only imparts technical skills but also develops critical thinking. This trend of moving employees directly into the workforce without graduating suggests a lack of skills, particularly leadership and problem-solving skill (Wong et al., 2015). This fact suggests the necessity of competency-based learning that emphasizes theoretical knowledge as much as practical skills. Through a focus on developing such skills, students stand a better chance of overcoming challenges and achieving dominance in their fields. Through scenario-based testing that provokes the mind, students can be prepared to address real-world problems effectively. Reforming schooling practices along the lines of the demands of the workforce is therefore crucial in creating future leaders capable of addressing the complexities in their areas (Figure 2.8).

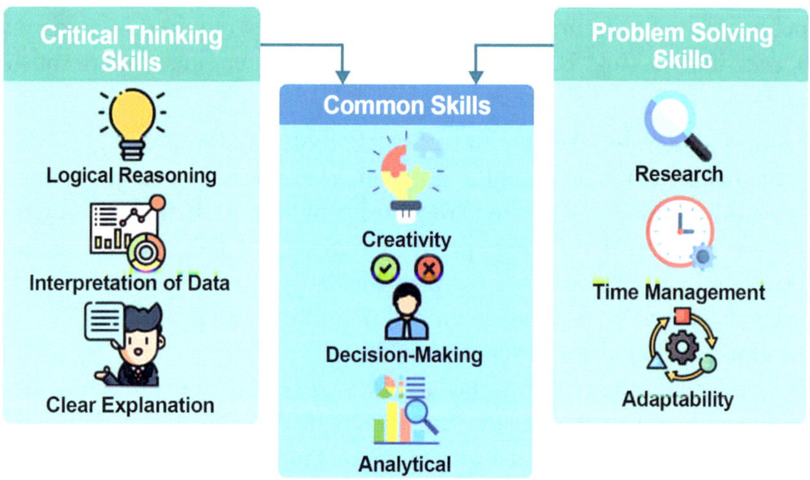

Figure 2.8. *Critical thinking in problem solving.*

Source: https://cdn.educba.com/academy/wp-content/uploads/2023/07/Critical-Thinking-and-Problem-Solving-Skills.jpg.

2.3.1. Definition of Critical Thinking

Critical thinking is usually defined as the cognitive process of analyzing, evaluating, and combining information to make rational decisions. Critical thinking comprises a range of skills, such as the ability to recognize prejudice, weigh evidence, and make logical conclusions. Problem-solving, critical thinking cannot be evaded because it enables individuals to resolve complex problems with a systematic organization. This systematic approach is very prevalent within project management, where having the ability to differentiate and balance technical competences against behavioural competences will make or break the success of a project. As recognised by Kanabar et al. (2018), present models of education now prioritize the acquisition of these competences in order to prepare students to address practical challenges effectively. Hence, critical thinking is a critical trait that not only enhances education quality but also professional skill in different environments. The development of skills in critical thinking generates creativity and innovative solutions to issues. In environments where innovation is essential, that is, technology and manufacturing, liberation from typical mental models is important. It is here best illustrated through methodologies like Total Quality Management (TQM) and Just-In-Time (JIT), which break paradigms and encourage new thinking on complex matters. As is noted in Mann et al. (2003), significant innovations are most likely to occur when individuals apply their critical thinking abilities towards resolving trade-off paradoxes in systems. Through critical inspection of current practice and probing assumptions, individuals can identify areas for improvement and rethink strategies with the potential to yield revolutionary results. Becoming critical thinkers, therefore, is not merely a pursuit of intellect but a fundamental element driving the construction of procedures for achieving innovative solutions in multifaceted circumstances. Further, integrating critical thinking into problem-solving procedures can potentially enhance collaborative working and team working. When people employ critical discourse, they tend to critique diverse opinions and merge differing points of view into their critiques. This becomes crucial in the context of group decision-making, as collective wisdom can make solutions stronger. By creating a culture where critical thinking prevails, organizations are able to overcome the challenges of group dynamics and enhance results in problem-solving exercises. The emphasis on behavioral competence in project management, as described in Kanabar et al. (2018), supports the idea, demonstrating how soft skills are employed to bridge gaps between technical know-how and social impact. In conclusion, critical thinking is a central component of effective problem-solving, allowing individuals and groups to effectively approach and resolve issues in constantly evolving contexts.

2.3.2. The Role of Critical Thinking in the Analysis of Problems

Critical thinking is an essential component in the process of problem analysis, enabling one to analyze issues using logic and clarity. In problem solving, critical thinking enables one to scrutinize information critically, differentiate between germane and non-germane information, and balance several perspectives. Being methodical in this way enhances one's capacity to solve problems methodically rather than employing shallow or intuitive responses. By using such evaluation methods, people are able to gain deeper insights into the complexities of the issues that they encounter, hence making decision-making processes more informed. Therefore, the use of critical thinking becomes imperative in learning institutions where learners are faced with complex challenges whose resolution demands serious analysis and reflective consideration before coming up with conclusions. The significance of critical thinking is also emphasized in engineering education, as students are generally short of required competences to carry out successful problem analysis.

Figure 2.9. *Role of critical thinking in analyzing problems.*

Source: https://thumbs.dreamstime.com/b/critical-thinking-components-diagram-outline-symbols-vector-illustration-reasoning-evaluating-positive-negative-problem-172885244.jpg.

According to recent studies, several critical capabilities—questioning, qualitatively modeling, and communicating—are most frequently absent from their capability set, which has been described as the missing basics (Goldberg et al., 2009). Through the establishment of a solid foundation in critical thinking, educators can help students become familiar with applying such skills to academic work, as well as helping them examine and deal effectively with real-world problems. In this manner, the encouragement of critical thinking not only helps the student develop analysis skills but also develops an appreciation of the complexity that characterizes most problems, essentially setting students up to solve problems in the real world. Furthermore, the integration of advanced educational technology has also been shown to promote critical thinking and problem-solving skills effectively. Systems like the Andes Intelligent Tutoring System and Microcomputer-Based Laboratory Tools provide students with interactive learning spaces that enable experimentation and conceptual change in physics instruction (Arons et al., 2007). Such platforms allow students to learn to think critically through hands-on means by actively solving problems, developing their ideas, and receiving real-time feedback. As students navigate these virtual worlds, they learn to apply critical thinking in the moment, which makes them adept at noticing, understanding, and resolving problems. This fusion of technology and critical thinking emphasizes the need to implement alternative pedagogical approaches in order to equip individuals with what they need to handle the increasingly complex problems they will encounter in their careers (Figure 2.9).

2.3.3. Techniques to Enhance Critical Thinking Skills

Enhancing critical thinking skill plays a fundamental role in effective problem-solving, and one of the influential approaches involves the integration of cross-disciplinary approaches in education. As highlighted in contemporary studies, utilizing a mix of different methodologies such as arts and information technologies in the teaching of science can significantly enhance creative and critical thinking. This multi-disciplinary approach not only enriches the learning process but also aligns with the Responsible Research and Innovation (RRI) agenda that is concerned with socially embedded knowledge and capabilities for generations to come. Students being involved in various disciplines compel them to think more broadly about things, allowing them to gain a comprehensive understanding of complex issues. Therefore, emphasizing interdisciplinary studies within academic curricula can create a culture where critical thinking thrives, ultimately leading to enhanced problem-solving skills among students (Torruella et al., 2020). Experiential learning experiences also signify a potent way for developing critical thinking skills. Participatory experience of real activity—such as that of gaming—could provide a unique domain for students to encounter problem-solving scenarios in controlled and reflective environments. Teachers might be able to harness the power of virtual worlds to recreate challenging dilemmas that can be simulated so that individuals can experiment with various strategies and outcomes employing constructs such as Revans learning equation. This mode of learning allows for contemplation of failure and success in a safe place, allowing for critical thinking and analysis. The learning from this experience can be translated to enhanced decision-making ability when confronted with actual problems, and thereby strengthening the pedagogical foundation necessary for maximum problem-solving (Gallagher et al., 2012). Secondly, it is important to promote the culture of questioning and inquiry in the learning environment in order to acquire critical thinking. By encouraging students to question, critically evaluate assumptions, and look for alternative perspectives, they become proficient at scrutinizing information and harmonizing conflicting opinions. This habit not only enables the students to critically analyze the information given to them but also prepares them for success in solving tough issues both within and outside of a learning environment. Teachers can facilitate this environment by fostering free discussion and promoting collaborative discussions, wherein the students are not held back to present their thoughts and opinions. Finally, growing an inquiring mentality assists in the development of critical thinking individuals who are well placed to handle challenges and devise innovative solutions to problems they encounter (Torruella et al., 2020).

2.4. PROBLEM SOLVING TOOLS AND TECHNIQUES

Effective problem solving in any field involves a toolkit of techniques and a repertoire of approaches to expand the ability of a solver to handle complexity. Central to this is an understanding that problem solving is a systematic process that adopts multiple methodologies to suit a variety of challenges. Classical techniques like brainstorming and decision matrices enable the generation of multi-faceted solutions and then screen them based on given standards. Equally, sophisticated techniques such as root cause analysis also lead to greater understanding of the root causes, thus more accurate solutions. The true power comes in integrating these practices so that there is a more comprehensive approach that considers that different aspects of a problem may be interrelated. By creating a multi-perspective view of problems, solvers can develop innovative solutions that may not always be apparent using one approach. One of the most important components of problem-solving today is computational thinking (CT), which frames problems within computer science principles. CT emphasizes breaking down hard problems into smaller and simpler components systemically, making solution pathways clearer. This is an approach that best suits the iterative process of programming, where grasping the nature of the data is crucial. Yet there is a critical challenge in successfully teaching CT, as expressed in recent works. The inclining disposition to focus on prescriptive methods rather than on creative problem-solving processes constrains the ability of students to exercise their analytical skills to the fullest extent. Thus, there ought to be a pedagogical shift toward incorporating CT along with traditional problem-solving frameworks to enhance learners capacity to effectively solve problems in various situations (Michaelson et al., 2015). Additionally, the application of specific algorithms and heuristics in problem-solving contexts symbolizes the flexibility of tools in the modern era. For instance, when producing plans for flexible manufacturing systems, the operations' nature leads to hierarchical subproblems that are tractable to solve with mathematical models like mixed-integer programming. Operations like Lagrangian relaxation and tabu search show some of the advanced techniques operational managers can employ to allocate resources efficiently and optimize maximization. By entering into these future-generation approaches, problem solvers do not just maximize operational outcomes but also maximize their analytical thinking skills. This proves that embracing a wide toolset, ranging from simple methods to current computational techniques, is critical in developing well-rounded problem solvers in a fast-evolving world (Chen et al., 1996) (Figure 2.10).

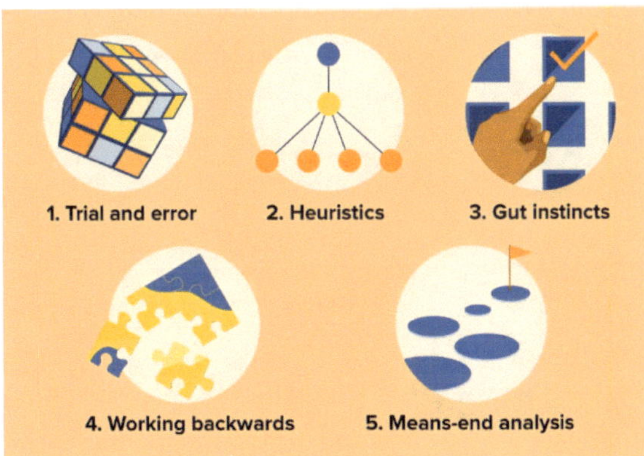

Figure 2.10. *Tools and techniques for problem solving.*

Source: https://post.psychcentral.com/wp-content/uploads/sites/4/2022/11/418979-5-effective-problem-solving-strategies-body-1296x1169-1-1024x924.jpg.

2.4.1. Brainstorming

Applying brainstorming as a problem-solving technique significantly enhances creativity and generates numerous ideas. Brainstorming as a group activity allows members to verbalize their ideas without immediate feedback, generating an environment in which unorthodox ideas have room to develop. By encouraging freewheeling exchange of ideas, brainstorming demultiples cognitive barriers and generates an environment conducive to creative thinking. Past research highlights that effective brainstorming has the ability to generate new ideas that might not be created through individual contemplation. The concentration on the number and not the quality in such sessions makes possible diverse input, which becomes the ground for probing complex problems. Therefore, brainstorming is a worthy element in the grand strategy of problem-solving because it allows teams to harness the collective wisdom of their members to find successful solutions. Brainstorming quality is nevertheless improved when paired with traditional methodologies like the Six Sigma approach. For instance, integrating the Define, Measure, Analyze, Improve, Control (DMAIC) approach into brainstorming can enable the problem-solving process to be optimized by solving each step of a problem systematically.

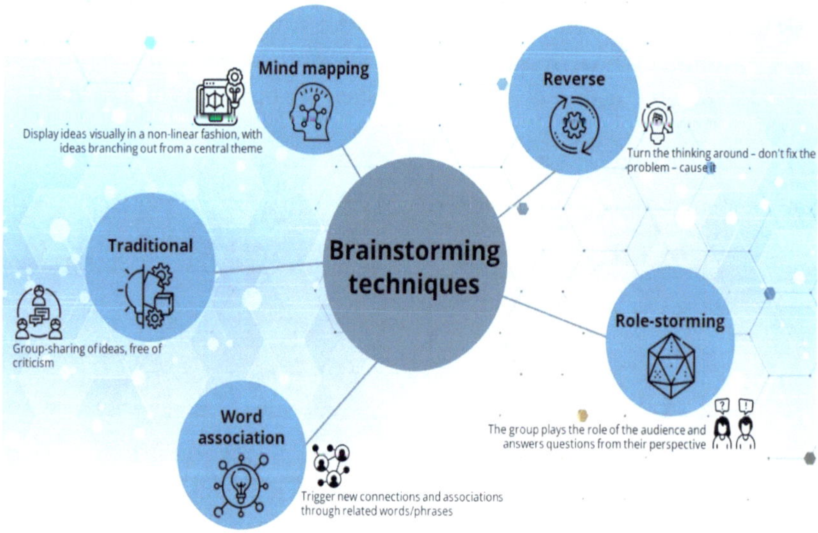

Figure 2.11. *Brainstorming as a problem-solving technique.*

Source: https://examples-of.net/wp-content/uploads/examples-of-brainstorming-techniques-for-innovation.jpg.

By defining key parameters and applying brainstorming to devise solutions, groups can focus their creative capabilities on a specific aspect of a problem, optimizing the impact of their ideation. Six Sigma literature depicts how this structured method can result in tangible outcomes, such as the eradication of casting defects using targeted brainstorming sessions informed by data analysis and empirical research (Antony et al., 2007). This synergy indicates that even though brainstorming generates ideas, it is by means of formal decision-making mechanisms that such ideas are translated into workable solutions. Nevertheless, success with brainstorming does not entirely depend on the methodology employed; it is equally reliant on the dynamics and composition of the group going through the process. Multicultural groups composed of members from varied backgrounds and expertise will come up with more innovative ideas due to the numerous perspectives. Moderation of brainstorming sessions also matters; an effective moderator will ensure everyone is heard and avoid loudmouths overriding quieter members. Research supported by European Regional Development Fund grants emphasizes the contribution of organized and inclusive brainstorming sessions towards significant problem-solving and creativity advances (Briscoe et al., 2016). Lastly, the interaction among participatory diversity, effective facilitation, and systematic methods results in an effective brainstorming process, ultimately determining problem-solving strategy effectiveness across various settings (Figure 2.11).

2.4.2. Root Cause Analysis

Root cause analysis (RCA) is a fundamental component in effective problem-solving techniques for various fields. It focuses on the identification of the root causes of a problem rather than merely its symptoms. Based on a systematic analysis of the causes of a problem, RCA discovers the root cause of a problem and thereby enables organizations to implement long-term solutions. Organizations tend to apply tools such as Five Whys or fishbone diagrams to facilitate this process of questioning. Due to the rigid examination of causes, RCA not only minimizes the likelihood of recurrence but also enhances operational efficiency and quality. By doing so in a preventive way, ultimately, a framework is developed that fosters continuous improvement and innovation. By prioritizing root cause identification, firms can establish a culture that promotes careful analysis and strategic planning essential to long-term achievement. Utilizing root cause analysis within organizational designs has tremendous dividends when combined with methods such as Six Sigma. This method enables teams to manage complex challenges while minimizing variance and enhancing quality. In a rare case, Six Sigma's use brought a remarkable increase in the manufacturing process of motor vehicle products with the first-pass yield increasing from 85% to 99.4% after applying RCA methods along with careful data analysis methodologies like regression analysis and hypothesis testing. This effectiveness stems from the fact that RCA is able to pinpoint exact inefficiencies so that teams can be able to successfully correct these inaccuracies. Consequently, the organizations utilizing RCA not only enhance their operational process but also gain substantial economic benefits, as evident in the application of Six Sigma technique that has generated a saving of approximately US$70,000 annually. This also emphasizes the key role played by RCA in decision-making. Moreover, the success stories resulting from root cause analysis demonstrate its application in various industries, hence further solidifying its significance as a problem-solving technique. For instance, in engineering, the development of special algorithms that are particularly applied to solve non-linear equations demonstrates how eliminating root causes can initiate revolutionary advancements. Researchers have come up with new convergence control algorithms to enhance the accuracy of numerical solutions to complex engineering challenges. These breakthroughs not only streamline processes but also minimize user intervention in traditional methods. Through rigorously testing these algorithms and demonstrating their practicability, companies value the outright necessity of investigating causes in product design and function. Through these examples, RCA becomes paramount to supporting innovation and increasing the resilience of solution methods in engineering and manufacturing, thus contributing to organisational goals (Figure 2.12).

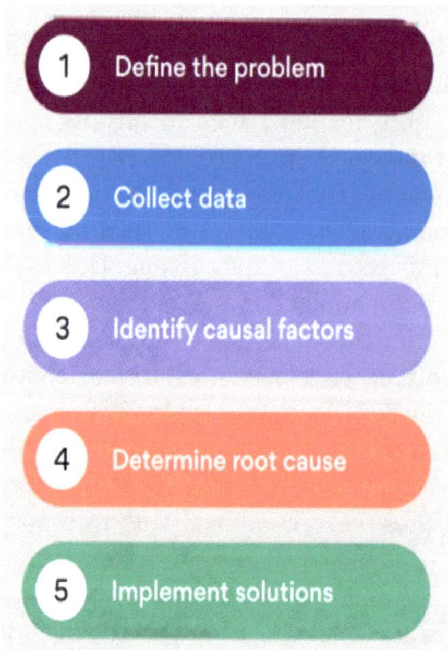

Figure 2.12. *Root cause analysis (RCA) serves.*

Source: https://assets.asana.biz/m/4966b31de0edb46d/original/inline-project-planning-root-cause-analysis-1-2x.jpg.

2.4.3. Decision-Making Matrices

Decision-making matrices are an effective tool in problem solving, providing a systematic approach to comparing multiple alternatives to a set of predetermined criteria. By quantitative and visual structuring of information, these matrices provide intensive scrutiny that can uncover the most plausible solutions. In complex circumstances where variables and consequences get intertwined, decision-making matrices allow individuals and organizations to analyze objectively the merits of each alternative. Such a process not only clarifies the meaning of each decision but also enhances transparency in decision-making, which lessens instances of bias.

Ultimately, such a structured process is closely in line with the bigger picture of effective problem-solving, where clear options result in informed decisions and calculated actions. In addition, utilizing decision-making matrices has been found to transcend even simple evaluations.

These can be used in various contexts, from individual choices to intricate business strategies with large teams and resources. An example is how the use of matrices in shared environments will help attain contributions from numerous various stakeholders, creating mutual consideration of potential solutions. Not only does this collaboration enrich the outcomes, but it also yields greater degrees of buy-in among team members, thereby making them accountable for the final decisions made. Coordinating shared goals through the collaborative matrices approach establishes a shared direction, essential in ensuring solutions are not only feasible, but more importantly, widely acceptable within the firm. Universality, combined with systematic analysis, highlights the efficacy of decision-making matrices in different contexts. Ultimately, introducing technology innovations to decision-making matrices makes them even more useful.

As worlds become more complicated—that is, an increasing number of wirelessly interconnected devices in network cooperation (Poorter et al., 2013)—effective and responsive structures are crucial. Automated systems in such cases can use matrices in real-time to support decision-making with the help of algorithms that execute pre-defined analytical strategies.

Additionally, the complexity of high-dimensional signal processing demonstrated in source separation issues (Asaei et al., 2013) stresses the importance of employing matrices in managing and simplifying daunting data sets. The future of decision-making matrices lies in the incorporation of sophisticated algorithms that will further refine decisions with an eye towards leading organizations to innovative problem-solving mechanisms.

2.5. BARRIERS TO EFFECTIVE PROBLEM SOLVING

In problem-solving, there are a number of barriers to effective resolution that can derail the process toward less-than-ideal solutions. The first and foremost stumbling block tends to be a lack of defining the problem itself. If the initial problem is not clearly articulated, then the more difficult it is to develop successful strategies toward its solution. This ambiguity may stem from opposing team member interpretations or insufficient data to determine the underlying variables involved. For instance, in the context of solving computational problems within parallel architectures, computer programmers may find it difficult to identify with clear precision the very nature of performance bottlenecks and thereby end up hindering the discovery of effective algorithms geared towards appropriate problems, as the theoretical partitioning framework for sparse triangular systems of equations (Saltz et al., 2025) illustrates. This demonstrates how a vague problem definition can propagate into even more extensive problems during the process of solving problems. Another major roadblock to effective problem solving is cognitive bias that contaminates judgment. Cognitive biases, such as confirmation bias or anchoring, have the potential to make individuals or groups favor evidence consistent with preconceptions and discount contradictory evidence.

This mental shortcut has the potential to significantly impede creative thinking and suppress open dialogue, critical components of effective problem solving. For instance, in process analysis of manufacturing, biases result in groups failing to objectively weigh facts relevant to defects or inefficiencies. Application of the Six Sigma approach helps demonstrate the virtue of having a systematic procedure that minimizes such biases through encouraging data-driven action with its DMAIC structure, which systematically identifies and addresses production process shortcomings (Antony et al., 2007). By recognizing and avoiding cognitive biases, teams can enhance their problem-solving capabilities.

Organizational culture, too, can be an enabler and a detractor from good problem-solving. A risk-taking, innovative, and open communication culture tends to result in creative solutions to tough problems. Hierarchical or fear-generating culture, by contrast, can discourage initiative and deter team members from offering ideas or issues. In high-performance contexts, such as those involving complex computational problems, collaborative settings that reward failure and experimentation as a learning process are more likely to yield more consolidated solutions. The paradox between the fineness of computational work, as treated in the case of parallel architectures, highlights the necessity for a tolerant culture that ultimately liberates workers to try several solutions without retribution (Saltz et al., 2025). Thus, adaptive organizational culture building is fundamental in dissipating barriers to problem-solving effectiveness.

2.5.1. Cognitive Biases

The effects of cognitive biases on problem-solving activities are extensive as the natural biases shape the decisions that people make and the alternatives they will evaluate. Cognitive biases are systematic tendencies to deviate from norm or rationality in judgment, leading to irrational interpretation and decision-making. Confirmation bias, for example, makes individuals like information that confirms their already existing beliefs and disregard opposing evidence.

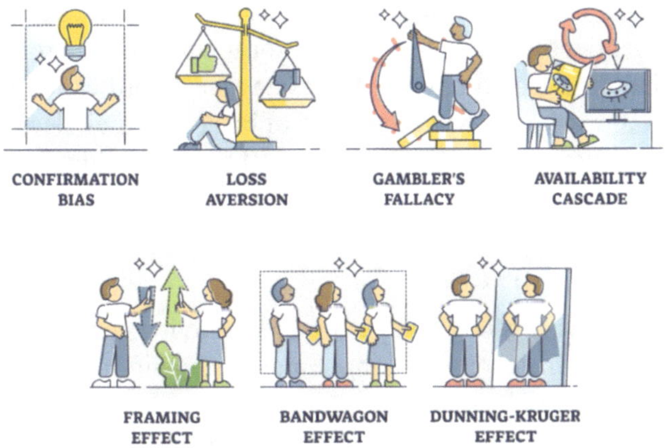

Figure 2.13. *Cognitive biases on problem-solving processes.*

Source: https://www.simplypsychology.org/wp-content/uploads/heuristics-cognitive-bias.jpg.

This can severely impede the decision-making process because individuals may overlook viable solutions or fail to thoroughly evaluate the issues. Awareness of cognitive biases is essential to effective problem-solving because it enables an individual to understand the limits of their cognitive processes and encourages them to engage more critically when evaluating the information and options. Cognitive biases and bounded rationality theory make the problem-solving environment more challenging as well. Bounded rationality theorizes that individuals' intellectual limitations confine their ability to process information, and thus they rely on simplifications that may not necessarily reflect reality. Since organizations have to address complex decision-making problems, the integration of more robust conceptions of bounded rationality is crucial. Incorporating knowledge from cognitive psychology, such as the identification of many of the cognitive biases, can assist with organizational effectiveness by allowing leaders to come up with strategies that mitigate such biases. Through the realization of how bounded rationality and cognitive bias interact, organizations and individuals can design better rules for overcoming challenges across numerous problem-solving scenarios (Nicolai, 2025). In addition, cognitive biases have implications that are long term and cross-decision-making by individuals and find expression in organizational actions. In group settings, bias leads to groupthink, in which consensus takes precedence over good thinking. This impact stifles experimentation and creativity with alternative solutions, ultimately weakening the overall problem-solving capacity. Organizations must develop a culture that encourages diverse opinion and constructive dissent to counterbalance the effects of cognitive biases. Awareness and mitigation training interventions can help groups form improved problem-solving routines. By building a culture that emphasizes the identification of cognitive biases, organizations would then be capable of bolstering their decision-making processes, with more positive outcomes and more healthy organizational dynamics (Dosi et al., 1996) (Figure 2.13).

2.5.2. Emotional Barriers

Emotional challenges severely hamper problem-solving success by impacting people's perceptions and choice-making. Emotions manifest themselves as fear, apprehension, and skepticism, and in most instances, lead to evasive behavior that hinders advancement. In situations of adversity, emotions are clouded thinking so that people are rendered incapable of looking at challenges objectively. Furthermore, the presence of unfavorable emotions chokes innovation, limiting the expression of novel solutions. As highlighted in the models of education, breaking such emotional barriers is critical as those learners with high anxiety or low self-efficacy are less engaged to be meaningfully involved in the learning process, which leads to their underachievement in academics and disengagement from the learning process (Adelman et al., 2018). Thus, emotional barriers need to be identified and dealt with for creating an appropriate environment to promote problem-solving. At the educational level, the impacts of emotional barriers extend beyond personal attainment to affect systemic problems on a broader scale. Schools that fail to provide students' emotional needs are likely to experience mounting achievement disparities, since those experiencing psychological distress can fail to participate vigorously in class activities or benefit from instructional methods. Research indicates that lack of emotional support would lead to chronic disengagement and increased dropout rates, particularly among marginalized student populations (Adelman et al., 2018). Successful problem-solving in schools thus hinges on a holistic approach that integrates systems of emotional support with academic reforms. By prioritizing the emotional well-being of students, schools have the ability to create the learning environment as an arena where all learners believe they can overcome challenges, hence enhancing problem-solving skills and grades. Moreover, lowering emotional obstacles involves fostering resilience and accountability culture among both instructors and learners. Instructors play a significant role in setting examples of emotional intelligence, hence enabling learners to have the tool for handling emotions constructively. Social-emotional learning (SEL) programs supporting self-awareness, emotional control, and interpersonal skills empower students to feel confident enough to defy adversity. Implementation of such models has wide-ranging advantages in the form of enhanced student engagement and academic performance, with emotional challenges being addressed in a systematic manner. The inclusion of SEL in school reform initiatives illustrates the importance of treating emotional health as a key component of sound problem-solving and overall academic achievement (Adelman et al., 2018) (Figure 2.14).

Figure 2.14. *Emotional barriers effective problem-solving.*

Source: https://clearinfo.in/wp-content/uploads/2023/06/Emotional-barriers-to-communication-examples.png.

2.5.3. Environmental Factors

Environmental factors are the ones accountable for affecting the parameters under which issues are defined and explored. Not just physical factors such as climate and geography, but socio-political and economic factors constituting decision-making patterns as well, fall within these factors. For example, the natural resources of a region and related economic models may dictate not just what types of solutions become feasible but also what types are prioritized. In problem-solving scenarios, awareness of these environmental variables makes interventions more specific and real. Forgetting such variables makes interventions theoretically possible but impossible in a given context.

Thus, holistic problem-solving should be aware and take into account such environmental variables to produce outcomes that are sustainable and real, as exemplified in existing studies of complex systems across research disciplines (Hall et al., 1959). Furthermore, the interaction of environmental conditions with human intervention also introduces a degree of complexity in problem-solving. Institutional issues, belief systems, and social values impose a significant impact on how perception and response to environmental conditions are viewed. For example, where environmental degradation is a serious problem in a given region, action at the community level becomes an effective countermeasure to counter such issues. Yet these efforts can be thwarted by regulatory systems and the availability of funds, thereby emphasizing the interrelatedness of various environmental conditions. Comprehending this interrelationship is needed for developing solutions that resonate with the local populace and tap into existing socio-political frameworks. Therefore, honoring these dynamics gives problem-solving interventions the reality grounding that exists in the surrounding environment, thus raising the likelihood of resolving complex problems (Amineh et al., 2017). Finally, environmental factors being integrated into problem-solving paradigms are increasingly recognized as an obligatory response to an external globalized threat such as climate change and resource scarcity. Systems thinking can potentially provide a framework for evaluating such complicated problems, and by doing so, promote an understanding of how environmental variables lead to outcomes at any scale. As an illustration, the evaluation of the automotive industry based on environmental variables supplies critical information about production processes, customer actions, and regulatory impacts on sustainability. With the development of a structural and hierarchical structure of environmental quality, witnessed in evolving methods of industrial production, stakeholders can better anticipate the implications of their decisions. Such an overarching structure is necessary to develop solutions that will work, as well as being sensitive to the constantly evolving state of the environment, and hence focusing on inserting these considerations into the solution process (Amineh et al., 2017).

2.6. APPLICATION OF PROBLEM SOLVING IN REAL LIFE

The practical usage of problem-solving is made vibrant through several real-life examples where individuals are required to handle complex problems in a step-by-step way. This is a process often used in working life, which needs a systematic approach to identifying problems, analyzing potential solutions, and making changes effectively. For instance, businesses often encounter complex issues that could impact their operational efficiency and customer satisfaction.

With the application of problem-solving strategies, organizations are able to transfer theoretical knowledge into concrete action plans, thus improving their potential. The relationship between identification and implementation of solutions mirrors a process of continuous improvement that mirrors discussions in the context of online game-playing, where users play out real-world problems in a game environment in order to test solutions at a low-risk level (Gallagher et al., 2012). This research illustrates the manner in which virtual experience can teach and sharpen real-world decision-making, ultimately for practical purposes. Problem-solving is a cornerstone in the educational arena for teaching critical thinking and analytical abilities to students. In the context of the classroom, the intricacies of problems in life are now being replicated, compelling instructors to design courses that challenge students to resolve problems in advance. For example, project-based learning encourages students to collaborate with real-life situations, which promotes cooperation and strategic thinking. In being faced with challenges that reflect real life, students not only acquire knowledge in the subject matter but also improve their skills at dealing with uncertainty and devising effective solutions. This is found in greatest light in activities to construct relationships via cooperative technology, which allows the learner to move through diverse perspectives as they work through common issues—a reflection of the interactive process found within digital environments (Briscoe et al., 2011). Therefore, problem-solving has consequences that extend far beyond pedagogical practice, encompassing the weave of everyday interaction and experience. Furthermore, the integration of problem-solving capability into individual training is essential. Individuals tend to be faced with day-to-day issues, which range from mere frustrations to major, life-altering decisions. The ability to employ systematic problem-solving methods provides room for effective coping measures and personal empowerment to encounter problems with confidence. For instance, individuals may employ problem-solving frameworks to make effective decisions in career changes, financial planning, or relationship patterns. These matters tend to call for serious thinking and innovative methods, demonstrating how varied problem-solving measures yield beneficial results. The practice of facing personal problems in orderly ways not only builds resilience but also generates adaptability—skills needed to thrive in a world that is ever in flux. Therefore, the transference of problem-solving carries over into personal domains and affects the way individuals comprehend and deal with daily and material things in their lives.

2.6.1. Problem Solving in Business

Effectiveness in problem-solving in business is increasingly recognized as a key competency that directly helps organizations become effective. In light of the escalating complexity of the business environment caused by globalization, technology, and shifting customer needs, companies must ready their people with appropriate skills to handle problems efficiently. This would involve producing technical and soft skills as the model of education based on outcomes-based education proposed. Prioritizing essential project-based behavioral competencies by companies allows their employees to manage resources more effectively, meet deadlines, and work with the team, ultimately leading to successful project delivery and effective outcomes (Kanabar et al., 2018). Overall training that includes such competencies prepares an individual to address real business problems in a dynamic business world, ensuring effectiveness and innovation within the company.

Figure 2.15. *Problem solving in business.*

Source: https://storage.googleapis.com/profit-prod/wp-content/uploads/2023/07/94097ffb-great-leaders-solve-problem.png.

Additionally, organizational operations need to include problem-solving practices to handle rapid change. Techniques such as action learning, evident in the gaming scenario, can be a new skill-building approach. By using simulated scenarios for workers, organizations have the ability to implement the strategic potential of gaming to drive experimentation and collective learning. This process allows participants to deal with real-world actual problems in a secure setting, experimenting with potential output and solutions without having to fear negative consequences. Interactive gaming and business problem-solving dynamic offers the exceptional opportunity to refine interpersonal skills and enhance team synergy, with improved working relations in the organization and promoting a spirit of continuous improvement (Gallagher et al., 2012). In addition, the implementation of collaborative problem-solving practices develops a positive organizational culture that is critical to long-term success. Organizations with open lines of communication and an acceptance of multiple perspectives are best equipped to solve challenges on an integrated level. When teams brainstorm, or utilize analytics tools in an effort to identify root issues, they create innovative solutions but also enhance employee morale and collaboration. This democratic problem-solving process fosters a culture in which every individual has a say, resulting in greater insights and more commitment to implementation of solutions. Focusing on collaboration not only enables companies to respond efficiently to current problems but also enables them to prepare for predicting future challenges, thereby improving organizational resilience and adaptability in a dynamic market environment (Figure 2.15).***2.6.2. Problem Solving in Education*** In the learning process, problem-solving is not just a skill but a central aspect of the learning process that affects the cognitive development of students. Problem-solving activities between students enhance critical thinking, creativity, and team work skills that are essential in today's world. Through the application of real-world scenarios and guided challenges, teachers can develop a platform where students experiment with multiple solutions and construct the resilience to handle failures. This process calls for educators to act as facilitators, guiding students through uncertainty, challenging assumptions, and assessing consequences. The use of problem-solving models in curriculum can therefore result in deeper understanding of subject matter while at the same time equipping students to handle challenges beyond the classroom. In addition, the use of technology in problem-solving education has opportunities and challenges. Since instruction employs digital technology in enhancing the learning process, the role of traditional problem-solving techniques is all the more relevant. For instance, even though computer-aided drafting (CAD) technology dominates in technical fields, studies have shown that traditional hand-on technical drawing instruction has a significant pedagogical role to play. This includes the development of overall transferable skills such as visualization, precision, and coordination, which significantly contribute toward enhancing a student's problem-solving capacity. The digital versus traditional differential captures major issues about the optimum methods for equipping students with various problem-solving methodologies, thereby increasing the learning process generally and added flexibilities in various settings. In order to effectively facilitate problem-solving skills, educators must be attuned to the broader education system that they are operating in. This involves an appreciation of some of the various pedagogical practices and the significance of cooperative learning experiences. Recent research claims problem-solving to be more than individual capability—its effectiveness is improved by collaboration and peer learning. By equipping learners with positive settings for collaboration, they can learn from each other's perspectives, improve their critical thinking, and acquire social skills. While instructors become better at their craft, there is need to value the inherent value of problem-solving activities that foster personal discipline and creative expression. In so doing, they equip the students with the tools needed to gain academic achievement, as well as prepare them for lifelong problem-solving endeavors in an ever-evolving society, as captured in findings in many studies in education (Hall et al., 1959; McLaren et al., 2007) (Figure 2.16).

Figure 2.16. *Problem solving in education.*

Source: https://cdn.edclass.com/wp-content/uploads/teaching-creative-problem-solving-class.jpg.

2.6.3. Problem Solving in Personal Life

At individual level, problem-solving is a necessary skill that contributes enormously to one's coping ability with daily challenges. Such an ability entails a range of cognitive processes from issue detection and possibility scrutiny to selecting good solutions. People have issues requiring solution through evaluative thinking, either managing interpersonal relationships or making life's crucial decisions. The importance of this capacity is emphasized by its relationship to achievement and personal growth, as efficient problem-solving generally leads to enhanced self-esteem and personal satisfaction. Working these mental exercises strengthens one's adaptability and resilience, enabling them to transfer lessons learned from previous obstacles to apply to new obstacles, thus enhancing their overall standard of living as they face new and unforeseen adversity (McLaren et al., 2007). In addition, problem-solving in daily life is often supported by social experience and external influence. Feedback and guidance from family and friends can exert significant influence on an individual's problem-solving repertoire. For instance, collaborative problem-solving can unveil diverse methods and solutions, with the final outcome being tighter. Including other people in making decisions welcomes debate, stimulates commentary, and fosters a sense of community, which is required during periods of stress. Furthermore, as is evident in various community forums, individuals are likely to share their difficulties and successes in a common platform, demonstrating the way peer support can develop problem-solving skills (Gallagher et al., 2012). This process of coming together not only broadens the knowledge about various matters but also cultivates a support system that can facilitate development as well as learning. Finally, effective problem-solving at the personal level also mirrors with the application of learned skills at the personal level. Those who play most insistently at problem-solving in their leisure hours are likely to transfer those skills over into other spheres of their life and enhance their ability to handle such on-the-spot crises. This adaptability is particularly visible in how people live their career, relationships, and personal development. Part of mastering this process for learning involves analyzing one's failures and successes and getting a better idea of what approaches will work under most conditions. As stated, the act of simulating real problems in virtual settings—such as through video gaming or role-playing—can further enhance problem-solving ability by offering subjects a means to try out solutions without real-life repercussions, leaving avenues open for growth and learning (Gallagher et al., 2012). Problem-solving thus has an impact that transcends momentary solutions; it basically decides a person's resilience and flexibility to cope with the complexity of life.

SUMMARY

In conclusion, problem solving is a complicated activity that transcends various fields and applications. With awareness of the fundamental principles sustaining effective problem-solving techniques, people can heighten their brainpower and produce improved outcomes in both individual and business contexts. The integration of such tactics as critical thinking, creativity, and analytical reasoning helps problem solvers solve complex problems more efficiently.

Moreover, building systematic methodologies encourages systematic thinking and innovative solutions, emphasizing the importance of flexibility in a dynamic environment. With the streamlining of practitioners' problem-solving expertise, the processes enhance better practices for all fields. Lastly, advances in technology and the strength of data analytics have revolutionized problem solving as a field, providing new tools and structures to practitioners. Artificial intelligence and machine learning-based methods offer never-before-seen functionality for the examination of big data, eventually leading to enhanced decision-making. For instance, techniques such as pyramid pooling module and pyramid scene parsing network (PSPNet) have demonstrated vast improvement in performance via common datasets, thereby increasing the potential of image classification and contextual understanding in problem-solving procedures (Zhao et al., 2017). With each increment of technological development, it is imperative that individuals are made aware of such developments and how they can enhance problem-solving efficiency. As a matter of fact, the worth of adopting an attitude of ongoing improvement and learning cannot be overstated. Expertise in problem-solving involves ongoing work towards enhancing one's abilities, measuring performance, and solidifying new knowledge. Embracing approaches such as the Parametric Rectified Linear Unit (PReLU) has been shown to facilitate enhanced model fitting and reduced risk of overfitting, with a pertinent example of how innovation significantly affects problem-solving outcomes (He et al., 2015). Encouraging such an environment, it is possible for organizations and individuals to generate value through effective solutions, thereby positioning themselves for long-term success. The coming together of advanced problem-solving processes and early technological advancement has before it a considerable potential for future investigation and use.

In problem-solving model studies, some prominent points emerge that project the complexities and multidimensionality of good solutions. Among the fundamental points reiterated time and again is the importance of proper identification and definition of the problem. A poorly defined statement of the problem can produce misguided efforts and unsatisfactory solutions, emphasizing the importance of detailed analysis in the initial stages. Also, diverse methodologies are often used to address issues, proving that multiple perspectives can generate diverse solutions. For example, using formal approaches like the scientific method or heuristics enables systematic research and experimentation of the solutions to enable a better understanding of the issues at hand. Thus, the first step of precisely defining the issue and researching alternative methodologies is crucial in the process of problem-solving. Key to sound problem-solving is the application of analytical tools that split complex problems into manageable portions. Methods such as data analysis, modeling, and simulation enable us to improve on the prediction of outcomes and assess probable impacts before taking specific measures. Stability in these methods is vital; for instance, even if some of the methods are seemingly ill-conditioned, as evidenced by the work on Fourier extensions, they could actually yield good solutions under finite computational constraints (Adcock et al., 2012). Such evidence goes against the assumption that ill-conditioning discourages effective problem-solving. It underscores evaluating not only the methods employed but also stability under realistic computational limitations. This understanding fosters a more advanced problem-solving approach in embracing uncertainty and variability. Macro-fundamentals' interaction with outside shocks also shows an important understanding in problem-solving exercises. For example, volatility in G3 bilateral exchange rates tends to diverge from traditional economic theories, hence making it challenging for traditional approaches to economic stability (Adam et al., 2025). These discrepancies serve to enhance the relevance of behavioral economics in shaping responses to market uncertainty, with the suggestion being that irrational or greed-based trader movements often add to uncertainty. Taking these prejudices into account allows problem solvers to enhance their strategies to counteract adverse effects. And lastly, the insights derived from both mathematical techniques and economic behavior only serve to reinforce the necessity that productive problem-solving must be flexible, attentive, and one that considers a full spectrum of surrounding influence and potential effects.

REFERENCES

1. Abu Naser, S. S. (2016). ITSB: An intelligent tutoring system authoring tool. https://core.ac.uk/download/131208699.pdf (accessed on 9th September 2025).
2. Adcock, B., Adcock, B., Adcock, B., Huybrechs, D., Huybrechs, D., Huybrechs, D., Martín–Vaquero, J., et al. (2012). On the numerical stability of Fourier extensions. http://arxiv.org/abs/1206.4111 (accessed on 9th September 2025).
3. Adelman, H. S., & Taylor, L. (2018). Improving school improvement. https://core.ac.uk/download/286362371.pdf (accessed on 9th September 2025).
4. Adelman, H. S., & Taylor, L. L. (2018). Addressing barriers to learning: In the classroom and schoolwide. https://core.ac.uk/download/286362370.pdf (accessed on 9th September 2025).
5. Albert, A., & Ross, N. (2023). 99 problems? PBL can help: An intro to problem-based learning. https://core.ac.uk/download/555220479.pdf (accessed on 9th September 2025).
6. Amineh, H., & Kosach, N. (2017). Development of the integrated model of the automotive product quality assessment. https://core.ac.uk/download/301580339.pdf (accessed on 9th September 2025).
7. Anderson, R. C., Atiyah, P. S., Barnett, R., Beck, U., Bloom, B. S., Boone, L. E., Buchanan, L., et al. (2009). Why, what, and how? Case study on law, risk, and decision making as necessary themes in built environment teaching. https://core.ac.uk/download/100186.pdf (accessed on 9th September 2025).
8. Antony, F. J., Antony, J., Kumar, M., Madu, C. N., et al. (2007). Winning customer loyalty in an automotive company through Six Sigma: A case study. https://core.ac.uk/download/9036406.pdf (accessed on 9th September 2025).
9. Arons, A. B., Dhillon, A. S., Mazur, E., Redish, E. F., Redish, E. F., Schoenfeld, E. H., Lemke, J., et al. (2007). Emerging technologies in physics education. https://core.ac.uk/download/44176944.pdf (accessed on 9th September 2025).
10. Asaei, A., Baldassarre, L., Cevher, V., Dinh, Q., et al. (2013). Convexity in source separation: Models, geometry, and algorithms. https://core.ac.uk/download/33110428.pdf (accessed on 9th September 2025).
11. Berrens Torruella, K., Heras López, M., & Ruiz Mallen, I. (2020). Responsible research and innovation in science education: Insights from

evaluating the impact of using digital media and arts-based methods on RRI values. https://core.ac.uk/download/322837097.pdf (accessed on 9th September 2025).

12. Breiman, L., Breyfogle, F. W., Bryman, A., Draper, N. R., Dudewicz, E. J., Gijo, E. V., Grant, E. L., et al. (2012). Case study in Six Sigma methodology: Manufacturing quality improvement and guidance for managers. https://core.ac.uk/download/9033636.pdf (accessed on 9th September 2025).
13. Briscoe, G. (2016). Creating cultures of innovation. https://core.ac.uk/download/30697505.pdf (accessed on 9th September 2025).
14. Briscoe, G., De Wilde, P., & Sadedin, S. (2011). Digital ecosystems: Ecosystem-oriented architectures. http://arxiv.org/abs/1112.0204 (accessed on 9th September 2025).
15. Chen, W. H., & Srivastava, B. (1996). Heuristic solutions for loading in flexible manufacturing systems. https://core.ac.uk/download/213082546.pdf (accessed on 9th September 2025).
16. De Poorter, E., Demeester, P., Moerman, I., Rovcanin, T., et al. (2013). An LSPI based reinforcement learning approach to enable network cooperation in cognitive wireless sensor networks. https://core.ac.uk/download/55782560.pdf (accessed on 9th September 2025).
17. Dosi, G., Fagiolo, G., & Marengo, L. (1996). Learning in evolutionary environments. https://core.ac.uk/download/11828776.pdf (accessed on 9th September 2025).
18. Ferreira, O. P., & Németh, S. Z. (2018). How to project onto extended second order cones. https://core.ac.uk/download/185504529.pdf (accessed on 9th September 2025).
19. Foss, N. J. (2025). Bounded rationality in the economics of organization: Present use and (some) future possibilities. https://core.ac.uk/download/pdf/6548402.pdf (accessed on 9th September 2025).
20. Fratzscher, M., & Bussiere, M. (2025). Towards a new early warning system of financial crises. https://core.ac.uk/download/pdf/6754973.pdf (accessed on 9th September 2025).
21. Gallagher, L. (2012). Gaming business communities: Developing online learning organizations to foster communities, develop leadership, and grow interpersonal education. https://core.ac.uk/download/29200559.pdf (accessed on 9th September 2025).
22. Goldberg, D. E. (2009). The missing basics & other philosophical reflections for the transformation of engineering education. https://core.ac.uk/download/11922212.pdf (accessed on 9th September 2025).

23. Hall, M. M. (1959). A study to determine the role of one mental health integrator as she functioned on the instructional staff responsible for the teaching of fundamentals of nursing, Block III, in "X" University School of Nursing. https://open.bu.edu/bitstream/2144/17954/1/Hall_Margaret_Mary_1959_web.pdf (accessed on 9th September 2025).
24. He, K., Zhang, X., Ren, S., & Sun, J. (2015). Delving deep into rectifiers: Surpassing human-level performance on ImageNet classification. https://doi.org/10.1109/iccv.2015.123 (accessed on 9th September 2025).
25. Johannes, J. D., & Macdonald, J. R. (2025). Artificial intelligence approaches to software engineering. https://core.ac.uk/download/pdf/42829921.pdf (accessed on 9th September 2025).
26. Kanabar, V., Messikomer, C., & Thomas, A. (2018). Enhancing project-related behavioral competence in education. https://open.bu.edu/bitstream/2144/29016/1/Enhancing%20Project-Related%20Behavioral%20Competence%20in%20Education.pdf (accessed on 9th September 2025).
27. Kotsiopoulos, P., Pachidis, V., Pilidis, P., Templalexis, A., et al. (2010). A dynamic convergence control scheme for the solution of the radial equilibrium equation in through-flow analyses. https://core.ac.uk/download/140423.pdf (accessed on 9th September 2025).
28. Low, S. H., Palaniswami, M., & Wang, W. H. (2006). Application-oriented flow control: Fundamentals, algorithms and fairness. https://core.ac.uk/download/4875885.pdf (accessed on 9th September 2025).
29. Mann, D., Duguay, R., Stratton, R., Silveira, G. J. C., Steyn, H., & Warburton, R. D. H. (2003). Systematic innovation and the underlying principles behind TRIZ and TOC. https://core.ac.uk/download/30629190.pdf (accessed on 9th September 2025).
30. Markov, Z., Neller, T. W., Russell, I., Zlatareva, N., et al. (2006). Pedagogical possibilities for the N-puzzle problem. https://cupola.gettysburg.edu/cgi/viewcontent.cgi?article=1004&context=csfac (accessed on 9th September 2025).
31. McLaren, S. V. (2007). Exploring perceptions and attitudes towards teaching and learning manual technical drawing in a digital age. https://core.ac.uk/download/9016897.pdf (accessed on 9th September 2025).
32. Michaelson, G. (2015). Teaching programming with computational and informational thinking. https://core.ac.uk/download/29822230.pdf (accessed on 9th September 2025).

33. Posen, A. S., & Kuttner, K. N. (2025). Inflation, monetary transparency, and G3 exchange rate volatility. https://core.ac.uk/download/pdf/6459114.pdf (accessed on 9th September 2025).

34. Rosen, D. W., & Sager, B. (2005). Use of parameter estimation for stereolithography surface finish improvement. https://core.ac.uk/download/287648766.pdf (accessed on 9th September 2025).

35. Saltz, J. H. (2025). Automated problem scheduling and reduction of synchronization delay effects. https://core.ac.uk/download/pdf/42835494.pdf (accessed on 9th September 2025).

36. Wong, C. S. (2015). Competency based learning in hospitality education and its impact on future leadership skills. https://digitalscholarship.unlv.edu/cgi/viewcontent.cgi?article=4206&context=thesesdissertations (accessed on 9th September 2025).

37. Zhao, H., Shi, J., Qi, X., Wang, X., & Jia, J. (2017). Pyramid scene parsing network. https://doi.org/10.1109/cvpr.2017.660 (accessed on 9th September 2025).

CHAPTER 3

ALGORITHMS AND FLOWCHARTS

Contents

INTRODUCTION

In computer science, the significance of algorithms and flowcharts cannot be overstated as they represent the fundamental basis for problem-solving approach. Algorithms are specific, step-by-step instructions written with the aim of achieving specific objectives, encapsulating the nature of computational process. Flowcharts, on the other hand, graphically display processes defined by algorithms, yielding a rational depiction of the sequence of operations required to resolve a problem. This equivalence between flowcharts and algorithms provides a synergistic linkage between the two, so that both the computing abstractions and their applications can be better understood. Given that millions of individuals are programming worldwide, the literature avers, it remains still the challenge to take these concepts and communicate them effectively to novices, highlighting the need for a pedagogic framework that interlaces these computing building blocks (Michaelson et al., 2015).

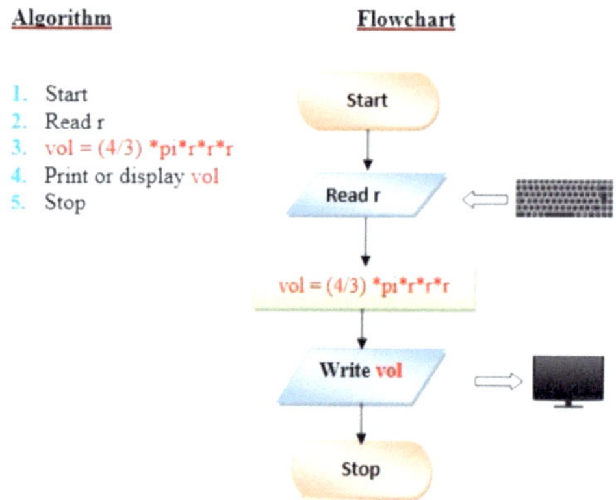

Figure 3.1. *Algorithms and flowcharts.*

Source: *https://engineerstutor.com/wp-content/uploads/2020/10/1.jpg.*

Algorithmic and flowchart knowledge is basic in several fields other than computer science, like engineering, finance, and data analysis, where process management and logical organization are critical. When students begin their computer science learning experience, they are likely introduced to these topics to use for developing computational thinking, a holistic approach that enhances problem-solving ability in addition to programming ability. Application of interactive methods in teaching has proven to work, with research indicating that active learning environments contribute significantly to improving the understanding and retention of complex content (Coffman-Wolph et al., 2019). Through application of practical examples and common scenarios, instructors can make abstract notions about algorithms and flowcharts more understandable, hence making learners confident as they handle more complicated problems. In addition, flowchart and algorithm interactions highlight an extended pedagogical need: the development of effective teaching methodologies that accommodate various learning modes. Granting that students have diverse experiences and backgrounds, instructors must adopt an expansive role promoting teamwork and ingenuity when it comes to learning flowcharts and algorithms. Traditional methods inevitably disregard the dynamic characteristics of problem-solving, where this process can be iterative and multilinear. Therefore, paradigms that are new and concentrate on the practical application of these principles in real-world circumstances are needed. With changing computer science educational dynamics, introducing computational thinking in combination with more precise methodologies can be helpful for programmers in the future, thereby enabling them to manage the complexity of algorithmic planning and flowchart designing (Michaelson et al., 2015) (Figure 3.1).

Definition of Algorithms

The concept of algorithms is a fundamental part in computer science and other fields of study. An algorithm can be defined as a collection of specified steps or regulations that are directed towards solving an issue or performing an activity. The systematic guidance implies the process can be performed logically and consistently regardless of complexity level. Algorithms are not merely significant in computer programming but also in decision-making in general, as it allows one to embrace systematic methods and achieve expected outcomes in a productive way. Algorithms are also classified into different kinds, namely recursive, iterative, or divide-and-conquer algorithms, with each having its respective characteristics and applications that show how versatile algorithms can be used when confronted with problems. In computer science, algorithms are often specified in terms of formal language or programming constructs that allow implementation. For example, more recent developments in algorithmic design have led to languages like EXEL that support synchronous and asynchronous mode and represent a full set of behavioral synthesis. This supports specifications of intricate structures with timing needs, again stressing the importance of algorithms for managing advanced computational processes. By providing an official way to represent chains of logic, these systems of algorithms not only provide increased efficiency but also enhance understanding of the process involved in solving problems. Traditionally, the development of such languages is a reflection of the growing significance of algorithms for navigating complex systems and hierarchies.

Moreover, the theoretical foundations of algorithms are based on algebraic theory that heightens their usefulness and understanding. For instance, synchronous dataflow network study led to the creation of the Basic Network Algebra (BNA), which captures the algebraic properties that networks require to interact. Such theoretical abstractions emphasize the inherent connection between algorithms and their running in various environments, besides offering models that examine distinctive operation traits. Through the study of these connections, we come to understand better how algorithms choose data flow and manage processes in various applications. The confluence of high-level theory and practical implementations is the stereotypical example of the constant evolution of algorithms, maintaining them at the forefront of both technological development and theoretical exploration in computer science and related areas, as illustrated in Bergstra et al. (2013) and Dutt et al. (1988).

Definition of Flowcharts

Flowcharts are indispensable tools in the process of visualization, serving to assist individuals in documenting procedures and algorithms step-by-step in a precise and sequential manner. Essentially, flowcharts consist of numerous symbols of various types interlinked through arrows with directions and illustrate the sequence of operations to achieve a specific outcome. Each symbol is assigned a specific role to fill, such as an oval for the start and end points, rectangles for processes, and diamonds for decision points. Not only does the official visual presentation easily make it possible to understand the flow of an algorithm, but easy communication among team members is also assured, hence easier problem-solving collaborative work. Flowcharts are thus inevitable in fields ranging from computer programming to project management, where clarity of process is extremely necessary. Flowcharts are particularly applicable in breaking complex algorithms into smaller parts that can be handled. Through step-by-step definition of processes, flowcharts allow one to test the logic and adequacy of an algorithm before implementation. This preliminary testing is crucial because it can identify errors or redundancy in a plan and consequently ensure better performance and efficiency. Moreover, flowcharts facilitate an iterative approach to algorithm development, where changes can be integrated smoothly based on stakeholder feedback, allowing a responsive project culture. With changing technology and ever-complex algorithms, the position of flowcharts in providing a complete understanding of the systems cannot be overstated, creating opportunities for innovative solutions across industries. Against the backdrop of today's technological innovation, the use of flowcharts in algorithmic design has become significantly important, particularly concerning telecommunications and network control. For instance, in the roll-out of sophisticated systems like LTE-advanced, flowcharts are critical planning and optimization tools for various network capabilities. Through visual representation of handover processes and variables in decision-making in multi-level networks, flowcharts assist in better understanding data flow and interdependence between such systems. Researchers and practitioners can use flowcharts to achieve enhanced performance while grappling with challenges like network complexity and resource management, as illustrated through studies of the efficiency of handover algorithms in heterogeneous networks (NA et al., 2014). Hence, with the dynamic landscape of technology, the reliance on flowcharts as a fundamental instrument for designing algorithms is as necessary as ever, allowing designers and implementers to navigate the complexities of contemporary systems with confidence (Figure 3.2).

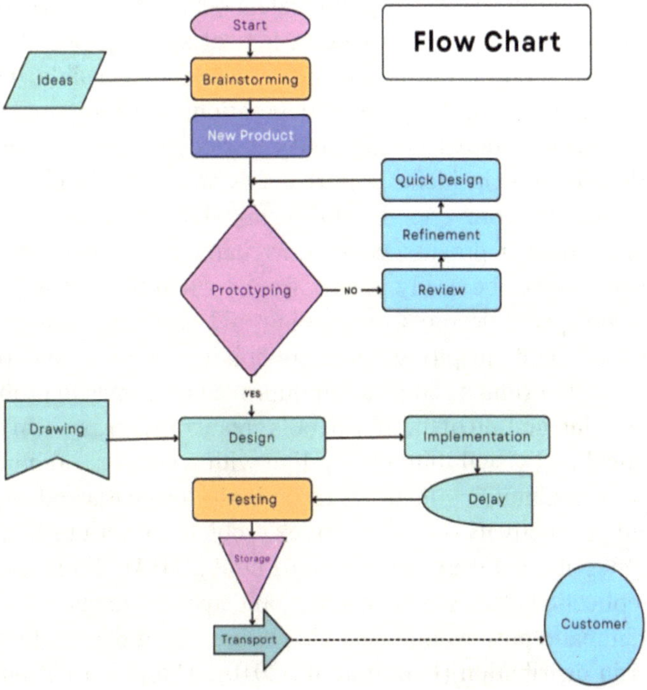

Figure 3.2. *Flowcharts serve as essential tools in the visualization of complex processes.*

Source*: https://qualityengineerstuff.com/wp-content/uploads/2022/11/Flow-chart-example.jpg.*

Importance of Algorithms and Flowcharts in Problem-Solving

In problem-solving, algorithms are a basis for systematic solutions to facilitate effective and organized solutions. An algorithm, as a clearly articulated set of instructions or regulations for solving a certain problem, allows individuals to break down complicated problems into subprocesses. This organized method enhances the transparency and strictness of problem-solving. Algorithms also reduce the mental load, allowing individuals not to be victims of fallacies of ad-hoc approaches to problem-solving. For example, in the case of huge datasets or intricate computations, a properly designed algorithm can deliver not only effective, but also efficient solutions, minimizing time and resources. With academia increasingly adopting data-based decision-making, the significance of algorithms becomes more pronounced, taking their status to the level of both theoretical and practical use across various domains. Flowcharts are also crucial in problem-solving since they are graphical models that assist in comprehending complicated processes. By representing logical steps graphically, flowcharts condense information in a form that is easily comprehensible. The graphical aspect is crucial, particularly in collaboration, whereby multidisciplinary groups have to collaborate under a shared knowledge of solutions and problems. Besides, flowcharts help identify bottlenecks and redundancies in processes, hence resulting in more effective problem-solving strategies. The step-by-step explanation of a process using flowcharts has a tendency of evoking insights that may not be easily visible from written texts. This aspect makes flowcharts indispensable tools in learning and working settings, sharpening communication and inspiring problem-solving ability. Incorporation of flowcharts and algorithms can result in improved outcomes in problem-solving activities. The integration of these two tools creates a strong system that supports both analytical and visual thinking. In line with recent research on plagiarism detection systems, building methods using both flowcharts and algorithms has been helpful in effectively solving complex problems in various fields, including academic integrity and data analysis (Afif et al., 2014). Similarly, in machine learning applications for computer intrusion detection, the union of algorithms with diagrammatic presentation aids navigation of big data and understanding of changes in distribution (Farran et al., 2010). The union not only increases precision but also develops a greater understanding of the dynamics at play, demonstrating the requirement for the use of both algorithms and flowcharts in modern problem-solving techniques.

3.1. HISTORICAL BACKGROUND

The development of algorithms and flowcharts has been shaped by the historical period under which they have been born. Structured approaches to solving mathematical problems were used by ancient civilizations, and this laid the foundation for contemporary algorithmic thought. The great mathematician Euclid, for example, came up with a set of steps to prove geometric concepts, which can be understood as primitive algorithmic processes. Over the centuries, these early techniques evolved, particularly during the Renaissance and the Enlightenment periods, when philosophers like Leibniz and Pascal formulated more formal systems of calculation and reasoning. To understand how algorithms eventually developed into sophisticated tools for problem-solving and so capable to be used in all aspects today, ranging from computer programming and data analysis, this foundation is a must. In the 20th century, computers played the role of catalysts to the invention and widespread use of algorithms. Theoretical computer science foundations of algorithmic design by visionary computer scientists such as Alan Turing and John von Neumann later paved the way for the formation of computational theory. These researchers' work brought insight into the system processes of computation, which provide the foundation to algorithms as well as flowchart design. Apart from this, the evolution of flowcharts also rose as a critical tool for the graphical depiction of complex algorithms, allowing for improved understanding and articulation of the underlying logic. This is an example of the interplay between theory and practice, how the major events in the past directly affected the tools and techniques used in contemporary algorithm design. The role of technology in the development of algorithmic forms can also be traced further through specific applications in medicine and civil engineering. The application of Decision Support Systems in medical care is a fine example wherein previous algorithmic contributions have been taken forward practically to improve patient outcomes. For instance, a triage system employed in health centers demonstrates how algorithms can effectively sort patients based on clinical needs, examining achievements made in the past history of computer science (Abelha et al., 2014). Similarly, the use of open-source technology for monitoring heritage buildings denotes the openness and fluidity of algorithmic application in civil engineering, showing the richness of history surrounding algorithms and flowcharts (Basto et al., 2017). The examples above show the continuous use of historical achievements, whereby they shape present-day practices and innovations across different sectors.

3.1.1. Origins of Algorithms in Mathematics

Algorithms date back to ancient times, where the early mathematical ideas started taking form. Mathematicians of the early times, including those in Babylon and Greece, applied algorithms for everyday problem-solving, especially in geometry and number theory. The term algorithm itself originated from the name of the Persian mathematician Muhammad ibn Musa al-Khwarizmi, who heavily advanced the subject in his works on arithmetic and algebra in the 9th century. His texts included systematic methods for equation solutions, providing the groundwork for subsequent algorithmic evolution. This history emphasizes the way in which algorithms arose from simple methods of computation to more formalized models that would eventually form a part of more complex mathematical systems to result in their modern applications in computer science and technology. With the passing centuries, algorithmic progress was based on progressively more sophisticated mathematical ideas. During the Renaissance era, mathematicians in Europe began to use algorithms to investigate more complex concepts such as calculus, which, by the work of Newton and Leibniz, led to the development of algorithms capable of handling infinitesimals and limits. This revolution demonstrated a significant shift in the use of algorithms—from being only problem-solving tools to ideas-coping instruments that were able to define complex mathematical ideas and procedures. Further, the creation of symbolic notation during this period enabled more concise algorithm descriptions and thereby made algorithms more useful. The abstractive and pragmatic mode of thinking that characterized algorithmic thinking attracted the attention of students and led the way for the application of mathematical algorithms in various scientific disciplines. In the modern era, algorithms play an even bigger role, especially with the advent of computer and digital computing. This era is a central convergence of mathematics and computer science, in which algorithms became the cornerstones of programming and software construction. Systematic approaches initially conceived in mathematical practice have now assumed an important role in the creation of effective algorithms for computation. Algorithmic processes have also increasingly been spoken of in terms of social and ethical concerns, as in data processing and artificial intelligence, for example. The cultural meaning of algorithms is increasingly discussed in terms of aesthetic programming, highlighting the necessity for a profound understanding of how these mathematical abstractions impact modern society. This shift in relationship reflects a richer comprehension of algorithms not only as technoscientific means but also as influential forces shaping the socio-political landscape, thereby requiring increased critical examination of their design and implementation (Cox et al., 2021) and (Chu et al., 2025).

3.1.2. Development of Flowcharts in Computer Science

In computer science evolution, the development of flowcharts is a watershed advancement in learning about algorithms and their implementation. Initially conceived in the 1920s, flowcharts produced visual representations of procedures that quickly became an essential element of both programming and systems development. The simplicity and beauty of flowcharts enable programmers to disassemble complex algorithms into discrete segments so that they can be better examined and communicated. As in contemporary literature on computational thinking, such visual aids are of primary importance in grasping intricate procedures and are a natural pedagogical approach to learning to code, a fascinating subject still grappling with pedagogy challenges (Michaelson et al., 2015). The use of flowcharts thus establishes an essential connection between theory and practice, facilitating a process of learning required for novices and seasoned professionals alike. As computer science as a field of study developed, the utilization of flowcharts grew more significant in numerous applications, representing their adaptability and usefulness. Outside of programming, flowcharts are increasingly utilized in business process modeling, software engineering, and instructional situations. That workflows and decision processes can be represented through flowcharts is a fact that allows technical and non-technical stakeholders to communicate with complex data systems effectively. Moreover, their integration into modern computational thinking emphasizes the necessity of visualizing information processing, which is often overlooked in traditional programming instruction. Evidence of this relevance is seen in ongoing studies and innovation on decision tables and applications, which directs the scholarly focus on enhancing the methodologies being applied in problem-solving and programming (Gacia et al., 2025).

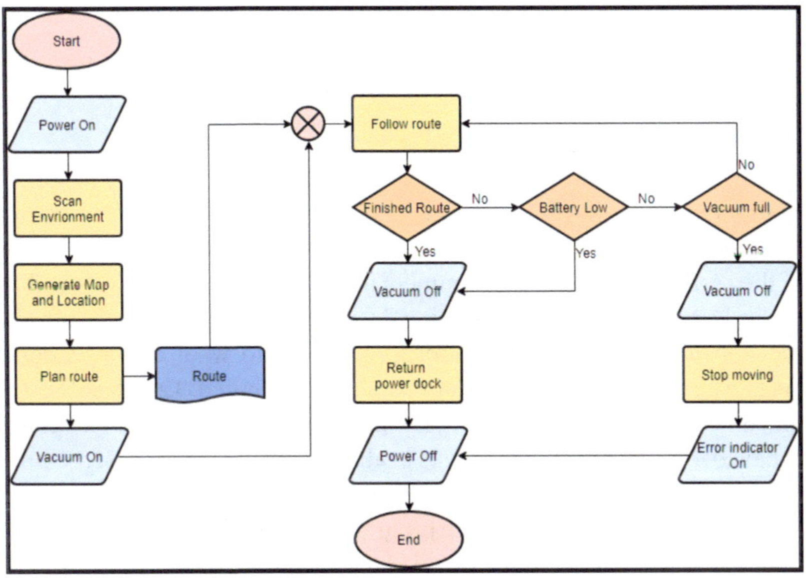

Figure 3.3. *Development of flowcharts in computer science.*

Source: *https://www.visual-paradigm.com/servlet/editor-content/tutorials/flow-chart-tutorial/sites/7/2018/09/flowchart-example.png.*

Hence, flowcharts remain as vital a tool for constructing theoretical models and real-world applications in the realm of computer science. Flowcharts' continued relevance as a part of computer science education reveals its impact on contemporary programming techniques. Emerging pedagogical models such as integrated pedagogy based on computational thinking have given fresh momentum to investigate the role of flowcharts in problem-solving competencies. So far, then, flowcharts are a double boon since they are not only a means of mapping out algorithms but also a means that encourages iterative, reflective, and imaginative problem-solving activity—qualities increasingly recognized to be central to would-be programmers. The problem remains to make sure that these diagrammatic aids are utilized effectively to facilitate deeper understanding and not superficial memorization of procedures. Positioning flowcharts at the intersection of computer science problem-solving and programming allows teachers to leverage their ability to rethink the way students think about and break down algorithms, and ultimately enhance a deeper understanding of computational practices and concepts (Michaelson et al., 2015). Thus, ongoing transformation and reconfiguration of flowcharts in computer science education curricula are essential to satisfy both the historical and contemporary requirements of computer science (Figure 3.3).

3.1.3. Key Figures in the Evolution of Algorithms and Flowcharts

The origin of algorithms and flowcharts can be traced back mainly to some key contributors whose contributions have largely shaped the fields of computer science and mathematics. One such contributor is Ada Lovelace, often known as one of the earliest computer programmers in the world. Lovelace's contribution to Charles Babbage's Analytical Engine during the mid-19th century introduced the concept of algorithmic calculations, looking into what could be done by machines as far as complex calculations were concerned. Lovelace's concept of a machine that is capable of doing not just arithmetic but also more complex things paved the way for advancements in algorithms in the future. Her comment on programming languages was a move from computers being only computation tools to computers that could execute programmed, precise processes, much like flowcharts that set up operations in a linear manner. Following Lovelace, Alan Turing was another key player in the creation of algorithms. Turing's definition of what is widely known as the Turing machine in the 1930s provided a clear model for understanding computation and algorithms. His work established basic principles that are equally applicable today in computer science, particularly when confronting the limits of computable functions. Turing's concept is crucial in assessing algorithms because it attempts to reconcile problems of efficiency and practicability. His impact extends to the realm of flowcharts as well, where the decision-making techniques he identified can be beautifully visualized. Familiarity with Turing's work enables researchers and practitioners to appreciate the power of algorithms and appreciate the well-organized dissemination of information exhibited through the application of flowcharts. In even more contemporary settings, Donald Knuth and Barbara Liskov have contributed greatly to the field of algorithmic study and the use of flowcharts as a method of describing process. Knuth's algorithm analysis work and his seminal book series The Art of Computer Programming provided meticulous methods for analyzing the efficiency of algorithms, which remain a proven foundation for computer science education. Liskov contributed significantly to programming languages and software engineering, particularly through her research on abstract data types. Her emphasis on robust program building locates an algorithmic form that is consistent with flowchart practice and keeps complicated systems tractable and comprehensible. The authors' work illustrates a constant dialogue between flowcharts and algorithms, emphasizing the pivotal position of systematic methods within knowledge of computational processes.

3.2. TYPES OF ALGORITHMS

Algorithms, so varied in number, are the very core of computational operations, breaking down into several large categories based on application and usage. Amongst these, sorting algorithms are one of the most elementary ones that put elements into a specified order, ascending or descending. Some of the most well-known algorithms in use are Quick Sort, Merge Sort, and Bubble Sort, differing by efficiency and mechanism. These are algorithms that play a crucial role where the rate at which data is fetched affects the performance of the system. For instance, efficient sorting may drastically reduce the time complexity of search algorithms, demonstrating the dependency of different types of algorithms on computation models. The efficiency of these algorithms is often found to directly correlate with flowcharts as diagrammatic representations of their procedures can greatly help in comprehending and implementation. For contrast, search algorithms play a central role in discovering distinctive data points in large collections. This category comprises several techniques, such as linear search and binary search, which differ greatly in approach to searching and efficiency. Linear search, as straightforward as it may be, becomes inefficient with increasing dataset size, necessitating advanced alternatives like binary search, taking advantage of ordered data to minimize comparisons. Their use is observed in database searching, where rapid access to data can be significant factors in both user satisfaction and system performance. Coupled with flowcharts, which illustrate search algorithm operations and decision points, this knowledge can be extended further, enabling practitioners to make appropriate choices based on the specific nature of the data they are handling. Another vital category of algorithms is the optimization algorithm, whose objective is to provide the optimal solution out of a list of acceptable solutions. Such algorithms, like Genetic Algorithms and Simulated Annealing, find immense application in complex problem-solving where numerous variables are involved and interact non-linearly, such as in operations research or machine learning applications. These algorithms optimize parameters to reach an optimal solution under a constraint and uncertainty-prone problem space. The application of flowcharts here helps explain the algorithms iterative processes and points of decision-making, facilitating enhanced conceptual awareness of driving forces. In addition, the need for innovation in algorithm efficiency study is highlighted within the current literature, as illustrated in efforts to design systems to detect plagiarism within flowcharts and algorithms, showing the evolving environment of algorithm consumption and study (Afif et al., 2014). Moreover, decision tables also clarify the systematic aspect of decision-making process in optimization algorithms that further enhances overall comprehension and real-world use, as highlighted in response studies to their application across various domains (Gacia et al., 2025) (Figure 3.4).

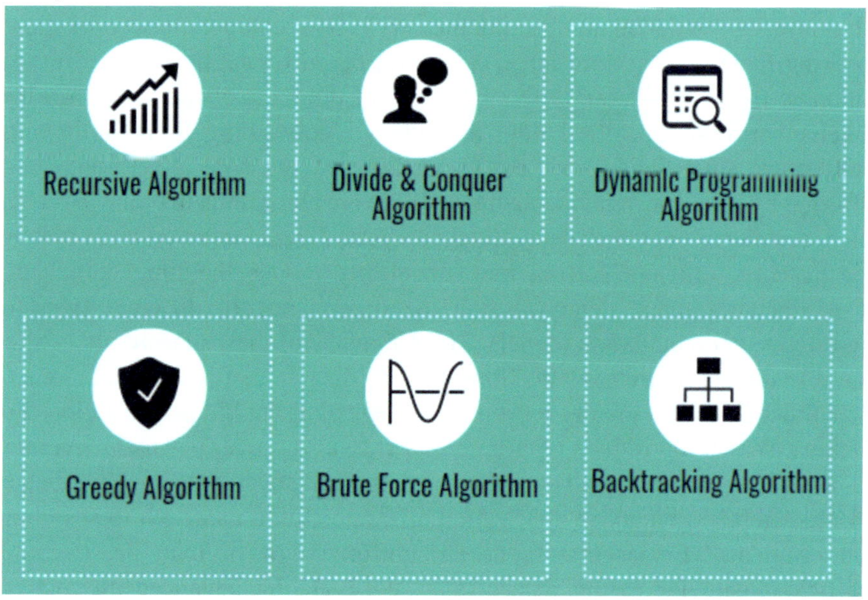

Figure 3.4. *Types of algorithms.*

Source: *https://images.edrawsoft.com/images2019/articles/flowchart/types-of-algorithm.png.*

3.2.1. Sorting Algorithms

Sorting algorithms in computer science are fundamental tools for data organization and access. Algorithms for sorting are applied to improve the efficiency of other applications, ranging from database management systems to real-time computing. Some well-known sorting algorithms include quicksort, mergesort, and bubble sort, with their respective functioning concepts and time complexities. Quicksort, for instance, uses a divide-and-conquer approach with a leaning towards achieving dramatic average-case behavior, while mergesort is stable and has consistent time complexity, leaning towards being optimal for huge data sets. Sort algorithm efficiency is an important aspect as it has a direct implication on the overall running time of programs in software, creating a reason for programmers to select the appropriate algorithm based on the context and nature of the data set. Studies of sorting algorithms using flowcharts reveal their inherent logical structure and execution sequence. Flowcharts are pictorial representations of sequential activities involved in sorting data.

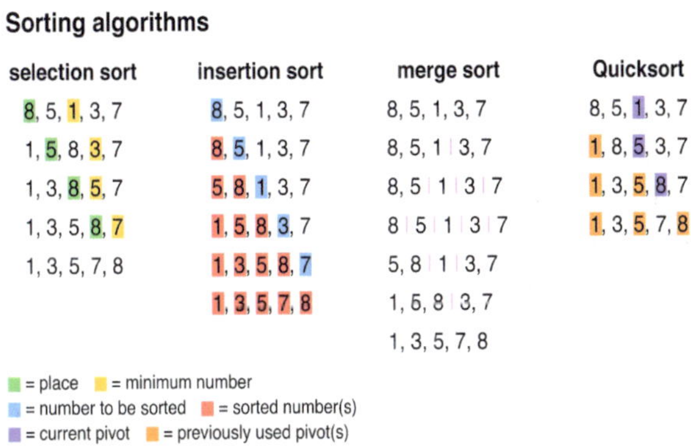

Figure 3.5. *Sorting algorithms.*

Source: *https://cdn.britannica.com/09/239909-050-573D293B/visualization-sorting-algorithms.jpg.*

They help in understanding algorithm actions better by breaking them up into individual operations such as comparisons, swaps, and recursive calls. By decomposing algorithms like heapsort or insertion sort into flowchart components, the sequence flow and decision points of the sorting are made comprehensible visually. This didactic approach not only enhances the conceptual insight but also algorithm design ability, as the professionals and students can learn and redesign already existing algorithms by simply reading through their flowchart depiction. Hence, the inclusion of flowcharts within studying sorting algorithms improves the learning process and allows for a deeper understanding of algorithmic design and efficiency. Even the theory behind the sorting algorithms extends to their application in real-world circumstances, particularly in the study of computational complexity. Knowledge of the efficiency of these algorithms is fundamental in developing scalable applications that can handle enormous amounts of data. Notably, time complexity is different for algorithms, where some are linearly scalable while others are polynomial or even worse. For example, a good sorting algorithm can have a significant effect on overall performance, especially where big datasets are involved, as indicated in the study that discusses ranking functions for termination of programs (Alias et al., 2010). Furthermore, presentation of ranking functions via flowcharts enables programmers to visualize potential chokepoints in the sorting algorithm, making it easier to spot opportunities for optimization. Effective sorting algorithms, therefore, not only make data management easier, but also have implications for computational approaches more broadly in software programming (Figure 3.5).

3.2.2. Search Algorithms

Search algorithms are involved in retrieval processes for data in the majority of computing environments. They come up with a structured approach to finding specific items in datasets based on applying different methodologies for different types of data and search requirements. The overall objective is to lower time complexity associated with accessing data and hence improve computations as a whole. For instance, binary search algorithms have significantly improved on retrieval speed when dealing with sorted data structures with a time complexity of O(log n). This performance is in sharp contrast to linear search algorithms that scan elements sequentially and therefore have a complexity of O(n). By making use of some strategies, developer communities can select search algorithms that not only map well onto the data model at hand but also serve system goals at a larger scale, such as minimizing operational costs or enhancing user satisfaction. Outside of the domain of more traditional data structures, search algorithms find themselves becoming increasingly common in more complex contexts, such as wireless sensor networks (WSNs). Evidence confirms the optimization of the lifetime of heterogeneous WSNs calls for effective search methods to manage resource allocation appropriately. An ACO-based method stands out because of the individual framework with a construction graph where ants travel paths towards maximizing the connected covers so that sensing coverage and network connectivity are guaranteed. This latest algorithm uses pheromone trails and heuristic information to manage the search process, showing how advanced search algorithms can be employed in highly complex environments. The possibility of network formation and energy conservation in WSNs emphasizes the importance of employing appropriate algorithms that facilitate connectivity as well as overall efficiency, unveiling the complexity of algorithm selection for specific computational problems (Chung et al., 2011). Besides, the evolution of search algorithms to multimodal databases highlights cross-modal correlation and efficient indexing as necessities in order to meet current retrieval demands in huge databases. The emergence of heterogeneous data types, that is, text, image, and audio, leads to a demand for a seamless hashing approach to ensure high retrieval accuracy between modalities. The CCQ model presents a new approach that unites different modalities within a single latent space and simultaneously encodes short binary codes for compact storage and search retrieval purposes. This saves reconstruction and quantization loss, thereby preserving the integrity of data relationships that is crucial for effective search outcomes. The ability of CCQ in quickly processing paired as well as partially paired data validates the adaptability of search algorithms in being able to manage ever more advanced data interactions, placing their role in the present evolution of indexing and retrieval systems within today's search engines and social networks (Besag et al., 2016) (Figure 3.6).

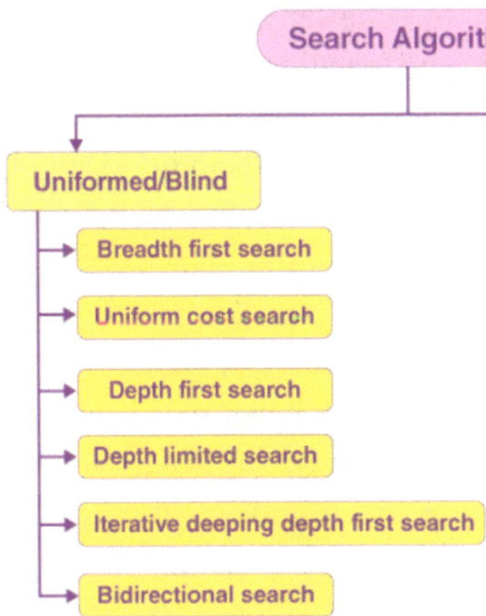

Figure 3.6. *Search algorithms.*

Source: *https://cdn1.byjus.com/wp-content/uploads/2022/07/search-algorithms.png.*

3.2.3. Recursive Algorithms

Recursive algorithms are one of the fundamental concepts of computer science and problem-solving approaches. Recursive algorithms are founded on the principle of recursion, that is, a function calling itself to find the solution for a smaller version of the same problem until a base case is reached. This method has tremendous advantages, especially in the breaking up of complex problems into solvable sub-problems to enable beautiful solutions to be obtained in problems such as tree traversals, sorting algorithms such as quicksort and mergesort, and searching problems. Recursion arranges the problem-solving process in a neat way, with the recursive call a level of abstraction that will abstract away the complexity of the initial iterative solution. By providing a divide-and-conquer strategy, recursive algorithms not just optimize the process of problem solving but also make the program more readable and maintainable. But recursive algorithms can also be troublesome with respect to efficiency and resource management. Each recursive call occupies space on the stack, which results in a stack overflow if the level of recursion exceeds a threshold value. In addition, recursive functions, while simpler to conceptualize, may have higher time complexity than their iterative counterparts since they entail duplicated computation. Methods such as memorization can prevent some of these inefficiencies but require understanding when and how to implement such methods. In classroom teaching, the challenge is finding the right balance between presenting recursive methods and learning how and when to circumvent them. As has been explained, there remains a necessity for a unified framework to teach programming and problem-solving methods in good stead, considering the intrinsic nature of recursion as a problem-solving technique (Michaelson et al., 2015). The utility of recursive algorithms far outweighs theoretical argument, since they do have practical applications that vindicate their inclusion in programming research. Whereas in fields such as artificial intelligence and data processing, recursive algorithms form the basis for numerous algorithms, allowing programs to analyze huge amounts of information in a resourceful way. Moreover, recursion is not just a programming model but also shares analogies in numerous scientific models, further vindicated by the analogy between concepts of complexity in computer science and energy in physics, as evidenced in recent research (Manin et al., 2013). This inter-disciplinary applicability shows the broader significance of recursion, so that both tutors and practitioners are motivated to lay greater stress on understanding these algorithms in the larger context of computational thinking. Thus, recursive algorithms not only constitute a powerful computational tool but also an introduction to better knowledge in algorithm design as well as theoretical aspects of complexity, thereby making it an essential subject of study in the field of algorithms and flowcharts.

3.3. TYPES OF FLOWCHARTS

Flowcharts are a basic tool when it comes to process documentation behind algorithms, with various types to describe various kinds of information in an effective way. The process flowchart is one of the common ones, which graphically describes steps taken in order to achieve a certain task or program. This is largely composed of standard symbols such as rectangles for actions, diamonds for decisions, and arrows to show the flow of control. Through the use of this graphical model, stakeholders can easily comprehend how an algorithm functions and track complex logic with ease, which is good for programmers as well as users. Process flowcharts can also enhance communication between members within a group so that every member comprehends agreed-on procedures and points of decision, making it easier to work together when developing as well as implementing an algorithm. Another significant variation is the data flowchart, which highlights the passage of data through a system. Contrary to process flowcharts, which revolve around the order of operations, data flowcharts shed light on how information gets passed around between elements of a system, like processes and databases.

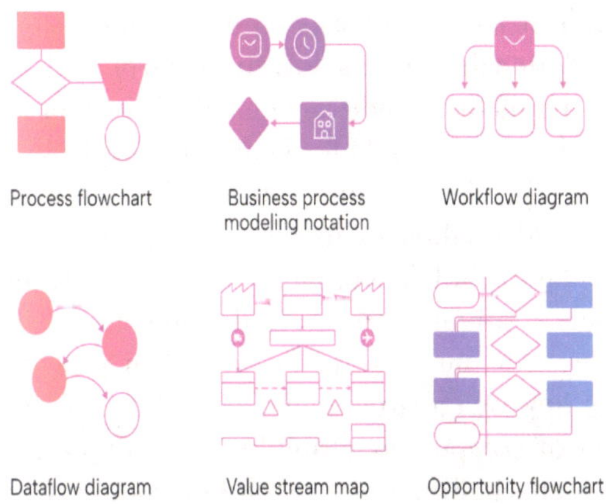

Figure 3.7. *Types of flowcharts.*

Source: *https://global-uploads.webflow.com/62fcfcf2e1a4c21ed18b80e6/649b22c357fc18bfe4a55550_different_types_of_flow_charts_xqz0.png.*

This variation comes in handy when considering how algorithms change data, determine where bottlenecks can occur, and discover redundancies. Data flowcharts employ symbols such as circles to represent processes, parallel lines to represent data stores, and arrows to represent direction of data flow. By clearly defining these relationships, data flowcharts not only aid in the designing of good algorithms but also aid in tracing down, enabling developers to enhance their designs, thereby reducing errors during the coding process significantly. Decision flowcharts are also a critical type of flowchart, primarily applied to decision-making steps in algorithms. In those fields where complex decisions are made on a regular basis, such as artificial intelligence and operational research, decision flowcharts have a significant role to play in representing the paths based on various conditions and results. This type utilizes conditional statements represented by diamond-shaped symbols that point to other branches showing possible decisions and their consequences. In the end, decision flowcharts make it easier to depict alternative situations and help programmers choose the optimal option, thereby improving algorithm efficiency and effectiveness. Decision flowcharts are priceless tools during algorithm design to ensure all possible outcomes are considered to produce more efficient and stable systems (Figure 3.7).

3.3.1. Process Flowcharts

In the realm of algorithms and flowcharts, process flowcharts are a wonderful source of assistance in observing processes and reducing complex series of actions. Process flowcharts define the process flow from one phase to another through the use of particular symbols that denote actions, decisions, or terminations. Using standardized symbols such as ovals for beginnings and endings, rectangles for tasks, and diamonds for choices, process flowcharts provide an easy-to-read and easy-to-understand method of understanding workflows. Not only does the visual representation aid in communicating with team members, but it also enhances problem-solving ability by allowing stakeholders more easily to review the workflow for unnecessary or redundant processes. Consequently, process flowcharts improve a structured approach to solving problems, under the overall concept of computational thinking, highlighting the importance of identifying key elements before software solution coding is done, as discussed in Michaelson et al. (2015). Further, process flowchart design is closely associated with algorithmic thinking. An algorithm, a series of steps followed in solving a problem, may be clearly laid down using a flowchart. The graphical method makes users view every step of the algorithm clearly, and therefore easier to track the logic and flow of the solution. The algorithmic iterative process is exposed using flowcharts, as they enable the users to see how one process can call back previous steps based on some conditions. This process of iteration is fundamental in fields like programming and systems analysis, where it's always a requirement to troubleshoot while honing and optimizing a solution. As noted in computer programming education and computational methods, application of flowcharts guarantees the efficiency of deciphering complex algorithms, thereby enhancing learning and application, as evidenced in Chung et al. (2011). In schools, the employment of process flowcharts as learning materials has become the trend since they assist in de-mystifying algorithms and making learning more efficient. Students also benefit by creating their own flowcharts of algorithms they have learned or developed, better understanding the principles behind them and exercising creativity in problem-solving. This education aligns with principles of computational thinking, where information structures are to be comprehended more than procedural use. Engaging students through visualizing algorithms is something that teachers can use to take advantage of diverse learning styles and increase general understanding. As such, process flowcharts not only serve as teaching tools but also as a bridge between theory and application, preparing students for real-world challenges in systems design and programming, as sustained by Michaelson et al. (2015) and Chung et al. (2011).

3.3.2. Data Flowcharts

Data flowcharts are critical in process representation and algorithm analysis to facilitate easier understanding of system processes and data flow. With the graphical representation of information processing, these charts make it easier for developers and stakeholders to comprehend intricate procedures. Their ability to show information movement from processes, data stores, and external inputs aids in determining inefficiencies and possible failure points within an algorithm. As learners find it difficult to grasp abstract concepts in computer science, employing interactive methods such as data flowcharts can simplify learning and enhance knowledge retention in alignment with studies that show interactive learning platforms have better education outcomes (Coffman-Wolph et al., 2019). Employing data flowcharts in algorithm development also enhances collaboration among team members by providing an ideal common visualization platform. This simplicity also promotes good communication because everyone on board will be in agreement regarding the goals and operations of the algorithm. Workflow consistency is extremely crucial in algorithm development because it prevents the repetition of tasks and allows for easy debugging. Data flowcharts are dynamic documents as they can be updated and refined incrementally alongside the project. They are particularly valuable in education, where students can utilize them in demonstrating their understanding of programming concepts and algorithms. By embracing these visual representations, students can easily reconcile theory and practice, hence enhancing coding skills (Basto et al., 2017). Moreover, data flowcharts can significantly contribute to the documentation of algorithms, offering an instantly accessible reference point for future development phases or new team members. Well-documented algorithms from clear flowcharts can expedite onboarding processes and foster knowledge sharing cultures of quality in organizations. Flowcharts also encourage critical thinking, as students and professionals alike have to think about how the information is flowing from one step to the next, which eventually results in dissecting the concepts of algorithmic building in more detail. With the emergence of technology, inclusion of data flowcharts in the computer science educational curriculum still takes precedence, as it guarantees that future developers can handle intricate systems efficiently and effectively, thereby placing emphasis on visual learning strategies in technical programs (Coffman-Wolph et al., 2019) (Figure 3.8).

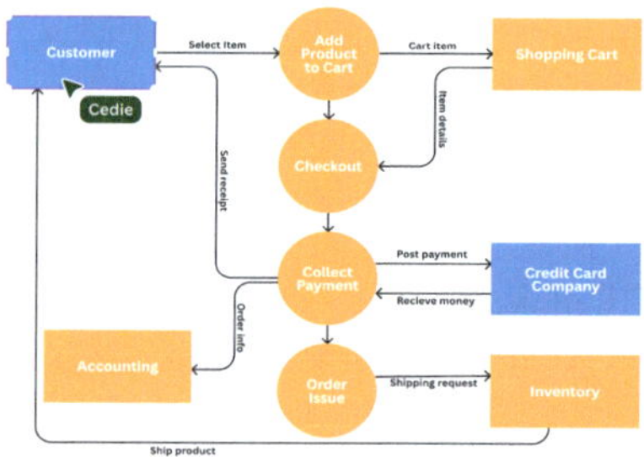

Figure 3.8. *Data flowcharts serve.*

Source: *https://static-cse.canva.com/blob/1420680/long-form_data-flow-diagram section-1_asset-1.png*

3.3.3. Workflow Flowcharts

Workflow flowcharts serve as essential tools in delineating processes, enabling organizations to visualize complex sequences of tasks or decisions in a simplified manner. By providing a graphical representation, these flowcharts enhance comprehension among team members and stakeholders, clarifying each step involved in a workflow. Particularly in environments where multiple workflows intersect, such as in project management or software development, flowcharts allow for immediate recognition of both tasks and their dependencies. This visual clarity is fundamental in identifying potential bottlenecks or redundancies, ensuring that stakeholders can swiftly adapt to changing circumstances or requirements. Furthermore, workflow flowcharts often improve communication and collaboration across departments, as they provide a common reference point that aligns the various perspectives of team members. The development and implementation of workflow flowcharts are informed by a systematic approach to design, integrating principles from both cognitive psychology and process engineering. The integration of these principles is crucial for understanding user interactions within a workflow, particularly when security mechanisms are involved. Research has indicated that usability issues frequently arise when security tasks impose undue friction on primary workflows, leading to user frustration or disengagement. By modeling the workload associated with specific tasks, including any necessary authentication measures, designers can more effectively align security protocols with user actions. This "best fit" approach not only ensures compliance with security standards but also enhances user satisfaction and productivity. Thus, workflow flowcharts become vital in depicting how user tasks interrelate with security mechanisms, guiding organizations toward more integrated and user-friendly designs (Glass et al., 2016). Moreover, the evolving landscape of workflows necessitates the continuous update and refinement of flowchart designs to accommodate technological advancements. In the context of artificial intelligence and software engineering, incorporating modern algorithms into workflow flowcharts can significantly enhance process efficiency and decision-making quality. For instance, algorithms can automate data processing within the flowchart, allowing for real-time adjustments based on user inputs or external variables. This adaptability adds a dynamic element to workflow flowcharts, transforming them from static representations into living documents that reflect changing organizational needs. Furthermore, the integration of best practices from knowledge engineering can lead to the development of intelligent workflow systems that learn from historical data and user interactions. Such advancements underscore the importance of interdisciplinary collaboration in creating optimized workflow flowcharts that truly serve their intended purpose (Baumeister et al., 2011).

3.4. THE RELATIONSHIP BETWEEN ALGORITHMS AND FLOWCHARTS

The link between flowcharts and algorithms is the building concept within computational operations study. Algorithms are lists of steps or mathematical equations applied to solve problems, and they outline the logical steps taken in executing tasks. Flowcharts, on the other hand, illustrate graphically the algorithms to offer a detailed comprehension by outlining how a step operates and impacts another. This visual representation facilitates the explanation of complex ideas, particularly to those outside of computing theory. By demystifying the hidden logic, flowcharts act as an educational tool that helps students grasp the algorithmic techniques employed in solving problems. In addition, the integration of algorithms and flowcharts is of most benefit in scholastic settings, particularly with computer science becoming more and more a part of high school and college curricula. For example, educators adopting computer science teaching must develop their pedagogical knowledge, which can be done through methods such as introducing flowcharts to algorithmic teaching. Studies reveal that these visual learning aids can actually improve student motivation and comprehension of computational assignments (Csizmadia et al.,

2018). By developing a system where algorithms are learned together with their flowchart equivalents, educators can then design a more stimulating learning environment where students can visualize and apply programming solutions in an efficient way. Additionally, the evolving demands for computational thinking also necessitate an improved comprehension of the interplay of algorithms and flowcharts in actual implementations. Increasing industries rely on best algorithms and their corresponding flowcharts for decision-making, such as in the area of computational fluid dynamics (CFD). Studies indicate that the ability of algorithm implementations can be optimized by optimal visualization techniques to enable better use of resources in high-performance computing environments (Bruno et al., 2025). This interdependence of each other underlines the significance of both representations in enhancing algorithms for specific applications and thereby organizational efficiency and scientific advancements. As both tools continue evolving, their interaction will likely play a crucial role in shaping the future trajectory of technological growth and learning.

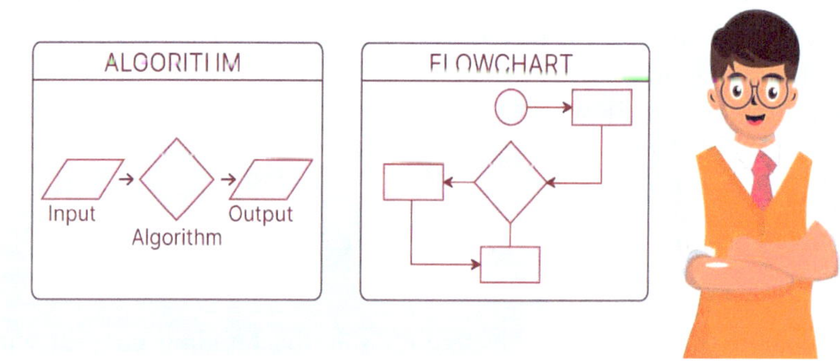

Figure 3.9. *The relationship between algorithms and flowcharts.*

Source: *https://images.shiksha.com/mediadata/ugcDocuments/images/wordpressImages/2023_01_difference-between-flowchart-and-algorithm.jpg.*

3.4.1. Visual Representation of Algorithms

The graphical modeling of algorithms is a very important part of making the understanding of complex computational processes more in-depth. Flowcharts, the most popular method of such graphical modeling, provide a systematic way of expressing the step-by-step development of an algorithm. By expressing abstract concepts in terms of graphical symbols and connecting them with arrow symbols, flowcharts make simple understanding of operations like conditional statements, loops, and handling variables possible. This visual representation caters to more than one learning style but particularly benefits those who grasp concepts better through pictures rather than words. Application of flowcharts is not only educational but also functional in everyday application within software coding, as computer programmers are able to visualize algorithmic logic before implementation, thereby minimizing potential errors as well as allowing for easier communication among team members. The effectiveness of these visual aids is also supported by research that interactive learning environments enable student learning (Coffman-Wolph et al., 2019). Additionally, the utilization of visual aids enables the connecting of theory to practice. In the creation of algorithms, the visualization of each item in a flowchart allows programmers to deconstruct and comprehend sophisticated logical configurations with ease. Formal notation of symbols—such as ovals to denote beginnings and endings, diamonds for decisions, and rectangles for processes—establishes a clear road map that guides programmers through the obscurity of their code. This visual method is even more important in large projects, as it allows more comprehensible communication about algorithm design and structure between groups of programmers. As algorithms become increasingly complicated, the requirement of effective visual communication is even more critical, thus supporting the role of flowcharts to reduce the complexity of the problem-solving approach in computer science learning (Hirata et al., 2017). Additionally, with advancing technology, the sophistication of visualizing algorithm tools also increases. The introduction of advanced approaches, such as object detection systems like Faster R-CNN, opens up interesting opportunities for enhanced accuracy and effectiveness in graphical representations, such as flowcharts. The use of such algorithms will make it feasible to automate symbol recognition in computer-drawn or hand-written graphics, thereby reducing the possibility of human error in interpretation. By examining data on the representation of flowcharts and mathematical equations, researchers have begun to identify the potential that machine learning provides in producing more interactive and dynamic algorithmic representations. This process underscores the ongoing utility of graphical representations not just for educating future computer science professionals, but for developing new software that pushes the boundaries of algorithmic use and knowledge (Hirata et al., 2017).

3.4.2. Enhancing Understanding Through Flowcharts

In the context of the educational field of algorithms, flowcharts are a valuable tool for enhancing the learning of students. By visually defining processes, flowcharts enable students to categorize and conceptualize complex algorithms more effectively. They translate ambiguous programming procedures into a comprehensible format that is simpler to process, and students can more readily follow the order of the execution of a program in linear and structured form. This visualization supports better comprehension of the interactions between various aspects of an algorithm and is especially beneficial for STEM students when solving problems. Most importantly, these visualization tools facilitate collaborative learning environments, and students can share ideas and approaches, hence maximizing their learning experiences (Bento et al., 2023). Consequently, the application of flowcharts in the teaching of algorithms transforms the traditional way of learning programming by bridging the gap between theory and practice. Furthermore, the application of flowcharts corrects the inclination by most students towards visual methods of learning. Research indicates that students learn significantly by imagining the logic of programming languages. Flowcharts do not only increase retention but also arouse interest, as the students can view the order of commands in an algorithm. Flowcharts are different from conventional written instructions, which have a tendency of limiting understanding for those with problems comprehending abstract programming concepts. By giving students a tangible means to partition and analyze algorithms, flowcharts allow them to explore programming at a more sophisticated level. Furthermore, the combination of flowchart practice with programming practice allows educators to create an extended learning environment that enhances skill retention and understanding (Godbole et al., 2014). Lastly, visual tools like flowcharts prove to be precious in establishing an active learning environment for algorithm learning. The use of flowcharts is not just relevant in the sense of visualization; they also encourage a problem-solving and logical thinking methodology. Through solving flowcharts, students are forced to consider the framework of algorithms, thus becoming more competent programmers. This process encourages critical thinking—not merely taking pre-defined paths, but also examining other potential solutions and debugging errors in their code. As researchers have shown, acquiring these abilities is essential to achieving success in technology-driven sectors (Bento et al., 2023). Moreover, reciprocal application of flowcharts in project-based situations accumulates team dynamics knowledge in programming, preparing students for feasible challenges in the real world. Finally, application of flowcharts in teaching algorithms not only enhances comprehension but also transfers abilities that enhance students' future education and professionalism.

3.4.3. Use Cases in Programming and Software Development

Use cases are significant in software development and programming to define how users and a system communicate. Use cases are a good means of documenting the requirements and making sure that all involved understand a clearly defined set of functionalities needed for successful software implementation.

Use cases help developers visualize how the end-users will use the software, enabling a user-centered way of working and designing. By highlighting real-life scenarios, these cases allow the closing of often significant gap between technical specifications and user needs, which is paramount in developing effective algorithms. By developing use cases, programmers can identify edge cases and pitfalls that may arise during the implementation of algorithms, leading to more robust and adaptable software solutions. Finally, this emphasis on user interaction creates products of better overall quality and usability. Furthermore, the use case incorporation into the software development process neatly fits with established practices that emphasize iterative development and stakeholder feedback.

Figure 3.10. *Use cases in programming and software development.*

Source: *https://blog.ionixxtech.com/wp-content/uploads/2018/04/01.14.2018-The-6-Basic-Steps-of-the-Software-Development-Process.jpeg.*

During agile development, as a case in point, use cases enable ongoing communication among developers and users, enabling incremental improvement based on immediate feedback. This circular process is necessary in algorithmic improvement because it allows for adaptation in line with evolving user needs and not being limited by rigid, pre-stipulated requirements. By the application of use cases, developers can create algorithms not just for functionality but also according to specific contexts where such algorithms will operate. This feedback loop is particularly important when dealing with complex systems, where unforeseen interactions are certain to arise, and thus there is a need for adaptability. Therefore, use cases are not merely a foundation for understanding requirements but also a dynamic tool for refining algorithmic design. Apart from their role of facilitating software-user interaction, use cases also have an important role to play in software documentation and subsequent software system maintenance. Well-documented use cases are used as an unequivocal point of reference for new project developers entering a project, giving continuity and consistency to development teams. This is especially applicable in environments where frequent rates of update and modification to algorithms are the standard, as they illuminate the intended functionality and the decision-making context within the software. Further, decision tables, also cited in literature, complement use cases by presenting a formalized structure of decision processes, enhancing the understandability of complex programmatic decisions (Gacia et al., 2025). By combining use cases with decision tables, developers create a comprehensive framework that not only places emphasis on user interaction but also eases the problem-solving involved in algorithm design. Use cases for programming and software development considerably enhance both initial development and subsequent evolution of software systems (Figure 3.10).

3.5. APPLICATIONS OF ALGORITHMS

Algorithm applications are not confined to theoretical abstract models; they constitute a crucial component of resolving real-life problems across diverse fields. An instance is the case of wireless sensor networks (WSNs), where enhancing network performance plays a crucial role in prolonging system lifespan. An ant colony optimization (ACO)-based strategy has proven to optimize the lifetime of heterogeneous WSNs. It involves constructing a graph where every node corresponds to assignment of a sensor device. Using pheromone and heuristic principle guidelines, ACO enables ants to search for optimal paths that meet sensing coverage and connectivity demands. From this realistic application, it is possible to observe how algorithms like ACO span the theorization of mathematics and actual problem solutions to significantly enhance network performance and survivability (Chung et al., 2011). The second field where algorithms are especially important in usage is computer security, that is, intrusion detection systems. Traditional machine learning techniques are normally incapable of processing large data that abound in cybersecurity, such as the KDD Cup '99 dataset that contains millions of observations and lots of features. In a bid to address this shortcoming, sophisticated algorithms like Voted Spheres have been developed. This parameter-free categorization method partitions the input space into overlapping hyperspheres and enables rapid voting procedures in testing. Moreover, by applying methods such as density weighting and kernel mean matching, the Voted Spheres approach dynamically counteracts distribution shifts in test and training data. This synergy of algorithms provides insight into how adaptability methods can significantly enhance machine learning models' performance in dynamically changing environments (Farran et al., 2010). Finally, the contribution of algorithms to modern technological advancements cannot be overstated. From maximization of resource allocation across networks to augmentation of predictive analytics in finance, algorithmic deployments determine the character of various industries. For instance, algorithms automate supply chain management by effectively assessing various variables such as demand volatility, transportation logistics, and inventory levels. With sophisticated algorithms, business can maximize operations, minimize costs, and respond faster to market swings. In addition, as data continues to propagate, increasingly sophisticated algorithms are increasingly crucial to develop, underlining their importance not only in business process productivity but also in innovation. As such, the continuous enhancement of algorithms is therefore a cornerstone of progress in most sectors, underscoring their fundamental importance in the modern age.

3.5.1. Algorithms in Everyday Technology

The integration of algorithms into everyday technology has changed the way human beings interact with electronic machines and processes. Algorithms are the very cornerstone of technological infrastructure, driving everything from web search engines to social media sites. For instance, the algorithms employed by web search engines scan enormous volumes of data to deliver the most appropriate information in answer to what users query. This capability not only enhances the efficacy of information lookup but also generates the shape of content users are presented with, affecting everything from consumer behavior to social interactions. Hence, the pervasiveness of algorithms necessitates assessing their importance regarding privacy, data protection, as well as ethical considerations in technology-enabled communication. In addition, algorithms increasingly become pervasive in education technology, enhancing personalized learning experiences. For example, adaptive learning systems employ algorithms to analyze a learner's current knowledge and adapt educational materials in response. Such targeted intervention allows learners to engage with content at their own speed, thereby maximizing learning return. As observed in recent trends, algorithmic guided generation of concept maps from open sources illustrates how algorithms can maximize user-initiated learning processes, through offering tailored recommendations and natural information seeking (Lahti et al., 2009). These works put more emphasis on the role of algorithms not only as technical objects but as constitutive elements of a broader pedagogy-friendly system supporting active learning. In addition to enhancing personal and learning lives, algorithms are relevant to interactive technology development, especially video games. An interesting research focus is gaming practice semiotics and how algorithms control player interaction in virtual spaces. Games can be viewed as interactive matrices where player interaction is controlled by algorithms, crafting a story that unfolds along the axes of action and choice. The communication between a games design—grounded in algorithmic paradigms—and players' actions can provide significant insights into user behavior and experience (Ferri et al., 2012). Such a relation is not only constructive in advancing the practice of game design but also in articulating the formation of ethical guidelines that address challenges to user interaction in algorithmic environments.

3.5.2. Algorithms in Data Analysis

In the analysis of data, algorithms are traditional tools which enable researchers and analysts to derive insights from vast amounts of data. The sophistication of contemporary data makes sophisticated algorithms which have ample capacity to process lots of data without compromising on accuracy a requirement. Algorithms find application in a wide range of activities, such as classification and regression, clustering, and learning of association rules. As researchers try to glean insights from disparate sources of data, the necessity of algorithms grows increasingly significant. If algorithms are well designed, the process of analysis becomes efficient, where one can have greater productivity and speedier decision-making, which is especially crucial in business spheres from advertising to medicine. Furthermore, the complexities involved in formulating and fine-tuning such algorithms reinforce the significance of building a firm understanding of both theoretical concepts and practical applications of data management and making it a core area of focus in the education of future data scientists and analysts (Michaelson et al., 2015). In the study of the relationship between flowcharts and algorithms in data analysis, it is necessary to study how flowcharts are a graphical representation of algorithmic steps. Flowcharts are best used to explain the algorithmic processes involved, thus facilitating a deeper understanding of complex procedures. Flowcharts enable analysts to map the courses on which data becomes processed and interpreted into operational intelligence. This visualization is educative in nature; flowcharts used for operations are also highly beneficial while designing algorithms since they bring out the likely inefficiencies and bottlenecks. Additionally, using flowcharts together with algorithms aids in debugging and process improvement through effective demonstration of data flow. With data-driven decision-making becoming more common in organizations, the union of flowcharts and algorithms becomes core, particularly in how algorithms are being carried out in an efficient and effective manner (Afif et al., 2014). Also, the pedagogical process of learning algorithms using flowcharts serves to enhance a greater overall understanding of data analysis among students. As already discussed in previous discussions on Computational Thinking (CT), it is necessary that students comprehend how problem-solving and algorithmic design relate to each other. Having flowcharts as part of the learning process enables students to acquire iterative thinking, and it also encourages them to think creatively while solving complex problems. This pedagogical shift is particularly relevant in that traditional pedagogy has a tendency to focus narrowly on programming proficiency without taking the problem-solving approaches that underlie the capacity to excel at data analysis seriously. Adopting a curriculum that incorporates both algorithms and flowcharts can thus enhance the skills of students and prepare them for the data analysis challenges in real-world applications, equipping them with the skills to deal with and make sense of the nuances of data spaces (Michaelson et al., 2015) (Figure 3.11).

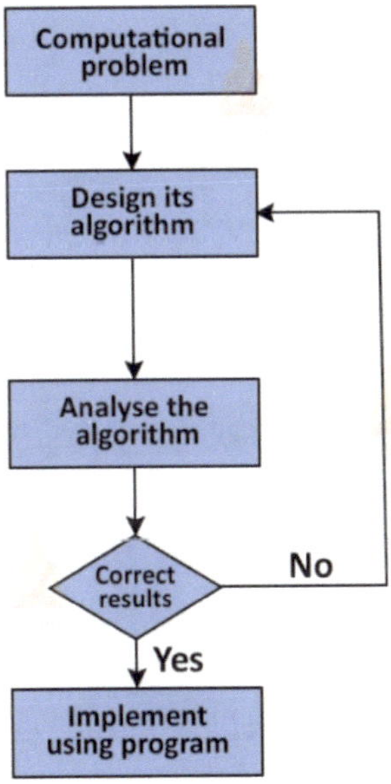

Figure 3.11. *Algorithms in data analysis.*

Source: *https://techvidvan.com/tutorials/wp-content/uploads/sites/2/2021/06/Algorithmic-Analysis.jpg.*

3.5.3. Algorithms in Artificial Intelligence

The use of algorithms in artificial intelligence (AI) has transformed how machines consume information and make decisions. At the core of this transformation are advanced algorithms that can sort through vast pools of data, learn from patterns, and improve over time. They are the foundation of most AI programs, from natural language processing to image recognition, enabling machines to decipher and understand human input more complexly. As AI evolves, the deployment of sophisticated algorithms becomes common, and their use in enabling sophisticated analytical capabilities and best decision-making processes is at the forefront. Algorithms of machine learning are central to developing sophisticated systems that learn from emerging information to facilitate innovation in fields as wide-ranging as healthcare, finance, and autonomous transportation.

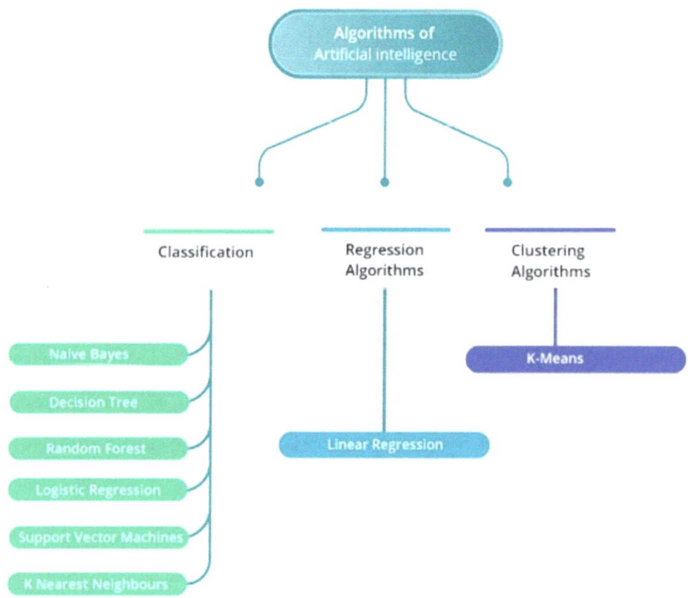

Figure 3.12. *Algorithms into artificial intelligence (AI).*

Source: *https://www.besanttechnologies.com/wp-content/uploads/2020/01/artificial-intelligence-algorithms.jpg.*

Furthermore, the use of algorithms transcends mere data analysis; they also make possible the development of decision support systems within various sectors. For instance, in the health sector, algorithms are key to formulating models to improve clinical decision-making. One such example is triage systems in emergency departments within hospitals, where smart algorithms prioritize patients based on their clinical needs. According to studies, not only do these systems streamline decision-making processes but also maximize the efficiency of medical personnel through facilitating balanced distribution of attention based on levels of urgency (Abelha et al., 2014). The practical implementations of such algorithms serve to indicate their relevance in operational settings, demonstrating the manner in which they can successfully reduce waiting times and improve patient outcomes when appropriately utilized. Further, the theoretical justifications for such algorithms illustrate their complexity and the need for ongoing research in the area. Decision tables, for example, illustrate a formal process of executing decisions based on given conditions and outcomes, a key tool for algorithm creation. Decision table literature records the widespread usage and adaptability of algorithms in domains other than computer science, illustrating the growing salience (Gacia et al., 2025). This is an important flexibility, as it allows for algorithms to be retooled based on new challenges and technology in order to remain relevant. As more and more industries adopt AI solutions, having an understanding of the algorithms behind them is becoming vital to fostering innovation and expanding system capabilities, making careful education and information-sharing in this rapidly changing field a requirement (Figure 3.12).

3.6. APPLICATIONS OF FLOWCHARTS

Flowcharts are a useful tool in most industries, providing a visual representation of processes that can make algorithms or workflows clear even in complex situations. Flowcharts are applied best in project management, as they enable groups to depict stages of projects, identify the pinch points, and ensure tasks are executed in a rational manner. Visualization assists groups to communicate since it generates a common consciousness of the workflow structure. Apart from that, flowcharts also serve the purpose of decision-making by clarifying things and enumerating choices and outcomes, showing how various paths can lead to varying results. Using flowcharts for these purposes, organizations can enhance efficiency and reduce the chances of mistakes at the implementation stage, leading to the successful completion of projects. In computer science, flowcharts are found to be very helpful in representing algorithms and their related workflows. They provide transparency in the interaction between algorithms and data and decision-making at runtime. For instance, in developing software, programmers use flowcharts regularly to specify coding logic for structures such as loops and conditionals. By grouping algorithms into graphs, flowcharts allow programmers to detect bugs or optimizations before they code. This can lead to improved code quality and reduced debugging time. As highlighted by recent studies, the use of visual aids like flowcharts can enhance understanding and communication between teams of software developers and, ultimately, improve the effectiveness of programming solutions (Farran et al., 2010). Flowcharts are also increasingly applied to data analysis and machine learning projects. They can be used to outline procedures in data preprocessing, model training, and model evaluation, which allows data scientists to systematically handle complex analysis tasks. For instance, for the field of computer intrusion detection, flowcharts could represent the various stages in the process of network traffic analysis to assist in identifying abnormal activity. Through representing complex algorithms in visual format, flowcharts enable researchers and practitioners to understand underlying mechanisms without compromising an appreciation of significant overall relationships. As evident in decision tables and algorithms literature, flowcharts' systematical style can be of invaluable assistance in explaining and decision-making across various fields, and further solidifying flowcharts as an essential tool in algorithmic design and implementation (Gacia et al., 2025).

3.6.1. Flowcharts in Business Processes

Flowcharts are important business process modeling tools because they assist companies in visualizing complicated processes in an orderly manner. It becomes simpler to understand the pictorial display of sequence and decision points, thus improving communication for stakeholders. The illustration of each process step assists in clarifying not just tasks but also monitoring possible inefficiencies as well as redundancy within procedure of operations. As defined in decision-making literature, and sharing and incorporation of decision tables, these graphical tools hold core explanation of the information flow and tasks between departments that end up leading to improved decision-making and strategic planning (Gacia et al., 2025). In this manner, flowcharts turn out to be a central component of assessing and streamlining business operations such that it becomes easier to explain current and desired states. The application of flowcharts extends past elementary process mapping; they facilitate continuous improvement approaches such as Six Sigma and Lean Thinking. Through the application of the models, organizations are able to identify process choke points successfully and optimize operations, thereby achieving higher overall productivity as well as quality. Flowcharts are foundational tools that allow these approaches by recording 'as-is' and 'to-be' process states, which allows practitioners to conduct gap analyses and implement necessary change accurately. Moreover, the combination of flowcharts with mathematical algorithms related to process improvement enables organizations to make rational choices; such a combination facilitates measuring improvement and testing the efficacy of proposed solutions (Polák et al., 2013). By making every member of a team familiar with processes in one manner, flowcharts promote a culture of transparency and responsibility, both of which are crucial for achieving long-term organizational goals. Furthermore, the dynamic nature of today's business settings demands flowcharts to also be flexible and adaptable with ease in order to reflect changing processes. As firms transform over the years, so may their processes, and thus constant readjustments may be necessary, with flowcharts having to accommodate this dynamism. This has been made possible by using electronic flowchart tools with easy revisions and quick communication among colleagues. This enhances the company's ability to respond quickly to changes in the outside market while maintaining a congruence with routine work on the inside. Thus, flowcharts not only enable quick problem-solving and process visualization but also serve as training and new employee orientation documents, which is key to helping an organization ensure its long-term survival. In conclusion, flowcharts encapsulate the intricacies of business processes, acting as fundamental aids for continuous improvement and operational adaptability (Gacia et al., 2025) (Figure 3.13).

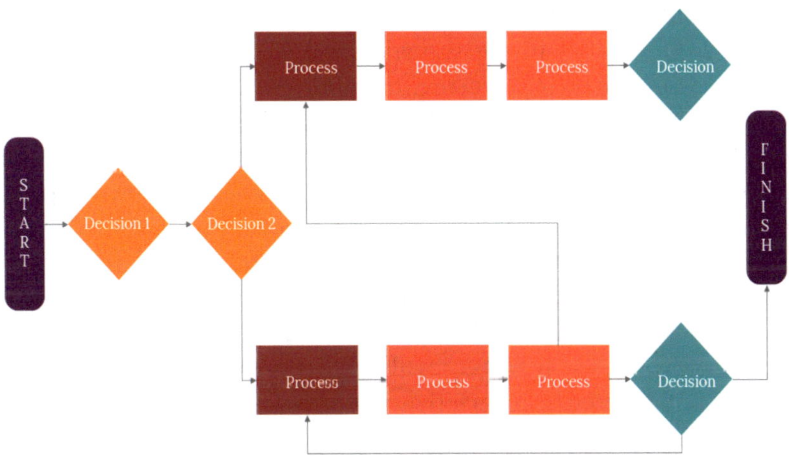

Figure 3.13. *Flowcharts serve as essential tools in the modeling of business processes.*

Source: *https://www.slideegg.com/image/catalog/60948-business-process-flowchart-template.png.*

3.6.2. Flowcharts in Education and Training

In an instructional and training setting, flowcharts are a useful tool to enhance comprehension and support learning. Flowcharts are graphical representations of procedures to be executed, which guide learners through knowledge and dissect complicated concepts into simple components. Such simplicity is particularly useful in instructional design, where educators can demonstrate algorithms and decision-making patterns. Teachers not only summarize information using flowcharts but also present it in a more visually captivating way, which enhances retention. In training sessions, flowcharts can be employed to chart work flows or procedural sequences so that trainees can follow their way through established procedures and best practices. Incorporating flowcharts into instructional materials, one emphasizes their versatility and practicality as tools for instruction and therefore invites learning-conducive environments. In addition, the use of flowcharts in classrooms is in line with the modern methods of active learning, where student participation is emphasized. By getting students to examine and construct flowcharts, teachers are able to facilitate critical thinking and problem-solving. The process of doing so forces learners to reduce information to its essential elements, leading to a better grasp of materials. For instance, students studying algorithms can map out the flow of steps in problem-solving scenarios and then ascertain efficiencies or different paths through their procedure. In training sessions, this active process not only establishes theoretical knowledge but also bridges the divide between theory and practical application. Flowcharts thus function dual-duty roles as learning tools and as active participation venues, proving their pivotal position within learning methodologies. Also, the pedagogical potential of flowcharts can be optimized through their integration with electronic platforms and group technologies. Modern learning spaces are progressively employing electronic tools to create and disseminate flowcharts, where students collaborate on the mapping of workflows and processes through flow mapping. This not only makes the learning process interactive but also is within the constructivist structure of learning, in which knowledge is developed through interaction and collaboration. Moreover, as educators learn about how decision tables have been presented and utilized across fields of study, what they learn can be transferred to the creation of flowcharts for a particular teaching environment and learners' requirements, which can reveal patterns of teaching practice that can contribute to improved outcomes (Gacia et al., 2025). By creating flowcharts for various learners based on their different learning style and preference, teachers can ultimately design a concessionary learning environment that maximizes the efficacy of education and training programs (Ambuel et al., 2015).

3.6.3. Flowcharts in Software Design

Flowcharts are essential software design tools, providing a simple-to-comprehend graphical representation of processes and algorithms. Through the description of control flow in terms of states and operations, flowcharts describe more complex systems and make them comprehensible to technical and nontechnical users. The graphical nature of flowcharts facilitates clearer communication between team members, allowing for problem-solving and even more effective design tuning. Besides, flowcharts provide a structured way of coding as they are a blueprint that will guide developers to carry out the respective algorithms. Not only does this serve to reduce errors but also make debugging easier as any discrepancies between the code and the flowchart may be readily identified and corrected.

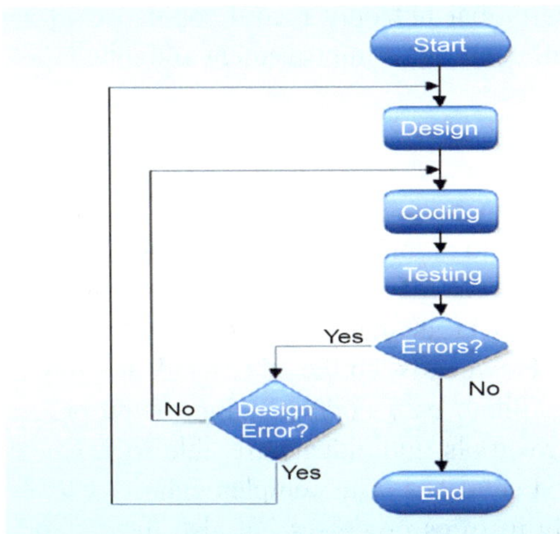

Figure 3.14. *Flowcharts serve as essential tools in software design.*

Source: *https://images.sampletemplates.com/wp-content/uploads/2015/04/29152927/Software-Development-Flow-Chart-Template.jpg.*

In software design, the use of flowcharts is more than just visualization; they also contribute towards systematic problem solving. By defining the steps of an algorithm, flowcharts enable designers to identify where there could be bottlenecks or inefficiencies within the process. The analysis is particularly valuable when considering how to apply decision tables, which are often used in conjunction with flowcharts to describe decision-making in a clear and logical manner (Gacia et al., 2025). Combining the two tools facilitates a thorough search across the design space such that major factors can be evaluated before development. Thus, the techniques facilitate thorough understanding of the manner in which various components communicate with one another in software systems and hence lead to more stable and efficient designs. Also, contemporary flowcharting tools have evolved to encompass advanced features that contribute to their effectiveness in designing software. With the advent of digital platforms, flowcharts can now be dynamically adjusted and shared effortlessly across teams to facilitate greater collaboration and responsiveness in the design process. This technological development parallels the developments observed in structural health monitoring of heritage buildings where open-source, low-cost solutions have transformed traditional practices (Basto et al., 2017). Similarly, the integration of sophisticated software tools in flowcharting is making software development more cost-effective and effective. Through these technologies, software designers are able to create sophisticated and responsive flowcharts that not only record sophisticated algorithms but also promote a culture of continuous improvement and innovation for their projects (Figure 3.14).

SUMMARY

In closing an inquiry into algorithms and flowcharts, it is evident that the two are core to problem-solving in nearly every discipline. Algorithms provide systematic methods to tasks that make it possible to systematically solve complex problems. Flowcharts, on the other hand, are graphical representation of algorithms to facilitate easy understanding of the processes involved. By combining these two tools, individuals are able to enhance problem-solving and delivering good solutions. The complementarity between flowcharts and algorithms not only justifies processes but also fosters collaboration in team settings, where they need to communicate ideas. Hence, knowledge of their relationship is critical in maximizing their use in technology fields. Furthermore, with advancing technology, the necessity for refining algorithmic techniques and flowchart systems cannot be overstated. For example, the recent innovation of plagiarism detection systems highlights the urgency for innovative techniques in algorithm design. The urgency for efficient systems to detect plagiarism in varying formats, such as figures and charts, highlights the paradigm shift in the application of algorithms. As noted, current procedures mainly overlook some elements of data representation, and by doing so, create loopholes that can be exploited. To address the loopholes, future research will be required to focus on creating robust algorithms that can account for the complexity of visual data, such as flowcharts, in order to offer comprehensive solutions to integrity within academic and work environments (Afif et al., 2014). Lastly, integrating algorithms and flowcharts into learning curricula can significantly enhance students' learning processes. Through studying both concepts simultaneously, teachers can help students learn the key concepts of computational thinking while allowing the students to develop creativity in solving problems. New topics such as heterogeneous wireless sensor networks demonstrate the need for adaptive and efficient algorithmic methods, as evidenced in recent research utilizing ant colony optimization to optimize network lifetime (Chung et al., 2011). As each new generation of engineers, scientists, and technologists emerges, a strong background in algorithms and flowcharts will prepare them to tackle ever more complex problems. Thus, the conclusion of this analysis points to the significance of these devices—not just for the purposes they are currently serving, but also for shaping future developments.

The flowchart versus algorithm debate acknowledges the fine balance between problem-solving and programming. As technologys influence expands along the vectors of society, the place of productive teaching methodology for learning to program has been brought into clearer relief. Traditional methods generally fall short, with an overly specialized focus on programming mechanisms and a corresponding lack of attention to the full richness of problem-solving as necessarily a many-sided, give-and-take activity. Current trends like Computational Thinking (CT) seemed to address these pedagogical loopholes. However, CTs predisposition to highlight methods over nuanced understanding can render creativity in coding stifled, and with it, the need for more integrated teaching methodologies so as to align problem-solving nuances with programming skills. To end, pedagogy has to shift its approach to meet the diversity programming embodies and its philosophical basis in instructing effective flowcharts and algorithms and therefore elevating the learner's capacity for innovative solutions in an ever-evolving digital era.

Shifting from pedagogical theory into practical application, how algorithms apply across various technological infrastructures is fundamental in optimizing functionalities. For instance, research in Wireless Sensor Networks (WSNs) is an excellent domain where novel algorithms demonstrate their capabilities. An ACO-based approach that focuses on maximizing the lifetime of heterogeneous WSNs is a strong indication of the utility of domain-specific algorithms in managing complex problems. In constructing disjoint connected covers, this method makes use of both heuristic and pheromone-based guidance, which is an indication of the convergence of algorithmic design and real-world application. Such algorithms not only address fundamental operational issues but also accurately capture the value of algorithms in enabling connectivity and efficiency of resources in technological systems. Accurate algorithm application is thus brought into focus as a fundamental principle that guarantees appropriate constructs are vital in the delivery of both efficiency and durability in technological systems. The interaction between algorithms and flowcharts is also underscored in the discussion of their role in process improvement in various sectors. Flowcharts are graphical aids that facilitate understanding and communication of algorithms, with complexities of procedure being made more comprehensible. By breaking down procedures into steps chronologically, flowcharts contain logic that is inherent in algorithms and enable students as well as professionals to trace decision-making paths of a process. Additionally, the combined application of flowcharts and algorithms can streamline activities, reduce errors, and enhance overall productivity, particularly in sectors that require accurate outputs, such as information technology and engineering. As industries increasingly rely on automation and data-driven answers, the union of algorithms and flowcharts will certainly continue to be a vital consideration in defining productive workflows and streamlined methods of problem-solving, cementing their status in contemporary technology.

REFERENCES

1. Abelha, A., Brandão, A., Machado, J. M., Pereira, A., et al. (2014). Simulating a multi-level priority triage system for maternity emergency. https://core.ac.uk/download/55631516.pdf (accessed on 9th September 2025).
2. Afif, F. N., Arrish, S., Maidorawa, A., Salim, A., et al. (2014). Shape-based plagiarism detection for flowchart figures in texts. http://arxiv.org/abs/1403.2871 (accessed on 9th September 2025).
3. Alias, C., Darte, A., Feautrier, P., Gonnord, C., et al. (2010). Multi-dimensional rankings, program termination, and complexity bound of flowchart programs. https://core.ac.uk/download/50051714.pdf (accessed on 9th September 2025).
4. Ambuel, B., Blackwood, B., Blackwood, B., Blackwood, B., Blackwood, B., Blackwood, B., Maloney, C., et al. (2015). The implausibility of 'usual care' in an open system: Sedation and weaning practices in pediatric intensive care units (PICUs) in the United Kingdom (UK). https://core.ac.uk/download/42138145.pdf (accessed on 9th September 2025).
5. Amirrudin, N. A., Azni, A. H., Behjati, M., Behjati, M., Bhattacharya, S., Chang, C. W., Chowdhury, M. Z., et al. (2014). Self-organizing comprehensive handover strategy for multi-tier LTE-advanced heterogeneous networks. https://core.ac.uk/download/29140722.pdf (accessed on 9th September 2025).
6. Basto, C., Chacón Flores, R. A., & Pelà, L. (2017). Open-source digital technologies for low-cost monitoring of historical constructions. https://core.ac.uk/download/81578722.pdf (accessed on 9th September 2025).
7. Baumeister, J., Cañadas Martínez, J. J., & Nalepa, G. J. (2011). At the 14th Conference of the Spanish Association for Artificial Intelligence (CAEPIA 2011). https://core.ac.uk/download/143455419.pdf (accessed on 9th September 2025).
8. Bento, F., Martinho, D., Vardasca, R., et al. (2023). Easy-Programming: Towards a web collaborating algorithmic and programming aid for early apprentices. https://core.ac.uk/download/614514536.pdf (accessed on 9th September 2025).
9. Bergstra, J. A., Middelburg, C. A., & Stefanescu, G. (2013). Network algebra for synchronous dataflow. https://core.ac.uk/download/489633137.pdf (accessed on 9th September 2025).
10. Besag, J., Wang, J., Wang, Q., Weiss, Y., Wu, B., Zhang, D., Zhang, T., et al. (2016). Composite correlation quantization for efficient multimodal

retrieval. http://arxiv.org/abs/1504.04818 (accessed on 9th September 2025).

11. Bruno, J. (2025). Feasibility of using the massively parallel processor for large eddy simulations and other computational fluid dynamics applications. https://core.ac.uk/download/pdf/42827496.pdf (accessed on 9th September 2025).
12. Chu, E., & George, A. (2025). Algorithms and software for solving finite element equations on serial and parallel architectures. https://core.ac.uk/download/pdf/42832105.pdf (accessed on 9th September 2025).
13. Chung, H. S. H., Ip, W. H., Li, Y., Lin, C., et al. (2011). An ant colony optimization approach for maximizing the lifetime of heterogeneous wireless sensor networks. https://core.ac.uk/download/9389323.pdf (accessed on 9th September 2025).
14. Coffman-Wolph, S., & Gray, K. (2019). Fun and interactive activities for an introductory computer science course of 200 students. https://core.ac.uk/download/287648661.pdf (accessed on 9th September 2025).
15. Cox, G., & Soon, W. (2021). Aesthetic Programming. https://core.ac.uk/download/478118089.pdf (accessed on 9th September 2025).
16. Csizmadia, A., Sentance, S., Simmons, C., Sinclair, J., et al. (2018). Classroom-based research projects for computing teachers: Facilitating professional learning. https://core.ac.uk/download/227096987.pdf (accessed on 9th September 2025).
17. Dutt, N. D., & Gajski, D. D. (1988). EXEL: A language for interactive behavioral synthesis. https://core.ac.uk/download/287623403.pdf (accessed on 9th September 2025).
18. Farran, B., Niranjan, M., & Saunders, C. (2010). Machine learning for intrusion detection: Modeling the distribution shift.
19. Ferri, G. (2012). Between procedures and computer games: Semiotics of practices as a unifying perspective. https://core.ac.uk/download/61912458.pdf (accessed on 9th September 2025).
20. Garov, K., & Radev, V. (2010). About learning discrete mathematics at Bulgarian school. https://core.ac.uk/download/62659855.pdf (accessed on 9th September 2025).
21. Glass, B., Jenkinson, G., Liu, Y., Sasse, M. A., et al. (2016). The usability canary in the security coal mine: A cognitive framework for evaluation and design of usable authentication solutions. https://core.ac.uk/download/157858010.pdf (accessed on 9th September 2025).

22. Godbole, S. (2014). Impact of a visual programming experience on the attitude toward programming of introductory undergraduate students. https://core.ac.uk/download/77951455.pdf (accessed on 9th September 2025).

23. Hirata, N. S. T., & Julca-Aguilar, F. D. (2017). Symbol detection in online handwritten graphics using Faster R-CNN. http://arxiv.org/abs/1712.04833 (accessed on 9th September 2025).

24. Lahti, L. (2009). Guided generation of pedagogical concept maps from the Wikipedia. https://core.ac.uk/download/80714249.pdf (accessed on 9th September 2025).

25. Manin, Y. I. (2013). Complexity vs energy: Theory of computation and theoretical physics. http://arxiv.org/abs/1302.6695 (accessed on 9th September 2025).

26. Michaelson, G. (2015). Teaching programming with computational and informational thinking. https://core.ac.uk/download/29822230.pdf (accessed on 9th September 2025).

27. Moreno Gacia, M. A., Vanthienen, J., & Verhelle, M. (2025). An overview of decision table literature. https://core.ac.uk/download/pdf/6468533.pdf (accessed on 9th September 2025).

28. Polák, L. (2013). Analysis and simulation of the signal's transmission in the DVB-H/SH standards. https://core.ac.uk/download/30311053.pdf (accessed on 9th September 2025).

29. Roper, W. J., Srisawat, C., & Thomas, P. A. (2020). MEGA: Merger graphs of structure formation. https://corc.ac.uk/download/305117890.pdf (accessed on 9th September 2025).

CHAPTER 4

PROGRAMMING FUNDAMENTALS

Contents

INTRODUCTION

The programming environment has transformed drastically over the past decades from simple coding practice to complex problem-solving tasks with real-life applications. This transformation emphasizes the need to recognize that programming is not merely a technical field but a core discipline of computer science. As argued by Michaelson et al. (2015), despite programming being essential to creating software that penetrates life dimensions, the educational process to educate this topic still remains under-developed. Problem-solving and programming's interdependence poses new challenges to educators since students still do not connect theory to practice. Hence, the need for an effective educational framework becomes evident; it must include programming knowledge as well as the creative aspects of problem solving in order to create a balanced foundation of knowledge for the subject. One potential solution to the complicated scenario of the interconnectedness of programming and problem solving is that of Computational Thinking (CT). As noted in Michaelson et al. (2015), CT not only emphasizes the programming abilities but also highlights the processes of creativity used when solving and analyzing complex problems. This blended approach has been popular in recent years, as it compels students to look at programming holistically.

Figure 4.1. *Programming fundamentals.*

Source: *https://technology.online.city.ac.uk/media/mageplaza/blog/post/c/i/city_programming_languages_1.jpg.*

But learning strategies tend to focus more on programming technicalities and less on problem-solving skill development in students, which leads to a superficial level of understanding. A good curriculum must find a balance between both domains to equip students with critical thinking of problems and generating innovative solutions through coding. It is here that an updated learning pedagogy can come into play to equip efficient programmers who are equally efficient problem solvers. In addition to the reformulation of pedagogical models, teachers also began to investigate gamification strategies to enhance student motivation and engagement in coding classes. Through, the inclusion of game mechanics in learning environments has been observed to create a more interactive learning environment for learners effectively. This action addresses the increasing trend of demotivation among students in traditional forms of teaching. By turning programming exercises into competitive challenges, instructors can effectively engage students with greater intellectual participation. Such methods not only make learning enjoyable but also enable students to practice and solidify their software engineering abilities. Lastly, blending new teaching methods with a focus on programming skills along with problem-solving can create a dynamic learning experience, paving the way for the future generation of talented programmers who can meet the demands of the virtual landscape (Figure 4.1).

Definition of Programming

Programming in its most fundamental sense can be defined as the process of developing and using a set of instructions by which a computer can perform a series of operations. This includes all types of activities ranging from typing simple scripts to the creation of complex software systems. The content of programming is more than the syntax of various programming languages to the problem-solving and reasoning ability that goes into the creation of effective algorithms. Students learning to code acquire the ability to methodically approach problems, often breaking down issues into discreet, single-focused components, a talent vital to software development. Adding design thinking to programming education enables future coders to more clearly visualize the worth of user experience and usability in their coding, bridging the gap between abstractions and the actual implementation. Additionally, programming is also closely related to computer science and software engineering disciplines and entails more than just coding. It also involves understanding principles for breaking down problems, abstraction, and modularity. As an illustration, programming learning projects such as courses focusing on the Internet of Things (IoT) highlight the pertinence of programming to real-world situations. These programs seek to demystify the technical nature of programming so that it is made understandable and interesting to students from various backgrounds, thus promoting inclusion in technological fields. Such programs reflect the idea that programming is not so much a technical skill but a multidisciplinary endeavor that involves creativity, design, and engineering principles. This broader vision is what effectively draws a whole picture of what programming is all about. In addition, programming is precisely in accord with computational models that direct functionality and object execution in software. The models developed that allow concurrent function execution are at a higher abstraction level, enhancing the functionality of programming. For example, the model of computational object execution, following the principles of object-oriented programming, illustrates how programming acts as the basis for developing strong and efficient software systems. The synergistic impact of programming and computational frameworks not only contributes to the developers' skill set but also highlights the utilization of core concepts in creating scalable applications. Thus, by understanding the definition and broader implications of programming, one can appreciate its value as a part of the ever-changing technology landscape.

Importance of Programming in Modern Society

Programming is a fundamental skill in this day and age, one that cuts across computer science. It plays an essential role in many areas of life, including medicine, finance, and education, and shapes the manner in which we utilize technology on a daily basis. The use of coding to other areas facilitates the development of innovative products for addressing challenging problems. For example, in medicine, programming allows algorithms to be developed that can process enormous data sets and enhance patient care as well as increase efficiency within hospitals. As technology progresses, the need for a workforce trained in programming grows more essential, highlighting the importance of programming instruction in readying students for the challenges of the current job market. Besides, programming unlocks the possibilities of innovation and problem-solving ability in a person. People learn the ability to develop customized applications and devise solutions to solve real-life problems by coding. The process of creation encourages critical thinking because programmers have to look at a problem from different points of view to develop practical solutions. The collaboration between academia and industry, as seen in work that explores education frameworks, shows a methodical effort to link theoretical knowledge to practical application (Angles et al., 2016). By building a strong understanding of programming fundamentals, not just do individuals enhance their professional skills but their capability to innovate as well, and this is essential in today's technology-driven world. Finally, the growing demand for programming proficiency identifies it as a language that has the capacity to overcome geographical and cultural barriers. With technology fast becoming part of daily life, the ability to read and write computer systems is a valuable expertise in any number of industries. Cooperative efforts, such as those funded by the National Science Foundation, aim to enhance educational outcomes by using machine learning and artificial intelligence within learning environments (Coleman et al., 2005). These innovations represent the merging of programming and modern uses of technology, confirming the necessity of educational programs that accommodate coding instruction. By incorporating programming basics into different working environments, society can better prepare itself for an increasingly more interconnected world where programming literacy becomes key to survival (Figure 4.2).

Figure 4.2. *Importance of programming in modern society.*

Source: https://thumbs.dreamstime.com/b/dynamic-scene-showing-hands-typing-laptop-vibrant-coding-data-screen-illustrating-modern-programming-digital-339452457.jpg.

Overview of Programming Languages

The programming language environment is dense and holds numerous paradigms that are used for numerous goals and depict the evolution of computational concepts. Programming languages are the core of programming, as they assist programmers in transforming algorithms and logical programming into a machine-readable form. Traditional programming languages had the divide between low-level and high-level. Low-level languages such as Assembly provide low-level hardware control and therefore can be utilized in systems programming, whereas high-level languages such as Python and Java simplify complex coding processes. The development of object-oriented programming, as discussed in Diertens et al. (2012), introduced models that enhanced code modularity and reusability, which in effect revolutionized the software development approach. This classification emphasizes the dependencies of language design, their aim, and their impact on the practice of software engineering. The past decades have seen the programming world transformed with the advent of new languages designed to meet specific purposes, such as JavaScript for web applications and R for statistical computing. Each programming language also has its syntax and semantics, which specify how the programmers communicate with computers and structure their solutions. The relationship between programming and problem-solving has also been of special interest, showing the necessity for sound pedagogical principles for teaching programming. Even though there are many teaching approaches, Michaelson et al. (2015) indicates that the relationship between programming and problem-solving remains a challenging problem. Teachers have begun to adopt holistic methodologies such as Computational Thinking (CT), which are concerned with problem space understanding as well as coding. This movement highlights the significance of an integrated strategy in teaching programming fundamentals. Essentially, a sound understanding of programming languages is essential not only to software engineering but also to an understanding of the overall technological framework that supports the digital world today. Those foundations of early programming languages form the basis of modern computing, foreshadowing the solution to and resolution of problems that will be faced. The development of programming paradigms, particularly object-oriented approaches to programming, has revolutionized notions of software design principles so abstraction and efficiency are promoted. However, as Diertens et al. (2012) proposes, continued endeavors to seek computational models will be important to being able to ensure programming languages can address ever-evolving technological problems. As such, knowledge about the significance of different programming languages in coming up with creative solutions is important to every person working in the programming sector. Such information forms the core of programming fundamentals and provides students and practitioners with the ability to resist harsh computing systems (Figure 4.3).

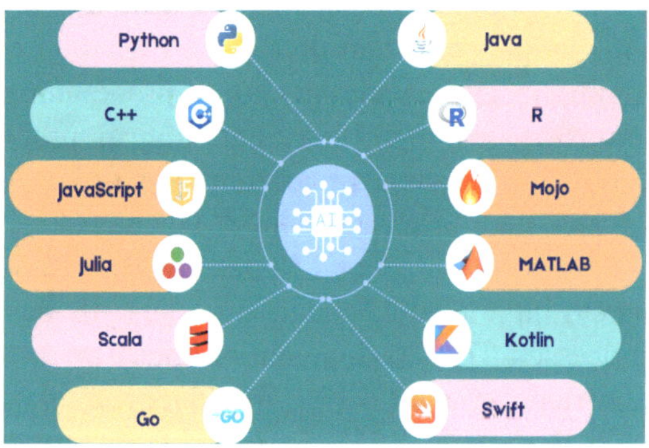

Figure 4.3. *Overview of programming languages.*

Source: https://external-content.duckduckgo.com/iu/?u=https%3A%2F%2Fstatic.seaflux.tech%2Fmedia%2Fblog%2F9124688b-fb34-4f72-8e40-376feeec1420-infographic.png&f=1&nofb=1&ipt=cfdf9408ac824004f90aef62f4493823a26609ddcf917c79ad2da27df9361e69.

4.1. BASIC CONCEPTS OF PROGRAMMING

In computer programming, the fundamentals form the pillars on which all software is built. In other words, programming is a systematic approach to problem-solving in the form of algorithmic design and programming languages. Variables, data types, control structures, and functions are the constructs that form the minimum vocabulary used by programmers to develop useful and effective code. In addition, an understanding of object-oriented programming (OOP) is essential due to its prevalent paradigm addressing concepts such as encapsulation, inheritance, and polymorphism. Such fundamental knowledge not only prepares learners to address complex issues but also enables them to work on various programming languages, providing them with a general skill set applicable to a broad spectrum of computing areas, based on the background of introductory programming courses (Chen et al., 2011). Coupled with core concepts, the role of methodologies in computer programming cannot be downplayed. Methods like procedural programming, functional programming, and logic programming each have their own advantages and can be applied to different programming needs. Procedural programming, for example, emphasizes the sequence of operations to be performed, while functional programming has a computation perspective of function evaluation of mathematical functions and does not alter state and mutable data. Logic programming, studied in the case of Prolog, applies formal logic to describe facts and rules about problems given. This flexibility in approaches allows programmers to choose the best paradigm for their project requirements and thus enhance the outcomes and facilitate better program maintenance and design. The historical context of such programming paradigms recognizes their evolution, and also enhances study and program application (Taltavull et al., 2015). Finally, practical use of these fundamental concepts is the entry point to proficiency in programming. Use of these principles through hands-on experience in labs or coding is what makes students transform theoretical models to useful skills. Problem-solving skills are also essential at this level, allowing students to break down complex programming issues into manageable pieces of work. Further, group assignments foster collaboration and communication skills, an important part of exposing students to real-world software development environments. The process of coding, debugging, and refining solutions becomes instrumental in reiterating learning, emphasizing the importance of perseverance in addressing challenges. By applying these basic principles within a supportive learning environment, students not only become capable of managing simple programming issues but are also motivated to innovate and tackle more sophisticated computing scenarios (Chen et al., 2011).

4.1.1. Variables and Data Types

Variables and data types form the essence of programming and are imperative for successful coding. Variables are named storage locations in a program, which make it possible for software engineers to store, retrieve, and manipulate information. A variable is associated with a data type, which determines the type of information it can hold and how the information can be operated on. Data types can vary from integers, floats, and strings to booleans. Choice of data type influences not only the storage of data in memory but also how data is processed. For example, the use of integers in counting operations usually proves more efficient than the use of strings because it will allow for faster computations and consume less memory. Hence, familiarity with variables and their corresponding data types is very crucial in writing optimized and efficient code for any given programming language. Apart from storage, variables and data types are used in more than one way.

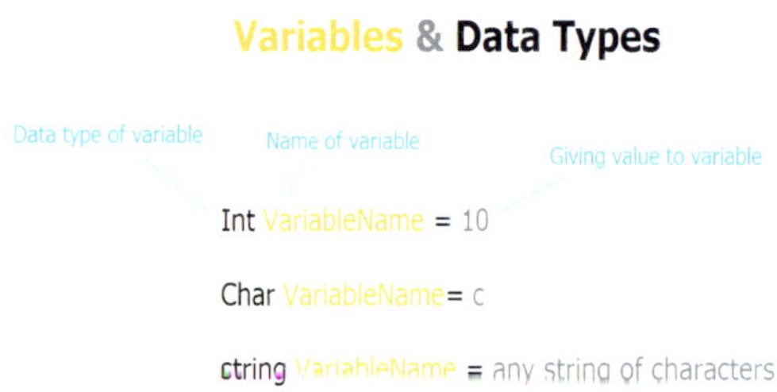

Figure 4.4. *Variables and data types.*

Source: https://1.bp.blogspot.com/-B9jLMmTdMGg/YOtchn9oe6I/AAAAAAAAB-KQ/jA3YuHqb3LMV28wrbqx-wdCFoQLh_LxDwCLcBGAsYHQ/s1246/Variables%2B%2526%2BData%2Btypes%2Bbloger.png.

They play a critical role in defining the control flow of computer programs and ensuring data integrity. With the use of various types of data, computer programmers can make use of specific logic that dictates how the data is accessed and manipulated. Strong type systems, for instance, require explicit conversions and reduce the likelihood of errors that occur when mixing incompatible types. Furthermore, advancements in programming practice and methodologies have led to the development of advanced frameworks that rely on common variables and data types for complex applications. Variable-based projects, such as the N-puzzle game, in an educational context, demonstrate collaboration between data types in algorithms. This allows for a clear understanding of programming concepts with a focus on the pedagogical value of coding hands-on experience (Markov et al., 2006). As the digital world evolved, so did the evolution in the demand for sophisticated data handling systems. The increase in qualitative data, especially of the sentiment analysis type, fueled the need to translate such data into quantifiable variables—essentially bridging the qualitative observation to quantitative analysis gap. Such an endeavor is called sentometrics, which best encapsulates the use of appropriate data types to accurately represent complex sentiment measures. Using powerful econometric techniques, programmers and data scientists can create meaningful variables that identify important correlations with other data sets. Ultimately, coding proficiency in the interactions between types of data and variables contributes to one's own coding skill and establishes an environment for data-driven innovation (Algaba et al., 2020) (Figure 4.4).

4.1.2. Control Structures (If Statements, Loops)

Control structures like if statements and loops are the foundation of programming because they control the flow of program execution within an application. If statement allows a programmer to specify conditions under which a specified blocks of code will be executed, hence making it possible to develop dynamic and responsive programs. This capability is most critical where decisions have to be made about user input or external data. As an example, a simple if statement can determine whether to provide a user with or without access depending on their credentials, illustrating the functional application of such control structures in determining software behavior and user interaction. Through proper application of if statements, programmers can create logical flows that enhance a programs responsiveness and interactivity, thereby laying the ground for more sophisticated programming paradigms. In addition to if statements, loops are control structures that are included in most programming languages to facilitate repetition of code according to given conditions. They are commonly used to repeat through lists or arrays to enable the management of many items using minimal code. Both of the two fundamental loop types—while loops and for loops—are used differently; while loops repeat indefinitely as long as a specified condition is true, while for loops iterate over a certain number of items or a given range. Repetition of this kind is important in data processing operations, for instance, reviewing huge datasets or performing calculations that entail repeated tasks. Through the use of loops, programmers can avoid redundancy and shorten the code, hence making the coding process more clear and controllable. In addition to syntax, control structures play a key role in forming the foundation for the construction of smart algorithms and decision-making in software construction. As illustrated in various fields, including bioinformatics and computational biology, controlling these structures is essential to unleashing complex functionalities that respond to real-time data and user command. For instance, in bioinformatics, if statements can be used to discover paths in genetic algorithms, while loops can search for genomic sequences to find specific patterns. This exchange between control structures and algorithmic design demonstrates how managing these fundamental programming tools can enhance solutions across applications to ultimately contribute to advances within domains reliant on computational methods, such as the ones defined in Ekmekci et al. (2016) and Chenouard et al. (2009).

4.1.3. Functions and Procedures

In software programming, the ideas of functions and procedures are essential in promoting code reusability and organization, which are core principles in software development. Functions may be described as pieces of code written to accomplish certain tasks, usually returning a value when execution ends. Through this modular programming, programmers are able to capture complexity, and their code becomes simpler and easier to manage. Procedures, however, execute a sequence of operations without necessarily having to yield a value. Both constructs allow for code reuse, minimizing redundancy and optimizing efficiency. Through the use of these constructs by developers, they are able to build libraries of reusable code elements that save time and reduce errors in many applications. This emphasis on structured programming is central to building solid software, and it emphasizes the importance of placing emphasis on the exact design and implementation of procedures and functions. Function and procedure implementation and design are not academic exercises; they have a great deal of influence over program reliability and development effectiveness. For instance, a language like PenDraw is created in order to surpass the weaknesses of mainstream languages and their extensions in computer graphics (CG) programming. By emphasizing compile-time testing over run-time debugging, PenDraw shows how a specialized language can simplify programming and lower development costs. Once the developers are better at working with functions and procedures in these types of languages, they are better able to create sophisticated graphical programs. Pen Draws easy-to-work-with syntax and design permit more users, not only professional developers, but users of various skill levels. This democratization of CG programming is indicative of the evolution of the software development world. In addition, the development processes for functions and procedures, especially with regards to an approach such as the cleanroom software development process, draw attention to the aspect of reliability in programming. The cleanroom process emphasizes defect prevention throughout the entire development process using structured specifications and statistical controls to achieve high reliability. Through following a systematic inclusion of procedures and functions within the strict framework, developers can systematically eliminate possible bugs and inefficiencies. Function design is a job more of art than of engineering; it is part of the process of creating software reliability, since each function added is approached in a statistical mindset that anticipates things to fail. A knowledge of how functions and procedures are built into overall development frameworks such as those in Dyer et al. (2025) demonstrates their role in producing quality software to very tight operation specifications.

4.2. PROGRAMMING LANGUAGES

The universe of programming languages is extensive and wide, each with differing purposes and applications in the universe of computer science. A first foray into programming shows that fundamental concepts like problem-solving and algorithm design are language-agnostic across languages. That universality allows students to have a learning foundation, where they can move on from rudimentary constructs to more complex programming paradigms. For instance, languages like Java have been popular in classrooms due to the portability and extremely widespread application. Students prefer solving examples based on the extensive scope of applications, which facilitate a thorough understanding of programming that does not remain limited within the boundaries of theory but also involves everyday application, as reflected in the course plan of Chen et al. (2011). This approach effectively lays the groundwork upon which future programmers may create, ultimately leading to the effective utilization of more intricate programming techniques. Of primary concern in programming language education is the approach used in educational settings. The choice of approach—either Objects-first, Fundamentals-first, or GUI-first—has a profound impact on students' comprehension and retention of programming concepts. Current research supports a Fundamentals-first approach, introducing students to fundamental programming concepts before advancing to more complex material. This method not only ensures greater understanding but also resonates with the cognitive advancement of students as they move through progressively more difficult material. By comparison of various pedagogies, researchers have established an ordered Java topic sequence aligned with the Fundamentals-first approach, as found in the evidence of Joy et al. (2004). Directed learning pathways are crucial to enable students by enabling them to have the necessary skills to tackle actual programming issues. In addition to instructional approaches, the programming language of choice can influence learning and learner engagement. Java as a primary language used in introductory programming instruction provides a strong foundation that appeals to both new programmers and veteran programmers returning to fundamentals. Java's object-oriented paradigm facilitates a good understanding of encapsulation, inheritance, and polymorphism, the building blocks of software development. Secondly, Java's excellent library support allows one to easily investigate a wide variety of applications, further embedding the learning experience of students with real, representative instances. With a framework that emphasizes core programming concepts, it is possible for teachers to educate students to become good programmers. Hence, a sound background in languages such as Java lays the foundations for a successful transition into more complex programming activities, creating a learning and application continuous cycle in the field of computer science, as pointed out in Chen et al. (2011) (Figure 4.5).

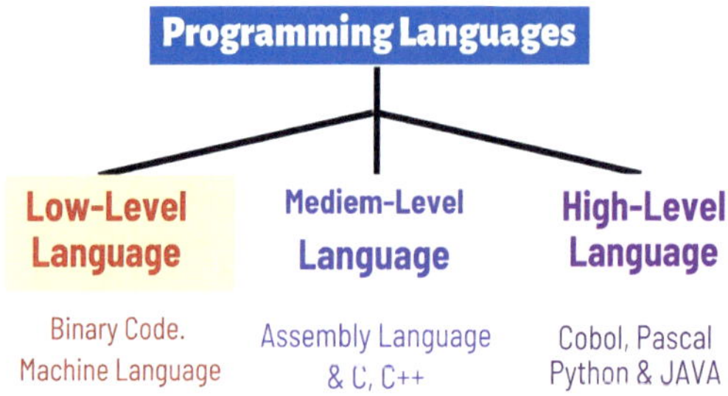

Figure 4.5. *Programming languages.*

Source: https://edukedar.com/wp-content/uploads/2021/09/3-Types-of-Programming-Languages.jpg.

4.2.1. High-Level Versus Low-Level Languages

The high-level and low-level separation is at the heart of understanding the world of programming. High-level languages, such as Python and Java, remove much of the complexity of the computer architecture so programmers can program more easily and with a more readable human format. They are more natural language-oriented and less hardware-defined management that must be accomplished. Hence, they are predisposed towards abbreviating the development cycle, making them extremely well suited for new programmers and also for software that has to be quickly prototyped. The increase in the application of high-level languages also finds its correlate with pedagogy for computer science instruction supporting their application in elementary programming courses aimed at uninstructing programming to students and encouraging expanded use of the field. On the other hand, low-level programming languages such as machine code and assembly offer a direct interaction with the hardware so that the programmer can create code which speaks directly to the machine language of the system. This can lead to maximum efficiency in terms of speed and resource consumption as there is negligible overhead due to abstraction. However, low-level programming is very hard to accomplish and is accompanied by increased complexity with a harder learning curve. As shown by research, a systematic review has been behind the importance of both visual and text programming languages in shaping the learning process in computer science. Understanding the strengths and limitations of these languages enables instructors to better design curriculum to meet student requirements and address the critical issue of retention in computer science education (Mooney et al., 2017). Besides that, programming language level, high or low level, can significantly influence student interest and performance in learning programming. For instance, after students understand basic programming concepts using high-level programming like Java, they are better placed to deal with more advanced ideas through the application of low-level programming (Joy et al., 2004). This sequential learning process helps enhance learning and retention by the students, thereby the low dropout rates characteristic of computer science classes. The combination of high-level abstractions with low-level machinery understanding helps students appreciate the entire range of programming. Finally, establishing a strong foundation in both high-level and low-level languages will not only prepare students to perform intricate programming tasks but also simplify the transition into various fields of technology.

4.2.2. Programming Language Trends (Python, Java, C++)

With the advancement of programming sciences, such programming languages as Python, Java, and C++ have become essential tools for programmers in the majority of industries. Python, which is simple to learn and readable, has been promoted as a first language among those who study the basics of programming. Its syntax in natural language is simplistic enough to make it suitable for new developers but robust enough to carry out challenging tasks in areas like data science and artificial intelligence (Ekmekci et al., 2016). Python's robust libraries also contribute to its usefulness, allowing users to accomplish anything from web development to data analysis without too much trouble. This blend of accessibility and strength ignites its popularity in learning environments as well as professional environments. Java with its platform independence enabled by the Java Virtual Machine (JVM) is still unbeatable in software development, particularly for enterprise and Android application development. The object-oriented nature of the language facilitates the creation of modular programs that increase code maintainability and scalability, which aligns with contemporary software engineering principles (Michaelson et al., 2015). Javas rigorous emphasis on security and performance also render it a favorite for highly robust-demanding applications, that is, e-commerce and financial services. Its extensive user base and deep documentation provide a wealth of materials for new users, making it a staple in both programming courses and business use. C++ distinguishes itself by being highly efficient and low in system resource usage, and therefore is the go-to choice for applications with high efficiencies required, for example, systems programming and game development. C++ builds upon the foundation of C, offering object-oriented features that allow for complex software development but, concurrently, offer low-level memory management, leaving a programmer with control not found anywhere else (Ekmekci et al., 2016). The language's flexibility and performance have earned it a firm footing in competitive programming and performance-critical applications. However, the C++ learning curve is intimidating for new users, demanding strong comprehension of programming concepts and solution strategies. As technology advances, C++ evolves to meet new demands from programmers across industries.

4.2.3. Choosing the Right Programming Language for a Project

Selecting the appropriate programming language for a project is a significant choice that can profoundly impact the development process as well as the ultimate success of the application. Various considerations come into play, such as the scope of the project, the expertise of the team, and the proposed application domain. For instance, some languages suit some assignments better; Python is a popular choice in fields such as bioinformatics due to its easy syntax and extensive libraries. As mentioned, "the ability to design and write computer programs is among the most indispensable skills that a modern researcher can cultivate" (Ekmekci et al., 2016). Selecting an appropriate language will raise productivity and allow more efficient team collaboration, particularly when the members have good grounding in the selected paradigms and syntax. Another deciding factor when selecting a programming language is the support and longevity of the language. Established languages like Java, Python, and JavaScript enjoy strong communities and extensive libraries that make it easier to learn and debug. This community support is invaluable, as it will allow developers to have access to shared knowledge and resources, thus leading to faster development cycles. As paraphrased, "online gaming provides opportunity to train a wide range of skills" (Gallagher et al., 2012), which can be directly related to learning a programming language through practicing and experimenting. Therefore, while comparing languages, coders must not only compare present trends but also the flexibility of the language to what will be changing in technology and frameworks in the future. Lastly, performance needs and system architecture significantly influence the programming language selection. For instance, if there is high-performance demand from the project, languages such as C or C++ would be necessary due to their near-hardware nature, making them more suitable for systems programming and applications where fast response is of paramount importance. For web application development, however, languages such as JavaScript or Ruby can be used due to the ease of use and speed of development they provide. Moreover, the potential to be integrated into other technologies or languages should not be overlooked because the interoperability can increase what a project can do. Therefore, there is an absolute requirement for in-depth examination of the specific project's goals and requirements in order to make an informed decision when choosing the appropriate programming language (Figure 4.6).

Figure 4.6. *Choosing the right programming language for a project.*

Source: https://i0.wp.com/www.webzin.in/wp-content/uploads/2023/09/Choosing-the-Right-Programming-Language-for-Your-Project.jpeg?resize=1200%2C674&ssl=1.

4.3. DEVELOPMENT ENVIRONMENTS

The concept of development environments lies at the core of programming fundamentals, as such environments are the basis on which software is developed, tested, and debugged. A development environment typically contains an integrated development environment (IDE), which provides developers with tools necessary to adequately coordinate their coding endeavors. Such environments usually include code editors, compilers, and debuggers that streamline the development process, allowing programmers not just to write code but also identify and correct errors with ease. Furthermore, the customization features in such environments allow developers to tailor their configurations based on individual preference, enhancing productivity and encouraging an experience-oriented approach. Hence, a well-chosen development environment can have a tremendous impact on students' programming learning curve and is an important stepping stone to their coding skill and subsequent endeavors. Beyond efficiency enhancement, development environments allow cooperative programming, which is essential in contemporary software development. The integration of version control systems into such settings enables teams to work on projects simultaneously, monitor changes in code, and roll back to previous versions if necessary. This aspect is crucial in establishing a collaborative learning environment where programming students can communicate with each other, share ideas, and resolve problems in groups. By learning to use platforms through which integration with tools like Git is possible, potential programmers gain critical teamwork skills in conjunction with familiarity with industry-standard practice. Digital collaboration factors found in such development environments appeal to perspectives reported in contemporary educational discussion, in which experiential learning methods are linked with effective skill development within programming environments and membership in a community is highlighted within enhanced educational outcomes from experiential participation (Gallagher et al., 2012). In addition, the trend towards gamified elements in development spaces is an adaptive approach to engaging learners. The integration of game-inspired teaching methods into coding spaces has the potential to transform the potentially daunting process of acquiring programming principles into an enjoyable activity. While students work through problems placed in a game format, they are able to develop critical thinking and problem solving skills in a safe space. Such a pedagogic method proves the hypothesis that interactive and immersive learning can significantly enhance comprehension and memory of complex topics, as evidenced by experiments on game-based learning (Cuinas et al., 2015). Such development environments that embrace these interactive features not only appeal to the palates of digital-native learners but also prepare them for real environments in which adaptability, innovation, and collaboration are essential. This shift reflects the potential of development environments to become driving forces of profound educational reform in programming fundamentals (Figure 4.7).

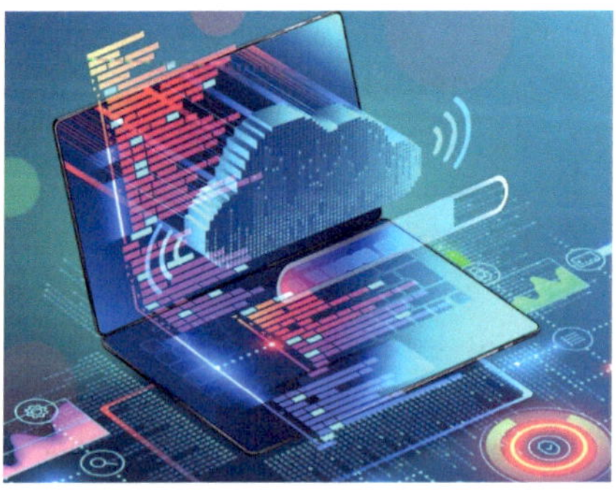

Figure 4.7. *Development environments.*

Source: https://www.mytutorialrack.com/wp-content/uploads/2021/07/Development-Environment-1024x768.jpg.

4.3.1. Integrated Development Environments (IDEs)

Integrated Development Environments (IDEs) are a vital collection of tools for software development, offering a complete package of capabilities that make programming less complicated. IDEs combine a code editor, debugger, and build automation capabilities within a single application, significantly enhancing overall productivity. Simple-to-use interfaces and included functionality allow developers to write, debug, and compile code more efficiently than using text editors or command-line interfaces. The integration of these aspects enables real-time feedback, which is required for detection and correction of errors at every stage of code development to develop an iterative and interactive coding environment that is crucial for novice as well as seasoned developers. Further, IDEs support a wide range of programming languages, adhering to the needs of various professions within the software development world.

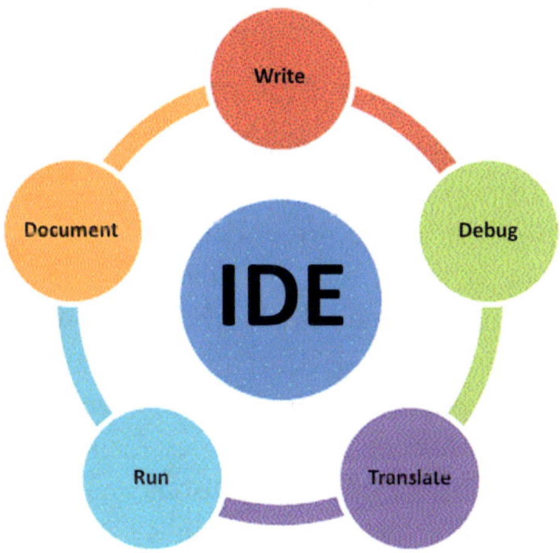

Figure 4.8. *Integrated development environments (IDEs).*

Source: https://2.bp.blogspot.com/-IUEBkv0M8Co/Vclh2sSw4CI/AAAAAAAAA-Go/phkpMJnuwmc/s1600/IDE.GIF.

The majority of modern IDEs include plugins and extensions, providing customization as well as the integration of specific language features or frameworks. For instance, platforms such as Visual Studio, Eclipse, and PyCharm are equipped with tailored functionalities that include support for languages such as C++, Java, and Python. Such adaptability is particularly advantageous in cross-disciplinary fields, as compatibility with other technologies—for example, computational biology or digital signal processing—is typically necessary. The ability to leverage expert libraries and tools within an IDE can greatly reduce setup and configuration time, enabling developers to focus their energies on solving complex problems more effectively (Angoletta et al., 2008). With evolving programming paradigms, the role of IDEs is increasing in fields like bioinformatics and computational biology, where data analysis complexity demands solid software solutions. Rising reliance on computer aids has placed emphasis on programming environments that can handle complex algorithms as well as large data sets. IDEs are not only convenient to use via their graphical interfaces but also support third-party libraries extending their built-in capabilities. These are the skills needed for carrying out high-level analyses, as seen in post-genomic biology, where researchers utilize programming languages like Python to develop applications that manage vast biological data (Ekmekci et al., 2016). Thus, studying the features and operations of various IDEs is essential for aspiring programmers because these environments lay the groundwork for effective coding habits and innovative problem-solving skills in a world and era of technology (Figure 4.8).

4.3.2. Text Editors and Their Features

Text editors are fundamental software in the programming world that not only aid in code writing but also testing and writing environments. That additional feature of a text editor can be the difference in the code writing experience, allowing programmers to write, edit, and navigate their code better. Major functions typically include syntax highlighting to differentiate keywords, variables, and commands by coding them visually. This feature is particularly helpful in reducing errors and readability because developers rummage through layers of code. Moreover, text editors can offer features like autocompletion, which foresees and proposes code completion, enabling faster coding and minimizing typographical errors. In turn, these enhancements allow new programmers and seasoned developers to be more efficient and clean in their programming tasks. In addition to basic skills, most of these text editors also possess debugging capabilities, which are crucial in identifying and correcting coding errors. Debugging facilities, such as line-by-line execution and breakpoints, allow developers to examine their code in real time in order to predict correct behavior. For instance, working with intricate algorithms or data structures, the software allows a detailed examination of a program's state at specific stages of execution. Furthermore, some editors include version control systems, such as Git, to enable users to track changes, collaborate perfectly, and revert to past code states in case of need. Such provision boosts productivity and collaboration among teams engaged in complex projects, according to the discussions on tools that simplify programming processes. With these features, developers can minimize the risk associated with coding, thus improving overall productivity and quality of output. Another characteristic of text editors is their level of configurability and extendability, which allows users to personalize the environment to specific requirements and tastes. Most modern editors come with plugins or extensions that accommodate an array of programming languages and frameworks. This flexibility enhances the coding experience by allowing developers to implement only the features that have a direct connection with their work process, ensuring a more tailored experience. Editors like PenDraw also manifest as a tailored approach to programming, offering alternatives to traditional languages while promoting efficiency and cost-saving in graphic programming. The continuous development of programming expert languages, as reflected in the works of others, illustrates the need to tailor tools to serve the increasing needs of programmers and the programming complexity of the times. This focus on tailored and productive programming environments justifies the assertion that there is a need for good text editors in the search for programming foundations.

4.3.3. Version Control Systems (Git, SVN)

One of the foundations of modern computer programming is the use of version control systems (VCS) as a requirement for monitoring code changes and allowing collaborative work between programmers. Examples of tools used include Git and Subversion (SVN), which offer a system for tracking changes, allowing multiple programmers to work concurrently on a project without interfering with one another's work. Historical file and log snapshots, checked periodically by such systems, not only track changes but also mirror developers patterns of practice within the development environment. For instance, the developers' habit of avoiding concurrent changes to the same files to avoid conflict demonstrates how VCS not only ensures code integrity but also impacts collaborative coding practices amongst members of a development team (Hattori et al., 2018). This dual mandate of version control systems underlines their importance in guaranteeing software quality as well as the efficiency of development processes. As software development teams have progressed towards more distributed forms, the implementation of version control systems has become increasingly important. Global software development is accompanied by particular issues such as communication barriers and cultural differences that can hinder collaboration and knowledge awareness among developers. With the application of systems like SVN and Git, developers can have visibility into each other's work regardless of location. Such systems facilitate fine-grained changes to be recorded, thus aiding developer knowledge through mechanisms like notification of simultaneous changes or revealing conflicts. Because collaboration degrades due to the lack of face-to-face communication in distributed teams, the application of VCS helps redistribute that sensitivity and support that normally exists in collocated situations (Hattori et al., 2012). Thus, version control systems have become enablers of effective collaboration, making potential drawbacks bearable challenges. In addition, the application of version control systems goes beyond simple change tracking since they are knowledge repositories that can significantly improve a team's collaborative work. The capacity to extract information from version history provides windows through which code ownership and expertize of developers can be understood. For example, instead of depending on developer recollection, it is possible to use version history to examine the contribution of a single team member with accuracy. Merging a model of memory retention with code ownership metrics adds a richer picture of responsibility-sharing within an organization. This advancement on data collection and awareness can result in improved decisions and resource commitment during development, achieving the highest potential for productiveness and quality output. By elevating version control systems in such a way, developers are able to leverage previous experiences to construct a culture of continuous improvement and collective learning (Hattori et al., 2018) (Figure 4.9).

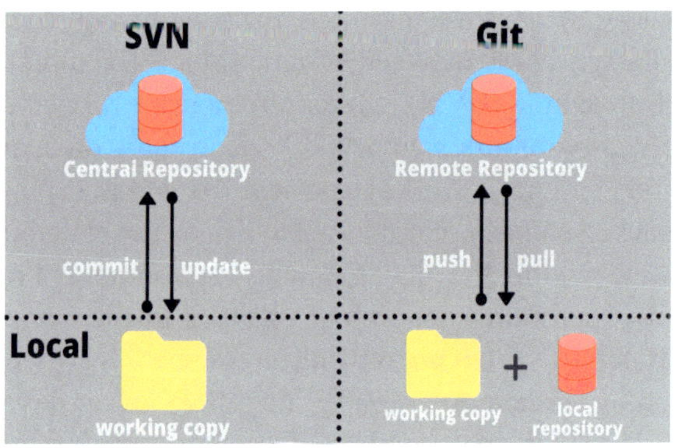

Figure 4.9. *Version control systems (Git, SVN).*

Source: https://engage.primeone.global/wp-content/uploads/anspress-uploads/5f0af8f5b0ad10853572f8fc4db69e121fd335ce_51.png.

4.4. DEBUGGING AND TESTING

The sophistication that is associated with modern-day programming calls for proficiency in debugging and testing processes. Debugging entails the identification and correction of errors or bugs in the program, which can significantly impair function. This intricate process calls for employing diversified methods, from eyeballing to automated debugging tools. Software development has included with it an emphasis on preventive debugging methods which try to eradicate problems during coding rather than following installation. This is not just a way to enhance the quality of software but also an optimization of the software development process so that developers can focus solely on functionality and innovation. Therefore, debugging competence is imperative for aspiring developers because it enables them to ascertain and improve software integrity throughout its lifespan. Testing complements debugging, which scrutinizes the performance of the softwares mercilessly against predetermined demands. It is a formal validation process that ensures the code performs as intended under various circumstances. The testing phase can be categorized into different types of testing, such as unit testing, integration testing, and system testing, which are utilized for specific reasons throughout the software development process. For instance, unit testing verifies the individual components individually to validate their accuracy when in isolation, while integration testing verifies the interaction among multiple components.

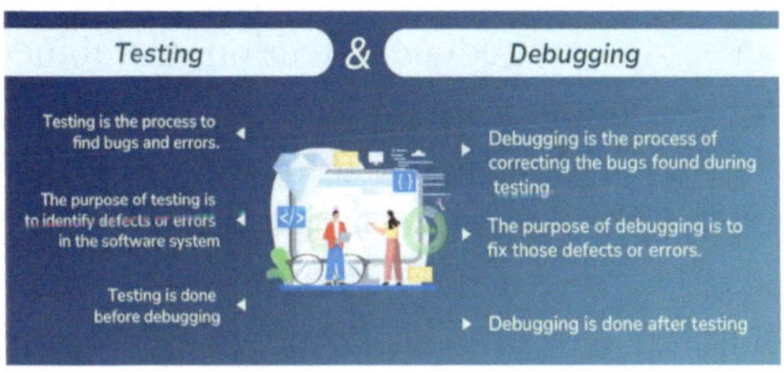

Figure 4.10. *Debugging and testing.*

Source: https://media.geeksforgeeks.org/wp-content/uploads/20240709184455/Differences-between-Testing-and-Debugging-copy.webp.

By combining these testing techniques, developers can detect potential weaknesses and performance problems early, even before the software is ready for delivery to the end-user, hence greatly improving user satisfaction and experience. Finally, adequate testing procedures are necessary for the guarantee that software not just fulfills functionality specifications but is likewise secure and trustworthy. The interdependence of debugging and testing is mutual, as both procedures inform and strengthen the other. Debugging could, in the process, reveal the testing phase, highlighting areas of the code that require further scrutiny based on faults realized. Conversely, rigorous testing could reveal hidden bugs that could not be detected while debugging. The nature of programming, especially with the emergence of multi-threaded programs, necessitates the need to have sophisticated debugging tools that are capable of drilling through concurrent threads effectively (Kathare et al., 2012). In addition, instructional practices integrating problem-solving in the field and theoretical knowledge—for example, those used in classes introducing software engineering as well as future technologies like the Internet of Things—promote end-to-end know-how of testing and debugging (Julien et al., 2019). These, and the continuous learning that they create, are integral to building sound software engineers capable of addressing the challenges of modern programming (Figure 4.10).

4.4.1. Common Debugging Techniques

Good debugging is a fundamental programming practice, through which programmers discover and eliminate bugs that stall the execution of their program. A standard technique is the use of print statements, which is a simple means of observing the data flow and determining the location of bugs. With the insertion of print statements into a program at key locations, programmers are able to track variable values at various stages of execution. This approach, while simple, is frequently worth its weight in gold in highly complex projects where logic bugs can escape immediate detection. Combined with other tools, including breakpoint debugging in integrated development environments (IDEs), programmers are able to halt execution and examine the program state, providing a deeper analysis of potential bugs that can emerge during execution. Another widely used debugging method is unit testing, which seeks to test the smallest program building blocks in isolation. By composing exact tests for single functions or methods, software developers can ensure that each part functions as anticipated before inclusion into the overall system. This proactive approach not only enables bugs to be discovered earlier but also improves code reliability and ease of maintenance. Moreover, continuous integration tools also offer built-in automated testing environments that run unit tests with each change, creating a safety net that minimizes the introduction of defects into evolving codebases. These steps highlight the significance of adopting rigorous testing practices in the overall programming process, building a healthy development ecosystem that is less susceptible to the introduction of defects. In addition to traditional debugging techniques, modern software development is more dependent on sophisticated tools, such as static analysis and code linters. These tools analyze source code without executing it, identifying likely errors and suggesting best practices for optimizing and readability of code. This forward-looking approach is aligned with contemporary software engineering pedagogy, as evident from practice-directed course subjects like the Internet of Things (IoT), which emphasize programming proficiency along with robust software engineering practices (Julien et al., 2019). By embracing such advanced debugging techniques in everyday development practices, developers can enhance their productivity significantly, create more quality software, and become more sensitive to the evolving demands of technology (Angoletta et al., 2008) (Figure 4.11).

Figure 4.11. *Common debugging techniques.*

Source: https://www.technostation.com/wp-content/uploads/2023/01/Debugging-techniques-1024x587.jpg.

4.4.2. Importance of Testing in Software Development

Comprehensive testing is an essential part of software development and forms the basis for producing quality products. Complete testing not only identifies defects but also ensures that the software fulfills specified requirements and user expectations. In today's high-pressure development cycle, clearly defined testing techniques such as unit testing, integration testing, and system testing have become imperative. Such techniques offer a formal approach to examining various function components in an application, allowing developers to detect errors early during development. Moreover, the use of several testing techniques ultimately improves the dependability and efficiency of the software, so that end-users receive an undisturbed experience with the product. Furthermore, testing assumes greater significance outside error detection within the software. It is critically important to establish user confidence and satisfaction, which can have a profound impact on the success of a product in the market. When users are presented with dependable and thoroughly tested software, they are more confident in how it will work, thus making their overall experience better. As recent studies have shown, putting into practice sound testing practices has been demonstrated to speed up development cycles by eliminating the need for long post-launch fixes. This ultimately leads to optimal use of resources and enables development teams to focus on innovation rather than continuous debugging. Besides improving quality and user satisfaction, testing is also important in instilling a culture of ongoing improvement among development teams. Making testing a part of the software development life cycle enables teams to adopt agile approaches, fostering an environment wherein iterative refinement is the standard. Engaging in hands-on, experiential testing methods—such as those used in software engineering and IoT technology courses—can nicely leverage students' interest while imparting the importance of testing in coding. Throughout the process of designing and implementing projects, students are kept in mind that software engineering involves something more than just programming. Instead, it is a process of planning, implementing, and evaluating cautiously, emphasizing that proper testing must be done to acquire resilient and adaptable software solutions (Julien et al., 2019; Comley et al., 2017) (Figure 4.12).

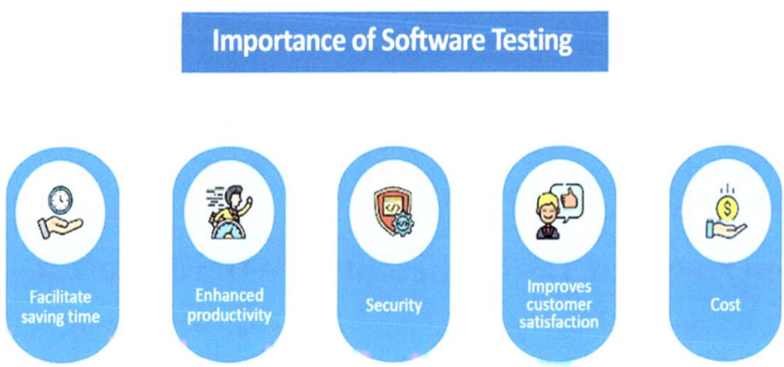

Figure 4.12. *Importance of testing in software development.*

Source: https://cdn.iplocation.net/assets/images/blog/articles/importance-of-software-testing.png.

4.4.3. Types of Testing (Unit Testing, Integration Testing)

The world of software testing comprises various methodologies, two of which are most critical, that is, unit testing and integration testing. Unit testing is the verification of individual component or function of a software program to ensure that each unit will function as expected separately. This is a crucial initial level of testing which is able to identify defects early in the development cycle, thus saving effort and cost in later stages. By concentrating on tiny pieces of code, developers can catch problems that would otherwise balloon into huge issues during the integration phase. Test-Driven Development (TDD) practices allow for unit testing by promoting first writing tests and subsequently the code itself, creating a disciplined habit that allows for cleaner, more maintainable code throughout the programming life cycle. Conversely, integration testing consists of combining single units to test how they work as part of the overall system. The objective is to detect issues that arise when various parts are interrelating with one another, for instance, data passing and dependency conflicts. Integration testing is essential in order to detect errors that do not appear during unit testing, such as interface incompatibility or unexpected module interaction. Integration testing can be performed in various modes, for example, big bang integration, wherein all units are integrated at once, or incremental integration, via which units are integrated one after another. Each mode has advantages and disadvantages, which must be considered thoroughly in the context of software under development. Integration testing rigorously guarantees that the system as a whole will function well and meet user requirements. Both unit testing and integration test important roles in software development, leading to overall program reliability and user satisfaction. While the debugging process becomes more efficient with the use of unit testing to solve solitary pieces of code, integration testing provides an overview by testing the interactions between such pieces of code. Together with other testing methods, for instance, system and acceptance testing, they create a robust framework that is directed towards ensuring the quality of software products. Since programming languages and frameworks, as in the case of the "Java Programming Speech Recognition Application" mentioned in cite39, evolve to include complex functionalities, the need for a structured testing methodology becomes more apparent. Most significantly, the inclusion of test approaches and tools facilitates more transparent transitions from development to deployment, leading to sustainable software development practices.

4.5. OBJECT-ORIENTED PROGRAMMING (OOP)

The arrival of Object-Oriented Programming (OOP) represents a major breakthrough in software development. OOP presents a paradigm that is all about the object concept, whereby objects contain both data and behavior, making it possible to write more modular, reusable, and manageable code. This encapsulation enables developers to represent entities in the real world in a more realistic way, making programming possible in a manner that reflects users' natural way of understanding entities and how they interact. Some of the most important features of OOP include inheritance, polymorphism, and encapsulation, each of which contributes to easier coding practices yet more clarity in code. The shift towards OOP not only adheres to the complexities of modern applications but also provides a platform for collaborative development, as many programmers can work on different portions of a program without hindering each other's progress. As OOP teaching becomes ever more prominent in computer science education, effective methodologies are vital. For instance, the Fundamentals-first teaching methodology for teaching OOP, particularly in languages like Java, has been shown to be promising to enhance the grasp and skill acquisition of students.

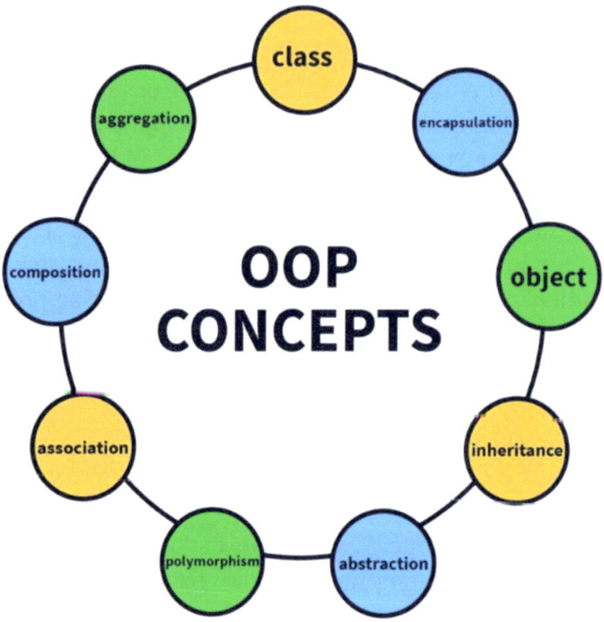

Figure 4.13. *Object-oriented programming (OOP).*

Source: https://www.scaler.com/topics/images/object-oriented-programming-concepts-1024x870.jpg.

Research indicates that beginners learning with the focus on basic ideas—class design and object interaction—grapple with the complexities of OOP more effectively. By establishing a well-defined order of topics, students are able to establish a solid foundation prior to the intricate OOP concepts being tackled. Real-life scenarios and problem-solving activities reinforce these underlying foundations, enabling students to engage with the learning material in an active sense. Through this, an emphasis on foundational knowledge has the potential to offer the foundation for students' long-term success in software development, aligning well with established pedagogical methods of programming education (Joy et al., 2004). In recent years, the inclusion of new tools and technologies on OOP courses has brought about deeper learning processes. One excellent example is the use of tangible user interfaces (TUIs) in teaching OOP principles. Experiments have shown that using interactive devices, like Sifteo cubes, significantly enhances student motivation and understanding. In a controlled test, students who were taught C# programming through such physical interfaces demonstrated high motivation and improved performance in grasping OOP. The interactive and sensor-based nature of TUIs provides a hands-on process which defamiliarizes challenging programming concepts, rendering learning an active process. Thus, integration of technology in the OOP learning process not only enhances the interest of learners but also has a beneficial effect on their learning of fundamental programming concepts, and it is an effective methodology in programming fundamentals (Balcells et al., 2014) (Figure 4.13).

4.5.1. Principles of OOP (Encapsulation, Inheritance, Polymorphism)

In computer programming, Object-Oriented Programming (OOP) concepts like encapsulation, inheritance, and polymorphism are some of the basic tenets that enable effective software design. Encapsulation is particularly significant in protecting an object's internal state by allowing access and modification only via declared methods. This avoids any unwanted interference and enhances code maintainability because developers can modify without undermining other areas of the system. Encapsulation is part of a broader systems theory, where modularity is seen as a design value, interaction being controlled within contained contexts. Controls thereby ensure not just data integrity but also cleaner interfaces, opening the path to more complex functions. Inheritance, another core principle of OOP, promotes code reuse and hierarchical structure. By allowing a new class to inherit attributes and behaviors from an existing class, programmers are able to create a well-organized structure that reflects the structures of the real world. The inheritance facilitates simple expansion of existing code without redundancy, allowing a more efficient coding process. Inheritance in its usage injects a paradigm that reflects classical systems theory, which emphasizes the significance of relationships in systems. Through this principle, programmers are able to create stable programs with common features and simplify the maintenance process, thereby improving productivity and performance in a broad spectrum of programming environments (Dominick et al., 2025). Polymorphism, the third fundamental principle, facilitates flexibility and response in code execution. Through the ability of objects to be used as instances of a parent class, polymorphism enables a single interface to manage several different data types and functionalities dynamically. This concept not only makes program tasks easier but also yields a more intuitive interface, as programmers can employ more general code capable of dealing with numerous types of objects with little modification. Polymorphism also proves its significance through its role in method overloading and overriding, leading further to better program control (Dominick et al., 2025). Lastly, polymorphism in OOP drives software development through the ability to develop scalable software that adapts to changing user needs and technologies.

4.5.2. Benefits of Applying OOP

One of the greatest strengths of Object-Oriented Programming (OOP) is that it enhances reusability of the code, and this consequently has a great impact on enhancing efficiency when writing software. Through the utilization of classes and objects, OOP allows programmers to write modules that can be used with ease in other programs or projects and, therefore, reduces the utilization of repetitive code to a great extent. Instead of needing to rewrite identical functions or algorithms, programmers can make new objects from existing classes, overlay and modify them as needed. Such modularity is suited to improved code organization, enabling ease of maintenance and collaboration for teams involved in large systems. Consequently, not only does OOP accelerate the development process, but it also facilitates easier maintenance and upgrading of existing applications, in line with software engineering best practices that promote sustainable programming methods and project longevity (Joy et al., 2004). Another key benefit of OOP is its inherent ability to model complex systems more effectively. By relating programming abstractions to real-world objects, OOP allows developers to construct simulations that are understandable and manageable. This is a shift away from procedural programming, where data and routines are more likely to be separated, to a paradigm where they are packaged together as objects. This packaging enables more specific expression of relationships and interactions among various parts of a system. This proves particularly helpful in areas such as computational biology, where simulation of biological behaviors usually entails knowing complicated relationships. Being able to define classes that create biological objects, such as their properties and behaviors, allows researchers to apply OOP toward developing computational software which directly adheres to their domain needs (Ekmekci et al., 2016). Lastly, OOP promotes greater collaboration among software development teams through emphasis on encapsulation and abstraction. These paradigms support division of labor, such that programmers can develop different sections of a system at the same time without interfering with each other's code. The abstraction layer supports hiding the implementation details so elaborate that team members can collaborate with each other's components in a smooth and integrated manner. This proves highly advantageous within educational environments, where systematic approaches encourage increased learning results. For instance, with an object-oriented methodology in first-year programming classes, it is easier to learn central concepts while, concurrently, conditioning the student for day-to-day programming issues. By presenting clean abstractions as teaching instruments, OOP exemplifies its unequaled capacity to support the learning process, and thus forms the ideal methodology in programming instruction (Joy et al., 2004) (Figure 4.14).

Figure 4.14. *Benefits of using object-oriented programming (OOP).*

Source: https://www.learncomputerscienceonline.com/wp-content/uploads/2021/01/Advantages-Of-Object-Oriented-Programming.jpg.

4.5.3. Real-World Applications of OOP

The use of object-oriented programming (OOP) in learning environments is a good example of its everyday use beyond mere software development. A new way of teaching OOP concepts includes the use of tangible user interfaces (TUIs), such as Sifteo cubes. The technology allows students to access OOP concepts physically and interactively. In a study on the effectiveness of this method, students in an experimental course with experience in Sifteo cubes demonstrated not only greater motivation but also enhanced understanding of key OOP concepts compared to control group students in a standard course. This shift in interest underscores the potential of OOP to enhance scholarly models, allowing students to confront real programming issues when working on interesting learning activities that resonate with their interests and cognitive processes (Balcells et al., 2014). Outside the classroom, OOP is at the heart of many industries, revolutionizing the software construction practice. Through its support of modularity and reusability, OOP enables developers to create well-constructed systems that are maintainable and can be easily changed. Companies in sectors such as healthcare and finance utilize OOP to manage intricate data structures and relationships better. For instance, an enterprise financial application can use object-oriented principles to encapsulate transactions, accounts, and audits as individual objects, which makes them easy to manage and reduces errors. This abstraction allows teams to focus on even more abstract business logic rather than being weighed down by difficult code, demonstrating how OOP can lead to improved operational efficiency and product quality in real-world applications (Diertens et al., 2010). In addition, the impact of OOP is not just on implementation but determines software solution design and structure. By emphasizing abstraction, encapsulation, inheritance, and polymorphism, OOP provides a theoretical foundation critical to today's software engineering practice. The use of these concepts throughout the software life cycle helps teams navigate through various phases, from requirement analysis to system design and testing. Object-oriented design patterns, for instance, can facilitate communication between stakeholders and developers by providing a vocabulary shared by all regarding system functionality. This agreement diminishes misinterpretations and cultivates collaboration, ultimately leading to improved project results. Since businesses continue to understand the significance of OOP in producing sustainable and scalable software, its uses in actual application will only expand (Diertens et al., 2010).

4.6. SOFTWARE DEVELOPMENT METHODOLOGIES

The landscape of software development methodologies is ever-changing as technology improves and project requirements adjust. Lying beneath these methodologies is the overall objective of providing structured approaches that enhance the effectiveness and efficiency of the software development cycle. Among the most popular methodologies, Agile stands out for its adaptability and iterative nature, allowing teams to react to changing demands in a timely manner. This method encourages collaboration among team members with open communication and feedback mechanisms, ultimately leading to a product that reflects user needs more clearly. In contrast, more traditional methods, such as the Waterfall model, emphasize a sequential design process where each phase must be completed before the next one begins. These different approaches mirror the diversity of approaches with which software developers can work, each offering its own advantages in accordance with the context and goals of the project. The debate regarding the viability of many software development approaches also reflects the worth of creativity in coding. As evidence suggests, creativity plays a significant role in a programmer's performance and is a critical skill which needs to be included in engineering curricula. By encouraging a creative mindset, instructors can help students approach coding challenges with innovative thought and adaptability—qualities that are aligned with modern Agile practices. As companies become increasingly committed to agility and responsiveness to customers, educators need to discuss how to instill these qualities in future software developers. Incorporating creative problem-solving into technical training can bridge the gap between programming fundamentals and the ever-changing nature of the software industry. Adopting such integrated learning approaches can potentially bring forth a generation of programmers who are technically competent as well as creatively capable. Furthermore, the current software development environment demands incessant reconsideration of existing methodologies in order to remain relevant in a fast-paced area. The development of new technologies and platforms, such as cloud computing and artificial intelligence, demands programmers to employ methodologies that can keep up with rapid changes. For instance, hybrid approaches that combine the best of both Agile and Waterfall provide a middle path, enabling teams to take advantage of the planned aspects of Waterfall with the flexibility in Agile. As organizations opt for more productivity through their processes, exploring hybrids can be the future of software development methodologies. Through the education of various methodologies, instructors can prepare students to handle the complexity of software projects in a way that they possess the versatility to perform well in various development environments (Figure 4.15).

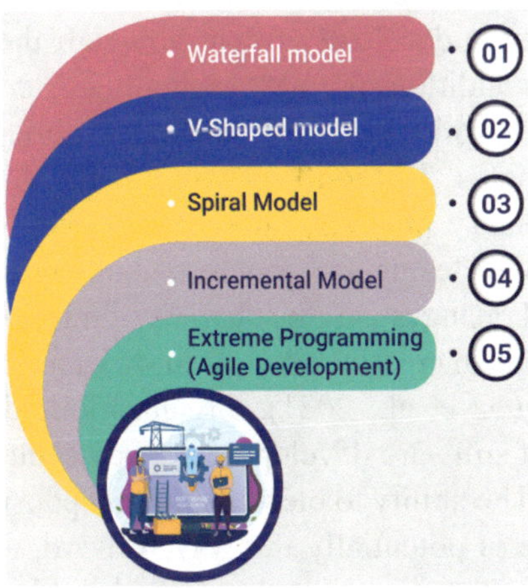

Figure 4.15. *Software development methodologies.*

Source: https://www.dreamsoft4u.com/wp-content/uploads/2022/05/5-Different-Software-Development-Methodologies-Models-Infomative-Image-968x1024.png.

4.6.1. Agile Versus Waterfall Methodologies

When it comes to software development, the choice of using the Agile or Waterfall model has a profound impact on project success. The Waterfall model, being linear and sequential in its phase nature of working, is a planned approach in which a phase must be completed before moving to the next. The model is highly commendable for being simple and having an orderly process, hence perfect for projects with established requirements. However, its inherent rigidity is a hindrance in cases where there is a changing user demand, a case of the inability to change. As companies are increasingly faced with the dynamism of software development, the shortcomings of Waterfall are eclipsed, and the industry is directed towards more adaptive methods such as Agile, whose emphasis is on iterative and incremental approaches to software development. Agile methods, by contrast, are more concerned with sensitivity to change and continuous stakeholder involvement. Using brief development cycles referred to as sprints, Agile systems such as Scrum enable teams to generate working software regularly, through which continuous user feedback and incremental refinement are acquired. Such adaptability not just encourages innovation but also optimizes project alignment with user and market demands. Analysis also shows that even though certain Agile practices like XP do not necessarily subscribe to standard rules, they also flourish in contexts with a high need for flexibility and stakeholder involvement (Mathew et al., 2016). Such evidence emphasizes the critical place of Agile in today's software development where demands for flexibility and velocity often outweigh the formal strictness of Waterfall methods. In addition, the new technologies enshrined in the fourth industrial revolution introduce more complexity into project management, fueling the Agile versus Waterfall debate. With shifting industries and extremely interdisciplinary projects, effective communication and teamwork among multi-disciplinary teams are immense challenges. Agile's incremental nature facilitates rapid changes and the sharing of multiple expertise, which is appropriate for the needs of creative projects in smart manufacturing and digital environments (Rodríguez et al., 2021). Organizations that are ready to deal with the complexity of software development today should consider these new approaches seriously. The ability to blend Agile's responsiveness with elements of Waterfalls structure is potentially the way forward, allowing for balanced management of projects that preserves the strengths of both models.

4.6.2. The Importance of Project Management in Programming

The role of project management in programming cannot be overstated, especially with increased complication of software development projects. Effective project management is the cornerstone of successful programming ventures because it guarantees all stages—time, money, and staff—are managed with utmost caution. Such a methodical approach promotes interaction between staff, streamlines processes, and delineates definite roles, which are imperative in keeping failures of lateness and cost blowouts at bay. By facilitating systematic planning, project management allows developers to anticipate challenges and adapt to the ever-evolving technological landscape. Project management is also aided by the necessity of having a solid project framework by the various stakeholders who demand transparency and accountability in the development process. Lastly, integrating principles of project management into programming activities makes them complement organizational goals and aspirations of stakeholders. Furthermore, project management methods such as Agile and Waterfall play crucial roles in determining programming processes, which promote adaptability and efficiency. Agile, for example, prioritizes customer feedback and incremental development, through which programmers can enhance features and adapt to user needs swiftly. Such ease of modification is vital in an environment where technology refreshes and user needs can alter unpredictably. Conversely, traditional methodologies like Waterfall provide a formal plan which, given the existence of well-established goals and timelines for a project, can be beneficial. Approach choice generally depends on some project and team-specific requirements and, finally, plays its role in the programmers' ability to utilize solutions effectively. Through encouraging an open structure of operational procedures, project management enables the programmer to devote energy to innovation and creativity, as seen in evidence to the extent that high creativity is linked to programming competence (López Álvarez et al., 2016). In addition to encouraging efficiency, project management minimizes risks entailed in programming projects, which are normally plagued by unforeseen obstacles. By incorporating risk management strategies, project managers can identify potential issues early in the development cycle and implement contingency plans to address them, thereby reducing the likelihood of project failure. The continuous evaluation of project health through metrics and performance indicators further reinforces this proactive approach. With programming increasingly encroaching upon other industries such as healthcare, finance, and education, the use of competent project management becomes increasingly relevant, making it a fundamental ability for programmers. Learning environments, as underscored in findings grounded on Latin America, indicate pressure towards curriculum alignment with industry demands, emphasizing the necessity of project managements in brokering between theoretical knowledge and practical application in programming (Angles et al., 2016). In conclusion, successfully applying project management principles into programming is essential to realizing successful, innovative, and sustainable outcomes (Figure 4.16).

Figure 4.16. *Importance of project management in programming.*

Source: https://media.geeksforgeeks.org/wp-content/uploads/20240619103030/Why-Is-Project-Management-Important.webp.

4.6.3. Role of Documentation in Software Development

Documentation serves as a cornerstone of effective software development, playing an indispensable role throughout the programming lifecycle. It acts not merely as a record of design decisions and technical specifications but also as a communication bridge among team members. Comprehensive documentation ensures that all stakeholders, including developers, project managers, and end users, have a shared understanding of the projects goals and requirements.

Moreover, well-organized documentation facilitates onboarding for new team members, allowing them to grasp complex systems and codebases more swiftly. In the contemporary landscape, where agile methodologies dominate, the emphasis on incremental development and swift iterations necessitates that documentation is accurate and up to date. This adaptability ensures that as projects evolve, the documentation evolves in tandem, thereby maintaining its relevance and utility. Furthermore, the significance of documentation extends beyond the mere recording of programming tasks; it is fundamentally linked to the quality of the software product itself. It has been observed that meticulous documentation practices lead to fewer defects and more maintainable codebases. This relationship emphasizes that documentation is not merely an extraneous exercise but rather a crucial element that enhances software reliability and functionality. While engaging with hands-on projects, such as those involving Internet of Things (IoT) devices, students are encouraged to grasp the applicability of good documentation. As detailed in relevant educational programs, students learn to incorporate robust documentation practices alongside technical competencies, ensuring that their projects not only fulfill requirements but also exhibit high standards of clarity and maintainability (Julien et al., 2019). Ultimately, the interplay between documentation and software quality cultivates an environment where innovation can thrive.

End-user involvement further enriches the context surrounding documentation within software development. Engaging end-users in the documentation process can lead to a more thorough understanding of their needs and expectations, which, in turn, results in user-centered designs. Research highlights that actively including end-users in requirement elicitation bolsters the development of more effective and usable systems (Graf et al., 2010). By allowing users to provide real-time insights, documentation can be continuously refined to reflect genuine needs rather than hypothetical scenarios. This iterative feedback loop not only improves the quality of the software but also empowers developers to create products that are closely aligned with user expectations. As software engineers increasingly adopt frameworks enabling end-user participation, the practice of thorough documentation evolves into a dynamic tool that captures valuable insights and adjustments, ensuring that the software remains relevant and user-friendly (Figure 4.17).

Figure 4.17. *Role of documentation in software development.*

Source: https://nix-united.com/wp-content/uploads/2022/09/1-3-1024x819.jpg.

SUMMARY

In concluding a review of computer programming fundamentals, it is relevant to acknowledge that successful learning of programming is influenced by countless factors more nuanced than intellectual capacity. Course design and social structures of peer interaction significantly shape what affects students' learning processes. The outcome of a statistical analysis of students' scores indicates a minimal negative relationship between mean course grades and score variance. This reveals that the courses with higher mean scores are those with lower variation in students' performances, thus supporting the requirement for effectively structured courses that promote divergent learning capabilities and styles. Through such analysis of these linkages, instructors can enhance curriculum organization in a manner that promotes comprehensive learning achievements and provides equal support to all learners across their programming activity (Chołoniewski et al., 2016). Moreover, stimulating the creativity of programming instruction is a factor of pivotal importance in the success of the students. As recently reported, research establishes that strong levels of creativity have a high positive correlation with programming success among college freshmen. This testifies to the need for curricula that include and honor thinking creatively, particularly in engineering domains where conventional approaches dominate. Thus, computer programming instruction must go beyond traditional practices and incorporate elements that enable creative and original thought. This is not only beneficial for students of diverse backgrounds, but also enhances classroom dynamics as a whole to pave the way for a more inclusive and rewarding learning environment (López et al., 2016). Lastly, the implications of the results of the determinants of programming education highlight the necessity of having a combined effort in approaching curriculum development. Policymakers and educators must collaborate to create a model that not only specializes in developing the technical skill required by programming but also the innovative capacities needed for problem-solving and innovation. Finding the correlation between learning architecture, creativity, and educational success can lead to curricula that not only learn traditional programming skills but also teach the next generation of thinkers and creators in the tech arena. By embracing such principles, the landscape of programming education can be transformed to suit the multi-faceted demands of students and the imperatives of an evolving rapidly changing technological landscape (Chołoniewski et al., 2016; López et al., 2016).

An understanding of programming fundamentals is essential to anyone interested in the study of computer science. At the heart of programming is the concept of an algorithm, which is a sequential process for achieving a specific solution. These algorithms can be written in numerous ways, including flowcharts, pseudocode, or outright code, depending on the level of abstraction necessary. So integral to programming are data structures, the means by which data is stored and manipulated. Arrays, linked lists, and trees are the most common data structures that have varying strengths and applications. Familiarity with these foundation stones enables programmers to develop efficient and effective code, opening doors to more advanced topics such as object-oriented programming and software design principles that form the basis in developing robust applications. Control structures are another fundamental concept in programming, providing a way to control the execution flow inside a program. Conditional statements, loops, and function calls are the most simple control structures, and they together make possible more flexible and dynamic code. Conditional statements, such as if and else, enable decision-making inside programs, checking for given conditions to execute particular blocks of code therefrom. Loops, for and while statements, allow for repetitive work, which allows programmers to execute code repeatedly without code duplication. Code encapsulation within functions promotes reusability and modularity so that it is easier to manage larger codebases. Hence, learning these control structures is essential to writing clean, efficient, and maintainable code in any programming paradigm. Apart from this, an awareness of programming principles also means being familiar with testing and debugging techniques. Debugging is the process of locating and correcting bugs or mistakes in a program, something every programmer has to do. Good debugging means using a methodical approach, for example, using tools such as debuggers or logging frameworks to follow back problems. Testing, on the other hand, involves checking the performance and reliability of code in different formats such as unit testing and integration testing. The procedures ensure that not only does the code perform as anticipated, but it is also reliable when there are upgrades and new developments. Collectively, these procedures enhance the software development process, promoting improved quality and more long-lasting software solutions. Hence, understanding debugging and testing in combination with essential programming fundamentals is important for aspiring programmers who wish to excel at the profession.

REFERENCES

1. Algaba, A., Ardia, D., Bluteau, K., Borms, S., et al. (2020). Econometrics meets sentiment: An overview of methodology and applications. https://core.ac.uk/download/323232776.pdf (accessed on 9th September 2025).
2. Allan, I., Go, J., Roberts, G., Stegemann, J. A., et al. (2006). Modelling and simulation framework for reactive transport of organic contaminants in bed-sediments using a pure Java object-oriented paradigm. https://core.ac.uk/download/1679532.pdf (accessed on 9th September 2025).
3. Angles, R., Curiel, M., Impagliazzo, J., Leger, C., et al. (2016). Latin American perspectives to internationalize undergraduate information technology education. https://core.ac.uk/download/86427281.pdf (accessed on 9th September 2025).
4. Angoletta, M. E. (2008). *Digital Signal Processor Fundamentals and System Design*. https://core.ac.uk/download/44195315.pdf (accessed on 9th September 2025).
5. Balabinis, G., Beavan, A., Beavan, L., Bondarchuk, Y., Bouchard, C., Brown, T., Brown, L., et al. (2010). New horizons for the methodology and physiology of training periodization: Block periodization: New horizon or a false dawn? https://core.ac.uk/download/9632216.pdf (accessed on 9th September 2025).
6. Cardona Taltavull, J. A. (2015). *Programación Lógica*. https://core.ac.uk/download/43549414.pdf (accessed on 9th September 2025).
7. Chan, A. T. S., Chan, S. C. F., Lau, C. K., Lu, X., et al. (2017). Problem-based learning: A teaching method to enhance learning experience for students in service-learning. https://core.ac.uk/download/78916481.pdf (accessed on 9th September 2025).
8. Chen, K. (2011). *CS 240: Computer Programming–I*. https://core.ac.uk/download/80832976.pdf (accessed on 9th September 2025).
9. Chenouard, R., Granvilliers, L., & Soto, R. (2009). Using ATL to define advanced and flexible constraint model transformations. https://core.ac.uk/download/53014824.pdf (accessed on 9th September 2025).
10. Chołoniewski, J., Gajewski, Ł., & Hołyst, J. (2016). Key courses of academic curriculum uncovered by data mining of students' grades. http://arxiv.org/abs/1604.07074 (accessed on 9th September 2025).
11. Civit Balcells, A., Ferreiro Ramos, M. J., Jiménez Moreno, G., Morgado Estévez, A., et al. (2014). A game-based approach to the teaching of object-oriented programming languages. https://core.ac.uk/download/286563814.pdf (accessed on 9th September 2025).

12. Coleman, S., Georgiopoulos, M., Markov, Z., Neller, T., et al. (2005). Unifying an introduction to artificial intelligence course through machine learning laboratory experiences. https://cupola.gettysburg.edu/cgi/viewcontent.cgi?article=1007&context=csfac (accessed on 9th September 2025).
13. Comley, R., Georgiadou, E., & White, A. (2017). CoFeD: A visualisation framework for comparative quality evaluation. https://core.ac.uk/download/83926120.pdf (accessed on 9th September 2025).
14. Cuinas, I., Vercauteren, L., & Verhaevert, J. (2015). Learning through play: An educational computer game to introduce radar fundamentals. https://core.ac.uk/download/55846939.pdf (accessed on 9th September 2025).
15. Diertens, B. (2010). On object-orientation. http://arxiv.org/abs/1010.3100 (accessed on 9th September 2025).
16. Diertens, B. (2012). From functions to object-orientation by abstraction. http://arxiv.org/abs/1209.6163 (accessed on 9th September 2025).
17. Dominick, W. D., & Moreau, D. R. (2025). *A Programming Environment Evaluation Methodology for Object-Oriented Systems*. https://core.ac.uk/download/pdf/42830116.pdf (accessed on 9th September 2025).
18. Dyer, M., & Mills, H. D. (2025). *Cleanroom Software Development*. https://core.ac.uk/download/pdf/42856656.pdf (accessed on 9th September 2025).
19. Ekmekci, B., McAnany, C. E., & Mura, C. (2016). An introduction to programming for bio scientists: A Python-based primer. http://arxiv.org/abs/1605.05419 (accessed on 9th September 2025).
20. Fischer, M. M., & Leung, Y. (2025). A genetic-algorithms based evolutionary computational neural network for modelling spatial interaction data. https://core.ac.uk/download/pdf/7045981.pdf (accessed on 9th September 2025).
21. Fotaris, P., Kheirkhahzadeh, A., & Sauer, C. (2016). Practice makes perfect–gamification of a competitive learning experience. https://core.ac.uk/download/146471246.pdf (accessed on 9th September 2025).
22. Gallagher, L. (2012). Gaming business communities: Developing online learning organizations to foster communities, develop leadership, and grow interpersonal education. https://core.ac.uk/download/29200559.pdf (accessed on 9th September 2025).
23. Gande, S. (2015). Developing Java programs on Android mobile phones using speech recognition. https://core.ac.uk/download/55333573.pdf (accessed on 9th September 2025).

24. Graf, F., Maiden, N., & Seyff, N. (2010). Using mobile RE tools to give end-users their own voice. https://core.ac.uk/download/9559634.pdf (accessed on 9th September 2025).

25. Hattori, L. P., & Lanza, M. (2012). Change-centric improvement of team collaboration. https://core.ac.uk/download/20658765.pdf (accessed on 9th September 2025).

26. Hattori, L., Lanza, M., & Robbes, R. (2018). Refining code ownership with synchronous changes. https://core.ac.uk/download/159156620.pdf (accessed on 9th September 2025).

27. Hendrickson, A. R., & Newman, W. A. (1996). The object-oriented paradigm as an implementation of systems theory in IS. https://core.ac.uk/download/55331824.pdf (accessed on 9th September 2025).

28. Joy, M., & Yau, J. Y. K. (2004). Introducing Java: The case for fundamentals-first. https://core.ac.uk/download/1381479.pdf (accessed on 9th September 2025).

29. Julien, C. (2019). Using the Internet of Things to teach good software engineering practice to high school students. https://core.ac.uk/download/287648521.pdf (accessed on 9th September 2025).

30. Kathare, S. (2012). Easier debugging of multithreaded software. https://core.ac.uk/download/70408307.pdf (accessed on 9th September 2025).

31. López Álvarez, D., Olmedo Torre, N., Pérez Poch, A., Salán Ballesteros, M., et al. (2016). On the influence of creativity in basic programming learning at a first-year engineering course. https://core.ac.uk/download/81571927.pdf (accessed on 9th September 2025).

32. Main, A. (2005). PenDraw–A language for improving take-up of SVG. https://core.ac.uk/download/75054.pdf (accessed on 9th September 2025).

33. Markov, Z., Neller, T. W., Russell, I., Zlatareva, N., et al. (2006). Pedagogical possibilities for the N-puzzle problem. https://cupola.gettysburg.edu/cgi/viewcontent.cgi?article=1004&context=csfac (accessed on 9th September 2025).

34. Mathew, S. K., & Rajagopalan, S. (2016). Choice of agile methodologies in software development: A vendor perspective. https://core.ac.uk/download/55336694.pdf (accessed on 9th September 2025).

35. Michaelson, G. (2015). Teaching programming with computational and informational thinking. https://core.ac.uk/download/29822230.pdf (accessed on 9th September 2025).

36. Mooney, A., & Noone, M. (2017). Visual and textual programming languages: A systematic review of the literature. https://core.ac.uk/download/297032078.pdf (accessed on 9th September 2025).

37. Ochoa, H. A., & Shirvaikar, M. V. (2018). A survey of digital systems curriculum and pedagogy in electrical and computer engineering programs. https://core.ac.uk/download/286777712.pdf (accessed on 9th September 2025).

38. Rodríguez Martínez, M. E. (2021). Project management in the Fourth Industrial Revolution. Beer production project. https://core.ac.uk/download/481423099.pdf (accessed on 9th September 2025).

CHAPTER 5

CONTROL STRUCTURES

Contents

INTRODUCTION

Control structures are ubiquitous building stones across fields, from computer science to biology, as blueprints for applying the structure and behavior of systems. In computer programs, control structures such as loops and conditionals rule data flow in a program so that things happen with efficiency and prudence. This hierarchical influence of control structures affects beyond programming, shaping the structure of biological systems at the molecular level. For instance, complex interactions of molecular motors show how control and design principles reach beyond artificial systems to also in nature, where dynamic molecular systems control important processes such as transport and energy conversion, thus demonstrating the underlying need for systematic order in essential functions (Bray et al., 2018). The ability to control these control structures effectively can lead to amazing breakthroughs in areas. On the molecular scale of biology, employing synthetic control mechanisms like molecular motors provides insights into fundamental biological processes.

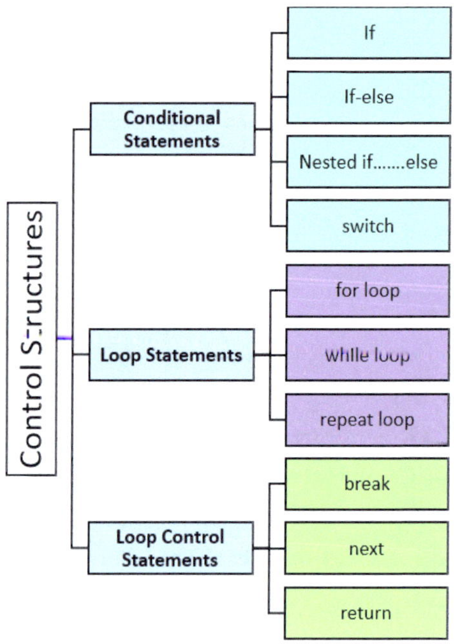

Figure 5.1. *Control structures.*

Source*: https://learnetutorials.com/assets/images/r/control/image2.png.*

This could range from understanding cell motions to the assembly of targeted drug delivery systems. The complementarity between programming theory and biology strengthens the multidisciplinary argument for control structures, as evidenced in the employment of responsive components that react to environmental conditions. This convergence results in innovation in the creation of smart materials and responsive systems that respond in real time, just like adaptive algorithms in computer systems, therefore emphasizing the dual importance of control structures in technological as well as biological systems (Ben, 2017). As we progress deeper into the essay on control structures, it is crucial to note the importance of control structures towards helping us understand the operation of complex systems. From an examination of the various applications, from molecular motors that constitute the basis of life processes to control systems in software, this study is poised to bring out the parallels and applications across fields. The dynamic interplay between adjustability, utility, and structure in control systems is a classic example of their role in driving innovation in science and engineering. Lastly, their focus on those very important building blocks paves the way for future work, with the potential for controlled, efficient, and dynamic systems in technology and biology being the basis of current-day research (Bray et al., 2018) (Figure 5.1).

Definition of Control Structures

Control structures are simple programming language building blocks used to control the order of execution in a program. In essence, they enable programmers to control the way instructions are executed in order to facilitate more sophisticated decision-making and repetitive operations. The primary control structures include sequential, selection, and iteration that are utilized differently in programming. As an example, sequential control structures execute statements in serial order, while selection structures, such as if-then statements, allow programs to branch based on specific conditions. Lastly, iteration control structures, such as loops, allow for repeated execution of a statement block and is thus priceless for tasks that have repetition or iteration over data sets. This control flow systematic organization enhances the expressiveness and efficiency of code while making it easier to handle complex logic in software construction. Control structures are most clearly demonstrated in computational biology, where the complexity of biological processes requires sophisticated programming paradigms. With computing having transformed bioscience research so much, control structures enable one to implement algorithms crucial to such activities as simulation and data analysis in bioinformatics. As previously discussed, computer programming skill is one of the most essential skills that a modern-day researcher can acquire (Ekmekci et al., 2016). For instance, Python's ease of syntax and rich libraries provide room for control structures to facilitate activities like sequence analysis and structural genomics. With the help of control structures, researchers can comfortably handle vast biological data, iterating through genomic sequences or making choices based on algorithmic models to investigate biological phenomena. Such combination of computer programming and biological research suggests that control structures should be known in creating good computational biology applications. Aside from their use in biosciences, control structures also extend to computational linguistics, though their use here is in building grammars for linguistic theories. Amalia abstract machine is one example and employs rigorously defined operational semantics to assist grammars as typed as specified with feature structures to be assigned explicit meaning (Wintner et al., 1997). Their use here allows for efficient compilation and execution of linguistic algorithms and affects performance results. Through structuring flows and operations of data, control structures allow linguists to create dynamic models responsive to language constraints. Their combination of theoretical basis and applied applications promotes innovation in various disciplines, as they prove versatile and unreplaceable in computation as well as analysis. Control structures are thus the fundamental components of programming languages and domain-specific programs, proving their prominence in modern scientific research.

Importance in Programming

Control structures form the nucleus of programming since they are fundamental in determining the flow and execution of code. The structures, including conditionals, loops, and branching, give programmers a way of introducing logic to their applications, enabling them to execute various paths depending on various input conditions. This flexibility is vital in the creation of dynamic applications that can respond to user input and calculate complex calculations. By effectively using control structures, developers can render their code more readable and maintainable and hence make it simpler to debug and modify in the future. In addition to that, knowledge of these fundamental constructions is important in impacting a programmer's productivity and problem-solving skills and gravitating toward deeper and refined code outputs. The effect of control structures is not limited to basic programming alone, and it extends to computer science education in terms of teaching strategies. For instance, in the creation of foundation computer programming courses, teaching methods must take into account how learners acquire knowledge. As explained under training of high school computer programming courses, certain teaching methods such as the Expert, Spiral, and Reading methods address the management of students cognitive loads during learning (Krammer et al., 1987). By incorporating control structures in the curriculum, instructors can emphasize top-down design and incremental learning that facilitate students to build their programming skills in a structured way. Not only does this approach to instruction impart a solid understanding of programming constructs, but it also prepares students to understand and employ control structures in building strong and efficient programs. Also, the significance of control structures arises from the way they respond to memory management, particularly when higher-level abstractions are being dealt with. For instance, heap memory is more complex compared to memory controlled by the stack because it is infinite and complex (Kanvar et al., 2015). This complexity demands meticulous planning and use of control structures to manage memory well or else programmers become prone to issues in the forms of memory leaks or fragmentation. Knowing how to use control structures allows programmers to take advantage of summarization methods and models that can accurately capture heap memory. This is ultimately what leads to more efficient programs that are able to utilize resources effectively and perform tasks with ease. Thus, understanding the role of control structures is not only crucial for writing effective code but also for ensuring the sustainability and expandability of programs in today's increasingly resource-intensive technology era (Figure 5.2).

Figure 5.2. *Control structures play a pivotal role in programming.*

Source: *https://www.siteuptime.com/blog/wp-content/uploads/2021/07/a70e-911d1e1f00197ebaa00b51c8519d.jpg.*

5.1. TYPES OF CONTROL STRUCTURES

Control structures are programming language building blocks that regulate the execution flow based on some condition. There are three types of control structures: sequential, selection, and iteration. The control structures that execute the statements sequentially, one following the other, as encountered and in the same order, make them the most basic and simplest in programming. Selection structures are those that offer decision-making features. These include constructs such as switch cases and if-else statements that enable programs to execute different code blocks based on given conditions. Finally, iteration structures, usually performed through loops such as do-while, while, and for, permit execution of code repeatedly until a given condition is met. Understanding these fundamental control structures is crucial to successful programming because they form the foundation on which more sophisticated logic and functionality are built. As more complex programs are developed, sophisticated control structures are crucial in handling program execution complexities. Agent-Based Modelling demonstrates how control structures are applied in supply chain simulations, particularly in minimizing logistics in the chemical industry. This model uses different types of agents with algorithms such as the Location Algorithm for logistics allocation and Clarke & Wrights Savings Algorithm for routing calculation. Regarding this, control structures not just state the sequence of operations but also govern the overall efficiency of supply chain activities. The System also has a variety of control mechanisms to manage stock levels through simulation procedures. By changing the control structures' parameters, it is possible to observe significant effects on distribution costs and thus highlight their importance for real-world usage (Dyntar et al., 2013). Ultimately, proper utilization of these structures promotes more developed and efficient systems. Control structures in embedded systems, especially real-time operating systems, are even more important as they help ensure reliability and safety. For instance, in aerospace systems, proper functioning of embedded software demands rigorous testing and validation of control structure to guarantee the elimination of future faults. One such technique using Prolog to analyze the abstract syntax tree of source code is an example of the needed requirement. By transforming code into Prolog facts, developers are able to calculate call graphs and execution traces, taking advantage of Prologs backtracking and non-determinism to try a range of program flows. This analysis simplifies the detection of bugs, such as the incorrect use of semaphores, which have significant effects on system performance. The communication between control structures in such scenarios underscores their pivotal role not only in programming but even in maintaining the integrity of complex systems (Flederer et al., 2017) (Figure 5.3).

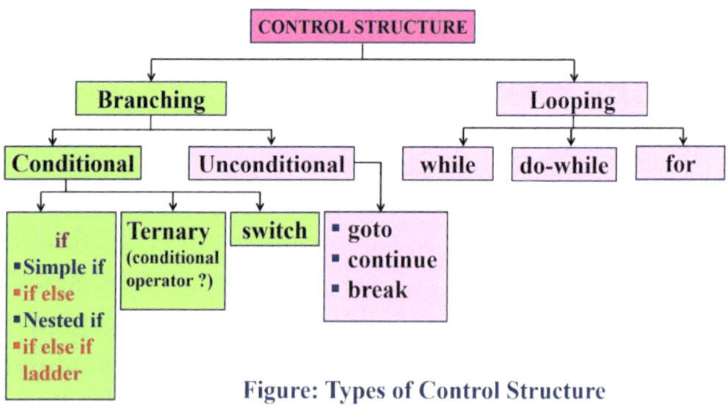

Figure 5.3. *Types of control structures.*

Source: https://i.ytimg.com/vi/dVsEcOj9G3I/maxresdefault.jpg.

5.1.1. Sequential Control Structures

Sequential control structures are the minimum programming logic building blocks, wherein commands are followed in a linear straightforward manner, each command following the previous one. In this direct flow control method, each step of a program is executed in the order in which they are programmed, so there is simplicity and simplicity. In the educational setting, especially in the classroom setting of first-year computer science courses, emphasizing sequential control structures is a good foundation for students to learn more sophisticated programming principles. Having the basic sequence of operations at hand, students are better equipped to handle the conditional and iterative control structures that introduce program flow branching and looping, respectively. This sequential growth not only develops logical reasoning but also problem-solving skills—essential skills that are advantageous in the technologically enhanced modern world.

The introduction of digital modules, as seen in the latest educational initiatives like Malaysia's Digital Education Policy (2023), has transformed the method by which students acquire programming content. Use of multimedia and interactive learning materials facilitates a more interactive learning process of successive control structures. By allowing students to see and manipulate code in an electronic environment, instructors are teaching a hands-on exercise that reinforces theoretical concepts. In studies comparing how effective these computer-based modules are, findings indicate that basic control structures are easier for students to learn when provided interactively. Hence, the implementation of technology-supported learning aids does not only increase engagement but also ensures greater understanding of programming principles by students, particularly at secondary school levels (Mansor et al., 2025). Furthermore, the use of control structures can be extended to early childhood education as more teachers are finding the potential of teaching computational thinking to early children. Research indicates that preschool children can begin to understand and apply simple control structures through the aid of programming tools that match their ages. Presenting this simple concept, teachers aim to give students the fundamental reasoning and problem-solving skills they will require for the remainder of their school years. An extensive review of literature has identified a number of tools that effectively teach control structures, given the imperative to select appropriate platforms with which children closely identify (Bakala et al., 2022). With increasing integrations of computer science in models of learning through the introduction of computational thinking, sequential control structures remain at the core, marking their widespread application and need at various levels of learning.

5.1.2. Selection Control Structures

Selection control structures are a cornerstone in programming because they determine how the program will be executed according to specified conditions. By executing specified chunks of code depending on whether conditions are true or false, they enhance the efficiency and functionality of the program. The primary selection control structures include basic if statements, if-else statements, and switch statements. These structures allow decision-making processes to be capable of altering automatically in accordance with various inputs, which is fundamental when building software to interact and respond to people accordingly and data alterations. To boot, understanding how to operate and apply these structures is very vital to programmers because they constitute the underlying principle behind simple scripts and complex programs. In applications involving lots of data, the correct selection of control structures is crucial in maximizing performance and making appropriate use of resources.

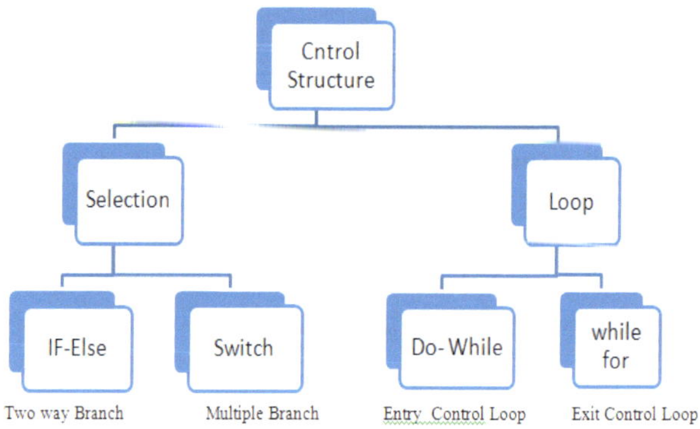

Figure 5.4. *Selection control structures.*

Source: https://2.bp.blogspot.com/-dDLiiSDIYIw/W4uSMbKQGmI/AAAAAAAAF-vA/J5LNjQNWWy4P2FFIEP4TUL2elyXOKWq8wCLcBGAs/s1600/loop.png.

For instance, the utilization of a switch statement is very useful when several conditions have to be tested against a single variable, hence making code readability simple as well as reducing execution time. This is especially true in environments like user interface programming, where the application must respond rapidly to diverse user actions and tastes. Such selection control structures not only make the programming simpler but also assist in making the application more responsive, thus providing a superior user experience. Programmers may apply such constructs in constructing good programs that support differing requirements without aggravating the codebase, demonstrating the significance of selection control structures in selection process. The virtue of selection control structures is not just in the mere coding practices; they reflect larger principles applied in computational theory and data management. In order to understand how such constructs operate, one must be conversant with terms such as branching and conditional execution, which find parallels in genetic and developmental processes in nature. For instance, it has been shown by research that selection processes similar to those applied in programming have been employed to maximize the genetic characteristics of crop wild relatives through methods such as landscape genomics (Emmanuel et al., 2024). In the same light, the growth of causality knowledge in gene selection can resonate with applying selection control structures to enhance decision-making processes (Huang et al., 2022). Hence, understanding selection control structures in a balanced manner invokes not only more effective programming expertise but also practical applications that center on adaptive responses to varying conditions (Figure 5.4).

5.1.3. Iteration Control Structures

Iteration control structures are imperative programming constructs utilized to execute a code block for repeated iterations. They allow programmers to execute tasks that require repetition without repeatedly writing the same code. Iteration control structures are loops such as for loops, while loops, and do-while loops. They have varying capabilities specific to the need of different programs. The ability to execute a list of statements repeatedly under a specific condition greatly enhances the efficacy of algorithms and facilitates more efficient and maintainable code. Also, knowledge about control structures of iteration is crucial for students, particularly high school students, where elementary programming concepts are established. Understanding these structures properly enables students to generate more advanced algorithms and enhances overall computational thinking skill. Iteration control structures are even more critical when set against the backdrop of distance learning. As indicated in current literature on education, the integration of technology in schools can serve to enhance the learning environment for computer science students. Specifically, the application of a control structure programming module has been shown to improve the comprehension and utilization of iteration control structures by Malaysian Form Four students (Mansor et al., 2025). Interactive computer modules allow the learning process to be more interactive, allowing the students to observe and even engage in the process of programming. This approach is a reaction to the need of educating future skilled programmers who can apply iteration effectively in their coding. This has necessitated schools and educators to align their learning modules with electronic material to meet modern learning paradigms. Further, technology innovation has paved the way for the establishment of adaptive learning software that incorporates iteration control structures in their features. For instance, in complex control systems, such as nonlinear Markov jump systems, iterative mechanisms play a crucial role in determining optimal control strategies (Lu et al., 2024). Such sophisticated algorithms typically depend on adaptive dynamic programming methods based on iterative policy improvement, demonstrating the versatility and inclusivity of iteration control structures as well as basic programming instruction. Since they are working with both fundamental concepts and sophisticated applications, students' comprehension of iterative processes becomes deeper, allowing them to tackle more sophisticated programming challenges. Therefore, embracing the iterative approach to programming not only makes learning more elementary feasible but also prepares students for real-world applications in a rapidly evolving environment of technology.

5.2. SEQUENTIAL CONTROL STRUCTURES

In programing and algorithm design, sequential control structures are fundamental building blocks that govern the flow of a program's execution. They establish a simple and linear path, whereby instructions are carried out in the given sequence they are written. This basic but straightforward form of control structure allows the programmer to specify a series of instructions for the computer to follow, encouraging determinism and clarity in the operation of the program. With an organized sequence, sequential control structures contribute significantly to the development process, serving as the basis for more complex structures and program functionality overall. Thus, understanding how they operate is vital to programmers who would want to develop effective and efficient software solutions that can manipulate data and perform tasks in a series of logic. In practical applications, sequential control structures are illustrated using simple programming concepts like conditionals and loops. For example, a loop may repeat a set of code repeatedly until a specific condition is met so that tasks could be repeated in multiples without duplication. Similarly, conditionals allow specific segments of code to be run based on logical tests so that the control flow can decide where it proceeds next. These data structures show how sequential control structures are flexible because they could easily fit into an extremely wide range of programming contexts. The ability to manage both repetition and conditional branching enables the effectiveness of sequential control structures, such that programmers can make effective programs that can solve diverse problems within computer systems. Furthermore, the use of sequential control structures enables improved code readability and maintainability. Through organizing the program logic in a way that is simple to understand, programmers can enable collaboration and reduce debugging complexity. Code that employs explicit sequential structures allows it to be simpler for teams to convey ideas and solve problems, as the logical flow of the computer mimics human patterns of thought. Moreover, programming languages have evolved, and most now accommodate specialized features that simplify using sequential control structures, such that they become more accessible to a broader audience of programmers. The sophistication of modern programming environments renders sequential, conditional, and iterative processes switchable with ease, thereby enhancing the power and usability of sequential control structures in complex programs in the dynamic world of software development (Figure 5.5).

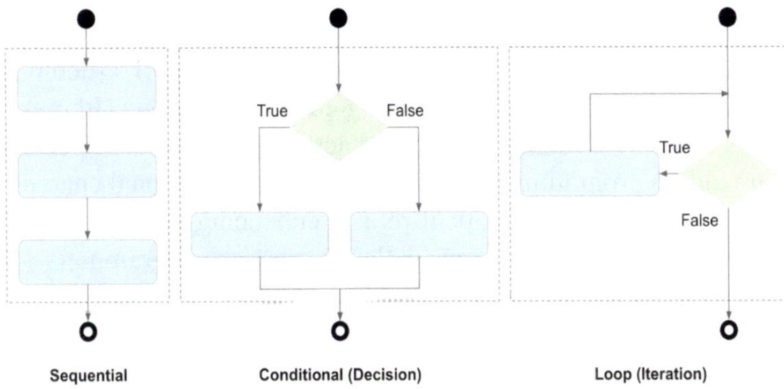

Figure 5.5. *Sequential control structures.*

Source: https://docs.scs.gg/assets/images/control-structures-f12e5bb66aed4ce-13d00a71e3563c928.png.

5.2.1. Definition and Characteristics

Control structures are the simple building blocks of programming that regulate the flow of execution of a software program. Essentially, control structures define how a program operates through controlling the way statements are executed, enabling decision, looping, and branching according to dynamic situations. These capabilities ensure that complex activities are broken down into feasible pieces, enhancing code simplicity and efficiency. As programming languages develop, so too have their control structures become more advanced, a response to the demand for higher abstraction and flexibility. The development of languages such as Blue, with its focus on object-oriented programming learning environments, shows the increasing preoccupation with developing environments conducive to learning effectively via simple control structures (Kölling et al., 1996). These developments not only assist beginning programmers in comprehending basic notions but also equip them with the skills to tackle more intricate programming paradigms. Moreover, control constructs play an important role in enhancing the expressiveness of programming languages so that they can accomplish a great variety of functions in different applications. For example, conditional statements enable a program to make decisions based on input, while loops allow repetitive operations to be executed efficiently. These abstractions play a key role in the development of algorithms that can solve sophisticated problems, particularly in computational biology. The increasingly intensive reliance on software in this field is a reflection of the importance of control structures as nearly all contemporary bioinformatics research depends on algorithms facilitated by these abstractions. For example, Python, with its syntax clarity and object-oriented nature, has also been on the ascendancy in bioinformatics, where control structures of rich expressiveness are at the heart of managing complex data sets (Ekmekci et al., 2016). The versatility of control structures across various areas speaks to their key role in modern programming. In addition to their functional characteristics, control structures also play a critical role in enhancing codes readability and maintainability. Well-designed control flows enhance programmers ability to follow logic and handle the code in an effective way, which is most crucial in team-based environments where numerous developers work on the same code repository. Moreover, explicit control structures reduce the possibility of errors, since they present logical paths that can be traced and debugged effectively. To conclude these benefits, instructional means emphasize teaching control structures at the start of programming instruction, ensuring students are familiar with these basic building blocks as they continue to more advanced material. Systematic understanding of control structures not only consolidates the fundamental programming skill but also extends to practical application across a wide variety of industries, enabling a new generation of skilled programmers well equipped to develop sophisticated systems (Kölling et al., 1996; Ekmekci et al., 2016).

5.2.2. Examples in Programming Languages

Control structures are intrinsic building blocks that regulate the flow of execution in programming languages. Examples are decision-making structures, that is, if-else statements, and looping constructs such as for and while loops. Control structures in programming languages such as Python are readable-oriented and therefore cause programmers to write understandable, serviceable code. For instance, the use of if-else statement makes it possible to implement conditional logic, and one can execute specific code blocks based on certain conditions. Not only does this enhance efficiency but also makes the code more readable, a factor that is particularly important when dealing with large projects in cooperation with other developers. This accessibility is pivotal in the biosciences field, where Python use in bioinformatics proves control structures' applicability to complex computational tasks (Ekmekci et al., 2016). Further, control structures are not merely just encompassing elementary decision and looping behavior; more complex constructs such as switch-case statements and exception handling are also paramount in controlling program run-time flow. In professional programming paradigms, they support richer decision-making and exception handling.

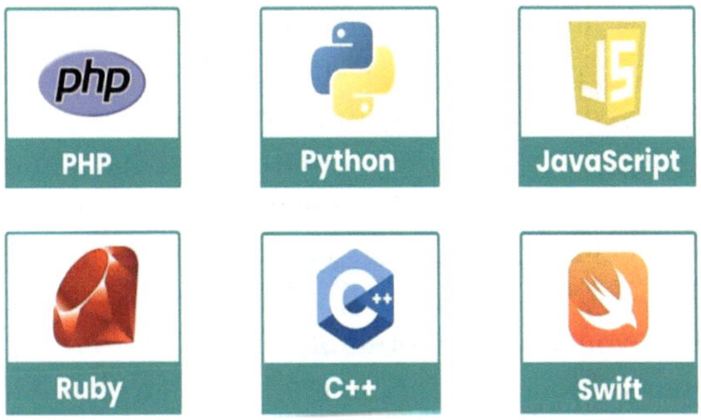

Figure 5.6. *Examples in programming languages.*

Source: https://cdn-ilcfkpn.nitrocdn.com/dYTvffvupnjxELJNiOzugpRXpwHkeglU/assets/images/optimized/rev-0f693f4/educatecomputer.com/storage/2024/06/Examples-of-Programming-Languages-image-1024x576.webp.

For example, in the C# and Java programming languages, the switch-case statement provides an elegant alternative to a group of if-else statements when dealing with many discrete values. Not only is it more readable but also more efficient. Furthermore, effective application of control structures can also render programs more efficient, as is the case in fields like bioinformatics, where enormous amounts of data necessitate optimized processing techniques (Krammer et al., 1987). As such, the structure of the control mechanisms will directly influence a program's capability to output the correct and timely results. Finally, with evolving teaching methodologies in programming courses, the necessity to teach control structures becomes ever more salient. Various pedagogical approaches, such as the Expert, Spiral, and Reading methods, emphasize various learning components in an effort to enable students to comprehend these significant concepts. For instance, the Reading method has been shown to improve the comprehension of control structures by using worked examples and practice exercises to reinforce declarative and procedural knowledge. This instructional design not only focuses on the theoretical foundations of control structures but also equips students with practical skills necessary for use in the real world. In light of the complicated nature of today's programming, particularly in emerging fields like computational biology, it becomes imperative for future programmers to learn and apply control structures (Krammer et al., 1987) (Figure 5.6).

5.2.3. Use Cases and Applications

In exploring the general theme of control structures, their application across various fields further attests to their general potential and significance. A clear use case is in genetic programming (GP), in which control structures allow programs to be evolved automatically to address complex problems. By means of GP, users are able to engage in a structured process that allows solutions to be created without having to know much about program structure. This has yielded tangible outcomes, including revolutionary scientific discoveries and patentable innovations, validating the overarching role of control structures in charting and navigating the evolution of algorithmic solutions. With explicit refinement of random programs through mutation and recombination, GP highlights the capacity of control structures to effectively manage decision-making processes within intricate contexts (Langdon et al., 2008). In addition, control structures are used in distributed systems, particularly those with concurrency control needs. Various types of mutual exclusion constructs, that is, semaphores and monitors, constitute a significant portion of managing concurrent access to common information in the systems. Transactions or linearizability use allows such systems to maintain integrity and consistency despite complex data operations. Also, the inclusion of virtual synchrony in distributed applications enables more predictable interaction between independently designed components. This is critical for consistency property-based applications relying on maintaining consistency properties between nodes. Having the ability to manage these concurrent computations using appropriate control structures denotes their importance in the formulation of computational architectures (Birman et al., 1991). The application of control structures has also reached advanced applications, such as data modeling and industrial process control. For instance, businesses apply control structures for controlling the automation and optimization of production processes and eliminating human mistakes and maximizing efficiency. Similarly, control structures are extremely critical in financial analysis, whereby risk assessment algorithms employ robust logical structures to take real-time decisions based on ever-varying market information. Besides, the control structure flexibility makes it possible to utilize them in new fields such as video game programming and graphic design for controlling user interfaces and environmental feedback. The wide range of applications reflects the relevance of control structures across many fields, enabling both innovation and maximizing performance (Langdon et al., 2008).

5.3. SELECTION CONTROL STRUCTURES

Selection control structures are programming paradigm building blocks because they allow programmers to direct the flow of execution based on certain conditions. If, else if, and switch constructs are used by programmers to create dynamic and interactive programs. Systems can test pre-defined conditions using these structures, which make decision-making processes mimic human logic. For instance, it may be necessary that a program validates input from users or checks readings from sensors in a robot system so that differential response can be made based on the latest data. Thus, selection control structures not only improve the efficiency of code during execution but also significantly contribute to creating interactive and user-centered applications. In education, the significance of teaching selection control structures becomes clear by considering how hard it is for students to become proficient in algorithmic thinking. Based on research, the skill to become proficient in these structures contributes significantly to a student's ability to produce clean and functioning code, filling the gap between abstract and concrete knowledge. Through the use of generative learning objects, teachers can encourage a deeper comprehension of selection structures, thus facilitating the students in overcoming general obstacles in their programming journey. The use of explicit instruction for the details of the control structures not only enhances learners' confidence but also equips them to deal with more advanced problem-solving situations in their professional life in computer science (García et al., 2016). Forward, programming language design continues to expand the variety and expressiveness of selection control structures. Contemporary languages now include more sophisticated forms, such as pattern matching and more expressive conditional expressions, that streamline coding and improve legibility. These advances allow programmers to code more lovely solutions to hard problems while establishing a context for best practices in maintenance and collaborative working on code. As businesses advance and computational requirements grow, the focus on proficiency in selection control structures is still critical for those who aspire to become software engineers, thus maintaining the skills they need to adapt to an increasingly complex digital world (Langdon et al., 2008) (Figure 5.7).

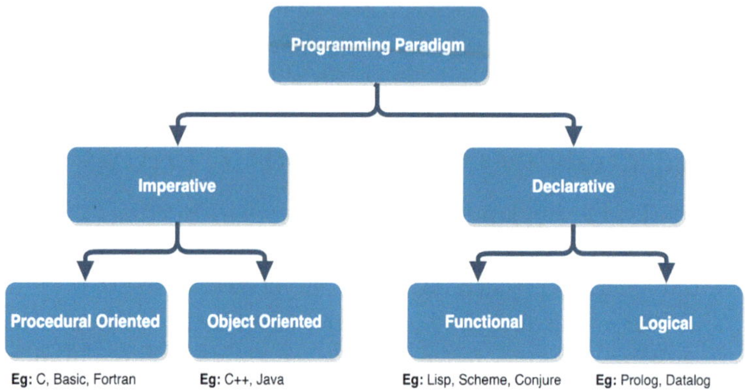

Figure 5.7. *Selection control structures of programming paradigms.*

*Source: https://miro.medium.com/v2/resize:fit:1200/1*vDV-PiKka-__11Vl1P_1_A.png.*

5.3.1. Definition and Characteristics

Control structures are fundamental constructs in programming that dictate the flow of execution within a program. These structures allow developers to manage how instructions are executed, enabling the implementation of complex logic and decision-making processes. At their essence, control structures can be categorized into three primary types: sequential, selection, and iteration. Sequential control structures execute instructions in a linear order, while selection structures facilitate decision-making through conditional statements, enabling branching paths within the code. Iteration structures, on the other hand, allow portions of code to be executed repeatedly based on specific conditions, fostering efficiency and reducing redundancy. The implementation of these control structures is essential for creating algorithms and, consequently, functional software applications. One defining characteristic of control structures is their impact on readability and maintainability of code. Well-structured control mechanisms enhance the clarity of intent behind a sequence of operations, thereby allowing programmers to infer the logic without extensive commentary. This is particularly crucial in collaborative environments where multiple developers may interact with the same codebase. For instance, languages designed with object-oriented principles, such as Python, incorporate sophisticated control structures that seamlessly integrate with object management features. Such integration boosts not only the quality of programming output but also encourages best practices in code structuring and design. As projects grow in complexity, maintaining a high level of readability through effective control structures becomes imperative, leading to reduced development time and minimized errors. Moreover, the evolution of programming paradigms has substantially affected how control structures are defined and utilized. The shift towards object-oriented programming embodies a more abstract approach, where control structures are often encapsulated within objects and classes. This abstraction allows for a more intuitive design, where behaviors are tied to the objects themselves, exemplifying a natural alignment with real-world systems. Consequently, programmers using object-oriented languages can benefit from encapsulated control structures that promote modularity and reuse, enhancing overall software architecture. As computational demands increase, optimizing control structures becomes vital; advancements in programming environments, such as Blue, emphasize tailored approaches to teaching object-oriented methods, highlighting the importance of selecting appropriate control structures for educational contexts. This alignment of control structures with contemporary programming practices underscores their significance in both academic and professional settings, reinforcing their role in shaping capable software developers (Kölling et al., 1996; Ekmekci et al., 2016).

5.3.2. Common Types (If, Switch, etc.)

Control structures are a key feature of programming since they allow the program to decide, based on control structures, which path of execution it takes. Most common control structures are the conditional statements, such as if statements, which allow a particular block of code to be executed depending on a given set of conditions. The simple structure checks a specified condition and, in the event that it is true, executes the associated block of code. Conversely, if the condition is not true, the program can bypass the block or execute another part through an else statement. This flexibility facilitates dynamic behavior in software programs, particularly in high-speed data processing and decision-making applications, such as data analysis or real-time systems, where responsiveness to varying inputs is vital. Another typical control structure is the switch statement, a replacement for several if statements when coping with a large number of conditions. This structure organizes code in a simpler way to read and understand, especially when the conditions require inspecting a given variable against multiple possible values. By combining a number of conditions in one statement, the switch structure minimizes the potential for error and increases program maintainability, especially where applications have to be scaled. As in other programming paradigms, for example, array programming in libraries such as NumPy, control structures like switch can lead to more efficient execution of algorithms to enable optimized workflows as well as improved performance in operations ranging from scientific simulations to financial modeling (Harris et al., 2020). Besides the above control structures, looping statements such as for and while loops are the backbone of program execution due to their ability to allow repeated execution of code blocks. Loops are even more specifically used in handling arrays and data collections where repetition is needed. For instance, effective iteration of arrays in array programming may simplify operations on extensive collections of data, for example, scientific calculations or business use cases (Harris et al., 2020). In addition, with control structures such as loops in conjunction with conditional statements, programmers are able to build more complex and interactive logic to respond to changing input conditions. This dynamic capability positions these constructs as elementary building blocks in the design of software systems, particularly in satisfying evolving requirements and intricacies of contemporary digital networking that can be seen in Software-Defined Networking (SDN).

5.3.3. Contribution to Decision-Making Processes

The importance of decision-making procedures in control structures cannot be emphasized enough, since these procedures are important in directing organizational actions and strategies. The success of such structures relies on the capacity to analyze and process information, which in the end affects the quality of decisions made. Control boards, for instance, are significant boards in making alternative project or system solutions, depending on the experience of speakers and board members to lead decision-making. This kind of scenario highlights the character of information flow, whereby the decision relies on the knowledge being offered while discussing. Furthermore, information theory models enable better understanding of this flow, serving as the foundation for optimal decision-making systems developed for specific organizational needs, as evidenced in Watson et al. (2025). The integration of control theory in decision-making also highlights the importance of extremely structured control processes within organizations. By means of a systematic decision process, control structures can contrast various data inputs and apply theoretical frameworks for establishing their implications. This similarity allows organizations to develop models that, aside from promoting more intellectual processing, allow collaboration among participants in decision-making to be promoted. Therefore, the understanding of information as a component of such control structures allows organizations to optimize decision-making processes continually. Mathematical relationships evolved from information theory are a basis to build coherent decision models in the sense that they depict the interrelatedness of information, control, and cognition, as seen in Watson et al. (2025). The convergence of control structures and effective decision-making processes eventually results in a stronger organizational resilience and adaptability. When decision-making bodies are able to process information effectively, they will be able to respond to change promptly, risk-manage, and exploit opportunities. The control mechanisms allow for feedback loops that allow refinement and correction of decision-making plans based on feedback, in order to stay aligned with general organizational goals. This ability for adaptability is essential in a more complex and dynamic world where decisions must be made from data and guided by specialist expertise. Thus, the importance of decision-making processes in control mechanisms is not just ensuring well-made decisions but also creating a culture of continuous improvement, innovation, and strategic adaptability consistent with the mission and vision of the organizations (Figure 5.8).

Figure 5.8. *Importance in decision-making processes.*

Source: https://www.barnesconti.com/programs/virttours/decisionProcess.png.

5.4. ITERATION CONTROL STRUCTURES

Amongst all control structures that programmers utilize, iteration control structures form the heart because they enable the programmer to execute a set of statements repeatedly subject to given conditions. They are also called loops and comprise the traditional for loop, while, and do-while structures. Using iteration enables programmers to handle repetitive activities in an effective way to avoid code duplication and improve maintainability. The significance of such control structures is also emphasized in computer programming education, especially in the context of developing students' computational thinking skills. For instance, in research conducted on Malaysian education, learning an online module with a focus on control structures was seen to impart greater understanding to students since it illustrated the practical importance of iteration in programming models (Mansor et al., 2025). Besides, iteration control structures are of different kinds, each suited to a different environment and context. The for loop, generally used for a definite iteration, allows programmers to loop through arrays or collections in a systematic way. On the other hand, while loops are useful when the number of iterations is indefinite, depending on the value of a Boolean expression. This variation offers greater variability in the flow of logic, permitting a range of programming activities from simple iteration to sophisticated algorithmic implementation. Integrating successful iteration structures into computer programming instruction is significant because these concepts not only cause code to be efficient but also enhance complex problem-solving approaches utilized in advanced computer science (Lu et al., 2024). The instructional approaches to the teaching of iteration control structures are a reflection of the broader shifts in instructional practices and incorporation of digital resources to enhance student interaction. As may be deduced from the ongoing development of the Malaysian Digital Education Policy, utilization of multimedia modules has proved to enhance learning by making abstract programming concepts more tangible and interactive for learners. These innovative pedagogies yield greater comprehension and retention of such important contents as iteration, ultimately enabling students to write effective control structure programs. Research has demonstrated that greater comprehension through integrated computer modules can significantly enhance teachers' efforts toward teaching programming literacy, paving the way for a more competent future population in technology and related fields (Mansor et al., 2025).

5.4.1. Definition and Characteristics

Control structures are fundamental programming constructs that regulate the flow of execution of a program. They provide the adequate structure for controlling decisions and operations in a program, thereby allowing developers to implement logical sequences crucial in getting certain outcomes. Control structures are usually categorized into three broad categories: selection, iteration, and sequential. This categorization highlights their application in governing the programs flow, where sequence structures execute statements sequentially, selection structures give decision-making by giving branching paths under conditions, and iteration structures give repetitive execution of blocks of code. Each serves a different role and is needed for efficient program writing. By using control structures, programmers can program more dynamic and robust programs that tackle varying inputs and scenarios more effectively. Aside from merely executing flow, control structures help make the program readable and maintainable as well. Well-structured code with control flow makes it simple for other programmers to clearly understand the logic and intent that go into the program. This is particularly useful in group settings where many programmers will share the same code base. In addition, abstraction of control structures makes program logic less complex, hence easy to debug and modify. Unpacking these characteristics reveals that control structures, by providing explicit execution paths, have a significant role in a program's overall structure, as the ongoing debate in programming pedagogy seems to suggest, especially for those languages that are being designed specifically to teach object-oriented principles, such as the new Blue language (Kölling et al., 1996). Also, the integration of sophisticated control structures into computer languages, particularly those targeting modern paradigms, reflects changing patterns of use of computing. Python is one language that reflects such change with its sophisticated but friendly control structures making automation of tasks and problem-solving across domains, such as the life sciences, more manageable. The seamless incorporation of basic control structures into sophisticated paradigms enables researchers and developers to solve intricate problems with efficacy and accuracy. The expanding application of computational methods across diverse domains requires proficiency in control structures to create efficient and dependable code. This growing reliance underscores their characteristic versatility, which not only enhances programming skills but also enhances the creativity of scientific research as well as technological advancement (Ekmekci et al., 2016).

5.4.2. Types of Loops (for, While, Do-While)

Loop statements are basic control structure building blocks of programming that allow code to be repeated under some specific condition. For loop, while loop, and do-while loop are among the most common loop types. For loop is typically employed when the number of iterations is constant, and it is best suited to iterate over arrays or other data structures. This loop constructs a counter, tests a condition before each iteration, and increments the counter accordingly, thereby delivering precise control over the iteration process. Such operation predictability aids robustness and efficiency in programming, which is critical in fields such as bioinformatics, where repetitive computation is used to form the basis of data analysis (Ekmekci et al., 2016). The while loop, on the other hand, is used where the number of iterations is unknown and determined by dynamic situations. The loop tests its condition before processing in each iteration, thereby accommodating flexible processing against runtime data. For instance, a while loop can continually process input until some terminative condition arises, say user input or signal from an input stream of data. This flexibility is essential in scenarios where data stream processing or continuous monitoring is required, with high performance being a requirement. Most significantly, the ability to tighten loops in such environments is key to reducing execution times and operations, something that shows how programming principles can have a direct impact on computation efficiency (ACM et al., 2016). The do-while loop introduces further disparity of loop action by providing at least one pass through the code block before the condition is evaluated. This syntax is most useful where at least one pass through the code block must occur at any cost, even if the conditions beginning point is not fulfilled. Menu-driven programs, where an initial-time prompt must be displayed to the user, are the best instances of where do-while loops are required. Through effective recording of user interaction, developers can make use of this control structure in order to ensure user interaction while managing flow control within programs. Finally, in identifying subtle differences between such loops, programmers are able to select the most appropriate construct for their specific requirements, consequently enhancing functionality and performance in code activities (ACM et al., 2016).

5.4.3. Performance Considerations

Performance issues in control structures must be assessed to ensure system responsiveness and efficiency are optimized. A major such area is communication between clients and servers, particularly in web applications. For instance, creating an interface for a deductive database necessitates that developers make sure HTTP handlers are employed to effectively map between client and server representations of data. Such handlers must also facilitate operations such as result pagination to improve user experience. Pengines introduce this dynamic by allowing clients to feed in a Prolog program directly to some data, hence improving flexibility and responsiveness of the API. Through simplification of logical data access, Pengines minimize the complexity common while developing strong web services, ultimately leading to faster performance in data retrieval and manipulation (Lager et al., 2014). Performance issues, however, take a more general context above and beyond web interface to encompass robotic system architecture itself, based on intricate control structures for managing coupled sub-systems. These programs are multi-complex by nature, demanding resource-intensive calculations typically that are often challenging to manage with one computational unit. Robot system hybrid algorithms typically call for resource-intensive cooperative work to generate desired outcomes. By promoting decoupled architectures, programmers can minimize impedance to leveraging distributed and parallel resources. This flexibility of design is most critical, enabling components to be reused and rearranged on an as-needed basis while retaining the interactions needed for coherent system behavior (Kloss et al., 2007). Such optimizations not only maximize performance but also enable maximum adaptability across varying operating environments within robotics. Proceeding with the discussion further regarding performance consideration, account must also be taken of the effects of service-oriented architectures (SOAs) towards maximizing system responsiveness. Interoperability among diverse software components through web services is highly advantageous, particularly for cases where platform independence as well as interoperability are crucial. The empirical data derived from the performance of web services, as evidenced from systems with response times below 50 milliseconds, indicates the possible application in time-critical robotic systems. Such performance takes center stage in environments where accuracy and speed are absolutely essential, guaranteeing control structures to effectively process real-time instructions. In a broad perspective, developments in the creation of performance-tuned control structures reap substantial returns, providing avenues for innovation across fields ranging from robotics and data access strategies (Kloss et al., 2007) (Figure 5.9).

Figure 5.9. *Assessment of performance considerations.*

Source: https://www.pageuppeople.com/wp-content/uploads/2016/09/5-key-Considerations-Performance-Management-Transformation-Thumbnail.jpg.

5.5. CONTROL STRUCTURES IN DIFFERENT PROGRAMMING LANGUAGES

Control structures are fundamental programming constructs that decide the control flow in a program. They are language constructs such as loops, conditionals, and branches that allow developers to execute certain pieces of code based on given conditions. Programming languages use different syntax and semantics to define these control structures, and this has implications on how programmers approach problems. For instance, imperative languages like C and Java employ explicit and immediate loop structures (e.g., for, while), whereas declarative languages like Haskell utilize recursion as a primary control structure. This difference not only signifies the underlying paradigms but also affects how programmers conceptualize tasks and organize their code, highlighting the pivotal role that control structures play in all programming languages. The practical relevance of control structures is particularly evident in complex systems, such as knowledge-based systems. Here, the intricacies of control of program flow are pertinent to performance, and to maintainability. Consider, for instance, the design of the abstract machine Amalia, which incorporates linguistic formalism implementations with properly designed control structures that preserve enhanced operational semantics. Through the use of a direct compilation methodology for unification grammars on typed feature structures, the performance of knowledge-based systems is significantly improved with the demonstration that thoughtful control structures are a major factor in high-level programming and computational linguistics. Such an achievement highlights the necessity to specialize control structures to the relative requirements and complexities of applications, as in the case of Amalias management of processing grammatical parsing effectively (Wintner et al., 1997). Besides, the dynamic nature of systems, especially in knowledge environments, demands robust control mechanisms to address the complexity of knowledge bases. Several specification languages are employed in describing this dynamic nature in an appropriate way, merging control structures with rich knowledge description. Control structures identified in conceptual modeling languages and logic programming frameworks are some that illustrate how dynamic reasoning can influence system behavior. With the help of abstract state machines and transactional models such as Transaction Logic, developers are equipped with mechanisms to systematically describe dynamic interactions of systems (Engelfriet et al., 2000). As programming paradigms evolve, research and development of control structures remain essential to shaping versatile, effective, and accurate programming solutions in multiple languages and domains.

5.5.1. Comparison of Control Structures in C++

Control structures are extremely basic building blocks in programming language and serve as the basis for controlling the flow of execution in a program. Sequence, selection, and iteration are the major control structures in C++. The structure of sequence executes statements one after the other in an order that is linear, hence every instruction is executed sequentially. Decision structures, such as if-else statements and switch cases, facilitate decision-making via alternative paths of execution based on logical values. Concurrently, iteration structures, such as for, while, and do-while loops, enable blocks of code to be executed repeatedly, which is crucial in the management of repetitive processing tasks. With these structures, one is able to observe the potential and versatility of C++ in managing program flow with clarity and effectiveness in structure coding. Additionally, the way these control structures are used in C++ varies extensively based on their function and complexity. For instance, selection structures allow programmers to make a decision between various alternative paths of execution, thus allowing effective decision-making in the code. In comparing if-else and switch-case statements, the latter is typically a better solution where there are numerous discrete decisions. However, iteration constructs can intentionally be applied to automatize routine work such that it is particularly valuable in data processing and algorithmic application. Correct application of the control structures will drastically enhance C++ program readability and maintainability, as well as result in more rational flow during program design. Choice of which structure to use may even direct the programming paradigm adopted, as in recent educational criticisms (Krammer et al., 1987). Lastly, the interplay of such control structures may influence the effectiveness of a program in solving complex problems. For instance, nested control structures can create intricate control flows that allow for in-depth problem-solving. But this introduces readability complications and increases cognitive load for programmers. As mentioned in discussions on pedagogical strategies for teaching programming, a number of strategies can be employed to ease this burden, guiding students through the intricacies of C++ control structures (Cameron et al., 2005). The comparison of such structures therefore not only identifies their unique features but also their combined impact on the realm of programming, illustrating how C++ allows programmers to construct robust and efficient programs (Figure 5.10).

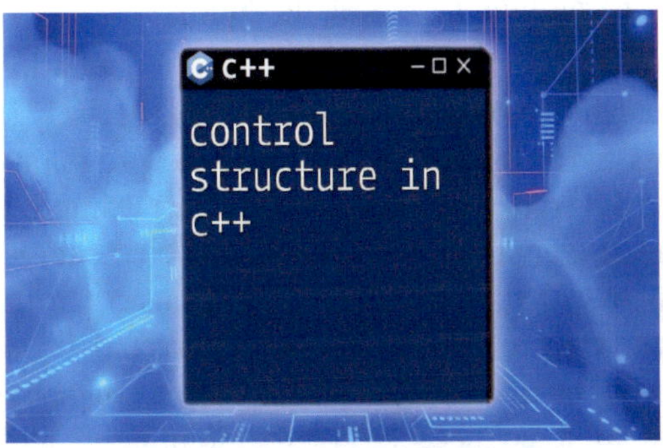

Figure 5.10. *Comparison of control structures in C++.*

Source: https://cppscripts.com/images/posts/c/control-structure-in-cpp.webp.

5.5.2. Control Structures in Python

Control structures in Python are literally the backbone of program flow, allowing programmers to decide under what conditions and how different chunks of code receive execution. One of the simplest forms of control structures are conditional statements, which permit a program to execute a specific action based on whether or not a specific condition is met. For example, the `if`, `elif`, and `else` syntax allow branching logic, which results in dynamic decision-making within programs. Branching function is most vital, especially in data-intensive fields such as bioinformatics, where the algorithm may need multiple branches depending on the input data and condition. Use of these constructs enhances the expressiveness and versatility of Python programs, essential to much modern scientific activity, because the ability to change execution paths is proportional to the dependability of the solution being developed (Ekmekci et al., 2016).

Looping constructs, the second essential category of control structures, provide for code repetition under specified conditions until a specified goal is achieved or a specified condition is no longer met. Python boasts various looping constructs, including `for` loops and `while` loops, that are pivotal in scenarios requiring repeated operations, such as iterating through sequences, processing input data, or performing calculations. The cost-benefits resulting from their use cannot be overemphasized, as they not only reduce code to be shorter but also make it more readable and maintainable. In robotics, for instance, where complex algorithms must interact with thousands of subsystems, well-designed loops enable concurrent data and operation processing. This is particularly important in time-critical programming, as illustrated in robotics where quick decision making is paramount (Kloss et al., 2007).

Python control structures also have an important function in code structuring, enhancing code readability and maintainability. By precisely identifying logical steps and activities performed by a program, the programmers construct an architecture that is layered, enabling debugging and improvement in a more streamlined manner. Indentation, the sole distinct element of Python syntax, is a prime example of marking blocks of code, and thus control structures become visually separate and easy to understand. This characteristic is especially useful when working on collaborative projects where there can be multiple developers for different parts of a codebase. As programming languages continue to evolve, the need for effective control structures becomes increasingly evident in an effort to create sophisticated software, particularly where computational approaches are employed in studies and application, such as in computational biology (Ekmekci et al., 2016). Therefore, being aware of these structures is vital for potential programmers and researchers (Figure 5.11).

Figure 5.11. *Control structures in Python serve.*

Source: *https://www.datapro.in/uploads/f680de23be25558a4ebb2d7dfcc945dd.jpg.*

5.5.3. Differences in Java Control Structures

In Java programming, an understanding of the distinctive characteristics of control structures is critical to efficient coding practices. Control structures in Java can be generally categorized into three: sequential, selection, and repetition. The sequential control structure executes statements sequentially, which forms the basis of programming logic. Selection constructs, including if, else, and switch, provide the developer with the ability to control the flow of the program based on certain conditions, which in turn makes decision-making mechanisms in the code easier to achieve. This set of control structures forms the basis for logical functions in Java, where developers can write more sophisticated and dynamic programs that can react to an extensive number of inputs, thereby creating dynamic user interactions in applications. On the other hand, repetition control structures like for, while, and do-while are essential in the performance of repetitive tasks with effectiveness. All the iteration structures possess their own unique abilities, which most appropriately meet a wide range of programming needs. The for loop is particularly well-suited for instances where iterations are predetermined and best suited for offering a concise syntax, making it easy to read. While and do-while loops are utilized when iteration is not definite, depending on dynamic computational scenarios to function. They enable Java programmers to execute intricate algorithms, ensuring highest performance and resource utilization under extensive data sets or complex calculations, an essential aspect of modern software development. Moreover, novel programming paradigms that have emerged after Javas time has started also brought innovations into Javas control structures that make the code more powerful and expressive. For instance, Javas innovation has integrated into its functions as novel elements such as lambda expressions, which transform the traditional use of control structures. Such a development in contemporary applications reinforces the expressiveness and legibility of code. Through the inclusion of such new attributes into control structures, Java continues to be relevant in various applications from web services and distributed computing to contemporary applications. Employing declarative programming paradigm, like that being displayed by Javas recent growth following JDK 8, allows developers to exploit the capabilities of control structures to a high degree, mirroring shifts in other languages like OCL and its recent equivalent like LINQ (Conrad et al., 2004; Akehurst et al., 2008). This combination of long-past and modern methods ultimately adds to the developers toolset, guaranteeing creativity and efficiency in solving problems.

5.6. BEST PRACTICES FOR USING CONTROL STRUCTURES

Control structures are building blocks of sound programming that enable programmers to control the flow of logic and affect decision-making operations. Control structure best practices enhance code quality and ease of maintenance. One basic practice is to favor structure choice clarity; programmers should choose the most minimal control structures that deliver the necessary functionality. This approach not only lowers the readability barrier but also lowers the possibility of code bugs. According to recent studies, communities that engage in collective media production will be inclined towards clarity and strategic direction, which can be related to the manner in which program decision-making must be addressed by developers (Johnson et al., 2007). By maintaining simplicity and transparency, programmers create systems that not only run optimally but also remain easy to understand for other programmers in the future who will have the ability to alter or extend the original code.

Another best practice is the repetition of the same indentation and structure when using control structures, thus making the code much cleaner and readable. Consistency of style facilitates the differentiation between various control statements to make it easier for the programmers to write out complex logical paths. Adherence to these style conventions provides a feeling of familiarity for the code, allowing faster comprehension and fewer errors. Additionally, in computer-based information systems (CBIS), organization of the control structure can directly affect usability (Iacono et al., 1989). An organized system helps with routine tasks without causing execution mismatches, thereby displaying the importance of neat coding. Therefore, by maintaining neat coding and organization standards, programmers enhance the usability and lifetime of their control structures. Finally, developers ought to have rigorous testing and refactoring as essential aspects in their best practices for control structures. Testing does not just allow the discovery of logical errors but also verifies that the outcomes sought are achieved. This process of enhancement through code refinement is helped by familiar testing patterns, which allow for less complicated control path and if statement analysis. Refactoring code also makes optimization simpler and can lead to the simplification of complex control structures. By continually examining and streamlining the control mechanisms, developers can create stable systems that adapt to user needs and demands. Lastly, these methodological processes, assisted by tactics within community media projects, allow control structures to operate effectively and responsively in various programming contexts (Johnson et al., 2007).

5.6.1. Writing Maintainable and Clear Code

In programming, readable and transparent code is most critical, particularly when utilizing control structures. Not only does transparent code make the code easier to read, but it also makes debugging and modification easier, which is crucial in intricate programs. Control structures such as loops and conditional statements are fundamental building blocks that decide the flow of the program. It is therefore crucial that such structures are written in clarity. Carefully annotated control structures allow for other developers, or even the original developer at a later time, to readily see why a decision was made in code, cutting down onboarding time for new developers or accommodating future needs. Making logic within control structures easier to understand leads to more flexible software and fewer chances of inserting bugs during subsequent development cycles. Another vital thing about writing code that can be maintained is the question of how one balances performance and scalability against portability and maintainability, a problem software engineering literature has described. Because software systems increasingly need to do complex things—such as large-scale simulations—code needs to be designed such that it not only performs well under load but also easily modified or transferred between platforms (Graziotin et al., 2016). This double-pronged strategy emphasizes the need to adopt best practices in code structure and organization. Writing with natural and readable control structures can be very much helpful in providing a codebases long-term viability and flexibility. Keeping maintainability at the highest level with performance constraints ensures that the applications created will not only adapt to new technologies but also to shifting user demands. Moreover, maintainability of code is generally facilitated by frameworks that enforce domain-specific control structures. For instance, when cloud computing came into popularity, frameworks like EbbRT illustrate that domain-specific operating systems are capable of furthering performance without jeopardizing tractability in code management (Appavoo et al., 2016). Such environments focus on crafting code that can seamlessly integrate into specialized environments without compromising its maintainability. These breakthroughs place in the spotlight the evolving nature of software development, where clean and sustainable code is not merely best practice but a necessity in producing high-performance programs. This ultimately contributes to the argument that programmers must continue to be mindful of coding clean code that has a balance of performance and sustainability, most particularly in the delicate domain of control structures (Figure 5.12).

Figure 5.12. *Writing clear and maintainable code.*

Source: https://thecrazyprogrammer.com/wp-content/uploads/2024/01/Best-Practices-for-Writing-Clean-and-Maintainable-Code.jpeg.

5.6.2. Avoiding Common Pitfalls

In control structures, understanding and prevention of frequent fallacies are essential for improving efficiency and effectiveness in system design and programming. The most typical problem results from inadequate understanding of logical structures such as loops and conditional statements. The programmer will often be stuck on creating overly complicated conditions that may lead to infinite loops or flawed blocks of code. These complications not only discourage people from performing well but also make debugging a nightmare. Using unambiguous and succinct reasoning, along with the practice of breaking down hard problems into pieces that are solvable, can make control structures a great deal more reliable. Without resorting to complex constructs, programmers can spend more time writing cleaner, better-organized code according to best practices, making collaboration and future modifications much easier. The second serious mistake involves incorrect application of variable scope and declaration inside control structures. Lack of proper comprehension of variable visibility can make it into unexpected access to or modification of data among different parts of an application. For instance, excessive use of global variables could insert unjustified side effects, lowering code predictability as well as testing difficulty. Ensuring variables are declared in the proper scope and how they act within loops and other control blocks is crucial.

Figure 5.13. *Avoiding common pitfalls.*

Source: https://external-content.duckduckgo.com/iu/?u=https%3A%2F%2Fexternal-preview.redd.it%2Favoiding-common-pitfalls-in-documenting-procedures-and-v0-Ubo6y6SwjZXYbNziQAV2jWo_bUh7LL3Y-ICVrSSp95hA.jpg%3Fauto%3Dwebp%26s%3Da849056f473f7934c9d356c679825b0cff928cc5&f=1&nofb=1&ipt=b20dcd7ee80f23cdd3e5a7937623a9dba8b069bcf45fcb5a0bf5630142fc4cee.

A developer needs to be cautious not to draw a blurry line of variable application so that no conflicts exist and integrity of the data is ensured. This interest in scope not only prevents bugs but also makes code more modular, which is most critical for collaborative programming and open-source development in an expanding inter-disciplinary world (Snyder, 2019). Finally, bad testing and verification often undermine the strength of control structures. Most programmers underestimate the strength of whole test cases since they can get programs to act in unpredictable manners during runtime. Without proper testing, tiny moments of weakness in the implementation of control structure can turn into catastrophes, particularly on large and complicated systems. To mitigate this risk, there must be a stringent testing process that includes unit tests, integration tests, and end-to-end system tests. Aside from displaying potential errors early on, such practices also enhance the general quality and dependability of the application. With the field of machine learning, in particular graph neural networks (GNNs), increasingly now incorporating control structures into their algorithms, proper validation becomes that much more critical in achieving desired outcomes (Wu et al., 2020). With structured testing approaches taking center stage, developers are able to fix issues prior to deployment, leading to more robust and working control structures (Figure 5.13).

5.6.3. Enhancing Performance Through Efficient Control Flow

Control flow constitutes an imperative element of computational process execution that directly influences performance optimization. With proper control flow construction, programmers can reduce latency by a significant extent and enhance throughput to its optimum value. Algorithms developed with a judicious focus on control structure allow effective utilization of resources available, especially in high-performance environments. For instance, the application of control flow structures such as conditionals and loops enables the programmer to add sequencing among operations without too much computational overhead. Optimizations are particularly effective in scenarios where quick processing and timely handling of tasks are required, proving that the way in which control structures are implemented in practice has a decisive influence on overall performance outcomes. Furthermore, the development in hardware technology calls for corresponding developments in software control methods. Data locality and caching techniques become significant while managing data flow to avoid performance bottlenecks. For example, new GPUs have unique characteristics that can be exploited with optimized control structures. In the case of the Lattice Boltzmann method, efficient data propagation methods need to be developed in order to maximize parallel computing potential. By exploiting shared memory and leveraging specialist hardware facilities, the programmer is able to eliminate typical bottlenecks in terms of data access and transfer. Optimizing control flow can thus confer considerable performance advantage, enabling systems to execute intricate calculations more quickly without sacrificing throughput levels (Mawson et al., 2013). For the broader case of distributed applications, good control flow maximizes responsiveness and exploitation of resources across networked systems. Factors such as computing infrastructure and communication structure have a significant influence on the performance of applications. For instance, with the transition of the bottleneck from network-centric considerations to the components of computing infrastructure, control flow optimization meant efficient application performance. Optimizing protocol processing operations and minimization of overhead lead to the effective processing of interaction among heterogeneous systems. This is in line with the dynamic nature of applications that require seamless communication and collaboration among nodes. Proper understanding and application of control structures have the power to significantly affect the efficiency and performance of such distributed systems to provide timely and accurate solutions to computational problems (Schmidt et al., 1992).

SUMMARY

In summarizing the subject of control structures, one can see that such underlying elements have a lot of importance in the provision of effectiveness and versatility to systems. Control structures allow companies and individuals to manage complexities by offering rules and frameworks that guide decision-making. Through the definition of paths of action, they bring about unity and consistency and hence allow stakeholders to overcome difficulties confidently. Besides, employment of robust control structures can facilitate ongoing improvement by providing feedback loops and adapting to changing environments, thereby optimizing overall operation efficiency. The role of control structures is not merely in mere regulation; they play a vital role in driving innovation and flexibility within defined parameters. In this era of necessity for flexibility, sound control structures guarantee a balance between stability and the need for dynamism in the face of disturbances. In other contexts, including technology and medicine, harnessing the potential of control structures allows one to optimize results and optimize resources. Such adaptability is particularly important in dynamic fields where the ability to pivot can lead to significant advancements and improved performance. Furthermore, the analysis of control structures highlights the ongoing need for research and refinement in their application. As supported by the latest finding on adversarial loss of image translation, the application of new methods to control structures can deliver more advantageous results compared to traditional means (Zhu et al., 2017). Further, lessons from risk factors in public health programs indicate how certain control measures can minimize important societal loads (Lindsey et al., 2015). Thus, the conclusion derived from this study emphasizes the necessity of constant evaluation and enhancement of control structures. This commitment not only guarantees their effectiveness but also paves the way for novel advancements across a variety of disciplines.

Control structures are basic building blocks of mathematical optimization and computational problem-solving, and particularly in the realm of polynomial minimization methods. Some new developments add to the significance of convergence rates within a hierarchy of upper bounds by Lasserre. More precisely, the rate of convergence of such bounds reaches Theta ($1/r^2$), which improves the efficiency of such an approach, particularly when solving problems bounded by the surface of the unit sphere. These findings are pivotal in enhancing the understanding of control structures within polynomial optimization, supporting more robust framework selection and research development in mathematical programming methods (de Klerk et al., 2019). This is based on current theory, demonstrating how control structures can leverage probabilistic models to establish optimal solutions within bounded environments. In addition to mathematical models, control structures underlie response to complex social issues, such as school violence against children. The Kampala, Uganda, Program Learning Event (PLE) indicates how controlled events can generate a larger community of stakeholders to produce a coordinated response toward prevention initiatives. The three-day conference brought together practitioners and policymakers from various countries to develop a common learning agenda on violence among children in and around schools. Such initiatives are indicative of effective control mechanisms' capacity to open up possibilities for conversation and activity, ultimately leading to frameworks that counterattack at the basic problems with robust responses. This convergence of mathematical abstractions and social constructions reveals the multidimensional nature of control structures that both encompass quantitative and qualitative dimensions of problem-solving (N/A, 2015).

Lastly, the dialectic of theoretical optimization methods and applied social uses discloses the flexibility of control structures. By forming evident hierarchies and procedural guidelines, these structures not only advance the mathematics but also enhance policy initiatives towards social welfare. The importance of understanding rates of convergence in polynomial minimization, along with the resolve towards transcending obstacles in learning environments, is evidence of the widespread application of control structures in a variety of disciplines. As we pool insights from mathematical and social arenas, it is apparent that effective control structures are an essential factor towards the realization of maximum outcomes, indicating the need for even more research and interdisciplinarity towards solving complex global issues.

REFERENCES

1. Akehurst, D. H., Howells, W. G., Mcdonald-Maier, K. D., Scheidgen, M., et al. (2008). C# 3.0 makes OCL redundant! https://core.ac.uk/download/16470463.pdf (accessed on 9th September 2025).
2. Appavoo, J., Cadden, J., Dong, H., Krieger, O., et al. (2016). EbbRT: A framework for building per-application library operating systems. https://open.bu.edu/bitstream/2144/21780/1/2016-002-ebbrt.pdf (accessed on 9th September 2025).
3. Bakala, E., Gerosa, A., Hourcade, J., Tejera, G., Peterman, K., & Trinidad, G. P. (2022). A systematic review of technologies to teach control structures in preschool education. *Frontiers in Psychology, 13*. https://www.semanticscholar.org/paper/41e3d4167de3cece386c0408bcaa2deb7e2afec7 (accessed on 9th September 2025).
4. Biboudis, A., Biboudis, A., Jones, S. P., Kiselyov, O., Pouzet, M., Prokopec, A., et al. (2016). Stream fusion, to completeness. http://arxiv.org/abs/1612.06668 (accessed on 9th September 2025).
5. Birman, K. P. (1991). Maintaining consistency in distributed systems. https://core.ac.uk/download/pdf/42815035.pdf (accessed on 9th September 2025).
6. Bray, F., Ferlay, J., Soerjomataram, I., Siegel, R. L., Torre, L. A., & Jemal, A. (2018). Global cancer statistics 2018: GLOBOCAN estimates of incidence and mortality worldwide for 36 cancers in 185 countries. *CA: A Cancer Journal for Clinicians, 68*, 394–424. https://doi.org/10.3322/caac.21492 (accessed on 9th September 2025).
7. Cameron, H., King, P., & Thompson, S. (2005). Modelling reactive multimedia: Design and authoring. https://core.ac.uk/download/30704203.pdf (accessed on 9th September 2025).
8. Conrad, M., & French, T. (2004). A gentle transition from Java programming to web services using XML-RPC. https://core.ac.uk/download/29820916.pdf (accessed on 9th September 2025).
9. de Klerk, E., & Laurent, M. (2019). Convergence analysis of a Lasserre hierarchy of upper bounds for polynomial minimization on the sphere. https://core.ac.uk/download/301632242.pdf (accessed on 9th September 2025).
10. Dyntar, J., & Škvor, J. (2013). Chemical industry supply chain optimization using agent-based modelling. https://core.ac.uk/download/14742047.pdf (accessed on 9th September 2025).

11. Ekmekci, B., McAnany, C. E., & Mura, C. (2016). An introduction to programming for bio scientists: A Python-based primer. http://arxiv.org/abs/1605.05419 (accessed on 9th September 2025).
12. Engelfriet, J., Fensel, D., van Eck, P., van Harmelen, F., et al. (2000). A survey of languages for specifying dynamics: A knowledge engineering perspective. https://core.ac.uk/download/pdf/11456853.pdf (accessed on 9th September 2025).
13. Evans, L., Rhodes, A., Alhazzani, W., Antonelli, M., Coopersmith, C. M., French, C., Machado, F. R., et al. (2021). Surviving sepsis campaign: International guidelines for management of sepsis and septic shock 2021. *Critical Care Medicine, 49*, e1063–e1143. https://doi.org/10.1097/ccm.0000000000005337 (accessed on 9th September 2025).
14. Feringa, B. L. (2017). The art of building small: From molecular switches to motors (Nobel Lecture). *Angewandte Chemie International Edition, 56*, 11060–11078. https://doi.org/10.1002/anie.201702979 (accessed on 9th September 2025).
15. Flederer, F., Montenegro, S., Ostermayer, L., Seipel, D., et al. (2017). Source code verification for embedded systems using Prolog. http://arxiv.org/abs/1701.00630 (accessed on 9th September 2025).
16. García Orozco, J., & Guerrero Posadas, M. (2016). Algorithmic thinking development with generative learning objects support. https://core.ac.uk/download/51407779.pdf (accessed on 9th September 2025).
17. Graziotin, D., Lindner, F., Mehl, M., Pfander, H., et al. (2016). The scalability-efficiency/maintainability-portability trade-off in simulation software engineering: Examples and a preliminary systematic literature review. http://arxiv.org/abs/1608.04336 (accessed on 9th September 2025).
18. Harris, C. R., Millman, K. J., van der Walt, S., Gommers, R., Virtanen, P., Cournapeau, D., Wieser, E., et al. (2020). Array programming with NumPy. *Nature, 585*, 357–362. https://doi.org/10.1038/s41586-020-2649-2 (accessed on 9th September 2025).
19. Huang, M., Ye, X., & Sakurai, T. (2022). Unveiling interpretable development-specific gene signatures in the developing human prefrontal cortex with ICGS. https://www.semanticscholar.org/paper/7cc994f7fb5b488270cab4b74fbf8d0df39fa91d (accessed on 9th September 2025).
20. Iacono, S., & Kling, R. (1989). The institutional character of computerized information systems. https://core.ac.uk/download/287623358.pdf (accessed on 9th September 2025).

21. Johnson, F., & Menichelli, K. (2007). What's going on in community media. https://core.ac.uk/download/71339790.pdf (accessed on 9th September 2025).

22. Kanvar, V., & Khedker, U. P. (2015). Heap abstractions for static analysis. http://arxiv.org/abs/1403.4910 (accessed on 9th September 2025).

23. Kloss, G. K. (2007). Performance evaluation of a distributed integrative architecture for robotics. https://core.ac.uk/download/148639212.pdf (accessed on 9th September 2025).

24. Kölling, M., & Rosenberg, J. (1996). Blue–A language for teaching object-oriented programming. https://core.ac.uk/download/63387.pdf (accessed on 9th September 2025).

25. Krammer, H. P. M., & van Merriënboer, J. J. G. (1987). Instructional strategies and tactics for the design of introductory computer programming courses in high school. https://core.ac.uk/download/pdf/11462350.pdf (accessed on 9th September 2025).

26. Kreutz, D., Ramos, F. M. V., Veríssimo, P. E., Rothenberg, C. E., Azodolmolky, S., & Uhlig, S. (2014). Software-defined networking: A comprehensive survey. *Proceedings of the IEEE, 103*, 14–76. https://doi.org/10.1109/jproc.2014.2371999 (accessed on 9th September 2025).

27. Lager, T., & Wielemaker, J. (2014). Pengines: Web logic programming made easy. http://arxiv.org/abs/1405.3953 (accessed on 9th September 2025).

28. Langdon, W. B., McPhee, N. F., & Poli, R. (2008). *A Field Guide to Genetic Programming*. https://core.ac.uk/download/214315022.pdf (accessed on 9th September 2025).

29. Lu, H., Xing, H., & Zhou, W. (2024). Adaptive event-triggered control and observer design for discrete-time nonlinear Markov jump systems with DoS attacks using policy iteration-based adaptive dynamic programming. *Optimal Control Applications and Methods, 45*, 2153–2175. https://www.semanticscholar.org/paper/15ba0d91785e5fbd061b8821cd19882473f86d19 (accessed on 9th September 2025).

30. Mansor, R., & Kamsin, I. F. (2025). The importance of creating a control structure programming module to improve students' understanding. *International Journal of Academic Research in Business and Social Sciences*. https://www.semanticscholar.org/paper/33b575a2442b6f88c6d606b96ea15055c7ac0ba0 (accessed on 9th September 2025).

31. Mawson, M., & Revell, A. (2013). Memory transfer optimization for a lattice Boltzmann solver on Kepler architecture NVIDIA GPUs. http://arxiv.org/abs/1309.1983 (accessed on 9th September 2025).

32. N/A. (2015). *Program Learning Event on Violence Against Children in and Around Schools in East Africa.* https://core.ac.uk/download/75782886.pdf (accessed on 9th September 2025).

33. Omondi, E. O., Lin, C. Y., Huang, S., Liao, C. A., Lin, Y. P., Oliva, R., & van Zonneveld, M. (2024). Landscape genomics reveals genetic signals of environmental adaptation of African wild eggplants. *Ecology and Evolution, 14.* https://www.semanticscholar.org/paper/e8d9bc4ef5a27645068b6e3cde16cec90bf2c4b0 (accessed on 9th September 2025).

34. Schmidt, D. C., & Suda, T. (1992). Computing infrastructure issues in distributed communications systems: A survey of operating system transport system architectures. https://core.ac.uk/download/287622717.pdf (accessed on 9th September 2025).

35. Snyder, H. (2019). Literature review as a research methodology: An overview and guidelines. *Journal of Business Research, 104*, 333–339. https://doi.org/10.1016/j.jbusres.2019.07.039 (accessed on 9th September 2025).

36. Torre, L. A., Bray, F., Siegel, R. L., Ferlay, J., Lortet-Tieulent, J., & Jemal, A. (2015). Global cancer statistics, 2012. *CA: A Cancer Journal for Clinicians, 65*, 87–108. https://doi.org/10.3322/caac.21262 (accessed on 9th September 2025).

37. Venkatasubramanian, V. (2018). The promise of artificial intelligence in chemical engineering: Is it here, finally? *AIChE Journal, 65*, 466–478. https://doi.org/10.1002/aic.16489 (accessed on 9th September 2025).

38. Watson, M. D. (2025). Information theory applied to decision making structures. https://core.ac.uk/download/pdf/161999880.pdf (accessed on 9th September 2025).

39. Wintner, S. (1997). An abstract machine for unification grammars. http://arxiv.org/abs/cmp-lg/9709013 (accessed on 9th September 2025).

40. Wu, Z., Pan, S., Chen, F., Long, G., Zhang, C., & Yu, P. S. (2020). A comprehensive survey on graph neural networks. *IEEE Transactions on Neural Networks and Learning Systems, 32*, 4–24. https://doi.org/10.1109/tnnls.2020.2978386 (accessed on 9th September 2025).

41. Zhu, J. Y., Park, T., Isola, P., & Efros, A. A. (2017). Unpaired image-to-image translation using cycle-consistent adversarial networks. https://doi.org/10.1109/iccv.2017.244 (accessed on 9th September 2025).

CHAPTER 6

FUNCTIONS AND MODULAR PROGRAMMING

Contents

INTRODUCTION

Successful programming in computer science forms the foundation for the development of sound applications. Programming functions and modularity are key concepts that make it easy to simplify the otherwise complex task of coding. Segmenting a program into smaller, easier units assists programmers in making code more readable, manageable, and reusable. Functions assist individuals in compartmentalizing some behaviors or calculations, making them foster structured coding practices. This encapsulation not only allows lone testing and debugging but also facilitates collaborative software development, where multiple programmers can work simultaneously on various modules without congesting each other. Modular programming takes advantage of the principles evolved by functions, encouraging large-scale application development through combining smaller, independent modules. Each module has a designated function and interface, enabling well-defined interaction with other components. This kind of organization is beneficial to project management in general, since teams can isolate and solve parts without disturbing the rest of the codebase. This flexibility present in modular setups is also evidenced through software setups like KALI, which enhances flexibility with multi-coordinated manipulators in intricate programmable setups, as presented in Backes et al. (2025). This modularity in designing optimizes programming methods and fosters innovation. Finally, the subject of functions and modularity provides entryways to understanding the broader implications of these concepts in other programming paradigms, for example, abstract state machines (ASMs). The underlying principles of modularity and function usage enable not just efficiency but also design conceptual simplicity. References such as in Boerger et al. (1998) illustrate how there remains ongoing research in the field as scientists continue to evaluate the meaning of ASMs with modular programming. One can observe from this initial overview of these fundamental principles how function integration and modular approaches are a key underlying factor in carrying forward programming approaches and optimizing developer productivity (Figure 6.1).

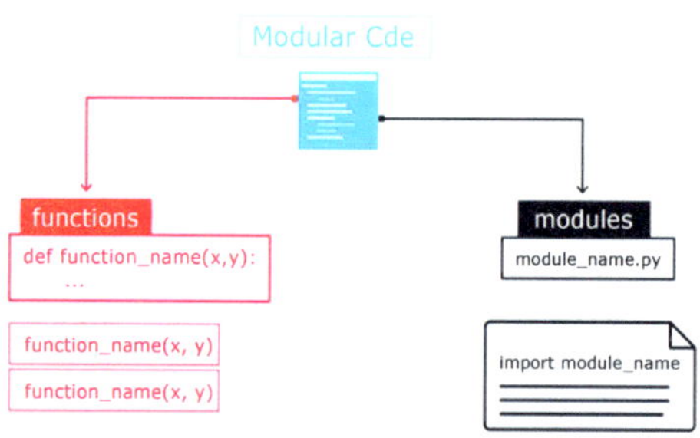

Figure 6.1. *Functions and modular programming.*

Source: https://media2.dev.to/dynamic/image/width=800%2Cheight=%2Cfit=scale-down%2Cgravity=auto%2Cformat=auto/https%3A%2F%2Fdev-to-uploads.s3.amazonaws.com%2Fuploads%2Farticles%2F1i9yfofdjt6glw87e6s5.jpg.

Definition of Functions

The concept of functions is fundamental to programming, particularly in the case of modular programming. Functions are pieces of code that are reusable and meant to accomplish a specific task and assist in maintaining code and avoiding redundancy. By encapsulating functions' behavior, programmers can make code more readable and maintainable, which are chief aspects in the creation of effective software. A function typically contains a list of parameters, a body with the code to execute, and a return value, all of which combined permit an easy definition of purpose. This structured style of coding allows programmers to deal easier with complicated systems by breaking them down into manageable smaller pieces that can be coded, tested, and debugged individually. Functions are typically the solution to ensuring code compatibility in modular programming. For instance, when different components or programming languages need to communicate with one another, how functions are defined and invoked makes integration easier. Multilingual systems, where coordination between several components is called for, rely heavily on precise definitions of functions to ensure compatibility among various programming languages. A classic example of addressing this issue can be seen in Baird et al. (2018), wherein it is elucidated how a light-weighted analysis architecture can assist in constructing call graphs for multilingual codebases. Such approaches stress the need for a clean function structure that allows developers to follow calls and interactions among functions in different programming environments without any glitch. In addition, functions can be specified further by not just encapsulating their functional behavior but also their non-functional behavior—such as performance and reliability. NoFun, a tool demonstrated in Guti et al. (1998), is one such advanced technique for handling functional as well as non-functional behavior in the context of component programming. By assigning hierarchies of properties to segments of software, programmers can order implementations by specific non-functional requirements, such as response time or resource usage. In doing so, complete appreciation of functions transcends simple code containment; it involves a broader context where performance is part of the very definition of functions and its applicability in the modular framework of software systems.

Definition of Modular Programming

Modular programming is a paradigm that emphasizes breaking down extensive programs into small, independent, and manageable modules. A module encapsulates a specific function to enable programmers to create an organized codebase with enhanced maintainability and reusability. The paradigm simplifies the organization of code in a clearer manner, and modules are simple to write, test, and understand independently before combining them into a broad system. Modular design not only allows for collaboration among software developers but also aids in the detection of and correction of bugs because each module can be inspected separately. Besides that, modular programming is very compatible with object-oriented concepts and effectively offers abstraction and encapsulation, which is a key element in developing stable software architectures. As a result, the module approach has become an intrinsic element of the majority of contemporary programming languages, maintaining the essence of the separation of concerns in software design. Modularity can be particularly useful in functional programming because it allows for multiple views of program entities to be built and transformed. For example, in investigating the expression problem in Haskell, programmers are able to deploy various architectures that embody many decomposition approaches.

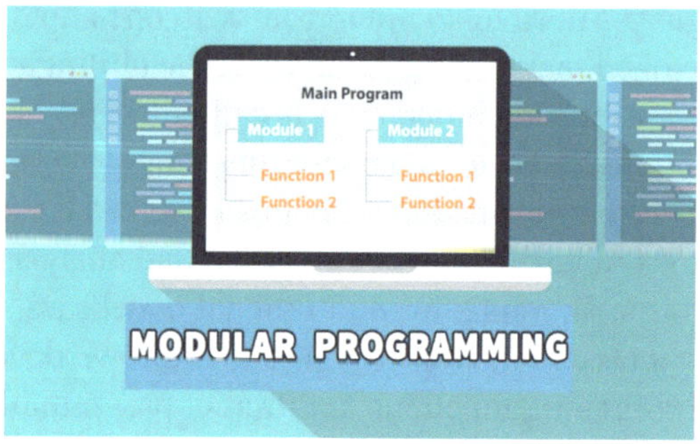

Figure 6.2. *Modular programming.*

Source: https://coditize.com/wp-content/uploads/2021/09/modular-cover-1024x658.jpg.

The Haskell Refactor is one such example of this ability by automatically performing the conversion from one modular perspective to another, demonstrating how modular programming can evolve to suit multiple requirements without requiring a new version of the original codebase to be written. Such flexibility not only maximizes the development process but also highlights the potential of modular programming to accommodate shifting software requirements, under which developers can improve and extend functionalities without changing underlying logic. Being able to do so captures the essence of modular programming in that it provides developers with the tools necessary to innovate over and over again. Further, modularity is a basis for the development of sophisticated programming languages with the ability to deal with high-level functionalities. The ability to embed extensions of semantic models, such as the subject matter of RAISE specification language

RSL, is one instance of the key role of modularity in integrating state-based properties and concurrency features into programming environments. By establishing a rigorous framework for relating elementary and extended models, developers can create languages that not only preserve fundamental properties but can readily accommodate additional functions. Modular composition in this case highlights the profound impact modular programming has on refining language definitions, thereby allowing for the development of languages that are optimized for specific application contexts. Hence, the addition of new functionality to established programming languages enhances their readability and efficiency, exemplifying the dynamic nature of modular programming in contemporary software engineering practices (Figure 6.2).

Importance of Functions and Modular Programming in Software Development

The utility of functions and modular programming in computer coding is primarily due to their capacity to enhance the readability and structure of the code. With the help of functions, the programmers can break down large segments of code into systematic and logical units. This modularized approach supports an open structure where the programmers can find it easier to understand and navigate through the code. Since programs tend to grow and develop over time, clearness in terms of effectively defined functions is crucial. Additionally, as Stein et al. (1999) explores, using a computational metaphor derived from community interaction can redefine our way of programming in a manner consistent with modular programming principles. This shift in perspective allows programmers to consider their products not as simple linear strings of instructions, but as intricate networks of interdependent items, which can significantly improve cognitive processing and problem-solving efficiency. Moreover, the technique of modular programming is susceptible to code reusability and maintainability principles. By designing functions that can be easily reused between projects or modules within the same project, developers save considerable time and resources that would be lost through repetition. This not only prevents redundancy but also reduces the potential for introducing inconsistencies or bugs because a change to a single function cascades throughout all locations where it is called. This approach eventually leads to more stable software systems. In addition, recent advances in multilingual software analysis have made modularity more critical. Techniques like those in Baird et al. (2018) demonstrate how modular programming assists in combining different programming languages into a single codebase, making interoperability and the potential for collaborative software engineering better. Finally, testing and debugging are immensely facilitated with functions and modular programming. Principles of modular design enable the developers to encapsulate individual pieces of code so that testing and debugging become easier. If a function is confronted by some problem or bug, it can be tested separately to determine its correctness without disturbing other components of the application. Encapsulation makes it easier to identify the errors and encourages the creation of useful unit tests so that every module works according to expectations prior to integration into large systems. By prioritizing modular structures as its first choice, programmers create a stronger software development environment within which issues can be corrected efficiently, observed by Stein et al. (1999). As the demand for agile and reactive software programs continues to grow, functions and modular programming's role will definitely remain one of the key drivers of efficient software development techniques.

6.1. HISTORICAL CONTEXT

The historical context of functions and modular programming is firmly rooted with the evolution of computer science and software engineering. Programming languages such as FORTRAN and COBOL were some of the first precursors to structured programming with their adoption of subroutines and procedures. These features, besides facilitating reuse of code, promoted greater organization in software applications. With increasing sophistication in software systems, the need was felt to create systematic means of dealing with this sophistication. Modular programming emerged as a result of reaction against issues such as code redundancy and the difficulties associated with dealing with large codebases, and it established the foundation for more advanced programming paradigms. Understanding this history is fundamental to an appreciation of how functions and modularity evolved to allow for greater productivity and collaborative software development. The development of object-oriented programming (OOP) further transformed the software's development and introduced a radical shift in the application of functions and modular components. The concepts of encapsulation, inheritance, and polymorphism brought by OOP enable the developers to write modular code that not just remains reusable but also becomes more flexible in nature to meet changing requirements. This shift in the past was driven by the growing need for more reliable software systems to run on a wide variety of platforms and languages. Interestingly, OOP languages such as C++ and Java had strong emphasis on modularity in designing systems that are easier to understand and modify. This trend mirrors the continued development of programming concepts that address the need to manage the complexity that exists in current computing environments. Professionals today can thus leverage both modular and functional programming methodologies towards creating scalable and maintainable software solutions. Over the past few years, modular programming emphasis has been reiterated by the appearance of software repositories and team-based development platforms enabling integration of multiform programming paradigms. These repositories serve as hubs for consolidation of isolated tools supplementing the development process, including defect tracking systems and project control tools. As the need for effective decision-making processes increases, techniques such as forecasting have become an integral aspect of software development to enable teams to anticipate project trajectories based on history. The development of an open-source modular forecasting service, as detailed in Mart et al. (2019), is a good representation of this trend, demonstrating how flexible tools can make software development increasingly linked. Additionally, efforts at dismantling multilingual codebases, as highlighted in Baird et al. (2018), indicate an enduring enthusiasm for furthering modularity in software design as a method of promoting interoperability as well as efficiency in a deepening program environment.

6.1.1. Evolution of Programming Languages

The evolution of programming languages has shaped the field of computer science and played a central role in making functions and modular programming possible. The first programming languages, such as assembly and machine code, entailed manipulating hardware directly by the programmer, which was difficult and laborious to do so. With the progression of times in the industry, there emerged higher-level languages that provided greater abstraction so developers could focus on solving problems rather than dealing with hardware specifics. Programming languages like FORTRAN and COBOL pioneered the way by simplifying syntax and providing access to functions that masked particular tasks. This changed the way for modern programming paradigms, highlighting modular programming's benefits of promoting reusability and maintainability of code, which are critical in modern software creation. Enhancements came with the introduction of object-oriented programming (OOP), which dramatically shifted the way developers conceived and structured code. OOP, popularized by programming languages like C++ and Python, was centered on encapsulation, inheritance, and polymorphism. These helped make programming more natural when simulating objects in the real world and also enabled more modular programming. OOP increased collaboration and avoided redundancy by allowing programmers to define reusable blocks of code via classes and objects. Moreover, the modularity of OOP is well-suited for contemporary software engineering that often consists of teams working on larger-scale systems requiring effective partition of labor and integration of functionalities of diverse natures. Hence, the study of numerous programming paradigms over the years has developed a robust intellectual heritage that directs software advancement and facilitates innovation. The drift towards functional programming languages such as Haskell and Scala has also contributed to ongoing development of programming. Functional programming emphasizes the use of pure functions, first-class functions, and immutable data structures that promote declarative programming. This paradigm has particularly helped concurrent and parallel programming by easily providing predictable and controlled code execution in multi-core systems. The capability to represent complex problems in a clear and concise form has resulted in wider usage in many areas, such as scientific computation and bioinformatics. Even better, tools like the Haskell Refactorer illustrate the value of functional programming through its capability to support arbitrary transformations between alternative program representations seamlessly, as Cohen et al. (2011) illustrates. Besides, the introduction of scripting languages like Python, known for their beautiful syntax and vast libraries, has brought into focus the importance of modularity and functionality in today's programming platforms, thereby influencing domains beyond computer science, including biology and data analysis, as mentioned in Ekmekci et al. (2016) (Figure 6.3).

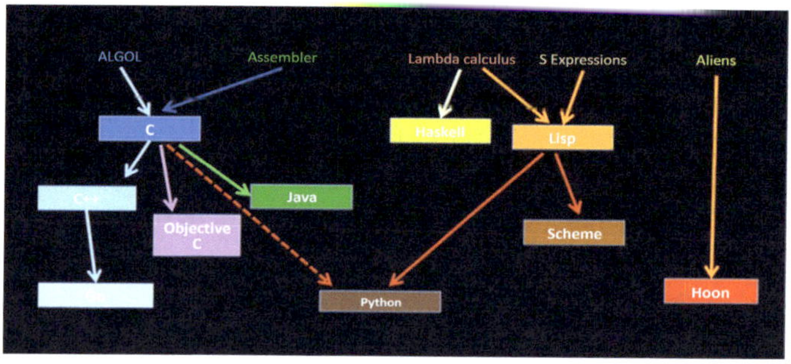

Figure 6.3. *Evolution of programming languages.*

Source: https://biblipole.com/wp-content/uploads/2016/06/evolution_of_programming_languages.png.

6.1.2. Early Use of Functions in Programming

The initial introduction of functions in computer programming was an essential move from procedural to modular thought, significantly changing the nature of how computer programmers approached intricate issues. Functions facilitated encapsulation of logic such that discrete operations could be abstracted from the general program framework. Encapsulation facilitated easier code reuse and maintenance since programmers could modify a function without interfering with other parts of the program. With a modular programming mindset, functions were not just a sequence of instructions, but as key building blocks that contributed towards cooperation among other programming entities. This shift in perspective justifies one key shift in programming cognitive practices, which justifies the thesis in Stein et al. (1999) with regard to the shifting metaphors in computation and their impact on programming as a co-operative activity. As programming languages evolved, the first use of functions reflected a growing consciousness of the contribution that abstraction made to the creation of software. Most programming environments at first did not support the notion of high-level function definitions and therefore limited programmers to writing blocks of long code. The discovery of functions allowed programmers to build sets of reusable code in the form of libraries, making it easier to develop programs and avoid redundancy. For instance, at the beginning, functions were not first-class citizens; however, as languages matured, they could be passed as parameters and returned from a second function. This capability enabled sophisticated operations to be broken down into sub pieces and thereby improved not only efficiency but also program logical structure. ENCOMPASS captures this modularity, providing development cycles that capitalize on earlier work and enhance systematically, as described in Campbell et al. (2025). Early programming functions' influence is not purely restricted to coding efficiency; it also affects an epistemological shift in terms of how one thinks about solving problems. Through imagining functions as objects that are acting within a community—their relationships structured through modules—programmers came to embrace a more integrated vision of software building. Such an image accords with the vision presented in Stein et al. (1999) which breaks from sequential computational metaphors towards more mature, interactive models and which resonates with present-day practice in software engineering. The modular paradigm, as exemplified through the use of programs like ENCOMPASS, not only promotes collaborative coding but also supports continual integration and incremental improvement between groups of programmers. Thus, the early applications of functions revolutionized programming practice, making software construction a more participatory community-based activity applicable today.

6.1.3. Evolution of Modular Programming Concepts

The history of modular programming concepts can be traced through the core emphasis placed on dividing complex software into smaller, manageable units. Modules, or units, allow code organization and allow programmers to encapsulate functionality, facilitating development and maintenance. By application of modular style, programmers can write and test independent parts of code independently, significantly reducing the ability to include errors within a system. This is good practice according to software engineering best practices, with separation of concerns being key so that readability can be enhanced and reusable components can be accommodated. This type of modularity is not all theory; it forms the foundation of actual applications across all types of industry, proving its fundamental role in contemporary programming practices. Furthermore, the addition of access control functionality into modular programming has become a crucial addition.

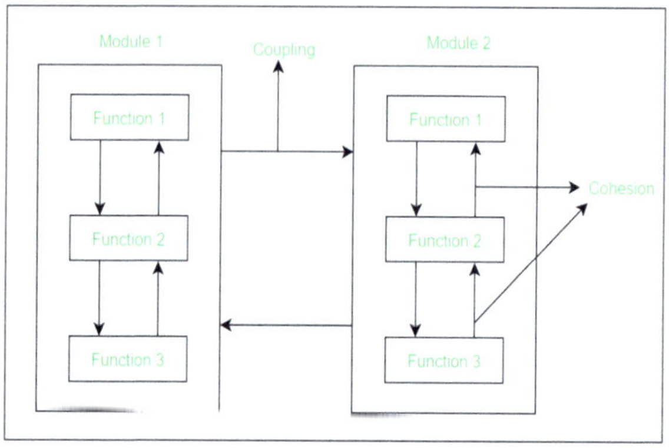

Figure 6.4. *Development of modular programming concepts.*

Source: https://media.geeksforgeeks.org/wp-content/uploads/20191218224936/ Screenshot-2994.png.

As software environments evolve to accommodate multi-user applications, static access policies must be translated dynamically to ensure security and operational integrity. Through abstract algebraic models formalizing access control policies, static parameters can be mapped within modular frameworks effectively. It is feasible to encapsulate access control operations as first-class citizens along with other functions using techniques such as monads in functional programming languages. This integration not only facilitates the modular programming philosophy but also addresses security issues in an increasingly networked world as envisaged in Pahl et al. (2000). The development of environments like KALI that are suited for the modular programming philosophy indicates the potential of dynamic and versatile robot control and programming systems. Here, KALI provides a software environment where user-level procedures can control complex operations in multiple robot arms. By allowing the software to be easily extended and modified, the platform makes it convenient to experiment with several programming concepts, such as sensor interfacing and multi-arm control. This feature is vital when developing applications that require real-time coordination and precision, illustrating how modular programming principles can be utilized in complex systems. By having the users author and revise trajectories in a single integrated environment, the potential for combining nearby path segments shows a perfect marriage of modular creation and real-world application, as mentioned in Backes et al. (2025). This trend highlights the flexibility and relevance of modular programming concepts to different domains and scenarios (Figure 6.4).

6.2. KEY CONCEPTS OF FUNCTIONS

Functions are low-level building elements in computer programming, and they serve many significant purposes that help in code reusability and modularity. A function is a bit of code that is independent and can be called to perform a specific function or operation. Through the mechanism of breaking down complex problems into simpler, manageable fragments, the programmer is in a better position to isolate, test, and debug individual units. This module-based structure is highly responsible for code non-redundancy, as functions allow the same operation to be carried out from various positions in a program without duplicating code. Functions also play a vital role in maintaining readability in programming logic, which improves comprehension and maintenance of code in the future, especially in massive systems where coherence has to be maintained. Thus, strategic use of functions needs to be applied for optimizing habits of programming and enhancing the overall efficiency of software development. The philosophy of higher-order functions further inserts advanced functionality into the traditional notion of functions. Higher-order functions can be given other functions as an argument or return them as a result, granting programmers access to a dynamic program paradigm supporting more abstract and flexible ways of coding. This feature is particularly useful in contexts like functional programming, where the function is a first-class citizen. Through the use of callbacks and function composition, coders can achieve rich behavior using more humble building blocks without compromising on readability. Besides, in the case of highly data-manipulative settings such as large data sets processing or real-time processing, passing and returning functions enable effective operations that can truly reduce the time complexity of algorithms. For this reason, higher-order functions are essential in enriching the expressiveness and flexibility of programs. In the area of modern programming challenges, functions' concepts are used on more complex systems such as those used in aviation and cryptography. For instance, for high-speed broadband data communications in aerospace, there is a great demand for dependable software solutions that apply modular functions. Specifically, technologies like software-defined radio (SDR) illustrate how functions must be adaptable in order to cater to changing needs, handling various communications protocols within one system (Pereira et al., 2025). Similarly, technologies like the Compact And Scalable Accelerator (CASA) for homomorphic encryption reveal the necessity of composite functions that can efficiently handle advanced operations within confined spaces with the potential to scale and optimize performance (He et al., 2024). These contemporary applications validate the relevance of the understanding and implementation of the basic concepts of functions in tackling the complex nature prevalent in today's technological world, demonstrating how they can produce innovation and efficiency in various applications.

6.2.1. Function Definition and Syntax

In computer programming, the function definition and syntax are important to continue improving readability, reusability, and modularity. Functions are naturally coded pieces of self-contained code with the purpose of performing a specific task. Their definition would typically include a function name, parameters, and a body that houses the coded instructions. This structured approach helps programmers encapsulate intricate operations into manageable pieces. Syntax varies between programming languages; for instance, Python employs the use of the def keyword to define functions whereas Java Script employs the function keyword. Such homogeneity in design ensures that it is easier to comprehend and enables collaborative projects where more than one programmer can work without inducing errors owing to syntactical differences. Also, the modularity of functions makes developers decompose bigger problems into smaller, simpler problems to solve, enhancing code organization in general. Such modularity not only simplifies testing, but also fosters code reuse, as functions may be called repeatedly in a program, reducing redundancy. The overall principle here is that the efficiency and simplicity of the code are of paramount importance; thus, functions are likely to be composed to do differentiated tasks with well-defined inputs and outputs. For example, in security programming, accessing the combination of access control facilities can be beneficial from modular abstractions where each operation can be focused on different things about security, that is, authentication or auditing. Syntactic and functional focus facilitates developers to maintain distinct domains of functionality distinct within compound programs, encouraging disciplined programming practice. The influence of well-specified functions is not only on the organization; it significantly contributes to software performance and security as well. In systems where advanced systems operate under routine conditions, such as multi-user systems, function definitions may incorporate dynamic security features. For instance, functions that are designed to regulate access control can utilize algebraic models to impose controls, hence minimizing security violations. In using these practices in a modular configuration, an effective response to security violations is achieved, as each function can be an admissible checkpoint in the security procedure. Thus, with precisely defined function syntax with the ability to support variegated operations, developers can enhance system integrity without inhibiting an efficient programming environment, eventually to develop safer and more trustworthy software solutions (Boerger et al., 1998; Pahl et al., 2000).

6.2.2. Parameters and Return Values

In modular and functional programming, parameters and return values are critical to properly design code. Parameters are representations of variables that allow functions to accept input values, making them reusable and flexible. Through parameter definition, a programmer can structure a function to manage different sets of data without altering the internal logic of the function. For instance, a function which will calculate the area of a rectangle can accept parameters as length and breadth so that it can be utilized for any size of the rectangle. This modular procedure not only eases coding but can make functions readily appropriate to various requirements, an exhibition of the code abstraction principle which is the foundation of software development. Return values fill out parameters by enabling functions to transmit outputs to the caller. When a function has completed execution, it can return a value that can be reused for other calculations later on or stored for later use. A function calculating an integer's factorial, for example, can return the calculated value, and other parts of the program can utilize this output without an issue. This parameter-return value relationship encourages programming modularity; functions are self-contained units that may be tested and supported independently. As highlighted in contemporary programming environments, a formal design method like this fosters teamworking as well as the quality of software products in general (Ekmekci et al., 2016). Furthermore, parameters and return values not only serve to manipulate data but also serve as explicit documentation and coding guidelines that support effective software development. Applying common conventions in parameter naming and return value types improves code readability and maintainability. For instance, having a uniform format for return values can prevent mistakes when another programmer calls a function. This practice comes from formal programming practices, where well-documented code is highlighted as evident in influential books on coding standards (Earnest et al., 2025). In this manner, not only do coders enhance their individual knowledge, but they also encourage a monolithic coding culture respectful of openness and thereby amplify the overall effectiveness of group programming (Figure 6.5).

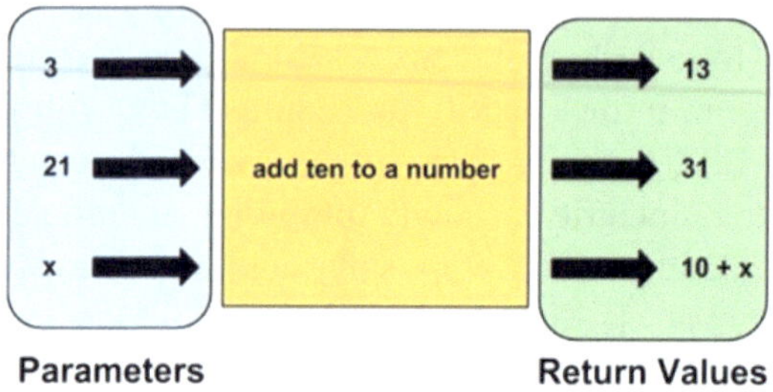

Figure 6.5. *Parameters and return values.*

Source: https://external-content.duckduckgo.com/iu/?u=https%3A%2F%2Fthfvnext.bing.com%2Fth%2Fid%2FOIP.PixtCHvUGj5eZS1NYqF84wHaDr%3Fcb%3Dthfvnext%26pid%3DApi&f=1&ipt=d5c023f8ff44df579bfa5291e44b5a40830b5582fd6e1e37381362498c37212c.

6.2.3. Scope and Lifetime of Variables

The concept of variable scope is foundational in programming, as it determines the accessibility of a variable within different parts of a program. In modular programming, functions serve as discrete modules of code, where variables can be classified as either local or global. Local variables, defined within a function, exist only for the duration of that functions execution. This limited visibility ensures that they do not interfere with variables in other functions, thus promoting modularity and reducing the risk of unintended side effects. Conversely, global variables, which are defined outside of all functions, are accessible throughout the entire program. While the convenience of global variables may seem appealing, their widespread accessibility can lead to complex debugging scenarios due to potential name collisions and unintended modifications from various function contexts. The lifetime of a variable refers to the duration for which a variable maintains its existence in memory. Local variables are created when a function is invoked and destroyed once the function execution completes. This ephemeral nature is advantageous, as it automatically reclaims memory resources, minimizing the risk of memory leaks. In contrast, global variables remain in memory for the entire lifespan of the program, which may lead to increased memory consumption if poorly managed. This distinction highlights the need for careful design when determining the location and lifetime of variables. When modular programming principles are applied, operators must consider both scope and lifetime to ensure that variables serve their intended purpose without introducing unnecessary complexity or memory overhead. Effective use of variable scope and lifetime directly affects software quality and maintainability. Programming methodologies that stress these principles often lead to clearer, more intuitive code, especially when functions are designed to perform specific tasks independently. For instance, the HEP computational roadmap emphasizes the importance of software effectiveness, which includes the judicious use of variables to prevent errors in high-volume data processing (Asai et al., 2015). Furthermore, as software engineering practices evolve, incorporating early aspects of variable management into the software development lifecycle can significantly enhance robustness (Araújo et al., 2004). Ultimately, understanding the intricacies of variable scope and lifetime is vital for developers aiming to build reliable and efficient software within modular programming frameworks.

6.3. ADVANTAGES OF USING FUNCTIONS

In the context of programming, functions are simple building units that enhance modularity and code reusability. Bounding specific functionality within a function enables developers to reduce redundancy, thereby ensuring efficient coding practices. Functions enable developers to break complex problems into tractable subproblems, thus focusing on addressing a part of the overall task at a time. Secondly, the modular nature enables collaboration as different members can work on individual functions individually before bringing together their work into the final program. It not only facilitates ease of development but also eliminates the risk of bugs that are normally characteristic of big codebases, leading to a more stable end result. In addition, employing functions facilitates easier debugging and code maintenance. When something is wrong with a program, it may be daunting to identify the source of the issue if it weren't for modularization. However, with functions, programmers can isolate and test isolated code blocks. This systematic process allows for easier troubleshooting because programmers know where the breakdown is taking place without having to dig through everything. Further, the application of functions encourages more formal organization of code, which significantly benefits documentation and readability of programs. The advantages gained with this organization make functions a very important component within the programming paradigm, which improves longevity and flexibility in software development. Functions also assist in providing better scalability in programming projects. With the growth in software applications and their advancement, the need to adjust and incorporate features becomes paramount. The use of functions allows programmers to introduce new functionality or enhance existing capabilities without having to replace the entire system. For instance, the modularity of functions can lead to systems that are capable of accommodating more measurement and display devices, as illustrated in terms of a modular approach in data acquisition systems, allowing for rapid configuration adjustment (Miller et al., 2025). Furthermore, just as in the functional programming environment, switching among various perceptions of a program can be automated and hence reduces the need for wholesale rewrites (Cohen et al., 2011). This flexibility makes software continue to be useful and efficient regardless of changing user requirements or technological advancements (Figure 6.6).

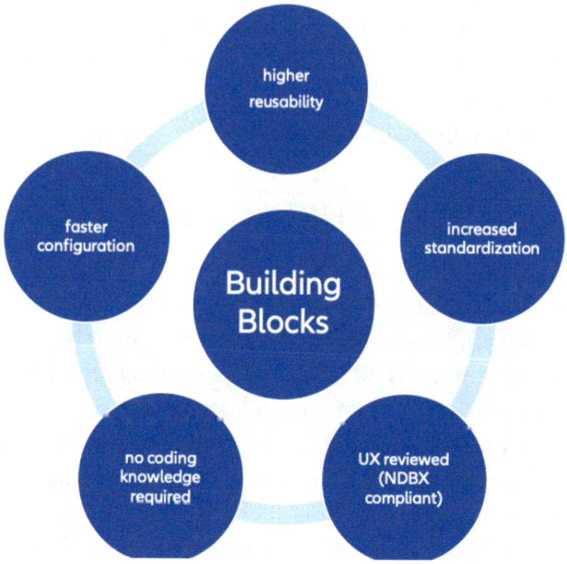

Figure 6.6. *Advantages of using functions of modular building blocks.*

Source: https://globaldigitalfactory.allianz.com/blog/building-blocks--gdf-s-modular-building-block-approach/_jcr_content/root/parsys/wrapper/wrapper/multi_column_grid/grid-0-par/image.img.82.3360.png/1592290966258/benefits-bb.png.

6.3.1. Code Reusability

In software development, code reusability is a highly significant principle that helps significantly in increasing efficiency and maintainability. By providing Developers the ability to utilize available code in new applications, reusability minimizes redundancy and makes development easier. Reusability is very critical with modular programming, where functions and components can be designed as standalone units of function. Each module can be used universally in various applications, promoting cleaner and more organized coding space. In addition, code reusability's harmony with modularity promotes a culture of sharing within teams, allowing libraries and parts to be shared. The final product not only accelerates the development cycle but also improves overall software quality, as reusable pieces are thoroughly tested and more stable than fresh, poorly coded code. The use of code reusability increases the scalability of the software solutions. Over time, the systems are sure to be upgraded and refined; reusable code allows these modifications without necessitating wholesale overhauls of existing systems. In essence, the developers can modify or upgrade isolated components while maintaining the larger architecture. This is essential in high-speed environments for development, where responsiveness and flexibility can become key differentiators. Furthermore, a modular architecture also supports multiple application contexts, where one code base can serve many different purposes across different projects. By establishing a common framework of components, corporations can offer consistency, reduce error rates, and facilitate easier maintenance, thereby creating a more sustainable and future-proof software environment. Most importantly, reusable code impacts several areas related to software quality, including design, efficiency, and vulnerability. Studies have shown that using reusable parts leads to systems that are better designed due to known, tried patterns and are more efficient because the programmers have the freedom to code at a higher level without being forced to reinvent the wheel. Additionally, studies point out that software systems would be at risk for issues like bug spread, but systematic use of reusable components can anticipate such vulnerabilities by adhering to established coding standards and design practices. The adoption of code reusability in modular programming frameworks enables the support of the need for comprehensive testing processes and quality control, as evidenced by model studies of software systems depicting the utilization of adopting network-based quality parameters to analyze the robustness and reliability of reusable modules (Guti Férrez et al., 1998; Bajec et al., 2012).

6.3.2. Improved Readability and Maintainability

The modular programming guidelines significantly enhance code readability by providing a clear and logical structure. It allows for the breaking up of complex programs into simpler, manageable functions or modules, decoupling the program function so that it is easier to understand the overall purpose of the program. Each module can be written, tested, and serviced independently, thereby allowing a single-point check-up of the code without complexity overload. Furthermore, modularity enables developers to use self-documenting function and variable names, which can lead to greater understanding for future programmers who may be using the code. Modular form ultimately leads to a more user-friendly interface, as it is easier to access and understand, crucial in collaborative programming scenarios. Maintainability is a natural consequence of adopting modular programming concepts. Since code is organized in independent modules, modifications can be done without compromising unexpected effects on other portions of the program. Not only is this less prone to bring new bugs when upgrading, but debugging becomes simpler. When things go wrong, it is easy to pinpoint the faulty module since developers can proceed to check each section individually without having to wade through a single blob of code. Besides, the potential for reuse of such modules in other applications encourages consistency, as well as maintainability. Through the case of C2Eif translation tool, translating complex C code to the modularized one in Eiffel, one can highlight the benefits of maintainability through the effective separation of functionality, especially in large-scale applications (Furia et al., 2013). In addition, established guidelines for software development of sophisticated systems, such as those proposed for the European Space Research Organizations Spacelab mission, stress readability and maintainability in high-risk environments. Such guidelines advocate the use of means that encourage structured programming with easy documentation and positive tools for managing code. By establishing concepts related to each project element, for example, data management and integration testing, these standards reinforce the importance of an efficient process towards software development. This organized framework not only reduces mistakes but also insures that the developed codebase is both readable and maintainable, allowing developers to collaborate smoothly and lengthen the lifecycle of software projects (Rose et al., 2025) (Figure 6.7).

Figure 6.7. *Improved readability of code by promoting and maintainability.*

Source: https://blog.pixelfreestudio.com/wp-content/uploads/2024/07/7-15-1024x683.jpeg.

6.3.3. Simplification of Complex Problems

Simplification of complex problems emerges as a governing principle in functions and module programming where programmers can cope with complex tasks effectively. Complex problems usually are characterized by numerous variables and potential solutions, and they may leave one in fear. Applying functions, programmers can wrap the complexities in nicely defined, tractable pieces of code. This encapsulation also makes the code more readable and facilitates reusability of code, hence eliminating duplication and the possibility of errors. Functions also facilitate testing and debugging because single components are testable separately. This modular approach adheres to the general objective of minimizing complexity so that the developers can tackle larger issues through smaller uniform units of effort. Such methodologies appeal to the broader discussion of computational effectiveness and accuracy in programming practice. Additionally, the tenet of modular programming in simplification along with applying it derives its focus on planning decomposition of problems into independent modules or parts. Every module is designed to address specific functionalities, thus adhering to the notion of separation of concerns. This separation makes it easier for developers to focus on individual aspects without losing sight of the system architecture as a whole. On close examination of automated formal verification processes as outlined in literature, one finds that breaking down complex protocols into higher-level abstractions simplifies not only comprehension but the verification loop as well (Bauer et al., 2014). The modular nature enables developers and researchers to concentrate on putting in application code without the effort of having to pre-validate libraries used for cryptographic operations. Thus, the capability to simplify problem-solving of intricate issues is considerably amplified by this methodical decomposition of problems into manageable, well-defined modules. Lastly, application of reduced complexity methods in solving complex issues is not only restricted to discrete programming tasks but also extended to broader fields, such as supply chain management. Being categorized in current research, the application of multiobjective optimization (MOO) techniques can serve as a decision-making aid within the build-to-order supply chain process to take advantage of logistics issues in reality with their complex nature (Askariazad et al., 2012). In illustrating these issues through the lenses of simplification, stakeholders can identify important aspects to target and simplify decision-making processes. Such systems reinforce the importance of developing effective, modular strategies that not only enable easier navigation through complex problems but also improve operational outcomes. Ultimately, the ability to render complexity simpler is a decisive advantage across multiple programming and decision-making fields, establishing itself as a required standard in efficient problem-solving.

6.4. INTRODUCTION TO MODULAR PROGRAMMING

Modular programming is a foundational technique of software development that keeps code manageable and expandable. This paradigm is characterized by partitioning a program into independent, interchangeable parts or modules that have specific functionality. Through compartmentalizing distinct pieces of the program, developers can focus on individual modules, and it becomes easier to debug, manage, and make future developments in the software. This results in more collaboration among the developers as different teams can work on different modules simultaneously without stopping the whole project. The modularity also makes code reuse possible, where the developers are able to utilize existing modules in other projects, thus improving the development process and increasing efficiency in software engineering practices. Central to modular programming is the use of functions as the building blocks of modules. Functions allow for the programming of specific tasks, and their use promotes simplicity and structure in the code base. A function can be written independently and tested independently, and this provides a more structured workflow. It not only makes reading easier but also facilitates simpler error detection and code refinement.

For instance, a complex task can be broken into minute functions, each of which solves a specific part of the problem. By combining these functions in modules, programmers render their code efficient and maintainable. Also, as the software grows, programmers can effectively modify or replace functions, reflecting the dynamic nature of modular programming and adaptation to changing technology needs. The value of modular programming extends beyond mere organization; it is founded on principles that are designed to facilitate collaboration and creative software development. As a result of such modularity, alterations in one module can be added without affecting other modules, providing an agile environment for development. This is particularly significant for large projects, where a variety of modules may work together in complex ways. Furthermore, the growing significance of Software-Defined Networking (SDN) highlights the relevance of modular programming in various technology disciplines. SDN's decoupling of control and data planes is a reflection of how modularity represents improved management of network resources as well as general performance enhancement (Kreutz et al., 2014). This shift in design philosophy emphasizes flexibility and sets the stage for improvements yet to come, placing foremost the absolute necessity of modular programming in the constantly evolving field of computer science (Figure 6.8).

Figure 6.8. *Introduction to modular programming.*

Source: https://assets-global.website-files.com/5e0f1144930a8bc8aace526c/66172fd271da805ec2117c9e_66162e5dc6ca02a816dff7af-a7ed0e8b5cf-48f7a449fb4b14fc6953c.jpeg.

6.4.1. Definition and Characteristics of Modular Programming

Modular programming in software design is a fundamental paradigm that comprises dividing a program into discrete, manageable components. A module represents a specific task, which allows for a less complex organization in complex systems. Not only does it provide developers with the ability to develop individual pieces apart from one another, but it also provides better reusability across diverse applications. By promoting separation of concerns, modular programming reduces the cognitive load on programmers, allowing them to focus on a single aspect of a problem at a time. This conscious separation lessens the risks of debugging and system maintenance, ultimately leading to more robust and easier-to-maintain software systems. Besides, modularity can facilitate programming teamwork because different team members are able to make, test, and enhance individual modules without mutual overlapping of work processes.

Apart from mere organization, the features of modular programming include encapsulation practices, abstraction, and interface design. Encapsulation hides what goes on inside a module and exposes just what is necessary for interaction with other modules. This abstraction promotes more polished interfaces and improved overall readability of the codebase, allowing developers to understand the software structure without being overwhelmed in the details of every module. Furthermore, particularly in settings like scientific programming, modular designs can lead to increased functionality through the use of highly standardized interfaces that allow for mixing heterogenous components. For instance, open-source projects like ImageJ use modular programming principles to allow developers to develop a range of plugins that extend the software's capabilities in a manner that is still congruent with the current framework (Rueden et al., 2017).

That said, the most significant advantage of modular programming is probably its versatility. The fact that it can be altered or replaced without redesigning the system as a whole is a testament to its versatility. It is especially so in high-speed fields like the identification of drugs, where ontologies like the Drug Target Ontology (DTO) illustrate how modular constructions could effectively integrate sets of disparate data and support collaborative research practices (Lin et al., 2017). Such flexibility also promotes software engineering innovation to allow developers to adapt to newly emerging challenges and needs in their respective fields. This is significant in environments where up-to-date functionality and interoperability are crucial. With modular programming becoming increasingly prevalent, it is an excellent example of an adaptable approach that suits the diverse needs of modern software development while fostering innovation and collaboration among developers.

6.4.2. Modular Versus Monolithic Programming Differences

It is vital to know the differences between monolithic and modular programming so that one can know how such methodologies influence program function and design. In monolithic programming, everything in the software is interfaced and tightly coupled within a single code base. This method has the ability to produce severe issues, particularly when there is the need for updates or debugging patches, as modifying one aspect of the code has the tendency to destabilize other functions by coincidence. On the other hand, modular programming isolates code in distinct, replaceable pieces or modules, each processing a specific functionality. This isolation facilitates maintenance and development because individual modules may be tested or updated independently without impacting the remaining software, making the overall software more stable.

Efficiency in addressing complexity and scalability is another major area where these programming paradigms vary. Monolithic programming is apt to lead to increasing complexity over time, particularly after additional features or functionalities have been included. This can lead to excessive interdependencies that make the codebase increasingly difficult and complex to understand and navigate through. Modular programming, by contrast, promotes better organization in the code so that developers can develop complex applications more reliably. By allowing use of well-defined module interfaces, new functionality can be added or old functionality changed without adverse effects on the overall program, something that might be less readily achieved with a monolithic framework. Considerations for performance also mark these programming paradigms, especially regarding resource management and analysis. Research has indicated that monolithic programs, although exhibit peak performance initially with their encapsulated form, collapse under drastic changes or scaling due to resource constraints (Garcia-Contreras et al., 2020). Modular programs, on the other hand, can leverage incremental global analysis techniques, which optimize further due to their modular nature, leading to improvement in time and memory consumption during updates or debugging (Schmidt et al., 1992). Such a module structure allows for better optimization approaches and better resource allocation, crucial in high-performance and adaptability applications within dynamic settings. In essence, the design philosophy of modules has serious advantages in comparison to monolithic approaches, particularly towards long-term software maintenance and development objectives (Figure 6.9).

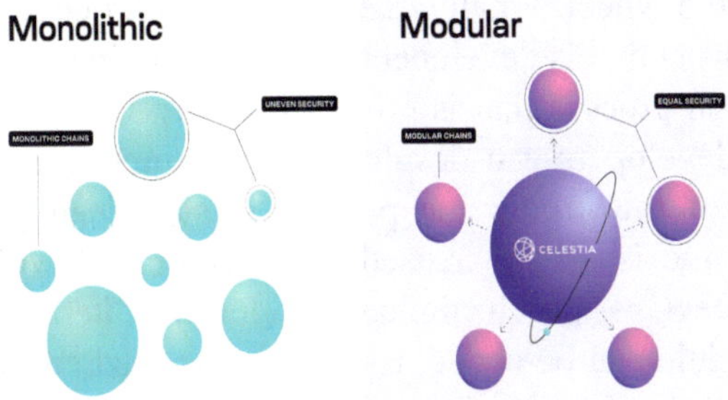

Figure 6.9. *Between modular and monolithic programming.*

Source: https://blog.celestia.org/content/images/2022/11/Monolithic-Modular-Aproach_2.jpg.

6.4.3. Benefits of Modular Design

Modular development, dividing complex systems into smaller and more manageable portions, is very advantageous as it favors both efficiency as well as effectiveness in programming. Separate division of each module allows programmers to focus on single functionalities without having to necessarily comprehend the entire system comprehensively. Not only does this organized methodology facilitate debugging, but it also facilitates updating and enhancing. For instance, within software architectures like the TUBA architecture, embedded software tools are programmed with a modular framework described by class objects, allowing easy integration of features like file handling and report writing without complete redesign of the entire application (Engmann et al., 1987). Modular design hence becomes an important paradigm for systems aspiring to maintain responsiveness in a constantly evolving technological landscape. Furthermore, the benefits of modular design exceed organizational advantage; they are essential elements in improving code reusability. As the theme of efficiency makes its presence felt in developers' minds, reusing already existing modules for new purposes gains greatest priority. More so is this the case when contemplating advanced methods of computing, such as Amorphous Data Parallelism, that demand robust modular design rules in order to keep complex algorithms at bay. Through the use of modular approach, algorithms such as the betweenness centrality algorithm applied in social network analysis can be coded with increased functionality and reduced redundancy, thus promoting an innovation and collaboration culture (Christianson et al., 2013). The developers are not only capable of saving time but also of enhancing the quality of what they develop through the utilization of already tried and tested modules rather than reinventing the wheel. Finally, the inbuilt parallel development potential of modular designs compels developers to collaborate in unison and allows for an agile production process that is critical in today's programming societies. Where multiple developers can develop different modules at the same time, the productivity of the production process is significantly improved. This cooperative dynamic is also increased when combined with methodologies such as Agile or DevOps, which emphasize velocity of iteration and reaction to change. Each module can be coded, tested, and iterated on in isolation before integration, so that the final product is not only consistent but high quality as well. By exploiting modular design strengths, programming teams can control complexities more flexibly and develop software solutions that are innovative yet dependable, thus attesting to the several benefits of modular design in contemporary programming practice.

6.5. MODULAR PROGRAMMING IMPLEMENTATION

Modular programming is an important technique in managing complexity in software development. Through dividing a program into separate, autonomous modules, programmers can organize code more effectively and manage it better. Segmentation allows developers to work on various modules at the same time, thus enhancing collaboration and speeding up the development process. Each module encapsulates some functionality, making it easier to test and debug as modules can be tested in isolation prior to integration with the core system. Modular programming also encourages code reuse; such modules may be reused by programmers in new applications, spending much time and effort to create from scratch, thus increasing productivity and efficiency as a whole. But the search for modularity tends to be an uphill battle, particularly when trying to optimize performance. While modular programming enhances readability and maintainability, it may inadvertently add inefficiencies when modules must communicate. In performance-critical programs, programmers sometimes resort to hand-optimized code at the expense of modularity in the program, creating brittle and unmanageable frameworks. Solving this paradox has given rise to research into methods that straddle the divide between performance demands and modular design. SQuOpt, for instance, offers a solution with promise as it allows for deep embedding of collection APIs that accommodate collection-specific optimizations, such as traversal unifications and indexing, but without compromising the modular programming model. This hybrid approach shows that innovative solutions preserve the integrity of modular structures without sacrificing efficiency, thereby contributing to building more robust software systems (Eichberg et al., 2012). In addition, the use of access control mechanisms in modular programming paradigms illustrates the adaptability required in complex software systems. Dynamic management of resources in multi-user environments necessitates sophisticated access control policies that can prevent violations during program execution. By using algebraic models combined with monads, developers are able to implement static access control in modular structure. The combination provides a boost in a safe environment since each module is independently evaluated and controlled, thereby guaranteeing access privileges and constraints explicitly enforced across the system. Hence, the marriage of modular programming and sophisticated security protocols not only enhances the softwares resistance to unauthorized access but also highlights the accommodation of modular design towards diverse system needs (Pahl et al., 2000) (Figure 6.10).

Figure 6.10. *Implementation of modular programming software development.*

Source: https://www.in-com.com/wp-content/uploads/2022/05/software-complexity.jpg.

6.5.1. Creating Modules and Interfaces

In modern software coding, module and interface construction is an essential function in function and modular programming. By separating complex programs into individual, manageable pieces, programmers facilitate easier code organization and better maintainability. Each module contains special functionalities that allow programmers to focus on distinct parts of a system without having to work with the overall codebase. This modularization is simple to debug and test, along with promoting team collaboration because different team members can work concurrently on different modules. Moreover, appropriate module construction adheres to best practices in software engineering to make components reusable and optimized. As discussed, reuse library or component reuse repository can make the task considerably easy, providing systematic guidelines to developers to follow while developing and maintaining reusable components efficiently (Sharma et al., 2010).

Interface design is also significant in the modular programming paradigm since this becomes the interface point among heterogeneous modules. An interface provides a contract for how various components interact so that loose coupling and flexibility in application design are guaranteed. This independence between implementation and the interface allows the inner workings to evolve without influencing other modules, making an agile development model feasible. Properly documented interfaces also enable improved code readability and ease of use, and other developers can easily work with a module without necessarily having to understand its inner workings. The emphasis on crafting solid interfaces is of chief significance since it allows even closer systems to be combined in a balanced manner, thus upholding the module programming paradigm (Bakar et al., 2020). Software products' efficient evolution while remaining at high performance and reliability is attainable through this strategic plan. Moreover, module usage and interfaces align perfectly with software performance enhancement as noted in certain engineering applications. Like a variable length intake manifold engine, for example—module design enables real-time performance optimization. The adaptive modules are able to be changed in isolation by variables like load and speed so that the system will always be at peak efficiency under different conditions. The performance profiles of these kinds of applications illustrate the material benefits of module programming, wherein stand-alone elements adapt to optimize overall performance. By focusing on developing modules and defining interfaces, programmers position themselves to design adaptable systems that are capable of responding effectively to changing requirements (Bakar et al., 2020). This back-and-forth dynamic reflects the significance of deliberate design in the development of scalable and sound software solutions in the overall framework of functions and modular programming.

6.5.2. Module Testing and Debugging

Effective module testing and debugging are essential components of software development, particularly in the modularity paradigm. Modular programming in this context emphasizes partitioning complex systems into smaller modules or units where each module serves a particular purpose and can be developed, tested, and maintained independently. This modularity simplifies the task for developers to isolate errors and faults, as errors can easily be detected in specific modules rather than the entire system. The testing usually begins with unit tests whose sole purpose is to ensure that these modules, in an isolated state, behave as expected before integrating them within the larger system. Further, debugging is an important iterative activity following initial testing, wherein developers fine-tune the functionality of each module.

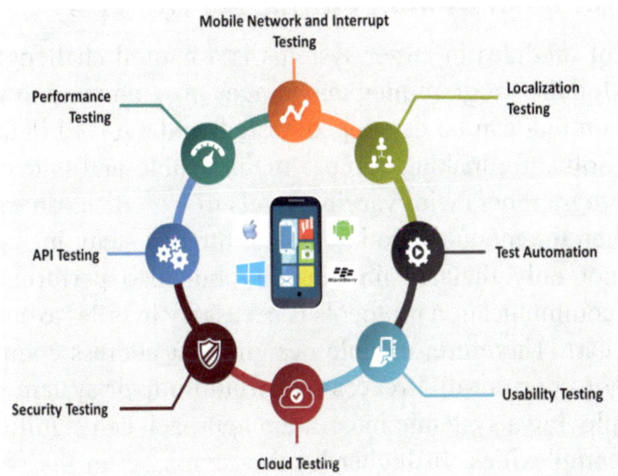

Figure 6.11. *Module testing and debugging.*

Source: https://www.frshr.tech/wp-content/uploads/2020/12/testing-1024x671.png.

While debugging requires finding and fixing faults, understanding how such mistakes arise within the paradigm of modular systems also falls within its scope. Practices and tools vary extensively; for instance, integrated development environments (IDEs) provide step-through execution debuggers and inspection of module states. Software tools like ENCOMPASS show such methods by providing specification, design, and verification of modular programs, which support efficient debugging methods (Campbell et al., 2025). Utilizing these tools significantly enhances the ability of a programmer to control individual modules so that faults can be quickly located and isolated. Furthermore, the extensibility by modular programming is further supported using elaborate support frameworks like SAGA, designed to support throughout the software life cycle. The modularity of the parts of SAGA permits customization with meta-tools so that the developers are able to modify some of these environments for maximum debugging and testing (Beckman et al., 2025). The systems support various configurations for various software development tasks and thus permit software developers to change their approaches to debugging according to the special needs of the modules that they are working with. Consequently, the harmony of effective module testing and dynamic debugging facilities yields robust software systems that are effective enough to meet high-quality requirements while being scalable and maintainable in the long term (Figure 6.11).

6.5.3. Integration of Modules in Larger Systems

The structure of modules in larger systems is a natural challenge in software engineering. Modular programming encourages programmers to write a single piece or function that can be developed, tested, and evolved independently. It simplifies the software, making it more maintainable and understandable, so that multiple programmers with varying levels of expertise can easily work on it together. When the modules are integrated into a system, interaction among the modules not only dictates functionality but also performance. Having interfaces and communication protocols is necessary in order to ensure modules operate in concert. Therefore, module design must address compatibility and interoperability to prevent differences that would impair system performance. Moreover, employing a systemic integration approach can significantly reduce development complexities. In higher-level systems, as in the case of hybrid architectures, voices of different methodologies assist in combining distinct modules. For example, as in early frameworks of integrating fuzzy logic to mix neural networks and knowledge-based systems, coordination among different paradigms of programming illuminates the strength of modularity. Here, fuzzy inference rules are employed to broaden symbolic processing capability, offering tighter links between modules. Thus, integration is a critical bridge, transforming specific functionalities to overall systemic operations in the overall system, enabling more efficient data processing and decision-making processes, as Yen et al. (2025) argued. Module integration assessment extends beyond initial development and testing. Monitoring and optimization of performance as modules interface within running applications is critical. Equipment like that with electronically controlled fuel injectors is a good example of this necessity for stringent testing, whereby performance attributes are thoroughly examined under different conditions. These types of equipment are dependent on the accuracy and flexibility of modules integrated into them to support maximum performance, particularly under loads and velocities that vary. Experimental arrangements enable designers to measure how the variability affects the efficiency and overall performance of the engine, with the dynamic relationship between modules being emphasized. This incremental approach not only enhances the usefulness of the system in the short term but also illuminates the approaches to future design, emphasizing the significance of module integration in complex applications as indicated by Bakar et al. (2020).

6.6. REAL-WORLD APPLICATIONS

In contemporary software development, functions and modular programming are essential in coding to enhance efficiency as well as ease of maintenance. Their application across real-world use is common across fields that range from data science to artificial intelligence, as well as web development. Modular programming allows developers to encapsulate code into discrete components, facilitating ease of test, debug, and modification. Such a practice not only speeds up the development cycle but also fosters teamwork, as modules can be developed at once without conflict. For instance, front-end and back-end operations within web applications are typically decoupled to maximize development procedures as well as overall performance, significantly improving user experience and application scalability. In computational research, functions play a significant role in reducing intricate mathematical problems. One of the most significant uses is in evolutionary computation techniques, which are very good at solving optimization problems with many variables. The techniques leverage modular programming ideas to construct solutions incrementally and search efficiently through complex solution spaces. This makes it easier for researchers to combine various search methods and mechanisms, hence improving the robustness of their results. By using clearly defined functions to depict various operations in evolutionary algorithms, scientists can design hybridized models that utilize neural networks in combination with conventional optimization methods. Such combinations illustrate the role of modular programming in enhancing the efficiency of solving traditional computing problems, demonstrating its application in sophisticated computational contexts (Hibbs et al., 1995). Moreover, their use in formal verification is another functional application of functions and modular programming. ASMs are also a way of algorithm and system design through programmers' ability to declare operations and states in a structured fashion. This is particularly beneficial for systems where reliability is the number one priority, such as aerospace and automotive software development. Modular programming makes it possible for programmers to encapsulate individual aspects of a systems behavior in separate functions, which impose more rigorous testing and analysis. The use of the modular approach with ASMs also promotes software specification documentation and use of industry standards. As observed in the annotated bibliographies that enclose ASM studies, integration into usable software solutions underscores the versatility and position of functions in real-world applications (Boerger et al., 1998) (Figure 6.12).

Figure 6.12. *Real-world applications.*

Source: https://www.appypie.com/blog/wp-content/uploads/2023/08/Real-world-Applications-of-LLMs.jpg.

6.6.1. Use of Functions and Modules in Software Development

Function and module application is essential in software development to create maintainable and efficient codebases. Functions, which group particular operations or computations, enable developers to segment complex operations into manageable units. Modularity not only makes code easier to read but also reduces duplication because functions can be called from other places in a program. Moreover, modules as sets of similar functions and variables improve this structure by bundling functionalities that share a common goal.

This theoretical model makes it easier to debug and test, as developers can identify problems within isolated functional blocks. As a result, modular programming not only simplifies the process of development but also improves the adaptability of the software to change, making it suitable for the long term in changing programming environments. In advanced software development contexts, frameworks such as Kronos depict the sophistication of modular implementations.

Figure 6.13. *Functions and modules in software development.*

*Source: https://miro.medium.com/v2/resize:fit:1000/1*ytZA6eAVs7-Ns3JAgYJ_Bw.png.*

Kronos is a framework for constructing and executing bioinformatics workflows and depicts the necessity of maintainable and modular components in deep analysis contexts. By facilitating the construction of configurable workflows that can be simply modified through text configuration files, Kronos depicts how more advanced abstractions can mask functionality without explicit coding. Moreover, the structure facilitates the parallel processing of tasks and fine-grain logging requirements inescapable in reproducible research outcomes. Application of such modular programming structures has a deep effect on software development practices, moving away from error-prone ad hoc analyses toward systematic sound analyses that can be exchanged, reused, and remixed by biologically oriented computational communities' developers, enhancing research productivity and collaboration overall. Also, the reuse of software components is a basis for efficient development, making the merit of functions and modules deserving. An organized reuse library or repository of reused components not only categorizes existing components, but also makes best practices in software engineering worth it. With adherence to coding standards and guidelines, programmers have it guaranteed that reusable components are built to enhance the functionality and efficiency of new applications. This approach is critical in today's fast-paced environments where rapid deployment and iteration are most crucial. Through instilling a culture of reuse, organizations can reduce development cycles and leverage existing resources, resulting in time and cost savings in software development. Ultimately, this practice will foster a working culture amongst the programming community that will once again increase the pool of reusable elements to be pulled from in case future projects are undertaken, such as in the study of developing and maintaining such reusable elements in software engineering (Sharma et al., 2010) (Figure 6.13).

6.6.2. Case Studies of Successful Modular Programs

In the investigation of successful modular programs, some case studies illustrate the utility of modular programming principles to make software more useful and maintainable. A good illustration is the development of a toolkit for distributed interaction, which embodies both modularity and flexibility as inherent design philosophies. The toolkit is designed to facilitate an extensible workbench to accommodate existing algorithms while providing doors of opportunity for future innovation. This feature is the pillar of modular programming because it offers a way by which new functionality is added without having to change the underlying codebase in huge ways. From this case study, the application of a modular design comes a long way in adaptive software development in developing environments that are capable of changing pace with technological advancements and user needs (Mycroft et al., 2011). Another such renowned instance of the achievement of modular programming's is that of using Abstract State Machines (ASMs), which have found successful implementation in several programming and verification tools. The constraints brought upon by the use of ASMs include the essential programming functionalities in individual, testable modules, thereby making the program generation easier. This module method allows developers to encapsulate and address unique computer tasks with precision, creating ease and reduced possibilities of errors along the way. As an annotated bibliography of ASM literature notes, ongoing exploration of these methods demonstrates the continued use and value of modular programming methods in academic and practical settings (Boerger et al., 1998). Moreover, the impact of modular programming is not just theoretical; it has practical applications that reveal its advantages. Organizations employing modular programming techniques experience smoother collaboration between development teams since individual modules are assigned to various members without constant communication. This segregation of work leads to increased productivity, quality software, and effective debugging. Effective utilization of modular frameworks has been identified to play a crucial role in systems of high complexities, where breaking down large codebases into tractable units renders maintenance possible along with adaptation to changing demands at high rates. Hence, the case studies presented from various industries attest to the fact that modular programming is a crucial method towards achieving scalable and resilient software systems and thus its central role in contemporary software development approaches.

6.6.3. Impact on Project Management and Team Work

Function integration and modular programming has a profound impact on collaboration in teams and project management, particularly in handling complex projects. By bundling individual functionalities in separate modules, teams are capable of providing an environment in which members can work on independent tasks without the burden of understanding the entire system at a time. This segmentation not only makes development simpler but also enhances responsibility and clarity within the team, since each member of the team is responsible for ownership in some of the components. Furthermore, as the HEP Forum for Computational Excellence highlights, by focusing on software effectiveness and infrastructure, teams are capable of adapting quickly to changes, which makes collaboration easy despite varying project requirements (Asai et al., 2015). As a result, modular programming encourages an iterative approach that enhances team coordination and overall project management efficiency. Furthermore, the modular programming paradigm benefits the mirroring hypothesis, which describes how organizational structures can mirror the system's technical interdependencies. Experimental studies show that when teams are structured around modular components, communication connections and social relationships mirror the modular organization of software. This connection not only facilitates effective project management but also reduces communications barriers and misunderstandings in teams (Carliss et al., 2025). As teams develop interdependent modules, they are capable of maintaining functional consistency when dealing with intricate dependencies. Thus, the mirroring hypothesis signifies the necessity of aligning organizational patterns with technical structures, again supporting the necessity of modular programming in enhancing teamwork and project outcomes. Secondly, actionable transparency is a fundamental concept that is intertwined with modular programming, where teams can manage complex interdependencies without reflecting exactly. Actionable transparency offers a means through which teams can work effectively irrespective of whether interaction patterns exactly mirror technical dependencies or not. Through enabling open information on status and individual responsibilities, groups can achieve coordination and high involvement without being held back by traditional hierarchies (Carliss et al., 2025). When organizations embrace modular programming, they can leverage actionable transparency in a way that enables them to construct a more responsive and flexible system for project management. Thus, such synergy not only facilitates team working but also innovation and is a must for today's project management practices (Figure 6.14).

Figure 6.14. *Impact on team collaboration and project management.*

Source: https://img.freepik.com/premium-photo/project-management-financial-report-strategy-consulting-team-collaboration-concept-with-collaborative-people_776674-1051172.jpg.

SUMMARY

In summarizing the discussion of modular programming and functions, it is apparent that the systematic approach significantly enhances code readability and maintainability. Functions are fundamental building blocks that encapsulate specific operations, and software developers can break down complex problems into manageable sub-problems. The modular approach, in addition to being simple to debug and test the code, allows for code reuse because it makes it simple for developers to utilize existing functions under new circumstances with minimal changes. The employment of functions is, therefore, no longer a convenience issue; it is an evolution towards more organized and efficient coding practices that align with the demands of contemporary software development. Additionally, the application of abstract separation logics within modular programming paradigms highlights the advanced character of this approach to efficient resource management. By employing propositional abstract separation logics (PASLs), developers are in a position to reason more effectively about programs and their manipulations of resources. Recent research, through the construction of a modular proof theory, has yielded an impenetrable foundation for constructing assertions that specify varied logics and thus resolving the inherent challenges that accompany resource administration in programming settings. Consequently, the work not only increases theoretical understanding but also obtains practical application that has strong relevance for software engineering practice (Clouston et al., 2017).

Finally, the intersection of evolutionary computation techniques and modular programming reveals new possibilities for problem-solving, especially in optimization problems where functions have several variables. Such techniques turn out to be adaptable and effective, particularly when applied in complex functional optimizations. As programmers seek more sophisticated solutions to today's programming problems, exploring the hybridization of evolutionary algorithms and modular programming techniques can be promising to lead to groundbreaking improvements in computational effectiveness. By employing these techniques, programmers not only stand a chance to enhance the ability of their programs but also design a system that is conducive to learning and adapting at all times in the rapidly evolving tech landscape (Hibbs et al., 1995).

In the research on the realm of functions and modular programming, there is a need to understand the structural advantages modularity brings to software design. Modular programming makes it possible to divide complex systems into manageable, independent fragments that can be developed, tested, and maintained independently. Not only does such segregation enhance code readability and controllability but also facilitates code reuse across different projects. For instance, in architectures like the TUBA architecture, where a package of integrated tools is used for application development, the modular structure represented by class objects demonstrates how such an approach could make development activities easier and increase overall efficiency in developing business-oriented applications (Engmann et al., 1987). By employing modular design, developers can develop innovation and flexibility so that they can promptly respond to changing requirements and technologies. Furthermore, the increasing complexity of modern networks emphasizes the use of modular programming strategies to address challenges like architectural ossification. Traditional Internet architectures suffer from an inability to be flexible due to their conventional designs emphasizing decentralized operations that can hinder rapid evolution and integration of new technology (Ahad et al., 2014).

Here, modular programming unlocks the door to more flexible systems, that is, programmable wireless networks, giving more management and flexibility. Such systems utilize technologies like software-defined networks and cognitive radio networks to build a more dynamic platform for network operation. By integrating the ideas of modular programming into these new architectures, programmers can better handle the complexities of contemporary technologies and are capable of fostering innovation in network architectures. Last but not least, development toward software and networking modular programming continues to offer scope for research and development. While the efforts to break through traditional limitations in network design, particularly for wireless technologies, are encouraging, they also identify a number of issues that need to be addressed in the future, that is, compatibility between heterogeneous modular components (Ahad et al., 2014). The challenge for next-generation programmable networks overcomes these issues by advocating one approach to design and implementation. By allowing interoperability among different network technologies and protocols using modular structures, the discipline will be able to gain from greater collaboration and a more homogenized infrastructure. Generally speaking, the concepts of functions and modular programming not only make the development process more sophisticated but also create new solutions to modern technological issues in the ever-changing environment of software engineering and network design.

REFERENCES

1. Abu Bakar, M. A., Ithsan, M. Z., Khalid, A., Manshoor, B., et al. (2020). Engine performance characteristics and evaluation of variation in the length of intake plenum. https://core.ac.uk/download/12007819.pdf (accessed on 9th September 2025).
2. Ahad, N., Ahmed, N., & Qadir, J. (2014). Building programmable wireless networks: An architectural survey. http://arxiv.org/abs/1310.0251 (accessed on 9th September 2025).
3. Aniba, R., Bashashati, A., Boutros, P. C., Grande, S. M., et al. (2017). Kronos: A workflow assembler for genome analytics and informatics. https://core.ac.uk/download/323080438.pdf (accessed on 9th September 2025).
4. Araújo, J., Clements, P., Moreira, A., Tekinerdogan, B., et al. (2004). Early aspects: Aspect-oriented requirements engineering and architecture design. https://core.ac.uk/download/pdf/11461066.pdf (accessed on 9th September 2025).
5. Asai, M., Bauerdick, L., Borgland, A., Calafiura, A., et al. (2015). High Energy Physics Forum for Computational Excellence: Working group reports (I. Applications Software II. Software Libraries and Tools III. Systems). http://arxiv.org/abs/1510.08545 (accessed on 9th September 2025).
6. Askariazad, M. H., Gallear, D., & Mansouri, S. A. (2012). Decision support for build-to-order supply chain management through multiobjective optimization. https://core.ac.uk/download/20496354.pdf (accessed on 9th September 2025).
7. Ayala Martínez, C. P., Gómez Seoane, C., López Cuesta, L., Manzano Aguilar, M., et al. (2019). A software service supporting software quality forecasting. https://core.ac.uk/download/288625464.pdf (accessed on 9th September 2025).
8. Backes, P., Hayati, S., Hayward, V., Tso, K., et al. (2025). The KALI multi-arm robot programming and control environment. https://core.ac.uk/download/pdf/42821887.pdf (accessed on 9th September 2025).
9. Baird, D., Bogar, A. M., & Lyons, D. M. (2018). Lightweight call-graph construction for multilingual software analysis. http://arxiv.org/abs/1808.01213 (accessed on 9th September 2025).
10. Bajec, M., & Šubelj, L. (2012). Software systems through complex networks science: Review, analysis and applications. http://arxiv.org/abs/1208.2518 (accessed on 9th September 2025).

11. Baldwin, C. Y., & Colfer, L. J. (2025). The mirroring hypothesis: Theory, evidence and exceptions. https://core.ac.uk/download/pdf/6508133.pdf (accessed on 9th September 2025).
12. Bauer, A., Pironti, A., Dolev, D., Otway, D., et al. (2014). Formal verification of security protocol implementations: A survey. https://core.ac.uk/download/pdf/11431672.pdf (accessed on 9th September 2025).
13. Beckman, C. S., Benzinger, L., Beshers, G., Campbell, J., et al. (2025). SAGA: A project to automate the management of software production systems. https://core.ac.uk/download/pdf/42835320.pdf (accessed on 9th September 2025).
14. Boerger, E., & Huggins, J. K. (1998). Abstract state machines 1988–1998: Commented ASM bibliography. https://core.ac.uk/download/304691565.pdf (accessed on 9th September 2025).
15. Campbell, R. H., & Terwilliger, R. B. (2025). ENCOMPASS: A SAGA based environment for the composition of programs and specifications, appendix A. https://core.ac.uk/download/pdf/42835319.pdf (accessed on 9th September 2025).
16. Clouston, R., Goré, R., Hóu, Z., et al. (2017). Modular labelled sequent calculi for abstract separation logics. http://arxiv.org/abs/1710.10805 (accessed on 9th September 2025).
17. Cohen, J., & Douence, R. (2011). Views, program transformations, and the evolutivity problem in a functional language. https://core.ac.uk/download/50018397.pdf (accessed on 9th September 2025).
18. Earnest, B. M. (2025). Guidelines for development structured FORTRAN programs. https://core.ac.uk/download/pdf/42845685.pdf (accessed on 9th September 2025).
19. Eichberg, M., Giarrusso, P. G., Kästner, C., et al. (2012). Reify your collection queries for modularity and speed! http://arxiv.org/abs/1210.6284 (accessed on 9th September 2025).
20. Ekmekci, B., McAnany, C. E., & Mura, C. (2016). An introduction to programming for bio scientists: A Python-based primer. http://arxiv.org/abs/1605.05419 (accessed on 9th September 2025).
21. Engmann, R., & van Hoeve, F. (1987). An object-oriented approach to application generation. https://core.ac.uk/download/pdf/11474345.pdf (accessed on 9th September 2025).
22. Franch Gutiérrez, J. (1998). Systematic formulation of non-functional characteristics of software. https://core.ac.uk/download/224976303.pdf (accessed on 9th September 2025).

23. Furia, C. A., Meyer, B., Nordio, M., et al. (2013). C to O-O translation: Beyond the easy stuff. http://arxiv.org/abs/1206.5648 (accessed on 9th September 2025).
24. Garcia-Contreras, I., Hermenegildo, M. V., & Morales, J. F. (2020). Incremental and modular context-sensitive analysis. http://arxiv.org/abs/1804.01839 (accessed on 9th September 2025).
25. He, P., Oliva Madrigal, S. C., Koç, Ç., Bao, T., & Xie, J. (2024). CASA: A compact and scalable accelerator for approximate homomorphic encryption. *IACR Transactions on Cryptographic Hardware and Embedded Systems, 2024*, 451–480. https://www.semanticscholar.org/paper/493579d68000818deff72a2cba1ab460ff76393c (accessed on 9th September 2025).
26. Hibbs, R. A., Jain, L. C., Veelenturf, L. P. J., et al. (1995). Integrating evolutionary computation with neural networks. https://core.ac.uk/download/pdf/11453924.pdf (accessed on 9th September 2025).
27. Kreutz, D., Ramos, F. M. V., Veríssimo, P. E., Rothenberg, C. E., Azodolmolky, S., & Uhlig, S. (2014). Software-defined networking: A comprehensive survey. *Proceedings of the IEEE, 103*, 14–76. https://doi.org/10.1109/jproc.2014.2371999 (accessed on 9th September 2025).
28. Lin, Y., Mehta, S., Küçük-McGinty, H., Turner, J. P., Vidović, D., Forlin, M., Koleti, A., et al. (2017). Drug target ontology to classify and integrate drug discovery data. *Journal of Biomedical Semantics, 8*. https://doi.org/10.1186/s13326-017-0161-x (accessed on 9th September 2025).
29. Miller, R. L. (2025). Escort: A data acquisition and display system to support research testing. https://core.ac.uk/download/pdf/42873926.pdf (accessed on 9th September 2025).
30. Mycroft, A., Alves, A., Cooper, D. C., Oppen, D. C., Tuosto, E., Lange, J., et al. (2011). A modular toolkit for distributed interactions. http://arxiv.org/abs/1110.4164 (accessed on 9th September 2025).
31. Pahl, C. (1999). Modular composition of language features through extensions of semantic language models. https://core.ac.uk/download/11309975.pdf (accessed on 9th September 2025).
32. Pahl, C. (2000). An algebraic basis for specifying and enforcing access control in security systems. https://core.ac.uk/download/11309986.pdf (accessed on 9th September 2025).
33. Pereira, J., Di Meo, G. A., Van Den Einden, B., & Sacré, P. (2025). Flexible multimode avionics enabled by hyper integrated software defined radio solutions. *2025 Integrated Communications, Navigation and Surveillance Conference (ICNS)*. https://www.semanticscholar.org/

paper/d5a8150637d6c0111888df0a0efd939f6ee7e60b (accessed on 9th September 2025).

34. Rose, P. L., & Willis, B. G. (2025). Spacelab software development and integration concepts study report, volume 1. https://core.ac.uk/download/pdf/42892541.pdf (accessed on 9th September 2025).
35. Rueden, C., Schindelin, J., Hiner, M., DeZonia, B. E., Walter, A. E., Arena, E. T., & Eliceiri, K. W. (2017). ImageJ2: ImageJ for the next generation of scientific image data. *BMC Bioinformatics, 18*. https://doi.org/10.1186/s12859-017-1934-z (accessed on 9th September 2025).
36. Schmidt, D. C., & Suda, T. (1992). Computing infrastructure issues in distributed communications systems: A survey of operating system transport system architectures. https://core.ac.uk/download/287622717.pdf (accessed on 9th September 2025).
37. Sharma, S. S. V. N., & Shireesha, P. (2010). Building reusable software component for optimization check in ABAP coding. http://arxiv.org/abs/1007.5123 (accessed on 9th September 2025).
38. Stein, L. A. (1999). Challenging the computational metaphor: Implications for how we think. https://core.ac.uk/download/pdf/84443.pdf (accessed on 9th September 2025).
39. Whelton, P. K., Carey, R. M., Aronow, W. S., Casey, D. E., Collins, K. J., Himmelfarb, C. D., DePalma, S. M., et al. (2017). 2017 ACC/AHA/AAPA/ABC/ACPM/AGS/APhA/ASH/ASPC/NMA/PCNA guideline for the prevention, detection, evaluation, and management of high blood pressure in adults: A report of the American College of Cardiology/American Heart Association Task Force on Clinical Practice Guidelines. *Hypertension, 71*. https://doi.org/10.1161/hyp.0000000000000065 (accessed on 9th September 2025).
40. Yen, J. (2025). Using fuzzy logic to integrate neural networks and knowledge-based systems. https://core.ac.uk/download/pdf/42818677.pdf (accessed on 9th September 2025).

CHAPTER 7

ARRAYS AND STRINGS

Contents

INTRODUCTION

Computer science depends primarily on the analysis of arrays and strings as vital data structures that underlie numerous applications. Arrays, as a collection of elements accessed by index or key, enable efficient data storage and retrieval. Strings, on the other hand, are an array of characters encoding textural data. Appreciation of the interaction among these data structures is most important while developing algorithms in other domains, like software development, bioinformatics, and database administration. The study of arrays and strings involves theoretical concepts and implementation in reality and thus contributing towards the performance and capability of computational solutions. In bioinformatics, strings and their associated structures are critical as a consequence of the exponential growth in sequence data generated by current sequencing technologies. Efficient managing of these huge data sets necessitates advanced algorithms and index data structures that can handle complex string problems.

As can be seen from the literature, sophisticated bioinformatics techniques have been conceived to manage the challenge of this flood of data and concentrate on utilizing strong data structures to achieve improved performance. The exposition of such index data structures and what they can bring to the table lies at the heart of understanding their use for biological sequence analysis and beyond that, computational biology as a whole, as seen in recent studies. In addition, the dependence of arrays and strings is not only practical; it reflects the essence of algorithmic design and data structure representation.

The concept of strings being query able by practical arrays and prefix tables, for instance, elucidates how strings can be divided into structured frameworks that enable matching and comparison to be efficient. According to recent studies, any potential array may be represented by a prefix table of an indeterminate string, pointing toward a fascinating intersection between mathematical theory and computer practice (Alatabbi et al., 2014). Under such circumstances, a thorough understanding of the properties, limitations, and trade-offs of varying string and array implementations not only enhances computation performance but also contributes to the body of knowledge in meaningful ways (Dawyndt et al., 2012) (Figure 7.1).

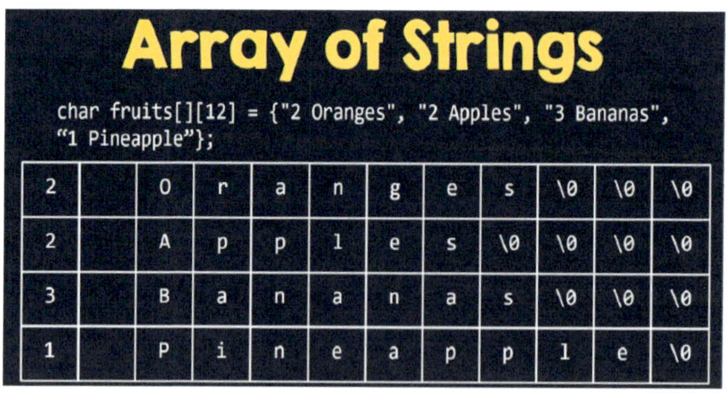

Figure 7.1. *Arrays and strings.*

Source: *https://i.ytimg.com/vi/AefKSoNpZtQ/maxresdefault.jpg.*

Definition of Arrays

Arrays are the fundamental data structure in computer programming that provide an efficient means of storing and managing collections of related data. Being an ordered collection of elements, each expressed by one or more array indexes or keys, arrays provide fast access to data with the expense of additional structures. This fixed-size data structure allows for data grouping through contiguous memory allocation, thus greatly improving performance, especially in programs that require rapid random access. Moreover, arrays are able to hold various kinds of data, from integers to complex objects, the foundation for higher-level data structures like lists and matrices. Their utilization and application cross a broad scope of programming paradigms, making arrays an unavoidable part of every programmer who needs efficiency in data solution management. The properties defined for arrays enable them to support numerous operations with efficiency, providing sequential as well as random access. For instance, accessing one element by its index is an operation conducted within a constant time, and thus arrays are particularly beneficial in programs where speed is the major concern. However, the fixed-size brittleness can become a limiting factor to dynamic usage, and therefore extra constructs, such as dynamic arrays or lists, accommodating different data sizes, are needed. Learning arrays also offers insight into more complex data structures and algorithms in learning environments, an important aspect for development of reliable programming skills. Current programming environments, such as those emphasized in object-oriented curricula, usually adopt array-based models for allowing students to effectively learn fundamental programming concepts (Kölling et al., 1996). Additionally, arrays have implications in data processing techniques, including compression algorithms that compress data redundancy in data sets. Data compression techniques usually employ arrays for managing and processing large amounts of data, with a view to optimizing communication efficiency and storage capacity. For this purpose, arrays allow parallel algorithms to execute complex compression tasks in parallel, and this leads to gigantic system enhancement (Hirschberg et al., 1991). Thus, learning arrays becomes essential not only to elementary programming, but to grasping the data analysis spaces and algorithm design. Such multipurpose array utilization reinforces their importance as a building block in the big picture of computer science and teaching programming, especially in regard to manipulating strings, which typically are character arrays used for a diverse range of purposes.

Definition of Strings

Strings, as fundamental data structures in programming and computer science, are the primary means of text information representation and manipulation. A string is just a group of characters that may include letters, numbers, symbols, and spaces. This definition forms strings independent of other data types, such as integers or floating-point, that are numeric data. String spatiality and temporality are most useful when operations such as string concatenation, slicing, and searching are called upon. Besides their usage in text processing, strings play a fundamental role in data storage, transmission, and representation in computer systems. As developers deal with strings across various programming languages, it is evident that the abstraction has its downfalls, especially when it comes to handling character encoding and special characters, leading to varying implementations in varied environments. Furthermore, strings are not always static; they are dynamic data structures that are managed and rearranged through various programming functions and techniques. For instance, the immutability of strings in programming languages like Java or Python is that once a string is created, it cannot be modified.

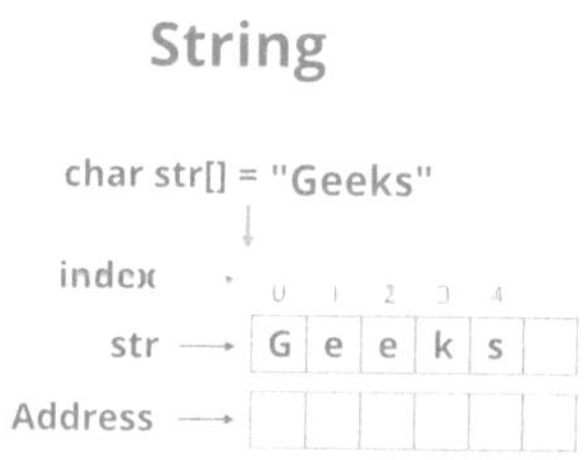

Figure 7.2. *Strings.*

Source: https://media.geeksforgeeks.org/wp-content/uploads/20220820132424/Strings-660x496.png.

That attribute aids programmers to understand memory management better as modification entails creating a fresh instance of a string. Programming languages also provide an extensive range of predefined functions to facilitate string manipulation, such as finding substrings, formatting output, and changing cases. Thus, strings are a foundational bridging element between machine processable and human readable text, which requires solid and flexible implementations. Their mild processing of textual information is essential for applications ranging from simple text display to complex natural language systems. In the overall array and string framework, how these two abstractions interact is particularly noteworthy. Arrays, an array of items indexed, are capable of holding strings as its items, illustrating how arrays and strings are associated with each other in programming. Arrays' own flexibility allows an array of strings to be manipulated, such as in applications handling lists, like names in address books or search keywords. In addition, the understanding of strings' definitions extends to their representation in array form, which treats individual characters as accessible and updatable. This interaction suggests a growing importance in computational linguistics and processing protocols. With enhanced software systems, the potential for efficient manipulation and management of strings in arrays can help pave the foundation for sophisticated algorithms and applications, creating a pressing field for ongoing development and research in both academic studies and daily implementations, such as in the use of ImageJ, a program developed on sophisticated data structures to scan images (Rueden et al., 2017) (Figure 7.2).

Importance of Arrays and Strings in Programming

Arrays and strings are fundamental data structures in computer programming that facilitate efficient means of storing and manipulating collections of data. Arrays give a structured way of storing elements in a manner that makes the elements easily accessible through index values. For instance, when a programmer needs to perform operations on a set of numeric values, an array facilitates simple iteration over elements without the need for other structures. This linear structure not only enables improved performance during access time but also supports the smoother application of complex algorithms. The significance of such data structures is displayed in professional fields, such as aerodynamic analysis, where computational fluid dynamics relies on arrays to deal with and manipulate geometric data effectively, illustrating the pivotal function of arrays in making possible advanced software solutions within engineering platforms (Gentry et al., 2025). Strings, a fixed collection of characters, extend the application of arrays into the domain of handling text data. Strings enable programmers to develop programs that require processing, searching, and manipulating strings efficiently. The nature of strings itself allows algorithms to perform operations such as concatenation and substring extraction with relative ease. Strings are important in a broad range of applications, from database management software to graphical user interface development, where manipulation of text data is routine. Furthermore, with advancing technology, the need for effective handling of strings becomes more and more emphasized, particularly in high-performance-oriented programming languages. These properties ensure that software is interactive and adaptable, an aspect crucial to seamless user experiences for programs with heavy interactivity (N/A). Beyond their utility benefits, arrays and strings also contribute significantly towards organization and code readability. By employing these data structures, programmers can achieve code readability and maintainability, thus facilitating teamwork in team settings. For instance, employing arrays to manage data sets can provide a clean separation of responsibility whereby individual components of a program handle specific tasks and mention shared datasets. This module approach not only enhances team efficiency but also reduces errors in development. Lastly, programming integration of arrays and strings not only serves the needs of technology but also improves good programming habits, making future software solutions stable, scalable, and easy to maintain, thereby improving their validity in the programming community.

7.1. CHARACTERISTICS OF ARRAYS

Arrays are elementary data structures that are the starting point for storing and manipulating collections of related data. One of the fundamental attributes of arrays is their ability to store multiple elements, each of which may be accessed by a separate index, which allows for data to be easily obtained. In contrast to other data structures like linked lists, arrays reserve a block of memory contiguously, so that fast access times are achieved—usually O(1) for accessing an element. This ordered arrangement makes it easy to iterate over the elements, so that arrays can be used effectively in many applications ranging from matrix implementation in mathematical calculations to storing lists of strings. Further, the fixed size of an array, while limiting in certain situations, encourages effective memory use, thus contributing to optimized performance in programs involving predictable data manipulation (Ashcroft et al., 2011). Another characteristic of arrays is that they are homogeneous in nature because they are designed to store elements of the same data type. This consistency provides several advantages, including type safety and the ability to benefit from optimized functions and algorithms tailored to a specific data type. For instance, arrays in programming languages like C or Java allow programmers to write improved performance code that minimizes possible runtime errors due to type mismatches. It also greatly enhances performance, especially when the array-specific operations are coded. But the necessity of consistency can also be a difficulty where flexibility is called for, prompting designers to look to alternatives like dynamic arrays or other data types when handling diverse collections (N/A). Having a fixed size property has both benefits and drawbacks in the area of applications for arrays. While the predetermined length of an array neatly enforces order and keeps memory efficiently used, it also limits flexibility. Once an array is declared, its size cannot be altered, and thus has to be foreseen beforehand at the programming design level. In situations where the size of elements on the top end is not specified, dynamic resizing techniques or other data structures like linked lists may have to be employed by programmers. Among these restrictions, arrays are highly employed due to their simplicity and naturally inheriting speed advantages for most standard operations. It is essential that developers and computer scientists understand the weaknesses and strengths of arrays to create efficient algorithms and data-processing systems (Ashcroft et al., 2011) (Figure 7.3).

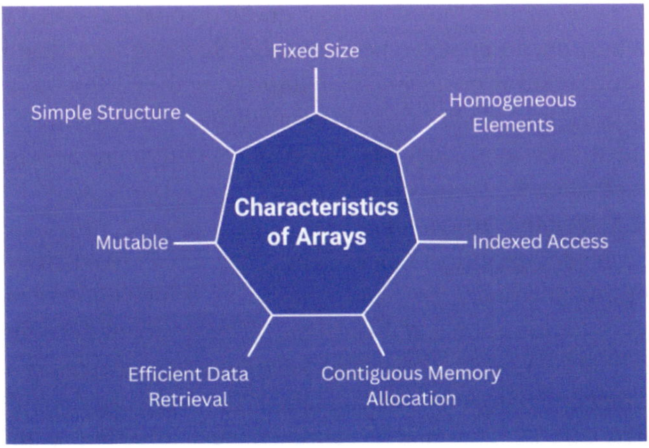

Figure 7.3. *Characteristics of arrays.*

Source: https://cdn.prod.website-files.com/670cbf146221ee06c3cdd761/6751a2b560be24be15ef474d_6751a2277de05ad4a91a7955_Characteristics%2520of%2520Arrays.webp.

7.1.1. Fixed Size Versus Dynamic Size

In programming, fixed-size versus dynamic-size data structures is crucial, particularly for arrays and strings. Fixed-size arrays are characterized by their fixed allocation of memory, done upon creation, which makes them predictable and consistent. Although it might be a plus, this inflexibility will prove to be a drawback when there is a need to alter size within the execution of the program. The consequence of restricted space is typically inefficient use of memory or the need for expensive data copying and relocation operations. This trade-off of speed versus flexibility is repeated in numerous different computational structures, where high accuracy and performance can impose unpractical costs on hardware and post-processing capability, as seen in related research examining the efficiency of optical processors (Athale et al., 1986). On the other hand, dynamic-size data structures, such as linked lists or dynamic arrays, offer flexibility, accommodating variable amounts of data without pre-set boundaries. This flexibility is particularly desirable in managing uncertain input sizes, which is a common condition in programming problems related to database handling and processing user content. However, while dynamic structures sidestep the disadvantages of fixed-size constraints, these also come with their own challenges, primarily in memory management and potential fragmentation. The use of dynamic arrays usually involves a constant resizing system, where new memory needs to be requested and data copied from an old location to a new one to preserve performance. Resizing is critical in allowing the structure to expand as necessary, then improving the performance efficiency of algorithms using arrays and strings. Recent advances in algorithmic efficiency place in context how vital selecting the best data structure according to real needs of an operation is. Techniques like the Gapped k-mer Kernel, which take advantage of associative arrays for enhanced performance, prove how dynamic techniques can dramatically outperform traditional fixed-size structures, especially in computational processes that work with volumes of data, like DNA sequence classification and text mining. The agility of dynamic structures allows algorithms to scale cost-effectively, meeting increased complexity with less computational overhead than their fixed-size analogs (Kowsari et al., 2017). The role of fixed and dynamic sizing interacting, with increasing programming language development, is still a determiner of best practice software development, showing the necessity of knowing both paradigms so that strengths of the paradigms can be leveraged effectively.

7.1.2. Homogeneous Data Types

Homogeneous data types are the key to the declaration and use of arrays and strings in programming languages. Homogeneous data types facilitate effective storage and handling of information in array or string form where every element within an array or string is of the same type. This is a key feature in optimizing the use of memory and performance as it allows for compilers to allocate the appropriate amount of memory and perform some operations that are applicable to the particular type, thereby minimizing overhead. Operations such as iteration, sorting, and filtering become efficient and can be performed easily, thereby making homogeneous collections ideal for applications with fast processing and accessing of large data sets. As for arrays, the use of homogeneous data types not only makes things easier but also makes things safer in terms of types. If an array is defined to hold a specific type of data—either integers, floats, or characters—then developers can prevent type-mismatching errors and guarantee that the data being held is correct. For instance, a numeric array will not allow any string or character inputs, thereby safeguarding the integrity of the data structure. This aspect of homogeneous data types is beneficial when following industry-standard coding practices since it enables cleaner, more maintainable code to be written up front. Through the application of more strict data type checks, programmers can minimize runtime errors, which is important especially in applications that have large data operations to undertake.

Furthermore, homogeneous data types have an impact on advanced data structures such as multi-maps or trie maps since they may utilize homogeneous elements to achieve higher efficiency and performance. Recent research shows that storage and retrieval of heterogeneous data in such structures optimized to a great degree leads to large application performance improvements. For example, those implementations that are aimed at supporting multiple data types usually have greater memory overhead that can become performance-affecting. Data structures to accommodate homogeneous data types allow for easier support with improved management of operations and type safety guarantee. The search for efficiency in data management parallels ongoing innovations in programming paradigms, more precisely in data manipulation and modeling, and drives the creation of tools for high-performance computing (Steindorfer et al., 2016; Fu et al., 2014).

7.1.3. Memory Allocation and Access

Memory allocation and access are fundamental concepts with significant implications in the manipulation of arrays and strings within various programming environments. Arrays, serving as contiguous memory blocks, necessitate efficient allocation to enhance performance, particularly in resource-constrained systems. When an array is declared, the memory allocator reserves a specified amount of space based on the data type and array size. Such allocation can occur on the stack or the heap; each has unique performance characteristics. For example, stack allocation is faster but limited in size and scope, whereas heap allocation offers flexibility but incurs overhead. Understanding these nuances is crucial for programmers, as inefficient memory handling can lead to performance bottlenecks, memory leaks, or even program crashes if the allocated memory is improperly managed. Accessing elements in arrays and strings is an equally essential aspect of memory management, significantly influencing computational efficiency. Each element in an array is accessed using its index, which directly translates to an offset from the base address of the array. This direct addressing method allows for constant-time complexity, O(1), when accessing or modifying elements, making arrays suitable for scenarios where rapid access is necessary. In contrast, strings, though based on character arrays, require careful indexing given their potential immutability in certain programming languages. Memory allocation strategies, such as dynamic resizing of strings through mechanisms like copy-on-write, are pivotal for optimizing memory usage. The interaction between memory allocation and access mechanisms shapes the performance characteristics of both data structures, emphasizing the importance of selection and implementation in software design. Moreover, modern programming paradigms have introduced sophisticated techniques to enhance memory access efficiency, especially in complex applications. For instance, the development of inter-process communication (IPC) mechanisms, such as TZC, demonstrates the innovative approaches taken to reduce overhead in data transmission while maintaining memory integrity. By partitioning message components between sockets and shared memory, TZC minimizes copying during message exchanges, fundamentally altering how data is shared across processes. This technique underscores the broader implication of memory allocation in system design, as optimized memory access can significantly enhance real-time performance in applications such as robotics and autonomous systems. Effective memory management, therefore, not only involves allocation but also how these memory blocks are accessed, manipulated, and shared across different program components, shaping overall application efficiency and reliability (Figure 7.4).

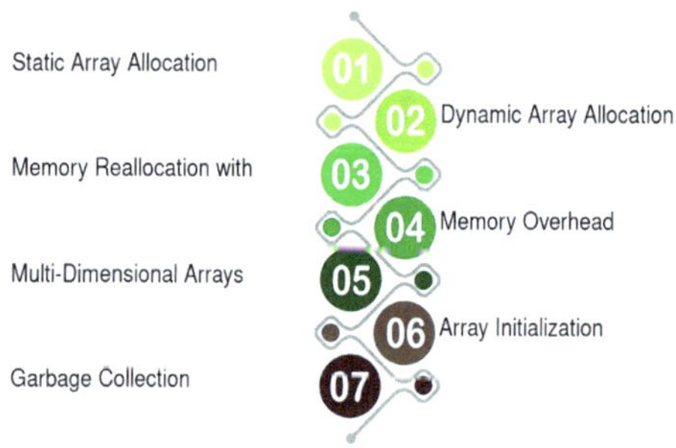

Figure 7.4. *Memory allocation and access.*

Source: https://fastercapital.co/i/Array-Memory-Management--Efficient-Coding--Array-Memory-Management-in-VBA--Understanding-VBAs-Memory-Allocation-for-Arrays.webp.

7.2. TYPES OF ARRAYS

Arrays are elementary data structures in programming with robust mechanisms for storing and organizing data. Out of all types of arrays, one distinguishes single-dimension and multi-dimension arrays. Single-dimension arrays are the simplest form, making it feasible to store elements in linear fashion. They are utilized in millions of applications, ranging from sorting functions to simple lists of data. Multi-dimensional arrays, as some might understand two-dimensional arrays, take this concept to another level by enabling more complex data organizations like matrices or tables. The application of these two types essentially defines the programs structure and dictates data handling and access, exemplifying the versatility and importance of arrays in programming. To further deconstruct the array types, there needs to be examination of static versus dynamic arrays. Static arrays are of a fixed size determined at the time of compilation and may prove to be inefficient if the data size is rapidly varying. Dynamic arrays, on the other hand, use the memory at runtime and can dynamically modify their size as per the need, thereby maximizing the use of resources. Similar flexibility is also needed in modern programming models where the data size cannot be predicted. In real-time system development environments, the nature of array used can be highly critical to performance and flexibility. In view of recent breakthroughs in real-time systems, the use of more flexible data structures like dynamic arrays can greatly enhance function and responsiveness of the system, which is a demonstration of their high relevance to programming effectiveness and efficiency (Li et al., 2016). Aside from the intrinsic differences between array types, context of application is also an important factor in their adoption. For instance, in schools, the adoption of arrays would be accompanied by pedagogical methodologies that enable students to understand programming principles more effectively. The choice of whether array types are to be employed depends on pedagogical approaches, that is, the Fundamentals-first approach, where the fundamentals are prior to discussing higher-level topics (Joy et al., 2004). Understanding array types using this teaching curriculum not only gives the learner essential programming concepts but also prepares them for real-world application where such structures are prevalent. Lastly, the various types of arrays, augmented by their context of application, draw out the crucial position occupied by arrays in programming and computer science (Figure 7.5).

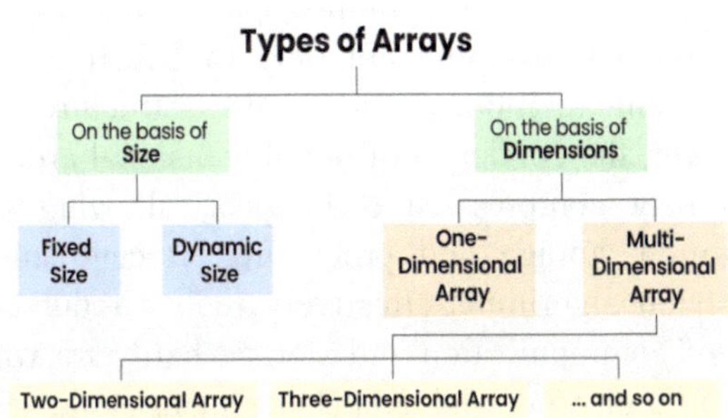

Figure 7.5. *Types of arrays.*

Source: https://media.geeksforgeeks.org/wp-content/uploads/20240731124259/Types-of-Arrays.webp.

7.2.1. One-Dimensional Arrays

One-dimensional arrays represent an elementary computer science idea that serves as an essential building block for manipulating and structuring data. One-dimensional arrays consist of linear sequences of elements, with each element accessed by a specific index, allowing efficient storage and retrieval of data in memory. One-dimensional arrays are simple to implement in most programming languages, such as lists of integers or strings of characters. Their applicability is ubiquitous in a variety of uses, ranging from storing user input to performing algorithms that require sequential data processing. They facilitate manageable memory management, which is essential in designing efficient programs, by providing an array of a fixed size. As simple as they are, one-dimensional arrays also have their own limitations, particularly in managing dynamic sizes for data and maintaining efficient indexing to avoid traps such as off-by-one errors.

The enormous real-world applications of one-dimensional arrays extend to areas like algorithm design and data processing. For instance, sorting algorithms usually employ one-dimensional arrays to obtain an ordered array of objects, and as such, they form a critical part of effective search functionality. One-dimensional arrays also allow for varied computational operations like mathematical computation, where all the items can be utilized as coefficients in a polynomial or components of a vector. Their ability to store related data elements together in memory encourages cache performance, thus accelerating execution. Moreover, these arrays can be used as a stepping stone to achieving more advanced structures, including stacks and queues, thus identifying their universality in various programming paradigms. Finally, mastery of one-dimensional arrays is essential not only to effective programming but also towards advancing to more advanced data structures and algorithmic techniques. Moreover, the efficiency of one-dimensional arrays also increases when used with data compression techniques, allowing programmers to minimize information storage and processing. Recent studies established that data compression algorithms effectively reduce redundancy, improving the effectiveness of communication and storage hardware while maintaining the integrity of stored or processed data (Hirschberg et al., 1991). In systems where memory space is small, as in the case of embedded systems or cell phone applications, the ability to leverage one-dimensional arrays for minimal storage of data makes perfect sense. This convergence of one-dimensional arrays and compression of data reflects a clear breakthrough in computational efficiency, indicating the applicability of traditional data structures in today's technological systems. Lastly, the competency in one-dimensional arrays not only provides one with a solid foundation in programming but also presents avenues for dealing with more sophisticated data processing techniques essential to today's software development (Figure 7.6).

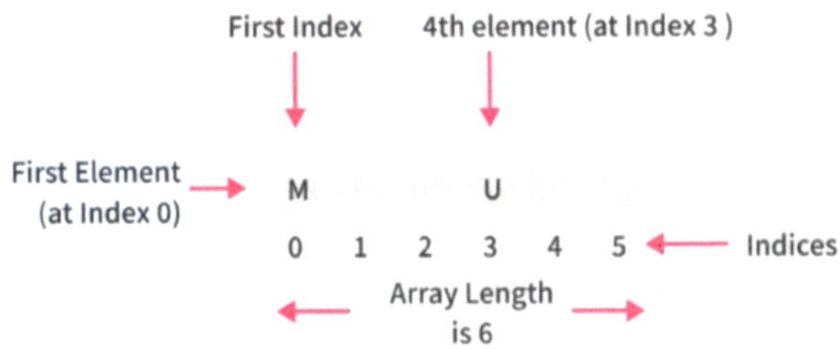

Figure 7.6. *One-dimensional arrays.*

Source: https://www.scaler.com/topics/c/one-dimensional-array-in-c/.

7.2.2. Multi-Dimensional Arrays

Multi-dimensional arrays are a significant improvement of regular lincar arrays, where information is actually stored in more than one dimension, so the representation of more complex data structures is achieved. Arrays in this case handle tables, matrices, and higher-order forms, presenting an effective way of handling multidimensional data. For instance, a multi-dimensional array can store an array of values in a grid form, typically used in programs like image processing where the image pixel is directly corresponding to some coordinate in the array. Multi-dimensional arrays also facilitate logical operations and computations that would otherwise be cumbersome with one-dimensional structures, thus enhancing the power and flexibility of data manipulation in programming languages. The application of multi-dimensional arrays in programming languages such as Java and C++ differs, demonstrating varied memory allocation and management policies. Java two-dimensional arrays are nothing but arrays of arrays, leading to a more complex memory structure that imposes overhead on performance. Yet, C++ does facilitate the utilization of contiguous memory allocation, allowing more efficient access patterns. This gap has practical implications in high-performance computing scenarios, where memory management and access speeds are critical. Secondly, data structures innovation—such as the Heterogeneous Hash-Array Mapped Trie (HHAMT)—allows for better means of encoding and encoding multi-dimensional data, demonstrating ongoing improvement of the means by which programmers can employ arrays to effectively handle intricate datasets (Steindorfer et al., 2016). While the presence of intrinsic advantages of multi-dimensional arrays is possible, they nevertheless are not free from disadvantages, notably ease of use and complexity. High dimensionality also may exacerbate problems of program readability and behavior influenced, notably for data sets of larger size. Programmers may often have to write supporting functions or libraries to perform basic operations, say, slicing or reshaping arrays. This issue is compounded in memory management and optimization for performance, particularly within the garbage collection environment, in which inefficient memory management reduces the speed of the application (Hawblitzel et al., 2009). As programming practices evolve, understanding multi-dimensional array strength and weakness remains paramount in effective data handling, in the long run leading to improved decision-making while designing algorithms and software (Figure 7.7).

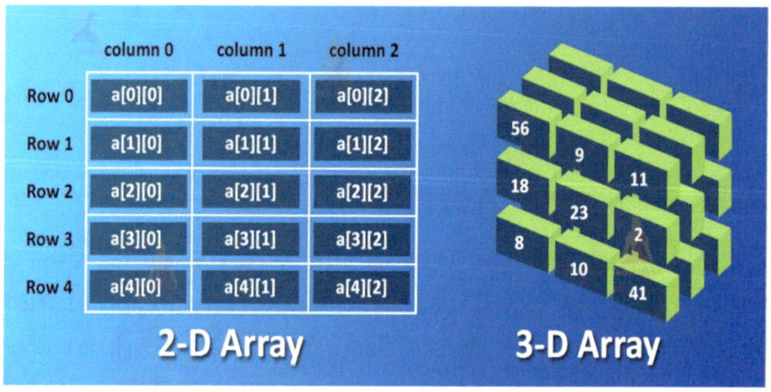

Figure 7.7. *Multi-dimensional arrays.*

Source: https://techvidvan.com/tutorials/wp-content/uploads/2021/06/Multidimensional-Arrays-in-C.jpg.

7.2.3. Associative Arrays

Associative arrays, also referred to as maps or dictionaries in other languages, are a generic data structure by their key-value pair storage method. They enable data to be retrieved efficiently by using an associated key to address its corresponding value. As opposed to the traditional arrays based on numeric indexing, associative arrays introduce the flexibility of using heterogenous data types as keys, hence the simplicity of representing complex data relationships. Implementing associative arrays is the foundation for the development of most applications, particularly in the dynamic domains of data management such as database indexing, data analysis, and web development. As applications usually call for scalability and responsiveness, associative arrays provide facilities for efficient insert and lookup quickly, significantly improving performance efficiency. One of the widely used implementations of associative arrays is achieved through the use of hash tables, where hashing functions transform keys into unique hash codes. This allows retrieval of associated values quickly, significantly increasing the efficiency of applications based on large data sets. But the design and performance of hash tables can in turn vary depending on the specific language and data structures in use. In multi-threaded scenarios, as highlighted by recent research, becoming thread-safe for multi-map data structures becomes a critical issue. Immutable multi-maps offer an appealing solution to this challenge, for instance, fixing race conditions at little extra cost and saving memory by employing compact encoding schemes. Although hash tables have the performance advantage, the implementation subtleties must be carefully weighed to best leverage their capabilities on high-level applications. Aside from that, advances in associative array data structures can be observed for Heterogeneous Hash-Array Mapped Tries (HHAMT). The new framework accommodates type-heterogeneous keys and values and has considerably lower memory overhead compared to simple encoding. The flexibility of HHAMT becomes useful in multi-map applications where dealing with many associations between keys and values is of utmost importance. By avoiding excess overhead of empty value sets and optimizing the storage process, HHAMT can minimize performance without compromising type safety. Such innovation indicates the continuous advancements of associative arrays as an ever-growing part of contemporary programming paradigms. Specifically, these constructs mirror contemporary constructs, such as Jasper, in highlighting a broad trend towards containing complex data interactions in amenable programming contexts (Steindorfer et al., 2016; Smith et al., 2012).

7.3. STRINGS' CHARACTERISTICS

Strings, being fundamental data structures, possess certain characteristics that distinguish them from other types of collections, including arrays. One such common characteristic of strings is their immutability in the majority of programming languages, that is, a string cannot be altered after its creation. This characteristic impacts memory management and performance, notably in languages like Java and Scala, where immutability imposes safety in concurrent programs. For instance, creating new strings through concatenation results in new instances rather than altering the original string, thus influencing the use of memory in programs that deal with big data sets. As such, acquiring the influence of string manipulation on performance and memory use becomes imperative in designing applications, particularly those dealing with big data. Another property that distinguishes strings is their ability to handle sequences of characters, wherein they provide a great level of flexibility in data representation. Strings can handle various encodings such as ASCII and UTF-

8, which accommodates the representation of international character sets and symbol sets. It is not only crucial for user interface but also for data interchange between systems with varying encoding schemes. Also, the possibility of treating strings as arrays of characters allows programmers to use a body of algorithms for search, comparison, and conversion. For example, patterns of strings are highly efficiently processed by sequence-processing algorithms that greatly enhance a program's ability to manipulate strings. The power and flexibility supplied by strings therefore make strings a programming mainstay, touching from trivial input/output functions to complex text manipulation. Finally, despite strings having some array-like properties, there are intrinsic differences programmers must be careful about. Strings, in contrast to arrays, tend to be immutable and do not easily allow changing of elements, so string manipulation can involve the creation of entirely new instances for optimization and data integrity reasons. Strings also carry the ability to incur tremendous overhead when employed in applications where many-to-many relationships are inevitable, as exposed through data structure efficiency debates in modern programming scenarios. Growth of data structures such as the Heterogeneous Hash-Array Mapped Trie (HHAMT) is a manifestation of ongoing innovations in efficient processing of diverse string types using minimal memory, thus helping programmers overcome issues related to various types of data in high-performance applications (Steindorfer et al., 2016). Because object-oriented programming is an emergent paradigm, the introduction of using primary instruction languages—such as Blue—can make the learning of strings and their complexities more in-depth for new students (Kölling et al., 1996) (Figure 7.8).

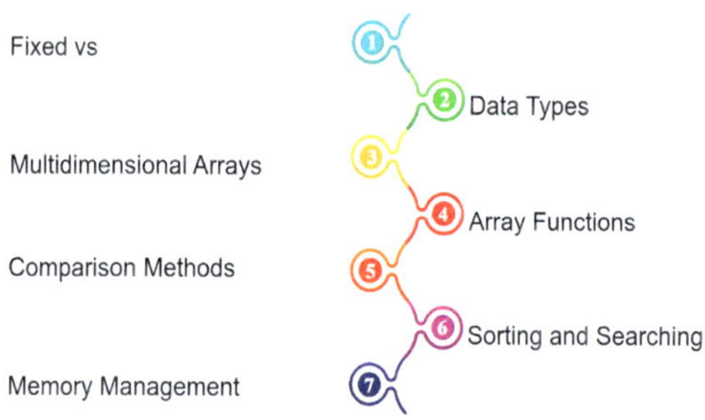

Figure 7.8. *Characteristics of strings.*

Source: https://fastercapital.co/i/String-Comparison--The-Fine-Line--Comparing-Strings-in-VBA-Arrays--Understanding-VBA-Arrays-and-Their-Characteristics.webp.

7.3.1. Immutable Versus Mutable Strings

The distinction between mutable and immutable strings is a very fundamental rule of programming, particularly among various programming languages. Immutable strings, such as in the examples of Java and Python, cannot be modified once created for the first time; any modification results in the creation of a new string object. The following are advantages of this property: enhanced memory integrity, ease of use in concurrent programming, and optimization potential by the compiler. For instance, immutable strings cannot be modified, so they can be cached and reused, which reduces memory overhead. By way of comparison, mutable strings in languages such as C++ and JavaScript allow for in-place change, providing flexibility and efficiency in string manipulation where size or contents may be subject to frequent change. Thus, choosing between immutable and mutable strings can have a significant impact upon performance and memory utilization within a program. The consequences of immutable and mutable strings are also known at the data handling and algorithmic level. With complex applications, especially those that involve intensive manipulation and data analysis, the overhead of applying immutable strings can lead to a bottleneck in performance. For example, if repeatedly concatenating strings or working on massive text strings, applying immutable strings could lead to gargantuan amounts of time and memory allocation issues. This raises a pertinent question because developers must establish the string nature based on the specific needs of their own applications. Knowledge of encapsulated efficiencies with mutable strings in heavy-lifting applications, thus, can go a long way in reducing performance drags. This dualism raises a delicate balance of needs in mobility against flexibility because developers apply these concepts in the process of creating their applications. Furthermore, the decision to employ immutable or mutable strings relates intimately to the general importance of programming paradigms and algorithm design. In performance-critical applications, such as scientific computing and real-time data processing, mutable strings may allow for required flexibility at the expense of string creation overheads. As highlighted in discussions around modern programming practices, achieving proficiency involves the balance between foundational concepts and advanced applications, bridging the gap between theoretical knowledge and real-world application (Hill, 2020). For developers, this balance informs not only string manipulation tactics but also shapes the overall architecture of software. As seen from the evolution of programming practices and tools, this information equips programmers with the ability to select an appropriate data structure to ensure effective efficient application performance effectively as per optimal software design practices (Barbosa et al., 2022).

7.3.2. String Length and Capacity

The length of a string and the capacity of it is an important subject of research in the research of data structures, particularly strings and arrays. The length of a string refers to how many characters the string contains, usually determining the amount of space required to store the string as well as the efficiency of string manipulation. This length in programming languages can also affect the behavior of algorithms, especially those string comparison- or concatenation-based algorithms. For instance, when an algorithm is dealing with strings of varying lengths, having each strings capacity allows programmers to optimize resources, for example, reduced memory fragmentation. Similarly, incorrect handling of string lengths can also lead to buffer overflows, a widespread software flaw. Hence, determination of accurate string lengths is critical not only for performance but also for application security and reliability. Capacity is equally a factor to be considered in string management as it defines the amount of reserved memory to hold a string and the available space for future growth. While length counts the number of existing characters, capacity encompasses the number of memory allocated to hold a string, which is most probably higher than the existing length of strings.

This division is critical when operations that change string content, like character insertion or appending, may require reallocation of memory if the existing capacity is not enough. Proper memory management practices are of utmost importance here. For example, when using a data structure like a dynamic array, programmers often use mechanisms for increasing capacity incrementally in anticipation of growth, as seen in the analysis of compressed tire data structures balancing space utilization without compromizing query performance (Pibiri et al., 2018). The relationship between string length and capacity ultimately plays a role in the effective construction of algorithms and data structures. Also, the practical issues of string length and capacity spill over into specific usage, especially in specific fields such as natural language processing and string approximate matching.

For these applications, being able to accommodate variations in length of string is critical to effective measuring of string similarity or dissimilarity, particularly when employing algorithms that take edit distances into account. Such. Such algorithms require a small representation of both strings to be compared and operation costs involved in transforming one string into another, which can be deletion, insertion, or substitution (Belazzougui et al., 2014). String lengths and capacities direct. This focus on string lengths and capacities impacts the design of effective data structures that would enable storage and querying of gigantic dictionaries and account for varied string sizes. Therefore, the combination of string length and capacity not only enhances algorithm efficiency but also makes it easy to develop robust applications in a variety of computational activities, underscoring their significance in the context of strings and arrays.

7.3.3. Encoding and Character Sets

The complexity of encoding and character sets is paramount in understanding how arrays and strings function within programming languages. Character encoding refers to the process of converting characters into a specific format that a computer can understand. This transformation relies on character sets, which consist of pre-defined mappings that associate characters with unique numeric values or code points. The most prevalent encoding system today is UTF-8, an extension of ASCII that supports a vast array of characters from various languages, allowing for global text representation. Understanding these encodings is crucial for handling strings correctly, ensuring that data transferred between systems, platforms, and applications is interpreted consistently and accurately. Without a proper grasp of character encodings, developers risk generating applications that fail to communicate effectively with different languages and locales, ultimately compromising user experience and data integrity. In the field of bioinformatics, the significance of efficient encoding becomes increasingly pronounced, particularly with the rise of genomic data. As sequencing technologies advance, they produce copious amounts of data, necessitating efficient string manipulation techniques. Bioinformatics tools frequently employ advanced data structures to encode biological sequences, allowing for rapid processing and retrieval. These solutions must navigate the intricacies of irregular data patterns and asynchronous updates, emphasizing the need for optimized encoding methodologies. For instance, applications designed for genetic alignment, profiling, and assembly require meticulous handling of character sets to ensure that genomic sequences are accurately represented and manipulated during analysis. The vast variety of index structures explored in the literature highlights the advancements made in adapting encoding systems to meet the unique challenges posed by bioinformatics applications (Dawyndt et al., 2012). Furthermore, the evolution of genomic data sets has led to a paradigm shift in how encoding and character sets are perceived in computational biology. With genomic databases expanding and becoming more accessible due to decreased sequencing costs, the demand for robust encoding systems has intensified. Developers are challenged to address distinct requirements for memory usage and processing power when designing software for large-scale genomic analysis. Notably, problems like clustering or assembly demand not only efficient algorithms but also precise character encoding to facilitate smooth data transitions. As computational patterns evolve in high-performance genomics, the integral relationship between encoding, character sets, and system architecture becomes evident. Such insights inform programming strategies that bolster data handling efficiency, ensuring that the rich data contained within genomic sequences contributes effectively to scientific discovery and innovation (Awan et al., 2020) (Figure 7.9).

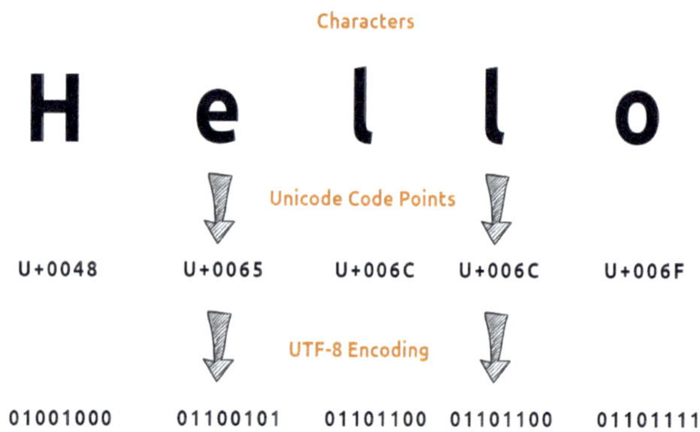

Figure 7.9. *Encoding and character sets.*

*Source: https://miro.medium.com/v2/resize:fit:2418/0*O2gVrncQJf55othp.*

7.4. STRING MANIPULATION TECHNIQUES

In computer science, string manipulation is a basic operation in most applications ranging from data processing to algorithms. Strings as strings of characters require various methods of manipulation, sorting, and analyzing their contents effectively. Basic operations like extracting substrings, string concatenation, and character replacement are some of the basic operations that form building blocks for more complex manipulations. For instance, the search for specific patterns within strings necessitates good algorithms, such as the Knuth-Morris-Pratt algorithm or the Boyer-Moore algorithm. Not only do these processes improve string operations, but also program efficiency in general via a reduction in time complexity. As such, control of string manipulation is absolute for any computer scientist aiming to maximize data processing and handling. Aside from routine operations, advanced string handling techniques can be applied to facilitate data compression, a valuable resource to deal with large data. Removal of redundant data through compression mechanisms leads to improved communication and storage that complements the functions of many systems. For example, applying parallel algorithms in compressing text-based data facilitates parallel processing, significantly improving system speed and performance. Through the application of dynamic codeword construction methods, programmers are able to adapt compression algorithms to enhance efficiency. Not only is resource consumption optimized but also the manner in which data is sent over networks. As a result, it becomes crucial to comprehend the interrelation between string manipulation and data compression in order to have successful data management solutions implemented in contemporary computing (Hirschberg et al., 1991). Moreover, actual implementation of string manipulation techniques is most often integration of programming languages that allow dynamic memory allocation and efficient data handling. For instance, Python and Java have built-in libraries and functions to manipulate strings for ease of use. This allows the programmer to focus on higher-level algorithm and design without getting mired in the complexity of memory management. Moreover, system interoperability, as highlighted in system interoperability research, enhances interoperability across a number of programming environments to facilitate the use of string manipulation functions across various platforms. The study of such interoperability identifies how simple functions are altered to fit various uses, making them even more functional and setting the stage for continued technological advancements (N/A). Thus, string manipulation abilities remain the basis of efficient programming and data management methods in the era of the internet (Figure 7.10).

Figure 7.10. *String manipulation techniques.*

Source: https://external-content.duckduckgo.com/iu/?u=https%3A%2F%2Ftse3.mm.bing.net%2Fth%2Fid%2FOIP.meG2IOCOO6b2dmoBDk4BAgH-aEO%3Fpid%3DApi&f=1&ipt=3f4a803e2b1c807aa4fb65edc2fefde0e22ff377809e435aa73397b9ba07802c.

7.4.1. Concatenation

Concatenation, a fundamental operation with respect to arrays and strings, is the act of combining two or more sequences into one new entity. Concatenation not only broadens the theoretical foundation of data structures but also has necessary applications in a large number of computational operations. For example, in the case of combining strings within programming languages, the efficiency of concatenation can heavily influence runtime performance, particularly in contexts of data processing and manipulation. The principle of concatenation becomes increasingly important in use within applications such as data compression, where information redundancy is eliminated to reduce storage. As discussed in Hirschberg et al. (1991), data compression methods employ concatenation along with parallel algorithms to remove redundancy effectively and enhance capabilities for data transmission. The complexity of concatenation can also be investigated in terms of its impact on computational efficiency. When concatenating strings of varying lengths, special care must be taken as far as time complexity is concerned, which must otherwise be typically linear in the sizes of the strings being concatenated. This efficiency is essential while doing tasks that require lots of concatenation since too much computational overhead could lead to performance degradation. Since the string lengths are dynamic in nature, efficient algorithms must be formulated in order to handle concatenation, particularly when handling heterogeneous data structures. For instance, the work in Andersson et al. (2011) explores an approximately string matching algorithm that, by nature, has the elements of concatenation through the alignment of substrings, thereby addressing its prominent position in string manipulation operations. Lastly, the role of concatenation becomes pivotal in various advanced algorithms utilized in computer science. Through the successful concatenation of different strings or arrays, it is possible to construct deep data structures that support complex operations, including searching and sorting. New approaches, such as the application of parallel computation models, have been devised to accelerate concatenation activities as well as improve efficiency. This applies with greatest emphasis in the case of huge datasets or high-speed databases, where the conventional methods of concatenation may fail. The research into such advanced techniques, as suggested in Hirschberg et al. (1991), serves to confirm the increasing role of concatenations in today's technology world, cementing its fundamental position in controlling and organizing arrays and strings.

7.4.2. Extraction of Substring

Substring retrieval is an extremely significant portion of the general application of arrays and strings, particularly in the processing and manipulation of textual data. The ability to obtain subsets of a string properly is the foundation of much application in such fields as data processing and bioinformatics, where substring application is utilized in the search for crucial information about genetic sequences. The importance of substring extraction is compounded in situations where there are large, repetitive sets of data since such tend to cause high performance problems. Advanced algorithms facilitating these extraction processes have been developed to maximize efficiency and often utilize such concepts as indexing, whose aim is to facilitate the retrieval of occurrences of substrings, especially in the case of large texts. Efficient substring extraction not only helps in simplifying advanced data queries but also complements the needs of having faster systems and quicker responses in data analysis models. Moreover, the relationship between compression and indexing is a major factor in optimizing substring extraction. Recent breakthroughs in dictionary compression algorithms indicate that all dictionary compressors can be understood from the string attractor point of view, which provides a collection of indices in a text with all distinct substrings. It was this groundbreaking insight that motivated the design of novel indexing data structures that reduce the space complexity compared to conventional substring extraction methods. Specifically, universal compressed self-indexes, following the string attractor theory, can effectively minimize the space for indexing large texts. As the universal indexing methods evidence indicates, the application of these algorithms makes substring extraction possible in considerably shorter periods, ultimately enhancing the overall efficiency of text processing software (Navarro et al., 2018). Particularly, the performance of substring extraction algorithms can be likened on the grounds of space and time complexity. The Run-Length FM-index is one such algorithm that balances both space and processing performance. It incorporates a measure of compressibility, denoted as r, that keeps run count in Burrows-Wheeler Transforms in repeated texts such that substrings can be simply enumerated and positioned. This algorithm allows substring extraction to be performed in optimal time under space restrictions, hence making real-time data analysis possible. The uses of such an efficient substring extraction algorithm are enormous, especially for areas dealing with massive strings such as genomic databases, where quick access to specific subsequences may bring about research and usage breakthroughs (Gagie et al., 2019).

7.4.3. String Comparison

String comparison is a fundamental computer science operation, particularly handy when working with arrays and strings. The efficiency of string comparison algorithms impacts vastly different applications from search engines to data processing systems. Traditional string comparison is usually done character for character, which can lead to performance that is variable in terms of the lengths of the strings being compared. By utilizing more sophisticated methods that utilize string-handling optimized data structures such as suffix trees, the comparison process can be significantly improved. The data structures allow search and comparison operations to be conducted in logarithmic time, thereby ensuring maximum efficiency on a whole. In contrast to conventional solutions, linear time complexity can be unavoidable. Yet, with advances in dynamic data structures come hopeful solutions that are more adept at handling keys of unbounded length than ever, enhancing the imperative of efficiency in optimized string comparison methods within the realm of data management and retrieval (Amir et al., 2013). In real-world usage, the significance of efficient string comparison goes beyond simplistic performance factors; it has a direct bearing on user experience and resource consumption.

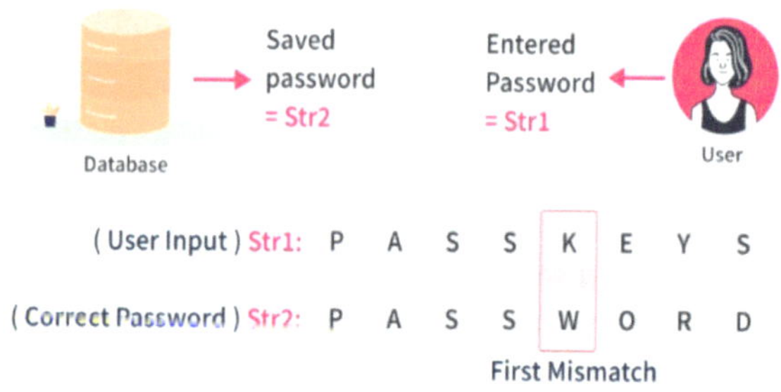

Figure 7.11. *String comparison.*

Source: https://external-content.duckduckgo.com/iu/?u=https%3A%2F%2Fscaler.com%2Ftopics%2Fimages%2Fcompare-two-strings-in-c.webp&f=1&nofb=1&ipt=9f9882461eb402a0816e5621f08235d39695d23d58f51a4e8d29dbbb819c7db5.

As data grew exponentially, systems that entail vast string operations need to be capable of sustaining fast and correct comparisons to satisfy users. The most prominent among such techniques is the transformation of elementary data structures to more advanced ones that support constant-time atomic comparison of keys. Such transformations turn out to be vital in scenarios where string data are persistently being updated, such as in databases or real-time processing environments. As illustrated in high-level algorithms, such transformations conclude with worst-case time complexities much superior to the traditional strategy. This shift towards more sophisticated data manipulation methods mirrors the ongoing advancement in string comparison algorithms that are essential in addressing modern scalability challenges (Amir et al., 2013). Moreover, the range of applications of string comparison algorithms is not limited to discrete data structures. Their usage can be applied in a range of areas including information retrieval, compiler optimizations, and natural language processing. For instance, in natural language processing, the comparison of strings in an efficient manner enables linguistic forms and patterns to be studied, assisting in tasks such as machine translation and automatic summarization. The brutal reality of static versus dynamic solutions to string comparison is evidenced in their efficiency; whereas static algorithms are good enough for small datasets, dynamic solutions become essential with growing data, particularly with approaches like those described in working with complex data interactions. As the technology continues to advance, such innovative methods will definitely make string comparisons more efficient up to a point of defining the future of data-intensive applications (Figure 7.11).

7.5. COMMON OPERATIONS ON ARRAYS

Arrays are fundamental data structures in computational programming, holding elements in efficient organization and enabling quick access to sets of elements. Basic operations on arrays include insertion, deletion, search, and sorting. All operations have a time complexity, which influences the efficiency of algorithm performance to a large extent. For instance, insertion and deletion at the end of an array can be performed in constant time, O(1), whereas operations that involve repositioning the elements, such as at the beginning or in the middle, could be in the order of O(n) time. Understanding the nuances of such complexities allows programmers to create better algorithms, particularly for programs dealing with vast amounts of data, for example, genomic analysis, where efficient data manipulation becomes critical for result interpretation and analysis. Sorting algorithms are also part of basic array operations, bringing meaning to accessing and organizing data. Among common algorithms deployed are Quick Sort, Merge Sort, and Bubble Sort, differing in their efficiency and suitability within the context. For example, Merge Sort's time complexity is O(n log n), and thus is most suitable for big data sets which are common to applications within bioinformatics. With the size of genomic data sets as large as debated within current studies, the need for effective sorting algorithms cannot be overstated. As genomics data generators are becoming increasingly complex, implementing advanced sorting algorithms into array operations is all the more relevant so that data can be processed efficiently, thereby enhancing both research outcomes as well as computational techniques (Dawyndt et al., 2012; Awan et al., 2020). Array searching takes myriad forms, linear and binary search being the most general approaches. Linear search, while simple and usable with any array structure, has a time complexity of O(n) and so is less suitable for large data. Binary search, which requires that the array is sorted, possesses a much improved O(log n) complexity, it's worth where efficiency counts. This is particularly relevant in genomic data analysis, where identification of genetic variants and patterns can be useful in gaining an understanding of biological processes. As real-time processing of data becomes increasingly vital, an understanding of such common operations on arrays becomes important not just for the performance of the algorithm but also for driving innovations in fields requiring rapid and fault-free data analysis (Awan et al., 2020; Dawyndt et al., 2012) (Figure 7.12).

Figure 7.12. *Common operations on arrays.*

Source: https://image4.slideserve.com/8300667/basic-array-operations-1-l.jpg.

7.5.1. Traversal

Traversal in arrays and strings is an elementary operation that enables the manipulation and access of data in such linear data structures. Whether it is with the simple one-dimensional array or with the more complex string data structure, traversal is a must for data searching, data modification, or data computation. Traversal in arrays has a tendency to employ iterative methods, taking advantage of loop constructs to access each element in sequential order. This method, while easy to follow, becomes resource-consuming with large data sets, highlighting the need for cost-effective methodologies. Greater insight into traversal practice not only equips one to be a better programmer but also supports the formulation of more complex algorithms, especially in the general framework of computational processes that seek to process and manipulate strings. In stringland, traversal is of sophisticated nature because of the complexity of these character strings. Operations normally done on strings, such as substring search, concatenation, and reversal, are reliant on traversal algorithms. Advance algorithms, such as the Aho-Corasick automaton, demonstrate the efficacy of traversal in string matching problems. This classical solution organizes the search process so that multiple patterns can be identified within a single scan of the input text, optimizing both time and space complexities. These intelligent traversal mechanisms underscore the critical role of data structures to enhance performance to a significant degree in matching problems such that effective search operations are facilitated with large volumes of data, as presented in recent research on index structures and their use in bioinformatics that emphasizes the emerging trends in the field (Dawyndt et al., 2012). Besides, traversal impacts go beyond the mere data retrieval; they belong to algorithm performance enhancement and resource efficiency. Specifically, as data topography increases in complexity, new traversal methods emerge to combat challenges presented by huge data sets. Analysis of current mechanisms reveals that novel algorithms are re-engineered to exploit the inherent properties of strings and arrays and sidestep confines in memory and CPU time. For instance, Aho-Corasick automaton construction optimizations mirror stunning space complexity improvements under optimal operation times (Aho et al., 2010). This optimization highlights the central synergy between traversal techniques and algorithmic efficiencies, placing traversal firmly on the map of technical skills far beyond the status of a simple building block of efficient data manipulation in modern-day computational paradigms.

7.5.2. Insertion and Deletion

Insert and delete operations are fundamental operations with respect to strings and arrays that heavily influence both performance and efficiency. With regard to arrays, insertion typically requires the rearrangement of elements to accommodate a new value and comes with a time complexity in the order of O(n) in its worst case. This limitation is particularly high in static arrays, where fixed sizes prohibit dynamic updates. Conversely, deletion also needs to relocate elements, making the process more complicated and subject to greater computational overhead. Dynamic arrays or linked lists are more accommodating, though they may alleviate the challenges of insertion and deletion, but introduce some complexities of their own, particularly in memory management and access time. Optimizing the insertion and deletion operations is critical, most importantly in applications where there is a need for high-performance, and therefore understanding how insertion and deletion work is crucial for computer scientists and developers. In data structures, enhancing the insertion and deletion process can be optimized by advanced techniques. For instance, linked lists prevent shifting of overlapping elements by allowing nodes to be added or removed irrespective of their position in the array. Not only is the time complexity for operations lowered to O(1) for lists but also memory allocation algorithms are optimized. Besides, associative data structures such as hash tables utilize linked lists in their implementation for handling collisions and thus combine fast lookup with efficient manipulation of data. Development of sophisticated structures, such as the frequent multi-map highlighted in Steindorfer et al. (2016), suggests further development in data management techniques. Such innovations illustrate that improved techniques can enhance not just insertion, but also deletion, thereby achieving superior performance in managing complex data relationships. The significance of insertion and deletion extends beyond theoretical application; it has practical relevance in different programming scenarios. Their effective handling renders them useful in actual practical applications of data processing, such as graph structure or XML data handling. Methods for optimization of dynamic data structures, as outlined in Amir et al. (2013), not only optimize insertion and deletion but also extend their applicability to keys of unlimited size, for example, strings. Understanding these operations aids programmers in selecting appropriate data structures that will enhance program performance and efficiently manage memory usage. As programs become more complex, the skill in insertion and deletion operations will remain a pillar of effective programming and systems design, supporting the ongoing need for novel algorithmic methods within the field.

7.5.3. Searching Algorithms

Searching algorithms are the backbone of data manipulation and retrieval of data that is stored in arrays and strings. The algorithms carry out the important task of locating individual elements or substrings efficiently, considering the vast volume of data that may be involved in today's applications. Linear search and binary search are the two most common searching algorithms. While linear search tests each element individually, making it easy but inefficient with large datasets, binary search decreases the process greatly by splitting the search space in half for each cycle. This reduction in potential comparisons makes binary search a highly viable option when searching within ordered arrays since it creates logarithmic time complexity, thereby drastically decreasing processing time when searching within large datasets. Notably, the new application of high-throughput sequencing to bioinformatics emphasizes the importance of specialized search algorithms in handling massive strings of genetic data. As the sequencing technologies continue to generate ever bigger sets of data, effective solutions to hard string problems come into prominence. Merging index structures would enhance the capabilities of standard search algorithms, offering a platform whereby rapid search of big arrays of string data becomes possible. The properties, advantages, and limitations of various index structures should be understood by bioinformaticians because controlling computational resources in research environments requires such an understanding in order to navigate the intricacy of genomic sequences efficiently. Over the last decade, there has been a revolution in discovering index structures with different memory-time trade-offs that are a basic requirement to control computational resources in research environments (Dawyndt et al., 2012). In contemporary times, new approaches such as adaptive sampling configuration interaction (ASCI) algorithms have emerged, again revealing the intersection of search algorithms with effective computation in fields of science. They apply fast sorting algorithms to enable more effective searching involved in quantum Hamiltonians, revealing an expanded application of searching principles in more sophisticated data beyond simple retrieval. The application of algorithms such as dynamic bit masking and quick diagonal matrix elements is a demonstration of how simple searching techniques can be adapted to solve advanced computational issues. With elaboration on established algorithms, new models offer result that is efficient and scalable, thus the implementation of searching algorithms in complicated problem-solving scenarios across different disciplines (Freeman et al., 2019) (Figure 7.13).

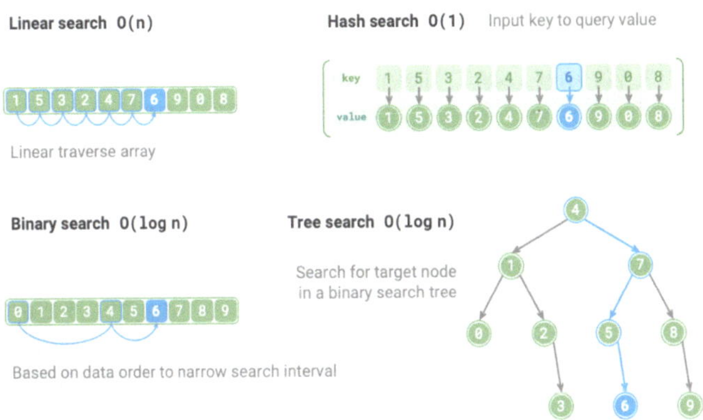

Figure 7.13. *Searching algorithms.*

Source: https://www.hello-algo.com/en/chapter_searching/searching_algorithm_revisited.assets/searching_algorithms.png.

7.6. APPLICATIONS OF ARRAYS AND STRINGS

The applications of arrays and strings are manifold and are at the core of most areas of computer science, particularly to computations and data processing. Arrays are the foundation for data structures, allowing for compact storage and retrieval of elements due to the fact that they are of fixed length and indexed. These factors allow for efficient searching, sorting, and manipulation of large datasets. In genomic studies, for instance, rapidly growing volumes of genomic data necessitate robust computational platforms that can handle complex queries and computations on arrays, including clustering and alignment. Such application validates the use of arrays in the processing of structured information so that scientists can derive meaningful conclusions from large volumes of data, ultimately leading to innovation in personalized medicine and genetic studies (Awan et al., 2020). Strings, on the other hand, have significant applications in text processing, which enables them to deal with character data for any kind of application, from natural language processing (NLP) to bioinformatics. The naturally flexible nature of strings has the potential to express a wealth of information ranging from user input to biological sequences. One of the very interesting application domains is the finding of palindromic substrings from a string, which is very important in genetic applications for matching patterns in DNA. More current advancements propose successful data structures for simple access to palindromic items that employ the methods of suffix tries and trees to provide strong solutions for an assortment of palindrome issues (Rubinchik et al., 2015). Consequently, the intricacy of string manipulation has far-reaching consequences in various areas, from computational linguistics to molecular biology. Second, the interplay between strings and arrays significantly enhances data analysis methodologies in computational science. As scientists tackle increasingly complicated problems, particularly in high-performance computing, awareness and tuning of the relational behaviors between these data structures are critical. For example, array-based algorithms for pre-processing strings effectively can lead to efficient pattern searching and string matching techniques. Similar to genomic data analysis, non-contiguous communication patterns and asynchronous data updates also complicate dealing with these structures by requiring expert programming support and software libraries in order to be computationally efficient. The combination of arrays and strings makes a versatile toolset that allows researchers to streamline their processing capabilities, paving the way for innovative solutions in both science and applied sectors (Awan et al., 2020).

7.6.1. Data Storage and Management

Given the increasing strength of information generated in storage and management of data, there is a need for sophisticated means to process and retrieve effectively. This is especially so in fields such as bioinformatics, where huge volumes of sequencing data are produced in real time. Efficient resolution of challenging string problems is essential for the management of data flow, and many bioinformatics tools exploit advanced data structures, which are commonly referred to as index structures. These data structures enhance the efficiency and speed of accessing and modifying data, which has been commonly sought after in the bioinformatics community. However, while the utility of index structures has already been acknowledged, the fineness of their design and operations is still less investigated. Knowledge of these characteristics, interdependencies, and workaday constraints is crucial for furthering data management techniques in this area, which is dependent on quick analysis of large datasets (Dawyndt et al., 2012). The progress of variant index structures over the past decade also underlines the development of data storage techniques specific to every dataset to overcome challenges posed by a particular dataset. The trade-offs between the use of memory and time efficiency in such structures are particularly important.

Figure 7.14. *Data storage and management.*

Source: https://www.dqglobal.com/wp-content/uploads/2017/07/Data-Management-1100x917.jpg.

These developments are done in preparation for the constantly increasing demand for faster retrieval times and enhanced query performance, a necessity in data spaces with high data growth rates. As these domain-specific structures become widespread, researchers and practitioners must thoroughly evaluate their use in real-world applications. Selecting the correct index structure can significantly influence the performance of bioinformatics applications, so keeping oneself abreast of the latest developments in such a scenario is crucial. Exploring these complex memory-time trade-offs eventually takes useful insights towards the development of data storage and management methods in various other situations (Dawyndt et al., 2012). In the realm of other technology, data storage will also be in keeping with being compatible with older systems, such as with software systems such as the Ground Support Software System (GSSS). Comparison of compatibility of such systems with different hardware platforms, say the

VAX 11/780 and ModComp IV/35, provides useful information about effective data management strategies. The compatibility testing not only confirms the smooth integration of data between platforms but also informs the developers about potential limitations and enhancements that are possible for greater efficiency and interoperability. As data storage systems become more integrated and dependent on one another, such knowledge of compatibility problems is vital. It serves as a reminder that data management is not just about storage space but also about ensuring data remains accessible and usable in evolving technological environments (Figure 7.14).

7.6.2. Algorithm Implementation

Efficient use of algorithms plays a crucial role in manipulating and managing arrays and strings given the complexity and amount of data handled in contemporary computing. Basic operations such as searching, sorting, and indexing must be done using high-performance algorithms. Some algorithmic strategies, such as divide-and-conquer or dynamic programming, tend to optimize the efficiency of these operations to the point where they result in huge time and resource savings. For instance, insertion of cutting-edge data structures, such as hash tables, can give immediate access and string and array data updates. A realization of the strengths and weaknesses of these structures allows developers to introduce the most suitable algorithms optimized for specific tasks, significantly improving data processing application performance in general. In bioinformatics, implementation of algorithms is particularly beneficial due to the enormous volumes of sequence data generated by advances in sequencing technology. The majority of bioinformatics tools rely on good solutions to hard string problems, where the algorithms play the starring role in managing large sets of data. Index structures, which are designed to facilitate efficient searching and data retrieval from strings, are a major area of research. The evolution of such structures in the last decade has seen many variants with differing memory-time trade-offs that enable researchers to sift through vast genomic data effectively. As mentioned, it is important to have a good understanding of the available index structures and their characteristics in coming up with effective bioinformatics applications that can execute complex string manipulations in an efficient manner (Dawyndt et al., 2012). In addition, algorithm use makes its way into high-level computational fields such as quantum chemistry, providing indications of the interdisciplinary origins of algorithms in computing complex datasets. The improvement of adaptive sampling configuration interaction (ASCI) algorithms provides information on how algorithm development promotes efficiency in computing quantum Hamiltonians, making processing of complicated datasets such as arrays of quantum states simple. By employing fast sorting algorithms—like the ones used in array and string searching and indexing—scientists can realize efficient and scalable computational models. The feasibility of employing such algorithms efficiently makes simulations of systems with complex behavior feasible, opening new avenues to massive scientific advancement for all sciences. Consequently, the continued advancement and application of algorithms across disciplines highlight their basis in managing both arrays and strings effectively in practical applications (Freeman et al., 2019).

7.6.3. Examples from Software Development in Real Life

In programming, strings and arrays are basic data structures that enable effective manipulation of data on different applications. An exemplary instance that best illustrates this feature is automatic translation of C code into Eiffel using the C2Eif tool, which utilizes existing codebases to rejuvenate outdated systems. The conversion utilizes arrays and strings in translation, which allows for data integrity in transitioning from an older style of programming to a more secure object-oriented system. With its translation of advanced C programs such as vim and libgsl, C2Eif demonstrates the flexibility and usability of arrays and strings in ensuring the seamless functioning of software when it is upgraded. These modifications not only enhance the readability and safety of code but also increase developers' efficiency in general, as suggested by the effective handling of large bodies of code in real life (Furia et al., 2013). Moreover, real-world applications of software frequently suggest the use of arrays and strings when it comes to defending against threats. For instance, manipulating sensitive information involves using string operations and array manipulations to ensure integrity, confidentiality, availability, and accountability. Software systems must be well crafted by developers to ensure they are not accessed without authorization but, at the same time, they allow authorized users to toy around with their information. As attackers favor threats and carry out attacks using well-crafted inputs, string validation and bounds checking arrays become useful when developing secure programs. This aspect of security is especially critical in preventing denial of service attacks, which pose a threat to system availability. With proper management of arrays and strings, software developers can make the software more resilient against such attacks, and thus more robust and reliable (Bardas, 2025).

Lastly, the cooperation among arrays, strings, and algorithm optimization in software development points towards the practical relevance of these data structures. For example, array-based sort algorithms are the foundation of efficient performance optimization of various applications from database management to real-time data processing. String manipulation algorithms, such as in the case of text parsing or search, are based on arrays to enable quick access to sequences of characters and substrings. Improvement of these algorithms is seen to have significant impact on system performance, culminating in the direct effect of appropriately designed arrays and strings on the user experience. With developers incessantly innovating and pushing these data structures to new heights, they will necessarily address the evolving challenges in software development, ensuring the continued relevance of arrays and strings in creating efficient, user-centric applications, culminating in shaping the future of technology (Figure 7.15).

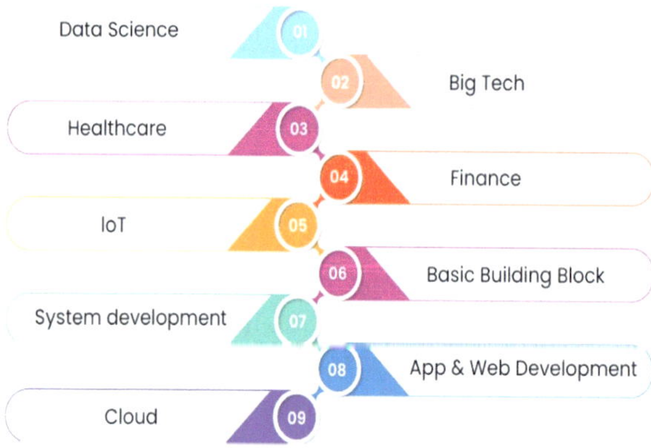

Figure 7.15. *Real-world examples in software development.*

Source: https://media.geeksforgeeks.org/wp-content/uploads/20240403164719/Real-world-applications-of-SDLC-(Software-Development-Life-Cycle).webp.

SUMMARY

In concluding the examination of arrays and strings, it is important to recognize their fundamental purposes in computational theory and application. Arrays are the building blocks for data structures that enable storing and accessing data in an orderly manner. Their efficiency in retrieving and modifying components makes for effective algorithms and reduces complexity of computation. On the other hand, strings, since they are arrays of characters, support the representation of text and symbols in coding. Such a fundamental relationship points out how these two structures support each other to create a solid framework for developing effective applications that demand sophisticated data management. With advancing technology, knowledge of these building blocks becomes more important for both new and experienced programmers. Besides, the effects of using arrays and strings extend beyond the mere representation of data; they also affect software organization and system performance. Arrays may be utilized to save memory space, while string handling has an array of functions that are required in modern programming models. For instance, the utilization of effective string operations enhances security through data integrity and confidentiality, which is essential in cases necessitating high-level security measures (Bardas, 2025). Next-generation methods, including functional and reactive programming, are utilized by the developers, yet effective handling of arrays and strings remains a necessity. These concepts not only constitute the foundation of application performance but also guide software construction paradigms in an ever-evolving technological landscape. Ultimately, the symbiotic relationship between strings and arrays lies at the heart of computer science theoretical and practical usage. Mastering these constructs is how programmers gain necessary tools for creating efficient and secure software programs. Future improvements in programming languages and methods can still further improve the utilization of arrays and strings, potentially to provide more performance and scalability for real-time systems (Li et al., 2016). With the continued development of the subject, research and education on these fundamental data structures will keep them useful and applicable in addressing emerging problems in computational theory and computer program construction. In short, a good grasp of arrays and strings enables both the development of robust systems and the foundation of new programming methods.

In array and string studies, one should emphasize their natural significance in data manipulation and programming. The two data structures perform distinct but complementary roles that facilitate efficient data organization and access. Arrays offer a fixed-size ordered collection of elements, which can be accessed by using indexed positions, making them ideal for operations with contiguous memory allocation. On the other hand, strings, typically implemented as character arrays, encapsulate collections of string data. The programmer's knowledge of how they operate allows him or her to benefit from their strengths, achieving a balance between efficiency and memory when designing algorithms. Moreover, the dynamic uses of arrays and strings range from utilization in straightforward data processing to advanced systems like multi-maps, illustrating their adaptability in computer contexts. The presence of advanced data structures, such as immutable multi-maps, also calls for the importance of strings and arrays in modern programming paradigms. Such multi-maps, to support many-to-many relationships, depend upon efficient array and string implementations to handle huge datasets. Specifically, the development of Hash-Array Mapped Tries (HAMT) is a critical development in this context. The Heterogeneous Hash-Array Mapped Trie (HHAMT) framework reduces storage overhead of type-heterogeneous keys and values while significantly reducing overhead. Specifically, the framework can represent multi-maps compactly by not wasting space for null value sets as well as inline singleton values. These improvements, as highlighted in the study, illustrate the record-breaking progress in data structure efficiency that attracts those dealing with large applications (Steindorfer et al., 2016). In addition, the issue of complicated data structures highlights the necessity of robust programming languages to manage such system requirements. The development of geometry programming languages to assist aerodynamicists is a classic example of the relationship between domain-specific tools and advanced data structuring. Programming languages must learn to deal with the complexities in computational fluid dynamics, thus allowing efficient construction and manipulation of geometrical information. This intersection of problem-solving capacity and data structure optimality underscores the core significance of arrays and strings across all areas of study, ranging from engineering and software design. As indicated by the Boeing Aero Grid and Paneling System, deliberate selection of programming tools can be a determinative influence on project success, promoting innovation and maximality in data-handling processes (Gentry et al., 2025).

REFERENCES

1. Aho, A. V., Munro, J. I., Sadakane, K., Elias, P., Fano, R. M., Dori, S., & Hon, W. K. (2010). Succinct dictionary matching with no slowdown. http://arxiv.org/abs/1001.2860 (accessed on 9th September 2025).
2. Alatabbi, A., Rahman, M. S., & Smyth, W. F. (2014). Inferring an indeterminate string from a prefix graph. https://core.ac.uk/download/77131001.pdf (accessed on 9th September 2025).
3. Amir, A., Franceschini, G., Grossi, R., et al. (2013). Managing unbounded-length keys in comparison-driven data structures with applications to on-line indexing. http://arxiv.org/abs/1306.0406 (accessed on 9th September 2025).
4. Andersson, A. H., Wright, D., Gusfield, D., Harel, D., Knuth, D. E., Ukkonen, E., et al. (2011). Faster approximate string matching for short patterns. http://arxiv.org/abs/0811.3490 (accessed on 9th September 2025).
5. Ashcroft, E. A., Paquet, J., Plaice, J., Mokhov, S. A., et al. (2011). Reasoning about a simulated printer case investigation with Forensic Lucid. https://core.ac.uk/download/211514110.pdf (accessed on 9th September 2025).
6. Athale, R. A., & Psaltis, D. (1986). High accuracy computation with linear analog optical systems: A critical study. https://core.ac.uk/download/4871743.pdf (accessed on 9th September 2025).
7. Awan, M., Azad, A., Brock, B., et al. (2020). The parallelism motifs of genomic data analysis. https://core.ac.uk/download/286729201.pdf (accessed on 9th September 2025).
8. Barbosa, H., Barrett, C., Brain, M., Kremer, G., Lachnitt, H., Mann, M., Mohamed, A., et al. (2022). cvc5: A versatile and industrial-strength SMT solver. *Lecture Notes in Computer Science*. https://doi.org/10.1007/978-3-030-99524-9_24 (accessed on 9th September 2025).
9. Bardas, A. G. (2025). *The Impact of Programming Languages on the Software's Security*. https://core.ac.uk/download/pdf/6662580.pdf (accessed on 9th September 2025).
10. Belazzougui, D., & Chegrane, I. (2014). Simple, compact and robust approximate string dictionary. http://arxiv.org/abs/1312.4678 (accessed on 9th September 2025).
11. Bharti, K., Cervera-Lierta, A., Kyaw, T. H., Haug, T., Alperin-Lea, S., Anand, A., Degroote, M., et al. (2022). Noisy intermediate-scale quantum algorithms. *Reviews of Modern Physics, 94*. https://doi.org/10.1103/revmodphys.94.015004 (accessed on 9th September 2025).

12. Dawyndt, P., De Baets, B., Fack, V., et al. (2012). Prospects and limitations of full-text index structures in genome analysis. https://core.ac.uk/download/55755713.pdf (accessed on 9th September 2025).
13. Doan Van, B., Huy, H. N., Quang, N. N., Phung, Q. N., Sanseverino, E. R., Romano, P., Tran Trong, T., et al. (2019). A hierarchical architecture for increasing efficiency of large photovoltaic plants under non-homogeneous solar irradiation. https://core.ac.uk/download/224993600.pdf (accessed on 9th September 2025).
14. Freeman, C. D., Hait, D., Head-Gordon, M., et al. (2019). Modern approaches to exact diagonalization and selected configuration interaction with the adaptive sampling CI method. https://core.ac.uk/download/323308715.pdf (accessed on 9th September 2025).
15. Fu, Y., Ong, K. W., & Papakonstantinou, Y. (2014). Declarative Ajax web applications through SQL++ on a unified application state. http://arxiv.org/abs/1308.0656 (accessed on 9th September 2025).
16. Furia, C. A., Meyer, B., Nordio, M., et al. (2013). C to O-O translation: Beyond the easy stuff. http://arxiv.org/abs/1206.5648 (accessed on 9th September 2025).
17. Gagie, T., Navarro, G., & Prezza, N. (2019). Fully-functional suffix trees and optimal text searching in BWT-runs bounded space. https://core.ac.uk/download/288645374.pdf (accessed on 9th September 2025).
18. Gentry, A. E. (2025). Requirements for a geometry programming language for CFD applications. https://core.ac.uk/download/pdf/42812596.pdf (accessed on 9th September 2025).
19. Hawblitzel, C., Dijkstra, E. W., Petrank, E., & Havelund, K. (2009). Automated verification of practical garbage collectors. http://arxiv.org/abs/1004.3808 (accessed on 9th September 2025).
20. Hill, C. (2020). *Learning Scientific Programming with Python*. https://doi.org/10.1017/9781108778039 (accessed on 9th September 2025).
21. Hirschberg, D. S., & Stauffer, L. M. (1991). Parallel data compression. https://core.ac.uk/download/287623249.pdf (accessed on 9th September 2025).
22. Hu, S. M., Hu, X. Q., Manocha, D., et al. (2020). TZC: Efficient inter-process communication for robotics middleware with partial serialization. http://arxiv.org/abs/1810.00556 (accessed on 9th September 2025).
23. Joy, M., & Yau, J. Y. K. (2004). Introducing Java: The case for fundamentals-first. https://core.ac.uk/download/1381479.pdf (accessed on 9th September 2025).

24. Kölling, M., & Rosenberg, J. (1996). Blue–A language for teaching object-oriented programming. https://core.ac.uk/download/63387.pdf (accessed on 9th September 2025).

25. Kowsari, K., Lanchantin, J., Qi, Y., et al. (2017). GaKCo: A fast gapped k-mer string kernel using counting. http://arxiv.org/abs/1704.07468 (accessed on 9th September 2025).

26. Li, M., McArdle, D. E., Murphy, J. C., et al. (2016). Adding real-time capabilities to a SML compiler. http://arxiv.org/abs/1601.03116 (accessed on 9th September 2025).

27. N/A. (2025). *Multimission Modular Spacecraft Ground Support Software System (MMS/GSSS) State-of-the-Art Computer Systems/Compatibility Study*. https://core.ac.uk/download/pdf/42855829.pdf (accessed on 9th September 2025).

28. N/A. (2025). *NASA Thesaurus Supplement: A Three-Part Cumulative Supplement to the 1982 Edition of the NASA Thesaurus (Supplement 2)*. https://core.ac.uk/download/pdf/42847159.pdf (accessed on 9th September 2025).

29. Navarro, G., & Prezza, N. (2018). Universal compressed text indexing. https://core.ac.uk/download/288645376.pdf (accessed on 9th September 2025).

30. Pibiri, G. E., & Venturini, R. (2018). Handling massive N-gram datasets efficiently. https://core.ac.uk/download/195746474.pdf (accessed on 9th September 2025).

31. Rubinchik, M., & Shur, A. M. (2015). EERTREE: An efficient data structure for processing palindromes in strings. http://arxiv.org/abs/1506.04862 (accessed on 9th September 2025).

32. Rueden, C., Schindelin, J., Hiner, M., DeZonia, B. E., Walter, A. E., Arena, E. T., & Eliceiri, K. W. (2017). ImageJ2: ImageJ for the next generation of scientific image data. *BMC Bioinformatics, 18*. https://doi.org/10.1186/s12859-017-1934-z (accessed on 9th September 2025).

33. Smith, J. (2012). The Jasper Framework: Towards a platform independent, formal treatment of web programming. http://arxiv.org/abs/1210.6112 (accessed on 9th September 2025).

34. Steindorfer, M. J., & Vinju, J. J. (2016). Fast and lean immutable multi-maps on the JVM based on heterogeneous hash-array mapped tries. https://core.ac.uk/download/301639457.pdf (accessed on 9th September 2025).

CHAPTER 8

SEARCHING AND SORTING TECHNIQUES

Contents

INTRODUCTION

The discipline of computer science is increasingly dominated by efficient searching and sorting algorithms, which are the foundations of data management, information retrieval, and algorithm design. These algorithms enable systems to process huge amounts of data, thus making them run more efficiently in a vast array of applications ranging from algorithmic trading to web searching. Understanding the principles that govern these algorithms needs an in-depth analysis of several various algorithms, their complexities, and the conditions in which they outperform. This finding is particularly relevant as data production increases exponentially, necessitating robust systems for organizing and finding information in an effective way. From the reading, there is a nimble structure for teaching nuanced subjects like sorting and searching, mirroring how subjects like machine learning can be intertwined to facilitate understanding and application (Coleman et al., 2005). Further, the development of sorting algorithms highlights the relationship between theoretical underpinnings and real-world applications.

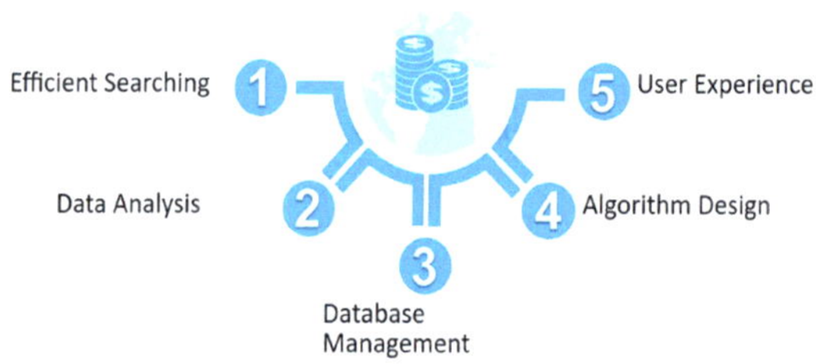

Figure 8.1. *Searching and sorting techniques.*

Source: *https://fastercapital.co/i/Sortinoratio--Exploring-the-Essence-of-Sorting-Techniques--Importance-of-Sorting-in-Computer-Science.webp.*

Advances in algorithms in recent times have resulted in quicker processes, usually building upon existing methodologies or creating new methods that utilize computational power efficiently. The evolution of paradigms on which algorithms are built, such as adaptive sampling configuration interaction, illustrates the capability of advanced computational method to enhance performance through focus on efficiency, illustrating a divide between theoretical application within academic forums and practical use in the world (Freeman et al., 2019). This dynamic supports increased investigation into the potential for constant refinement of searching and sorting functions in algorithmic design, highlighting the importance of these throughout disciplines. Finally, the requirement for searching and sorting techniques transcends mere efficiency. It reaches into deeper connotations such as data structure administration, resource distribution, and forecast processing capability in AI. With artificial intelligence technologies being everywhere, the use of far-reaching searching and sorting techniques becomes necessary in creating intelligent systems with learning and improving abilities over time. This intertwinement of searching methodologies and machine learning represents a revolutionary turning point in how we realize data analysis and decision-making operations. The union of innovative frameworks and efficient algorithms validates a pattern in more learning systems capable of facilitating intricate tasks in the majority of fields. This essay, therefore, will undertake a closer examination of specific searching and sorting algorithms and their respective impact on contemporary computational practices (Figure 8.1).

Definition of Searching and Sorting Techniques

Computer science has developed a large number of methods of searching and sorting information, simple operations which are vital to efficient information management and retrieval. Searching techniques are algorithms utilized to locate specific information within data structures, for instance, arrays or linked lists, with different approaches depending on the form of data and demands. For instance, linear search entails checking each element in turn, whereas more advanced approaches, including binary search, take advantage of ordered data to minimize time complexity by a substantial margin. These methods differ not only based on their running time but also according to their appropriateness to particular situations, emphasizing the need to grasp their operating principles and performance indicators. Sorting algorithms, on the other hand, refer to programs that place data in a specific order, ascending or descending. The performance of sorting algorithms is typically analyzed with regards to time complexity, memory, and stability, with a number of algorithms present, including quicksort, mergesort, and heapsort, each with different advantages and disadvantages. Choice of a sorting algorithm is a function of the size of the dataset, the nature of the data, and the needs of the application. To acquire more information on how sorting algorithms work, it is crucial to learn about their elementary principles with regard to their historical development and upcoming research trends, as this determines future use and optimizations in algorithmic design (Bhalchandra et al., 2009). Moreover, the interaction between search and sort techniques provides a rich interaction that can significantly enhance computation efficiency. For instance, sorted information makes search algorithms more efficient, as evidenced by the efficiency of binary search when applied against sorted data sets. The interaction of such techniques is behind numerous applications across database management systems to algorithmic problem-solving in competitive programming. Recent studies focus on optimizing both searching and sorting algorithms to further improve their performances because the development of one usually triggers the development of the other (Barbay et al., 2008) (Figure 8.2). The constant pursuit of efficiencies and complexities not only improves the fundamental concepts of searching and sorting but also lays the gates open to innovative algorithm constructs capable of addressing ever-growing data issues (Figure 8.2).

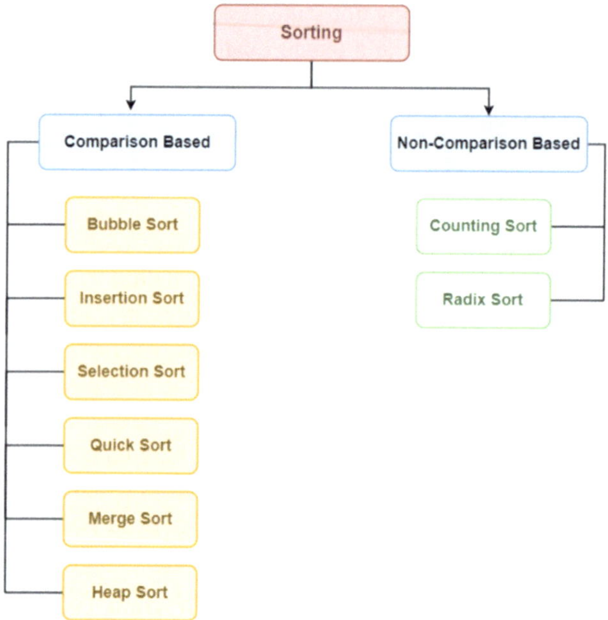

Figure 8.2. *Searching and sorting techniques.*

Source: *https://media.geeksforgeeks.org/wp-content/uploads/20220916131621/SortingTYPE.png.*

Importance in Computer Science and Data Management

The importance of efficient search and sort algorithms in computer science and data management cannot be overemphasized, especially in an era where gigantic amounts of data are generated daily. Effective algorithms not only make data retrieval easier but also accelerate the performance of databases and software programs. By using advanced sorting techniques, information is arranged in a manner such that browsing time is reduced to the minimum when dealing with huge data sets. For instance, traditional linear search methods become extremely impractical with the growth of data; hence, algorithms like binary search significantly enhance speed and efficiency. Finally, the effective use of search and sort algorithms is crucial for the creation of robust data management systems that can readily respond to requests from users in order to provide a smooth process in information retrieval operations. Further, incorporation of highly sophisticated search interfaces may transform the user interface of data management significantly. Complex question-holders may be unable to utilize simple keyword-based search mechanisms, which may act as a hindrance for them to fetch related information. Faceted browsing and result clustering, enhanced search capabilities, significantly improve the overall effectiveness of information seeking. These interfaces offer scalable solutions that adapt with several users' requirements, demonstrating user-centric design's significance in search tool development. Analysis of these user interfaces also becomes challenging due to the large number of variables involved, for which strict frameworks are vital to their effectiveness evaluation. Utilizing such frameworks can ultimately lead to improved quality search interfaces that are more effective and intuitive for supporting diverse search methods (Schraefel et al., 2009). In computer science, knowledge of the value of importance in data retrieval operations can ultimately lead to innovations in information searching and indexing. For large sets of data, limiting search scopes to include only the documents of highest relevance can greatly increase performance with still-intact retrieval precision. Systems can limit the processing load of handling large sets of data by classifying and prioritizing documents based on importance. This not only maintains intact the fundamental characteristics of effective retrieval but also greatly enhances the scalability of data management systems as a whole. Notably, the studies for large document collections show how meticulous priorization and sorting methodologies can yield enormous efficiency gains. The innovations illustrate an uninterrupted innovation in data handling in accordance with the need for constant innovations in search and sorting techniques owing to a rising level of complexity in information systems (Alan et al., 2012).

8.1. FUNDAMENTALS OF SEARCHING

The secret to effective searching lies in the understanding of the basic principles that govern how information is stored and retrieved. One must learn about what types of databases and search engines exist before proceeding with a search, which can make or break a search. For instance, subject-specific databases may provide more specialized information in specific fields of study, such as scientific or historical studies, while general search engines may provide more general information. Search effectiveness is enhanced by applying Boolean operators, such as AND, OR, and NOT, which allow users to limit their searches, thereby creating results most likely to satisfy their research needs. Thus, a good grasp of these patterns of thinking and practices dictates effective search strategies that maximize the relevance of one's results and minimize irrelevant distractions. Moreover, the awareness of the priority of keyword selection cannot be overemphasized when it comes to searching. Keyword selection particularly dictates the amount and quality of search results, as a particular term is often used in a particular setting and subject. Researchers need to undergo a reflective exercise of mind-mapping and examining different keywords to come up with their effects on search results. The process tends to take an iterative approach, whereby adjustments are made based on the preliminary search results to target the most applicable information. In addition, considering synonyms, variations, and technical terms in the target domain can also widen the search web even further, capturing subtle concepts that would otherwise pass unnoticed. All these methods are a part of learning basic concepts of search, ultimately resulting in more informed and comprehensive research results. Lastly, the organization of search results aids immensely in processing and retrieving beneficial information. Upon conducting searches, users are presented with an enormous number of results that require methodical sorting and analysis. The application of sorting methods in terms of relevance, date, or credibility of the source can simplify the process so that researchers may be able to sift through important information effectively. Also, visual aids like mind maps or spreadsheets can help identify findings, establish relationships between ideas, and enable better understanding. The application of network visualization in peer-to-peer learning research also better indicates how structuring information can enhance searching and understanding of complex content (Alevizou et al., 2010). Constantly being detailed and systematic in seeking not only advances one's own scholarship but also fosters an informed and collaborative scholarly community, which is indicative of well-coordinated efforts outlined in education paradigms (Schatz et al., 2012).

8.1.1. Definition of Searching in Computer Science

The concept of searching in computer science fundamentally refers to the process of locating specific data within a collection of information. This process serves as a foundational element in various computational applications, where efficient data retrieval is paramount. Searching techniques are essential in databases, file systems, and data structures such as arrays and linked lists. The efficiency of these techniques can greatly affect overall performance, particularly in large datasets, where quick access to information is necessary for effective data manipulation and analysis. As the volume of digital information grows, understanding searching techniques becomes critical for computer scientists and developers who design algorithms optimized for speed and accuracy in data retrieval tasks. Key to the understanding of searching is the distinction between structured and unstructured search methods. Structured searches operate within well-defined data formats, leveraging index-based systems such as binary search or hash tables. These methods provide considerable time efficiencies, enabling quicker access to data than linear search approaches, particularly in sorted datasets. In contrast, unstructured searches must sift through data without predefined organization, often utilizing heuristic or algorithmic approaches to identify relevant information. Such methods are crucial for handling varied data types, from social media posts to unindexed databases, demonstrating the breadth of searching applications in contemporary computing contexts. Each approach has its own advantages, indicating that the choice of searching algorithm significantly influences performance outcomes. Recent advancements in algorithmic techniques, particularly in relation to the 3SUM problem, extend the boundary of searching methodologies. The 3SUM problem, which inquires whether three numbers in a given set sum to zero, illustrates the complexity and real-world application of searching algorithms. Notably, the conjectured complexity surrounding this problem has stimulated the exploration of decision tree complexities and their implications for broader searching tasks. Efforts to refine the time complexity of this problem have yielded enhancements in searching efficiency, showcasing the relevance of understanding searching at an algorithmic level. As researchers continue to investigate these complexities, the interplay between searching and sorting techniques remains central to the evolution of computer science, shaping how data is accessed and utilized across numerous disciplines (Barbay et al., 2008; Gold et al., 2017) (Figure 8.3).

Figure 8.3. *Searching in computer science.*

Source: https://static.vecteezy.com/system/resources/previews/002/189/427/large_2x/a-hand-using-a-laptop-computer-searching-for-information-in-the-internet-with-a-search-box-icon-free-photo.jpg.

8.1.2. Types of Data Structures Used for Searching

An important element of search algorithms is the data structures employed in storing and querying information efficiently. The most popular structure employed is the binary search tree (BST), a tree-based structure that allows efficient insertion, deletion, and searching of data. Each node in a BST contains one key and pointers to its left child and right child such that all keys in the left subtree are less than the key of the parent node, and all keys in the right subtree are greater. This is what provides BSTs with logarithmic time complexity for search in average case, and hence it becomes an appropriate choice for dynamic data sets.

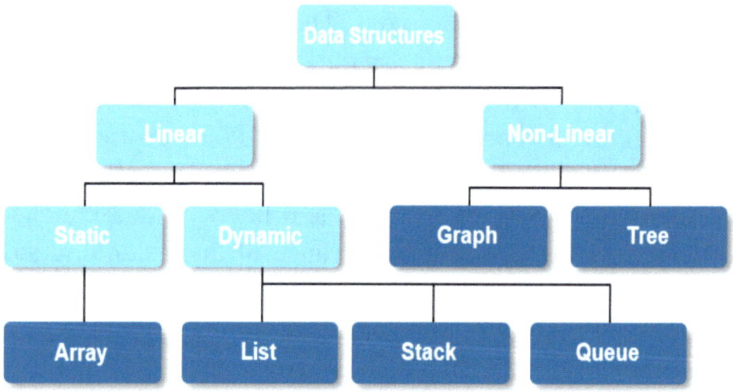

Figure 8.4. *Types of data structures used for searching.*

Source: https://phoenixnap.com/kb/wp-content/uploads/2022/10/data-structures-types-classification.png.

But the performance is compromised when data is unbalanced, leading to degenerate cases in which the tree comes close to being a linked list; hence, balancing techniques and self-balancing trees like AVL and Red-Black trees are typically employed to maintain performance optimal. Another critical data structure employed for search is the hash table, yielding average-case constant time complexity for lookup. Hash tables depend on a hash function to map keys onto index values, allowing for almost immediate access to related values. This makes them very useful in applications where there is a requirement for continuous lookups, such as databases and memory cache systems. However, they have their own disadvantage, which is mostly the handling of collision resolution when different keys land in the same index. Chaining and open addressing are some techniques employed to handle these issues. When searching for individual entries, both well-designed hash function and load factor play critical roles in ensuring efficiency—if too many collisions occur, hash table performance diminishes, rendering value to well-designed hash table implementations. Search trees with arrangement such as B-trees and tries present new ways for organization of data in query-efficient scenarios. B-trees are particularly suitable for use in large block read and write systems, and hence they find a wide variety of applications in file and database systems. B-trees store sorted data and support search, sequential access, insertion, and deletion in logarithmic time. Tries, however, exhibit a different kind of searching by storing strings in such a structure that it facilitates prefix querying. By storing common prefixes once in a place, tries efficiently utilize space where there are plenty of overlapping string keys in datasets. The effectiveness of such data structures, especially in applications such as autocomplete systems and routing IP addresses, shows the versatility of search data structures. The use of approaches based on data structures like (Amir et al., 2013) and (Cavoretto et al., 2014) may enhance searching efficiencies in various areas (Figure 8.4).

8.1.3. Importance of Efficiency in Searching Algorithms

In computer science, the efficiency of search algorithms plays a central role in determining the performance result for various applications. Efficient search algorithms permit quicker retrieval of data, which is directly responsible for the efficacy of software systems. With the volume of information still growing in the digital age, the necessity of algorithms with a capacity to quickly and efficiently locate related information can hardly be overstated. Methods such as binary search and hash tables provide frameworks for optimizing search efficiency and, therefore, minimizing resources such as time and computational resources. Greater focus on scalability in applications corresponds directly to the performance of these algorithms, where efficient methods of searching can significantly affect user experience and system ability. The marriage of new algorithms, including those derived from new breakthroughs in configuration interaction methods, illustrates the importance of efficiency for search algorithms. The adaptive sampling configuration interaction (ASCI) algorithm, for instance, leverages efficient selected CI/exact diagonalization algorithms powered by fast sorting algorithms. Employing fast sorting algorithms, researchers have been able to determine new ASCI search procedures that lead to more efficient computation in many applications. This paradigm shift demonstrates not only that efficiency not only makes the search process smoother but also offers means for solving complex problems in a more practical form, as the successful simulation directly leading to their use in quantum Hamiltonians clearly indicates. These enhancements justify the hypothesis that algorithm choice and construction can significantly contribute to research efficiency. In addition, efficiency's use is no longer restricted to traditional computing to new schemes, as seen in recent data-driven fuzzy modeling paradigms. The paradigms endeavor to balance model interpretability and accuracy, resulting in prediction models that are improved in robustness with very few data points. The paradigms employed, such as Pareto-optimal prediction models, demonstrate how effective searching schemes can enhance knowledge in intricate systems, such as FSW behaviors in aluminum alloys. The efficiency gained by these systems indicates that efficient searching techniques are not only essential to data retrieval but also serve as a supporting aspect of decision-making processes in high-end scientific applications. As the technology environment keeps evolving, it is apparent that the quest for efficiency within search algorithms will be a basis for creating beneficial and innovative solutions in the future (Figure 8.5).

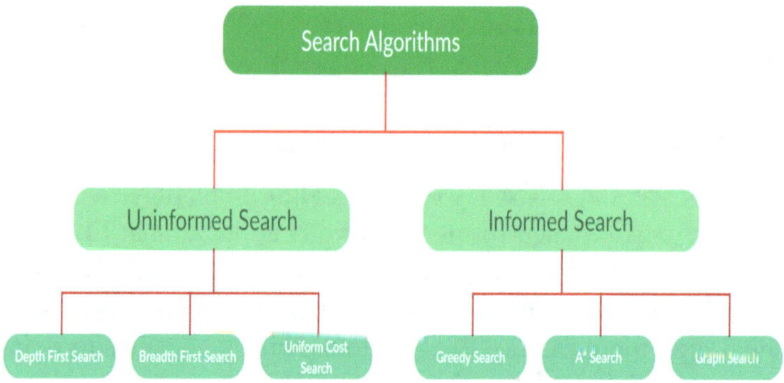

Figure 8.5. *Importance of efficiency in searching algorithms.*

Source: https://media.geeksforgeeks.org/wp-content/uploads/AI-algos-1-e1547043543151.png.

8.2. LINEAR SEARCH TECHNIQUE

Linear Search Technique is a fundamental algorithm in computer science to locate a specific element in an array or list. It is based on the checking of one element after the other from the starting element to the last element until the desired item is found or the whole set is searched. Though its application is easy to comprehend and use, linear search is inefficient when dealing with large datasets due to its time complexity of O(n). That means the algorithm may have to go through every element in the worst-case scenario, thereby leading to huge performance bottlenecks in applications where rapid access to data is required. Therefore, it is important to understand its working principles and limitations in determining when this technique is most appropriate for use. The inefficiency in linear search is most evident when compared to sophisticated searching techniques such as binary search, the uses of which can appreciably reduce search time for ordered data. This is not to detract from the utility of linear search in certain applications. For instance, when the dataset is either unsorted or relatively small, linear search remains a viable and, indeed, convenient choice. Additionally, linear search can also process no preprocessing of data at all, hence being particularly suited to applications dynamic in nature where items are being added and removed continuously and it would not be feasible to have them sorted. Such. situations underscore the necessity of accommodating. searching techniques. to the. specific. needs. and. constraints. of a. given. application. in one's possession. Furthermore, improvements in the. data. structure. manipulations. have. spurred the. study. of. alternative. searching. techniques. based. on. the. roots. of. linear. search. as a point of departure. For example, techniques utilizing dynamic structures. can be capable of improving efficiency. and. versatility. in various. situations. Search function optimization has not only been a matter of efficiency but also the preservation of functional integrity in changing data environments. Techniques such as those described in Amir et al. (2013) show the ways in which transformation techniques can enhance traditional linear search models to accommodate more efficient processing of complex data types. Thus, though linear search may seem primitive when taken in the context of searching and sorting algorithms, it is an elementary building stone upon which other more sophisticated approaches can be founded (Figure 8.6).

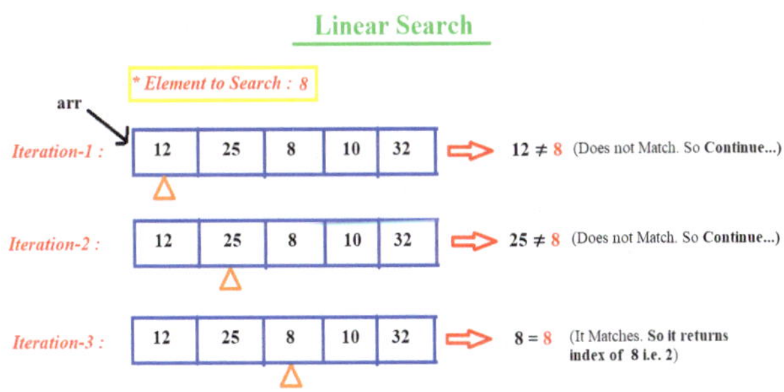

Figure 8.6. *Linear search technique a fundamental algorithm.*

Source: https://utkarsh1504.github.io/DSA-Java/static/e3fa513b23c9d1e51f-3c6f58ef6a9bfc/c1b63/linear-search.png.

8.2.1. Description of the Linear Search Algorithm

The linear search algorithm represents one of the simplest methods for locating a specific element within an unsorted list or array. This algorithm operates under a straightforward premise: it sequentially checks each element in the collection until the desired element is found or all options are exhausted. In practice, this means starting from the first element and proceeding to the last one, effectively comparing each current element against the target value. This process is inherently simple and does not require any prior organization or sorting of the data, making linear search a useful technique for small datasets or scenarios where quick implementation is required. By its nature, however, the linear search exhibits a time complexity of O(n), where n represents the number of elements examined, underscoring its inefficiencies with larger datasets when compared to more sophisticated searching techniques. Despite its simplicity, the linear search algorithm has notable limitations primarily associated with its computational efficiency. As the size of the input array increases, the number of comparisons required to locate an element grows proportionally, which can lead to sluggish performance. In situations where numerous searches occur on large datasets, this inefficiency becomes increasingly pronounced. Advanced searching algorithms, such as binary search, can provide significant performance improvements under specific conditions, notably when the data is sorted. Nonetheless, linear search remains relevant by serving as an introductory concept in algorithm analysis, illustrating fundamental principles of efficiency and serving as a baseline for understanding more complex algorithms. Such insights are crucial in grasping larger themes in algorithm design and performance optimization, as highlighted in the exploration of adaptive algorithms which optimize performance based on input distributions (Ailon et al., 2010). In certain contexts, though, linear search can be preferred due to its ease of implementation and lack of prerequisite conditions. For example, in programming environments where quick and straightforward solutions are preferred, or in applications dealing with small, frequently changing datasets, linear search stands out as a practical option. Moreover, its straightforward approach allows it to be easily adapted for various scenarios, such as searching for multiple occurrences or efficiently handling dynamic data that does not require sorting. While it may not achieve the optimal average-case time complexity of more advanced techniques, its adaptability and low overhead make it a viable choice in many practical situations. Thus, the linear search algorithm, despite its limitations, provides foundational knowledge essential for understanding both simple and complex searching techniques within the broader framework of algorithm design and implementation (Barbay et al., 2008).

8.2.2. Advantages and Disadvantages of Linear Search

In the field of searching algorithms, linear search is one of the simplest algorithms to search for an element in a list, that is, array or list. Its greatest advantage is its simplicity of implementation; the algorithm searches every element in the list individually until it obtains the given value or reaches the end. This simplicity makes linear search suitable for beginners and therefore a great option for teaching purposes. Additionally, linear search doesn't need any particular data structure and can be used on unsorted or sorted arrays equally. As such, in the case of limited data sets or situations where there are not enough computational resources available, linear search is still a practical solution. However, this should not be forgotten when it is used with larger datasets where high performance is critical. Conversely, the limitations of linear search become more pronounced with a larger dataset. The algorithm executes with a time complexity of O(n), which shows that in the worst possible case, all of the elements must be searched before one comes to the realization that the target is there or not there. Such inefficiency can lead to huge delays, especially in those applications that need faster response times or real-time processing of data. The linear search method becomes even more impractical as the amount of data increases, and so it is not recommended for large datasets where other ways of searching, such as binary search, would offer huge performance benefits. For example, the recursive or iterative binary search algorithms offer logarithmic time complexity, O(log n), that considerably enhances the execution speed in sorted data environments. Moreover, linear search is also constrained for real use through its sequential checking dependency, which renders it incapable of serving requirements for environments where repeating or high-speed searches are a necessity. Thus, while linear search can be a fundamental algorithm in studying concepts of search, it is frequently employed less in advanced computing applications since superior alternatives are designed. An example is search techniques like hashed data structures that can bring constant time complexity, O(1), in searching, surpassing linear techniques capabilities. Additionally, research of more advanced implementations or frameworks is essential towards boosting search operations in complex software programs, as evident in the realization of intuitive interfaces for sparse matrix management through computational operations and thus opening the door for adaptation of research in real-world environments (Curtin et al., 2019). In essence, even though linear search is a pedagogical aid, the transition to superior approaches to search is crucial in terms of efficiently handling big data queries (Perkins et al., 1999).

8.2.3. Use Cases for Linear Search in Real-World Applications

Linear search, while being comparatively inefficient when compared with other searching algorithms of higher complexity, is usable in many real-life situations where the data sets are small or of low complexity. A typical application is in basic data retrieval exercises, such as looking for names or numbers out of a list where the dataset is not large enough to justify the overhead of applying higher-order searching algorithms. Also, linear search comes in handy in scenarios involving highly dynamic data environments in which items are constantly added or removed and the need for a simple mechanism of searching arises. Under such conditions, the simplicity of code and the ease of implementation of linear search make it an apt choice, particularly for educational or introductory programming assignments where students are learning basic ideas in algorithms and data structures.

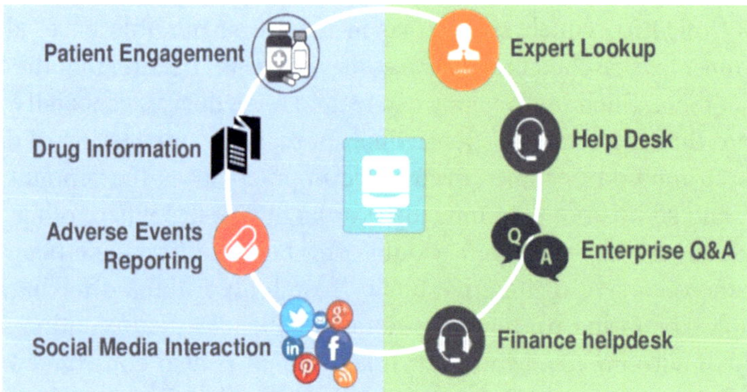

Figure 8.7. *Use cases for linear search in real-world applications.*

Source: https://research.aimultiple.com/wp-content/uploads/2017/10/Screen-Shot-2020-05-09-at-18.57.42.png.

Linear search also finds its application in real use cases where the data are not sorted and immediate feedback needs to be generated without pre-processing. For instance, certain user interfaces apply linear search for receiving immediate feedback when users search in search boxes, especially in systems with limited data. Additionally, websites like Yelp and AirBnB, which enable user-driven searching on large datasets, in theory optimize for good searching strategies. They will use linear searching algorithms in some internal processes, particularly when they query data with non-complex query criteria, thus confirming the balance between backend complexity and user interface complexity (Asudeh et al., 2017). Adding linear search to such systems further confirms its continued applicability in handling real-world datasets effectively. Also, linear search is priceless in certain algorithmic uses where one needs to have instant prototyping. In data and machine learning, specifically, practitioners often need checks to be verified quickly over datasets. Linear search-based methods are able to scan through unstructured data to allow for preliminary evaluation before a complex sorting or searching algorithm is employed, like locality-sensitive hashing (Cozzolino et al., 2016). In this way, linear search is a first aid to make an assessment of the type of data or outliers in specialized applications. Thus, even though there are better algorithms for large data sets, the versatility of linear search in handling various real-world situations proves its ageless value and aptness in the field of search algorithms (Figure 8.7).

8.3. BINARY SEARCH TECHNIQUE

The Binary Search Technique is a simple algorithm that is employed for the search of a target value in an array with ascending order in an efficient manner. This technique begins by examining the mid-element of the array; if the target value occurs here, the search is successful. However, if the target is lower than the mid-point, the algorithm looks for its target in the left part of the array. Conversely, if the target is larger, the search continues in the right half. This divide-and-conquer approach reduces the number of comparisons significantly with a time complexity of O(log n), where n represents the array size. Efficiency of binary search is a stark contrast to linear search, which has O(n) time complexity, and thus its application becomes indispensable in scenarios where quick data access is paramount, particularly in applications that make use of big datasets and demand speedy accessing mechanisms.

One interesting aspect of the Binary Search Technique is its adaptability to other data structures apart from arrays. For instance, it can be utilized with great effect in data structures such as binary search trees, with each comparison producing a comparable partitioning effect, enabling the optimal possible search times. Furthermore, the potential for combining binary search with more advanced data manipulation methods allows for improved performance in dynamic environments. For instance, multi-dimensional data-supported structures, for example, suffix trees, can utilize the efficiency of binary search in order to enable pattern searching with speed. The development of sophisticated algorithms from binary search principles is best demonstrated with recent advancements in dynamic data structures that accommodate unbounded-length keys, highlighting the universality and the importance of the algorithm in different computational spaces (Amir et al., 2013).

Moreover, as applications make their way towards the management of more advanced data types, binary search continues to be an integral component within broader sorting and searching designs. For example, hardness in permuting or complicated data formats has spurred innovative techniques that leverage the benefit of binary search. Some compression schemes use binary search ideas to access succinctly elements in a compressed permutation, reflecting the character of ordered sequences. This synergy of binary search and advanced data structures enhances not only the search operation but also enables functionalities like inverse operations and iterated searches (Barbay et al., 2008). With researchers continuing to look into optimizing search algorithms, the binary search algorithm is a cornerstone due to its simplicity, efficiency, and adaptability, which makes it relevant in the context of computer science (Figure 8.8).

Figure 8.8. *Binary search technique is a fundamental algorithm.*

Source: https://www.geeksforgeeks.org/wp-content/uploads/Binary-Search.png.

8.3.1. Explanation of the Binary Search Algorithm

The binary search algorithm is a highly efficient method used for finding a target value within an ordered list. Its efficiency comes from its divide-and-conquer approach of continuously dividing the remaining space by half at every step. It begins by initializing two pointers, typically referred to as the low and high indices, to represent the beginning and the end of the search space. By locating the midpoint of these indices, the algorithm is comparing the target value with the element at this midpoint. If the target value matches the midpoint element, the search is successful; otherwise, the search space is reduced to the upper or lower half of it, depending on whether the target value is higher or lower than the midpoint element. This is continued until the target is found or the search space is exhausted. Perhaps the greatest advantage of the binary search algorithm is its time complexity. As opposed to linear search algorithms, which have O(n) time complexity, binary search has O(log n) time, so it is exponentially faster in time for larger sets. This gain in efficiency is particularly valuable in computational contexts where the objective is to be efficient, such as database indexing and information retrieval systems. The dependency of the algorithm on an ordered dataset is fundamental because it makes it less efficient if being applied to unsorted data. As a result, when combined with efficient sorting algorithms, binary search is a pivotal component in the grand design of optimal searching, optimizing both time and resource usage in algorithm design (Ailon et al., 2010). In addition, binary search is a standard education example in algorithms, which illustrates basic problems of recursion, looping, and analysis of time. Teachers tend to use binary search in order to expose students to algorithmic complexity and the significance of the choice of data structure. In understanding the binary search algorithm, students gain essential problem-solving skills that they can use in other aspects of real life. The principles of binary search also show through in more advanced subjects, such as search algorithms for multi-dimensional data structures and applications in more sophisticated mathematical problems like the 3SUM problem, which examines the interactions of numerical sets within computational systems (Gold et al., 2017). Thus, skilled proficiency in binary search not only enhances students' understanding of algorithms but also gives them analytical tools to solve sophisticated programming problems.

8.3.2. Binary Search Implementation Requirements

The application of the binary search does entail the pre-ordering of the data set in an ordered form, a fundamental requirement that is the anchor for the effectiveness of the algorithm. The disciplined reduction of half of the search space is rendered useless without the main requirement, where the algorithm is able to make informed decisions as to which half to discard, against ordered input data. As far as implementation goes, there can be sorting done through several algorithms such as quicksort or mergesort that accept an array not in order and transform it into an orderly meaningful sequence. Not only does this order allow binary search to be performed, but retrieval operations are also optimized in general. Knowing sorting algorithms is crucial because search and sort techniques significantly interlink, highlighting that the choice of sort method can significantly impact binary search performance and scalability. The other requirement for binary search is that the data structure utilized must support random access to its elements. This requirement is important because binary search utilizes index-based probing and examines the target key versus the middle element of the current range. An array, which is a typical data structure to use for binary search, is a fine illustration of this requirement because it is capable of supporting constant time complexity for direct access to its indexed elements. However, linked lists are a drawback as they necessitate sequential searching for accessing elements, thereby compromising the efficiency binary search aims to offer. It then becomes imperative to identify the nature of data structures so as to optimize search operations because certain structures inherently support the needs of binary search operations whereas others do not, and this renders the approach practically feasible in varying contexts. Finally, the consideration when applying binary search is how to handle edge cases, such as duplicate values and empty structures. In the presence of duplicates, the design should return either an arbitrary instance, the first, or the last occurrence of the search key based on the needs of the application. These are significant factors as they affect both the precision and user impression of search results. The algorithm must also deal with empty data set cases smoothly so that it ideally conveys the absence of results. Aside from the theoretical application, such practical applications indicate the flexibility of the algorithm towards real applications, for example, domains with complex searches over large datasets, where querying and retrieval performance is essential, like the breakthroughs in bioinformatics data structures (Dawyndt et al., 2012) and the general techniques for dynamic data structures (Amir et al., 2013) (Figure 8.9).

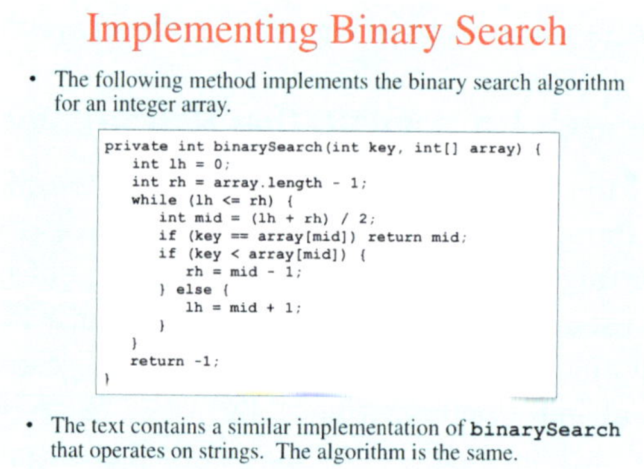

Figure 8.9. *Requirements for implementing binary search.*

Source: https://image3.slideserve.com/6024166/implementing-binary-search-l.jpg.

8.3.3. Comparison of Binary Search with Linear Search

Among search algorithms, two principal methods that are compared and contrasted are binary search and linear search. Linear search does this by reading through each item in a list sequentially until the target value is found or the end of the list is reached. The approach is straightforward and appropriate for unsorted data, providing a straightforward way of checking each entry. However, its time complexity is O(n), which means that it is not effective to employ it on large lists. As the datasets become larger, the linear search slows more to show the limitations. This slowing is most applicable when searching is performed over large sets of unordered data, where performance and responsiveness are required in the best search methods.

Binary search has a more efficient alternative though with limited preconditions. This algorithm requires the dataset to be sorted prior to searching, and this allows it to halve the search range in each step. This halving reduces the amount of comparison operations needed to find the target item, making its time complexity to be O(log n). The binary search is very clear in large, ordered datasets, where its logarithmic efficiency is distinctly better than the linear method. The initial sorting requirement does introduce overhead, though, particularly where data continues to change dynamically and consistent sorting is impractical. Thus, while the binary search algorithm does come faster than linear search, the requirement that it depend on the pre-sorted state can present trade-offs depending on data operation contexts. It is important to know where each of the search methods excels to maximize performance. For instance, in scenarios where the data set is fixed and sorted, binary search is greatly superior considering its efficiency. However, in dynamic environments where data are in constant flux and possibly not sorted, the linear search would be more expedient in the event that searches are not frequently conducted. In addition, the creation of more advanced data structures such as trees and hash tables contributes to these comparisons as they provide additional efficiency options. As is evident from research on dynamic data structures, application of search techniques together with data management through optimization enables enhanced search performance overall compared to naive applications, demonstrating the extent of searching and sorting techniques as well as their scope for optimization in advanced applications (Barbay et al., 2008; Amir et al., 2013).

8.4. INTRODUCTION TO SORTING

Sorting algorithms are a pillar of computer science and an essential part of data organization, manipulation, and retrieval. Sorting is simply the process of putting data into some order, ascending or descending, numeric or lexicographical. Sorting not only optimizes searching algorithms but also improves overall data handling. There are numerous sorting techniques, ranging from simple to complex, where algorithms like Bubble Sort, Quick Sort, and Merge Sort all have their own advantages and disadvantages. Choosing which algorithm to implement can exert a significant impact on the performance, particularly in dealing with large databases or constrained system resources. It is through insight into these varied techniques that programmers are able to optimize systems for planned purpose and facilitate smooth processing of information in modern computer systems. In both theoretical and practical situations, sorting algorithms are commonly ranked based on computational complexity, the time and space required by them to run. For example, simple algorithms like Bubble Sort with time complexity O(n2) renders them inappropriate for larger data use. In contrast, more sophisticated algorithms such as Quick Sort or Merge Sort have an average time complexity of O(n log n), which provides stunning performance improvements. Stability versus non-stability also becomes significant; stable sorting algorithms maintain the relative record positions for equivalent keys, which may be required in certain applications. Furthermore, as the world of science depicts, algorithms of sorting are not mere theory but are accompanied by practical uses in various fields, including the analysis of data in science research, whereby resources like NumPy facilitate effective numerical computation and data management (Harris et al., 2020). Moreover, advances in programming languages and libraries, particularly Python using libraries such as NumPy and the Atomic Simulation Environment (ASE), have heavily influenced the evolution of sorting algorithms. Such libraries enhance sorting operations by providing optimized functions based on efficient underlying algorithms. For instance, interweaving array programming paradigms makes complex operations of sorting possible with concise syntax and great performance potential. ASE, being atomistic simulation-focused, shows how a higher-level programming environment can render processes efficient, allowing the user to possess effective data handling functionalities like sorting, optimization, and analysis of humongous datasets (Larsen et al., 2017). The integration of sorting algorithms with modern programming libraries, therefore, highlights the importance of possessing effective data organization in the broader context of searching and sorting methods (Figure 8.10).

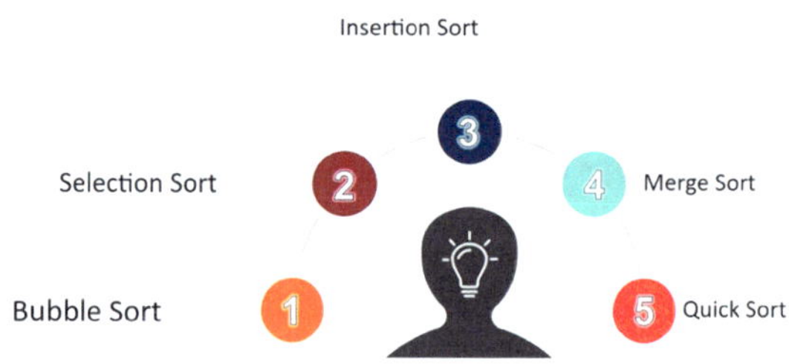

Figure 8.10. *Sorting algorithms are fundamental.*

Source: https://fastercapital.co/i/Selection-Sortinoratio--Selecting-the-Right-Order-in-Sortinoratio--Introduction-to-Sorting-Algorithms.webp.

8.4.1. Definition of Sorting in Computer Science

Sorting in computer science is the process of arranging data in a specific order, typically ascending or descending, based on a given key. This key could be numerical, alphabetical, or even in more complex data types, and it is accomplished through various algorithms that facilitate the process in an efficient manner. The requirement for sorting comes from its immense utility in data searching and data management, where ordered data can provide quicker access and easier manipulation. Sorting algorithms vary by time and space complexities that characterize their performance based on the size and nature of data. For instance, while basic algorithms like bubble sort are easier to program, they are usually inefficient with large sets compared to more sophisticated algorithms like quicksort or mergesort, which are used in actual applications due to their improved efficiency. Computational complexity of sorting is an important factor in comprehending its theoretical foundation. Lower bounds are familiar for sorting algorithms, that is, any comparison-based sort algorithm performs at least $\Omega(N \log N)$ comparisons in the worst case when N is the size of the items to be sorted. The immediate result establishes the fundamental limitation of sorting methods as they scale with data size. Furthermore, algorithms have varying strengths and weaknesses depending on the type of data and application requirements. The complications must be known to computer scientists so that they can select the most appropriate sort method for a given situation so that processing is maximized in data processing as well as application development (Borodin et al., 2001). Moreover, advances in research in data structures around sorting have witnessed new algorithms for enhancing the process. For instance, self-adjusting heaps and BSTs demonstrate a novel relationship that enhances sorting efficiency. By finding heap algorithms with isomorphic BST algorithms, researchers began to develop a theory of dynamic optimality for heaps, similar to one that was firmly established for BSTs. Not only does this enrich the arsenal at hand for sorting but also it signals the sensitive connection between data structures and sorting algorithms. Algorithms such as the smooth heap, which are founded upon algorithms of BSTs, have real-world application potential and provide efficient and easy-to-implement sorting mechanisms. In the future, these developments will significantly increase computation efficiency and usage of resources in the design of algorithms and software engineering (Kozma et al., 2018).

8.4.2. Importance of Sorting in Data Organization

The importance of sorting in the organization means data cannot be overemphasized because it significantly enhances the efficiency of data retrieval as well as the use of data sets overall. Sorting data ensures easy searching towards and retrieving information, which is paramount in numerous fields including academics as well as business. Sorting means transforming disorganized data into a tidy arrangement that makes it easy to find particular information. This process not only minimizes the time and effort invested in searching for data but also works to increase the level of efficiency of information systems and digital libraries. Following the usability study results' emphasis, interlocking relationship of effectiveness, efficiency, and satisfaction suggests that a best-sorted data structure supports a quality user experience, which in turn leads to enhanced engagement and productivity in the long term (Jeng et al., 2005). Moreover, the method of sorting may impact learnability for data systems.

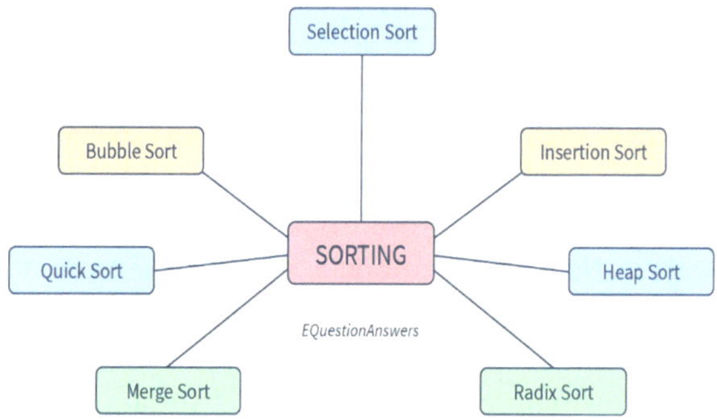

Figure 8.11. *The importance of sorting in data organization.*

Source: https://external-content.duckduckgo.com/iu/?u=https%3A%2F%2Fscaler.com%2Ftopics%2Fimages%2Ftypes-of-sorting-algorithms.webp&f=1&nofb=1&ipt=45b5245c7221675883b59c78765c7b682d3f0c1317f4f670c42fd9e568152ecb.

In those settings where users need to be proficient in navigating complex sets of information, an organized and meaningful structure facilitates learning. Sorting algorithms are fundamental techniques that simplify data organization and how the data is presented, thereby simplifying consumption for users unfamiliar with the system. Through effective sorting mechanisms, organizations are able to minimize cognitive load so that users only need to devote their attention to the task of analyzing and interpreting information instead of struggling with its built-in disorganization. Through matching sorting functionality with organizational goals, especially in digital libraries, institutions are better able to maximize overall user satisfaction and drive a sustainable loop of learning and skill acquisition (Jeng et al., 2005). In addition to providing improved usability and learnability, sorting is critical towards maintaining great performance in data management systems. For instance, when the data is sorted appropriately, it stabilizes and optimizes searching operations, which is of great importance in real-time information lookup environments. Effective sorting algorithms have a great potential to shorten the times of search, resulting in an increase in job performance and a decrease in job errors. Staff satisfaction and retention research emphasizes the importance of good data retrieval systems; those being easy to use are positively correlated with staff job satisfaction and reduced attrition. In essence, a systematic method of sorting enhances the integrity of data structure, building an effective and rewarding working environment (Figure 8.11).

8.4.3. Overview of Sorting Algorithms

Sorting algorithms are computer science fundamentals employed to sort data in a specific order, which is usually ascending or descending. Beyond the mere organization process, sorting has a significant impact on other computational procedures, particularly search algorithms. Various sorting algorithms, such as Quick Sort, Merge Sort, and Bubble Sort, exhibit varying performance under varying conditions, necessitating the selection of the appropriate algorithm based on the specific data set and application context. Surprisingly, Quick Sort, with its average-case complexity, has a time complexity of O(n log n) and is applied to large data sets, whereas the O(n2) worst-case complexity of Bubble Sort renders it typically relegated to instruction or when working with small data sets. Whether or not to employ a sorting algorithm can be important to computation resource usage, thereby determining the choice of a sorting algorithm essential in software engineering and algorithmic optimization. One of the major recent advancements in sorting algorithms is in the adaptive sampling configuration interaction (ASCI) method, which has been shown to greatly enhance efficiency in quantum simulations. The ASCI algorithm takes advantage of efficient sorting algorithms as a fundamental part of its process, indicating the dependency of other computational methods. This new paradigm facilitates efficient selected configuration interaction and exact diagonalization, leading to faster computations in quantum chemistry. With reduced computational overhead with improved sorting algorithms, researchers can now perform complex simulations of chemical systems, such as simulating 34 electrons in 152 orbitals of Si_2H_6, demonstrating the scalability and effectiveness of these new sorting-based algorithms (Freeman et al., 2019). Such advancements not only show the performance benefit that arises from better sorting algorithms but also open up new avenues for research in cross-disciplinary fields. The theoretical underpinnings of sorting algorithms also coincide with algorithmic problems such as the 3SUM problem, whereby determining whether or not any three numbers in a list sum to zero has significant implications in computational complexity. Recent studies have explored more efficient randomized complexities of decision trees for such operations in addition to the previously established limits with emphasis on the interrelationship between sorting and global paradigms in problem-solving (Gold et al., 2017). The bounded complexities inherent within sorting affect a variety of computational problems and hint at the broader importance of efficient sorting methods beyond their specific applications. With this realization of the complexities and the implications of the same in similar mathematical problems, one comes to admire sorting algorithms not just as a way of organizing data but as a significant component of the intricate picture of algorithm design and computational theory. Such interdependencies between seemingly independent algorithmic problems emphasize the significance of sorting techniques in the grand scheme of computer science.

8.5. BUBBLE SORT ALGORITHM

The Bubble Sort Algorithm is a simple sorting technique widely quoted in first-year computer science classes. Its steps are easy, founded on repeated element comparison of next items in a list, known as bubbling effect. In each pass, the algorithm looks for pairs of elements and switches their places if they are in the wrong order. This process continues until the entire pass is done without any swaps, meaning that the list is now sorted. Intuitively straightforward as it is, this algorithm's performance is severely inferior in real-world scenarios compared to other sorts. With worst-case and average-case time complexity of $O(n^2)$, the Bubble Sort is most appropriate in small data sets or teaching where arriving at the inner mechanisms of sorting algorithms is more important but is susceptible to inefficiency in larger data sets. While being simplistic, the Bubble Sort Algorithm raises important concepts relating to the discussion about algorithms. For instance, the act of iterating over the list time and again not only instills the idea of sorting but also evokes the essence of algorithmic complexity in the context of programming. While other algorithms achieve quicker sorting times—like Quick Sort or Merge Sort—Bubble Sort is a decent place for beginning programmers and students to examine performance metrics like time complexity and the importance of choosing appropriate algorithms based on the data set. Furthermore, the Bubble Sort discussion also often includes optimization possibilities, such as whether to add a flag to detect whether any swaps occurred on a pass so that one might perhaps gain efficiency by early termination if the list actually was sorted, and this helps to demonstrate the dynamic nature of algorithm design and optimization in computer science (Rahman et al., 2023). In practice, the Bubble Sort Algorithm, while mainly tutorial in nature, does bear deeper relevance to algorithm performance and choice. As computational needs for modern computing increasingly become more sophisticated, an awareness of basic algorithms like Bubble Sort allows developers an appreciation of limitations of simple solutions to more advanced ones. This is critical in making appropriate selections of the kind of sorting to use in applications with increasing dataset sizes in real-world usage. Also, algorithmic discourse entails issues like flexibility and stability; Bubble Sort has been found to be stable, that is, it preserves the relative order of similar elements, an issue of relevance in certain applications. Thus, while not otherwise used routinely in modern optimized sorting operations, Bubble Sort is a crucial study case in the broader paradigm of searching and sorting algorithms, as well as the dependency of computational theories on real-world uses in programming (Cuomo et al., 2022).

8.5.1. The Process Description of Bubble Sort

Bubble sort is one of the simplest algorithms in computer science that is easy to use. Bubble sort revolves around cycling through a list of items more than once, traversing it to look at each pair of next-to elements and swap them if they are not in the right order. This continues until the list is sorted, hence the name bubble, as smaller elements gradually bubble up to their correct positions at the top of the list. While bubble sort is simple to understand, it is normally not effective for big datasets due to its $O(n^2)$ time complexity. This inefficiency comes as a result of the repetition of passes through the data in order to no longer require making swaps, hence a less desirable choice to more sophisticated sorting algorithms for day-to-day use (Bell et al., 2014).

In decomposing the mechanics of bubble sort, it is understood that the efficiency of the algorithms can be improved using optimization techniques. One common modification is to insert a flag that keeps track of whether or not any swaps were made in a complete pass through the list. If there were no swaps, then the list is sorted and the algorithm can terminate early. These kinds of optimizations, without losing sight of the underlying bubble sort algorithm, can save unnecessary iterations and display a real-world appreciation for optimization. Nevertheless, although these small improvements, bubble sorts average time complexity remains quadratic, and is normally judged less efficient for big data sets. Therefore, bubble sort is primarily utilized as a pedagogical device to learn elementary ideas in sorting rather than being a core sorting algorithm in real applications (Gond et al., 2020). Despite its limitations, the bubble sort algorithm is of educational importance when it comes to introducing the basic principles of sorting and algorithm analysis. It gives a foundation upon which students can understand how the efficiency of algorithms is crucial when it comes to computation. Bubble sort also illustrates the concept of stability in sort algorithms in that identical elements remain in their relative positions after the sorting. This concept is often built on top of more advanced algorithms that add the same stability characteristics. Lastly, while bubble sort will never be the best sort out there, its simple methodology provides a beneficial stepping stone for students in the field of computer science, highlighting the importance of learning numerous various sorting techniques within the broader scheme of searching and sorting algorithms (Bell et al., 2014) (Figure 8.12).

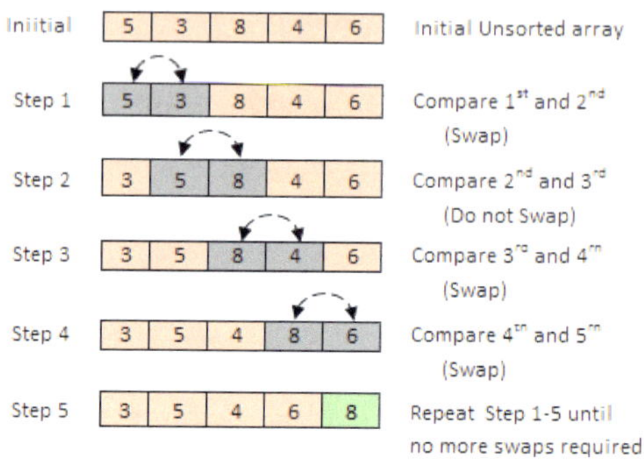

Figure 8.12. *Bubble sort process is a fundamental algorithm.*

Source: https://atechdaily.com/resources/images/posts/2020/4/275/bubbleSortExample.png.

8.5.2. Time Complexity and Performance Analysis

Time complexity is essential in studying the performance of various searching and sorting algorithms. Time complexity provides a theoretical framework by which computer scientists and developers are able to predict the efficiency of an algorithm relative to its input size. This estimate, usually in Big O notation, categorizes algorithms based on how their requirement for resources grows when their input size grows. For instance, linear search, in which each element is searched individually, takes O(n) time, while more efficient algorithms like quicksort or mergesort can operate in O(n log n) time on average. By studying the time complexity, practitioners can make smart decisions regarding the algorithm to employ in a given situation to achieve optimal performance and use of resources within computational power. Aside from time complexity, performance analysis is also conducted to other significant factors like space complexity and real runtime measurements. Space complexity considers how much memory an algorithm uses, which can have a profound impact on its viability on devices with limited resources. In addition, real performance can vary from theoretical analysis due to constant factors, overhead, and variations in hardware and input data distributions. As an example, an algorithm may theoretically enjoy improved time complexity but exhibit longer running times in practice due to inefficiencies in the cache or extra overhead for certain operations. Thus, understanding both theoretical and empirical performance figures is important in making useful searching and sorting approaches in various computationally different environments. Recent advances in algorithm design have enabled the development of new techniques that improve efficiency and performance analysis. For instance, advanced algorithms such as locality-sensitive hashing-based ones, which address data component ordering, can potentially enhance searchability in unstructured data very much. The algorithm in Cozzolino et al. (2016) demonstrates how data vector classification and resultant partitioning of search space can be leveraged in order to achieve state-of-the-art performance. Similarly, the effective utilization of interpolation methods as illustrated by the partition of unity method in Cavoretto et al. (2014) also emphasizes the necessity of combining local and global methods with the aim of optimizing computational efficiency. With such sophisticated methods combined, performance analysis is not only a tool to measure efficiency but also a catalyst in pushing the boundaries of search and sort algorithm design.

8.5.3. The Role of Bubble Sort in Certain Situations

Among sorting algorithms, bubble sort, while criticized often for its inefficiency in huge amounts of data, has specific relevance in provided situations. For instance, in educational use, where students are introduced to the fundamental concept of sorting. The ease of the algorithm to comprehend—driven by its simple philosophy of comparing adjacent elements and exchanging them—facilitates a rudimentary understanding of algorithmic steps without overwhelming the student. This complements the focus on interactive and integrated learning materials within computer science, for example, the NZ Computer Science Field Guide, which presents subjects alongside programming exercises to enhance the learning experience (Bell et al., 2014). The bubble sort is taught at introductory programming levels as a stepping stone to later more complex algorithms so that learners appreciate issues related to algorithm efficiency and performance. Also, bubble sort is beneficial in case of nearly sorted data. If the data sets are nearly sorted, bubble sort may be quicker than sophisticated algorithms like quicksort or mergesort since it possesses an early termination property. If during the entire pass through the data there is no swap, the algorithm will recognize that the list is sorted and will terminate further activity. This property gives rise to a best-case time complexity of O(n), which can be generally advantageous in situations involving working with data sets that sporadically experience minor disorganization (Carzaniga et al., 2017). This effectiveness indicates bubble sort's usability in scenarios where information needs to be maintained sorted, so minor disorganization can be more quickly rectified than through the implementation of more complex sorting algorithms. Furthermore, bubble sort is useful in environments with limited computing resources, in which the ease of implementation takes precedence over performance considerations. In embedded systems or microcontrollers, with low processing power and limited memory, the convenience of the algorithm's implementation is appealing. Its in-place sort characteristic with no requirement for additional storage capacity than in the input list makes the bubble sort algorithm the ideal candidate for such environments. This aligns with general software engineering practices toward reliability and simplicity of design, so that systems are functional under varying constraints. As software systems are increasingly adding complexity, learning to implement effective sorting algorithms like bubble sort, especially in niche applications, shows the diversity of application area of algorithm selection suitable for particular work (Carzaniga et al., 2017).

8.6. QUICK SORT ALGORITHM

Quick Sort is a widely applied method of sorting that is well known for high efficiency and performance in most cases compared to other forms of sorting, such as Bubble Sort or Insertion Sort. Quick Sort achieves this by using a divide-and-conquer strategy where the array is separated into smaller sub-arrays based on a pivot element. Once a pivot is selected, the algorithm arranges the elements in such a manner that elements smaller than the pivot are placed on one side and elements greater are placed on the other side. The operation is further iterated for ensuing sub-arrays. Quick Sort has average-case time complexity $O(n \log n)$, which renders Quick Sort extremely favorable where big sets of data have to sort rapidly. Nonetheless, the worst-case time complexity degrades to $O(n^2)$ if a bad pivot is constantly picked. In spite of its possible demerits, Quick Sort is still a top contender in the realm of sorting across numerous applications from databases to systems programming. One of the major advantages of Quick Sort is its in-place sorting capability, which considerably reduces the extra memory expense typically paid by other algorithms like Merge Sort. Also, because it uses contiguous memory segments, Quick Sort can more effectively use CPU cache hierarchies and so achieve superior actual performance. However, practitioners need to consider also its vulnerability to algorithmic complexity attacks as well. Flawed buggy implementations or suboptimal choice of pivots can expose systems to denial-of-service attacks wherein adversaries can design inputs leading to the worst-case time complexity of Quick Sort, thereby exploiting its efficiency vulnerabilities (Betts et al., 2017). In big data, wherein the amount of information may leave performance scalability in a state of limbo, seamless integration of efficient algorithms is a necessity. Quick Sort can particularly be valuable in the case of rapid processing and analysis of data. With evolving data frameworks, the development of means for optimizing sorting algorithms—for example, storing frequently queried elements in caches or using parallel computing—becomes imperative. The use of sorting algorithms in dealing with large data also intersects with security elements in that their execution vulnerabilities can be attacked. Hence, awareness and paying heed to potential algorithmic intricacies associated with Quick Sort is essential in order to guard against potential attacks to allow the algorithm to stay intact and functional in adverse environments (Cortés-Núñez et al., 2015) (Figure 8.13).

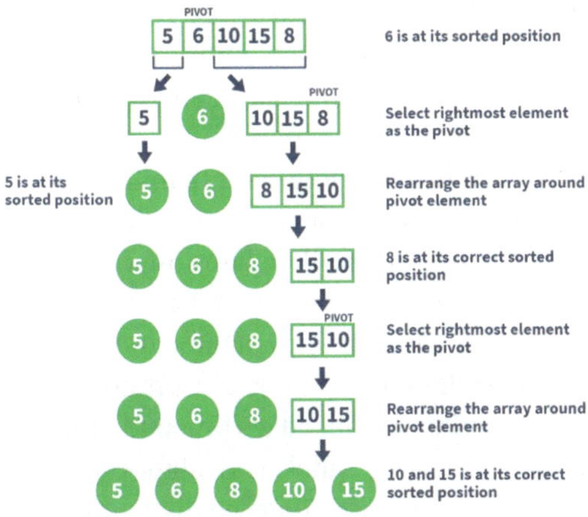

Figure 8.13. *Quick sort algorithm.*

Source: https://www.scaler.com/topics/media/Flowchart-for-working-of-quick-sort-algorithm-1024x950.webp.

8.6.1. Explanation of the Quick Sort Method

Quick sort is a speedy sorting algorithm prevalent in the realm of computer science due to its use of the divide-and-conquer technique. Quick sort, essentially, partitions an array by selecting a pivot item and splitting the rest of the items into sub-arrays that hold items below the pivot and items above. This partition is crucial because it positions the pivot in the right place within the sorted array, thus reducing the problem size. This process is then applied recursively to the sub-arrays so that quick sort can efficiently sort large amounts of data. Its average time complexity is O(n log n) and thus suitable for most applications where optimal performance is required, especially over that of less efficient algorithms like bubble sort, less efficient in larger data sets. One of the secrets to quick sort's efficiency is its best use of in-place sorting, with reduced usage of additional memory space allocation. Unlike other sorting techniques which may be greatly space-intensive in terms of auxiliary arrays, quick sort primarily sorts in terms of the original array, relocating items to their respective positions. This minimizes not just memory overhead but also cache performance, which is a significant factor in modern computing machines where resources need to be efficiently managed. While the worst-case time complexity of quick sort is up to $O(n^2)$ because of poor pivot selection that leads to unbalanced partitions, techniques such as random pivot selection and median-of-three can significantly eliminate this potential. Moreover, quick sort's versatility in handling various data types and distributions also further solidifies its reputation as a go-to sorting algorithm in performance-critical code. Secondly, flexibility of implementation of quick sorts pervades many programming applications, recursion and iteration both being available. Modern implementations have availed themselves of multi-threading and parallel processing to further enhance the performance of sorting speed, particularly in applications where the data sets are large. The use of parallel algorithms and adaptive indexing, as mentioned in contemporary studies, illustrates the ongoing evolution of sorting methods, relating quick sort to computer architecture and algorithm design of today. Such dynamic interrelation makes quick sort not only viable but also an elementary concept in learning advanced sorting and searching algorithms. As illustrated by research, the use of quick sort algorithms increases efficiency in related processes, further demonstrating the diversified application of quick sort in sophisticated computational procedures, emphasizing its applicability to the growing data processing field (Freeman et al., 2019; Alvarez et al., 2014) (Figure 8.14).

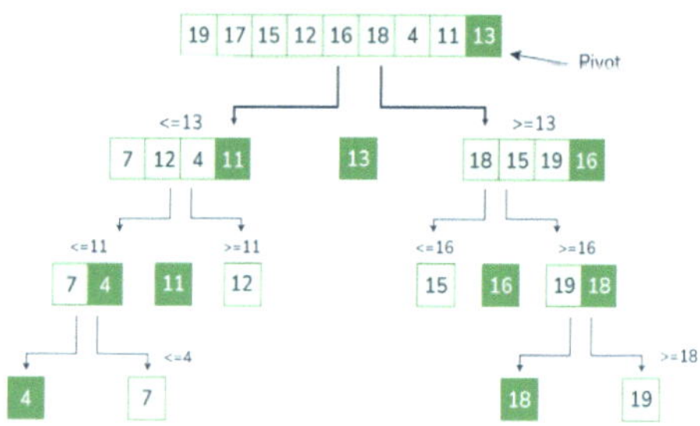

Figure 8.14. *Quick sort method is an efficient sorting algorithm.*

Source: https://media.geeksforgeeks.org/wp-content/uploads/20231219164812/Quick-Sort-Algorithm.png.

8.6.2. Advantages of Quick Sort Over Other Sorting Techniques

Among the sorting algorithms, quick sort is most distinguished for being efficient and exceedingly versatile, such that it is the preferred choice among a vast number of applications. Its biggest plus point perhaps lies in its O(n log n) time complexity in the average case, which brings it on par with other fast sorting algorithms like merge sort and heap sort. But what distinguishes quick sort is its real-world performance, whereby it typically outperforms these alternatives. This is in large part due to its in-place sort method, in the sense that it merely requires to have a small, constant volume of additional storage space. In turn, quick sort minimizes memory overhead as much as possible, and thus is particularly valuable for machines where memory use is a factor to be taken into account. Therefore, quick sorts combination of speed and efficiency makes it clearly superior to most other sorting algorithms in real-world application. Quick sort also employs a divide-and-conquer method that renders it even more efficient when working with enormous datasets. The algorithm proceeds by subdividing the data into smaller sub-arrays that can be sorted separately before merging the outcomes.

This approach not only optimizes the sorting algorithm but also improves cache performance due to the local access patterns it engenders. Unlike merge sort, which needs additional space for holding temporary arrays, quick sort sorts at minimal additional memory, thus reducing the data-to-insight time in scenarios where big data is common. The approach is particularly priceless in the realm of current data processing, where fast examination is crucial, as shown by the QUASII algorithm utilizing similar concepts to reduce data-to-insight time significantly (Ailamaki et al., 2018). Rapid sorts superior features in such cases emphasize better sorting methodology, particularly in environments where speed and resource allocation are imperative factors to take into consideration. Moreover, the ability of quick sort to be easily implemented on various data types and structures only adds to its appeal as a sorting algorithm. Not only is it ideally suited for sorting arrays, but it is also highly effective when applied in combination with linked lists and other data structures. Such flexibility is crucial to the management of the diverse forms of datasets that appear in the context of data science and software development. On top of that, quick sort is optimizable under other approaches such as changing pivot selection methods, all coded in a particular design to maximize performance under specific conditions. Such flexibility allows programmers to optimize the algorithm o the particular character of their data even with added complexity. In rapidly evolving domains, such as those involving real-time information gathering and processing like the information search and retrieval systems in past research (Wilson et al., 2007), this adaptability further supports the significance of quick sort among sorting algorithms.

8.6.3. Quick Sort Applications in Real Life

The effectiveness of quick sort algorithms has found its way into many real-world applications, particularly in software systems that process large amounts of data. For instance, operating systems will require effective process scheduling, whereby the quick sort algorithm can be used to schedule processes based on arrival time or CPU burst time. The process scheduling ensures more significant processes are run efficiently, thereby enhancing system performance. Also, database management software uses quick sort for rapid retrieval and sorting data to access data quickly, reducing access times to a significant degree. Such an implementation supports the fact that quick sort performance does not only reduce the computing load but also enhances the responsiveness of application user interfaces in general.

Quick sort is a significant feature in transaction processing and large amounts of financial data in the finance and banking sector. For instance, stock trading websites use quick sort to quickly and efficiently sort order trades to ensure buy and sell orders are handled with minimal latency. Such responsiveness is paramount in tumultuous market conditions when it can yield significant financial rewards through fast decision-making. Financial analysts also use quick sort when sorting large data sets while performing predictive modeling such as predicting stock prices or analyzing risk associated with various investment products.

The inherent efficiency of quick sort in handling such vast datasets proves its relevance in high-risk environments where time is of the essence. Furthermore, the development of advanced computational methods has also utilized quick sort within research fields in quantum chemistry calculations. Recent breakthroughs in computational algorithms have demonstrated that quick sort has the ability to enhance specifically selected configuration interaction algorithms, a fundamental aspect of solving complex quantum Hamiltonians.

By integrating quick sort with other methods such as adaptive sampling configuration interaction (ASCI), researchers can minimize the process of configuration selection, hence speeding up simulations of intricate molecular systems. This innovation attests to the versatility of quick sort in entirely disparate applications, demonstrating that it can execute fast calculations on diverse applications from analysis of stock market to groundbreaking quantum simulations (Freeman et al., 2019). With the development in technologies, the demand for quick sort continues to expand even broader, making its position as a fundamental part of sorting and search algorithms.

SUMMARY

In summary, a thorough appreciation of searching and sorting methods reinforces their importance in information searching and data management. As online libraries become more widespread, the need for efficient methods becomes more glaring. Bradfordizing, being an established method of producing core sets of documents, emphasizes the promise of greater relevance in search results. Evaluated by rigorous experiments such as in the social sciences and in the medical literature, Bradfordizing demonstrates an excellent potential to improve search outcomes, more specifically through significant re-ranking of document categories on the basis of relevance judgments. This empirical observation justifies the proposition that clearly defined searching techniques have a significant effect on users' capability to locate pertinent information in a timely and accurate manner, placing a heavy focus on advanced techniques in the rapidly evolving data accessibility environment (Marcia et al., 2008).

Moreover, the study of sorting algorithms reveals valuable conclusions in terms of the balancing act between algorithmic complexity and practical application. Sorting is central to effective searching and retrieval, allowing quicker access to large sets of data. Analysis of various algorithms, as remembered in computer science folklore, shows the natural trade-offs between complexity and performance. By comparing empirical results and theoretical models, it's apparent that folklore knowledge enhances our understanding of sorting methods. Engagement with such perspectives allows us to test and tune sorting procedures to realize better algorithms that can adapt to different settings of data. Such fusion of folklore and conceptual models thus aids in facilitating contemporary practices in sorting to achieve optimal search functionality (Bhalchandra et al., 2009).

The implications of such research extend beyond debates at the theoretical level, reflecting on real-world applications at the technological, educational, and research levels. As the infrastructures become more digital, the ability to leverage efficient searching and sorting techniques will be crucial to dealing with the overwhelming wealth of information available in the world today. By combining knowledge from empirical assessments and algorithmic engineering, practitioners can optimize user experiences such that individuals are able to get access to the most relevant information with minimal lag time. The future of information retrieval is predicated on ongoing study of approaches, opening an ever-changing dance between established approaches and new breakthroughs. Therefore, developers and researchers alike must continue to make this field a high priority, as improved searching and sorting techniques not only improve information access, but also towards the ultimate goal of making knowledge more accessible and usable in our increasingly data-driven culture.

The research on search and sort algorithms encompasses a broad variety of techniques addressing the intrinsic issues of data retrieval and organization. The significance of optimum data structures when comparing dynamic keys, particularly when there are unbounded-length keys, is one of the major topics addressed. A good example here is constructing an online suffix tree, which has been shown to have O(log n) worst-case time complexity per input symbol.

Not only this outperforms the amortized O(log n) time of previous proven algorithms but also enhances the efficiency of pattern searching in these trees. The ability to process and sort dynamic data structures efficiently affects the performance of numerous applications, hence towards ongoing attempts at enhancing algorithmic solutions and data handling techniques, as observed in Amir et al. (2013).

In addition, complexity of user interaction with search interfaces emphasizes the challenge in responding to poorly defined information-seeking goals. Traditional keyword searching often does not provide adequate support to users, and hence the development of more sophisticated searching models is essential. New interfaces with capabilities like faceted browsing and result clustering help achieve an improved match for diverse user requirements. However, evaluation of these advanced interfaces is fraught with enormous difficulties owing to the sheer number of independent factors on which user behavior is influenced. As introduced in Schraefel et al. (2009), the formulation of a standardized framework to analyze these interfaces can encourage better comprehension of their effectiveness, influence improvements and guide proper selection of interfaces for specific user environments. As a conclusion, the argument of search and sort approaches mirrors the ongoing advancement of methods towards improving retrieval and organization of information. The development of algorithms such as those supporting efficient management of suffix trees is a big step towards streamlining search procedures. Furthermore, as the needs of the users become more sophisticated, developing intricate search interfaces shows the necessity for technological advancements to be more adaptable and user-friendly. The ongoing development of such techniques not only enhances our understanding of data structures and their utilization but also dictates the paths of forthcoming research, bridging the gap between theory-based practices and actual-user experiences, exemplified by the varied results of Amir et al. (2013) and Schraefel et al. (2009).

REFERENCES

1. Ailamaki, A., Heinis, T., Pavlovic, M., et al. (2018). QUASII: QUery-aware spatial incremental index. https://core.ac.uk/download/156739007.pdf (accessed on 9th September 2025).
2. Ailon, N., Chazelle, B., Clarkson, K. L., et al. (2010). Self-improving algorithms. http://arxiv.org/abs/0907.0884 (accessed on 9th September 2025).
3. Alevizou, P., & De Liddo, A. (2010). A method and tool to support the analysis and enhance the understanding of peer-to-peer learning experiences. https://core.ac.uk/download/18785.pdf (accessed on 9th September 2025).
4. Alvarez, V., Dittrich, J., Richter, S., et al. (2014). Main memory adaptive indexing for multi-core systems. http://arxiv.org/abs/1404.2034 (accessed on 9th September 2025).
5. Amir, A., Franceschini, G., Grossi, R., et al. (2013). Managing unbounded-length keys in comparison-driven data structures with applications to on-line indexing. http://arxiv.org/abs/1306.0406 (accessed on 9th September 2025).
6. Asudeh, A., Das, G., Koudas, N., et al. (2017). Efficient computation of subspace skyline over categorical domains. http://arxiv.org/abs/1703.00080 (accessed on 9th September 2025).
7. Barbay, J., & Navarro, G. (2008). Compressed representations of permutations, and applications. https://core.ac.uk/download/62913856.pdf (accessed on 9th September 2025).
8. Bates, M. J., Bonitz, M., Brookes, B. C., Buckland, M. K., Garfield, E., Harman, D. K., et al. (2008). An evaluation of Bradfordizing effects. https://core.ac.uk/download/11884476.pdf (accessed on 9th September 2025).
9. Bell, T., Duncan, C., Jarman, S., et al. (2014). Presenting computer science concepts to high school students. https://core.ac.uk/download/35472287.pdf (accessed on 9th September 2025).
10. Betts, A., Crosby, S. A., Godefroid, P., Haller, I., & Shenoy, G. S. (2017). SlowFuzz: Automated domain-independent detection of algorithmic complexity vulnerabilities. http://arxiv.org/abs/1708.08437 (accessed on 9th September 2025).
11. Bhalchandra, P., Deshmukh, N., Khamitka, S., et al. (2009). The folklore of sorting algorithms. https://core.ac.uk/download/pdf/87301.pdf (accessed on 9th September 2025).

12. Borodin, A., Bennet, C. H., Zalka, Ch., Grigoriev, D., Buhrman, H., Grover, L. K., Choi, M. D., et al. (2001). Quantum complexities of ordered searching, sorting, and element distinctness. http://arxiv.org/abs/quant-ph/0102078 (accessed on 9th September 2025).

13. Carzaniga, A., Mattavelli, A., & Pezzè, M. (2017). Software redundancy: What, where, how. https://core.ac.uk/download/79427261.pdf (accessed on 9th September 2025).

14. Cavoretto, R. (2014). Two-dimensional interpolation using a cell-based searching procedure. http://arxiv.org/abs/1408.0183 (accessed on 9th September 2025).

15. Chauvin, B., Reed, B., Knuth, D. E., Dean, D. S., Ben-Naim, E., et al. (2004). Understanding search trees via statistical physics. http://arxiv.org/abs/cond-mat/0410498 (accessed on 9th September 2025).

16. Chu, T. C., Coello Coello, C. A., El-Danaf, E. A., Panoutsos, G., Norris, I., Beamish, K., Mahfouf, M., et al. (2012). Knowledge discovery for friction stirs welding via data driven approaches: Part 2–multiobjective modelling using fuzzy rule-based systems. https://core.ac.uk/download/30710032.pdf (accessed on 9th September 2025).

17. Coleman, S., Markov, Z., Neller, T. W., et al. (2005). Enhancing undergraduate AI courses through machine learning projects. https://cupola.gettysburg.edu/cgi/viewcontent.cgi?article=1002&context=csfac (accessed on 9th September 2025).

18. Cortés-Núñez, C. A. (2015). Algorithms and tools of big data: A bibliographic review. https://core.ac.uk/download/71896546.pdf (accessed on 9th September 2025).

19. Cozzolino, D., Poggi, G., & Verdoliva, L. (2016). A reliable order-statistics-based approximate nearest neighbor search algorithm. http://arxiv.org/abs/1509.03453 (accessed on 9th September 2025).

20. Cuomo, S., Schiano Di Cola, V., Giampaolo, F., Rozza, G., Raissi, M., & Piccialli, F. (2022). Scientific machine learning through physics–informed neural networks: Where we are and what's next. *Journal of Scientific Computing, 92*. https://doi.org/10.1007/s10915-022-01939-z (accessed on 9th September 2025).

21. Curtin, R., & Sanderson, C. (2019). Practical sparse matrices in C++ with hybrid storage and template-based expression optimization. https://core.ac.uk/download/224800384.pdf (accessed on 9th September 2025).

22. Dawyndt, P., De Baets, B., Fack, V., et al. (2012). Prospects and limitations of full-text index structures in genome analysis. https://core.ac.uk/download/55755713.pdf (accessed on 9th September 2025).

23. Freeman, C. D., Hait, D., Head-Gordon, M., et al. (2019). Modern approaches to exact diagonalization and selected configuration interaction with the adaptive sampling CI method. https://core.ac.uk/download/323308715.pdf (accessed on 9th September 2025).

24. Gold, O., & Sharir, M. (2017). Improved bounds for 3SUM, *k*-SUM, and linear degeneracy. https://core.ac.uk/download/132422547.pdf (accessed on 9th September 2025).

25. Gond, J. P., Mena, S., & Mosonyi, S. (2020). The performativity of literature reviewing: Constituting the corporate social responsibility literature through re-presentation and intervention. https://core.ac.uk/download/323306231.pdf (accessed on 9th September 2025).

26. Harris, C. R., Millman, K. J., van der Walt, S., Gommers, R., Virtanen, P., Cournapeau, D., Wieser, E., et al. (2020). Array programming with NumPy. *Nature, 585*, 357–362. https://doi.org/10.1038/s41586-020-2649-2 (accessed on 9th September 2025).

27. Heybatzade, G. (2019). Investigation on the relationship between business performance and business satisfaction: Company example. https://media.neliti.com/media/publications/297443-investigation-on-the-relationship-betwee-ebdf214a.pdf (accessed on 9th September 2025).

28. Jeng, J. (2005). What is usability in the context of the digital library and how can it be measured? https://core.ac.uk/download/70426219.pdf (accessed on 9th September 2025).

29. Kozma, L., & Saranurak, T. (2018). Smooth heaps and a dual view of self-adjusting data structures. http://arxiv.org/abs/1802.05471 (accessed on 9th September 2025).

30. Larsen, A. H., Mortensen, J. J., Blomqvist, J., Castelli, I. E., Christensen, R., Dułak, M., Friis, J., et al. (2017). The atomic simulation environment—a Python library for working with atoms. *Journal of Physics: Condensed Matter, 29*, 273002. https://doi.org/10.1088/1361-648x/aa680e (accessed on 9th September 2025).

31. Perkins, E. D. (1999). *Spatial Reasoning for Generalized N-Body Physics: Discrete Element Algorithms*. https://core.ac.uk/download/16521071.pdf (accessed on 9th September 2025).

32. Rahman, M. M., & Watanobe, Y. (2023). ChatGPT for education and research: Opportunities, threats, and strategies. *Applied Sciences, 13*, 5783. https://doi.org/10.3390/app13095783 (accessed on 9th September 2025).

33. Schatz, M. C. (2012). Computational thinking in the era of big data biology. https://core.ac.uk/download/33026256.pdf (accessed on 9th September 2025).

34. schraefel, m. c., White, R. W., & Wilson, M. L. (2009). Evaluating advanced search interfaces using established information-seeking model.
35. Smeaton, A. F., et al. (2012). Index ordering by query-independent measures. https://core.ac.uk/download/11310899.pdf (accessed on 9th September 2025).
36. Wilson, M. L. (2007). *A Nine-Month Report on Progress Towards a Framework for Evaluating Advanced Search Interfaces Considering Information Retrieval and Human Computer Interaction.*

CHAPTER 9

PROBLEM SOLVING WITH DATA STRUCTURES

Contents

INTRODUCTION

A solid introduction to the topic of problem solving with data structures lays a groundwork for learning how various structures affect computational efficiency and algorithmic construction. Data structures are basic building blocks in computer science that underpin software development because they determine structure, management, and storage of data. With the selection of data structure, programmers are able to attain performance optimality, raising the speed and effectiveness of algorithms. The field of programming develops by demanding a productive grasp of how to best apply data structures in many applications, from software engineering and databases to artificial intelligence. Thus, an examination of data structures as a significant tool for problem-solving is not merely pertinent but also an integral component of computer science education today. In order to explore further into this subject, it is possible to investigate the pedagogical significance of incorporating data structures in educational systems.

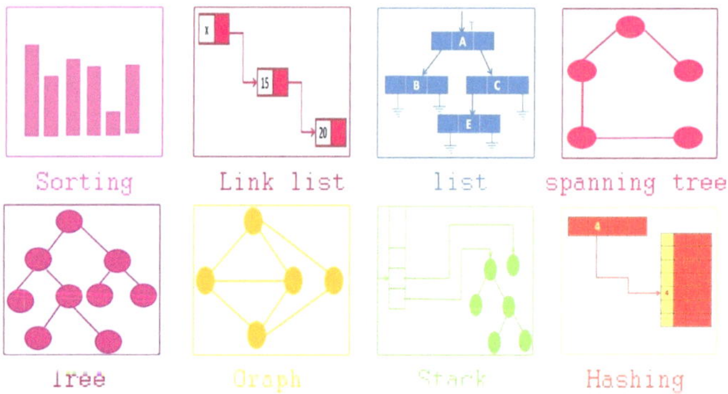

Figure 9.1. *Problem solving with data structures.*

Source: *https://miro.medium.com/v2/resize:fit:3000/1*Dyu63sMUVL-gYEZISOE-2BQ.jpeg.*

The National Science Foundation has funded projects that have sought to integrate the learning of computer science concepts around practical applications with an increased focus on machine learning and data structures for problem-solving skills acquisition. Through the use of experiential laboratory projects that engage students with practical problems, pedagogical frameworks can enhance learning and student activity, building greater understanding of core computation principles. In addition to enabling learners to understand theoretical concepts, this approach can enable students to tackle real-world problems in the workplace, bridging academia and the technological requirements of the business environment (Coleman et al., 2005). In addition, their great application in artificial intelligence (AI) proves their high applicability across fields. Integration of data structures in AI teaching through activities like the N-puzzle game is an example of convergence of computational theory into actual problem-solving. Such learning activities expose students to the direct impact of well-structured data on algorithmic efficiency and performance within AI processes. By fostering engagement with such real-world problems, students are taught underlying AI concepts as well as problem-solving skills. This integrated method embodies the essence of modern computational education, with data structure understanding being more than a mere pedagogic exercise but a valuable set of competences in preparing good problem solvers in the field (Markov et al., 2006) (Figure 9.1).

Definition of Data Structures

The concept of data structures is the essence of computer science, being a building block that allows for efficient design of algorithms and solving problems. A data structure can be defined as a systematic way of storing and organizing data so that it can be accessed and manipulated effectively. This structuring of data becomes the basis of numerous distinct algorithms and how they perform and run. Linear data structures, such as arrays and linked lists, allow easy data manipulation, while non-linear structures, such as trees and graphs, allow complex relationships between data. The choice of a data structure directly affects the running time of algorithms and their ability to solve specific computational problems. Thus, it is imperative to understand the complexity of multiple data structures in order to optimize software engineering and computational theory approaches. Data structures in practical applications provide for efficient processing of large sets of data with retrieval and manipulation methods. Databases, for instance, use various data structures to enhance response time to queries as well as maintain data consistency, while predictive models in machine learning heavily rely on structured data to train algorithms. The data structure variability also enables the programmers to select the most appropriate type based on the problems constraint and demands. With progress in software programming paradigms, reusable pieces of software have been an urgent necessity. New data structures supporting reusability are able to manage a variety of programming needs, being flexible to traditional as well as knowledge-based situations. This capacity for change is critical in modern application building, as indicated by research on reusable software components (Cuena et al., 1999).

The development of algorithms has also highlighted the importance of data structures tailored to special problems that can address specific kinds of problems better. For example, in mathematical optimization, recognition of special problem structure can significantly enhance the algorithms employed with substantially increased speed of solutions. Techniques such as branch-and-cut optimization apply sophisticated data structures to recognize and exploit concealed patterns within complex optimization problems (Ceccon et al., 2016). With the spotlight on data structure recognition across various settings, researchers and developers can leverage particular heuristics and techniques to optimize problem-solving procedures. Hence, a firm understanding of data structures not only assists in the construction of algorithms but also leads to intelligent decision-making in solving diverse computational issues in the contemporary digital era.

Importance of Problem Solving in Computer Science

The application of problem-solving in computer science cannot be overstressed as it acts as the foundation for developing creative solutions as well as efficient algorithms. In computer science, problem-solving skills contextualize the application of theoretical concepts into practical solutions. As a result of an interaction with data structures, students and experts alike learn to deal with complex problems in stages, which gives rise not only to technical skills but also logistical thinking. Dividing a problem into tractable pieces makes it possible to analyze and strategically use algorithms more accurately. It is similar to Simons symbolic information processing (SIP) approach in which designers use intellectual processes for refining solutions. The method relies on iterative construction and building of representations such that each step is both rational and effective (Visser et al., 2006). Besides this, the interactive and dynamic nature of problem-solving exhibited through embracing certain tools and methodologies guarantees active engagement with the topic. For instance, the application of representations guarantees theorctical understanding and practical application, thereby creating a relationship between concepts and concrete outcomes. Tools that guarantee active learning environments ensure that prospective computer scientists can build their understanding by experimentation and exploration. In particular, the emphasis on affective aspects can lead to increased ownership of problems in question. This is an approach that encourages students to be responsible and question their strategies, leading to a deeper learning process emphasizing understanding rather than memorization (LeBlanc et al., 2004). Problem-solving is in this regard both an art and a skill that relies on the individual's capacity for navigating intricate systems. Worth mentioning is that the capacity to build effective problem-solving skills in computer science directly impacts the industry's capacity to address real problems of the world. As technology advances further, so does the complexity of problems encountered by engineers and software developers. Through the honing of their skills at problem-solving with data structures, computer scientists prepare themselves to handle these emerging challenges. This skill not only enhances their employability in the competitive job markets but also enables them to be better skilled with the skills needed for innovation and critical thinking. Dealing with intricate problems develops a culture of resilience and adaptability, which are vital competencies in the rapidly changing world of technology. Lastly, computer science problem-solving is worth more than academic achievement alone; it creates a community of thinkers capable of contributing to making the world a better place through the implementation of computational methods and knowledge (Figure 9.2).

Figure 9.2. *Problem solving in computer science.*

Source: https://www.eschoolnews.com/files/2018/05/computational-thinking.jpg.

9.1. TYPES OF DATA STRUCTURES

The significance of data structures cannot be overstated in computer science, particularly in problem-solving. Data structures are formatted data forms used for storing, manipulating, and retrieving data efficiently. Some of the most common examples include arrays, linked lists, stacks, and queues, each with different advantages that are appropriate for specific purposes. Arrays provide quick access to elements by using indices, thus they are suitable for repeated element access situations. On the other hand, linked lists are particularly good with dynamic memory allocation and enable insertions and deletions to be made more easily, hence supporting a more dynamic data handling methodology. Familiarization with these basic structures is important for developers as they form the basis of more advanced structures and algorithms that directly affect the efficiency of solutions implemented in software applications. Apart from basic data structures, sophisticated types like trees and graphs enable more sophisticated problem-solving needs. Trees, in the shape of binary search trees or AVL trees, enable structuring data hierarchically and efficient searching, therefore being an indispensable application in usage scenarios like database indexing and hierarchy-based information representation. Graphs, however, are used to represent relationships in data sets and are invaluable in use cases like network analysis and pathfinding algorithms. The significance of picking the right data structure cannot be overstated; it really does make a huge difference in the performance and scalability of an application. Recent trends in programming paradigms have also placed emphasis on constructing reusable building blocks of data structures, which are essential in software and knowledge engineering and thus enhancing flexibility in application construction (Cuena et al., 1999). Despite the many available data structures, the issue lies in deciding which to employ in a given scenario. This decision-making process is associated with the computational thinking values, so that the problem design will decide upon the representation of the data to be chosen. The solution building entails understanding how different data structures interact with each other and how much computation it takes to perform operations like searching, adding, or deleting information. This interaction highlights the significance of problem characterization and structural representation for the education of computer programming (Michaelson et al., 2015). Finally, a balanced understanding of data structures improves problem-solving capability since the ability to handle and optimize data in an efficient manner is paramount in today's software-centric environment (Figure 9.3).

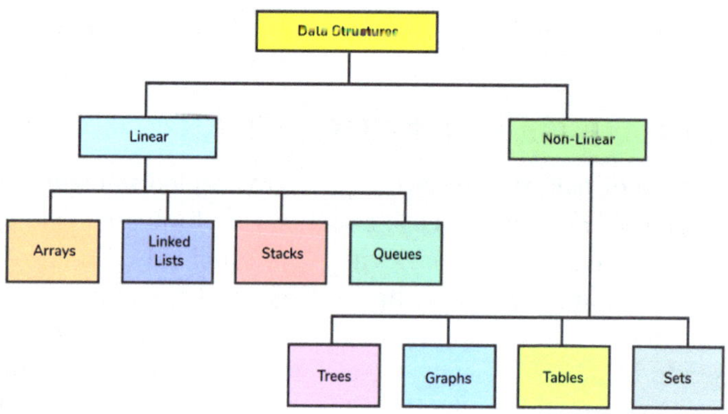

Figure 9.3. *Types of data structures.*

Source: https://assets.interviewbit.com/assets/skill_interview_questions/data-structure/data-structure-types-8ca6352dd895aab5ced64c3339408031b70c-5faaaa443aaa6c246981c694b841.png.gz.

9.1.1. Primitive Data Structures

Primitive data structures in computer science are the foundations of more complex data structures. They include integers, floating-point numbers, characters, and boolean values, which are utilized to store elementary forms of information. Their utility is their simplicity and effectiveness in providing immediate representation of the data types that the machine structure can understand. By using these primitive data types, developers can perform simple operations, such as arithmetic operations and logical operations, in efficient and fast manners. Knowledge of these primitive data structures is also essential in the algorithmic process of optimization and ensuring that complex data manipulations take place with little overhead, thus providing the stage for advanced programming and problem-solving strategies in many computational situations. The significance of primitive data structures extends much further than storage; they are also the foundation for data organization and manipulation. For instance, the sorting and searching operations heavily depend on the manner in which these basic types are processed and combined. The progression of newer programming models has fueled exploring higher-level abstractions, but most of the time, the basic operations can be traced back to these fundamental structures. Today, promotion of reusable parts in software development emphasizes having to incorporate a large set of reusable elements known as the primitive of representation, which is based on the knowledge-based approach. It supports reusability in application development and further establishes the position of primitive data structures as unavoidable components of code and as contributors to broad software engineering practices (Cuena et al., 1999). Additionally, the advent of genetic programming demonstrates the potential for evolution of problem solving in terms of data structures, and it particularly emphasizes the role of representation. Genetic programming begins with a diverse set of random programs formed from these primitive building blocks, subjecting them to actions like mutation and recombination to evolve incrementally improving solutions. This process of evolution is comparable to the manner in which primitive data structures come together to create more intricate structures and algorithms, from basic computations to advanced decision-making algorithms. The impact of such primitive forms can be seen, as they not only lay the foundation for hybrid applications blending conventional and knowledge-based approaches but also reveal their adaptability and usability across different domains (Langdon et al., 2008). There is more to the mastery of primitive data structures in this regard than merely academic exercise. It is a necessary skill set for problem-solving within the field of computer science.

9.1.2. Non-Primitive Data Structures

The understanding of non-primitive data structures is important in problem-solving skill development in computer science. Compared to primitive data types that provide descriptions of single values, non-primitive data structures accommodate complex data sets' management and manipulation. Examples such as arrays, linked lists, stacks, and queues demonstrate how data storage and retrieval can be performed in an effective way using these structures. These data structures carry out unique functions; for example, stacks utilize a Last In, First Out (LIFO) principle and are suited to usage in areas where reversal functions are needed, such as recursive function calls. With knowledge of these fundamental structures, programmers are better placed to select the appropriate form of data support for their particular algorithmic needs, thereby optimizing performance and resource handling in software programs. Further, the significance of non-primitive data structures extends into the realm of more complex constructs like trees and graphs. Trees enable hierarchical representation of data, which can prove very useful to utilize in applications like file systems and organization hierarchies where parent-child relationships are essential. Or, conversely, graphs enable a structure with which to represent relationships between disparate entities, including applications like social networks and transportation systems. As the structures become more complex, their utility in supporting robust data manipulation and representation becomes increasingly evident. Moreover, as has been discussed in software component literature, the combinations of varieties of these structures can generate a wide range of reusable and effective solutions for particular programming paradigms, hence making hybrid approaches increasingly viable in software and knowledge engineering, as indicated in Cuena et al. (1999). The emerging field of genetic programming (GP) also poses the new application of non-primitive data structures within problem-solving methodologies. GP, employing natural evolution-based algorithms, manipulates complex structures to represent possible solutions in a search space for automatic program generation. As described in Langdon et al. (2008), GP begins with a diverse initial population of solutions that get progressively enhanced through operations like mutation and crossover. This paradigm points to the generality of non-primitive data structures to learn and integrate complex responses to unstable problems, broadening a lot the horizons of computing task automation. Through the utilization of these structures, the practitioners have been in a position to address complicated issues that not only encompass the storage of information but also evolve and adapt solutions in real time.

9.1.3. Abstract Data Types

Abstract Data Types (ADTs) is a fundamental computer science concept that encapsulates data structures and their operations in a strict, rigorous definition. Programmers are not worried about the nitty-gritty of how data types are implemented when they are abstractly defined but rather how data is used. Abstraction in this regard simplifies problem-solving to a great extent because developers can utilize and manipulate data without necessarily understanding structural complexity. For instance, stacks and queues are examples of ADTs which provide varying operations like pushing, popping, enqueuing, and dequeuing without revealing the inner implementation details. Encapsulation is critical in large software development where the reduction of complexity leads to increased productivity and clearer identification of high-level problems closer to user requirements and system functionality (Cuena et al., 1999). The reusability of ADTs is another compelling benefit that makes the process of software engineering more efficient.

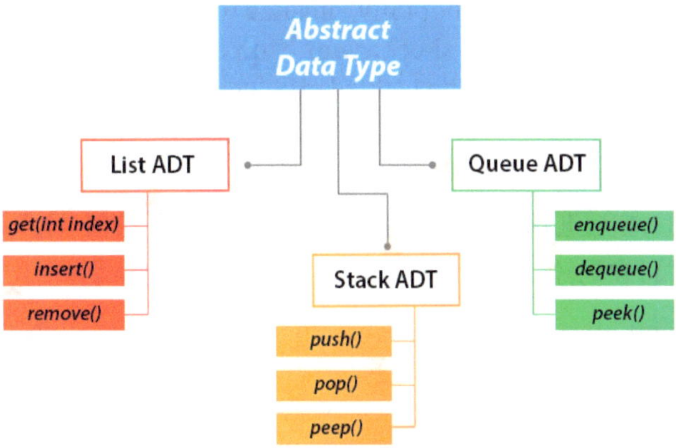

Figure 9.4. *Abstract data types.*

Source: https://techvidvan.com/tutorials/wp-content/uploads/sites/2/2020/03/various-java-abstract-data-types.jpg.

With shifting paradigms in software, the need for pieces that can be readily combined and rearranged or tailored becomes a key requirement (Cuena et al., 1999). ADTs facilitate this reusability in the form of standardized interfaces and their operations, which can be made applicable for several applications and frameworks. This modularity promotes cleaner code and enables programmers to be capable of thinking about how to implement a particular problem rather than reinventing the wheel with each project. Furthermore, as ADTs may shift between implementations—such as arrays versus linked lists to implement queues—programmers have flexibility when designing the most effective structure for their particular use. This adaptability speaks highly of the importance of learning and utilizing ADTs in dealing with different computational operations within contemporary programming platforms (Cuena et al., 1999). Incorporating ADTs in educational curricula can potentially change the manner in which upcoming programmers approach problem-solving within programming. Traditional programming education gravitates toward emphasizing more the syntax and mechanics of programming and less the inherent logic and organizational structure of data handling (Cuena et al., 1999). By focusing on ADTs, teachers can enhance their understanding of the relationship between problem-solving strategies and data types. Students can critically examine the different structures and understand how they might be applied to optimize solutions. This educational model nicely addresses the emerging emphasis on Computational Thinking that demands a wide-based approach to problem-solving (Michaelson et al., 2015). As they become proficient in ADTs, they will not only enhance their programming abilities but also become expert problem slicers who can carve large issues into smaller manageable pieces which can be tackled efficiently through abstraction (Figure 9.4).

9.2. FUNDAMENTAL OPERATIONS ON DATA STRUCTURES

The exploration of fundamental operations on data structures is essential in understanding how to effectively solve problems using computational methods. Data structures serve as the backbone of algorithms, allowing for efficient storage and retrieval of information. Fundamental operations—such as insertion, deletion, searching, and traversal—facilitate these interactions. Mastery of these operations is crucial for optimizing performance and ensuring that algorithms run efficiently under various conditions. Additionally, these operations provide a framework for approaching complex problems, integrating systematic methodologies essential in programming. By emphasizing these core functionalities, learners can develop a more profound comprehension of how to apply data structures to real-world scenarios, which directly supports their coding and problem-solving skills, ultimately augmenting their computational thinking abilities as underscored in discussions of pedagogy and programming in various educational contexts (Michaelson et al., 2015). Incorporating an understanding of fundamental operations into programming education not only enriches students technical skills but also enhances their problem-solving capabilities. Fundamental operations on data structures enable programmers to abstractly model real-world problems, translating complex requirements into manageable increments. For instance, knowing how to efficiently access data in a structure—be it through arrays, linked lists, or trees—can dramatically influence the efficacy of an algorithm. This understanding aligns with the broader educational goal of fostering a creative approach to problem-solving, as learners are encouraged to explore distinct pathways to solution development. Such skills play a vital role in navigating the evolving landscape of technology that emphasizes adaptability and resourcefulness, which are critical traits in today's fast-paced tech environment (N/A, 1982). Moreover, the relationship between fundamental operations and problem-solving extends beyond mere technical application; it fosters a more holistic understanding of programming as an iterative process. As students engage with data structures, they not only learn how to implement these operations but also how to conceptualize problems in various contexts. This iterative learning process resonates with the idea of computational thinking, where understanding the structure of information becomes paramount. The ability to manipulate data structures dynamically, assessing their strengths and weaknesses in different scenarios, cultivates critical analytical skills. Such insights empower students to devise more innovative solutions and enhances their overall efficacy as problem solvers in the realm of computer science, echoing the need for progressive educational methodologies aimed at melding problem-solving with programming (Michaelson et al., 2015).

9.2.1. Insertion and Deletion

Insertion and deletion are primitive operations within the field of data structures that significantly impact the overall performance and efficiency of most algorithms. The efficiency of such an operation can vary depending on the data structure utilized, that is, arrays, linked lists, or trees. For instance, insertion may be an easy task in a linked list due to its dynamic structure but is an issue in arrays where resizing may be needed. Deletion is not just the deletion of an item but also ensuring the integrity and order of the remaining elements. Understanding these nuances allows programmers to successfully manage data and optimize performance in algorithms critical to application in databases via real-time data processing. Insertion and deletion operations become even more intricate when dynamic data structures are brought into the mix. These structures adapt to changing data requirements and thus must provide for regular updates. For example, in dynamic graph data structures, removal and addition of edges and vertices must be efficiently handled for maintaining the graphs integrity. The recent breakthroughs highlight the efficiency of such structures, achieving insertion rates that are significantly greater than the traditional method, with the improvement in performance varying from 3.4 to 14.8 times over existing solutions. This shows how the improvement of insertion and deletion operations in dynamic settings can lead to massive performance advantages, serving as an essential tool for providing solutions to complex problems with data structures (Ashkiani et al., 2020). New techniques have also been developed to enhance the functionality of dynamic data structures, particularly when dealing with non-atomic keys such as strings and multi-dimensional points. An important technique facilitates the transformation of a standard data structure into one that may handle unbounded-length keys independently without relying on the intrinsic properties of the structure, thereby broadening the scope of usage. For instance, the construction of an online suffix tree has been notably improved with worst-case time complexity of O(log n) per input symbol, as opposed to the previous amortized time complexities. These advances enable developers to manage complex sets of information such that insertion and deletion not only become feasible but also efficient and responsive to changing demands across different computational environments (Amir et al., 2013).

9.2.2. Traversal Techniques

Traversal algorithms are elementary techniques employed in data structures to visit and treat each entity systematically. Such algorithms—depth-first search (DFS) and breadth-first search (BFS)—are elementary problem-solving devices for most computational issues. By employing these techniques, one can navigate trees, graphs, and other complex data structures and hence acquire useful data, detect cycles, or find the best paths. The applicability of these traversal approaches extends beyond algorithmic coding alone; they serve as the foundation for the focus on computational thinking, which underlines the importance of understanding the structure and nature of the problem. As highlighted in ongoing discussions, the programming and problem-solving competences must be comprehensively integrated into pedagogical models that are supportive of effective learning and implementation (Michaelson et al., 2015). In the decision of how to traverse, the utility of one method over others can vary based on the data structure used and the problem solved inherently. For instance, while depth-first search is particularly suited to traveling paths in trees and sparse graphs, breadth-first search is optimal for finding shortest paths in unweighted graphs due to its layer-by-layer approach. Existing research on hybrid disordered networks demonstrates how such techniques can be influenced by the presence of shortcuts in a network, ultimately influencing access times upon random walking. Such information is important in determining how to optimize traversal strategy, most notably in complex or partially disordered networks (Candia et al., 2008). Thus, it is essential that the interaction between traversal methods and data structure properties be understood by both the instructors and the students. Moreover, learning traversal methods offers a pedagogical viewpoint by which students are able to learn more about core programming concepts. Integrating the understanding of data structures into the framework of computational thinking helps the students view the iterative and creative elements of problem-solving. Unlike rote learning, under which methods are practiced as a habit, a deep understanding of traversal algorithms can produce innovative ways of solving problems. Teachers must therefore concentrate not just on the mechanism of such algorithms but also on their principles and potential applications. By embracing this cumulative method, the complexity involved in problem-solving and programming can be deconstructed, leading to a richer pedagogical experience that is closer to current computational demands (Michaelson et al., 2015) (Figure 9.5).

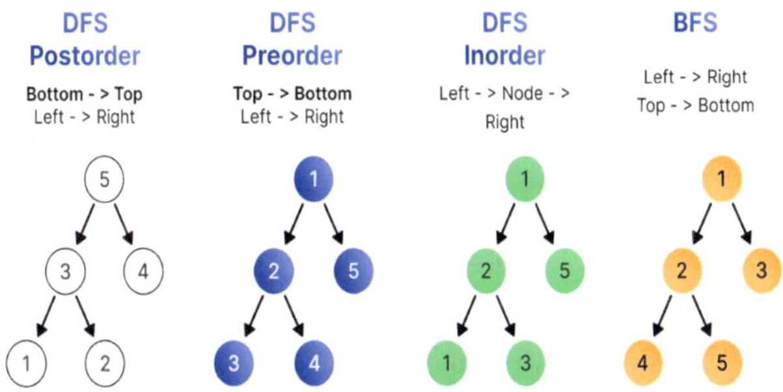

Figure 9.5. *Traversal techniques are fundamental methods.*

Source: https://deen3evddmddt.cloudfront.net/uploads/content-images/breadth-first-traversal.webp.

9.2.3. Searching Algorithms

The revelation of search algorithms constitutes an integral part of the broader category of problem-solving with data structures because they are predisposed to determine the efficiency and capability of data search processes. Linear search and binary search are some of the basic methods for locating accurate data in lists. Linear search operates through a simple process, searching the element individually until the object is located. However, this method is not very effective for large data sets. On the other hand, binary search, which requires sorted data, also brings down the performance considerably by halving the search space in each step. This is a fundamental difference that proves the significance of apt selection of data structures together with these algorithms. These decisions form the nucleus of effective algorithm design, emphasizing the mutualism between search methods and data structures. Advanced search algorithms extend beyond simple methods, typically marrying complex data structures that enhance query speed. For instance, data structures like hash tables and trees can greatly improve search operations. Hash tables provide average-case constant-time complexity for search operations, given well-spread keys, whereas tree data structures like Binary Search Trees (BSTs) allow search operations to be efficient using hierarchical structure. Moreover, the efficiency of these data structures is subject to their implementation and context of use, such that some configurations can result in improved average or worst-case performance. As algorithms get better, researchers are still exploring enhanced models that combine these data structures with novel searching techniques. For example, localitiesensitive hashing innovation in recent years has been quite promising at reducing search time across high-dimensional space, showing just how combining searching algorithms and data structures yields better problem-solving approaches (Laarhoven et al., 2017). The need for good search algorithms arises anytime one is working with intricate data search issues. When geometric data structures are involved, say, specialized searching algorithms can efficiently manage queries on colored point sets or intersecting geometric objects. Techniques used to report distinct colors of intersected objects impose constraints on the data structure in order to minimize query response time. Such advanced algorithms, based on robust data structures, not only improve performance but also help widen the application of searching methods to numerous fields, including computer graphics and spatial analysis. Increased query complexity to data requires researchers to keep improving searching algorithms in such a way that they are able to deal with these issues, demonstrating that the construction of searching algorithms plays an essential role in enhancing our power of using data structures (Gupta et al., 1996) (Figure 9.6).

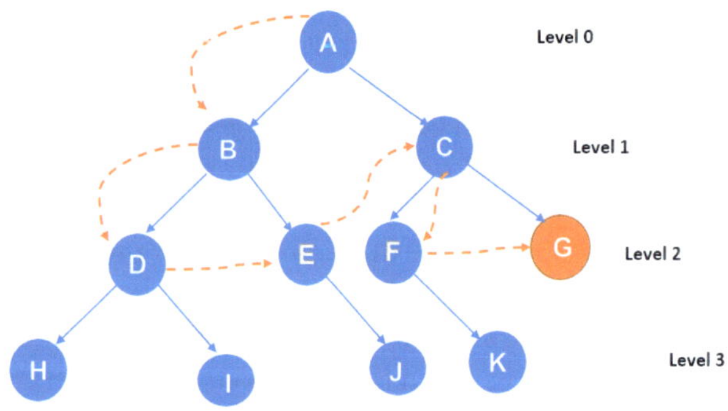

Figure 9.6. *Searching algorithms.*

Source: https://learnetutorials.com/assets/images/ai/searching/dls.png.

9.3. CHOOSING THE RIGHT DATA STRUCTURE

Picking the appropriate data structure is pivotal to achieving the optimum efficiency and effectiveness of computation problem-solving. Data structures that hold and arrange data in a way such that easy access and changes can be made can significantly influence the algorithms' performance. For instance, in the case of dynamic sets where insertion and elimination are frequently done, linked lists or dynamic arrays may be useful since they possess flexible memory allocation. Conversely, when search or sort operations are frequent, data structures such as hash tables or binary search trees will enhance performance due to quicker retrieval times. Careful consideration of the specific requirements of a specific problem, for example, frequency and type of operations, is essential for ensuring that the chosen data structure further enhances the operational requirements, guiding developers toward the optimal solution. Furthermore, the inherent nature of different data structures also needs to be known intimately from their trade-offs. For example, while arrays give constant time complexity for accessing elements using indices, they have a trade-off in the insertion and deletion operations with linear time complexity. On the other hand, certain data structures like heaps offer efficient retrieval of minimum or maximum elements but might require additional overhead in the maintenance of the heap property following updates. The capacity to appreciate these differences allows developers to actively take into account the strengths and weaknesses of each data structure in their own application, influencing critical design decisions in software development. Furthermore, the advances in other artificial intelligence techniques as outlined in existing literature can enhance deployment of suitably appropriate data structures for specific operations, hence constituting an emergent field of research in contemporary computing (Kobbacy et al., 2007). The selection of data structures also encompasses their maintainability and scalability, especially with the age of big data. When datasets are doubling in size and complexity exponentially, the quality of the chosen data structures is proportionally enhanced. For instance, the Graphical Lasso (GL) optimization problem shows the need for efficient data representation when dealing with high-dimensional data—here, the choice of data structure can significantly affect computational tractability (Agrawal et al., 2017). From this view, data structures not only have to serve the current data needs but also accommodate future scalability issues. Thus, adopting this double focus on operational efficiency in the current and future flexibility can drive developers to create sustainable data structure choices ultimately sharpening problem-solving ability in diverse computing environments.

9.3.1. Factors Influencing Choice

In determining the influencing factors on choice during problem-solving with data structures, an account should be taken of the intricacy of the decision environment. Decision-making is not linear but rather one entrenched in various factors such as personal experience, familiarity with some of the data structures, and the character of the problem to be solved. The starting point is identification of the particular needs of the problem that could set the choice of data structure. As an example, operations involving constant changes can be optimized with linked lists or dynamic arrays, and operations involving quick access can utilize hash tables. The interplay between these elements gives rise to an environment where a programmer has to navigate successfully in order to maximize the performance of the data structures within the constraints. Additionally, extrinsic factors such as technological advancements and algorithmic plans can dramatically realign the set of options.

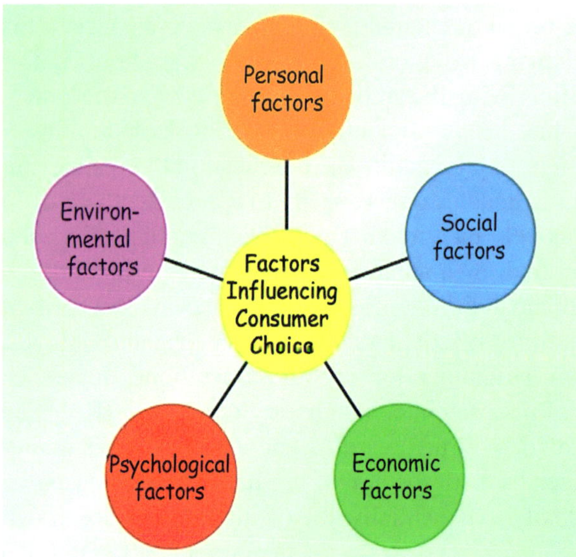

Figure 9.7. *Factors influencing choice.*

Source: https://image.slidesharecdn.com/factors-130525225001-phpapp01/95/factors-which-influnce-the-consumer-choice-4-638.jpg?cb=1369522239.

For instance, the evolution of hybrid methods such as the Fuzzy Logic-Genetic Algorithm structure illustrates an interface of innovation in algorithm design. This methodology not only facilitates planning of assembly sequence planning but also dynamically interacts with solution methods in real-time. With regard to responding to adapting significant parameters such as mutation probability and crossover rates, the process exhibits a high-level decision-making process where coders possess the ability to mold the output based on evolving requirements (Galantucci et al., 2004). Therefore, the interaction between technological advancements and underpinning knowledge determines the decisions by coders in making use of data structures. Social considerations also determine choice in a fundamental manner under collaborative coding scenarios. Sharing of experience through social networks can drive the adoption of one data structure against another as developers would aim to harness collective experience to maximize their work. For example, marketers can utilize a model of Online Influence Maximization to prioritize the most influential nodes to make available for universal uptake certain algorithms or processes. With this model, the cyclical process of feedback allows developers to refine their decisions by making adjustments based on feedback, sharpening their expertise in influence on coding (Cheng et al., 2015). This dynamic impacts individual decisions and is fed back into industry-wide patterns, rendering choice within data structure problem-solving a multifaceted phenomenon (Figure 9.7).

9.3.2. Time Complexity Considerations

Time complexity examination is crucial in evaluating how efficient data structure manipulator and problem-solving algorithms are. From time complexity, developers can predict how the performance of an algorithm will change with increased input sizes of data. Time complexities such as O(n), O(log n), and O(n^2) usually fall under the category of Big O notation and are a standard way of describing an algorithms efficiency. By isolating these complexities, it is possible to select the most appropriate data structure or algorithm for a given problem's specific needs. For instance, while lookup operations in a hash table are likely to be average-case O(1) time complexity, a linear search on an array that is not sorted may take O(n) time, highlighting the fundamental impact of choice in data structures on overall computational efficiency. In addition, time complexity issues become increasingly relevant when working with more complex data structures. Trees and graphs, for instance, are likely to require closer examination due to their hierarchical and relational nature. Algorithms such as insertion, deletion, and traversal of data structures like binary trees vary in complexity primarily based on the depth or balance of the tree. In a well-balanced binary search tree, operations generally provide a time complexity of O(log n), while the same operations in a skewed tree may fall to O(n). So, structure design not only affects unit performance measures but also the problem-solving approach as a whole. Where algorithmic efficiency wanes, time complexity can lead to resource shortages or an inability to scale well with different input size and thus requires an explicit familiarity with these measures in the real-world situation.

Finally, real-world examples of usage of time complexity implications involve applications in distributed artificial intelligence, as in the case with the ARCHON project. It is here that interaction between several solution producers comes to highlight the paramount importance of efficiency in algorithm performance. Techniques that enable communication and collaboration between solutions illustrate how time complexity influences not only individual algorithms but the entire community of problem solvers as well. As has been argued regarding legal pedagogy, the ability to explain and teach critical thinking using such algorithms can improve practical problem-solving capability in various areas. This relationship emphasizes that our approach to time complexity not only trains students in technological competence but also promotes increased sensitivity to integrative problem-solving strategies in real-life contexts, thus enhancing overall computational efficiency (Galloway et al., 2016; Jennings et al., 1991) (Figure 9.8).

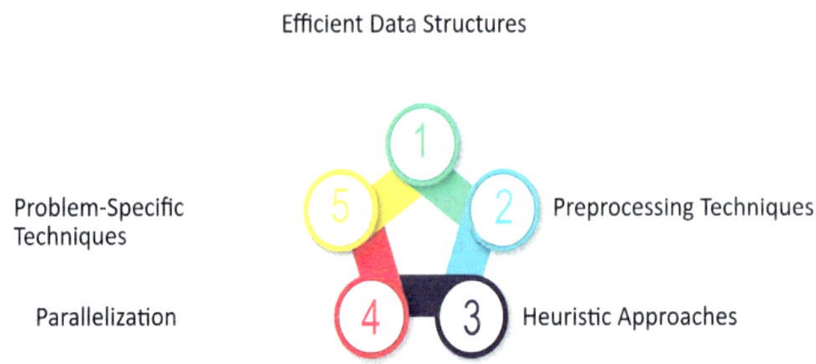

Figure 9.8. *Time complexity considerations.*

Source: https://fastercapital.co/i/Linear-programming--Solving-assignment-problems-efficiently--Optimizing-Time-and-Space-Complexity-in-Assignment-Problem-Solutions.webp.

9.3.3. Space Complexity Considerations

The space complexity is a critical term used within the analysis of algorithms, particularly in assessing data structure efficiency. Space complexity refers to the amount of memory an algorithm uses to execute as a function of the input size. Analysis accommodates both the auxiliary space, or computation temporary space, and the space used by the input. By comprehending the distinction between the types of data structures such as arrays, linked lists, and trees, people are in a position to make choices that optimize memory use. Under circumstances where memory is limited, selecting a data structure whose space complexity is smaller can significantly optimize the performance of an application, placing it at the core of problem-solving in computer science. Moreover, the relationship between space complexity and computational efficiency cannot be exaggerated. For instance, algorithms of greater time complexity may not be viable if they need excessive space, particularly where dealing with large datasets. Such a trade-off is observed in situations of processing large data or real-time processing where memory is a major consideration. As shown in recent research, enhancing machine learning and artificial intelligence refers to the contribution of space requirements on algorithm efficiency. As computer strength grows and improves, achieving efficient algorithms must sacrifice space consumption against other parameters of performance, further demonstrating the importance of space complexity in algorithm design and selection because it impacts overall effectiveness in solving problems (Ben-David et al., 2018). In practice, space complexity is achieved in real situations, where sudden demands for memory may lead to system breakdown or crippling loss of performance. For example, in distributed systems where varying data structures collaborate, as outlined in research on the ARCHON project, both the communication overhead and the storage requirements locally need to be considered in order to enable the integration of several problem solvers harmoniously (Jennings et al., 1991). To overcome such challenges calls for a proper grasp of space complexity, and thus developers and researchers set out to devise innovative solutions that use memory optimally without compromising algorithmic efficiency. In the advancement of the field, the necessity of balancing space and time complexity continues to push the development of theoretical concepts as well as working implementations that focus on maximizing resource utilization in the context of data structures.

9.4. COMMON DATA STRUCTURES AND THEIR APPLICATIONS

Data structures are the cornerstone of efficient algorithm design and implementation, offering a framework for the manipulation and organization of data in a manner that optimizes computational efficiency. Among the various data structures that exist, arrays, linked lists, stacks, queues, trees, and graphs are some of the most widely used. Each of these structures has unique attributes that address specific application needs. For example, arrays give constant-time access to elements using indexing, making them suitable for those applications where quick data access is important. However, linked lists give dynamic memory allocation and element insertion or deletion, which is useful in programs that have continuous changes. It is important to know the nature of these data structures in software programming because the choice of structure impacts significantly the program's performance and scalability. Data structures extend beyond regular software programs and are used across various fields, including data science, where data structure is crucial for analysis and insight. Data structures are central to algorithms processing large amounts of data, such as searching and sorting, which are fundamental operations in data analysis. Further, as put forward by recent guidelines of the Park City Math

Institute, a formal way of learning about such data structures must exist for aspiring data scientists and computer scientists. Such focus on pedagogical frameworks allows students to develop a strong conceptual knowledge of how best to apply different data structures in real-world contexts (Agarwal et al., 2017). By linking theory to practice, institutions of education can equip students to more effectively deal with the complexities of modern data issues. Besides, the increased demand for hybrid applications that merge conventional software approaches with knowledge-based solutions highlights the need for robust data structures with the ability to support such hybrids. The concept of reusable components, in particular, the representation primitive, presents itself as a suitable solution in order to increase reusability in software engineering (Cuena et al., 1999). This approach enables developers to combine various data structures with greater simplicity, thereby facilitating the development of intricate systems that can handle and analyze a broad range of data types. With the ever-changing aspect of the software engineering environment, the need to choose appropriate data structures does not diminish. With the enhanced understanding of data structures and their correlation, developers will be in a better place to address present challenges in technology and data management (Figure 9.9).

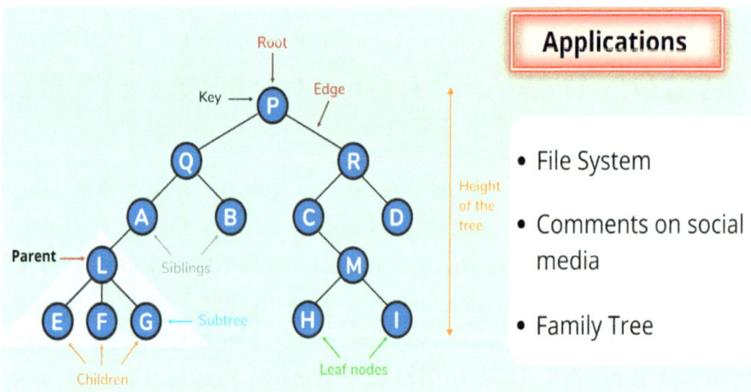

Figure 9.9. *Common data structures and their applications.*

Source: https://logicmojo.com/assets/dist/new_pages/images/tree_ds.png.

9.4.1. Arrays and Lists

The study of data structures such as arrays and lists forms the core of computer science, due primarily to their efficiency and adaptability in dealing with collections of data. Arrays, collections of elements located at contiguous areas of memory, offer an efficient and easy way to access elements by indexing. Arrays are thus appropriate for any scenario in which constant-time access is necessary. For example, while implementing algorithms that include searching or sorting, the predictable memory pattern of arrays allows optimized performance to be achieved. The fixed size of the array can also be beneficial where the data volume is known beforehand to avoid overhead and ensure maximum usage of memory. Thus, arrays form a fundamental data structure which is employed for more advanced implementations in most fields. Conversely, lists, particularly linked lists, provide a more dynamic solution to arrays. Lacking a preallocated size, like arrays, linked lists support dynamic memory allocation and deallocation. This dynamicity comes in very handy in applications involving much insertion or deletion of the dataset, such as adding or removing elements. Linked lists are able to carry out these operations efficiently without having to pay for expensive reallocations or element shifting, as opposed to arrays. The node-based form of linked lists, in which each node contains a reference to the next one, lends itself logically to operations like traversal, insertion, and deletion in linear time. Understanding these characteristics puts developers in a more advantageous position to choose the right data structure for an issue at hand, allowing effective problem-solving methodologies within computer software development. Arrays and lists are applied in more complex manners in modern software development by integrating newer methods such as symbolic execution as well as testing methodologies. For instance, CLP-based approaches have been encouraging in generating test cases (TCG) for object-oriented software that often relies on complex data structures like lists and arrays. Symbolic values are used in place of explicit numerical inputs in these approaches to be able to traverse more than one execution path and edge cases to ensure exhaustive testing of data structure behavior. Importantly, such a testing paradigm embraces the subtleties of data structure management, including heap-allocated arrays or lists management. Such advanced testing methods inclusion is a testament to the revolutionizing role of software verification and problem-solving via data structures, highlighting their relevance in theoretical as much as in practical contexts (Albarghouthi et al., 2015; Albert et al., 2010).

9.4.2. Stacks and Queues

Stacks and queues in data structures are fundamental concepts that play important roles in problem-solving strategies. Stacks, as characterized by their last-in-first-out (LIFO) paradigm, offer the sequential retrieval and storage of information. The structure is particularly used where the most recent information is to be accessed instantly while older information is not modified for future access if needed. This property of stacks makes them very significant in programming function calls and facilitates tasks such as tracing program execution and memory management for temporary variables. Implication of efficient push and pop functionalities enables numerous computing applications and highlights the need to grasp this data structure to ensure effective algorithm design and analysis in modern-day programming applications. On the other hand, queues exhibit the first-in-first-out (FIFO) model, which supports various computational requirements different from those offered by stacks. Queues allow for the sequential processing of tasks and are thus essential in usage like scheduling algorithms for operating system resource management. Since tasks come in one order, they are dispatched in the same manner, which is critical for fairness and efficiency where there are competing processes vying for scarce resources.

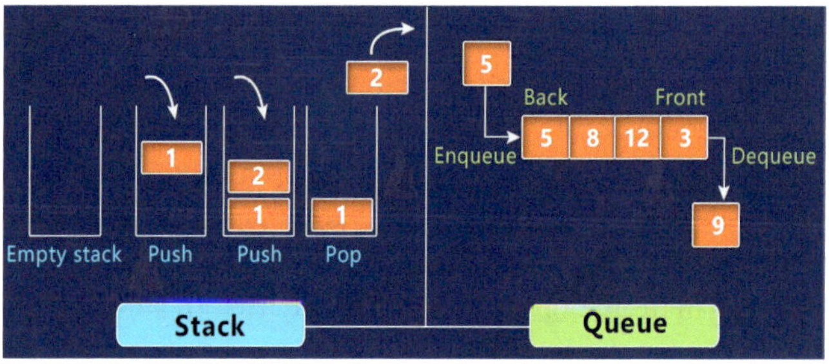

Figure 9.10. *Stacks and queues.*

Source: https://techvidvan.com/tutorials/wp-content/uploads/sites/2/2021/07/Stack-and-Queues-in-C-1.jpg.

The ease of enqueueing and dequeuing makes it an easy paradigm for breadth-first search algorithms, event-driven programming, and network system buffer management. Becoming familiar with queues is not merely a matter of functionality but also reflects how they are a key factor in making activities execute smoothly essential to system reliability and performance. Stacks and queues, as inherent constituents of data structures, the interaction between them reflects their complementary natures in solving problems across various disciplines.

Not only do both structures enhance algorithms with greater efficiency but also provide essential support for even higher-level data management systems. For instance, data mapping between types can be greatly improved by the systematic use of stacks and queues, as demonstrated through computational modeling (Lawrence et al., 1975). The combination only becomes more evident in such advanced fields as machine learning and data analysis at the large scale, where algorithmic efficiency and replicability are issues at hand (Anjos et al., 2017). By learning stacks and queues, students and professionals can hone their problem-solving skills while facilitating advancements in data processing and handling technologies critical to practical applications (Figure 9.10).

9.4.3. Trees and Graphs

The significance of graphs and trees in data structures cannot be exaggerated as they enable effective problem-solving in various fields of study, ranging from computer science to biology and social sciences. Trees with their hierarchical structure are the foundation of many algorithms which require effective data access, such as searching and sorting. For example, binary search trees offer logarithmic time complexity in searching because they are able to offer direct access to the elements with a maintained sorted order. Further, the hierarchical data representation reduces complexity in structures ranging from file systems to organizational charts. Conversely, graphs better capture relationships and interactions between different entities and hence are required for network analysis, social interactions, and transportation logistics. As a native data structure, trees and graph research enable scholars and practitioners to discern patterns and determine optimized solutions in complex systems. Statistical methodological enhancement also facilitates the process of making inferences from relationships using trees. Current studies focus on developing efficient algorithms for reliably inferring tree structures from data, particularly when there is limited data availability. Using techniques such as the imprecise Dirichlet model, the posterior interval expectations of mutual information can be derived to further improve the reliability of tree structure inference. The algorithm in Chow et al. (2005) has significant improvement in time complexity and presents a robust method for identifying common substructures among sets of potential trees. This capability not only enhances theoretical understanding but also makes practitioners capable of applying these findings in actual data sets where traditional techniques may fail. Accordingly, the intersection of statistical modeling and trees reveals profound meaning for good data inference.

Graph structures play an essential role in determining what is alike and what is not alike between various data sets, particularly in the case of comparing trees. Introduction of maximum agreement subtree-computation algorithms offers a more nuanced understanding of labeled tree relationships regardless of their form. As explained in Kao et al. (2001), refinement of arbitrary labeling algorithms enhances the speed of tree comparison and opens up areas for study. Of particularly notable importance is handling node-unbalanced or weight-unbalanced graphs to facilitate hierarchical bipartite matching problems, easing complex analysis. This focus on computational efficiency is important because it enables scientists to handle larger data sets and extract useful information without incurring prohibitive computational costs. Studying trees and graphs is thus at the heart of overcoming modern data challenges, laying the groundwork for a variety of applications in numerous scholarly and applied domains (Figure 9.11).

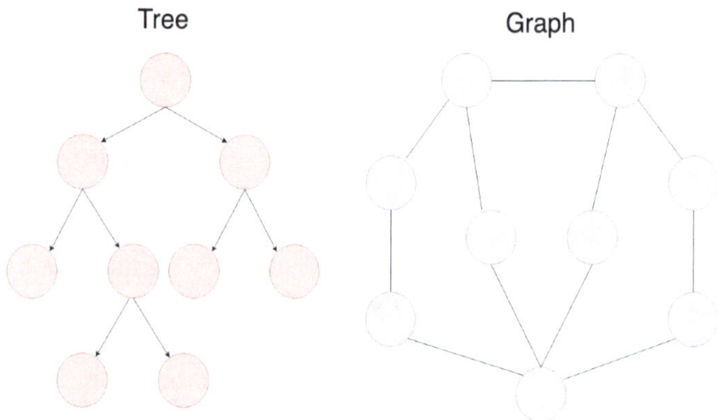

Figure 9.11. *Trees and graphs.*

Source: https://www.educative.io/api/edpresso/shot/6304047290646528/image/6393961088811008.

9.5. PROBLEM-SOLVING TECHNIQUES USING DATA STRUCTURES

Usage of the right data structures significantly enhances problem-solving techniques in various disciplines. By using appropriate data structures such as trees, graphs, and arrays, programmers can handle data and work on it efficiently, thereby allowing for more complex problem-solving mechanisms. This efficiency becomes critical while solving complicated problems involving numerous aspects. For instance, in optimization problems, an adequately implemented data structure can organize data retrieval and storage processes in a way that is efficient, allowing algorithms to operate more efficiently. Furthermore, libraries that incorporate specialized data structures provide researchers with tools that allow them to easily understand their respective problems so that the manipulations and operations performed on the data fit perfectly with the requirement of each individual task (Constantino et al., 2016). This tailored approach promotes a culture of innovation and advancement in solution paradigms. Furthermore, the use of sophisticated data structures is also extended to high-dimensional data scenarios, such as in genomics and chemometrics, where data complexity requires sophisticated dimensionality reduction techniques. Through methods such as Regularized Partial Least

Squares (PLS), it is shown how flexible data structures can be at the core of making key conclusions from high-dimensional data. The application of Sparse PLS, for example, illustrates the capacity to manage data variance well without sacrificing interpretability of output, significant in working with intricate datasets (Allen et al., 2012). To this end, these approaches not only facilitate better computation performance but also allow researchers to cope with data correlation nuances, leading to more accurate and reliable problem-solving solutions. In this context, designing bespoke application program interfaces (APIs) that are specific to certain problem domains facilitates proper utilization of performance-oriented data structures for research and development. These APIs can handle problem specification files and conduct structured memory management with new techniques like solution dispensers, which are more effective than traditional garbage collectors. The strategy has obvious advantages, such as enhancing problem comprehension, ensuring fairness when comparing results, and optimizing pertinent data structures for solving methodologies (Constantino et al., 2016). Through creating a framework that integrates problem-specific data handling with efficient algorithmic strategies, researchers are able to solve complex problems faster, eventually reaching solutions that are not only new but also dependable and scalable in actual applications.

9.5.1. Divide and Conquer

Divide and Conquer is a fundamental technique of problem-solving optimization in data structures. It is a way of breaking down large, complicated problems into smaller, simpler, independent, and parallel sub-problems that can be solved separately. Efficiency is highly improved by the use of this process, particularly in large data sets where direct methods are computationally expensive. For instance, sorting algorithms such as Merge Sort and Quick Sort use this approach to its maximum capacity, splitting the data into smaller and smaller parts recursively, sorting them, and then merging them. Not only does this enhance the sorting capacity but also reduces the time complexity throughout the entire process compared to traditional sorting methods, proving the prowess of Divide and Conquer when dealing with huge data. In addition, the hierarchical organization of Divide and Conquer allows for consistent representation of cases in problem spaces. As shown in Perera et al. (1997), problems can be decomposed into sub-problems that connect loosely conceptualized cases at higher abstract levels with concrete solutions at the lowest level in the hierarchy. By representing cases in this consistent manner, systems can exploit contextual commonalities in retrieving information more accurately. The retrieval techniques displayed here highlight how hierarchical case representation maximizes access to optimal solutions through contextual features, thereby maximizing the use of the Divide and Conquer concept in not only improving problem-solving but also achieving accuracy in solutions. Furthermore, the Divide and Conquer method is extended beyond traditional problems to new domains such as evolutionary algorithms in circuit design, as discussed in Kalganova et al. (2012). Here, circuit synthesis means a method in which incremental evolutions and substructures are employed strategically to construct efficient designs. Through dividing the circuit design problem into smaller, evolutionary steps, the complexity of the entire task is kept at bay, making it simpler to search for solutions in a more convenient manner. The effectiveness of the approach proves the malleability of Divide and Conquer across many fields and indicates how easily this strategic approach can adapt to different problem-solving hurdles in data structures. Through this process, not only is the problem-solving process simplified but innovation in its many applications is also encouraged (Figure 9.12).

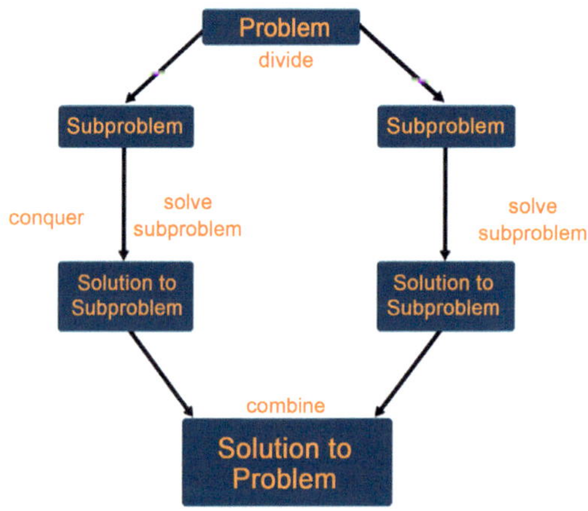

Figure 9.12. *Divide and conquer.*

Source: https://favtutor.com/resources/images/uploads/Divide_and_Conquer_Algorithm.png.

9.5.2. Dynamic Programming

Dynamic programming (DP) is a popular algorithmic technique that breaks down hard problems into subproblems, solves each subproblem only once, and stores their solutions. This approach contrasts with naive recursion, which may lead to exponential time complexity due to repeated calculations. The heart of dynamic programming lies in its principle of optimality, where a best solution is constructed cheaply from the best solutions of its subproblems. Not surprisingly, this technique is used widely throughout operations research, economics, and computer science. Dynamic programming employs arrays or tables for storing the computed values, which can be accessed very quickly and facilitate efficient recursive problem-solving for problems like the knapsack, Fibonacci sequence, and shortest path calculations in graphs. Dynamic programming is also at the core of enhancing algorithm efficiency, particularly when there are overlapping subproblems and optimal substructure.

By the employment of memorization or tabulation, dynamic programming decreases the amount of computational work and enhances efficiency. For instance, in the classic problem of generating the nth Fibonacci number, a naive recursive function recalculates again and again, while a dynamic programming solution stores previously computed values, decreasing the time complexity from exponential to linear. Moreover, this optimization is not only limited to Fibonacci numbers but is also the key to solving optimally the traveling salesman problem and other scheduling problems, demonstrating the remarkable versatility across application domains. The effectiveness of dynamic programming establishes its fame as one of the fundamental algorithms within the overarching category of data structures and algorithms. In practical applications, dynamic programming has also been successfully integrated into learning websites to teach individuals problem-solving.

For example, an interactive online system developed for the Italian Olympiads in Informatics has proved the effectiveness of dynamic programming through a structured training system, primarily increasing the number of secondary school participants. By utilizing a grading system that captures the principles of dynamic programming, students are encouraged to solve problems iteratively, and hence develop a clearer conceptual idea of algorithmic thinking. These applications inscribe the importance of dynamic programming not just in theoretical settings but also as an applied skill for prospective computer scientists, ultimately transferring an atmosphere of creativity and computational proficiency into educational contexts (Luigi et al., 2016). Furthermore, application of dynamic programming in design optimization indicates its core role in a majority of engineering disciplines, where it aids in the creation of safer and more efficient products (Perdahcioglu et al., 2009). This indicates the multifaceted significance of dynamic programming in current problem-solving paradigms dependent on data structures (Figure 9.13).

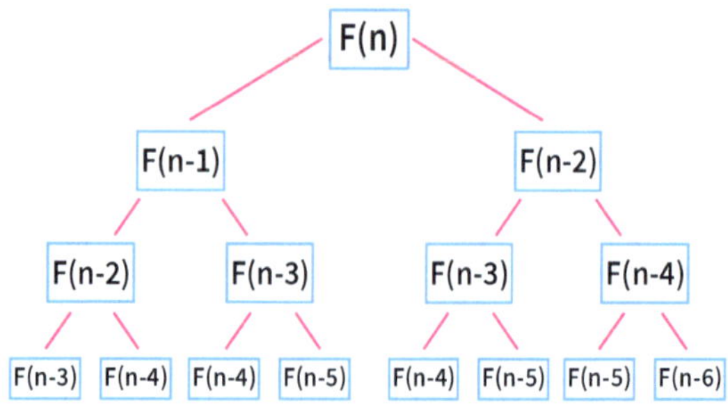

Figure 9.13. *Dynamic programming.*

Source: https://external-content.duckduckgo.com/iu/?u=https%3A%2F%2Fscaler.com%2Ftopics%2Fimages%2Fexample-of-dynamic-programming.webp&f=1&nofb=1&ipt=82d7b8289e3e1ac6930a8e76ab510d49d7525f17bad1c66fbe96a416116761a4.

9.5.3. Greedy Algorithms

Greedy algorithms are one of the basic problem-solving methods in the field of data structures and algorithms. Greedy algorithms make locally optimal choices at every stage with the hope that they might lead to a global optimum solution. For most problems, the greedy algorithm provides a method of reaching a solution efficiently without the exhaustive search normally needed in dynamic programming or backtracking algorithms. It is, however, necessary to consider problem structure to test whether a greedy solution will result in an optimal solution.

Where optimality does not work, understanding the limitations of this approach is important in the decision of which algorithmic approach will work best for a given problem. Greedy algorithms are applied to a broad variety of problems, ranging from optimization problems through resource allocation problems. For instance, for finding the minimum spanning tree in graph theory, Kruskal's and Prim's algorithm are commonly applied. They focus on the choice of edges by weight, such that at every decision point, the lowest-weight edge is chosen to construct a tree spanning all the vertices with minimum total weight. These methods focus on the greediness of greedy methods; they will typically give solutions quickly with manageable computational complexity. However, the requirement for careful implementation is increased when dealing with NP-hard problems, since greedy approaches can quite frequently fail to deliver optimal outcomes, and that is why it is necessary to dig deeper and establish their correctness (Quanrud et al., 2018).

Despite how excellent greedy algorithms may be, issues with intricate structures not being able to accommodate greedy ideas are an issue. As the example of combinatorial optimization illustrates, certain problems such as the minimum weight k-cut problem illustrate the limitations of a greedy approach. Although greedy algorithms have approximation approaches and can generate close-to-optimal solutions, in most instances they require complementary mechanisms or other approaches in order to be correct and efficient. For example, familiarity with the background concepts behind probabilistic graphical models and the relationship with greedy methods can enhance algorithmic design. The challenge of defining efficient data structures in parallel computation scenarios makes greedy strategies challenging to apply, as seen in the design of parallel computational intelligence-based algorithms based on contemporary programming technologies (Borchani et al., 2016). Hence, while greedy algorithms are wonderful solutions to countless scenarios, careful examination and understanding of their suitability is still necessary in effective problem-solving through data structures (Figure 9.14).

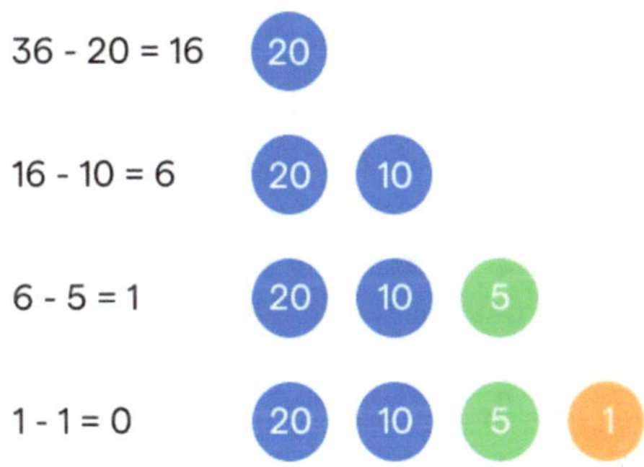

Figure 9.14. *Greedy algorithms.*

Source: https://cdn.botpenguin.com/assets/website/Greedy_Algorithm_19 db6 70e50.webp.

9.6. REAL-WORLD APPLICATIONS OF DATA STRUCTURES

Data structures are the building blocks for use in many real-world applications, facilitating efficient problem-solving in different domains. As an example, trees and graphs can be used to optimize the routing algorithms of contemporary networks such that data packets are delivered in a timely manner and without congestion. Heaps are also crucial in the application of priority queues, which form the basis of important functionalities like task scheduling in operating systems. Such courses demonstrate how choosing an appropriate data structure directly affects the efficiency of algorithmic solutions, thereby enhancing system performance. Proper usage of abstractions like these not only demonstrates theoretical knowledge but also fosters concrete skills that can be applied in the industry to improve developers' capacity to design scalable and efficient software solutions. The arrival of massive data environments rendered the use of complex data structures necessary to store and examine lots of data. For instance, databases extensively utilize hash tables and B-trees in order to support fast data retrieval and storage. Hash tables have O(1) average-case time complexity for lookups, and thus are suited in applications where quickly accessing is required of big data sets. At the same time, B-trees present an efficient way of data sorting and accessing, on which the performance of most database management systems is built. Additionally, the software application complexity growth requires the use of reusable components. Herein, the idea of the primitive representation, as described in Cuena et al. (1999), promotes program modularity and reusability, such that such applications become not only more efficient but easier to scale and maintain. Educational institutions increasingly come to understand the contribution value that data structures hold in preparing future data science and other professional practitioners. Suggestions from the Park City Math Institute in 2016 following the identification of best practices show a collective effort to streamline undergraduate data science curricula, integrating core data structure content into the curriculum (Agarwal et al., 2017). By equipping students with fundamental proficiency in data structures, such programs enable students to effectively solve complex data-oriented problems. Through acquired knowledge and skills built up through practice sessions and practical applications of data structures, graduates become competent problem solvers with the ability to provide services to various industries ranging from finance to healthcare. Emphasizing this intersection not only improves learning in the classroom but also aligns learning objectives with industry requirements so that the next generation of data scientists is properly prepared to solve real-world issues.

9.6.1. Data Management Systems

In data management systems, the significance of well-organized and efficient processing of data is crucial. The systems form the groundwork for several applications through which organizations are able to collect, store, process, and retrieve massive amounts of data. With the help of some data structures such as arrays, linked lists, and trees, data management systems facilitate efficient organization of data, which is very important for quick access and analysis.

With an increase in data-driven decision-making among organizations, the need to possess good data management solutions arises. Moreover, technologies integrated within these systems allow for the development of robust features such as data integrity, security, and real-time analytics, which play substantial roles in maintaining competitive advantage in today's information-based environment. All such underlying frameworks are vital to learn because they assist organizations in utilizing their data to the fullest.

Figure 9.15. *Data management systems.*

Source: https://www.hostinger.com/tutorials/wp-content/uploads/sites/2/2022/05/Database-Management-System-DBMS-components-reporting-data-utilities-monitoring-query-language-storage-engine-and-access-controls.jpg.

The evolution of data management systems has been marked by their adaptability to emerging technologies and changing organizational needs. The necessity of timely information processing has raised the levels of traditional systems to higher architectures that can accommodate enormous data complexities. Forefront among these advances are autonomous world model-based information systems, which have played an instrumental role in navigating extensive databases without sacrificing contextual expertise and usefulness (N/A, 1982). These advancements make it possible for data management systems to go beyond simple data storage capabilities, playing a focal role in decision support and management programs. The integration of more than one data structure has made it possible to create such advanced systems, illustrating how elementary knowledge can transform into comprehensive solutions that tap the maximum efficiency and resilience in complex environments. The integration of reasoning systems even more emphasizes the potential of data management systems to solve complex problems. The RIMSAT project is indicative of the trend, which aims at enhancing decision-making capability through the application of Case Based Reasoning and Model Based Reasoning paradigms (Merida-Campos et al., 2003). With the integration of the two paradigms of reasoning, the project aims to build an intelligent decision support system capable of solving complex, safety-critical situations. Utilization of such hybrid paradigms of reasoning in data management systems not only improves the quality of critical decisions but also makes it possible for organizations to respond to emergent threats in time. This strategy places emphasis on the critical role played by data structures and management systems in equipping decision-makers with the necessary tools to deal successfully with the complexities of the modern operating environments (Figure 9.15).

9.6.2. Networking and Communication

The intricate interdependence of communication and networking is key in addressing computationally intensive problems, especially data structures. Effective networking facilitates information exchange between heterogeneous systems and components, enabling ease of communication. In data structures, efficient networking protocols facilitate data to be structured and accessed in a manner that optimizes time and resources. As system architectures change—such as to cloud radio access networks (C-RANs)—high-capacity fronthaul connectivity becomes more critical. Not only do they enhance spectral efficiency but also support novel techniques such as compression and quantization, which are required to prevent the restrictions imposed by limited fronthaul on C-RANs (Lau et al., 2015). Thus, a robust networking platform enhances solutions in data-intense applications. The incorporation of advanced communication strategies in network models also increases the problem-solving process within data structures. These communication strategies facilitate distributed computing scenarios under which the components must cooperate even with potential failures. For example, in exa-scale computers where failures are bound to increase, new resilience techniques are employed to maintain computation integrity. Algorithm-based recovery processes' adaptive control mechanisms are a classic example of this coordination, making the system continue operations notwithstanding faults (Huber et al., 2018). Through coordination among healthy and faulty components of the computing process, communication protocols ensure reliability in data processing for effective use, ultimately influencing data structure usage effectiveness. Moreover, the evolving nature of networking and communication technologies underscores the constant need to formulate adaptive solutions to counter evolving data structure issues. As demand for computational power and efficiency rises, so does demand for innovative solutions to communication within networked environments. Combining system resources with sophisticated techniques like large-scale coordinated processing not only improves performance but is also compliant with the greater complexity and scale of datasets that have to be processed (Lau et al., 2015). It is this flexibility that ensures data structures continue to be relevant and useful amidst shifting technological environments. The cross-pollination of concept between data structure optimization and networking builds a strong base for overcoming the current computing issues, which opens up future prospects in both areas.

9.6.3. Artificial Intelligence and Machine Learning

The union of Machine Learning (ML) and Artificial Intelligence (AI) has revolutionized the problem-solving methods in various fields. The union enables sophisticated methods for processing complex data structures, leading to more effective solutions of real-time problems. Precisely, AI employs data structures to emulates complex patterns and relations and enables breakthroughs in predictive analytics, computer vision, and natural language processing. The capacity to handle vast volumes of data with algorithms programmed in ML gives systems the capability to learn and adapt from new data, enhancing their performance and precision. Adaptive learning systems not only provide processable problem-solving processes but also prepare users to tackle historically challenging tasks with increased confidence and efficiency, marking a paradigm shift in solving computational problems. In addition, educational models for AI and ML put a lot of emphasis on using data structures to solve real-world issues. Research projects sponsored by institutions such as the National Science Foundation have been at the forefront of incorporating core AI topics into lab experiments, offering a balanced learning experience. Students learn through interactive methods by experiencing first-hand the interaction of data structures with AI. For instance, the N-puzzle game is a state-of-the-art arena where students can acquire knowledge on search algorithms and heuristics in an ordered and engaging context. Not only does a strategy like this foster a deeper understanding of theoretical ideas, but it also sharpens critical thinking and problem-solving abilities, equipping future professionals with necessary tools for tackling the challenges of AI-imposed situations (Markov et al., 2006). The applications of the integration of AI and ML, in the context of data structures, extend beyond the academic domain; they also have implications for software engineering and industrial practices. Having a firm foundation in AI concepts, students will better be able to design intelligent systems that will be able to solve key issues in their field. Emphasis on the machine learning as a common thread underscores the importance of robust paradigms in problem-solving integrating AI technology and engineering principles. With business markets further leaping into the productivity advantages of smart automation, understanding these interfaces will be essential for future professionals. Through the adaptive learning and collaborative project work programs, the learning system is being transformed, ultimately resulting in a generation of learners who can handle the intricacies of problem-solving in data-intensive environments (Coleman et al., 2005) (Figure 9.16).

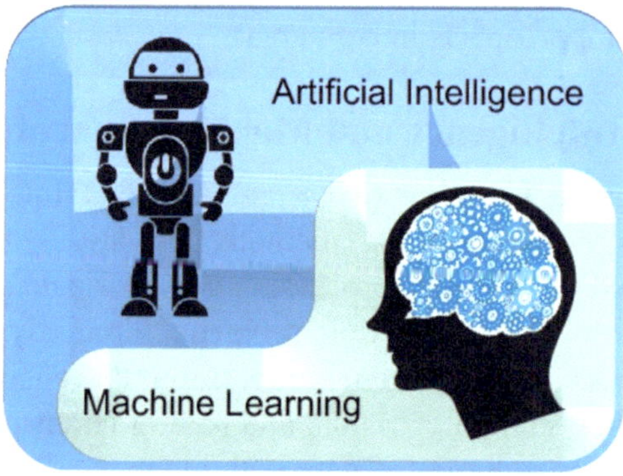

Figure 9.16. *Artificial intelligence and machine learning.*

Source: https://jeyedu.co.in/wp-content/uploads/2021/12/ai-vs-machine-learning.png.

SUMMARY

In concluding an examination of problem-solving with data structures, one should be mindful of the fundamental role that these structures play in providing potent design and thinking approaches. As demonstrated through this essay, data structures are the backbone of information management and organization, enabling efficient algorithm execution as well as the development of solutions to complex problems. The various properties and performance of data structures—ranging from arrays to trees and graphs—demonstrate their adaptability towards fulfilling diverse computational requirements. The same adaptability also reflects the basic principles of human cognition where the designers have to construct representations of the world in the light of real-world situations, bridging the gap between theory and practice (Visser et al., 2006). In addition, recognizing the cognitive material involved in data structuring solidifies our understanding of design complexity. The relationship between representations and cognitive processes shapes design practices within computer science. Different designs involve diverse data structuring strategies with significant impacts on problem conceptualization and solution. For instance, the constructive character of representation typically informs the strategies followed by designers, which influence their selection of data structures based on the specifics of the artefact or problem situation at hand. This alignment of cognitive process and data structuring confirms the importance of situational awareness in design and emphasizes the role of context in determining the best strategies for problem-solving (Akin et al., 2009). Lastly, summarizing the threads of this analysis, it is evident that there is a need for an intuitive understanding of both data structures as well as cognitive design processes in order to be able to solve problems successfully in computer science. Their interplay is to show how cognitive theory can be applied to enhance real-world results within data structures. By mapping different types of design and the high similarity levels between diverse problem situations, researchers and practitioners can generate a more advanced style of problem-solving. Future research must continue questioning the functional relationships between data structures and cognitive processes to provide ways for new solutions and research in the field (Akin et al., 2009).

Throughout problem-solving with data structures, there are several key points that demonstrate their significance in the computational world. One of the most vital points is the ability of data structures to manage, access, and manipulate data in efficient manners, and that is the foundation of algorithm performance. Surprisingly, the data structure selection can dramatically decrease both time complexity and space usage when programming algorithms. For example, the decision between a linked list and an array can determine the efficacy of operations like insertions and deletions. As observed in many applications, including databases and search engines, these data structures constitute the core of data handling, supporting rapid data access and manipulation that are in harmony with the needs of users. Equally vital is applying backcasting as a strategic decision-making key, particularly in data structures and their application in planning over the long term. Backcasting as a concept has its foundation based on identifying minimum steps towards given future objectives. Backcasting is indispensable in developing effective data strategies. By applying backcasting, interested parties are able to outline short-term measures that are in line with general data management objectives. This method encourages a reflective critique of current practices and calls forth critical revisions to promote innovation and design more sophisticated algorithms with the capability to utilize data structures effectively in solving intricate problems from various disciplines (Bärlund et al., 2010). Further, the guidelines provided for undergraduate Data Science programs encapsulate the revolutionizing nature of learning models meant to address contemporary challenges in problem-solving using data structures. These recommendations aim to give shape to institutions that desire to enhance their curricula, allowing for the better understanding of the interdisciplinary nature of data science. Through the use of math, statistics, and computer science, students gain the fundamental abilities to work with and take advantage of different data structures efficiently. This pedagogical method caters to the needs of the industry, making future professionals equipped to handle practical problems using data structures as a central part of data science strategies (Agarwal et al., 2017).

REFERENCES

1. Agarwal, M., Averett, M., Baumer, B., et al. (2017). Curriculum guidelines for undergraduate programs in data science. https://core.ac.uk/download/287356701.pdf (accessed on 9th September 2025).
2. Agrawal, R., Banerjee, A., Coffrin, C., Fattahi, S., Hsieh, C. J., Mazumder, R., Sojoudi, S., et al. (2017). Sparse inverse covariance estimation for chordal structures. http://arxiv.org/abs/1711.09131 (accessed on 9th September 2025).
3. Akcay Perdahcioglu, D., de Boer, A., Ellenbroek, M. H. M., et al. (2009). An optimization method for dynamics of structures with repetitive component patterns. https://core.ac.uk/download/pdf/11473336.pdf (accessed on 9th September 2025).
4. Akin, A., Akin, A., et al. (2009). Design: One, but in different forms. http://arxiv.org/abs/0708.1725 (accessed on 9th September 2025).
5. Albarghouthi, A., Bouajjani, A., Brillout, A., Reynolds, A., Stump, A., Bradley, A. R., Barrett, C., et al. (2015). On deciding local theory extensions via E-matching. http://arxiv.org/abs/1508.06827 (accessed on 9th September 2025).
6. Albert, E., Puebla, G., Gómez-Zamalloa, M., et al. (2010). Test case generation for object-oriented imperative languages in CLP. http://arxiv.org/abs/1007.5195 (accessed on 9th September 2025).
7. Allen, G. I., Maletic-Savatic, M., Peterson, C., et al. (2012). Regularized partial least squares with an application to NMR spectroscopy. https://core.ac.uk/download/77960813.pdf (accessed on 9th September 2025).
8. Amir, A., Franceschini, G., Grossi, R., et al. (2013). Managing unbounded-length keys in comparison-driven data structures with applications to on-line indexing. http://arxiv.org/abs/1306.0406 (accessed on 9th September 2025).
9. Anjos, A., El-Shafey, L., & Marcel, S. (2017). BEAT: An open-source web-based open-science platform. https://core.ac.uk/download/148029759.pdf (accessed on 9th September 2025).
10. Ashkiani, S., Awad, M. A., Owens, J. D., et al. (2020). Dynamic graphs on the GPU. https://core.ac.uk/download/287624095.pdf (accessed on 9th September 2025).
11. Bärlund, I., Dubel, A., Kok, K., et al. (2010). Pan-European back casting exercise, enriched with regional perspective, and including a list of short-term policy options. https://core.ac.uk/download/pdf/29235489.pdf (accessed on 9th September 2025).

12. Ben-David, S., Bishop, C. M., Bottou, L., Breuer, H. P., Chiang, C. F., Getoor, L., Golub, G. H., et al. (2018). Quantum machine learning: A classical perspective. https://core.ac.uk/download/154747677.pdf (accessed on 9th September 2025).
13. Borchani, H., Martinez, A. M., & Masegosa, A. R. (2016). Probabilistic graphical models on multi-core CPUs using Java 8. https://core.ac.uk/download/60655105.pdf (accessed on 9th September 2025).
14. Candia, J., Kenkre, V. M., & Parris, P. E. (2008). Random walk access times on partially-disordered complex networks: An effective medium theory. https://core.ac.uk/download/229209514.pdf (accessed on 9th September 2025).
15. Ceccon, F., Kouyialis, G., & Misener, R. (2016). Using functional programming to recognize named structure in an optimization problem: Application to pooling. https://core.ac.uk/download/77012258.pdf (accessed on 9th September 2025).
16. Cheng, R., Lei, S., Maniu, S., et al. (2015). Online influence maximization (extended version). http://arxiv.org/abs/1506.01188 (accessed on 9th September 2025).
17. Chow, C. K., Wolpert, D. H., Kleiter, G. D., Jeffreys, H., Papadimitriou, H., Yaman, H., Aron, I. D., et al. (2005). Robust inference of trees. http://arxiv.org/abs/cs/0511087 (accessed on 9th September 2025).
18. Coleman, S., Georgiopoulos, M., Markov, Z., Neller, T. W., et al. (2005). Unifying an introduction to artificial intelligence course through machine learning laboratory experiences. https://cupola.gettysburg.edu/cgi/viewcontent.cgi?article=1007&context=csfac (accessed on 9th September 2025).
19. Constantino, A. A., Landa-Silva, D., Pinheiro, R. L., Qu, R., et al. (2016). Towards an efficient API for optimization problems data. https://core.ac.uk/download/76971896.pdf (accessed on 9th September 2025).
20. Cuena, J., Molina, M., & Sierra, J. L. (1999). Reusable knowledge-based components for building software applications: A knowledge modelling approach. https://core.ac.uk/download/148662638.pdf (accessed on 9th September 2025).
21. Di Luigi, W., Farina, G., Laura, L., Nanni, L., et al. (2016). Oii-web: An interactive online programming contest training system. https://core.ac.uk/download/80310279.pdf (accessed on 9th September 2025).
22. Galantucci, L. M., Percoco, G., & Spina, R. (2004). Assembly and disassembly planning by using fuzzy logic & genetic algorithms. http://arxiv.org/abs/cs/0412054 (accessed on 9th September 2025).

23. Galloway, K., Heath, M., Hewitt, A., Israel, M., et al. (2016). Working the nexus: Teaching students to think, read and problem-solve like a lawyer. https://core.ac.uk/download/196605025.pdf (accessed on 9th September 2025).

24. Gupta, P., Janardan, R., & Smid, M. (1996). A technique for adding range restrictions to generalized searching problems. https://core.ac.uk/download/210674374.pdf (accessed on 9th September 2025).

25. Huber, M., Rüde, U., & Wohlmuth, B. (2018). Adaptive control in roll forward recovery for extreme scale multigrid. http://arxiv.org/abs/1804.06373 (accessed on 9th September 2025).

26. Jennings, N. R. (1991). *Cooperation in Industrial Systems.*

27. Kalganova, T. G. (2012). Open-ended evolution to discover analogue circuits for beyond conventional applications. https://core.ac.uk/download/20496288.pdf (accessed on 9th September 2025).

28. Kao, M. Y., Lam, T. W., Sung, W. K., Ting, H. F., et al. (2001). An even faster and more unifying algorithm for comparing trees via unbalanced bipartite matchings. http://arxiv.org/abs/cs/0101010 (accessed on 9th September 2025).

29. Kobbacy, K. A. H., Rasmy, M. H., & Vadera, S. (2007). AI and OR in management of operations: History and trends. https://core.ac.uk/download/104325.pdf (accessed on 9th September 2025).

30. Laarhoven, T. (2017). Faster tuple lattice sieving using spherical locality-sensitive filters. https://core.ac.uk/download/577052622.pdf (accessed on 9th September 2025).

31. Langdon, W. B., McPhee, N. F., & Poli, R. (2008). *A Field Guide to Genetic Programming.* https://core.ac.uk/download/214315022.pdf (accessed on 9th September 2025).

32. Lau, V., Peng, M., Poor, H. V., Wang, Y., et al. (2015). Fronthaul-constrained cloud radio access networks: Insights and challenges. http://arxiv.org/abs/1503.01187 (accessed on 9th September 2025).

33. Lawrence, R. A., & Tonge, F. M. (1975). Data representation and synthesis. https://core.ac.uk/download/237710844.pdf (accessed on 9th September 2025).

34. LeBlanc, M. D., & Russell, S. W. (2004). Learning by seeing by doing: Arithmetic word problems. https://core.ac.uk/download/215523709.pdf (accessed on 9th September 2025).

35. Markov, Z., Neller, T. W., Russell, I., Zlatareva, N., et al. (2006). Pedagogical possibilities for the N-puzzle problem. https://cupola.gettysburg.edu/cgi/

viewcontent.cgi?article=1004&context=csfac (accessed on 9th September 2025).

36. Merida-Campos, C., & Rollón Rico, E. (2003). CBR and MBR techniques: Review for an application in the emergency's domain. https://core.ac.uk/download/81578179.pdf (accessed on 9th September 2025).
37. Michaelson, G. (2015). Teaching programming with computational and informational thinking. https://core.ac.uk/download/29822230.pdf (accessed on 9th September 2025).
38. N/A. (1982). *Technology Assessment of Advanced Automation for Space Missions*. https://core.ac.uk/download/pdf/10364615.pdf (accessed on 9th September 2025).
39. Perera, S., & Watson, I. (1997). Context guided retrieval. https://core.ac.uk/download/17298854.pdf (accessed on 9th September 2025).
40. Quanrud, K. (2018). Fast and deterministic approximations for *k*-cut. https://core.ac.uk/download/231819152.pdf (accessed on 9th September 2025).
41. Visser, W. (2006). Designing as construction of representations: A dynamic viewpoint in cognitive design research. https://core.ac.uk/download/50349731.pdf (accessed on 9th September 2025).

CHAPTER 10

DEBUGGING AND ERROR HANDLING

Contents

INTRODUCTION

Programming is the realm of inherent complexity, with algorithms, data structures, and application logic displaying complex interactions. Error handling and debugging are fundamental to software development in this context. These processes not only identify and resolve errors in code but also enhance the intrinsic robustness and reliability of applications. As programming software continues to become more and more sophisticated, developers are confronted with a variety of types of errors ranging from syntax to logical fallacy which can significantly impede functionality. Therefore, it is essential that both novices and experts understand the underlying principles of debugging and error control. By traversing these fields, one can observe the extent to which meticulously crafted debugging methods serve as a blueprint to cross the barriers created by various coding environments and frameworks. Furthermore, the use of methodical debugging methods brings about a quality and responsibility culture within software development teams.

Figure 10.1. *Debugging and error handling.*

Source: https://www.connectinfosoft.com/uploads/post/3581debugging-and-error-handling-in-golang.webp.

Debugging is not only a reactive process performed to fix issues after development but a part of the software development life cycle in itself that focuses on preventive problem-solving. An organized debugging process can significantly reduce the debugging time and effort, which allows the developers to focus on feature enhancement and user experience. With the addition of appropriate error handling techniques, these techniques enable developers to anticipate potential errors before they even happen in production environments. Thus, the inclusion of rigorous debugging techniques results in better quality software, minimized downtime, and increased user satisfaction, validating the argument that effective error management plays a key role in effective software development. The implementation of new programming languages and frameworks has introduced several tools and processes to make the error handling and debugging easier. For instance, Python and JavaScript programming languages have built-in error reporting mechanisms that enable programmers to identify problems in the code efficiently and fix them. In addition, next-generation IDEs also provide high-end debugging tools like breakpoints and variable watches that enhance the ability to investigate code behavior in real-time. Similarly, external libraries and frameworks can add capability through previous functions for error handling, which can make the development process easier. With such state-of-the-art technology at their fingertips, programmers are repeatedly compelled to modify their error-handling and debugging protocols to adjust for revolutionary software development methodologies and achieve code stability in a fluid online setting. The focus on including advanced methodologies ensures that software solutions remain efficient, robust, and user-friendly in a competitive market (Figure 10.1).

Definition of Debugging

Debugging is a part of the software development process, the systematic approach via which programmers identify, analyze, and fix flaws in their codes. This is not merely a question of detecting errors; it is an intimate familiarity with the underlying structure and logic of the software systems. Debugging can never be done successfully without a proper understanding of the softwares intended purpose as well as the identification of anomalies that can take place when it is run. It is the consensus of the research community in software engineering that many techniques have been developed over time that are intended to enhance fault removal efficiency in programs. However, the inherent complexity and dynamics in software systems make it a challenging task to remove all faults, a reflection of ongoing demands for ingenuity in debugging methods (Alansari et al., 2018). The word debugging is also made more complex by the broad range of faults to which software systems may be subject. Bugs may be caused by syntax errors, logic faults, or even breakdown in external systems, each requiring disparate diagnostic methods. For instance, debugging involves functions like code tracing where programmers employ tools to execute the program line by line with the purpose of figuring out where the logic has gone astray from what is desired. In addition, as programs grow in complexity, debugging strategies can fall short. Studies on new models of fault localization, such as value-based or dependencies-based ones, have been at the forefront of this, however. These models allow for more systematic analysis of code behavior under various conditions, which allows developers to better understand the impact of various variables on software behavior (Alansari et al., 2018). While debugging is a necessity within normal software environments, the principles of debugging also penetrate more technical areas, such as in the use of sensor networks. Transitions from simulated to actual testbeds generally lead to characteristic failures and necessitate rapid cycles between the two testbeds. To counteract such failures, new methods such as sensor network checkpointing have been created. This technique is a hybrid approach by combining the non-intrusiveness of simulation and realism of testbeds of operation, so to speak, closing the gap between these two approaches. With the capture and porting of checkpoints from simulations to real deployments, programmers can ascertain consistency and reduce time lost in debugging faults, thereby further highlighting the dynamic nature of debugging in contemporary software engineering practices.

Role of Error Handling in Programming

Good error handling is crucial in programming since, besides ensuring the reliability of software, it supports good user experiences. When programmers adopt effective error-handling measures, they are able to anticipate issues beforehand and deal with them elegantly without making applications crash suddenly. The anticipation supports easier debugging and aids in resolving underlying causes effectively. In those instances where user interaction is continuous, such as web applications, improper handling of errors can lead to frustration and lost trust from the user. Hence, the ability to properly capture, log, and display error messages assures users that the software is stable. Caught and addressed errors while developing, rather than after deployment, reinforces a sense of responsibility from developers and encourages the adoption of best practices for code quality management. In addition, while programming paradigms mature with the introduction of multicore and multi-processor platforms, the need for sophisticated error-handling methods comes to the fore even more strongly. Modern computing environments tend to stretch the limits of conventional sequential programming models, requiring a move towards more complex architectures. This sophistication increases the threat of errors emerging from parallel processing, and careful attention to error handling becomes a prerequisite. While the sequential programming guidelines may be employed for building durable applications, hardware diversification introduces factors for consideration that require innovative measures. Systems need to have in place mechanisms not only for dealing with errors but also for facilitating their effective transmission through systems. This is particularly achieved in multicore/multi-processor systems, where an independent error can result in cascading failure throughout interdependent elements at the expense of system integrity and performance (Bekooij et al., 2009). Incorporating strong error-handling structures is also an essential aspect of ensuring maintainable codebases. Developers benefit by adopting practices such as exception handling, allowing for error classification and fallback implementation without halting program execution. This approach, besides simplifying debugging, also promotes code clarity and maintainability by isolating error control. Moreover, well-organized error handling can also promote team-working among development teams since good error-reporting mechanisms instill communication of failure and solution. As observed through systems like Arcturus, integration of errors and debugging within one framework enhances the development process while promoting better understanding of the code base. Therefore, error handling as a priority aligns with the overall quality of software development and is essential for navigating the intricacies of modern coding platforms (Standish et al., 1983).

10.1. THE MAJORITY OF ERROR TYPES

The identification of common error types is a critical component of effective debugging and error control in software programming. Syntax errors, for instance, occur whenever the code violates the grammatical rules of the programming language and, as a result, compilations fail. These are typically simple to identify since the compiler provides immediate feedback on where the offense occurred. But for logical errors, although they are not immediately evident at compile time, they can cause erratic software behavior at runtime. Unlike syntax errors, logical errors can require stricter testing and debugging to expose since they primarily occur when the software is executed under specific circumstances that expose its faulty logic. The fine line between these mistakes underscores the need for a systematic debugging approach that realistically addresses each kind of error's unique problems. Another significant category of errors is runtime errors, which take place at run time. These are typically the result of unforeseen user inputs or environmental conditions for which the program has not been designed to handle, and thus they create application crashes or unacceptable behavior. For instance, if a program attempts to read an array index greater than its specified size, it may result in a runtime exception. To handle these issues, there must be robust error handling facilities to manage such scenarios gracefully without leading to the crashing of the application. The employment of correct assertion checking techniques is one method to determine potential runtime errors, as explored in current industrial practice, that can significantly enhance the robustness of software systems (Clarke et al., 2006). By actively utilizing these methods in advance, developers can greatly minimize the occurrence and impact of runtime errors. Last but not least, semantic errors are a less apparent category of error that can greatly impact a programs functionality. These are errors which arise when the code is syntactically correct but does not execute the operation intended, usually as a consequence of incorrect comprehension of the needs of the programs. For instance, if a developer incorrectly reads a requirement and inserts an algorithm that produces incorrect results, then the code will execute without error, hence making debugging all the more troublesome. As indicated in Arcturus system discussion, the addition of features such as template-assisted editing and command completion can facilitate a greater grasp of complex programming abstractions (Standish et al., 1983). Accordingly, the enhancement of the development environment to facilitate deeper semantic analysis lessens the frequency of semantic errors, eventually leading to more reliable software products (Figure 10.2).

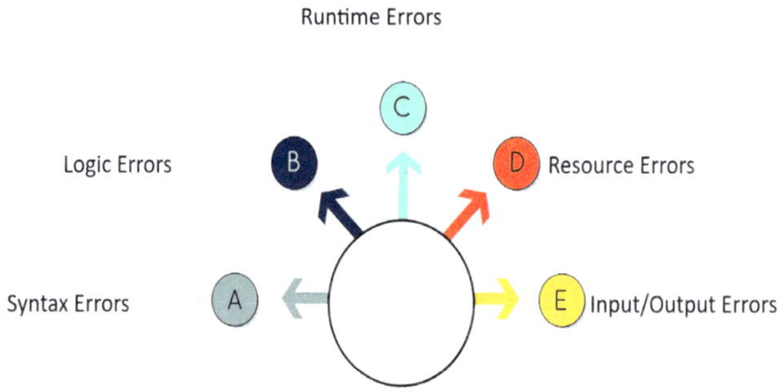

Figure 10.2. *Common types of errors.*

Source: https://fastercapital.co/i/Error-handling--Error-Handling-101--Key-Steps-to-Successful-Resolution--Understanding-Common-Errors.webp.

10.1.1. Syntax Errors

Syntax errors are a basic type of error in programming where the code breaks the given rules of a programming language. Errors can be caused by typographical errors, incorrect application of punctuation, or other incorrect usage of language constructs, all of which result in code interpretational failure. Rectification of syntax errors is critical, as they lead to programs failing compilation or run-time, bringing development processes to a halt. Programmers must hence be cautious in writing code, employing the best practices to prevent these errors. The significance of syntax error detection and rectification indicates the criticality of robust debugging tools that provide immediate feedback on the coding practice, thus speeding up the programming process. In modern development environments, syntax error checking has advanced to the extent of interactive functionality that streamlines the process of coding. There are tools that give real-time syntactic and semantic feedback that aid programmers in their endeavor to create well-forged applications. For instance, there are embedded debuggers that not only indicate syntax errors but also make programmers understand the impact of various changes to the code. This immediate feedback helps improve a superior environment for learning by novice programmers and assists experienced developers in maintaining codebases functioning properly.

The Rational Environment is a specific example of how interactive syntactic feedback improves comprehension of functioning programs and program organization, thereby reducing the burden of ongoing maintenance and making code more resilient as described in Archer et al. (2025). Moreover, syntax error paradigms can be improved upon by understanding how coding practices are intermingled and examined within higher-level programming environments. The Arcturus environment, for example, illustrates how syntax analysis and debugging facilities would be applied in combining streamlined software construction processes. With the introduction of features like template-assisted editing and command completion, programmers can gain control over complex codebases and minimize the prevalence of syntax errors. The integration of these traits allows for better integrated coding, facilitating quick and effective diagnosis and error correction by coders. Integration of these concepts does a great deal in programming education, enhancing coder efficiency and effectiveness and velocity in parsing and erroring out syntax errors as revealed in Standish et al. (1983).

10.1.2. Runtime Errors

Runtime errors are a crucial category of programming errors that occur during the run time of a program. Unlike compile-time errors, which are identified during code compilation, runtime errors have a tendency to appear as unexpected behavior, crashes, or system crashes. They are caused by diverse sources such as invalid input data, unavailability of system resources, or programming logic faults. Thus, mistakes like these are found to be very challenging for the developers to identify and correct properly. Rigorous debugging mechanisms, like the use of logging mechanisms and interactive debuggers, must then become relevant to diagnose effectively the source of runtime errors. The need for strong error handling procedures takes center stage as these procedures, besides making programs more reliable, also result in better user experiences through the elimination of sudden crashes and encouragement of graceful failure from unforeseen issues. In software development, the early evolution of error handling procedures has heavily contributed to the evolution of how runtime errors are handled. Initially, error-checking procedures were simple, but today's methodologies employ complex assertion checking techniques that track executing programs for reliability and compliance on an ongoing basis. Assertion checking, according to recent research, represents a proactive technique to identify likely runtime faults before they emerge as significant issues in sophisticated software systems (Clarke et al., 2006). This trend mirrors the increasing awareness in the profession of integrating advanced debugging practices into the software development life cycle with emphasis on the process of anticipating errors as an inherent part of coding. Given today's trends, emphasizing agile methodologies and accelerated iteration, embracing stringent error-checking processes ensures runtime errors are minimized to the highest extent, thus advocating for software products' overall quality. Furthermore, the requirements of performance and reliability within distributed computer systems accentuate the requisite effectiveness of appropriate measures in handling errors. As computing systems mature in terms of more complex architectures, such as with aerospace systems, high performance with runtime error handling becomes increasingly complex. The situation is compounded by the requirement for timely error recovery, particularly in situations where time-dependent operations are of critical nature (Berman et al., 2025). Thus, developers must practice caution while applying error handling best practices that are sensitive to concurrency, resource management, and exception handling. Giving precedence to such protocols, software engineers can develop more stable and efficient systems that can counter the unexpected nature of runtime errors, thus facilitating the reliability of modern-day technological applications (Figure 10.3).

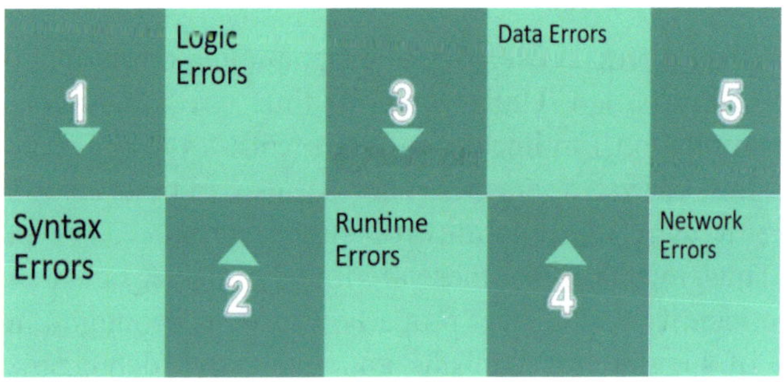

Figure 10.3. *Runtime errors.*

Source: https://fastercapital.co/i/Error-Resolution-101--A-Comprehensive-Beginner-s-Guide--Understanding-Different-Types-of-Errors.webp.

10.1.3. Logic Errors

Logic errors represent a pervasive challenge within the realm of programming and software development, often leading to unexpected behavior in software applications. These errors occur when a developers implementation diverges from their intended logic, causing the application to operate incorrectly, even though the code runs without any syntactical issues. This discrepancy can arise from misconceptions about algorithm design, incorrect assumptions about input data, or even oversight in handling edge cases. As a result, the outcomes produced by the software may not align with the expectations set forth by the developer, necessitating a careful debugging approach to identify and rectify the underlying flaws in logic. The methodologies employed in debugging logic errors are crucial for effective software maintenance. Techniques such as unit testing and assertion checking play a prominent role in identifying faults early in the development cycle. For instance, automated testing frameworks facilitate the creation of test cases that can systematically evaluate the expected outputs against the actual outputs of the software components. This proactive approach not only aids in detecting logic errors but also provides a safety net for future code modifications. Furthermore, implementing runtime assertion checking enables developers to catch erroneous logic in real time, promoting the development of more robust applications. Such practices are particularly highlighted in findings from the Software Engineering Impact Project, which emphasizes the importance of testing and analysis in refining software quality (Clarke et al., 2006). Additionally, sophisticated tools have emerged to specifically address logic errors within complex systems. One notable approach involves employing grammar-based black-box fuzz testing, which has proven effective in exposing various defects such as unsound behaviors in answer set solvers. This technique is designed to manipulate inputs indiscriminately, helping to uncover instances where the implemented logic does not align with intended behaviors, such as returning invalid answer sets or failing to identify existing solutions (Brummayer et al., 2010). Moreover, the application of delta debugging techniques can significantly enhance the debugging process by isolating failure-inducing inputs, thus simplifying the task of pinpointing logic errors. As developers continue to navigate the complexities of software design, these advanced debugging strategies remain vital for ensuring that logic errors are systematically identified and resolved, ultimately enhancing the reliability of software products.

10.2. DEBUGGING TECHNIQUES

Debugging strategies are essential to application development, whose function is to identify and solve problems in code in order to enable the application to operate at best. Effective debugging requires a close familiarity with the programming language and the environment where the program is executing. Strategies such as code review, paired programming, and systematic testing are at the heart of identifying issues. Of these, testing frameworks that are automated have gained significance as they can quickly identify discrepancies between anticipated and real behavior. The Arcturus system demonstrates the integration of debugging tools written specially for the Ada programming language with an approach to conceptual simplicity and effective coupling among tools that makes both analysis and debugging possible. Such a setting aids the development process since it enables robust support for the detection and correction of errors as and when they arise in the application lifecycle, hence minimizing debugging time and making software development efficient (Standish et al., 1983). Another fundamental debugging practice is that of using fault localization techniques, especially crucial when handling complex multi-threaded programs. The non-deterministic nature of thread scheduling introduces a degree of complexity that makes debugging extremely challenging. Traditional methods of debugging fail in multi-threaded environments because they may not be capable of accounting for the intricate interactions between threads.

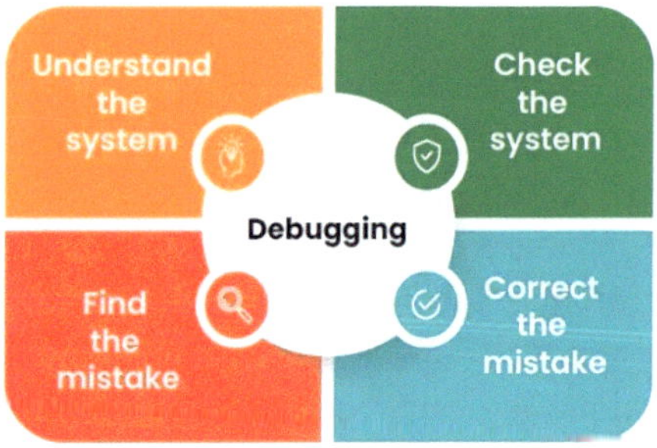

Figure 10.4. *Debugging techniques.*

Source: https://media.geeksforgeeks.org/wp-content/uploads/20240611174446/Debugging.webp.

In recent years, new methods have emerged that propose new ways of addressing these issues in efficient manners. For instance, one new fault-localization technique transforms multi-threaded programs to their sequential forms, giving a simpler method of utilizing established fault-diagnosis methods. By leveraging counterexamples generated by bounded model checkers, faults are identified more precisely and debugging time for multi-threaded programs is reduced (Alves et al., 2015). This approach demonstrates the dynamic nature of debugging and the necessity of adapting methods to cater to the challenges that newer software architecture presents. Last but not least, documentation and logging play a vital role in debugging. Documentation in detail not only benefits debugging but also promotes maintainability and future development. By having their code well organized with good comments and good documentation, programmers make it easier for themselves and fellow programmers to comprehend intricate systems. Logging, on the other hand, allows tracking of the behavior of an application during run time, an excellent insight into the execution path of the programs and the identification of untreatable bugs which are even not identifiable by static analysis. All these practices come under an efficient debugging scheme. By intertwining robust documentation with adequate logging mechanisms, developers can foster an error handling and fixing culture, thereby producing better software in increasingly complicated programming environments (Figure 10.4).

10.2.1. Print Debugging

Print debugging, an ancient yet sure method employed by developers, is a method where print statements are inserted in code to print variable data and program flow to the console or log. This technique provides immediate feedback regarding the state of a program during execution, and programmers can achieve discrepancies between expected and actual behavior. Sticking these print statements in the right places in the code permits developers to trace along programs execution and identify issues when they occur. Print debugging is easy, but it can provide insight into program behavior that doesn't quite reveal itself with other debugging methods, so it is a helpful tool during early development and debugging. One of the advantages of print debugging is its availability to programmers regardless of their experience. It has minimal setup and can be applied in almost any programming environment, making it a good choice for beginning programmers who may not have access to more sophisticated debugging capabilities. In addition, the direct output of print statements makes program logic and areas of error easier to understand. Print debugging is not without its faults, however; excessive print output can obscure code, decrease its readability, and add to its maintenance burden. Consequently, though it is an invaluable stepping stone in the debugging process, programmers would do well to balance this technique with other methods of debugging that offer more formal observations on program behavior. The evolution of debugging techniques demonstrates an increasing sophistication in how software bugs are dealt with. Advanced tools such as automated debuggers have emerged to complement traditional approaches such as print debugging. These tools add support for contracts and assertions, which define what is expected to occur within a program, to improve the accuracy of fault detection and repair. For instance, AutoFix tools utilize pre- and postconditions to provide outstanding fix suggestions, which significantly reduced the load of debugging for the developers. With further development of software engineering, combining traditional methods with modern technologies can bring a full image of error handling techniques. Effectively integrating print debugging within this broader context can enhance the learning curve for beginners and enhance the efficiency of experienced developers, as numerous studies of debugging methods demonstrate (Clarke et al., 2006; Furia et al., 2014).

10.2.2. Utilizing a Debugger Tool

The application of debugger tools lies at the core of enhancing the software development process, particularly in debugging and fault correction. Debuggers facilitate monitoring of program execution such that programmers are able to identify and correct issues that arise during the running of the programs. By granting control over the flow of execution, for example, setting breakpoints and stepping through lines of code, debuggers allow programmers to see the values of variables and the behavior of the programs at any point in time. This high-granularity visibility is essential in pin-pointing challenging problems, particularly in multi-thread or concurrent programs where the communication among various threads can introduce complex bugs that are difficult to reproduce in the absence of such tools. Ultimately, the ability to utilize debugging tools efficiently fosters code quality and reliability in order to provide more robust software solutions. In the matter of high-level debugging techniques, programs have evolved to not only identify runtime errors but also evaluate code quality and performance. As an example, environments like those described in the Arcturus system are concerned with template-guided editing and command completion tailored to Ada programming. These features depict how modern debugging tools are developed to enhance the development environment, streamlining the debugging process as well as promoting better coding practices throughout the software life cycle. Integration of debugging tools into a programming environment promotes productivity because the programmer can navigate code easily and correct errors with minimal effort. Implementing holistic debugging practices made possible by sophisticated tools has the potential to significantly boost the overall development process. In addition, the availability of automated testing and debugging techniques has transformed the process that programmers use to address error detection and repair. Application of black-box testing tools that are grammar-based, as highlighted in the most recent research, enables thorough examination of potential defects in software programs. The tools are especially good at identifying unsound or incomplete semantics since they can reveal differences in answer set solver implementations (Brummayer et al., 2010). Further, the use of delta debugging methods even further improves the process of debugging through separating and reducing failure-causing inputs, enabling developers to concentrate their efforts on the particular areas of their code that require improvement. Not only does this optimization make the workflow more efficient, but it also reinforces the necessity of integrating advanced debugging tools into the process to guarantee the correctness and effectiveness of software in the increasingly complicated world of programming.

10.2.3. Code Reviews and Pair Programming

One of the main processes involved in error correction and debugging is code review and pair programming, both intended to enhance the quality and reliability of code. Code review, which entails a peer review of code by one or more peers, allows experienced professionals to identify possible defects before the deployment of software. This collaborative process brings about different ideas and experience, ultimately leading to better software craftsmanship. Participation in the code review can detect not only syntactical mistakes but also logical mistakes that could arise when it is run. This method's success is bolstered by the findings of recent research, which show its massive contribution in producing trustworthy software by means of managing and structured programming methods utilized when reviewing (Foshee et al., 2025). In contrast, pair programming, whereby two programmers share a single workstation, is employed to facilitate dynamic real-time problem-solving as well as optimize learning capacity.

Figure 10.5. *Code reviews and pair programming.*

Source: https://wawand.co/blog/posts/enhancing-team-productivity-through-collaborative-coding-the-power-of-pair-programming-and-code-reviews/og.png.

The inherent interaction between the pair allows instant feedback, which facilitates the unfettered discussion of potential improvement or error in the code. The dynamic pair optimizes the understanding of the code and the debugging process since one programmer pilots while the other navigates. Most significantly, the practice, in addition to detecting bugs early, also assists in best practices and design conventions that come in handy for the overall development process. With teams adopting pair programming, the combined expertise of members is being utilized, which is likely to decrease defects found later in the development process. For the sake of automatic debugging techniques, such as the one demonstrated by AutoFix, pair programming and code reviews can be helpful to these technologies by making them more efficient. AutoFix uses contracts to improve fault detection so that there are speedy and correct fixes. Such automated debugging, combined with traditional coding practices such as pair programming and code reviews, can be highly useful in mitigating the debugging burden on developers. Combined with human control by way of reviews and interactive programming and by automated techniques, a sound basis for ensuring software reliability is ensured. As attested to by their use in a majority of deployments, the methods are capable of producing fantastic results such that automatic systems are able to come up with the same quality of fixes as expert programmers (Furia et al., 2014) (Figure 10.5).

10.3. ERROR HANDLING STRATEGIES

Error handling methods are the linchpin to the world of software programming where the randomness of execution environments brings surprises to the fore. Effective error handling not just ensures the dependability of software applications but also enhances the user experience through insightful feedback during the failure of execution. Logging, exception handling, and input validation are essential in this regard. By detecting errors in real time through logging controls, coders can look at patterns and fix errors in advance. Having good exception handling also allows a system to manage uncommon states without over-interfering with user processes. Being careful with input checking also helps reduce the threats of malicious data bringing down the system or exposing the system. All these methods comprise a sound methodology for developing sound software systems. Fundamental to error handling procedures is the principle of automated testing, an underlying procedure for their detection and healing before faults in the early part of the software life cycle. Automated testing environments can systematically test code under different circumstances so that programmers can discover latent bugs present only under exceptional circumstances. For instance, using fuzz testing, as provided in Brummayer et al. (2010), finds various types of defects through the production of invalid or malformed inputs and thus revealing problems in code flow and logic. Through these cycles of making their systems better by developers, probabilities of discovering unhandled errors in the live environment are significantly minimized. By incorporating automated testing with effective debugging tools, the developers not only facilitate quick problem identification but also simplify the entire debugging process, ultimately making software more efficient and reliable. Moreover, incorporating sophisticated tools in development environments significantly improves the error handling features. Templates programmed programming and context-sensitive help incorporated in systems, as elucidated by Standish et al. (1983), simplify the job for developers by simplifying debugging and error fixing. These advanced settings may offer direct connectivity to sophisticated debugging functionality such as step-through execution and live viewing, enabling developers to monitor and understand the root causes of anomalies more efficiently. Consequently, the alliance of intuitive interfaces with systematic analytic capability ensures an error-handling procedure with higher efficiency, offering a platform in which developers are not bogged down by undeclared errors but rather can focus on resolving intricate issues. This fusion of utilities not only boosts productivity but also promotes best practices in error handling and debugging techniques across a wide variety of software development life cycles.

10.3.1. Try-Catch Blocks

In programming, try-catch blocks are fundamental blocks of exception handling through which programmers can handle exceptions in an advanced way. Using these blocks, a programmer can execute a section of code anticipating what can go wrong. On encountering an error, the control is transferred from the try block to the catch block where the error can be addressed properly instead of causing program failure. This structured approach not only maintains the continuity of execution but also facilitates efficient diagnosis of problems. By employing try-catch blocks, programmers are thus able to put in place effective error handling mechanisms that provide insights into the root causes within the software, enhancing system reliability and user experience as a whole. Further, try-catch blocks facilitate the use of multiple error handling mechanisms tailored to exceptions. For example, a programmer can utilize individual catch clauses to handle different types of exceptions, such as input validation exceptions or resource availability exceptions. The use of such specificity not only results in more clearer code organization but also provides more accurate debugging. During exception throwing, the relevant catch block may supply a wealth of information about the type of exception, such as the error message and program state at failure. This kind of diagnostic information is particularly important in advanced systems, whereby it gets cumbersome to determine the exact location of failure, thus underscoring the need for using try-catch blocks for debugging. Moreover, not only are try-catch blocks more than error handling; they are also crucial to software quality improvement through the provision of the capability to detect bugs and correct them in a timely manner. Through the addition of advanced techniques such as statistical oracles and micro-oracles, this capability can be further developed. As noted in automatic diagnosis and repair discussion, these oracles can provide further information regarding the type of errors, thus improving the debugging process (Monperrus et al., 2016).

Null pointer exceptions, for example, which are so rampant in most programs, can be best handled by employing other execution semantics that mitigate such failures at runtime, as is evident in the NPEfix tool (Cornu et al., 2015). Lastly, the intentional use of try-catch blocks, complemented with sophisticated error handling techniques, provides programmers a robust toolset to support robust software systems (Figure 10.6).

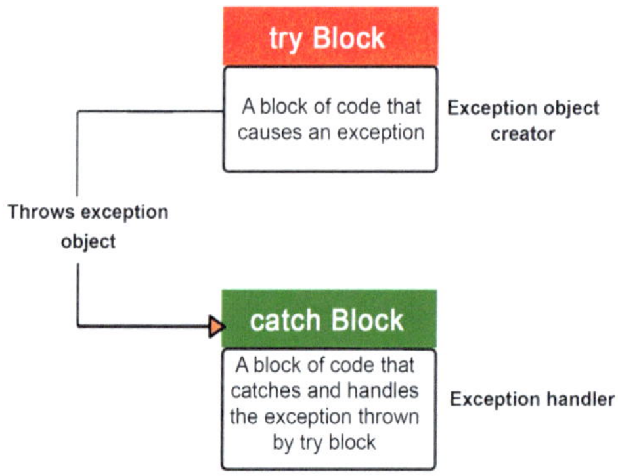

Figure 10.6. *Try-catch blocks.*

Source: https://www.scientecheasy.com/wp-content/uploads/2020/02/try-catch-block.png.

10.3.2. Error Logging

Error logging is a foundational element in the field of debugging and error handling that facilitates a systematic approach to discovering, capturing, and examining faults in software systems. Effective error logging provides proactive debugging in such a way that developers can gain useful information about the circumstances in which an error took place, such as the timestamp, error message, and stack trace. This information is valuable because it allows developers to trace back to the source of an issue more accurately, eventually resulting in a higher quality software product. Also, detailed error logs are not just an analysis tool after an event has occurred but also assist in improving new feature design and implementation by indicating recurring issues and vulnerabilities in existing code. The worth of error logging extends beyond mere data collection; it becomes a key to handling the increase in sophistication of software systems today. As software gets more entrenched in cloud computing and complex integration situations, programmers are inundated with alarms and warnings during system testing. For instance, more automation of testing can lead to the creation of an excessive number of test alarms so that engineers will struggle to find the root cause of issues (Jiang et al., 2017). Automating analysis of logs has the potential to dramatically reduce the workload for engineers so they can focus on correcting severe bugs rather than sifting through masses of data. By utilizing systems that have robust error logging capabilities, organizations can significantly maximize their debugging process to offer more efficiency and improved accuracy in fixing software failures. Proper error logging is a tactic that requires meticulous planning in the tools and methodologies utilized. Proper training in best practices is needed for developers to ensure logs capture the appropriate information needed for troubleshooting. Also, having automated scanners check logs in real-time and provide feedback allows for a higher level of efficiency. As an illustration, advanced logging tools utilize machine learning to identify patterns of error occurrence, and this leads developers down the path of preventive rather than reactionary solutions. This pre-emptive mechanism for dealing with errors not only enhances software reliability but also establishes a culture for ongoing improvement in development teams. By improving the process for error logging, organizations set themselves up to build more robust software systems that can easily cope with constantly evolving technological environments.

10.3.3. Graceful Degradation

In error handling and debugging, graceful degradation is an important concept that allows systems to operate even with failure of the components. When a program is at fault, instead of stopping everything, graceful degradation permits it to provide a reduced level of service. In real-time systems, this approach is unavoidable because continuous service is not only a luxury but a necessity in most situations. For instance, failure-responsive behavior can minimize disruption to end-users, preserving key functionalities while healing or compensating for the source of the failure. This technique not only enhances user experience but also enhances system resilience, increasingly valuable in a networked digital world with systems often subject to variable and uncontrolled stresses. The use of graceful degradation can also be of particular utility in overcoming vulnerabilities typical of software programs. By actually treating code execution as a transaction, systems are able to detect failures due to buffer overflow or other types of exploitative attacks (Keromytis et al., 2004). When such a breach is detected, the system's capacity to abort only the faulty components and continue running allows for security and performance enhancements to be applied. Developers can thus guarantee overall system integrity while selectively limiting risk of unhandled vulnerabilities and outside attack. This solution is a textbook case of proactive error handling, which places a premium on user access and operation continuity. Organizations can thus employ fewer resources in error mitigation while, at the same time, enhancing security infrastructure, finding a balance between functionality and reliability. Moreover, graceful degradation principles are also necessary to improve software safety in a case where the risks are extremely high in life-critical applications, like healthcare or aeronautical technology (Leveson et al., 1981). In such fields, whose failures lead to disastrous consequences, it is imperative that systems fail in a safe manner without generating further complications. By embracing practices that facilitate graceful degradation, it becomes possible for developers to build systems not only responding to failure but also equipped with the recovery mechanisms without undermining security. The approach supports the development of software that is more resilient and capable of maintaining critical functions under adverse conditions. Lastly, the application of graceful degradation helps enhance user faith in software systems and reinforce the entire framework for effective debugging and error handling (Figure 10.7).

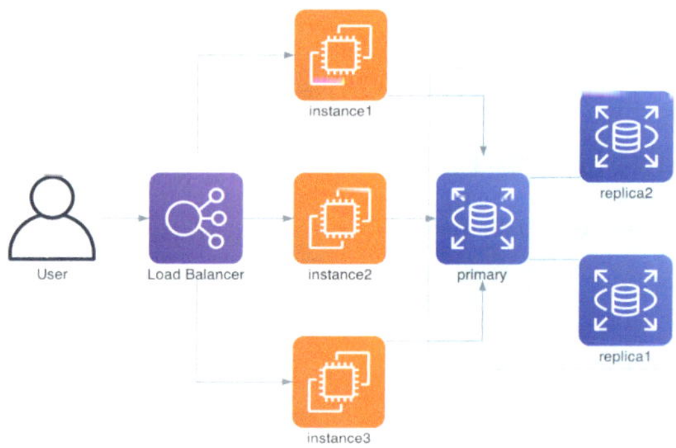

Figure 10.7. *Graceful degradation.*

Source: https://substackcdn.com/image/fetch/$s_!pTjG!,f_auto,q_auto:good,fl_progressive:steep/https%3A%2F%2Fsubstack-post-media.s3.amazonaws.com%2Fpublic%2Fimages%2Fc1c40c39-996d-4863-b6b8-a50b037ecf0b_1365x704.png.

10.4. BEST PRACTICES IN DEBUGGING

Effective debugging is a process-oriented approach that requires an understanding of the environment in which errors are being created and following best practices to minimize their impact. Maintaining a clean and organized codebase is one of the fundamental principles because it allows for easier identification and isolation of issues. Using standard naming conventions and comments makes it more readable, which means programmers are able to navigate through the code swiftly. Also, the incorporation of version control systems enables the tracking of changes to be able to know precisely when a bug was introduced. Modular programming incorporated also enables debugging by breaking the code into sections which can be tested independently. This is consistent with the guidelines of good software development support environments, such as those outlined in the Arcturus system, where it is emphasized that essential debugging tools and templates are key to helping programmers analyze errors (Standish et al., 1983). Testing is a fundamental aspect of good debugging practice, mirroring anticipatory steps. Adopting a multi-test model, that is, unit tests, integration tests, and system testing, helps developers identify bugs at various stages of software development. The multi-faceted model guarantees that individual pieces work right before getting integrated into larger systems to prevent chain failures. Practices involving continuous integration also foster a culture where code changes are thoroughly tested on a periodic basis, allowing rapid feedback and faster bug fixes. As software evolves towards complex architectures, particularly for multicore/multiprocessor system-on-chip systems, programmers must also sync their test paradigms. Designing these systems requires novel models and tools to deal with the parallelism in an efficient manner and guarantee parallel software bug-freeness (Bekooij et al., 2009). Finally, when fighting with repeated bugs, using a systematic debugging technique can greatly enhance the debugging process. Debugging practices such as the scientific method encourage developers to produce hypotheses about potential error causes, validate them in a controlled environment, and analyze the result. Not only does this help in resolving current issues, but it also allows for an understanding of the underlying software structure. Instrumentation added that allows real-time monitoring and logging throughout development can provide invaluable information about functional discrepancies. As argued in the adoption of debugging paradigms in software support environments, the combination of good test and analysis can greatly improve fault tolerance in concurrent programming. Such a holistic approach to debugging guarantees that software is maintainable and reliable throughout its whole lifecycle, adhering to optimal debugging practices (Standish et al., 1983).

10.4.1. Test Case Writing

In the complex world of software programming, the process of writing test cases is essential to enhancing the process of debugging and error handling. Test cases refer to structured documents that outline the manner in which a particular feature is expected to function. They spell out the inputs needed, the execution conditions, and the expected outcome, thus enabling programmers to verify that their code will conform to the design specifications. By systematically setting these parameters, developers can more effectively isolate and pick up faults. Debugging typically involves isolating the cause of a flaw, and in this case, good test cases act as a guide framework that directs the debugging process, indicating what areas of the code are at fault or need fixing. This approach not only facilitates early intervention in the software development process but also promotes a proactive quality assurance culture, ultimately leading to more stable software solutions. Automated testing frameworks significantly improve the efficiency of test case writing. These facilities allow programmers to execute a set of test cases quickly and often, ensuring that new changes to the codebase don't introduce regressions, or repeat previously fixed bugs. As software systems become more complex, especially in multi-threaded environments, the necessity for these automated utilities cannot be emphasized enough. This process alone can take its toll; however, automating test case execution lessens a lot of this weight. Techniques such as reducing a multi-threaded program into a single thread have been observed to enhance fault localization, as evidenced in the techniques proposed by recent research, and have the potential to lead to significant debugging time savings (Alves et al., 2015). This systematic approach provides the programmers with valuable feedback so that they can iteratively enhance. Type errors being the most crucial aspect to resolve in debugging, particularly in relation to logical errors found at runtime. Effective error handling begins with reasonable, explanatory test cases that can explain the type of error when the test fails. For instance, most beginner coders struggle with understanding type errors for programming languages. Through expression-specific error messages, as shown in user studies, programmers can construct a more user-friendly interface for users to learn and recover from type-related issues in code (Asai et al., 2014). The openness provides not only for debugging today but also for creating a better learning environment for programming concepts among beginner developers. Time thus spent in writing elaborate test cases benefits not only debugging but also creates a better learning environment for programmers and thus better software quality overall.

10.4.2. Keeping Code Clean and Organized

A key part of successful debugging and exception handling is the discipline of writing clean, organized code. An organized codebase is easier to read and maintain, making it possible for developers to quickly spot errors when they occur. Practices like using consistent naming conventions, modular design, and thorough documentation are important to obtaining this readability. By adhering to these conventions, programmers not only simplify their debugging but also provide an atmosphere where collaboration becomes effective and silky. For example, if variables and functions are named descriptively, a programmer encountering a problem can readily identify the purpose and origin of the code, reducing the time spent in locating and resolving bugs. Thus, writing good-looking code is not everything; it is part of having good error-handling strategy, which reaps benefits for the development process as a whole, as highlighted in the presentation of software engineering principles in Hartmann et al. (2001). Code structure, too, is more than mere visual beauty; it is a philosophy that lessens the chances of errors that arise during development. Modular programming techniques, that promote breaking down complex processes into simpler, reusable components, can significantly enhance error detection and correction. Each module is a standalone item, so developers can isolate problems more easily when they arise.

Figure 10.8. *Keeping code clean and organized of software development.*

*Source: https://miro.medium.com/v2/resize:fit:1358/1*aIUbD5L0PXymX5LQ7E54CQ.png.*

This removes interdependencies that complicate debugging so much. Additionally, employing the same commenting standard across enables developers to leave behind comments regarding the concepts and intention behind the code, simplifying it to return to in the future. Such a disciplined structure not only benefits individual programmers but also teams, as it is easier for new members to join. As illustrated in computational simulations research where clean coding is the foundation, disciplined techniques produce more robust error-handling functions (Hartmann et al., 2001). Incorporating error-handling capabilities into a clean code system further signifies its significance when it comes to coding. Through the use of structured code, the developer can implement systematic error-checking mechanisms, such as try-catch blocks or logging procedures, that get seamlessly integrated into the code base overall. In this manner, error handling is less likely to appear to be an afterthought and more like something inherent in the coding process. Debugging tools are more effective when applied to well-written code, allowing the instant identification of issues that remain and speeding up solution processes. Additionally, with attacks becoming more nefarious with capabilities to target poorly written code, cleanliness is also now the key to security. PowerShell attack research illuminates the ways in which code that is structured can be beneficial in detecting and repairing flaws, emphasizing the importance of a structured method in terms of the performance and security of the code (Figure 10.8).

10.4.3. Documenting Code Changes

Recording code changes is an essential practice in software development that significantly facilitates debugging and error management. Thoroughly documented records are not only a record of changes but also a valuable communication tool between team members. Rationally documenting the reason for code changes allows developers to make it simpler for maintenance and debugging in the future. It makes a significant impact while returning to code after many months or even years. If the developers understand why those changes were made, they will be able to identify instantly the likely sources of bugs or errors and thus debug faster. More importantly, detailed documentation avoids the knowledge transfer problem that happens when team members leave or join projects so that critical institutional knowledge is retained within the teams shared resources. Besides, adequate documentation of code change enhances the chances of applying automated software repair methods, as underscored by recent discussions on behavior and state repairs in software engineering. Developers are able to automate defect detection and fixing with little human intervention, thanks to various bug oracles and repair operators. This proves particularly relevant in the contemporary software infrastructure where high-end updates and continuous integration practices are the norm. Documentation provides a foundation for software behavior, allowing automated tools to calculate variations between desired and actual results when they cross-compare runtime states or test cases. This methodical approach to code change documentation aligns with recent trends in software reliability, eventually designing a more robust debugging model that can cope with varying codebases and deployment environments (Monperrus et al., 2016). Besides its impact on automated procedures, documentation of code changes aids in the creation of reliable software by employing systematic methods that analyze many factors, including verification aids and testing techniques. By maintaining detailed records of all changes, including the reason, test procedures, and results observed, developers are able to construct a logical framework for knowing reliable software practices. This data integration is critical when considering the validity of different coding techniques and dealing with the complexity of intricate software systems. As indicated in comprehensive research conducted on the determinants of software reliability, proper documentation can serve as a key factor in constructing methodologies that prioritize error prevention and the successful resolution of issues as they arise (Foshee et al., 2025). This anticipatory mindset not only improves the quality of the software but also optimizes the entire development process by allowing teams to react faster and be more nimble to problems that crop up in the software life cycle (Figure 10.9).

Figure 10.9. *Documenting code changes.*

Source: https://s9.easternpeak.com/wp-content/uploads/2023/09/Types-of-Source-Code-Documentation.png.

10.5. TOOLS FOR DEBUGGING

Debugging has developed significantly with the advent of sophisticated tools with the aim of simplifying fault localization and overall code quality. One of the major developments in this regard is the development of automatic debugging methods, which help developers locate bugs in multi-threaded systems. Debugging multi-threaded systems has been famously challenging for long due to their non-deterministic behavior caused by race conditions and thread scheduling. By transforming such complex programs into their sequential equivalents, automatic tools can apply established fault-localization techniques that are usually easier. This approach significantly reduces debugging time and improves the reliability of multi-threaded programs, emphasizing the importance of continued innovation in debugging technologies (Alves et al., 2015). In addition to automatic fault localization, runtime assertion checking has been an effective tool to prevent mistakes during a program's execution. The method allows programmers to place assertions within the code that will check conditions at runtime such that such problems are identified prior to them becoming serious faults. The history of developing mechanisms for assertion checking continues to identify their significant contribution towards modern software engineering practice.

Figure 10.10. *Tools for debugging.*

Source: https://media.geeksforgeeks.org/wp-content/uploads/20240612131423/Debugging-Tools.webp.

Trends continue to indicate the increasing industrial application of runtime assertion checking, which infers the effectiveness of assertion checking in improving the reliability of software. This ongoing integration of assertion facilities into software development processes not only enables early error detection but also enhances software system maintainability (Clarke et al., 2006).

Moreover, the addition of diagnostic tools and runtime assertions into contemporary integrated development environments (IDEs) has bolstered the debugging landscape. IDEs now incorporate sophisticated debugging features such as code analyzers, interactive debuggers, and performance profilers, providing developers with rich environments to detect and resolve issues in an efficient way. They have features such as breakpoints, watch variables, and live error logs, which in combination enable a systematic approach to debugging. With increasing complexity in software systems, use of such bundled platforms is important for developers who are interested in minimizing downtime and developing sound coding practices. Where these sophisticated tools converge illustrates the continued evolution of debugging methodologies towards more robust software applications (Figure 10.10).

10.5.1. Integrated Development Environments (IDEs)

Integrated Development Environments (IDEs) are at the core of today's software development, particularly in debugging and error fixing. IDEs have a primary feature that they allow programmers with enhanced tooling that simplifies the process of detecting and correcting code errors. By incorporating code editors, compilers, and test facilities, IDEs create a consolidated environment that makes debugging easier. Such an integrated process allows real-time feedback on the coding errors, and developers are able to rectify errors in real time without waiting for individual compilation or testing steps. Such a quick method not only promotes efficiency but also optimizes the learning environment for the beginners who are able to see the real-time effects of their coding decisions within the IDE itself. Furthermore, robust IDEs often come equipped with superior debugging facilities that can perform extensive code analysis. Breakpoints, step-through debugging, and dynamic variable observation are only a few of the capabilities that enable developers to analyze their code behavior extensively. For instance, a rich tracing facility may furnish information on complex algorithms by mirroring the hierarchical structure of executions. Such functionalities are especially useful in cases where complicated computations are called for, as programmers can trace down invisible bugs that would otherwise go unnoticed in less interactive contexts. Incorporating these characteristics within IDEs makes them indispensable tools, particularly in cases where precision and accuracy in coding are of the highest significance, such as projects with formal verification needs or the requirement to satisfy stringent operational requirements, like those outlined in Aspinall et al. (2014). Apart from improving the debugging process, IDEs also cater to handling errors through comprehensive reporting and logging functionality. When runtime errors are detected, IDEs are able to automatically give detailed error messages indicating not only the nature of the error but also ways to rectify it. This forward-looking effort prompts developers to learn more about potential errors in their code, thus fostering a learning culture in software development teams. As more developers begin adopting methods like Test-Driven Development (TDD) or behavior-driven development (BDD), the role of IDEs in enabling these approaches becomes increasingly valuable. By providing seamless integration with test frameworks and libraries required for testing, IDEs allow efficient development in which testing and debugging naturally coexist, ultimately leading to the creation of robust and efficient code. Examples such as secure application building in hardware environments are made possible through IDEs that provide developers with access to simulated environments as seen in tools like Open-TEE that enhance debugging even in complex environments, as cited in Asokan et al. (2015) (Figure 10.11).

Figure 10.11. *Integrated development environments (IDEs).*

Source: https://multiqos.com/blogs/wp-content/uploads/2023/09/Key-Features-of-IDEs.jpg.webp.

10.5.2. Static Analysis Tools

Static analysis tools are an indispensable part of the software development cycle as they analyze code automatically without executing it. Static analysis tools assist in identifying potential bugs, enforcing coding guidelines, and enhancing code quality overall. They are distinct from dynamic analysis, which executes the code at runtime, since static analysis scrutinizes source code or intermediate forms to detect vulnerabilities or code smells early in the development cycle. Early identification of issues leads to less work on debugging and maximizes the efficiency of error handling mechanisms. Programmers can then devote more time to optimizing their code as well as utilize proactive feedback offered by these tools to ultimately create more stable software design. Development of sophisticated static analysis tools has been guided by principles which are intended towards efficient software development. For instance, the integration of command completion and template-based editing in programming environments automates the coding experience while providing best practices in real time (Standish et al., 1983). In creating a culture that promotes proper coding practices and reduces the likelihood of introducing defects, static analysis tools allow programmers to maintain high-quality software standards. Apart from this, these tools can even analyze multi-programmed code, coping with the complexity of multi-threading and concurrency, which is usually a causality of sophisticated bugs. Thus, static analysis not only assists in debugging but also enhances error avoidance techniques since it makes developers aware of information through which they can make better decisions while developing software. Moreover, static analysis tools have also been extended, increasingly, with frameworks allowing for dynamic analysis steps, further enriching the debugging environment. Leveraging committed hardware architectures that offer virtualization support, such frameworks can track and analyze program behavior transparently without altering the running system (Fattori et al., 2010). This offers an isolated setting for extensive examination, such that any potential bugs in the tools do not interfere with the core systems operation. These developments point toward the complementarity of static and dynamic analysis tools because collectively they present an overall strategy for debugging as well as error management. With both of these approaches, developers will likely have more confidence in their products, so they can set themselves up to make more resilient manufacturing pieces of software in an ever-evolving technological universe.

10.5.3. Profiling Tools

Profiling tools play a key role to the debugging and error-handling process because they provide details regarding software performance and resource consumption. By providing systematic analysis of application behavior during run time, the tools allow programmers to locate bottlenecks and inefficiencies that can lead to unexpected errors. Profiling tools are able to monitor various aspects, such as CPU usage, memory, and execution time, that enable developers to determine some optimization hotspots. This is especially vital in diagnosing complex issues that arise from large codebases since understanding the intrinsic performance characteristics has a direct correlation with possessing excellent error handling strategies. Consequently, profiling tools support the development process while ensuring easier software maintenance in the long term through the provision of consistent application performance. In addition, the inclusion of particular profiling tools in the development cycle promotes an environment for active fault detection. For instance, advanced frameworks may leverage hardware virtualization to perform extensive, dynamic analyses without modifying underlying operating systems, as highlighted in Fattori et al. (2010). This methodology enables developers to execute profiling tools in parallel with production systems so that analyses are non-invasive and transparent. With live systems under observation, developers can detect faults as they appear, which facilitates an instant response to possible failures. This ahead-of-time approach to profiling focuses on the inclusion of robust error handling methods into the process of development since it allows for teams to address problems regarding performance early enough before they are significant faults that shape end-user impression. Another important technique within the confines of profiling and error handling is runtime assertion checking. This technique allows developers to verify assumptions in software at runtime, thereby detecting logical errors at an initial phase of the testing process. The Software Engineering Impact Project research results point to the previous development of runtime assertion checking as proof of its relevance in modern software engineering practices and integration in various sectors, as observed in Clarke et al. (2006). Through the utilization of runtime assertions, along with profiling tools, the reliability of programs is enhanced by creating a universal safety net. The integrated environment ensures the correctness and performance are ever-checked, which contributes to a robust error-handling framework for software development. In general, profiling tools, along with techniques like runtime assertion checking, constitute an introductory strategy for high-quality software delivery in buggy environments.

10.6. THE ROLE OF DEBUGGING IN SOFTWARE DEVELOPMENT

Debugging is a key activity in the software development process that serves as a systematic method of detecting and fixing faults in a program. Debugging not only enhances the quality of the final software product but also has a significant impact on the overall functionality and user experience. Correct debugging methods enable programmers to identify various types of bugs—logical bugs, syntax bugs, and runtime bugs—and assist in creating a more secure and stable application. Besides, debugging technologies and tools have improved immensely, from manual code inspection to the evolution of sophisticated environments that enable swift fault detection and correction. As argued in modern programming models, a comprehensive debugging environment makes these processes easier and enables a proactive development culture that emphasizes quality assurance at each level of the coding process (Standish et al., 1983). Besides emphasizing the importance of debugging, it can be seen as a continuous learning process that assists not only in the creation of the software but also in the development of the developers themselves. Through the process of debugging, developers learn about coding habits, the nature of errors, and optimization techniques that can be used later in other projects. Recent research indicates that debugging is not merely a reactive process but an integral part of software engineering that encourages best practices in application design and code maintenance. By grasping the nature of software anomalies—an extremely important aspect of debugging—programmers are able to start approaching error correction more preventively. Fault categorization and the employment of fault localization models could lead to greater efficiency in problem diagnosis, thus shaping a stronger codebase (Alansari et al., 2018). Generally, the inclusion of efficient debugging practices in the software development process is important to preventing risks associated with software failure. It provides an environment in which software quality can be measured and improved continuously, thus making programs more functional and usable. Debugging is at best a low description of its function; it is not only an approach to the correction of faults but also a way of organized scrutiny that influences future design and development choice. By placing highest emphasis on debugging as a phase of high priority in the software development life cycle, developers can handle the complex issues of software maintenance more effectively, leading to more reliable applications that function flawlessly under all situations and benefit the users accordingly (Standish et al., 1983) (Figure 10.12).

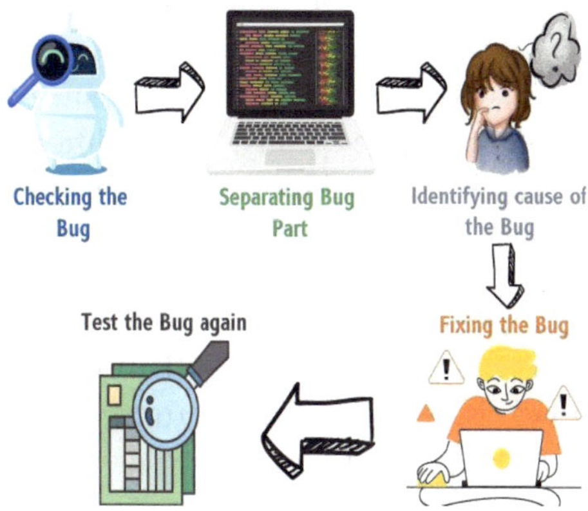

Figure 10.12. *Role of debugging in software development.*

Source: https://files.codingninjas.in/article_images/debugging-in-software-engineering-2-1693365203.webp.

10.6.1. Impact on Software Quality

In the realm of software development, the impact of error handling and debugging is very much related to the overall quality of software being produced. Applying efficient debugging methods in software development ensures that the bugs in the code can be identified and fixed efficiently, thus reducing errors in the final product. Specifically, debugging allows developers to understand the progression of execution and identify areas in the code that are faulty. Effective debugging practices also create a culture of quality assurance throughout the development life cycle. As teams get proficient at discovering and repairing errors early in the process, the softwares innate reliability increases, ultimately resulting in increased user satisfaction and fewer problems following deployment. Moreover, error handling-focused practices are equally significant in shaping software quality. With strong error management models, programs can deal with unexpected circumstances nicely without crashing or exhibiting unwanted behavior. This is particularly applicable in current computing environments where user expectation puts high value on smooth performance. Having well-designed error handling mechanisms can avoid the pitfalls of system collapse. Indeed, industry practice analysis, which Clarke et al. (2006) puts forward, underlines runtime assertion checking as critical to ensuring software integrity. Not only do such mechanisms enable proactive error detection, but also encourage developers to uphold better standards in coding methodology. Evolution in software architecture has also influenced how debugging and error management are addressed, particularly with the introduction of multicore and multiprocessor platforms. With increasing complexity in software systems, led by developments in computer hardware, software developers face new challenges while ensuring software quality. The traditional sequential models of programming are being left behind by embracing more advance approaches that require understanding of parallel execution. As advocated by Bekooij et al. (2009), the transition towards multicore programming demands evolving innovative tools specifically suited to this environment. These advancements are a crucial milestone not just in realizing the optimum use of hardware capabilities but also towards achieving sound, error-free software development. The meeting point of contemporary programming models and sound debugging methodology, therefore, holds great potential for enhancing software quality in diverse fields.

10.6.2. Debugging in Agile Methodologies

Agile methodologies debugging is defined by its iterative and collaborative nature compared to the traditional way of debugging. Agile development frameworks like Scrum or Kanban allow for an environment that is constantly in motion, where developers regularly have open discussions regarding bugs and problems that they encounter. The collaboration tends to result in a common understanding of the issues, eventually improving the team's capability to diagnose and fix the errors in a timely manner. In agile settings, continuous integration and continuous delivery practices build a culture in which feedback is immediate, and developers are able to identify changes that may cause bugs early. The emphasis on regular retrospectives builds an environment of self-reflection on the debugging process itself, perpetuating a culture of ongoing improvement in error-handling methodologies. Further, inclusion of automated testing as a part of agile practices is crucial for debug processes. Automated tests like unit tests, integration tests, and acceptance tests form a line of defense for bugs. By testing as part of the development process, agile teams can catch bugs early while iterating on their code in a fast pace. Not only does this technique reduce the complexity of debugging larger codebases, but it also incurs responsibility on team members because broken tests do not leave anyone wondering where the issues lie. Thus, testing is indeed integrated as part of the definition of done for a user story such that debugging is not something to be considered after implementation but is part of the core of the development process. Agile practices also foster a culture of ownership and quality code responsibility among the team members, which necessarily affects debugging work. Here, all developers are encouraged to learn bug fixing skills with the understanding that bug fixes not only benefit the individual but also the team. This shared ownership leads to more robust error handling techniques since developers actually seek to be better coders so that bugs do not form. The collaborative approaches witnessed in agile models help teams capitalize on diverse input on problem-solving since mutual information around errors can lead to innovative solutions. Collaboration also fosters an environment where developers openly discuss failures, again improving the teams overall debugging capability and strengthening overall software quality according to practice defined in projects making use of AI/ML development environments (Matthias et al., 2020) (Figure 10.13).

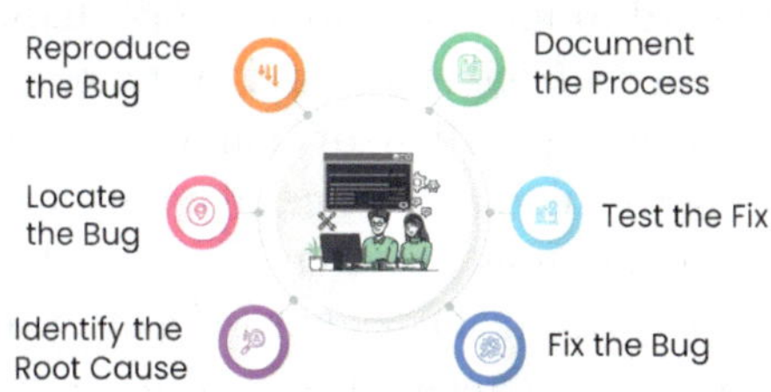

Figure 10.13. *Debugging in agile methodologies is characterized.*

Source: https://media.geeksforgeeks.org/wp-content/uploads/20240612131318/Process-of-Debugging-.webp.

10.6.3. Continuous Integration and Debugging

The application of continuous integration (CI) indeed transformed the software development universe, particularly with regard to debugging and error handling.

By inserting the new code automatically into a shared repository, CI enables developers to detect errors before the development cycle. The discovery early on is crucial in debugging because it allows for immediate feedback and easy determination of potential causes of failures. Thus, when faults do develop, they are able to be fixed in a short amount of time, hence lowering the technical debt that may be accumulated if faults are postponed. With testing systems still generating huge levels of alarms, proactive debugging strategies within CI environments become important in solving such problems, making code stable, and improving project trajectories overall. The emphasis placed on real-time error correction also creates a culture where the state of having a stable build is paramount, ultimately manifesting in improved user satisfaction and trust in software created. Of the various developments in the area of debugging in CI pipelines, the application of automated utilities to help with cause analysis is a major one. Traditional manual debugging methods are painstaking, particularly when engineers are bogged down with far too many test alarms from round-the-clock testing.

Based on recent research, automated cause analysis tools came to the rescue to lighten this burden with sophisticated information retrieval mechanisms pinpointing the causes of alarms from test logs. These tools significantly improve the precision and speed of fault localization, and studies have established a phenomenal accuracy rate of up to 72% when employed in real-world applications. Incorporating such cutting-edge tools into CI practice, organizations can reduce the time wasted in manual inspection immensely and free developers to proceed to more important work, further symbolizing the cohesive synergy between continuous integration and best debugging practice. In addition, the combined application of automated verification tools and systematic programming techniques enhances the reliability of software based on continuous integration. From intensive studies carried out on the tools, it is clear that the application of systematic testing and management practices forms a robust context of error management. Through the streamlining of tasks as well as enabling higher levels of collaboration among the development team members, these methods instill a fertile environment for feedback, which is perfect for effective debugging. The combination of continuous integration and incremental debugging methodologies not only supports detection and repair of bugs quicker but also makes the overall software development process more efficient. Hence, companies that embrace strict error management systems along with CI are well placed to provide good-quality, reliable software, with advantages in reduced time to market and improved product integrity (Jiang et al., 2017; Foshee et al., 2025) (Figure 10.14).

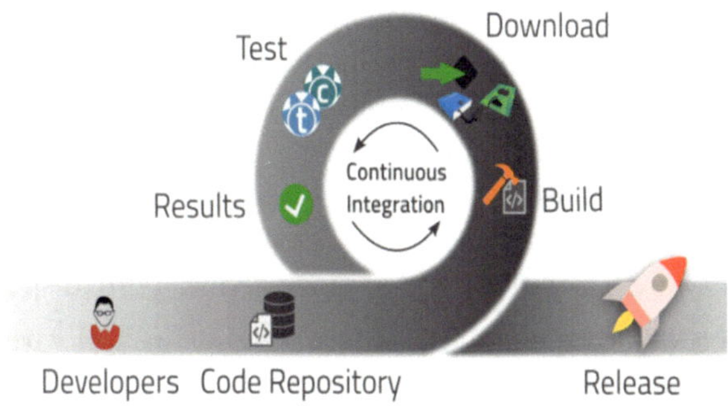

Figure 10.14. *Continuous integration and debugging.*

Source: https://www.isystem.com/files/content/img/blog_posts/CI_circle.png.

SUMMARY

In short, debugging and error handling is crucial in software development as it directly contributes towards program reliability and end-user satisfaction. With software systems becoming more complex, particularly when dealing with multi-threaded programming, even traditional debugging methodologies may prove to be inadequate. Complexity not only introduces the scope for errors but also complicates the identification and remediation of errors. The application of automated fault localization methods, as noted hereinbefore, is a significant breakthrough in evading this limitation. Sincere focus has been placed on translating multi-threaded programs into their sequential equivalents to enable developers to utilize proven debugging techniques with maximum efficiency and accuracy in locating and correcting faults (Alves et al., 2015). Moreover, the use of leading-edge programming support environments, such as the one under discussion with respect to Ada programming, is promising in terms of error handling. By leveraging functionality such as command completion and template-assisted editing, software developers can make coding more straightforward while simultaneously minimizing potential errors at the same time during the coding process from the start. Besides facilitating easier work with large codebases, such environments also support effective debugging techniques unique to concurrent programming. The benefits derived through such a combined approach are critical to the encouragement of a culture of rigorous error management and better software quality (Standish et al., 1983). Lastly, emphasis on proactive debugging techniques and higher-level error handling capabilities reflects the changing nature of software engineering. With the constant evolution of techniques and tools, it is evident that an integrated debugging model will result in more resilient systems. With automatic techniques and intelligent support environments increasing popularity, developers will be better enabled to tackle the inherent challenges of modern programming paradigms. In this, the future of debugging is not only about augmenting methodologies but also in establishing a scenario wherein error handling becomes an inherent aspect of the software development process so that solidity and dependability are assured for applications across a broad spectrum.

The significance of error handling and debugging in software development cannot be overstated since they play a very important role in delivering stable and dependable programs. A strong understanding of various debugging techniques results in proper identification and correction of software bugs, which is directly related to code quality as well as system stability. Advanced tools and support environments, as seen in the Ada programming example, show how template-supported editing, command completion, and the blending of interpretation and compilation can enhance debugging efficiency. These systems not only simplify the process of debugging but also improve the structure of the development environment.

This serves to highlight the necessity of using sophisticated debugging tools to counter the problematic nature of modern-day software construction, which aids in increasing the reliability and maintainability of programs (Standish et al., 1983).In referring to error handling methodologies, one learns that the incorporation of logical constructs within code can handle runtime issues beforehand. The development of runtime assertion checking, highlighted in recent news releases, represents a significant milestone toward software reliability through the enforcement mechanism for specific program states at run time. Through the inclusion of assertion checks, developers can proactively observe the application state, allowing for anomaly detection before it occurs. Debugging is not just useful to debug but also provides support to the general ethos of software engineering, that is, designing solid applications that can handle unforeseen circumstances with grace. Robust error handling practices, in line with current industrial practice, are hence important towards achieving better software quality (Clarke et al., 2006).

Ultimately, error handling and debugging affect the resilience of software systems. With advances in new tools and techniques, programmers are able to better counterprogram faults' inherent pitfalls. Through an adaptive mix of debugging techniques and error correction strategies, developers can better enhance software resilience as well as user satisfaction. The understanding gleaned from past practice and the latest innovations, like those introduced in the domain of runtime assertion checking and advanced programming environments, is essential to software practitioners who intend to soar high.

Familiarity with these key aspects not only helps improve near-term software, but also paves the way for future advancements in the field of software engineering based on continuous improvement of best practices in debugging and error recovery.

REFERENCES

1. Alansari, Z., Belgaum, M. R., Miraz, M. H., Soomro, S., et al. (2018). Fault localization models in debugging. http://arxiv.org/abs/1803.03673 (accessed on 9th September 2025).
2. Archer, J. E., & Devlin, M. T. (2025). Rationale's experience using Ada for very large systems. https://core.ac.uk/download/pdf/42829694.pdf (accessed on 9th September 2025).
3. Asai, K., & Ishii, Y. (2014). Report on a user test and extension of a type debugger for novice programmers. http://arxiv.org/abs/1412.4877 (accessed on 9th September 2025).
4. Asokan, N., Dettenborn, T., McGillion, B., Nyman, L., et al. (2015). Open-TEE–An open virtual trusted execution environment. http://arxiv.org/abs/1506.07367 (accessed on 9th September 2025).
5. Aspinall, D., Blanchette, J. C., Sterling, L., Alpuente, M., Ducassé, M., Wenzel, M., et al. (2014). Interactive simplifier tracing and debugging in Isabelle. http://arxiv.org/abs/1406.0292 (accessed on 9th September 2025).
6. Bekooij, M., Domer, R., Leupers, R., Nohl, A., et al. (2009). Programming MPSoC platforms: Road works ahead. https://core.ac.uk/download/pdf/11473351.pdf (accessed on 9th September 2025).
7. Berman, W. J., Bynum, W. L., Foudriat, E. C., Will, M., et al. (2025). An operating system for future aerospace vehicle computer systems. https://core.ac.uk/download/pdf/42848866.pdf (accessed on 9th September 2025).
8. Bishop, M. (1990). A proactive password checker. https://core.ac.uk/download/pdf/42812140.pdf (accessed on 9th September 2025).
9. Book, M., Charlotte, C., Jantunen, S., Sharp, H., & Washizaki, H. (2020). Sensemaking practices in the everyday work of AI/ML software engineering. https://core.ac.uk/download/294625305.pdf (accessed on 9th September 2025).
10. Brummayer, R., & Järvisalo, M. (2010). Testing and debugging techniques for answer set solver development. http://arxiv.org/abs/1007.3223 (accessed on 9th September 2025).
11. Buslaev, A. V., Iglovikov, V., Khvedchenya, E., Parinov, A., Druzhinin, M., & Kalinin, A. A. (2020). Albumentations: Fast and flexible image augmentations. *Information, 11*, 125. https://doi.org/10.3390/info11020125 (accessed on 9th September 2025).

12. Cara, F., Giacinto, G., Maiorca, D., Ugarte, M., et al. (2019). PowerDrive: Accurate de-obfuscation and analysis of PowerShell malware. https://core.ac.uk/download/220682597.pdf (accessed on 9th September 2025).
13. Clarke, L. A., & Rosenblum, D. S. (2006). A historical perspective on runtime assertion checking in software development. https://core.ac.uk/download/1673306.pdf (accessed on 9th September 2025).
14. Cornu, B., Durieux, T., Monperrus, M., Seinturier, L., et al. (2015). NPEFix: Automatic runtime repair of null pointer exceptions in Java. http://arxiv.org/abs/1512.07423 (accessed on 9th September 2025).
15. da Alves, E. H. S., Cordeiro, L. C., & de Filho, E. B. L. (2015). Fault localization in multi-threaded C programs using bounded model checking (extended version). http://arxiv.org/abs/1509.02490 (accessed on 9th September 2025).
16. Dunkels, A., Eriksson, J., Finne, N., Tsiftes, N., et al. (2009). Sensornet checkpointing: Enabling repeatability in testbeds and realism in simulations. https://core.ac.uk/download/11434667.pdf (accessed on 9th September 2025).
17. Fattori, A., Martignoni, L., Monga, M., Paleari, R., et al. (2010). Dynamic and transparent analysis of commodity production systems. http://arxiv.org/abs/1006.5845 (accessed on 9th September 2025).
18. Foshee, G., Kirchoff, M., Moranda, P. B., Omre, E., et al. (2025). A methodology for producing reliable software, volume 1. https://core.ac.uk/download/pdf/42881989.pdf (accessed on 9th September 2025).
19. Furia, C. A., Meyer, B., Nordio, M., Pei, Y., et al. (2014). Automated fixing of programs with contracts. http://arxiv.org/abs/1403.1117 (accessed on 9th September 2025).
20. Hartmann, A. K., & Rieger, H. (2001). *A Practical Guide to Computer Simulations*. http://arxiv.org/abs/cond-mat/0111531 (accessed on 9th September 2025).
21. Jiang, H., Li, X., Xuan, J., Yang, Y., et al. (2017). What causes my test alarm? Automatic cause analysis for test alarms in system and integration testing. http://arxiv.org/abs/1703.00768 (accessed on 9th September 2025).
22. Keromytis, A. D., & Sidiroglou, S. (2004). Using execution transactions to recover from buffer overflow attacks. https://core.ac.uk/download/161437268.pdf (accessed on 9th September 2025).
23. Leveson, N. G. (1981). Software safety: A definition and some preliminary thoughts. https://core.ac.uk/download/287623574.pdf (accessed on 9th September 2025).

24. Monperrus, M. (2016). Automatic software repair: A bibliography. https://core.ac.uk/download/49477621.pdf (accessed on 9th September 2025).
25. Monperrus, M. (2016). On oracles for automated diagnosis and repair of software bugs. https://core.ac.uk/download/46807431.pdf (accessed on 9th September 2025).
26. Roca Navarro, F. J., Ruiz Gironès, E., & Sarrate Ramos, J. (2009). Management, design and development of a mesh generation environment using open-source software. https://core.ac.uk/download/41784544.pdf (accessed on 9th September 2025).
27. Standish, T. A., & Taylor, R. N. (1983). Steps to an advanced Ada programming environment. https://core.ac.uk/download/287623545.pdf (accessed on 9th September 2025).
28. Sun, Q., Berkelbach, T. C., Blunt, N. S., Booth, G. H., Guo, S., Li, Z., Liu, J., et al. (2017). *PySCF: The Python-based simulations of chemistry framework. Wiley Interdisciplinary Reviews: Computational Molecular Science, 8*. https://doi.org/10.1002/wcms.1340 (accessed on 9th September 2025).

INDEX

Q

R

S

T

U

V

W

This book series support the global efforts towards sustainability by providing timely coverage of the progress, opportunities, and challenges of sustainable food production and consumption in Asia and Africa. The series narrates the success stories and research endeavors from the regions of Africa and Asia on issues relating to SDG 2: Zero hunger. It fosters the research in transdisciplinary academic fields spanning across sustainable agriculture systems and practices, post- harvest and food supply chains. It will also focus on breeding programs for resilient crops, efficiency in crop cycle, various factors of food security, as well as improving nutrition and curbing hunger and malnutrition. The focus of the series is to provide a comprehensive publication platform and act as a knowledge engine in the growth of sustainability sciences with a special focus on developing nations. The series will publish mainly edited volumes but some authored volumes. These volumes will have chapters from eminent personalities in their area of research from different parts of the world.

Sustainability Sciences in Asia and Africa

Sustainable Agriculture and Food Security

Series Editor

Rajeev K Varshney, International Chair-Agriculture & Food Security, Food Futures Institute, Murdoch University, Australia

Ndakalimwe Naftal Gabriel • Edosa Omoregie •
Kenneth Prudence Abasubong
Editors

Emerging Sustainable Aquaculture Innovations in Africa

Springer

Editors
Ndakalimwe Naftal Gabriel
Department of Fisheries and Ocean Science
University of Namibia
Henties Bay, Namibia

Edosa Omoregie
Department of Natural and Applied Sciences
Namibia University of Science and Technology
Windhoek, Namibia

Kenneth Prudence Abasubong
Nanjing Agricultural University
Nanjing, China

ISSN 2730-6771 ISSN 2730-678X (electronic)
Sustainability Sciences in Asia and Africa
ISSN 2730-6798 ISSN 2730-6801 (electronic)
Sustainable Agriculture and Food Security
ISBN 978-981-19-7450-2 ISBN 978-981-19-7451-9 (eBook)
https://doi.org/10.1007/978-981-19-7451-9

© The Editor(s) (if applicable) and The Author(s), under exclusive license to Springer Nature Singapore Pte Ltd. 2023
This work is subject to copyright. All rights are solely and exclusively licensed by the Publisher, whether the whole or part of the material is concerned, specifically the rights of translation, reprinting, reuse of illustrations, recitation, broadcasting, reproduction on microfilms or in any other physical way, and transmission or information storage and retrieval, electronic adaptation, computer software, or by similar or dissimilar methodology now known or hereafter developed.
The use of general descriptive names, registered names, trademarks, service marks, etc. in this publication does not imply, even in the absence of a specific statement, that such names are exempt from the relevant protective laws and regulations and therefore free for general use.
The publisher, the authors, and the editors are safe to assume that the advice and information in this book are believed to be true and accurate at the date of publication. Neither the publisher nor the authors or the editors give a warranty, expressed or implied, with respect to the material contained herein or for any errors or omissions that may have been made. The publisher remains neutral with regard to jurisdictional claims in published maps and institutional affiliations.

This Springer imprint is published by the registered company Springer Nature Singapore Pte Ltd.
The registered company address is: 152 Beach Road, #21-01/04 Gateway East, Singapore 189721, Singapore

Preface

The global food production systems require expanding their capacity to produce almost twice the current levels to safeguard the food security of the burgeoning population worldwide. More than 800 million suffering from undernourishment worldwide pose a great risk to the attainment of sustainable development goal (SDG) 2 of the UN that targets "End hunger, achieve food security and improved nutrition and promote sustainable agriculture" within the next 7 years. The challenge is further exacerbated by the rising weather extremities and unpredictability in rainfall patterns and pest-pathogen dynamics associated with global climate change that has profound negative impact on the agricultural productivity and farm incomes worldwide. Also, the future targets of food production should be secured in a resource-constrained agricultural setting and with least environment footprint, thus calling for sustainable innovations in agri-farming systems and enhanced participation of women in agriculture. The challenge to reduce hunger is alarming in the case of developing nations particularly in Asia and Africa that house the largest proportion of people suffering from malnutrition and other nutrition-related issues. Furthermore, the agri-food systems in Asia and Africa are severely constrained by subsistence nature of farming, declining land and other agricultural resources, increasing environmental pollution, soil and biodiversity degradation, and climate change. Therefore, this book series, "Sustainable Agriculture and Food Security," has been planned to support the global efforts towards sustainability by providing timely coverage of the progress, opportunities, and challenges of sustainable food production and consumption in Asia and Africa. The series narrates the success stories and research endeavours from the regions of Africa and Asia on issues relating to SDG 2: Zero hunger. It fosters research in transdisciplinary academic fields spanning across sustainable agriculture systems and practices, post-harvest and food supply chains. The focus of the series is to provide a comprehensive publication platform and act as a knowledge engine in the growth of sustainability sciences with a special focus on developing nations.

As per the UN's Food and Agriculture Organization (FAO), aquaculture is defined as the '*farming of aquatic organisms including fish, molluscs, crustaceans and aquatic plants. Farming implies some sort of intervention in the rearing process to enhance production, such as regular stocking, feeding, protection from predators, etc. Farming also implies individual or corporate ownership of the stock being cultivated, the planning, development and operation of aquaculture systems, sites, facilities and practices, and the production and transport.*' Although aquaculture has been around for millennia, it started to contribute significantly to the global food supply and rural livelihoods about 30–40 years ago. In the context of target geographic regions of the book series, Asia dominates global aquaculture accounting for 92% of global production, and Africa has <2% share in global production. However, in the last 20 years, aquaculture production in sub-Saharan Africa (SSA) has grown by 11% annually on average, almost twice as fast compared with the rest of the world, and some African countries with a growth of 12–23% per year. However, due to fish disease triggered by poor water and farm management practices in the beginning of 2015, the high cost of local production, competition from cheap fish imports, and then the recent addition of the COVID-19 pandemic, the production level has been stagnated. As per an estimate, the projected increase in demand for aquatic foods in SSA required that aquaculture produces an additional 5 million tonnes by 2030 and 10.6 million tonnes by 2050. However, such growth must not come at the cost of aquatic ecosystem health, increased pollution, animal welfare, biodiversity, or social equality. This requires new, sustainable and equitable aquaculture development strategies.

According to a joint report of Agence Française de Développement (AFD), European Commission, and German International Development Agency (GIZ), '*the aquaculture value chain—whether it be the primary production stage or the subsequent product supply chain—can contribute to achieving SDGs at both national and regional levels.*'

Among different kind of aquaculture types—subsistence aquaculture, small-scale commercial aquaculture, SME aquaculture, and industrial aquaculture—the subsistence aquaculture has the potential to contribute to most of the relevant SDGs. This is due to the family level of operations, where work is well distributed, meaningful, and empowering. Small-scale commercial aquaculture in terms of its contribution to the SDGs also has a greater opportunity to directly contribute to family income, and thus address poverty issues. This will assist to achieve other SDGs at community level, including good health and education opportunities. It can also generate some jobs, and being local, can be undertaken on a part-time basis by women. In the majority of the aquaculture sector in Africa, the above-mentioned two types of aquaculture farming are more common in Africa, and therefore improving aquaculture in Africa will significantly contribute to achieving SDGs.

In view of this, the present book, *Emerging Sustainable Aquaculture Innovations in Africa,* provides a platform to appreciate current efforts and plan future work on this important topic. The book contains 26 chapters written by various experts and practitioners in aquaculture in Africa. The chapters are written under four parts: Aquaculture Nutrition and Feed Management, Water Quality Management, Aquaculture Development and Innovations in Africa, and Aquaculture Animal Welfare. I would like to congratulate the editors, Ndakalimwe Naftal Gabriel, Edosa Omoregie, and Kenneth Prudence Abasubong, and all authors for their valued contributions. I am sure that this book is a great resource for students, researchers, aquaculture farmers, aquaculture educators and extension agents, policy makers, and other stakeholders engaged in transforming aquaculture in Africa and possibly other parts of the world.

I wish to extend my sincere thanks and gratitude to the Springer staff, particularly Aakanksha Tyagi, Senior Editor (Books), Life Sciences, and Naren Aggarwal, Editorial Director, Medicine, Biomedical and Life Sciences Books Asia, for their constant support for the accomplishment of this compendium. The cooperation received from my senior colleagues and research leaders such as David Morrison, Peter Davies, and Daniel Murphy and my laboratory colleagues Anu Chitikineni, Abhishek Bohra, and Vanika Garg from Murdoch University (Australia) is also gratefully acknowledged. I would like to thank my family members Monika Varshney, Prakhar Varshney, and Preksha Varshney for their love and support to discharge my duties as Series Editor.

Perth, WA, Australia Rajeev K. Varshney

Contents

About the Editors

Ndakalimwe Naftal Gabriel is a senior lecturer in the Department of Fisheries and Ocean Sciences at the University of Namibia (UNAM). He has a PhD in Fisheries and Aquatic Sciences from UNAM. From 2013 to 2015, he attended Nanjing Agricultural University in Jiangsu, China (MSc-aquaculture) and UNAM for his bachelor's degree in Biological Sciences. He has received numerous awards, including a Fulbright scholarship, TWAS fellowship, Nanjing Municipal People's Government international student scholarship, Distinguished Foreign Student Scholarship–2015, Chinese Government Scholarship, and recognition as one of the best students at Nanjing Agricultural University in 2014 and 2015. He has over 10 years of expertise as a researcher in aquaculture and 7 years as a lecturer at UNAM. He has over 30 published research pieces, including book chapters and 2 books. He has also evaluated numerous peer-reviewed articles from renowned journals and supervised several graduate students in the area of aquaculture and fishery sciences.

Edosa Omoregie obtained his PhD degree in Zoology (Fisheries) from the University of Jos, Nigeria, in 1995. He is an NSRIC (Nature Science Research and Innovation Centre, Canada) distinguished professor of fisheries and currently with the Namibia University of Science and Technology. His academic career started in 1990 with the Department of Zoology, University of Jos, Nigeria, where he rose to the rank of professor of fisheries in 2004. From 2005 to 2008, he was FAO expert lecturer in fisheries for the University of The Gambia. Between 2011 and 2015, he was the director of the Sam Nujoma Marine and Coastal Resources Research Centre, University of Namibia. He is actively involved in fisheries and aquatic science research on the African continent and has supervised over 50 postgraduate research students. He has served as a review editor for several journals with focus on fisheries and aquatic sciences and has contributed to over 150 scholarly works, including more than 75 peer-reviewed research papers.

Kenneth Prudence Abasubong holds an MSc in Animal Nutrition and Feed Science in 2018 and is a final year PhD candidate at Nanjing Agricultural University (NAU), China. His specialisation areas are aquaculture nutrition, molecular biology, feed science, animal and aquatic physiology, and nutrient metabolism. He has attended several international conferences and symposiums in aquaculture and fisheries sciences. He studied at the University of Uyo, Uyo, Nigeria (PGD Aquatic Environmental Management) from 2012 to 2013 and at the University of Calabar for his bachelor's degree in Animal Sciences. He has published more than 20 articles and reviewed several high-impact international journals in aquaculture. He has received several awards, including the best international student in NAU in 2018. He has supervised several undergraduate and graduate students in fisheries and aquaculture. He has over 8 years of experience as a researcher in aquaculture.

Part I
Aquaculture Nutrition and Feed Management

Chapter 1
Fish Nutrition: An African Aquaculture Perspective

Samwel Mchele Limbu

Abstract Aquaculture production is an essential industry in many African countries as a source of protein, income, and employment. The industry is expected to grow because the demand for fish products is increasing while the supply from natural sources is decreasing or has stagnated. Therefore, aquaculture in Africa is required to increase production while ensuring industry sustainability. One of the most important aspects required to increase aquaculture production and ensure the sustainability of the industry in Africa is fish nutrition. Fish nutrition plays a critical role in the expansion of aquaculture because it influences not only production costs but also fish growth, health and waste production. Under current production economics, feed is the most expensive item in African fish production, frequently amounting to more than 50% of the total variable costs depending on the intensity of culture. Accordingly, the success of African aquaculture partly depends on formulating affordable feeds, which guarantee fast growth and survival of cultured fish without causing environmental pollution. Extensive research has been conducted on African aquaculture on various aspects of fish nutrition by using various feeding strategies and technologies, ingredients to replace expensive and limited availability fishmeal and soybean meal by using cheap alternatives, use of affordable locally available feed ingredients and supplementation by using different feed additives for various purposes. The effects of these approaches on growth performance, feed utilization, organ indices, water quality, immunity and economic benefits have been documented. However, information is currently scattered and unorganized. This chapter critically analyses and discusses the available information in the literature on fish nutrition in cultured fish species in Africa. The chapter findings pave the way towards aquaculture development in Africa through proper fish nutrition to meet the needs of the industry for increased production and environmental sustainability in the era of blue economy.

S. M. Limbu (✉)
Department of Aquaculture Technology, School of Aquatic Sciences and Fisheries Technology, University of Dar es Salaam, Dar es Salaam, Tanzania

© The Author(s), under exclusive license to Springer Nature Singapore Pte Ltd. 2023
N. N. Gabriel et al. (eds.), *Emerging Sustainable Aquaculture Innovations in Africa*, Sustainable Agriculture and Food Security,
https://doi.org/10.1007/978-981-19-7451-9_1

Keywords Fish nutrition · African aquaculture · Growth performance · Immunity response · Feed additives

1.1 Introduction

One of the critical aspects required for future human development is food security. The unprecedented human population growth has caused increasing pressure on human food sources (Dunbar et al. 2014). Across the world, hunger and malnutrition are still challenging to tackle by 2030 (FAO 2022). Asia and Sub-Saharan Africa currently have many people who are food and nutrition insecure (Beveridge et al. 2013). Most inhabitants in the two Asia and Sub-Saharan Africa depend on fish as a rich source of protein, micronutrients and essential fatty acids. Fish is among the aquatic foods, which are increasingly recognized as significant contributors to the food security and nutrition (FAO 2022). Accordingly, one of the objectives of Africa is to increase the dietary intake of fish to provide the energy and protein sufficient to fight against wasting and stunting (Delarue 2019). Fish contributes to Africa's food and nutrition security, but future directions for the wild fish sector remain uncertain (Chan et al. 2019). Therefore, aquaculture is the potential industry to narrow the gap between fish demand and supply in Africa.

Aquaculture is the primary fish production sector projected to contribute largely to the expected increase in fishery products by a further 15% in the year 2030 (FAO 2022). Such projections are based on the intensification and expansion of sustainable aquaculture production. For the African aquaculture industry to meet the projected growth sustainably, effective feeding at affordable cost is a prerequisite. Affordable feed is important to the African aquaculture industry because fish feed constitutes 40% to 60% of the total operational costs depending on intensity of production (Limbu and Jumanne 2014). Accordingly, the African aquaculture has been using various methods and technologies to produce fish.

One of the potential approaches used in African aquaculture is the development of appropriate feeding methods and technologies for improved fish growth performance and general health at a reasonable cost. Indeed, the African aquaculture industry uses various approaches to achieve the production of high-quality fish for food consumption. These include mixed protein levels, restriction and re-feeding (Limbu and Jumanne 2014; El-Araby et al. 2020), on-farm made feeds (Limbu 2020b) and supplemental feeds with fertilization (Limbu et al. 2016; Lundeba et al. 2022). Moreover, feed supplementation by using different additives has also been reported as an important approach to sustain the African aquaculture industry (Abdel-Tawwab et al. 2021c). The projected expansion and diversification of aquaculture (FAO 2022) is expected to cause stress and compromise fish immunity, leading to disease outbreaks (Awad and Awaad 2017). Such effects require supplementation by using growth and immunity stimulants as antioxidant agents for protecting fish against xenobiotics (Abdel-Tawwab et al. 2020b). Extensive studies have been conducted in African aquaculture, covering an array of functional feed additives for various purposes. However, information on the feeding methods, technologies and feed additives used in African aquaculture is currently scattered and unorganized, consequently limiting the industry's growth.

This chapter organizes and synthesizes the available information in the literature on the African aquaculture industry feeding perspectives. The chapter first analyses the various methods used in the feeding of cultured fish in various African countries. Second, it discusses the feeding technologies used in the African aquaculture industry. Third, the chapter explains the approaches undertaken by the African fish nutritionists to solve feed costs by focusing on replacing expensive and limited access ingredients. Lastly, the chapter explores the various feed additives used in African aquaculture for feed production to ensure enhanced fish growth performance, immunity and general health. On each of the four aspects, future perspectives are highlighted. The information generated could transform the African aquaculture industry fish production for sustainable food production required by the continent and global population in the blue economy era.

1.2 The Feeding Practices Used in African Aquaculture

Feeding practices aim to ensure optimum growth rates, feed efficiencies and cost-effective utilization of feeds. These are essential aspects for increased production and revenue generation. African aquaculture uses various feeding practices to achieve the above objectives (Table 1.1). One such approach is mixed feeding schedules with different dietary crude protein levels designed as low protein, medium protein and high protein. Such a practice was conducted in African Sharp tooth catfish, *Clarias gariepinus* fingerlings (Morenike and Akinola 2010). Feeding the *C. gariepinus* on high protein resulted in higher growth, and feed utilization consequently led to more economic returns. Other feed practices used in African aquaculture are feed restriction and re-feeding. Restriction and re-feeding strategy has been reported in Nile tilapia, *Oreochromis niloticus* in Tanzania (Limbu and Jumanne 2014) and Egypt (El-Araby et al. 2020). In both studies, fish fasted compensated for weight during re-feeding. Furthermore, restricted feeding improved antioxidant status (El-Araby et al. 2020) and reduced feed cost up to 20% (Limbu and Jumanne 2014). This feeding strategy is simple, easy, practically applicable and affordable means of reducing feeding costs in African aquaculture.

Locally produced fish feed has long been recognized as potential for aquaculture development in Sub-Saharan Africa (Gabriel et al. 2007). Therefore, another approach commonly used in African aquaculture is to formulate cost-effective feeds at the farm level by using locally available ingredients. This approach was evident in Uganda in the culture of *C. gariepinus* (Limbu 2020b). The on-farm formulated diet reduced feed cost up to 30%, leading to better protein retention and healthier fish. Moreover, fish farmers in Africa feed the supplemental feeds and fertilization in semi-intensive production due to unaffordable commercial feeds. Accordingly, *O. niloticus* farmers in Tanzania fed their fish on mixed ingredients and rice bran alone (RB) diets complemented with fertilization in earthen ponds

Table 1.1 The feeding practices used in African aquaculture

Feeding approach; country	Species and growth stage; study time	Effects	References
Mixed feeding schedules with low and high protein; Nigeria	*Clarias gariepinus* fingerling; 8 weeks	Feeding continuously with high protein was more economical	Morenike and Akinola (2010)
Different feeding regimes; Egypt	*Oreochromis niloticus* fingerling; 10 weeks	Fasted and re-fed once or twice every other day and fasted and re-fed twice every third day compensated for growth Fasting improved antioxidant status	El-Araby et al. (2020)
Restricted and re-feeding regime; Tanzania	*Oreochromis niloticus* fingerling; 8 weeks	Reduced feeding cost by 10 and 20% for depriving feed for 1 and 2 days, respectively	Limbu and Jumanne (2014)
On-farm and industrially manufactured feeds; Uganda	*Clarias gariepinus* juveniles; 8 weeks	On-farm feed reduced feed cost up to 30%, had better protein retention and healthier fish	Limbu (2020b)
Mixed ingredients and rice bran alone diets; Tanzania	*Oreochromis niloticus* and *Clarias gariepinus* juveniles; 38 weeks	No effect on performance in semi-intensive earthen ponds with fertilization	Limbu et al. (2016)
Three different feeding regimes; Zambia	*Oreochromis macrochir*; 34 weeks	Feed and manure increased fish growth	Lundeba et al. (2022)

(Limbu et al. 2016). In this study, no differences on growth and feed utilization were evident, indicating that semi-intensively cultured fish can be reared on simple feeds when fertilization is conducted. In a relatively related fashion, Lundeba et al. (2022) conducted a participatory on-field study on tilapia, *Oreochromis macrochir* in Zambia utilizing three feeding regimes namely formulated feed only, fertilization and formulated feed and fertilization together. The fish maintained by feeding and fertilization increased survival rate, weight gain, specific growth rate, total amount of fish harvested and yield.

In a nutshell, these studies show that aquaculture in Africa uses various feeding practices aimed at ensuring optimum growth of cultured fish, enhanced feed efficiencies and reduced feed cost for the sustainability of the industry. The effective utilization of feeding practices, such as restricted and re-feeding, could improve growth and production upon re-feeding and save substantial feed costs for sustainable fish production to feed the ever-increasing human population in Africa.

1.3 Feeding Technologies Used in African Aquaculture

Feeding technology is one of the most important aspects for increased growth performance, survival rate and ultimately production of cultured species. The ability to use appropriate feeding technology also determines the profitability of aquaculture due to enhanced utilization of nutrients. The African aquaculture also uses various technologies to improve utilization of plant-based ingredients, which have limited nutritional value in fish. One such approach is to ferment the ingredients used to enhance the nutritional availability. Accordingly, the fermentation process has been used for sunflower by using *Saccharomyces cerevisiae* or *Bacillus subtilis* (Hassaan et al. 2018), palm seed meal fermented with *Aspergillus oryzae* (Dawood et al. 2020d) and poultry by-product meal by using yeast (Dawood et al. 2020i) in Nile tilapia and Common carp (*Cyprinus carpio*) (Dawood et al. 2020h).

Moreover, rice bran fermented by using *Bacillus subtilis* was used in white leg shrimp (*Litopenaeus vannamei*) reared at different salinities (Abdel-Tawwab et al. 2020a). In these studies, fermentation greatly increased the nutritional quality and value of plant by-products in practical diets (Hassaan et al. 2018), improved growth, digestion activity and immune response (Dawood et al. 2020d, h) and enhanced growth performance and health condition (Dawood et al. 2020i) of the cultured fish. In crustaceans, fermentation enhanced growth performance, antioxidant systems and innate immunity (Abdel-Tawwab et al. 2020a).

Apart from fermentation process, various technologies have also been used in African aquaculture for improving growth and health. These include dietary supplementation with lactic acid bacteria-produced nanoselenium spheres (Dawood et al. 2020m) and xylanase (Hassaan et al. 2019b) in Nile tilapia and heat-killed *Lactobacillus plantarum* (HK L-137) in genetically improved farmed tilapia (GIFT) (Dawood et al. 2019). Expectedly, lactic acid supplementation improved growth, oxidative status and immune-related gene expression (Dawood et al. 2020m), enhanced growth, protein digestibility and digestive enzymes activities (Hassaan et al. 2019b) and heat-killed *L. plantarum* promoted growth performance, feed utilization, digestive enzyme activity, fish health and modulated nutrients metabolism (Dawood et al. 2019).

It is clear from these studies that fermentation as a feeding technology holds potential application in African aquaculture for improved growth, nutrients digestion and health of cultured fish and crustaceans. This might be one of the strategies for improving utilization of plant-based ingredients for sustainable African aquaculture. Moreover, supplementation of different treated bacteria, such as heat killed, is an effective strategy to enhance growth, nutrients utilization and health for sustainable fish production in Africa.

1.4 Fishmeal and Soybean Replacement in African Aquaculture

Historically, fishmeal has been used as an important high-quality animal protein ingredient for aquaculture feeds production for most commercially farmed fish species (Luthada-Raswiswi et al. 2021; Limbu et al. 2022). However, fishmeal as a source of protein for aquafeed industry is expensive and has limited supply. The high prices and limited supply have tempted research in African aquaculture for alternatives to replace fishmeal (Dawood and Koshio 2020). Indeed, several studies have been conducted on fishmeal replacement in African aquaculture (Table 1.2). Most studies on fishmeal replacement were conducted in Egypt on *O. niloticus* with a few on European sea bass, *Dicentrarchus labrax* (Sallam et al. 2022), Grey mullet, *Mugil cephalus* (Abo-Taleb et al. 2021a, b; Ashour et al. 2021a), Common sole, *Solea solea* (Saleh et al. 2021) (Table 1.2). This is not surprising because Egypt is the leading country in African aquaculture production (FAO 2020, 2022) and it is the third producer of *O. niloticus* in the world (Dawood et al. 2020c). Moreover, a few studies on fishmeal replacement have also been conducted in other countries, such as Kenya (Kirimi et al. 2017; Ogello et al. 2017), Nigeria (Solomon et al. 2010; Olude and Badmus 2015), Zambia (Yossa et al. 2021) and Tanzania (Limbu et al. 2022). Results from these studies indicated total fishmeal replacement without adverse effect on *O. niloticus* fingerlings performance by using soybean meal (El-Saidy and Gaber 2002), shrimp meal, meat and bone meal, bone meal and poultry by-products meal (El-Sayed 1998) and plant protein mixture in *O. niloticus* juveniles in Egypt (El-Saidy and Gaber 2003). Moreover, complete replacement of fishmeal was reported in Grey mullet, *Mugil cephalus,* fry by using zooplankton biomass meal in Egypt (Abo-Taleb et al. 2021b) and a single cell protein feedstuff for *O. niloticus* fingerlings in Zambia (Yossa et al. 2021). The findings from these studies pinpoint at the possibility of replacing total fishmeal for sustainable African aquaculture industry.

Notwithstanding the above findings, several other ingredients partially replaced fishmeal in the diets for various fish species in African aquaculture, such as earthworm, *Eisenia fetida*, bedding meal in *O. niloticus* fingerlings in Kenya (Musyoka et al. 2020), *Daphnia magna* meal up to 75 to 100% for *M. cephalus* larvae in Egypt (Abo-Taleb et al. 2021a), black soldier fry larvae diet up to 75 to 84% for *O. niloticus* fry in Tanzania (Limbu et al. 2022) and methylated soy protein isolates at 66% in *O. niloticus* fingerlings in Egypt (Amer et al. 2020). Furthermore, partial fishmeal replacement of up to 50% has been reported by using amphipod meal, *Gammarus pulex* for *M. cephalus* fry (Ashour et al. 2021a) and broad bean meal for *O. niloticus* fry both in Egypt (Gaber 2006) and blood meal in *O. niloticus* juveniles in Kenya (Kirimi et al. 2017). Moreover, further lower partial fishmeal replacement has been reported by using whey protein of up to 45% in *D. labrax* juveniles (Sallam et al. 2022), soybean protein concentrate of up to 35% in Common sole, *Solea solea* post-larvae (Saleh et al. 2021) and whey protein concentrate up to 27.7% in *O. niloticus* fingerlings in Egypt (Amer et al. 2019), a mixture of moringa (*Moringa oleifera*) leaf

Table 1.2 The ingredients used for fishmeal and soybean replacement in African aquaculture

Ingredient used; country	Species and growth stage; study time	Effects	References
Fishmeal replacement			
Soybean meal; Egypt	*Oreochromis niloticus* fingerlings; 10 weeks	• Improved growth performance, feed utilization, nutrients digestibility and food intake	El-Saidy and Gaber (2002)
Shrimp meal, blood meal, meat and bone meal, their mixture and poultry by-product meal; Egypt	*Oreochromis niloticus* fingerlings; 21 weeks	• No difference on growth and body composition • Reduced feed utilization • Higher ash contents • Economically superior to fishmeal	El-Sayed (1998)
A plant protein mixture; Egypt	*Oreochromis niloticus* juveniles; 16 weeks	• No difference on growth and body composition • Reduced apparent protein digestibility for 100% fishmeal replacement • Economically superior to fishmeal	El-Saidy and Gaber (2003)
Three plant protein sources extruded soybean meal, extruded full-fat soybean and corn gluten meal; Egypt	*Oreochromis niloticus* and tilapia galilae *Sarotherodon galilaeus* fingerlings; 17 weeks	• Reduced growth performance and feed intake for Nile tilapia fed on plant protein • Increased growth performance for *Tilapia galilae* fed on soybean meal diet • Better feed conversion ratio for Nile tilapia and *Tilapia galilae* fed on soybean meal diet	Goda et al. (2007)
Methylated soy protein isolates; Egypt	*Oreochromis niloticus* fingerlings; 10 weeks	• Increased growth performance, phagocytic index, immunoglobulin M level and lysozyme activity post-bacterial challenge • Increased liver and intestine histomorphological structures with an increased level of replacement • Increased the total return, net profit, and performance index % for methylated soy protein	Amer et al. (2020)

(continued)

Table 1.2 (continued)

Ingredient used; country	Species and growth stage; study time	Effects	References
Whey protein concentrate; Egypt	*Oreochromis niloticus* fingerlings; 10 weeks	• Increased immunity parameters as whey concentrate replacement increased • Increased liver damage as whey concentrate replacement increased • Total return increased with whey protein replacement increased • Increased cysteine-aspartic acid protease 3 activity	Amer et al. (2019)
Whey protein; Egypt	European sea bass, *Dicentrarchus labrax* juveniles; 10 weeks	• No difference on growth, feed utilization and survival up to 45% fishmeal replacement • Total immunoglobulin and complement 3 increased up to 15% and 30% replacement of FM by whey protein • Increased liver and kidney function enzymes with increasing whey protein incorporation levels • Enhanced histopathological signs at high fishmeal substitution by whey protein	Sallam et al. (2022)
Zooplankton biomass meal; Egypt	Grey mullet, *Mugil cephalus* fry; 8 weeks	• Increased growth performance and feed utilization for fish fed on 100% zooplankton biomass meal • Improved intestinal villus length, crypts depth and muscle thickness with zooplankton biomass meal inclusion • No histopathological changes on fish fed on zooplankton biomass meal • Reduced diet cost formulation by 18% and the price per kg weight gain by about 40%	Abo-Taleb et al. (2021b)
Daphnia magna meal; Egypt	Grey mullet, *Mugil cephalus* larvae; 8 weeks	• Higher growth, and feed utilization parameters for fish fed on 75%	Abo-Taleb et al. (2021a)

(continued)

Table 1.2 (continued)

Ingredient used; country	Species and growth stage; study time	Effects	References
		Daphnia magna • Improved intestinal histomorphometric indices and goblet cell number with increasing *Daphnia magna* inclusion levels. • Reduced feed cost and incidence cost, and the increased profit index and economic efficiency ratio for fish fed on 100 *Daphnia magna*	
Amphipod meal, *Gammarus pulex*; Egypt	Grey mullet, *Mugil cephalus* fry; 8 weeks	• Increased growth performance and survival rate of fish fed on 50% amphipod meal • Enhanced feed utilization of diets for fish fed on 50% amphipod meal • Increased number of goblet cells and intestinal villi for fish fed on 50% amphipod meal • Better economic conversion ratio for fish fed on 50% amphipod meal	Ashour et al. (2021a)
Cotton seed meal; Egypt	*Oreochromis niloticus* juveniles; 10 weeks	• Improved growth performance, feed utilization efficiency and digestibility for fish fed on 2:1 and 1.1 fishmeal: cotton seed meal	Hassaan et al. (2019a)
Soybean protein concentrate; Egypt	Common sole, *Solea solea* post-larvae; 6 weeks	• No difference in growth and survival up to 50% replacement • Increased aspartate and alanine aminotransferases activities • Increased oxidative stress biomarkers • Increased hepatocyte infiltration and massive lipid accumulations in fish fed with 75% and 100% soybean protein diets	Saleh et al. (2021)
Poultry offal silage; Egypt	*Oreochromis niloticus* fingerlings; 16 weeks	• No differences on growth performance • Increased feed	Eissa et al. (2022)

(continued)

Table 1.2 (continued)

Ingredient used; country	Species and growth stage; study time	Effects	References
		efficiency on fish fed on poultry offal silage and fishmeal with betaine supplementation	
Sunflower cake and corn oil; Kenya	*Oreochromis niloticus* fingerlings; 10 weeks	• Higher linoleic acid on fish fed on sunflower cake	Maina et al. (2003)
Earthworm, *Eisenia fetida*, bedding meal; Kenya	*Oreochromis niloticus* fingerlings; 16 weeks	• No differences in mortalities, growth and feed efficiency • Superior amino acid profile, low fibre content and fish carcass crude protein • Higher mean weight gain and biomass for fish fed on 30% earthworm and fishmeal, respectively • Higher crude lipids content, economic returns and profit index for fish fed on 100% earthworm	Musyoka et al. (2020)
Broad bean meal; Egypt	*Oreochromis niloticus* fry; 16 weeks	• Comparable growth performance between fish fed on 50% broad meal and fishmeal • Decreased protein, energy and lipid digestibility of fish fed on broad bean meal above 50%	Gaber (2006)
Soybean meal; Egypt	*Oreochromis niloticus* fingerlings; 10 weeks	• Improved growth rate, feed utilization and food intake for fish fed on 55% soybean meal • Enhanced protein content of fish fed on 55% soybean meal	El-Saidy and Gaber (2002)
Sunflower seed meal; Kenya	*Oreochromis niloticus* juveniles; 14 weeks	• Similar growth for sunflower up to 25% • Similar nutrient utilization parameters in all diets except for sunflower 100%	Ogello et al. (2017)
Blood meal; Kenya	*Oreochromis niloticus* juveniles; 14 weeks	• Reduced essential amino acid levels	Kirimi et al. (2017)
A mixture of moringa (*Moringa oleifera*) leaf and kernel meal; Nigeria	*Clarias gariepinus* juveniles; 8 weeks	• Increased weight gain and specific growth rate of fish reared on control and	Olude and Badmus (2015)

(continued)

Table 1.2 (continued)

Ingredient used; country	Species and growth stage; study time	Effects	References
		20% moringa leaf and kernel meal • Better protein efficiency ratio for fish fed on control and 20% moringa leaf and kernel meal	
Silkworm caterpillar (*Anaphe infracta*) meal; Nigeria	*Heterobranchus bidorsalis* fingerlings; 8 weeks	• Better weight gain, specific growth rate, food conversion ratio and protein efficiency ratio for fish fed on 50% silkworm caterpillar meal	Solomon et al. (2010)
Duckweed, *Lemna minor* meal; Nigeria	*Oreochromis niloticus* fry; 10 weeks	• Comparable growth performance between fish fed on fishmeal and 15% duckweed diet meal	Ofojekwu et al. (2010)
A single cell protein feedstuff; Zambia	*Oreochromis niloticus* fingerlings; 12 weeks	• No effect on weight gain or gut length and weight for fish fed on 2 to 100% single cell protein • Improved feed and nutrient utilization for fish fed on 2 to 100% single cell protein • No gastrointestinal tract histopathology	Yossa et al. (2021)
Black soldier fry larvae meal; Tanzania	*Oreochromis niloticus* fry; 12 weeks	• Increased specific growth rate, total weight gain, Zihler's index of fry and nitrate in the culture water for fish fed on 75% black soldier fry larvae meal • Reduced feed conversion ratio of diet and total suspended solids in the culture water for fish fed on 75% black soldier fry larvae meal • Reduced incidence cost by 32% and 29% and increased profit index by 4% and 3%, respectively, for fry fed on 75% and 100% black soldier fry larvae meal	Limbu et al. (2022)

(continued)

Table 1.2 (continued)

Ingredient used; country	Species and growth stage; study time	Effects	References
Soybean meal replacement			
Cottonseed meal; Egypt	*Oreochromis niloticus* fingerlings; 14 weeks	• No difference on growth up to 75% replacement of soy bean meal with cottonseed meal • Reduced feed utilization efficiency at higher cottonseed meal levels • No difference on moisture, lipid and ash content in whole body and muscle	El-Saidy and Saad (2011)
Leaf protein concentrate from Sugar beet, *Beta vulgaris* and carrot, *Daucus carota*; Egypt	*Oreochromis niloticus* fingerlings; 12 weeks	• No differences in the growth, feed intake and feed conversion ratio indices • No differences on blood biochemical and haematological parameters • Increased condition factor for fish fed on carrot and sugar beet meal • Depleted crude lipid in fish fed on 50% sugar concentrate • Lower feeding cost and best profit margin for fish fed on 100% carrot protein	Ayyat et al. (2021)
Cassia fistula seed meal; Nigeria	*Oreochromis niloticus* fingerlings; 10 weeks	• Reduced growth, diet utilization efficiency, survival rate, digestibility, protein content in fish fed *Cassia fistula* seed meal at varying inclusion levels • Similar feed conversion ratio, specific growth rate and protein efficiency ratio of fish fed on 170 g kg^{-1} to the control diet • Fish fed on 170 g kg^{-1} had efficient cost per unit weight gain	Adebayo et al. (2004)
Shrimp by-products; Egypt	African catfish, *Clarias lazera* fingerlings; 12 weeks	• Increased growth and nutrient utilization parameters, plasma proteins and immunity in fish fed on 50% shrimp by-products • Increased body dry	Abu-Alya et al. (2021)

(continued)

Table 1.2 (continued)

Ingredient used; country	Species and growth stage; study time	Effects	References
		matter and crude protein for fish fed on shrimp by-products • Decreased diet costs and diet costs per 1 kg of weight gain	
Black soldier fry larvae meal; Kenya	*Oreochromis niloticus* juveniles; 12 weeks	• Increased final body weight, body weight gain, specific growth rate, feed conversion ratio, survival rate and condition factor • Increased phenylalanine, threonine, isoleucine, lysine, proline and glutamic acid amino acids • Reduced cost of production	Shati et al. (2022)

and kernel meal (1:1) of up to 20% in *C. gariepinus* juveniles (Olude and Badmus 2015) and 15% dietary duckweed meal in *O. niloticus* fry (Ofojekwu et al. 2010) in Nigeria. These studies suggest partial fishmeal replacement is possible by using various plant-based ingredients. To achieve complete fishmeal replacement, feeding techniques are required to increase plant-based proteins utilization in African aquaculture.

Various approaches have been used to improve the utilization of plant-based protein sources to replace fishmeal. Accordingly, 55% soybean meal supplemented with 0.5% L-lysine totally replaced fishmeal in *O. niloticus* fingerlings (El-Saidy and Gaber 2002). Furthermore, both extruded soybean meal and extruded full-fat soybean supplemented with DL-methionine and L-lysine completely replaced dietary fishmeal in *Sarotherodon galilaeus* fingerlings in Egypt (Goda et al. 2007). Moreover, poultry offal silage supplemented with 0.7% betaine replaced fishmeal in *O. niloticus* fingerlings in Egypt (Eissa et al. 2022), while an exogenous protease enzyme improved growth, nutrient assimilation and haematology of *O. niloticus* juveniles fed on cotton seed meal (Hassaan et al. 2019a). These studies suggest that the nutritional quality of plant-based protein contained in various ingredients for fishmeal replacement can be improved by various techniques. Fully utilization of these techniques at farm level holds the potential for increased aquaculture production in Africa.

Interesting, most ingredients used to replace fishmeal in African aquaculture resulted in reduced feed costs and thus increased economic returns (Table 1.2). Such studies were evident in *O. niloticus* when fishmeal was replaced by shrimp meal, blood meal, meat and bone meal, their mixture and poultry by-product meal

(El-Sayed 1998), a plant protein mixture (El-Saidy and Gaber 2003), methylated soy protein isolates (Amer et al. 2020), whey protein concentrate (Amer et al. 2019) and black soldier fry larvae diet (Limbu et al. 2022). Moreover, reduced diet cost was reported after fishmeal was replaced by zooplankton biomass meal (Abo-Taleb et al. 2021b), amphipod meal (Ashour et al. 2021a) and *Daphnia magna* meal (Abo-Taleb et al. 2021a) in *Mugil cephalus*. These studies highlight that feeding cost can be reduced in aquafeed industry by using various ingredients in African aquaculture to ensure sustainable production.

Despite the existence of studies using soybean meal to replace fishmeal, the former is also expensive and requires replacement. Therefore, several studies have been conducted in African aquaculture to replace soybean meal in various species without any adverse effects on growth and feed utilization efficiency. Indeed, carrot leaf protein concentrate replaced 100% of soybean meal in *O. niloticus* fingerlings without any negative effects on growth and blood constituents in Egypt (Ayyat et al. 2021), while black soldier fly meal replaced soybean meal up to 100% without negative effect on growth and carcass body composition (Shati et al. 2022). Moreover, up to 41.25% cotton seed mean replaced 75% of soybean protein in Nile tilapia fingerlings without any adverse effects on the growth performance, feed utilization, body composition and haematological indices (El-Saidy and Saad 2011). Furthermore, sugar beet leaf concentrate replaced 50% of soybean in *O. niloticus* fingerlings without any negative effects on growth and blood constituents (Ayyat et al. 2021). In addition, 25% duckweed replaced soybean meal protein obtaining the best growth performance and feed utilization in *O. niloticus* fingerlings (Ibrahim et al. 2017). Despite growth performance and feed utilization efficiency, various ingredients replaced soybean meal in African aquaculture to reduce feed cost and improve economic performance. Accordingly, 50% acid-treated shrimp by-products positively influenced productive and economic performances of African catfish, *Clarias lazera* fingerlings in Egypt (Abu-Alya et al. 2021) and 17% *Cassia fistula* seed meal was the most efficient diet in terms of cost per unit weight gain of *O. niloticus* fingerlings in Nigeria (Adebayo et al. 2004). Moreover, 50 and 100% black soldier fly reduced production cost in *O. niloticus* juveniles in Kenya (Shati et al. 2022). These findings indicate that soybean meal can be replaced by various ingredients in African aquaculture without adverse effects on growth performance and nutrients utilization at a lower cost for sustainability of the industry.

In general, fishmeal is limited and its price is prohibitively expensive in most African countries. Therefore, many African countries are investigating ingredients for complete and/or partial replacement of fishmeal by using low-cost and locally available plant by-products for use in fish grow-out facilities (Obirikorang et al. 2015). Moreover, although soybean holds the qualities as a potential plant-based ingredient for fishmeal replacement, it is also expensive and sources are limited. Accordingly, several studies have been conducted in African aquaculture for replacing soybean. Fishmeal and soybean are both expensive feedstuff in the aquafeed, which limit aquaculture development. The future of African aquaculture development should be directed towards overcoming the dependency on fishmeal and soybean by using other ingredients while ensuring environmental sustainability

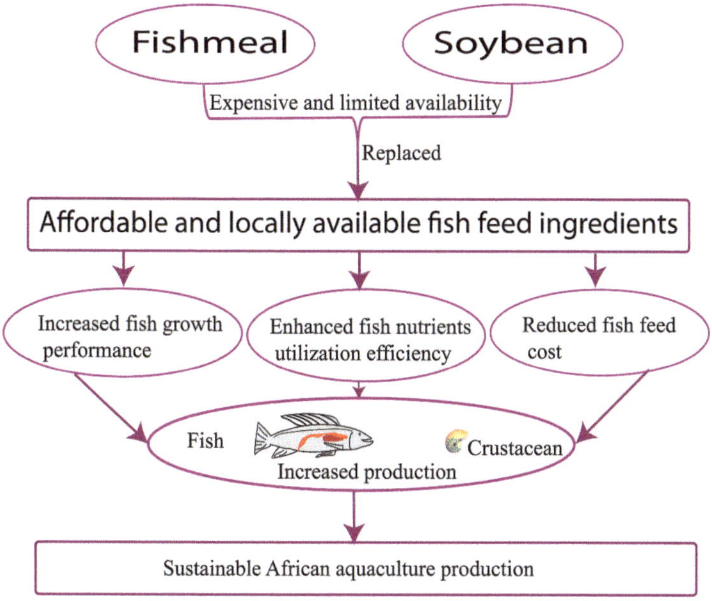

Fig. 1.1 Hypothetical consequences of replacing expensive and limited availability fishmeal and soybean by using cheap and locally available feed ingredients in African aquaculture

to provide enough protein for the increasing human population in the continent (Fig. 1.1). African aquaculture nutritionists should explore various ingredients, including edible crickets, which lacks information on its potential utilization as an ingredient in the aquaculture industry (Magara et al. 2021).

1.5 Feed Additives Used in African Aquaculture

The use of additives as growth enhancers, immunostimulants, disease-controlling agents and anaesthetics in African aquaculture is a common practice (Ashry et al. 2022; Gabriel et al. 2022). Most studies on feed additives were conducted in Egypt by using *O. niloticus* similar to fishmeal and soybean replacement above due to the reasons given before in this chapter. Additives are used for various purposes in African aquaculture production as discussed in the following sections (Table 1.3).

Table 1.3 The various feed additives used in African aquaculture for numerous functions

Feed additive and country	Species, growth stage and time	Purpose	Effect	References
Triticale; Egypt	*Oreochromis niloticus* juveniles; 8 weeks	Dietary feed additive as protein and carbohydrate source	• No effect on growth performance indices up to 20% • Increased lipid content for fish fed on 20% • Decreased amylase, lipase and protease for fish fed on 20% • No effect on haematological and biochemical blood parameters • Increased superoxide dismutase and glutathione peroxidase	Dawood et al. (2020c)
Inorganic, organic, and elemental nanoselenium; Egypt	*Oreochromis niloticus* fingerlings; 9 weeks	Selenium nanoparticles	• Enhanced growth performance • Increased haematological and immunity parameters • Reduced lipid peroxidation	Ghaniem et al. (2022)
Oregano essential oil; Egypt	Common carp, *Cyprinus carpio* fingerlings; 8 weeks	Dietary feed additive as a phytobiotic growth promoter	• Improved growth parameters and feed intake • No effects on body composition and haematological parameters • No histological damages on kidney and intestine	Abdel-Latif et al. (2020)
Curcumin; Egypt	*Oreochromis niloticus* juveniles; 8 weeks	Alleviate negative effects of melamine toxicity	• Alleviated the negative effect on growth performance and lipid composition • Enhanced haematological reduced by melamine • Improved antioxidant capacity • Increased survival rate of fish after bacteria challenge	Abd El-Hakim et al. (2020)

Turmeric powder alone or plus black pepper powder; Egypt	*Clarias gariepinus* juveniles; 4 weeks	Alleviate negative effects of cadmium toxicity	• Alleviated adverse effects on growth rate for fish fed on turmeric and pepper powders • Reduced kidney and liver toxicity on fish fed on turmeric and pepper powders • Improved antioxidant capacity and reduced lipid peroxidation for fish fed on turmeric and pepper powders • Restored depleted ATP for fish fed on turmeric and pepper powders • Normal hepatic histomorphological structures for fish fed on turmeric and pepper powders	El-Houseiny et al. (2019)
Curcumin; Egypt	*Oreochromis niloticus* fingerlings; 12 weeks	Dietary feed additive for growth performance and general fish health	• Inhibited *Aeromonas hydrophila* and *A. sobria* • Increased growth performance and survival rate indices • Better feed conversion and protein efficiency ratios • Increased catalase and reduced glutathione content • Decreased malondialdehyde level	Mahmoud et al. (2017)
Cucurbita mixta seed meal	*Oreochromis mossambicus* juveniles; 4 weeks	Immunostimulant	• Enhanced survival rate, weight gain, protein efficiency ratio, specific growth rate, feed conversion ratio and feed efficiency • Enhanced complement activity, phagocytic activity, respiratory burst activity and lysosome activity	Musthafa et al. (2017)

(continued)

Table 1.3 (continued)

Feed additive and country	Species, growth stage and time	Purpose	Effect	References
Curcumin; Egypt	*Oreochromis niloticus* fingerlings; 10 weeks	Immunostimulant	• Enhanced feed conversion ratio, fish body protein and ash contents but decreased body fat content • Increased villus height and width and upregulated tumor necrosis factor alpha and cysteine-aspartic acid protease 3 • Increased serum catalase activity and reduced glutathione level • Boosted serum superoxide dismutase activity and reduced the malondialdehyde level • Increased lysosome, complement 3, interleukin 10 and immunoglobulin M levels • Increased fish survival rate challenged with *Aeromonas hydrophila*	Amer et al. (2022)
Glycyrrhiza glabra extract and protexin concentrate; Egypt	*Oreochromis niloticus* fingerlings; 12 weeks	High stocking density stressor attenuator	• Increased growth, antioxidant, immunity and bacterial disease resistance of fish	Mahmoud et al. (2021)
Moringa oleifera seeds and leaves; Egypt	*Oreochromis niloticus* juveniles; 4 weeks	Ameliorative of chlorpyrifos health disturbances	• Counteracted the chlorpyrifos-induced adverse impacts on growth performance and health	Ibrahim et al. (2019)
Natural clay, coumarin, curcumin, vitamin C, probiotics and prebiotics; Egypt	*Oreochromis niloticus* fingerlings; 14 weeks	Safe feed additives for alleviating aflatoxin B_1 toxicity	• Higher growth rate for fish fed on vitamin C and aflatoxin • Better feed conversion ratio for fish fed on bentonite and Bio-Mos® • Increased haemoglobin, total erythrocyte, total protein, albumin	Ayyat et al. (2018)

			and globulin in fish fed on feed additives	
Lemongrass (*Cymbopogon citratus*) and geranium (*Pelargonium graveolens*) essential oils; Egypt	*Oreochromis niloticus* fry; 12 weeks	Immunostimulant	• Improved growth indices and feed utilization • Increased protein content of the whole body • Increased catalase activity and reduced glutathione and malondialdehyde levels • Increased lysozyme activity and total immunoglobulin M levels • Increased survival rate after *Aeromonas hydrophila* challenge	Al-Sagheer et al. (2018)
Moringa oleifera aqueous extract; Egypt	*Oreochromis niloticus* fingerlings; 12 weeks	Growth and immunity stimulator	• Enhanced final weight, weight gain, specific growth rate, red blood cells, haemoglobin, packed cell volume, white blood cells and total serum protein in fish fed 200 mg moringa/kg diet • Severe histological degenerative changes in the gills and liver of fish fed 400 mg moringa/kg diet • Positive cysteine-aspartic acid protease 3 cells in fish fed 400 mg moringa/kg diet	Emam et al. (2021)
Oregano essential oil; Egypt	*Oreochromis niloticus* juveniles; 8 weeks	Ameliorative of long-term acute heat stress	• Enhanced final weight, weight gain and specific growth rate • Increased villi length and width • Reduced aspartate aminotransferase and alanine aminotransferase • Increased total protein, albumin and globulin levels	Magouz et al. (2022)

(continued)

Table 1.3 (continued)

Feed additive and country	Species, growth stage and time	Purpose	Effect	References
			• Increased superoxide dismutase, catalase, phagocytic index and lysozyme activity • Decreased malondialdehyde content and relative expression of heat shock protein 70	
Mannan oligosaccharides and β-glucans; Egypt	*Oreochromis niloticus* juveniles; 8 weeks	Ameliorate lead reproductive toxicity	• Increased body weight, gonadal somatic index, estradiol, testosterone, gonadal antioxidant enzymes • Reduced cortisol, glucose and gonadal malondialdehyde	El-Fahla et al. (2022)
Aspergillus oryzae; Egypt	*Oreochromis niloticus* juveniles; 12 weeks	Alleviating salinity stress	• Decreased glucose, cortisol, alanine transaminase, aspartate transaminase and malondialdehyde • Increased albumin, globulin, total protein, lysozyme activity, phagocytic activity, phagocytic index, glutathione peroxidase, catalase and superoxide dismutase • Downregulated mRNA expression values of heat shock protein 70 and interferon-gamma genes, and upregulated interleukin 1 beta and interleukin 8 genes	Shukry et al. (2021)
Zinc sulphate; Egypt	*Oreochromis niloticus* juveniles; 3 weeks	Ameliorate nonylphenol toxicity	• Reduced haemolytic anaemia, leukocytosis, hyperbilirubinaemia, hyponatraemia, hyperkalaemia, azotemia, hyperproteinaemia, hypoalbuminaemia, hyper alpha1-	Mohamed et al. (2019)

			globulinaemia, hyper alpha2- and beta-globulinaemia, and hypogammaglobulinaemia • Reduced aspartate aminotransferase and alanine aminotransferase • Reduced lactate dehydrogenase, ammonia, cholesterol, creatinine, malondialdehyde, myeloperoxidase and tumor necrosis-alpha • Increased alkaline phosphatase, immunoglobulin M, complement 3, lysozyme activity and nitric oxide • Reduced hepatic and renal structural damages	
Silybum marianum and/or coenzyme Q10; Egypt	*Clarias gariepinus* adults; 8 weeks	Alleviate fluoride negative effects	• Increased weight gain and specific growth rate and reduced hepatosomtic index • Reduced leukopaenic and anaemic condition • Decreased serum, hepatic enzymes and kidney damage • Enhanced non-enzymatic and enzymatic antioxidants and reduced lipid peroxidation product • Enhanced lysozyme activity, complement 3, nitric oxide, total proteins, albumin and γ globulin contents in the serum • Reduced pathological alterations in the liver, kidney, and spleen • Increased survival rate	El-Houseiny et al. (2022)

(continued)

Table 1.3 (continued)

Feed additive and country	Species, growth stage and time	Purpose	Effect	References
			percentage after 14 days of *Aeromonas sobria* challenge	
Coenzyme Q10 and vitamin C; Egypt	*Oreochromis niloticus* juveniles; 8 weeks	Feed additive to improve growth performance and health	• Increased feed intake, amylase, lipase and protease activities • Decreased glucose, cortisol, total cholesterol, triglycerides and increased total protein • Increased superoxide dismutase and catalase activities and genes expression • Increased percentage survival rate of fish after *Streptococcus agalactiae* challenge	El Basuini et al. (2021)
Yucca extract; Egypt	*Cyprinus carpio* juveniles; 4 weeks	Ammonia absorbent	• Increased growth performance, survival rate, total protein, albumin and globulin • Reduced feed conversion ratio, uric acid, urea, creatinine, aspartate aminotransferase, alkaline phosphatase and alanine aminotransferase • Downregulated mRNA expression of heat shock protein, interleukin 8, tumor necrosis factor alpha, interferon gamma and interleukin 1 beta	Dawood et al. (2021b)
Sodium butyrate; Egypt	*Oreochromis niloticus* juveniles; 8 weeks	Nanoparticles dietary feed additives	• Increased final body weight, weight gain percentage, specific growth rate, feed intake, serum amylase, lipase and protease	Abdel-Tawwab et al. (2021c)

			activities • Increased villi length/width, crypt depth, surface absorption area and goblet cells	
Ziziphus mauritiana leaf powder; Egypt	*Oreochromis niloticus* fingerlings; 12 weeks	Dietary feed additive for growth and general health	• Increased body weight, weight gain percentage, feed intake, feed efficiency ratio, protein efficiency ratio and apparent protein utilization • Increased serum ion Na+ and Ca ++ • Upregulated insulin-like growth factor and ghrelin genes expression • Increased intestinal mucosal folds, heights, widths, area and perimeter of the villi and thickness of muscular layers	Amin et al. (2019)
Phosphorus supplemented with phytase enzyme; Egypt	*Oreochromis niloticus* juveniles; 8 weeks	Mineral supplement with digestive enhancer	• Increased final body weight, total body gain, average daily gain and weight gain for fish fed on 50% phosphorus and 500 or 1000 phytase units/kg • Improved immune response parameters • Reduced pathological lesions in the liver, spleen, stomach and intestine	Abo Norag et al. (2018)
Lycopene and/or resveratrol; Egypt	*Oreochromis niloticus* juveniles; 4 weeks	Ameliorate nanozinc oxide toxicity	• Reduced aspartate aminotransferase, alanine aminotransferase, alkaline phosphatase, cholesterol, urea and creatinine • Increased total proteins and albumin serum levels	Abdel-Daim et al. (2019)

(continued)

Table 1.3 (continued)

Feed additive and country	Species, growth stage and time	Purpose	Effect	References
			• Decreased malondialdehyde and increased reduced glutathione levels and superoxide dismutase and catalase activities	
Aspergillus oryzae and β-glucan; Egypt	*Oreochromis niloticus* fingerlings; 8 weeks	Synbiotic functional feed additive	• Increased growth performance and feed efficiency • Enhanced blood haematocrit, haemoglobin, red and white blood cells, total protein and digestive enzymes • Decreased blood triglyceride • Enhanced glutathione peroxidase and reduced malondialdehyde • Enhanced nitro blue tetrazolium, immunoglobulin M, lysozyme, bactericidal and phagocytosis	Dawood et al. (2020f)
Pyrazole derivatives; Egypt	*Clarias gariepinus* adult; 4 weeks	Ameliorate lead nitrate toxicity	• Reversed alterations in biochemical parameters, antioxidant biomarkers, lipid peroxidation, hepatic DNA damage and histopathological changes in liver	Soliman et al. (2019)
Green tea (*Camellia sinensis*) extract; Egypt	*Clarias gariepinus* adults; 2 weeks	Protective against 4-nonylphenol toxicity	• Increased serum glucose, aspartate aminotransferase, alanine aminotransferase, total protein, total lipids, cholesterol, glucose-6-phosphate dehydrogenase and cortisol • Increased serum acetylcholinesterase, alkaline phosphatase and lactate dehydrogenase	Sayed and Soliman (2018)

			• Increased superoxide dismutase, catalase, glutathione S-transferase and total antioxidant capacity • Reduced hepatic lipid peroxidation, DNA fragmentation and apoptosis • Reduced liver histopathological effects	
Anise (*Pimpinella anisum*); Egypt	*Dicentrarchus labrax* juveniles; 17 weeks	Dietary feed additive for fish growth and health	• Enhanced growth performance and reduced feed conversion ratio • Increased haematocrit, red blood cell, haemoglobin and white blood cells	Ashry et al. (2022)
Spirulina platensis; Egypt	*Clarias gariepinus* fingerlings; 2 weeks	Protection against hydroxychloroquine toxicity	• Normal haematological and biochemical indexes as well as antioxidant levels and the histological architecture	Sayed et al. (2021)
Spirulina platensis; Egypt	*Clarias gariepinus* adults; 4 weeks	Protection against lead nitrate toxicity	• Dietary inclusion of *Spirulina platensis* ameliorated cytotoxic and genetic changes in a time and dose dependent	Hamed et al. (2019)
Spirulina platensis; Egypt	*Clarias gariepinus* adults; 2 weeks	Protection against sodium dodecyl sulphate toxicity	• Dietary *Spirulina platensis* restored hepatic and renal dysfunction, electrolytes imbalance, as well as enzymatic and non-enzymatic antioxidants disruption, and micronuclei and apoptosis percentages in erythrocytes close to control treatment	Sayed and Authman (2018)
Spirulina platensis; Egypt	*Oreochromis niloticus* fry; 2 weeks	Bioremediation agent against ethidium bromide	• Increase total antioxidant capacity and decreased superoxide	El-Din et al. (2021)

(continued)

Table 1.3 (continued)

Feed additive and country	Species, growth stage and time	Purpose	Effect	References
			dismutase and catalase activities • Reduced DNA fragmentation	
Spirulina platensis; Egypt	*Oreochromis niloticus* juveniles; 8 weeks	Protection against gibberellic acid toxicity	• *Spirulina platensis* supplementation restored biochemical, antioxidants and histological changes near to control levels	Sayed et al. (2020)
Single- and multi- strain *Bacillus* species; Egypt	*Oreochromis niloticus* fry; 8 weeks	Probiotics additive	• Increased growth performance • Improved intestinal villi length and goblet cell number • Enhanced haemoglobin, haematocrit percentage and monocyte and leukocyte, lymphocyte and neutrophil contents • Better phagocytic activity, phagocytic index and lysozyme activity	Ghalwash et al. (2022)
Seaweeds mixture extract; Egypt	Striped catfish (*Pangasianodon hypophthalmus*) fry; 8 weeks	Antibacterial agents	• Increased growth performance • Enhanced haematological parameters and serum protein profile • Decreased serum alanine and aspartate aminotransferases and hepatic malondialdehyde and serum nitrous acid levels • Increased hepatic superoxide dismutase, catalase and glutathione peroxidase levels and serum lysozyme, total immunoglobulin and complement C3 activities	Abdelhamid et al. (2021)

			• Higher survival rate of fish after *Aeromonas hydrophila* infection	
Quillaja saponaria and linseed oil; Egypt	*Oreochromis niloticus* fingerlings; 8 weeks	Synergetic feed additives	• Improved growth performance and feed utilization efficiency, water quality and welfare indices • Increased serum total protein and globulin and reduced the cholesterol and triglycerides, increased catalase, superoxide dismutase and reduced malondialdehyde values • Improved lipase and amylase activities and expression of insulin growth factor I, superoxide dismutase and tumor necrosis factor-alpha	Elkaradawy et al. (2022)
Quillaja saponaria and *Yucca schidigera*; Egypt	*Oreochromis niloticus* adults; 8 weeks	Synergetic feed additives	• Improved water quality parameters • Increased growth performance and reduced feed conversion ratio • Improved gill health, increased intestinal villi length and goblet cell number • Increased lymphocytes, total protein, globulin and lysozyme activity and reduced cholesterol, triglycerides, glucose and creatinine • Increased lipase, amylase, superoxide dismutase, catalase activities and reduced malondialdehyde content	Abozeid et al. (2021)
Quillaja saponaria and Vitamin E; Egypt	*Oreochromis niloticus* fingerlings; 8 weeks	Synergetic feed additives	• Decreased total ammonia nitrogen and unionized ammonia	Elkaradawy et al. (2021)

(continued)

Table 1.3 (continued)

Feed additive and country	Species, growth stage and time	Purpose	Effect	References
			• Improved growth and feed utilization indices • Increased total protein, albumin, globulin, A/G ratio, cholesterol and triglycerides • Increased lipase, amylase and oxidative parameters superoxide dismutase and catalase activities • Improved villi length, villi surface area and goblet cells count	
Rice straw and zeolite; Egypt	*Oreochromis niloticus* juveniles; 4 weeks	Bioadsorbents for the removal of pollutants	• Better blood biochemistry, biochemical and histologic architecture	El Saidy et al. (2020)
Dunaliella algae; Egypt	*Oreochromis niloticus* juveniles; 8 weeks	Protection against lead acetate toxicity	• Increased growth performance parameters, serum antioxidant enzyme activities, fish body crude protein and liver antioxidant enzymes gene expression • Decreased degeneration and necrosis of hepatocytes	Fadl et al. (2021)
Spirulina platensis; Egypt	*Oreochromis niloticus* juveniles; 10 weeks	Dietary feed additive for growth performance and general health	• Increased final body weight, average daily weight gain, total weight gain and specific growth rate • Enhanced intestinal morphometric measures with increased hepatopancreatic acinar secretory activities • Increased serum catalase and superoxide dismutase activity and reduced glutathione and malondialdehyde levels	El-Araby et al. (2022)

			• Improved interleukin 10, lysozyme activity, complement 3 and immunoglobulin M serum levels	
Vitamin E and chitosan vitamin E nanocomposite; Egypt	*Oreochromis niloticus* fingerlings; 10 weeks	Nanoparticles to alleviate stress induced by high stocking density	• Improved final body weight, total weight gain, feed intake, specific growth rate and average daily weight gain • Decreased aspartate aminotransferase and alanine aminotransferase • Improved lysozyme activity, nitric oxide, phagocytic index and interleukin 10 • Improved serum and hepatic antioxidant enzymes and decreased lipid peroxidation • Increased survival rates of fish after *Aeromonas sobria* challenge	Ahmed et al. (2021)
Chitosan-vitamin C nanocomposite; Egypt	*Oreochromis niloticus* fingerlings; 10 weeks	Nanoparticle feed additive	• Increased final body weight, body weight gain, feed conversion efficiency, protein efficiency ratio, specific growth rate and daily weight gain • Increased serum and hepatic superoxide dismutase and glutathione, and decreased serum malondialdehyde • Increased serum lysozyme, nitric oxide, survival rate and phagocytic activity • Increased villus height, goblet cell count and lymphocytes	Ibrahim et al. (2021b)

(continued)

Table 1.3 (continued)

Feed additive and country	Species, growth stage and time	Purpose	Effect	References
Vitamin C; Egypt	*Oreochromis niloticus*; fingerlings; 10 weeks	Dietary feed additive for growth performance and general health	• Increased final body weight, total weight gain, specific growth rate and daily weight gain • Enhanced serum and hepatic antioxidant activities, lysozyme, nitric oxide and interleukin 10, phagocytic and survival rate of fish against *Aeromonas sobria* • Increased intestinal villus height and width	Ibrahim et al. (2020)
Seaweed liquid extract; Egypt	*Oreochromis niloticus* fingerlings; 10 weeks	Natural agent to rearing water	• Increased growth performance, feed intake and feed utilization • Improved total protein, albumin, globulin levels and lysozyme activity and antioxidant enzyme activities • Improved survival rate of fish after *Aeromonas hydrophila* challenge • Improved zooplankton community, diversity and abundance	Ashour et al. (2021b)
Potassium diformate and *Lactobacillus acidophilus*; Egypt	*Oreochromis niloticus* fingerlings; 12 weeks	Synergistic effects of probiotic and potassium diformate	• Improved growth and feed efficiency • Improved haemoglobin, red blood cells and white blood cells count • Decreased serum alanine and aspartate aminotransferase • Improved serum total protein, albumin, phosphorus and calcium content	Hassaan et al. (2021a)

			• Increased superoxide dismutase, total antioxidant capacity and catalase • Increased villi length width and goblet cells	
Arthrospira platensis; Egypt	Pacific white shrimp, *Litopenaeus vannamei* post-larvae; 13 weeks	Nanoparticle feed additive	• Improved all growth indices, survival and feed utilization parameters • Upregulated insulin growth-like factor I and II mRNA expression	Sharawy et al. (2022)
Arthrospira platensis; Egypt	*Oreochromis niloticus* fingerlings; 10 weeks	Nanoparticle feed additive	• Improved final weight, weight gain and feed conversion ratio • Enhanced total protein, albumin, globulin, lowered serum glucose and aspartate aminotransferase and alanine aminotransferase • Improved catalase, superoxide dismutase and glutathione peroxidase, lysozyme and respiratory burst activities alleviated inflammation induced by *Aeromonas hydrophila* challenge	Mabrouk et al. (2022)
Spirulina platensis; Egypt	*Oreochromis niloticus* juveniles; 8 weeks	Alleviate sodium sulphate toxicity	• Increased glutathione peroxidase, catalase, superoxide dismutase and total antioxidant capacity	Awed et al. (2020)
β-glucan; Egypt	*Oreochromis niloticus* juveniles; 4 weeks	Alleviate chlorpyrifos toxicity	• Increased final body weight, weight gain, specific growth rate, survival rate and feed intake • Decreased alkaline phosphatase, aspartate aminotransferase, alanine aminotransferase and cortisol levels	Dawood et al. (2020a)

(continued)

Table 1.3 (continued)

Feed additive and country	Species, growth stage and time	Purpose	Effect	References
			• Increased lysozyme levels and phagocytic activity and phagocytic index	
Copper nanoparticles; Egypt	Common carp, *Cyprinus carpio* fry; 8 weeks	Nanoparticle feed additive	• Increased growth performance and reduced feed conversion ratio • Increased carcass protein, lipid and ash contents • Increased haemoglobin, red blood cells, total protein, albumin and globulin levels • Increased Immunoglobulin M level, phagocytic, lysozyme, superoxide dismutase, catalase and glutathione peroxidase activities and decreased malondialdehyde content	Dawood et al. (2020e)
β-glucan and heat-killed *Lactobacillus plantarum*; Egypt	*Oreochromis niloticus* juveniles; 4 weeks	Synbiotics to alleviate deltamethrin toxicity and low water temperature	• Downregulated mRNA expression of heat shock protein 70 and cysteine–aspartic acid protease-3 genes • Reduced expression of interleukin 1 beta and interleukin 8 • Regular, normal and protected histopathological damages on gills, intestine, spleen and liver tissues	Gewaily et al. (2021a)
Lactobacillus plantarum; Egypt	*Oreochromis niloticus* juveniles; 4 weeks	Probiotic to alleviate deltamethrin and *Aeromonas hydrophila* effects	• Improved survive rate of fish after *Aeromonas hydrophila* infection • Elevated serum total protein,	Gewaily et al. (2021b)

			albumin, globulin, phagocytic index, phagocytic, and lysozyme activities, but reduced urea, uric acid bilirubin, creatinine, glucose, aspartate aminotransferase, alkaline phosphatase and alanine aminotransferase activities • Upregulated levels of superoxide dismutase, catalase and glutathione peroxidase genes • Relieved the inflammatory features in liver, spleen, gills and intestine	
Isatis; Egypt	*Oreochromis niloticus* juveniles; 4 weeks	Alleviate atrazine toxicity	• Enhanced final body weight, weight gain and specific growth rate • Improved feed conversion ratio • Increased survival rate of fish • Enhanced branching of the intestinal villi • Reduced uric acid, urea, creatinine, aspartate and alanine aminotransferase, and increased total protein, globulin and albumin • Increased superoxide dismutase, catalase, and glutathione peroxidase activities and decreased malondialdehyde content	Ali et al. (2022)
Propolis nanoparticles; Egypt	*Oreochromis niloticus* fingerlings; 4 weeks	Alleviate glyphosate toxicity	• Decreased malondialdehyde in the liver and gill and acetylcholinesterase activity • Increased glutathione concentration and white blood cell and red blood cell counts	Abdelmagid et al. (2022b)

(continued)

Table 1.3 (continued)

Feed additive and country	Species, growth stage and time	Purpose	Effect	References
Foeniculum vulgare; Egypt	*Oreochromis niloticus* fingerlings; 4 weeks	Alleviate glyphosate toxicity	• Decreased alanine aminotransferase, aspartate aminotransferase and alkaline phosphatase activities • Decreased malondialdehyde and DNA fragmentation and increased antioxidant enzyme activities • Downregulated mRNA expression tumor necrosis factor-alpha and interleukin-1 beta	Abdelmagid et al. (2021)
Ziziphus mauritiana leaf powder; Egypt	*Oreochromis niloticus* fingerlings; 6 weeks	Control *Aeromonas hydrophila* infection	• Upregulated lysozyme, interleukin 1 beta and superoxide dismutase genes expression • Improved serum lysozyme and liver antioxidant enzymes activities • Increased survival rate of fish after *Aeromonas hydrophila* infection • Reduced histopathological alterations in the liver, spleen, kidney and muscle of the fish	El Asely et al. (2020)
A mixture of taurine and medium-chain fatty acids; Egypt	*Oreochromis niloticus* fingerlings; 13 weeks	Digestive enhancer dietary feed additive	• Increased growth performance, feed intake, lipase, amylase and protease activities and reduced feed conversion ratio • Increased villus length, width and goblet cells • Improved phagocytic and lysozyme activities	Magouz et al. (2020a)
Azolla meal; Egypt		Dietary feed additive as an ingredient for fish	• Decreased final body weight, weight gain and specific growth rate	Magouz et al. (2020b)

	Genetically-improved farmed tilapia, *Oreochromis niloticus* fingerlings; 13 weeks		and increased feed conversion ratio • Increased villus length in mid and hind gut • Increased goblet cells in foregut and hindgut	
Lactobacillus plantarum and β-glucan; Egypt	Genetically-improved farmed tilapia *Oreochromis niloticus* fingerlings; 12 weeks	Synergetic effects of probiotics	• Increased final body weight and weight gain • Enhanced specific growth rate and feed efficiency ratio • Increased mucosal and villi lengths and muscle thickness • Improved lipase and protease enzymes activities • Upregulated insulin-like growth factor 1 and glucose-6-phosphate dehydrogenase genes expression • Increased haematocrit, haemoglobin and white blood cells and decreased triglyceride and glucose levels	Dawood et al. (2020j)
Lactobacillus plantaruml-137; Egypt	*Oreochromis niloticus* fingerlings; 4 weeks	Probiotic to alleviate deltamethrin toxicity	• Decreased blood creatinine, urea and bilirubin and increased hepatic enzymes aspartate aminotransferase, alkaline phosphatase and alanine aminotransferase • Increased blood total protein, globulin, albumin, white blood cells red blood cells, haemoglobin, phagocytic index, phagocytic and lysozyme activities • Upregulated immunity and downregulated stress genes	Dawood et al. (2020l)

(continued)

Table 1.3 (continued)

Feed additive and country	Species, growth stage and time	Purpose	Effect	References
			• Increased catalase and glutathione peroxidase	
Fenugreek; Egypt	*Oreochromis niloticus* fingerlings; 8 weeks	Alleviate *Aeromonas hydrophila* toxicity	• Increased growth performance parameters and decreased feed conversion ratio • Improved lysozyme, immunoglobulin and respiratory burst activity and superoxide dismutase and glutathione peroxidase and malondialdehyde • Upregulated immune-related genes expression in liver and kidney, interleukin 1 beta and tumor necrosis factor alpha • Reduced blood aspartate aminotransferase and alanine aminotransferase • Alleviated intestine, hepatopancreas, spleen and kidney damage • Increased survival rate of fish after *Aeromonas hydrophila* challenge	Moustafa et al. (2020)
Clenbuterol; Egypt	*Oreochromis niloticus* adults; 4 weeks	Dietary supplement	• Increased body weight, decreased liver, spleen and abdominal fat weights, and decreased total circulatory cholesterol and triacylglycerol levels • Downregulated fatty acid synthase gene expression and enhanced lipolysis	Mohamed et al. (2020)

Menthol essential oil; Egypt	*Oreochromis niloticus* fingerlings; 8 weeks	Alleviate ammonia toxicity	• Enhanced final body weight, weight gain, and feed conversion ratio • Enhanced protease activity • Increased lysozyme, phagocytic activities, phagocytic index, superoxide dismutase, catalase and glutathione peroxidase • Decreased cortisol, glucose and malondialdehyde • Reduced interleukin 8, tumor necrosis factor alpha and interleukin 1 beta • Reduced heat shock protein 70	Magouz et al. (2021b)
A mixture of *Bacillus amyloliquefaciens*, sodium butyrate, zinc methionine and digestive enzymes; Egypt	Common carp, *Cyprinus carpio* fry; 8 weeks	Multi-stimulants blend	• Enhanced fish growth and feed intake • Increased intestinal amylase, lipase and protease • Increased superoxide dismutase, catalase and glutathione peroxidase activities • Decreased malondialdehyde • Increased fish survival rate after ammonia exposure	Abdel-Tawwab et al. (2020c)
β-glucan; Egypt	*Oreochromis niloticus* fingerlings; 8 weeks	Alleviate high stocking density stress	• Increased growth for fish reared in low and medium stocking density • Reduced feed conversion ratio of fish reared in low and medium stocking density • Increased villus length, villus width and goblet cell count in fish reared on medium and high stocking	Dawood et al. (2020k)

(continued)

Table 1.3 (continued)

Feed additive and country	Species, growth stage and time	Purpose	Effect	References
			density • Increased haemoglobin levels and red blood cells counts • Reduced cortisol and glucose levels in fish reared in low and medium stocking density • Increased lysozyme activity, phagocytic activity and phagocytic index • Upregulated interferon-gamma, tumor necrosis factor alpha and interleukin 1 beta and downregulated heat shock protein 70 transcription levels	
Mannan oligosaccharide; Egypt	Thinlip grey mullet, *Liza ramada* juveniles; 8 weeks	Dietary feed additive for growth and general health	• Increased final body weight, protein gain and protein retention • Increased blood total protein, albumin globulin, lysozyme, phagocytic activity and phagocytic index • Increased superoxide dismutase, glutathione peroxidase and, catalase activities and decreased malondialdehyde concentration	Magouz et al. (2021a)
Zinc oxide, zinc methionine and zinc oxide nanoparticles; Egypt	Marbled spinefoot rabbitfish, *Siganus rivulatus* fry; 8 weeks	Zinc nanoparticles for alleviating ammonia toxicity	• Improved growth performance and protein utilization for fish fed on zinc methionine, and zinc oxide nanoparticles • Increased catalase, superoxide dismutase and glutathione peroxidase and decreased in	Sallam et al. (2020)

			malondialdehyde content • Improved lysozyme and phenoloxidase activities • Increased survival rate of fish after ammonia challenge	
Cinnamaldehyde and thymol; Egypt	*Oreochromis niloticus* fingerlings; 10 weeks	Dietary essential oils feed additives	• Increased growth performance for fish fed on thymol • Reduced malondialdehyde formation • Increased glutathione reductase in the muscle, lysozyme activity, immunoglobulin M, immunoglobulin G levels and catalase activity	Amer et al. (2018)
Doum palm, *Hyphaene thebaica*; Egypt	African catfish, *Clarias gariepinus* adults; 10 weeks	Feed additive for alleviating *Aeromonas hydrophila* infection	• Improved final body weight, body weight gain, specific growth rate, feed conversion ratio and protein efficiency ratio • Increased intestinal villi height, goblet cells and intraepithelial lymphocytes • Decreased glucose, cholesterol and triglyceride levels in serum • Increased catalase, superoxide dismutase and reduced glutathione content • Increased phagocytic percent and index, lysozyme activity, nitric oxide production and reduced myeloperoxidase • Increased survival rate of fish after *Aeromonas hydrophila* infection	Al-Khalaifah et al. (2020)

(continued)

Table 1.3 (continued)

Feed additive and country	Species, growth stage and time	Purpose	Effect	References
Taurine; Nigeria	African catfish, *Clarias gariepinus* fingerlings; 12 weeks	Feed additive for growth and general health as a plant protein source	• Improved growth performance • Increased serum glucose, cholesterol, total protein, albumin, globulin, aspartate aminotransferase, alanine aminotransferase, alkaline phosphatase, urea and creatinine • Increased lysozyme and respiratory burst activities and superoxide dismutase and catalase activities	Adeshina and Abdel-Tawwab (2020)
Chlorella vulgaris; Egypt	*Oreochromis niloticus* fingerlings; 10 weeks	Dietary feed additive as protein source for growth and general health	• Increased feed intake, specific growth rate and weight gain • Increased serum protease, amylase, lipase enzyme, total proteins, total lipids and globulin levels • Increased glutathione peroxidase, superoxide dismutase and catalase activities and serum lysozyme and respiratory burst activities, and total immunoglobulin M levels and reduced malondialdehyde levels • Upregulated hepatic growth hormone, insulin-like growth factor 1, interleukin 1 beta and tumor necrosis factor alpha genes	Abdel-Tawwab et al. (2022b)
Spirulina platensis, *Tetraselmis chuii* and decapsulated artemia cysts; Egypt	Common sole, *Solea solea* larvae; 4 weeks	Dietary novel feed additives for growth and survival rate	• Increased growth rate • Increased body protein contents • Increased survival rate	Shawky et al. (2021)
Tetraselmis suecica; Egypt	Pacific white shrimp, *Litopenaeus vannamei* post-larvae; 13 weeks	Dietary feed additive	• Increased survival rate of shrimps • Increased weight gain, and	Sharawy et al. (2020)

			specific growth rate and reduced feed conversion ratio • Increased protein, lipid and ash contents • Increased superoxide dismutase and glutathione peroxidase	
Miswak, *Salvadora persica*; Egypt	*Oreochromis niloticus* juveniles; 8 weeks	Nutraceutical immunostimulant dietary feed additive	• Increased immune and biochemical parameters such as white blood cell counts • Decreased malondialdehyde content • Increased antioxidant enzyme activities • Increased survival rate of fish	El-latif et al. (2021)
Pomegranate, *Punica granatum* peel; Egypt	*Oreochromis niloticus* fingerlings; 6 weeks	Alleviate silver nanoparticles toxicity	• Reduced fish performance for pomegranate alone but enhanced antioxidant and immunological activities • Attenuated hepato-renal damage, oxidative stress and immunity parameters	Hamed and Abdel-Tawwab (2021)
Yucca schidigera and/or *Saccharomyces cerevisiae*; Egypt	*Oreochromis niloticus* juveniles; 8 weeks	Water additive probiotic synergetic effects	• Reduced pH and NH_3 levels • Improved growth performance • Decreased aspartate aminotransferase, uric acid and creatinine • Increased superoxide dismutase, catalase, and glutathione peroxidase and reduced malondialdehyde values	Abdel-Tawwab et al. (2021b)
Chamomile, *Matricaria chamomilla* oil; Egypt	Indian shrimp, *Penaeus indicus* juveniles; 8 weeks	Immunostimulant feed additive	• Improved final weight, weight gain, specific growth rate and feed	

(continued)

Table 1.3 (continued)

Feed additive and country	Species, growth stage and time	Purpose	Effect	References
			intake • Improved total protein, albumin, and globulin, antioxidant and immunity variables • Reduced aspartate and alanine aminotransferase, creatinine, urea, malondialdehyde and nitric oxide • Improved survival rates after *Vibrio parahaemolyticus* infection	Abdel-Tawwab et al. (2022a)
Basil, *Ocimum basilicum* oil; Egypt	Indian shrimp, *Penaeus indicus* juveniles; 13 weeks	Dietary feed additive for growth and general health	• Increased final weight, weight gain, specific growth rate and feed intake • Increased total protein, albumin and globulin values • Decreased aspartate, alanine aminotransferases creatinine and urea levels • Increased superoxide dismutase, catalase, glutathione peroxidase, lysozyme and phenol oxide activities • Decreased malondialdehyde and nitrous oxide levels • Improved survival rates after *Vibrio parahaemolyticus* infection	Abdel-Tawwab et al. (2021a)
Tridax procumbens leaves extract; Nigeria	*Oreochromis niloticus*, juvenile; 8 weeks	Chemotherapy to kill *Dactylogyrus vastator* parasites	• Increased growth and feed consumption • Enhanced villi length/width and absorption area • Elevated antioxidant and immunity responses	Adeshina et al. (2021)

			• Increased survival rate of fish after *Dactylogyrus vastator* infestation	
β-carotene and phycocyanin extracted from *Spirulina platensis*; Egypt	*Oreochromis niloticus* fry; 10 weeks	Immunostimulant feed additive	• Increased weight gain, specific growth rate and survival rate and reduced feed conversion ratio • Increased chymotrypsin, trypsin, lipase and amylase • Improved haematology parameters • Increased phagocytic, lysozyme, immunoglobulin M, superoxide dismutase, catalase, glutathione peroxidase and total antioxidant capacity activities • Upregulated interferon gamma and interleukin 1 beta genes • Downregulated heat shock protein 70 gene	Hassaan et al. (2021b)
Zinc oxide nanoparticles using *Ulva fasciata*; Egypt	*Oreochromis niloticus* fingerlings; 8 weeks	Zinc oxide nanoparticles as anti-fungal agent against *Candida albicans*	• Improved growth performance, survival rate and lysozyme, phagocytic, phagocytic index and respiratory burst activities • Improved interleukin 1 beta, tumor growth, transforming growth factor beta, tumor necrosis factor alpha, digestive enzyme activity and histopathological	Diab et al. (2022)
Bulk zinc oxide or zinc oxide nanoparticles; Egypt	*Oreochromis niloticus* fingerlings; 12 weeks	Dietary zinc nanoparticles	• Increased growth and digestive enzyme activity • Improved intestinal topography • Enhanced haematological indices	Ibrahim et al. (2022)

(continued)

Table 1.3 (continued)

Feed additive and country	Species, growth stage and time	Purpose	Effect	References
			• Reduced alanine and aspartate aminotransferase • Increased total serum protein, albumin and globulin contents	
Natural clay nanozeolite; Egypt	*Oreochromis niloticus* fingerlings; 12 weeks	Alleviate aflatoxin B_1 toxicity	• Increased growth performance and feed utilization • Increased amylase and chymotrypsin activities • Enhanced haemoglobin, haematocrit, red blood cells and white blood cells count • Decreased alanine and aspartate aminotransferase, alkaline phosphatase, total protein, albumin and globulin • Increased superoxide dismutase, catalase, lysozyme activities and DNA fragmentation, and reduced malondialdehyde content	Hassaan et al. (2020b)
Bulk selenium or selenium nanoparticles; Egypt	*Oreochromis niloticus* fingerlings; 12 weeks	Nanoparticle feed additive	• Improved growth performance and amylase and lipase enzymes activities • Increased villi height and width and goblet cells • Increased mucosal-to-serosal amplification ratio and villous absorption area • Increased haemoglobin, haematocrit, red blood cells and white blood cell count	Ibrahim et al. (2021a)

			• Reduced alanine and aspartate aminotransferases, while increased total serum protein, albumin and globulin contents • Increased superoxide dismutase, catalase, glutathione peroxidase, glutathione, glutathione-S-transferase and glutathione reductase activity accompanied with the lower malondialdehyde content	
Selenium nanoparticles; Egypt	European sea bass, *Dicentrarchus labrax* fingerlings; 13 days	Nanoparticle feed additive	• Increased final body weight, weight gain and specific growth rate • Haemoglobin, haematocrit, red blood cell counts and white blood cells • Increased protein and globulin contents • Enhanced phagocytic index, phagocytic and lysozyme activities • Increased superoxide dismutase and catalase activities • Reduced malondialdehyde content • Upregulated growth hormone, insulin-like growth factor 1, interleukin 8, and interleukin 1 beta • Downregulated heat shock protein 70	Abd El-Kader et al. (2021)
Selenium nanoparticles and *Spirulina platensis*; Egypt	*Oreochromis niloticus* juveniles; 8 weeks	Selenium nanoparticles and *Spirulina platensis* synergistic effects	• Improved weight gain, specific growth rate and decreased feed conversion ratio • Increased total protein and	Al-Deriny et al. (2020)

(continued)

Table 1.3 (continued)

Feed additive and country	Species, growth stage and time	Purpose	Effect	References
			immunoglobulin M • Upregulated superoxide dismutase and tumor necrosis factor alpha genes • Downregulated heat shock protein 70	
Fucoidan; Egypt	*Oreochromis niloticus* juveniles; 4 weeks	Alleviate aflatoxin B_1 toxicity	• Decreased alanine and aspartate aminotransferases, alkaline phosphatase, cholesterol, urea and creatinine • Increased blood protein, glutathione, glutathione peroxidase, superoxide dismutase and catalase activities	Abdel-Daim et al. (2020)
Zinc oxide; Egypt	*Oreochromis niloticus* adults; 4 weeks	Mineral feed additive	• Increased hepatosomatic index and gonadosomatic index • Increased total absolute relative fecundity and fry survival • Increased pH, motility and sperm concentration • Enhanced triglyceride cholesterol and high density lipoprotein • Increased catalase, glutathione peroxidase and superoxide dismutase enzymes	Soaudy et al. (2021)
Silicate clay; Egypt	*Oreochromis niloticus* fingerlings; 10 weeks	Mineral feed additive	• Improved final body weight, weight gain, specific growth rate and feed conversion ratio and protein efficiency ratio	Hassaan et al. (2020a)

			• Increase alkaline phosphatase, amylase, trypsin, chymotrypsin and lipase enzymes • Improved white blood cells, monocytes and lymphocytes • Increased total protein and immunoglobulin M	
Citrus limon peels; Egypt	*Oreochromis niloticus* and *Clarias gariepinus*; 6 weeks	Chemotherapeutics	• Decreased glucose but increased nitric oxide • Enhanced catalase, glutathione, lysozymes, myeloperoxidase in both fish • Enhanced superoxide dismutase in *Clarias gariepinus* • Increased survival rate after *Aeromonas hydrophila* challenge	Abdel Rahman et al. (2019)
Mannan oligosaccharide; Egypt	Red sea bream, *Pagrus major* juveniles; 8 weeks	Prebiotic feed additive to alleviate low salinity stress	• Increased final body weight, weight gain, and specific growth rate with decreased feed conversion ratio • Enhanced haematocrit level and total serum protein • Decreased glutamic pyruvic transaminase • Increased biological antioxidant potential and reactive oxygen metabolites, lysozyme, bactericidal, peroxidase, blood nitro blue tetrazolium assay and alternative complement pathway • Enhanced tolerance against low salinity stress	Dawood et al. (2020g)

(continued)

Table 1.3 (continued)

Feed additive and country	Species, growth stage and time	Purpose	Effect	References
Ginger nanoparticles; Egypt	*Oreochromis niloticus* juveniles; 4 weeks	Alleviate glyphosate toxicity	• Reduced alanine and aspartate aminotransferases activities, glucose and cortisol levels, and malondialdehyde levels • Reduced urea and creatinine levels and higher total protein, albumin and globulin • Increased reduced glutathione, lysozyme activity and immunoglobulin levels	Abdelmagid et al. (2022a)

1.5.1 The Use of Feed Additives for Growth Performance and General Fish Health

The primary goal of commercial aquaculture production is to produce bigger fish in the shortest possible period. Therefore, growth performance is the main target for fish farmers in Africa. Indeed, various additives are used in African aquaculture as dietary feed for growth enhancement and general health management for various development stages of cultured species. Feed additives used in African aquaculture on *O. niloticus* fingerlings include curcumin (*Curcuma longa*) (Mahmoud et al. 2017), *Ziziphus mauritiana* leaf powder (Amin et al. 2019), vitamin C (Ibrahim et al. 2020), a mixture of taurine and medium-chain fatty acids (Magouz et al. 2020a), Azolla meal (Magouz et al. 2020b) and *Chlorella vulgaris* (Abdel-Tawwab et al. 2022b). Moreover, triticale (Dawood et al. 2020c) and *Spirulina platensis* (El-Araby et al. 2022) have been used as feed additives for growth and general body health in *O. niloticus* juveniles, whereas only clenbuterol was used in *O. niloticus* adults (Mohamed et al. 2020). In other cultured fish species, taurine was used in *C. gariepinus* fingerlings (Adeshina and Abdel-Tawwab 2020), oregano essential oil in *C. carpio* fingerlings (Abdel-Latif et al. 2020) and Anise (*Pimpinella anisum*) in *D. labrax* juveniles (Ashry et al. 2022).

Results from these studies indicated that appropriate feed additive doses improved growth performance (Mahmoud et al. 2017; Amin et al. 2019; Abdel-Latif et al. 2020; Ibrahim et al. 2020; Magouz et al. 2020b; Mohamed et al. 2020; Abdel-Tawwab et al. 2022b; Ashry et al. 2022), feed utilization efficiency (Mahmoud et al. 2017), antioxidant capacity (Mahmoud et al. 2017; Abdel-Tawwab et al. 2022b; El-Araby et al. 2022), immune responses (Mahmoud et al. 2017; Ibrahim et al. 2020; Magouz et al. 2020b; Abdel-Tawwab et al. 2022b; El-Araby et al. 2022) and disease resistance against *A. hydrophila* (Mahmoud et al. 2017; Abdel-Tawwab et al. 2022b; El-Araby et al. 2022), *A. sobria* (Ibrahim et al. 2020) and *Pseudomonas fluorescens* and *Vibrio anguillarum* (Abdel-Tawwab et al. 2022b). Moreover, feed additives improved intestinal health (Amin et al. 2019; Abdel-Latif et al. 2020; Magouz et al. 2020b), hepatic and intestinal structures (Ibrahim et al. 2020), enhanced well-being (Ashry et al. 2022) and improved general fish health (El-Araby et al. 2022). Some additives, such as Azolla meal, was beneficial on the digestive enzymes (Magouz et al. 2020b), while clenbuterol reduced fat deposition rates (Mohamed et al. 2020). These studies indicate that additives are a feeding strategy for sustainable African aquaculture production (Dawood et al. 2020c). However, research must be taken to ensure appropriate doses are used because higher inclusion levels of dietary taurine limited growth, immunity, and antioxidant responses of *C. gariepinus* (Adeshina and Abdel-Tawwab 2020).

In addition to the use of single additives, multiple blends of feed additives are also used in African aquaculture due to their synergetic effects. Accordingly, more than one feed additives have been used in *O. niloticus* fingerlings by using *Quillaja saponaria* and vitamin E (Elkaradawy et al. 2021) and *Quillaja saponaria* and linseed oil (Elkaradawy et al. 2022). Moreover, coenzyme Q10 and vitamin C were used in *O. niloticus* juveniles (El Basuini et al. 2021), while *Quillaja saponaria* and *Yucca schidigera* were used in *O. niloticus* adults (Abozeid et al. 2021). For other species than *O. niloticus*, *S. platensis*, *Tetraselmis chuii* and decapsulated artemia cysts were used in *S. solea* larvae (Shawky et al. 2021). Expectedly, the feed additives interacted to improve growth performance (Abozeid et al. 2021; El Basuini et al. 2021; Elkaradawy et al. 2021, 2022), feed efficiency (El Basuini et al. 2021), digestive enzymes activities (Abozeid et al. 2021; El Basuini et al. 2021), biochemical blood indices (El Basuini et al. 2021), immune response (Abozeid et al. 2021; El Basuini et al. 2021; Elkaradawy et al. 2022) and antioxidant capacity (Abozeid et al. 2021; El Basuini et al. 2021; Elkaradawy et al. 2022). Moreover, feed additives interacted synergistically to improve water quality (Abozeid et al. 2021; Elkaradawy et al. 2021, 2022), gills and intestine health (Abozeid et al. 2021; Elkaradawy et al. 2021) and general health welfare profile of fish (Elkaradawy et al. 2021, 2022). They also interacted to increase resistance against *Streptococcus agalactiae* infection (El Basuini et al. 2021). A mixture of dietary additives has also been reported as an effective diet in the weaning of post-larvae stages in *S. solea*) (Shawky et al. 2021). Moreover, a mixture of taurine and medium-chain fatty acids was effective for *O. niloticus* reared at suboptimal temperatures to maintain normal growth rates without a decrease in the physiological and immunological status (Magouz et al. 2020a).

Interestingly, feed additives for growth and general health are also used in crustacean African aquaculture, although to a limited level. Accordingly, *T. suecica* were used in Pacific white shrimp, *Litopenaeus vannamei* post-larvae (Sharawy et al. 2020), while Basil, *Ocimum basilicum,* oil was used in Indian shrimp, *Penaeus indicus* juveniles (Abdel-Tawwab et al. 2021a). In these studies, the highest inclusion level of dried *T. suecica* improved growth and nutrient utilization (Sharawy et al. 2020), whereas appropriate dietary Basil oil enhanced growth performance, antioxidant capacity and innate immunity (Abdel-Tawwab et al. 2021a). Moreover, Basil oil also increased resistance of *P. indicus* against *Vibrio parahaemolyticus* infection (Abdel-Tawwab et al. 2021a).

In general, feed additives whether used singly or in combination provide valuable resources for improving growth performance, immunity and general health of fish and crustaceans. The diversity of feed additives resources for feeding fish and crustacean to improve growth performance and general health makes the African aquaculture viable for sustainable production. Discovering novel feed additives and improving the technology for higher inclusions are further required to ensure a sustainable African aquaculture for enhanced blue economy development.

1.5.2 Use of Feed Additives to Alleviate Toxicity of Various Xenobiotics and Stressful Conditions

The importance of feed additives in African aquaculture has led to their use in alleviating various xenobiotics effects during fish farming in the continent. Metal contamination is a common phenomenon in aquatic environment. Several feed additives are used in African aquaculture to alleviate the toxicity caused by metal contamination. They include pyrazole derivatives (Soliman et al. 2019) and *S. platensis* (Hamed et al. 2019), which were used in *C. gariepinus* adults to ameliorate lead nitrate toxicity. Moreover, Pomegranate, *Punica granatum,* peel and *Dunaliella* algae have been used in *O. niloticus* fingerlings and juveniles to alleviate silver nanoparticles toxicity (Hamed and Abdel-Tawwab 2021) and lead acetate toxicity (Fadl et al. 2021), respectively. The use of such feed additives minimized the effects of lead toxicity (Hamed et al. 2019; Soliman et al. 2019; Fadl et al. 2021; Hamed and Abdel-Tawwab 2021) on various pathological changes in organs (Fadl et al. 2021), cytotoxic and genotoxic effects (Hamed et al. 2019) and oxidative stress and immune suppression (Hamed and Abdel-Tawwab 2021). Moreover, various feed additives, including fennel extract, *Foeniculum vulgare,* and Isatis, have been used to alleviate herbicides toxicity caused by glyphosate and atrazine in *O. niloticus* fingerlings (Abdelmagid et al. 2021) and juveniles (Ali et al. 2022), respectively. Furthermore, zinc sulphate and green tea (*Camellia sinensis*) extract were used in *O. niloticus* juveniles (Mohamed et al. 2019) and *C. gariepinus* adults (Sayed and Soliman 2018) to ameliorate nonylphenol toxicity as an environmental endocrine disruptor. In addition, *M. oleifera* seeds and leaves (Ibrahim et al. 2019) and β-glucan (Dawood et al. 2020a) were used to ameliorate chlorpyrifos insecticide toxicity, while curcumin was used to alleviate melamine toxicity as a nitrogenous industrial material (Abd El-Hakim et al. 2020), all in *O. niloticus* juvenile.

In these studies, feed additives alleviated the toxicity of xenobiotics on growth retardation (Ibrahim et al. 2019; Ali et al. 2022), antioxidant capacity (Sayed and Soliman 2018; Ibrahim et al. 2019; Abd El-Hakim et al. 2020; Abdelmagid et al. 2021; Ali et al. 2022), nephrotoxicity (Mohamed et al. 2019; Ali et al. 2022), hepatotoxicity (Ibrahim et al. 2019; Mohamed et al. 2019; Dawood et al. 2020a; Abdelmagid et al. 2021), immunity (Ibrahim et al. 2019; Mohamed et al. 2019; Abd El-Hakim et al. 2020; Dawood et al. 2020a; Abdelmagid et al. 2021), haematotoxicity (Ibrahim et al. 2019; Mohamed et al. 2019; Abd El-Hakim et al. 2020), lipotoxicity (Ibrahim et al. 2019), spleen toxicity (Abd El-Hakim et al. 2020), gills and intestinal toxicity (Dawood et al. 2020a) and genotoxicity (Sayed and Soliman 2018; Ibrahim et al. 2019; Abdelmagid et al. 2021). The results from these studies suggest the great potential of feed additives as innovative approach for improving growth and general health for enhanced production and economic benefit for sustainable African aquaculture industry.

Feed additives are also used in African aquaculture to alleviate stress caused by various conditions. The available literature indicates studies conducted on

O. niloticus at various developmental stages. These include β-glucan for alleviating high stocking density stress (Dawood et al. 2020k), menthol essential oil for protecting against ammonia toxicity (Magouz et al. 2021b) in *O. niloticus* fingerlings, *A. oryzae* for alleviating salinity stress (Shukry et al. 2021) and oregano essential oil for ameliorating long-term acute heat stress (Magouz et al. 2022) in *O. niloticus* juveniles. The feed additives used alleviated the various stress factors by improving growth performance (Dawood et al. 2020k; Magouz et al. 2021b, 2022), digestive enzyme activity (Magouz et al. 2021b), intestinal morphometry (Dawood et al. 2020k), haemato-biochemical parameters (Shukry et al. 2021; Magouz et al. 2022), antioxidant responses (Magouz et al. 2021b, 2022; Shukry et al. 2021) and immunity (Dawood et al. 2020k; Magouz et al. 2021b, 2022; Shukry et al. 2021). These studies suggest that feed additives used in African aquaculture counteract the potential negative stressful conditions during production for sustainable aquaculture.

Bacteria diseases are a common challenge in intensively cultured fish production, which is the future for the industry to tackle shortage of food due to increasing population. Luckily, several feed additives are used in African aquaculture to alleviate toxicity of bacteria and other pathogenic organisms. Such studies have been conducted by using fenugreek for alleviating *A. hydrophila* toxicity (Moustafa et al. 2020), fucoidan for alleviating aflatoxin B_1 toxicity (Abdel-Daim et al. 2020) in *O. niloticus* fingerlings and juveniles, respectively. Moreover, Doum palm, *Hyphaene thebaica,* was used in African catfish, *C. gariepinus* adults for alleviating *A. hydrophila* infection (Al-Khalaifah et al. 2020). In these studies, the feed additives used were protective against the pathogenic organisms by enhancing growth performance (Al-Khalaifah et al. 2020; Moustafa et al. 2020), feed efficiency (Moustafa et al. 2020), biochemical parameters (Abdel-Daim et al. 2020), intestinal histomorphology (Al-Khalaifah et al. 2020; Moustafa et al. 2020), hepatic, hepatopancreas, spleen and kidney health (Moustafa et al. 2020), antioxidant capacity (Abdel-Daim et al. 2020; Al-Khalaifah et al. 2020), immune response (Al-Khalaifah et al. 2020) and disease resistance against *A. hydrophila* challenge (Al-Khalaifah et al. 2020; Moustafa et al. 2020). These studies indicate that the feed additives used in African aquaculture are beneficial as natural alternatives for alleviating toxicity caused by pathogenic organisms. Extending the available studies to species other than *O. niloticus* and *C. gariepinus* and selecting effective feed additives in alleviating toxicity caused by disease-causing organisms in African aquaculture could provide the extent of their use. In fact, the feed additives differ in their efficiency when used in African aquaculture. For instance, dietary β-carotene had a superior impact on growth performance, haemato-biochemical and immune-oxidative stress biomarkers (Taalab et al. 2022), phycocyanin was more effective for improving antioxidant capacity and immunity compared to β-carotene (Hassaan et al. 2021b) and thymol stimulated more growth and immune responses than cinnamaldehyde as essential oils in Nile tilapia nutrition (Amer et al. 2018) in *O. niloticus*. Therefore, further studies are required to designate effective additives, which can be used for multiple purposes in African aquaculture.

Indeed, a few feed additives, such as *Spirulina platensis,* has been used in African aquaculture to alleviate toxicity caused by multiple xenobiotics in various fish species. *Spirulina platensis* has been used as a feed additive to protect against fluorescent tag ethidium bromide (El-Din et al. 2021), gibberellic acid, a fungus metabolic by-product (Sayed et al. 2020) and sodium sulphate used in home detergents (Awed et al. 2020) in *O. niloticus* fry and juveniles. Moreover, *Spirulina platensis* has been used to protect against toxicity caused by an antibiotic hydroxychloroquine (Sayed et al. 2021) and sodium dodecyl sulphate, a surfactant used in houses (Sayed and Authman 2018) in *C. gariepinus* fingerlings and adults. *Spirulina platensis* alleviated toxicity induced by the xenobiotics by scavenging reactive oxygen species (ROS) (Sayed and Authman 2018), sustaining the antioxidant status (Sayed and Authman 2018; Awed et al. 2020; Sayed et al. 2020, 2021; El-Din et al. 2021), rendering haematological and biochemical indices (Sayed et al. 2021), reducing hepatotoxicity (Sayed et al. 2020, 2021), nephrotoxicity (Sayed et al. 2020) and genotoxicity (Sayed and Authman 2018; El-Din et al. 2021). These results offer a promising role of using certain well-studied feed additives in African aquaculture industry to protect fish against multiple xenobiotics and stressors.

Another potential use of feed additives in African aquaculture is a combination of more than one additive in order to benefit from their synergistic effects in alleviating toxicity and stressful conditions in captivity. Evidently, *Glycyrrhiza glabra* extract and protexin concentrate (Mahmoud et al. 2021) and natural clay, coumarin, curcumin, vitamin C, probiotics and prebiotics (Ayyat et al. 2018) were used in *O. niloticus* fingerlings for alleviating high stocking density stress and aflatoxin B_1 toxicity, respectively. Moreover, mannan oligosaccharides and β-glucans (El-Fahla et al. 2022) and lycopene and/or resveratrol (Abdel-Daim et al. 2019) were used to ameliorate lead reproductive and nanozinc oxide toxicity in *O. niloticus* juvenile, respectively. Furthermore, turmeric powder alone or plus black pepper powder (El-Houseiny et al. 2019) and *Silybum marianum* and/or coenzyme Q10 (El-Houseiny et al. 2022) were used in *C. gariepinus* juveniles and adults for alleviating negative effects of cadmium and fluoride toxicity, respectively. Clear synergetic effects were reported in alleviating toxicity and stress by enhancing growth performance (Ayyat et al. 2018; El-Houseiny et al. 2019, 2022; Mahmoud et al. 2021) and reducing hepatotoxicity (Ayyat et al. 2018; El-Houseiny et al. 2019, 2022), nephrotoxicity (El-Houseiny et al. 2019, 2022), haematotoxicity (Ayyat et al. 2018; El-Houseiny et al. 2022) and reprotoxicity effects (El-Houseiny et al. 2019; El-Fahla et al. 2022), improving antioxidant capacity (Abdel-Daim et al. 2019; Mahmoud et al. 2021; El-Fahla et al. 2022; El-Houseiny et al. 2022), immunity (Mahmoud et al. 2021; El-Houseiny et al. 2022) and bacterial disease resistance of fish (Mahmoud et al. 2021). In a nutshell, the use of feed additives in combination in African aquaculture is beneficial for alleviating toxicity of multiple xenobiotics and stressful factors for enhanced fish growth and immunity, resulting in increased production. Such an approach offers a means to ensure sustainable African aquaculture production required during this blue economy era.

1.5.3 The Use of Feed Additives as Prebiotics, Probiotics and Synbiotics

Probiotics, prebiotics and synbiotics use in African aquaculture production are considered a viable, safe and environmentally friendly alternative for enhancing growth performance, feed utilization, immunity, disease resistance and fish survival against pathogens and environmental stress (Dawood et al. 2020b; Mugwanya et al. 2022). Probiotics, prebiotics and synbiotics are used in African aquaculture as alternative to antibiotics (Dawood et al. 2020b), which have been shown to affect fish health globally (Limbu et al. 2021) and African aquaculture (Limbu 2020a).

Prebiotics are non-digestible food ingredients, which enhance proliferation of beneficial microbiota in the intestines. The existing limited information in African aquaculture indicates the use of mannan oligosaccharide prebiotic in Thinlip grey mullet, *Liza ramada* juveniles (Magouz et al. 2021a), and Red sea bream, *Pagrus major* juveniles, to alleviate low salinity stress (Dawood et al. 2020g). Expectedly, mannan oligosaccharide enhanced growth rate (Dawood et al. 2020g; Magouz et al. 2021a), feed efficiency, digestive enzyme activity and blood chemistry (Magouz et al. 2021a), antioxidant capacity (Dawood et al. 2020g; Magouz et al. 2021a) and immunity (Dawood et al. 2020g; Magouz et al. 2021a). Contrary to prebiotics, several probiotics as live beneficial microbiota are widely used in African aquaculture as single or multi-strains for their useful qualities, including alleviating toxicity effects. They promote good health by enhancing the internal microbiota balance (El-Saadony et al. 2021). Accordingly, single- and multi-strain *Bacillus* species were used in *O. niloticus* fry as feed additive for improving growth and immunological parameters (Ghalwash et al. 2022). *Lactobacillus plantarum* were used to alleviate deltamethrin toxicity in *O. niloticus* fingerlings (Dawood et al. 2020l) and juveniles (Gewaily et al. 2021b) and for reducing *A. hydrophila* adverse effects in *O. niloticus* juveniles (Gewaily et al. 2021b). Results showed that *L. plantarum* relieved toxicity and adverse effects by improving antioxidant capacity (Dawood et al. 2020l; Gewaily et al. 2021b), biochemical responses (Dawood et al. 2020l), immunity (Dawood et al. 2020l; Gewaily et al. 2021b), reducing inflammation (Gewaily et al. 2021b) and histopathological effects (Dawood et al. 2020l). These studies highlight the importance of prebiotics and probiotics in improving growth and immunity of cultured fish in African aquaculture.

Some probiotics are either used in African aquaculture in combination with other additives or multiple species in order to benefit their interactive effects. Evidently, potassium diformate and *Lactobacillus acidophilus* were used in *O. niloticus* fingerlings (Hassaan et al. 2021a); *Yucca schidigera* and/or *Saccharomyces cerevisiae* were used in *O. niloticus* juveniles as water additive (Abdel-Tawwab et al. 2021b). Conceivably, additives worked synergistically to improve growth performance (Abdel-Tawwab et al. 2021b; Hassaan et al. 2021a), intestine morphology (Hassaan et al. 2021a) and antioxidant capacity (Abdel-Tawwab et al. 2021b; Hassaan et al. 2021a). To further optimize the benefits of prebiotics and probiotics, African aquaculture practitioners mix them in the form of synbiotics. Evidently,

L. plantarum and β-glucan (Dawood et al. 2020j) and *A. oryzae* and β-glucan (Dawood et al. 2020f) were used together as synbiotics functional feed additives in *O. niloticus* fingerlings. This form of mixture has been used to ameliorate toxicity of xenobiotics in a few studies. Accordingly, natural clay, coumarin, curcumin, vitamin C, prebiotics and probiotics were used in *O. niloticus* fingerlings for alleviating aflatoxin B_1 (Ayyat et al. 2018), whereas β-glucan and heat-killed *L. plantarum* were used in *O. niloticus* juveniles to alleviate deltamethrin toxicity and low water temperature (Gewaily et al. 2021a). Results from these studies showed clear that the synbiotics improved growth performance (Dawood et al. 2020f, j), condition factor (Ayyat et al. 2018), feed efficiency, digestive capacity, nutrients metabolism (Dawood et al. 2020j), antioxidant status (Dawood et al. 2020f; Gewaily et al. 2021a), haematological parameters (Dawood et al. 2020j), immunity (Dawood et al. 2020f; Gewaily et al. 2021a), ameliorated histopathological damages (Dawood et al. 2020j; Gewaily et al. 2021a) and inflammation (Gewaily et al. 2021a).

In general, prebiotics, probiotics and synbiotics application in African aquaculture improve growth performance through increased nutrients metabolism, enhancing antioxidant capacity and immunity for improved health of cultured fish. They offer beneficial effects for the industry either singly or in combination or added to other feed additives for alleviating toxicity of various xenobiotics. Therefore, prebiotics, probiotics and synbiotics provide potential solution as functional feed additives for improving African aquaculture industry to ensure its sustainability for protecting fish against stressful conditions.

1.5.4 The Use of Nanoparticles as Feed Additives in African Aquaculture

Nanoparticles are increasingly used in different animal nutrition systems for enhancing physical and chemical properties of feeds. The African aquaculture industry also uses them for improving growth and health of cultured fish, especially *O. niloticus* at various development stages. Accordingly, chitosan-vitamin C nanocomposite (Ibrahim et al. 2021b), *Arthrospira platensis* nanoparticles (Mabrouk et al. 2022), nanozinc oxide particles (Ibrahim et al. 2022), and nanoselenium particles (Ibrahim et al. 2021a; Ghaniem et al. 2022) were used in *O. niloticus* fingerlings, while sodium butyrate nanoparticles (Abdel-Tawwab et al. 2021c) were used in *O. niloticus* juveniles as dietary feed additives. Limited studies are available on other species, including *C. carpio* fry (Dawood et al. 2020e) and *D. labrax* fingerlings (Abd El-Kader et al. 2021), in which copper and selenium nanoparticles were used, respectively. The nanomaterials used enhanced growth performance (Dawood et al. 2020e; Abd El-Kader et al. 2021; Abdel-Tawwab et al. 2021c; Ibrahim et al. 2021a, b, 2022; Ghaniem et al. 2022; Mabrouk et al. 2022), feed efficiency (Dawood et al. 2020e; Abdel-Tawwab et al. 2021c; Ibrahim et al. 2021a, 2022), digestive enzymes (Abdel-Tawwab et al. 2021c; Ibrahim et al. 2021a, 2022), nutrients body composition (Dawood et al. 2020e), intestinal histomorphology (Abdel-Tawwab et al. 2021c; Ibrahim et al. 2021a, b, 2022), haemato-biochemical parameters (Abd El-Kader et al. 2021; Ibrahim et al. 2021a, 2022; Ghaniem et al. 2022; Mabrouk et al. 2022), antioxidant capacity (Dawood et al. 2020e; Abd El-Kader et al. 2021; Ibrahim et al. 2021a, b, 2022; Ghaniem et al. 2022; Mabrouk et al. 2022), liver, kidney, and spleen health (Mabrouk et al. 2022), immunity response (Dawood et al. 2020e; Abd El-Kader et al. 2021; Ibrahim et al. 2021b; Ghaniem et al. 2022) and disease resistance (Ibrahim et al. 2021b). These studies indicate that nanoparticles are beneficial in African aquaculture for enhancing growth, immunity and general health of cultured fish species.

Limited studies have explored the synergetic effects of nanoparticles in African aquaculture. The available literature point to a study conducted by Al-Deriny et al. (2020) on selenium nanoparticles and *S. platensis* in *O. niloticus* juveniles (Al-Deriny et al. 2020). In this study, the mixture of selenium nanoparticles and *S. platensis* interacted to improve growth performance, feed efficiency, haemato-biochemical parameters, immunity, antioxidant capacity and reduced stress (Al-Deriny et al. 2020). Interestingly, several nanoparticles have been used in African aquaculture to alleviate xenobiotics toxicity in fish. Most studies have been used in *O. niloticus* fingerlings by using chitosan vitamin E nanocomposite to alleviate stress induced by high stocking density (Ahmed et al. 2021), natural clay nanozeolite to alleviate aflatoxin B_1 toxicity (Hassaan et al. 2020b), propolis nanoparticles to alleviate glyphosate toxicity (Abdelmagid et al. 2022b), zinc oxide nanoparticles using *Ulva fasciata* as anti-fungal agent against *Candida albicans* (Diab et al. 2022) and *A. platensis* nanoparticles to protect against *A. hydrophila* (Mabrouk et al. 2022). Moreover, ginger nanoparticles were used in *O. niloticus* juveniles to alleviate glyphosate toxicity (Abdelmagid et al. 2022a) and zinc oxide nanoparticles were utilized in Marbled spinefoot rabbitfish, *Siganus rivulatus* fry to alleviate ammonia toxicity (Sallam et al. 2020).

The nanoparticles used ameliorated toxicity and stress to promote growth performance (Hassaan et al. 2020b; Sallam et al. 2020; Ahmed et al. 2021; Diab et al. 2022), feed utilization (Hassaan et al. 2020b), survival rate (Diab et al. 2022), digestive enzymes activities (Hassaan et al. 2020b; Diab et al. 2022), antioxidant status (Hassaan et al. 2020b; Sallam et al. 2020; Ahmed et al. 2021; Abdelmagid et al. 2022b) and immune response (Sallam et al. 2020; Ahmed et al. 2021; Abdelmagid et al. 2022b; Diab et al. 2022). The nanoparticles also reduced genotoxicity (Hassaan et al. 2020b), enhanced fish resistance to *A. sobria* infection (Ahmed et al. 2021) and *C. albicans* (Diab et al. 2022) and alleviated the inflammation induced by *A. hydrophila* (Mabrouk et al. 2022). Limited studies have been conducted in crustaceans on nanoparticles in African aquaculture. The available study was conducted on *L. vannamei* post-larvae by using *A. platensis* nanoparticle feed additive (Sharawy et al. 2022). In this study, *A. platensis* nanoparticle improved growth, survival rate and feed utilization (Sharawy et al. 2022). Taken together, the utilization of nanoparticle in African aquaculture as feed additives improve production, and general health of fish and crustaceans. The nanoparticles used are beneficial for eliminating toxicity and stress induced by xenobiotics. Studies exploring the production of nanoparticles by using technologies accessible to small-scale farmers could further ensure the sustainability of the industry.

1.5.5 The Use of Feed Additives as Immunostimulants in African Aquaculture

Several feed additives are used in African aquaculture due to their immunostimulant effects on fish health because of the presence of various bioactive compounds. They act as natural immunostimulants and antioxidants, thereby improving growth performance and general health of cultured fish (El Basuini et al. 2021). The immunostimulators applied in African aquaculture include curcumin (Amer et al. 2022) and *M. oleifera* aqueous extract (Emam et al. 2021) used in *O. niloticus* fingerlings. Moreover, miswak, *Salvadora persica* as nutraceutical immunostimulant was used in *O. niloticus* juveniles (El-latif et al. 2021), while *Cucurbita mixta* seed meal was applied in *O. mossambicus* juveniles (Musthafa et al. 2017). Evidently, appropriate doses of the immunostimulants used improved growth performance (Musthafa et al. 2017; Emam et al. 2021; Amer et al. 2022), antioxidant capacity (El-latif et al. 2021; Amer et al. 2022), immunity (Musthafa et al. 2017; El-latif et al. 2021; Amer et al. 2022), intestinal histology (Amer et al. 2022), liver and kidney functions (Emam et al. 2021), haematological parameters (El-latif et al. 2021; Emam et al. 2021) and disease resistance against *A. hydrophilla* (Musthafa et al. 2017; El-latif et al. 2021). Clearly, these studies indicate the stimulation of immune system of cultured fish upon application of immunostimulants in African aquaculture. However, the application of immunostimulants as feed additives in African aquaculture should be guided by specific research because high doses (Emam et al. 2021; Amer et al. 2022) used for longer periods affect fish health (Amer et al. 2022).

Some of the bioactive compounds contained in immunostimulants function synergistically to influence growth and health of cultured fish (Dawood et al. 2021a). To this end, several immunostimulants have been used in African aquaculture to benefit from their synergistic actions. These include lemongrass (*Cymbopogon citratus*) and geranium (*Pelargonium graveolens*) as essential oils (Al-Sagheer et al. 2018), β-carotene and phycocyanin extracted from *Spirulina platensis* (Hassaan et al. 2021b) applied in *O. niloticus* fry and cinnamaldehyde and thymol also as essential oils used in *O. niloticus* fingerlings (Amer et al. 2018). A mixture of *Bacillus amyloliquefaciens*, sodium butyrate, zinc methionine and digestive enzymes as multi-stimulants blend was also used in *C. carpio* fry (Abdel-Tawwab et al. 2020b). The results obtained clearly indicated the synergetic effects of immunostimulants on improving growth performance (Al-Sagheer et al. 2018; Abdel-Tawwab et al. 2020b), feed utilization (Al-Sagheer et al. 2018; Abdel-Tawwab et al. 2020b), digestive enzymes (Abdel-Tawwab et al. 2020b; Hassaan et al. 2021b), antioxidant capacity (Al-Sagheer et al. 2018; Amer et al. 2018; Abdel-Tawwab et al. 2020b; Hassaan et al. 2021b), haematology parameters (Hassaan et al. 2021b), immune responses (Al-Sagheer et al. 2018; Amer et al. 2018; Hassaan et al. 2021b), disease resistance (Al-Sagheer et al. 2018) and survival against ammonia stress (Abdel-Tawwab et al. 2020b). In crustaceans, limited studies have been conducted in African aquaculture with only one report on the use of Chamomile, *Matricaria chamomilla* oil in *P. indicus* juveniles (Abdel-Tawwab et al. 2022a). The results also indicated improved growth performance, antioxidant capacity, immunity and resistance to *V. parahaemolyticus* infection (Abdel-Tawwab et al. 2022a).

In summary, immunostimulators are useful resources for improving growth performance, antioxidant capacity and immunity, which are all important for enhanced general health and control of infectious diseases in African aquaculture. Immunostimulators offer an alternative to antibiotics for controlling bacterial pathogens in the African aquaculture industry for the expected intensive production systems in the near future. Such an approach promises the sustainable future of the industry considering that antibiotics affect severely fish health (Limbu et al. 2018, 2019, 2020, 2021; Zhou et al. 2018; Limbu 2020a) and are currently threatening global human health (Zhang et al. 2022). Therefore, concerted efforts are required to explore immunostimulants uses in African aquaculture for several species cultured, particularly to control pathogenic organisms.

1.5.6 The Use of Feed Additives for Controlling Pathogenic Organisms

Diseases are known as one of the challenges for sustainable aquaculture globally. The African aquaculture is also threatened by diseases in cultured fish. Interestingly, several feed additives have been used for controlling pathogenic organisms in African aquaculture. These include *Z. mauritiana* leaf powder to control *A. hydrophila* infection in *O. niloticus* fingerlings (El Asely et al. 2020), *Tridax procumbens* leaves extract as chemotherapy to kill *Dactylogyrus vastator* parasites in *O. niloticus* juveniles (Adeshina et al. 2021), *Citrus limon* peels in *O. niloticus* and *C. gariepinus* chemotherapeutic against *A. hydrophila* (Abdel Rahman et al. 2019) and seaweeds mixture extract as antibacterial agents in Striped catfish (*Pangasianodon hypophthalmus*) fry (Abdelhamid et al. 2021). Expectedly, the feed additives used controlled pathogenic organisms by enhancing antioxidant capacity (Abdel Rahman et al. 2019; El Asely et al. 2020; Abdelhamid et al. 2021; Adeshina et al. 2021) and immunity (Abdel Rahman et al. 2019; El Asely et al. 2020; Abdelhamid et al. 2021; Adeshina et al. 2021), resulting in improved well-being of fish. The results from these studies highlight the importance of using feed additives to control pathogenic organisms, which cause significant economic loss in African aquaculture. Feed additives are potential functional supplements that could be successfully used as cheap curative agents in aquaculture to enhance disease resistance and avoid economic losses for sustainable African aquaculture industry.

1.5.7 The Use of Minerals as Feed Additives in African Aquaculture

Most minerals used in aquaculture are currently applied as nanoparticles as indicated above in this chapter. However, a few minerals are also used as feed additives in African aquaculture for *O. niloticus* at various development stages. These include silicate clay used in *O. niloticus* fingerlings (Hassaan et al. 2020a), phosphorus supplemented with phytase enzyme as digestive enhancer in *O. niloticus* juveniles (Abo Norag et al. 2018) and zinc oxide in *O. niloticus* adults (Soaudy et al. 2021). The use of the minerals as feed additives enhanced growth rate (Abo Norag et al. 2018; Hassaan et al. 2020a), reproduction performance (Soaudy et al. 2021), immunity (Abo Norag et al. 2018; Hassaan et al. 2020a), feed utilization and digestive enzymes activities (Hassaan et al. 2020a), antioxidant capacity (Soaudy et al. 2021), modulated lipid metabolism (Abo Norag et al. 2018; Soaudy et al. 2021) and gut microbiota of *O. niloticus* (Hassaan et al. 2020a). In short, minerals used as feed additives in aquaculture improve growth performance and health status of cultured fish for protein production required by the growing African population.

1.5.8 Feed Additives as Water Quality Cleaning Agents

The growth and general health in aquaculture are also affected by water quality parameters in the culture systems. Water quality parameters influence feeding, immunity and disease risk due to stress. Accordingly, several feed additives are used in African aquaculture to improve water quality parameters. Indeed, seaweed liquid extract (Ashour et al. 2021b), and *Y. schidigera* and/or *S. cerevisiae* (Abdel-Tawwab et al. 2021b) were used as natural agents to rearing water in *O. niloticus* fingerlings and juveniles, respectively. Moreover, rice straw and zeolite were used water for rearing *O. niloticus* juveniles as bioadsorbents for removing pollutants (El Saidy et al. 2020), while yucca extract was used as water additive for *C. carpio* juveniles as ammonia absorbent (Dawood et al. 2021b). The feed additives used were effective to removal most pollutants in water, thereby improved growth performance (Abdel-Tawwab et al. 2021b; Ashour et al. 2021b; Dawood et al. 2021b), nutrients metabolism (Abdel-Tawwab et al. 2021b), biochemical parameters (El Saidy et al. 2020; Dawood et al. 2021b), histologic architecture (El Saidy et al. 2020; Dawood et al. 2021b), antioxidant capacity (Dawood et al. 2021b), health status (El Saidy et al. 2020; Ashour et al. 2021b), immunity (Dawood et al. 2021b), and resistance of fish against pathogenic bacteria challenge and modulated natural microbiota in the

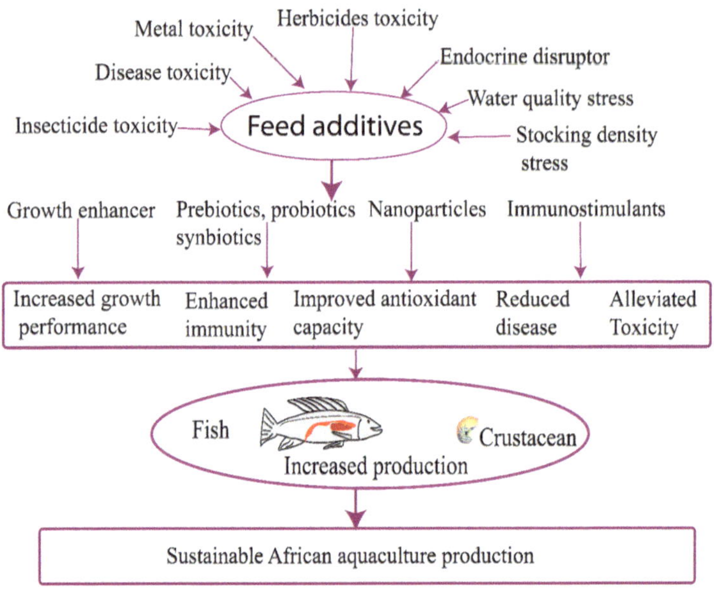

Fig. 1.2 The types and roles of feed additives used in African aquaculture

water (Ashour et al. 2021b). Overall, feed additives provide a solution for water contamination in aquaculture for improved fish growth, immunity and general health for enhanced production and sustainability of the African aquaculture industry.

Taken together, the African aquaculture uses several feed additives as growth promoters, prebiotics, probiotics and synbiotics, nanoparticles and immunostimulants to alleviate toxicity of various xenobiotics and stressful conditions, control pathogenic organisms and water cleaning purposes (Fig. 1.2). Ultimately, feed additives used improve production, and general health of fish and crustaceans for sustainable African aquaculture industry.

1.6 Conclusion

The African aquaculture industry feeds fish by using mixed protein levels, restriction and re-feeding, on-farm feeds and supplemental feeds with fertilization. The industry utilizes and array of technologies, including fermentation, supplementing with various nutrients modulators to ensure optimum growth of cultured fish, enhanced feed efficiencies and reduced feed cost for sustainability of the industry. Fish nutritionists in Africa are working tirelessly to replace the limited and expensive ingredients, such as fishmeal and soybean through various feed additives, whether singly or in combination for improving growth performance, immunity, and general health of fish and crustaceans. Feed additives are used for various purposes, including alleviating toxicity of multiple xenobiotics and stressful factors, functional feed, nanoparticles, immunostimulators, mineral sources and for cleaning water used in aquaculture for improved fish growth performance, immunity and general health for enhanced production and sustainability of the African aquaculture industry. The African aquaculture holds potential for supplying aquatic products for the blue economy.

References

Abd El-Hakim YM, El-Houseiny W, El-Murr AE et al (2020) Melamine and curcumin enriched diets modulate the haemato-immune response, growth performance, oxidative stress, disease resistance, and cytokine production in *Oreochromis niloticus*. Aquat Toxicol 220:105406. https://doi.org/10.1016/j.aquatox.2020.105406

Abd El-Kader MF, Fath El-Bab AF, Abd-Elghany MF et al (2021) Selenium nanoparticles act potentially on the growth performance, hemato-biochemical indices, antioxidative, and immune-related genes of European seabass (*Dicentrarchus labrax*). Biol Trace Elem Res 199(8):3126–3134. https://doi.org/10.1007/s12011-020-02431-1

Abdel Rahman AN, ElHady M, Shalaby SI (2019) Efficacy of the dehydrated lemon peels on the immunity, enzymatic antioxidant capacity and growth of Nile tilapia (*Oreochromis niloticus*) and African catfish (*Clarias gariepinus*). Aquaculture 505:92–97. https://doi.org/10.1016/j.aquaculture.2019.02.051

Abdel-Daim MM, Eissa IAM, Abdeen A et al (2019) Lycopene and resveratrol ameliorate zinc oxide nanoparticles-induced oxidative stress in Nile tilapia, *Oreochromis niloticus*. Environ Toxicol Pharmacol 69:44–50. https://doi.org/10.1016/j.etap.2019.03.016

Abdel-Daim MM, Dawood MAO, Aleya L et al (2020) Effects of fucoidan on the hematic indicators and antioxidative responses of Nile tilapia (*Oreochromis niloticus*) fed diets contaminated with aflatoxin B1. Environ Sci Pollut Res 27(11):12579–12586. https://doi.org/10.1007/s11356-020-07854-w

Abdelhamid AF, Ayoub HF, Abd El-Gawad EA et al (2021) Potential effects of dietary seaweeds mixture on the growth performance, antioxidant status, immunity response, and resistance of striped catfish (*Pangasianodon hypophthalmus*) against *Aeromonas hydrophila* infection. Fish Shellfish Immunol 119:76–83. https://doi.org/10.1016/j.fsi.2021.09.043

Abdel-Latif HMR, Abdel-Tawwab M, Khafaga AF et al (2020) Dietary oregano essential oil improved the growth performance via enhancing the intestinal morphometry and hepato-renal functions of common carp (*Cyprinus carpio* L.) fingerlings. Aquaculture 526:735432. https://doi.org/10.1016/j.aquaculture.2020.735432

Abdelmagid AD, Asely AME, Said AM (2021) Evaluation of *Foeniculum vulgare* impact on glyphosate hepato-toxicity in Nile tilapia: biochemical, molecular and histopathological study. Aquac Res 52(11):5397–5406. https://doi.org/10.1111/are.15409

Abdelmagid AD, Said AM, Abd El-Gawad EA et al (2022a) Glyphosate-induced liver and kidney dysfunction, oxidative stress, immunosuppression in Nile tilapia, but ginger showed a protection role. Vet Res Commun. https://doi.org/10.1007/s11259-022-09961-0

Abdelmagid AD, Said AM, Gawad EAA et al (2022b) Propolis nanoparticles relieved the impacts of glyphosate-induced oxidative stress and immunosuppression in Nile tilapia. Environ Sci Pollut Res 29(13):19778–19789. https://doi.org/10.1007/s11356-021-17201-2

Abdel-Tawwab M, Khalil RH, Nour AM et al (2020a) Effects of *Bacillus subtilis*-fermented rice bran on water quality, performance, antioxidants/oxidants, and immunity biomarkers of White leg shrimp (*Litopenaeus vannamei*) reared at different salinities with zero water exchange. J Appl Aquacult 34:332–357. https://doi.org/10.1080/10454438.2020.1844110

Abdel-Tawwab M, Monier MN, Abdelrhman AM et al (2020b) Effect of dietary multi-stimulants blend supplementation on performance, digestive enzymes, and antioxidants biomarkers of common carp, *Cyprinus carpio* L. and its resistance to ammonia toxicity. Aquaculture 528: 735529. https://doi.org/10.1016/j.aquaculture.2020.735529

Abdel-Tawwab M, El-Ashram AM, Tahoun AA et al (2021a) Effects of dietary sweet basil (*Ocimum basilicum*) oil on the performance, antioxidants and immunity welfare, and resistance of Indian shrimp (*Penaeus indicus*) against *Vibrio parahaemolyticus* infection. Aquac Nutr 27(4):1244–1254. https://doi.org/10.1111/anu.13265

Abdel-Tawwab M, Mounes HAM, Shady SHH et al (2021b) Effects of yucca, Yucca schidigera, extract and/or yeast, *Saccharomyces cerevisiae*, as water additives on growth, biochemical, and antioxidants/oxidant biomarkers of Nile tilapia, *Oreochromis niloticus*. Aquaculture 533: 736122. https://doi.org/10.1016/j.aquaculture.2020.736122

Abdel-Tawwab M, Shukry M, Farrag FA et al (2021c) Dietary sodium butyrate nanoparticles enhanced growth, digestive enzyme activities, intestinal histomorphometry, and transcription of growth-related genes in Nile tilapia juveniles. Aquaculture 536:736467. https://doi.org/10.1016/j.aquaculture.2021.736467

Abdel-Tawwab M, Abdel-Razek N, Tahoun A-A et al (2022a) Effects of dietary supplementation of chamomile oil on Indian shrimp (*Penaeus indicus*) performance, antioxidant, innate immunity, and resistance to *Vibrio parahaemolyticus* infection. Aquaculture 552:738045. https://doi.org/10.1016/j.aquaculture.2022.738045

Abdel-Tawwab M, Mousa MAA, Mamoon A et al (2022b) Dietary *Chlorella vulgaris* modulates the performance, antioxidant capacity, innate immunity, and disease resistance capability of Nile tilapia fingerlings fed on plant-based diets. Anim Feed Sci Technol 283:115181. https://doi.org/10.1016/j.anifeedsci.2021.115181

Abo Norag MA, El-Shenawy AM, Fadl SE et al (2018) Effect of phytase enzyme on growth performance, serum biochemical alteration, immune response and gene expression in Nile tilapia. Fish Shellfish Immunol 80:97–108. https://doi.org/10.1016/j.fsi.2018.05.051

Abo-Taleb HA, Ashour M, Elokaby MA et al (2021a) Effect of a new feed *Daphnia magna* (Straus, 1820), as a fish meal substitute on growth, feed utilization, histological status, and economic revenue of grey mullet, *Mugil cephalus* (Linnaeus 1758). Sustainability 13(13):7093. https://doi.org/10.3390/su13137093

Abo-Taleb HA, El-feky MMM, Azab AM et al (2021b) Growth performance, feed utilization, gut integrity, and economic revenue of grey mullet, *Mugil cephalus*, fed an increasing level of dried zooplankton biomass meal as fishmeal substitutions. Fishes 6(3):38. https://doi.org/10.3390/fishes6030038

Abozeid AM, Abdel-Rahim MM, Abouelenien F et al (2021) *Quillaja saponaria* and/or *Yucca schidigera* ameliorate water quality, growth performance, blood health, intestine and gills histomorphology of Nile tilapia, *Oreochromis niloticus*. Aquacult Res 52(12):6117–6131. https://doi.org/10.1111/are.15474

Abu-Alya IS, Alharbi YM, Fathalla SI et al (2021) Effect of partial soybean replacement by shrimp by-products on the productive and economic performances in African catfish (*Clarias lazera*) diets. Fishes 6(4):84. https://doi.org/10.3390/fishes6040084

Adebayo OT, Fagbenro OA, Jegede T (2004) Evaluation of *Cassia fistula* meal as a replacement for soybean meal in practical diets of *Oreochromis niloticus* fingerlings. Aquac Nutr 10(2):99–104. https://doi.org/10.1111/j.1365-2095.2003.00286.x

Adeshina I, Abdel-Tawwab M (2020) Dietary taurine incorporation to high plant protein-based diets improved growth, biochemical, immunity, and antioxidants biomarkers of African catfish, *Clarias gariepinus* (B.). Fish Physiol Biochem 46(4):1323–1335. https://doi.org/10.1007/s10695-020-00791-y

Adeshina I, Abdel-Tawwab M, Tijjani ZA et al (2021) Dietary Tridax procumbens leaves extract stimulated growth, antioxidants, immunity, and resistance of Nile tilapia, *Oreochromis niloticus*, to monogenean parasitic infection. Aquaculture 532:736047. https://doi.org/10.1016/j.aquaculture.2020.736047

Ahmed SAA, Ibrahim RE, Farroh KY et al (2021) Chitosan vitamin E nanocomposite ameliorates the growth, redox, and immune status of Nile tilapia (*Oreochromis niloticus*) reared under different stocking densities. Aquaculture 541:736804. https://doi.org/10.1016/j.aquaculture.2021.736804

Al-Deriny SH, Dawood MAO, Elbialy ZI et al (2020) Selenium nanoparticles and Spirulina alleviate growth performance, hemato-biochemical, immune-related genes, and heat shock protein in Nile tilapia (*Oreochromis niloticus*). Biol Trace Elem Res 198(2):661–668. https://doi.org/10.1007/s12011-020-02096-w

Ali MF, Soliman AA, Gewaily MS et al (2022) Isatis phytogenic relieved atrazine induced growth retardation, hepato-renal dysfunction, and oxidative stress in Nile tilapia. Saudi J Biol Sci 29(1): 190–196. https://doi.org/10.1016/j.sjbs.2021.08.072

Al-Khalaifah HS, Khalil AA, Amer SA et al (2020) Effects of dietary doum palm fruit powder on growth, antioxidant capacity, immune response, and disease resistance of African catfish, *Clarias gariepinus* (B.). Animals 10(8):1407. https://doi.org/10.3390/ani10081407

Al-Sagheer AA, Mahmoud HK, Reda FM et al (2018) Supplementation of diets for *Oreochromis niloticus* with essential oil extracts from lemongrass (*Cymbopogon citratus*) and geranium (*Pelargonium graveolens*) and effects on growth, intestinal microbiota, antioxidant and immune activities. Aquac Nutr 24(3):1006–1014. https://doi.org/10.1111/anu.12637

Amer SA, Metwally AE, Ahmed SAA (2018) The influence of dietary supplementation of cinnamaldehyde and thymol on the growth performance, immunity and antioxidant status of monosex Nile tilapia fingerlings (*Oreochromis niloticus*). Egypt J Aquat Res 44(3):251–256. https://doi.org/10.1016/j.ejar.2018.07.004

Amer SA, Osman A, Al-Gabri NA et al (2019) The effect of dietary replacement of fish meal with whey protein concentrate on the growth performance, fish health, and immune status of Nile tilapia fingerlings, *Oreochromis niloticus*. Animals 9(12):1003. https://doi.org/10.3390/ani9121003

Amer SA, Ahmed SAA, Ibrahim RE et al (2020) Impact of partial substitution of fish meal by methylated soy protein isolates on the nutritional, immunological, and health aspects of Nile tilapia, *Oreochromis niloticus* fingerlings. Aquaculture 518:734871. https://doi.org/10.1016/j.aquaculture.2019.734871

Amer SA, El-Araby DA, Tartor H et al (2022) Long-term feeding with curcumin affects the growth, antioxidant capacity, immune status, tissue histoarchitecture, immune expression of proinflammatory cytokines, and apoptosis indicators in Nile tilapia, *Oreochromis niloticus*. Antioxidants 11(5):937. https://doi.org/10.3390/antiox11050937

Amin A, El Asely A, Abd El-Naby AS et al (2019) Growth performance, intestinal histomorphology and growth-related gene expression in response to dietary *Ziziphus mauritiana* in Nile tilapia (*Oreochromis niloticus*). Aquaculture 512:734301. https://doi.org/10.1016/j.aquaculture.2019.734301

Ashour M, Abo-Taleb HA, Hassan A-KM et al (2021a) Valorization use of amphipod meal, *Gammarus pulex*, as a fishmeal substitute on growth performance, feed utilization, histological and histometric indices of the gut, and economic revenue of grey mullet. J Mar Sci Eng 9(12): 1336. https://doi.org/10.3390/jmse9121336

Ashour M, Mabrouk MM, Abo-Taleb HA et al (2021b) A liquid seaweed extract (TAM®) improves aqueous rearing environment, diversity of zooplankton community, whilst enhancing growth and immune response of Nile tilapia, *Oreochromis niloticus*, challenged by *Aeromonas hydrophila*. Aquaculture 543:736915. https://doi.org/10.1016/j.aquaculture.2021.736915

Ashry AM, Habiba MM, El-Zayat AM et al (2022) Dietary anise (*Pimpinella anisum* L.) enhances growth performance and serum immunity of European sea bass (*Dicentrarchus labrax*). Aquacult Rep 23:101083. https://doi.org/10.1016/j.aqrep.2022.101083

Awad E, Awaad A (2017) Role of medicinal plants on growth performance and immune status in fish. Fish Shellfish Immunol 67:40–54. https://doi.org/10.1016/j.fsi.2017.05.034

Awed EM, Sadek KM, Soliman MK et al (2020) *Spirulina platensis* alleviated the oxidative damage in the gills, liver, and kidney organs of Nile tilapia intoxicated with sodium sulphate. Animals 10(12):2423. https://doi.org/10.3390/ani10122423

Ayyat MS, Ayyat AMN, Al-Sagheer AA et al (2018) Effect of some safe feed additives on growth performance, blood biochemistry, and bioaccumulation of aflatoxin residues of Nile tilapia fed aflatoxin-B1 contaminated diet. Aquaculture 495:27–34. https://doi.org/10.1016/j.aquaculture.2018.05.030

Ayyat MS, Abdel-Rahman GA, Ayyat AMN et al (2021) Evaluation of leaf protein concentrate from *Beta vulgaris* and *Daucus carota* as a substitute for soybean meal in *Oreochromis niloticus* fingerlings diets. Aquac Res 52(7):3256–3269. https://doi.org/10.1111/are.15171

Beveridge MCM, Thilsted SH, Phillips MJ et al (2013) Meeting the food and nutrition needs of the poor: the role of fish and the opportunities and challenges emerging from the rise of aquaculture. J Fish Biol 83(4):1067–1084. https://doi.org/10.1111/jfb.12187

Chan CY, Tran N, Pethiyagoda S et al (2019) Prospects and challenges of fish for food security in Africa. Glob Food Sec 20:17–25. https://doi.org/10.1016/j.gfs.2018.12.002

Dawood MAO, Koshio S (2020) Application of fermentation strategy in aquafeed for sustainable aquaculture. Rev Aquacult 12(2):987–1002. https://doi.org/10.1111/raq.12368

Dawood MAO, Magouz FI, Salem MFI et al (2019) Modulation of digestive enzyme activity, blood health, oxidative responses and growth-related gene expression in GIFT by heat-killed *Lactobacillus plantarum* (L-137). Aquaculture 505:127–136. https://doi.org/10.1016/j.aquaculture.2019.02.053

Dawood MAO, Abdel-Razik NI, Gewaily MS et al (2020a) β-glucan improved the immunity, hepato-renal, and histopathology disorders induced by chlorpyrifos in Nile tilapia. Aquacult Rep 18:100549. https://doi.org/10.1016/j.aqrep.2020.100549

Dawood MAO, Abo-Al-Ela HG, Hasan MT (2020b) Modulation of transcriptomic profile in aquatic animals: probiotics, prebiotics and synbiotics scenarios. Fish Shellfish Immunol 97: 268–282. https://doi.org/10.1016/j.fsi.2019.12.054

Dawood MAO, Amer AA, Elbialy ZI et al (2020c) Effects of including triticale on growth performance, digestive enzyme activity, and growth-related genes of Nile tilapia (*Oreochromis niloticus*). Aquaculture 528:735568. https://doi.org/10.1016/j.aquaculture.2020.735568

Dawood MAO, Eweedah NM, Khalafalla MM et al (2020d) Evaluation of fermented date palm seed meal with *Aspergillus oryzae* on the growth, digestion capacity and immune response of Nile tilapia (*Oreochromis niloticus*). Aquac Nutr 26(3):828–841. https://doi.org/10.1111/anu.13042

Dawood MAO, Eweedah NM, Moustafa EM et al (2020e) Copper nanoparticles mitigate the growth, immunity, and oxidation resistance in common carp (*Cyprinus carpio*). Biol Trace Elem Res 198(1):283–292. https://doi.org/10.1007/s12011-020-02068-0

Dawood MAO, Eweedah NM, Moustafa EM et al (2020f) Synbiotic effects of *Aspergillus oryzae* and β-glucan on growth and oxidative and immune responses of Nile tilapia, *Oreochromis niloticus*. Probiotics Antimicrob Proteins 12(1):172–183. https://doi.org/10.1007/s12602-018-9513-9

Dawood MAO, Koshio S, Fadl SE et al (2020g) The modulatory effect of mannanoligosaccharide on oxidative status, selected immune parameters and tolerance against low salinity stress in red sea bream (*Pagrus major*). Aquacult Rep 16:100278. https://doi.org/10.1016/j.aqrep.2020.100278

Dawood MAO, Magouz FI, Essa M et al (2020h) Impact of yeast fermented poultry by-product meal on growth, digestive enzyme activities, intestinal morphometry and immune response traits of common carp (*Cyprinus carpio*). Ann Anim Sci 20(3):939–959. https://doi.org/10.2478/aoas-2020-0021

Dawood MAO, Magouz FI, Mansour M et al (2020i) Evaluation of yeast fermented poultry by-product meal in Nile tilapia (*Oreochromis niloticus*) feed: effects on growth performance, digestive enzymes activity, innate immunity, and antioxidant capacity. Front Vet Sci 6:516. https://doi.org/10.3389/fvets.2019.00516

Dawood MAO, Magouz FI, Salem MFI et al (2020j) Synergetic effects of *Lactobacillus plantarum* and β-glucan on digestive enzyme activity, intestinal morphology, growth, fatty acid, and glucose-related gene expression of genetically improved farmed tilapia. Probiotics Antimicrob Proteins 12(2):389–399. https://doi.org/10.1007/s12602-019-09552-7

Dawood MAO, Metwally AE-S, El-Sharawy ME et al (2020k) The role of β-glucan in the growth, intestinal morphometry, and immune-related gene and heat shock protein expressions of Nile tilapia (*Oreochromis niloticus*) under different stocking densities. Aquaculture 523:735205. https://doi.org/10.1016/j.aquaculture.2020.735205

Dawood MAO, Moustafa EM, Gewaily MS et al (2020l) Ameliorative effects of *Lactobacillus plantarum* L-137 on Nile tilapia (*Oreochromis niloticus*) exposed to deltamethrin toxicity in rearing water. Aquat Toxicol 219:105377. https://doi.org/10.1016/j.aquatox.2019.105377

Dawood MAO, Zommara M, Eweedah NM et al (2020m) The evaluation of growth performance, blood health, oxidative status and immune-related gene expression in Nile tilapia (*Oreochromis niloticus*) fed dietary nanoselenium spheres produced by lactic acid bacteria. Aquaculture 515: 734571. https://doi.org/10.1016/j.aquaculture.2019.734571

Dawood MAO, Basuini MFE, Zaineldin AI et al (2021a) Antiparasitic and antibacterial functionality of essential oils: an alternative approach for sustainable aquaculture. Pathogens 10(2):185. https://doi.org/10.3390/pathogens10020185

Dawood MAO, Gewaily MS, Monier MN et al (2021b) The regulatory roles of yucca extract on the growth rate, hepato-renal function, histopathological alterations, and immune-related genes in common carp exposed with acute ammonia stress. Aquaculture 534:736287. https://doi.org/10.1016/j.aquaculture.2020.736287

Delarue J (2019) Fatty acids: a role for Africa? Proc Nutr Soc 78(4):532–539. https://doi.org/10.1017/s0029665119000508

Diab AM, Shokr BT, Shukry M et al (2022) Effects of dietary supplementation with green-synthesized zinc oxide nanoparticles for candidiasis control in *Oreochromis niloticus*. Biol Trace Elem Res 200(9):4126–4141. https://doi.org/10.1007/s12011-021-02985-8

Dunbar BS, Bosire RV, Deckelbaum RJ (2014) Omega 3 and omega 6 fatty acids in human and animal health: an African perspective. Mol Cell Endocrinol 398(1–2):69–77. https://doi.org/10.1016/j.mce.2014.10.009

Eissa AE, Yusuf MS, Younis NA et al (2022) Effect of poultry offal silage with or without betaine supplementation on growth performance, intestinal morphometry, spleen histomorphology of Nile tilapia (*Oreochromis niloticus*) fingerlings. J Anim Physiol Anim Nutr 106(5):1189–1195. https://doi.org/10.1111/jpn.13655

El Asely A, Amin A, Abd El-Naby AS et al (2020) *Ziziphus mauritiana* supplementation of Nile tilapia (*Oreochromis niloticus*) diet for improvement of immune response to *Aeromonas hydrophila* infection. Fish Physiol Biochem 46(4):1561–1575. https://doi.org/10.1007/s10695-020-00812-w

El Basuini MF, Shahin SA, Teiba II et al (2021) The influence of dietary coenzyme Q10 and vitamin C on the growth rate, immunity, oxidative-related genes, and the resistance against *Streptococcus agalactiae* of Nile tilapia (*Oreochromis niloticus*). Aquaculture 531:735862. https://doi.org/10.1016/j.aquaculture.2020.735862

El Saidy NR, El-Habashi N, Saied MM et al (2020) Wastewater remediation of heavy metals and pesticides using rice straw and/or zeolite as bioadsorbents and assessment of treated wastewater reuse in the culture of Nile tilapia (*Oreochromis niloticus*). Environ Monit Assess 192(12):779. https://doi.org/10.1007/s10661-020-08760-x

El-Araby DA, Amer SA, Khalil AA (2020) Effect of different feeding regimes on the growth performance, antioxidant activity, and health of Nile tilapia, *Oreochromis niloticus*. Aquaculture 528:735572. https://doi.org/10.1016/j.aquaculture.2020.735572

El-Araby DA, Amer SA, Attia GA et al (2022) Dietary *Spirulina platensis* phycocyanin improves growth, tissue histoarchitecture, and immune responses, with modulating immunoexpression of CD3 and CD20 in Nile tilapia, *Oreochromis niloticus*. Aquaculture 546:737413. https://doi.org/10.1016/j.aquaculture.2021.737413

El-Din AE-DS, Abdullah S, Sayed AE-DH (2021) Antioxidant capacity and DNA damage in Nile tilapia (*Oreochromis niloticus*) exposed to ethidium bromide: a protective role for *Spirulina platensis*. Sci Afr 13:e00961. https://doi.org/10.1016/j.sciaf.2021.e00961

El-Fahla NA, Khalil KAA, Dessouki AA et al (2022) Dietary Beta-MOS® ameliorated lead induced reproductive toxicity and stress in Nile tilapia. Aquaculture 548:737711. https://doi.org/10.1016/j.aquaculture.2021.737711

El-Houseiny W, Khalil AA, Abd-Elhakim YM et al (2019) The potential role of turmeric and black pepper powder diet supplements in reversing cadmium-induced growth retardation, ATP depletion, hepatorenal damage, and testicular toxicity in *Clarias gariepinus*. Aquaculture 510: 109–121. https://doi.org/10.1016/j.aquaculture.2019.05.045

El-Houseiny W, Abd El-Hakim YM, Metwally MMM et al (2022) The single or combined *Silybum marianum* and co-enzyme Q10 role in alleviating fluoride-induced impaired growth, immune suppression, oxidative stress, histological alterations, and reduced resistance to *Aeromonas sobria* in African catfish (*Clarias gariepinus*). Aquaculture 548:737693. https://doi.org/10.1016/j.aquaculture.2021.737693

Elkaradawy A, Abdel-Rahim MM, Albalawi AE et al (2021) Synergistic effects of the soapbark tree, *Quillaja saponaria* and vitamin E on water quality, growth performance, blood health, gills and intestine histomorphology of Nile tilapia, *Oreochromis niloticus* fingerlings. Aquacult Rep 20:100733. https://doi.org/10.1016/j.aqrep.2021.100733

Elkaradawy A, Abdel-Rahim MM, Mohamed RA (2022) *Quillaja saponaria* and/or linseed oil improved growth performance, water quality, welfare profile and immune-oxidative status of Nile tilapia, *Oreochromis niloticus* fingerlings. Aquacult Res 53(2):576–589. https://doi.org/10.1111/are.15602

El-latif AMA, El-Gawad EAA, Soror EI et al (2021) Dietary supplementation with miswak (*Salvadora persica*) improves the health status of Nile tilapia and protects against *Aeromonas hydrophila* infection. Aquacult Rep 19:100594. https://doi.org/10.1016/j.aqrep.2021.100594

El-Saadony MT, Alagawany M, Patra AK et al (2021) The functionality of probiotics in aquaculture: an overview. Fish Shellfish Immunol 117:36–52. https://doi.org/10.1016/j.fsi.2021.07.007

El-Saidy DMSD, Gaber MMA (2002) Complete replacement of fish meal by soybean meal with dietary L-lysine supplementation for Nile tilapia *Oreochromis niloticus* (L.) fingerlings. J World Aquacult Soc 33(3):297–306. https://doi.org/10.1111/j.1749-7345.2002.tb00506.x

El-Saidy DMSD, Gaber MMA (2003) Replacement of fish meal with a mixture of different plant protein sources in juvenile Nile tilapia, *Oreochromis niloticus* (L.) diets. Aquac Res 34(13): 1119–1127. https://doi.org/10.1046/j.1365-2109.2003.00914.x

El-Saidy DMSD, Saad AS (2011) Effects of partial and complete replacement of soybean meal with cottonseed meal on growth, feed utilization and haematological indexes for mono-sex male Nile tilapia, *Oreochromis niloticus* (L.) fingerlings. Aquac Res 42(3):351–359. https://doi.org/10.1111/j.1365-2109.2010.02629.x

El-Sayed A-FM (1998) Total replacement of fish meal with animal protein sources in Nile tilapia, *Oreochromis niloticus* (L.), feeds. Aquac Res 29(4):275–280. https://doi.org/10.1046/j.1365-2109.1998.00199.x

Emam MA, Shourbela RM, El-Hawarry WN et al (2021) Effects of *Moringa oleifera* aqueous extract on the growth performance, blood characteristics, and histological features of gills and livers in Nile tilapia. Aquacult Fish. https://doi.org/10.1016/j.aaf.2021.12.011

Fadl SE, El-Habashi N, Gad DM et al (2021) Effect of adding *Dunaliella* algae to fish diet on lead acetate toxicity and gene expression in the liver of Nile tilapia. Toxin Rev 40(4):1–17. https://doi.org/10.1080/15569543.2019.1652652

FAO (2020) The state of world fisheries and aquaculture 2020. In: Sustainability in action, 206 pp

FAO (2022) The state of world fisheries and aquaculture 2022. In: Towards blue transformation, 236 pp

Gaber MM (2006) Partial and complete replacement of fish meal by broad bean meal in feeds for Nile tilapia, *Oreochromis niloticus*, L., fry. Aquac Res 37(10):986–993. https://doi.org/10.1111/j.1365-2109.2006.01517.x

Gabriel UU, Akinrotimi OA, Bekibele DO et al (2007) Locally produced fish feed: potentials for aquaculture development in sub-Saharan Africa. Afr J Agric Res 2(7):287–295. https://doi.org/10.5897/AJAR.9000470

Gabriel NN, Iitembu JA, Hasimuna OJ et al (2022) Medicinal plants: a perspective on their application in the African smallholder aquaculture farms. In: Food security for african smallholder farmers, pp 191–217

Gewaily MS, Abdo SE, Moustafa EM et al (2021a) Dietary synbiotics can help relieve the impacts of deltamethrin toxicity of Nile tilapia reared at low temperatures. Animals 11(6):1790. https://doi.org/10.3390/ani11061790

Gewaily MS, Shukry M, Abdel-Kader MF et al (2021b) Dietary *Lactobacillus plantarum* relieves Nile tilapia (*Oreochromis niloticus*) juvenile from oxidative stress, immunosuppression, and inflammation induced by deltamethrin and *Aeromonas hydrophila*. Front Mar Sci 8:621558. https://doi.org/10.3389/fmars.2021.621558

Ghalwash HR, Salah AS, El-Nokrashy AM et al (2022) Dietary supplementation with *Bacillus* species improves growth, intestinal histomorphology, innate immunity, antioxidative status and expression of growth and appetite-regulating genes of Nile tilapia fingerlings. Aquac Res 53(4): 1378–1394. https://doi.org/10.1111/are.15671

Ghaniem S, Nassef E, Zaineldin AI et al (2022) A comparison of the beneficial effects of inorganic, organic, and elemental nano-selenium on Nile tilapia: growth, immunity, oxidative status, gut morphology, and immune gene expression. Biol Trace Elem Res 200:5226–5241. https://doi.org/10.1007/s12011-021-03075-5

Goda AMA-S, Wafa ME, El-Haroun ER et al (2007) Growth performance and feed utilization of Nile tilapia *Oreochromis niloticus* (Linnaeus, 1758) and tilapia galilae *Sarotherodon galilaeus* (Linnaeus, 1758) fingerlings fed plant protein-based diets. Aquac Res 38(8):827–837. https://doi.org/10.1111/j.1365-2109.2007.01731.x

Hamed HS, Abdel-Tawwab M (2021) Dietary pomegranate (*Punica granatum*) peel mitigated the adverse effects of silver nanoparticles on the performance, haemato-biochemical, antioxidant, and immune responses of Nile tilapia fingerlings. Aquaculture 540:736742. https://doi.org/10.1016/j.aquaculture.2021.736742

Hamed M, Soliman HAM, Sayed AE-DH (2019) Ameliorative effect of *Spirulina platensis* against lead nitrate–induced cytotoxicity and genotoxicity in catfish *Clarias gariepinus*. Environ Sci Pollut Res 26(20):20610–20618. https://doi.org/10.1007/s11356-019-05319-3

Hassaan MS, Soltan MA, Mohammady EY et al (2018) Growth and physiological responses of Nile tilapia, *Oreochromis niloticus* fed dietary fermented sunflower meal inoculated with *Saccharomyces cerevisiae* and *Bacillus subtilis*. Aquaculture 495:592–601. https://doi.org/10.1016/j.aquaculture.2018.06.018

Hassaan MS, El-Sayed AIM, Soltan MA et al (2019a) Partial dietary fish meal replacement with cotton seed meal and supplementation with exogenous protease alters growth, feed performance, hematological indices and associated gene expression markers (GH, IGF-I) for Nile tilapia, *Oreochromis niloticus*. Aquaculture 503:282–292. https://doi.org/10.1016/j.aquaculture.2019.01.009

Hassaan MS, Mohammady EY, Soaudy MR et al (2019b) Exogenous xylanase improves growth, protein digestibility and digestive enzymes activities in Nile tilapia, *Oreochromis niloticus*, fed different ratios of fish meal to sunflower meal. Aquac Nutr 25(4):841–853. https://doi.org/10.1111/anu.12903

Hassaan MS, Mohammady EY, Soaudy MR et al (2020a) The effect of dietary sericite on growth performance, digestive enzymes activity, gut microbiota and haematological parameters of Nile tilapia, *Oreochromis niloticus* (L.) fingerlings. Anim Feed Sci Technol 262:114400. https://doi.org/10.1016/j.anifeedsci.2020.114400

Hassaan MS, Nssar KM, Mohammady EY et al (2020b) Nano-zeolite efficiency to mitigate the aflatoxin B1 (AFB1) toxicity: effects on growth, digestive enzymes, antioxidant, DNA damage and bioaccumulation of AFB1 residues in Nile tilapia (*Oreochromis niloticus*). Aquaculture 523:735123. https://doi.org/10.1016/j.aquaculture.2020.735123

Hassaan MS, El-Sayed AMI, Mohammady EY et al (2021a) Eubiotic effect of a dietary potassium diformate (KDF) and probiotic (*Lactobacillus acidophilus*) on growth, hemato-biochemical indices, antioxidant status and intestinal functional topography of cultured Nile tilapia *Oreochromis niloticus* fed diet free fishmeal. Aquaculture 533:736147. https://doi.org/10.1016/j.aquaculture.2020.736147
Hassaan MS, Mohammady EY, Soaudy MR et al (2021b) Comparative study on the effect of dietary β-carotene and phycocyanin extracted from *Spirulina platensis* on immune-oxidative stress biomarkers, genes expression and intestinal enzymes, serum biochemical in Nile tilapia, *Oreochromis niloticus*. Fish Shellfish Immunol 108:63–72. https://doi.org/10.1016/j.fsi.2020.11.012
Ibrahim M, Eid A, Mohamed K et al (2017) Effect of replacement of soybean meal with duckweed (*Lemna minor*) meal on the growth performance and feed utilization in Nile tilapia fingerlings. J Anim Poult Fish Prod 6(1):7–12. https://doi.org/10.21608/japfp.2017.7415
Ibrahim RE, El-Houseiny W, Behairy A et al (2019) Ameliorative effects of *Moringa oleifera* seeds and leaves on chlorpyrifos-induced growth retardation, immune suppression, oxidative stress, and DNA damage in *Oreochromis niloticus*. Aquaculture 505:225–234. https://doi.org/10.1016/j.aquaculture.2019.02.050
Ibrahim RE, Ahmed SAA, Amer SA et al (2020) Influence of vitamin C feed supplementation on the growth, antioxidant activity, immune status, tissue histomorphology, and disease resistance in Nile tilapia, *Oreochromis niloticus*. Aquacult Rep 18:100545. https://doi.org/10.1016/j.aqrep.2020.100545
Ibrahim MS, El-gendy GM, Ahmed AI et al (2021a) Nanoselenium versus bulk selenium as a dietary supplement: effects on growth, feed efficiency, intestinal histology, haemato-biochemical and oxidative stress biomarkers in Nile tilapia (*Oreochromis niloticus* Linnaeus, 1758) fingerlings. Aquac Res 52(11):5642–5655. https://doi.org/10.1111/are.15439
Ibrahim RE, Amer SA, Farroh KY et al (2021b) The effects of chitosan-vitamin C nanocomposite supplementation on the growth performance, antioxidant status, immune response, and disease resistance of Nile tilapia (*Oreochromis niloticus*) fingerlings. Aquaculture 534:736269. https://doi.org/10.1016/j.aquaculture.2020.736269
Ibrahim MS, El-Gendi GMI, Ahmed AI et al (2022) Nano zinc versus bulk zinc form as dietary supplied: effects on growth, intestinal enzymes and topography, and hemato-biochemical and oxidative stress biomarker in Nile tilapia (*Oreochromis niloticus* Linnaeus, 1758). Biol Trace Elem Res 200(3):1347–1360. https://doi.org/10.1007/s12011-021-02724-z
Kirimi JG, Musalia LM, Munguti JM (2017) Effect of replacing fish meal with blood meal on chemical composition of supplement for Nile tilapia (*Oreochromis niloticus*). East Afr Agric For J 82(1):1–9. https://doi.org/10.1080/00128325.2016.1158898
Limbu SM (2020a) Antibiotics use in African aquaculture: their potential risks on fish and human health. In: Abia ALK, Lanza GR (eds) Current microbiological research in Africa: selected applications for sustainable environmental management. Springer International Publishing, Cham, pp 203–221
Limbu SM (2020b) The effects of on-farm produced feeds on growth, survival, yield and feed cost of juvenile African sharptooth catfish (*Clarias gariepinus*). Aquacult Fish 5(1):58–64. https://doi.org/10.1016/j.aaf.2019.07.002
Limbu SM, Jumanne K (2014) Effect of restricted and re-feeding regime on feeding cost, growth performance, feed utilization and survival rate of mixed sex Nile tilapia *Oreochromis niloticus* cultured in tanks. Int J Fish Aquat Stud 2(1):118–123
Limbu SM, Shoko AP, Lamtane HA et al (2016) Supplemental effects of mixed ingredients and rice bran on the growth performance, survival and yield of Nile tilapia, *Oreochromis niloticus* reared in fertilized earthen ponds. Springerplus 5(1):1–13. https://doi.org/10.1186/s40064-015-1643-x
Limbu SM, Zhou L, Sun S-X et al (2018) Chronic exposure to low environmental concentrations and legal aquaculture doses of antibiotics cause systemic adverse effects in Nile tilapia and provoke differential human health risk. Environ Int 115:205–219. https://doi.org/10.1016/j.envint.2018.03.034

Limbu SM, Ma Q, Zhang M-L et al (2019) High fat diet worsens the adverse effects of antibiotic on intestinal health in juvenile Nile tilapia (*Oreochromis niloticus*). Sci Total Environ 680:169–180. https://doi.org/10.1016/j.scitotenv.2019.05.067

Limbu SM, Zhang H, Luo Y et al (2020) High carbohydrate diet partially protects Nile tilapia (*Oreochromis niloticus*) from oxytetracycline-induced side effects. Environ Pollut 256:113508. https://doi.org/10.1016/j.envpol.2019.113508

Limbu SM, Chen L-Q, Zhang M-L et al (2021) A global analysis on the systemic effects of antibiotics in cultured fish and their potential human health risk: a review. Rev Aquacult 13(2):1015–1059. https://doi.org/10.1111/raq.12511

Limbu SM, Shoko AP, Ulotu EE et al (2022) Black soldier fly (*Hermetia illucens*, L.) larvae improves growth performance, feed efficiency and economic returns of Nile tilapia (*Oreochromis niloticus*, L.) fry. Aquacult Fish Fish 2:167–178. https://doi.org/10.1002/aff2.48

Lundeba M, Cole SM, Mekkawy W et al (2022) On-farm participatory evaluation of feeding approaches used by farmers for tilapia (*Oreochromis macrochir*) production in northern Zambia. Aquaculture 549:737747. https://doi.org/10.1016/j.aquaculture.2021.737747

Luthada-Raswiswi R, Mukaratirwa S, O'Brien G (2021) Animal protein sources as a substitute for fishmeal in aquaculture diets: a systematic review and meta-analysis. Appl Sci 11(9):3854. https://doi.org/10.3390/app11093854

Mabrouk MM, Ashour M, Labena A et al (2022) Nanoparticles of Arthrospira platensis improves growth, antioxidative and immunological responses of Nile tilapia (*Oreochromis niloticus*) and its resistance to *Aeromonas hydrophila*. Aquac Res 53(1):125–135. https://doi.org/10.1111/are.15558

Magara HJO, Niassy S, Ayieko MA et al (2021) Edible crickets (Orthoptera) around the world: distribution, nutritional value, and other benefits—a review. Front Nutr 7:537915. https://doi.org/10.3389/fnut.2020.537915

Magouz FI, Dawood MAO, Salem MFI et al (2020a) The role of a digestive enhancer in improving the growth performance, digestive enzymes activity, and health condition of Nile tilapia (*Oreochromis niloticus*) reared under suboptimal temperature. Aquaculture 526:735388. https://doi.org/10.1016/j.aquaculture.2020.735388

Magouz FI, Dawood MAO, Salem MFI et al (2020b) The effects of fish feed supplemented with Azolla meal on the growth performance, digestive enzyme activity, and health condition of genetically-improved farmed tilapia (*Oreochromis niloticus*). Ann Anim Sci 20(3):1029–1045. https://doi.org/10.2478/aoas-2020-0016

Magouz FI, Bassuini MI, Khalafalla MM et al (2021a) Mannan oligosaccharide enhanced the growth rate, digestive enzyme activity, carcass composition, and blood chemistry of Thinlip grey mullet (*Liza ramada*). Animals 11(12):3559. https://doi.org/10.3390/ani11123559

Magouz FI, Mahmoud SA, El-Morsy RAA et al (2021b) Dietary menthol essential oil enhanced the growth performance, digestive enzyme activity, immune-related genes, and resistance against acute ammonia exposure in Nile tilapia (*Oreochromis niloticus*). Aquaculture 530:735944. https://doi.org/10.1016/j.aquaculture.2020.735944

Magouz FI, Amer AA, Faisal A et al (2022) The effects of dietary oregano essential oil on the growth performance, intestinal health, immune, and antioxidative responses of Nile tilapia under acute heat stress. Aquaculture 548:737632. https://doi.org/10.1016/j.aquaculture.2021.737632

Mahmoud HK, Al-Sagheer AA, Reda FM et al (2017) Dietary curcumin supplement influence on growth, immunity, antioxidant status, and resistance to *Aeromonas hydrophila* in *Oreochromis niloticus*. Aquaculture 475:16–23. https://doi.org/10.1016/j.aquaculture.2017.03.043

Mahmoud HK, Reda FM, Alagawany M et al (2021) Ameliorating deleterious effects of high stocking density on *Oreochromis niloticus* using natural and biological feed additives. Aquaculture 531:735900. https://doi.org/10.1016/j.aquaculture.2020.735900

Maina JG, Beames RM, Higgs D et al (2003) Partial replacement of fishmeal with sunflower cake and corn oil in diets for tilapia *Oreochromis niloticus* (Linn): effect on whole body fatty acids. Aquac Res 34(8):601–608. https://doi.org/10.1046/j.1365-2109.2003.00848.x

Mohamed WAM, El-Houseiny W, Ibrahim RE et al (2019) Palliative effects of zinc sulfate against the immunosuppressive, hepato- and nephrotoxic impacts of nonylphenol in Nile tilapia (*Oreochromis niloticus*). Aquaculture 504:227–238. https://doi.org/10.1016/j.aquaculture.2019.02.004

Mohamed RA, Elbialy ZI, Latif ASAE et al (2020) Dietary clenbuterol modifies the expression of genes involved in the regulation of lipid metabolism and growth in the liver, skeletal muscle, and adipose tissue of Nile tilapia (*Oreochromis niloticus*). Aquacult Rep 17:100319. https://doi.org/10.1016/j.aqrep.2020.100319

Morenike AA, Akinola JA (2010) Effect of mixed feeding of varying dietary crude protein levels on the growth and feed utilization of *Clarias gariepinus* (Burchell, 1822) fingerlings. J Anim Vet Adv 9(10):1415–1419. https://doi.org/10.3923/javaa.2010.1415.1419

Moustafa EM, Dawood MAO, Assar DH et al (2020) Modulatory effects of fenugreek seeds powder on the histopathology, oxidative status, and immune related gene expression in Nile tilapia (*Oreochromis niloticus*) infected with *Aeromonas hydrophila*. Aquaculture 515:734589. https://doi.org/10.1016/j.aquaculture.2019.734589

Mugwanya M, Dawood MAO, Kimera F et al (2022) Updating the role of probiotics, prebiotics, and synbiotics for tilapia aquaculture as leading candidates for food sustainability: a review. Probiotics Antimicrob Proteins 14(1):130–157. https://doi.org/10.1007/s12602-021-09852-x

Musthafa MS, Jawahar Ali AR, Arun Kumar MS et al (2017) Effect of *Cucurbita mixta* (L.) seed meal enrichment diet on growth, immune response and disease resistance in *Oreochromis mossambicus*. Fish Shellfish Immunol 68:509–515. https://doi.org/10.1016/j.fsi.2017.07.050

Musyoka SN, Liti D, Ogello EO et al (2020) Earthworm, *Eisenia fetida*, bedding meal as potential cheap fishmeal replacement ingredient for semi-intensive farming of Nile tilapia, *Oreochromis niloticus*. Aquacult Res 51(6):2359–2368. https://doi.org/10.1111/are.14579

Obirikorang KA, Amisah S, Fialor SC et al (2015) Local agro-industrial by-products with potential use in Ghanaian aquaculture: a review. Aquacult Int 23(2):403–425. https://doi.org/10.1007/s10499-014-9831-1

Ofojekwu P, Amali E, Keke I et al (2010) Substitution of fish meal by duckweed *Lemna minor* meal in diets for Nile tilapia *Oreochromis niloticus*. J Aquat Sci 25(1):1–7

Ogello EO, Kembenya EM, Githukia CM et al (2017) Substitution of fish meal with sunflower seed meal in diets for Nile tilapia (*Oreochromis niloticus* L.) reared in earthen ponds. J Appl Aquac 29(1):81–99. https://doi.org/10.1080/10454438.2016.1275074

Olude O, Badmus O (2015) An evaluation of mixture of Moringa (*Moringa oleifera*) leaf and kernel meals as partial replacement for fish meal in the diet of *Clarias gariepinus* juveniles. J Aquat Sci 30(2):391–397. https://doi.org/10.4314/jas.v30i2.10

Saleh NE, Mourad MM, El-Banna SG et al (2021) Soybean protein concentrate as a fishmeal replacer in weaning diets for common sole (*Solea solea*) post-larvae: effects on the growth, biochemical and oxidative stress biomarkers, and histopathological investigations. Aquaculture 544:737080. https://doi.org/10.1016/j.aquaculture.2021.737080

Sallam AE, Mansour AT, Alsaqufi AS et al (2020) Growth performance, anti-oxidative status, innate immunity, and ammonia stress resistance of *Siganus rivulatus* fed diet supplemented with zinc and zinc nanoparticles. Aquacult Rep 18:100410. https://doi.org/10.1016/j.aqrep.2020.100410

Sallam AE, El-feky MMM, Ahmed MS et al (2022) Potential use of whey protein as a partial substitute of fishmeal on growth performance, non-specific immunity and gut histological status of juvenile European seabass, *Dicentrarchus labrax*. Aquacult Res 53(4):1527–1541. https://doi.org/10.1111/are.15688

Sayed AE-DH, Authman MMN (2018) The protective role of *Spirulina platensis* to alleviate the sodium dodecyl sulfate toxic effects in the catfish *Clarias gariepinus* (Burchell, 1822). Ecotoxicol Environ Saf 163:136–144. https://doi.org/10.1016/j.ecoenv.2018.07.060

Sayed AE-DH, Soliman HAM (2018) Modulatory effects of green tea extract against the hepatotoxic effects of 4-nonylphenol in catfish (*Clarias gariepinus*). Ecotoxicol Environ Saf 149:159–165. https://doi.org/10.1016/j.ecoenv.2017.11.007

Sayed AE-DH, AbdAllah EA, Hamed M et al (2020) Hepato-nephrotoxicity in late juvenile of *Oreochromis niloticus* exposed to gibberellic acid: ameliorative effect of *Spirulina platensis*. Pestic Biochem Physiol 167:104600. https://doi.org/10.1016/j.pestbp.2020.104600

Sayed AE-DH, Hamed M, Soliman HAM (2021) *Spirulina platensis* alleviated the hemotoxicity, oxidative damage and histopathological alterations of hydroxychloroquine in catfish (*Clarias gariepinus*). Front Physiol 12:683669. https://doi.org/10.3389/fphys.2021.683669

Sharawy ZZ, Ashour M, Abbas E et al (2020) Effects of dietary marine microalgae, *Tetraselmis suecica*, on production, gene expression, protein markers and bacterial count of Pacific white shrimp *Litopenaeus vannamei*. Aquac Res 51(6):2216–2228. https://doi.org/10.1111/are.14566

Sharawy ZZ, Ashour M, Labena A et al (2022) Effects of dietary *Arthrospira platensis* nanoparticles on growth performance, feed utilization, and growth-related gene expression of Pacific white shrimp, *Litopenaeus vannamei*. Aquaculture 551:737905. https://doi.org/10.1016/j.aquaculture.2022.737905

Shati S, Opiyo M, Nairuti R et al (2022) Black soldier fly (*Hermetia illucens*) larvae meal improves growth performance, feed utilization, amino acids profile, and economic benefits of Nile tilapia (*Oreochromis niloticus*, L.). Aquat Res 5(3):238–249. https://doi.org/10.3153/AR22023

Shawky WA, El-Sayed HS, Saleh NE et al (2021) Evaluation of microalgae-supplemented diets and enriched decapsulated artemia cyst powder as novel diets for post-weaned common sole (*Solea solea*) larvae. Aquac Nutr 27(4):1042–1051. https://doi.org/10.1111/anu.13245

Shukry M, Abd El-Kader MF, Hendam BM et al (2021) Dietary *Aspergillus oryzae* modulates serum biochemical indices, immune responses, oxidative stress, and transcription of HSP70 and cytokine genes in Nile tilapia exposed to salinity stress. Animals 11(6):1621. https://doi.org/10.3390/ani11061621

Soaudy MR, Mohammady EY, Ali MM et al (2021) Potential effects of dietary ZnO supported on kaolinite (ZnO-K) to improve biological parameters, reproduction indices, lipid profile and antioxidant enzymes activities for broodstock of Nile tilapia (*Oreochromis niloticus*). Anim Feed Sci Technol 281:115117. https://doi.org/10.1016/j.anifeedsci.2021.115117

Soliman HAM, Hamed M, Lee J-S et al (2019) Protective effects of a novel pyrazolecarboxamide derivative against lead nitrate induced oxidative stress and DNA damage in *Clarias gariepinus*. Environ Pollut 247:678–684. https://doi.org/10.1016/j.envpol.2019.01.074

Solomon S, Sadiku S, Tiamiyu L (2010) Replacement of fishmeal by silkworm caterpillar (*Anaphe infracta*) meal in the practical diets of *Heterobranchus bidorsalis*. J Aquat Sci 25(1):66–72

Taalab HA, Mohammady EY, Hassan TMM et al (2022) β-Carotene of *Arthrospira platensis* versus vitamin C and vitamin E as a feed supplement: effects on growth, haemato-biochemical, immune-oxidative stress and related gene expression of Nile tilapia fingerlings. Aquac Res 53:4832–4846. https://doi.org/10.1111/are.15977

Yossa R, Greiling AM, Basiita RK et al (2021) Replacing fishmeal with a single cell protein feedstuff in Nile tilapia *Oreochromis niloticus* diets. Anim Feed Sci Technol 281:115089. https://doi.org/10.1016/j.anifeedsci.2021.115089

Zhang Z, Zhang Q, Wang T et al (2022) Assessment of global health risk of antibiotic resistance genes. Nat Commun 13(1):1553. https://doi.org/10.1038/s41467-022-29283-8

Zhou L, Limbu SM, Qiao F et al (2018) Influence of long-term feeding antibiotics on the gut health of zebrafish. Zebrafish 15(4):340–348. https://doi.org/10.1089/zeb.2017.1526

Chapter 2
Feed Restriction as a Feed Management Strategy in Tilapia and Catfish Culture: An African Perspective

Ndakalimwe Naftal Gabriel, Kenneth Prudence Abasubong, and Benjamin U. Akpoilih

Abstract Aquaculture is recognised throughout Africa as an option with the ability to contribute significantly to food security, job development, wealth generation, and community empowerment, just as elsewhere in the world. However, the high feed cost and the limited availability of feed components prevent this industry from reaching its full potential. Diverse feed management strategies have been investigated and developed in various aquaculture systems to reduce feed costs without sacrificing fish production performance by reducing feed ration. This chapter reviewed feeding rate (% body weight per day), feeding frequency, and cyclic feeding (feed deprivation and refeeding cycles) as feed management strategies in tilapia and catfish species, focusing on their applicability in African aquaculture. The optimal feeding rates and frequency at various stages and temperatures have been determined for tilapia and catfish species; these feeding strategies reduce feed ration, enhance feed utilisation, and promote fish growth. Cyclic feeding appears to be a relatively novel concept, yet it has the potential to save feed without impacting fish production in the studied species, mainly when the feeding regime is not severe (feeding days are more than starvation days). These feed management solutions are suitable for African farmers since they do not necessitate additional financial resources or technologically advanced equipment beyond competent labour. However, information on the influence of these feeding strategies on fish physiological

N. N. Gabriel (✉)
Department of Fisheries and Ocean Sciences, Faculty of Agriculture, Engineering and Natural Science, Sam Nujoma Campus, University of Namibia, Henties Bay, Namibia
e-mail: ngabriel@unam.na

K. P. Abasubong
Key Laboratory of Aquatic Nutrition and Feed Science of Jiangsu Province, College of Animal Science and Technology, Nanjing Agricultural University, Nanjing, China

B. U. Akpoilih
Department of Fisheries, Faculty of Agriculture, University of Port Harcourt, Port Harcourt, River State, Nigeria

© The Author(s), under exclusive license to Springer Nature Singapore Pte Ltd. 2023
N. N. Gabriel et al. (eds.), *Emerging Sustainable Aquaculture Innovations in Africa*, Sustainable Agriculture and Food Security,
https://doi.org/10.1007/978-981-19-7451-9_2

responses, water quality, and economic parameters in various aquaculture systems worldwide is still needed for better optimisation.

Keywords Aquaculture · Cyclic feeding · Cichlid · Catfish · Feeding rate · Feeding frequency

2.1 Introduction

Aquaculture is one of the world's fastest-growing food-producing industries. It is recognised as one of the options in Africa and elsewhere in the world that can significantly contribute to food security, poverty alleviation, job development, and community empowerment, among other things. Between 1995 and 2018, Africa's aquaculture production climbed from 110,200 to 2,196,000 tonnes, representing a compound annual growth rate of 15.5% (FAO 2020). Although small compared to other parts of the world, Africa's extraordinary production performance is due to several factors, including capacity growth in key aquaculture sectors, good governance, private sector involvement, and intensification of production aquaculture systems (Satia 2017). Nonetheless, more work needs to be done for aquaculture to be sustainable, as difficulties, such as high reliance on formulated feed, poor water quality, increased disease susceptibility, high energy demand, and chemical use, among others, make intensification both a blessing and a curse.

Aquaculture's long-term viability depends on cost-effective production strategies with little environmental impact. Feeding is one of the activities in aquaculture that needs to be optimised because overfeeding can result in more significant production costs and water pollution, whilst underfeeding can result in poor growth performance and economic loss (Yogev et al. 2020). Feed costs often account for 40–60% of overall aquaculture production costs, making it challenging to translate the benefits of higher productivity associated with commercial feeds into economic gains when fed fish are fed according to conventional procedures. To improve aquaculture earnings, fish farmers have devised numerous feeding management systems that reduce feed inputs, water quality problems, and labour costs. Mixed feeding, such as commercial pellets mixed with farm-made feed (Akinwole and Faturoti 2007), and restricted feedings, such as feeding rate, feeding frequency, and cyclic feeding, are some strategies (Ali et al. 2003) (Fig. 2.1).

Feed restriction is a generally practised feed management approach in aquaculture (Maciel et al. 2018; Assis et al. 2020). This strategy is based on evidence that, in nature, fish may go without food for a long time and survive by utilising stored energy and can compensate for growth when feeding is resumed (de Souza e Silva et al. 2019; Assis et al. 2020). Feeding after starvation can result in overcompensation growth (higher growth than typically fed fish) (Hayward et al. 1997), complete/total compensation (same growth as typically fed fish) (Jobling and Johansen 1999), or partial compensation (lower growth than typically fed fish) (Hayward et al. 1997; Paul et al. 1995). Feed restriction is a feed management method because in addition to boosting fish growth, it also improves fish health (de Souza e Silva et al. 2019),

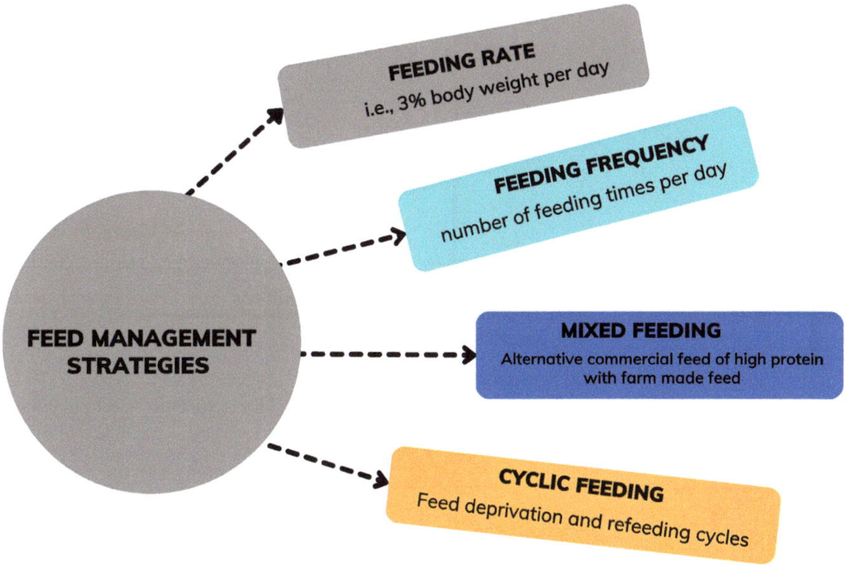

Fig. 2.1 A schematic representation of some feed management strategies in fish farming

water quality (Turano et al. 2008), and economic benefits (Turano et al. 2008; Khan et al. 2009). Moreover, this feed management strategy has been widely reported in a range of fish species, including tambaqui, *Colossoma macropomum* (Assis et al. 2020), actinopteri, *Brycon amazonicus* (Urbinati et al. 2014), marine shrimp (Maciel et al. 2018), common carp, *Cyprinus carpio* (Tiogué et al. 2017), and tilapia species (Abdel-Tawwab et al. 2006; Bolivar et al. 2006; Tiogué et al. 2017; Gabriel et al. 2018).

Therefore, this chapter covers several feed management strategies, such as feeding rate, feeding frequency, and cyclic feeding, as feed management measures in aquaculture, with particular focus on tilapia and catfish species; these are Africa's most popular aquaculture fish species (Adeleke et al. 2020). The chapter also discusses their present advancements and perspectives on their application in African aquaculture.

2.2 Feed Restriction in Aquaculture

Several feed restriction strategies are part of the critical knowledge necessary to improve productivity when adopting a fish in aquaculture. Feeding strategies are influenced by various parameters, including fish species, size, health, culture environment, feed, and the type of culture system (Schram et al. 2009). Fish fed until they are satiated or at a high feeding rate have been demonstrated to develop poorly due to low feed utilisation efficiency (Yakupitage 2013) (Fig. 2.2). As a result, the

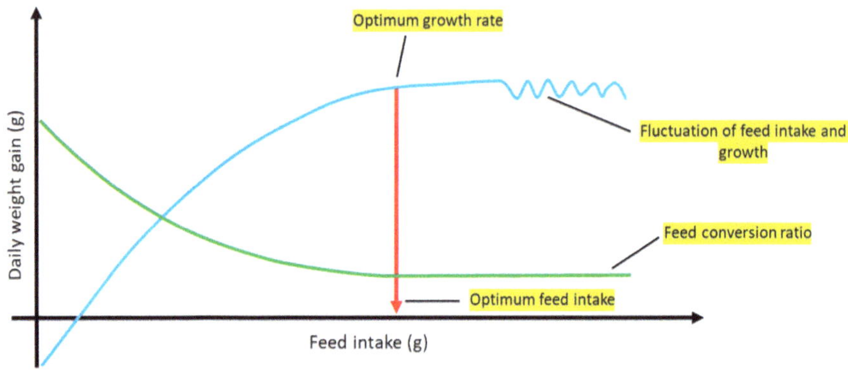

Fig. 2.2 A schematic illustration of fish growth and feed intake for a specific size (Yakupitage 2013)

feeding rate, feeding efficiency, and various cyclic feeding regimes in various fish species have been extensively studied, with some of them being used in aquaculture to maximise growth and profit.

2.2.1 *Feeding Rate and Feeding Frequency*

The feeding rate estimates how much feed should be delivered depending on the animal's body weight, total fish biomass in the culture pond, and water temperature (Goddard 1996). For example, if a fish farmer stocks a pond with 100 kg of fish biomass, the quantity of daily feed that can be supplied if they must be fed at 4% of their body weight may be calculated as follows (Wurts 2015):

$$\begin{aligned} \text{Daily feed ration} &= \text{biomass}(\text{kg}) \times \text{feeding rate}(\%) \\ &= 100\,\text{kg} \times 4\% \\ &= 4\,\text{kg of feed}. \end{aligned} \tag{2.1}$$

Additionally, the feeding rate should consider the relationship between the specific growth rate and the ration for that size at a given temperature (De Silva and Anderson 1994). In general, the feeding rate of most fish species studied decreases as the fish grows larger (Halver and Hardy 2003). Feeding frequency, on the other hand, refers to how many times per day a feed is supplied (Davis and Hardy 2022). Most fish are fed many times, and the frequency of feeding also decreases as the fish develops; feeding is mainly controlled by the stomach's ability to hold feeds, as well as the fish's nutritional demand, growth, and other physiological processes (Craig et al. 2017). The feeding frequency may also be impacted by the quality of the water, the feeding technique, the expectation of increased production, and the size uniformity of the fish (Davis and Hardy 2022). Nonetheless, understanding when and how much to feed promotes good fish growth, feed efficiency, a reduced feed conversion ratio, and the preservation of culture water quality.

2.2.1.1 Feeding Rate and Frequency in Some Tilapia Species

The feeding regime of genetically improved farmed Nile tilapia, *Oreochromis niloticus,* has been established in non-circulating and non-biofiltered systems. Huang et al. (2015) studied the effects of different feeding frequencies (two and three meals per day) and feeding rates (2, 4, 6, 8, 10%) on the growth and physiological response of GIFT fry fed a 34% crude protein (CP) diet at 28.2 °C water temperature for over 70 days. According to this research, a 6% feeding rate at two and three meals per day resulted in a more significant weight gain rate, specific growth rate, and better physiological performance (Huang et al. 2015). Hisano et al. (2021) reported that when Nile tilapia fingerlings (5.36–1.45 g) were fed a 32% (CP) diet at 5–3% of their body weight in the biofloc system in a water temperature range of 22.20–22.47 °C, they exhibited more significant weight gain and protein efficiency ratio, with no impact on general health. Chowdhury (2011) reported in a comprehensive study on Nile tilapia that the optimal daily feeding rate of juveniles (1.1 g) was 10–8% in the first week and 8–6% in the second week, and 3% for fish between 80 and 115 g and 1.2% for fish larger than 260 g when fed a 34.2% CP diet at 25–26 °C and subjected to mixed feeding frequencies. This is in accordance with the published guides for feeding tilapia species at different stages, such as fingerlings (Table 2.1) and grow-out (Table 2.2) by Min (2015). Furthermore, recommended

Table 2.1 Feeding rations (g/10000 fish) for tilapia fingerlings of various sizes at various temperatures (Min 2015)

Water temp (°C)	Fingerlings size (cm)					
	<2	2–4	4–6	6–8	8–10	>10
20–22	5–15	10–50	100–250	200–1000	500–1200	1500–3000
23–24	10–28	40–120	150–400	400–1500	800–1500	2000–4500
25–26	18–50	60–180	300–800	800–2000	1800–3000	3500–6000
27–28	22–65	100–300	450–1000	1500–3000	2500–5000	5000–7000
29–30	40–100	200–600	550–1500	40,000–7000	6000–8000	12,000–16,000

Table 2.2 Tilapia feeding rations (percentage of body weight/100 kg fish) in the grow-out culture stage (Min 2015)

Water temp (°C)	Fish size (g)			
	<50	50–200	200–500	>500
16–18	1–2	1–2	0.5–1	0.1–0.5
18–20	2–4	2–3	1–2	0.5–1
20–25	4–6	3–4	2–3	1–1.5
25–30	6–8	4–6	3–4	1.5–2
Above 30	4–6	3–4	2–3	1–1.5

tilapia feeding practices should be carried out with common sense, for example, (1) the feeding rate should be adjusted depending on the weather condition, water temperature, and water quality. For instance, the feed amount should be reduced when the water temperature is above 30 °C, as failure to do so will result in the decomposition of uneaten feed, which degrades water quality; (2) feeding should also be reduced when the water temperature is below 20 °C, due to the fish's poor appetite; (3) improved fish performance may be gained by feeding fish twice a day between 8:00 a.m. and 10:00 a.m., and 2:00 p.m. and 4:00 p.m.; and (4) fries and fingerlings should be fed in shallow water near the pond dike (Min 2015).

2.2.1.2 Feeding Rate and Frequency in Catfish Production

Similar to other fish species, the feeding regime required for optimising feed efficiency and growth performance in catfish is influenced by the interaction of several factors, including feed composition (Li et al. 2004; Marimuthu et al. 2011), ratio size (Dada et al. 1998), fish species (Li et al. 2005; Akomoda et al. 2019), size (Robinson and Li 2007), and environmental factors (e.g. temperature and dissolved oxygen) and experimental conditions (e.g. photoperiod) (Almazán-Rueda et al. 2004). If feeding level and frequency are not optimised, they impact fish nutrient utilisation (Nwanna et al. 2012; Elesho et al. 2021) and, ultimately, growth performance (Li et al. 2005). For example, Okomoda et al. (2019) investigated the effect of different feeding frequencies on the growth and nutrient utilisation of African catfish (*Clarias gariepinus*) fry and fingerlings by feeding the fry ad libitum with decapsulated *Artemia* cysts 1, 2, 3, 4, 5, or 6 times per day. The fingerlings were fed an equal daily ration (15% body weight per day) of a commercial diet administered in one, two, three, or four meals per day. This study discovered that fry fed five or six rations per day and fingerlings fed three or four meals of the same ration per day grew faster than those fed less frequently (Okomoda et al. 2019). Similarly, feeding African catfish (44 g) a methionine adequate diet once daily for 32 days resulted in lower feed intake and nutrient digestibility than providing two or six meals per day (Elesho et al. 2021). *Heterobranchus bidorsalis* (Clariidae family) fry (30 mg) can be fed as many as 40 meals per day (Dada et al. 1998), and *H. bidorsalis* fingerlings (about 10 g) had the best growth performance when provided 4–6 meals per day (Dada 2012). Ndome et al. (2011) reported that when fed a compounded diet (42% CP) two–three times daily, fingerling (4.12 g) of hybrid catfish (*C. gariepinus* × *H. longifilis*) showed the lowest feed conversion ratio (FCR) and the highest feed efficiency when compared to other feeding frequencies (one, four, or five meals a day). *Clarias gariepinus* and *H. bidorsalis* feeding frequency could reflect variability in culture conditions, diet composition, and fish species (Dada and Olarenwaju 2002; Marimuthu et al. 2011).

Studies concluded that catfish post-fry (0.10–1.3 g) could be fed two to three times per day at an 8% body weight rate (Asiwaju et al. 2014), whereas advanced fingerling reared in grow-out ponds can be fed compounded feed (40–42% CP) at a 5–10% body weight/day rate in three equal meals per day (Aderolu et al. 2010; Ajani

Table 2.3 African catfish, *Clarias gariepinus,* feeding rate (% body weight/ day) at different temperatures (Hecht 2013)

	Fish size (g)					
Water temp (°C)	1–10	10–25	25–50	50–100	100–300	300–800
16–18	1.0–3.0	0.6–1.6	0.4–1.0	0.3–0.8	0.2–0.6	0.2–0.5
18–20	3.0–5.0	1.6–3.0	1.0–2.0	0.8–1.5	0.6–1.2	0.5–1.0
20–22	5.0–6.8	3.0–4.5	2.0–3.0	1.5–2.4	1.2–2.0	1.0–1.7
24–26	6.8–8.1	4.5–6.0	3.0–4.0	2.4–3.0	2.0–2.5	1.7–2.2
26–28	8.1–9.5	6.0–6.6	4.0–5.1	3.0–3.6	2.5–3.2	2.2–2.8
28–30	9.5–10.0	6.6–7.0	5.1–5.5	3.6–4.0	3.2–3.5	2.8–3.1
30–32	9.5–9.8	6.5–6.8	5.0–5.3	3.5–3.7	3.0–3.2	2.8–2.9

et al. 2011; Lawan et al. 2017; Akomoda et al. 2019; Abanikannda et al. 2019; Marimuthu et al. 2011) (Table 2.3). But, depending on the experimental rearing conditions, limiting feed intake (>5% of body weight) may make fish eat more often per day because they are not getting as many nutrients (Akomoda et al. 2019), especially for smaller fish (0.88–0.98 g) (Arshad Hossain et al. 2010). Interestingly, fish that are fed at night do better than fish that are fed during the day because they swim more (Arshad Hossain et al. 2010). Larger catfish can optimise feed intake and growth with two meals per day as opposed to three to four meals per day (Pantazis and Neofitou 2003; Ayisi et al. 2021).

2.3 Feeding Deprivation and Refeeding Cycles in Aquaculture

As briefly mentioned above, many aquatic animals in the wild go hungry for short periods due to seasonal changes, reproduction, and spawning migration (McCue 2010; Li et al. 2018). To deal with this type of short-term starvation, aquatic animals have evolved compensatory mechanisms. The activation of acute-phase protein production, which protects the fish from oxidative stress, is one of these (Sakyi et al. 2020). Fish growth in captivity has increased with feed deprivation and refeeding programs (Mohanta et al. 2017). This is because fish have increased hyperphagia (high feed appetite) after starvation and during the refeeding period, which could help aquatic animals achieve higher growth efficiency by increasing food intake, improving digestion and absorption, and decreasing total feed consumption (Abdel-Tawwab et al. 2006; Mohanta et al. 2017; Shao et al. 2020; Py et al. 2022). Depending on the species, compensatory growth may be partial, complete, overcompensation, or absent entirely (Jobling and Johansen 1999; Mohanta et al. 2017). Feed restrictions can occur for various reasons, including low fish prices, economic pressure from high commercial feed prices, or farm disease outbreaks (Bosworth and Wolters 2005).

2.3.1 Feeding Deprivation and Refeeding Cycles in Tilapia Species

In a study by Gabriel et al. (2017), *O. mossambicus* (5.53 g) was subjected to a variety of short-term feeding, starvation, and refeeding cycles, including 2 days of starvation followed by 2 days of refeeding, 2 days of starvation followed by 3 days of refeeding, 2 days of starvation followed by 4 days of refeeding, and daily feeding (control) for 60 days. According to this study, the growth of fish that went without food for 2 days and then ate again for 4 days did not differ much from the growth of fish that ate every day (complete compensation). At the end of the trial, however, the starved fish had eaten a lot less feed than the other fish. This means that feed can be saved without hurting the performance of the fish being raised. Gabriel et al. (2018) found the same results when they fed hybrid tilapia (*O. mossambicus* × *O. niloticus*) on the exact schedules.

Similarly, Nile tilapia, *O. niloticus* juveniles that were starved for one week and then fed for another 13 weeks were found to have fully compensated for their starvation (Abdel-Tawwab et al. 2006; Gao and Lee 2012). It is interesting to note that overcompensation was observed in Nile tilapia following 2–4 days of feed deprivation and long-term feeding (80 and 185 days) (Gao et al. 2015). Feed deprivation was also successfully used to induce total compensatory growth in Nile tilapia raised in a biofloc system (6 days of feeding/one day of deprivation; 5 days of feeding/2 days of deprivation; 4 days of feeding, 3 days of deprivation) (Correa et al. 2020).

Moreover, some studies showed that feeding a combination of low- and high-protein feed for a set period causes compensatory growth in fish. For example, Liu et al. (2020) investigated whether feeding a low-protein diet (25%) once a day for 10 days or 20 days and then refeeding a high-protein diet (35%) thrice daily for 30 days or 20 days, respectively, would elicit compensatory growth in genetically improved farmed tilapia (GIFT), *O. niloticus* (11.02 0.05 g), compared to those fed 35% (control). Fish fed low-protein feed for 10 days and high-protein feed for 30 days grew similarly to controls, but the weight of those fed low-protein feed for 20 days and high-protein feed for 20 days was lower at day 20. Nonetheless, this significant difference vanished at the end of the experiment.

On the other hand, starving fish can harm their growth and other health-related factors. However, only those that have not experienced a prolonged period of severe feed deprivation can recover after refeeding (Abdel-Tawwab et al. 2006; Gao et al. 2015). Based on the evidence, it can be said that feed deprivation and refeeding regimens (such as 6 days of feeding followed by a starvation cycle lasting 1–2 days or one week of starvation followed by a long period of refeeding) can be effective for tilapia species, but caution should be used when selecting these regimens.

2.3.2 *Feeding Deprivation and Refeeding Cycles in Catfish Production*

Studies of feed deprivation and refeeding cycles in catfish species have also been reported, and the effects on fish vary depending on the species and length of feed deprivation, as was seen in tilapia species. Neotropical catfish (0.9 g) fed in a recirculating system for 45 days showed complete growth in fish starved for 1 or 2 days a week (de Souza e Silva et al. 2019). Li and Robinson (2005) found that fingerling channel catfish (*Ictalurus punctatus*) (14.4 g) raised in a flow-through system and fed once daily to satiation gained significantly more weight than groups that were starved for one, two, or three consecutive days per week, or one day per 5-day period, or three consecutive days per 10-day period, and fed to satiation for 82 days. Gaylord and Gatlin III (2001) found that starving channel catfish for three days and then refeeding them for 11 days to satiation for three cycles resulted in weight gain comparable to that of those fed daily to satiation. Chatakondi and Yant (2001) also found that channel catfish fingerlings (2.5 g) fed a floating diet (36% CP) for 1–3 days and then re-fed for 10 weeks to satiation gained the same weight as fish fed daily. Reigh et al. (2006) compared the production performance of channel catfish (22 g) raised in tanks and exposed to three cycles of 5 days of fasting and refeeding (57 days of feeding and 15 days of fasting) or 10 days of fasting and refeeding (42 days of feeding and 30 days of fasting) to the group that was fully fed for 72 days. They found that weight gain was 25% and 41% lower, respectively, than the body weight of fully fed fish (Reigh et al. 2006).

Similarly, Ali and Jauncey (2004) found that 13.05 g of *C. gariepinus* fed a 35% CP diet that included repeated cycles of feed restriction and feeding until satiation (14, 7, 3, and 2 days) showed some compensatory growth. Reduced growth in the starved group could be attributed to lower levels of lipid and protein in the liver and muscle, indicating decreased liver metabolism and nutrient deposition in the flesh (Luo et al. 2009). Similar to tilapia species, it is evident that feed deprivation and refeeding regimes could also work in catfish species, and a longer duration of refeeding could maximise growth and reduce feeding costs, as demonstrated by Ofor and Ukpabi (2013).

2.4 Conclusion and Perspectives

The importance of feed management in aquaculture cannot be emphasised, especially in an era of scarce resources. Different feed management strategies, such as restricted feeding levels, feeding frequency, and feeding deprivation/refeeding cycles, are being investigated in numerous fish species, including tilapia and catfish. Most of the research indicate that certain levels of feeding rate, feeding frequency, and feeding deprivation and refeeding cycles tend to lower the amount of feed, enhance feed utilisation, and, ultimately, increase fish growth performance. African fish farmers at all levels may be able to implement these tactics for improved feed management, given that they do not necessitate additional financial resources other than skilled staff. However, there is still much work before feed management systems can be broadly implemented. For example, the economic question (i.e. feed cost savings and profit) and water quality are not well addressed for various restricted feeding management strategies in various aquaculture production systems. As the response can be species-specific (Schram et al. 2009), the feeding management strategies highlighted in this chapter should be applied to a broader range of tilapia and catfish species cultivated in Africa. For better optimisation, future research should further elaborate on the impact of restricted feeding as a feed management approach on the physiological parameters of fish in various culture systems.

Overall, regulated feeding is a crucial aspect of feed management that contributes to the sustainability of the aquaculture industry.

References

Abanikannda OTF, Jimoh AA, Bakare KO, Shitta SA, Shopeyin ZF (2019) Influence of feeding regimen on growth parameters of African catfish (*Clarias gariepinus* Burchell 1822). Niger J Anim Prod 46:192–204

Abdel-Tawwab M, Khattab YAE, Ahmad MH, Shalaby AME (2006) Compensatory growth, feed utilization, whole body composition, and hematological changes in starved juvenile Nile tilapia, *Oreochromis niloticus* (L.). J Appl Aquac 18(3):17–36

Adeleke B, Robertson-Andersson D, Moodley G, Taylor S (2020) Aquaculture in Africa: a comparative review of Egypt, Nigeria, and Uganda vis-a-vis South Africa. Rev Fish Sci Aquac 29:167–197

Aderolu AZ, Seriki BM, Apatira AL, Ajaegbo CU (2010) Effects of feeding frequency on growth, feed efficiency and economic viability of rearing African catfish (*Clarias gariepinus*, Burchell 1822) fingerlings and juveniles. Afr J Food Sci 4:286–290

Ajani F, Dawodu MO, Bello-Olusoji OA (2011) Effects of feed forms and feeding frequency on growth performance and nutrient utilization of *Clarias gariepinus* fingerlings. Afr J Agric Res 6: 318–322

Akinwole AO, Faturoti EO (2007) Biological performance of African Catfish (*Clarias gariepinus*) cultured in recirculating system in Ibadan. Aquac Eng 36:18–23

Akomoda VT, Aminem W, Hassan A, Martins CO (2019) Effects of feeding frequency on fry and fingerlings of African catfish *Clarias gariepinus*. Aquaculture 511:734232

Ali MZ, Jauncey K (2004) Evaluation of mixed feeding schedules with respect to compensatory growth and body composition in African catfish *Clarias gariepinus*. Aquac Nutr 10:39–45

Ali M, Nicieza A, Wootton RJ (2003) Compensatory growth in fishes: a response to growth depression. Fish Fish 4:147–190

Almazán-Rueda P, Schrama JW, Verreth JA (2004) Behavioural responses under different feeding methods and light regimes of the African catfish (*Clarias gariepinus*) juveniles. Aquaculture 231:347–359

Arshad Hossain M, Almatar SM, James CM (2010) Optimum dietary protein level for juvenile silver pomfret, *Pampus argenteus* (Euphrasen). J World Aquac Soc 41:710–720

Asiwaju FF, Onyeche VO, Ogbuebunu KE, Moradun HF, Robert EA (2014) Effect of feeding frequency on growth and survival rate of *Clarias gariepinus* fingerlings reared in plastic bowls. J Fish Aquat Sci 9:425–429

Assis YPAS, de Assis Porto L, de Melo NFAC, Palheta GDA, Luz RK, Favero GC (2020) Feed restriction as a feeding management strategy in *Colossoma macropomum* juveniles under recirculating aquaculture system (RAS). Aquaculture 529:735689

Ayisi CL, Debra G, Alhassan EH (2021) Effects of feeding frequency on growth performance of the juvenile Bagrid catfish, *Chrysichthys nigrodigitatus*. Egypt J Aquat Biol Fish 25:513–527

Bolivar RB, Jimenez EBT, Brown CL (2006) Alternate-day feeding strategy for Nile tilapia grow out in the Philippines: marginal cost-revenue analyses. N Am J Aquac 68:192–197

Bosworth BG, Wolters W (2005) Effects of short-term feed restriction on production, processing and body shape traits in market-weight channel catfish, *Ictalurus punctatus* (Rafinesque). Aquac Res 36:344–351

Chatakondi NG, Yant RD (2001) Application of compensatory growth to enhance production in channel catfish *Ictalurus punctatus*. J World Aquac Soc 32:3

Chowdhury DK (2011) Optimal feeding rate for Nile tilapia (*Oreochromis niloticus*). MSc, Norwegian University of Life Sciences

Correa ADS, Pinho SM, Molinari D, Pereira KDR, Gutiérrez SM, Monroy-Dosta MDC, Emerenciano MGC (2020) Rearing of Nile tilapia (*Oreochromis niloticus*) juveniles in a biofloc system employing periods of feed deprivation. J Appl Aquac 32:139–156

Craig SR, Helfrich LA, Kuhn D, Schwarz MH (2017) Understanding fish nutrition, feeds, and feeding. College of Agriculture and Life Sciences, Virginia Tech, pp 420–256

Dada AA (2012) Effect of four feeding rations on the growth performance of African giant catfish *Heterobranchus bidorsalis* fingerlings. Int J Biol Chem Sci 6:6069–6074

Dada AA, Olarenwaju O (2002) The influence of feeding frequency on the growth and feed utilization of catfish (*Clarias gariepinus*) fry in outdoor concrete tanks. Biosci Res Commun 14:431–435

Dada AA, Fagbenro OA, Ita EO (1998) Effect of different feeding levels on the production of *Heterobranchus bidorsalis* in outdoor concrete tanks. Fisheries Society of Nigeria, pp 217–221

Davis DA, Hardy RW (2022) Feeding and fish husbandry. In: Fish nutrition. Academic, pp 857–882

De Silva SS, Anderson TA (1994) Fish nutrition in aquaculture, vol. 1. Springer Science & Business Media

de Souza e Silva W, Hisano H, Mattioli CC, Torres IFA, de Oliveira Paes-Leme F, Luz RK (2019) Effects of cyclical short-term fasting and refeeding on juvenile *Lophiosilurus alexandri*, a carnivorous Neotropical catfish. Aquaculture 505:12–17

Elesho FE, Krockel S, Ciavoni E, Sutter DAH, Verreth JAJ, Schrama JW (2021) Effect of feeding frequency on performance, nutrient digestibility, energy and nitrogen balances in juvenile African catfish (*Clarias gariepinus*) fed diets with two levels of crystalline methionine. Anim Feed Sci Tech 281:115098

FAO (2020) FAO aquaculture newsletter no. 61 (April). Rome

Gabriel NN, Omoregie E, Tjipute M, Kukuri L, Shilombwelwa L (2017) Short-term cycles of feed deprivation and refeeding on growth performance, feed utilisation, and fillet composition of hybrid tilapia (*Oreochromis mossambicus* x *O. niloticus*). Isr J Aquac 69:7

Gabriel NN, Omoregie E, Martin T, Kukuri L, Shilombwelwa L (2018) Compensatory growth response in *Oreochromis mossambicus* submitted to short-term cycles of feed deprivation and refeeding. Turk J Fish Aquat Sci 18:161–166

Gao Y, Lee JY (2012) Compensatory responses of Nile tilapia *Oreochromis niloticus* under different feed-deprivation regimes. Fish Aquatic Sci 15:305–311

Gao Y, Wang Z, Hur JW, Lee JY (2015) Body composition and compensatory growth in Nile tilapia *Oreochromis niloticus* under different feeding intervals. Chin J Oceanol Limnol 33:945–956

Gaylord TG, Gatlin DM III (2001) Dietary protein and energy modification to maximize compensatory growth of channel catfish (*Ictalurus punctatus*). Aquaculture 194:337–348

Goddard S (1996) Feeding, temperature, and water quality. In: Feed management in intensive aquaculture. Springer, Boston, pp 51–74

Halver JE, Hardy RW (2003) Nutrient flow and retention. In: Fish nutrition. Academic, pp 755–770
Hayward RS, Noltie DB, Wang N (1997) Use of compensatory growth to double hybrid sunfish growth rates. Trans Am Fish Soc 126:316–322
Hecht T (2013) A review of on-farm feed management practices for North African catfish (*Clarias gariepinus*) in sub-Saharan Africa. In: Hasan MR, New MB (eds) On-farm feeding and feed management in aquaculture. FAO fisheries and aquaculture technical paper no. 583. FAO, Rome, pp 463–479
Hisano H, Barbosa PTL, de Arruda Hayd L, Mattioli CC (2021) Comparative study of growth, feed efficiency, and hematological profile of Nile tilapia fingerlings in biofloc technology and recirculating aquaculture system. Trop Anim Health Prod 53:1–7
Huang Q, Huang K, Ma Y, Qin X, Wen Y, Sun L, Tang L (2015) Feeding frequency and rate effects on growth and physiology of juvenile genetically improved farmed Nile Tilapia. N Am J Aquac 77:503–512
Jobling M, Johansen SJS (1999) The lipostat, hyperphagia and catch-up growth. Aquac Res 30: 473–478
Khan S, Hossain MS, Haque MM (2009) Effects of feeding schedule on growth, production and economics of pangasiid catfish (*Pangasius hypophthalmus*) and silver carp (*Hypophthalmichthys molitrix*) polyculture. J Bangladesh Agric Univ 7:175–181
Lawan I, Hassan M, Yusuf A (2017) Effects of feeding frequency on growth and feed efficiency of rearing African catfish (*Clarias gariepinus,* Burchell 1822) fingerlings. ARC Int J Agribusiness Innov 4:1–8
Li MH, Robinson EH (2005) Effects of periodic peed deprivation on growth, feed efficiency, processing yield, and body composition of channel catfish *Ictlaurus puncrarus*. J World Aquac Soc 36:4
Li MH, Manning BB, Robinson EH (2004) Effect of daily feed intake on feed efficiency of juvenile channel catfish. N Am J Aquac 66:100–104
Li MH, Manning BB, Oberle DF, Robinson EH (2005) Effects of maintenance feeding regimens on weight gain, feed efficiency, and body condition of pond raised channel catfish. N Am J Aquac 67(2):129–132
Li H, Xu W, Jin J, Yang Y, Zhu X, Han D, Liu H, Xie S (2018) Effects of starvation on glucose and lipid metabolism in gibel carp (*Carassius auratus gibelio* var. CAS III). Aquaculture 496:166–175
Liu X, Shi H, He Q, Lin F, Wang Q, Xiao S, Dai Y, Zhang Y, Yang H, Zhao H (2020) Effect of starvation and refeeding on growth, gut microbiota and non-specific immunity in hybrid grouper (*Epinephelus fuscoguttatus*♀×*E. lanceolatus*♂). Fish Shellfish Immunol 97:182–193
Luo Z, Tan XY, Wang WM, Fan QX (2009) Effects of long-term starvation on body weight and body composition of juvenile channel catfish, *Ictalurus punctatus*, with special emphasis on amino acid and fatty acid changes. J Appl Ichthyol 25:184–189
Maciel JC, Francisco CJ, Miranda-Filho KC (2018) Compensatory growth and feed restriction in marine shrimp production, with emphasis on biofloc technology. Aquac Int 26:203–212
Marimuthu K, Umah R, Muralikrishnan S, Xavier R, Kathiresan S (2011) Effect of different feed application rate on growth, survival and cannibalism of African catfish, *Clarias gariepinus* fingerlings. Emir J Food Agric 23:330–337
McCue MD (2010) Starvation physiology: reviewing the different strategies animals use to survive a common challenge. Comp Biochem Physiol A Mol Integr Physiol 156:1–18
Min K (2015) Major aquaculture species and culture techniques for Africa. Zhejiang Science and Technology and Njala University Press
Mohanta KN, Rath SC, Nayak KC, Pradhan C, Mohanty TK, Giri SS (2017) Effect of restricted feeding and refeeding on compensatory growth, nutrient utilization and gain, production performance and whole body composition of carp cultured in earthen pond. Aquac Nutr 23: 460–469. https://doi.org/10.1111/anu.12414

Ndome CB, Ekwu AC, Ateb AA (2011) Effect of feeding frequency on feed consumption, growth and feed conversion of *Clarias gariepinus* X *Heterobranchus longifilis h*ybrids. Am Eurasian J Sci Res 6:6–12

Nwanna LC, Lemme A, Metwally A, Schwarz FJ (2012) Response of common carp (*Cyprinus carpio* L.) to supplemental DL-methionine and different feeding strategies. Aquaculture 356: 365–370

Ofor CO, Ukpabi C (2013) Effect of short-term cyclic feed deprivation on growth and economic limit of commercial feed based-indoor grow out of *Clarias gariepinus* (Burchell, 1822). Int J Fish Aquac 5:303–309

Okomoda VT, Aminem W, Hassan A, Martins CO (2019) Effects of feeding frequency on fry and fingerlings of African catfish *Clarias gariepinus*. Aquaculture 511:734232

Pantazis PA, Neofitou CN (2003) Feeding frequency and feed intake in the African catfish C*larias gariepinus* (Burchell 1822). Isr J Aquac 55:160–168

Paul AJ, Paul JM, Smith RL (1995) Compensatory growth in Alaska yellowfin sole, *Pleuronectes asper*, following food deprivation. J Fish Biol 46:442–448

Py C, Gonzalez RE, Pena-Rodriguez A (2022) Fitness cost in farmed fish and crustaceans. Rev Aquacult 14:1389–1477

Reigh RC, Williams MB, Jacob BJ (2006) Influence of repetitive periods of fasting and satiation feeding on growth and production characteristics of channel catfish, *Ictalurus punctatus*. Aquaculture 254:506–516

Robinson EH, Li MH (2007) Effects of fish size and feeding frequency on channel catfish production. Mississippi Agricultural and Forestry Experiment Station. https://thefishsite.com/articles/effects-of-fish-size-and-feeding-frequency-on-channel-catfish-production

Sakyi ME, Cai J, Tang J, Abarike ED, Xia L, Li P, Kuebutornye FKA, Zou Z, Liang Z, Jian J (2020) Effects of starvation and subsequent re-feeding on intestinal microbiota, and metabolic responses in Nile Tilapia, *Oreochromis niloticus*. Aquacult Rep 17:100370

Satia PB (2017) Regional review on status and trends in aquaculture development in sub-Saharan Africa—2010/ Revue regionale sur la situation et les tendances dans l'aquaculture en afrique subsaharienne—2010. FAO Fisheries and Aquaculture Circular, I, III, IV, V, 1-7, 9-23, 25-33, 35-41, 43-45, 47-51, 53-59, 61-67, 69-117, 119-137, 139-161, 163-191

Schram E, Verdege MCJ, Widjaja RTOBH, Kloet CJ, Foss A, Schelvis-Smit R, Imsland AK (2009) Impact of increased flow rate on specific growth rate of juvenile turbot (*Scophthalmus maximus,* Rafinesque 1810). Aquaculture 292:46–52

Shao JC, Zhu WC, Liu M, Wang L, Zhao W (2020) Cyclical fasting and refeeding is not an advisable feeding strategy for white shrimp (*Penaeus vannamei*). Aquacult Rep 18:100429

Tiogué CT, Kendi SFN, Tekou G, Tomedi-Tabi ME (2017) Compensatory responses of *Cyprinus carpio* (Linnaeus, 1758) fry under different feed-deprivation regimes in Happas in the Western–Cameroon. Annu Res Rev Biol 17:1–11

Turano MJ, Borski RJ, Daniels HV (2008) Effects of cyclic feeding on compensatory growth of hybrid striped bass (*Morone chrysops* × *M. saxitilis*) foodfish and water quality in production ponds. Aquac Res 39:1514–1523

Urbinati EC, Sarmiento SJ, Takahashi LS (2014) Short-term cycles of feed deprivation and refeeding promote full compensatory growth in the Amazon fish matrinxã (*Brycon amazonicus*). Aquaculture 433:430–433

Wurts W (2015) Using equations to improve feeding and growth of channel catfish. World Aquaculture 46:58–60

Yakupitage A (2013) On-farm feeding and feed management strategies in tropical aquaculture. In: Hasan MR, New MB (eds) On-farm feeding and feed management in aquaculture. FAO fisheries and aquaculture technical paper no. 583. FAO, Rome, pp 361–376

Yogev U, Barnes A, Giladi I, Gross A (2020) Potential environmental impact resulting from biased fish sampling in intensive aquaculture operations. Sci Total Environ 707:135630. https://doi.org/10.1016/j.scitotenv.2019.13563

Chapter 3
Black Soldier Fly (*Hermetia illucens*) Larvae Meal as a Sustainable Protein Source for Fish Feed Production in Kenya

Mary A. Opiyo, Rita N. Nairuti, Charles C. Ngugi, and Gladys Mwaka Holeh

Abstract Aquaculture has been ranked as one of the fastest-growing food sub-sectors, providing quality protein to better the livelihoods of rural communities alongside curbing malnutrition and food security globally. Nonetheless, the industry's sustainability has been threatened by the high cost of fish feeds, which account for approximately 60–70% of the total operational costs. Fish meal (FM) has been extensively utilised as the main source of protein in the diets of farmed finfishes. However, due to declining capture fisheries and competing uses from other animal feed producers, the ingredient has become a scarce resource with limited availability and high prices. Black soldier fly larvae (BSFL) have been identified as a promising alternative protein source in fish feeds. BSFL are documented to have high nutritional content: crude protein (of up to 64% dry matter), essential amino acids, fatty acids, and other micro-nutrients which are vital for the growth of fish. BSFL meal has the potential success of replacing FM in the diets of various fish species. This chapter focuses on analysing recent research work in BSFL proximate and chemical composition, its current utilisation in fish feeds and gaps to be filled in its complete utilisation as an ingredient in commercial feed production. This information is expected to help both cottage and commercial fish feed producers utilise BSFL in feed production in Kenya and further will promote the sustainability of the aquaculture industry.

Keywords Aquaculture · Black soldier fly larvae · Fish feeds · *Oreochromis niloticus*

M. A. Opiyo (✉) · R. N. Nairuti
Kenya Marine and Fisheries Research Institute, National Aquaculture Research Development and Training Center, Sagana, Kenya

C. C. Ngugi
Karatina University, School of Natural Resources and Environmental Studies, Karatina, Kenya

G. M. Holeh
Kenya Marine and Fisheries Research Institute, Mombasa Centre, Mombasa, Kenya

© The Author(s), under exclusive license to Springer Nature Singapore Pte Ltd. 2023
N. N. Gabriel et al. (eds.), *Emerging Sustainable Aquaculture Innovations in Africa*, Sustainable Agriculture and Food Security,
https://doi.org/10.1007/978-981-19-7451-9_3

3.1 Introduction

The aquaculture industry is faced with the challenge of the high cost of feeds which represents up to 60–70% of operational costs in fish production (Holeh et al. 2020). Fishmeal and fish oil have been the main source of protein and essential fats in the aquatic feed production (Betancor et al. 2016). This is due to the high nutritional value of fishmeal, balanced essential amino acids profile, high essential fatty acids, and phospholipids near to requirement levels of most cultivated aquatic organisms (Tacon 2018). However, high global demand and competition for fish meal (FM) from other animal feed manufacturers have increased the prices of the products, and the global supplies are on the decline (Montoya-Camacho et al. 2019; FAO 2020). These economic and sustainability concerns have led to the search for non-conventional ingredients from both plant and animal sources to replace fishmeal in fish diets (El-Sayed and Tacon 1997; El-Sayed 1998; Hasan and Chakrabarti 2009; Katya et al. 2017; Khalifa et al. 2018; Alfaro et al. 2019).

Research on insects focuses on various species of Coleoptera and Diptera, including the Black soldier fly (*Hermetia illucens*) (Burtle et al. 2012), common houseflies (*Musca domestica)* (Awoniyi 2007) and beetles (*Tenebrio molitor*) (Khosravi et al. 2018) as a potential replacement of fishmeal in aquaculture nutrition have gained attention in the recent years. This is attributed to the fact that they contain high protein levels with high availabilities since they can be reared on low-grade bio-wastes to effectively convert organic wastes into high-quality proteins (Veldkamp et al. 2012; Shumo et al. 2019a, b). Black soldier fly larvae (BSFL) appear to be superior among other insects as a potential source of animal protein for use in fish feed formulations (Henry et al. 2015). BSFL contains up to 50% crude protein (CP) and up to 35% lipids and has an amino acid profile that is similar to that of the FM (Elwert et al. 2010; Henry et al. 2015; Katya et al. 2017; Shumo et al. 2019a, b). Its sustainability is due to ease in production using organic wastes (Barragan-Fonseca et al. 2017; Ewald et al. 2020). Moreover, the Black soldier fly (BSF) is neither a non-vector nor a pest, and it is known to reduce the presence of harmful bacteria, especially *Escherichia coli* and *Salmonella enterica,* from food substrates (Liu et al. 2017; Shumo et al. 2019a, b). In most studies, dietary inclusion of BSFL in fish diets has improved fish growth, yields and reduced production cost, thus promoting profitability and resource utilisation (Kroeckel et al. 2012; Li et al. 2017; Fawole et al. 2020; Wachira et al. 2021).

3.2 Basic Culture Method of Black Soldier Fly

3.2.1 Life History and Culture Conditions

The BSF occurs in the tropical and sub-tropical regions of the world and possesses holometabolous metamorphosis (Nairuti et al. 2022). Their life cycle starts from an

Table 3.1 Abiotic factors requirements for rearing black soldier fly larvae (Barragan-Fonseca et al. 2017)

Parameter	Minimum	Optimal	Maximum
Temperature (°C)	12	26–27	36
Relative humidity (%)	25	60–70	99
Substrate moisture (%)	40	52–70	70
Light intensity/m^2/s	60	135–200	–

egg, which marks the end of the previous life stage, i.e. the female dies after laying eggs (Shumo et al. 2019a, b). A female fly lays 400–800 eggs in tiny, dry and well-sheltered cavities and close to a food source, preferably decomposing organic matter. After hatching, the cream-like larvae take up large amounts of decomposing organic matter and increase from a few millimetres to approximately 2.5 cm in length and 0.5 cm in width (Dortmans et al. 2017). Larval development takes 14–16 days under optimal conditions (Shumo et al. 2019a, b) (Table 3.1).

The pupae stage is symbolised by replacing the larval mouthparts with a hook-shaped structure and changing colour from cream to dark brown-charcoal grey. The pupation stage takes 2–3 weeks and is marked by the transformation of the pupa into a fly. The emergent fly does not feed and is only dependent on water for development along the life cycle (Dortmans et al. 2017; Zurbrügg et al. 2018). During this phase, the adult searches for a partner and copulates and the female lays eggs. The flies have been found to prefer copulating during the morning light, and females lay their eggs in well-shaded areas near substrates. Light intensity affects mating and egg fertilisation of BSF (Zurbrügg et al. 2018). The insects have higher mating activities in shaded areas, with the females ovipositing eggs in dark crevices (Shumo et al. 2019a, b).

3.2.2 *Culture Substrates for BSF Larvae*

The growth, production and maturation of *H. illucens* are highly dependent on the quantity and nutritional quality of the culture substrate. Adult BSF does not take up any food (Tomberlin et al. 2002) but instead survives on the food reserves built up during the larval stage and water (Diener et al. 2011; Nguyen et al. 2015). The larvae of the BSF require food that is obtained from suitable substrates. Previous studies indicate that substrates rich in protein and carbohydrates result in good larval growth and translate to larvae with high Crude protein and fat content (Dortmans et al. 2017). However, culture substrates with high oily amounts produce larvae with high lipid levels, which subsequently translates to lower protein content, because of the inverse relation of proteins and lipids in animal tissues (Mohanta et al. 2016).

Naturally, the BSF is found in faecal waste piles of livestock, poultry, swine and humans (Dortmans et al. 2017). Further, they are found colonizing domestic and wastes from industrial by-products, including kitchen vegetable and fruit wastes, decaying coffee pulp wastes and municipal organic wastes (Barragan-Fonseca et al. 2017). The presence of bacterial and fungal communities in these wastes acts as

Table 3.2 Nutritional composition of BSFL cultured in the different substrates in Kenya (Shumo et al. 2019a, b)

Parameters (% dry matter)	Chicken manure	Kitchen waste	Spent grain
Dry matter	80.7	87.7	83.1
Ash	9.3	9.6	11.6
Crude protein	41.1	33	41.3
Neutral detergent fibre	21.9	20.4	28.6
Acid detergent fibre	12.6	13.2	15
Ether extract	30.1	34.3	31

decomposition aids to further breakdown of organic matter making it easier for the larvae to access the nutrients (Dortmans et al. 2017). For the culture of BSF, the larvae can be fed on a wide range of organic food substrates rich in nitrogen and calcium (Ca) (Dortmans et al. 2017) and has a moisture content between 52 and 70% (Sophie et al. 2007; Shumo et al. 2019a, b). However, the wastes used as substrates should be free from potential pathogens, which can be harmful to human beings. They should not have food safety hazards as per the EU regulation of 2017 and must contain "products of non-animal origin" with those substrates made of flesh and manure (human food waste) explicitly excluded (EU Commission Regulation of 2017). In the United States of America, the Food and Drug Administration (FDA) also approved dried larvae of *Hermetia illucens* cultured in substrates comprising exclusively of feed grade materials containing not less than 34% CP and 32% fat for use in feeding salmonid fishes. These restrictions were implemented to fulfil the safety conditions for insect production for farmed fish and animal feed (Wang and Shelomi 2017). However, in Kenya, no regulations have been implemented to regulate the substrate used for BSFL production. The nutritional composition of cultured BSFL differs depending on the culture substrate. Substrates documented for use for BSFL culture include chicken manure, kitchen waste and spent grains (Table 3.2).

3.3 Biochemical Composition of BSF Larvae as a Feed Ingredient

3.3.1 Crude Protein and Fat Content

The protein and fat content of BSFL depends highly on the quality and quantity of the substrate used for the culture of the larvae (Nguyen et al. 2015; Barragan-Fonseca et al. 2017; Shumo et al. 2019a, b; Ewald et al. 2020). A study by Spranghers et al. 2017 reported significantly higher CP levels in larvae reared in restaurant waste (43.1%) compared to chicken feed and vegetable waste. Nguyen et al. (2015) also recorded higher protein and low fat in larvae fed on kitchen waste than those fed chicken feed. Previous studies have also reported higher fat content in

Table 3.3 Content of crude protein and crude fat (CF) of BSF larvae reared on different substrates. (Modified from Barragan-Fonseca et al. (2017)

Substrate	% Crude protein[a]	% Crude fat
Cattle manure	42.1	34.8
Chicken manure	40.1; 41.1	27.9
Swine manure	43.6; 43.2	26.4
Palm kernel meal	42.1; 45.8	27.5
Restaurant waste	43.1	39.2
Chicken feed	47.9	14.6
Liver	62.7	25.1
Fruits and vegetables	38.5; 30.84	26.63; 33.10
Fish	57.9	34.6

[a] All values are expressed on a dry matter basis

larvae reared on cattle manure (34.8%) in comparison to chicken (27.9%) and swine manure (26.4%) (Table 3.3).

3.3.2 *Amino Acid Content*

Essential amino acids (AA) are important in fish feeds and should be considered when selecting a fish feed ingredient. The AA content in BSFL is mainly influenced by the processing efficiency of the larvae. Defatting, which involves the mechanical or chemical removal of fat from the larvae, has been found to help increase the amino acid content of dried BSFL meal (Renna et al. 2017). Most studies have shown that the amino acid contents of the BSFL do not differ much based on the culture substrate (Table 3.4). However, some AA, like methionine, have been reported to be relatively low in BSFL meal compared to FM. Generally, BSFL meal has a good protein quality compared to FM and has higher contents of arginine, isoleucine, alanine, valine histidine and tryptophan (Barragan-Fonseca et al. 2017).

3.3.3 *Fatty Acids Content of BSF Larvae*

The BSF larvae meal is rich in monounsaturated fats but has lower polyunsaturated fatty acid percentages compared to other insects, such as housefly maggots, mealworms and adult crickets used in animal feed (Ghosh et al. 2017). BSFL contain between 58 and 72% saturated fatty acids and 19 and 40% mono- and polyunsaturated fatty acids (Table 3.5) (Larouche 2019). The quality and quantity of fatty acid content in the BSFL are highly influenced by the type of substrate used. They tend to accumulate more lipids when the larvae are fed on a lipid-rich animal diet (Wang and Shelomi 2017). Larvae fed on fish by-products and fish wastes have increased levels of n-3 polyunsaturated fatty acids (n-3 PUFA), a-linolenic acid (ALA), eicosapentaenoic acid (EPA) and docosahexaenoic acid (DHA) in their tissues

Table 3.4 Amino acid profile of the BSF larvae. (Source: Spranghers et al. (2017)

Parameter (g/kg dry matter)	Chicken feed	Digestate	Vegetable waste	Restaurant waste
Essential amino acids				
Isoleucine	17.2	18.4	17.3	19.1
Leucine	28.6	29.5	28	30.6
Lysine	23.4	25.7	22.6	23
Arginine	20.3	20.3	20	19.9
Methionine	7.6	8.7	7.6	7.1
Histidine	13.6	13.5	12.4	3.8
Phenylalanine	17	18.7	16.3	16.4
Threonine	16.4	16.8	15.4	16.2
Non-essential amino acids				
Alanine	25.2	24.3	24.2	27.8
Cystine	2.5	2.4	2.1	2.2
Glutamic acid	41.9	39.8	41.3	45.8
Glycine	22.6	22.6	22.2	25.2
Proline	22.5	22.1	21.4	25.1
Serine	16.6	15.5	15	15.9
Aspartate	37.8	33.6	35.9	36.9
Tryptophan	6.7	6.2	5.8	5.4
Valine	24.1	24.9	24.8	28.2

Table 3.5 Fatty acid profile of the black soldier fly larvae. (Data adapted and modified from (Larouche 2019))

Parameter (% lipid)	Content in BSF larvae (Oonincx et al. 2015; Liu et al. 2017)
Lauric (C12:0)	29–61
Myristic (C14:0)	7–10
Palmitic (C16:0)	8–17
Palmitoleic (C16:1n-7)	3–7
Stearic (C18:0)	1–3
Oleic (C18:1n-9)	8–18
Linoleic (C18:2n-6)	4–17
Alpha-linolenic (C18:3n-3)	0–2
Unsaturated fatty acid	18–37
Saturated fatty acid	58–80

(Sophie et al. 2007; Renna et al. 2017). This indicates that BSFL provide the necessary fatty acids requirements to meet the different nutritional requirements of different fish species, which is 0.5–1% (Andersen et al. 2016).

3.3.4 Mineral Content of BSF Larvae

The mineral content of the BSFL larvae is profoundly influenced by the type of substrate used for feeding the larvae and the stage of development (Table 3.6). For instance, a study by Shumo et al. (2019a, b) reported higher phosphorus levels in BSFL reared on spent grain compared to kitchen waste and cattle manure. High Ca has been reported in larvae fed on digestate compared to chicken feed, vegetable and restaurant waste. The high Ca concentration and ash contents (9 and 28% dry matter, respectively) reported in the larvae were attributed to the secretion of calcium carbonate ($CaCO_3$) by the epidermis (Finke 2013). On the other hand, the low Ca content (0.03%) in the newly emerged adults has been attributed to the fact that the pupal cuticle that is concentrated with Ca is shed off to give rise to the adult fly, indicating that the Ca levels are affected by the larvae stage of development (Finke 2013; Spranghers et al. 2017).

3.4 Utilisation of BSF Larvae in Fish Feed Formulation

Earlier studies have documented the utilisation of BSFL in fish feed formulation (Henry et al. 2015; Barragan-Fonseca et al. 2017; Katya et al. 2017; Dietz and Liebert 2018; Fawole et al. 2020; Wachira et al. 2021). BSFL have attracted enormous attention due to their higher reproductive capacity, short life cycle, ability to convert organic matter into high-quality protein and their capacity to thrive in a wide array of environments (Barragan-Fonseca et al. 2017). Additionally, the high protein content, digestibility, and amino acid profiles of the BSFL have been the selling point for this meal in fish diets. The BSFL meal has successfully replaced conventional protein sources in the diets of salmon (*Salmo salar*) (Weththasinghe et al. 2021), African catfish (*Clarias gariepinus*) (Fawole et al. 2020), European sea bass (*Dicentrarchus labrax*) (Moutinho et al. 2021), Nile tilapia (*Oreochromis*

Table 3.6 Mineral composition of BSF larvae reared on three different rearing substrates. (Data adapted and modified from Tschirner and Simon (2015) and Shumo et al. (2019a, b))

Mineral composition g/kg DM)	Cattle manure	Kitchen waste	Spent grain	Sugar beet pulp	Requirements by fish (National Research Council (NRC) 2011)
Phosphorus	3.9	4.1	4.6	1.3	7 g
Potassium	4.9	5.7	4.4	1.9	1–3 g
Calcium	3.2	2.0	1.7	6.2	5 g
Magnesium	4.0	3.3	3.5	0.5	500 mg
Iron	0.6	2.2	0.3	0.02	50–100 mg
Copper	0.4	0.2	0.5	1.2	1–4 g
Manganese	1.4	0.9	1.1	0.05	20–50 mg
Zinc	0.3	0.3	0.3	0.01	30–100 mg

niloticus) (Nairuti et al. 2021; Wachira et al. 2021), rainbow trout (*Oncorhynchus mykiss*) (Sophie et al. 2007) and turbot (*Psetta maxima*) (Kroeckel et al. 2012).

3.5 BSF Larvae Meal Effect on Fish Growth Performance

The inclusion of BSFL meals in the diets of *O. niloticus* do not lead to any negative effect on the body weight gain (BWG) and specific growth rate (SGR) of the fish (Devic et al. 2018; Toriz-Roldan et al. 2019). Similarly, a partial or total dietary replacement of FM with BSFL meal did not lead to differences in the BWG and SGR of juvenile Japanese bass (*Lateolabrax japonicus)* and rainbow trout (*Oncorhynchus mykiss*), respectively (Wang and Shelomi 2017). A study carried out by Fawole et al. (2020) recorded better final weight and BWG when 50% FM was replaced by BSFL meal in the diets of *C. gariepinus*. Similarly, Muin et al. (2017) reported the highest weight gain and SGR values when BSFL meal was used to replace 50% FM in the diets of Nile tilapia (Table 3.7). Additionally, BSFL meal has been demonstrated to be a promising FM replacement in the diets of the pacific white shrimp (*Litopenaeus vannamei*) at a 25% inclusions level (Cummins et al. 2017).

3.6 Cost Reduction of Fish Feeds Using Black Soldier Fly Larvae Meal

Reducing feed costs is critical to the profitability and sustainability of aquaculture production since fish feeds account for more than half of the operating cost (Holeh et al. 2020). BSF larvae have lower prices than other animal-based products, like fish and soybean meals in Kenya. The cost of dry BSFL ranges from 0.5 to 0.7 USD, while the FM is from 0.9 to 1.2 USD and soybean meal is from 1.5 to 1.7 USD in Kenya (Nairuti et al. 2022). These low costs of BSFL could be because they are produced and fed on low-value organic wastes, which are readily available (Shumo et al. 2019a, b). Previous studies have reported a reduction in the cost of feed when BSF meal was used to replace primary conventional sources of proteins, especially soybean meal and FM (Onsongo et al. 2018; Wachira et al. 2021). Abdel-Tawwab et al. (2020) reported decreased diet costs at increasing levels of BSFL meal in European sea bass diets from 0.71 to 0.60 USD kg^{-1}. Similarly, Wachira et al. (2021) recorded 14.4% cost reduction in feed production when the FM was replaced by a BSFL meal at 100% for Nile tilapia diets and a cost–benefit ratio of 2.172 when 33% of FM was replaced with BSFL meal. This indicates that the utilisation of BSFL reduces the cost of feeds used in fish production.

Table 3.7 Growth performance of different species of fish fed diets with different BSFL meal levels. (Adapted and modified from Nairuti et al. (2022))

Fish species	Attribute/element tested	Replacement levels (%)
Jian carp (*Cyprinus carpio*) (Li et al. 2017)	Substitution of 100% FM by defatted BSFL meal in diets for Jian carp had a negative effect on growth performance and feed utilisation efficiencies	0, 25, 50, 75, **100**
Meagre (*Argyrosomus regius*) juveniles (Guerreiro et al. 2020)	10% of *Hermetia illucens* can be included in Meagre diets without major adverse effects on growth, feed utilisation, whole-body composition and fatty acid profile; further increase in the substitution rates leads to negative effects on the growth performance parameters	**10,** 20, 30
Nile tilapia (*Oreochromis niloticus*) (Dietz and Liebert 2018)	Replacement of soy protein concentrate by partly defatted BSFL meal up to a level of 50% had no negative effect on growth performance and improved the dietary protein quality of tilapia feeds under study	25, **50,** 100
Siberian sturgeon (*Acipenser baerii*) (Caimi et al. 2020)	Overall, this study showed that it is possible to replace up to 25% of FM with BSFL meal in the diet of Siberian sturgeons (equal to 18.5% HIM inclusion level) without affecting the growth performance	**25**, 50, 100
Rainbow trout (*Oncorhynchus mykiss*) (Dumas et al. 2018) Nile tilapia (*Oreochromis niloticus*) (Muin et al. 2017)	The maximum inclusion of BSFL meal recommended in rainbow trout diets is 13%; further increase in the substitution leads to a decrease in the growth parameters The study suggests that substitution of FM with BSFL up to 100% is possible without any negative effects on the growth performance, feed utilisation efficiency, body composition	0, 6.6, **13.2,** 26.4 0, 25, 50, 75, **100**
European sea bass (*Dicentrarchus labrax*) (Abdel-Tawwab et al. 2020)	With the 3 substitution levels of FM with BSFL meal at (25, 35 and 50%), BSF larvae meal can effectively replace FM up to 50% without any negative effects on the growth performance	25, 35, **50**
Rice field eel (*Monopterus albus*) (Hu et al. 2020)	Lower substitution rates (5.26, 10.52%) of FM by BSFL meal in the diets of Rice field eel exhibited low values of the growth performance parameters as compared to higher substitution rates of FM by BSF larvae meal made at 15.78%	5.26, 10.52, **15.78**
African catfish (*Clarias gariepinus*) (Fawole et al. 2020)	Substitution of FM by BSFL up to 75% leads to no negative effects on the growth performance and nutrient utilisation	0, 25, 50, **75**
Juvenile turbot (*Psetta maxima*) (Kroeckel et al. 2012)	The maximum inclusion of BSFL meal recommended in Juvenile turbot diets is 33%; further increase in the substitution	0, 17, **33,** 49, 64, 76

(continued)

Table 3.7 (continued)

Fish species	Attribute/element tested	Replacement levels (%)
	leads to a decrease in the growth performance parameters and nutrient utilisation	

*Values in bold represent the recommended replacement or inclusion levels

3.7 Conclusion

The BSF larvae have shown very promising results in aquaculture due to their high levels of CP, balanced amino acid profile and fatty acid profile, together with high mineral contents, which makes them suitable as a dietary component in fish feed. Different studies have reported that it can replace FM up to100% in diets of several fish species. However, in some cases, levels above 50% have resulted in a negative effect on growth performance. This is probably due to the high chitin and fat content of the larvae. Therefore, proper culture systems for the BSFL and further processing by defatting and removing the chitin contents can improve the utilisation of BSFL by a wide range of fish species to improve fish growth performance and reduce aquaculture production costs. Further work to promote BSFL rearing and commercialisation in Kenya is needed to achieve the full potential of its use as a protein feed ingredient. BSFL rearing will also provide additional ecosystem services through municipal and organic waste management leading to environmental ecological balance.

References

Abdel-Tawwab M, Khalil RH, Metwally AA et al (2020) Effects of black soldier fly (*Hermetia illucens* L.) larvae meal on growth performance, organs-somatic indices, body composition, and hemato-biochemical variables of European sea bass, *Dicentrarchus labrax*. Aquaculture 522: 735136. https://doi.org/10.1016/j.aquaculture.2020.735136

Alfaro AO, Núñez WL, Marcia J, Fernández IM (2019) The cricket (*Gryllus assimilis*) as an alternative food versus commercial concentrate for tilapia (*Oreochromis* sp.) in the nursery stage. J Agric Sci 11:97. https://doi.org/10.5539/jas.v11n6p97

Andersen SM, Waagbø R, Espe M (2016) Functional amino acids in fish health and welfare. Front Biosci (Elite Ed) 8:143–169. https://doi.org/10.2741/757

Awoniyi TAM (2007) Health, nutritional and consumers' acceptability assurance of maggot meal inclusion in livestock diet: a review. Int J Trop Med 2:52–56

Barragan-Fonseca KB, Dicke M, van Loon JJA (2017) Nutritional value of the black soldier fly (*Hermetia illucens* L.) and its suitability as animal feed—a review. J Insects Food Feed 3:105–120. https://doi.org/10.3920/JIFF2016.0055

Betancor MB, Sprague M, Montero D et al (2016) Replacement of marine fish oil with de novo Omega-3 oils from transgenic *Camelina sativa* in feeds for Gilthead Sea bream (*Sparus aurata* L.). Lipids 51:1171–1191. https://doi.org/10.1007/s11745-016-4191-4

Burtle G, Newton GL, Sheppard DC (2012) Mass production of black soldier fly prepupae for aquaculture diets. 6. engormix.com/Aquaculture

Caimi C, Renna M, Lussiana C et al (2020) First insights on black soldier fly (*Hermetia illucens* L.) larvae meal dietary administration in Siberian sturgeon (Acipenser baerii Brandt) juveniles. Aquaculture 515:734539. https://doi.org/10.1016/j.aquaculture.2019.734539

Cummins VC, Rawles SD, Thompson KR et al (2017) Evaluation of black soldier fly (*Hermetia illucens*) larvae meal as partial or total replacement of marine fish meal in practical diets for Pacific white shrimp (*Litopenaeus vannamei*). Aquaculture 473:337–344. https://doi.org/10.1016/j.aquaculture.2017.02.022

Devic E, Leschen W, Murray F, Little DC (2018) Growth performance, feed utilization and body composition of advanced nursing Nile tilapia (Oreochromis niloticus) fed diets containing Black Soldier Fly (Hermetia illucens) larvae meal. Aquac Nutr 24:416–423

Diener S, Zurbrügg C, Gutiérrez FR, Zurbrügg C, Tockner K (2011) Black soldier fly larvae for organic waste treatment – prospects and constraints. In: Proceedings of the WasteSafe 2011 – 2nd international conference on solid waste management in the developing countries, p 275

Dietz C, Liebert F (2018) Does graded substitution of soy protein concentrate by an insect meal respond on growth and utilization in Nile tilapia (*Oreochromis niloticus*)? Aquac Reports 12: 43–48. https://doi.org/10.1016/j.aqrep.2018.09.001

Dortmans B, Diener S, Verstappen B, Zurbrügg C (2017) Black soldier fly biowaste processing—a step-by-step guide. Swiss Federal Institute of Aquatic Science and Technology, Dübendorf

Dumas A, Raggi T, Barkhouse J et al (2018) The oil fraction and partially defatted meal of black soldier fly larvae (*Hermetia illucens*) affect differently growth performance, feed efficiency, nutrient deposition, blood glucose and lipid digestibility of rainbow trout (*Oncorhynchus mykiss*). Aquaculture 492:24–34. https://doi.org/10.1016/j.aquaculture.2018.03.038

El-Sayed AFM (1998) Total replacement of fish meal with animal protein sources in Nile tilapia, *Oreochromis niloticus* (L.), feeds. Aquac Res 29:275–280. https://doi.org/10.1046/j.1365-2109.1998.00199.x

El-Sayed A-FM, Tacon AGJ (1997) Fishmeal replacers for tilapia: a review. Cah Options Méditerranéennes 22:205–224

Elwert C, Knips I, Katz P (2010) A novel protein source: Maggot meal of the Black Soldier fly (Hermetia illucens) in broiler feed. 11 Tagung Schweine- und Geflügelernährung 140–142

Ewald N, Vidakovic A, Langeland M et al (2020) Fatty acid composition of black soldier fly larvae (*Hermetia illucens*)—possibilities and limitations for modification through diet. Waste Manag 102:40–47. https://doi.org/10.1016/j.wasman.2019.10.014

FAO (2020) The state of world fisheries and aquaculture 2020. In: Sustainability in action. Food and Agriculture Organization of the United Nations, Rome

Fawole FJ, Adeoye AA, Tiamiyu LO et al (2020) Substituting fishmeal with *Hermetia illucens* in the diets of African catfish (*Clarias gariepinus*): effects on growth, nutrient utilization, haemato-physiological response, and oxidative stress biomarker. Aquaculture 518:734849. https://doi.org/10.1016/j.aquaculture.2019.734849

Finke MD (2013) Complete nutrient content of four species of feeder insects. Zoo Biol 32:27–36. https://doi.org/10.1002/zoo.21012

Ghosh S, Lee SM, Jung C, Meyer-Rochow VB (2017) Nutritional composition of five commercial edible insects in South Korea. J Asia Pac Entomol 20:686–694. https://doi.org/10.1016/j.aspen.2017.04.003

Guerreiro I, Castro C, Antunes B et al (2020) Catching black soldier fly for meagre: growth, whole-body fatty acid profile and metabolic responses. Aquaculture 516:734613. https://doi.org/10.1016/j.aquaculture.2019.734613

Hasan MR, Chakrabarti R (2009) Use of algae and aquatic macrophytes as feed in small-scale aquaculture. Food and agriculture Organization of the United Nations (FAO), Rome

Henry M, Gasco L, Piccolo G, Fountoulaki E (2015) Review on the use of insects in the diet of farmed fish: past and future. Anim Feed Sci Technol 203:1–22. https://doi.org/10.1016/j.anifeedsci.2015.03.001

Holeh GM, Appenteng P, Opiyo MA et al (2020) Effects of intermittent feeding regimes on growth performance and economic benefits of Amur catfish (*Silurus asotus*). Aquat Res 3:167–176. https://doi.org/10.3153/ar20015
Hu Y, Huang Y, Tang T et al (2020) Effect of partial black soldier fly (*Hermetia illucens* L.) larvae meal replacement of fish meal in practical diets on the growth, digestive enzyme and related gene expression for rice field eel (*Monopterus albus*). Aquac Reports 17:100345. https://doi.org/10.1016/j.aqrep.2020.100345
Katya K, Borsra MZS, Ganesan D et al (2017) Efficacy of insect larval meal to replace fish meal in juvenile barramundi, *Lates calcarifer* reared in freshwater. Int Aquat Res 9:303–312. https://doi.org/10.1007/s40071-017-0178-x
Khalifa NSA, Belal IEH, El-Tarabily KA et al (2018) Evaluation of replacing fish meal with corn protein concentrate in Nile tilapia, *Oreochromis niloticus* fingerlings commercial diet. Aquac Nutr 24:143–152. https://doi.org/10.1111/anu.12542
Khosravi S, Kim E, Lee YS, Lee SM (2018) Dietary inclusion of mealworm (*Tenebrio molitor*) meal as an alternative protein source in practical diets for juvenile rockfish (Sebastes schlegeli). Entomol Res 48:214–221. https://doi.org/10.1111/1748-5967.12306
Kroeckel S, Harjes AGE, Roth I et al (2012) When a turbot catches a Fly: evaluation of a pre-pupae meal of the black soldier fly (*Hermetia illucens*) as fish meal substitute—growth performance and chitin degradation in juvenile turbot (*Psetta maxima*). Aquaculture 364–365:345–352. https://doi.org/10.1016/j.aquaculture.2012.08.041
Larouche J (2019) Processing methods for the black soldier fly (*Hermetia illucens*) larvae: from feed withdrawal periods to killing methods
Li S, Ji H, Zhang B et al (2017) Defatted black soldier fly (*Hermetia illucens*) larvae meal in diets for juvenile Jian carp (*Cyprinus carpio* var. Jian): growth performance, antioxidant enzyme activities, digestive enzyme activities, intestine and hepatopancreas histological structure. Aquaculture 477:62–70. https://doi.org/10.1016/j.aquaculture.2017.04.015
Liu X, Chen X, Wang H et al (2017) Dynamic changes of nutrient composition throughout the entire life cycle of black soldier fly. PLoS One 12:e0182601. https://doi.org/10.1371/journal.pone.0182601
Mohanta KN, Subramanian S, Korikanthimath VS (2016) Potential of earthworm (*Eisenia foetida*) as dietary protein source for rohu (*Labeo rohita*) advanced fry. Cogent Food Agric 2:1138594. https://doi.org/10.1080/23311932.2016.1138594
Montoya-Camacho N, Marquez-Ríos E, Castillo-Yáñez FJ et al (2019) Advances in the use of alternative protein sources for tilapia feeding. Rev Aquac 11:515–526. https://doi.org/10.1111/raq.12243
Moutinho S, Pedrosa R, Magalhães R et al (2021) Black soldier fly (*Hermetia illucens*) pre-pupae larvae meal in diets for European seabass (*Dicentrarchus labrax*) juveniles: effects on liver oxidative status and fillet quality traits during shelf-life. Aquaculture 533:736080. https://doi.org/10.1016/j.aquaculture.2020.736080
Muin H, Taufek NM, Kamarudin MS, Razak SA (2017) Growth performance, feed utilization and body composition of Nile tilapia (*Oreochromis niloticus*) fed with different levels of black soldier fly, *Hermetia illucens* (Linnaeus, 1758) maggot meal diet. Iran J Fish Sci 16:567–577
Nairuti RN, Munguti JM, Waidbacher H, Zollitsch W (2021) Growth performance and survival rates of Nile tilapia (*Oreochromis niloticus* L.) reared on diets containing Black soldier fly (*Hermetia illucens* L.) larvae meal. Die Bodenkultur J Land Manag Food Environ 72:9–19. https://doi.org/10.2478/boku-2021-0002
Nairuti RN, Musyoka SN, Yegon MJ, Opiyo MA (2022) Utilization of black soldier fly (*Hermetia illucens* Linnaeus) larvae as a protein source for fish feed: a review. Aquac Stud 22: AQUAST697. https://doi.org/10.4194/AQUAST697
National Research Council (NRC) (2011) Nutrient requirements of fish and shrimp. National Academies Press, Washington

Nguyen TTX, Tomberlin JK, Vanlaerhoven S (2015) Ability of Black Soldier Fly (Diptera: Stratiomyidae) larvae to recycle food waste. Environ Entomol 44:406–410. https://doi.org/10.1093/ee/nvv002

Onsongo VO, Osuga IM, Gachuiri CK et al (2018) Insects for income generation through animal feed: effect of dietary replacement of soybean and fish meal with black soldier fly meal on broiler growth and economic performance. J Econ Entomol 111:1966–1973. https://doi.org/10.1093/jee/toy118

Oonincx DGAB, Van Broekhoven S, Van Huis A, Van Loon JJA (2015) Feed conversion, survival and development, and composition of four insect species on diets composed of food by-products. PLoS One 10:1–21. https://doi.org/10.1371/journal.pone.0144601

Renna M, Schiavone A, Gai F et al (2017) Evaluation of the suitability of a partially defatted black soldier fly (*Hermetia illucens* L.) larvae meal as ingredient for rainbow trout (Oncorhynchus mykiss Walbaum) diets. J Anim Sci Biotechnol 8:1–13. https://doi.org/10.1186/s40104-017-0191-3

Shumo M, Khamis FM, Tanga CM et al (2019a) Influence of temperature on selected life-history traits of black soldier fly (*Hermetia illucens*) reared on two common urban organic waste streams in Kenya. Animals 9:79. https://doi.org/10.3390/ani9030079

Shumo M, Osuga IM, Khamis FM et al (2019b) The nutritive value of black soldier fly larvae reared on common organic waste streams in Kenya. Sci Rep 9:1–13. https://doi.org/10.1038/s41598-019-46603-z

Sophie S-H, Sheppard DC, Tomberlin JK et al (2007) Fly prepupae as a feedstuff for rainbow trout, *Oncorhynchus mykiss*. J World Aquac Soc 38:59–67

Spranghers T, Ottoboni M, Klootwijk C et al (2017) Nutritional composition of black soldier fly (*Hermetia illucens*) prepupae reared on different organic waste substrates. J Sci Food Agric 97:2594–2600. https://doi.org/10.1002/jsfa.8081

Tacon AGJ (2018) Global trends in aquaculture and compound aquafeed production. World Acquaculture 49:33–46

Tomberlin JK, Sheppard DC, Joyce JA (2002) Selected life-history traits of black soldier flies (Diptera: Stratiomyidae) reared on three artificial diets. Ann Entomol Soc Am 95:379–386

Toriz-Roldan A, Ruiz-Vega J, García-Ulloa M et al (2019) Assessment of dietary supplementation levels of black soldier Fly, *Hemertia illucens* L, pre-pupae meal for Juvenile Nile Tilapia, *Oreochromis niloticus*. Southwest Entomol 44:251. https://doi.org/10.3958/059.044.0127

Tschirner M, Simon A (2015) Influence of different growing substrates and processing on the nutrient composition of black soldier fly larvae destined for animal feed. J Insects Food Feed 1:249–259. https://doi.org/10.3920/JIFF2014.0008

Veldkamp T, van Duinkerken G, van Huis A et al (2012) Insects as a sustainable feed ingredient in pig and poultry diets—a feasibility study. Rep 38:48195

Wachira MN, Osuga IM, Munguti JM et al (2021) Efficiency and improved profitability of insect-based aquafeeds for farming Nile tilapia fish (*Oreochromis niloticus* L.). Animals 11:2599. https://doi.org/10.3390/ani11092599

Wang Y-S, Shelomi M (2017) Review of black soldier Fly (*Hermetia illucens*) as animal feed and human food. Foods 6:91. https://doi.org/10.3390/foods6100091

Weththasinghe P, Hansen J, Nøkland D et al (2021) Full-fat black soldier fly larvae (*Hermetia illucens*) meal and paste in extruded diets for Atlantic salmon (*Salmo salar*): effect on physical pellet quality, nutrient digestibility, nutrient utilization and growth performances. Aquaculture 530:735785. https://doi.org/10.1016/j.aquaculture.2020.735785

Zurbrügg C, Dortmans B, Fadhila A et al (2018) From pilot to full scale operation of a waste-to-protein treatment facility. Detritus 1:18–22. https://doi.org/10.26403/detritus/2018.22

Chapter 4
Waste to Feed: An Emerging Technology to Improve Aquaculture in Africa

Kenneth Prudence Abasubong, Ndakalimwe Naftal Gabriel, Jean-Jacques Yao Adjoumani, and Aniefiokmkpong Okokon Okon

Abstract As a result of globalization, the quantity and generation rate of solid waste in Africa have increased tremendously. This calls for the need to salvage the situation before it gets out of hand. Most African countries dump waste in landfills where there is overflow and burnt, causing severe health and safety concerns. Therefore, instead of taking this waste to landfills, it is significant to reuse it to culture animal feed. From waste to feed might be an alternative feed ingredient to boost the African aquaculture industry. On the other hand, it enables sustainable aquaculture production with less reliance on fish meals. As a result, the aquaculture industry must ramp up its quest for alternative components made from renewable natural resources. Microbial and insect protein have been considered long-term components, owing to their ability to convert non-food lignocellulosic biomass into significant protein resources. This chapter outlined the importance of microbial and insect meals to aquatic animals and the steps involved in turning wastes into proteins. Furthermore, we discuss their nutritional capacity, growth promoters, and the immunoregulatory functions of these resources in aquaculture. However, several advancements in aquaculture nutrition and considerations for the future development of sustainable and safe aquaculture production are also discussed.

Keywords Aquaculture industry · Aquatic products · Fish meal replacement · Waste · Microbial resources · Insect

K. P. Abasubong (✉) · J.-J. Y. Adjoumani
Key Laboratory of Aquatic Nutrition and Feed Science of Jiangsu Province, College of Animal Science and Technology, Nanjing Agricultural University, Nanjing, China

N. N. Gabriel
Department of Fisheries and Ocean Sciences, Faculty of Agriculture, Engineering, and Natural Science, Sam Nujoma Campus, University of Namibia, Henties Bay, Namibia

A. O. Okon
Department of Animal and Environmental Biology, University of Uyo, Uyo, Akwa Ibom State, Nigeria

© The Author(s), under exclusive license to Springer Nature Singapore Pte Ltd. 2023
N. N. Gabriel et al. (eds.), *Emerging Sustainable Aquaculture Innovations in Africa*, Sustainable Agriculture and Food Security,
https://doi.org/10.1007/978-981-19-7451-9_4

4.1 Introduction

Aquaculture is the only way to meet the growing need for animal protein as wild fish and crustaceans become scarce (Daniel 2018; Stankus 2021). Therefore, it is significant to expand aquaculture to improve food security. However, aquaculture relies heavily on a steady source of fish meal (FM), a vital ingredient in commercial fish feeds. Aquaculture has put growing pressure on wild fish to support farmed fish, causing wild fish supplies to fall rapidly (Stankus 2021). The rising costs of aquafeeds, such as meat meals, and FM, representing 60–70% of the total production expenses, impede further aquaculture development. To alleviate this pressure, an alternative protein source that is low cost and ecologically friendly could provide additional nutritional positive health effects without affecting fish growth and health. However, plant-based protein sources have been suggested as possible FM substitutes. However, their major setbacks, such as detrimental consequences on microbial community and intestine structure, high anti-nutrient content, low digestibility, and lower feed intake, have made their utilization unacceptable in fish diets (Table 4.1) (Farhangi and Carter 2015; Øverland et al. 2009; Francis et al. 2001). Although animal protein by-products, such as fish blood meal (El-Haroun et al. 2012), processing wastes (Hardy et al. 2007), meat, bone, and feather meal (Bureau et al. 2000), have some unique features over plant-based alternatives, including better digestibility and the non-availability of anti-nutrient elements, they seem to be expensive and have limited availability (Karimi et al. 2018). However, using human food as an ingredient for fish could pose some challenges that could affect the standard of living.

In 2015, fish and other aquatic items comprised roughly 26% of animal protein consumption in the least developed countries (LDCs), compared to 11% in developed countries (FAO 2018). So, by 2050, when the world's population reaches nine billion people, Africa, Latin America, and Asia will need to boost food production by 300%, 80%, and 70%, respectively, to feed the estimated populations of two billion, 810 million, and 5.4 billion people in their respective regions (Anon 1997). So, fish consumption and demand for a cheap protein source are rising due to the rapid growth of the human population and increasing standard of living. Rapid urbanization, rising economic activity, and population increase in Africa have produced unprecedented levels of waste. Since the waste pollution from these sites has reached an emergency level across Africa, this has consequently expanded hazardous waste material sites. Waste generation in Africa is predicted to quadruple by 2050, rising from 174 million tonnes annually in 2016 to roughly 516 million tonnes annually (UNEP (2018). However, Africa's average rate of rubbish collection is just about 55% of the total amount of waste. Notably, more than 90% of waste in Africa is disposed of in unregulated dumps and landfills, frequently with open burning in the aftermath. Most significantly, 19 of the 50 largest dumpsites in the world are in Africa, particularly in Sub-Saharan Africa. According to composition, roughly 13% of the municipal solid trash produced in Africa is plastic, while 57% is organic waste (OECD 2016). Currently, landfills are where most of the organic

Table 4.1 The advantages and disadvantages of an alternative fish diet

Alternative feed	Advantages	Disadvantages	References
Soybean meal	• EAA profile is favourable, and the protein level is high • Possibility of making soy protein concentration (low in anti-nutritional factors, soluble carbohydrates)	• Contains saponins, phytic acid • Some processing techniques (solvent extraction) leave anti-nutrient molecules in the food	Bandara (2018)
Wheat gluten meals	• On a dry matter basis, it comprises 85% protein • Most fish species, such as Atlantic salmon, Coho salmon, and Rainbow trout, have a higher digestibility • Fish distal intestine tissues show no morphological alterations	• Deficiency in lysine, methionine, and arginine	Bandara (2018)
Sunflower meal	• Dehulling and other preprocessing processes remove a greater amount of fibre	• Higher content of fibre • Higher in protease inhibitors, arginase inhibitors, and phytic acids	Bandara (2018)
Canola/ Rapeseed	• Ability to produce canola protein concentrate by aqueous extraction of fibre (higher protein content) • Good source of linolenic acid and low levels of linoleic acid in rapeseed oil	• It contains a higher amount of fibre and glucosinolates • Higher content of phytic acids and glucosinolates	Bandara (2018)
Pulses	• Possibility of producing protein concentrates to boost protein intake	• Higher carbohydrate content than protein • Higher content of phytic acid and tannins	Bandara (2018)
Lupins	• Arginine and glutamic acid levels are high, but anti-nutritional factors are low	• Deficiency in methionine and lysine • Presence of alkaloids	Bandara (2018)
Rice protein concentrate	• High protein and lipid content	• Deficiency in lysine	Abasubong et al. (2018)
Guar meal	• Guar meal can be used in place of soy meal without affecting the growth of some fish	• Anti-nutritional and anti-digestive chemicals, such as phytate, protease, residual gum, saponin, and inhibitor tannin, are present • Gastrointestinal evacuation takes time • Indigestible amino acids • Guar meal availability is influenced by oil output and guar gum utilization	Nidhina and Muthukumar (2015); Ullah et al. (2016)

(continued)

Table 4.1 (continued)

Alternative feed	Advantages	Disadvantages	References
Wheat	• Cheaper to obtained	• Starch content is higher (usually more than 70%) • A lysine deficit is seen • The protein content is low (11%)	Draganovic et al. (2013); Sørensen et al. (2011)
Blood meal (Cow blood)	• Higher protein content • Relatively rice in lysine content	• They are deficiency Methionine content • Heat sensitivity and drying conditions have a big impact on protein digestion	Aladetohun and Sogbesan (2013); Hussain et al. (2011)
Feather meal (Hydrolysed)	• They are rich in cystine (74–61%) and protein content	• Very hard to digest • Low in lysine and methionine • During processing with application heat typically deteriorates hemoglobin and causes low palatability	Grazziotin et al. (2008); Yu et al. (2020)
Poultry by-products	• Free from anti-nutrient	• Expensive feed ingredient in aqua diets • Low level of lysine, methionine, and histidine	Bandara (2018)

waste is disposed of. However, producing insect and microbial proteins for feed through organic waste could offer the enormous socioeconomic potential for African nations to continue aquaculture operations.

In this situation, making use of waste could serve as a protein source that could be used in animal feed. Insect and microbial proteins have attracted much attention as animal feed ingredients (Matassa et al. 2016). However, waste proteins are similar to FM in protein concentration and amino acid composition, which are widely consumed by fish and crustaceans. Many wastes protein is considered good because they do not impair the host's health but have some biological activities that help the host thrive. Therefore, this chapter assessed the understanding of microbial resources as a future feed ingredient for sustainable FM replacement. Thus, the utilization of various microbial resources in the aquafeed industry was thoroughly discussed. Therefore, having a rudimentary understanding of how waste nutrients are used in aquatic species culture can be beneficial.

4.2 Waste Production in Africa

A rapid increase in municipal solid waste (MSW) is anticipated in Africa due to population growth, urbanization, and shifting consumption habits. By 2040, the population of Africa is projected to reach approximately two billion people.

Approximately 40% of Africa's population currently resides in cities (as of 2014). In 2040, the number of people living in urban areas is projected to double to over 1 billion, growing at a rate of 3.5% annually, faster than on any other continent (UNEP 2018). In 2015, urban Africa produced 124 million tonnes of garbage annually. It is anticipated to reach 368 million tonnes by 2040 (UNEP 2018). In other words, by 2040, urban waste will have increased by about 200%. South Africa and North African nations produce significantly more daily waste per person (UNEP 2018). This is mainly caused by these countries' higher consumption and purchasing power levels. However, the amount of trash created and the patterns of consumption and production in Africa are starting to shift. More individuals adopt Western consumption habits as their affluence rises, which raises the quantity of waste produced. Africa now produces more waste than it did in the past due to rising global waste trade and illegal waste trafficking from high-income nations to the continent (UNEP 2018).

Due to the informal nature of recycling, there is a severe lack of factual data on recycling in Africa. Only a few formal recycling programmes are in operation, and the average recycling rate in Sub-Saharan Africa is only thought to be around 4% (UNEP 2018). Additionally, there are significant differences between country to country and region to region. There is excellent potential for zero-waste management, given the considerable proportion of African organic waste. Dumping rubbish is one of the most popular waste disposal techniques. The ecology and locals' health are harmed by open waste burning, which usually occurs in conjunction with dumping (Wael Fahmi and Sutton 2010). Waste disposal facilities are frequently dangerously overloaded and insufficient in many cities. However, many towns prioritize landfill site improvement and expansion over waste reduction, reuse, and recycling as part of an integrated waste management strategy. In fact, a 2014 evaluation of the two main dumpsites in Freetown, Sierra Leone, revealed that people who lived there or nearby were exposed to diseases and contamination of their air, soil, streams, and sea. Without sorting the waste first, it is burned, which causes significant air pollution and the release of poisons into the environment. The urgent need for a redesigned and integrated waste management system in Africa is demonstrated by the hazardous situations many landfills and dumps are in and the harm they inflict to the environment and public health.

Therefore, to prevent this waste from being dumped in landfills, which would increase climate change, increased circular systems that reuse feed nutrients can also lessen other adverse environmental effects of growing feed crops, such as those related to energy, water, and land use. Due to the rising cost of FM production and growing public awareness of FM's adverse environmental effects, it is imperative to develop sustainable alternatives to FM to satisfy the rising protein demands from the world's fastest-growing food-producing industry (Kim et al. 2019). Insect and microbial protein, which can be generated in vast quantities and possibly has a low carbon footprint, has proven to be a successful FM replacement for the latter (Jones et al. 2020; Matassa et al. 2016; Pikaar et al. 2017; Spalvins et al. 2018; Spalvins and Blumberga 2018). This is because low-value agricultural waste (such as waste from fruit, soy protein and rice concentrates, and dairy production) and

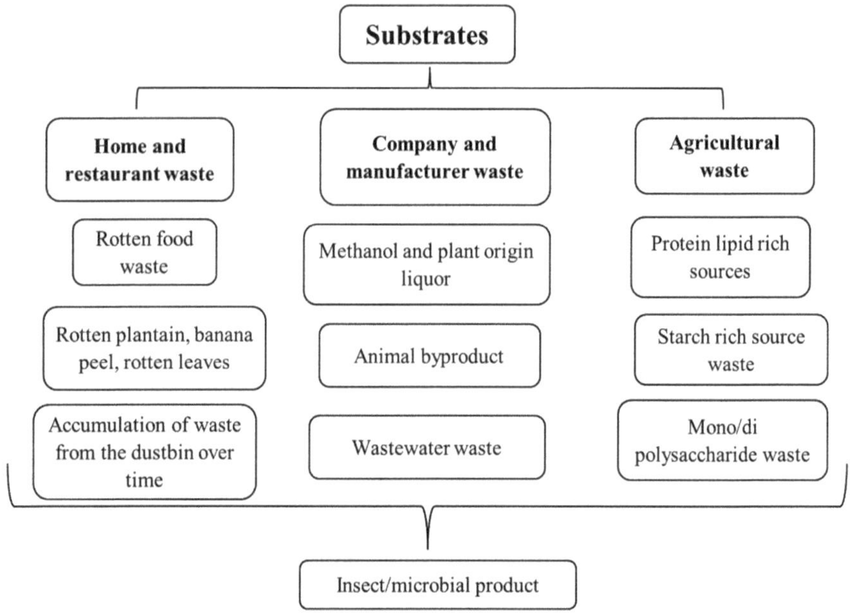

Fig. 4.1 Substrates are used for the culturing of insect and microbial species. (Adopted from Jannathulla et al. (2017))

industrial biomass residues (such as sulphite waste liquor, and lignin waste) can be inoculated and fermented to produce insect and microbial protein (Spalvins et al. 2018; Spalvins and Blumberga 2018) as shown in Fig. 4.1. It offers a strategy for developing a stable feed supply that regulates and turns waste from other industrial sectors into a valued commodity (Spalvins et al. 2018).

4.2.1 Waste to Microbial Resources

Microbial resources are the protein extracted from a single-cell protein or whole biomass from different single or mixed microbe cultures, such as algae, bacteria, fungi, and yeast from waste (home, restaurant, companies, etc.), that often have a crude protein (CP) content of about 40% by dry weight (Rajkumar et al. 2017; Matassa et al. 2016; García-Garibay et al. 2003). Compared to plant-based alternatives, the conversion of organics, nitrogen, and phosphorus to proteins is particularly effective (Matassa et al. 2016). Microbial resources are an excellent protein source and feed in aquaculture, and they help alleviate environmental issues caused by waste accumulation (Patil and Jadhav 2014). These substances are non-pathogenic to plants, humans, and animals, may be used for food and feed, have high nutritional value, are free of hazardous chemicals, and are inexpensive to produce. Overall, microbial components can potentially alleviate the strain on human food supplies. However, the production of microbial components is commercially under construction, and several start-up companies have been established, while current output quantities are unknown.

According to available data, Africa generated 125 million tonnes of MSW each year in 2012, with Sub-Saharan Africa accounting for 81 million tonnes (65%). This number is expected to increase to 244 million tonnes by 2025. With a waste collection rate of only 55% (68 million tonnes) (Scarlat et al. 2015), nearly half of all MSW generated in Africa is thrown on open fields, sidewalks, stormwater drains, and waterways. The issue is significantly worse in rural areas since formal waste collection services are frequently unavailable. This waste includes plastics, rotten food items, paper, wood, metal, etc. The waste from food and rotten greens accounted for roughly 44% (Scarlat et al. 2015). Therefore, biodegradable agro-industrial wastes and by-products should be considered sources of nutrients as potential substrates for microorganism cultivation to reduce environmental hazards and lower production costs.

The production of microbial resources is attained by submerged or solid-state fermentation to obtain microbial isolates and whole-cell biomass from various microorganisms, such as bacteria, fungus, and yeast. At the end of the process, the corresponding microorganisms' spores or cells are taken and subjected to multiple downstream operations, such as cell wall disruption washing, protein extraction, and purification (Rumsey et al. 2010). However, algae can be produced in indoor/outdoor, open/closed, axenic/non-axenic, and batch/continuous/semi-continuous methods. Although many factors influence the development of microbial resources, the substrates needed and the microorganisms used in this process must be standardized to achieve the best yield. For instance, fungus and yeast species thrive on lignocellulosic materials, including cellulose, hemicellulose, and lignin, primarily cultured in paper and wood waste, Corn cobs, maize, cotton stalk, plant, and animal wastes (Jannathulla et al. 2017). Carbon dioxide and sunlight are the essential parameters for culturing algal species, such as *Chlorella pyrenoidosa*, *Chlorella sorokiniana*, *Porphyrium sp*., etc. (Rumsey et al. 2010). However, specific fungi can be selected for this process according to dominant components present in the waste. By-products of industrial waste are mainly used for the cultivation of bacterial species.

4.3 Importance of Microbial Resources in Aquaculture

Microbial resources have been recommended as a viable ingredient in the worldwide feed business based on research on the compatibility of microbial resources in the diets of diverse aquatic species conducted over the last two decades (Pike et al. 1990; Bob Manuel and Alfred-Ockiya 2011). In aquaculture, microbial resources act as potential feed ingredients and serve as viable immunostimulants and probiotics, which improve growth, health, disease resistance, and immunity (Bharti et al. 2014). Microbial resources play a significant role in aquaculture by (1) changing the host-associated microbial ecology, (2) facilitating better feed utilization or increasing its nutritional value, such as biotin, fatty acids, and vitamin B12, which benefits an animal's health, (3) strengthening the host's disease resistance, and/or (4) improving the quality of its surrounding environment. On the other hand, this substance can be fed to the animal or added to the rising water, benefiting the host by boosting immunity and antioxidants capacities, improving health, growth performance, and feed utilization, as shown in Fig. 4.2. This is accomplished partly by enhancing the microbial balance of the host or the surrounding environment. According to Kolndadacha et al. (2011), one of the aquaculture's disease control options is using bacterial species as a probiotic, particularly gram-positive bacteria (Lactobacillus sp.), as an alternative to antibiotics. According to Fish Site (2019), using microbial products enhanced farmed animals' capability to absorb protein, resulting in a significant feed conversion ratio in aquaculture. Furthermore, according to Bharti et al. (2014), microbial resources play an essential role in ornamental fish farming by regulating the colour and size of the fish, primarily sourced from algae and bacteria rich in pigments, predominantly carotenoids.

The nutritional content of microbial resources is determined by the species, fermentation conditions, and post-harvest processing (Spalvins et al. 2018; Hansen et al. 2021; Lapea et al. 2020). Yeast has a CP level ranging from 38 to 60% DM, depending on yeast species and strains and the type of downstream processing employed after fermentation (Sharma et al. 2018). Yeast has a good amino acid composition than fish requirements; however, it is deficient in methionine and cysteine content (Agboola et al. 2020; Mahnken et al. 1980). Low lipid content is also associated with yeast, with unsaturated fatty acids predominating in the fatty acid composition (Halasz and Lasztity 1991), except for oleaginous yeast. The carbohydrate content of yeast contains a polysaccharide compound, with monosaccharides and oligosaccharides at a lower level. Fungi have a CP content of 55–63% and digestibility content of 87%. This was reported in monogastric animals. Their cell wall is rich with minerals and vitamin and comprises around one-third of the total biomass. Bacterial flour contains approximately 70% CP and 10% crude fat and is similar to a macronutrient composition of FM. The amino acid profile is comparable to that of the FM but with lower levels of lysine and methionine and higher levels of tryptophan. Microalgae can collect large amounts of n-3 PUFAs, accounting for 30–50% of their total fatty acid content and 50–65% of their CP biomass. Microalgae proteins have a similar amino acid content across species and

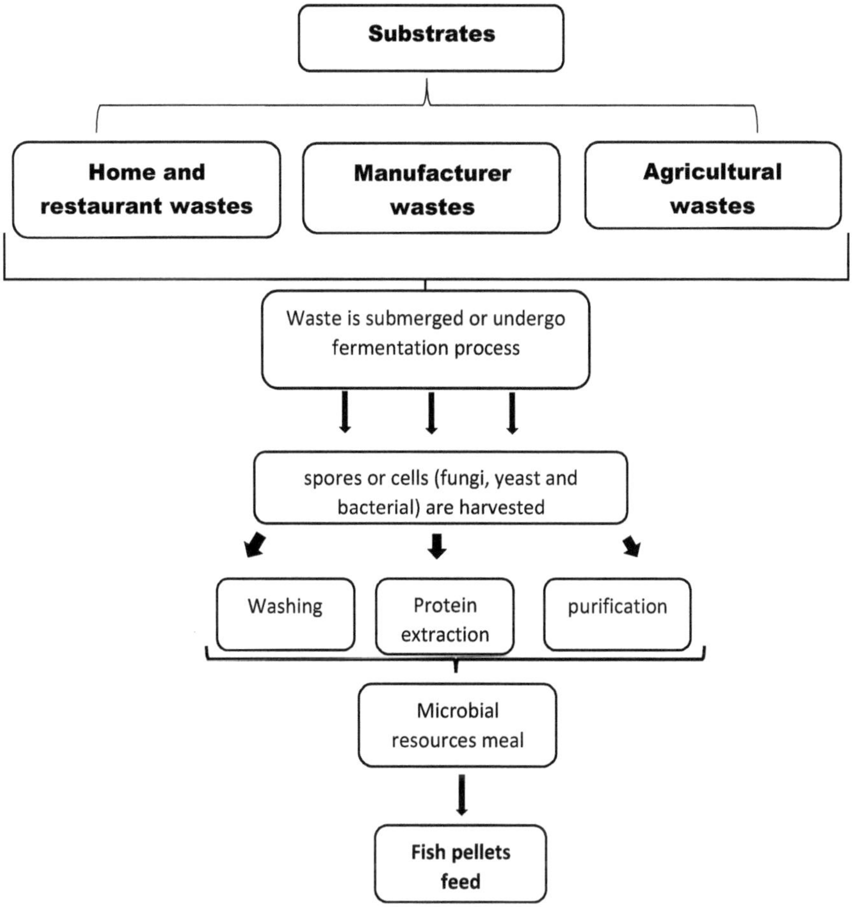

Fig. 4.2 Turning wastes into proteins using the microbial resources (bacterial fungi and yeast) to produce microbial meals to replace FM in aquafeeds for fish culture

are equivalent to traditional food and feed proteins, like soybean (Becker 2007). Algae were found to have lower nucleic acid content 4.0–6.0% dry weight. However, bacteria, fungal, and yeast species have 15.0–16.0, 9.7, and 7.1–12.0% dry weight, respectively. Of all the microbial species, fungi have a higher limiting amino acid content, particularly lysine (Jannathulla et al. 2017) (Fig. 4.3).

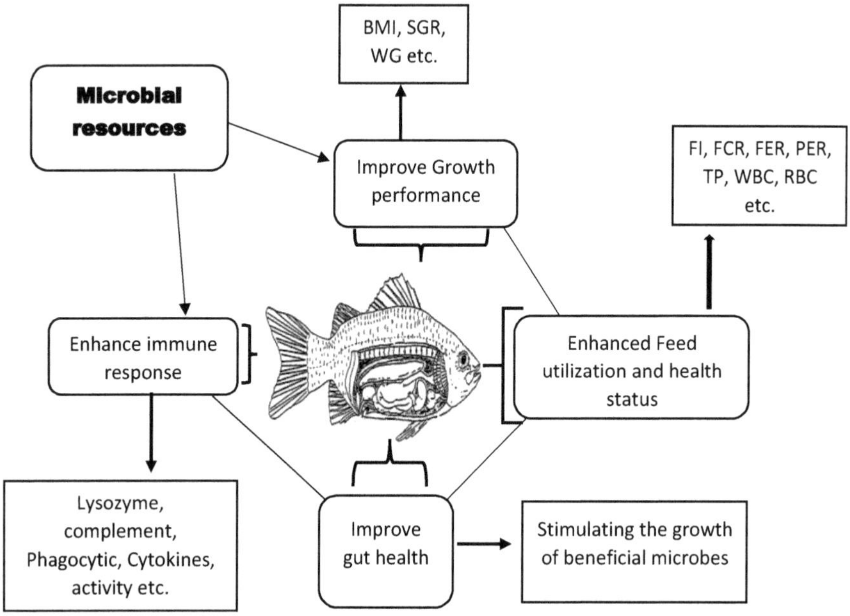

Fig. 4.3 The mode of action of microbial resources comprises of improved growth performance, feed utilization (macro-and micronutrients), health status, and enhanced immune and gut health. *BMI* body mass index, *SGR* specific growth rate, *WG* weight gain, *FI* feed intake, *FCR* feed conversion ratio, *FER* feed efficiency ratio, *PER* protein efficiency ratio, *TP* total protein, *WBC* white blood cell, *RBC* red blood cell

4.3.1 Stimulate Intestinal Enzymes to Promote a Growth Performance

The GI microbiota assists the host in a variety of ways. In mammals, their role in the nutritional provision, avoiding infectious agent colonization, energy balance, and maintaining adequate mucosal immunity is well recognized (Xu et al. 2003; Nicholson et al. 2005; Delzenne and Cani 2008). Fish GI tract microbial colonization, establishment, composition, and diversity is a complex process that is thought to reflect the microbial composition of the rearing water, nutrition, and environment (Korsnes et al. 2006; Fjellheim et al. 2007). Like mammals, hydrobionts' GI microbiota have been shown to promote physiological and nutritional health functions of the host by creating digestive enzymes, amino acids, vitamins, and metabolites (Skrodenyte Arbaeiauskiene 2000; Skrodenyte-Arbaciauskiene et al. 2006). When various chemicals, antibiotics, and pollutants enter an aquatic animal's digestive tract, they can drastically alter the composition of the dominant GI microbiota, potentially resulting in the extinction of individual species from the entire microbial community (Mickeniene and Syvokiene 2008; Navarrete et al. 2008). As a result, the composition of a fish's GI microbiota is strongly influenced by the meal and feeding conditions.

Fig. 4.4 Insect species used in producing meals to replace FM in aquafeeds. (**a**) Black soldier fly (*Hermetia illucens*), (**b**) Silkworms (*Bombyx mori*), (**c**) Jamaican field cricket (*Gryllus assimilis*), (**d**) housefly (Musca domestica) (Malik et al. 2007), (**e**) yellow mealworm (*Tenebrio molitor*), (**f**) house cricket (*Acheta domesticus*), (**g**) lesser mealworm (*Alphitobius diaperinus*)

A complex and integrated interaction of the modulation of GI enzymes is associated with nutrient absorption, and immune components are responsible for the fish's health and growth performance. On the other hand, feeding microbial resources is a better strategy for establishing and populating the probiont in fish's GI tract (Robertson et al. 2000). When microbial resources are fed to animals or added to water, they dramatically alter the gut microbiota composition by stimulating gastrointestinal bacteria to produce more enzymes. These enzymes can help increase nutrient digestibility and mineral absorption to enhance the host's growth performance, as seen in Fig. 4.4. However, besides enhancing enzymatic activities, it could stimulate B cell proliferation in gut-associated lymphoid tissues (GALT) or directly stimulate the innate immune system by increasing phagocytosis and antibacterial activity. This immune cell defends against harmful bacteria through competitive exclusion, the production of organic acids, and various other compounds, such as antibiotics (Gildberg et al. 1997; Gibson 1999; Gram et al. 1999). However, studies have shown that β-glucans (by-products from fungi and yeast), when digested, could stimulate the intestinal level via the production of cytokines, which influence fish's systemic immune response, thus hindering poisons, viruses, and harmful microorganisms from multiplying in the host (Volman et al. 2008).

The significance of microbial resources intake arises from their ability to selectively stimulate the growth and multiplication of indigenous bifidobacteria and lactobacilli in the intestine. For example, the Lactobacillus family of probiotics can produce lactase (which is responsible for breaking down lactose from dairy products), while the Bifidobacterium species can help break down fibre. The increase in healthy gut microflora is accompanied by several changes in the gut, including improved digesting enzyme activity. An increase in the synthesis of short-chain fatty acids (SCFAs) is frequently targeted and is the energy source of the colonocytes (van Immerseel et al. 2003). However, improved gut health in the host has been linked to increased SCFA production. As a result of the increased energy supply, the animal is stronger and more resistant to diseases. Besides, enhanced intestinal cell proliferation allows for improved uptake of nutrients from the meal, resulting in a higher feed uptake ratio and better growth (Vine et al. 2006). Nevertheless, there are reports concerning the interactive effect of microbial products on the digestive enzymes, growth performance, and immune response.

4.3.2 Improve Immune Response in Fish

The non-specific immune system, also known as the innate immune system, is the first line of defense, consisting of cells and mechanisms that protect the host from infection by other organisms. Immunomodulation can take several forms at the systemic level, including enhanced complement activity, increased lysozyme formation, phagocytic activity, peroxidase production, and respiratory burst activity. The GALT, a significant contributor to intestinal immune functions, have been revealed to be tightly connected with microbial resources bioactive chemicals or their metabolites (Saad et al. 2013). For example, the immunostimulatory capabilities of fungi and yeast is due to components, such as glucan, mannoproteins, and nucleic acids present in them (Ortuno et al. 2002) Meanwhile, β-glucans have been utilized in aquaculture to promote fish survival by regulating their innate immune system until adaptive immune responses develop enough to build effective anti-infection responses (Bricknell and Dalmo 2005; Meena et al. 2013). Suppose the β-glucans are administered as feed additives; they can exert their primary effects at the intestinal level through the induction of cytokines, affecting the systemic immune response in fish. As a result, its mode of action is dependent on dectin-1. β-glucan interacts with the dectin-1 receptor and activates NF-B via intracellular signaling, generating cytokines, phagocytosis, and respiratory burst (Volman et al. 2008). However, probiotics interact with immune cells, such as mononuclear phagocytes, neutrophils, and natural killer (NK) cells, to boost innate immune responses, thus increasing the number of erythrocytes, granulocytes, lymphocytes, and macrophages in different fishes (Kim and Austin 2006; Nayak et al. 2007). In fact, in fish fed microbial resources, a rise in the number of acidophilic granulocytes, T cells, Ig+

cells, and enhanced lysozyme synthesis and phagocytic activity has been noted at the gut level. Therefore, the immunomodulatory properties of these products could be achieved in the host by (1) stimulating specific and non-specific immune systems; (2) promoting phagocytic and lysozyme activities; (3) increasing the expression of various cytokines related to immunity; and (4) increasing immunoglobulin cells and acidophilic granulocytes in the fish's gut (Allameh et al. 2015).

4.3.3 *Prevent Spoilage in Aquatic Products*

Aquatic items have high water and protein content, making them tasty, nutritious, and prone to spoiling. Every year, the rotting of aquatic items causes significant economic losses and poses a health concern to consumers. As a result, many chemical preservatives have been created to preserve aquatic items during storage. According to Wang et al. (2020), their use may pose secondary health and environmental risks, and their application is limited to specific product categories and storage methods. Beneficial bacteria can prevent spoilage bacteria and diseases of aquatic animals through similar processes. As a result, it can be employed in addition to conventional preservatives. Fermentation is a widespread and traditional food processing method for aquatic goods that can help avoid spoiling and generate a distinct flavour. Because of the hypertonic or anaerobic environment, fermentation generally inhibits the growth of most spoilage microorganisms. Furthermore, the anti-spoilage effect is aided by the helpful microorganisms engaged in fermentation. These bacteria produce various products, primarily organic acids, alcohol, and CO_2, by oxidizing carbohydrates during metabolism. These products dramatically impact the environment and serve as a preservative by preventing the spread of pathogenic flora and/or deterioration in the food product (Ray and Montet 2015).

4.3.4 *Improve Water Quality*

Good water quality is essential to aquaculture as any deterioration in water quality causes stress and makes the cultured organism more vulnerable to deadly pathogens. Intensification in aquaculture, poor feed management, and indiscriminate disposal of fish waste is associated with improper mineralization of excess nutrients, affecting water quality (Edwards 2015). These poor water conditions threaten aquatic organisms' survival and render ground and surface water unsafe for other organisms. Notwithstanding the exact aquaculture system, sustaining balanced water quality levels is fundamental for farmed aquatic species' health and growth. However, water exchange/supplementation and chemicals, such as Biolite plus, Bio-tuff, Geotox, Green zeolite, JV zeolite, Pontox plus (Shamsuzzaman and Biswas 2012), Well Zeolite, and Aquazet (Faruk et al. 2008), have been the traditional methods used in solving those problems. Besides, this method is usually accompanied by pond-contaminated effluence directly discharging into adjacent water, thus causing a scrics of issues such as pollution diffusion, water environment deterioration, and water eutrophication. As a result, it is critical to maintaining water quality characteristics that allow for disease-free fish production.

Improving water quality and avoiding the accumulation of organic, nitrogen, ammonia, and nitrite waste are continual challenges. However, high concentrations of these compounds can be highly damaging and cause massive mortalities (Das et al. 2017). The oxidizing bacteria of ammonia (ammonia to nitrite) and nitrites (nitrite to nitrate) turn these hazardous compounds into less harmful forms in nature (Qi et al. 2009). Microbial resources, such as probiotic bacteria, have been proposed as ecological biocontrol or bioremediation agents in aquaculture (Dimitroglou et al. 2011; Iribarren et al. 2012). Benefits attributed to probiotics include increased bacterial populations, suppression of possible pathogens, and increased dissolved oxygen concentration (Ibrahem 2015). For instance, Bacillus bacteria have been considered probiotics in water treatment due to their unique ability to convert organic waste to CO_2 (Dalmin et al. 2001). Lalloo et al. (2010) found that three *Bacillus* isolates reduced the amounts of nitrite, nitrate, and ammonium in ornamental fish water. Probiotics can be administered in several ways, including (1) directly to the culture water or mixed with the inoculum of "green water", a high concentration of microalgae often employed in fish culture for food consumption in the early stages of larval development (2 days after hatching); (2) by live feed given to rotifers (up to day 19 after hatching), followed by the addition of Artemia (until about day 25 of culture after hatching). Probiotics can colonize the surface layer of the fish's skin and then infiltrate through it. As a result, probiotics can be discovered in water, sediment, and cultured organisms after inoculation in culture systems.

4.3.5 Several Advancements in Aquaculture Nutrition

Furthermore, the bacteria can produce flocculated material, providing an extra food supply while improving water quality and increasing breeding density (Schryver et al. 2008). In Pacific white shrimp (Litopenaeus vannamei), dry bioflocculant material obtained from aquaculture can partially replace FM; replacing more than 20% of FM with biofloc meal may facilitate faster growth of shrimp (Dantas et al. 2016). Other aquatic animals, such as flatfish (*Paralichthys olivaceus*) and sea cucumber (*Apostichopus japonicus*), have also shown better growth performance in similar tests and applications (Chen et al. 2018).

In Nile and blue tilapia, Viola (1984) discovered that up to 50% FM inclusion using a commercial bacterial-based microbial product (Pruteen with 70% protein) created from *Methylophilus methylotrophus* produced equal growth to the control group (no FM substitute). *Penaeus chinensis*, on the other hand, had a similar outcome (Daniel 2018). Rainbow trout fed a diet that replaced 25% of the dietary FM with a bacterial-based microbial product exhibited no negative impacts on growth, feed intake, or absorption efficiency (Perera et al. 1995). A similar outcome was seen in Atlantic salmon using bacterial and algal-based microbial products (*Desmodesmus sp.*) (Storebakken et al. 2004; Aas et al. 2006; Kiron et al. 2016). In Cobia fish, a commercial yeast (*S. cerevisiae*) derived source (NuPro) at a level of 40% may replace a control diet with 65.9% FM. Nevertheless, the percentage of FM substituted in the diet was increased to 50%, while a control diet made up of 54.4% FM was being fed (Lunger et al. 2007). When *P. vannamei* was fed an algal-based microbial product made from *Spirulina platensis*, it was found to partially replace FM similarly (Hanel et al. 2007).

For instance, *M. rosenbergii,* given *Turbinaria ornate,* and *Gracilaria corticata*-included diet, had higher activity of digestive enzymes, such as amylase, protease, and lipase, than the control group (Rajkumar et al. 2017). The addition of *Bacillus sp.* to *P. indicus* boosted the specific activity of amylase, protease, and lipase (Ziaei-Nejad et al. 2006). This enhanced enzyme activity could be attributable to exogenous enzyme release by microbes, which aids in growth and survival by improving food absorption and digesting. In the intestine of *P. vannamei* fed basic meal supplemented with *Rhodobacter sphaeroides* and *B. coagulans* at various doses of 0.1, 1, and 2%, Wang (2008) discovered a steady rise in protease and amylase activity. Although there was no difference in lipase or cellulose activity between the treated groups, the groups fed a bacteria-supplemented meal had a much greater value than the control group. Rengpipat et al. (1998) found that using the appropriate probiotics and administering them accurately improved the intestinal microbiota balance, resulting in improved digestion and absorption of cultivated species and positive results in farmed species growth.

Compared to oral supplementation, Taoka et al. (2006) study of *O. niloticus* revealed considerably higher levels of lysozyme in the skin mucosa when commercial probiotics were added to the water. These findings imply that fish given probiotic supplements can afford to resist bacterial illnesses due to enhanced lysozome activity. After 30 days of ingesting Epinephelus coioides grouper, blood C3 levels of probiotic treated group, according to Sun et al. (2010), were considerably greater than those of the control. The maximum activity against *Vibrio anguillarum* was seen in rainbow trout 2 weeks after the probiotic feeding, and after 4 weeks, there was an increase in activity compared to the control (Sharifuzzaman and Austin 2009). Yuan et al. (2019) indicated that dietary replacement of FM by 3% YH (yeast hydrolysate) could improve antioxidant capability and enhance the non-specific immunity of juvenile Jian carp. Purified β-glucan product fed to Atlantic cod (Gadus morhua L.) for 5 weeks increased the expression of IL-1 β in the anterior intestine and rectum when challenged with *V. anguillarum* (Lokesh et al. 2012). Schizochytrium fed to Atlantic salmon for 12 weeks improved goblet cell proliferation, mucus production, and inducible nitric oxide synthase activity in those given the control diet. Brewer's yeast and Spirulina increased serum proteins, notably albumin and globulin, after exposure to Aeromonas hydrophila challenge in Rohu Labeo rohita after 60 days when compared to the control group.

4.4 Waste to Insect Feed Meal

Insects are the most diverse group of animals, and a natural food source for fish, especially for carnivorous and omnivorous fish, as these fish species need a relatively high number of proteins in their diets (van Huis 2019). For more than 2000 years, people have used insects as a food source in numerous nations. For thousands of years, numerous societies have engaged in entomophagy, gathering insects for nourishment (Evans et al. 2015). Insect rearing was practiced thousands of years ago when silkworms (*Bombyx mori*) were first cultivated in China to produce silk. During the collection of the silk, the pupae by-product was fed to carp fish in ponds. Insects are a relatively recent method of producing high-quality protein for animal feeds from food waste or cow feces and pee slurry. Since then, increased research efforts and sector expenditures have resulted in more industrialized insect breeding for food and feed (van Huis 2019). Insect output is currently insufficient for the widespread use of insects in aquafeed production in Africa, despite significant research advancements and an increase in insect productivity. Numerous areas, like handling insects, production automation, and raw materials, require greater attention (Liland et al. 2017).

In Africa, Orders, including Lepidoptera, Orthoptera, Coleoptera, Isoptera, Hymenoptera, and Hemiptera, contain the greatest diversity of edible insect species. According to recent studies, the protein and calorie content of insects may be comparable to that of traditional meat sources. In Africa, crickets and acridians are the Orthoptera species most frequently ingested. More than 850 insect farms that produce food and feed are already present in Africa, along with hydroponic farms. Africa may produce up to $2.6 billion in CP and $19.4 billion in biofertilizers per year from insect farming using agricultural waste as feed. The protein meal would be sufficient to provide up to 14% of the CP required to raise fish in Africa.

The following insect species have been studied and used to produce industrial aquafeed: silkworms (*Bombyx mori*) (Duan et al. 2010); black soldier fly (*Hermetia illucens*) (Barry 2004); Jamaican field cricket (*Gryllus assimilis*) (Masson et al. 2020); housefly (*Musca domestica*) (Malik et al. 2007); yellow mealworm (*Tenebrio molitor*) (Li et al. 2013); house cricket (*Acheta domesticus*) (Hessler Frelinckx 2019), and lesser mealworm (*Alphitobius diaperinus*) (Rumbos et al. 2019). The ideal dietary inclusion varies considerably depending on the fish or crustacean species and their nutrient requirements. Therefore, insect meals are unquestionably a good substitute for animal protein in aquaculture feed.

In nature, insects are responsible for converting rotting food into high-quality nutrients. The larvae of some species, like the black soldier fly (BSF) species, can ingest low-quality feed and function at scales that traditional mechanical systems have not yet attained. These initiatives improve regional food security by focusing on local reuse, which lowers the pollution brought on by transportation.

4.4.1 The Nutritional Capacity of Insect Meals

The nutritional value of insect proteins is widely known. According to feeding experiments with various fish and crab species, insect meal additions do not negatively affect development and performance. Adding insect protein to aquafeeds has improved FCRs in several aquatic species. Most insect species have high CP levels, ranging from 42.1 to 63.3%. Although it is like soybean meal (SM), this level of CP is lower than that in FM (Allegretti et al. 2017; Henry et al. 2015). Various insects in these species had different amino acid profiles. Except for silkworms, sulphur amino acid concentrations in insects are lower than those in FM. While other insect species have equal quantities of threonine, silkworms have higher levels (Henry et al. 2015; Sanchez-Muros et al. 2014). Tryptophan concentrations in other insect species are often lower than those in silkworms and housefly maggot meal. Depending on the fish species' specific needs, synthetic amino acid supplements may be advised for optimum growth. An amino acid profile superior to SM is found in silkworms, black army flies, and houseflies. These insects are, therefore, preferable to SM for replacing FM in aquafeeds (Henry et al. 2015; Sanchez-Muros et al. 2014).

In comparison to FM, these species contain less fat. After researching various insect species, van Huis stated in 2020 that the fat content ranged from 8% for mature locusts to 36% for mealworm larvae. The development stage and the food that insects consume are two aspects that impact the fat content (Barros-Cordeiro et al. 2014; Barroso et al. 2019). Omega-3 fatty acids are substantially more prevalent in fish oil than in insect meals (Makkar et al. 2014); however, there are significant amounts of saturated fatty acids in insect meals. Compared to other insect species, mealworm, and housefly maggot diets have higher quantities of unsaturated fatty acids (between 60 and 70%). At the same time, approximately 19–37% of black soldier fly larvae (BSFL) contain unsaturated fatty acids (Gasco et al. 2020; Hawkey et al. 2021; van Huis 2019). These insects have lower concentrations of EPA (eicosapentaenoic acid 20:5n-3) and DHA (docosahexaenoic acid 22:6n-3) than fish oil but greater concentrations of polyunsaturated fatty acids (PFA), specifically n-6 PFA (Gasco et al. 2020; Hawkey et al. 2021; van Huis 2019). Therefore, their usefulness as an oil source in aquafeeds is restricted by the dearth of EPA and DHA in the five insect species.

4.4.2 Insect Meal as an Immunostimulant

In addition, there is growing interest in the naturally occurring bioactive compounds found in insects and the nutritional advantages of eating insects. Insect chitin in food has been linked to beneficial effects on intestinal health in rainbow trout, Jian carp, Siberian sturgeon, and marron crayfish. The precise function of chitin in fish diets is still up for debate and is dependent on the amount of chitin present in the diet; chitin may act as a prebiotic, immunostimulant, and anti-inflammatory molecule in fish when present at low levels, but when present in high doses, it may inhibit fish growth and induce intestinal inflammation. More than 50 potential active peptides have been found in BSF larvae, indicating that insects are a significant source of antimicrobial peptides (AMPs) (Pastor et al. 2015). A wide range of bacteria, fungi, certain parasites, and viruses can be attacked by AMPs, which are essential parts of the innate immune system in most animals. Due to their immunostimulant, antioxidant, and antibacterial qualities, insect meals can improve the health and performance of fish and crustaceans even at modest inclusion levels. The functionalities of premium insect meal can be used in particular formulations targeting high-value species, like sturgeons, shrimp, salmonids, juveniles, or broodstock with distinct needs.

4.4.3 Production of Insect Meal

Insect farming in a controlled or indoor environment is a suitable technique to make them available all year round because many insects are only present in nature during specific seasons or months (Cadinu et al. 2020; van Huis 2019; Hawkey et al. 2021). Collecting significant amounts of organic matter, preserving progenitors, and ensuring efficient egg production in number and quality are all crucial steps in insect farming (Pastor et al. 2015). Indoor rearing of insects necessitates the management of ambient environmental conditions (temperature, relative humidity, photoperiod), premium feed, and avoidance of parasites and diseases for the best possible insect growth and development (Hawkey et al. 2021; van Huis 2019). Long-term intensive insect farming can be carried out under technical supervision in such cases.

Various crucial phases are involved in producing insect meals (van Huis 2019). Since the nutrient composition of growing substrates significantly impacts crucial production factors, like total larvae yield, individual larva body weight, and nutrient composition of yielded insect larvae, the first step is to ensure biomass availability, which should be continuously available (Tschirner and Simon 2015). Decontamination, which involves thermal or radiation techniques, is the next phase. The final phase involves drying the insect pupa or entire body through convection, contact, and radiation. The fourth stage involves crushing the insects or pupa into tiny pieces. Defatting, the fourth step in extracting fat from insects, is crucial for particular insect species (like yellow mealworms). Defatting is often accomplished by mechanical pressing, aqueous solutions, and solvents (Soxhlet and supercritical carbon dioxide) (Rumpold et al. 2017). Numerous methods for extracting proteins include enzyme-, microwave-, ultrasound-, pulsed electric energy-, and high-pressure-aided extraction methods (Pojić et al. 2018). It is crucial to eliminate chitin from meals for some species since their bodies contain chitin. Chitin can be extracted chemically or biologically in various ways; one illustration is fermentation using microbes and enzymes (Rumpold et al. 2017). Energy costs are a significant problem for preparing insect meals. Modern technologies, such as automation with IOT, must be used to maximize every stage of the processing (Yue and Shen 2021).

4.5 Several Advancements in Aquaculture Nutrition

The effects of including insect meals into aquafeeds on various aquaculture species have recently been the subject of an increasing number of research that involved feeding trials. Here, we provide a concise summary of what is currently known about employing the eight insects as aquafeeds.

Studies have demonstrated that it is theoretically possible to grow insects on a big scale and use them as a sustainable protein substitute in the diet of birds, pigs, cattle, and aquatic animals (Veldkamp et al. 2012). However, several uses of insects to feed fish have been thoroughly studied. These include house fly larvae (*Musca domestica*) (Ogunji et al. 2008a, b; Ezewudo et al. 2015), larvae of butterflies (*Bematistes macaria*) (Nwamba and Ogunji 2012); and *Tenebrio molitor* (Ng et al. 2001; Piccolo et al. 2014; Belforti et al. 2015; Gasco et al. 2016; MªJ et al. 2016; Freccia et al. 2016).

Silkworm pupae meal can replace FM in common carp and Japanese sea bass (*Lateolabrax japonicus*) without sacrificing growth performance (Jeyachandran and Paulraj 1976). Feeding trials showed that Silkworm pupae meal might replace up to 30% of FM in the diet of rainbow sharks (*Epalzeorhynchos frenatum*) (Raja et al. 2020). When the two amino acids Lys and Met were added to the meals containing Silkworm pupae meal, the growth performance of olive flounder (*Paralichthys olivaceus*) was unaffected (Lee et al. 2012). The results of an eight-week feeding experiment on juvenile yellow catfish (*Pelteobagrus fulvidraco*) showed that BSFL meal could replace 20% of the FM in the fish feed without negatively affecting growth outcomes, including weight gain, FCR, as well as a whole body and proximate muscle composition. Dry matter, CP, crude lipids, gross energy, and ADCs (amino acid's apparent digestibility coefficients) remained unchanged among the other metrics. According to feeding research on Atlantic salmon, the quality of the fillets was unaffected when FM was replaced entirely with BSFL meal. For example, in the fillets of Atlantic salmon fed diets containing BSFL meal, neutral n-3 PUFA (polyunsaturated fatty acids) increased considerably. The impact of BSFL meal on diets was examined in African catfish (*Clarias gariepinus*). FM can be substituted with BSFL meal up to 50% without harming the growth, nutrient uptake, survival rate, or welfare of *C. gariepinus* fingerlings (Adeoye et al. 2020).

Numerous feeding studies have been conducted on two catfish species (*Clarias gariepinus* and *Heterobranchus longifilis*) and their hybrids to explore the impact of adding housefly maggots to their meals on their growth performance. Overall, the results of feeding trials for catfish species are favourable. However, maggot meal inclusion cannot exceed 30% because greater inclusion rates tend to reduce growth performance (Aniebo et al. 2009; Fasakin et al. 2003; Okore et al. 2016; Saleh 2020). A study substituted housefly maggots grown from chicken waste for FM in aquafeeds at varied inclusion levels of 0, 25, 50, 75, and 100% of maggot inclusions. The study suggests that *C. gariepinus* juveniles can effectively consume wet maggots; 75% of them should be utilized in commercial fish feed (Ipinmoroti et al. 2019). The best growth performance and survival rate were seen at 34% substitution of FM, with no adverse effects on homeostasis, when maggot meal was substituted for FM in the diet at a rate of 15–68%. It was discovered that n-6 and n-3 fatty acids must be included in the diet and maggot meal to improve fish's fatty acid profile (Ogunji et al. 2008a, b).

Using up to 25% mealworm as a meal replacement for FM demonstrated no detrimental effects on weight gain in European sea bass (*Dicentrarchus labrax*). While protein efficiency, feed consumption, and body composition were unaffected, growth and feed consumption ratios were reduced when FM was replaced with mealworm meal to 50%. Tenebrio meal at a 25% inclusion rate had no adverse effects on young European sea bass (*D. labrax*), but at a 50% inclusion rate, the specific growth rate was decreased (Gasco et al. 2014). With an outstanding replacement value of 25%, which equates to the inclusion of 7.5% of giant tenebrio meal in the diet, studies testing the replacement of FM with giant tenebrio (*Zophobas morio*) for Nile tilapia obtained a better feed conversion ratio and weight gain than the control (Abd Rahman Jabir et al. 2012).

According to Elia et al. (2018), eating BSFL meals increased the oxidative stress biomarkers SOD and CAT levels in rainbow trout (*Oncorhynchus mykiss*). The activity of serum immune-related enzymes, such as LZM and SOD in yellow catfish (*P. fulvidraco*), increased when BSF meals were included in the diet. The fish's serum levels of SOD, nitric acid, malondialdehyde (MDA), ceruloplasmin, myeloperoxidase, and glutathione peroxidase (GPx) could cause all rise if yellow meal worm is added to their diet (Su et al. 2017; Sankian et al. 2018; Henry et al. 2018). When treated with dietary supplementation of Silkworm pupae meal, *O. mykiss'* WBCs were considerably high, according to Shakoori et al. (2015) in another investigation on the innate immunity of finfish. WBC production would boost the body's defenses against viruses as they become more prevalent (Shakoori et al. 2015).

4.6 Conclusion

Although novel ingredients are required to bridge the gap in aquaculture feed resources, several obstacles must be overcome before these can be implemented in the African aquaculture industry. Aside from nutritional value, technical quality, accessibility, affordability, and environmental sustainability must all be considered. Most novel protein sources discussed in this paper are currently unavailable to the aquaculture feed industry, and several factors limit their immediate use as feed ingredients. It is significant to note that the use of these proteins (insect and microbial) may be associated with contamination with allergens and toxins (such as enterotoxins and cytotoxins) during the production process (Linder 2019; Ritala et al. 2017). So, they should not be widely used until more study and testing is finished. However, such contaminations can be managed and avoided in a closed fermentation system by following industrial verification and validation, adhering to food safety production standards (for instance, HACCP systems and ISO standards), and maintaining traceability throughout the production cycle. As a result, before large-scale industrial applications, credible and adequate examinations of resource's potential side effects, including hazardous consequences, should be conducted.

References

Aas TSV, Hatlen B, Grisdale-Helland B, Terjesen BF, Bakke-Mckellep AM, Helland SLJ (2006) Effects of diets containing a bacterial protein meal on growth and feed utilisation in rainbow trout (*Oncorhynchus mykiss*). Aquaculture 261:357–368

Abasubong KP, Liu WB, Adjoumani Y, Xia SL, Xu C, Li XF (2018) Xylooligosaccharides benefits the growth, digestive functions and TOR signaling in *Megalobrama amblycephala* fed diets with fish meal replaced by rice protein concentrate. Aquaculture 500:417–428

Abd Rahman Jabir MD, Abd Rahman Jabir SA, Vikineswary S (2012) Nutritive potential and utilization of super worm (*Zophobas morio*) meal in the diet of Nile tilapia (*Oreochromis niloticus*) juvenile. Afr J Biotechnol 11:6592–6598

Adeoye AA, Akegbejo-Samsons Y, Fawole FJ, Davies SJ (2020) Preliminary assessment of black soldier fly (*Hermetia illucens*) larval meal in the diet of African catfish (*Clarias gariepinus*): impact on growth, body index, and hematological parameters. J World Aquac Soc 51:1024–1033

Agboola JO, Verland M, Skrede A, Hansen JV (2020) Yeast as major protein-rich ingredient in aquafeeds: a review of the implications for aquaculture production. Rev Aquac 13:949–970

Aladetohun N, Sogbesan O (2013) Utilization of blood meal as a protein ingredient from animal waste product in the diet of *Oreochromis niloticus*. Int J Fish Aquac 5:234–237

Allameh SK, Ringø E, Yusoff FM, Daud HM, Ideris A (2015) Dietary supplement of *Enterococcus faecalison* digestive enzyme activities, short-chain fatty acid production, immune system response and disease resistance of Javanese carp (*Puntius gonionotus*, Bleeker 1850). Aquac Nutr 23:331–338

Allegretti G, Schmidt V, Talamini E (2017) Insects as feed: species selection and their potential use in Brazilian poultry production. Worlds Poult Sci J 73:928–937

Aniebo AO, Erondu ES, Owen OJ (2009) Replacement of fish meal with maggot meal in African catfish (Clarias gariepinus) diets. Revista Científica UDO Agrícola 9:666–671

Anon (1997) Communication from the Commission to the council and the European parliament commission European Commission Brussels, p 20

Bandara T (2018) Alternative feed ingredients in aquaculture: opportunities and challenges. J Entomol Zool Stud 6:3087–3094

Barros-Cordeiro KB, Bao SN, Pujol-Luz JR (2014) Intra-puparial development of the black soldier-fly, *Hermetia illucens*. J Insect Sci 14:83

Barroso FG, Sanchez-Muros MJ, Rincon MA, Rodriguez-Rodriguez M, Fabrikov D, Morote E, Torres A, Ramos R, Gui JL (2019) Production of n-3-rich insects by bioaccumulation of fishery waste. J Food Compos Anal 82:103237

Barry T (2004) Evaluation of the economic, social, and biological feasibility of bioconverting food wastes with the black soldier fly (Hermetia illucens). University of North Texas, Denton, Texas

Becker EW (2007) Micro-algae as a source of protein. Biotechnol Adv 25:207–210

Belforti M, Gai F, Lussiana C, Renna M, Malfatto V, Rotolo L (2015) *Tenebrio molitor* meal in rainbow trout (*Oncorhynchus mykiss*) diets: effects on animal performance, nutrient digestibility and chemical composition of fillets. Ital J Anim Sci 14:4170

Bharti V, Pandey PK, Koushlesh SK (2014) Single cell proteins: a novel approach in aquaculture systems. World Aquacult 45:62–63

Bob Manuel FG, Alfred-Ockiya JF (2011) Evaluation of yeast single cell protein (SCP) diets on growth performance, feed conversion and carcass composition of Tilapia *Oreochromis niloticus* (L.) fingerlings. Afr J Biotechnol 10:9473–9478

Bricknell I, Dalmo RA (2005) The use of immunostimulants in fish larval aquaculture. Fish Shellfish Immunol 19:457–472

Bureau DP, Harris AM, Bevan DJ, Simmons LA, Azevedo PA, Cho CY (2000) Feather meals and meat and bone meals from different origins as protein sources in rainbow trout (*Oncorhynchus mykiss*) diets. Aquaculture 181:281–291

Cadinu LA, Barra P, Torre F, Delogu F, Madau FA (2020) Insect rearing: potential, challenges, and circularity. Sustainability 12:4567

Chen J, Liu P, Li Y, Li M, Xia A (2018) Effects of dietary biofloc on growth, digestibility, protein turnover and energy budget of sea cucumber *Apostichopus japonicus* (Selenka). Anim Feed Sci Technol 241:151–162

Dalmin G, Kathiresan K, Purushothaman A (2001) Effect of probiotics on bacterial population and health status of shrimp in culture pond ecosystem. Indian J Exp Biol 39:939–942

Daniel N (2018) A review on replacing fish meal in aqua feeds using plant protein sources. Int J Fish Aquat Stud 6:164–179

Dantas EM, Valle B, Brito C, Calazans N, Peixoto S, Soares RB (2016) Partial replacement of fishmeal with biofloc meal in the diet of postlarvae of the Pacific white shrimp *Litopenaeus vannamei*. Aquac Nutr 22:335–342

Das S, Mondal K, Haque S (2017) A review on application of probiotic, prebiotic and synbiotic for sustainable development of aquaculture. J Entomol Zool Stud 5:422–429

Delzenne NM, Cani PD (2008) Gut micro£ora is a key player in host energy homeostasis. Med Sci (Paris) 24:505–510

Dimitroglou A, Merrifield DL, Carnevali O, Picchietti S, Avella M, Daniels C, Güroy D, Davies SJ (2011) Microbial manipulations to improve fish health and production—a Mediterranean perspective. Fish Shellfish Immunol 30:1–16

Draganovic V, van der Goot A, Boom R, Jonkers J (2013) Wheat gluten in extruded fish feed: effects on morphology and on physical and functional properties. Aquac Nutr 19:845–859

Duan J, Li R, Cheng D, Fan W, Zha X, Cheng T et al (2010) SilkDB v2. 0: a platform for silkworm (Bombyx mori) genome biology. Nucleic Acids Res 38:D453–D456

Edwards P (2015) Aquaculture environment interactions: past, present and likely future trends. Aquaculture 447:2–14

El-Haroun ER, Azevedo PA, Bureau DP (2012) High dietary incorporation levels of rendered animal protein ingredients on performance of rainbow trout *Oncorhynchus mykiss* (Walbaum, 1972). Aquaculture 290:269–274

Elia AC, Capucchio MT, Caldaroni B, Magara G, Dörr AJM, Biasato I, Gai F (2018) Influence of *Hermetia illucens* meal dietary inclusion on the histological traits, gut mucin composition and the oxidative stress biomarkers in rainbow trout (*Oncorhynchus mykiss*). Aquaculture 496:50–57

Evans J, Alemu MH, Flore R (2015) ‘Entomophagy’: an evolving terminology in need of review. J Insects Food Feed 1:293–305

Ezewudo BI, Monebi CO, Ugwumba AAA (2015) Production and utilization of Musca domestica maggots in the diet of *Oreochromis niloticus* (Linnaeus, 1758) fingerlings. Afr J Agric Res 10: 2363–2371

FAO (2018) The state of world fisheries and aquaculture 2018. FAO, Rome

Farhangi M, Carter CG (2015) Growth, physiological and immunological responses of rainbow trout (*Oncorhynchus mykiss*) to different dietary inclusion levels of dehulled lupin (*Lupinus angustifolius*). Aquac Res 32:329–340

Faruk MAR, Ali MM, Patwary ZP (2008) Evaluation of the status of use of chemicals and antibiotics in freshwater aquaculture activities with special emphasis to fish health management. J Bangladesh Agric Univ 6:381–390

Fasakin EA, Balogun AM, Ajayi OO (2003) Evaluation of full-fat and defatted maggot meals in the feeding of clariid catfish *Clarias gariepinus* fingerlings. Aquac Res 34:733–738
Fjellheim AJ, Playfoot KJ, Skjermo J, Vadstein O (2007) Vibrionaceae dominates the microflora antagonistic towards *Listonella anguillarum* in the intestine of cultured Atlantic cod (*Gadus morhua* L.) larvae. Aquaculture 269:98–106
Francis G, Makkar H, Becker K (2001) Antinutritional factors present in plant-derived alternate fish feed ingredients and their effects in fish. Aquaculture 199:197–227
Freccia A, Meurer ES, Jerônimo GT, Emerenciano MGC (2016) Insect meal in diets of tilapia fingerlings. Zootechn Arch 65:541–547
García-Garibay M, Gómez-Ruiz L, Cruz-Guerrero AE, Bárzana E (2003) Single-cell proteinl algae. In: Encyclopedia of food sciences and nutrition, 2nd edn. pp 5269–5276
Gasco L, Gai F, Piccolo G, Rotolo L, Lussiana C, Molla P (2014) Substitution of fish meal by *Tenebrio molitor* meal in the diet of *Dicentrarchus labrax* juveniles. In: Insects to feed the world, vol. 80. The Netherlands, pp 14–17
Gasco L, Henry M, Piccolo G, Marono S, Gai F, Renna M (2016) *Tenebrio molitor* meal in diets for European sea bass (*Dicentrarchus labrax* L.) juveniles: growth performance, whole body composition and in vivo apparent digestibility. Anim Feed Sci Technol 220:34–45
Gasco L, Biancarosa I, Liland NS (2020) From waste to feed: a review of recent knowledge on insects as producers of protein and fat for animal feeds. Curr Opin Green Sustain Chem 23:67–79
Gibson LF (1999) Bacteriocin activity and probiotic activity of *Aeromonas* media. J Appl Microbiol 85:2445–2485
Gildberg A, Mikkelsen A, Sandaker E, Ring E (1997) Probiotic effect of lactic acid bacteria in the feed on growth and survival of fry of Atlantic cod (*Gadus morhua*). Hydrobiology 352:279–285
Gram L, Melchiorsen J, Sanggard B, Hubber I, Nielsen T (1999) Inhibition of *Vibrio anguillarum* by *Pseudomonas fuorescens* AH2 a possible probiotic treatment of fish. Appl Environ Microbiol 65:969–973
Grazziotin A, Pimentel FA, Jong EVD (2008) Poultry feather hydrolysate as a protein source for growing rats. Braz J Vet Res Anim Sci 45:61–67
Halasz A, Lasztity R (1991) Use of yeast biomass in food production, 1st edn. CRC Press, Boca Raton
Hanel R, Broekman D, Graaf SD, Schnack D (2007) Partial replacement of fishmeal by lyophylized powder of the microalgae Spirulina platensis in Pacific white shrimp diets. Open Mar Biol J 1:1–5
Hansen JV, Lagos L, Peng L, Reveco F, Verland M (2021) Down-stream processing of baker's yeast (*Saccharomyces cerevisiae*)—effect on nutrient digestibility and immune response in Atlantic salmon (*Salmo salar*). Aquaculture 530:735707
Hardy RW, Sealey WM, Gatlin DM (2007) Fisheries by-catch and by-product meals as protein sources for rainbow trout *Oncorhynchus mykiss*. J World Aquacult Soc 36:393–400
Hawkey KJ, Lopez-Viso C, Brameld JM, Parr T, Salter AM (2021) Insects: a potential source of protein and other nutrients for feed and food. Annu Rev Anim Biosci 9:333–354
Henry M, Gasco L, Piccolo G, Fountoulaki E (2015) Review on the use of insects in the diet of farmed fish: Past and future. Anim Feed Sci Technol 203:1–22
Henry MA, Gasco L, Chatzifotis S, Piccolo G (2018) Does dietary insect meal affect the fish immune system? The case of mealworm, *Tenebrio molitor* on European sea bass, *Dicentrarchus labrax*. Dev Comp Immunol 81:204–209
Hessler Frelinckx J-C (2019) Behavioural study of the house cricket (*Acheta domesticus*): behavioural study of the house cricket (*Acheta domesticus*). Swedish University of Agricultural Science, Uppsala
Hussain SM, Afzal M, Salim M, Javid A, Khichi TAA, Hussain M, Raza SA (2011) Apparent digestibility of fish meal, blood meal and meat meal for *Labeo rohita* fingerlings. J Anim Plant Sci 21:807–811

Ibrahem MD (2015) Evolution of probiotics in aquatic world: potential effects, the current status in Egypt and recent prospective. J Adv Res 6:765–791

Ipinmoroti M, Akanmu O, Iyiola A (2019) Utilisation of house fly maggots (Musca domestica) as replacement for fish meal in the diets of *Clarias gariepinus* juveniles. J Insects Food Feed 5:69–76

Iribarren D, Dagá P, Moreira MT, Feijoo G (2012) Potential environmental effects of probiotics used in aquaculture. Aquacult Int 20:779–789

Jannathulla R, Dayal JS, Vasanthakumar D, Ambasankar K, Muralidhar M (2017) Effect of fermentation methods on amino acids, fiber fractions and anti-nutritional factors in different plant protein sources and essential amino acid index for Penaeus (*Litopenaeus) vannamei.* Indian J Fish 64:40–44

Jeyachandran P, Paulraj S (1976) Experiments with artificial feeds on Cyprinus carpio fingerlings. J Inland Fish Soc India 8(1976):33–37

Jones SW, Karpol A, Friedman S, Maru BT, Tracy BP (2020) Recent advances in single cell protein use as a feed ingredient in aquaculture. Curr Opin Biotechnol 61:189–197

Karimi S, Soofiani NM, Mahboubi A, Taherzadeh M (2018) Use of organic wastes and industrial by-products to produce filamentous fungi with potential as aqua-feed ingredients. Sustainability 10:1–19

Kim DH, Austin B (2006) Cytokine expression in leucocytes and gut cells of rainbow trout, *Oncorhynchus* mykiss Walbaum, induced by probiotics. Vet Immunol Immunopathol 114: 297–304

Kim SW, Less JF, Wang L, Yan T, Kiron V, Kaushik SJ, Lei XG (2019) Meeting global feed protein demand: challenge, opportunity, and strategy. Annu Rev Anim Biosci 7:221–243

Kiron V, Sørensen M, Huntley M, Vasanth GK, Gong Y, Dahle D, Palihawadana AM (2016) Defatted biomass of the microalga, *Desmodesmus sp*., can replace fishmeal in the feeds for Atlantic salmon. Front Mar Sci 3:67

Kolndadacha OD, Adikwu IA, Okaeme AN, Atiribom RY, Mohammed A, Musa YM (2011) The role of probiotics in aquaculture in Nigeria-a review. Cont J Fish Aq Sci 5:8–15

Korsnes K, Nicolaisen O, Skar CK, Nerland AH, Bergh Ø (2006) Bacteria in the gut of juvenile cod *Gadus morhua* fed live feed enriched with four different commercial diets. Front Mar Sci 63: 296–301

Lalloo R, Ramchuran S, Rgens JG, Gardiner N, Maharajh D (2010) Isolation and selection of *Bacillus* spp. as potential biological agents for enhancement of water quality in culture of ornamental fish. J Appl Microbiol 103:1471–1479

Lapea D, Olsen PM, Arntzen M, Kosa G, Passoth V, Eijsink V, Horn SJ (2020) Spruce sugars and poultry hydrolysate as growth medium in repeated fed-batch fermentation processes for production of yeast biomass. Bioprocess Biosyst Eng 43:723–736

Lee J, Choi I, Kim K, Cho S, Yoo J (2012) Response of dietary substitution of fishmeal with various protein sources on growth, body composition and blood chemistry of olive flounder (Paralichthys olivaceus, Temminck & Schlegel, 1846). Fish Physiol Biochem 38(2012):735–744

Li L, Zhao Z, Liu H (2013) Feasibility of feeding yellow mealworm (Tenebrio molitor L.) in bioregenerative life support systems as a source of animal protein for humans. Acta Astronaut 92(2013):103–109

Liland NS, Biancarosa I, Araujo P (2017) Modulation of nutrient composition of black soldier fly (*Hermetia illucens*) larvae by feeding seaweed-enriched media. PLoS One 12:e0183188

Linder T (2019) Making the case for edible microorganisms as an integral part of a more sustainable and resilient food production system. Food Security 11:265–278

Lokesh J, Fernandes JMO, Korsnes K, Bergh O, Brinchmann MF, Kiron V (2012) Transcriptional regulation of cytokines in the intestine of Atlantic cod fed yeast derived mannan oligosaccharide or beta-glucan and challenged with *Vibrio anguillarum*. Fish Shellfish Immunol 33:626–631

Lunger AN, McLean E, Craig SR (2007) The effects of organic protein supplementation upon growth, feed conversion and texture quality parameters of juvenile cobia (*Rachycentron canadum*). Aquaculture 264:342–352
Mahnken C, Spinelli J, Waknitz FW (1980) Evaluation of an alkane yeast (Candida sp.) as a substitute for fish meal in Oregon moist pellet: feeding trials with coho salmon (*Oncorhynchus kisutch*) and rainbow trout (*Salmo gairdneri*). Aquaculture 20:41–56
MªJ SM, Haro C, Sanz A, Braided CE, Villareces S, Barroso FG (2016) Nutritional evaluation of *Tenebrio molitor* meal as fishmeal substitute for tilapia (*Oreochromis niloticus*) diet. Aquac Nutr 22:943–955
Makkar HPS, Tran G, Henze V, Ankers P (2014) State-of-the-art on use of insects as animal feed. Anim Feed Sci Tech 197:1–33
Malik A, Singh N, Satya S (2007) House fly (Musca domestica): a review of control strategies for a challenging pest. J Environ Sci Health Part B 42:453–469
Masson MV, de Souza Tavares W, Alves JM, Ferreira-Filho PJ, Barbosa LR, Wilcken CF et al (2020) Bioecological aspects of the common black field cricket, *Gryllus assimilis* (Orthoptera: Gryllidae) in the laboratory and in Eucalyptus (Myrtaceae) plantations. J Orthop Res 29:83
Matassa S, Boon N, Pikaar I, Verstraete W (2016) Microbial protein: future sustainable food supply route with low environmental footprint. Microb Biotechnol 9:568–575
Meena DK, Das P, Kumar S, Mandal SC, Prusty AK, Singh SK (2013) Beta-glucan: an ideal immunostimulant in aquaculture (a review). Fish Physiol Biochem 39:431–457
Mickeniene L, Syvokiene J (2008) The impact of zinc on the bacterial abundance in the intestinal tract of rainbow trout (*Oncorhynchus mykiss*) larvae. Ekologija 54:5–9
Navarrete P, Mardones P, Opazo R, Espejo R, Romero J (2008) Oxytetracycline treatment reduces bacterial diversity of intestinal microbiota of Atlantic salmon. J Aquat Anim Health 20:177–183
Nayak SK, Swain P, Mukherjee SC (2007) Effect of dietary supplementation of probiotic and vitamin C on the immune response of Indian major carp, *Labeo rohita* (Ham.). Fish Shellfish Immunol 23:892–896
Ng WK, Liew FL, Ang LP, Wong KW (2001) Potential of mealworm (*Tenebrio molitor*) as an alternative protein source in practical diets for African catfish, *Clarias gariepinus*. Aquac Res 32:273–280
Nicholson JK, Holmes E, Wilson ID (2005) Gut microorganisms, mammalian metabolism and personalized health care. Nat Rev Microbiol 3:431–438
Nidhina N, Muthukumar S (2015) Antinutritional factors and functionality of protein-rich fractions of industrial guar meal as affected by heat processing. Food Chem 173:920–926
Nwamba H, Ogunji JO (2012) Evaluating butterfly larvae (*Bematistes macaria*) meal as fishmeal substitute in diets of African catfish hybrid (*Heteroclarias*). Indian J Soc Nat Sci 1:78–84
OECD (2016) The cost of air pollution in Africa. https://www.oecd-ilibrary.org/development/thecost-of-air-pollution-in-africa_5jlqzq77x6f8-en
Ogunji JO, Kloas W, Wirth M, Neumann N, Pietsch C (2008a) Effect of housefly maggot meal (magmeal) diets on the performance, concentration of plasma glucose, cortisol and blood characteristics of *Oreochromis niloticus* fingerlings. J Anim Physiol Anim Nutr 92:511–518
Ogunji J, Schulz C, Kloas W (2008b) Growth performance, nutrient utilization of Nile tilapia *Oreochromis niloticus* fed housefly maggot meal (magmeal) diets. Turk J Fish Aquat Sci 8:141–147
Okore O, Ekedo C, Ubiaru P, Uzodinma K (2016) Growth and haematological studies of African catfish (*Clarias gariepinus*) juveniles fed with Housefly larva (*Musca dometica*) as feed supplement. Int J Agric Earth Sci 2:21–30
Ortuno J, Cuesta A, Rodriguez A, Esteban MA, Meseguer J (2002) Oral administration of yeast, *Saccharomyces cerevisiae,* enhances the cellular innate immune response of gilt-head seabream (*Sparus aurata* L.). Vet Immunol Immunopathol 85:41–50
Øverland MS, Rensen M, Storebakken T, Penn M, Krogdahl Å, Skrede A (2009) Pea protein concentrate substituting fish meal or soybean meal in diets for Atlantic salmon (*Salmo salar*)-

effect on growth performance, nutrient digestibility, carcass composition, gut health, and physical feed quality. Aquaculture 288:305–311
Pastor B, Velasquez Y, Gobbi P, Rojo S (2015) Conversion of organic wastes into fly larval biomass: bottlenecks and challenges. J Insects Food Feed 1:179–193
Patil NS, Jadhav JP (2014) Single cell protein production using penicillium ochrochloron chitinase and its evaluation in fish meal formulations. J Microb Biochem Technol S4:005
Perera W, Carter CG, Houlihan DF (1995) Apparent absorption efficiencies of amino acids in rainbow trout, *Oncorhynchus mykiss* (Walbaum), fed diets containing bacterial single-cell protein. Aquac Nutr 2:95–103
Piccolo G, Marono S, Gasco L, Iannaccone F, Bovera F, Nizza A (2014) Use of Tenebrio Molitor larvae meal in diets for Gilthead Sea bream Sparus aurata juveniles. In: Insects to feed the world. The Netherlands, pp 14–17
Pikaar I, Matassa S, Rabaey K, Bodirsky BL, Popp A, Herrero M, Verstraete W (2017) Microbes and the next nitrogen revolution. Environ Sci Technol 51:7297–7303
Pike IH, Andorsdottir G Mundheim H (1990) The role of fishmeal in diets for salmonids. International association of fishmeal manufacturers. https://www.iffo.net/es/system/files/TB24%20FM%20Salmon.PDF. Accessed 23 Aug 2019
Pojić M, Mišan A, Tiwari B (2018) Eco-innovative technologies for extraction of proteins for human consumption from renewable protein sources of plant origin. Trends Food Sci Technol 75:93–104
Qi Z, Zhang XH, Boon N, Bossier P (2009) Probiotics in aquaculture of China—current state, problems and prospect. Aquaculture 290:15–21
Raja PK, Aanand S, Sampathkumar JS, Padmavathy P (2020) Effect of silkworm (*Bombyx mori*) pupae on the growth and maturation of rainbow shark *Epalzeorhynchos frenatum* (Fowler, 1934) under captive rearing. Indian J Fish 67:89–96
Rajkumar G, Bhavan PS, Srinivasan V, Udayasuriyan R, Satgurunathan T (2017) Partial replacement of fishmeal with marine algae *Turbinaria ornata* and *Gracilaria corticata* for sustainable culture of the freshwater prawn *Macrobrachium rosenbergii*. Int J Res Stud Zool 3:32–44
Ray RC, Montet D (eds) (2015) Microorganisms and fermentation of traditional foods. CRC Press, New York
Rengpipat S, Phianphak W, Piyatiratitivorakul S, Menasveta P (1998) Effects of a probiotic bacterium on black tiger shrimp *Penaeus monodon* survival and growth. Aquaculture 167: 301–313
Ritala A, Häkkinen ST, Toivari M, Wiebe MG (2017) Single cell protein—state-of the-art, industrial landscape and patents 2001–2016. Front Microbiol 8:2009
Robertson PAW, Dowd CO, Burrels C, Williams P, Austin B (2000) Use of *Carnobactrium sp.* as a probiotic for Atlantic Salmon (*Salmo salar* L.) and rainbow trout (*Oncorhynchus mykiss*, Walbaum). Aquaculture 18:235–243
Rumbos CI, Karapanagiotidis IT, Mente E, Athanassiou CG (2019) The lesser mealworm Alphitobius diaperinus: a noxious pest or a promising nutrient source? Rev Aquac 11 (2019):1418–1437
Rumpold BA, Klocke M, Schluter O (2017) Insect biodiversity: underutilize bioresource for sustainable applications in life sciences. Reg Environ Chang 17:1445–1454
Rumsey GL, Hughes SG, Kinsella JL (2010) Use of dietary yeast *Saccharomyces cerevisiae* nitrogen by Lake trout. J World Aquacult Soc 21:205–209
Saad N, Delattre C, Urdaci M, Schmitter JM, Bressollier P (2013) An overview of the last advances in probiotic and prebiotic field. LWT Food Sci Technol 50:1–16
Saleh HH (2020) Effect of feeding on fresh (wet) housefly maggots (*Musca domestica*) with or without artificial diet on water quality and growth rates of African catfish (*Clarias gariepinus* Burchell, 1822) fry under laboratory conditions. J Zool Res 2:2053
Sanchez-Muros MJ, Barroso FG, Manzano-Agugliaro F (2014) Insect meal as renewable source of food for animal feeding: a review. J Clean Prod 65:16–27

Sankian Z, Khosravi S, Kim YO, Lee SM (2018) Effects of dietary inclusion of yellow mealworm (*Tenebrio molitor*) meal on growth performance, feed utilization, body composition, plasma biochemical indices, selected immune parameters and antioxidant enzyme activities of mandarin fish (*Siniperca scherzeri*) juveniles. Aquaculture 496:79–87

Scarlat N, Motola V, Dallemand JF, Monforti-Ferrario F, Mofor L (2015) Evaluation of energy potential of municipal solid waste from African urban areas. Renew Sust Energ Rev 50:1269–1286

Schryver PD, Crab R, Defoirdt T, Boon N, Verstraete W (2008) The basics of bio-flocs technology: the added value for aquaculture. Aquaculture 277:125–137

Shakoori M, Gholipour H, Naseri S (2015) Effect of replacing dietary fish meal with silkworm (*Bombyx mori*) pupae on hematological parameters of rainbow trout *Oncorhynchus mykiss*. Comp Clin Path 24:139–143

Shamsuzzaman MM, Biswas TK (2012) Aqua chemicals in shrimp farm: a study from south-west coast of Bangladesh. Egypt J Aquat Res 38:275–285. https://doi.org/10.1016/j.ejar.2012.12.008

Sharifuzzaman SM, Austin B (2009) Influence of probiotic feeding duration on disease resistance and immune parameters in rainbow trout. Fish Shellfish Immunol 27:440–445

Sharma S, Hansen LD, Hansen JØ, Mydland LT, Horn SJ, Øverland M, Eijsink VGH, Vuoristo KS (2018) Microbial protein produced from brown seaweed and spruce wood as a feed ingredient. J Agric Food Chem 66:8328–8335

Skrodenyte-Arbaeiauskiene V (2000) Proteolytic activity of the roach (Rutilus rutilus L.) intestinal micro£ora. Acta Zool Litu 10(3):69–77

Skrodenyte-Arbaciauskiene V, Sruoga A, Butkauskas D (2006) Assessment of microbial diversity in the river trout *Salmo trutta fario* L. intestinal tract identified by partial 16S rRNA gene sequence analysis. Fish Sci 72:597–602

Sørensen M, Morken T, Kosanovic M (2011) Pea and wheat starch possess different processing characteristics and affect physical quality and viscosity of extruded feed for Atlantic salmon. Aquac Nutr 17:326–336

Spalvins K, Blumberga D (2018) Production of fish feed and fish oil from waste biomass using microorganisms: overview of methods analyzing resource availability. Environ Clim Technol 22:149–164

Spalvins K, Ivanovs K, Blumberga D (2018) Single cell protein production from waste biomass: review of various agricultural by-products. Agron Res 16:1493–1508

Stankus A (2021) State of world aquaculture 2020 and regional reviews: FAO webinar series. In: FAO aquaculture newsletter, pp 17–18

Storebakken T, Baeverfjord G, Skrede A, Olli JJ, Berge GM (2004) Bacterial protein grown on natural gas in diets for Atlantic salmon, *Salmo salar*, in freshwater. Aquaculture 241:413–425

Su J, Gong Y, Cao S, Lu F, Han D, Liu H, Xie S (2017) Effects of dietary *Tenebrio molitor* meal on the growth performance, immune response and disease resistance of yellow catfish (Pelteobagrus fulvidraco). Fish Shellfish Immunol 69:59–66

Sun YZ, Yang HL, Ma RL, Lin WY (2010) Probiotic applications of two dominant gut *Bacillus* strains with antagonistic activity improved the growth performance and immune responses of grouper *Epinephelus coioides*. Fish Shellfish Immunol 29:803–809

Taoka Y, Maeda H, Jo JY, Kim SM, Park S, Yoshikawa T (2006) Use of live and dead probiotic cells in tilapia Oreochromis niloticus. Fish Sci 72:55–66

Tschirner M, Simon A (2015) Influence of different growing substrates and processing on the nutrient composition of black soldier fly larvae destined for animal feed. J Insects Food Feed 1: 249–259

Ullah Z, Ahmed G, Nisa MU (2016) Standardized ileal amino acid digestibility of commonly used feed ingredients in growing broilers. Asian Australas J Anim Sci 29:1322

UNEP (2018) Africa waste management outlook. UN Environment Programme, Nairobi, p 153

van Huis A (2019) Insects as food and feed, a new emerging agricultural sector: a review. J Insects Food Feed 6:27–44 van Immerseel F, de Buck J, Pasmans F, Velge P, Bottreau E, Fievez V (2003) Invasion of Salmonella enteritidis in avian intestinal epithelial cells in vitro is influenced by short-chain fatty acids. Int J Food Microbiol 85:237–248

Veldkamp T, Van Duinkerken G, Van Huis A, Lakemond CMM, Ottevanger E, Bosch G (2012) Insects as a sustainable feed ingredient in pig and poultry diets—a feasibility study. In: Wageningen UR livestock research, pp 1570–8616

Vine NG, Leukes WD, Kaiser H (2006) Probiotics in marine larviculture. FEMS Microbiol Rev 30:404–427

Viola SGZ (1984) Nutrition studies with market size hybrids of tilapia (*Oreochromis*) in intensive culture. Isr J Aquacult 36:3–15

Volman JJ, Ramakers JD, Plat J (2008) Dietary modulation of immune function by β-glucans. Physiol Behav 94:276–284

Wael Fahmi W, Sutton K (2010) Cairo's contested garbage: sustainable solid waste management and the Zabaleen's right to the city. Sustainability 2:1174

Wang YB (2008) Effect of probiotics on growth performance and digestive enzyme activity of the shrimp *Penaeus vannamei*. Aquaculture 269:259–264

Wang C, Chuprom J, Wang Y, Fu L (2020) Beneficial bacteria for aquaculture: nutrition, bacteriostasis and immunoregulation. J Appl Microbiol 128:28–40

Xu J, Bjursell MK, Himrod J, Deng S, Carmichael LK, Chiang HC, Hooper LV, Gordon JI (2003) A genomic view of the human- Bacteroides thetaiotaomicron symbiosis. Science 299:2074–2076

Yu R, Cao H, Huang Y, Peng M, Kajbaf K, Kumar V, Tao Z, Yang G, Wen C (2020) The effects of partial replacement of fishmeal protein by hydrolysed feather meal protein in the diet with high inclusion of plant protein on growth performance, fillet quality and physiological parameters of Pengze crucian carp (*Carassius auratus* var. Pengze). Aquac Res 51:636–647

Yuan XY, Jiang GZ, Wang CC, Abasubong KP, Zou Q, Zhou YY, Liu WB (2019) Effects of partial replacement of fish meal by yeast hydrolysate on antioxidant capability, intestinal morphology, and inflammation-related gene expression of juvenile Jian carp (*Cyprinus carpio* var. Jian). Fish Physiol Biochem 45:187–197

Yue K, Shen Y (2021) An overview of disruptive technologies for aquaculture. Aquac Fish 7:111–120

Ziaei-Nejad S, Rezaei MH, Takami GA, Lovett DL, Mirvaghefi AMS (2006) The effect of Bacillus spp. bacteria used as probiotics on digestive enzyme activity, survival and growth in the Indian white shrimp *Fenneropenaeus indicus*. Aquaculture 252:516–524

Chapter 5
Prebiotics as Functional Ingredients in Aquafeed: Trends and Prospects in African Aquaculture

Kaulo Salushando and Ahmad Cheikhyoussef

Abstract The aquaculture sector is growing exponentially and has certainly gained popularity in the international economics and development agenda across the world. The challenges in aquaculture intensification can be solved by establishing sustainable technologies that could boost the rapid growth rate while minimizing disease outbreaks. Host physiology is influenced by the microbiome; thus, its modulation can improve human and animal health. This can be achieved through the introduction of beneficial microorganisms (probiotics), a supply of substrates to support the growth of commensal microorganisms (functional additives) and fecal transplants. Functional additives include prebiotics, immunostimulants, and short-chain fatty acids (SCFAs). Prebiotics have been reported to improve growth performance, feed utilization, survival, carcass composition, health status, disease resistance, immune functions, microbiota modulation, and reduced oxidative stress in aquaculture. Prebiotics confer benefits in fish through changes in bacterial communities; they act as energy sources for beneficial bacterial species that ferment prebiotics. The by-products of this fermentation (SCFAs, vitamins, and peptides) are responsible for the beneficial effects of prebiotics in fish. In this chapter, we summarize the effect of prebiotics and their application in aquaculture as functional feed ingredients for fish nutrition and provide perspectives on the potential application of prebiotics in aquaculture in Africa.

K. Salushando
Department of Biochemistry, Microbiology, and Biotechnology, Faculty of Agriculture, Engineering and Natural Sciences, University of Namibia, Windhoek, Namibia

Ministry of Fisheries and Marine Resources, Hardap Inland Aquaculture Center, Hardap, Namibia

A. Cheikhyoussef (✉)
Science and Technology Division, Multidisciplinary Research Service, Centre for Research Services, University of Namibia, Windhoek, Namibia
e-mail: acheikhyoussef@unam.na

© The Author(s), under exclusive license to Springer Nature Singapore Pte Ltd. 2023
N. N. Gabriel et al. (eds.), *Emerging Sustainable Aquaculture Innovations in Africa*, Sustainable Agriculture and Food Security,
https://doi.org/10.1007/978-981-19-7451-9_5

Keywords Aquaculture · Fish nutrition · Functional ingredient · Inulin · Mushroom · Prebiotics · Probiotics

5.1 Introduction

The aquaculture sector is expanding rapidly and has gained prominence in the international economics and development agendas around the world, as well as among small-scale farmers in Sub-Saharan African countries, such as Namibia (Salushando 2022). The oceans are regarded as the world's most significant nutrient reservoirs, with fish and marine organisms well known as rich sources of bioactive compounds and new valuable ingredients for nutraceutical and pharmaceutical formulations (Ngo et al. 2012; Sardari and Nordberg Karlsson 2018). One of the goals of aquaculture is to meet the growing demand for fish as a food source, considering the fact that fish stocks in natural water systems, such as oceans, are depleting.

In developing countries, challenges in aquaculture include lack of quality fish seeds and feeds; high cost of fish feeds; losses due to poor fish health management interventions, sometimes leading to disease outbreaks; food safety and quality of products; and slow growth of some farmed species (Hongskul 1999; Nsonga and Simbotwe 2014). Nevertheless, production can be increased through expansion, intensification, diversification, and improved integration of fish production into current land and water use (Nsonga and Simbotwe 2014; Benedict 2017). Moreover, there is a need to establish sustainable technologies that could boost rapid increase in growth rate, while minimizing disease outbreaks in aquaculture (Bharathi et al. 2019).

The microbiome greatly influences host physiology, and its composition is affected by host, environmental, and diet factors (Romero et al. 2014; Wang et al. 2018). Thus, improving human and animal health via modulation of the microbiome is an evolving strategy that is part of a comprehensive, holistic approach to lifestyle awareness (Gibson et al. 2017). This can be achieved through the introduction of consortia or single beneficial microorganisms (probiotics), supply of substrates to support growth of commensal microorganisms (functional additives) and fecal transplants (Enam and Mansell 2019). Typical examples of functional additives include prebiotics, immunostimulants, and short-chain fatty acids which have been found to improve immunity, feed efficiency, and growth performance of fish through the modulation of the gut microbiota (Ganguly et al. 2013).

Prebiotics are defined as substrates that are selectively utilized by host microorganisms conferring a health benefit (Gibson et al. 2017). Prebiotics can be included in foods, drinks, animal feeds, as well as supplements (Gibson et al. 2010). There are many types of prebiotics, and sources include honey, banana, onion, wheat, human's and cow's milk, barley, tomato, asparagus, garlic, peas, and beans (Davani-Davari et al. 2019). Prebiotics cause shifts in the gut microbiota by supporting the growth of beneficial communities, as well as serving as substrates to produce biologically active metabolites, resulting in positive systemic and specific health outcomes

(Krumbeck et al. 2016). Moreover, they enhance the bioavailability and uptake of minerals, including calcium, magnesium, and possibly iron (Slavin 2013).

In aquaculture, prebiotics have been reported to improve growth performance, feed utilization, survival, carcass composition, health status, disease resistance, immune functions, microbiota modulation, and reduced oxidative stress (Ganguly et al. 2013; Ringø et al. 2014; Akhter et al. 2015; Guerreiro et al. 2018). This chapter aims to review prebiotics and their application in aquaculture as functional feed ingredients for fish nutrition and provide perspectives on the potential application of prebiotics in aquaculture in Africa.

5.2 Prebiotics and Their Functions in Fish

The current aquaculture intensification may lead to water quality deterioration and subsequently to disease outbreaks (Dawood and Koshio 2016). In the past, disease outbreaks were controlled using antibiotics and vaccines, but due to the widespread emergence of antibiotic resistance in fish pathogens, they were banned by the European Union (EU) (Pérez-Sánchez et al. 2018). Prebiotics, together with probiotics, offer a distinct strategy for avoiding disease outbreaks in aquaculture and positive impacts have been reported, such as enhancing growth, survival, intestinal absorption, the well-being of fish and immunomodulation (González-Félix et al. 2018). However, prebiotics present an alternative way of manipulating endogenous microbes to improve host health and as well as overcome issues of biosecurity associated with probiotics (Ringø et al. 2010; Dimitroglou et al. 2011).

Most prebiotics (oligosaccharides) are made up of beta-glycosidic bonds that resist hydrolysis by endogenic enzymes of animals (which only recognize the alpha-glycosidic linkages) and are fermented or hydrolyzed by beneficial microbiota (Lauzon et al. 2014). Common prebiotics in aquaculture include inulin, fructooligosaccharides (FOS), galactooligosaccharides (GOS), xylooligosaccharides (XOS), isomaltooligosaccharides (IMO), short-chain fructooligosaccharides (sc-FOS), oligofructose, mannanoligosaccharides (MOS), trans-galactooligosaccharides (TOS), arabinoxylooligosaccharides (AXOS), and different commercial prebiotic mixtures (Ringø et al. 2014; Zoumpopoulou et al. 2018).

Furthermore, they stimulate selected favorable indigenous microbial populations by altering conditions in favor of beneficial species which potentially enhance fish growth efficiency and reduce disease susceptibility (Ringø et al. 2010; Dimitroglou et al. 2011). Ringø et al. (2010) further hypothesized the potential of prebiotics in increasing efficiency and sustainability of aquaculture production. In fact, several studies (Table 5.1) have documented the benefits of prebiotics in aquaculture (Ortiz et al. 2013; Eshaghzadeh et al. 2015; Tiengtam et al. 2015). However, few studies could be found in the literature from African countries; therefore, further studies are required to elucidate prebiotic's role in aquaculture in Africa and Namibia is not an exception.

Table 5.1 Examples on documented studies on the benefits of prebiotics in aquaculture

Prebiotic	Fish species	Dosage (%)	Size of fish	Duration (weeks)	Results	References
Inulin and Jerusalem artichoke tuber	Nile tilapia (*Oreochromis niloticus*)	0.25, 0.5, and 1	Juveniles (42–47 g)	8	Positive effects on growth performance and health parameters	Tiengtam et al. (2015)
XOS, GOS, FOS, and MOS	Hybrid catfish (*Pangasianodon gigas* × *Pangasianodon hypophthalmus*)	0.6	Fingerlings (5.50 ± 0.04 g)	10	Improved growth performance, gut health, and immune response	Hahor et al. (2019)
Corncob derived XOS	Nile tilapia (*O. niloticus*)	0.5, 1, 2	Fingerlings (20.72 ± 0.02 g)	4 and 8	Improved growth performance and health status	van Doan et al. (2018)
GroBiotic®-A (yeast-based prebiotic)	Totoaba (*Totoaba macdonaldi*)	2	Juvenile (215.6 ± 9.3 g)	16	No effect on growth performance, reduced lysozyme activity, and significant effect on transient intestinal microbiota	González-Félix et al. (2018)
Prebiotic mixtures (inulin and GOS; GOS and D-sorbitol; and inulin, GOS and D-sorbitol)	Juvenile chu's croaker (*Nibea coibor*)	1	Juvenile (13.58 ± 0.07 g)	8	Improved growth performance, increased intestinal microbiota diversity, and improved immune parameters	Li et al. (2019b)
GOS	Caspian roach (*Rutilus rutilus*)	1 and 2	Fry (1.36 ± 0.03 g)	7	Improved growth performance, stress resistance, and modulated intestinal microbiota by increasing lactic acid bacteria	Hoseinifar et al. (2013)
β-glucan; GOS; MOS	Snakehead (*Channa striata*)	0.2, 1, and 0.5	Fingerlings (22.46 ± 0.17 g)	15.5	Improved growth performance, and no effect on hepatosomatic index (HSI)	Munir et al. (2016)
Dietary Fiber Concentrates	Jundiá (*Rhamdia quelen*)	0.5 and 1	Fingerlings (7.16 ± 0.06)	8	Improved growth and intestinal villus height	Goulart et al. (2018)

FOS	Common carp (*Cyprinus carpio*)	1, 2 and 3	Fry (3.23 ± 0.14)	7	No effect on growth performance and hematological parameters, significant increase in total viable heterotrophic aerobic bacteria and lactic acid bacteria, and increased the survival rate and stress resistance	Hoseinifar et al. (2014)
Inulin	Common carp (*C. carpio*)	1	Fry (0.55 ± 0.02 g)	7	No significant effect on the growth performance, increased survival rate and lipid content, and no effects on digestive lipase, protease and amylase activities	Eshaghzadeh et al. (2015)
MOS	Nile tilapia (*O. niloticus*)	0.2, 0.4, and 0.6	Juveniles (49.6 ± 10.8)	8.5	No effect on the growth performance, immune parameters, and intestinal morphology	Yuji-Sado et al. (2015)
sc-FOS	Common carp (*C. carpio*)	0.5 and 1	Larvae (0.55 ± 0.02 g)	7	No significant effect on growth performance and total viable counts of heterotrophic aerobic bacteria (TVC) and lactic acid bacteria, and increased digestive enzyme activities and survival rate	Hoseinifar et al. (2016)

Over the past decades, the definition of what constitutes a prebiotic has evolved; in particular, the prebiotic concept has expanded applications to include not only humans but also other animals and other target sites apart from the gastrointestinal (GI) tract (Gibson et al. 2017). Previously, prebiotics were defined and characterized based on human applications; this has been the case with the criteria to classify an ingredient as a prebiotic. Defining, using, and setting up criteria for prebiotics in aquaculture is complex; Lauzon et al. (2014) suggested criteria for classifying prebiotics in aquaculture (aquatic organisms) as follows:

- Resistance to hydrolysis by the host's enzymes and GI absorption,
- Improvement in intestinal microbial balance, and
- Conferring host benefits (such as improved disease resistance, nonspecific immunity, gut morphology, growth, survival, and/or nutrient digestibility).

The fact that mammals and aquatic organisms significantly vary physiologically justifies the need to define the criteria specific to groups of organisms and consensus on classifying prebiotics is needed to enable correct applications of prebiotics in different animals. Specifically, aquatic organisms lack a well-defined colon, and some fish species have a distinct stomach while some do not (Lauzon et al. 2014). Moreover, pyloric ceca numbers can vary from nil to 1000 for some species, intestinal length ranges from short or up to 20 times the body length, and some species have a hindgut (fermentation) chamber (Lauzon et al. 2014). The criteria by Lauzon et al. (2014) are very similar to the established criteria except they are more applicable to aquatic animals.

5.3 Benefits and Mode of Action of Prebiotics in Aquaculture

Reported benefits of prebiotics in aquaculture are improved growth performance, survival, feed utilization, carcass composition, health status, disease resistance, gut morphology, digestibility, GI enzyme activities, immune functions, glucose and lipid metabolism, microbiota modulation, and reduced oxidative stress (Ganguly et al. 2013; Ringø et al. 2014; Akhter et al. 2015; Guerreiro et al. 2018). Due to the several modes of actions and synergies that often occur, elucidating the mechanisms by which the benefits of prebiotics are conferred is often difficult to explain (Guerreiro et al. 2018). Nevertheless, Merrifield et al. (2010) suggested that the mechanism by which prebiotics confer benefits in fish is through changes in bacterial communities increasing beneficial bacteria that promote the production of inhibitory compounds. What is more, prebiotics act as energy sources for selective (beneficial) bacterial species in the gut that ferment these prebiotics and the end products of this fermentation (short-chain fatty acids (SCFAs), vitamins, and peptides) are responsible for the majority of the beneficial effects of prebiotics in fish (Lauzon et al. 2014; Caipang and Lazado 2015; Guerreiro et al. 2018; Lieke et al. 2020).

Furthermore, mechanisms of action include competition for chemicals, available energy, and adhesion sites; inhibition of virulent gene expression; or disruption of quorum sensing (Merrifield et al. 2010). This chapter will further explain the mechanism of selective stimulation of intestinal microbiota and SCFAs provide and how prebiotics affect health (immunomodulation) and growth performance of fish. Since the major mode of action of prebiotics is through changes in microbiota, it is of outmost importance to elucidate the role of gut microbiota in fish health and growth.

5.3.1 Role of Fish Gut Microbiota

Intestinal microbiota performs a major function in nutrition, development of immunity, disease resistance, health, and well-being of fish similarly to terrestrial animals (Lauzon et al. 2014; Romero et al. 2014; Montalban-Arques et al. 2015). The microbial community of the fish GI tract is made up of viruses, Archae, protozoa, yeast, and bacteria (Guerreiro et al. 2018). However, bacteria are the most abundant in the gut (Guerreiro et al. 2018). Llewellyn et al. (2014) summarized the general lifecycle of a teleost and accessory indigenous microbiota as follows:

1. immediately when the eggs are laid, the interactions and colonization of fish progeny occurs and the diversity of the microbiota that develops reflects the microbial composition of the water;
2. once the egg hatches, environmental microbiota colonizes the larvae;
3. once the larvae begins to feed, early digestive tract colonization occurs with microbial taxa resembling those associated with feed;
4. development of the microbiome occurs, accumulating diversity, and reaching maturity; and finally
5. the adult microbiome is a diverse assemblage of microbial taxa.

Furthermore, gut microbiota of fish is to a greater extent fluidic compared to terrestrial vertebrates on account of the fluctuating environmental conditions, variational factors, high influx of microbe-laden aqueous media and dietary changes (Ringø et al. 2016; Li et al. 2019a). The factors affecting the composition of the gut microbiota can be divided into three categories, namely, host, environmental and diet factors (Romero et al. 2014). Host factors include species, genetics, gender, weight, age, immunity, and different regions of the GI tract (Li et al. 2012; Romero et al. 2014; Ringø et al. 2016). However, environmental factors include seasonal changes, water quality, temperature, salinity, stress, and cultured versus wild (Romero et al. 2014; Ringø et al. 2016; Wang et al. 2018). Diet factors include dietary form, dietary lipid, protein sources, functional glycomic ingredients, nutraceuticals (prebiotics, probiotics, synbiotics, and immunostimulants), antibiotics, dietary iron, and chromium (Li et al. 2012; Romero et al. 2014; Ringø et al. 2016; Wang et al. 2018; Tapia-Paniagua et al. 2019).

Diet is the chief source of energy for microbial growth, making it a significant factor in modulating the GI microbiota composition of fish (Davani-Davari et al. 2019; Enam and Mansell 2019). Among fish gut microbiota *Proteobacteria, Bacteroidetes, Actinobacteria, Firmicutes,* and *Fusobacterium* are the dominant phyla (Wang et al. 2018). Fish gut microbiota potentially has a positive impact in digestive processes of fish. In fact, a broad variety of enzyme-producing microbiota have been isolated and identified in the GI tract of fish (Romero et al. 2014). The enzymes produced by gut microbiota have a significant role in digestion through hydrolysis of feed components and they include amylase, cellulase, lipase, proteases, chitinase, and phytase (Wang et al. 2018; Tapia-Paniagua et al. 2019). In addition, intestinal microbiota participate in epithelial renewal, enhances the stability of β-catenin in intestinal epithelial cells, and promotes cell proliferation in the developing vertebrate intestine (Wang et al. 2018; Tapia-Paniagua et al. 2019). Moreover, the gut microbiota stimulates nutrient uptake of cholesterol and regulates fat storage by stimulating fatty acid uptake in intestinal epithelium leading to the buildup of dietary fatty acids in extraintestinal tissues (Wang et al. 2018).

Furthermore, gut microbes have a vital role in the development, maturation, and modulation of the immune response, which in turn mediate a variety of host immune functions (Wang et al. 2018; Tapia-Paniagua et al. 2019). Gut microbiota and derived products stimulate systemic and mucosal immune response through microbe-associated molecular patterns (MAMPs) interaction with pattern recognition receptors (Tapia-Paniagua et al. 2019). In addition, fish gut-associated lymphoid tissues (GALT) have significant numbers of antigen-presenting cells that participate in the initial stages of the immune response (Tapia-Paniagua et al. 2019). They further modulate the levels of cytokine and immunoglobulin as well as activate cellular response including B and T cells (Tapia-Paniagua et al. 2019). Equally important, the gut microbiota prevents pathogenic microbes from colonizing the GI tract by competitive exclusion or production of toxic secondary metabolites (Llewellyn et al. 2014).

Finally, some species in the phylum *Fusobacteria* are capable of excreting butyrate or synthesizing vitamins which positively affect the health of the fish (Romero et al. 2014). Although there is an increase in research studying the GI microbiota communities of fish Wang et al. (2018), fewer studies have been done on *O. mossambicus* in general and particularly in Namibia. Wang et al. (2018) postulated that the lack of gut microbiota in aquatic organisms could result in damaged physiological functions, for instance, intestinal epithelial cell dysfunction, compromised nutrient absorption, metabolism, and weaker immune responses. Therefore, investigating the role gut microbiota play in metabolism is useful in improving the development of commercial feeds, fish feed efficiency, and overall health and well-being of fish in aquaculture (Li et al. 2014).

5.3.2 Selective Stimulation of Intestinal Microbiota

Gut microbiota plays an important role in host health and immunity as discussed above, and most times can be considered an "extra organ" of the fish due to their significance in development, homeostasis, and protection of the GI tract (Nawaz et al. 2018). Diet plays a significant role in modulating gut microbiota. To sustain beneficial microbe homeostasis, the provision of substrates (prebiotics) that stimulate the proliferation of beneficial microbes, such as bifidobacterial and lactic acid bacteria, is of paramount importance as the basic mechanism of action of prebiotics is via its impact on the gut microbiota (Guerreiro et al. 2018; Nawaz et al. 2018). The key mode of action of prebiotics on the selective modulation of gut microbiota is as a result of the fermentation of prebiotics by advantageous bacteria, such as LAB and Bifidobacteria (Huynh et al. 2017; Guerreiro et al. 2018). These bacteria hydrolyze prebiotics using enzymes into respective sugars and use them as a carbon source to increase biomass of bacteria and therefore become favored compared to less beneficial (pathogenic) bacteria in the gut (Huynh et al. 2017; Guerreiro et al. 2018). Moreover, some species (*Lactobacillus*) have adopted various transport mechanisms and catabolic pathways together with intracellular and extracellular hydrolysis of specific oligosaccharide substrates (Goh and Klaenhammer 2015).

Studies have shown that prebiotics increase lactic acid bacteria, such as Firmicutes (*Lactobacillus* and *Enterococcus*); however, they decrease the abundance of pathogenic bacteria, for instance, Proteobacteria (*Aeromonas* and *Vibrio* spp.) (Boyd et al. 2020). According to Huynh et al. (2017) the mechanism with which prebiotics decrease the abundance of pathogens is through competitive adhesion where prebiotics either bind to receptors on the opportunistic pathogens or bind to the target sites of opportunistic bacteria. Moreover, pathogens have a complex metabolism making them unlikely to take advantage of prebiotics as substrates because they do not possess the necessary enzymes to hydrolyze them (Caipang and Lazado 2015). However, caution needs to be taken because supplying the substrate constantly in the gut could bring about a risk of pathogens acquiring the ability to use either the substrate or its degraded product (Caipang and Lazado 2015). Equally important, because prebiotics are able promote the growth of beneficial microbes, they can be combined with beneficial live microorganisms (probiotics) to facilitate their colonization in the gut to ensure the benefits of the probiotic (Huynh et al. 2017).

5.3.3 SCFAs Production

SCFAs are carboxylic acids made up of aliphatic tails of less than six carbons and are the end products of fermentation of prebiotic carbohydrates that escape digestion in the upper GI tract by anaerobic microbiota (Montalban-Arques et al. 2015; Tran et al. 2020). The most abundant SCFAs in the fish GI tract are acetate, propionate, and butyrate (Lauzon et al. 2014). Among fish and gut regions within a species, differences in the concentration of SCFAs, such as acetate, propionate, and butyrate, are evident (Tran et al. 2020).

The factors that influence the production of SCFAs according to Tran et al. (2020) are as follows: composition of the gut microbiota, environmental conditions (such as pH, hydrogen partial pressure, and available substrates), and species of fish. For instance, freshwater herbivorous fish are reported to have lower SCFAs levels compared to marine herbivorous fish, while carnivorous fish generally have higher concentrations of SCFAs than herbivorous and omnivorous fish (Hao et al. 2017). Other factors include living environments, seasons, intestinal morphology, intestinal regions, gut transit time, and rate of SCFA transport across the gut epithelium; however, in aquatic animals, limited data are available on the biosynthesis of SCFAs (Tran et al. 2020).

Furthermore, SCFAs play a crucial role in maintaining energy homeostasis, metabolism, and gut health (Tran et al. 2020). Nearly all SCFAs produced are absorbed in the hindgut as an energy source and aids in various biosynthetic processes within the vicinity of the gut (Tran et al. 2020). Nonetheless, small proportions of propionate and acetate reaches the liver and is used as substrates for the energy-producing tricarboxylic acid cycle and gluconeogenesis (Tran et al. 2020). Moreover, in fish, acetate is carried into the portal blood and utilized as energy source for skeletal muscle or lipid synthesis and butyrate is attributed for most of the oxygen requirements for gut (Lauzon et al. 2014; Tran et al. 2020).

SCFAs production leads to the modulation of blood lipid metabolism, gastrointestinal/systemic immunomodulation, energy sources resulting in intestinal cell proliferation, and improved intestinal barrier function (Lauzon et al. 2014). In addition, their synergistic stimulation of commensal and symbiotic bacteria grants competitive exclusion of pathogens, incidentally heightening pathogen resistance, decreasing toxic microbial metabolites, and repressing intestinal inflammation (Lauzon et al. 2014; Llewellyn et al. 2014). Specifically, SCFA production leads to a lowered pH in the GI tract which aids in mineral absorption and general nutritional support by enhancing digestive enzymes and the bioavailability of dietary minerals cells (Lauzon et al. 2014; Hoseinifar et al. 2017). To add, SCFAs inhibit the growth of pathogenic microbes; for instance, Gram-positive bacteria are inhibited by dissociating acids and the anions produced in bacterial cells (Ebrahimi et al. 2017; Hoseinifar et al. 2017).

SCFAs contribute significantly to the energy requirements of fish; they are absorbed and metabolized by the enterocytes, accounting for a large proportion of enterocyte energy needs and stimulating growth of gut beneficial bacteria, resulting in proliferation of epithelia and maintenance of gut health homeostasis (Ebrahimi et al. 2017; Hoseinifar et al. 2017; Guerreiro et al. 2018; Nawaz et al. 2018). In mammals SCFAs (mostly acetate, butyrate and propionate) seem to act as signaling molecules in cellular activities via the binding of receptors, G-protein-coupled receptors 41 (GPR41), GPR43, GPR109A, and Olfactory receptor 78 (OLFR78) (Tran et al. 2020).

The expression of these receptors in different tissues and cell types indicates that SCFAs have a role in modulating substrate and energy metabolism together with the immune response of the host by leading to a rise in immune components and improved regulation of immune-related gene expression (Tran et al. 2020). While these receptors have not been substantiated in fish to date, it is likely that the fish mucosal immune response is regulated in the same way (Hoseinifar et al. 2017).

The dietary supplementation of SCFAs and their salts led to the immunomodulation of fish and shrimp ensuing the up-regulation of favorable immune components, at the same time matching a reduction in immune components that are harmful to the host, subsequently aiding fish in the fight against pathogens (Hoseinifar et al. 2017). Therefore, consideration should also be taken to incorporating SCFAs as dietary supplements due to their positive impact on growth performance and feed utilization and the health status of the fish as well as in maintaining intestinal homoeostasis, acting as energy sources and anti-inflammatory agents (Hoseinifar et al. 2017; Tran et al. 2020).

5.3.4 Immunomodulation

The fish immune system is a sophisticated network made up of genes, proteins, and cells that perform a vital role in protecting the fish against invading pathogens and stress (Caipang and Lazado 2015). In fish, cellular and humoral immunity consists of phagocytic cells, neutrophils, natural killer cells, lymphocytes, lysozyme, hemolysin, immunoglobulin, and complement molecules (Wang et al. 2017; Dawood et al. 2018).

There are four mechanisms of fish immunity: Firstly, phagocytosis, whereby neutrophils, monocytes, and macrophages engulf pathogens and then secrete degradative enzymes and antimicrobial peptides, which helps destroy pathogens (Song et al. 2014; Akhter et al. 2015; Caipang and Lazado 2015; Carbone and Faggio 2016). Secondly, respiratory burst, the invigorated release of reactive oxygen species (hydrogen peroxide, superoxide anions, and hydroxyl radicals) by phagocytic cells responsible for degrading engulfed material and measured by nitro blue tetrazolium (NBT) or myeloperoxidase (MPO) tests (Song et al. 2014; Akhter et al. 2015; Caipang and Lazado 2015; Carbone and Faggio 2016). Thirdly, lysozyme, responsible for the degradation of peptidoglycan in bacterial cell walls by hydrolyzing of β-(1, 4) glycosidic linkages in N-acetylmuramic acid and N-acetylglucosamine; they are synthesized by macrophages and neutrophils and are found in mucus, plasma, and lymphoid tissues (Song et al. 2014; Akhter et al. 2015; Caipang and Lazado 2015; Carbone and Faggio 2016). Lastly, cytokines, produced by macrophages, lymphocytes, and other cells, include chemokines, interferons, interleukins, lymphokines, and tumor necrosis factors, and they regulate and link innate and adaptive immune responses for maximum immunity as well as stimulate hematopoiesis (Song et al. 2014; Akhter et al. 2015; Caipang and Lazado 2015; Carbone and Faggio 2016).

Prebiotics modulate the immune system by directly stimulating the innate immune system or indirectly by enhancing the growth of beneficial microbiota (Song et al. 2014). The mucosal immune response is the line of defense where pathogens may enter the host and is vital in securing the host immunity for better health (Nawaz et al. 2018). Prebiotics directly impact the epithelial barrier by interlinking epithelial cells via tight junctions reducing the penetration of pathogens; they block pathogen adhesion on mucus lowering the number of pathogens that invade the mucosa; they as well bind the active site of pathogens to decrease their activity; and they facilitate the initiation of immunoglobulin A (IgA) and dendritic cells increasing permeability (Nawaz et al. 2018). Furthermore, prebiotics directly activate the innate immunity by interacting with pattern recognition receptors (PRR) (β-glucan or dentin-1) expressed on macrophages (Song et al. 2014; Hoseinifar et al. 2015).

On the other hand, prebiotics indirectly effect immunity by promoting the growth of beneficial bacteria which hinder the adhesion and invasion of pathogens in the epithelia by competing for adhesion sites in epithelia, lowering the pH, enhancing mucus production, producing SCFAs and antimicrobial peptides, and stimulating cytokine production (Akhter et al. 2015). The SCFAs produced by fermentation of prebiotics seem to be a significant mechanism of this indirect impact on immunity. SCFAs provide energy to epithelial cells and they positively impact anti-inflammatory properties and cytokine expression (Nawaz et al. 2018). To add, because they lower the pH in the intestine, they prevent pathogen growth. Prebiotics may also associate with MAMPs (teichoic acid, peptidoglycan, glycosylated protein, or the capsular polysaccharide of bacteria), resulting in the activation of innate immune cells (Song et al. 2014; Hoseinifar et al. 2015). Other indirect effects include the stimulation of natural killer cells, stimulation of phagocytosis, stimulation of neutrophils, stimulation of the alternative complement system, an increase in lysozyme activity, and antibody response in the host (Akhter et al. 2015). Without a doubt, a boosted immune status will bring about a heightened immune response, manifested in higher survival rates post-bacterial or environmental challenges, disease resistance, and improved growth performance and feed utilization (Guerreiro et al. 2018). The effects of prebiotics may vary depending on the fish species investigated; hence, effects should not be extrapolated between species; rather, the actual effect should be primarily demonstrated before claiming its potential use (Caipang and Lazado 2015; Hoseinifar et al. 2015).

5.3.5 Growth Performance and Feed Utilization

Several elements influence the growth of the fish, such as nutrient digestion, assimilation rate, or feed conversion efficiency (Torrecillas et al. 2014). The mechanism of action of prebiotics' effect on growth performance and feed utilization is closely linked to greater nutrients availability owing to changes in digestive enzymes activities or in gut morphology (Guerreiro et al. 2018). The improvement in growth performance could be related to prebiotics that stimulate beneficial microbes that produce digestive enzymes and SCFAs that aid in improving nutrient availability and intermediary metabolism (Huynh et al. 2017; Guerreiro et al. 2018). Prebiotics also improve gut morphology by enhancing gut integrity, for example, microvilli density, intestinal fold height, enterocyte height, and absorption area, resulting in heightened functioning of enterocytes and transport of nutrients across the intestine (Gatlin III and Peredo 2012). Moreover, they improve immune response, confer disease resistance, and positively affect oxidative status in fish by either reducing oxidative damage or improving antioxidant potential (Gatlin III and Peredo 2012; Huynh et al. 2017; Guerreiro et al. 2018; Boyd et al. 2020).

All these effects lead to increased nutrient absorption, resulting in improved nutrient utilization and enhanced metabolism culminating in increased weight gain and feed efficiency (Gatlin III and Peredo 2012). Prebiotic effects on growth and feed utilization varies based on numerous factors, for example, prebiotic source, supplementation level, fish species and age, rearing conditions, and diet composition, with some having positive effects, no effects, and sometimes negative effects on the growth of fish supplemented with prebiotics (Das et al. 2017; Guerreiro et al. 2018). Henceforth, Caipang and Lazado (2015) proposed the prospect that growth-promoting properties of prebiotics in fish encompass complex underlying mechanisms which might be random in nature and greatly manipulated by the maturity of the physiological status of the host.

5.4 Conclusions and Future Perspectives

Prebiotics play a significant role in fish quality, and their use in aquaculture has been shown to enhance growth performance and control fish gut microbiota, which in turn improves fish production and health. Numerous elements that affect fish growth performance and gut microbiota diversity may be responsible for the variations in prebiotics application results. This offers the opportunity for prebiotics and other useful additives to be used in African aquaculture systems. Studies focusing on enhancing the growth and general health of farmed fish leading to improved production are of utmost importance as aquaculture develops in Africa and the world. More research is required to examine various prebiotic percentage/ratio inclusion levels and methods of incorporation, such as adding prebiotics to the feed formulation before pelleting, as well as functional feed additives and prebiotics, like mushrooms and MOS in aquaculture diets. Studies on common pathogens (bacteria and parasites) and stress, along with the administration of prebiotics, should also be encouraged to better optimize the positive effects. This will help maximize fish growth and increase fish production to meet national demands for African countries and ensure food security in Africa.

References

Akhter N, Wu B, Memon AM, Mohsin M (2015) Probiotics and prebiotics associated with aquaculture: a review. Fish Shellfish Immunol 45:733–741. https://doi.org/10.1016/j.fsi.2015.05.038

Benedict PS (2017) Regional review on status and trends in aquaculture development in sub-Saharan Africa—2015. Rome

Bharathi S, Antony C, Rajagopalasamy C et al (2019) Functional feed additives used in fish feeds. Int J Fish Aquat Sci 7:44–52

Boyd CE, D'Abramo LR, Glencross BD et al (2020) Achieving sustainable aquaculture: historical and current perspectives and future needs and challenges. J World Aquac Soc 51:578–633. https://doi.org/10.1111/jwas.12714

Caipang CMA, Lazado CC (2015) Nutritional impacts on fish mucosa: immunostimulants, pre- and probiotics. In: Beck Benjamin H, Peatman E (eds) Mucosal health in aquaculture, 1st edn. Academic, London, pp 211–272

Carbone D, Faggio C (2016) Importance of prebiotics in aquaculture as immunostimulants. Effects on immune system of *Sparus aurata* and *Dicentrarchus labrax*. Fish Shellfish Immunol 54:172–178. https://doi.org/10.1016/j.fsi.2016.04.011

Das S, Mondal K, Haque S (2017) A review on application of probiotic, prebiotic and synbiotic for sustainable development of aquaculture. J Entomol Zool Stud 5:422–429

Davani-Davari D, Negahdaripour M, Karimzadeh I et al (2019) Prebiotics: definition, types, sources, mechanisms, and clinical applications. Foods 8:1–27. https://doi.org/10.3390/foods8030092

Dawood MAO, Koshio S (2016) Recent advances in the role of probiotics and prebiotics in carp aquaculture: a review. Aquaculture 454:243–251. https://doi.org/10.1016/j.aquaculture.2015.12.033

Dawood MAO, Koshio S, Esteban MÁ (2018) Beneficial roles of feed additives as immunostimulants in aquaculture: a review. Rev Aquac 10:950–974. https://doi.org/10.1111/raq.12209

Dimitroglou A, Merrifield DL, Carnevali O et al (2011) Microbial manipulations to improve fish health and production—a Mediterranean perspective. Fish Shellfish Immunol 30:1–16. https://doi.org/10.1016/j.fsi.2010.08.009

Ebrahimi M, Daeman NH, Chong CM et al (2017) Comparing the effects of different dietary organic acids on the growth, intestinal short-chain fatty acids, and liver histopathology of red hybrid tilapia (*Oreochromis* sp.) and potential use of these as preservatives. Fish Physiol Biochem 43:1195–1207. https://doi.org/10.1007/s10695-017-0365-0

Enam F, Mansell TJ (2019) Prebiotics: tools to manipulate the gut microbiome and metabolome. J Ind Microbiol Biotechnol 46:1445–1459. https://doi.org/10.1007/s10295-019-02203-4

Eshaghzadeh H, Hoseinifar SH, Vahabzadeh H, Ringø E (2015) The effects of dietary inulin on growth performances, survival and digestive enzyme activities of common carp (*Cyprinus carpio*) fry. Aquac Nutr 21:242–247. https://doi.org/10.1111/anu.12155

Ganguly S, Dora KC, Sarkar S, Chowdhury S (2013) Supplementation of prebiotics in fish feed: a review. Rev Fish Biol Fish 23:195–199. https://doi.org/10.1007/s11160-012-9291-5

Gatlin DM III, Peredo AM (2012) Prebiotics and probiotics: definitions and applications. Southern Regional Aquauclture Center, pp 1–8

Gibson GR, Scott KP, Rastall RA et al (2010) Dietary prebiotics: current status and new definition. Food Sci Technol Bull 7:1–19. https://doi.org/10.1616/1476-2137.15880

Gibson GR, Hutkins R, Sanders ME et al (2017) The International Scientific Association for Probiotics and Prebiotics (ISAPP) consensus statement on the definition and scope of prebiotics. Nat Rev Gastroenterol Hepatol 14:491–502. https://doi.org/10.1038/nrgastro.2017.75

Goh YJ, Klaenhammer TR (2015) Genetic mechanisms of prebiotic oligosaccharide metabolism in probiotic microbes. Annu Rev Food Sci Technol 6:137–156

González-Félix ML, Gatlin DM, Urquidez-bejarano P et al (2018) Effects of commercial dietary prebiotic and probiotic supplements on growth, innate immune responses, and intestinal microbiota and histology of *Totoaba macdonaldi*. Aquaculture 491:239–251. https://doi.org/10.1016/j.aquaculture.2018.03.031

Goulart FR, Lovatto NM, Klinger AC et al (2018) Effect of dietary fiber concentrates on growth performance, gut morphology and hepatic metabolic intermediates in jundiá (*Rhamdia quelen*). Arq Bras Med Vet Zootec 70:1633–1640. https://doi.org/10.1590/1678-4162-10218

Guerreiro I, Oliva-Teles A, Enes P (2018) Prebiotics as functional ingredients: focus on Mediterranean fish aquaculture. Rev Aquac 10:800–832. https://doi.org/10.1111/raq.12201

Hahor W, Thongprajukaew K, Suanyuk N (2019) Effects of dietary supplementation of oligosaccharides on growth performance, gut health and immune response of hybrid catfish (*Pangasianodon gigas* × *Pangasianodon hypophthalmus*). Aquaculture 507:97–107. https://doi.org/10.1016/j.aquaculture.2019.04.010

Hao YT, Wu SG, Jakovlić I et al (2017) Impacts of diet on hindgut microbiota and short-chain fatty acids in Grass carp (*Ctenopharyngodon idellus*). Aquac Res 48:5595–5605. https://doi.org/10.1111/are.13381

Hongskul V (1999) Into the next millennium: fishery perspective. Bangkok

Hoseinifar SH, Khalili M, Khoshbavar Rostami H, Esteban MÁ (2013) Dietary galactooligosaccharide affects intestinal microbiota, stress resistance, and performance of Caspian roach (*Rutilus rutilus*) fry. Fish Shellfish Immunol 35:1416–1420. https://doi.org/10.1016/j.fsi.2013.08.007

Hoseinifar SH, Soleimani N, Ringø E (2014) Effects of dietary fructo-oligosaccharide supplementation on the growth performance, haemato-immunological parameters, gut microbiota and stress resistance of common carp (*Cyprinus carpio*) fry. Br J Nutr 112:1296–1302. https://doi.org/10.1017/S0007114514002037

Hoseinifar SH, Esteban MÁ, Cuesta A, Sun YZ (2015) Prebiotics and fish immune response: a review of current knowledge and future perspectives. Rev Fish Sci Aquac 23:315–328. https://doi.org/10.1080/23308249.2015.1052365

Hoseinifar SH, Eshaghzadeh H, Vahabzadeh H, Peykaran Mana N (2016) Modulation of growth performances, survival, digestive enzyme activities and intestinal microbiota in Common carp (*Cyprinus carpio*) larvae using short chain fructooligosaccharide. Aquac Res 47:3246–3253. https://doi.org/10.1111/are.12777

Hoseinifar SH, Sun YZ, Caipang CM (2017) Short-chain fatty acids as feed supplements for sustainable aquaculture: an updated view. Aquac Res 48:1380–1391. https://doi.org/10.1111/are.13239

Huynh TG, Shiu YL, Nguyen TP et al (2017) Current applications, selection, and possible mechanisms of actions of synbiotics in improving the growth and health status in aquaculture: a review. Fish Shellfish Immunol 64:367–382. https://doi.org/10.1016/j.fsi.2017.03.035

Krumbeck JA, Maldonado-Gomez MX, Ramer-Tait AE, Hutkins RW (2016) Prebiotics and synbiotics: dietary strategies for improving gut health. Curr Opin Gastroenterol 32:110–119. https://doi.org/10.1097/MOG.0000000000000249

Lauzon HL, Dimitroglou A, Merrifield DL et al (2014) Probiotics and prebiotics: concepts, definitions and history. In: Merrifield D, Ringø E (eds) Aquaculture nutrition: gut health, probiotics and prebiotics, 1st edn. Wiley, West Sussex, pp 383–390

Li X, Yu Y, Feng W et al (2012) Host species as a strong determinant of the intestinal microbiota of fish larvae. J Microbiol 50:29–37. https://doi.org/10.1007/s12275-012-1340-1

Li J, Ni J, Li J et al (2014) Comparative study on gastrointestinal microbiota of eight fish species with different feeding habits. J Appl Microbiol 117:1750–1760. https://doi.org/10.1111/jam.12663

Li X, Ringø E, Hoseinifar SH et al (2019a) The adherence and colonization of microorganisms in fish gastrointestinal tract. Rev Aquac 11:603–618. https://doi.org/10.1111/raq.12248

Li Z, Tuan N, Ji P et al (2019b) Effects of prebiotic mixtures on growth performance, intestinal microbiota and immune response in juvenile Chu's croaker, *Nibea coibor*. Fish Shellfish Immunol 89:564–573. https://doi.org/10.1016/j.fsi.2019.04.025

Lieke T, Meinelt T, Hoseinifar SH et al (2020) Sustainable aquaculture requires environmental-friendly treatment strategies for fish diseases. Rev Aquac 12:943–965. https://doi.org/10.1111/raq.12365

Llewellyn MS, Boutin S, Hoseinifar SH, Derome N (2014) Teleost microbiomes: the state of the art in their characterization, manipulation and importance in aquaculture and fisheries. Front Microbiol 5:1–17. https://doi.org/10.3389/fmicb.2014.00207

Merrifield DL, Dimitroglou A, Foey A et al (2010) The current status and future focus of probiotic and prebiotic applications for salmonids. Aquaculture 302:1–18. https://doi.org/10.1016/j.aquaculture.2010.02.007

Montalban-Arques A, De Schryver P, Bossier P et al (2015) Selective manipulation of the gut microbiota improves immune status in vertebrates. Front Immunol 6:1–14. https://doi.org/10.3389/fimmu.2015.00512

Munir MB, Hashim R, Suhaimee M et al (2016) Dietary prebiotics and probiotics influence the growth performance, feed utilisation, and body indices of snakehead (*Channa striata*) fingerlings. Trop Life Sci Res 27:111–125. https://doi.org/10.21315/tlsr

Nawaz A, Bakhsh Javaid A, Irshad S et al (2018) The functionality of prebiotics as immunostimulant: evidences from trials on terrestrial and aquatic animals. Fish Shellfish Immunol 76:272–278. https://doi.org/10.1016/j.fsi.2018.03.004

Ngo DH, Vo TS, Ngo DN, Wijesekara I, Kim SK (2012) Biological activities and potential health benefits of bioactive peptides derived from marine organisms. Int J Biol Macromol 51:378–383. https://doi.org/10.1016/j.ijbiomac.2012.06.001

Nsonga A, Simbotwe M (2014) Challenges and emerging opportunities associated with aquaculture development in Zambia. Int J Fish Aquat Sci 2:232–237

Ortiz LT, Rebolé A, Velasco S et al (2013) Effects of inulin and fructooligosaccharides on growth performance, body chemical composition and intestinal microbiota of farmed rainbow trout (*Oncorhynchus mykiss*). Aquac Nutr 19:475–482. https://doi.org/10.1111/j.1365-2095.2012.00981.x

Pérez-Sánchez T, Mora-Sánchez B, Balcázar JL (2018) Biological approaches for disease control in aquaculture: advantages, limitations and challenges. Trends Microbiol 26:896–903. https://doi.org/10.1016/j.tim.2018.05.002

Ringø E, Olsen RE, Gifstad T et al (2010) Prebiotics in aquaculture: a review. Aquac Nutr 16:117–136. https://doi.org/10.1111/j.1365-2095.2009.00731.x

Ringø E, Dimitroglou A, Hoseinifar SH, Davies SJ (2014) Prebiotics in finfish: an update. In: Merrifield D, Ringø E (eds) Aquaculture nutrition: gut health, probiotics and prebiotics, 1st edn. Wiley, West Sussex, pp 360–399

Ringø E, Zhou Z, Vecino JLG et al (2016) Effect of dietary components on the gut microbiota of aquatic animals. A never-ending story? Aquac Nutr 22:219–282. https://doi.org/10.1111/anu.12346

Romero J, Ringø E, Merrifield DL (2014) The gut microbiota of fish. In: Merrifield D, Ringø E (eds) Aquaculture nutrition: gut health, probiotics and prebiotics. Wiley, West Sussex, pp 75–100

Salushando K (2022) Investigation of the effects of prebiotics on the growth performance and gastro intestinal microflora modulation in *Oreochromis mossambicus* in Hardap region, Namibia. Thesis, University of Namibia

Sardari R, Nordberg Karlsson E (2018) Marine poly- and oligosaccharides as prebiotics. J Agric Food Chem 66:11544–11549. https://doi.org/10.1021/acs.jafc.8b04418

Slavin J (2013) Fiber and prebiotics: mechanisms and health benefits. Nutrients 5:1417–1435. https://doi.org/10.3390/nu5041417

Song SK, Beck BR, Kim D et al (2014) Prebiotics as immunostimulants in aquaculture: a review. Fish Shellfish Immunol 40:40–48. https://doi.org/10.1016/j.fsi.2014.06.016

Tapia-Paniagua ST, Fumanal M, Anguís V et al (2019) Modulation of intestinal microbiota in *Solea senegalensis* fed low dietary level of *Ulva ohnoi*. Front Microbiol 10:1–16. https://doi.org/10.3389/fmicb.2019.00171

Tiengtam N, Khempaka S, Paengkoum P, Boonanuntanasarn S (2015) Effects of inulin and Jerusalem artichoke (*Helianthus tuberosus*) as prebiotic ingredients in the diet of juvenile Nile tilapia (*Oreochromis niloticus*). Anim Feed Sci Technol 207:120–129. https://doi.org/10.1016/j.anifeedsci.2015.05.008

Torrecillas S, Montero D, Izquierdo M (2014) Improved health and growth of fish fed mannan oligosaccharides: potential mode of action. Fish Shellfish Immunol 36:525–544. https://doi.org/10.1016/j.fsi.2013.12.029

Tran NT, Li Z, Wang S et al (2020) Progress and perspectives of short-chain fatty acids in aquaculture. Rev Aquac 12:283–298. https://doi.org/10.1111/raq.12317

van Doan H, Hoseinifar SH, Faggio C et al (2018) Effects of corncob derived xylooligosaccharide on innate immune response, disease resistance, and growth performance in Nile tilapia (*Oreochromis niloticus*) fingerlings. Aquaculture 495:786–793. https://doi.org/10.1016/j.aquaculture.2018.06.068

Wang W, Sun J, Liu C, Xue Z (2017) Application of immunostimulants in aquaculture: current knowledge and future perspectives. Aquac Res 48:1–23. https://doi.org/10.1111/are.13161

Wang AR, Ran C, Ringø E, Zhou ZG (2018) Progress in fish gastrointestinal microbiota research. Rev Aquac 10:626–640. https://doi.org/10.1111/raq.12191

Yuji-Sado R, Raulino-Domanski F, de Freitas PF, Baioco-Sales F (2015) Growth, immune status and intestinal morphology of Nile tilapia fed dietary prebiotics (mannan oligosaccharides-MOS). Lat Am J Aquat Res 43:944–952. https://doi.org/10.3856/vol43-issue5-fulltext-14

Zoumpopoulou G, Kazou M, Alexandraki V et al (2018) Probiotics and prebiotics: an overview on recent trends. In: Di Gioia D, Biavati B (eds) Probiotics and prebiotics in animal health and food safety. Springer International Publishing AG, Cham, pp 1–34

Chapter 6
The Potential Benefits of *Aloe vera* Products in Aquafeed: Current Knowledge and Prospects

Ndakalimwe Naftal Gabriel, Kenneth Prudence Abasubong, Sahya Maulu, Ghasem Rashidian, and Wilhelm Haihambo

Abstract There has been an increasing effort to use medicinal plants as alternative pharmaceutical drugs, primarily to improve production in intensive aquaculture systems sustainably. Similarly, the potential of aloe vera *(Aloe vera)* in aquaculture has recently received much attention due to its biological properties, such as anti-inflammatory, immune stimulating, antioxidant, gut health enhancement, and hepatoprotective. This study reviewed the progress of research on the use of *A. vera* products in aquaculture, as well as the limitations of existing knowledge and prospects. Many studies have shown that some concentrations of *A. vera* products (especially less than 2%) significantly increase fish growth and appetite, improve general health, and increase resistance to physiological stressors. However, these findings are insufficient to recommend the use of *A. vera* products in aquaculture because of toxicological studies and validation of growth and immune-stimulating effects in different fish species, as well as improved research designs incorporating various vital factors, are still required.

N. N. Gabriel (✉) · W. Haihambo
Department of Fisheries and Ocean Sciences, Faculty of Agriculture, Engineering and Natural Science, Sam Nujoma Campus, University of Namibia, Henties Bay, Namibia
e-mail: ngabriel@unam.na

K. P. Abasubong
Key Laboratory of Aquatic Nutrition and Feed Science of Jiangsu Province, College of Animal Science and Technology, Nanjing Agricultural University, Nanjing, China

S. Maulu
Centre for Innovative Approach Zambia (CIAZ), Lusaka central Business Area, Lusaka, Zambia

Faculty of Science and Engineering, School of Biological and Marine Sciences, University of Plymouth, Drake Circus, Plymouth, United Kingdom

G. Rashidian
Faculty of Fisheries and Protection of Waters, South Bohemian Research Center of Aquaculture and Biodiversity of Hydrocenoses, Institute of Aquaculture and Protection of Waters, University of South Bohemia, České Budějovice, Czech Republic

© The Author(s), under exclusive license to Springer Nature Singapore Pte Ltd. 2023
N. N. Gabriel et al. (eds.), *Emerging Sustainable Aquaculture Innovations in Africa*, Sustainable Agriculture and Food Security,
https://doi.org/10.1007/978-981-19-7451-9_6

This review will encourage the optimisation of various *A. vera* products in the aquaculture industry, as well as future studies to maximise production and improve fish welfare.

Keywords Aloe Vera · Intensive aquaculture · Feed additives · Growth promoters · Immune stimulants · Medicinal plants

6.1 Introduction

Aquaculture has been the fastest growing food-producing sector for decades, contributing significantly to meeting global seafood demand. Intensification is one of the factors that contribute to aquaculture's success. Yields are typically higher in intensive and extensive systems, owing to high stocking density. Higher fish stocking density, on the other hand, can be stressful to the fish and create an environment conducive to pathogen proliferation (i.e. viruses, bacteria, and parasites); fish reared in intensive systems are susceptible to diseases and death if not treated (Amal et al. 2018; Kibenge 2019; Maulu et al. 2021; Vaseeharan and Thaya 2014). Nonetheless, the aquaculture industry as a food-producing sector has yet to reach its full potential.

Farmers in the past began to use pharmaceutical and chemical drugs to maintain the excellent health of farmed fish to reap the economic benefits associated with intensive farming systems in aquaculture. The use of these drugs in aquaculture was later shown to be unsustainable for a variety of reasons, including pathogens developing drug resistance, such as *Vibrio harveyi* to trimethoprim-sulfamethoxazole, chloramphenicol, erythromycin, and streptomycin (Miller and Harbottle 2018), immunosuppression, environmental pollution, and the accumulation of potentially hazardous chemical residues (Bojarski et al. 2020). As a result, many countries, including the United States, the European Union (Bulfon et al. 2015), and some Asian countries, have a high demand for aquatic products free of synthetic pharmaceutical drugs (Rico et al. 2013). As a result, it has become increasingly important to replace pharmaceutical drugs with ingredients or additives that can improve fish health, growth, feed utilisation ability, and ensure safe and high-quality aquatic products from aquaculture.

The number of studies on the application of herbal extracts in aquaculture has increased over the last three decades, with the majority concluding that herbs have the potential to eliminate the use of synthetic pharmaceutical drugs in fish farming. Herbs contain a variety of biologically active metabolites, including polysaccharides, alkaloids, flavonoids, volatile oils, organic acids, tannins, and nutrients (amino acids, carbohydrates, minerals, and vitamins) (Pu et al. 2017). These metabolites, if properly administered, could boost growth and feed intake, improve antioxidative capacity, antidepressants, and modulate immunity in fish (Gabriel et al. 2015a; Pu et al. 2017; Raissy et al. 2022; Reverter et al. 2014), and improve meat quality (Ning et al. 2021). Other advantages of using herbs in aquaculture include their ease of access, low cost for small-scale rural fish farmers, and biodegradability and eco-friendliness (Reverter et al. 2014). However, the current challenges of using herbs in aquaculture may be difficulties with standardisation because they are diverse (with complex bioactive compounds), and their biological metabolites may not be consistent (Pu et al. 2017) for a variety of reasons, including geographical location, extraction methods, and storage/post-harvest treatments (Baptiste Hzounda Fokou et al. 2020), and their modes of action are not fully understood. As a result, more research is required before medicinal herbs can be fully implemented in aquaculture worldwide.

Thus, the current study reviewed the research progress on applying aloe vera (*Aloe vera*) products in aquaculture and presents the gaps in existing knowledge and prospects.

6.2 The Composition of *Aloe vera*

Aloe vera (synonym *A. barbadensis* Miller) is a stemless, drought-resistant cactus-like herb from the genus *Aloe* of the Aloeaceae family native to South and East Africa (Reynolds and Dweck 1999). *Aloe vera* is the most studied and commercially important *Aloe* species, and it is used as traditional medicine by many nations worldwide (Maan et al. 2018). *Aloe vera* is best known for its high water content, which accounts for 99–99.5% (Hamman 2008), with the remaining 0.5–1.0% containing approximately 70 biologically active compounds such as water-soluble and fat-soluble vitamins, minerals, enzymes, simple/complex polysaccharides, phenol compounds, and organic acids (Radha and Laxmipriya 2015) (Fig. 6.1). These bioactive compounds are found in the *A. vera* leaf's gel (inner transparent mucilaginous jelly-like tissues), latex (middle layer), and/or rind (outer thick layer) (Fig. 6.1).

The gel contains active ingredients such as polysaccharides (glucomannans, xylose, rhamnose, galactose, and arabinose), vitamins (A, C, E, B1, B2, B12, niacin, choline, and folic acid), minerals (potassium, chloride, sodium, calcium, magnesium, copper, zinc, chromium, and iron), enzymes (catalase, amylase, oxidase) (Radha and Laxmipriya 2015). Anthraquinones can be found in the leaf's latex (Hamman 2008) (Fig. 6.1). The rich composition of aloe vera justifies its widely recognised pharmacological properties, which include anti-inflammatory, antioxidant, immune-boosting (Sánchez-Machado et al. 2017), wound-healing properties (Reynolds and Dweck 1999), intestinal absorption enhancement, and hepatoprotective effects (Baruah et al. 2016).

6.3 Applications of *Aloe vera* Extracts in Aquaculture

Aloe vera studies in humans have already progressed from the experimental phase to the application phase (i.e. cosmetics, food, and beverages). However, *A. vera* research in aquaculture has yet to fully translate into practical applications. Kim

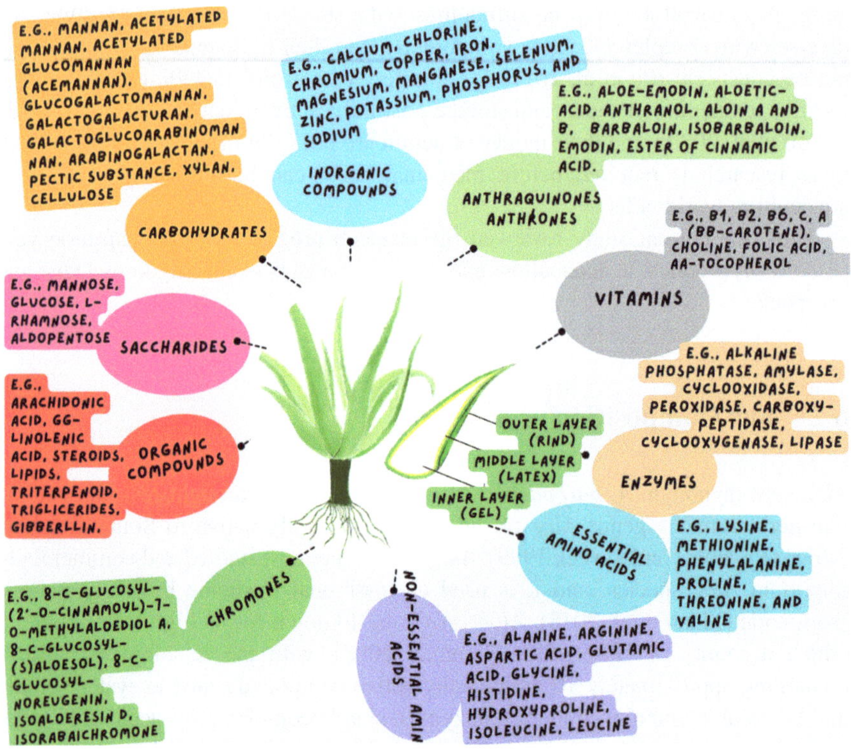

Fig. 6.1 *Aloe vera* plant, leaf cross-sectional view, and bioactive ingredients present in the leaf gel and latex (Boudreau and Beland 2006; Gupta and Malhotra 2012)

et al. (1999) were the first to report on the effects of *A. vera* on nonspecific immune response and disease resistance in rockfish (*Sebastes schlegeli*). Aquaculture research interest in *A. vera* has only recently increased. Several authors have investigated various *A. vera* extracts, including crude powder (Gabriel et al. 2015a, b, 2017; Zanuzzo et al. 2015a, b, 2017; Mehrabi and Firouzbakhsh 2020), gel (Fehrmann-Cartes et al. 2019; Golestan et al. 2015; Mehrabi et al. 2019; Soltanizadeh and Mousavinejad 2015), solvent extracts (Mahdavi et al. 2013), nanoparticles (Pati 2021; Rohani et al. 2017), aloin (Srivastava et al. 2018), and eloe-emodin (Devi et al. 2019) in fish for different purposes (Fig. 6.2). Overall, these studies concluded that *A. vera* extracts have the potential to be used as aquaculture remedies.

6.3.1 Growth Performance and Feed Utilisation

Several studies have found that various *A. vera* products improve growth and feed utilisation efficiency in various fish species (Table 6.1). Different levels of different

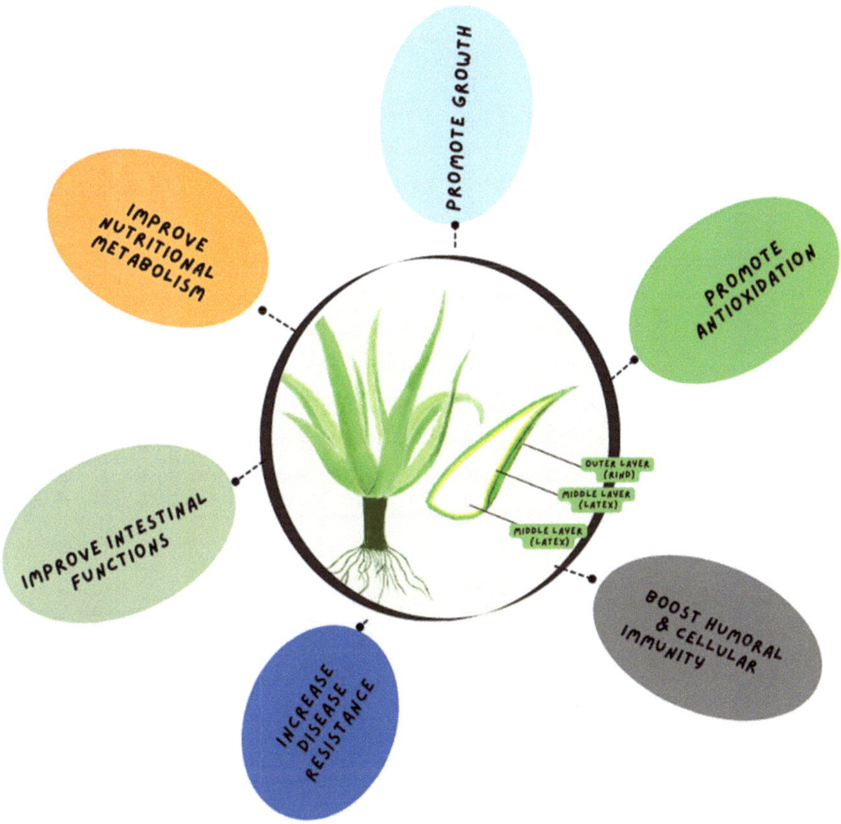

Fig. 6.2 The benefits of *A. vera* in aquaculture

A. vera products, ranging from 0.5 to 4.0%, have been tested with varying results. For example, after 84 days, *A. vera* leaf paste (10 g/kg diet) significantly improved growth performance parameters such as final weight (FW), weight gain, specific growth rate (SGR), and feed utilisation indices such as feed conversion ratio (FCR), protein efficiency ratio (PER), and apparent net protein utilisation (ANPU) in *C. gariepinus* fingerlings (Adegbesan et al. 2018). When *Cyprinus carpio* juveniles were fed a diet supplemented with *A. vera* ethanolic extract (25 g/kg diet) for 56 days, the same parameters improved significantly (Mahdavi et al. 2013). According to Alishahi and Abdy (2013), feeding *C. carpio* juveniles a diet supplemented with *A. vera* gel (5 g/kg) resulted in a significant improvement in growth and feed utilisation parameters. After 42 days, aloe vera gel (1.0–10 g/kg diet) increased growth and feed utilisation indices in *Oncorhynchus mykiss* juveniles (Heidarieh et al. 2013). Diets supplemented with *A. vera* leaf powder (10–20 g/kg diet) were also found to improve growth and feed utilisation efficiency in juvenile *Oreochromis niloticus* (Gabriel et al. 2015a; Syed et al. 2021). This implies that *A. vera* could be used to improve fish growth performance and increase farmed fish

Table 6.1 The effects of various *A. vera* products on fish growth performance and feed utilisation indices in aquaculture

Types of *A. vera* extracts	Dosages (g/kg diet)	Optimum dosage/s	Experiment duration	Growth/Feed utilisation	Fish species	Initial wt. (g)	References
Gel	0.1, 1.0, 10,	1.0–10	42 days	SGR (>), WG (>), IVL (>) IVW (>), FCR (<)	*O. mykiss*	50.3	Heidarieh et al. (2013)
Ethanolic extract (EE)	1, 5, 25	5–25	56 days	FW (>), SGR (>), FL (>) PE (>), FCR (<), FCE (>)	*C. carpio*	29.74	Mahdavi et al. (2013)
EE	2, 4, 8, 16	4–8	90 days	WG (>), SGR (>), FCR (<) FER (>), PER (>)	*C. carpio*	1.73	Khanal et al. (2021)
Gel	0.5, 1.0, 2.0	(–)	56 days	FW (=), SGR (=), WG (=) RGR (=), CF (=), FCR (=)	*O. mykiss*	9.5	Golestan et al. (2015)
Gel	1, 5, 10	5	60 days	GR (>), SGR (>), FCR (<)	*C. carpio*	45	Alishahi and Abdy (2013)
Leave paste	10, 20, 30	10	84 days	FW (>), SGR (>), WG (>) FI (>), FCR (>), PER (<) ANPU (>)	*C. gariepinus*	2.33	Adegbesan et al. (2018)
Powder	5	(–)	42 days	WG (=), SSI (=),	*O. mykiss*	133.9	Zanuzzo et al. (2015a)
Powder	5, 10, 15	15	28 days	WG (>), SGR (>), FW (>) FCR (<), FER (>)	*O. mykiss*	10.80	Mehrabi and Firouzbakhsh (2020)
Nanoparticles	5, 10, 15	10–15	60 days	FW (>), FL (>), WG (>)	*Acipenser baerii*	10.95	Rohani et al. (2017)

				SGR (>), FCR (<), PER (>)			
Aqueous crude extract	5, 10, 15	15	56 days	WG (>), SGR (>), FCR (>)	*O. mykiss*	10.89	Mehrabi et al. 2019)
Powder	2%	(–)	30 days	WG (=), SGR (=)	*C. auratus*	4–7 cm	Palermo et al. (2013)
Powder	5, 10, 20, 40	10–20	60 days	WG (>), SGR (>), AGR (>) FI (<), VSI (=), HSI (=) FCR (<), FER (>)	GIFT-*O. niloticus*	4.83	Gabriel et al. (2015a)
Methanol extracts	1, 2, 3%	1–2%	105 days	WG (>), SGR (>), FW (>) FCR (>), FCE (=)	*O. niloticus*	4.04	Syed et al. (2021)
Powder	0.5, 1, 2, 4%	1–2%	60 days	WG (>), FW (>), SGR (>) FCR (<), FER (=), PER (>)	*C. gariepinus*	3.16	Gabriel et al. (2019)

SGR Specific growth rate, *WG* Weight gain, *FL* Fish length, *IVL* Intestinal villus length, *IVW* Intestinal villus width, *FCE* Feed conversion efficiency, *RGR* Relative growth rate, *CF* condition factor, *VSI* Viscerosomatic index, *HSI* Hepatosomatic index, *wt* Weight, *FI* feed intake, *FW* Final weight, *ANPU* Apparent net protein utilisation protein, *PER* Protein efficiency ratio, *FCR* Feed conversion ratio, *FI* Feed intake, *FER: FCE* Feed conversion efficiency: Feed efficiency ratio, *(–)* Not available, *(>)* Significantly increased, *(<)* Significantly decreased, *(=)* Not affected production. However, some studies have found that dietary *A. vera* extracts do not affect fish growth. Following a 42-day feeding trial, dietary *A. vera* crude powder supplementation (5 g/kg basal diet) did not affect the WG and SSI (spleen somatic index) in *O. mykiss* (Zanuzzo et al. 2015a). Similarly, after 30 days of administration, 2% *A. vera* powder did not affect the WG and SGR of goldfish (*Carassius aurata*) (Palermo et al. 2013).

The presence of compounds in the leaves, such as complex polysaccharides and phenolic compounds, may be responsible for improved growth in fish following *A. vera* supplementation (Hamman 2008; Radha and Laxmipriya 2015). The polysaccharides in medicinal herbal extracts have been linked to growth-promoting effects in fish (Tremaroli and Bäckhed 2012; Zahran et al. 2014). Polysaccharides aid fish in maintaining the balance of their gut microbial community in favour of health-promoting microbes (Tremaroli and Bäckhed 2012), as well as promoting health status by increasing resistance to bacterial and viral infection (Chen et al. 2003) or directly influencing pathogenic gut microbiota (Yu et al. 2018). All of this improves feed digestibility and nutrient availability from feedstuffs, as well as shortens the feed transition time, which may have a beneficial effect on digestive enzymes (Platel and Srinivasan 2004) and reduces the amount of feed substrate available for pathogenic bacteria proliferation (Citarasu 2010). In order to be certain that the growth-promoting effects of *A. vera* are due to their polysaccharide, more research is needed.

6.3.2 *Effects of* A. vera *on Fish Health*

Blood is the most commonly examined tissue to assess the health or physiological status of fish after the administration of herbal extracts. Oxygen-carrying capacity, for example, has been determined directly using primary haematological indices such as red blood cell (RBC), haemoglobin concentration (Hb), percentage of blood volume made up of red blood cells, and haematocrits (Hct). Secondary health indices such as Mean Corpuscular Volume (MCV) = (Hct × 10/RBC), Mean Corpuscular Haemoglobin (MCH) = (Hb × 10/RBC), and Mean Corpuscular Haemoglobin Concentration (MCHC) = (Hb × 100/Hct) could be deduced from primary indices for the classification of anaemia conditions, as illustrated by Gabriel et al. (2015a). Other indices such as white blood cell (WBC) and a number of their differential counts (i.e. leucocyte counts such as lymphocytes, neutrophils, eosinophils, monocytes, and basophils) as well as expression of immune-related genes have been assessed to measure the immune status of fish supplemented with herbs, particularly during stressful conditions (Zanuzzo et al. 2015a). Aside from promoting growth, various *A. vera* extracts have been shown to significantly improve immune indices and, to a lesser extent, specific immune responses in fish (Table 6.2). Mehrabi et al. (2019) discovered that feeding *A. vera* extract to O. mykiss fingerlings for 56 days could significantly increase haematological parameters (RBC, WBC, Hct, and Hb) as well as some blood serum parameters (the total protein, albumin, globulin,

Table 6.2 The effects of *A. vera* extracts on health indices of some of aquaculture fish species

Aloe products	Delivery	Dosages (g/kg diet)	Duration of exposure	Health indices	Fish species	References
Gel	Oral	0.5, 1.0, 2.0	56 days	FRA (>), MDA (<)	*O. mykiss*	Golestan et al. (2015)
Crude powder	Immersion	0.02, 0.2, 2.0 mg/L	9 h	Glu. (=), RBA (>)	*B. amazonicus*	Zanuzzo et al. (2015b)
Gel	Oral	1.0, 5.0, 10.0	60 days	SBA (<), NBT (>), CSA, TP (>) IgM (>), PCV (>), Hb (>), MCV (=) MCHC (=), MCH (=), RBC (>), HETR (=) LYMP (=), MON (=), EOS (=), LYZ (>)	*C. carpio*	Alishahi and Abdy (2013)
Leave paste	Oral	10.0, 20.0, 30.0	84 days	PCV (>), Hb (>), RBC (>), MCH (=); MCV (=), MCHC (=), WBC (>) NEU (<), LYMP. (>), EOS (<) MON (=), BASO (>)	*C. gariepinus*	Adegbesan et al. (2018)
Gel	Injection	100 μL added 5 mL TSB 0.1 mL injected into a fish	42 days	ACH50 (>), LYZ (>), BCIDAL (<)	*C. carpio*	Abdy et al. (2017)
Gel	Oral	5.0	56 days	CL (>), PHAGO (>)	*Sebastes schlegeli*	Kim et al. (1999)
Powder	Oral	5.0	42 days	RBA (=), LYZ (=), CSA (=) Ferritin heavy chain (>), IRF-1 (>) TNFα-1 (>), TNFα-2 (>), IL-8 (>) CATH-1 (>), CATH-2 (>), IL-1β) (>)	*O. mykiss*	Zanuzzo et al. (2015a)
		4.0	28 days	MR (=), MO2 (8% lower), CORT (=)		Zanuzzo et al. (2015b)
Aloin	Injection	1 mg/body wt.	7 days	LYZ (>), Protease (>), CARBOX. (>) ALP (>) AP (>) CAT (>), PEROX (>)	*L. rohita*	Srivastava et al. (2018)

(continued)

Table 6.2 (continued)

Aloe products	Delivery	Dosages (g/kg diet)	Duration of exposure	Health indices	Fish species	References
Aqueous extracts	Oral	0.5, 1.0, 2.0 (w/w)	10 days	RBA (>), Glu. (<), NBT (>), LYZ (>) CSA (>)	*P. mesopotamicus*	Zanuzzo et al. (2017)
Aqueous extracts	Oral	5.0	42 days	WBC (>), IgM (>), LYZ (>), BCIDAL (>) RBC (=), PVC (=), CSA (=)	*C. carpio*	Alishahi et al. (2010)
Aloe-emodin	Oral	0.001, 0.005, 0.01 (mg/kg diet)	Days interval (14, 28, 42, 56)	ALB (>), GLOB (>), PHAGO (>), RBA (>) CC3 (>), LYZ. Act. (>)	*L. rohita*	Devi et al. (2019)
Aqueous extracts	Oral	5,10, 15	56 days	RBC (=), WBC (>), Hct (>), Hb (>) TP (>), ALB (>), GLOB (>), RBA (>) LYZ (>). CSA (>)	*O. mykiss*	Mehrabi et al. (2019)
Crude powder	Oral	2 mg/g diet	30 days	CHOL (<), LDL (=), HDL (=), TG (=)	*C. auratus*	Palermo et al. (2013)
Crude powder	Oral	5, 10, 20, 40	60 days	WBC (>), RBC (>), Hb (>), Hct (>), MON (=), LYMP (<), NEU (>), EOS (>)	*O. niloticus*	Gabriel et al. (2015a)
Crude powder	Oral	5, 10, 20, 40	60 days	TCHO (<), TG (<), LDL (=), HDL (>) CAT (>), GSH-Px (>), SOD (=)	*O. niloticus*	Gabriel et al. (2015b)
Powder	Oral	10, 20, 30	105 days	Hb (>), NEU (>), LYMP (>), MON (>), EOS (>) RBC (=), MCV (>), MCHC (=), WBC (>), ALB (=) GLOB (=), TP (>)	*O. niloticus*	Syed et al. (2021)
Powder	Oral	5, 10, 20, 40	60 days	RBC (=), Hct (=), Hb (=), MCV (=), MCHC (=) WBC (>) LYMP (=), MON (=), ALT (<), AST (<) Glu (=), TCHO (=), TG (=)	*C. gariepinus*	Gabriel et al. (2019)

Nature's oil (Batch no 24228)	Oral	5, 10, 20	7 days	RBA (>), LYZ (>), CSA (>), TG (<), TCHO (<)	*P. mesopotamicus*	de Assis and Urbinati (2020)
Powder	Oral	1	72 h	TCTP (<), SOD (>), HSP 70 (>)	*Penaeus vannamei*	Trejo-Flores et al. (2018)

FRA Ferric-reducing ability, *CAT* Catalase, *MDA* Malondialdehyde, *SBA* Serum bactericidal, *CL* Chemiluminescent response, *CORT* Cortisol, *TG* Triglycerides, *TCHO* Total cholesterol, *CHOL* Cholesterol, *NBT* Nitroblue tetrazolium, *CSA* Complement system activity, *Hct* Hematocrits, *Hb* Haemoglobin, *WBC* White blood cells, *MCV* Mean corpuscular volume, *SOD* Superoxide dismutase, *LYZ* Lysozyme activity, *GSH-Px* Glutathione peroxidase, *Glu* Glucose, *MR* Metabolic rate, MO_2 Oxygen consumption, *HDL* High-density lipoprotein, *LDL* Low-density lipoproteins, *PEROX* Peroxidase, *CARBOX* Carboxylesterase, *ALP* Alkaline phosphatase, *AP* Acid phosphatase, *IgM* Immunoglobulin M, *PCV* Packed cell volume, *HETR* Heterophil, *ACH50* Serum-alternative complement activity, *TP* Total protein, *CC3* Complement C3, *ALB* Albumin, *GLOB* Globulin, *RBC* Red blood cells, *MCH* Mean corpuscular haemoglobin, *MCHC* Mean corpuscular haemoglobin concentrate, *NEU* Neutrophils, *LYMP* Lymphocytes, *AST* Aspartate aminotransferase, *ALT* Alanine aminotransferase, *PHAGO* Phagocytic activity, *RBA* Respiratory burst activity, *MON* Monocytes, *(>)* Significantly increased, *(<)* Significantly decreased, *(=)* Not affected, *BASO* Basophils, *TCTP* Translationally controlled tumour protein, *HSP 70* Heat shock protein 70 respiratory burst activity, and lysozyme, and complement system activity). For only 7 days, *A. vera* extracts in pacu (*Piaractus mesopotamicus*) reduced stress, stimulated innate immunity, protected triglyceride levels in the blood, lipid depots in the liver and muscle, and directed energy mobilisation to visceral depots (de Assis and Urbinati 2020). Moreover, aloin (*A. vera* extract) has been shown to improve innate immunity (increased lysozyme activity) and antioxidant activity (increased catalase activity) in *Labeo rohita* 7 days after a 1 mg aloin/kg fish body weight injection (Srivastava et al. 2018). *Aloe vera* extracts, including emodin in *L. rohita* (Devi et al. 2019), aqueous extracts in *C. carpio* (Abdy et al. 2017), and *P. mesopotamus* (Zanuzzo et al. 2017), crude powder in *O. mykiss* (Zanuzzo et al. 2015a, b), *Carassius auratus* (Palermo et al. 2013), and *O. niloticus* (Gabriel et al. 2015a, b; Syed et al. 2021) were also reported to improve the overall health status of target species significantly. Based on these findings, *A. vera* extracts have the potential to be used as immunostimulants in aquaculture.

Previous research has shown that supplementing *A. vera* extracts improves haematological indices in fish, indicating that *A. vera* can stimulate erythropoiesis (the generation of mature red blood cells), increasing oxygen-carrying capacity and strengthening the body to better tolerate physiological stresses. Iji et al. (2010) reported erythropoietin effects of *A. vera* extracts in hematopoietic cells of bone marrow. The assumption is that these effects are due to the presence of vitamins (beta carotene, C, E, B12, riboflavin, thiamine, and folic acid), minerals (calcium, chromium, copper, selenium, manganese, potassium, sodium, and zinc), and essential and non-essential amino acids in *A. vera* that are required for haemoglobin synthesis (Olaifa 2016). The presence of polysaccharides in *A. vera* leaves has also been linked to erythropoiesis and leukopoiesis (the formation of white blood cells in bone marrow) (Hamman 2008; Im et al. 2005; Tai-Nin Chow et al. 2005). Some immunomodulatory effects have been linked to lectins, glycoproteins found in *A. vera* gel (Reynolds and Dweck 1999). *Aloe vera* extracts have been shown to elicit specific immune responses in fish, in addition to innate immune responses. Diets supplemented with *A. vera* powder, for example, reportedly resulted in a robust immune response following bacterial antigen exposure, which was expressed by all eight selected antibacterial biomarker genes (i.e. ferritin heavy chain, IRF-1, TNF-1, TNF-2, IL-8 CATH-1, CATH-2, IL-1) in *O. mykiss* (Zanuzzo et al. 2015a). Abdy et al. (2017) also found that 0.5% dietary *A. vera* increased serum bactericidal activity and immunoglobulin M (IgM) antibody levels in *C. carpio* infected with *Aeromonas hydrophila*. *A. vera* has been shown to boost fish resistance to various physical and biological stressors. For example, *A. vera* (0.2 mg/L of water) was found to significantly increase the innate immune response (respiratory burst activity) in *Brycon amazonicus* after transport stress (Zanuzzo et al. 2015b). Gabriel et al. (2015a) found that *O. niloticus* (GIFT strain) juveniles fed a diet supplemented with *A. vera* powder had significantly lower glucose levels, cortisol levels, and neutrophil/lymphocyte ratios after *Streptococcus inae* experimental challenge than control fish. Similarly, *Oreochromis* sp. (Raina Manaf and Mohd Daud 2016) and *P. mesopotamicus* (Zanuzzo et al. 2017) were fed an *A. vera* supplemented diet exposed to pathogenic bacteria of *Streptococcus agalactiae* and *A. hydrophila*, respectively; similar results were obtained. Following *A. hydrophila*, *S. agalactiae*, and *Saprolegnia parasitica* (parasite) exposure, dietary *A. vera* supplementation increased the survival probability in *C. carpio* (Abdy et al. 2017) and *O. mykiss* (Heidarieh et al. 2013; Mehrabi et al. 2019). According to the literature review, dietary supplementation with *A. vera* extracts can improve fish health and produce animals that are more resistant to physiological stresses. This suggests that *A. vera* can help prevent disease outbreaks and negative fish reactions to other types of stresses in aquaculture.

Medicinal herbs, on the other hand, have been reported to be toxic to fish and even fatal in high doses (Ponnusamy et al. 2011). Anaemia and tissue necrosis are two of the adverse effects of *A. vera* reported in fish following dietary supplementation by Gabriel et al. (2015a, b) and Taiwo et al. (2006). In mice supplemented with *A. vera* extracts, spermatogenesis dysfunction decreased central nervous system activity, and a decrease in red blood cell count was observed (Boudreau et al. 2013). Anaemia in animals is thought to be caused by herbal extracts' ability to disrupt some biological functions such as erythropoiesis, haemoglobin synthesis, and osmoregulation (Gabriel et al. 2015a). In animals, *A. vera* has also been linked to haematuria (the presence of red blood cells in the urine), metabolic acidosis (an acid–base imbalance in the blood), malabsorption (the inability to absorb nutrients and fluids), and electrolyte disturbance (mineral imbalance) (Müller-Lissner 1993). These adverse effects could explain why somc studies found poor hemato-biochemical parameters and a decrease in growth (Adegbesan et al. 2018; Gabriel et al. 2015a; Zanuzzo et al. 2015b). As a result, an upper limit dosage of *A. vera* supplementation is critical for improving immune responses and resistance to physiological stressors.

6.4 Limitations in Current Knowledge and Perspectives for the Future

This review has presented strong evidence that *A. vera* is becoming more popular in aquaculture for various uses, but mainly as a feed supplement. However, the following issues have been noted in the literature:

It is difficult to compare and substantiate the effects of this herb in fish because of the following factors: (1) this herb was only studied in a small number of fish species, and conclusions were sometimes drawn using insufficient doses or testing durations; (2) different *A. vera* products, such as powder, gel, methanolic, and ethanolic extracts, were presented in the literature; and (3) many studies repeatedly failed to characterise the composition of the used *A. vera* products or quantify the beneficial compounds. Furthermore, (4) there are insufficient studies on the toxicological effects of *A. vera* in fish, the durability of the herb in the water (culture environment), digestibility in fish, and product quality, which would help determine the ideal incorporation levels of *A. vera*; and (5) there is a lack of in-depth understanding on the physiology of how *A. vera* and other herbs affect growth performance, immune function, and their tolerance to stressors.

This study recommends that future studies include the following topics: (1) investigating the interactive effects of *A. vera* on fish growth and immune response; (2) herbal extracts have been praised for their ability to improve the intestinal microbiota, which improves fish growth and health. To confirm this mechanism, future research should look at the composition and diversity of bacterial communities in the fish gut after herbal product administration. (3) Furthermore, since *A. vera* has antimicrobial activity, future research should investigate its protective and reparative effects in fish against harmful bacteria that are problematic in aquaculture. (4) Because *A. vera* is known to have bitter tastes, future studies should include a sensory test to determine the sensory quality in *A. vera* supplemented fish. (5) Future research should include a cost-benefit analysis of using *A. vera* extracts in aquaculture versus pharmaceutical drugs. (6) Since many *A. vera* products used in the literature are crude, effective extraction and screening methods for the primary components must be investigated to develop a better understanding of their functions. (7) Finally, to ensure the long-term development of the aquaculture industry, mass production of these herbs should be investigated, as their use in aquaculture could double the tension already imposed by agricultural sectors and humans.

In conclusion, this study demonstrated that *A. vera* has the potential to improve growth and immune parameters in fish. However, a lack of sufficient knowledge may limit the practical and industrial application of this herb in aquaculture. More research, as recommended in this paper, is needed to better optimise the use of *A. vera* products without endangering farmed fish, consumers, or the environment.

References

Abdy E, Alishahi M, Tollabi M, Ghorbanpour M, Mohammadian T (2017) Comparative effects of *Aloe vera* gel and Freund's adjuvant in vaccination of common carp (*Cyprinus carpio* L.) against *Aeromonas hydrophila*. Aquac Int 25:727–742. https://doi.org/10.1007/s10499-016-0074-1

Adegbesan SI, Obasa SO, Abdulraheem I (2018) Growth performance, haematology, and histopathology of African catfish (*Clarias gariepinus*) fed varying levels of *Aloe barbadensis* leaves. J Fish 6:553–562. https://journal.bdfish.org/index.php/fisheries/article/view/JFish_245

Alishahi M, Abdy E (2013) Effects of different levels of *Aloe vera* L. extract on growth performance, hemato-immunological indices of *Cyprinus carpio* L. Iran J Vet Sci Technol 5:33–44. https://doi.org/10.22067/veterinary.v5i2.16908

Alishahi M, Ranjbar M, Ghorbanpoor M, Peyghan R, Mesbah M, Razi Jalali M (2010) Effects of dietary *Aloe vera* on some specific and nonspecific immunity in the common carp (*Cyprinus carpio*). Int J Vet Res 4:189–195

Amal MNA, Koh CB, Nurliyana M, Suhaiba M, Nor-Amalina Z, Santha S, Diyana-Nadhirah KP, Yusof MT, Ina-Salwany MY, Zamri-Saad M (2018) A case of natural co-infection of Tilapia Lake Virus and *Aeromonas veronii* in a Malaysian red hybrid tilapia (*Oreochromis niloticus*×*O. mossambicus)* farm experiencing high mortality. Aquaculture 485:12–16. https://doi.org/10.1016/j.aquaculture.2017.11.019

Baptiste Hzounda Fokou J, Michel Jazet Dongmo P, Fekam Boyom F (2020) Essential oil's chemical composition and pharmacological properties. In: El-Shemy HA (ed) Essential oils—oils of nature. IntechOpen. https://doi.org/10.5772/intechopen.86573

Baruah A, Bordoloi M, Deka Baruah HP (2016) *Aloe vera*: a multipurpose industrial crop. Ind Crop Prod 94:951–963. https://doi.org/10.1016/j.indcrop.2016.08.034

Bojarski B, Kot B, Witeska M (2020) Antibacterials in aquatic environment and their toxicity to fish. J Pharm 13:189. https://doi.org/10.3390/ph13080189

Boudreau MD, Beland FA (2006) An evaluation of the biological and toxicological properties of *Aloe barbadensis* (miller), *Aloe vera*. J Environ Sci Health C Environ Carcinog Ecotoxicol Rev 24:103–154. https://doi.org/10.1080/10590500600614303

Boudreau MD, Beland FA, Nichols JA, Pogribna M (2013) Toxicology and carcinogenesis studies of a nondecolorized [corrected] whole leaf extract of *Aloe barbadensis* Miller (*Aloe vera*) in F344/N rats and B6C3F1 mice (drinking water study). NTP Technical Reports 577:1–266

Bulfon C, Volpatti D, Galeotti M (2015) Current research on the use of plant-derived products in farmed fish. Aquac Res 46:513–551. https://doi.org/10.1111/are.12238

Chen HL, Li DF, Chang BY, Gong LM, Dai JG, Yi GF (2003) Effects of Chinese herbal polysaccharides on the immunity and growth performance of young broilers. Poult Sci 82:364–370. https://doi.org/10.1093/ps/82.3.364

Citarasu T (2010) Herbal biomedicines: a new opportunity for aquaculture industry. Aquac Int 18: 403–414. https://doi.org/10.1007/s10499-009-9253-7

de Assis RWS, Urbinati EC (2020) Physiological activity of *Aloe vera* in pacu (*Piaractus mesopotamicus*) inoculated with *Aeromonas hydrophila*. Fish Physiol Biochem 46:1421–1430

Devi G, Harikrishnan R, Paray BA, Al-Sadoon MK, Hoseinifar SH, Balasundaram C (2019) Effects of aloe-emodin on innate immunity, antioxidant and immune cytokines mechanisms in the head kidney leucocytes of *Labeo rohita* against *Aphanomyces invadans*. Fish Shellfish Immunol 87: 669–678. https://doi.org/10.1016/j.fsi.2019.02.006

Fehrmann-Cartes K, Coronado M, Hernández AJ, Allende ML, Feijoo CG (2019) Anti-inflammatory effects of aloe vera on soy meal-induced intestinal inflammation in zebrafish. Fish Shellfish Immunol 95:564–573. https://doi.org/10.1016/j.fsi.2019.10.075

Gabriel NN, Qiang J, He J, Ma XY, Kpundeh MD, Xu P (2015a) Dietary *Aloe vera* supplementation on growth performance, some haemato-biochemical parameters and disease resistance against *Streptococcus iniae* in tilapia (GIFT). Fish Shellfish Immunol 44:504–514. https://doi.org/10.1016/j.fsi.2015.03.002

Gabriel NN, Qiang J, Ma XY, He J, Xu P, Liu K (2015b) Dietary *Aloe vera* improves plasma lipid profile, antioxidant, and hepatoprotective enzyme activities in GIFT-tilapia (*Oreochromis niloticus*) after Streptococcus iniae challenge. Fish Physiol Biochem 41:1321–1332. https://doi.org/10.1007/s10695-015-0088-z

Gabriel NN, Qiang J, Ma XY, He J, Xu P, Omoregie E (2017) Sex-reversal effect of dietary *Aloe vera* (Liliaceae) on genetically improved farmed Nile Tilapia fry. N Am J Aquac 79:100–105. https://doi.org/10.1080/15222055.2016.1236046

Gabriel NN, Wilhelm MR, Habte-Tsion HM, Chimwamurombe P, Omoregie E, Iipinge LN, Shimooshili K (2019) Effect of dietary *Aloe vera* polysaccharides supplementation on growth performance, feed utilization, hemato-biochemical parameters, and survival at low pH in African catfish (*Clarias gariepinus*) fingerlings. Int Aquat Res 11:57–72. https://doi.org/10.1007/s40071-019-0219-8

Golestan G, Salati AP, Keyvanshokooh S, Zakeri M, Moradian H (2015) Effect of dietary aloe vera on growth and lipid peroxidation indices in rainbow trout (*Oncorhynchus mykiss*). Vet Res Forum 6:63–67. https://www.ncbi.nlm.nih.gov/pmc/articles/PMC4405687/

Gupta VK, Malhotra S (2012) Pharmacological attribute of *Aloe vera*: revalidation through experimental and clinical studies. AYU 33:193–196. https://doi.org/10.4103/0974-8520.105237

Hamman JH (2008) Composition and applications of *Aloe vera* leaf gel. Molecules 13:1599–1616. https://doi.org/10.3390/molecules13081599

Heidarieh M, Mirvaghefi AR, Sepahi A, Sheikhzadeh N, Shahbazfar AA, Akbari M (2013) Effects of dietary *Aloe vera* on growth performance, skin and gastrointestine morphology in rainbow trout (*Oncorhynchus mykiss*). Turk J Fish Aquat Sci 13:367–373. https://doi.org/10.4194/1303-2712-v13_2_20

Iji OT, Oyagbemi AA, Azeez OI (2010) Assessment of chronic administration of *Aloe vera* gel on haematology, plasma biochemistry, lipid profiles and erythrocyte osmotic resistance in Wistar rats. Niger J Physiol Sci 25:107–113

Im SA, Oh ST, Song S, Kim MR, Kim DS, Woo SS, Jo TH, Park YI, Lee CK (2005) Identification of optimal molecular size of modified *Aloe* polysaccharides with maximum immunomodulatory activity. Int Immunopharmacol 5:271–279. https://doi.org/10.1016/j.intimp.2004.09.031

Khanal M, Lamichhane S, Bhattarai A, Kayastha BL, Labh SN (2021) Extract of *Aloe vera* (*Aloe barbadensis* Miller) enhances the growth, protein contents, and gastrosomatic index (GaSI) of common carp *Cyprinus carpio*. J Nutr Metab 2021:8029413. https://doi.org/10.1155/2021/8029413

Kibenge FS (2019) Emerging viruses in aquaculture. Curr Opin Virol 34:97–103. https://doi.org/10.1016/j.coviro.2018.12.008

Kim KH, Hwang YJ, Bai SC (1999) Resistance to *Vibrio alginolyticus* in juvenile rockfish (*Sebastes schlegeli*) fed diets containing different doses of aloe. Aquaculture 180:13–21. https://doi.org/10.1016/S0044-8486(99)00143-X

Maan AA, Nazir A, Khan MKI, Ahmad T, Zia R, Murid M, Abrar M (2018) The therapeutic properties and applications of *Aloe vera*: a review. J Herb Med 12:1–10. https://doi.org/10.1016/j.hermed.2018.01.002

Mahdavi M, Hajimoradloo A, Ghorbani R (2013) Effect of *Aloe vera* extract on growth parameters of common carp (*Cyprinus carpio*). World J Med Sci 9:55–60. https://doi.org/10.5829/idosi.wjms.2013.9.1.75128

Maulu S, Hasimuna OJ, Mphande J, Munang'andu HM (2021) Prevention and control of *Streptococcosis* in tilapia culture: a systematic review. J Aquat Anim Health 33:162–177. https://doi.org/10.1002/aah.10132

Mehrabi Z, Firouzbakhsh F (2020) Short-term effects of feeding powdered *Aloe vera* (*Aloe barbadensis*) and nettle (*Urtica dioica*) on growth performance and stimulation of innate immune responses in rainbow trout (*Oncorhynchus mykiss*). Comp Clin Pathol 29:441–449

Mehrabi Z, Firouzbakhsh F, Rahimi-Mianji G, Paknejad H (2019) Immunostimulatory effect of *Aloe vera* (*Aloe barbadensis*) on non-specific immune response, immune gene expression, and experimental challenge with *Saprolegnia parasitica* in rainbow trout (*Oncorhynchus mykiss*). Aquaculture 503:330–338. https://doi.org/10.1016/j.aquaculture.2019.01.025

Miller RA, Harbottle H (2018) Antimicrobial drug resistance in fish pathogens. Microbiol Spectr. https://doi.org/10.1128/microbiolspec.ARBA-0017-2017

Müller-Lissner SA (1993) Adverse effects of laxatives: fact and fiction. Pharmacology 47:138–145. https://doi.org/10.1159/000139853

Ning L, Zhang X, Zhang D, Hu Y, Li Y (2021) The benefits of blend essential oil for GIFT tilapia on the digestion, antioxidant, and muscle quality during cold storage. Aquaculture 533:736097. https://doi.org/10.1016/j.aquaculture.2020.736097

Olaifa A (2016) Effects of aloe vera gel application on epidermal wound healing in the domestic rabbit. Int J Med Sci 5:101–105. https://doi.org/10.18203/2320-6012.ijrms20164531

Palermo FA, Cocci P, Angeletti M, Felici A, Polzonetti-Magni AM, Mosconi G (2013) Dietary *Aloe vera* components' effects on cholesterol lowering and estrogenic responses in juvenile goldfish, *Carassius auratus*. Fish Physiol Biochem 39:851–861. https://doi.org/10.1007/s10695-012-9745-7

Pati P (2021) The use of *Aloe vera* gel functionalized biogenic zinc-oxide nanoparticles against fish putative pathogens. Aquat Sci Eng 36:101–108. https://doi.org/10.26650/ASE2020773014

Platel K, Srinivasan K (2004) Digestive stimulant action of spices: a myth or reality? Indian J Med Res 119:167–179

Ponnusamy P, Govindaraj D, Mallikaraj D, Bhuvaneshwari N, Natarajan GM (2011) Haematological changes of fresh water food fish, *Channa striata* on exposure to *Cleistanthus collinus* suicidal plant extract. Res J Pharm Biol Chem 2:812–816

Pu H, Li X, Du Q, Cui H, Xu Y (2017) Research progress in the application of Chinese herbal medicines in aquaculture: a review. Engineering 3:731–737. https://doi.org/10.1016/J.ENG.2017.03.017

Radha MH, Laxmipriya NP (2015) Evaluation of biological properties and clinical effectiveness of *Aloe vera*: a systematic review. J Tradit Complement Med 5:21–26. https://doi.org/10.1016/j.jtcme.2014.10.006

Raina Manaf S, Mohd Daud H (2016) The effects of *Vitex trifolia, Strobilanthes crispus* and *Aloe vera* herbal-mixed dietary supplementation on growth performance and disease resistance in red hybrid tilapia (*Oreochromis sp.*). J Aquac Res Dev 7:2. https://doi.org/10.4172/2155-9546.1000425

Raissy M, Ghafarifarsani H, Hoseinifar SH, El-Haroun ER, Shahbazi Naserabad S, Van Doan H (2022) The effect of dietary combined herbs extracts (oak acorn, coriander, and common mallow) on growth, digestive enzymes, antioxidant and immune response, and resistance against *Aeromonas hydrophila* infection in common carp, *Cyprinus carpio*. Aquaculture 546:737287. https://doi.org/10.1016/j.aquaculture.2021.737287

Reverter M, Bontemps N, Lecchini D, Banaigs B, Sasal P (2014) Use of plant extracts in fish aquaculture as an alternative to chemotherapy: current status and future perspectives. Aquaculture 433:50–61. https://doi.org/10.1016/j.aquaculture.2014.05.048

Reynolds T, Dweck AC (1999) *Aloe vera* leaf gel: a review update. J Ethnopharmacol 68:3–37. https://doi.org/10.1016/s0378-8741(99)00085-9

Rico A, Phu TM, Satapornvanit K, Min J, Shahabuddin AM, Henriksson PJG, Murray FJ, Little DC, Dalsgaard A, Van den Brink PJ (2013) Use of veterinary medicines, feed additives and probiotics in four major internationally traded aquaculture species farmed in Asia. Aquaculture 412(413):231–243. https://doi.org/10.1016/j.aquaculture.2013.07.028

Rohani MS, Haghighi M, Moghaddam SB (2017) Study on nanoparticles of *Aloe vera* extract on growth performance, survival rate and body composition in Siberian sturgeon (*Acipenser baerii*). Iran J Fish Sci 12

Sánchez-Machado DI, López-Cervantes J, Sendón R, Sanches-Silva A (2017) *Aloe vera*: ancient knowledge with new frontiers. Trends Food Sci Technol 61:94–102. https://doi.org/10.1016/j.tifs.2016.12.005

Soltanizadeh N, Mousavinejad MS (2015) The effects of *Aloe vera* (*Aloe barbadensis*) coating on the quality of shrimp during cold storage. J Food Sci Technol 52:6647–6654. https://doi.org/10.1007/s13197-015-1747-x

Srivastava A, Nigam AK, Mittal S, Mittal AK (2018) Role of aloin in the modulation of certain immune parameters in skin mucus of an Indian major carp, *Labeo rohita*. Fish Shellfish Immunol 73:252–261. https://doi.org/10.1016/j.fsi.2017.12.014

Syed R, Masood Z, Hassan H, Khan W, Mushtaq S, Ali A, Gul Y, Jafari H, Habib A, Ishaq Ali Shah M, Gabol K, Gul H, Ullah A (2021) Growth performance, haematological assessment and chemical composition of Nile tilapia, *Oreochromis niloticus* (Linnaeus, 1758) fed different levels of *Aloe vera* extract as feed additives in a closed aquaculture system. Saudi J Biol Sci 29:296–303. https://doi.org/10.1016/j.sjbs.2021.08.098

Tai-Nin Chow J, Williamson DA, Yates KM, Goux WJ (2005) Chemical characterization of the immunomodulating polysaccharide of *Aloe vera* L. Carbohydr Res 340:1131–1142. https://doi.org/10.1016/j.carres.2005.02.016

Taiwo V, Olukunle O, Ozor I, Oyejobi A (2006) Consumption of aqueous extract of raw *Aloe vera* leaves: histopathological and biochemical studies in rat and tilapia. Afr J Biomed Res 8:169–178. https://doi.org/10.4314/ajbr.v8i3.35746

Trejo-Flores JV, Luna-González A, Álvarez-Ruiz P, Escamilla-Montes R, Fierro-Coronado JA, Peraza-Gómez V, Rubio-Castro A (2018) Immune-related gene expression in *Penaeus vannamei* fed *Aloe vera*. Lat Am J Aquat Res 46(4):756–764

Tremaroli V, Bäckhed F (2012) Functional interactions between the gut microbiota and host metabolism. Nature 489:242–249. https://doi.org/10.1038/nature11552

Vaseeharan B, Thaya R (2014) Medicinal plant derivatives as immunostimulants: an alternative to chemotherapeutics and antibiotics in aquaculture. Aquac Int 22:1079–1091. https://doi.org/10.1007/s10499-013-9729-3

Yu Y, Shen M, Song Q, Xie J (2018) Biological activities and pharmaceutical applications of polysaccharide from natural resources: a review. Carbohydr Polym 183:91–101. https://doi.org/10.1016/j.carbpol.2017.12.009

Zahran E, Risha E, AbdelHamid F, Mahgoub HA, Ibrahim T (2014) Effects of dietary *Astragalus* polysaccharides (APS) on growth performance, immunological parameters, digestive enzymes, and intestinal morphology of Nile tilapia (*Oreochromis niloticus*). Fish Shellfish Immunol 38: 149–157. https://doi.org/10.1016/j.fsi.2014.03.002

Zanuzzo FS, Urbinati EC, Rise ML, Hall JR, Nash GW, Gamperl AK (2015a) *Aeromonas salmonicida* induced immune gene expression in *Aloe vera* fed steelhead trout, *Oncorhynchus mykiss* (Walbaum). Aquaculture 435:1–9. https://doi.org/10.1016/j.aquaculture.2014.09.010

Zanuzzo FS, Zaiden SF, Senhorini JA, Marzocchi-Machado CM, Urbinati EC (2015b) *Aloe vera* bathing improved physical and humoral protection in breeding stock after induced spawning in matrinxã (*Brycon amazonicus*). Fish Shellfish Immunol 45:132–140. https://doi.org/10.1016/j.fsi.2015.02.017

Zanuzzo FS, Sabioni RE, Montoya LNF, Favero G, Urbinati EC (2017) *Aloe vera* enhances the innate immune response of pacu (*Piaractus mesopotamicus*) after transport stress and combined heat killed *Aeromonas hydrophila* infection. Fish Shellfish Immunol 65:198–205. https://doi.org/10.1016/j.fsi.2017.04.013

Chapter 7
Use of Plant Extracts to Control Reproduction in Tilapia Production Systems: An Emerging Eco-Friendly Innovation

Ivan Abaho, Ndakalimwe Naftal Gabriel, and Andrew Arinaitwe Izaara

Abstract This chapter gives an account of the usage of plant extracts to control-prolific spawning in tilapia production systems. The culture of mixed-sex tilapia results in overcrowding, leading to stunted fish that attract low market price, hence, making the investment less profitable. All-male tilapia has, however, proven to be a viable option towards solving this challenge. Besides, all-male sex individuals grow faster and bigger than females. Currently, farmers mainly use 17-α-methyltestosterone (MT) synthetic hormone to convert newly hatched fish into males. There is, however, increasing public concern on use of chemicals and drugs in aquaculture, accompanied by the increasing demand for safe food fish. For example, MT is a known carcinogenic substance; thus, prolonged exposure by fish farmers during application processes can adversely affect their health. Research has now embarked on the search for potential alternatives focusing on use of organic, plant-based products for control of tilapia reproduction. Contrary to synthetic hormones, plant extracts are easily accessible, safe, eco-friendly, and affordable. Presently extracts from several plant species mainly *Tribulus terrestris, Mucuna pruriens, Carica papaya, Asparagus racemosus, Aloe vera,* and *Pinus tabulaeformis,* have shown positive results towards controlling unwanted breeding in tilapia production systems. However, *C. papaya* and *Azadirachta indica* extracts have been more utilized in Africa at experimental level, which represent 31% and 17% of the

I. Abaho (✉)
National Agricultural Research Organization, Bulindi Zonal Agricultural Research and Development Institute, Hoima, Uganda

N. N. Gabriel
Department of Fisheries and Ocean Sciences, Faculty of Agriculture, Engineering and Natural Science, Sam Nujoma Campus, University of Namibia, Henties Bay, Namibia
e-mail: ngabriel@unam.na

A. A. Izaara
National Agricultural Research Organization, Mukono Zonal Agricultural Research and Development Institute, Mukono, Uganda

© The Author(s), under exclusive license to Springer Nature Singapore Pte Ltd. 2023
N. N. Gabriel et al. (eds.), *Emerging Sustainable Aquaculture Innovations in Africa*,
Sustainable Agriculture and Food Security,
https://doi.org/10.1007/978-981-19-7451-9_7

reviewed studies, respectively. The commercialization of the plant extracts is limited by lack of a standard application protocol. In-depth studies on extraction and refining of extracts, optimal dosages, mechanism of action, and likely effects on fish and human health are required to facilitate the commercial adoption of plant extracts in tilapia aquaculture.

Keywords All-male Tilapia · Aquaculture · Bioactive compounds · Phytochemicals · Synthetic hormones · 17α-methyltestosterone

7.1 Introduction

Tilapia are freshwater cichlids, which are native to Africa (Tibihika et al. 2018; Lind et al. 2019), despite with a wide distribution across tropics, subtropics, and in some temperate regions (Baroiller and D'Cotta 2019). Amongst the tilapia species, Nile tilapia (*Oreochromis niloticus*) is the widest distributed tilapia appearing on all continents except the Antarctica (Zambrano et al. 2006). It is presently the most farmed species of all tilapia, grown in 78 countries (Lind et al. 2019) and accounted for 4.5 million tons valued at $8.2 billion in 2018 (FAO 2020). In Africa, Nile tilapia and Mozambique tilapia (*Oreochromis mossambicus)* are the most cultured tilapia species (Hishamunda 2007; Moyo and Rapatsa 2021). Egypt contributes 71% of Africa's tilapia production (FAO 2017, 2020), with Nigeria, Uganda, Ghana, Tunisia, Kenya, Zambia, Madagascar, Malawi, and South Africa also contributing significantly to the overall production (Adeleke et al. 2021; Mapfumo 2022). The success of tilapia in aquaculture is attributed to its ability to breed easily in captivity, obtain nutrition at different trophic levels; readily grow on diets formulated using a wide range of feed raw materials, tolerate a wide range of environmental conditions, as well as technological advances such as the development of intensive culture systems, formulated feeds, and fast-growing strains (Pandit and Nakamura 2010; Wang et al. 2017; Mustapha and Atolagbe 2018; Baroiller and D'Cotta 2019; El-Sayed 2019; Rahmah et al. 2020; Levina et al. 2021).

However, for all its positive attributes, tilapia exhibits precocious maturation and prolific spawning, with a tendency to attain sexual maturity before realizing harvestable size (Abdel-Tawwab 2005). Hence, when left unchecked, the female individuals produce fry continuously in monthly batches, which result in overpopulation of the culture units. Overpopulation leads to crowding, which in turn induces stress and depresses growth of fish. In order to improve the economic returns from tilapia production enterprises, it is imperative that unwanted reproduction is controlled. Several approaches have been proposed: periodic harvesting of fry and fingerlings, biological control (polyculture), sterilization, and all-male culture for control of prolific spawning in the tilapia production systems (Mair and Little 1991; Beardmore et al. 2001; Abdel-Tawwab 2005; Fortes 2005; Wang and Lu 2016). Amongst these methods, all-male production is considered ideal, deriving its importance from the ability to reduce sex-directed territorial behavior and overall ensuring higher average growth rate of fish (Beardmore et al. 2001; Baroiller and D'Cotta 2019). The male individuals are desirable over female ones because they tend to reduce size variation at harvest and gain more weight than females of the same cohort (Beardmore et al. 2001; Toguyeni et al. 2002; Ridha 2011; Srisakultiew 2013; Mukti et al. 2020).

Presently, most tilapia hatcheries produce all-male individuals through feeding tilapia fry with diets mixed with synthetic hormones, especially 17-α-methyltestosterone hormone (MT), for a period of 3–4 weeks after hatching (Vera Cruz and Mair 1994; Mateen and Ahmed 2007). However, the use of synthetic hormones continues to attract public criticism of their after-use effects on humans and, overall, on environmental health (Jegede 2010; Baroiller and D'Cotta 2019). For example, MT is a carcinogenic substance, and therefore, prolonged exposure by fish farmers during fish feeding processes can adversely affect their health (Velazquez and Alter 2004; Megbowon and Mojekwu 2014). Some reported adverse health effects include hepatotoxicity, menstrual irregularities, and prostatic hypertrophy (Hartleb and Nowak 1990; Vick and Hayton 2001). Furthermore, the likely leakages of MT into the aquatic environment from uneaten or un-metabolized food pose a risk to non-target organisms, especially eliciting reproductive abnormalities, hence, disrupting aquatic ecosystem robustness (Hulak et al. 2008; Ramirez-Godinez et al. 2013; Abo-Al-Ela et al. 2017; Abo-Al-Ela 2018). With the indiscriminate use of different synthetic hormones associated with inexperienced fish farmers and weak aquaculture regulatory systems, adverse health and environmental effects are likely to increase in Africa (Fortes 2005; Gabriel et al. 2017).

Consequently, studies have focused on exploring the possibility of utilizing plant extracts as alternatives to synthetic hormones in the production of all-male tilapia. Plant extracts are envisioned as plausible alternatives since they are more biodegradable, with less minimal adverse. Various research efforts have generated promising results from using plant extracts for population control in tilapia aquaculture. However, this information remains scattered and sometimes reports inconsistent results. Therefore, the present chapter reviewed and compiled results from various studies on the application of plant extracts to control-prolific spawning in tilapia production systems in Africa. The information from other continents has been included, too, in order to generate a comprehensive inventory of phyto-extracts, which will play a key role in sustainable aquaculture production.

7.2 Plant Extracts Used to Control Tilapia Reproduction, Their Bioactive Compounds, and Used Extractants

Due to the increasing demand for chemical-free fish products, many countries are advocating for organic fish production and, hence, have banned use of synthetic chemicals in some aquaculture operations (Leet et al. 2011; Chakraborty et al. 2014; Mlalila et al. 2015). As a result, the interest in using organic plant extracts has recently increased. For instance, owing to the adverse effects of synthetic hormones in the production of all-male tilapia, various interventions are exploring plant-based products as alternatives (Table 7.2). In Africa, aquaculture is still in its infancy stage, despite on a steady growth trajectory, and hence, the adoption of sustainable production practices is vital. A significant increase in various studies exploring the use of plant extracts to control unwanted breeding in tilapia production systems is noticeable (Ampofo-Yeboah 2013; Gabriel et al. 2015; Omeje 2016; Kapinga et al. 2018; Kapinga et al. 2019; Linda 2019; Abaho et al. 2021). The extracts are easily accessible, less costly and safe for the environment and humans since they are more biodegradable compared to synthetic hormones (Logambal et al. 2000; Chakraborty et al. 2014; Reverter et al. 2014; Gabriel et al. 2015; Gabriel 2019; Abaho et al. 2021). Consequently, plant extracts are considered economically viable and eco-friendly alternatives to synthetic hormones for smallholder tilapia farmers in Africa.

The present review noted 20 plant species that have been studied for possible utilization in the control tilapia reproduction globally (Tables 7.1 and 7.2). However, only 12 species, mainly *C. papaya* and *A. indica,* have been explored in Africa (Fig. 7.1), with more research studies in Nigeria (45.7%), followed by Egypt (17.1%). The other African countries that have explored this innovation are Cameroon, Ivory Coast, Tanzania, Kenya, South Africa, and Namibia (Fig. 7.2; Gabriel 2019; Abaho et al. 2021). Regarding fish species, Nile tilapia and Mozambique tilapia have been studied.

In all studies, a significant shift in sex ratio from the normal 1:1 tilapia sex ratio, favoring male individuals, was observed (Table 7.2). Generally, results from the reviewed studies showed higher levels of tilapia masculinization by methanolic and ethanolic extracts from Velvet bean (*Mucuna pruriens*) and Shatavari (*Asparagus racemosus*) (Mukherjee et al. 2018), Red kwao krua (*Butea superba*) (Kiriyakit 2014), and Puncture vine (*Tribulus terrestris*) (El Deen et al. 2020; Ghosal et al. 2021; El-Kady et al. 2022). Comparable results were obtained when Nile tilapia was fed diets supplemented with pollen from pine tree (*Pinus tabulaeformis*) (Nian et al. 2017; Nieves 2017). Pawpaw (*C. papaya*), the mostly utilized plant extract in Africa, also induced 77.8% masculinization of Mozambique tilapia-fed diets supplemented with 20 g kg^{-1} of feed (Omeje et al. 2018). In addition to these findings, supplementation of tilapia diets with lower doses of *C. papaya* and *Moringa. oleifera* seed extracts (2.0–5.0 g kg^{-1} of diet) in both sexually immature and mature tilapia disintegrates gonadal cells, thus, altering their development and subsequently resulting in anti-fertility (Jegede and Fagbenro 2008; Ampofo-yeboah 2013; Solomon et al. 2017; Ugonna et al. 2018). However, higher doses of C. papaya (120 g kg^{-1} of diet) can result in permanent sterility in Nile tilapia (Abdelhak et al. 2013). Notably, however, the findings of reviewed studies were not consistent, even for similar doses of the same plant extract and treatment periods (Table 7.2; Stadtlander et al. 2008; Ampofo-Yeboah 2013; Olusola et al. 2013; Mukherjee et al. 2015a, b; Ghosal et al. 2016; Nian et al. 2017; Nieves 2017; Mukherjee et al. 2018).

From the reviewed literature, extracts are obtained from different parts of the plant, i.e., seeds, roots, leaves, and flowers, although leaf and seed extracts are mostly used (Table 7.1). The extraction yield and biological activity of the extracts greatly depend on the extraction technique as well as the extraction solvent used

Table 7.1 Plant species, used parts, and their respective bioactive compounds hypothesized to be responsible for reproduction control in tilapia

Family	Common and scientific names	Plant part used	Bioactive agent	References
Anacardiaceae	Mango, *Mangifera indica*	Leaves	Saponins	Obaroh and Nzeh (2013)
Asparagaceae	Shatavari, *Asparagus racemosus*	Roots	Steroidal saponins	Thakur et al. (2009); Aloka et al. (2013)
Asphodelaceae	True aloe, *Aloe vera*	Leaves	Saponins and flavonoids	Patel et al. (2012)
Basellaceae	Indian spinach, *Basella alba*	Leaves	Steroids	Moundipa et al. (2005); Nantia et al. (2011); Ghosal et al. (2015)
Caricaceae	Pawpaw, *Carica papaya*	Seeds	Saponin (oleanolic acid 3-glucoside)	Ampofo-Yeboah (2013); Waweru et al. (2019)
Clusiaceae	Bitter kola, *Garcinia kola*	Seeds	Flavonoids (apigenin)	Sulem-Yong et al. (2018)
Compositae	Aspilia plant, *Aspilia mossambicensis*	Leaves	Saponins and flavonoids	Musyimi et al. (2008); Kapinga et al. (2018, 2019)
Fabaceae	Fenugreek, *Trigonella foenum-graecum*	Seeds	Steroidal saponins (Diosgenin)	Murakami et al. (2000); Raju et al. (2004)
Leguminosae	Red kwao krua, *Butea superba*	Roots	Flavonol and flavonoid glycoside	Manosroi and Manosroi (2005); Cherdshewasart et al. (2008)
Leguminosae	Velvet bean, *Mucuna pruriens*	Seeds	Steroid	Mukherjee et al. (2018); Abaho et al. (2021)
Malvaceae	Cotton, Gossypium herbaceum	Seeds	Polyphenol (gossypol)	Akin-Obasola and Jegede (2016); Tope-Jegede et al. (2019)
Malvaceae	Red hibiscus, *Hibiscus rosa-sinensis*	Roots, leaves and flowers	Flavonoids	Jegede (2010)
Meliaceae	Neem tree, *Azadirachta indica*	Leaves	Saponins and flavonoids	Atangwho et al. (2009); Kapinga et al. (2018, 2019)
Meliaceae	Honeysuckle tree, *Turraea heterophylla*	Roots, leaves and flowers	Steroids	El Deen et al. (2020)

(continued)

Table 7.1 (continued)

Family	Common and scientific names	Plant part used	Bioactive agent	References
Moringaceae	Moringa, *Moringa oleifera*	Leaves and roots	Triterpenoids (oleanolic acid-3-glucoside and β-sitosterol)	Lambole and Kumar (2011); Ampofo-yeboah (2013)
Myrtaceae	Guava, Psidium guajava	Leaves	saponins and flavanoids	Uboha et al. (2010); Tarigan et al. (2016)
Pinaceae	Pine trees, *Pinus spp.*	Pollen from male cones	Steroids (testosterone, epitestosterone, and androstenedione)	Jones and Roddick (1988); Adenigba et al. (2017); Velasco et al. (2018)
Simaroubaceae	Jack plant, *Eurycoma longifolia*	Roots	Phytosterol (stigmasterol)	Low et al. (2013b); Abubakar et al. (2017)
Quillajaceae	Soapbark tree, *Quillaja saponaria*	Stems	Triterpenoidal saponins (triterpene glycoside)	Francis et al. (2005); Stadtlander et al. (2008)
Zygophyllaceae	Puncture vine, *Tribulus terrestris*	Seeds	Steroidal saponin (protodioscin)	Ganzera et al. (2001); Dinchev et al. (2008); Yılmaz et al. (2013)

(Ajanal et al. 2012; Mahdi-Pour et al. 2012). Therefore, a technique, especially using a solvent with appropriate polarity, to maximize the desired bioactive compound is crucial (Dhanani et al. 2017). Solvent extraction of bioactive compounds from various plant materials is the widely used method with the following solvents: methanol, dichloromethanol, ethanol, ethyl acetate, hexane, ether, chloroform, and water utilized (Sasidharan et al. 2011; Bulfon et al. 2015; Gabriel et al. 2015; Van Hai 2015; Nik et al. 2022). Notably, the present review revealed that extracts obtained with organic solvents, mainly ethanol and methanol, induced higher masculinization of tilapia compared to water-based aqueous extracts (Table 7.2).

The phyto-compounds, i.e., phytoandrogens and phytoestrogens, from plant extracts, mimic the action of the natural sex steroids (testosterone and 17β- estradiol) in animals (Glazier and Bowman 2001). The saponins, flavonoids, and steroids are the main bioactive compounds in plant extracts, which have been hypothesized to induce sex masculinization and fertility impairment in fish (Table 7.1; Musyimi et al. 2008; Lee et al. 2009; Obaro et al. 2012; Gabriel et al. 2017; Kapinga et al. 2018; Velasco et al. 2018; Tarkowska 2019; Ghosal et al. 2021; Abaho ct al. 2021). In contrast, the plant extracts may stimulate feminization of tilapia rather than the desired masculinization. For example, the inclusion of soybean in fish diets before gonadal differentiation is known to significantly reduce male individuals (El-Sayed et al. 2012). Soybean contains phytoestrogens, mainly genistein and daidzein, which induce ovarian development in fish (Pelissero et al. 1991). Particularly, the presence of anti-nutritional factors in some plant extracts may also inhibit the growth of

Table 7.2 Effect of plant extracts on the sex ratio, gonadal histology, spawning, and number of hatchlings of tilapia towards reproduction control (Adopted from Abaho et al. 2021, with modifications)

Plant species	Treatment	Doses tested	Duration (days)	Delivery	Tilapia species	Study	Best dose	Summary of results	References
Aloe vera	Crude powder extract	0, 1.0, 2.0, and 4.0% of feed	30	Oral	*O. niloticus*	Sex ratio	4.0% of feed	Induced 67.62 ± 4.37% male individuals after the treatment period	Gabriel et al. (2017)
	Aloe vera latex	0, 0.5, 1.0, 1.5, and 2.0 mL kg^{-1} feed	60	Oral	*O. niloticus*	Gonadal histology	2.0 mL kg^{-1}	Disintegration of spermatids in males, ruptured follicles, and gonadal necrosis in females	Jegede (2011); Kushwaha (2013)
Asparagus racemosus	Root methanol extract	0.1, 0.15, and 0.2 g kg^{-1} of feed	30	Oral	*O. niloticus*	Sex ratio	0.2 g kg¯1 of feed	Induced 92.24 ± 0.13% male individuals	Mukherjee et al. (2018)
	Root aqueous extract	0.01, 0.015, and 0.02 g L^{-1}	30	Immersion	*O. niloticus*	Sex ratio	0.015 g L^{-1}	Sex inversion results produced 90.60 ± 1.56% males	Mukherjee et al. (2015a)
Aspilia mossambicensis	Leaf powder	1.0, 2.0, 4.0, and 8.0 g kg^{-1} feed	90	Oral	*O. niloticus*	Hatchlings production	8 g kg^{-1}	Low hatchlings number (101.9 ± 19.7)	Kapinga et al. (2018)
	Leaf powder	1.0, 2.0, 4.0, and 8.0 g kg^{-1} of diet	90	Oral	*O. niloticus*	Gonadal histology	2.0 g kg^{-1}	Degenerated of seminiferous tubules and atretic follicles	Kapinga et al. (2019)
Azadirachta indica	Crude ethanol extract	0.0, 0.5, 1.0, 2.0, 4.0, and 8.0 g kg^{-1} diet	56	Oral	*O. niloticus*	Hatchlings number	1.0 g kg^{-1}	No breeding from the 5th week of the treatment	Obaroh and Achionye-Nzeh (2011)

(continued)

Table 7.2 (continued)

Plant species	Treatment	Doses tested	Duration (days)	Delivery	Tilapia species	Study	Best dose	Summary of results	References
	Leaf crude extract (Saponin)	0.0, 0.5, 2.0, 4.0, and 8.0 g kg^{-1} feed	56	Oral	*O. niloticus*	Hatchlings number	4.0 and 8.0 g kg^{-1}	No spawning observed	Obaro et al. (2012)
	Leaf powder	0.0, 0.5, 1.0, 2.0, 4.0, and 8.0 g kg^{-1} feed	56	Oral	*O. niloticus*	Hatchlings number	1.0, 2.0, 4.0, and 8.0 g kg^{-1}	No spawning observed	Obaroh and Nzeh 2013)
	Leaf powder	0, 0.5, 1.0, 1.5, and 2.0 g kg^{-1} diet	60	Oral	*Tilapia zilli*	Gonadal histology	2.0 g kg^{-1}	Rendered the testes and ovaries devoid of spermatids and oocytes	Jegede and Fagbenro (2008)
	Leaf powder	1.0, 2.0, 4.0, and 8.0 g kg^{-1} feed	90	Oral	*O. niloticus*	Hatchlings production	8 g kg^{-1}	Low hatchlings number (62.5 ± 6.2)	Kapinga et al. (2018)
Basella alba	Leaf powder of aqueous, methanol, ethanol, dichloromethane, hexane, and successive methanol extracts	0.5, 1.0, and 1.5 g kg^{-1} of feed	30	Oral	*O. niloticus*	Sex ratio	1.0 g of ethanol extract kg^{-1} of feed	Sex inversion with 83.2 ± 0.7% males were observed	Ghosal et al. (2015)
	Leaf aqueous extract	0.00, 0.05, 0.10, and 0.15 g L^{-1}	30	Immersion	*O. niloticus*	Sex ratio	0.1 g L^{-1}	Skewed sex ratio with 70.3 ± 1.9% males obtained	Ghosal and Chakraborty (2014a)
	Leaf powder	0.0, 5.0, 10.0, and 15.0 g kg^{-1} of feed	30	Oral	*O. niloticus*	Sex ratio	10.0 g kg^{-1} of feed	Triggered sex inversion to 70.3 ± 1.2% males	Ghosal et al. (2016)
	Leaf aqueous extract	0.05, 0.10 and 0.15 g L^{-1}	30	Immersion	*O. niloticus*	Sex ratio	0.1 g L^{-1}	Sex masculinization producing 71.9 ± 1.9% males observed	Ghosal et al. (2016)

Butea superba	Root powder	100, 200, and 300 g kg^{-1} of feed	30	Oral	*O. niloticus*	Sex ratio	200 g kg^{-1} of feed	Male individuals increased to 72.2 ± 25.5% from the normal 1:1 sex ratio	Mengumphan et al. (2006)
	Root powder ethanol extract	0.00, 0.04, 0.08, 0.12, 0.16, and 0.20 g kg^{-1} of feed	21	Oral	*O. niloticus*	Sex ratio	0.20 g kg^{-1} of feed	Induced 100% testicular development	Kiriyakit (2014)
Carica papaya)	Seed powder	15 g kg^{-1} of feed	30	Oral	*O. mossambicus*	Sex ratio	15 g kg^{-1} of feed	Low level of masculinization observed with 65% male individuals	Ampofo-Yeboah (2013)
	Seed powder	10, 15, 20, 25, and 30 g kg^{-1} of feed	120	Oral	*O. mossambicus*	Sex ratio	20 g kg^{-1} of feed	The treatment sex inversed tilapia producing 77.8% males	Omeje (2016)
	Seed powder	6 g kg^{-1} of feed	45	Oral	*O. niloticus*	Sex ratio	6 g kg^{-1} of feed	68% male individuals observed at the end of the study	Mehrim et al. (2019)
	Seed powder	0, 0.5, 1.0, 2.0, 5.0, and 10.0 g kg^{-1} diet	60	Oral	*O. mossambicus*	Gonadal histology	2.0 g kg^{-1}	Anti-fertility effect, preventing reproduction in both genders of sexually immature fingerlings	Ampofo-Yeboah (2013)
	Seed powder	0, 0.5, 1.0, 5.0, 10.0, 15.0 g kg^{-1} diet	60	Oral	*O. mossambicus*	Gonadal histology	5.0 g kg^{-1}	Anti-fertility effect, preventing reproduction in both genders of sexually mature juveniles	Ampofo-Yeboah (2013)

(continued)

Table 7.2 (continued)

Plant species	Treatment	Doses tested	Duration (days)	Delivery	Tilapia species	Study	Best dose	Summary of results	References
	Seed powder	0, 4, 8, and 12 g kg^{-1} feed	60	Oral	*O. niloticus*	Gonadal histology	8 g kg^{-1}	Atretic follicles in ovaries and degenerated spermatozoa in testes	Waweru et al. (2019)
	Seed powder	3 and 6 g kg^{-1} of diet	30	Oral	*O. niloticus*	Gonadal histology	6 g kg^{-1}	Permanent sterility in mature male tilapia	Abbas and Abbas (2011)
	Seed powder	0, 2, 4, 6, and 8 g kg^{-1} of feed	28	Oral	*O. niloticus*	Gonadal histology	4 g kg^{-1}	Gonadal deformity resulting into sterility of female individuals	Solomon et al. (2017)
	Seed powder	4.9, 9.8 g kg^{-1} of feed per day	30	Oral	*O. niloticus*	Gonadal histology	9.8 g kg^{-1} per day	Permanent sterility	Ekanem and Okoronkwo (2003)
	Seed powder	0, 0.5, 1.0, 1.5, and 2.0 g kg^{-1} diet	60	Oral	*O. niloticus*	Gonadal histology	2.0 g kg^{-1}	Disintegration of gonadal cells, rendering the testes, and ovaries devoid of spermatids and oocytes, respectively	Jegede and Fagbenro (2008)
	Seed powder	60, 90, and 120 g kg^{-1} of feed	60	Oral	*O. niloticus*	Gonadal histology	120 g kg^{-1}	Permanent sterility	Abdelhak et al. (2013)
Eurycoma longifolia	Root methanol extract	0.00, 0.03, 0.06, and 0.09 g kg^{-1} of feed	30	Oral	*O. niloticus*	Sex ratio	0.06 g kg^{-1} of feed	82.10% male individuals were obtained	Yusuf et al. (2019)

	Root powder ethanol extract	0.00, 0.02, 0.04, and 0.06 g L^{-1}	60	Immersion	*O. niloticus*	Sex ratio	0.06 g L^{-1}	Altered gonadal differentiation to 67.44% males	Rinaldi et al. (2017)
Garcinia kola	Seed powder	0, 6, and 10% feed	70	Oral	*O. niloticus*	Gonadal histology	6%	Impaired gonadal development in female individuals	Nyadjeu et al. (2019)
	Seed powder	0, 1, 3, and 6% diet	44	Oral	*O. niloticus*	Number of eggs spawned	83.45%	Significantly reduced fecundity	Sulem-Yong et al. (2018)
	Seed powder	0, 10, 20, and 30 g kg^{-1} of feed	28	Oral	*O. niloticus*	Sex ratio	30 g kg^{-1} of feed	Treatment resulted in 65.75 ± 4.19% males individuals	Tigoli et al. (2018)
Gossypium (Herbaceum)	Root bark powder	0, 5, 10, 15, and 20 g kg^{-1} diet	70	Oral	*O. niloticus*	Gonadal histology	20 gkg^{-1}	Disintegration in seminiferous lobule and oocytes damaged plus connective tissue	Akin-Obasola and Jegede (2016)
	Cotton seed meal	0, 25, 50, 75, and 100% of soybean meal protein substituted	90	Oral	*O. niloticus*	Gonadal histology	25, 50, 75, and 100%	Destroyed spermatocytes and distorted vitellogenic stages	Tope-Jegede et al. (2019)
Hibiscus rosa-sinensis	Leaf powder	0, 1.0, 2.0, 3.0, and 4.0 g kg^{-1} feed	60	Oral	*O. niloticus*	Gonadal histology	3.0 and 4.0 g kg^{-1}	Induced sterility by destructing testes and ovary tissues	Jegede (2010)
Mangifera indica	Leaf powder	0.0, 0.5, 1.0, 2.0, 4.0, and 8.0 g kg^{-1} feed	56	Oral	*O. niloticus*	Hatchlings number	2.0, 4.0, and 8.0 g kg^{-1}	No spawning observed during the experiment	Obaroh and Nzeh (2013)

(continued)

Table 7.2 (continued)

Plant species	Treatment	Doses tested	Duration (days)	Delivery	Tilapia species	Study	Best dose	Summary of results	References
Moringa oleifera Lam.	Seed powder	15 g kg^{-1} of feed	30	Oral	*O. mossambicus*	Sex ratio	15 g kg^{-1} of feed	Induced sex masculinization producing 65.5% males	Ampofo-Yeboah (2013)
	Seed powder	0.0, 0.5, 1.0, 2.0, 5.0, and 10.0 g kg^{-1} diet	60	Oral	*O. mossambicus*	Gonadal histology	2.0 g kg^{-1}	Anti-fertility effect, preventing reproduction in both genders of sexually immature fingerlings	Ampofo-Yeboah (2013)
	Seed powder	0.0, 0.5, 1.0, 5.0, 10.0 15.0 g kg^{-1} diet	60	Oral	*O. mossambicus*	Gonadal histology	5.0 g kg^{-1}	Anti-fertility effect, preventing reproduction in both genders of sexually mature juveniles	Ampofo-Yeboah (2013)
	Leaf powder	0%, 5%, 10%, and 15% of total dietary protein	90	Oral	*O. niloticus*	Gonadal histology	5% of total dietary protein	Severe oocyte cytoplasm degeneration with normal hepatocytes	Nwankpa (2017)
Mucuna pruriens	Seed methanol extract	0.1, 0.15, and 0.2 g kg^{-1} of feed	30	Oral	*O. niloticus*	Sex ratio	0.2 g kg^{-1} of feed	Masculinization producing 93.79 ± 0.95% males observed	Mukherjee et al. (2018)
	Seed powder	0.0, 2.0, 3.5, and 5.0 g kg^{-1} of feed	30	Oral	*O. niloticus*	Sex ratio	5.0 g kg^{-1} of feed	73.33 ± 0.67% of males were obtained	Mukherjee et al. (2015b)
	Seed aqueous extract	0.02, 0.035, and 0.05 g L^{-1}	30	Immersion	*O. niloticus*	Sex ratio	0.05 g L^{-1}	Induced sex masculinization producing 74.67 ± 0.33% males	Mukherjee et al. (2015b)

Pinus tabulaeformis	Pollen powder	0.00, 0.08, 0.16, 0.32, and 0.64 g kg^{-1} of feed	60	Oral	*O. niloticus*	Sex ratio	0.32 g kg^{-1} of feed	Increased male individuals to 89.1 ± 3.6% from the ideal 50%	Nian et al. (2017)
Pinus kesiya	Pollen powder	(0.5 g of pine pollen +0.5 g MT) kg^{-1} of feed and 1.0 g of pine pollen kg^{-1} of feed	28	Oral	*O. niloticus*	Sex ratio	1.0 g of pine pollen kg^{-1} of feed	Sex inversion with 88% males was observed	Nieves (2017)
Psidium guajava	Crude leaf extract	0.0, 0.5, 1.0, 2.0, 4.0, and 8.0 g kg^{-1} diet	56	Oral	*O. niloticus*	Gonadal histology	4 .0, 8.0 g kg^{-1}	Atrophy of the testicular tissues and ripe oocytes	Obaroh et al. (2018)
Quillaja saponaria	Saponin (QS; Sigma, St. Louis, MO, USA)	0.05, 0.15, 0.30, 0.50, and 0.70 g kg^{-1} of feed	60	Oral	*O. niloticus*	Sex ratio	0.70 g kg^{-1} of feed	69% male individuals obtained	Francis et al. (2002)
	Saponin methanol extract	40, 60, and 80% QS (0.15 and 1.00 g kg^{-1} of feed)	120	Oral	*O. niloticus*	Sex ratio	80% QS (0.15 g kg^{-1} of feed)	Sex masculinization with 73% male individuals was observed	Stadtlander et al. (2008)
Tribulus terrestris	Seed powder aqueous, methanol, ethanol, dichloromethane, hexane, and successive methanol extracts	0.5, 1.0, and 1.5 g kg^{-1} of feed	30	Oral	*O. niloticus*	Sex ratio	1.5 g of ethanol extract kg^{-1} of feed	Altered the normal 1:1 sex ratio producing 88.9 ± 1.1 % male individuals	Ghosal et al. (2015); Ghosal and Chakraborty (2020)
	Trib 60 Extract (Tonvara Premium Natural Supplements, UK)	0.0, 1.0, 1.5, 2.0, and 2.5 g kg^{-1} of feed	42	Oral	*O. niloticus*	Sex ratio	2.5 g kg^{-1} of feed	Induced sex inversion producing 83.67 ± 4.04% males	Omitoyin et al. (2013)

(continued)

Table 7.2 (continued)

Plant species	Treatment	Doses tested	Duration (days)	Delivery	Tilapia species	Study	Best dose	Summary of results	References
	Seed powder	0.0, 5.0, 10.0, and 15.0 g kg^{-1} of feed	30	Oral	*O. niloticus*	Sex ratio	15.0 g kg^{-1} of feed	76.6 ± 0.5% male fish were obtained	Ghosal et al. (2016)
	Seed aqueous extract	0.05, 0.1, and 0.15 g L^{-1}	30	Immersion	*O. niloticus*	Sex ratio	0.15 g L^{-1}	Sex inversion producing 81.4 ± 0.5% males observed	Ghosal et al. (2016)
	Seed aqueous extract	0.00, 0.05, 0.10, and 0.15 g L^{-1}	30	Immersion	*O. niloticus*	Sex ratio	0.15 g L^{-1}	81.4 ± 0.5% male individuals obtained	Ghosal and Chakraborty (2014b)
	Seed powder ethanol extract	0.0, 2.0, 2.5, and 3.0 g kg^{-1} of feed	30	Oral	*O. niloticus*	Sex ratio	2.0 g kg^{-1} of feed	Sex masculinization resulting in 91.85 ± 0.38% males observed	Ghosal et al. (2021)
	N/S	1.0 and 2.0 g kg^{-1} of feed	28	Oral	*Oreochromis sp.* (Red tilapia)	Sex ratio	2.0 g kg^{-1} feed	Altered gonadal differentiation producing 84.4% male individuals	Zaki et al. (2021)
	Root, flower, and leaf aqueous extract	0.0, 1.0, 2.0, and 3.0	28	Oral	*O. niloticus*	Sex ratio	2.0 g kg^{-1} feed	Sex inversion was effective producing 97.43 ± 0.13% males	El Deen et al. (2020)
Trigonella foenum-graecum	Saponin methanol extract	0.15 and 0.30 g kg^{-1} of feed	30	Oral	*O. niloticus*	Sex ratio	0.30 g kg^{-1} of feed	Low levels of masculinization with 56 ± 12.6% males	Stadtlander et al. (2013)
	Saponin methanol extract	40, 60, and 80% TS (0.15	120	Oral	*O. niloticus*	Sex ratio	80% TS (0.15 g	Induced sex change to mainly males at 73% at	Stadtlander et al. (2008)

		and 1.00 g kg^{-1} of feed)					kg^{-1} of feed)	the end of the experiment	
Turraea heterophylla	Root powder	0, 10, 20, and 30 g kg^{-1} of feed	28	Oral	*O. niloticus*	Sex ratio	30 g kg^{-1} of feed	Resulted in 76.82 ± 3.34% male individuals	Tigoli et al. (2018)

MT 17α-methyltestosterone, *N/S* Not specified, *QS Quillaja saponaria* saponin, *TS Trigonella foenum-graecum* saponin

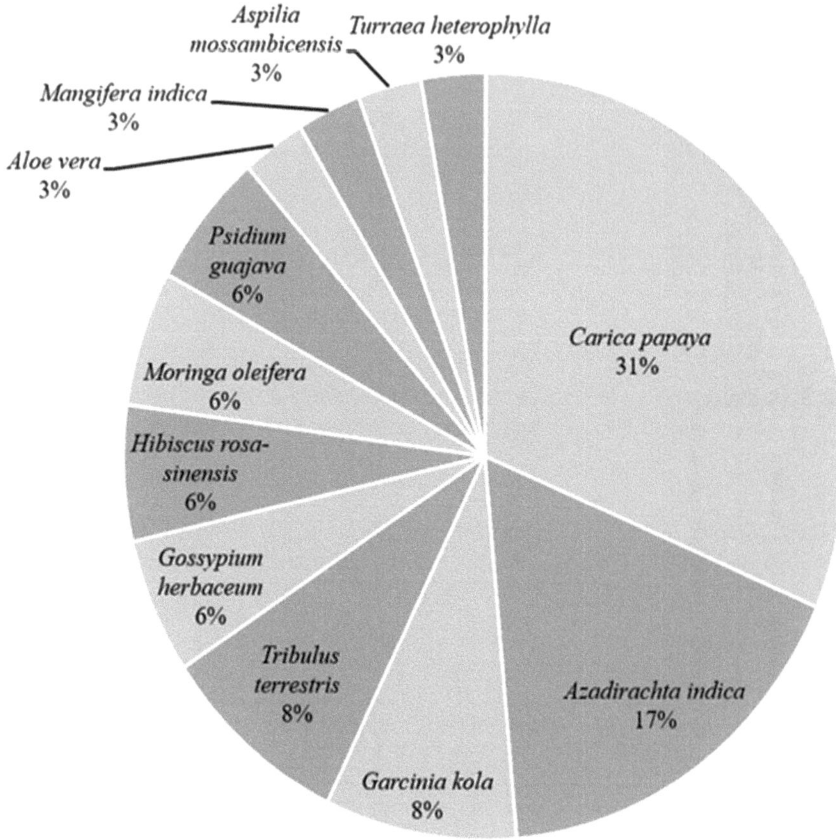

Fig. 7.1 Commonly utilized plant extracts to control-prolific breeding of tilapia in Africa

tilapia. Gossypol, a natural phenolic compound in cotton, is reported to be an anti-nutritional factor and hence, elicits retarded growth of fish (Mbahinzireki et al. 2001). It is, therefore, necessary to exclude extracts with feminization agents and anti-nutritional factors in the ingredients while formulating diets to be fed tilapia fry during sex inversion period.

Besides sex masculinization potential, the phyto-extracts have innate immunity enhancement properties and can improve the parameters of the culture water and survival rate, as well as stimulate the appetite of the fish, which ultimately boosts fish growth (Citarasu 2010; Chakraborty and Hancz 2011; Gabriel et al. 2015; Nian et al. 2017; Nieves 2017; Baluran et al. 2018; Baldove et al. 2019; Gharaei et al. 2020; Ghosal et al. 2021; Zaki et al. 2021). As such, the benefits from the plant extracts are twofold, which make them a better alternative to synthetic hormones in the production of all-male tilapia (Logambal et al. 2000; Olusola et al. 2013; Reverter et al. 2014; Nian et al. 2017; Baluran et al. 2018; Abaho et al. 2021; Gabriel et al. 2022).

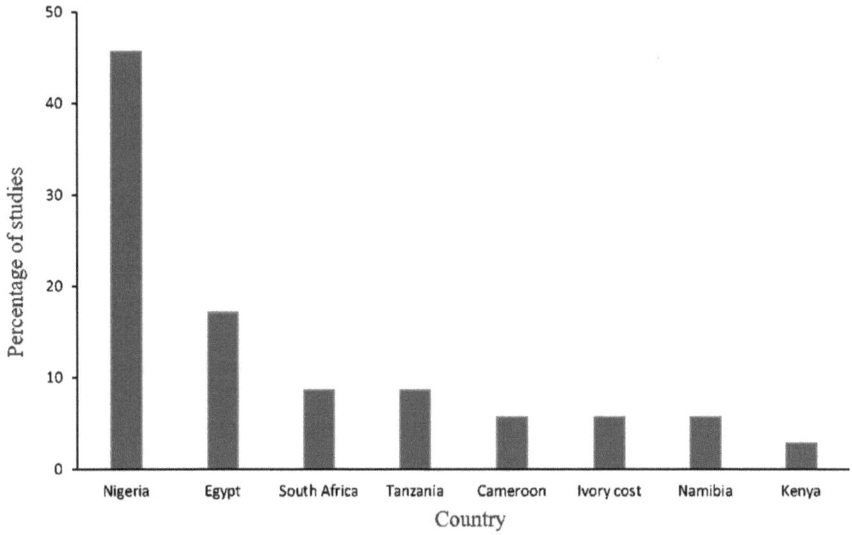

Fig. 7.2 Number of studies on plant extracts used to control tilapia reproduction by country in Africa

Despite the potential of plant extracts to control tilapia reproduction and the associated benefits, the discrepancy observed in the results continues to cause uncertainty over their application. This inconsistency in results is attributed to (1) variations in the composition of bioactive compounds due to plant growing stage, locations, and season, (2) extraction technique, solvent, and storage conditions of the extract; and (3) varied conditions during the experiment such as environment, age of fish, genetics, basal diets, and the health status of fish (Dinchev et al. 2008; Akula and Ravishankar 2011; Dhanani et al. 2017; Isah 2019; Nhu et al. 2019). Research focused on addressing these limitations will be a step forward towards improving their biological activity, and hence, commercial application of the plant extracts in tilapia hatcheries.

7.2.1 Route of Administration of Plant Extracts

Overall, three approaches, i.e., oral, immersion/baths, and injection (intraperitoneal), are utilized to administer plant extracts to the fish in aquaculture (Reverter et al. 2014, 2017; Gabriel 2019; Abaho et al. 2021). The injection method of administering extracts is considered to be rapid and efficient (Reverter et al. 2014). However, it is stressful to the fish, laborious, especially for small-sized fish and is costly (Yoshida et al. 1995; Beardmore et al. 2001; Reverter et al. 2014, 2017). Hence, oral and immersion administration methods are mostly used. For reproduction control in tilapia production systems, 88.5% of the reviewed studies utilized the oral method, while 11.5% used the immersion approach. No study used the injection technique (Table 7.2).

Generally, the immersion technique resulted in inferior sex inversion of tilapia compared to the oral method. As such, the incorporation of plant extracts in fish diets is mostly preferred administration method. This method is less costly and more practical since it allows for treatment of large numbers of fish at the same time, with either reduced or no stress (Sakai 1999; Bulfon et al. 2015; Awad and Awaad 2017). Besides, this method is effective with reports of up to 95% sex masculinization (Phelps and Popma 2000; El-Greisy and El-Gamal 2012). Nevertheless, the oral method can be relatively ineffective due to the slow absorbance of bioactive compounds from the extract. In addition, the targeted phytocompound may not be uniformly distributed in the diet during feed mixing, which leads to variations in the amounts of the bioactive compound accessed by the fish. This further reduces the effectiveness of the extracts (Budd et al. 2015; Bulfon et al. 2015).

7.2.2 Mechanism of Reproduction Control in Tilapia by Plant Extracts

In tilapia, the labile period for gonadal differentiation is from 10 days post fertilization (dpf) after the fish has absorbed yolk sac, to 25–30 dpf (Kobayashi et al. 2008). Research has demonstrated that the application of androgenic and estrogenic treatments during this period alters the sex differentiation pathway (Pandian and Sheela 1995; D'Cotta et al. 2001; Devlin and Nagahama 2002; Leet et al. 2011; Baroiller and D'Cotta 2019; Muniasamy et al. 2019). As such, plant extracts should be applied during this critical period while exploring how they modify the sex differentiation pathway in tilapia. The current knowledge on the precise mechanism of plant extracts in the control of tilapia reproduction is not clear. They are, however, thought to follow a similar pathway like natural sex steroids during the process of sex differentiation of fish. For instance, the bioactive compounds in the extracts induce either sex masculinization acting as phytoandrogens (Turan and Akyurt 2005), or fertility impairment by obstruction of gonadal functions, mainly through disintegration and rupturing of gonad cells (Table 7.2). The induction of testicular development involves interference with the endocrine system of the fish and, subsequently, the normal gonadal differentiation. Therefore, the bioactive compounds, which re-direct the sex of tilapia, are termed "endocrine disrupting compounds (EDCs)" (Omeje 2016). These phyto-compounds are believed to alter reproduction by changing the levels and activities of hormones involved in reproduction along the hypothalamus–pituitary–gonadal (HPG) axis. They interfere with the androgen–to-estrogen ratio in fish, which ultimately determines the direction of sex differentiation. Since the fate of gonads in fish is influenced by the ratio between endogenous estrogens and androgens, with excess steroids determining the final sex (Devlin and Nagahama 2002; Barannikova et al. 2004; Sandra and Norma 2010; Yarmohammadi et al. 2017), it is hypothesized that plant extracts act on this pathway to modify sex differentiation in tilapia.

Like the synthetic hormones, the phyto-compounds are hypothesized to alter the androgen-to-estrogen concentrations via (1) inhibition of aromatase activity, (2) blocking or altering estrogen nuclear receptors, and (3) activation of androgen receptors (Francis et al. 2002; Rempel and Schlenk 2008; Chakraborty et al. 2014; Golan and Levavi-Sivan 2014; Lee et al. 2017). Firstly, aromatase inhibition averts the aromatization of androgens to estrogens, thus, reducing estrogen levels in the differentiating gonad, which otherwise would elicit ovarian development. Consequently, the androgens are in higher concentrations promoting the development of male gonads (Cheshenko et al. 2008; Takatsu et al. 2013; Golan and Levavi-Sivan 2014). Second, the phyto-compounds can mimic and antagonize the estrogen nuclear receptors by blocking or altering their nuclear binding sites in the cytoplasm. The end result is blocking or attenuating estrogen production, favoring male sex differentiation (Ososki and Kennelly 2003; Matozzo et al. 2008). Third, the bioactive compounds can act as androgen receptor activators. The compounds bind and activate the androgen receptor to function as a transcription factor, which facilitates the expression of the target gene in response to the androgen, subsequently initiating masculinization (Carson-Jurica et al. 1990; O'Malley and Tsai 1992; Golshan et al. 2019). This is facilitated by the structural and binding affinity similarities of these phytochemicals and the natural androgen receptor ligands, i.e., testosterone and 11-ketotestosterone. For instance, treatment of Zebra fish (*Danio rerio*) with *Tribulus terrestris* extract yielded a considerable number of males, corresponding with an increase in testosterone levels in the treated fish. The study concluded that the masculinization capacity of *T. terrestris* was probably due to the presence of protodioscin, a phytochemical that is reported to stimulate testosterone production (Ahmad Gharaei et al. 2020). In rats, it was demonstrated that Eurycomanone, the primary bioactive compound from the root extracts of *E. longifolia,* improved fertility by increasing testosterone and spermatogenesis through the HPG axis (Low et al. 2013a, b). Similarly, *E. longifolia* extracts induced masculinization in tilapia (Table 7.2). Whether the extracts also attenuate 17β-estradiol concentration, hence, altering the androgen-to-estrogen ratio, remains to be confirmed. The flavonoids and saponins, present in many of plant extracts, have been reported to inhibit both the aromatase activity and act as anti-estrogenic compounds (Miyahara et al. 2003; Chen and Chang 2007; Golan et al. 2008; Green and Kelly 2009; Tarigan et al. 2016). Notably, some phyto-compounds such as genistein and daidzein, the phytoestrogens from soya, can modify sex differentiation in fish by promoting the development of female sex characteristics. The plant extracts that contain these phytochemicals should, thus, be avoided while formulating diets for tilapia fry, which are to be inversed to males.

The phytochemicals are also believed to differentially modulate the expression of sex genes in the ovary and testis of fish (Sarasquete et al. 2020). The sex-related genes such as cytochrome P450 (*cyp19a1a*) and forkhead transcriptional factor 2 (*foxl2*) promoted female development, while double-sex/mab-3-related transcription factor 1 (*dmrt1*) and anti-mullerian hormone (*amh*) promoted male development

(Ijiri et al. 2008; Tao et al. 2013; Chen et al. 2016). No previous study has attempted to investigate the effect of phyto-compounds on the expression of sex genes in tilapia. Considering the role of these genes in gonadal differentiation, further research is needed to clearly understand how plant extracts induce sex inversion or fertility impairment at a molecular level.

Lastly, the bioactive compounds from plant extracts stimulate histological changes in tilapia gonads, such as rupture of seminiferous lobules and follicles, and disintegration of spermatids and oocytes. The normal functioning of the gonads is disrupted, thereby inhibiting reproduction fertility (Table 7.2). Saponins from *C. papaya, P. guajava,* and *A. indica* were found to degenerate the gonadal cells of Nile tilapia and Mozambique tilapia, subsequently impairing fertility (Jegede and Fagbenro 2008; Khalil et al. 2011; Ampofo-Yeboah 2013; Solomon et al. 2017; Obaroh et al. 2018; Waweru et al. 2019).

7.3 Conclusions and Recommendations

Considering the findings of this review, it is clear that plant extracts present a promising alternative to synthetic hormones to control unwanted reproduction in tilapia culture. Undoubtedly, the application of plant extracts by tilapia farmers in Africa is still low, attributed to low research into their use and lack of standardized application protocol. The lack of holistic research continues to undermine the transition from trials to full-scale commercialization in aquaculture production systems. To maximize plant extracts, research should focus on identifying the active ingredients in different plant extracts, responsible for reproduction control in tilapia. This would facilitate the optimization of extraction procedures, identification of the most potent ingredient, determination of the optimal doses, and their mode of action. Likewise, sufficient data to support the growth, as well as safety benefits of plant extracts on fish are required. Given that studies at the endocrine and molecular levels provide more precise data, it is imperative that research incorporates these aspects, focusing on the expression of genes associated with sex differentiation and sex steroid profiles. Subsequently, effective extracts should be certified and a standard protocol to guide their application by tilapia farmers generated.

References

Abaho I, Masembe C, Akoll P, Jones CLW (2021) The use of plant extracts to control tilapia reproduction: current status and future perspectives. J World Aquac Soc 2021:1–27. https://doi.org/10.1111/JWAS.12863

Abbas H, Abbas WT (2011) Assessment study on the use of Pawpaw; *Carica papaya* seeds to control *Oreochromis niloticus* breeding. Pak J Biol Sci 14:1117–1123. https://doi.org/10.3923/pjbs.2011.1117.1123

Abdelhak EM, Madkour FF, Ibrahim AM, Sharaf SM, Sharaf MM, Mohammed DA (2013) Effect of pawpaw (*Carica papaya*) seeds meal on the reproductive performance and histological characters of gonads in Nile tilapia (*Oreochromis niloticus*). Indian J Appl Res 3:34–37. https://doi.org/10.15373/2249555x/dec2013/177

Abdel-Tawwab M (2005) Predation efficiency of Nile Catfish, *Clarias gariepinus* (Burchell, 1822) on fry Nile tilapia, *Oreochromis niloticus* (Linnaeus, 1758): effect of prey density, predator size, feed fupplementation and Submerged vegetation. Turk J Fish Aquat Sci 5:69–74

Abo-Al-Ela HG (2018) Hormones and fish monosex farming: a spotlight on immunity. Fish Shellfish Immunol 72:23–30. https://doi.org/10.1016/j.fsi.2017.10.038

Abo-Al-Ela HG, El-Nahas AF, Mahmoud S, Ibrahim EM (2017) The extent to which immunity, apoptosis and detoxification gene expression interact with 17α-methyltestosterone. Fish Shellfish Immunol 60:289–298. https://doi.org/10.1016/j.fsi.2016.11.057

Abubakar BM, Salleh FM, Wagiran A (2017) Chemical composition of *Eurycoma longifolia* (Tongkat Ali) and the quality control of its herbal medicinal products. J Appl Sci 17:324–338. https://doi.org/10.3923/jas.2017.324.338

Adeleke B, Robertson-Andersson D, Moodley G, Taylor S (2021) Aquaculture in Africa: a comparative review of Egypt, Nigeria, and Uganda vis-a-vis South Africa. Rev Fish Sci Aquac 29:167–197. https://doi.org/10.1080/23308249.2020.1795615

Adenigba I, Tumbokon BLM, Serrano AE (2017) Androgenic and anabolic effects of *Pinus tabulaeformis* carr. Pollen in *Clarias gariepinus*. Isr J Aquac 69:1388–1396. https://doi.org/10.46989/001c.21053

Ajanal M, Gundkalle M, Nayak S (2012) Estimation of total alkaloid in Chitrakadivati by UV-spectrophotometer. Anc Sci Life 31:198–201. https://doi.org/10.4103/0257-7941.107361

Akin-Obasola B, Jegede T (2016) Reproduction control of male *Oreochromis niloticus* (Nile Tilapia) using *Gossypium herbaceum* (Cotton) root bark meals as fertility inhibitor. Eur Sci J 12:1857–7881. https://doi.org/10.19044/esj.2016.v12n12p218

Akula R, Ravishankar GA (2011) Influence of abiotic stress signals on secondary metabolites in plants. Plant Signal Behav 6:1720–1731. https://doi.org/10.4161/psb.6.11.17613

Aloka S, Jain SK, Verma A, Kumar M, Mahor A, Sabharwal M (2013) Plant profile, phytochemistry and pharmacology of *Asparagus racemosus* (Shatavari): a review. Asian Pac J Trop Dis 3: 242–251

Ampofo-Yeboah A (2013) Effect of phytogenic feed additives on gonadal development in Mozambique tilapia (*Oreochromis mossambicus*). Stellenbosch University

Atangwho IJ, Ebong PE, Eyong EU, Williams IO, Eteng MU, Egbung GE (2009) Comparative chemical composition of leaves of some antidiabetic medicinal plants: Azadirachta indica, *Vernonia amygdalina* and *Gongronema latifolium*. African J Biotechnol 8:4685–4689

Awad E, Awaad A (2017) Role of medicinal plants on growth performance and immune status in fish. Fish Shellfish Immunol 67:40–54. https://doi.org/10.1016/J.FSI.2017.05.034

Baldove AB, Tumbokon BLM, Serrano AE (2019) Effects of different levels of *Pinus tabulaeformis* pollen on growth and ammonia stress resistance of milkfish fry (*Chanos chanos*). Isr J Aquac 71:1–7. https://doi.org/10.46989/001c.20975

Baluran SMDL, Quiazon KMA, Garcia GG, Fernando SID, Velasco RR (2018) Immunostimulatory effect of Benguet (*Pinus kesiya*) pollen on Nile tilapia (*Oreochromis niloticus L*). Int J Biol Pharm Allied Sci 7:1652–1663

Barannikova IA, Bayunova LV, Semenkova TB (2004) Serum levels of testosterone, 11-ketotestosterone and oestradiol-17b in three species of sturgeon during gonadal development and final maturation induced by hormonal treatment. J Fish Biol 64:1330–1338. https://doi.org/10.1111/j.0022-1112.2004.00395.x

Baroiller J, D'Cotta H (2019) Sex control in tilapias. In: Wang H-P, Piferrer F, Chen S-L, Shen Z-G (eds) Sex control in aquaculture. Wiley, New Jersey, pp 191–234

Beardmore JA, Mair GC, Lewis RI (2001) Monosex male production in finfish as exemplified by tilapia: applications, problems, and prospects. Aquaculture 197:283–301. https://doi.org/10.1016/S0044-8486(01)00590-7

Budd AM, Banh QQ, Domingos JA, Jerry DR (2015) Sex control in fish: approaches, challenges and opportunities for aquaculture. J Mar Sci Eng 3:329–355. https://doi.org/10.3390/jmse3020329

Bulfon C, Volpatti D, Galeotti M (2015) Current research on the use of plant-derived products in farmed fish. Aquac Res 46:513–551. https://doi.org/10.1111/are.12238

Carson-Jurica MA, Schrader WT, O'Malley BW (1990) Steroid receptor family: structure and functions. Endocr Rev 11:201–220. https://doi.org/10.1210/EDRV-11-2-201

Chakraborty SB, Hancz C (2011) Application of phytochemicals as immunostimulant, antipathogenic and antistress agents in finfish culture. Rev Aquac 3:103–119. https://doi.org/10.1111/J.1753-5131.2011.01048.X

Chakraborty SB, Horn P, Hancz C (2014) Application of phytochemicals as growth-promoters and endocrine modulators in fish culture. Rev Aquac 6:1–19. https://doi.org/10.1111/raq.12021

Chen JJ, Chang HC (2007) By modulating androgen receptor coactivators, daidzein may act as a phytoandrogen. Prostate 67:457–462. https://doi.org/10.1002/PROS.20470

Chen L, Jiang X, Feng H, Shi H, Sun L, Tao W, Xie Q, Wang D (2016) Simultaneous exposure to estrogen and androgen resulted in feminization and endocrine disruption. J Endocrinol 228: 205–218. https://doi.org/10.1530/JOE-15-0432

Cherdshewasart W, Bhuntaku P, Panriansaen R, Dahlan W, Malaivijitnond S (2008) Androgen disruption and toxicity tests of *Butea superba* Roxb., a traditional herb used for treatment of erectile dysfunction, in male rats. Maturitas 60:131–1137. https://doi.org/10.1016/j.maturitas.2008.04.011

Cheshenko K, Pakdel F, Segner H, Kah O, Eggen RIL (2008) Interference of endocrine disrupting chemicals with aromatase CYP19 expression or activity, and consequences for reproduction of teleost fish. Gen Comp Endocrinol 155:31–62. https://doi.org/10.1016/J.YGCEN.2007.03.005

Citarasu T (2010) Herbal biomedicines: A new opportunity for aquaculture industry. Aquac Int 18: 403–414. https://doi.org/10.1007/s10499-009-9253-7

D'Cotta H, Fostier A, Guiguen Y, Govoroun M, Baroiller JF (2001) Aromatase plays a key role during normal and temperature-induced sex differentiation of tilapia *Oreochromis niloticus*. Mol Reprod Dev 59:265–276. https://doi.org/10.1002/mrd.1031

Devlin RH, Nagahama Y (2002) Sex determination and sex differentiation in fish: an overview of genetic, physiological, and environmental influences. Aquaculture 208:191–364. https://doi.org/10.1016/S0044-8486(02)00057-1

Dhanani T, Shah S, Gajbhiye NA, Kumar S (2017) Effect of extraction methods on yield, phytochemical constituents and antioxidant activity of Withania somnifera. Arab J Chem 10: S1193–S1199. https://doi.org/10.1016/j.arabjc.2013.02.015

Dinchev D, Janda B, Evstatieva L, Oleszek W, Aslani MR, Kostova I (2008) Distribution of steroidal saponins in Tribulus terrestris from different geographical regions. Phytochemistry 69:176–186. https://doi.org/10.1016/j.phytochem.2007.07.003

Ekanem SB, Okoronkwo TE (2003) Pawpaw seed as fertility control agent on male Nile tilapia. NAGA 26:8–10

El Deen AIN, Zaki MS, Shafi ME (2020) Assessment *Tribulus terrestris* on sex-reverse on Nile tilapia with respect to its chemical composition. Researcher 12:6–11. https://doi.org/10.2165/00128415-201113400-00147

El-Greisy ZA, El-Gamal AE (2012) Monosex production of tilapia, *Oreochromis niloticus* using different doses of 17α-methyltestosterone with respect to the degree of sex stability after one year of treatment. Egypt J Aquat Res 38:59–66. https://doi.org/10.1016/j.ejar.2012.08.005

El-Kady MA, Hussein MS, Abd-Elghany MF, Mabrouk MM (2022) Effect of adding *Tribulus terrestris* extract to the diets of Nile tilapia *Oreochromis niloticus* larvae on sex ratio and growth performance. Indian J Agric Res 47:123–132

El-Sayed A-FM (2019) Tilapia culture, 2nd edn. CABI Publishing, Wallingford

El-Sayed A-FM, Abdel-Aziz ESH, Abdel-Ghani HM (2012) Effects of phytoestrogens on sex reversal of Nile tilapia (*Oreochromis niloticus*) larvae fed diets treated with

17α-Methyltestosterone. Aquaculture 360–361:58–63. https://doi.org/10.1016/j.aquaculture.2012.07.010

FAO (2017) Social and economic performance of tilapia farming in Africa. FAO Fish Aquac Circ No 1130, pp 1–158

FAO (2020) The state of world fisheries and aquaculture 2020. Sustain action 1–224. https://doi.org/10.4060/ca9229en

Fortes RD (2005) Review of techniques and practices in controlling tilapia populations and identification of methods

Francis G, Levavi-Sivan B, Avitan A, Becker K (2002) Effects of long term feeding of *Quillaja saponins* on sex ratio, muscle and serum cholesterol and LH levels in Nile tilapia (*Oreochromis niloticus* (L)). Comp Biochem Physiol Toxicol Pharmacol 133:593–603. https://doi.org/10.1016/S1532-0456(02)00167-9

Francis G, Makkar PS, Becker K (2005) *Quillaja saponins*—a natural growth promoter for fish. Anim Feed Sci Technol 121:147–157. https://doi.org/10.1016/j.anifeedsci.2005.02.015

Gabriel NN (2019) Review on the progress in the role of herbal extracts in tilapia culture. Cogent Food Agric 5:1619651. https://doi.org/10.1080/23311932.2019.1619651

Gabriel NN, Qiang J, Kpundeh MD, Xu P (2015) Use of herbal extracts for controlling reproduction in tilapia culture: trends and prospects—A review. Isr J Aquac 67:29

Gabriel NN, Qiang J, Ma XY, He J, Xu P, Omoregie E (2017) Sex-reversal effect of dietary Aloe vera (Liliaceae) on genetically improved farmed Nile tilapia fry. N Am J Aquac 79:100–105. https://doi.org/10.1080/15222055.2016.1236046

Gabriel NN, Iitembu JA, Hasimuna OJ, Rashidian G, Mbokane EM, Moyo NAG, Hlophe-Ginindza SN (2022) Medicinal plants: a perspective on their application in the African smallholder aquaculture farms. In: Mupambwa HA, Nciizah AD, Nyambo P, Muchara B, Gabriel NN (eds) Food security for African smallholder farmers. Sustainability sciences in Asia and Africa. Springer, Singapore, pp 191–217

Ganzera M, Bedir E, Khan IA (2001) Determination of steroidal saponins in *Tribulus terrestris* by reversed-phase high-performance liquid chromatography and evaporative light scattering detection. J Pharm Sci 90:1752–1758

Gharaei A, Jorjani HE, Harijani JM, Miandare HK (2020) Effects of *Tribulus terrestris* extract on masculinization, growth indices, sex determination and steroid hormones level in Zebra fish (Danio rerio). Int Aquat Res 12:22–29. https://doi.org/10.22034/IAR(20).2020.670992

Ghosal I, Chakraborty SB (2014a) Effects of the aqueous leaf extract of *Basella alba* on sex reversal of Nile tilapia, *Oreochromis niloticus*. IOSR J Pharm Biol Sci 9:162–164

Ghosal I, Chakraborty SB (2014b) Effects of the aqueous seed extract of *Tribulus terrestris* on sex reversal of Nile tilapia, *Oreochromis niloticus*. Indian J Appl Res 4:459–461

Ghosal I, Chakraborty SB (2020) Production of monosex all-male nile tilapia using ethanol extract of *Tribulus terrestris* seeds. Proc Zool Soc 73:188–191. https://doi.org/10.1007/s12595-017-0254-7

Ghosal I, Mukherjee D, Hancz C, Chakraborty SB (2015) Efficacy of *Basella alba* and T*ribulus terrestris* extracts for production of monosex Nile tilapia, *Oreochromis niloticus*. J Appl Pharm Sci 5:152–158. https://doi.org/10.7324/JAPS.2015.50824

Ghosal I, Mukherjee D, Hancz C, Chakraborty SB (2016) Production of monosex Nile tilapia, *Oreochromis niloticus* by dietary and immersion treatment with Basella alba leaves and Tribulus terrestris seeds. Int J Fish Aquat Stud 4:358–363

Ghosal I, Mukherjee D, Chakraborty SB (2021) The effects of four plant extracts on growth, sex reversal, immunological and haemato-biochemical parameters in Nile tilapia, *Oreochmomis niloticus* (Linnaeus, 1758). Aquac Res 52:559–576. https://doi.org/10.1111/are.14914

Glazier MG, Bowman MA (2001) A review of the evidence for the use of phytoestrogens as a replacement for traditional estrogen replacement therapy. Arch Intern Med 161:1161–1172. https://doi.org/10.1001/ARCHINTE.161.9.1161

Golan M, Levavi-Sivan B (2014) Artificial masculinization in tilapia involves androgen receptor activation. Gen Comp Endocrinol 207:50–55. https://doi.org/10.1016/j.ygcen.2014.04.026

Golan M, Avitan A, Qutob M, Dweik H, Abu-Lafi S, Focken U, Francis G, Becker K, Kerem Z, Levavi-Sivan B (2008) *Quillaja saponins* inhibit tilapia aromatase activity in vitro. Cybium 32: 80–82

Golshan M, Mohammad S, Alavi H (2019) Androgen signaling in male fishes: examples of anti-androgenic chemicals that cause reproductive disorders. Theriogenology 139:58–71. https://doi.org/10.1016/j.theriogenology.2019.07.020

Green CC, Kelly AM (2009) Effects of the estrogen mimic genistein as a dietary component on sex differentiation and ethoxyresorufin-O-deethylase (EROD) activity in channel catfish (*Ictalurus punctatus*). Fish Physiol Biochem 35:377–384. https://doi.org/10.1007/s10695-008-9260-z

Hartleb M, Nowak A (1990) Severe jaundice with destructive cholangitis after administration of methyltestosterone. Am J Gastroenterol 85:766–767

Hishamunda N (2007) Aquaculture in Africa: reasons for failures and ingredients for Success. In: Leung PS, Cheng-Sheng Lee PJO (eds) Species and system selection for sustainable aquaculture. Wiley, Iowa City, pp 103–115

Hulak M, Paroulek M, Simek P, Kocour M, Gela D, Rodina M, Linhart O (2008) Water polluted by 17α-methyltestosterone provides successful male sex inversion of common carp (*Cyprinus carpio* L.) from gynogenetic offspring. J Appl Ichthyol 24:707–710. https://doi.org/10.1111/j.1439-0426.2008.01107.x

Ijiri S, Kaneko H, Kobayashi T, Wang DS, Sakai F, Paul-Prasanth B, Nakamura M, Nagahama Y (2008) Sexual dimorphic expression of genes in gonads during early differentiation of a teleost fish, the Nile tilapia *Oreochromis niloticus*. Biol Reprod 78:333–341. https://doi.org/10.1095/biolreprod.107.064246

Isah T (2019) Stress and defense responses in plant secondary metabolites production. Biol Res 52: 39. https://doi.org/10.1186/s40659-019-0246-3

Jegede T (2010) Control of reproduction in *Oreochromis niloticus* (Linnaeus 1758) using Hibiscus Rosa-sinensis (Linn.) leaf meal as reproduction inhibitor. J Agric Sci 2:149–154. https://doi.org/10.5539/JAS.V2N4P149

Jegede T (2011) Effects of *Aloe vera* (Liliaceae) on the gonad development in Nile tilapia, *Oreochromis* niloticus (Linnaeus 1758). In: Liping L, Fitzsimmons K (eds) Proceedings of the ninth international symposium on Tilapia in aquaculture. AquaFish Collaborative Research Support Program, Shanghai, China, p 295

Jegede T, Fagbenro O (2008) Histology of gonads in *Tilapia zillii* (gervais) fed neem (*Azadirachta indica*) leaf meal diets. In: 8th international symposium on tilapia in aquaculture, pp 119–1134

Jones JL, Roddick JG (1988) Steroidal estrogens and androgens in relation to reproductive development in higher plants. J Plant Physiol 133:510–518. https://doi.org/10.1016/S0176-1617(88)80047-6

Kapinga IB, Limbu SM, Madalla NA, Kimaro WH, Tamahtamah RA (2018) Aspilia mossambicensis and *Azadirachta indica* medicinal leaf powders modulate physiological parameters of Nile tilapia (*Oreochromis niloticus*). Int J Vet Sci Med 6:31–38. https://doi.org/10.1016/j.ijvsm.2018.03.003

Kapinga IB, Limbu SM, Madalla NA, Kimaro WH, Mabiki FP, Lamtane HA, Tamatamah RA (2019) Dietary Aspilia mossambicensis and Azadirachta indica supplementation alter gonadal characteristics and histology of juvenile Nile tilapia (*Oreochromis niloticus*). Aquac Res 50: 573–580. https://doi.org/10.1111/are.13931

Khalil WKB, Hasheesh WS, Marie M-AS, Abbas HH, Zahran EA, Khalil WKB (2011) Assessment the impact of 17α-methyltestosterone hormone on growth, hormone concentration, molecular and histopathological changes in muscles and testis of Nile tilapia; *Oreochromis niloticus*. Life Sci J 8:1097–8135

Kiriyakit A (2014) Efficacy of red kwao krua (*Butea superb* Roxb.) crude extract for all male production of Nile tilapia (*Oreochromis niloticus*). J Agric Technol 10:391–398

Kobayashi T, Kajiura-Kobayashi H, Guan G, Nagahama Y (2008) Sexual dimorphic expression of DMRT1 and Sox9a during gonadal differentiation and hormone-induced sex reversal in the teleost fish nile tilapia (*Oreochromis niloticus*). Dev Dyn 237:297–306. https://doi.org/10.1002/dvdy.21409

Kushwaha MP (2013) Effects of *Aloe vera* (Liliaceae) on Gonad development in Nile tilapia, *Oreochromis niloticus* (L.) during intensive aquaculture. Int J Fish Aquat Stud 1:56–60

Lambole V, Kumar U (2011) Phytochemicals and acute toxicity of *Moringa oleifera* barks in rats. Int J Biomed Res 2:548–553

Lee K-H, Kim A-J, Choi E-M (2009) Antioxidant and antiinflammatory activity of pine pollen extract in vitro. Phytother Res 23:41–48. https://doi.org/10.1002/ptr.2525

Lee SLJ, Horsfield JA, Black MA, Rutherford K, Fisher A, Gemmell NJ (2017) Histological and transcriptomic effects of 17α-methyltestosterone on zebrafish gonad development. BMC Genomics 18:1–19. https://doi.org/10.1186/s12864-017-3915-z

Leet JK, Gall HE, Sepulveda MS, Sepúlveda MS (2011) A review of studies on androgen and estrogen exposure in fish early life stages: effects on gene and hormonal control of sexual differentiation. J Appl Toxicol 31:379–398. https://doi.org/10.1002/jat.1682

Levina AD, Mikhailova ES, Kasumyan AO (2021) Taste preferences and feeding behaviour in the facultative herbivorous fish, Nile tilapia *Oreochromis niloticus*. J Fish Biol 98:1385–1400. https://doi.org/10.1111/JFB.14675

Lind CE, Agyakwah SK, Attipoe FY, Nugent C (2019) Genetic diversity of nile tilapia (*Oreochromis niloticus*) throughout West Africa. Sci Rep 9:16767. https://doi.org/10.1038/s41598-019-53295-y

Linda NI (2019) Effect of pawpaw (*Carica papaya*) seed meal on growth performance, feed utilization, survival and masculinization of sexually undifferentiated three spotted tilapia (*Oreochromis andersonii*) fry. MSc thesis, University of Namibia, pp 1–109

Logambal SM, Venkatalakshmi S, Michael RD (2000) Immunostimulatory effect of leaf extract of *Ocitnum sanctum* Linn. in *Oreochromis mossambicus* (Peters). Hydrobiologia 430:113–120. https://doi.org/10.1023/A:1004029332114

Low BS, Choi SB, Abdul Wahab H, Kumar Das P, Chan KL (2013a) Eurycomanone, the major quassinoid in *Eurycoma longifolia* root extract increases spermatogenesis by inhibiting the activity of phosphodiesterase and aromatase in steroidogenesis. J Ethnopharmacol 149:201–207. https://doi.org/10.1016/J.JEP.2013.06.023

Low BS, Das PK, Chan KL (2013b) Standardized quassinoid-rich *Eurycoma longifolia* extract improved spermatogenesis and fertility in male rats via the hypothalamic-pituitary- gonadal axis. J Ethnopharmacol 145:706–714. https://doi.org/10.1016/J.JEP.2012.11.013

Mahdi-Pour B, Jothy SL, Latha LY, Chen Y, Sasidharan S (2012) Antioxidant activity of methanol extracts of different parts of Lantana camara. Asian Pac J Trop Biomed 2:960–965. https://doi.org/10.1016/S2221-1691(13)60007-6

Mair GC, Little DC (1991) Population control in farmed tilapias. NAGA 4:8–13

Manosroi A, Manosroi J (2005) Determination of bioactive compounds in roots of different ages *Pueraria mirifica*, airy shaw suvatabhandhu and *Butea superba*, roxb. from various locations in Thailand. Acta Hortic 680:135–138. https://doi.org/10.17660/ActaHortic.2005.678.18

Mapfumo B (2022) Regional review on status and trends in aquaculture development in sub-Saharan Africa—2020. FAO Fish Aquac Circ N 1232/4 Rome, FAO. https://doi.org/10.4060/cb8400en

Mateen A, Ahmed I (2007) Effect of androgen on sexreversal and growth of Nile tilapia (*Oreochromis niloticus*). Pak J Agric Sci 44:272–276

Matozzo V, Gagne F, Marin MG, Ricciardi F, Blaise C (2008) Vitellogenin as a biomarker of exposure to estrogenic compounds in aquatic invertebrates: a review. Environ Int 34:531–545. https://doi.org/10.1016/J.ENVINT.2007.09.008

Mbahinzireki GB, Dabrowski K, Lee K, El-saidy D, Wisner ER (2001) Growth, feed utilization and body composition of tilapia (*Oreochromis* sp.) fed with cottonseed meal-based diets in a recirculating system. Aquac Nutr 7:189–200

Megbowon I, Mojekwu TO (2014) Tilapia sex reversal using methyltestosterone (MT) and its effect on fish, man and environment. Biotechnology 13:213–216. https://doi.org/10.3923/biotech.2014.213.216

Mehrim AI, Khalil FF, Farrag FH, Refaey MM (2019) 17α-methyltestosterone and some medicine plants as reproductive controller agents of *Oreochromis niloticus*. J Biol Sci 19:407–417. https://doi.org/10.3923/jbs.2019.407.417

Mengumphan K, Samitasiri Y, Carandang R (2006) The potential of red kwao kreua (*Butea superba*) in inducing sex reversal on three strains (Red, Ghana, Chitralada) of Nile Tilapia (*Oreochromis niloticus* L.) and the effect of 17-α-methyltestosterone (MT). Asian Fish Sci 19: 271–279. https://doi.org/10.33997/j.afs.2006.19.3.007

Miyahara M, Ishibashi H, Inudo M, Nishijima H, Iguchi T, Guillette LJ, Arizono K (2003) Estrogenic activity of a diet to estrogen receptors -a and -b in an experimental animal. J Health Sci 49:481–491. https://doi.org/10.1248/JHS.49.481

Mlalila N, Mahika C, Kalombo L, Swai H, Hilonga A (2015) Human food safety and environmental hazards associated with the use of methyltestosterone and other steroids in production of all-male tilapia. Environ Sci Pollut Res 22:4922–4931. https://doi.org/10.1007/s11356-015-4133-3

Moundipa PF, Beboy NSE, Zelefack F, Ngouela S, Tsamo E, Schill WB, Monsees TK (2005) Effects of *Basella alba* and *Hibiscus macranthus* extracts on testosterone production of adult rat and bull leydig cells. Asian J Androl 7:411–417. https://doi.org/10.1111/j.1745-7262.2005.00056.x

Moyo NAG, Rapatsa MM (2021) A review of the factors affecting tilapia aquaculture production in Southern Africa. Aquaculture 535:736386. Contents. https://doi.org/10.1016/j.aquaculture.2021.736386

Mukherjee D, Ghosal I, Chakraborty SB (2015a) Application of *Asparagus racemosus* roots for production of monosex Nile tilapia, *Oreochromis niloticus*. Int J Adv Res 3:828–833

Mukherjee D, Ghosal I, Chakraborty SB (2015b) Production of monosex Nile tilapia, *Oreochromis niloticus* using seed of *Mucuna pruriens*. IOSR J Pharm Biol Sci 10:55–59. https://doi.org/10.9790/3008-10145559

Mukherjee D, Ghosal I, Hancz C, Chakraborty SB (2018) Dietary administration of plant extracts for production of monosex tilapia: searching a suitable alternative to synthetic steroids in Tilapia culture. Turk J Fish Aquat Sci 18:267–275. https://doi.org/10.4194/1303-2712-v18

Mukti AT, Carman O, Alimuddin A, Zairin M, Suprayudi MA (2020) Growth performance, survival rate, flesh, and proximate composition of sex-grouped triploid and diploid Nile tilapia (*Oreochromis niloticus*). Turk J Vet Anim Sci 44:290–298. https://doi.org/10.3906/VET-1905-79

Muniasamy S, Allen Benziger PS, Ananth Kumar Y, Haniffa MA, Paray BA, Albeshr MF, Al-Umri S (2019) Effect of 17α-methyl testosterone incorporated diets on growth of spotted snakehead, *Channa punctatus* and white carp, *Cirrhinus mrigala*. Saudi J Biol Sci 26:541–546. https://doi.org/10.1016/j.sjbs.2018.07.006

Murakami T, Kishi A, Matsuda HYM (2000) Medicinal foodstuffs. XVII. Fenugreek seed. (3): structures of new furostanol-type steroid saponins, trigoneosides Xa, Xb, XIb, XIIa, XIIb, and XIIIa, from the seeds of Egyptian *Trigonellafoenum-graecum* L. Chem Pharm Bull 48:994–1000. https://doi.org/10.1248/cpb.48.994

Mustapha MK, Atolagbe SD (2018) Tolerance level of different life stages of Nile tilapia *Oreochromis niloticus* (Linnaeus, 1758) to low pH and acidified waters. J Basic Appl Zool 79:46. https://doi.org/10.1186/s41936-018-0061-3

Musyimi DM, Ogur JA, Muema PM (2008) Phytochemical compounds and antimicrobial activity of extracts of aspilia plant (*Aspilia mossambicensis*) (Oliv) wild. Int J Bot 4:56–61. https://doi.org/10.3923/ijb.2008.56.61

Nantia EA, Travert C, Manfo FPT, Carreau S, Monsees TK, Moundipa PF (2011) Effects of the methanol extract of *Basella alba* L (Basellaceae) on steroid production in Leydig cells. Int J Mol Sci 12:376–384. https://doi.org/10.3390/ijms12010376

Nhu TQ, Bich Hang BT, Bach LT, Buu Hue BT, Quetin-Leclercq J, Scippo ML, Phuong NT, Kestemont P (2019) Plant extract-based diets differently modulate immune responses and resistance to bacterial infection in striped catfish (*Pangasianodon hypophthalmus*). Fish Shellfish Immunol 92:913–924. https://doi.org/10.1016/j.fsi.2019.07.025

Nian CT, Tumbokon BLM, Serrano AE (2017) *Pinus tabulaeformis* pollen as replacement for 17-alpha-methyltestosterone in the diet of *Oreochromis niloticus* larvae for sex reversal and growth. Isr J Aquac 69. https://doi.org/10.46989/001c.21042

Nieves PM (2017) On-farm trials of phytoandrogen for sex inversion of tilapia. Kuroshio Sci 11:8–13

Nik N, Nek M, Natrah I, Loh J, Kumar F, Ranzil E, Gina M, Lim SE, Lai K, Chong C (2022) Phytocompounds as an alternative antimicrobial approach in aquaculture. Antibiotics 11:469. https://doi.org/10.3390/antibiotics11040469

Nwankpa K (2017) The histological evaluation of the efects of *Moringa oleifera* leaf meal inclusions on the liver and ovaries of female *Oreochromis niloticus*. Int J Fish Aquat Res 2: 22–26

Nyadjeu P, Angoun J, Ndasi NP, Tabi-Tomedi ME (2019) Effect of *Garcinia kola* seeds supplemented diet on growth performance and gonadal development of *Oreochromis niloticus* juveniles breed in ponds. Fish Aquat Sci 22:20. https://doi.org/10.1186/s41240-019-0136-1

O'Malley BW, Tsai MJ (1992) Molecular pathways of steroid receptor action. Biol Reprod 46:163–167. https://doi.org/10.1095/BIOLREPROD46.2.163

Obaro IO, Nzeh CG, Oguntoye SO (2012) Control of reproduction in *Oreochromis niloticus* (L) using crude extract of *Azadirachta indica* saponin. Adv Environ Biol 6:1353–1356

Obaroh IO, Achionye-Nzeh GC (2011) Effects of crude extract of *Azadirachta indica* leaves at controlling prolific breeding in *Oreochromis niloticus* (Linnaeus, 1758). Asian J Agric Res 5: 277–282

Obaroh IO, Nzeh GC (2013) Antifertility effect of some plant leaf extracts on the prolific breeding of *Oreochromis niloticus*. Acad J Interdiscip Stud 2:87–94. https://doi.org/10.5901/ajis.2013.v2n12p87

Obaroh IO, Adamu I, Dikko OC, Joseph EK, Arilewo FV, Sani KA (2018) Changes in gonad of Nile Tilapia (Oreochromis niloticus) fed with crude extract of guava (*Psidium guajava* Linnaeus) leaves. J Appl Sci Environ Manag 22:895–889. https://doi.org/10.4314/jasem.v22i6.9

Olusola SE, Emikpe BO, Olaifa FE (2013) The potentials of medicinal plant extracts as bio-antimicrobials in aquaculture. Int J Med Aromat Plants 3:404–412

Omeje VO (2016) Effect of Pawpaw (*Carica papaya*) seed meal on the reproductive, endocrine and immune system of Mozambique tilapia (*Oreochromis mossambicus*). Stellenbosch University

Omeje VO, Lambrechts H, Brink D (2018) Effect of pawpaw (*Carica papaya*) seed meal on sex determination, growth, and survival, of *Oreochromis mossambicus* fry. Isr J Aquac 70:1–12. IJA_70.2018.1494

Omitoyin BO, Ajani EK, Omitoyin BO, Ajani EK, Sadiq HO (2013) Preliminary investigation of Tribulus terrestris (Linn., 1753) extracts as natural sex reversal agent in *Oreochromis niloticus* (Linn., 1758) Larvae. Int J Aquac 3:133–137. https://doi.org/10.5376/ija.2013.03.0023

Ososki AL, Kennelly EJ (2003) Phytoestrogens: a review of the present state of research. Phytother Res 17:845–869. https://doi.org/10.1002/PTR.1364

Pandian TJ, Sheela SG (1995) Hormonal induction of sex reversal in fish. Aquaculture 138:1–22. https://doi.org/10.1016/0044-8486(95)01075-0

Pandit NP, Nakamura M (2010) Effect of high temperature on survival, growth and feed conversion ratio of Nile Tilapia, *Oreochromis niloticus*. Our Nat 8:219–224. https://doi.org/10.3126/ON.V8I1.4331

Patel DK, Patel K, Dhanabal S (2012) Phytochemical standardization of *Aloe vera* extract by HPTLC techniques. J Acute Dis 1:47–50. https://doi.org/10.1016/s2221-6189(13)60011-6

Pelissero C, Le Menn F, Kaushick S (1991) Estrogenic effect of dietary soya bean meal on vitellogenesis in cultured siberian sturgeon *Acipenser baeri*. Gen Comp Endocrinol 83:447–457. https://doi.org/10.1016/0016-6480(91)90151-U

Phelps RP, Popma TJ (2000) Sex reversal of Tilapia. Tilapia Aquac Am 26:34–59

Rahmah S, Liew HJ, Napi N, Rahmat SA (2020) Metabolic cost of acute and chronic salinity response of hybrid red tilapia *Oreochromis* sp. larvae. Aquac Rep 16:100233. https://doi.org/10.1016/J.AQREP.2019.100233

Raju J, Patlolla JMR, Swamy MV, Rao CV (2004) Diosgenin, a steroid saponin of Trigonella foenum graecum (Fenugreek), inhibits azoxymethane-induced aberrant crypt foci formation in F344 rats and induces apoptosis in HT-29 human colon cancer cells. Cancer Epidemiol Biomarkers Prev 13:1392–1398

Ramirez-Godinez J, Beltran-Hernandez RI, Coronel-Olivares C, Contreras-Lopez E, Quezada-Cruz M, Vázquez-Rodriguez G (2013) Recirculating systems for pollution prevention in aquaculture facilities. J Water Resour Protect 5:5–9. https://doi.org/10.4236/jwarp.2013.57a002

Rempel MA, Schlenk D (2008) Effects of environmental estrogens and antiandrogens on endocrine function, gene regulation, and health in fish. Int Rev Cell Mol Biol 267:207–252. https://doi.org/10.1016/S1937-6448(08)00605-9

Reverter M, Bontemps N, Lecchini D, Banaigs B, Sasal P (2014) Use of plant extracts in fish aquaculture as an alternative to chemotherapy: current status and future perspectives. Aquaculture 433:50–61. https://doi.org/10.1016/j.aquaculture.2014.05.048

Reverter M, Tapissier-Bontemps N, Sasal P, Saulnier D (2017) Use of medicinal plants in aquaculture

Ridha MT (2011) Evaluation of monosex culture of GIFT and non-improved strains of Nile tilapia *Oreochromis niloticus* in recirculating tanks. Int Aquat Res 3:189–195

Rinaldi, Zairin M Jr, Tri Soelistyowati D, Imron (2017) Masculinization of tilapia *Oreochromis niloticus* using extract of pasak bumi plant Eurycoma longifolia through larval immersion. Int J Fish Aquat Stud 5(3):248–252

Sakai M (1999) Current research status of fish immunostimulants. Aquaculture 172:63–92

Sandra GE, Norma MM (2010) Sexual determination and differentiation in teleost fish. Rev Fish Biol Fish 20:101–121. https://doi.org/10.1007/s11160-009-9123-4

Sarasquete C, Ubeda-Manzanaro M, Ortiz-Delgado JB (2020) Soya isoflavones, genistein and daidzein, induce differential transcriptional modulation in the ovary and testis of zebrafish *Danio rerio*. Aquat Biol 29:79–91. https://doi.org/10.3354/ab00726

Sasidharan S, Chen Y, Saravanan D, Sundram KM, Yoga LL (2011) Extraction, isolation and characterization of bioactive compounds from plants' extracts. African J Tradit Complement Altern Med 8:1–10. https://doi.org/10.1007/978-3-642-56936-4_2

Solomon SG, Ugonna BO, Olufeagba SO, Okomoda VT (2017) Haematology and gonad histology of *Oreochromis niloticus* (Linnaeus, 1758) fed *Carica papaya* seed meal. Braz J Aquat Sci Technol 21:8–15. https://doi.org/10.14210/bjast.v21n1

Srisakultiew P (2013) Immersion of 17α-methyltestosterone dose & duration on tilapia masculinization. J Fish Sci 7:302–308. https://doi.org/10.3153/jfscom.2013033

Stadtlander T, Focken U, Levavi-Sivan B, Dweik H, Qutob M, Abu-Lafi S, Kerem Z, Becker K (2008) Treatment with saponins from *Trigonella foenum-graecum* and *Quillaja saponaria* influences sex ratio in Nile Tilapia (*Oreochromis niloticus*) larvae. In: Fitzsimmons K, Liping L (eds) Proceedings of the eighth international symposium on tilapia aquaculture. AquaFish Collaborative Research Support Program. Corvallis, pp 355–364

Stadtlander T, Levavi-Sivan B, Kerem Z, Dweik H, Qutob M, Abu-Lafi S, Francis G, Focken U, Becker K (2013) Effects of a saponin fraction extracted from *Trigonella foenum-graecum* L. and two commercially available saponins on sex ratio and gonad histology of Nile tilapa fry, *Oreochromis niloticus* (L.). J Appl Ichthyol 29:265–267. https://doi.org/10.1111/jai.12002

Sulem-Yong NN, Sandjoh R, Angoun J, Nzoko AF, Mounjouenpou P, Agbor KE, Yong- Sulem S (2018) Effect of varied dietary bitter kola (*Garcinia Kola*) seeds levels on spawning of nile tilapia (*Oreochromis niloticus* L.). Int J Fish Aquat Stud 6:507–510

Takatsu K, Miyaoku K, Roy SR, Murono Y, Sago T, Itagaki H, Nakamura M, Tokumoto T (2013) Induction of female-to-male sex change in adult zebrafish by aromatase inhibitor treatment. Sci Rep 3:1–7. https://doi.org/10.1038/srep03400

Tao W, Yuan J, Zhou L, Sun L, Sun Y, Yang S, Li M, Zeng S, Huang B, Wang D (2013) Characterization of gonadal transcriptomes from Nile Tilapia (*Oreochromis niloticus*) reveals differentially expressed genes. PLoS One 8:e63604. https://doi.org/10.1371/journal.pone.0063604

Tarigan RVB, Nasution MP, Widjaja SS (2016) The activities of antifertility ethanol extract guava leaves (*Psidium Guajava* L.) based on the analysis of cement and display of immunohistochemistry cyclooxygenase-2 in testis of mice (*Mus musculus* L.). J Ilmu Kefarmasian Indones 14: 219–225

Tarkowska D (2019) Plants are capable of synthesizing animal steroid hormones. Molecules 24:1–13. https://doi.org/10.3390/molecules24142585

Thakur M, Bhargava S, Dixit VK (2009) Effect of Asparagus racemosus on sexual dysfunction in hyperglycemic male rats. Pharm Biol 47:390–395. https://doi.org/10.1080/13880200902755234

Tibihika PD, Waidbacher H, Masembe C, Curto M, Sabatino S, Alemayehu E, Meulenbroek P, Akoll P, Meimberg H (2018) Anthropogenic impacts on the contextual morphological diversification and adaptation of Nile tilapia (*Oreochromis niloticus*, L. 1758) in East Africa. Environ Biol Fishes 101:363–381. https://doi.org/10.1007/S10641-017-0704-0

Tigoli K, Cisse M, Kone M, Ouattara M, Ouattara A, Gourene G (2018) Effects of two African aphrodisiatic plants *Garcinia kola* and *Turraea heterophylla* on zooetchnic performances and sexual inversion rate in *Oreochromis niloticus*

Toguyeni A, Fauconneau B, Fostier A, Abucay J, Mair G, Baroiller JF (2002) Influence of sexual phenotype and genotype, and sex ratio on growth performances in tilapia, *Oreochromis niloticus*. Aquaculture 207:249–261. https://doi.org/10.1016/S0044-8486(01)00747-5

Tope-Jegede O, Fagbenro A, Olufayo M (2019) Histology of gonads in *Oreochromis niloticus* (Linnaeus 1757) fed cottonseed meal-based diets. Int J Fish Aquat Stud 7:269–274

Turan F, Akyurt I (2005) Effects of androstenedione, a phytoandrogen, on growth and body composition in the African catfish *Clarias gariepinus*. Isr J Aquac 57:62–66

Uboha FE, Okon IE, Ekong MB (2010) Effect of aqueous extract of *Psidium Guajava* leaves on liver enzymes, histological integrity and hematological indices in rats. Gastroenterol Res 3:32–38. https://doi.org/10.4021/GR2010.02.174W

Ugonna BO, Solomon SG, Olufeagba SO, Okomoda VT (2018) Effect of pawpaw *Carica papaya* seed meal on growth and as a natural sex-reversal agent for Nile Tilapia. N Am J Aquac 80:278–285. https://doi.org/10.1002/naaq.10032

Van Hai N (2015) The use of medicinal plants as immunostimulants in aquaculture: a review. Aquaculture 446:88–96

Velasco RR, Dollente DJM, Natividad LR, Abella TA (2018) Benguet pine pollen as (*Pinus kesiya*) a natural source of phytoandrogen. Int J Biol Pharm Allied Sci 7:1121–1132

Velazquez I, Alter BP (2004) Androgens and liver tumors: Fanconi's anemia and non-Fanconi's conditions. Am J Hematol 77:257–267. https://doi.org/10.1002/ajh.20183

Vera Cruz EM, Mair GC (1994) Conditions for effective androgen sex reversal in *Oreochromis niloticus* (L.). Aquaculture 122:237–248. https://doi.org/10.1016/0044-8486(94)90513-4

Vick AM, Hayton WL (2001) Methyltestosterone pharmacolinetics and oral bioavailability in Rainbow trout (*Oncorhynchus mykiss*). Aquat Toxicol 52:177–188. https://doi.org/10.1016/S0166-445X(00)00146-6

Wang M, Lu M (2016) Tilapia polyculture: a global review. Aquac Res 47:2363–2374. https://doi.org/10.1111/are.12708

Wang X-X, Chen M-Y, Wang K, Ye J-D (2017) Growth and metabolic responses in Nile tilapia (*Oreochromis niloticus*) subjected to varied starch and protein levels of diets. Ital J Anim Sci 16: 308–316. https://doi.org/10.1080/1828051X.2016.1275953

Waweru JN, Raburu PO, Odhiambo EA (2019) Gonad histology, proximate composition and growth efficiency of Nile Tilapia fed with Pawpaw (*Carica papaya*) seeds powder. Asian J Fish Aquat Res 3:1–9. https://doi.org/10.9734/ajfar/2019/v3i430041

Yarmohammadi M, Pourkazemi M, Kazemi R, Sadati YAM, Hallajian A, Saber MH (2017) Sex steroid level and sexual dimorphism expression of genes in gonads of the great sturgeon Huso huso Linneaus, 1758 during maturity developmental stages. Aquac Res 48:1413–1429. https://doi.org/10.1111/ARE.12977

Yılmaz E, Cek S, Mazlum Y (2013) Effects of synthetic and natural steroids on the growth, sex reversal and gonadal development of Rainbow trout, *Oncorhynchus mykiss* (Walbaum). Ege J Fish Aquat Sci 30:123–131. https://doi.org/10.12714/egejfas.2013.30.3.06

Yoshida T, Kruger R, Inglis V (1995) Augmentation of non-specific protection in African catfish, *Clarias gariepinus* (Burchell), by the long-term oral administration of immunostimulants. J Fish Dis 18:195–198. https://doi.org/10.1111/j.1365-2761.1995.tb00278.x

Yusuf NS, Andayani S, Risjani Y, Rahem Faqih A (2019) Feed enriched with methanol extract of tongkat ali *Eurycoma longifolia* Jack root for masculinization of Nile tilapia *Oreochromis niloticus*. AACL Bioflux 12:1481–1492

Zaki FM, Said MM, Tahoun AA, Amer M (2021) Evaluation of different sex reversal treatments in red tilapia hybrid. Egypt J Aquat Biol Fish 25:279–292. https://doi.org/10.21608/ejabf.2021.140630

Zambrano L, Martínez-Meyer E, Menezes N, Peterson AT (2006) Invasive potential of common carp (*Cyprinus carpio*) and Nile tilapia (*Oreochromis niloticus*) in American freshwater systems. Can J Fish Aquat Sci 63:1903–1910. https://doi.org/10.1139/F06-088

Chapter 8
Pawpaw (*Carica papaya*) Extracts as Potential Growth Promoters and Sex Reversal Agents in Aquaculture

Linda Nuushona Iipinge, Ndakalimwe Naftal Gabriel, and Johannes Angala Iitembu

Abstract Aquaculture is the rearing, breeding, and harvesting of aquatic organisms in a controlled environment for commercial, recreational, or public purposes, such as fish, shellfish, algae, and aquatic plants. Fish in captivity are frequently subjected to various stressors that affect their production performance parameters. Furthermore, fish species such as tilapia are plagued by prolific breeding, which reduces their yield in captivity. Antibiotics, hormones, vitamins, and chemotherapeutics are chemicals used in aquaculture to improve overall health and increase culture fish production. Highly effective chemicals, however, may be hazardous to human health and the environment. *Carica papaya* is one of the medicinal plants used in aquaculture as an alternative to chemicals. Pawpaw crude extracts contain saponins and flavonoids, which have antibacterial, antifertility, antifungal, and pesticide properties. Growth-promoting and sex reversal effects of pawpaw seed powders have been reported in freshwater fish species, according to research. Masculinity is usually required in tilapia species because male fish grow faster than females, and monosex population culture prevents tilapia species from reproducing uncontrollably. More research, however, is necessary to understand the various effects of *C. papaya* extracts in different fish species for better aquaculture optimisation. The properties of pawpaw crude extracts are discussed in this chapter, as well as their potential benefits in aquaculture.

Keywords Aquaculture · Growth promoter · Phytochemicals · 17 α methyltestosterone · Pawpaw extracts · Sex reversal

---

L. N. Iipinge (✉) · N. N. Gabriel · J. A. Iitembu
Department of Fisheries and Ocean Sciences, Sam Nujoma Campus, University of Namibia, Henties Bay, Namibia

© The Author(s), under exclusive license to Springer Nature Singapore Pte Ltd. 2023

N. N. Gabriel et al. (eds.), *Emerging Sustainable Aquaculture Innovations in Africa*, Sustainable Agriculture and Food Security,
https://doi.org/10.1007/978-981-19-7451-9_8

8.1 Introduction

Aquaculture is the rearing, breeding, and harvesting of aquatic organisms such as fish, shellfish, algae, and plants in a controlled aquatic environment for commercial, recreational, or human consumption. Aquaculture is the world's fastest-growing food sector, accounting for approximately 50% of global food fish production in 2014 (FAO 2014) and projected to contribute 41% of global fish production by 2020. (Krishen et al. 2009). Similarly, FAO (2012) reported a substantial increase in aquaculture production (an average growth of 6%) between 1990 and 2010. Aquaculture is also essential in developing countries because it employs poor rural communities, thereby alleviating poverty.

Since the ocean world's fish yields have reached their maximum production level, fish culture (which is expanding in new directions, increasing, and diversifying) has become an essential agricultural business industry (Cruz-Garcia et al. 2009; Bud et al. 2009). Tilapia is one of the most important fish species in freshwater aquaculture, serving as a significant source of protein and alleviating food security in rural communities in developing countries such as Sub-Saharan Africa (FAO 2002; FAO 2012). According to FAO statistics, global tilapia production increased from 1.5 million tonnes in 2001 (FAO 2002) to 4.51 million in 2012 (FAO 2014). Although tilapia is ranked second in production after carps, its output in 2010 exceeded 3.2 million metric tonnes, outperforming salmon and catfish (Omeje 2016).

Tilapia species is widely cultured throughout the world because it exhibits desirable characteristics such as rapid growth, acceptance of natural and inexpensive artificial feed, efficient food conversion, adaptability to a wide range of environmental conditions, and disease resistance under cultured conditions (Phelps and Popma 2000; El-Sayed 2006). Furthermore, unlike other species such as African catfish, *Clarias gariepinus* (Reed et al. 1967), which requires exogenous hormones to induce spawning in captivity, tilapia species are hardy, highly prolific, and spawn naturally in captivity. Despite the preceding characteristics, studies have shown that tilapia cultures are negatively impacted by the onset of precocious sexual maturity and uncontrolled spawning, which frequently results in overcrowding of ponds and consequently stunted growth, production of variable fish sizes, more extended culture periods, and low marketable sized fish (Popma and Masser 1999; Toguyeni et al. 2002; Ekanem and Okoronkwo 2003).

The concept of tilapia monosex culture production (preferably male) provides an opportunity to overcome the limitation of precious breeding, which minimises stunted growth, shortens culture duration, and thus, improves yield and economic return (Omeje 2016). All male tilapia cultures are preferred because they grow faster (Beardmore et al. 2001) and spend less energy on reproduction (Popma and Masser 1999). Several techniques, including sex sorting by hand, hybridisation, genetic manipulation, temperature control, and hormonal induction, were developed to produce an all-male population of marketable size (Beardmore et al. 2001). Because it saves time and produces precise results, synthetic sex reversal hormone (17 methyltestosterone) appears to be the most effective and widely used technique

(Toguyeni et al. 2002; Phelps and Popma 2000). To achieve phenotypic sex reversal, synthetic hormones are incorporated into the diet and administered to sexually undifferentiated fry about 2 weeks after hatching (Fuentes-Silva et al. 2013; Baras et al. 2000). The fry-fed steroid hormones (17 methyltestosterone) incorporated in a diet at the appropriate time and dosage (during the fish's undifferentiated gonadal development stage) will be converted from genotypic females to phenotypic males (Omeje 2016; Toguyeni et al. 2002; Pandian and Sheela 1995). Furthermore, fish-farming enterprises use a variety of chemicals, hormones, chemotherapeutics, and vitamins to combat problems such as infectious diseases, health issues, and economic losses (Yılmaz et al. 2013).

Besides the effectiveness of synthetic hormones, concerns have been raised about the health consequences for fish farmers who come into contact with the hormone during feeding (Guerrero III 2008) and the environment when the effluent is discharged into the environment (Heberer 2002). As a result, countries such as India have prohibited using synthetic hormones and antibiotics as feed additives (White et al. 2006). With this ban, the use of natural plant extracts as feed additives has emerged as a promising alternative approach for controlling bacterial diseases, promoting growth performance, and manipulating sex to obtain all-male tilapia production. The World Health Organization also supports using medicinal plants to replace steroid hormones, which pose no health risk to humans, are environmentally friendly, less expensive, and biodegradable for commercial aquaculture use (Farrag et al. 2013).

8.2 Pawpaw (*Carica papaya*) Extracts

One of the medicinal plants used in aquaculture as an infectious disease preventative, stress resistance booster, and growth promoter is the pawpaw. The term "pawpaw" refers to a short-lived, evergreen, tropical herbaceous plant with a height of up to 10 metres (m) (Verma et al. 2017). The *Carica papaya* is primarily native to southern Mexico, Central America, and South America (Carvalho and Renner 2014). It is regarded as one of the Caricaceae family's most economically significant fruits (Oliveira and Almada 1996) (Fig. 8.1). In Sub-Saharan Africa, tropical and subtropical regions, pawpaw is widely available all year around. It is grown for its delicious and nutritious fruit and medicinal purposes (Carvalho and Renner 2014). The plant's various parts, such as the seeds, unripe pulp, latex, and leaves, offer an alternative for controlling diseases and the sex ratio in aquaculture. The fruits were said to contain dietary fibre, calcium, iron, and sodium as well as carbohydrates, protein, fat, vitamin A, B, and C, carotene, and lycopene (Krishna et al. 2008). Other plant parts, including the seed, roots, unripe pulp, flowers, bark, latex, and leaves, have been found to contain vitamins A, B1, B2, and C, as well as chymopapain A and B and papain (Mitchel et al. 1970), all of which support muscle growth and function and aid in the metabolism of protein, fat, and carbohydrates (Su et al. 2009).

Fig. 8.1 Pawpaw (*Carica papaya*) tree and its fruits

8.3 Administration Methods in Aquaculture

Depending on the purpose of administration, herbal extracts are administered via three methods: oral, immersion, and injection. Oral administration is the most common method for incorporating extracts into diets, and animals can access the extracts through feeding. This method is commonly used when farmers want to improve fish growth, reverse sex, or improve the overall health of culture fish (Gabriel 2019). The immersion method is also helpful in aquaculture, where it is used for sex reversal, parasites treatment, and anaesthesia (Mukherjee et al. 2015; de Oliveira Hashimoto et al. 2016; Hoseini et al. 2019). Injection, on the other hand, is thought to be an effective method of administration; however, it can cause a high level of stress in fish, is labour intensive, expensive, and may require high-level technology that may not be available in other parts of the world (Mastan 2015).

8.3.1 Potential Health Benefits of Pawpaw Crude Extracts in Fish

Plant extracts are an essential resource in aquaculture for promoting growth, increasing stress resistance, and combating severe and infectious diseases. It is estimated that 80% of the world's population relies on traditional medicine, and a significant portion of traditional therapies involve using plant extracts or active ingredients (Ekor 2014; World Health Organization 2004). Furthermore, studies have shown that pawpaw products in their crude form contain a high concentration of bioactive compounds (such as saponins, flavonoids, phenols, alkaloids, terpenoids, glycosides, steroids, and cardenolides (Lohiya et al. 2000; Ezike et al. 2009; Oloyede 2005), which have antioxidant, antifungal, antifertility, anti-inflammatory, antimicrobial, and antifungal (Mansura et al. 2009). According to Awad and Awaad (2017), the presence of compounds with antibacterial, antifungal, and antiviral

Table 8.1 Health benefits response of fish-fed diet enriched with pawpaw crude extracts

Type of plant extract	Type of phytochemicals	Function	References
Root	Benzyl iso-thiocyanate, glucosinolatescarposide	Pawpaw root extracts were used to treat wound infections and gastroenteritis diseases in fish caused by pathogenic bacteria	Doughari et al. (2007)
Seed	Phenolics compounds, vanillic acid, vitamin C, caricain, alkaloids, steroids, flavonoids, saponins, and tannins	Pawpaw seed powder credited with molluscicidal activities against freshwater snail (*Lymnaea acuminata*) Pawpaw seeds exhibited significant inhibitory activity against cowpea weevil (*Callobruchus macalatus*)	Jaiswal and Singh (2008) Farias et al. (2007)
Fruit	Ferulic, p-coumaric, vitamin C, caffeic acid, carotenoids	Promote wound healing and skin repair	Emeruwa (1982)
Leaves	Folic acid, saponins, glycosides, tannins, flavonoids, vitamin B12, A, and C	Source of antimicrobial agent against fish pathogens	Fakoya et al. (2019)
Unripe pulp	Saponins, alkaloids, terpenoids, flavonoids, glycoside, stereoids, cardcnolides	Responsible for medicinal properties in fish	Oloyede (2005); Ezike et al. (2009)

properties in the fish system may directly inhibit pathogen growth. Several studies have shown that compounds extracted from the pawpaw plant can inhibit pathogen growth in fish (Table 8.1). Emeruwa (1982), for example, discovered that pawpaw fruit and seed extracts have antibacterial properties. Furthermore, Doughari et al. (2007) reported that bioactive compounds in pawpaw root extracts were used to treat pathogenic bacteria-caused diseases in fish, such as wound infections and gastroenteritis. According to Jaiswal and Singh (2008), pawpaw seed powder has molluscicidal properties against the freshwater snail *Lymnaea acuminata*. Similarly, Farias et al. (2007) discovered that pawpaw seed crude extract had significant inhibitory activity against the cowpea weevil *Callosobruchus maculatus*.

Furthermore, studies have shown that mature unripe pawpaw pulp contains phytochemicals such as saponins, alkaloids, terpenoids, flavonoids, glycosides, steroids, and cardenolides, all of which are responsible for medicinal properties (Oloyede 2005; Ezike et al. 2009). According to Emeruwa (1982), whole fruit extracts contain ferulic, p-coumaric, vitamin C, caffeic acid, and carotenoids, all of which promote wound healing and skin repair. Folic acid, saponins, glycosides, tannins, flavonoids, vitamin B12, A, and C have been reported to be present in leaf extracts, and they serve as a source of an antimicrobial agent against fish pathogens (Fakoya et al. 2019). Pawpaw seeds have been found to contain anti-oxidants, anti-cancer, and antibacterial active ingredients such as phenolic compounds, vanillic acid, vitamin C, caricain, alkaloids, steroids, flavonoids, saponins, and tannins.

Ampofo-Yeboah (2013) reported that benzyl iso-thiocyanate in the crushed pawpaw seeds is thought to have activity against helminthic intestinal parasites.

8.3.2 *Sex Reversal Effects of Pawpaw Crude Extracts in Fish*

The adoption of natural plant extract practices that produce fish that are environmentally sound and free of pollutants has been prompted by a rise in consumer demand for safe and high-quality fish products (Chakraborty et al. 2014). This has led to the promotion of fish to satisfy new market demands. In tilapia culture systems, pawpaw crude extracts like seed meal have been used to reduce prolific spawning. According to reports (Udoh and Kehinde 1999; Verma et al. 2006), pawpaw seeds contain essential bioactive substances like saponins and oleanolic acid 3-glucoside with antifertility properties. Additionally, pawpaw seeds have been used to control fertility in a variety of animal models, including fish (Omeje 2016; Ampofo-Yeboah 2013; Iipinge 2019), rabbits (Pathak et al. 2000), rats (Udoh et al. 2005), and langur monkeys (Verma et al. 2006) (Table 8.2). Other studies have shown that the active components in pawpaw seeds, such as oleanolic glycoside and carpasemine (a plant growth inhibitor), caused sterility in male rats (Kobayashi et al. 2008) and were used to control *O. niloticus* breeding by changing the sex of fish in favour of males (Ekanem and Okoronkwo 2003; Ayotunde and Ofem 2008). According to Ampofo-Yeboah (2013), the potential use of pawpaw seed meal in fish feed resulted in a 65% masculinisation rate in *O. mossambicus*. Omeje (2016) found that *O. mossambicus* had a masculinization rate of 77.8%. In the study on the

Table 8.2 The sex ratio response of fish-fed diet incorporated with pawpaw seed powder

Type of plant product	Function	Fish species	References
Seed	Pawpaw seed meal incorporated into fish feed produced 65% masculinization rate	Mozambique tilapia (*Oreochromis mossambicus*)	Ampofo-Yeboah (2013)
	Pawpaw seed meal produced 77.8% masculization rate	Mozambique tilapia (*O. mossambicus*)	Omeje (2016)
	A high percentage of male fish (82%) was produced when fish fed with pawpaw seed powder	Three spotted tilapia (*O. andersonii*)	Iipinge (2019)
	A significant reduction in the sperm parameters in fish fed with pawpaw seed powder	Sharp-tooth catfish (*Clarias gariepinus*)	Ekpo et al. (2018)
	Pawpaw seeds at high dosage disintegrated the testes and ovaries leading to the devoid of spermatids and oocytes	Nile tilapia (*O. niloticus*)	Ekanem and Okoronkwo (2003); Jegede and Fagbenro (2008)

impact of pawpaw seed powder on the growth performance, feed utilisation, and masculinisation of sexually undifferentiated *O. andersonii* fry, a high proportion of male fish (82%) was noted (Iipinge 2019).

Furthermore, pawpaw seeds have been linked to a decrease in the quantity and quality of male rats' sperm (Nkeiruka and Chinaka 2013). Ekpo et al. (2018) discovered that C. *papaya* seed powder significantly reduced the sperm parameters of sharp-tooth catfish. A historical observation of gonads in *O. niloticus*-fed diets containing pawpaw seed powder revealed that glucoside in the seeds showed antifertility properties at high dosage as they disintegrate the testes and ovaries, respectively, devoid of spermatids and oocytes (Ekanem and Okoronkwo 2003; Jegede and Fagbenro 2008). The phytochemicals in pawpaw seed meal may contribute to tilapia masculinisation by lowering 17 estradiol levels in female fish while increasing testosterone levels (Ampofo-Yeboah 2013).

8.3.3 Growth Benefits of Pawpaw Crude Extracts in Fish

Pawpaw crude extracts are predominantly used in aquaculture to improve fish growth, boost innate immune response, and control a variety of diseases (Logambal et al. 2000). Pawpaw crude extracts have been used as feed additives in aquaculture to improve fish survival rates, feed utilisation efficiency, and productive performance of fish (Lević et al. 2008) (Table 8.3). Numerous studies on applying pawpaw products in crude form in various fish species have been reported, with impressive results. A study by Farrag et al. (2013) found that feeding *O. niloticus* a diet containing pawpaw seed meal at 6 g/PSP/kg diet for 45 days improved growth performance. Irabor et al. (2016) discovered that feeding *Clarias gariepinus* fingerlings 80% pawpaw seed powder meal improved their growth performance. According to studies, an increase in growth performance and feed utilisation in fish is attributed to a wide range of immune-nutritional constituents, including complex sugars such as polysaccharides (Zahran et al. 2014), which are believed to contain prebiotic properties (Kumar et al. 2016), which can increase an animal's nutrient digestibility, absorption, and assimilation capacity through improved

Table 8.3 Growth performance and feed utilisation response of different fish species-fed diet containing pawpaw seed powder

Types of plant extract	Function	Fish species	References
Seed	An improved growth performance was observed in fish-fed pawpaw seed meal incorporated at the level of 6 g/PSP/kg diet for 45 days	Nile tilapia (*Oreochromis niloticus*)	Farrag et al. (2013)
	An increased in growth performance was reported in fish fed with 80% of pawpaw seed powder meal	Sharp-tooth catfish (*Clarias gariepinus*)	Irabor et al. (2016)

gastrointestinal morphology or digestive system (Heidarieh et al. 2013; Gabriel et al. 2015).

8.4 Conclusion

The potential benefits of pawpaw crude extracts as alternatives to pharmaceutical drugs in boosting fish growth, preventing infectious diseases, and controlling undesirable reproduction in tilapia production systems were revealed in this chapter. Pawpaw crude extracts contain phytochemicals that are used to treat bacterial, viral, and parasitic diseases, as well as to control fish breeding in growing ponds. Because pawpaw is locally available, accessible, biodegradable, cheap, and diverse in nature, it could be used as a medicinal and economically beneficial plant by poor small-scale fish farmers and aquaculture scientists in tropical, subtropical, and sub-Saharan Africa. Even though the number of studies on the application of pawpaw crude extracts in aquaculture is increasing, more research is still needed to collect adequate information, particularly immune parameters, sex reversal effects, and toxicological effects in different fish species for better aquaculture optimisation.

References

Ampofo-Yeboah A (2013) Effect of phytogenic feed additives on gonadal development in Mozambique tilapia (*Oreochromis mossambicus*). PhD (Agric) thesis, University of Stellenbosch, South Africa

Awad E, Awaad A (2017) Role of medicinal plants on growth performance and immune status in fish. Fish Shellfish Immuno 67:40–54

Ayotunde EO, Ofem BO (2008) Acute and chronic toxicity of pawpaw (*Carica papaya*) seed powder to adult Nile tilapia (*Oreochromis niloticus* Linne 1757). Afr J Biotechnol 7(13): 2265–2274

Baras E, Prignon C, Gohoungo G, Méalard C (2000) Phenotypic sex differentiation of blue tilapia under constant and fluctuating thermal regimes and its adaptive and evolutionary implications. J Fish Biol 57(1):210–223

Beardmore JA, Mair GC, Lewis RI (2001) Monosex male production in finfish as exemplified by tilapia: applications, problems, and prospects. In: Reproductive biotechnology in finfish aquaculture, pp 283–301

Bud I, Boaru MA, Petrescu-Mag IV (2009) Influence on food and age on breeding and reproduction perfomances in a rainbow trout population. AACL Bioflux 2:239–247

Carvalho FA, Renner SS (2014) The phylogeny of the Caricaceae. In: Genetics and genomics of papaya. Springer, New York, pp 81–92

Chakraborty SB, Horn P, Hancz C (2014) Application of phytochemicals as growth-promoters and endocrine modulators in fish culture. Rev Aquac 6(1):1–19

Cruz-Garcia L, Minghetti M, Navarro I, Tocher DR (2009) Molecular cloning, tissue expression and regulation of liver X receptor (LXR) transcription factors of Atlantic salmon (*Salmo salar*) and rainbow trout (*Oncorhynchus mykiss*). Comp Biochem Physiol B Biochem Mol Biol 153(1):81–88 de Oliveira Hashimoto GS, Neto FM, Ruiz ML, Acchile M, Chagas EC, Chaves FCM, Martins ML (2016) Essential oils of *Lippia sidoides* and *Mentha piperita* against monogenean parasites and their influence on the haematology of Nile tilapia. Aquaculture 450:182–186

Doughari JH, Elmahmood AM, Manzara S (2007) Studies on the antibacterial activity of root extracts of *Carica papaya* L. Afr J Microbiol Res 1(3):37–41

Ekanem SB, Okoronkwo TE (2003) Pawpaw seed as fertility control agent on male Nile tilapia. NAGA 26:8–10

Ekor M (2014) The growing use of herbal medicines: issues relating to adverse reactions and challenges in monitoring safety. Front Pharmacol 4:177

Ekpo PB, Uno UU, Adilieje CM, Umoyen AJ, Okey FO (2018) Reproduction performance of *Carica papaya*, *Hibiscus rosa-sinensis* and *Ipomoea batatas* on Female African Catfish(*Clarias gariepinus*). Biotechnol J Int 21(2):1–8

El-Sayed AFM (2006) Tilapia culture. CABI Publishing, Cambridge

Emeruwa AC (1982) Antibacterial substance from *Carica papaya* fruit extract. J Nat Prod 45(2): 123–127

Ezike AC, Akah PA, Okoli CO, Ezeuchenne NA, Ezeugwu S (2009) *Carica papaya* (Paw-Paw) unripe fruit may be beneficial in ulcer. J Med Food 12(6):1268–1273

Fakoya S, Aderoboye O, Olusola S (2019) Phytobiotics effects of pawpaw (*Carica papaya*) leaves and fluted pumpkin (*Telferia ocidentalis*) leaves extracts against certain aquatic pathogens. Med Aromat Plants (Los Angeles) 8:1–7

FAO (2002) The role of aquaculture in rural development. Committee on Fisheries Sub- committee on aquaculture. Beijing, China, pp 18–22

FAO (2012) The state of the world fish and aquaculture. FAO, Rome, p 209

FAO (2014) The state of world fisheries and aquaculture. FAO, Rome, p 223

Farias LR, Costa FT, Souza LA, Pelegrini PB, Grossi-de-Sá MF, Neto SM, Bloch C Jr, Laumann RA, Noronha EF, Franco OL (2007) Isolation of a novel *Carica papaya* α-amylase inhibitor with deleterious activity toward *Callosobruchus maculatus*. Pestic Biochem Physiol 87(3): 255–260

Farrag FH, Khalil FF, Mehrim AI, Refaey MMA (2013) Pawpaw (*Carica papaya*) seeds powder in Nile Tilapia (*Oreochromis niloticus*) diet 1-growth performance, survival, feed utilization, carcass composition of fry and fingerlings. J Anim Poult Prod 4(6):363–379

Fuentes-Silva C, Soto-Zarazúa GM, Torres-Pacheco I, Flores-Rangel A (2013) Male tilapia production techniques: a mini-review. Afr J Biotechnol 12(36):5496–5502

Gabriel NN (2019) Review on the progress in the role of herbal extracts in tilapia culture. Cogent Food Agric 5(1):1619651

Gabriel NN, Qiang J, He J, Ma XY, Kpundeh MD, Xu P (2015) Dietary *Aloe vera* supplementation on growth performance, some haemato-biochemical parameters and disease resistance against *Streptococcus iniae* in tilapia (GIFT). Fish Shellfish Immunol 44(2):504–514

Guerrero RD III (2008) Tilapia sex. reversal.www.agribusinessweek.com/tilapia-sex-reversal

Heberer T (2002) Occurrence, fate, and removal of pharmaceutical residues in the aquatic environment: a review of recent research data. Toxicol Lett 131(1–2):5–17

Heidarieh M, Mirvaghefi AR, Sepahi A, Sheikhzadeh N, Alishahbazfar A, Akbari M (2013) Effects of dietary *Aloe vera* on growth performance, skin and gastrointestinal morphology in rainbow trout (*Oncorhynchus mykiss*). Turk J Fish Aquat Sci 13(2):367–373

Hoseini SM, Taheri Mirghaed A, Yousefi M (2019) Application of herbal anaesthetics in aquaculture. Rev Aquacult 11(3):550–564

Iipinge LN (2019) Effect of pawpaw (*Carica papaya*) seed meal on growth performance, feed utilization, survival and masculinization of sexualy undifferentiated three spotted tilapia (*Oreochromis andersonii*) fry (Doctoral dissertation, University of Namibia)

Irabor AE, Ekokotu PA, Nwachi OF (2016) Effects of pawpaw seed powder as an additive on growth of catfish fingerlings reared in indoor tanks. J Northeast Agric Univ 23(4):55–60

Jaiswal P, Singh DK (2008) Molluscicidal activity of *Carica papaya* and *Areca catechu* against the freshwater snail *Lymnaea acuminata*. Vet Parasitol 152(3-4):264–270

Jegede T, Fagbenro O (2008) Histology of gonads in *Oreochromis niloticus* (Trewavas) fed pawpaw (*Carica papaya*) seed meal diets. In 8th international symposium on Tilapia in aquaculture, vol. 11, pp 1135–1141

Kobayashi H, Wang C, Pomper KW (2008) Phenolic content and antioxidant capacity of pawpaw fruit (*Asimina triloba* L.) at different ripening stages. Hortscience 43(1):268–270

Krishen JR, Sunil S, Mohammad RH (2009) Impact of rising feed ingredient prices on aqua feeds and aquaculture production. FAO fisheries and aquaculture technician paper no. 541. issn:2070-7010

Krishna KL, Paridhavi M, Patel JA (2008) Review on nutritional, medicinal and pharmacological properties of papaya (*Carica papaya* Linn.). Indian J Nat Prod Resour 7:362–373

Kumar S, Auroshree P, Mishra J (2016) Mushroom polysaccharides as potential preboitics with immunomodulating properties: a review. Bioact Carbohydr Diet Fibre 7:1–14

Lević J, Siniša M, Djuragić O, Slavica S (2008) Herbs and organic acids as an alternative for antibiotic-growth-promoters. In: 5th international symposium of IBNA (National Research. Development Institute for Animal Biology and Nutrition), Balotesti, pp 28–29

Logambal SM, Venkatalakshmi S, Dinakaran Michael R (2000) Immunostimulatory effect of leaf extract of *Ocimum sanctum* Linn. in *Oreochromis mossambicus* (Peters). Hydrobiologia 430(1): 113–120

Lohiya NK, Pathak N, Mishra PK, Manivannan B (2000) Contraceptive evaluation and toxicological study of aqueous extract of the seeds of *Carica papaya* in male rabbits. J Ethnopharmacol 70(1):17–27

Mansura AA, Amen DA, Ibrahim S, Ayo J, Ambali SF (2009) Effect of fermented and unfermented seed extracts of *Carica papaya* on pre-implantation embryo development in female Wistar rats (*Rattus norvegicus*). Sci Res Essay 4(10):1080–1084

Mastan SA (2015) Use of immunostimulants in aquaculture disease management. Int J Fish Aquat Stud 2(4):277–280

Mitchel RE, Chaiken IM, Smith EL (1970) The complete amino acid sequence of papain: additions and corrections. J Biol Chem 245(14):3485–3492

Mukherjee D, Ghosal I, Chakraborty SB (2015) Application of *Asparagus racemosus* roots for production of monosex Nile tilapia, *Oreochromis niloticus*. IJAR 3:828–833

Nkeiruka UE, Chinaka NO (2013) Anti-fertility effects of *Carica papaya* linn: Methanol leaf extracts in male wistar rats. J Pharmacol Toxicol 8(1):35–41

Oliveira RF, Almada VC (1996) Dominance hierarchies and social structure in captive groups of the Mozambique tilapia *Oreochromis mossambicus* (Teleostei Cichlidae). Ethol Ecol Evol 8(1): 39–55

Oloyede OI (2005) Chemical profile of unripe pulp of *Carica papaya*. Pak J Nutr 4(6):379–381

Omeje VO (2016) Effect of Pawpaw (*Carica papaya*) seed meal on the reproductive, endocrine and immune system of Mozambique tilapia (*Oreochromis mossambicus*) (Doctoral dissertation, Stellenbosch: Stellenbosch University, South Africa)

Pandian TJ, Sheela SG (1995) Hormonal induction of sex reversal in fish. Aquaculture 138(1–4): 1–22

Pathak N, Mishra PK, Manivannan B, Lohiya NK (2000) Sterility due to inhibition of sperm motility by oral administration of benzene chromatographic fraction of the chloroform extract of the seeds of *Carica papaya* in rats. Phytomedicine 7(4):325–333

Phelps RP, Popma TJ (2000) Sex reversal of Tilapia. Aquaculture 2:34–59

Popma T, Masser M (1999) Tilapia life history and biology. Southern Regional Aquaculture Centre No: 283

Reed W, Burchard J, Hopson AJ, Jenness J, Yaor I (1967) Fish and fisheries of Northern Nigeria. Gaskia Corporation, Zaria, p 13

Su SN, Nie HL, Zhu LM, Chen TX (2009) Optimization of adsorption conditions of papain on dye affinity membrane using response surface methodology. Bioresour Technol 100(8):2336–2340

Toguyeni A, Fauconneau B, Fostier A, Abucay J, Mair G, Baroiller JF (2002) Influence of sexual phenotype and genotype, and sex ratio on growth performances in tilapia, *Oreochromis niloticus*. Aquaculture 207(3–4):249–261

Udoh P, Kehinde A (1999) Studies on antifertility effect of pawpaw seeds (*Carica papaya*) on the gonads of male albino rats. Phytother Res 13(3):226–228

Udoh FV, Udoh PB, Umoh EE (2005) Activity of alkaloid extract of Carica papaya. Seeds on reproduction functions in male wistar rats. Pharm Biol 43:563–567

Verma RJ, Nambiar D, Chinoy NJ (2006) Toxicological effects of *Carica papaya* seed extract on spermatozoa of mice. J Appl Toxicol 26(6):533–535

Verma S, Varma RK, Singh S (2017) Medicinal and pharmacological parts of *Carica papaya*: a review. Indian J Drugs 5(3):88–93

White JR, Belmont MA, Metcalfe CD (2006) Pharmaceutical compounds in wastewater: wetland treatment as a potential solution. ScientificWorldJournal 6:1731–1736

World Health Organization (2004) WHO guidelines on safety monitoring of herbal medicines in pharmacovigilance systems. World Health Organization, Geneva

Yılmaz E, Çek Ş, Mazlum Y (2013) Effects of synthetic and natural steroids on the growth, sex reversal and gonadal development of rainbow trout, *Oncorhynchus mykiss* (Walbaum). Su Ürünleri Dergisi 30(3):123–131

Zahran E, Risha E, AbdelHamid F, Mahgoub HA, Ibrahim T (2014) Effects of dietary *Astragalus* polysaccharides (APS) on growth performance, immunological parameters, digestive enzymes, and intestinal morphology of Nile tilapia (*Oreochromis niloticus*). Fish Shellfish Immunol 38(1):149–157

Chapter 9
Microbial-Based Systems and Single-Cell Ingredients: Exploring Their Role in Sustainable Aquaculture Production

Benjamin U. Akpoilih

Abstract Nearly 20% of all animal protein comes from seafood, which is often a good source of vitamins, minerals, and omega-3 fatty acids. Since the beginning of the 1990s, the production of marine fisheries has stayed the same. This is because of the massive fishing pressure on wild fish stocks and human activities. The increasing scarcity of fish meal (FM), the most expensive feed ingredient in aqua feed, may pose a future threat to aquaculture expansion. This chapter examines the role of single-cell ingredients (SCI) and microbes (microbial-based systems, MBS) in circular economy-based sustainable aquaculture production of farmed fish and shellfish. Single-cell organisms (e.g. bacteria, yeasts, and microalgae) and microbial-based systems (MBS) such as biofloc and periphyton play critical roles in reducing nitrogen (N) and phosphorus (P) loss from fish diets to the environment by volarising aquaculture wastes. Single-cell protein (SCP) and single-cell oil (SCO) are derived from microbial biomass that contains a high concentration of antioxidants and other bio-active components such as amino acids, long-chain polyunsaturated fatty acids (LC-PUFA), carotenoids, glucan, mannan, pullulan, xylitol, polyhydroxy butyrate (PHB), and polyhydroxyalkanoate (PHA). These dietary compounds stimulate the immune system, improve reproductive performance, and increase disease resistance in farmed fish species. With zero-water exchange and a low ecological footprint, biofloc technology can support intensive fish or shrimp production at a lower cost. To ensure that the aquaculture industry takes advantage of SCP and MBS, advanced but affordable technology to produce these agents must be developed to improve production, reduce feed costs, and minimise the harmful effects of SCP anti-nutritional factors.

Keywords Aquaculture · Biofloc · Single-cell protein · Microalgal oil · Periphyton · Biofilm

---

B. U. Akpoilih (✉)
Department of Fisheries, Faculty of Agriculture, University of Port Harcourt, Port Harcourt, River State, Nigeria

© The Author(s), under exclusive license to Springer Nature Singapore Pte Ltd. 2023
N. N. Gabriel et al. (eds.), *Emerging Sustainable Aquaculture Innovations in Africa*, Sustainable Agriculture and Food Security,
https://doi.org/10.1007/978-981-19-7451-9_9

9.1 Introduction

Fish contributes essentially to human nutrition, providing various health benefits in terms of protein, essential fatty acids (EFA), long-chain polyunsaturated fatty acids (LC-PUFA), and eicosapentaenoic acid (EPA) and minerals (Gephart et al. 2020; Kok et al. 2020). Fish and other aquatic foods from marine environments are central to meeting food and nutrition security goals, providing more than 3.3 billion people with 20% of their animal protein intake (FAO 2020; Gephart et al. 2020). However, fish production from the marine environment has been static since the late 1980s (Tacon and Metian 2018; FAO 2020). In contrast, aquaculture production has increased, with inland and fin fish aquaculture accounting for 51.3 Mt and 54.3 Mt, respectively, of the total fish production from all sectors (FAO 2020). In 2018, fed aquaculture represented more than 70% of global aquaculture production (Hua et al. 2019; Naylor et al. 2021), with carp, shrimp, tilapia, catfish, and salmon accounting for about 75–80% of farmed fish and shellfish combined (FAO 2020; Naylor et al. 2021). Freshwater fish species represented about 75–83.6% of total global edible farmed fish production, mainly under intensive net cage systems, including lakes, reservoirs, and rivers (FAO 2020; Naylor et al. 2021). The rapid growth of aquaculture makes it one of the fastest food-producing sectors globally (FAO 2020). According to Waite et al. (2014), fish production from the sector will increase to 140 Mt in 2050 and provide a source of high-quality protein in the future. Engle et al. (2017) estimated that aquaculture could close roughly 14% of the "gap" between global animal protein consumption today and the animal protein requirement in 2050.

However, aquaculture is heavily reliant on fish meal (FM) to fuel growth, particularly for major farmed species such as catfish, shrimp, and salmon (Cottrell et al. 2020), which accounted for 18% (15 Mt) of total aquaculture production in 2018 (FAO 2020). According to Boyd et al. (2022), formulated feed containing FM and fish oil (FO) accounts for roughly two thirds of fin fish and crustacean production. Concerns about the sustainability of aquaculture have recently arisen because of a decline in FM and FO production from capture fisheries (Costello et al. 2020). This decline may impact global aquaculture production of carnivorous fish such as salmon, trout, sea bream, sea bass, and shrimp, which rely on FM and FO to meet stringent requirements (Chatvijitkul et al. 2016; Kok et al. 2020). The shift from reliance on marine products to crop-based aquaculture increases competition for land and water (Fry et al. 2016; Chatvijitkul et al. 2016; Hua et al. 2019) via crop production (maize, rapeseed, wheat, soya bean) (Fry et al. 2016). Despite the declining use of FM and FO in aqua feed, feed accounts for 50–70% of the production cost of fish farming operations (Waite et al. 2014); it is also responsible for approximately 90% of the cumulative environmental impact of aquaculture supply chains (Kok et al. 2020; Naylor et al. 2021). The rapid growth rate of human populations (Engle et al. 2017; Hua et al. 2019) will increase aquaculture competition for natural resources and their ecological limits (Engle et al. 2017; Costello et al. 2020; Naylor et al. 2021) through habitat loss or degradation, mainly for shrimp farming (Carvalho Pereira et al. 2021), and through discharge of waste and nutrient-rich sludge (Carvalho Pereira et al. 2021).

The rapid expansion of the aquaculture sector is also associated with environmental issues such as greenhouse gas (GHG), carbon dioxide (CO_2), methane (CH_4), and nitrous oxide (NO_2) emissions, which contribute to climate change (Boyd and McNevin 2015; Boyd et al. 2022; Fang et al. 2022; Luo et al. 2018). Other aspects of aquaculture production's environmental impacts include toxic and ecotoxic effects (Camargo and Alonso 2006); toxic residue in fish and antimicrobial resistance due to chemical use (antibiotics, hormones, pesticides, fertilisers Kawsar et al. 2022); increasing land, water, and energy requirements for feed production (Chatvijitkul et al. 2016; Fry et al. 2016); and global incidences of disease outbreaks in aquaculture systems (FAO 2020; Gephart et al. 2020; Kok et al. 2020). The impressive growth rate of aquaculture (11%, 2000–2019) in Sub-Saharan Africa is hampered by fish disease (e.g. Ghana), high production costs, and prohibitive feed prices, combined with the impact of the COVID-19 pandemic (Ragasa et al. 2022a, b), and the unavoidable threat to food security posed by Ukraine's ongoing war.

Chemical treatment and recirculating aquaculture systems (RAS) are two methods for reducing the environmental impact of aquaculture (Badiola et al. 2018). However, the risks of chemical contamination of water and fish, the high cost of RAS operation, and the discharge of nutrient-rich sludge have significant environmental consequences (Badiola et al. 2018; Carvalho Pereira et al. 2021). Practices that improve environmental performance include reducing feed conversion ratio (FCR) and increasing productivity with fewer inputs (water, land, and energy) required per tonne of production to reduce aquaculture's impact on resource use and the environment (Chatvijitkul et al. 2016; Costello et al. 2020). To achieve the goal of sustainable aquaculture, researchers tested several novel protein sources: Food and feed-processing wastes (Boyd et al. 2019; Jones et al. 2020); microbial-based food systems (Martínez-Córdova et al. 2017; Viau et al. 2020; Muthoka et al. 2021); and single-cell organisms (Martínez-Córdova et al. 2017; Viau et al. 2020; Muthoka et al. 2021). (Maizatul et al. 2017; Shah et al. 2018; Boyd et al. 2019; Costello et al. 2020; Carter and Codabaccus 2022). Single-cell organisms (e.g. bacteria, yeasts, and microalgae) and microbial-based systems (MBS) such as biofloc and periphyton play critical roles in reducing nutrient loss to the environment by recycling nutrients and volatilising waste from aquaculture (Chavan and Mutnuri 2019). The process can produce protein-rich biomass (SCP) and microalgae biomass (MAB) with an excellent nutritional profile (Azim and Little 2008; Goncalves et al. 2017; Gullian-Klanian et al. 2020; Pacheco et al. 2020; Adeoye et al. 2021; Ahmad et al. 2022; Maizatul et al. 2017; Han et al. 2019; Ansari et al. 2021; Muthoka et al. 2021; Tinh et al. 2021, Liao et al. 2022). This chapter reviewed the contributions of single-cell ingredients (SCI) to circular economy-based sustainable aquaculture production of farmed fish and shellfish. The current literature on the nutritive and feeding value of microbial-based systems and single-cell ingredients in aquaculture was reviewed.

9.2 Overview of Sustainable Alternative Protein Sources

Several researchers have reviewed some nutritional approaches in the literature to improve the sustainability of aquaculture and reduce its associated environmental impact (reduced P and N) (Gasco et al. 2019; Costello et al. 2020; Naylor et al. 2021; Albrektsen et al. 2022); namely, plant protein (PP), and plant by-product derived from the fermentation industry (e.g. distillers dried grains and solubles—DDGS) (El-Husseiny et al. 2018; Amer et al. 2019). These innovative approaches can help create a circular economy by making better use of food waste and natural resources (Ragasa et al. 2022a, b). Nonetheless, several factors limit their use in aquaculture: high anti-nutritional factors (for example, phytic acid in PP, Krogdahl et al. 2010), low essential amino acids (EAA) (Makkar et al. 2014), deficiencies of EFA and LC-PUFAs (Fry et al. 2016; Malcorps et al. 2019), low nutritional quality (Hua et al. 2019), and sustainability issues related to aquaculture.

9.3 Microbial-Based Food Systems and Single-Cell Proteins as Novel Ingredients in Aquaculture

For sustainable aquaculture production, MBS and single-cell organisms (e.g. bacteria, yeasts, and microalgae) represent a valuable feed protein (SCP) and lipid or single-cell oil (SCO) (Crab et al. 2007; Azim and Little 2008; Tibbetts et al. 2017; Sillman et al. 2019). They can also reduce the environmental impact of intensive aquaculture production through nutrient cycling (Martiınez-Cordova et al. 2014; Martínez-Córdova et al. 2017; Huang 2020; Campanati et al. 2022) and waste removal (e.g. bacteria and microalgae Goncalves et al. 2017; Jung et al. 2017; Spalvins et al. 2019; Huang 2020). SCP and MBS (for example, biofloc) may also offer an alternative to antibiotics in aquaculture production by reducing the negative impact of disease on fish health and increasing fish immunity (Durigon et al. 2019; Wang et al. 2019; Agboola et al. 2020; Wang et al. 2022a, b). Dietary SCP can also reduce global feed demand, closing the gap between fish production and demand in aquaculture (Shah et al. 2018; Ahmad et al. 2022; Campanati et al. 2022).

9.3.1 Microbial-Based Food Systems in Aquaculture: Nutritional Composition and Feeding Value

Microbial-based food systems are a collection of microscopic organisms that live in a matrix (bacteria, fungi, rotifer, zooplankton, and microalgae). A biofloc is an aggregation of microorganisms such as algae, fungi, ciliates, flagellates, rotifers, and detritus that contain essential amino acid (EAA) comparable to commercial

Table 9.1 Overview of the nutritional composition of some microbial-based systems in aquaculture

Microbial systems	Culture system	Proximate composition (g/kg DM)	References
Periphyton	Mixed-sex tilapia farming in earthen ponds	CP: 272.6; L: 35.9; CF: 5.5; Ash: 359	Muthoka et al. (2021)
Biofloc	BFT using indoor tanks for Pacific white shrimp (*Litopenaeus vannamei*)	CP:292–303; E: 12.7–14.4; Ash: 361–401; TN: 47–49	Tinh et al. (2021)
Biofilm	Enclosures of shrimp with artificial substrates	CP: 4.30; biomass: 1.76–4.23 mg cm^{-2}; L: 12.1	Martiınez-Cordova et al. (2014)
Biofilm	Enclosures of shrimp with artificial substrates in zero-water system	CP: 3.4–6.90; L: 6.0–9.10; CHO: 8.8–14.1; Biomass: 2.9–15.6 g cm^{-2}	Viau et al. (2016)
Biofloc	Indoor internal minimum water exchange BFT internal tanks given with restricted protein	CP: 293.4–297.6, L: 250–500	Gullian-Klanian et al. (2020)

CP Crude protein (g/kg), *L* lipid, *CF* Crude fibre (g/kg), *E* Energy (kJ/g), *DW* dry weight, *CHO* Carbohydrates, *DM* Dry matter

shrimp feed (Najdegerami et al. 2015; Ju et al. 2008). Reportedly, biofloc enhances growth in fish species (Ekasari et al. 2015; Dauda et al. 2017, 2018a, b; Aboseif et al. 2022). Microbial floc and MBSs provide essential nutrients and increase digestive enzymes in fish (Najdegerami et al. 2015; Viau et al. 2016); however, the nutritional composition of these food sources is dependent on several factors, including the type of microbial system (Table 9.1, periphyton, biofilms, and bioflocs), their association with organic and inorganic materials (detritus, sludge) and the carbon (C) source ((Nevejan et al. 2016). Protein concentration in bioflocs, for example, can range from 140 to 500 g/kg of dry matter (DM), with greater levels observed for bioflocs created in shrimp tanks utilising aquaculture wastewater (Martiınez-Cordova et al. 2014). Ekasari et al. (2014a, b) found that the >100 m biofloc group had more protein and fat content than the other size categories. In contrast, the 0.48 m biofloc group had the most excellent amino acid (AA) content. According to Dauda et al. (2017), the crude protein (CP) of biofloc generated from various C sources ranged from 113.9 g/kg DM (rice bran) to 312.7 g/kg DM (sucrose).

9.3.2 *Biofloc Systems*

Increasing the abundance of heterotrophic bacteria in the biofloc system reduces the toxic inorganic N species and P in the system (Tinh et al. 2021; Aboseif et al. 2022). It also increases biomass yield compared to that of C added by algae (Avnimelech et al. 2014) and in tanks without C (Tinh et al. 2021). The addition of a carbon source lowers the concentrations of potentially toxic total ammonia nitrogen (TAN) and nitrate–nitrogen (NO_2–N) in biofloc systems (Debbarma et al. 2022), allowing for greater reuse of biofloc-derived aquaculture wastewater (up to 100%) (Figueroa-Espinoza et al. 2022). Crab et al. (2007) reported that the inclusion of carbohydrate (CHO) reduced CP from 400 to 250 g/kg of dry matter (DM) without compromising shrimp production. Biofloc replaced 500–1000 g/kg of DM of the FM in fish and crustacean diets, according to Martínez-Córdova et al. (2017). According to Kumar et al. (2015), rice flour added to a culture tank of black tiger shrimp *Penaeus monodon* (Fabricius, 1978) in a biofloc technology (BFT) system resulted in better growth in shrimp fed a 32% CP diet than in shrimp fed a 40% CP diet. Debbarma et al. (2022) found that adding C at 0 mL/L, 1.7 mL/L (C/N 10), 6 mL/L (C/N 15), 13 mL/L (C/N 20), and 14.6 mL/L (C/N 25) increased floc volume and improved fish growth performance when comparing the potential of biofloc in the production of panda (*Ompok bimaculatus*, 0.082 g). The authors also observed increases in digestive enzymes (lipase, amylase, and protease) in the gut, liver, and muscle in the biofloc group, with a C/N of 20, showing overall improvement in production performance and water quality compared to other groups.

These observations show that applying a C source in an aquaculture system stimulates microbial growth and improves access to nutrient-rich microbial floc, effectively enhancing growth performance (Wang et al. 2015). The magnitude of growth response depends on the type of C source with biofloc produced from glycerol (Dauda et al. 2017) and tapioca resulting in better growth and feed utilisation (Ekasari et al. 2014a, b). The daily feeding rate (e.g. common carp fed up with 75% biofloc (Najdegerami et al. 2015), fish stocking density (Table 9.2, Fauji et al. 2018), and the amount of biofloc used (Wang et al. 2015) are all factors that influence fish growth. Biofloc technology (BFT) enables a decrease in the amount of feed applied for fish feeding (Kaya et al. 2019). A study carried out by Aboseif et al. (2022) showed that in addition to increased growth and feed utilisation, biofloc enhanced carcass protein content and increased the population of lactic acid bacteria (LABs) in the gut, demonstrating the probiotic effect of biofloc; the authors concluded that increasing the C/N facilitated higher assimilation of nutrients (EAA, LC-PUFA, and protein) and decreased total N discharge in the water.

9.3.3 Periphyton Systems

Periphyton is a type of MBS that serves as an important natural food source for aquatic animals due to its high concentration of essential dietary nutrients (Martiınez-Cordova et al. 2014). Bacteria, fungi, protozoa, snails, chironomids, oligochaetes, and crustaceans comprise periphyton which is attached to submerged substrates (Azim et al. 2002). These organisms provide live food for cultured fish (Azim et al. 2002; Miao et al. 2021;Muthoka et al. 2021; Saikia and Das 2014), reduce feed input in the system (Garcia et al. 2016), and improve water quality (Garcia et al. 2016). (Li et al. 2019; Muthoka et al. 2021; Saikia and Das 2014).

Table 9.2 Overview of some factors that influence growth performance, feed utilisation, and physiology of fish that are raised in BFT system

Parameters	Treatments	Experimental diet	Chemical composition (g/kg dry matter)	Feeding strategy	Culture system	Fish/shrimp species	Size (g)	Duration (days)	Response (best diet)	References
C/N	9.5:1 (control), 15:1, 20:1, 25:1	Control (basic feed); Exp diet (Basic feed + added glucose)	Comm diet: CP, 300; L, L, 120; CF, 120; Ash, 15%	Fixd ration (3–5% body weight)	Zero-water exchange	Crucian carp, *Carassius auratus*	5.01 ± 0.13	56	Improved WG, SGR; reduced FCR compared to control (20:1 and 25:1)	Wang et al. (2015)
	0 (control), 10:1, 15:1, 20:1	Control (comm..feed); Exp diet: (comm. feed + added glycerol)	Comm diet: CP, 430; L, 60	Fixed ration (3% body weight)	Zero-water exchange	African catfish (*Clarias gariepinus*)	11.77 ± 0.01	42	Higher WG, body protein, chymotrypsin, and lower muscle cholesterol, lipid peroxidation compared to control (15:1)	Dauda et al. (2018a, b)
Feeding rate	100% DFR, BFT+ 75% DFR, BFT + 50% DFR and BFT + 25% DFR	Control (comm.. diet); Exp diet (BFT+ comm. diet). C source: Beet molasse (24% C; CP,	Comm. Diet: CP, 350; L, 70; Ash, 90	Fixed ration Control: 3.5% body weight (100% DFR), BFT(+75%, 50%, 25% DFR)	Zero-water exchange	Common carp (*Cyprinus carpio* L.) fingerlings	58.6 ± 0.2	30	Improved WG, SGR, and digestive enzymes (pepsin, lipase activities (BFT + 75%)	Najdegerami et al. (2015)

(continued)

Table 9.2 (continued)

Parameters	Treatments	Experimental diet	Chemical composition (g/kg dry matter)	Feeding strategy	Culture system	Fish/shrimp species	Size (g)	Duration (days)	Response (best diet)	References
C source	Control, Sucrose, glycerol, rice bran	Control (Comm diet); Exp diet (biofloc with sucrose, glycerol and rice bran)	Comm diet; CP, 430	Apparent satiation	Zero-water exchange	African catfish *C. gariepinus* fingerlings	5.06	42	Improved WG, SGR, biomass gain, biofloc volume, survival and plasma glucose and triglycerides (glycerol)	Dauda et al. (2017)
	Control, molasses, tapioca, tapioca by-products, and rice bran	Control (comm. Diet), exp. diet: control with C sources added to the system	Comm diet: 300 CP	Fixed ration (7% body weight)	Zero-water exchange	Pacific white shrimp (*Litopenaeus vannamei*) juveniles	2.02 ± 0.05	49	Improved SGR, FCR, survival, yield, and protein assimilation, and immunity in C sources (Tapioca)	Ekasari et al. (2014a, b)
Biofloc level	0, 50 g/kg, 100 g/kg, 150 g/kg, and 200 g/kg diet	Control (comm.. diet); Exp. Diet (comm.. diet with biofloc)	Comm. Diet: CP, 350; L, 54.5; Exp. Diet: CP, 351–357; L, 52.2–56.3	Fixed ration (3.5–5% body weight)	Zero-water exchange	Crucian carp, *C. auratus*	3.24 ± 0.27	56	Improved WG, WGR, SGR and reduced FCR compared to control (10 g/kg)	Wang et al. (2015)

Biofloc size	Un-sieved, <48 μm, 48–100 μm, >100 μm	Control (comm.. diet); Exp. diet (comm.. diet with biofloc sizes)	Comm diet: 400 CP	Fixed ration (8% body weight)	Zero-water exchange	White shrimp (*Litopenaeus vannamei*), red tilapia (*O. niloticus*) and mussels (*Perna viridis*)	5	4	Nitrogen uptake, recovery were in higher in >100 μm, while biofloc consumption as well as amino acid was higher in <48 μm than un-sieved (<48 μm)	Ekasari et al. 2014a, b
Dietary protein level	Control (32C and 40C), 32R, 32 M, 40R, 40 M	32C (practical diets with 32% CP) and 40C (practical diets with 40% CP); Exp diets 32R and 32 M (32C + rice flour (R) and molasse (M); 40R and 40 M (40C + R and 40C + M)	32R/32M: CP, 318; L, 58; CF,121; Ash, 137 40R/ 40M: CP: 405; L, 6%; CF, 121; Ash, 152	Fixed ration (4–6% body weight)	Partial (30%) water exchange	black tiger shrimp *Penaeus monodon* (Fabricius, 1978)	3.37 ± 0.04	75	Higher FW, SGR and lower FCR, catalase, serum protein and glucose in 40R, 40M and 32 R than 32 C and 40C (32 R)	Kumar et al. (2015)

(continued)

Table 9.2 (continued)

Parameters	Treatments	Experimental diet	Chemical composition (g/kg dry matter)	Feeding strategy	Culture system	Fish/shrimp species	Size (g)	Duration (days)	Response (best diet)	References
Stocking density	Control, low (LD), medium (MD), and high density (HD)	Control, 333 fish m^{-3}; Exp.: 166 fish m^{-3} (LD), 333 fish m^{-3} (MD), and 600 fish m^{-3} (HD)	Control had no glucose in water, while exp. groups all had glucose	Apparent satiation	Zero-water exchange	Nile tilapia (*O. niloticus*) fingerlings	0.51 ± 0.05	120	Higher FBW, DWG, SGR, and lower FCR; higher immunity in LD and MD than control (LD&MD)	Liu et al. (2018)
Feeding habit	BFT + LFBH, BFT + ACF	Triplicate group of each fish (20) were fed Comm. diet in 25 L BFT	Comm. diet: CP, 400; L, 60	Fixed ration (3% body weight)	Zero-water exchange	Lemon fin barb hybrid (LFBH) & African cat-fish (ACF)	1.77 ± 0.02 (LFBH) 0.98 ± 0.05 (ACF)	56	Higher WG, SGR, and PER as well as higher biofloc volume and protein for LBFT than ACF	Dauda et al. (2018a, b)

C/N carbon/nitrogen ratio, *Comm* commercial diet, *Exp Diet* experimental diet, *WG* weight gain (g), *FCR* feed conversion ratio, *SGR (% /day)* specific growth rate, *FBW* Final body weight, *CP* crude protein, *L* lipid, *CF* crude fibre, *BFT* biofloc technology

When compared to a control without periphyton, a source of C is added to the system to maintain an optimum C/N of 10–20, which increases the growth of the microbial community and improves fish growth performance and yield (Guo et al. 2020; Tinh et al. 2021). (Asaduzzaman et al. 2008; Garcia et al. 2017). Muthoka et al. (2021) reported that Nile tilapia (12 g) raised in the periphyton technology (PPT) system in a fertilised pond (1 m deep) and fed at 3% body weight for 3 months exhibited higher WG, SGR, and lower FCR than non-PPT systems; the abundance of diatom and zooplankton communities was higher with reduced cyanobacteria and decreased ammonia (NH3), Fish raised in PPT-based systems in cages grew faster than fish raised in periphyton-based systems (Garcia et al. 2016; Tammam et al. 2020). However, David et al. (2021) reported that PPT in a cage system did not benefit from feed restriction when compared to a system with full feeding but no periphyton; this was due to the study's low N/P ratio when compared to previous research with PPT (27:1, Garcia et al. 2017).

9.3.4 *Biofilm Systems*

A biofilm is a microbial consortium consisting of microalgae, bacteria, protozoans, fungi, and metazoans that are attached to a submerged substrate. It is critical for fish species whose diet does not consist of plant matter (Martiınez-Cordova et al. 2014). Dar and Bhat 2020; Dar et al. 2020). Biofilms are made up of microorganisms from various domains held together by EPS on surfaces (Dar et al. 2020), whereas biofloc is made up of heterotrophic bacteria (HB), phytoplankton, zooplankton, and protozoa attached to a floating surface (Porchas-Cornejo et al. 2017). Biofilms are high in protein, lipids, and LC-PUFA, which are beneficial to fish, particularly tilapia (Martínez-Córdova et al. 2017). Biofilms are critical to the live food sources of many farmed fish species (Garibay-Valdez et al. 2019; Ortiz-Estrada et al. 2019).

Viau et al. (2016, 2020) reported improved growth and reproductive success of pink shrimp in a zero-water system with biofilm as a single feed source, as well as reduced N loss. According to Lara et al. (2017), biofilm reduced feed input by 35% compared to the group reared in biofloc without artificial feed or biofilm. Wang et al. (2022a, b) found that augmentation of microalgae–bacteria with biofilm carriers increased fish production in recirculating ponds; bacteria–microalgae–biofilm decreased total ammonia-N (TAN) and nitrite–N by 51.28% and 33.48%, respectively. FM can be replaced in a fish diet by a biofilm-based single-cell protein (SCP) derived from purple phototrophic bacteria (PPB) (Delamare-Deboutteville et al. 2019). MBS is a powerful bioremediation tool for heavy metals and other contaminants in aquatic environments (Dar et al. 2020; Dar and Bhat 2020).

9.3.5 Microbial-Based Systems as Immunostimulants in Aquaculture

In addition to enhancing growth, the incorporation of MBS, such as biofloc, in aquaculture production systems improves water quality (Crab et al. 2007; Ekasari et al. 2014a, 2015; Dauda et al. 2018b); controls harmful pathogens (Crab et al. 2007; Martínez-Córdova et al. 2017); and increases beneficial gut microbiota (Crab et al. 2007). (Clenfuegos-Martinez et al. 2022). Biofloc minimises the environmental effect of aquaculture when compared to other aquaculture production technologies (Dauda et al. 2018a, b). Biofloc includes beneficial components such as EFA, carotenoids, chlorophylls (Ju et al. 2008), poly-hydroxybutyrate (PHB), Gulian-Klanian et al. 2020), and polyhydroxyalkanoate (PHA). These chemicals have been shown to promote immunological response and reproductive performance in farmed fish species (Ekasari et al. 2014a, b, 2015; Bossier and Ekasari 2017), as well as suppress pathogenic microorganisms (Supono et al. 2014; Matassa et al. 2015). Biofloc has several value-added components, such as antioxidants that boost aquatic animal immunity (Ekasari et al. 2014a, b; Yu et al. 2020). (Liu et al. 2018). Simultaneously, biofloc stimulates fish immune systems (Ekasari et al. 2014a, b; Liu et al. 2018; Karimi et al. 2019; Yu et al. 2020), effectively overcoming the problem of antibiotic abuse in aquaculture (Martínez-Córdova et al. 2017; Durigon et al. 2019; Wang et al. 2019) by enhancing disease resistance (Dauda et al. (Bentzon-Tilia et al. 2016). Biofloc promoted innate immunity (phenoloxidase and respiratory burst activity) and improved resistance to infectious myonecrosis virus (IMNV) in Pacific white shrimp (*L. vannamei*) juveniles, according to Ekasari et al. (2014a, b).

9.4 Single-Cell Protein and Their Application in Aquaculture

9.4.1 Production of Single-Cell Protein (SCP)

Several researches have shown that SCP and microbial consortia might be used in biomass and feed production (Overland et al. 2013; Bakhshi et al. 2018; Vidakovic et al. 2019). Protein obtained from yeast, fungus, microalgae, and bacteria may be used to make SCP or microbial protein (MP) (Nasseri et al. 2011; Bharti et al. 2014; Glencross et al. 2020). These microbes are grown on agricultural and industrial wastes (cassava waste, bran, bagasse, paper pulp, sucrose, ethanol, polysaccharides, industrial by-products, dairy waste, Jach et al. 2022) via solid/semi-solid state fermentation (SSF, Sharif et al. 2021) or submerged fermentation (SMF) using free-flowing liquid substrates (molasses, broth) (Bharti et al. 2014; Upadhyaya et al. 2016; Kuzniar et al. 2019). The following steps are involved in SCP production, depending on the culture technique and microorganism used (Ritala et al.

2017): preparation of nutrient media, possibly from waste; enzymatic hydrolysis (for yeast production, Overland and Skrede 2016); cultivation, including SSF; separation and concentration of SCP, in some cases drying; and final processing of SCP into ingredients and products (Ritala et al. 2017; Jach et al. 2022). In contrast to yeast SCP, bacterial SCP (Spirulina, Methylococcus, or Methylophilus) undergoes a secondary drying process (Overland et al. 2010). The drying phase in SCP processing allows for incorporation in extruded/pelleted feeds (Glencross et al. 2020). Microalgae, a high-protein source (510–740 g/kg), may be cultivated in various conditions and organic substrates (Han et al. 2019; Acquah et al. 2021). Microalgae farming yields more biomass (4–15 tonnes per acre per year) than traditional protein sources (0.6–2 hectare per year, Acquah et al. 2021). Microalgal extraction produces biopeptides, animal feed, and feed additives (Ahmad et al. 2022; Campanati et al. 2022). However, depending on the species, microalgae's solid cell wall composition limits its usage as feed (Raji et al. 2020). As a result, multiple techniques (for example, mechanical disruption) that assist in protein extraction, concentration, isolation, or purification of various products, including feed, are used to improve protein extraction efficiency (Amorim et al. 2021). SCP-manufacturing techniques for many microorganisms have been examined by Anupama and Ravindra (2000), Nasseri et al. (2011), Upadhyaya et al. (2016), Sharif et al. (2021), Albrektsen et al. (2022), and Jach et al. (2022) (yeast, bacteria, and fungi).

A recent trend in SCP production has seen an increase in the usage of different by-products (off-gas biogas and syngas) (Teixeira et al. 2018) derived from a variety of sources such as dairy wastes (whey, biogas, biohydrogen, bioethanol, protease, and bio-active substances, Sar et al. 2022); fruit and potato-processing wastewater (Sharif et al. 2021); and alkane wastewater (Sharif et al. 2021), agro-industrial waste, and industrial residue (Jones et al. 2020; Overland and Skrede 2016; Ritala et al. 2017; Jach et al. 2022; Leeper et al. 2022). Recent improvements in microbial technology have resulted in better and enhanced MB production using gas bioreactor fermentation technology (Matassa et al. 2016; Sillman et al. 2019; Albrektsen et al. 2022). Many new businesses are manufacturing MP from natural gas, primarily CH4)-using methanotrophic bacteria (Ritala et al. 2017; Teixeira et al. 2018; Kuzniar et al. 2019; Jones et al. 2020). Banks et al. (2022) predicted a $24 billion growth in alternative proteins by 2024, thus, lowering operational costs in the future owing to economies of scale. Compared to FM, SCP has a higher production volume and market value (Table 9.3). Industries that use current microbial biotechnology and better downstream processes have a bright future (Matassa et al. 2016; Ritala et al. 2017).

9.4.2 Nutritional Composition of SCP

SCP derived from bacteria has a high-protein content that ranges from 500 to 800 g protein kg^{-1} dry weight (DW) (Table 9.4). In comparison to yeast and microalgae SCP, bacterial meals (BM) have the most methionine (Overland et al. 2010).Protein

Table 9.3 Overview of production volumes and market sizes for different MPs

SCP	Production by volume (tonne/y)	Production costs (Euro/kg DM)	Economic value (Billion Euro)	Growth rate (% per year)
Yeast[a]	3,000,000 (Frost and Sullivan 2018)	–	9.2 (Jach et al. 2022)	8 (Jach et al. 2022)
Microalgae[b]	9000 (Frost and Sullivan 2018), 40,000 (Hua et al. 2019)	4–25 (Matassa et al. 2016)	1.6–2.4 (Matassa et al. 2016), 4.4–6.2 (Chang et al. 2017)	
Microalgae (Spirulina)[c]	10000 (Upadhyaya et al. 2016)		1.49 (Ahmad et al. 2022)	7.9 (Ahmad et al. 2022)
Bacteria (FeedKind)[d]	80,000, 200000 (Frost and Sullivan 2018)	–	–	–
ValProMic[e]	5000 (Matassa et al. 2016)			
Mycoprotein (Quorn)[f]	25000 (Matassa et al. 2016)	–	0.214 (Matassa et al. 2016)	20 (Matassa et al. 2016)
Bacteria (ProFloc™)[g]	5000	1–1.1 (Matassa et al. 2016)	–	–
Fish meal	171Mt (FAO 2018)	0.81–0.98[h], 1.303BC (Alloul et al. 2021)		

[a] Produced by LeSaffre® in France under different product names such as Lynside®Nutri, Lynside®ProteYn and related products (Lesaffre Human Care products), as well as yeast-based flavour ingredients (Biospringer products), with a turnover of 1.6 billion Euro in 2013
[b] Produced and marketed by E.I.D Parry Ltd., Parry Nutraceuticals Division, which is part of the 4.4 billion US$ Murugappa Group that produce Chlorella and Spirulina (Ritala et al. 2017)
[c] Produced and marketed by Cyanotech Corporation, USA;, with turnover of almost 32 million US$ and a GRAS status by FDA (Ritala et al. 2017)
[d] Produced by Calysta Inc, Menlo Park, Canada
[e] ValProMic is an MP grown on wastewater from the potato- processing industry (Ritala et al., 2017)
[f] Produced by Marlow Foods Ltd, and sold to Monde Nissin Corporation
[g] Nutrinsic, based in USA with subsidiaries in China, it used waste water for SCP
[h] Based of 2018 market price and a CP of 65%, according to Delamare-Deboutteville et al. (2019)

levels in dietary microalgae range from 500 g/kg (*Nannochloropsis oculata*, Sarker et al. 2020) to 600 g/kg (Pavlova sp., Wei et al. 2022) and 700–710 g/kg (*Spirulina maxima*), depending on the species (Maizatul et al. 2017; Shah et al. 2018; Hua et al. 2019). The nutritional profile of microalgae meal (MAM) was superior to that of fish meal (FM) (Bharti et al. 2014; Shah et al. 2018). Microalgae are rich sources of docosahexanoic acid DHA (300 g/kg, Schizochytrium sp., Sarker et al. 2020), with high ADC of protein (83%), lipids (91%), omega-6 6-PUFA (94%), omega-3 PUFA

Table 9.4 Nutrient composition of SCP source used in aquaculture production

Composition (g/kg DW)	Microorganisms			
	Fungi	Microalgae	Yeasts	Bacteria
Crude protein	300–450[k], 300–700[a], 400–500,[f] [h]300–500 350–500[i]	400–600[a], 550–700[b], [e]710, [h]600–700, 400–600[i], 540[q]	450–550,396–539*,462–598¶, 544#	500–650, 500–830[a],800[b], [c]500–830, [d] 500–650,[g]780,[h]500–800, 600–800[i]
Crude lipid	20–80, 200–250[f], 50–130[i], 560[o], 501[p]	70–200[a], [e]400, 50–100[i], 110[q]	20–60, 5–80*, 3.2–24¶,9#, 580[l], 650[m], 720[n]	10–30, [g]25–90, 80–100[i]
Ash	90–140	80–100, 100[q]	50–100, 45–103*, 58–95¶, 81	30–70
Nucleic acid	70–100, 97[i]	30–80[h], 40–60[i]	6–120, 48–90*, 15–99¶, 109#	80–120, 150–160[i]
Bioactive compounds[a]	Carbohydrates	Microbial oil	Amino acids, glucan & mannan[r]	PHB Ectoine
	Pullulan	Carbohydrates	Alcohols (1-butanol and isobutanol)£	Lipids Coenzyme Q8[j]
	Xylitol	Vitamins	Sesquiterpenes (farnesene and bisabolene) £	Extracellular polysaccharides

[a] Matassa et al. (2016)
[b] Upadhyaya et al. (2016)
[c] Sillman et al. (2019)
[d] Delamare-Deboutteville et al. (2019)
[e] Hua et al. (2019)
[f] Karimi et al. (2019)
[g] Nevejan et al. (2016)
[h] Ritala et al. (2017)
[i] Anupama and Ravindra (2000)
[j] Overland et al. (2010)
[k] Bharti et al. (2014)
[l] *Candida curvata*
[m] *Cryptococcus albidus*
[n] *Cryptococcus albidus*
[o] *Fusarium equiseti*
[p] *Mortierella isabellina (*Szczepańska et al. 2022)
[q] *Pavlova sp.* 459 (Tibbetts and Patelaskis, 2022)
[r] Agboola et al. (2020)
* *S. cerevisiae*
¶ *Candida utilis*
\# *Kluyveromyces marxianus* (Overland and Skrede 2016)
£ Ekpeni et al. (2015). *PHB* poly-hydroxybutyrate

(99%), and (EPA + DHA, 99%) recorded for marine microalgae (Pavlova sp. 459, Tibbetts and Patelakis 2022).

The nutritional content of yeast SCP is affected by the fermentation technique, species, and downstreaming procedure (Hansen et al. 2021). Yeast SCP protein content varied between 380 and 600 g/kg (Albrektsen et al. 2022). C. utilis and Kluyveromyces marxianus have lately sparked attention as possible protein sources in aqua feed (Overland and Skrede 2016; Jones et al. 2020). These yeasts have been granted "generally recognized as safe" (GRAS) classification by the US Food and Drug Administration (FDA), which is given to drugs that are not detrimental to health (Overland and Skrede 2016). Despite higher contents of non-protein N in the form of nucleic acids in yeast (10–15%, Overland and Skrede 2016; Ritala et al. 2017; Albrektsen et al. 2022), the analysis of nutrients in yeast protein and FM reveals similar contents of most indispensable AA on a CP basis (Glencross et al. 2020; Albrektsen et al. 2022). Yeast protein has more lysine, leucine, and isoleucine than FM, but less methionine, tryptophan, arginine, and lysine (Glencross et al. 2020). Yeast, on the other hand, has a better FAO protein scoring pattern than FM (Anupama 2000; Glencross et al. 2020), based on human EAA needs to quantitatively assess protein quality (Matassa et al. 2016). The CP and lipid of five yeast S. cerevisiae, *Cyberlindnera jadinii*, *Kluyveromyces marxianus*, *Blastobotrys adeninivorans*, and *Wickerhamomyces anomalous* are 380–520 g/kg and 7–89 g/kg, respectively (Agboola et al. 2020), with a comparable chemical score (a ratio of the individual digestible AA in each yeast product and the (Agboola et al. 2020). *S. cerevisiae*, on the other hand, contains more methionine and cysteine but less lysine than other yeast species (Agboola et al. 2020).

9.4.3 Nutritional Feeding Value of SCP in Aquaculture

The potential of SCP as a future feed ingredient in aqua feed production for larval and adult fish/shellfish with opportunities for future expansion and commercialisation has recently been realised (Carter and Codabaccus 2022). Beal et al. (2018) reported that it is possible to substitute 30% of world FM and FO with microalgae MP, which can improve the sustainability of fisheries and aquaculture. On the other hand, while performing a 10-year FM and FO replacement meta-analysis, Cottrell et al. (2020) reported that dietary SCP can reduce forage fish demand to 8–10 Mt based on projected aquaculture growth scenarios of faster growth rate and global shifts in consumer preferences in 2030, which is below the ecosystem-based fisheries management limit of fish supply (8.65–10.27Mt). Studies with marine and freshwater fish species show that dietary MP is essential for the growth and physiology of aquatic species (Crab et al. 2007; Azim and Little 2008; Vidakovic et al. 2019; Gullian-Klanian et al. 2020; Mahmoud et al. 2020).

9.4.4 Yeast SCP

Yeasts and many co-products of ethanol-fermented yeast, such as dry distiller grains with solubles, DDGS (Overland et al. 2013; Overland and Skrede 2016; Shurson 2018; Glencross et al. 2020; Rimoldi et al. 2020) improve fish growth (Overland et al. 2013; Goda et al. 2019) and protein availability (88–98%, Overland et al. 2013; Langeland et al. 2016). Fayeofori and Bob-Manuel (2014) reported good growth and FCR for Nile tilapia fed up to 500 g/kg YM compared to the FM diet. In contrast, including 328 g/kg YM in the diet was ideal for African catfish (*Clarias gariepinus*). The replacement of FM with YM (200–300 g/kg) improved protein digestibility (80%) in *O. niloticus* fry (Olvera-Novoa et al. 2002), and rainbow trout fed a practical diet (Martin et al. 1993). According to Olvera-Novoa et al. (2002), it is possible to replace up to 650 g/kg of animal protein with a mixture of SBM (200 g/kg), alfalfa leaf protein concentrate (150 g/kg), and torula yeast *C. jadinii* (300 g/kg) in tilapia fry diets without adverse effects on fish performance. Gumus et al. (2016) reported good growth and improved feed utilisation in the goldfish-fed diet supplemented with brewer's YM (350 g/kg diet) than in other yeast diets (0, 150, 250, and 450 g/kg). Compared to FM, dietary supplementation of non-saccharomyces enhanced growth in Nile tilapia (*Rhodotorula mucilaginosa*, Chen et al. 2019), rainbow trout (*Wickerhamomyces anomalous*, Vidakovic et al. 2019), shrimp (*C. aquaetextoris*, Babu et al. 2013), and Atlantic salmon (*Kluyveromyces marxianus*, Overland et al. 2013; *C. utilise*, Overland et al. 2013; Sahlmann et al. 2019).

A recent study by Leeper et al. (2022) showed that torula yeast (*C. jadinii*) cultivated on wood hydrolysates can replace 200 g/kg FM without affecting the growth performance of Atlantic salmon. However, the authors reported that while dietary yeast (100 g/kg) supplementation promoted growth by enhancing LAB associated with host fish, the population of *Staphylococcus* increased in the gut as the dietary yeasts increased in the diet to 200 g/kg, suggesting that a plant-based diet could alter the gut microbiome and reduce intestinal function. Differences between the single and combined yeast substitution levels in the mix might be due to dietary composition and CP level, which for Atlantic salmon, is met mainly by FM supply (Costello et al. 2020; Naylor et al. 2021). Current research has shown that a protein-rich solid fermentation culture method is suitable for yeast production, which can be a source of feed in aquaculture. After 8 weeks of culture, Wang et al. (2022a, b) discovered that supplementing the hybrid grouper (*Epinephelus fuscoguttatus* × *Ephelus lanceolatus*) diet with dietary yeast culture (YC, ESTAQUA®) (20 and 40 g/kg) stimulated growth and improved antioxidant and immune (immunoglobulin) response parameters. The post-challenge test against *Vibrio harveyi* infection revealed that YC enhanced disease resistance and improved fish survival. The authors found higher intestinal microflora (*Blautia* and *Lactobacillus*) than in the control group without YC. After 12 weeks, Hao et al. (2022) discovered that replacing dietary FM with *S. cerevisiae*-derived YC (200 g/kg diet) increased WG and decreased FCR in channel catfish (*Ictalurus punctatus*). The expression of the intestinal HIF1 gene increased while intestinal Nf-kB gene expression was down-regulated in the group that fed on YC. The authors reported a higher relative abundance of *Firmicutes* and *Turicibacter* in fish with YC than in control fish. Fish survival improved in fish challenged with *Aeromonas veronii* Hm091 and *A. hydrophila* NJ2.

The high nucleic acid and indigestible cell wall contents (Rimoldi et al. 2020) in yeast protein products constrain their use as a dietary protein source in aqua feed because they limit digestive enzymes and nutrient digestibility in fish (Nasseri et al. 2011; Glencross et al. 2020). Homogenisation (centrifugation), cell wall crushing and spray drying (Hansen et al. 2021), enzymatic treatment (Rimoldi et al. 2020), and extrusion (Overland et al. 2013) are applied to reduce the high cell wall content (Glencross et al. 2020) and enhance protein solubility and digestibility in fish (Atlantic salmon, Hansen et al. 2021). Fish can tolerate nucleic acid due to their efficient hepatic uricase activity that degrades plasma uric acid (Karimi et al. 2019).

9.4.5 Bacterial SCP

Protein derived from BM in aquaculture is gaining popularity due to its high nutritive value and palatability in aqua feed with the potential to improve the growth and welfare of several fish species (Biswas et al. 2020; Adeoye et al. 2021), and reduce plant-induced enteritis in the intestine (Romarheim et al. 2013). Table 9.5 presents the results from various studies that evaluated the use of BM in fish production. The response varied with the type of bacteria and fish species used. For example, FM substitution (100–200 g/kg diet) by the bacteria *Corynebacterium ammoniagenes* SCP in the diet of white leg shrimp resulted in good growth, nutrient utilisation and whole-body protein compared to FM control (Hamidoghli et al. 2018). The use of *C. autoethanogenum* in the diet of largemouth bass (*Micropterus salmoides*) indicated that dietary levels up to 156–204 g/kg could replace FM without affecting fish growth, haemato-biochemistry, digestive capacity, as well as protein digestibility and intestinal morphology (Zhu et al. 2022). A similar response in black sea bream (*Acanthopagrus schlegelii*) fed a diet with *C. autoethanogenum* has been reported previously (Chen et al. 2019a, b).

A study with an Atlantic salmon-fed diet supplemented with *Methylococcus* BM improved growth performance and reduced soybean-induced distal enteritis and intestinal inflammation (Romarheim et al. 2013; Vasanth et al. 2015), suggesting the potential of *Methylococcus* bacteria in enhancing gut health and immune protection as well as replacing SBM in the fish diet. Chen et al. (2022), while evaluating the performance of Pacific white shrimp (*L. vannamei*) fed a diet supplemented with methanotroph (*M. capsulatus*, Bath), observed no significant impact on growth performance and feed utilisation. Similarly, a recent study with Pacific white shrimp (*L. vannamei*) showed that dietary substitution of FM (25%) with *M. capsulatus* Bath (15, 30, and 45%) did not affect the growth performance and feed utilisation of shrimp compared to the FM reference control group, which indicated the possibility

Table 9.5 Overview of the effect of dietary SCP supplementation on growth performance and nutrient utilisation/ digestibility in fish and shrimp

MP source	Treatments	FM/ SBM replacement (g/kg)	Chemical composition	Feeding strategy (bw)	Culture system	Fish/shrimp species	Size (g)	Duration (days)	Response (Optimum requirement)	Reference
Bacteria *Corynebacterium ammoniagenes*	0%, 10%, 20%, 30%, and 40%	0 g/kg, 20 g/kg, 40 g/kg, 60 g/kg, and 80 g/kg FM (200 g/kg)	All diets contained 45% CP, 7% L, and 16KJ/g GE The PROC contained 63% CP, 8.77% L	Fixed ration (7% body weight)	RAS	Whiteleg shrimp (*L. vannamei*)	0.15 ± 0.02	63	WG, SGR, and FCR were improved for PRO 0 and PRO2 than for other diets (10% and 20%)	Hamidoghli et al. (2018)
Rhodopseudomonas palustris and mix culture *Rhodobacter capsulatus*	0, *Rps. palustris* (50 g/kg and 110 g/kg), *Rb. capsulatus* (50 g/kg and 110 g/kg), and mix culture *Rb. capsulatus* (110 g/kg)	50 and 110 g/kg, 50 and 110 g/kg, and 110 g/kg protein, respectively, from SBM and FM	Practical diets contained 35% CP and 7% L	Fixed ration (based on FCR of 1.6 and SGR of 15% / day	RAS	*L. vannamei* postlarvae	9.33 g	28	WG, SGR, and FCR were significantly improved in fish fed 50 g/kg *Rps. Palustris*, 110 g/kg *capsulatus* and 50 g/kg *Rb. capsulatus* (50 g/kg *Rps. Palustris*) diet	Alloul et al. (2021)
Purple phototrophic bacteria (PPB)	0%, 33%, 66%, and 100%	100, 200, and 300 g/kg PPB grown in synthetic wastewater	Practical diet contained 56.3% CP, 12.5% L. PPB contained 58% CP, 3.4% L	Restrictive pair fed	RAS	Asian sea bass (*Lates calcarifer*)	6.11 ± 0.10* g (4 tanks)–4.23 ± 0.21 (8 tanks)	47	WG, SGR, and FCR were not affected by PPB substitution (33% and 66% PPB)	Delamare-Deboutteville et al. (2019)
Marichromatium sp. & *Rhodopseudomonas sp.*	*Rhodopseudomonas sp* + control (diet 1), *Marichromatium sp.* + control (diet 2), Control (comm.. diet) diet 1	Exp diets were mixed with control diet at 2:1	Commercial diet contain 39.55–42.7% CP, 4.77–8.13% L	Apparent satiation	RAS	Malaysian Mahseer or Kelah (*Tor tambroides*)	12.27 ± 0.25 g	70	Higher WG, SGR, and lower FCR in diet 2 than diet 2 and diet 1 (*Marichromatium sp*)	Chowdhury et al. (2016)
Microalgae *Chlorella*	0% (RCM0), 25% (RCM25), 50% (RCM50), 75% (RCM75), and 100% (RCM100)	Control (520 g/g FM), RCM 25 (390 g/kg FM +99.6 g/kg RCM), RCM50 (260 g/kg FM + 199.2 g /kg RCM), RCM 75 (130 g/kg + 298.8 g/kg RCM), RCM100 398.4 g/kg RCM).	The diets were equal for CL = 38%, L = 9%	4%–7% body weight	Static renewal (30% daily)	Crucian carp (*C. auratus gibelio*)	1.77 ± 0.04 g	42	WG, SGR, FCR and ADC of protein, lipid, and energy as well as digestive enzyme activities (amylase, trypsin, and lipase) in intestine were unaffected by RCM inclusion (100% RCM)	Shi et al. (2017)

(continued)

Table 9.5 (continued)

MP source	Treatments	FM/ SBM replacement (g/kg)	Chemical composition	Feeding strategy (bw)	Culture system	Fish/shrimp species	Size (g)	Duration (days)	Response (Optimum requirement)	Reference
Chlorella	0, 60, 120, 180, 240, and 300 g/kg of whole-cell or cell-ruptured *C. vulgaris* meals	The practical diet (100: 0, reference diet) was blended (w/w) with test diets containing *C. vulgaris* at 94:6, 88: 12, 82:18, 76:24, and 70:30 for whole-cell or cell-ruptured *C. vulgaris* meals	Reference diet: CP = 50.2, L = 17.8 Test diet: CP = 43.5–49.3%, L = 18–18.6%	Apparent satiation	Flow through	Atlantic salmon (*Salmo salar L*	40.4 ± 2.7 g	25	Lower ADC of lipid and protein at >60 g/kg for whole cell. Protein ADC was unaffected by cell-ruptured *C. vulgaris* (60–240 g/kg). Levels (>120 g/kg) reduced ADC of leucine whole cell. Cell ruptured *C. vulgaris* did not affect ADC of all 10 AA (240–300 g/kg	Tibbetts et al. (2017)
Scenedesmus obliquus	Standard diet (control), whole *S. obliquus* biomass and control) + whole microalgal biomass (50:50) diets	Half the diet (FM and peanut based) was mixed with microalgae at equal ratio (diet2); whole microalgae was used as diet 3	Control: CP = 30%, L = 3.5%, 40% + CHO *S. obliquus* biomass 53.2%CP, 12.5% L, and 22% CHO	Fixed ration (2% body weight)	Static renewal (80% daily)	Rohu (*Labeo rohita*), mrigal (*Cirrhinus mrigala*) and catla (*Catla catla*)	4.5–4.9 g	90	Higher WG and SGR in 50:50 diet than control and *S. obliquus*biomass (50:50)	Patnaik et al. (2019)
Nannochloropsis oceanic	Control (0%), 25%, 50%, 75%, and 100% algae biomass	57.5 g/kg (25%), 115 g/kg (50%), 175 g/kg (75%), and 230 g/kg (100%) of SBM (230 g/kg diet)	All diets were equal for CP (30%), L (6%) and CHO (55%)	n.a	n.a	Red tilapia larvae	0.32 ± 0.1 g	30	FI, WG, SR increased while FCR declined in fish-fed diet up to 75% replacement (75% algae biomass)	Abugrara et al. (2019)
Chlorella	Control, CL-25, CL-50, CL-75, CL-100	62.5, 125, 187.5, and 250 g/kg of FM (250 g/kg diet)	The diets were equal for CP (40%) and L (20%)	Fixed ration (10% bw)	Static renewal	*M. rosenbergii* postlarvae	2.20 ± 0.39 g	90	Higher WG, SGR, and lower FCR in PL fed 75% CL (CL-50) than control diet	Radhakrishnan et al. (2015)

Yeast *Saccharomyces cerevisiae* and *Wickerhamomyces anomalus*	FM control, S20, S40, S60, S60 (meth), W20, W40, W60	*S. cerevisiae* replaced 107 g /kg (20%, S20), 214 g/kg (40%, S40), and 321 g/kg (60% (S60) of FM (300 g/kg) and a 70:30 biomass ratio of the yeasts *W. anomalus* and *S. cerevisiae* replaced 118 g/kg (20%, W20), 239 g/kg (40%, W40), and 355 g/kg (60%, W60) of FM. No methionine in S60meth	The diets were equal for CP (42.5–46.3%); L (18.6–20.8%)	Near-satiation fixed rations of 1.5% body weight	Flow through	Rainbow trout (*O. mykiss*)	144.7 ± 25 g	70	Replacement of FM with W60 and S60 produced lower SGR and abnormal (oedematous mucosal fold) than other diets, respectively. ADC of AA and P were similar for FM and W20 (.S40)	Vidakovic et al. (2019)
S. cerevisiae	0% (control), 15%, 25%, 35%, and 45% yeast	88.7 g/kg (15%), 147.8 g/kg (25%), 207.1 g/kg (35%), and 266.3 g/kg (45%) of FM (400 g/kg)	All diets had similar CP (37%) and L (8%)	Apparent satiation	Static renewal (50% daily)	Goldfish (*C. auratus*)	0.56 ± 0.01 g	84	WG, SGR, FCR and PER of fish fed 35% of yeast diet were better than other diets (35% yeast)	Gumus et al. (2016)
Candida utilis	FW and SW (Control), FW and yeast-based diet in SW (Control/Yeast), yeast-based diet in FW and SW (Yeast/yeast), and yeast-based FW and control SW (Yeast/ Control)	Two diets (a plant-based control diet and an experimental diet with 25% or 106.5 g/kg *C. utilis* (replaced 29% FM (150 g/kg) in control were given to fish in two periods: FW (0–28 days) and SW (28–56 days)	Both diets contained equal CP (50%), L (16%)	Fixed ration 2% (FW) and 0.5–1% (SW)	Flow through	Atlantic salmon (*Salmo salar* L.	80–85 g (FW) 115–129 g (after 56 days)	56	Higher WG and RWG was found for yeast diet than control (Yeast)	Sahlmann et al. (2019)

FI feed intake, *WG* weight gain, *SR* survival rate, *FCR* feed conversion ratio, *SGR* specific growth rate, *PER* protein efficiency ratio, *PPB* purple phototrophic bacteria, *VFA* volatile fatty acid, *CL* Chlorella, *RAS* recirculation aquaculture system, *SBM* soya bean meal, *FM* fish meal, *CP* crude protein, *L* lipid, *Exp diet.* experimental diet, *comm diet* commercial diet, *ADC* apparent digestibility coefficient, *FW* fresh water, *SW* salt water, *n.a* not available of incorporating BM as an alternative protein source in fish diets (Chen et al. 2022). Recent studies have revealed that PPB, a novel protein-rich MP source (670–737 g/kg CP), grows exclusively on wastewater under anaerobic conditions in light (Alloul et al. 2021). Delamare-Deboutteville et al. (2019) reported that PPB replaced 660 g FM/kg in the diet of Asian sea bass (*Lates calcarifer*), a high-value carnivorous fish, without affecting growth and feed utilisation. A recent study by Alloul et al. (2021) reported that white leg shrimp (*P. vannamei*) fed a diet supplemented with purple non-sulphur bacteria (a PPB): The shrimp fed with *Rhodobacter capsulatus* (110 g/kg feed protein) and *Rhodopseudomonas palustris* (50 g/kg feed protein) displayed higher WG (5–25% and 26%), respectively, compared to commercial feed. The authors also found that dietary inclusion of PPB enhanced resistance against *Vibrio* infection and reduced NH_3 stress compared to the control diet, indicating the suitability of PPB in sustainable fish production.

9.4.6 Microalgae SCP

9.4.6.1 Effect on Fish Growth

Several kinds of literature have reported the aquaculture potential of microalgae meal (MAM) as a replacement for FM in the fish diet with a positive impact on growth and feed utilisation in fish (Mahmoud et al. 2020; Raji et al. 2020). In several pieces of literature on aqua feed formulations, the most commonly used microalgae are *Chlorella spp.* (Tibbetts et al. 2017; Raji et al. 2020), *Scenedesmus sp.* (Skalli et al. 2020), and *Spirulina* (Olvera-Novoa et al. 1998). It is possible to incorporate 300 or 600 g/kg of MAM into the diet without affecting growth performance (Sørensen et al. 2016). However, the effect of dietary supplementation of MAM varies with the source of microalgae species used, the composition of the diet, as well as fish species and fish size. While Hajiahmadian et al. (2012) reported significantly higher growth in Golden Barb (*Puntius gelius*) fed a diet with *Spirulina* meal (200 g/kg diet) as a replacement for FM, the dietary inclusion of 500 g/kg *Spirulina* meal produced comparable FCR and WG in silver seabream (*Rhabdosargus sarba*) fed an FM-based diet. Cardinaletti et al. (2018) evaluated the performance of European sea bass, *Dicentrarchus labrax*, fed a diet with a blend of 18% of freeze-dried microalgae (*Tisochysis lutea* and *Tetraselmis suecica*) meal and 15% FM and found no difference in growth performance with fish fed the control diet (27.5% FM). Radhakrishna et al. (2015) showed that *C. vulgaris* meal substituted about 500 g FM/kg in the diet of postlarvae freshwater prawns. *Macrobrachium rosenbergii* without affecting growth and survival.

Olvera-Novoa et al. (1998) reported improved growth and feed utilisation of 20–40% *Spirulina* meal (104.7–314.1 g/kg) substituted FM in the diet of *O. mossambicus* (Peters) fry, whereas the supplementation of the diet with de-fatted biomass of *N. oculata* (80 g/kg) or whole cells of *Schizochytrium sp.* (32 g/kg) enhanced WG and SGR of Nile tilapia (34.5 g). The economic conversion ratio ($0.95/kg of fish) of Nile tilapia was reduced relative to fish that fed on the reference diet with FM and FO ($1.03/kg) (Sarker et al. 2020). However, Tibberts et al. (2017) found that feeding Atlantic salmon with whole-cell *C. vulgaris*-enriched diets reduced WG and increased FCR compared to a reference diet with FM. However, MAB combined with PP (e.g. rapeseed and *Chlorella*) replaced FM in the diet without affecting growth and feed utilisation (Shi et al. 2017).

9.4.6.2 Effect on Nutrient Digestibility in Fish

Dietary microalgae supplementation improves growth by enhancing nutrient availability in fish (Gamble et al. 2021). Gamble et al. (2021) reported that dietary *Schizochytrium sp, Chlorella and Spirulina* had a significantly higher apparent digestibility coefficient (ADC, 74.02–81.53%) of phosphorus (P) in Nile tilapia than FM control group (71.7%). Shah et al. (2018) reported that the high ADC of nutrients in *Spririulina* (*Arthrospira,* 86.1% of CP) and *Chlorella* (80.0% of EAA) compared well with conventional feed stuff. Feeding European sea bass (*D. labrax*) and rainbow trout (*Oncorhynchus mykiss*) with freeze-dried *Isochrysis sp.* (14%, Tibaldi et al. 2015) and whole cells of *Schizochytrium sp.* (30%, Bélanger et al. 2021) improved the ADC of CP (92.6% and 90.8%), lipid (87.6% and 85.9%), and energy (85% and 84.3%). Similarly, Nile tilapia and African catfish-fed dietary *Schizochytrium sp* meal (Sarker et al. 2016; Teuling et al. 2017) and *C. vulgaris* and *S. maxima* meal (Teuling et al. 2017), respectively, showed high lipid ADC of 80–98% and >80%, respectively. Raji et al. (2020) evaluated the performance of *C. gariepinus* fed diet supplemented with *Chlorella* and *Spirulina* for 42 days. The study showed that higher ADC of protein (98.64–98.66% vs 97.71%), lipid (96.51–96.67% vs 92.77%), energy (93.2–94.66% vs 86.04%, lysine (99.05–99.34% vs 98.59%), and PUFA (98.92–99.01% vs 97.51%) were higher than the fish that fed on FM diet.

Some studies showed that dietary microalgae supplementation did not improve ADC of essential nutrients in some species (Shi et al. 2017; Roy et al. 2011). For example, while dietary *Nannochloropsis, Phaeodactylum, and Isochrysis* up to 240 g/kg in the diet did not affect feed intake, nutrient digestibility of *Nannochloropsis* and *Isochrysis* was reduced compared to control (Skrede et al. 2011). These findings are consistent with a study which showed that the combination of dried *Nannochloropsis sp.* and *Isochrysis sp.* reduced feed intake, nutrient utilisation, and somatic indices in algae-fed (15–30%) Atlantic cod as compared to the control group. The reduced feed utilisation could be attributed to palatability issues related to the rigid cell wall content of microalgae.(Shah et al. 2018; Acquah et al. 2021). A recent study with Atlantic salmon-fed whole-cell *Pavlova* 459 meal (20 g/kg) showed that ADC of protein (90.1% vs 92.3%) and lipid (91% vs 94.4%) were lower than that of the FM-based reference diet (Tibbetts and Patelakis 2022). The reduced ADC of nutrients observed in these findings might be related to microalgae cell composition, microalgae source, diet composition, processing techniques used, and fish species and experimental conditions.

Homogenisation (Tibbetts et al. 2017), acid hydrolysis (Patnaik et al. 2019), pasteurisation (Agboola et al. 2019), bead milling (Agboola et al. 2019), and spray drying (Raji et al. 2020) can reduce the cell wall content and improve the feeding value of MAM. Tibbetts et al. (2017) found that dietary inclusion of cell-ruptured *C. vulgaris* biomass did not affect protein ADC at 60, 120, 240, and 300 g/kg diet (Table 9.5). However, dietary whole-cell MAB significantly reduced protein ADC at >60 g/kg diet. Similarly, ADC of all AA was unaffected by cell-ruptured MAB compared to reduced ADC of whole-cell biomass. Teuling et al. (2019) observed that cell wall ruptured *N. gaditana* meal improved the availability of nutrients in the diet of juvenile Nile tilapia, *O. niloticus*. Agboola et al. (2019) reported higher ADC of protein (83.8% vs 77.4%) and lipid (81.8% vs 65.4%) of *C. gariepinus* fed the diet supplemented with bead-milled *N. gaditana* meal (300 g/kg) compared to untreated microalgae. A blend of MAB with PP can enhance microalgae utilisation. In this instance, Shi et al. (2017) fed crucian carp (*C. auratus gibelio*) a diet based on a mixture of rapeseed meal and *Chlorella* meal (0, 25%, 50%, 75%, and 100%) as a replacement for FM for 6 weeks. In contrast, dietary de-fatted *N. oculata* and DHA-rich *Schizochytrium sp* improved the ADC of protein, lipid, and AA in Nile tilapia (34.5 g). The enhanced digestive enzyme activities in the fish-fed *Schizochytrium sp* meal diet may have improved nutrient availability in the fish (Sarker et al. 2020).

9.4.6.3 Effect on Fish Carcass Quality and Reproductive Performance

Studies show that dietary microalgae improve the carcass quality of aquatic animals (Roy and Pal 2014; Chang et al. 2017) through enrichment with LC-PUFAs (Stoneham et al. 2019). Dietary MAM in fish diets can replace or supplement FO (Haas et al. 2015; Allen et al. 2019; Guimaraes et al. 2019; Stoneham et al. 2019) and FM in aqua feed (Adel et al. 2017; Shi et al. 2017; Abugrara et al. 2019; Patnaik et al. 2019) without affecting growth performance, suggesting that microalgae contribute to nutrient-sensitive fish production in aquaculture. Stoneham et al. (2019) evaluated the effect of FO (10, 30, 50 g/kg diet) replacement with *Schizochytrium sp* meal (17.5, 52.6, 87.7 g/kg diet). They observed no significant difference in WG and carcass FA amongst the diets after 8 weeks of feeding juvenile Nile tilapia (160 g). However, compared to the group fed the 50 g/kg FO diet (165% and 232%), the diet supplemented with 87.7 g/kg *Schizochytrium sp* showed higher fillet n-3 (189%) and LC-PUFA (298%) (Stoneham et al. 2019). Dietary supplementation with 10–20% *Pav* 459 meal (2.86% EPA and 1.45% DHA) exhibited no significant differences in carcass DHA, EPA, and most FAs compared to Atlantic salmon fed the control diet based on FM after 12 weeks of culture, which indicates that MAM from *Pav* 459 is a good source of protein and n-3 LC-PUFA in farmed fish species (Wei et al. 2022). For 21 days, Carvalho et al. (2022) studied the performance of gilthead sea bream (*Sparus aurata*, 0.48 mg) fed dietary marine heterotroph *Schizochytrium limacinum* (19% DHA), alga fermentation-derived *Crypthecodinium cohnii* (39.5% DHA), and *S. limacinum* (49% DHA). The authors found that it is possible to replace FO with microalgae oil in the diet with increased DHA in the fillet of gilthead sea bream (*S. aurata*, 0.48 mg).

Cardona et al. (2022) showed that the carcass quality of female rainbow trout (*O. mykiss*) fed a plant-based diet containing *Schizochytrium sp.* meal (69 g/kg diet) or *Schizochytrium sp.* oil (26 g/kg) as a replacement for FM or FO in commercial feed, respectively, for 8 weeks, showed high PUFA n-6 and n-3 levels compared to the control group that had no MAM in the diet. The authors, however, reported that the reproductive success of females, as measured by egg weight, absolute fecundity, and relative fecundity, was similar to that of brood stock females fed a commercial diet. Kohal et al. (2018) and Zhang et al. (2020) also reported improved reproductive performance and survival of red cherry shrimp (*Neocaridina davidi*) and yellow tail cichlids (*Pseudotropheus acei*) fed a diet containing *Spirulina* meal when compared with a control diet without microalgae.

9.4.6.4 Effect on Immunomodulation in Fish

Studies reveal that dietary microalgae plays a positive role in fish immunomodulation. For example, Zhang et al. (2014) reported improved physiology and enhanced innate immunity of gibel carp (*C. auratus gibelio*) fed a diet containing *Chlorella* meal. Similarly dietary supplementation of *C. Vulgaris* (60–80 g/kg diet) enhanced immune response and improved resistance of *M. rosenbergii* postlarvae against *A. hydrophila* infection (Maliwat et al. 2017). A recent study with pacu (*Piaractus mesopotamicus*) exposed to 2.5 mg/L NH_3 for one hour after a 45-day feeding with dietary *Spirulina* (*A. platensis*, 40–60 g/kg diet) in place of FM indicated that microalgae stimulated the immune system and enhanced antioxidant enzymes as compared to control fish that did not feed on *Spirulina* (Carneiro et al. 2022). According to the authors, these effects seem to be attributable to antioxidant compounds present in *Arthrospira*, which mitigated NH_3 toxicity. Ma et al. (2022) found that dietary supplementation with microalgae (*Schizochytrium sp., A. platensis, C. sorokiniana, Chromochloris zofingiensis, Dunaliella salina*) enhanced the immune status and intestinal health of zebrafish (*Danio rerio*), comparing groups fed non-microalgae supplemented diets.

9.5 Application of Single-Cell Oil (SCO) in Aqua Feed: Effect on Fish Growth and Nutrient Digestibility

Single-cell oils (lipids derived from microorganisms) are a potential nutrient source in aqua feed, providing fish with a cheap source of lipid and EFA (Glencross et al. 2020; Lee et al. 2022). Oleaginous microbes can be grown on organic wastes with high lipid biomass recovery, ranging from 560 g/kg DW (*Fusarium exquisite,* Yang and Hu 2019) to 750 g/kg DW of lipid *(Schizochytrium sp*, Spalvins et al. 2019). Compared to dietary FM, SCO is more efficient at reducing FO inclusion in the diet, which reduces aquaculture demand for forage fish (Cottrell et al. 2020). According to Cottrell et al. (2020), dietary microalgae oil can replace 100% FO without affecting carcass quality (DHA + EPA) compared to 20%, 10%, and 25% soy oil or soy oil blend replacement for salmonids, shrimps, and marine fishes, respectively.

The majority of research has focused on *Schizochytrium* SCO products, which have a high protein (91.4%) and lipid digestibility (94.2%) for rainbow trout (Lee et al. 2022). A study conducted by Sarker et al. (2020) revealed that whole-cell *Schizochytrium* (6.2%) and de-fatted *N. oculata* (8% without FM) completely replaced FO in Nile tilapia after 184 days of feeding. The study concluded that the microalgae blend enhanced fillet macro-minerals and DHA deposition in the fillet of the group that fed on FM- and FO-free feed (5.15 mg/g) compared to the reference diet (2.47 mg/g). In contrast, Carvalho et al. (2020) reported that a dietary blend of microalgae oil, poultry oil, and rapeseed oil enhanced the EPA/DHA profile and fillet quality of gilthead seabream (*S. aurata*) when compared with fish fed with poultry oil or rapeseed oil. The authors concluded that microalgae oil replaced 52.8 g/kg of FO and 150 g/kg of FM in a PP-based diet of gilthead seabream. Sarker et al. (2016) reported that dietary *Schizochytrium* enhanced growth performance, fillet DHA and LC-PUFA of Nile tilapia, compared to fish fed with an FO diet. Lee et al. (2022) found that *Schizochytrium* (80%) replaced FO in rainbow trout without affecting growth, fillet quality, or lysozyme activity. In a post-challenge test against bacteria (*Lactococcus garvieae* 1×10^8 CFU/mL), microalgae outperformed FM in terms of fish survival. Katerina et al. (2020) evaluated the lifelong performance and fillet quality of Atlantic salmon reared from tank phase (18 g in freshwater to 800 g in salt water) on FO, *or S. limacinum* biomass (SLB) or a mix (FO + SLB) to slaughter stage (3 kg) in sea cages on FO or SCL for 11 months. At the end of the trial, the fish fed on SCB had higher body weight (3.3 kg vs 2.8 kg), fillet DHA + EPA, and higher ADC of LC-PUFA and DHA when compared to the FO and FO + SLB groups. There was no difference in fillet colour or odour between the FO and SCB groups, even though the SCB group had more astaxanthin than the FO group. Hossain et al. (2022) reported that the feeding of sobaity sea bream (*Sparidentex hasta*) with a high DHA algae meal diet containing 9.34% DHA improved fish growth, fillet DHA, serum lysozyme activities, and superoxide dismutase when compared with commercial finisher feed and basal diet (no added DHA). However, the fish fed the high DHA algae diet were similar to FO with similar DHA as the algal meal, suggesting the possibility of replacing FO in the diet.

9.6 Sustainability and Environmental Performance of SCP and Microbial-Based Systems

Dietary SCP can enhance aquaculture sustainability (Overland et al. 2010; Hua et al. 2019; Sillman et al. 2019). Compared to conventional agriculture, Pikaar et al. (2017) claim that MP or SCP can increase overall nutrient efficiency by 2.5 times, with 3 to 10 times lower nitrogen loss (43% improved protein efficiency). This significant ecological function makes MB, a sustainable third-generation protein source after FM and soy protein (Matassa et al. 2015, 2016; De Vrieze et al. 2019; Sillman et al. 2019). A recent study that linked the absolute planetary boundary to the sustainable environmental performance of MP showed that aerobic HB grown on potato-processing waste in a bioreactor emitted lesser N and P and caused reduced land-use change than FM and SBM, which suggests the sustainability of MP as an alternative to conventional protein sources (Owsianiak et al. 2022). Linder (2019) estimates that by 2050, replacing 10–19% of conventional crop-based protein feed with MP can reduce global cropland area, N loss, and greenhouse gas emissions.

Unlike terrestrial crops (Schlechtriem et al. 2016), microorganisms do not require pesticides or insecticides (Sillman et al. 2019) for cultivation. They demand less space, water, and land than conventional agriculture (Swain et al. 2018) and terrestrial PP production (Matassa et al. 2015; Sillman et al. 2019). In comparison to conventional proteins such as SBM, MP requires 128 times less land and five times less water to produce 1 kg of protein (Matassa et al. 2016; Sillman et al. 2019). Sakarika et al. (2022) reported that MP requires 40,000 less land (0.05 m^2/kg protein vs 2279 m^2/kg protein) and 20 times less water (282 L/kg protein vs 5516 L/kg protein), and higher N efficiency (430 g N consumed/kg N supplied vs 40 g N consumed/kg N supplied) than meat.

Several studies have reported significantly reduced GHG, water, and land requirements with MP from renewable energy sources like the wind (Sillman et al. 2019), electricity (Jourdin et al. 2018), and solar (Matassa et al. 2016; De Vrieze et al. 2019).The production of MP through innovative continuous fermentation culture processes allows high volumetric productivities (3–4 kg MP/m^3 per hour, Matassa et al. 2016), with a physical footprint that is a factor of 1000 smaller than any conventional vegetable protein production system (Matassa et al. 2015). Despite the small amount of land required for FM processing (Matassa et al. 2016), the C footprint analysis shows that MP emits less CO_2 (1.7-tonne CO_2eq/tonne MP) than FM (CO_2 eq/tonne protein). Besides achieving feasible industrial-scale production and cost competitiveness with FM, the final MP product is comparable to FM in terms of EAA profile and overall nutritive value (Overland et al. 2010; Kuzniar et al. 2019). Durigon et al. (2019) found that MBSs require little or no water exchange and have a low environmental impact (Dauda et al. 2018a, b; Liu et al. 2018). While conventional aquaculture ponds require approximately 20,000 L of water per kg of fish or shrimp produced, Martínez-Córdova et al. (2017) reported that the water demand in biofloc systems could be as low as 200 L per kg and that the cost of raising fish in biofloc systems is lower than in conventional RAS systems (Crab et al. 2007).

9.7 Conclusion, Future Perspectives, and Opportunities

Given that future farming systems will have to be increasingly more self-contained, not only in terms of farm biosecurity and potential disease exclusion/impacts but also in terms of water reuse and minimising nutrient discharge, improving the functionality of aqua feeds will be of paramount importance in guiding the long-term sustainable development of the fed fin fish and crustacean aquaculture sector toward the development of a more environmentally friendly and nutrient-sensitive production system. Novel techniques (for example, aerobic/anaerobic fermentation technology, gas bioreactor fermentation, and microbial electrosynthesis, Jourdin et al. 2018; Jones et al. 2020) will be required to up-scale production and improve the nutritional value of SCP feed ingredients. Using anaerobic digestion to exploit the C content of microalgae from high organic load wastewater for MP without dewatering (drying) can reduce the high cost and environmental footprint of microalgae production. Harvesting, dewatering, and lipid extraction from MAB pose challenges due to the high energy requirements. Batch, fed-batch, continuous bioreactors, and semi-continuous cultivation are all examples of anaerobic fermentation (AnF) that can improve the production performance of microalgae, particularly in relation to high-rate sludge systems. Co-cultivation of bacteria and microalgae in bioreactors can reduce energy demand associated with the production process, which could reduce the climate change and ozone depletion impact potential of MP and support the United Nations' sustainable development goals (Owsianiak et al. 2022). Novel approaches like heat shock treatment and alkaline hydrolysis (Sakarika et al. 2022) can mitigate ANF (trypsin inhibitors, heavy metals, nucleic acid, and cell wall contents) associated with low nutritional value and acceptance of SCP (Ahmad et al. 2022). Bioreactors can also remove suspended solids (95–99.5%) and nutrients (>90% for NO_3-, NO_2-, and NH_3) from aquaculture wastewater (Avnimelech et al. 2014). Large-scale biofloc production in external bioreactors (ex situ biofloc) can ensure MP availability and reduce aquaculture's environmental impact.

A good selection of microbes with improved nutritional quality or growth characteristics could improve their efficiencies and reduce the cost of production through metagenomics (Diwan et al. 2021). Metagenomics can be applied to evaluate the potential for isolation and culture of aquaculture-relevant microbial species. Post-genomic and cutting-edge technologies like transcriptomics and shotgun proteomics can provide insights into microbial cellular processes and function (Kumar et al. 2016; Diwan et al. 2021). The application of proteomic techniques, including the gel-based techniques like two-dimensional gel electrophoresis (2-DE or 2D PAGE, Schrama et al. 2018), sequential window acquisition of all theoretical spectra (SWATH) technology (for quantifying and distinguishing strains of MP, Kumar et al. 2016), electrospray ionisation mass spectrophotometry (ESI-MS, Graham et al. 2007), gel-free nano liquid chromatography electrospray ionisation (LC-ESI, Kumar et al. 2016), liquid chromatography coupled to tandem mass spectrophotometry (LC-MS/MS, Timmins-Schifman et al. 2018), label-based isobaric tag for relative and absolute quantitation (iTRAQ, Rodrigues et al. 2017), stable isotope labelling by/with amino acids in cell culture (SILAC, Rodrigues et al. 2017), quantitative real-time polymerase chain reaction (qRT-PCR, for detecting, identifying, and quantifying pathogens, (Kumar et al. 2016), and matrix-assisted laser desorption ionisation time of flight mass spectrophotometry (MALDI-TOF MS, Singhal et al. 2015), will advance knowledge about the physiology and metabolism of microorganisms in aquaculture through changes in proteome (complete set of protein expressed by a genome, tissue, or organism. These methods will also facilitate the rapid identification of mass microbial samples consisting of diverse microorganisms of different strains, species, and genera.

References

Aboseif AM, Flefil NS, Taha MKS, Tahoun UM, Abdel Mola HR, El Haroun E, Van Doan H, Goda AMS-A (2022) Influence of dietary C: N: P ratios on Nile tilapia *Oreochromis niloticus* growth performance and formation of water biotic communities within a biofloc system containment. Aquac Rep 24(4):101136. https://doi.org/10.1016/j.aqrep.2022.101136

Abugrara AM, El-Sayed HS, Zaki MAA, Nour AE-AM (2019) Utilization of *Nannochloropsis oceanica* alga for biodiesel production and the de-lipidated biomass for improving Red tilapia aquaculture. Egypt J Aquatic Biol Fish 23(4):421–436

Acquah C, Ekezie, FG, Udenigwe CC (2021) Potential applications of microalgae-derived proteins and peptides in the food industry. In: Cultured microalgae for the food industry. https://doi.org/10.1016/B978-0-12-821080-2.00011-3

Adel M, Lazado CC, Safari R, Yeganeh S, Zorriehzahra MJ (2017) Aqualase®, a yeast-based in-feed probiotic, modulates intestinal microbiota, immunity and growth of rainbow trout *Oncorhynchus mykiss*. Aquac Res 48:1815–1826

Adeoye AA, Akegbejo-samsons Y, Fawole FJ, Olatunji PO, Muller N, Wan AH, Davies SJ (2021) From waste to feed, dietary utilisation of bacterial protein from fermentation of agricultural wastes in African catfish (*Clarias gariepinus*) production and health. Aquaculture 531:735850. https://doi.org/10.1016/j.aquaculture.2020.35850

Agboola JO, Teuling E, Wierenga PA, Grupen H, Schrama JW (2019) Cell wall disruption: an effective strategy to improve the nutritive quality of microalgae in African catfish (*Clarias gariepinus*). Aquac Nutr 25(4):783–797. https://doi.org/10.1111/anu.12896

Agboola JO, Overland M, Skrede A, Hansen JO (2020) Yeast as major protein-rich ingredient in aquafeeds: a review of the implications for aquaculture production. Rev Aquac 13(2):949–970. https://doi.org/10.1111/raq.12507

Ahmad A, Hassan SW, Banat F (2022) An overview of microalgae biomass as a sustainable aquaculture feed ingredient: food security and circular economy. Bioengineered 13(4): 9521–9547. https://doi.org/10.1080/21655979.2022.2061148

Albrektsen S, Kortet R, Skov PV, Ytteborg E, Gitlesen S, Kleinegris D, Mydland L-T, Hansen JO, Lock E-J, Mørkøre T, James P, Wang X, Whitaker RD, Vang B, Hatlen B, Daneshvar E, Bhatnagar A, Jensen LB, Øverland M (2022) Future feed resources in sustainable salmonid production: a review. Rev Aquac 14:1790–1812. https://doi.org/10.1111/raq.12673

Allen KM, Habte-Tsion HM, Thompson KR, Filer K, Tidwell JH, Kumar V (2019) Freshwater microalgae (*Schizochytrium sp.*) as a substitute to fish oil for shrimp feed. Sci Rep 9:6178. https://doi.org/10.1038/s41598-019-41020-8

Alloul A, Wille M, Lucenti P, Bossier P, Van Stappen G, Vlaeminck SE (2021) Purple bacteria as added-value protein ingredient in shrimp feed: *Litopenaeus vannamei* growth performance, and tolerance against *Vibrio* and ammonia stress. Aquaculture 530:735788. https://doi.org/10.1016/j.aquaculture.2020.735788

Amer SA, Osman A, Al-Gabri NA, Elsayed SAM, El-Rahman GIA, Elabbasy MT, Ahmed SAA, Ibrahim RE (2019) The effect of dietary replacement of fish meal with whey protein concentrates on the growth performance, fish health, and immune status of Nile tilapia Fingerlings, Oreochromis niloticus. Animals 9:1003. https://doi.org/10.3390/ani9121003

Amorim ML, Soares J, Coimbra JSD, Leite MD, Albino LFT, Martins MA (2021) Microalgae proteins: production, separation, isolation, quantification, and application in food and feed. Crit Rev Food Sci Nutr 61(12):1976–2002. https://doi.org/10.1080/10408398.2020.1768046

Ansari FA, Guldhe A, Gupta SK, Rawat I, Bux F (2021) Improving the feasibility of aquaculture feed by using microalgae. Environ Sci Pollut Res 28:43234–43257

Anupama RP (2000) Value-added food: single cell protein. Biotechnol Adv 18:459–479

Asaduzzaman M, Wahab MA, Verdegem MCJ, Huque S, Salam MA, Azim ME (2008) C/N ratio control and substrate addition for periphyton development jointly enhance freshwater prawn *Macrobrachium rosenbergii* production in ponds. Aquaculture 280:117–123

Avnimelech Y, De Scryver P, Emerenciano M, Kuhn D, Ray A, Taw N (2014) A practical guide book, 3rd edn. Avnimelech Y (ed) The World Aquaculture Society, Baton Rouge, LA

Azim ME, Little DC (2008) The bioflocs technology (BFT) in indoor tanks: water quality, bioflocs composition, and growth and welfare of Nile tilapia (*Oreochromis niloticus*). Aquaculture 283: 29–35

Azim ME, Verdegem MCJ, Khatoon H, Wahab MA, van Dam AA, Beveridge MCM (2002) A comparison of fertilization, feeding and three periphyton substrates for increasing fish production in freshwater pond aquaculture in Bangladesh. Aquaculture 212:227–243

Babu DT, Antony SP, Joseph SP, Bright AR, Philip R (2013) Marine yeast *Candida aquaetextoris* S527 as a potential immunostimulant in black tiger shrimp *Penaeus monodon*. J Invertebr Pathol 112:243–252

Badiola M, Basurko OC, Piedrahita R, Hundley P, Mendiola D (2018) Energy use in recirculating aquaculture systems (RAS): a review. Aquac Eng 81:57–70

Bakhshi F, Najdegeramib EH, Manaffarc R, Tukmechid A, Farah KR (2018) Use of different carbon sources for the biofloc system during the grow-out culture of common carp (Cyprinus carpio L.) fingerlings. Aquaculture 484:259–267

Banks M, Johnson R, Giver L, Bryant G, Guo M (2022) Industrial production of microbial protein products. Curr Opin Biotechnol 75:102707. https://doi.org/10.1016/j.copbio.2022.102707

Beal CM, Gerber LM, Thongrod S, Phromkunthong W, Kiron V, Granados J, Archibald I, Greene CH, Huntley ME (2018) Marine microalgae commercial production improves sustainability of global fisheries and aquaculture. Sci Rep 8:15064. https://doi.org/10.1038/s41598-018-33504-10

Bélanger A, Sarker PK, Bureau DP, Chouinard Y, Vandenberg GW (2021) Apparent digestibility of macronutrients and fatty acids from microalgae (*Schizochytrium sp.*) fed to rainbow trout (*Oncorhynchus mykiss*): a potential candidate for fish oil substitution. Animals 11(2):456. https://doi.org/10.3390/ani11020456

Bentzon-Tilia M, Sonnenschein EC, Gram L (2016) Monitoring and managing microbes in aquaculture—towards a sustainable industry. Microb Biotechnol 9:576–584

Bharti V, Pandey PK, Koushlesh SK (2014) Single cell proteins: a novel approach in aquaculture systems. World Aquac: 62–63. www.was.org

Biswas A, Takakuwa F, Yamada S, Matsuda A, Saville RM, Leblanc A, Silverman JA, Sato N, Tanaka H (2020) Methanotroph (*Methylococcus capsulatus*, Bath) bacteria meal as an alternative protein source for Japanese yellowtail, *Seriola quinqueradiata*. Aquaculture 529:735700. https://doi.org/10.1016/j.aquaculture.2020.735700

Bossier P, Ekasari J (2017) Biofloc technology application in aquaculture to support sustainable development goals. Microb Biotechnol 10(5):1012–1016

Boyd CE, McNevin AA (2015) Aquaculture, resource use, and the environment. Wiley. 368pp

Boyd CE, D'Abramo LR, Glencross BD, Huyben DC, Juarez LM, Lockwood GS, McNevin AA, Tacon AGJ, Teletchea F, Tomasso JR Jr, Tucker CS, Valenti C (2019) Achieving sustainable aquaculture: historical and current perspectives and future needs and challenges. J World Aquac Soc 51:578–633

Boyd CE, McNevin AA, Davis RP (2022) The contribution of fisheries and aquaculture to the global protein supply. Food Secur 14(3):805–827. https://doi.org/10.1007/s12571-021-01246-9

Camargo JA, Alonso A (2006) Ecological and toxicological effects of inorganic nitrogen pollution in aquatic ecosystems: a global assessment. Environ Int 32:831–849

Campanati C, Willer D, Schubert J, Aldridge DC (2022) Sustainable intensification of aquaculture through nutrient recycling and circular economies: more fish, less waste, blue growth. Rev Fish Sci Aquac 30(2):143–169

Cardinaletti G, Messina M, Bruno M, Tulli F, Poli BM, Giorgi G, Chini-Zittelli G, Tredici M, Tibaldi E (2018) Effects of graded levels of a blend of *Tisochrysis lutea* and *Tetraselmis suecica* dried biomass on growth and muscle tissue composition of European sea bass (*Dicentrarchus labrax*) fed diets low in fish meal and oil. Aquaculture 485:173–182

Cardona E, Segret E, Cachelou Y, Vanderesse T, Larroquet L, Hermann A, Surget A, Corraze G, Cachelou F, Bobe J, Skiba-Cassy S (2022) Effect of microalgae *Schizochytrium sp.* supplementation in plant diet on reproduction of female rainbow trout (*Oncorhynchus mykiss*): maternal programming impact of progeny. J Anim Sci Biotechnol 13:33. https://doi.org/10.1186/s40104-022-00680-9

Carneiro WF, Castro TFD, Reichel T, Uzeda PL, Palacios CAM, Murgus LDS (2022) Diets containing *Arthrospira platensis* increase growth, modulate lipid metabolism, and reduce oxidative stress in pacu (*Piaractus mesopotamicus*) exposed to ammonia. Aquaculture 547: 737402. https://doi.org/10.1016/jj.aquaculture.2021.737402

Carter CG, Codabaccus MB (2022) Assessing the value of single cell ingredients in aqua feeds. Curr Opin Biotechnol 76:102734. https://doi.org/10.1016/j/copbio.2022.102734

Carvalho Pereira J, Lemoine A, Neubauer P, Junne S (2021) Perspectives for improving circular economy in brackish shrimp aquaculture. Aquac Res 53:1169–1180

Carvalho M, Montero D, Rosenlund G, Fontanillas R, Ginés R, Izquierdo M (2020) Effective complete replacement of fish oil by combining poultry and microalgae oils in practical diets for gilthead sea bream (*Sparus aurata*) fingerlings. Aquaculture 529:735696. https://doi.org/10.1016/j/aquaculture.2020.735696

Carvalho M, Marotta M, Xu H, Geraert P-A, Kaushik S, Montero D, Izquierdo M (2022) Complete replacement of fish oil by three microalgal products rich in n-3 long-chain polyunsaturated fatty acids in early weaning micro diets for gilthead sea bream (*Sparus aurata*). Aquaculture 558: 738354. https://doi.org/10.1016/j.aquaculture.2022.738354

Chang JS, Show PL, Ling TC, Chen CY, Ho SH, Tan CH, Nagarajan D, Phong WN (2017) Photobioreactors. In: Current developments in biotechnology and bioengineering: bioprocesses, bioreactors and controls, pp 313–352. https://doi.org/10.1016/B978-0-444-63663-8.00011-2

Chatvijitkul S, Boyd CE, Davis DA, McNevin AA (2016) Embodied resources in fish and shrimp feeds. J World Aquac Soc 48:7–19

Chavan R, Mutnuri S (2019) Tertiary treatment of domestic wastewater by *Spirulina platensis* integrated with microalgal biorefinery. Biofuels 10:33–44

Chen XQ, Zhao W, Xie SW, Xie JJ, Zhang ZH, Tian LX et al (2019a) Effects of dietary hydrolyzed yeast (*Rhodotorula mucilaginosa*) on growth performance, immune response, antioxidant capacity and histomorphology of juvenile Nile tilapia (*Oreochromis niloticus*). Fish Shellfish Immunol 90:30–39

Chen Y, Sagada G, Xu B, Chao W, Zou F, Ng W, Sun Y, Wang L, Zhong Z, Shao Q (2019b) Partial replacement of fish meal with *Clostridium autoethanogenum* single-cell protein in the diet for juvenile black sea bream (*Acanthopagrus schlegelii*). Aquac Res 51(3):1000–1011

Chen Y, Chi S, Zhang S, Dong X, Yang Q, Liu H, Tan B, Xie S (2022) Evaluation of Methanotroph (*Methylococcus capsulatus,* Bath) bacterial meal on body composition, lipid metabolism, protein synthesis and muscle metabolites of Pacific white shrimp (*Litopenaeus vannamei*). Aquaculture 547:737517. https://doi.org/10.1016/j.aquaculture.2021.737517

Chowdhury AJK, Zakaria NH, Abidin ZAZ, Rahman MM (2016) Phototrophic purple bacteria as feed supplement on the growth, feed utilization and body compositions of Malaysian mahseer *Tor tambroides* Juveniles. Sains Malays 45(1):135–140

Clenfuegos-Martinez K, Monroy-Dosta MDC, Hamdan-Partida A, Hernandez-Vergara MP, Aguirre-Garrido JF, Bustos-Martinez J (2022) Effect of the probiotic *Lactococcus lactis* on the microbial composition in the water and in the gut of freshwater prawn (*Macrobrachium rosenbergii*) cultivate in biofloc. Aquac Res 53:3877–3889. https://doi.org/10.1111/are.15889

Costello C, Cao L, Gelcich S, Cisneros-Mata MA, Free CM, Froehlich HE, Golden CD, Ishimura G, Maier G, Macadam-Somer I, Mangin T, Melnychuk MC, Miyahara M, Moor CLD, Naylor R, Nøstbakken N, Ojea E, O'Reilly E, Parma AM, Plantinga AJ, Thilsted SH, Lubchenco J (2020) The future of food from the sea. Nature 588:95–100. https://doi.org/10.1038/s41586-020-2616-y

Cottrell RS, Blanchard JL, Halpern BS, Metian M, Froehlich HE (2020) Global adoption of novel aquaculture feeds could substantially reduce forage fish demand by 2030. Nat Food 1:301–308

Crab R, Avnimelech Y, Defoirdt T, Bossier P, Verstraete W (2007) Nitrogen removal techniques in aquaculture for a sustainable production. Aquaculture 270:1–14

Dar SA, Bhat RA (2020) Aquatic pollution stress and role of biofilms as environment clean-up technology. In: Qadri H, Bhat RA, Dar GH, Mehmood MA (eds) Freshwater pollution dynamics and remediation. Springer Nature, Singapore, pp 293–318

Dar SA, Lone FA, Dar SA, Bhat RA, Bashir I, Mir SA, Dar ZA (2020) Biofilm: an innovative modern technology for aquatic pollution remediation. In: Bhat RA et al (eds) Bioremediation and biotechnology, vol. 2, pp 207–219. https://doi.org/10.1007/978-3-030-40333-1_12

Dauda AB, Romano N, Ebrahimi M, Karim M, Natrah I, Kamarudin MS, Ekasari J (2017) Different carbon sources affects biofloc volume, water quality and the survival and physiology of African catfish *Clarias gariepinus* fngerlings reared in an intensive biofoc technology system. Fish Sci. https://doi.org/10.1007/s12562-017-1144-7

Dauda AB, Romano N, Chen WW, Natraha I, Kamarudin MS (2018a) Differences in feeding habits influence the growth performance and feeding efficiencies of African catfish (*Clarias gariepinus*) and lemon fin barb hybrid (*Hypsibarbus wetmorei* ♂ × *Barboides go nionotus* ♀) in a glycerol-based biofloc technology system versus a recirculating system. Aquac Eng 82:31–37

Dauda AB, Romano N, Ebrahimi M, Teh JC, Ajadi A, Chong CM, Karim M, Natrah I, Kamarudin MS (2018b) Influence of carbon/nitrogen ratios on biofloc production and biochemical composition and subsequent effects on the growth, physiological status and disease resistance of African catfish (*Clarias gariepinus*) cultured in glycerol-based biofloc systems. Aquaculture 483:120–130

David LH, Campos DWJ, Pinho SM, Romera DM, Garcia F (2021) Growth performance of Nile tilapia reared in cages in a farm dam submitted to a feed reduction strategy in a periphyton-based system. Aquac Res 53(3):1147–1150

De Vrieze J, Verbeecka K, Pikaar I, Boered J, Wijk AV, Rabaey K, Verstraete W (2019) The hydrogen gas bio-based economy and the production of renewable building block 3 chemicals, food and energy. N Biotechnol 55:12–18. https://doi.org/10.1016/j.nbt.2019.09.004

Debbarma R, Meena DK, Biswas P, Meitei MM, Singh SS (2022) Portioning of microbial waste into fish nutrition via frugal biofloc production: a sustainable paradigm for greening of environment. J Clean Prod 334:130246. https://doi.org/10.1016/jclepro.2021.130246

Delamare-Deboutteville J, Batstone DJ, Kawasaki M, Stegman S, Salini M, Tabrett S, Smullen R, Barnes AC, Hülsen T (2019) Mixed culture purple phototrophic bacteria is an effective fishmeal replacement in aquaculture. Water Res X 4:100031. https://doi.org/10.1016/j.wroa.2019.100031

Diwan AD, Harke SN, Krishna G, Panche AN (2021) Aquaculture industry prospective from gut microbiome of fish and shellfish: an overview. J Anim Physiol Anim Nutr 106(2):441–469

Durigon EG, Almeida APG, Jerônimo GT, Baldisserotto B, Emerenciano MGC (2019) Digestive enzymes and parasitology of Nile tilapia juveniles raised in brackish biofloc water and fed with different digestible protein and digestible energy levels. Aquaculture 506:35–41

Ekasari J, Azhar MH, Surawidjaja EH, Nuryati S, De Schryver P, Bossier P (2014a) Immune response and disease resistance of shrimp fed biofloc grown on different carbon sources. Fish Shellfish Immunol 41:332–339

Ekasari J, Angela D, Waluyo SH, Bachtiar T, Surawidjaja EH, Bossier P, De Schryver P (2014b) The size of biofloc determines the nutritional composition and the nitrogen recovery by aquaculture animals. Aquaculture 426:105–111

Ekasari J, Rivandi DR, Firdausi AP, Surawidjaja EH, Zairin M, Bossier P, De Schryver P (2015) Biofloc technology positively affects Nile tilapia (*Oreochromis niloticus*) larvae performance. Aquaculture 441:72–77

Ekpeni LEN, Benyounis KY, Aboderheeba AKM, Nkem-Ekpeni FF, Stokes J, Olabi AG (2015) Yeast: a potential biomass substrate for the production of cleaner energy (biogas). The 6th International Conference on Applied Energy – ICAE2014. Energy Procedia 61:1718–1731

El-Husseiny OM, Hassan MI, El-Haroun ER, Suloma A (2018) Utilization of poultry by-product meal supplemented with L-lysine as fish meal replacer in the diet of African catfish *Clarias gariepinus* (Burchell, 1822). J Appl Aquac 30(1):63–75. https://doi.org/10.1080/10454438.2017.1412844

Engle C, Abramo LR, Slater MJ (2017) Global aquaculture 2025: editorial. J World Aquac Soc 48(1):1–4

Fang X, Zhao J, Wu S, Yu K, Huang J, Ding Y, Hu T, Xiao S, Liu S, Zou J (2022) A two-year measurement of methane and nitrous oxide emissions from freshwater aquaculture ponds: affected by aquaculture species, stocking and waste management. Sci Total Environ 813: 151863. https://doi.org/10.1016/j.scitotenv.2021.151863

FAO (2018) The state of world fisheries and aquaculture 2018-meeting the sustainable development goals. Rome, 227 pp.

FAO (2020) The state of world fisheries and aquaculture 2020: sustainability in action. Rome, 227pp. https://doi.org/10.4060/ca9229en

Fauji H, Budiardi T, Ekasari J (2018) Growth performance and robustness of African catfish *Clarias gariepinus* (Burchell) in biofloc-based nursery production with different stocking densities. Aquac Res 49:1339–1346

Fayeofori GB-M, Bob-Manuel FG (2014) A comparative study of the effect of yeast single cell protein on growth, feed utilization and condition factor of the African catfish *Clarias gariepinus* (Burchell) and tilapia, *Oreochromis niloticus* (Linnaeus) fingerlings. Afr J Agric Res 9:2005–2011

Figueroa-Espinoza J, Rivas-Vega ME, Mariscal-Lopez MDLA, Emerenciano MGC, Martinez-Porchas M, Miranda-Baeza A (2022) Reusing water in a biofloc culture system favours the productive performance of the Nil tilapia (*Oreochromis niloticus*) without affecting the health status. Aquaculture 558:738363. https://doi.org/10.1016/j.aquaculture.2022.738363

Frost and Sullivan (2018) Emerging protein sources for fish feed. Frost and Sullivan

Fry JP, Love DC, MacDonald GK, West PC, Engstrom PM, Nachman KE, Lawrence RS (2016) Environmental health impacts of feeding crops to farmed fish. Environ Int 91:201–214

Gamble MM, Sarker PK, Kapuscinski AR, Kelson S, Fitzgerald DS, Schelling B, De Souza AVB, Tsukui T (2021) Toward environmentally sustainable aquafeeds: managing phosphorus discharge from Nile tilapia (*Oreochromis niloticus*) aquaculture with microalgae-supplemented diets. Elem Sci Anth 9:1. https://doi.org/10.1525/elementa.2020.00170

Garcia F, Romera DM, Sousa NS, Paiva-Ramos I, Onaka EM (2016) The potential of periphyton-based cage culture of Nile tilapia in a Brazilian reservoir. Aquaculture 464:229–235

Garcia F, Sabbag OJ, Kimpara JM, Romera DM, Sousa NS, Onaka EM, Ramos IP (2017) Periphyton-based cage culture of Nile tilapia: an interesting model for small-scale farming. Aquaculture 479:838–844

Garibay-Valdez E, Martínez-Córdova LR, Vargas-Albores F, GollasGalván T, Lago-Leston A, Calderón K, Martínez-Porchas M (2019) Biofilm consumption shapes the intestinal microbiota of shrimp (*Penaeus vannamei*). Aquac Nutr 25:427–435

Gasco L, Biasato I, Dabbou S, Schiavone A, Gai F (2019) Animals fed insect-based diets: state-of-the-art on digestibility, performance and product quality. Animals 9(4):170. https://doi.org/10.3390/ani9040170

Gephart JA, Golden CD, Asche F, Belton B, Brugere C, Froehlich HE, Fry JP, Halpern BS, Hicks CC, Jones RC, Klinger DH, Little DC, McCauley DJ, Thilsted SH, Troell M, Allison EH (2020) Scenarios for global aquaculture and its role in human nutrition. Rev Fish Sci Aquac 29:122–138. https://doi.org/10.1080/23308249.2020.1782342

Glencross BD, Huyben D, Schrama JW (2020) The application of single-cell ingredients in aquaculture feeds—a review. Fishes 5:22. https://doi.org/10.3390/fishes5030022

Goda AA-S, Srour TM, Omar E, Mansour AT, Baromh MZ, Mohamed SA, El-Haroun E, Davies SJ (2019) Appraisal of a high-protein distiller's dried grain (DDG) in diets for European sea bass, *Dicentrarchus labrax* fingerlings on growth performance, haematological status and related gut histology. Aquac Nutr 25(4):808–816. https://doi.org/10.1111/anu.12898

Goncalves AL, Pires JCM, Simoes M (2017) A review on the use of microalgal consortia for waste water treatment. Algal Res 24(Part B):403–415. https://doi.org/10.1016/j.algal.2016.11.008

Guimaraes AM, Schleder DD, Nagata M, Nóbrega RO, Fracalossi DM, Seiffert WQ, Vieira FDN (2019) *Aurantiochytrium sp.* meal can replace fish oil in practical diets for the juvenile Pacific white shrimp. Aquac Nutr 25:798–807

Gullian-Klanian M, Díaz MD, Solís MJS, Aranda J, Moral PM (2020) Effect of the content of microbial proteins and the poly-β-hydroxybutyric acid in biofloc on the performance and health of Nile tilapia (*Oreochromis niloticus*) fingerlings fed on a protein-restricted diet. Aquaculture 519:734872. https://doi.org/10.1016/j.aquaculture.2019.734872

Gumus E, Aydin B, Kanyilmaz M (2016) Growth and feed utilization of goldfish (Carassius auratus) fed graded levels of brewers yeast (Saccharomyces cerevisiae). Iran J Fish Sci 15 (3):1124–1133

Guo H, Huang L, Hu S, Chen C, Huang X, Liu W, Wang S, Zhu Y, Zhao Y, Zhang D (2020) Effects of carbon/nitrogen ratio on growth, intestinal microbiota and metabolome of shrimp (*Litopenaeus vannamei*). Front Microbiol 11:652. https://doi.org/10.3389/fmicb.2020.00652

Haas S, Bauer JL, Adakli A, Meyer S, Lippemeier S, Schwarz K, Schulz C (2015) Marine microalgae *Pavlova viridis* and *Nannochloropsis sp.* as n-3 PUFA source in diets for juvenile European sea bass (*Dicentrarchus labrax* L.). Environ Biol Fish 28:1011–1021

Hajiahmadian M, Vajargah MF, Farsani HG, Chorchi MM (2012) Effect of *Spirulina platensis* meal as feed additive on growth performance and survival rate in golden barb fish, *Punius gelius* (Hamilton, 1822). J Fish Int 7:61–64

Hamidoghli A, Yun H, Won S, Kim S, Farris NW, Bai SC (2018) Evaluation of a single-cell protein as a dietary fish meal substitute for whiteleg shrimp *Litopenaeus vannamei*. Fish Sci. https://doi.org/10.1007/s12562-018-1275-5

Han P, Lu Q, Fan L, Zhou W (2019) A review on the use of microalgae for sustainable aquaculture. Appl Sci 9:2377. https://doi.org/10.3390/app9112377

Hansen JO, Lagos L, Lei P, Reveco-Urzuaa FP, Morales-Lange B, Hansen LD, Schiavone M, Mydland LT, Arntzen MO, Mercado L, Benicio RT, Øverland M (2021) Down-stream processing of Baker's yeast (*Saccharomyces cerevisiae*)—effect on nutrient digestibility and immune response in Atlantic salmon (*Salmo salar*). Aquaculture 530:535707. https://doi.org/10.1016/j.aquaculture.2020.735707

Hao Q, Xia R, Zhang Q, Xie Y, Ran C, Yang Y, Zhou W, Chu F, Zhang X, Wang Y, Zhang Z, Xhou Z (2022) Partially replacing dietary fish meal by *Saccharomyces cerevisiae* improve growth performance, immunity, disease resistance, composition and function of intestinal microbiota in channel catfish (*Ictalurus punctatus*). Fish Shellfish Immunol 125:220–229

Hossain MA, Al-Adul-Elah K, Alzalzalah ISAA, Alnuiami S (2022) High DHA algae meal as cost-effective alternative to high DHA fish oil in finisher feed for sobaity sea bream (*Sparidentex hasta*). Anim Feed Sci Technol 284:115209. https://doi.org/10.1016/j.anifeedsci.2022.115209

Hua K, Cobcroft JM, Cole A, Condon K, Jerry DR, Mangott A, Praeger C, Vucko MJ, Zeng C, Zhenger K, Strugnell JM (2019) The future of aquatic protein: implication for protein sources in aquaculture diets. One Earth 1(3):316–329. https://doi.org/10.1016/j.oneear.2019.10.018

Huang HH (2020) Novel biofloc technology (bft) for ammonia assimilation and reuse in aquaculture *in situ*. In: Lu Q, Serajuddin M (eds) Emerging technologies, environment and research for sustainable aquaculture. Intech Open, London, pp 3–22. https://doi.org/10.5772/intechopen.82887

Jach ME, Serefko A, Ziaja M, Kieliszek M (2022) Yeast protein as an easily accessible food source. Metabolites 12:63. https://doi.org/10.3390/metabo12010063

Jones SW, Karpol A, Friedman S, Maru BT, Tracy BT (2020) Recent advances in single cell protein use as a feed ingredient in aquaculture. Curr Opin Biotechnol 61:189–197

Jourdin L, Raes SMT, Buisman CJN, Strik PBTB (2018) Critical biofilm growth throughout unmodified carbon felts allows continuous bioelectrochemical chain from CO_2 up to caproate at high current density. Front Energy Res 6:7. https://doi.org/10.3389/fenrg.2018.00007

Ju ZY, Forster I, Conquest L, Dominy W, Kuo WC, Horgen FD (2008) Determination of microbial community structures of shrimp floc cultures by biomarkers and analysis of floc amino acid profiles. Aquac Res 39:118–133

Jung J-Y, Damusaru JH, Park Y, Kim K, Seong M, Je HW, Kim S, Bai SC (2017) Autotrophic biofloc technology system (ABFT) using *Chlorella vulgaris* and *Scenedesmus obliquus* positively affects performance of Nile tilapia (*Oreochromis niloticus*). Algal Res 27:259–264

Karimi S, Soofiani NM, Mahboubi A, Taherzadeh MJ (2019) Use of organic wastes and industrial by-products to produce filamentous fungi with potential as aqua-feed ingredients. Sustainability 10:3296. https://doi.org/10.3390/su10093296

Katerina K, Berge GM, Turid M, Aleksei K, Grete B, Trine Y, Mats C, John S, Bente R (2020) Microalgal *Schizochytrium limacinum* biomass improves growth and filet quality when used long-term as a replacement for fish oil, in modern salmon diets. Front Mar Sci 7:57. https://doi.org/10.3389/fmars.2020.00057

Kawsar MA, Alam MT, Pandit D, Rahman MM, Mia M, Talukdar A, Sumon TA (2022) Status of disease prevalence, drugs and antibiotics usage in pond-based aquaculture at Narsingdi district, Bangladesh: a major public health concern and strategic appraisal for mitigation. Heliyon 8(3): e09060. https://doi.org/10.1016/j.heliyon.2022.e09060

Kaya D, Genc MA, Aktas M, Yavuzcan H, Ozmen O, Genc E (2019) Effect of biofloc technology on growth of speckled shrimp, *Metapenaeus monoceros* (Fabricus) in different feeding regimes. Aquac Res 50(10):2760–2768

Kohal MN, Fereidouni AE, Firouzbakhsh F, Hayati I (2018) Effects of dietary incorporation of *Arthrospira* (*Spirulina*) *platensis* meal on growth, survival, body composition, and reproductive performance of red cherry shrimp *Neocaridina davidi* (Crustacea, Atyidae) over successive spawnings. J Appl Phycol 30:431–443

Kok B, Malcorps W, Tlusty MF, Eltholth MM, Auchterlonie NA, Little DC, Harmsen R, Newton RW, Davies SJ (2020) Fish as feed: using economic allocation to quantify the Fish In: Fish Out ratio of major fed aquaculture species. Aquaculture 528:735474. https://doi.org/10.1016/j.aquaculture.2020

Krogdahl A, Penn M, Thorsen J, Refstie S, Bakke AM (2010) Important antinutrients in plant feedstuffs for aquaculture: an update on recent findings regarding responses in salmonids. Aquac Res 41:33–44

Kumar S, Anand PSS, De D, Deo AD, Ghoshal TK, Sundaray JK, Ponniah AG, Jithendran KP, Raja RA, Biswas G, Lalitha N (2015) Effects of biofloc under different carbon sources and protein levels on water quality, growth performance and immune responses in black tiger shrimp *Penaeus monodon* (Fabricius, 1978). Aquac Res 48(3):1168–1182. https://doi.org/10.1111/are.12958

Kumar G, Hummel K, Ahrens M, Menanteau-Ledouble S, Welch TJ, Eisenacher M, Razzazi-Fazeli E, El-Matbouli M (2016) Shotgun proteomic analysis of *Yersinia ruckeri* strains under normal and iron-limited conditions. Vet Res 47:100. https://doi.org/10.1186/s13567-016-0384-3

Kuzniar A, Furtak K, Włodarczyk K, Stepniewska Z, Wolinska A (2019) Methanotrophic bacterial biomass as potential mineral feed ingredients for animals. Int J Environ Res Public Health 16: 2674. https://doi.org/10.3390/ijerph16152674

Langeland M, Vidakovic A, Vielma J, Lindberg JE, Kiessling A, Lundh T (2016) Digestibility of microbial and mussel meal for Arctic charr (*Salvelinus alpinus*) and Eurasian perch (*Perca fluviatilis*). Aquac Nutr 22:485–495

Lara G, Honda M, Poersch L, Wasielesky W Jr (2017) The use of biofilm and different feeding rates in biofloc culture system: the effects in shrimp growth parameters. Aquac Int 25:1959–1970. https://doi.org/10.1007/s10499-017-0151-0

Lee S, Park C-O, Choi W, Bae J, Kim J, Choi S, Katya K, Kim K-W, Bai SC (2022) Partial substitution of fish oil with microalgae (*Schizochytrium* sp.) can improve growth performance, non-specific immunity and disease resistance in rainbow trout, *Oncorhynchus mykiss*. Animals 12:1220. https://doi.org/10.3390/ani12091220

Leeper A, Ekmay R, Knobloch S, Skírnisdóttir S, Varunjikar M, Dubois M, Smárason BO, Árnason J, Koppe W, Benhaïm D (2022) Torula yeast in the diet of Atlantic salmon *Salmo salar* and the impact on growth performance and gut microbiome. Sci Rep 12:567. https://doi.org/10.1038/s41598-021-04413-2

Li Z, Wang G, Yu E, Zhang K, Yu D, Gong W, Xie J (2019) Artificial substrata increase pond farming density of grass carp (*Ctenopharyngodon Idella*) by increasing the bacteria that participate in nitrogen and phosphorus cycles in pond water. PeerJ 7:e7906. https://doi.org/10.7717/peerj.7906

Liao H, Liu P, Yongyan D, Zhang W, Pan C, Jia Y, Long F, Tang H (2022) Feeding effects of low-level fish meal replacements by algal meals of *Schizochytrium limacinum* and *Nannochloropsis salina* on largemouth bass (*Micropterus salmoides*). Aquaculture 557: 738311. https://doi.org/10.1016/j.aquaculture.2022.738311

Linder T (2019) Making the case for edible microorganisms as an integral part of a more sustainable and resilient food production system. Food Secur 11:265–278. https://doi.org/10.1007/s12571-019-00912-3

Liu G, Ye Z, Liu D, Zhao J, Sivaramasamya E, Deng Y, Zhu S (2018) Influence of stocking density on growth, digestive enzyme activities, immune responses, antioxidant of *Oreochromis niloticus* fingerlings in biofloc systems. Fish Shellfish Immunol 81:416–422

Luo Z, Hu S, Chen D (2018) The trends of aquacultural nitrogen budget and its environmental implications in China. Sci Rep 8:10877. https://doi.org/10.1038/s41598-018-29214-y. pp. 1–9

Ma K, Chen S, Wu Y, Ma Y, Qiao H, Fan J, Wu H (2022) Dietary supplementation with microalgae enhances the zebrafish growth performance by modulating immune status and gut microbiota. Appl Microbiol Biotechnol 106:773–788

Mahmoud E, El-Sayed B, Mahsoub Y, El-Murr A, Neamat-Allah A (2020) Effect of *Chlorella vulgaris* enriched diet on growth performance, hemato-immunological responses, antioxidant and transcriptomics profile disorders caused by deltamethrin toxicity in Nile tilapia (*Oreochromis niloticus*). Fish Shellfish Immunol 102:422–429

Maizatul AY, Mohamed RMS, Al-Gheethi A, Amir HMK (2017) An overview of the utilization of microalgae biomass derived from nutrient cycling of wet market waste water and slaughterhouse wastewater. Int Aquat Res 9(2):177–193

Makkar HPS, Tran G, Heuze V, Ankers P (2014) State-of-the-art on use of insects as animal feed. Anim Feed Sci Technol 197:1–33. https://doi.org/10.1016/j.anifeedsci.2014.07.008

Malcorps W, Kok B, Land MV, Fritz M, Doren DV, Servin K, Heijden PV, Palmer R, Auchterlonie NA, Rietkerk M, Santos MJ, Davies SJ (2019) The sustainability conundrum of fish meal substitution by plant ingredients in shrimp feeds. Sustainability 11:1212. https://doi.org/10.3390/su11041212

Maliwat GC, Velasquez S, Robil JL, Chan M, Traifalgar RF, Tayamen M, Ragaza JA (2017) Growth and immune response of giant freshwater prawn *Macrobrachium rosenbergii* (De Man) postlarvae fed diets containing *Chlorella vulgaris* (Beijerinck). Aquac Res 48:1666–1676

Martiınez-Cordova LR, Mauricio Emerenciano MGC, Miranda-Baeza A, Martiınez-Porchas M (2014) Microbial-based systems for aquaculture of fish and shrimp: an updated review. Rev Aquac 6:1–18

Martin AM, Goddard S, Bemibster P (1993) Production of *Candida utilis* biomass as aquaculture feed. J Sci Food Agric 61:363–370

Martínez-Córdova LR, Martínez-Porchas M, Emerenciano MGC, Miranda-Baeza A, Gollas-Galván T (2017) From microbes to fish the next revolution in food production. Crit Rev Biotechnol 37(3):287–295. https://doi.org/10.3109/07388551.2016.1144043

Matassa S, Boon N, Verstraete W (2015) Resource recovery from used water: the manufacturing abilities of hydrogen-oxidizing bacteria. Water Res 68:467–478. https://doi.org/10.1016/j.watres.2014.10.028

Matassa S, Boon N, Pikaar I, Verstraete W (2016) Microbial protein: future sustainable food supply route with low environmental footprint. Microb Biotechnol 9(5):568–575. https://doi.org/10.1111/1751-7915.12369

Miao L, Wang C, Adyel TM, Zhao J, Yan N, Wu J, Hou J (2021) Periphytic biofilm formation on natural and artificial substrates: comparison of microbial compositions, interactions, and functions. Front Microbiol 12:684903. https://doi.org/10.3389/fmicb.2021.684903

Muthoka M, Ogello EO, Ouma H, Obiero K (2021) Periphyton technology enhances growth performance and delays prolific breeding of Nile tilapia, *Oreochromis niloticus* (Linnaeus, 1758), juveniles. Asian Fish Sci 34:290–300

Najdegerami EH, Bakhshi F, Lakani FB (2015) Effects of biofloc on growth performance, digestive enzyme activities and liver histology of common carp (*Cyprinus carpio* L.) fingerlings in zero-water exchange system. Fish Physiol Biochem 42(2):457–465. https://doi.org/10.1007/s10695-015-0151-9

Nasseri AT, Rasoul-Amini S, Morowvat MH, Ghasemi Y (2011) Single cell protein: production and process. Am J Food Technol 6(2):103–116

Naylor RL, Hardy RW, Buschmann AH, Bush SR, Cao L, Klinger DH, Little DC, Lubchenco J, Shumway SE, Troell M (2021) A 20-year retrospective review of global aquaculture. Nature 591:551–573

Nevejan N, De Schryver P, Wille M et al (2016) Bacteria as food in aquaculture: do they make a difference? Rev Aquac 10(1):180–212. https://doi.org/10.1111/raq.12155

Olvera-Novoa MA, Domnguez-Cen LJ, Olivera-Castillo L, Martínez-Palacios CA (1998) Effect of the use of the microalga *Spirulina maxima* as fish meal replacement in diets for tilapia, *Oreochromis mossambicus* (Peters), fry. Aquac Res 29:709–715

Olvera-Novoa MA, Martinez-Palacios AA, Olivera- Castillo L (2002) Utilization of torula yeast (*Candida utilits*) as a protein source in diets for tilapia (*Oreochromis niloticus*) Peters fry. Aquac Nutr 8(4):257–264

Ortiz-Estrada AM, Gollas-Galván T, Martínez-Córdova LR, BurgosHernández A, Scheuren-Acevedo SM, Emerenciano M, Martínez-Porchas M (2019) Diversity and bacterial succession of a phototrophic biofilm used as complementary food for shrimp raised in a super-intensive culture. Aquac Int 27:581–596

Overland M, Skrede A (2016) Yeast derived from lignocellulosic biomass as a sustainable feed resource for use in aquaculture. J Sci Food Agric 97(3):733–742. https://doi.org/10.1002/jsfa.8007

Overland M, Tauson A-H, Shearer K, Skrede A (2010) Evaluation of methane-utilising bacteria products as feed ingredients for monogastric animals. Arch Anim Nutr 64:171–189. https://doi.org/10.1080/17450391003691534

Overland M, Karlsson A, Mydland LT, Romarheim OH, Skrede A (2013) Evaluation of *Candida utilis, Kluyveromyces marxianus* and *Saccharomyces cerevisiae* yeasts as protein sources in diets for Atlantic salmon (*Salmo salar*). Aquaculture 402–403:1–7

Owsianiak M, Pusateri V, Zamalloa C, de Gussem E, Verstraete W, Ryberg M, Valverde-Perez B (2022) Performance of second-generation microbial protein used as aquaculture feed in relation to planetary boundaries. Resour Conserv Recycl 180:106158. https://doi.org/10.1016/j.resconrec.2022.106158

Pacheco D, Rocha AC, Pereira L, Verdelhos T (2020) Microalgae water bioremediation: trends and hot topics. Appl Sci 10:1886. https://doi.org/10.3390/app10051886

Patnaik R, Singh NK, Bagchi SK, Rao PS, Mallick N (2019) Utilization of *Scenedesmus obliquus* protein as a replacement of commercially- available fish meal under an algae refinery approach. Front Microbiol 10:2114. https://doi.org/10.3389/fmicb.2019.02114

Pikaar I, Matassa S, Rabaey K, Bodirsky BL, Popp A, Herrero M, Verstraete W (2017) Microbes and the next nitrogen revolution. Environ Sci Technol 51(13):7297–7303. https://doi.org/10.1021/acs.est.7b00916

Porchas-Cornejo MA, Vargas-Albores F, Martnez-Porchas M (2017) What is yet to e known about microbial-based systems for aquaculture? J Aquac Mar Biol 5(1):00108. https://doi.org/10.15406/jamb.2017.05.00108

Radhakrishnan S, Saravana BP, Seenivasan C, Muralisankar T (2015) Effect of dietary replacement of fishmeal with Chlorella vulgaris on growth performance, energy utilization and digestive enzymes in Macrobrachium rosenbergii postlarvae. Int J Fish Aquat 7(5):62–70

Ragasa C, Agyakwah SK, Asmah R, Mensah ET-D, Amewu S, Oyih M (2022a) Accelerating pond aquaculture development and resilience beyond COVID: ensuring food and jobs in Ghana. Aquaculture 547:737476. https://doi.org/10.1016/j.aquaculture.2021.73746

Ragasa C, Charo-Karisa H, Rurangwa E, Tran N, Shikuku KM (2022b) Sustainable aquaculture development in sub-Saharan Africa. Nat Food 3:92–93

Raji AA, Jimoh WA, Bakar NHA, Taufek NHM, Muin H, Alias Z, Milow P, Razak SA (2020) Dietary use of *Spirulina* (*Arthrospira*) and *Chlorella* instead of fish meal on growth and digestibility of nutrients, amino acids and fatty acids by African catfish. J Appl Phycol 32: 1763–1770. https://doi.org/10.1007/s10811-020-02070-y

Rimoldi S, Gini E, Koch JFA, Iannini F, Brambilla F, Terova G (2020) Effects of hydrolyzed fish protein and autolyzed yeast as substitutes of fish meal in the gilthead sea bream (*Sparus aurata*) diet, on fish intestinal microbiome. Vet Res 16:118. https://doi.org/10.1186/s12917-020-02335-1

Ritala A, Hakkinen ST, Toivari M, Wiebe MG (2017) Single cell protein: state-of-the-art industrial landscape and patents. Front Microbiol 8:2009. https://doi.org/10.3389/fmicb.2017.02009

Rodrigues PM, Campos A, Kuruvilla J, Schrama D, Cristobal S (2017) Proteomics in aquaculture: quality and safety. In: Colgrave ML (ed) Proteomics in food science, from farm to fork. Elsevier, London, pp 279–290. https://doi.org/10.1016/B978-0-12-804007-2.00017-5

Romarheim OH, Landsverk T, Mydland LT, Skrede A, Overland M (2013) Cell wall fractions from *Methylococcus capsulatus* prevent soybean meal-induced enteritis in Atlantic salmon (*Salmo salar*). Aquaculture 402:13–18

Roy SS, Pal R (2014) Microalgae in aquaculture: a review with special references to nutritional value and fish dietetics. Proc Zool Soc 68:1–8

Roy SS, Chaudhuri A, Mukherjee S, Home Chauduri S, Pal R (2011) Complete algae supplementation in nutrition of *Oreochromis mossambicus*. J Algal Biomass Util 2(1):10–20

Sahlmann C, Djordjevic B, Lagos L, Mydland LT, Morales-Lange B, Hansena JO, Ånestad R, Mercado L, Bjelanovic M, Press CM, Overland M (2019) Yeast as a protein source during smoltification of Atlantic salmon (*Salmo salar* L.), enhances performance and modulates health. Aquaculture 513:734396. https://doi.org/10.1016/j.aquaculture.2019.734396

Saikia SK, Das DN (2014) Sustainable aquaculture: agro-ecological role of periphyton in ricefish farming. Rev Aquac 6:1–15

Sakarika M, Ganigué R, Rabaey K (2022) Methylotrophs: from C1 compounds to food. Curr Opin Biotechnol 75:102685. https://doi.org/10.1016/j.copbio.2022.102685

Sar T, Harirchi S, Pandey MA, Taherzadeh MJ (2022) Potential utilization of dairy industries by-products and wastes through microbial processes: a critical review. Sci Total Environ 810: 152253. https://doi.org/10.1016/j.scitotenv.2021.152253

Sarker PK, Gamble MM, Kelson S, Kapuscinski AR (2016) Nile tilapia (*Oreochromis niloticus*) show high digestibility of lipid and fatty acids from marine *Schizochytrium sp.* and of protein and essential amino acids from freshwater *Spirulina sp.* feed ingredients. Aquac Nutr 22:109–119

Sarker PK, Kapuscinski AR, McKuin B, Fitzgerald DS, Nash HM, Greenwood C (2020) Microalgae-blend tilapia feed eliminates fshmeal and fsh oil, improves growth, and is cost viable. Sci Rep 10:19328. https://doi.org/10.1038/s41598-020-75289-x

Schlechtriem C, Pucher J, Michalski B (2016) Dietary burden calculations relating to fish metabolism studies. J Sci Food Agric 96:1415–1419

Shah MR, Lutzu GA, Alam A, Sarker P, Chowdhury MAK, Parsaeimehr A, Lian Y, Daroch M (2018) Microalgae in aqua feeds for a sustainable aquaculture industry. J Appl Phycol 30:197–213. https://doi.org/10.1007/s10811-017-1234-z

Sharif M, Zafar MH, Aqib AI, Saeed M, Farag MR, Alagawany M (2021) Single cell protein: sources, mechanism of production, nutritional value and its uses in aquaculture nutrition. Aquaculture 531:735885. https://doi.org/10.1016/j.aquaculture.2020.735885

Shi X, Chen F, Chen G-H, Pan Y-X, Zhu X-M, Liu X, Luo Z (2017) Fish meal can be totally replaced by a mixture of rapeseed meal and *Chlorella* meal in diets for crucian carp (*Carassius auratus gibelio*). Aquac Res 48(11):5481–5489

Shurson CG (2018) Yeast and yeast derivatives in feed additives and ingredients: sources, characteristics, animal responses, and quantification methods. Anim Feed Sci Technol 235:60–76

Sillman J, Nygren L, Kahiluoto H, Ruuskanen V, Tamminen A, Bajamundib C, Nappa M, Wuokko M, Lindha T, Vainikka P, Pitkänen JP, Ahola J (2019) Bacterial protein for food and feed generated via renewable energy and direct air capture of CO_2: can it reduce land and water use? Global Food Secur 22:25–32

Singhal N, Kumar M, Kanaujia PK, Virdi JS (2015) MALDI-TOF mass spectrometry: an emerging technology for microbial identification and diagnosis. Front Microbiol 6:791. https://doi.org/10.3389/fmicb.2015.00791

Skalli A, Firmino JP, Andree KB, Salomón R, Estévez A, Puig P, Sabater-Martínez M, Hechavarria T, Gisbert E (2020) The inclusion of the microalga *Scenedesmus sp.* in diets for rainbow trout, *Onchorhynchus mykiss*, juveniles. Animals 10:1656. https://doi.org/10.3390/ani10091656

Skrede A, Mydland L, Ahlstrøm Ø, Reitan K, Gislerød H, Overland M (2011) Evaluation of microalgae as sources of digestible nutrients for monogastric animals. J Anim Feed Sci 20: 131–142

Sørensen M, Berge GM, Reitan KI, Ruyter B (2016) Microalga *Phaeodactylum tricornutum* in feed for Atlantic salmon (*Salmo salar*)—effect on nutrient digestibility, growth and utilization of feed. Aquaculture 460:116–123

Spalvins K, Vamza I, Blumberga B (2019) Single cell oil production from waste biomass: review of applicable industrial by-products. Environ Clim Technol 23(2):325–337. https://doi.org/10.2478/rtuect-2019-0071

Stoneham TR, Kuhn DD, Taylor DP, Neilson AP, Smith SA, Gatlin DM III, Chu HSS, O'Keefe SF (2019) Production of omega-3 enriched tilapia through dietary algae meal or fish oil. PLoS One 13(4):e0194241. https://doi.org/10.1371/journal.pone.0194241

Supono HJ, Prayitno SB, Darmanto YS (2014) White shrimp (*Litopenaeus vannamei*) culture using heterotrophic aquaculture system on nursery phase. Int J Waste Resour 4:1–4. https://doi.org/10.4172/2252-5211.1000142

Swain M, Blomqvista L, McNamara J, Ripple WJ (2018) Reducing the environmental impact of global diets. Sci Total Environ 610–611:1207–1209

Tacon AGJ, Metian M (2018) Food matters: fish, income, and food supply—a comparative analysis. Rev Fish Sci Aquac 26(1):15–28

Tammam MS, Wassef EA, Toutou MM, El-Sayed AFM (2020) Combined effects of surface area of periphyton substrates and stocking density on growth performance, health status, and immune response of Nile tilapia (*Oreochromis niloticus*) produced in cages. J Appl Phycol 32(5): 3419–3428

Teixeira LV, Moutinho LF, Romao-Dumaresq AS (2018) Gas fermentation of C1 feedstocks: commercialization status and future prospects. Biofuels Bioprod Biorefin 12(6):1105–1117. https://doi.org/10.1002/bbb

Teuling E, Schrama JW, Gruppen H et al (2017) Effect of cell wall characteristics on algae nutrient digestibility in Nile tilapia (*Oreochromis niloticus*) and African catfish (*Clarias gariepinus*). Aquaculture 479:490–500

Teuling E, Wierenga PA, Agboola JO, Gruppen H, Schrama JW (2019) Cell wall disruption increases bioavailability of *Nannochloropsis gaditana* nutrients for juvenile Nile tilapia (*Oreochromis niloticus*). Aquaculture 499:269–282

Tibaldi E, Zittelli GC, Parisi G, Bruno M, Giorgi G, Tulli F, Venturini S, Tredici M, Poli B (2015) Growth performance and quality traits of European sea bass (D. labrax) fed diets including increasing levels of freeze-dried Isochrysis sp.(T-ISO) biomass as a source of protein and n-3 long chain PUFA in partial substitution of fish derivatives. Aquaculture 440:60–68

Tibbetts SM, Patelakis SJJ (2022) Apparent digestibility coefficients (ADCs) of intact-cell marine microalgae meal (*Pavlova* sp. 459) for juvenile Atlantic salmon (*Salmo salar* L.). Aquaculture 546:737236. https://doi.org/10.1016/j.aquaculture.2021.737236

Tibbetts SM, Mannb J, Dumas A (2017) Apparent digestibility of nutrients, energy, essential amino acids and fatty acids of juvenile Atlantic salmon (*Salmo salar* L.) diets containing whole-cell or cell-ruptured *Chlorella vulgaris* meals at five dietary inclusion levels. Aquaculture 481:25–39

Timmins-Schifman E, Mikan MP, Ting YS, Harvey HR, Nunn BL (2018) MS analysis of a dilution series of bacteria: phytoplankton to improve detection of low abundance bacterial peptides. Sci Rep 8:9276. https://doi.org/10.1038/s41598-018-27650-4

Tinh TH, Momoh TA, Kokou F, Hai TN, Schrama JW, Verreth JAJ, Verdegem MCJ (2021) Effects of carbohydrate addition methods on Pacific white shrimp (*Litopenaeus vannamei*). Aquaculture 543:736890. https://doi.org/10.1016/j.aquaculture.2021.736890

Upadhyaya S, Tiwari S, Arora NK, Singh DP (2016) Microbial protein: a valuable component for future food security. In: Singh JS, Singh DP (eds) Microbes and environmental management. Studium Press, Houston. https://doi.org/10.13140/RG.2.1.1775.8801

Vasanth G, Viswanath K, Kulkarni A, Dahle D, Lokesh J, Kitani YA (2015) Microbial feed additive abates intestinal inflammation in Atlantic salmon. Front Immunol 6:409. https://doi.org/10.3389/fimmu.2015.00409

Viau VE, Marciano A, Iriel A, Greco LSL (2016) Assessment of a biofilm-based culture system within zero water exchange on water quality and on survival and growth of the freshwater shrimp *Neocaridina heteropoda heteropoda*. Aquac Res 47:2528–2542

Viau VE, Pérez JG, Tomas AL, Fracas PA, Veira FB, Vatnick I, Greco LSL (2020) Breeding and life cycle of the ornamental freshwater shrimp *Neocaridina davidi* in a biofilm-based culture system. Aquac Res 51(9):3847–3864

Vidakovic A, Huyben D, Sundh H, Nyman A, Vielma J, Passoth V, Kiessling A, Lundh T (2019) Growth performance, nutrient digestibility and intestinal morphology of rainbow trout (*Oncorhynchus mykiss*) fed graded levels of the yeasts *Saccharomyces cerevisiae* and *Wickerhamomyces anomalus*. Aquac Nutr 26(2):275–286. https://doi.org/10.1111/anu.12988

Waite R, Beveridge MCM, Brummett R, Castine S, Chaiyawannakarn N, Kaushik S, Mungkung R, Nawapakpilai S, Phillips M (2014) Improving productivity and environmental performance of aquaculture: installment 5 of "creating a sustainable food future". World Resources Institute, Washington, DC, pp 1–60. https://doi.org/10.5657/FAS.2014.0001

Wang GJ, Yu EM, Xie J, Yu DG, Li ZF, Luo W, Qiu LJ, Zheng ZL (2015) Effect of C/N ratio on water quality in zero-water exchange tanks and the biofloc supple mentation in feed on the growth performance of crucian carp *Carassius auratus*. Aquaculture 443:98–104. https://doi.org/10.1016/j.aquaculture.2015.03.015

Wang C, Chuprom J, Wang Y, Fu L (2019) Beneficial bacteria for aquaculture: nutrition, bacteriostasis and immunoregulation. J Appl Microbiol 128:28–40

Wang Q, Ayiku S, Liu H, Tan B, Dong X, Chi S, Yang Q, Zhang S, Zhou W (2022a) Effects of dietary ESTAQUA® yeast culture supplementation on growth, immunity, intestinal microbiota and disease-resistance against *Vibrio harveyi* in hybrid grouper (♀*Epinephelus fuscoguttatus* × ♂*E. lanceolatus*). Aquac Rep 22:100922. https://doi.org/10.1016/j.aqrep.2021.100922

Wang C, Jiang C, Gao T, Peng X, Ma S, Sun Q, Xia B, Xie X, Bai Z, Xu S, Zhuang X (2022b) Improvement of fish production and water quality in a recirculating aquaculture pond enhanced with bacteria-microalgae association. Aquaculture 547:737420. https://doi.org/10.1016/j.aquaculture.2022.737420

Wei M, Parrish CC, Guerra NI, Tibbetts SM, Colombo SM (2022) Dietary inclusion of a marine microalgae meal for Atlantic salmon (*Salmo salar*): impact of *Pavlova* sp. 459 on growth performance and tissue lipid composition. Aquaculture 553:738084. https://doi.org/10.1016/j.aquaculture.2022.738084

Yang Y, Hu B (2019) Investigation on the cultivation conditions of a newly isolated fusarium fungal strain for enhanced lipid production. Appl Biochem Biotechnol 187(4):1220–1237

Yu Z, Li L, Zhu R, Li M, Duan J, Wang J-Y, Liu Y-J, Wu L-F (2020) Monitoring of growth, digestive enzyme activity, immune response and water quality parameters of Golden crucian carp (*Carassius auratus*) in zero-water exchange tanks of biofloc systems. Aquac Rep 16: 100283. https://doi.org/10.1016/j.aqrep.2020.100283

Zhang Q, Qiu M, Xu W, Gao Z, Shao R, Qi Z (2014) Effects of dietary administration of *Chlorella* on the immune status of gibel carp, *Carassius auratus gibelio*. Ital J Anim Sci 13:3. https://doi.org/10.4081/ijas.2014.3168

Zhang F, Man YB, Mo WY, Wong MH (2020) Application of *Spirulina* in aquaculture: a review on wastewater treatment and fish growth. Rev Aquac 12(2):582–599

Zhu S, Gao W, Wen Z, Chi S, Shi Y, Hu W, Tan B (2022) Partial substitution of fish meal by *Clostridium autoethanogenum* protein in the diets of juvenile largemouth bass (*Micropterus salmoides*). Aquac Rep 22:100938. https://doi.org/10.1016/j.aqrep.2021.100938

Chapter 10
Ferulic Acid as Feed Additives in Aquaculture: A Review on Growth, Immune Response, and Antioxidant Status of Finfish

Kenneth Prudence Abasubong, Ndakalimwe Naftal Gabriel, and Jean-Jacques Yao Adjoumani

Abstract Producing protein through aquaculture is the solution to the world's protein needs. Aquaculture feed additives boost fish growth, immunology, and antioxidant status and prevent diseases. Among these feed additives, phytochemicals draw the most attention. Phytochemicals are considered harmless for humans, fish, and the environment because they are natural products. Ferulic acid (FA) is a phenolic substance with numerous advantages linked to its antioxidant, cytoprotective, antibacterial, and anabolic activities, generating particular interest in aquaculture. The stimulation and favouring of these systems lead to the stimulation of physiological and metabolic processes, promoting aquatic animals' development and reproduction. Therefore, the administration of FA could enhance the growth of muscle fibres, immunological response, inflammatory response, and antioxidant capacity in fish. This is a product that African aquaculture farmers can incorporate into their fish feed formulas; however, more research is required to fully understand the dietary potential of FA application, particularly in Africa. Therefore, this chapter reviewed recent studies that utilize ferulic acid (FA) as feed additives in cultured fish species.

Keywords Ferulic acid · Phytochemicals · Phenolic substance · Growth performance · Feed additives · Metabolic processes

K. P. Abasubong (✉) · J.-J. Y. Adjoumani
Key Laboratory of Aquatic Nutrition and Feed Science of Jiangsu Province, College of Animal Science and Technology, Nanjing Agricultural University, Nanjing, China

N. N. Gabriel
Department of Fisheries and Ocean Sciences, Faculty of Agriculture, Engineering, and Natural Science, Sam Nujoma Campus, University of Namibia, Henties Bay, Namibia

© The Author(s), under exclusive license to Springer Nature Singapore Pte Ltd. 2023
N. N. Gabriel et al. (eds.), *Emerging Sustainable Aquaculture Innovations in Africa*, Sustainable Agriculture and Food Security,
https://doi.org/10.1007/978-981-19-7451-9_10

10.1 Introduction

Aquaculture has grown into a large industry and the world's fastest-growing agricultural and commercial sector, generating significant economic activity in several countries (Kumari and Sahoo 2010; Villa-Cruz et al. 2009; Karga et al. 2020). In the last year, global aquaculture production has increased massively for the protein requirement of humans (Özçelik et al. 2020; Salem et al. 2021). However, aquaculture practices have intensified to meet demand as wild fish sources become scarcer by the day. With this intensification, problems and threats associated with high production costs, diseases, stress, environmental impact, animal welfare issues, and organic production demand are increasing to inhibit sustainable aquaculture production (Sönmez 2017; Arslan et al. 2018; Elbesthi et al. 2020). Due to this perspective, chemical additives and drugs from veterinary medicines such as antibiotics have been the only effective way to enhance growth, prevent and treat the occurrence of diseases in animals. However, these drugs are often considered expensive and unhealthy to improve growth and treat an infection. Secondly, these drugs are generally associated with considerable public health hazards by encouraging bacterial-resistant strains' selection, multiplication, and survival in the host (Dawood et al. 2020). Indeed, antibiotic resistance can be acquired through chromosomal mutation or plasmid acquisition. Resistance plasmids can be moved very rapidly, producing a high percentage of pathogenic bacteria that develop mediated plasmid resistance in a short period (Lazdins et al. 2015). At the same time, chromosomal mutations are non-transferable to other bacteria. For instance, multidrug resistance was transferred during the cholera epidemic in Ecuador between 1991 and 1992, spread by shrimp farmworkers. Although the original epidemic strain, *Vibrio cholerae* 01, was susceptible to all 12 antimicrobial medications tested, it gained multidrug resistance along the Ecuadorian coast due to resistance genes transferred from other *Vibrio* species that are fatal to shrimp (Faruque and Albert 1992).

Also, the scrutiny for high-performance alternative feedstuffs has gained much attention. For instance, Soy protein has been a primary source of fishmeal replacement in the plant protein field, providing a high protein alternative at a reasonable price (Sales 2009). The administration of diets based on soybean meal has received attention for its connection to intestinal enteritis, particularly in fish. The distal intestine is most susceptible to enteric inflammation due to the inclusive antinutritional factors (ANFs) and alcohol-soluble components of the feed ingredients (Romarheim et al. 2008), thus resulting in immune dysfunction. The immune system function is closely related to fish health and is usually associated with nutrition. Immune dysfunction causes a wide range of unanticipated effects. Intestinal mucosal immune dysfunction, for instance, can impair the equilibrium of the intestinal microbiota and cause the host to contract several diseases (Williams et al. 2017), causing death in fish species. As a result, immunological dysfunction is a component of many fish disease pathogens. So, instead of using growth promoters, synthetic antimicrobials, or hormones as a natural technique to boost animal production output or to enhance immunity in aquaculture, it is of significance to explore additives suitable for improving feed utilization by fish as use of these additives aims to increase feed digestion rates as well as immunity and resilience to oxidative stress and inflammation (Kothari et al. 2019). Recently, the benefits of phytochemicals in boosting immunological activation and promoting growth through diet and feed have received more attention (Hashem et al. 2020; Macías-Cruz et al. 2018; Marquardt and Li 2018). Phytochemicals are plant-derived bioactive molecules with a wide range of therapeutic effects, including antiviral, growth-promoting, antioxidant, immune-stimulating, and anti-inflammatory activities (Mani et al. 2020; Choudhari et al. 2020; Terzi et al. 2021).

Ferulic acid (FA) is presently a phytochemicals phenol compound with antioxidant, antibacterial, and anabolic qualities, potentially enhancing farm animals' health, productivity, and reproduction (González-Ríos et al. 2016; Macías-Cruz et al. 2018; Wang et al. 2019). Ferulic acid, also known as hydroxyl cinnamic acid, is the most prevalent phenolic acid found in plants, including grains, fruits, vegetables, herbs, and spices (Zhang et al. 2018). FA exists as esters attached covalently to monosaccharides, disaccharides, and polysaccharides and is broadly used in food, industry, and medicine as a natural antioxidant (Yildiztugay et al. 2018). In addition, FA aids in scavenging reactive molecules like hydroxyl, superoxide radicals, nitric oxide, and peroxynitrite and suppressing lipid peroxidation (Dulong et al. 2018). In this regard, some researchers have explored utilizing FA as a nutritional supplement used in domestic animal feed to increase productive qualities. These were reported in livestock species such as beef cattle, pigs, and ewe lamb (Kroon and Williams 1999; González-Ríos et al. 2016; Macías-Cruz et al. 2014). Hence, this chapter aims to summarize current knowledge of FA's modes of action and its advantages on animal production. Also, the potential regulatory impacts of FA as an additive on growth performance, immune stimulation, and antioxidant capacities in aquaculture were discussed.

10.2 Ferulic Acid: Structural Properties and Importance as a Functional Ingredient

Ferulic acid ([E]-3-[4-hydroxy-3-methoxy-phenyl] prop-2-enoic acid) (Fig. 10.1) belongs to the family of phenolic acids that are frequently present in plant tissues (Mattila and Kumpulainen 2002). Ferulic acids are secondary metabolites of varying chemical structures and biological properties. The plants are mainly bound as ester or glycosides, lignin components, and hydrolysis tannins (Bezerra et al. 2017), as shown in Table 10.2. They can be separated into cinnamic and benzoic acid derivatives, which differ in the amount and substitution of hydroxyl and methoxy groups, and phenolic acids of a peculiar character, based on their chemical structure. Ferulic acid is the most frequent cinnamic acid derivative, alongside caffeic, p-coumaric, synapine, syryte, and vanillin (Bezerra et al. 2017). The physical properties of FA are listed in Table 10.1.

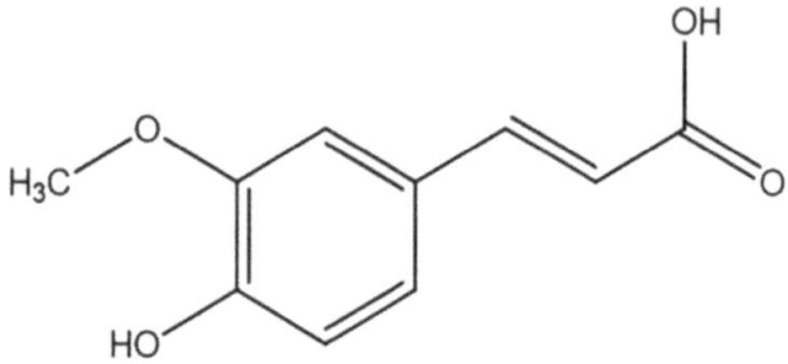

Fig. 10.1 Chemical structure of ferulic acid

Table 10.1 Chemical properties of ferulic acid

Properties	Value/nature
Common name	Ferulic acid
Synonym	trans-4-Hydroxy-3-methoxycinnamic acid
Molecular formula	$C_{10}H_{10}O_4$
Chemical family	Phenolic acids
Molecular weight	194.18
Physical status	Amber coloured solid
Odour	Nil
Melting temperature	174 °C1 λmax: 234 nm, 322 nm^2
Vapour pressure	0.00000269 [mmHg]
Melting Point	168–172 °C (L)
Density	1.3 ± 0.1 g/cm^3
Boiling Point	372.3 ± 27.0 °C at 760 mmHg
Decomposition temperature	~55 °C
Solubility	Soluble in water 0.78 g/L
pH stability	3–4.5
Relative sweetness	Nil
Molar mass	194.18 g/mol
Appearance	Crystalline powder
Carcinogenicity	Nil
Flavour enhancer	Monosodium glutamate (MSG)
Absorbability in the gastro-intestinal tract	FA can be absorbed along the entire gastrointestinal tract and metabolized mainly by the liver

The antioxidant activity of phenolic acids, particularly cinnamic acid derivatives, is determined by the quantity of hydroxyl and methoxy groups connected to the phenyl ring (Bezerra et al. 2017; Aguilar-Hernández et al. 2017). The absorption capacities of ferulic acid are significantly higher in the body and could remain in the bloodstream longer than other phenolic acids. Compared to other phenolic compounds, ferulic acid is an effective antioxidant (Tee-Ngam et al. 2013). Ferulic acid is low in toxicity and has many physiological effects, including anti-inflammatory, antibacterial, nerve-cell damaging properties and the potential to restore broken cells. It is also a sports supplement since it can neutralize free radicals in muscle tissue (alleviating muscle fatigue). It has been utilized in pharmaceutics and food for a long time. Additionally, research in mouse models indicates that FA may aid in treating obesity and infertility in humans (Kuppusamy et al. 2019; Salazar-Lopez et al. 2017). In addition, research in mouse models suggests that FA could effectively treat obesity and infertility in humans (Kuppusamy et al. 2019; Salazar-Lopez et al. 2017). It has also been used to produce pharmaceuticals, cosmetics, and nutraceuticals. Using FA as a nutraceutical supplement, numerous research teams have been researching this phenolic molecule to increase animal production in the past ten years (Macías-Cruz et al. 2018; Wang et al. 2021).The chemical properties of ferulic acid are shown in Table 10.1.

FA is a secondary metabolite produced by plants in the shikimate and phenylpropanoid pathways that provides stiffness and protection to the host (de Oliveira Silva and Batista 2017). As a result, it is found unbound, dimerized, and coupled by ester and ether linkages with lipids, carbohydrates, and lignin in the cell wall's structural composition (de Paiva et al. 2013). Different extraction methods release free and bound FA from natural sources (Mancuso and Santangelo 2014). While free FA can be extracted using aqueous or organic solvents (e.g. methanol), bound FA requires chemical alkalinity or enzymatic hydrolysis to break covalent connections with the other cell wall components. Free FA or other bioactive derivatives can be released depending on the extraction process and operational parameters (such as room temperature, pH, and time) (Bento-Silva et al. 2018). The levels of ferulic acid in grains, fruits, and vegetable sources are presented in Table 10.2.

Due to its widespread use as a component in pharmaceuticals, functional foods, and nutraceuticals, FA extraction offers accessible business opportunities as well as significant environmental and economic support for enterprises. In the literature, various alkaline, acidic, and enzymatic techniques for extracting FA from various sources have been proposed (Buranov and Mazza 2009; Kim et al. 2006; Mathew and Abraham 2005; Feng et al. 2005), as shown in Table 10.3. However, optimizing important parameters for FA isolation, such as extraction duration, pH, and temperature, for a high yield is necessary. The study was conducted with the help of response surface methodology, which showed 1.3-fold increases in the production of FA compared to the unoptimized conventional extraction technique (Tilay et al. 2008). At room temperature, FA is insoluble in water. However, it is soluble in hot water, ethyl acetate, ethanol, and ethyl ether, and it has been discovered that ethanol (60%) is ideal for FA extraction (Guo et al. 2003). Although FA is abundant in the cell walls of hardwoods, grasses, and maize husks, it is difficult to obtain from these natural sources because it is covalently attached to various carbohydrates as a glycosidic conjugate, ester, or amide. As a result, alkaline hydrolysis is the only way to get it out of these natural products (Tilay et al. 2008). FA created through a chemical technique cannot be regarded as natural; therefore, numerous efforts have been made to release FA from natural sources enzymatically. However, most FA contents in plants are covalently bonded with lignin and other biopolymers, isolating

Table 10.2 The levels of ferulic acid in grains, fruits, and vegetable sources

Sources	FA contents (%)	References
Carbohydrate		
Refined maize bran	2.61–3.3	Zhao and Moghadasian (2008); Zhao et al. (2005)
Maize, dehulled kernels	0.174	Adom and Liu (2002)
Whole grain rye flour	0.086	Zhao and Moghadasian (2008); Mattila et al. (2005)
Whole brown rice	0.042	Zhao and Moghadasian (2008); Adom and Liu (2002)
Maize flour	0.038	Mattila et al. (2005)
Whole grain barley flour	0.025–0.034	Mattila et al. (2005)
Oat bran	0.033	Zhao and Moghadasian (2008); Mattila et al. (2005)
Rye bran	0.28	Zhao and Moghadasian 2008; Mattila et al. (2005)
Fruits		
Grapefruit	0.0107–0.0116	Mattila and Hellström (2007)
Rhubarb	0.00147	Mattila and Hellström (2007)
Apples	0.00027–0.00085	Mattila and Hellström (2007)
Banana	0.0054	Mattila and Hellström (2007)
Orange	0.0092–0.0099	Mattila and Hellström (2007)
Berries	0.00025–0.0027	Mattila and Hellström (2007)
Vegetables		
Eggplant	0.0073–0.035	Mattila and Hellström (2007)
Tomato	0.00029–0.006	Bourne and Rice-Evans (1998); Mattila and Hellström (2007)
Carrot	0.0012–0.0028	Mattila and Hellström 2007
Chinese cabbage	0.0014	Mattila and Hellström (2007)
Broccoli	0.00409	Mattila and Hellström (2007)
Red cabbages	0.0063–0.0065	Mattila and Hellström (2007)
soybeans	0.012	Mattila and Hellström (2007)
Green bean/fresh	0.0012	Mattila and Hellström (2007)

Source: Zhao and Moghadasian 2008; Boz 2015; Kumar and Pruthi 2014

FA for commercial production by enzymatic techniques seems challenging. Extraction of ferulic acid from various by-products are presented in Table 10.3.

10.3 Absorption and Metabolism Effect of FA in Animal

Compared with other phenolic compounds, ferulic acid is quickly absorbed from the stomach (Zhao and Moghadasian 2008). Following absorption, ferulic acid quickly transforms into a conjugation product in the liver when combined with glucuronides,

Table 10.3 Extraction of ferulic acid from various by-products

Name of raw materials	Method of Extraction	Yield	Reference
Sugar beet pulp	Three extraction solvents, sodium hydroxide (0.5, 1, 2 M), methanol, and their mixture (alkaline methanolic solvent)	957.4 mg/L	Aarabi (2016)
The root of Angelica sinensis	Ethanol with supercritical CO_2	0.35–0.37%	Sun et al. (2006)
Palm pressed fibre	Deep eutectic solvent (DES) of choline chloride-acetic acid (ChCl-AA) and choline chloride-citric acid (ChCl-CA)	41,155 ± 940 mg/kg	Mei and Hadi (2022)
Sweet corn cob (SCC)	Chemical or enzymatic hydrolysis	1.69 ± 0.02 $g\,kg^{-1}$	
Flax shives, wheat bran, and corn bran	Non-pressurized alkaline hydrolysis (0.5 M NaOH) and pressurized solvents (0.5 M NaOH, water, ethanol, and ammonia)	Flax shives 25 mg/100 g FA Wheat 391 mg/100 FA Corn bran 2510 mg/100 g FA	Buranov and Mazza (2009)
Wheat-bran	Enzymatic hydrolysate	2000–3000 mg/L	Liu et al. (2004)
Corn fibre	Alkaline	2.10 ± 0.09 g. L^{-1} and 11.14 ± 1.00 kg Ton^{-1}	Valério et al. (2021)
Rice Bran oil	Ultrasonic method	10–20%	Arumsari et al. (2019)
Sweet potato stem	Enzymatic treatment	>2.0%/g dry weight	Min et al. (2006)
A recombinant strain of Saccharomyces cerevisiae	Eugenol and coniferyl alcohol	90%	Lambert et al. (2013)
Defatted rice bran	Enzymatic production	22%	Uraji et al. (2013)
A recombinant strain of *Ralstonia eutropha* H16	Eugenol hydroxylase	93.8 mol%	Overhage et al. (2002)

sulfate, and sulfoglucuronide (Zhao and Moghadasian 2008). FA can be quickly absorbed from the stomach and is likely metabolized mainly in the liver. Ferulic acid taken orally was distributed at 4% in gastric mucosa and 10% in the blood pool and liver, kidney, and 53% in other tissues (Zhao and Moghadasian 2008). However, free ferulic acid bioavailability is very low due to the rapid conjugation process in the liver (Zhao and Moghadasian 2008). It is more bioavailable than other dietary flavonoids and phenolics studied. Furthermore, the intestinal microflora metabolizes FA into hydroxyphenyl propionic acid through reduction, demethylation, and dihydroxylation at C4 (Chesson et al. 1999). FA's absorption and metabolism effect in the animal has been demonstrated, owing to its cytoprotective effects. Studies have shown that FA could improve animal carbohydrate utilization; this was observed in several studies. Extensive research in sheep shows that FA could increase cellular glucose absorption while preserving euglycemia (Macías-Cruz et al. 2018; Wang et al. 2019). A similar result was also observed in mice fed FA diet (de Oliveira Silva and Batista 2017; Ramar et al. 2012; Roy et al. 2014). However, the authors attributed the improved glucose metabolism to the increase in the circulation of insulin concentration and translocation of gluco-transporters (GLUT4) towards the cell membrane (Kumar and Goel 2019; Naowaboot et al. 2018). This positively affects glucose metabolism fed FA diet, which promotes energy metabolism in tissues such as skeletal muscle (Chen et al. 2019; Chodkowska et al. 2018). Macías-Cruz et al. (2018) discovered alterations in the glucose–insulin system, including lower serum glucose levels and enhanced insulin secretion in pre-pubertal lambs fed free FA diet. Notably, this is a crucial response for animal reproduction and growth because glucose is the primary energy source used by gonads and muscles

The anti-hyperlipidemic effects of FA were observed in obese farm animals as it decreases the biosynthesis of fatty acids, triglycerides, and cholesterol esters. This study was carried out with mouse C2C12 myoblasts exposed to hydrogen peroxide (Chodkowska et al. 2018) and rats fed a high-fat diet (Melo et al. 2017; Salazar-Lopez et al. 2017). Lipid synthesis was significantly improved in obese rats fed a high-fat diet supplemented with FA. This suggests that dietary FA could stimulate lipolysis to hinder dyslipidemia by exerting an anti-insulin resistance effect in rats administered a high diet (Naowaboot et al. 2018). In contrast, no change was observed in serum TG and TC concentrations when fattening lambs received free FA supplementation (Macías-Cruz et al. 2014; Wang et al. 2019). At the same time, FA-fed pigs (Li et al. 2015) and steers (González-Ríos et al. 2016) ´show decreased meat lipid peroxidation rates. These findings suggest that FA modulates lipid metabolism only in dyslipidemia. Overall, FA seems to act as a modulator of energy metabolism in animals with carbohydrate and lipid metabolic disorders.

However, studies have shown that FA did not affect serum total protein and urea concentrations in hair ewe lambs under heat stress or thermoneutral settings (Macías-Cruz et al. 2014; Macías-Cruz et al. 2018). However, an increase in serum total protein concentrations in cold-stressed male lambs (Wang et al. 2019). Increased blood total protein concentrations have also been seen in lambs fed feruloyl oligosaccharides (Wang et al. 2019). According to both studies, FA raises total protein in the blood because it enhances microbial protein production and/or enzymatic antioxidant activity, preventing protein oxidation (Wang et al. 2019). FA may enhance protein metabolism in ruminants by increasing protein synthesis while lowering catabolism (cytoprotective effect). The mechanism of action for FA's beneficial effect on protein metabolism in ruminants and other producing animals needs further investigation.

Therefore, with the findings above, it can be inferred that FA affects metabolic routes of the major nutrients and consequently favours both animal reproduction and growth than those present in fish species

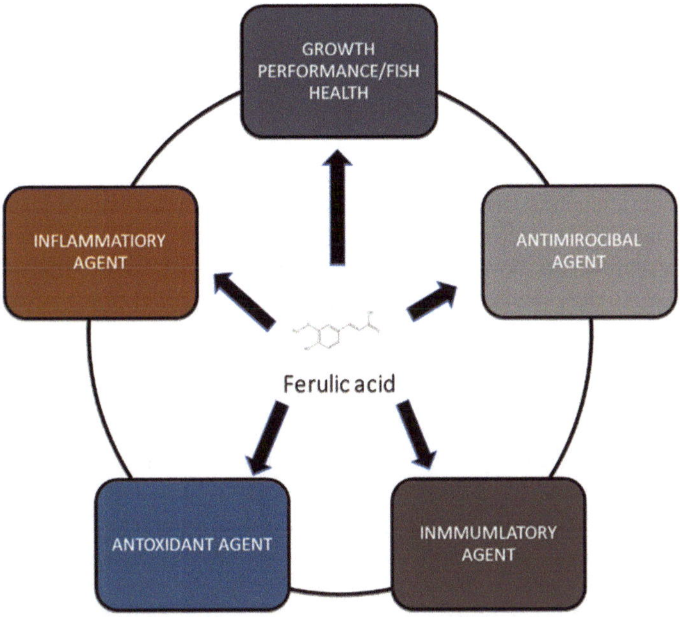

Fig. 10.2 The role of ferulic acid in fish

10.4 Overview of the Use of Ferulic Acid in Aquaculture

Providing sustainable seafood for human consumption is best accomplished through aquaculture. Several criteria, like environmental considerations, dietary practices, and disease control, are necessary for aquaculture to succeed (Abdel-Tawwab et al. 2020; Dawood and Koshio 2019). Ferulic acid (FA) is one of the most crucial additions to increase immunity and enhance an animal's physiological state (Ahmadifar et al. 2019; Kroon and Williams 1999; Nomura et al. 2003). Therefore, the role of ferulic acid in improving growth, fish health, antioxidant capacities, and anti-inflammatory and immune response has thoroughly been investigated and reported in fish, as shown in Fig. 10.2.

10.4.1 Ferulic Acid Improves Growth Performances and Biochemical Parameters

The change in length and weight of a fish or any organism due to nutrition metabolism is called growth. As a result, growth is the ability to provide healthy food. The cost of aquaculture has led business owners to desire to harvest the maximum yield per unit area. In contrast, the scarcity of natural resources has driven scientists to do the same. Both situations have the same objective: faster fish growth with fewer costs. Hence, growth promotion is among the essential purposes of recent studies.

FA is successfully demonstrated to promote growth in various fish species. For instance, studies in fish have shown that weight gain in genetically improved farmed tilapias fed FA derivative diet at 0.52 mmol kg^1 was much higher than those fed the control diet. In contrast, the opposite pattern was observed in feed conversion ratio, hepatosomatic and viscerosomatic index (Yu et al. 2017, 2018). This was accompanied by significantly lower TCHO, LDLC and TG, LDL, AST, ALT, and higher HDL contents than the control. Similarly, Yu et al. (2017) noted a significantly higher WGR with lower FCR, VSI and HSI in GIFT (*Oreochromis niloticus*) fed dietary FA at a 100 mg/kg in diet. This was connected with a substantial reduction in serum TG, TC, LDL contents, AST and ALT activities, whereas serum HDL content was significantly higher. The growth performance was significantly affected by the inclusion of FA, and the highest rates were reported in an 80 mg/kg diet after 60 days of feeding in Nile tilapia (Dawood et al. 2020). Also, weight gain rate (WGR) and specific growth rate (SGR) of oriental river prawn (*Macrobrachium nipponense*) fed FA diet for 10 weeks were significantly higher with the opposite trend seen in FCR than those of the control group (Liu et al. 2022). After 8 weeks of feeding, common carp fed with an FA diet registered a significantly higher SGR, FBW, WGR, white blood cells (WBCs), red blood cells (RBCs), haematocrit (HCT), and haemoglobin (Hb), compared to those in control. Yu et al. (2020) noted a considerable improvement in serum ALB, TP and ALP, BUN, AST and LDH in genetically improved farmed tilapia (*Oreochromis niloticus*) administered with an oxidized fish oil diet supplemented with FA for 12 weeks as compared to the control. At 10 weeks of feeding, FA inclusion level at 80 mg/kg obtained noticeable growth performance and feed utilization compared to the control. However, serum TC, TG, LDL, ALT, AST, and AKP were significantly decreased, and HDL levels increased following the FA-containing (80–160 mg/kg) diets. Additionally, it was shown that the expression of genes involved in growth (GH, IGF-1, GHR1, GHR2) was significantly increased in the liver. Dietary FA at 20 g/g enhanced growth and feed absorption and increased PPAR-α, a gene linked to fat metabolism, and lowered the expression of PPAR-β and PPAR-γ in male adult zebrafish (Yin et al. 2002). These alterations in gene expression improved fatty acid production and metabolism and decreased fat deposition. This suggests that FA may be necessary for lipid metabolism.

10.4.2 Ferulic Acid Improves Molecular Mechanisms Associated with Muscle Hypertrophy

Skeletal muscle is a flexible tissue that aids movement and energy metabolism (King et al. 2004). Muscle hypertrophy, defined by a rise in muscle mass and an expanded cross-sectional area due to the proliferation of myofibers, is the most common pattern of skeletal muscle growth in adults (Hernandez and Kravitz 2003). The myofiber is the skeletal muscle's basic unit, consisting of bundles of myofibrils, each of sarcomeric units (Sanger et al. 2004). FA, like β-AA, can regulate signaling pathways and myogenic gene expression, which may promote muscle hypertrophy in obese animals. Due to the activation of the Sirt1/AMPK/PGC-1 pathway and improved mitochondrial function, supplemental FA increases the proportion of slow-twitch fibres in the animal's Longissimus thoracic muscle (LTM) (Wang et al. 2021). FA also activates the 3 kinase/protein B kinase (PI3K/PKB or Akt) pathway in a manner comparable to insulin-like growth factor I (IGF-I), resulting in increased muscle fibre diameter (Kuppusamy et al. 2019; Yeh et al. 2014). In zebrafish, a diet supplemented with FA increased transcription of myogenic regulatory factors (i.e. MyoD, Myogenin, and SRF), resulting in improved hypertrophic growth of rapid skeletal muscle for increased body weight (Wen and Ushio 2017).

On the other hand, FA has been shown to increase sarcomeric unit proteins in zebrafish by increasing the expression of sarcomeric unit proteins, which are the primary components of the myofiber. FA dramatically boosted the expression of genes involved in myogenic development (myod1, myog, and myf5) and increased the breadth of skeletal muscle fibres (Yin et al. 2002). However, because these findings are still preliminary, more research with fish species is required to confirm the efficiency of FA on transcription, translation, and expression of sarcomeric proteins, and hence on muscle hypertrophy.

10.4.3 Ferulic Acid as an Antimicrobial Agent

A substance known as an antimicrobial prevents the growth or kills germs (Citarasu 2012). By functioning as a fermentation substrate, FA, whether in free form or bound to oligosaccharides, promotes the population expansion of the intestinal beneficial family *Bifidobacteriaceae*. Due to this alteration in the microbiota, FA also reduces the number of bacteria from the Enterobacteriaceae family, which are linked to GIT disorders and the breakdown of amino acids. FA was demonstrated to improve GIT health, increase microbial protein production, and provide a natural option for treating common bacterial and viral illnesses in animal models (Wang et al. 2019). According to Yin et al. (2002), zebrafish fed 20 g/g FA exhibited a higher number of goblet cells in intestinal tissue, and the makeup of the gut microbiota also changed. Also, the authors updated that the 16s rRNA gene sequences showed that 20 g/g FA increased *Bacteroides* and decreased *Firmicutes*, indicating that FA had an antibacterial effect. However, further research will be needed to fully comprehend the intricate connections between the FA and GIT microbiota and how these affect the well-being and output of aquatic animals.

10.4.4 Ferulic Acid as an Anti-apoptotic Agent

Cells have a built-in cell death program, apoptosis (programmed cell death), which protects the organism by removing potentially damaged cells and unnecessary cells after differentiation. Apoptosis occurs when internal monitors recognize damage or malfunction and initiate signaling cascades that eventually activate caspases and endonucleases that kill the cell (Gao et al. 2013). Apoptosis is induced in a wide range of physiological settings regulated by cell growth and differentiation in normal biological processes and pathogenesis in vertebrates (Ellis et al. 1991; Steller 1995; Jacobson et al. 1997). The two primary forms of apoptosis pathways are "extrinsic pathways", where a cell receives a signal to begin apoptosis from other cells in the organism, and "intrinsic pathways", where a cell receives a signal to start apoptosis from one of its genes or proteins owing to the detection of DNA damage (Elmore 2007). A thorough understanding of the mechanism between apoptosis and diseases has excellent potential for treating diseases. Additionally, studies have connected stress and diet to be associated with apoptosis. For instance, common carp fed a high-fat diet exhibited higher Caspase-8 and Caspase-9 than the control (Abasubong et al. 2022). A similar result was also observed in blunt snout bream (Dai et al. 2018). Recent studies have found that FA can take an anti-apoptotic part by mediating different targets. Fu et al. (2022) noted the ameliorating effect of hepatic morphology coupled with the downregulated gene expression of apoptosis (Caspase-3 and p53) and keap1bin juvenile hybrid grouper (*Epinephelus fuscoguttatus*♀ × *Epinephelus polyphekadion*♂) fed FA 80–160 mg/g.

10.4.5 Ferulic Acid as an Anti-inflammatory Agent

Inflammation, which involves the recruitment of phagocytes (macrophages and neutrophils) and the release of numerous cytokines, is essential to defend against tissue damage, infection, or toxic substances (Medzhitov 2008). Macrophages are one of the most significant phagocytes during an inflammatory process and can contribute to the emergence of a range of diseases by secreting a massive number of cytokines, such as TNF-, IL-6, and IL-1. Such inflammatory mediators can influence immune and non-immune cells to activate an immunological response that defends the body against pathogens and toxic chemicals (Medzhitov 2008). The inflammation process is usually tightly regulated, comprising signals that initiate and sustain inflammation and those that impede it. When the two signals are out of balance, inflammation can develop unchecked and cause damage to cells and tissue. The mononuclear phagocyte system strongly depends on macrophages as one of its essential components and is composed of closely related bone marrow-derived cells, including blood monocytes and tissue macrophages. The three primary functions of macrophages in inflammation are antigen presentation, phagocytosis, and immunomodulation by producing various cytokines and growth factors.

Macrophages have a vital role in initiating, continuing, and resolving inflammation. During the inflammatory process, they are both activated and deactivated. Some activation signals include interferon-gamma, granulocyte-monocyte colony-stimulating factor, tumor necrosis factor-alpha, bacterial lipopolysaccharide, extra-cellular matrix proteins, and other chemical mediators. The host can repair damaged tissues when inflammation is suppressed by removing or inactivating mediators and inflammatory effector cells. Anti-inflammatory cytokines (such as interleukin 10 and transforming growth factor-beta) and cytokine antagonists, primarily produced by macrophages, deactivate active macrophages.

Numerous studies have demonstrated that FA has a potent anti-inflammatory effect in many disorders. In order to reduce and combat inflammation, FA primarily suppresses the production and expression of associated inflammatory components via numerous molecular pathways, and multiple types of mediators (cytokines, chemokines, and eicosanoids) are released by strengthened immune cells, (Rinaldi et al. 2011). These inflammation-related mediators are in charge of removing the pathogen that has invaded and establishing the recovery procedures. Therefore, in response to infection, ferulic acid inhibited the synthesis of macrophage inflammatory protein-2 (Sakai et al. 1999). The control of inflammation depends on preventing the synthesis or activity of inflammatory cytokines and mediators (Vinegar et al. 1969). As a result, a requirement for an anti-inflammatory substance may be the capacity to control inflammatory mediators.

Several studies have been conducted to prove these in fish species. For instance, compared to controls, juvenile hybrid grouper (*Epinephelus fuscoguttatus, Epinephelus polyphekadion*) fed diets containing 80–160 mg/kg FA had significantly higher transcriptional levels of immune-related genes (IL-1, IL-8, TNF-, and IFN-) in the liver, head, kidney, and spleen (Fu et al. 2022). Additionally, following FA administration of LPS, the contents of pro-inflammatory cytokines gene expression, including TNF- and IL-1, under LPS stimulation at 96 hpi in Megalobrama amblycephala were considerably decreased (Chen et al. 2021). Additionally, Fish fed diets containing 80–160 mg/kg FA had significantly higher transcriptional levels of immune-related genes in their liver, head kidney, and spleen. These genes include IL-1, IL-8, TNF-, and IFN-. Fish offered dietary FA upregulated the HSP70 gene before and after high stress while upregulating the INF-, TNF-, and IL-1 gene expression (Dawood et al. 2020).

10.4.6 Ferulic Acid Immunostimulatory Agent

The mucosal layer, epithelium, and lamina propria are the three defence lines of the gut's innate immune system. The mucosal layer is the initial line of defence against foreign infections in the host digestive tract (Xu et al. 2014). The immune system comprises various humoural and cellular components that protect the body from foreign invaders (Biller-Takahashi and Urbinati 2014). Immunostimulation is a phenomenon in which an organism's immune response is stimulated beforehand so that it must face a strengthened immune system when an extraneous substance enters the body. Immune responses are the main controlling elements for the emergence and spread of numerous chronic diseases. In studies, numerous compounds, besides ferulic acid, have successfully activated the immune response in finfish (Mohamed et al. 2018; Bilen et al. 2020). Ferulic acid is a bioactive compound class that enhances intestinal health through various processes, including mucosal immunity and inflammatory modulation. Many investigations on the regulatory effects of ferulic acid on intestinal immune function have produced compelling evidence, necessitating more research.

Present studies in aquatic animals show that FA supplemented with 163.99–183.33 mg/kg level significantly improves albumin/globulin ratio (A/G), the complement 3 (C3)) with down-regulated *Toll* and *Dorsal*, immune deficiency (*IMD*), and heat shock protein (*HSP70*) and disease resistance against non-O1 *Vibrio* cholera GXFL1-X infection of *M. nipponense* (Liu et al. 2022). Similarly, higher lysozyme was observed in improved farm tilapia (Yu et al. 2017). After 8 weeks of feeding, lysozyme activity and the serum respiratory burst were enhanced in common carp given a 100 mg/kg FA diet. However, after the challenge with pathogenic *A. hydrophila,* fish fed FA added diet had a higher survival rate than those in the control group (Ahmadifar et al. 2019). According to the results, FA could be employed as a valuable feed supplement to enhance immune responses and disease resistance in common carp culture's initial phases. The serum nitric oxide (NO), complement 3 (C3), complement 4 (C4), and lysozyme (LSZ) were all significantly increased in tilapia (*Oreochromis niloticus*) fed oxidized fish oil supplemented with 400 mg/kg FA for 12 weeks (Yu et al. 2020). Fu et al. (2022) noted that fish fed dietary 80–160 mg/kg FA increased the contents of complement 3, immunoglobulin M, and lysozyme compared to the control.

10.4.7 Ferulic Acid as Antioxidant Agents

When oxidation and antioxidation in the body are out of balance, this is referred to as oxidative stress (OS) (Mustafa et al. 2020), and it causes the body's general state to lean toward oxidation. When the body's antioxidant mechanism and ROS generation are imbalanced, they promote a significant amount of ROS (Kikuzaki et al. 2002; Birben et al. 2012). This ROS results in neutrophil infiltration, an increase in protease secretion, and the development of many oxidation intermediates (Halliwell 1994), which ultimately cause tissue degeneration, steatosis, cell transformation, apoptosis, and host death (Abasubong et al. 2022). Additionally, the synthesis of NO and nuclear factor kappa B (NFkB), along with other mediators, control the expression of cyclooxygenase (COX)-2 and induced nitric oxide synthase when ROS levels rise above physiological levels (iNOS). Oxidative stress is associated with improper dietary formation. In the body, there are two types of antioxidant systems: non-enzyme antioxidants (lipoic acid (LA), glutathione, vitamin C, vitamin E); and enzyme antioxidants (catalase (CAT), superoxide dismutase (SOD), glutathione peroxidase (GPx) (Mustafa et al. 2020). ROS, an oxygen-containing material, is constantly created in the body because the body continually obtains oxygen for a long time Williams (Williams et al. 2004)(Mustafa et al. 2020). With this, the body's antioxidation mechanism can resist oxidation, limiting the body's production of reactive oxygen species (ROS) and repairing the harm they produce.

An antioxidant is a substance that inhibits oxidation. Oxidation, a chemical reaction, results in the production of free radicals (Williams et al. 2004). Atoms or clusters of atoms containing an unpaired electron are referred to as free radicals. Since unpaired electrons are likely to form pairs with other electrons, they are typically unstable and reactive. The occurrence of metabolism in a living organism causes oxygen molecule (O_2) to undergo reduction by four electrons. In this process, reactive oxygen metabolites are produced, which interact with transition elements, the excitation of electrons, or the input of energy. These oxygen-reactive metabolites are called active oxygen species because they are far more reactive than oxygen molecules. Active oxygen species include hydroxyl radicals (OH*), hydrogen peroxide (H_2O_2), superoxide (O_{2-}), and singlet oxygen ($_1O^2$) (Bors et al. 1990). Free radicals are formed in live cells due to photolysis, homolysis, chemical bond fission, radiolysis, and redox processes. In a live organism, free radicals start a chain reaction that damages cells and causes disease. Antioxidants are chemicals that stop a chain reaction in a live organism that free radicals have formed (Rizzo et al. 2010). In other words, antioxidants prevent the detrimental effects of reactive oxygen species (free radicals) by neutralizing or deactivating their impact. Oxidative stress is a term that describes the distinction between the creation of antioxidant defenses and very reactive oxygen groups.

Ferulic acid's antioxidant effect is multifaceted, involving both the prevention of the production of reactive oxygen species (ROS) or nitrogen as well as the neutralization ("sweeping") of free radicals. This acid also chelates protonated metal ions, including copper and iron ions (Rice-Evans et al. 1996, 1997). Ferulic acid is a free radical scavenger, an inhibitor of free radical generating enzymes, and increases the activity of scavenging enzymes (Kumar and Pruthi 2014). The mechanism of antioxidative activity is the capacity of ferulic acid to create persistent phenoxyl radicals due to the radical molecule reacting with the antioxidant molecule. It is therefore inhibiting the occurrence of chemical chain reaction that generates free radicals. This chemical could also operate as a hydrogen donor, supplying atoms to radicals directly. This is crucial for protecting lipid acids in cell membranes from unwanted autoxidation reactions. This reduces the generation of harmful hydroxyl radicals, which cause the peroxidation of cell membranes.

According to studies, oxidized fish oil was shown to induce oxidative stress, destroy the liver, and dysregulate the lipid metabolism of tilapia fed for 12 weeks. However, a diet supplemented with 400 mg/kg of ferulic acid offsets these adverse effects by increasing SOD, CAT, and GPx activities and reducing malondialdehyde (MDA) content (Yu et al. 2020). Chen et al. (2021) reported that FA gavage (50 mg/kg BW and 100 mg/kg BW) significantly increased GSH, GST, SOD, GR, and GPx activity. This was associated with increased SOD, CAT, and GPX mRNA expression, suggesting that FA administration could inhibit the LPS-induced oxidative stress in *Megalobrama amblycephala*. Ahmadifar et al. (2019) reported a noticeable increase in serum antioxidant enzymes (CAT, GPX SOD) activity in common carp (*Cyprinus carpio*) fed FA for 8 weeks as compared to the control. Nile tilapia (*O. niloticus*) fed 80 mg kg^{-1} for 60 days significantly increased SOD, CAT, and GPx activity and reduced MDA levels before and after heat stress (Dawood et al. 2020). The antioxidant-related parameters of SOD, CAT, GPx, and total antioxidant capacity were elevated. At the same time, MDA content was significantly reduced in 80–160 mg/kg FA treatment with a significant antioxidant gene expression Nrf2, Cu/ZnSOD, and MnSOD) as compared with control (Fu et al. 2022). Studies have also shown that European sea brass fed XOS diet obtained higher SOD, CAT, and GPX activities than the control (Guerreiro et al. 2015). The authors attributed this improvement to their composition of ester-linked phenolic acids such as ferulic in XOS. Abasubong et al. (2022) also obtained a similar result when an XOS was given to common carp fed the high-fat diet for 8 weeks. Finally, iNOS, NO, SOD, GPx, and MDA were dramatically decreased in the FA groups fed oriental river prawn (*Macrobrachium nipponense*) compared to the control group after ten weeks of feeding (Liu et al. 2022).

10.5 Conclusion

Current research indicates that FA can boost growth, anti-inflammation, immunological response, and antioxidant capacity in fish. However, knowledge is lacking, which has resulted in the opening of a vast field of research into the application of this phytochemical. Future research should examine environmental variables, species, the animal's oxidative status, bioavailability, modes of action, and product dosage. The information acquired thus far and findings from future studies will allow management methods to be developed to make this natural material viable for ensuring food safety while protecting animal welfare and human health.

References

Aarabi A (2016) Extraction and purification of ferulic acid as an antioxidant from sugar beet pulp by alkaline hydrolysis. Ital J Food Sci 28:362–375

Abasubong KP, Li XF, Adjoumani JJY, Jiang GZ, Desouky HE, Liu WB (2022) Effects of dietary xylooligosaccharide prebiotic supplementation on growth, antioxidant and intestinal immune-related genes expression in common carp *Cyprinus carpio* fed a high-fat diet. J Anim Physiol Anim Nutr 106(2):403–418

Abdel-Tawwab M, Khalil RH, Metwally AA, Shakweer MS, Khallaf MA, Abdel Latif HMR (2020) Effects of black soldier fly (*Hermetia illucens* L.) larvae meal on growth performance, organs-somatic indices, body composition, and hemato-biochemical variables of European sea bass, *Dicentrarchus labrax*. Aquaculture 522:735136

Adom KK, Liu RH (2002) Antioxidant activity of grains. J Agric Food Chem 50:6182–6187

Aguilar-Hernández I, Afseth NK, López-Luke T, Contreras-Torres FF, PetterWold J, Ornelas-Soto N (2017) Surface enhanced Raman spectroscopy of phenolic antioxidants: a systematic evaluation of ferulic acid, p -coumaric acid, caffeic acid and sinapic acid. Vib Spectrosc 89:113–122

Ahmadifar E, Moghadam MS, Dawood MAO, Hoseinifar SH (2019) Lactobacillus fermentum and/or ferulic acid improved the immune responses, antioxidative defence and resistance against *Aeromonas hydrophila* in common carp (*Cyprinus carpio*) fingerlings. Fish Shellfish Immunol 94:916–923

Arslan G, Sönmez AY, Yanık T (2018) Effects of grapeVitis vinifera seed oil supplementation on growth, survival, fatty acid profiles, antioxidant contents andblood parameters in rainbow trout *Oncorhynchus mykiss*. Aquac Res 49:2256–2266

Arumsari AG, Nugrahani RA, Hendrawati TY (2019) The Extraction of Ferulic Acid from the phenolic fraction from rice bran oil using ultrasonic methods and analysis of antioxidant effectiveness:third international conference on sustainable innovation. Adv Health Sci Educ Theory Pract. 15:37–39

Bento-Silva A, Vaz Patto MC, do Rosário Bronze M (2018) Relevance, structure and analysis of ferulic acid in maize cell walls. Food Chem 246:360–378

Bezerra GSN, Pereira MAV, Ostrosky EA, e e Barbosa EG, de Moura M, Ferrari M, Arago CFS, Gomes APB (2017) Compatibility study between ferulic acid and excipients used in cosmetic formulations by TG/DTG, DSC and FTIR. J Therm Anal Calorim 127: 1683-1691.

Bilen S, Karga M, Altunolu YE, Ulu F, Biswas G (2020) Immune responses and growth performance of the aqueous methanolic extract of malva sylvestris in *Oncorhynchus mykiss*. Bull Mar Sci 9:159–167

Biller-Takahashi JD, Urbinati EC (2014) Fish Immunology. The modification and manipulation of the innate immune system: Brazilian studies. Anais Acad Bras Cien 86:1484–1506

Birben E, Sahiner UM, Sackesen C, Erzurum S, Kalayci O (2012) Oxidative stress and antioxidant defense. World Allergy Organ 5:9–19

Bors W, Heller W, Michel C, Saran M (1990) Flavonoids as antioxidants: determination of radical-scavenging efficiencies. Methods Enzymol 186:343–355

Bourne LC, Rice-Evans C (1998) Bioavailability of ferulic acid. Biochem Biophys Res Commun 253:222–227

Boz H (2015) Ferulic acid in cereals—a review. Czech J Food Sci 33:1–7

Buranov AU, Mazza G (2009) Extraction and purification of ferulic acid from flax shives, wheat and corn bran by alkaline hydrolysis and pressurised solvents. Food Chem 115:1542–1548

Chen X, Guo Y, Jia G, Zhao H, Liu G, Huang Z (2019) Ferulic acid regulates muscle fiber type formation through the Sirt1/AMPK signaling pathway. Food Funct 10:259–265

Chen S, Lin Y, Miao L, Pan W, Ge X (2021) Ferulic acid alleviates lipopolysaccharide-induced acute liver injury in *Megalobrama amblycephala*. Aquaculture 532:735972

Chesson A, Provan GJ, Russell WR, Scobbie L, Richardson AJ, Stewart C (1999) Hydroxycinnamic acids in the digestive tract of livestock and humans. J Sci Food Agric 79: 373–378

Chodkowska K, Ciecierska A, Majchrzak K, Ostaszewski P, Sadkowski T (2018) Simultaneous miRNA and mRNA transcriptome profiling of differentiating equine satellite cells treated with gamma-oryzanol and exposed to hydrogen peroxide. Nutrients 10:1871

Choudhari AS, Mandave PC, Deshpande M, Ranjekar P, Prakash O (2020) Corrigendum: phytochemicals in cancer treatment: from preclinical studies to clinical practice. Front Pharmacol 11: 175

Citarasu T (2012) Natural antimicrobial compounds for use in aquaculture. In: Infectious disease in aquaculture, pp 419–456

Dai YJ, Jiang GZ, Yuan XY, Liu WB (2018) High-fat-diet-induced inflammation depresses the appetite of blunt snout bream (*Megalobrama amblycephala*) through the transcriptional regulation of leptin/mammalian target of rapamycin. Br J Nutr 120(12):1422–1431

Dawood M, Koshio S (2019) Application of fermentation strategy in aquafeed for sustainable aquaculture. Rev Aquac 12:1–16

Dawood M, Metwally ES, El-Sharawy ME, Ghozlan AM, Ali M (2020) The influences of ferulic acid on the growth performance, haemato-immunological responses, and immune-related genes of Nile tilapia (*Oreochromis niloticus*) exposed to heat stress. Aquaculture 525:735320
de Oliveira Silva E, Batista R (2017) Ferulic acid and naturally occurring compounds bearing a feruloyl moiety: areview on their structures, occurrence, and potential health benefits. Compr Rev Food Sci Food Saf 16:580–616
de Paiva LB, Goldbeck R, Santos WDD, Squina FM (2013) Ferulic acid and derivatives: molecules with potential application in the pharmaceutical field. Braz J Pharm Sci 49:395–411
Dulong V, Kouassi MC, Labat B, Le Cerf D, Picton L (2018) Antioxidant properties and bioactivity of carboxymethylpullulan grafted with ferulic acid and of their hydrogels obtained by enzymatic reaction. Food Chem 262:21–29
Elbesthi RTA, Zdemir KY, Tatan Y, Bilen S, Snmez AY (2020) Effects of ribwort plantain (*Plantago lanceolata*) extract on blood parameters, immune response, antioxidant enzyme activities, and growth performance in rainbow trout (*Oncorhynchus mykiss*). Fish Physiol Biochem 46:1295–1307
Ellis RE, Yuan J, Horvitz HR (1991) Mechanisms and functions of cell death. Annu Rev Cell Biol 7:663–698
Elmore S (2007) A review of programmed cell death. Toxicol Pathol 35:495–516
Faruque S, Albert J (1992) Genetic relation between *Vibrio cholerae* O1 strains in Ecuador and Bangladesh. Lancet 339:740–741
Feng X, Sun RC, Sun JX, Liu CF, He BH, Fan JS (2005) Determination of cell wall ferulic and p-coumaric acids in sugarcane bagasse. Anal Chim Acta 552:207–217
Fu W, Amenyogbe E, Yang E, Luo J, Huang J-S, Xie R-T, Chen G (2022) Effects of dietary supplementation of ferulic acid on growth performance, antioxidant ability, non-specific immunity, hepatic morphology and genes expression related to growth and immunity in juvenile hybrid grouper (*Epinephelus fuscoguttatus*♀ × *Epinephelus polyphekadion*♂). Aquaculture 552:737988
Gao D, Xu Z, Zhang X, Wang H, Wang Y, Min W (2013) Molecular cloning, immunohistochemical localization, characterization and expression analysis of caspase-9 from the purse red common carp (*Cyprinus carpio*) exposed to cadmium. Aquat Toxicol 142–143:53–62
González-Ríos H, Dávila-Ramírez J, Peña-Ramos EA, Valenzuela-Melendres M, Zamorano-García L, Islava-Lagarda TY, Valenzuela-Grijalva NV (2016) Dietary supplementation of ferulic acid to steers under commercial feedlot feeding conditions improves meat quality and shelf life. Anim Feed Sci Technol 222:111–121
Guerreiro I, Couto A, Pérez-Jiménez A, Oliva-Teles A, Enes P (2015) Gut morphology and hepatic oxidative status of European sea bass (*Dicentrarchus labrax*) juveniles fed plant feedstuffs or fishmeal-based diets supplemented with short-chain fructo-oligosaccharides and xylo-oligosaccharides. Br J Nutr 114:1975–1984
Guo T, Yi S, Yin S, Li F (2003) Determination of ferulic acid and adenosine in Angelicae Radix by micellar electrokinetic chromatography. Anal Bioanal Chem 375:840–843
Halliwell B (1994) Free radicals, antioxidants, and human disease: curiosity, cause, or consequence? Lancet 344:721–724
Hashem NM, Gonzalez-Bulnes A, Simal-Gandara J (2020) Polyphenols in farm animals: source of reproductive gain or waste? Antioxidants 9:1023
Hernandez RJ, Kravitz L (2003) The mystery of skeletal muscle hypertrophy. ACSMs Health Fit J 7:18–22
Jacobson M, Weil M, Raff MC (1997) Programmed cell death in animal development. Cell, 88: 347–354
Karga M, Kenanolu ON, Bilen S (2020) Investigation of antibacterial activity of two different medicinal plants extracts against fish pathogens. J Prod Agric 1:5–7
Kikuzaki H, Hisamoto M, Hirose K, Akiyama K, Taniguchi H (2002) Antioxidant properties of ferulic acid and its related compounds. J Agric Food Chem 50:2161–2168

Kim KH, Rong T, Yang R, Cui SW (2006) Phenolic acid profiles and antioxidant activities of wheat bran extracts and the effect of hydrolysis conditions. Food Chem 95:466–473

King AM, Loiselle DS, Kohl P (2004) Force generation for locomotion of vertebrates: skeletal muscle overview. IEEE J Ocean Eng 29:684–691

Kothari D, Patel S, Kim SK (2019) Probiotic supplements might not be universally-effective and safe: a review. Biomed Pharmacother 111:537–547

Kroon PA, Williams G (1999) Hydroxycinnamates in plants and food: current and future perspectives. J Sci Food Agric 79:355–361

Kumar N, Goel N (2019) Phenolic acids: natural versatile molecules with promising therapeutic applications. Biotechnol Rep 24:e00370

Kumar N, Pruthi V (2014) Potential applications of ferulic acid from natural sources. Biotechnol Rep 4:86–93

Kumari J, Sahoo PK (2010) Dietary levamisole modulates the immune response and disease resistance of Asian catfish *Clarias batrachus* (Linnaeus). Aquac Res 37:500–509

Kuppusamy P, Soundha Rr Ajan I, Kim DH, Hwang IH, Choi KC (2019) 4-hydroxy-3-methoxy cinnamic acid accelerate myoblasts differentiation on C2C12 mouse skeletal muscle cells via AKT and ERK 1/2 activation. Phytomedicine 60:152873

Lambert F, Zucca J, Ness F, Aigle M (2013) Production of ferulic acid and coniferyl alcohol by conversion of eugenol using a recombinant strain of *Saccharomyces cerevisiae*. Flavour Fragr J 29:14–21

Lazdins A, Miller C, Thomas CM (2015) Plasmids and the spread of antibiotic resistance. Biochemist 37:12–17

Li Y, Li L, Li J, ZhangL GF, Zhou G (2015) Effects of dietary supplementation with ferulic acid or vitamin E individually or in combination on meat quality and antioxidant capacity of finishing pigs. Asian-Australas J Anim Sci 28:374–381

Liu Z, Ou S, Huang X, Luo Y, Jiang D (2004) Extraction of ferulic acid from enzymatic hydrolysate by ion-exchange adsorption. J Chin Clin Med 27:910–913

Liu XH, Jiang S, Liu B, Zhou Q, Cunxin S, Zheng S, Han Y (2022) Dietary effect of ferulic acid on growth performance, physiological response, non-specific immunity and disease resistance of oriental river prawn (*Macrobrachium nipponense*). Aquac Rep 24:101162

Macías-Cruz U, Perard S, Vicente R, Lvarez FD, Torrentera-Olivera NG, González-Ríos H, Soto-Navarro SA, Rojo R, Meza-Herrera CA, Avendao-Reyes L (2014) Effects of free ferulic acid on productive performance, blood metabolites, and carcass characteristics of feedlot finishing ewe lambs. J Anim Sci 92:5762–5768

Macías-Cruz U, Vicente-Pérez R, López-Baca MA, González-Ríos H, Correa-Calderón A (2018) Effects of dietary ferulic acid on reproductive function and metabolism of pre-pubertal hairbreed ewes during the anestrous season. Theriogenology 119:220–224

Mancuso C, Santangelo R (2014) Ferulic acid: pharmacological and toxicological aspects. Food Chem Toxicol 65:185–195

Mani JS, Johnson JB, Steel JC, Broszczak DA, Neilsen PM, Walsh KB, Naiker M (2020) Natural product-derived phytochemicals as potential agents against coronaviruses: a review. Virus Res 284:197989

Marquardt RR, Li S (2018) Antimicrobial resistance in livestock: advances and alternatives to antibiotics. Anim Front 8:30–37

Mathew S, Abraham TE (2005) Studies on the production of feruloyl esterase from cereal brans and sugar cane bagasse by microbial fermentation. Enzyme Microb Technol 36:565–570

Mattila P, Hellström MJ (2007) Phenolic acids in potatoes, vegetables, and some of their products. J Food Compost Anal 20:152–160

Mattila P, Kumpulainen J (2002) Determination of free and total phenolic acids in plant-derived foods by HPLC with diode-array detection. J Agric Food Chem 50:3660–3667

Mattila P, Pihlava JM, Hellström MJ (2005) Contents of phenolic acids, alkyl and alkenylresorcinols, and avenanthramides in commercial grain products. J Agric Food Chem 53:8290–8295

Medzhitov R (2008) Review article: origin and physiological roles of inflammation. Nature 454: 428–435

Mei HN, Hadi NA (2022) Extraction of ferulic acid from oil palm pressed fiber by a choline chloride based deep eutectic solvent. J Am Oil Chem Soc 4:100155

Melo TD, Lima PR, Carvalho K, Fontenele TM, Solon F, Tomé A, Lemos TD, Fonseca SC, Santos FA, Rao VS (2017) Ferulic acid lowers body weight and visceral fat accumulation via modulation of enzymatic, hormonal and inflammatory changes in a mouse model of high-fat diet-induced obesity. Braz J MedBiol Res 50:e5630

Min JY, Kang SM, Park DJ, Kim YD, Jung HN, Yang JK, Seo WT, Kim SW, Karigar CS, Choi MS (2006) Enzymatic release of ferulic acid from *Ipomoea batatas* L. (sweet potato) stem. Biotechnol Bioprocess Eng 11:372–376

Mohamed GA, Amhamed ID, Almabrok AA, Barka A, Elbeshti RT (2018) Effect of celery (*Apium graveolens*) extract on the growth, haematology, immune response and digestive enzyme activity of common carp (*Cyprinus carpio*). Bull Mar Sci 7:51–59

Mustafa SK, Oyouni A, Aljohani M, Ahmad MA (2020) Polyphenols more than an antioxidant: role and scope. J Pure Appl Microbiol 14:47–61

Naowaboot J, Piyabhan P, Tingpej P, Munkong N, Parklak W, Pannangpetch P (2018) Anti-insulin resistant effect of ferulic acid on high fat diet-induced obese mice. Asian Pac J Trop Biomed 8: 604–608

Nomura E, Kashiwada A, Hosoda A, Nakamura K, Morishita H, Tsuno T, Taniguchi H (2003) Synthesis of amide compounds of ferulic acid, and their stimulatory effects on insulin secretion in vitro. Bioorg Med Chem 11:3807–3813

Overhage J, Steinbuchel A, Priefert H (2002) Biotransformation of eugenol to ferulic acid by a recombinant strain of Ralstonia eutropha H16. Appl Environ Microbiol 68:4315–4321

Özçelik H, Taştan Y, Terzi E, Sönmez AY (2020) Use of onion (*Allium cepa*) and garlic (*Allium sativum*) wastes for the prevention of fungal disease (*Saprolegnia parasitica*) on eggs of rainbow trout (*Oncorhynchus mykiss*). J Fish Dis 43:1325–1330

Ramar M, Manikandan B, Raman T, Priyadarsini A, Palanisamy S, Velayudam M, Munusamy A, Prabhu NM, Vaseeharan B (2012) Protective effect of ferulic acid and resveratrol against alloxan-induced diabetes in mice. Eur J Pharmacol 690:226–235

Rice-Evans CA, Miller NJ, Paganga G (1996) Structure-antioxidant activity relationships of flavonoids and phenolic acids. Free Radic Biol Med 20:933–956

Rice-Evans C, Miller N, Paganga G (1997) Antioxidant properties of phenolic compounds. Trends Plant Sci 2:152–159

Rinaldi SF, Hutchinson JL, Rossi AG, Norman JE (2011) Anti-inflammatory mediators as physiological and pharmacological regulators of parturition. Expert Rev Clin Immunol 7:675–696

Rizzo AM, Berselli P, Zava S, Montorfano G, Negroni M, Corsetto P, Berra B (2010) Endogenous antioxidants and radical scavengers. Springer, New York

Romarheim OH, Zhang C, Penn M, Liu YJ, Tian LX, Skrede A, Krogdahl Å, Storebakken T (2008) Growth and intestinal morphology in cobia (*Rachycentron canadum*) fed extruded diets with two types of soybean meal partly replacing fish meal. Aquac Nutr 14:174–180

Roy S, Metya SK, Rahaman N, Sannigrahi S, Ahmed F (2014) Ferulic acid in the treatment of post-diabetes testicular damage: relevance to the down regulation of apoptosis correlates with antioxidant status via modulation of TGF-β1, IL-1β and Akt signalling. Cell Biochem Funct 32:115–124

Sakai S, Kawamata H, Kogure T, Mantani N, Terasawa K, Umatake M, Ochiai H (1999) Inhibitory effect of ferulic acid and isoferulic acid on the production of macrophage inflammatory protein-2 in response to respiratory syncytial virus infection in RAW264.7 cells. Mediat Inflamm 8: 173–175

Salazar-Lopez N, Astiazaran-García H, Gonzalez-Aguilar G, Loarca-Pina G, Ezquerra-Brauer J, Domínguez-Avila J (2017) Ferulic acid on glucose dysregulation, dyslipidemia, and inflammation in diet-induced obese rats: an integrated study. Nutrients 9:1–13

Salem MOA, Salem TA, Yürüten Zdemir K, Snmez AY, Bilen S, Güney K (2021) Antioxidant enzyme activities and immune responses in rainbow trout (*Onchorhynchus mykiss*) juveniles fed diets supplemented with dandelion (*Taraxacum officinalis*) and lichen (*Usnea barbata*) extracts. Fish Physiol Biochem 47:1053–1062

Sales J (2009) The Effect of fish meal replacement by soybean products on fish growth: ameta-analysis. Br J Nutr 102:1709–1722

Sanger J, Sanger J, Franzini-Armstrong C (2004) Assembly of the skeletal muscle cell. Myology 3: 35–65

Sönmez A (2017) Evaluating two different additive levels of fully autolyzed yeast, Saccharomyces cerevisiae, on rainbow trout (*Oncorhynchus mykiss*) growth, performance, liver histology and fatty acid composition. Turk J Fish Aquat 17:379–385

Steller H (1995) Mechanisms and genes of cellular suicide. Science 267:1445

Sun Y, Li S, Song H, Tian S (2006) Extraction of ferulic acid from Angelica sinensis with supercritical CO2. Nat Prod Res 20:835–841

Tee-Ngam P, Nunant N, Rattanarat P, Siangproh W, Chailapakul O (2013) Simple and rapid determination of ferulic acid levels in food and cosmetic samples sing paper-based platforms. Sensors (Basel, Switzerland) 13:13039–13053

Terzi E, Kucukkosker B, Bilen S, Kenanolu ON, Corum O, Özbek M, Parug SS (2021) A novel herbal immunostimulant for rainbow trout (*Oncorhynchus mykiss*) against *Yersinia ruckeri*. Fish Shellfish Immunol 110:55–66

Tilay A, Bule M, Kishenkumar J, Annapure U (2008) Preparation of ferulic acid from agricultural wastes: its improved extraction and purification. J Agric Food Chem 56:7644–7648

Uraji M, Kimura M, Inoue Y, Kawakami K, Hatanaka T (2013) Enzymatic production of ferulic acid from defatted rice bran by using a combination of bacterial enzymes. Appl Biochem Biotechnol 171:1085–1093

Valério R, Cadima M, Crespo JG, Brazinha C (2021) Extracting ferulic acid from corn fibre using mild alkaline extraction: apilot scale study. Waste Biomass Valor 13:287–297

Villa-Cruz V, Davila J, Viana MT, Vazquez-Duhalt R (2009) Effect of broccoli (*Brassica oleracea*) and its phytochemical sulforaphane in balanced diets on the detoxification enzymes levels of tilapia (*Oreochromis niloticus*) exposed to a carcinogenic and mutagenic pollutant. Chemosphere 74:1145–1151

Vinegar R, Scrheiber W, Hugo R (1969) Biphasic development of carragenin edema in rats. J Pharmacol Exp Ther 166:96–103

Wang Y, Wang W, Wang R, Meng Z, Duan Y, An X, Qi J (2019) Dietary supplementation of ferulic acid improves performance and alleviates oxidative stress of lambs in a cold environment. Can J Anim Sci 99:705–712

Wang Y, Chen X, Huang Z, Chen D, Yu B, Chen H (2021) Effects of dietary ferulic acid supplementation on growth performance and skeletal muscle fiber type conversion in weaned piglets. J Sci Food Agric 101(12):5116–5123

Wen Y, Ushio H (2017) Ferulic acid promotes hypertrophic growth of fast skeletal muscle in zebrafish model. Nutrients 9:E1066. https://doi.org/10.3390/nu9101066

Williams RJ, Spencer J, Rice-Evans C (2004) Flavonoids: antioxidants or signalling molecules? Free Radic Biol Med 36:838–849

Williams AR, Lukasz K, Hajar FA, Peter N, Kerstin S, Nielsen DS, Thamsborg SM, Aroian RV (2017) A polyphenol-enriched diet and Ascaris suum infection modulate mucosal immune responses and gut microbiota composition in pigs. Plos One 12:e0186546

Xu XR, Liu CQ, Feng BS, Liu ZJ (2014) Dysregulation of mucosal immune response in pathogenesis of inflammatory bowel disease. World J Gastroenterol 20:3255

Yeh TS, Hsu CC, Yang SC, Hsu MC, Liu JF (2014) Angelica Sinensis promotes myotube hypertrophy through the PI3K/Akt/mTOR pathway. BMC Complement Altern Med 14:144–144

Yildiztugay E, Ozfidan-Konakci C, Karahan H, Kucukoduk M, Turkan I (2018) Ferulic acid confers tolerance against excess boron by regulating ROS levels and inducing antioxidant system in wheat leaves (*Triticum aestivum*). Environ Exp Bot 161:193–202

Yin X, Liu W, Chen H, Qi C, Chen H, Niu H, Yang J, Kwok K, Dong W (2002) Effects of ferulic acid on muscle development and intestinal microbiota of zebrafish. J Anim Physiol Anim Nutr 106(2):429–440. https://doi.org/10.1111/jpn.1363

Yu L, Wu F, Liu W, Tian J, Lu X, Wen H (2017) Semisynthetic ferulic acid derivative: an efficient feed additive for genetically improved farmed tilapia (*Oreochromis niloticus*). Aquac Res 48: 5017–5028

Yu LJ, Wu F, Jiang M, Yang CG, Liu W, Tian J, Lu X, Wen H (2018) Ferulic acid: a natural compound as an efficient feed additive for GIFT (*Oreochromis niloticus*). Aquacult Nutr 24:27–35

Yu L, Wen H, Jiang M, Wu F, Liu W (2020) Effects of ferulic acid on intestinal enzyme activities, morphology, microbiome composition of genetically improved farmed tilapia (*Oreochromis niloticus*) fed oxidized fish oil. Aquaculture 528:735543

Zhang X, Han B, Feng ZM, Yang YN, Jiang JS, Zhang PC (2018) Ferulic acid derivatives from *Ligusticum chuanxiong*. Fitoterapia 125:147–154

Zhao Z, Egashira Y, Sanada H (2005) Phenolic antioxidants richly contained in corn bran are slightly bioavailable in rats. J Agric Food Chem 53:5030–5035

Zhao Z, Moghadasian MH (2008) Chemistry, natural sources, dietary intake and pharmacokinetic properties of ferulic acid: a review. Food Chem 109:691–702

Chapter 11
The Importance and Utilization of Palm Oil as a Fish Oil Replacement in Aquaculture

Kenneth Prudence Abasubong, Ndakalimwe Naftal Gabriel, Jean-Jacques Yao Adjoumani, AniefiokmkpongOkokon Okon, and Mfon T. Udo

Abstract The oil palm tree is a centuries-old tropical plant native to West Africa. Palm oil has been used as a food and medicine for centuries. Crude palm oil (CPO) is extracted from the oil palm tree's fruit (*Elaeis guineensis*). Palmitic acid, carotene, and vitamin E are abundant in the oil. This chapter reviewed the progress made in using palm oil as an alternative lipid source in aquafeeds. This section discusses the most recent significant materials discovered in the literature on palm oil processing, refining, and distribution compared to other vegetable oils. Furthermore, palm oil in aquafeeds may or may not compromise fish growth and feed utilization composition. Finally, the effect of replacing fish oil with palm oil on immune and antioxidant capacity was discussed. This could be an additional good source of aquafeed oil for African aquaculture. More research in the African setting, however, is required to optimize this ingredient in different culture species.

Keywords Oil palm · Growth performance · Fatty acid profile: body composition: inflammation: antioxidant capacity

---

K. P. Abasubong (✉) · J.-J. Y. Adjoumani
Key Laboratory of Aquatic Nutrition and Feed Science of Jiangsu Province, College of Animal Science and Technology, Nanjing Agricultural University, Nanjing, China

N. N. Gabriel
Department of Fisheries and Ocean Sciences, Faculty of Agriculture, Engineering, and Natural Science, Sam Nujoma Campus, University of Namibia, Henties Bay, Namibia

A. Okon
Department of Animal and Environmental Biology, University of Uyo, Uyo, Akwa Ibom State, Nigeria

M. T. Udo
Department of Fisheries and Environmental Management, University of Uyo, Uyo, Akwa Ibom State, Nigeria

© The Author(s), under exclusive license to Springer Nature Singapore Pte Ltd. 2023
N. N. Gabriel et al. (eds.), *Emerging Sustainable Aquaculture Innovations in Africa*, Sustainable Agriculture and Food Security,
https://doi.org/10.1007/978-981-19-7451-9_11

11.1 Introduction

The world's fastest expanding industry for producing food is aquaculture. It makes up almost half of the world's fish consumption. According to estimates, aquaculture presently provides 50% of the food fish need, and by 2030, this percentage is expected to increase to 60–70% (Subsinghe et al. 2009). Over the past few decades, aquaculture has expanded, and farmed fish consumption has increased globally (FAO 2018). Global fisheries production increased by 174.0 Mt in total, of which 83.6 Mt came from aquaculture and 90.4 Mt from capture (Hodar et al. 2020). The demand for aqua feeds rises as worldwide aquaculture production expands. Fish feeds to give them the nutrients they need for rapid growth, survival, and maintaining a healthy existence. It accounts for between 30 and 70% of the overall operating expenses in an aquaculture production system. Overall, aquaculture feed output increased by around 4% from the previous year to 40.1 million tons in 2018. The primary research areas in recent years have concentrated on identifying substitute raw materials due to the rising expense of fishmeal and marine oils and their restricted availability. Since feed can account for 50% or more of the production costs of most aquaculture systems, artificially designed diets (also known as aquafeed) are essential to maintaining the ongoing expansion of aquaculture production. Fish oil, which provides vital fatty acids and dietary energy, is crucial in aquafeed formulation.

Fish oil (FO) is a crucial source of omega-3 long-chain polyunsaturated fatty acids (n-3 LC-PUFA), particularly docosahexaenoic acid (DHA) and eicosapentaenoic acid (EPA) (Fukada et al. 2020). They are estimated to give 8.5 kcal of metabolizable energy (ME) per gram, making them the biological product with the highest energy density per unit weight. Fish oil is a great provider of lipids, specifically HUFAs and PUFAs (Rice 2009). Triacylglycerols (TAGs), most stored fats and typically make up more than 90% of the total fatty acid makeup, are abundant in fish oil. Particularly in aquaculture diets, the fatty acid profile of fish oils determines a significant portion of their nutritional content.

Additionally, FO includes several lipid-soluble additives, flavorings, and additives that improve palatability and essential nutrients for fish (Turchini et al. 2009). FO has thus emerged as the top lipid source for fish feed (Nasopoulou and Zabetakis 2012). However, the global supply of FO is constrained due to declining marine catches and cannot keep up with the fast-increasing demand for aquafeed production (Turchini et al. 2011). As a result, there is a significant shortage of FO, which drives up FO prices. After fish meal replacement, fish oil replacement in aquafeeds is a top international research focus (Torstensen et al. 2005). Although using vegetable oils in commercial feed formulations for farmed fish has mixed results, this alternative method for creating aquafeeds offers promising results. This is generally attributed to the inconsistent nutritional quality and types of oils (Benedito-Palos et al. 2008; Fountoulaki et al. 2009; Abbasi et al. 2020; Alvarez et al. 2020; Tseng and Lin 2020). Therefore, adequate lipid sources must be found to replace FO to support the sustainable development of aquaculture.

With the global production of roughly 66 million tons in 2017, palm oil (PO) is one of the most widely used vegetable oils. It is found in between 34 and 50% of frequently used food and consumer products (Kushairi et al. 2019). The nutritional and health benefits of PO have been determined for human ingestion and are well established (Sun et al. 2015). The oil is rich in C16:0 and C18:1n-9 FA but has comparatively low levels of C18:2n-6, despite having a higher level of saturated fatty acids (SFA) than other edible vegetable oils (Balbuena-Pecino et al. 2021). PO has stronger resistance to rancid because of its high SFA level, which could produce long-lasting fish meals (Ng et al. 2007; Riera-Heredia et al. 2020). As a result, significant efforts have been made to utilize PO as a viable FO substitute in aquafeeds (Bell et al. 2002), and numerous studies have demonstrated that PO can replace FO in diets at a range between 40 and 100% without negatively impacting fish growth performance (Ng et al. 2004; Fonseca-Madrigal et al. 2015; Balbuena-Pecino et al. 2021). However, when fish were fed a high PO diet, the fatty acids (FA) profile of the muscle was significantly different from that of the FO treatment in various fish species (Fonseca-Madrigal et al. 2015; Aliyu-Paiko and Hashim 2012; Ahmad et al. 2013; Ma et al. 2019). This could have an impact on the quality of fish meat. As a result, while considering whether to include PO in the fish diet, the evaluation of the quality of the flesh may be crucial (Mock et al. 2019; Gudid et al. 2020; Balbuena-Pecino et al. 2021; Guo et al. 2021). In this chapter, we review the use of palm oil in aqua feeds, considering its availability, distribution, significance, growth performance, fatty acid and body composition, and antioxidant and inflammatory and immune response in fish.

11.2 Palm Oil

The ripening mesocarp of the oil palm tree's fruits is where palm oil is obtained (*Elaeis guineensis*). The fruit of the oil palm is a drupe that develops in spikey, compact bunches (Fig. 11.2). The oil palm tree is a member of the Palmae family and has an unbranched stem. The tree has a 25-to-30-year economic life span and can reach a height of 20–30 m. The female bunch can weigh up to 30–40 kg and contain up to 2000 fruits, which are initially black before becoming orange-red when they are ripe (Vincent et al. 2014). After germination, which takes about 3 months, the seedlings are planted in plastic bags, moved into the field at almost a year old, and begin to bear fruit in less than 2 years (Abdullah and Sulaiman 2013). At 5–6 years, the number of leaves in an oil palm plant increases from 30 to 40 per year. After that, just 20–25 leaves each year are produced on average (Abdullah and Sulaiman 2013). Palm oil is one of the top 17 oils and fats now produced and traded worldwide. The fastest-growing oil in the world during the last 40 years has been palm oil. Despite presently ranking second behind soybean oil, palm oil is predicted to become the most produced oil in the world (Carter et al. 2007). Compared to three million tons of soybean oil, only 1.5 million tons were produced in 1961. However, in 2006, palm oil production overtook soybean oil for the first time, and by 2011, there were 48.6

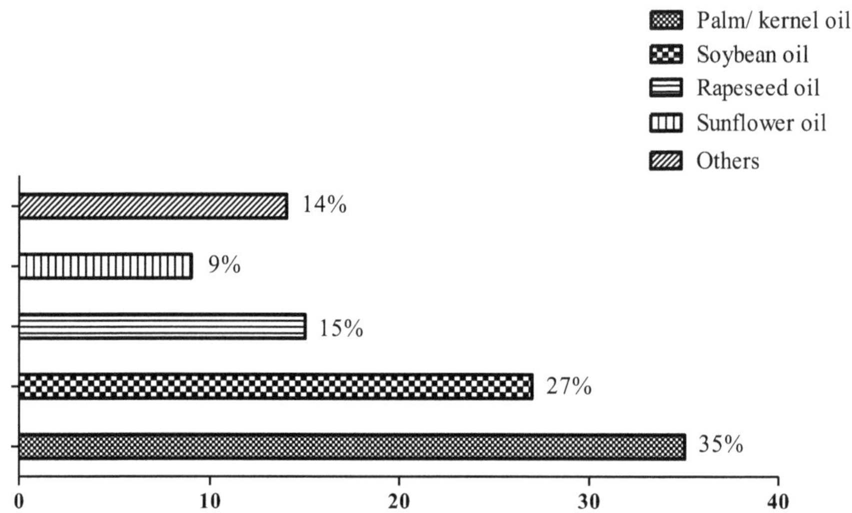

Fig. 11.1 Global vegetable production in 2011. (Adopted from Koushki et al. 2015)

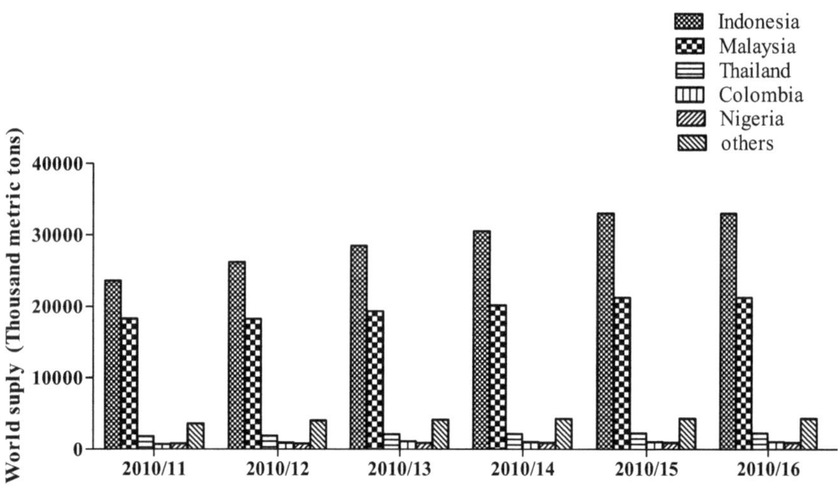

Fig. 11.2 World supply and distribution (Thousand Metric Tons). (Source: Adopted from Koushki et al. 2015)

million tons of palm oil produced globally, compared to 41.6 million tons of soybean oil, as shown in Fig. 11.1. Also, a detailed summary of the physiochemical analysis of palm oil is shown in Table 11.1.

A single hectare of an oil palm plantation can yield up to ten times as much oil as other essential oilseed crops. The mesocarp of the palm fruit yields crude palm oil (CPO), and the kernel yields palm kernel oil (PKO) (Röbbelen 1990). In global trade, CPO and PKO are both significant (Schroeder et al. 2006). CPO and PKO

Table 11.1 Physiochemical analysis of palm oil

Characteristics	Range
Apparent density at 50 1 °C (g/mL)	0.892–0.899
AOM stability (h)	53.0–60.0
Melting point (°C)	33.0–45.0
Oxidative stability index at 110 °C (h)	16.6–19.0
Refractive index at 50 °C	1.449–1.456
Smoke point (°C)	230.0–235.0
Solidification point (°C)	35.0–42.0
Specific gravity at 50 °C	0.888–0.889
Viscosity (cP)	45.0–49.0
Iodine value (g/100 g)	46.0–56.0
Free fatty acid (% FFA as palmitic)	3.17–5.0
Peroxide value (meqO_2/kg)	0.1–10.0
Anisidine value (mg KOH/g)	0.6–4.65
Saponification value (mg KOH/g)	190.0–209.0
Unsaponifiable matter (%)	0.15–0.99
Total polar compounds (%)	9.47–19.50
Total polymer materials (%)	0.4–15.0
Saturated fatty acids SFA (%)	49.9–54.7
Monounsaturated fatty acids MUFA (%)	37.1–39.2
Polyunsaturated fatty acids PUFA (%)	8.1–10.5
Crystal habit	–

Source: adopted from Mba et al. (2015)

produced 32% of the world's fats and oils in 2012. The most significant vegetable oil in the world now is palm oil, which has replaced soybean oil (Oil world 2013). Due to its high carotene concentration, CPO is also known as red palm oil. It contains high levels of sterols (325–365 mg/kg), coenzyme Q10 (ubiquinone) (18–25 mg/kg), and vitamin E (600–1000 ppm) (Tyagi and Vasishtha 1996). About 90% of palm oil is used in the production of edible foods, and the remaining 10% is used in producing soap and oleochemicals (Oil World 2013).

Pisifera, Dura, and Tenera are the three main varieties of oil palm. The dura kinds are distinguished by their thin mesocarp content (35–55% of the fruit weight), thick endocarp shells (2–8 mm), and big kernels. Pisifera kinds are distinguished by thick, 95% mesocarps (with limited oil content), no endocarp, and small kernels (Baryeh 2001). The Tenera is a single-factorial hybrid of Dura and Pisifera (Baryeh 2001). It has a decent kernel size, a 60–95% thick mesocarp, and an endocarp between 0.5 and 3 mm thin. The carotenoids in the CPO are thermally destroyed to generate the appropriate colour for refined, bleached, deodorized (RBD) palm oil during the refining process, in addition to removing any remaining contaminants in the oil (Ping and May 2000). To expand the range of their applications, RBD palm oil can be fractionated by thermomechanical processes to produce RBD palm stearin and RBD palm olein, primarily used as culinary oils (used mainly in margarine and shortenings). Carotenoids, tocopherols, tocotrienols, sterols, phospholipids, triterpene alcohols, squalene, aliphatic alcohols, and aliphatic hydrocarbons are minor constituents in crude palm oil (Hof et al. 2000). The main substances of interest are the carotenes, tocopherols, tocotrienols, sterols, and squalene. Antioxidants that protect the oil from oxidation are carotenoids and tocopherols. During refining, the bleaching and steam deodorization processes partially remove several vital components. The circumstances of refining determine the quantity kept in the refined oils.

11.3 Global Oil Palm Production

Palm oil production has increased rapidly over the past 50 years. In 1970, the world was producing only two million tons. This is now 35 times higher: in 2018, the world produced 71 million tons. The change in global production is shown in the chart (Wahid et al. 2005). The rise of palm oil follows the rapid increase in demand for vegetable oils more broadly. The stacked area chart shows the breakdown of global vegetable oil production by crop. Global production increased ten-fold since the 1960s, from 17 to 170 million tons in 2014. As we will see later in this article, more recent data for 2018 comes to 218 million tons. The story of palm oil is less about it as an isolated commodity but more about the story of the rising demand for vegetable oils. Palm oil is a very productive crop; as we will see later, it produces 36% of the world's oil but uses less than 9% of croplands devoted to oil production. It has therefore been a natural choice to meet this demand.

After being planted, the palm begins to produce fruit in the third year and continues for roughly 25 years. The oil palm fruit yields two different forms of oil: palm oil from the mesocarp and kernel oil from the nut's kernel. Fruit bunches are routinely picked throughout the year following the plantations' established criteria. They are then delivered to the palm oil mills, where raw palm oil and kernels are extracted mechanically and physically. Fruits are carefully picked at their peak of ripeness, handled as little as possible during shipping, and processed under ideal conditions to preserve oil quality.

A tropical plant species is the oil palm. The finest growing regions are located along a confined band around the equator because it thrives in environments with heavy rainfall, sufficient sunlight, and humidity (Wahid et al. (2005). As a result, palm oil is grown in numerous nations throughout Southeast Asia, South America, and Africa. Although several nations have grown some palm oil, only two—Indonesia and Malaysia—dominate the global market. Wahid et al. 2005 reported that 72 million tons of oil palm was produced globally in 2018. Malaysia generated 27% of this, and Indonesia produced 57% (41 million tons) (20 million tons). Indonesia and Malaysia produce 84% of the world's palm oil. Thailand, Colombia, Nigeria, Guatemala, and Ecuador are additional producers as shown in Fig. 11.2.

11.3.1 Oil Palm Processing and Production

The "wet" or "dry" processes are the most popular ways to extract palm oil (Fig. 11.3). The oil from the milled palm fruits is extracted using a liquid, typically

Fig. 11.3 (**a**) Palm tree, (**b**) Palm tree with bunch of fruits, (**c**) Palm friut, (**d**) Sectioned oil palm fruits showing the mesocarp, (e) Palm oil

water, in the so-called "wet" process. Oil is extracted from ruptured oily cells of palm fruits using hot water or steam. In addition to coagulating proteins, the hot water treatment hydrolyses any starch, glue, or gum that may be present. During frying, the gums and resins cause the oil to foam. During oil clarifying, the hydrolyzed and coagulated byproducts are eliminated. After the moisture has been evaporated, the extracted oil is recovered (Obibuzor et al. 2012; Poku 2002). The "dry" approach uses a hydraulic press, a screw press, or centrifugation. Continuous extraction systems are generally more suited for the screw press, while batch or semi-batch extraction systems are more frequently utilized with the hydraulic press (Poku 2002). The fibrous mesocarp is pressed to extract the crude palm oil, leaving behind fiber components containing roughly 5–6% of the oil. The pressure is often decreased, and oil retention rises to 10–12% to prevent the palm kernels' cracking (Corley and Tinker 2003; Obibuzor et al. 2012).

The final press liquor is a blend of various amounts of water, oil, dirt, and fruit fragments. The liquor is further treated to increase oil yield and lower the moisture percentage of the CPO to 10% (Poku 2002). Along with being crucial to the CPO's quality, this process also results in oil loss and environmental contamination. Palm oil mill effluent (POME) is what has left over after the majority of the oil has been extracted. POME can yield more oil when using food-grade solvents for oil extraction, such as hexane and petroleum ether (Obibuzor et al. 2012). Centrifugation and drying are used to purify the CPO stock further. To prevent further deterioration of the oil quality, particularly the FFA concentration, vacuum drying has been recommended. After cooling, the dried oil is poured into storage tanks or other appropriate containers (Bassim et al. 2003; Obibuzor et al. 2012). The viability of using the supercritical carbon dioxide extraction method for the extraction of CPO was reported by Norhuda and Omar in Norhuda and Omar 2009. This is more appropriate when PKO is extracted from crushed kernels. Similar to this, high-capacity mills extract PKO using a solvent extraction technique. Kernel pre-treatment, oil extraction, and solvent recovery from the oil and meal are the three basic unit operations involved. According to Poku (2002) the beginning oil and moisture contents, operation temperature, heating time, and the applied pressure affect the yields and quality of the extracted oil (Fig. 11.4).

11.3.2 Nutritive Component of Palm Oil

11.3.2.1 Sources of Carotenoids and Vitamin

Minor components found in palm oil significantly positively affect nutrition and health. Table 11.2 is a list of the micronutrients. Carotenoids, tocopherols, tocotrienols, sterols, phospholipids, glycerolipids, and squalene are some of these micronutrients (O'Brien (2010). The carotenoids, tocopherols, and tocotrienols operate as biological antioxidants in addition to preserving the stability and quality of palm oil (Wu and Ng 2007). According to Wu et al. (2008), tocopherols and

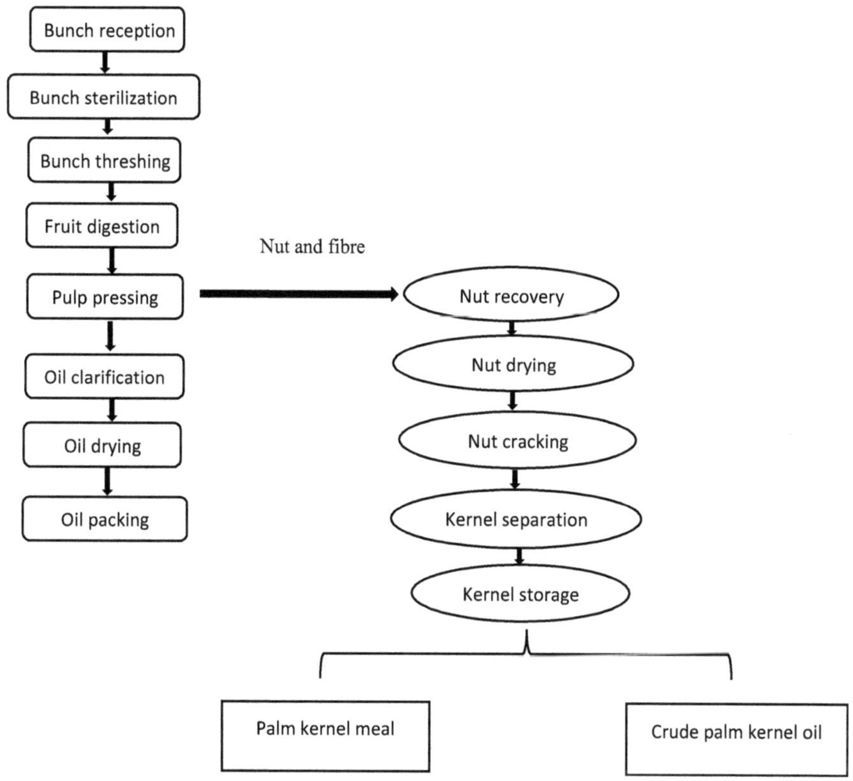

Fig. 11.4 Palm oil processing unit operations. (Source: Koushki et al. 2015)

tocotrienols have anti-cancer, anti-inflammatory, atherosclerosis-controlling, and cholesterol-lowering properties (Das et al. 2007).

The variety of colors found in nature is due to carotenoids. Provitamin A activity has been reported in alpha-, beta-, and cryptoxanthin. The strongest provitamin A carotenoid is beta-carotene. The physiologic processes of cell differentiation, development, and eyesight all require vitamin A (Hof et al. 2000). CPO is the richest natural source of carotenoids since it contains 500–700 ppm of carotenoids. 33%, 65%, and 2% of other carotenoids, such as lycopene and carotene, are found in CPO (Edem et al. 2002). The deep orange-red hue of CPO is a result of the carotenes. Securing free radicals, neutralizing thiyl radicals, chelating peroxy radicals, and quenching singlet oxygen in lipids serve as antioxidants. Carotenoids protect the oil from oxidation by first becoming oxidized themselves before being attacked by oxidants that attack the triacylglycerols (Edem et al. 2002; Gunstone (2011). The use of CPO as a substitute therapy for vitamin A insufficiency has been suggested. The bioavailability of the beta- and gamma-carotene present in CPO is increased by the high digestibility of these compounds (Benadé 2003; Edem et al. 2002).

Lycopene is the pigment that gives fruits and vegetables, including tomatoes, red grapes, watermelon, and pink grapefruit, its red color. Crude oil's deep orange-red

Table 11.2 Micronutrient components of palm oil

Micronutrient/component	Range (ppm)
Carotenoids	
α-Carotene	30.0–35.16
β-Carotene	50.0–56.02
Lycopene	1.0–1.30
Lycopene	500–700
Tocopherol	
α-Tocopherol	129–215
α-Tocopherol	19–32
γ-Tocopherol	19–32
δ-Tocopherol	10–16
Total tocopherol	500–600
Tocotrienols	
α-Tocotrienol	44–73
β-Tocotrienol	44–73
γ-Tocotrienol	262–437
δ-Tocotrienol	70–117
Total tocotrienols	1000–1200
Phytosterols	326–527
Phospholipids	5–130
Squalene	200–500
Ubiquinones	10–80
Aliphatic alcohols	100–200
Triterpene alcohols	40–80
Methyl sterols	40–80
Aliphatic hydrocarbons	50

Source: Mba et al. (2015)

color is from its high carotene content (700–800 ppm) (Sundram et al. 2003). The mechanisms of reactions that the pigment in palm oil goes through inside the plant include antioxidation, photooxidation, and oxidation. Carotene is light and oxygen sensitive. Hydroperoxides produced from lipid oxidation accelerate the oxidation of carotene, causing browning and bleaching (Sambanthamurthi et al. 2000).

Tocopherols and tocotrienols, also known as tocochromanols, are frequently referred to as vitamin E. They can dissolve in fat. The most prevalent form of tocopherol is alpha. The tocopherols and tocotrienols vary depending on the type of vegetable oil and where it comes from (Gunstone 2011). One of the most abundant natural sources of vitamin E is palm oil. Since tocopherols and tocotrienols are both present in palm oil's vitamin E, it is unique. There is 600–1200 ppm of vitamin E in CPO. Tocotrienols make up 78–82%, while tocopherols make up 18–22%. The three main tocotrienols are alpha, beta, and gamma tocotrienols (O'Brien 2010; Ping and May 2000; Zou et al. 2012). Processing and refining CPO causes some vitamin E to be lost. Tocopherols and tocotrienols, which act as antioxidants and free radical quenchers, help keep palm oil stable. Tocopherols can stop lipid oxidation by preventing the chain propagation step's production of peroxide, or they can stop the decomposition process by preventing the production of aldehydes. According to reports, alpha-tocopherol is exceptionally reactive with singlet oxygen and shields the oil from photooxidation (Sundram et al. 2003).

The unsaponifiable fraction of palm oil also contains sterols, higher aliphatic alcohols, and hydrocarbons, which are minor ingredients. Palm oil has very little cholesterol, like all edible oils of vegetable origin. Wax, methyl esters, phytosterols, and ketones are all reduced during refinement (Edem et al. 2002; Sambanthamurthi et al. 2000). Low concentrations of phenolic compounds (100 mg/L) are also present in palm oil. During frying, the phenolic chemicals are to blame for the early darkening of palm oil (Sundram et al. (2003). CPO, palm olein, and their refined derivatives contain a variety of sterols, much like all other vegetable oils. Avenesterols, stigmasterols, campesterols, and sitosterols are among the sterols present in palm oil. Avenesterols have antioxidant properties (Gunstone 2011).

In general, palmitic acid's detrimental effects on health are not demonstrated (Fattore and Fanelli 2013). Palmitic acid is only one of the numerous components of CPO, an intricate alimentary medium. In specific ways, nutritional balance is provided by palm oil's oleic acid content and the presence of several antioxidant chemicals.

11.3.2.2 Source of Fatty Acid

Crude palm oil (CPO) is naturally semi-solid at room temperature due to the almost equal proportion of saturated fatty acids (SFA) and unsaturated fatty acids (UFA). CPO contains much palmitic acid (C16:0), which makes up about 44% of the FAC. Oleic acid (C18:1), linoleic acid (C18:2), and stearic acid (C18:0) are the other three primary fatty acids, making up 40%, 10%, and 5% of the total fat, respectively (Tan and Man 2000). Like other vegetable oils, CPO comprises mixed triacylglycerols (TAGs) and partial acylglycerols such as diacylglycerols (DAGs) and monoacylglycerols as shown in Table 11.3. These fractions include palm olein, palm stearin, and superolein (MAGs). The hydrolysis products of TAGs, known as DAGs and MAGs, can alter the oil's melting point and crystallization behavior (Foster et al. 2009). At concentrations above 10%, partial acylglycerols can produce cloudiness, significantly when temperatures drop below 20 °C (Berger 2007). Table 11.3 displays the fatty acid and glyceride content of palm oil. Its makeup determines the physical and chemical characteristics of the oil. Red palm oil's fatty acid content has been chemically analyzed, and the results show that it comprises roughly 50% saturated fat, 40% monounsaturated fat, and 10% polyunsaturated fat. Palm oil is more stable and less prone to oxidation at high temperatures, while having more saturated fatty acids than soya oil.

Table 11.3 Fatty acid profile of crude palm oil

Compound	Typical	Range
Fatty acid composition (%)		
Lauric acid (C12:0)	0.0	0.1–1.0
Myristic acid (C14:0)	1.1	0.9–1.5
Palmitic acid (C16:0)	44.0	41.8–46.8
Palmitoleic acid (C16:1)	0.1	0.1–0.3
Stearic acid (C18:0)	4.5	4.5–5.1
Oleic acid (C18:1)	39.2	37.3–40.8
Linoleic acid (C18:2)	10.1	9.1–11.0
Linolenic acid (C18:3)	0.4	0.4–0.6
Arachidic acid (C20:0)	0.4	0.2–0.7
Triglyceride composition (%)		
Trisaturated (SSS)	9.8	0.8–9.0
Disaturated (SUS)	48.8	38.5–50.3
Monosaturated (SUU)	36.5	31.8–44.4
Triunsaturated (UUU)	4.8	4.8–9.8
Diglycerides (%)	4.9	3.0–7.6

Source: Mba et al. (2015)

11.4 Uses of Palm Oil

Palm oil, produced from oil palm fruit, has many uses in residential and industrial settings. The debris, which includes palm bunches, trunks, palm fronds, and palm kernel cakes, can be used in home and commercial settings. They make food and non-food products like margarine, shortening, compound cooking fat, soap, detergent manufacture, candles, cosmetics, lubricant grease, confectionery fat, vanaspati (vegetable ghee), and frying fat. In addition to their use in an industry, these oils are also employed locally in antidotes for poisoning, surface protectors for minor wounds, and body treatments and cooking oils (Akpanabiatu et al. 2001).

11.5 Oil Palm Utilization in Aquaculture Nutrition as Fish Oil Replacement

Using palm oil in aquafeeds adds excellent value to the feed produced. It possesses different properties, making it a better oil source concerning its effect on feed quality. Rancidity, the chemical decomposition of fats, oils, and other lipids (this degradation also occurs in mechanical cutting fluids), is a normal phenomenon found in aquafeeds. The level of feed rancidity in aquafeeds made of palm oil is substantially lower in aquafeeds made of palm oil than in other vegetables. This is an advantage of the use of palm oil in aquafeeds over the use of other oils with fish oil inclusive. This is because palm oil contains vitamin E and carotenoids, potent antioxidants in the natural states, and protective values against rancidity.

11.5.1 Effects on Growth Performances and Feed Utilization

Growing performance is one factor that can be used to determine if a particular nutrient or nutrient formulation impacts aquatic animals, such as fish or crustaceans. However, the development of fish is influenced by a variety of favorable and unfavorable influences. According to studies, the quantity and quality of feed play a significant role in how fish species grow. Numerous research has documented the positive effects of palm oil as a good substitute for various fish species.

The findings demonstrated that growth and feed utilization were not compromised when palm oil (PO) was used in place of fish oil (FO) either partially or totally in Nile tilapia (Christain et al. 2018). Weight gain and specific growth rate (SGR) were significantly lower in fish fed 8PO and 10PO diets. The increase in PO levels did not affect fish survival, feed intake, and feed conversion ratio in Juvenile Chu's Croaker, *Nibea coibor* (Huang et al. 2016). Fish fed the diet with 100% PO showed significantly lower growth performance with higher FER and FCR content than those in the control group in large yellow croaker (*Larimichthys crocea*) (Li et al. 2019). Five isonitrogenous diets containing 32% crude protein and increasing amounts of palm oil, 2%, 4%, 6%, and 8% and control (FO) were employed as the primary lipid sources. The findings revealed that at 6% dietary palm oil levels, the animals gained the most weight, had the highest specific growth rate, and had the highest protein efficiency ratio. However, compared to the control group, the feed conversion ratio (FCR) exhibited a reverse pattern (Ayisi et al. 2017). A different study on Japanese catfish found that although there was no discernible difference in the fish's final weight, fish fed with diet PO had numerically higher total weight gain and specific growth rate, as well as higher feed consumption than fish fed with the control diet. While feed efficiency, protein efficiency ratio, apparent protein retention, and apparent lipid retention were comparable across all fish groups. Throughout the 8-week feeding trial, there was no mortality in the diet PO group, and survival rates were reasonable, with at least 96% (Asdari et al. 2014).

Fish fed a 50% PO diet had final weights (FW) and weight gains (WG) that were considerably higher than those of fish fed a 25% PO diet but not significantly higher than those of the control, 75% PO, and 100% PO groups. There was no discernible difference between the groups regarding the condition factor and specific growth rate (SGR). Additionally, in Nile tilapia, feed intake and conversion ratio were comparable across all groups (Ayisi et al. 2017). The growth performance of fish given the crude palmoil (CPO) and palm fatty acid distillate (PFAD) dietary treatments was observed, and both were significantly better than the control (FO). Additionally, feed intake was comparable between the CPO and PFAD treatments and much higher than in the FO treatment. However, it was shown that FCR in the PFAD was superior to that in the other two treatments (Aliyu-Paiko and Hashim 2012). Following 13 weeks of feeding, dietary CPO in rainbow trout had no impact on growth performance or feed efficiency (Fonseca-Madrigal et al. 2015). Fish fed with 10F0P and 8F2P showed no discernible variations in SGR, but both treatments had SGR much higher than 4F6P. Red Sea Bream *Pagrus major* fed 6F4P and 4F6P, after 50 days of feeding, showed significantly lower FI compared to diet groups 10F0P and 8F2P (Komilus et al. 2008). While replacing fish oil with palm oil up to 25%, *C. mrigala* growth performance and survival were unaffected. However, inclusion rates above this threshold significantly slowed the fish's growth. Though, at all levels of dietary PO inclusion, no appreciable improvements in feed efficiency were seen (Singh et al. 2012).

Except for TL and FC, including 3 and 6% of palm oil in the diet resulted in better results than the diet containing only soybean oil. Diets containing 3, 4.5, and 6% of palm oil increased total fish length, while for CF, higher results were observed compared to the control diet for fish fed with a diet containing 100% palm oil in Nile tilapia (*Oreochromis niloticus*) post-larvae (de Souza Alves et al. 2021). FBW, WG, and SGR values were considerably more significant in crabs fed the FO diet than those provided the PO and PO + VA diets. Compared to crabs fed a PO diet alone, adding vitamin A to the diet increased crabs' FBW, WG, and SGR (Huang et al. 2022). African catfish's growth performance significantly improved in response to palm oil additions of up to 8%, while higher levels of palm oil supplementation in the diet had no further effect on growth. RBDPO or CPO was included at the same inclusion level in the diets of African catfish, and neither significantly affected growth or protein utilization efficiency. Compared to catfish fed diets with 4% RBDPO or the control diet, nitrogen retention was considerably higher in catfish fed diets with 8%, 12%, or 16% deodorized palm olein (RBDPO) (Lim et al. 2001). African catfish grew noticeably more when fed a diet containing 25% PFAD than fish fed a control diet with fish oil as the only lipid source. Catfish growth performance did not further increase with higher dietary PFAD supplementation doses (Ng et al. 2003).

Nevertheless, mRNA expression of Capn-3 of fish fed 75% PO was significantly higher than those fed 0% PO, 25% PO, and 100% PO. Also, fish fed 25% PO downregulated Pax-7 mRNA expression, significantly lower than all other groups and the FO group. However, no noticeable differences were observed in the mRNA expression of Psma-5, MyoG, MyoD, IGf-I, IGF-II, and GH (Ayisi et al. 2019).

11.5.2 Effects on Fatty Acid Composition

The body needs triglycerides, a lipid, to store energy, and fatty acids are one of their primary components. A lipid, in the simplest terms, is a type of molecule that includes fatty acids (Lupiañez-Perez et al. 2015). Omega-6 fatty acids linoleic acid and alpha-linolenic acid are complex for many animals to synthesize (an omega-3 fatty acid). On the other hand, those fatty acids are required for cellular processes and synthesizing more critical omega-3 and omega-6 fatty acids. However, studies have shown that palm oil could replace FO without adverse effects on fatty acid profile. For example, in tilapia, after 20 days of feeding, palm oil had considerably higher levels of saturated and monounsaturated fatty acids, but lower levels of polyunsaturated fatty acids (PUFA) than fish fed the FO diet. However, those fed the FO diet had much higher quantities of EPA (eicosapentaenoic acid) and DHA (docosahexaenoic acid) than the PO group. In an 8-week feeding trial, Ng et al. (2001) found that fish fed diets based on palm oil had considerably lower amounts of polyunsaturated fatty acids (PUFA) than those fed the CLO diet. However, their levels of saturated fatty acids did not change. Dietary PUFA concentrations significantly impacted the levels of each PUFA in muscle lipids.

After 8 weeks of feeding, (Asdari et al. 2014) discovered that Japanese Catfish *Silurus asotus* Juveniles fed on PO and MCT diets had significantly greater total levels of saturated and monounsaturated fatty acids in their muscles, notably oleic acid, than fish fed on FO diets, while the inverse was true for total n-3 fatty acids. Additionally, fish fed a PO, and MCT diet had lower n-3/n-6 ratios and total polyunsaturated fatty acid levels than fish fed a control diet. Finally, fish fed the FO diet also had the muscle's highest levels of total n-3 fatty acids. These levels were primarily made up of DHA, with fish on the PO and MCT diets having significantly lower levels of EPA. Similarly, fish treated with crude palm oil (CPO) and palm fatty acid distillate (PFAD) had considerably higher muscle SFA content than fish in control, although muscle MUFA level showed the reverse tendency. Compared to the control diet, fish given the CPO and PFAD diet had considerably lower levels of n-3 PUFA and higher levels of n-6 PUFA in their muscle Channa striatus (Aliyu-Paiko and Hashim 2012).

Additionally, differing quantities of palm oil significantly impacted the total saturates, total n-3 polyunsaturated fatty acids (PUFA), total n-6 PUFA, and DHA/EPA in muscle in Nile tilapia. Docosahexaenoic acid (DHA) levels in the fish fed the 6% palm oil level were the highest and were substantially higher than those in the control group (Ayisiet al. 2017). Liver 18:2n-6, SFAs, MUFAs, SFAs/PUFAs, and n-6 were markedly elevated when PO was substituted for FO. Conversely, PUFAs, n-3: n-6 and n-3 were dramatically reduced with increasing PO levels. These were 20:4n-6, 20:5n-3, and 22:6n-3. Additionally, Nile tilapia liver lipid rose along with dietary PO inclusion levels (Ayisi et al. 2018). Another study also shows that 18:3n-3 (LNA) and 20:4n-3 considerably rose with increasing PO inclusion levels in Nile tilapia, but 20:5n-3 (EPA), 20:4n-6 (ARA), and 22:6n-3 (DHA) dramatically reduced with increasing PO inclusion levels. Additionally, as PO inclusion levels rose compared to the control, n-3 PUFA declined while total saturated fatty acid (SFA) increased (Ayisi et al. 2019).

According to a two-week study by Christain et al. (2018) in Oreochromis niloticus, liver total saturated fatty acids (SFA), monounsaturated fatty acids (MUFA), and 18:2n-6 (LA) increased as PO inclusion levels increased. In contrast, EPA, DHA, and total polyunsaturated fatty acids (PUFA) decreased as PO inclusion levels increased. As opposed to the control, increasing PO levels in the muscle led to an increase in EPA, DHA, total n-3 PUFA, total PUFA, n-3: n-6 ratio, and 20:2n-6. After 56 days of feeding, replacing FO with PO in *Nibea coibor* led to higher levels of saturates and monoene like 16:0, 18:1n-9, 18:2n-6, and C18:3n-3 but lower levels of n-3 HUFA like 20:5n-3, 20:5n-3, 22:6n-3, and n-3/n-6 FA ratio (Huang et al. 2016). The ratios of 18:1n-9 and 18:2n-6 increased with increasing CPO content, while the ratios of n-3HUFA, 20:5n-3, and 22:6n-3 decreased. However, the pyloric ceca and muscle exhibited higher levels of palmitic acid (16:0) but not the liver. Compared to the control, the capacity of HUFA synthesis from 18:3n-3 in the hepatocytes and enterocytes of rainbow trout rose three times when dietary CPO was gradually increased (Fonseca-Madrigal et al. 2015). The amounts of EPA and DHA in the dorsal and ventral muscles both decreased steadily as the amount of dietary palm oil rose. Red sea bream showed no symptoms of EFA shortage throughout the trial, but there was a similar gradient decline in the n-3/n-6 ratio in both the dorsal and ventral muscles compared to the control (Komilus et al. 2008). Concentrations of monounsaturated, polyunsaturated, and saturated fatty acids in palm oil were observed, and the most prominent fatty acids were palmitic (C16: 0), oleic (C18: 1n-7), and linoleic acid (C18: 2n-6) as compared to the control (Alves et al. 2021).

Crabs fed diets of PO and PO + VA showed lower ΣSFA content and SFA, including C14:0, C16:0, C18:0, C20:0, and C22:0, compared to those fed FO and decreased the C12:0 and C16:0) content in hepatopancreas compared to those fed PO diet alone. C14:1n-9, C18:1n-7, C18:1n-9, and C20:1n-9 in the hepatopancreas of crabs fed PO and PO + VA were significantly lower than those fed a diet of FO. Crabs fed diets of PO showed higher C18:1n- 9 content in hepatopancreas than those fed FO, whereas crabs fed PO + VA showed decreased C18:1n-9 content in hepatopancreas. ΣMUFA in the hepatopancreas of crabs fed PO and PO + VA diet was significantly higher than those fed FO, but the opposite was found in Σn-6 PUFA and C18:2n-6 levels in hepatopancreas but showed lower levels of Σn-3 PUFA, C20:4n-6, C20:5n-3, C22:5n-3, and C22:6n-3 in hepatopancreas than that fed FO diet (Huang et al. 2022). PO inclusion showed that the concentrations of 16: 0, 18:1(n-9), 18:2(n-6), total saturated fatty acids, and total monoenoic fatty acids increased linearly with increasing dietary PO. The concentration of eicosapentaenoic acid [20:5(n-3)] was reduced significantly with increasing levels of dietary PO, but the concentration of docosahexaenoic acid [22:6(n-3)] was significantly reduced only in fish fed 100% PO, compared with the other three treatments in Atlantic Salmon (*Salmo salar*) (Bell et al. 2002).

11.5.3 Effects on Hematological Profile

The physiological status and health of fish cultivation can be determined by its hematological profile, so hematology, in conjunction with other standard diagnostic techniques, could be used to identify the effect of dietary nutrition formulation, evaluate stress-causing conditions and/or diseases that have an impact on production performance (Tavares-Dias and Moraes 2006). Based on its nutritional value, palm oil is added to animal feed to replace expensive fish oil and enhance physiological and health-related aspects of animal production. For instance, the highest total serum protein level was seen in fish given 20% palm oil, which was significantly higher than fish fed 60% palm oil, the control, and 40% palm oil. Red blood cells (RBC), hematocrit (Hct), and total bilirubin did not substantially differ across groups. Fish fed with 60% palm oil had the lowest RBC levels compared to the control group (Han et al. 2015). According to the results, glucose, hemoglobin, and red blood cells were all significantly influenced by OF level, whereas Glu and RBC were influenced considerably by factor PO. Despite their interaction, OF and P had no significant impact on the serum level of GOT (glutamic oxaloacetic transaminase). The treatment with the highest RBC was 6F4P, which had a much greater RBC than the oxidized groups (Han et al. 2012). Compared to fish given FO, those fed PO and LO showed a substantial rise in blood levels of TG, NEFA, TNF, ALT, and AST activity. However, there was no discernible difference in the concentration of IL6 in fish serum between treatments (Mu et al. 2019). Elevated dietary PO significantly impacted triglycerides, cholesterol, and total protein levels. The fish fed 8% PO had the most significant mean cholesterol concentrations. At the same time, total protein and triglycerides rose with increasing dietary PO and were considerably higher than those in the control group (Ayisi et al. 2017). Additionally, the plasma levels of the enzymes alanine transaminase (ALT) and aspartate aminotransferase (AST) were also significantly higher in fish fed a meal containing 100% PO than in the control group (Li et al. 2019). Moreover, 8 weeks of feeding by Christain et al. (2018) revealed that Oreochromis niloticus groups fed larger amounts of PO had significantly higher levels of AST, total protein, triacylglycerol (TAG), and low-density lipoprotein cholesterol (LDL-C) than the control group.

11.5.4 Effects on Body Composition

The proximate composition of fish includes the determination of moisture, protein, fat, and ash contents, which constitute about 96–98% of the total constituents of the fish body. Studying these components gives us a clear understanding of assessing the energy value of the fish. The chemical composition of fish flesh is regarded as a reliable predictor of the fish's quality, nutritional value, physiological state, and habitat (Ravichandran et al. 2011). Nowadays, appropriate knowledge about the proximate composition of fish is increasingly finding application in various profound areas. Knowing the chemical composition of fish help nutritionists determine readily available sources of high-protein, low-fat food sources for human food (Foran et al. 2005; Mozaffarian and Rimm 2006).

There were no apparent differences between the groups regarding fish body moisture, crude lipid, ash, or crude protein. Despite this, juvenile Japanese flounders fed the control diet had a slightly greater crude protein content than those feed with different levels of PO (Han et al. 2015). The crude protein of the fish's entire body was significantly impacted by both OF (oxidized fish oil) and P (palm oil), and interactions between the two diets were significant compared to the control. However, crude protein (CP) in the group fed the 10F diet was significantly higher than in oxidized groups (10OF, 6OF4P, and 4OF6P), as well as in the 10P and 4F6P, which were regarded as high substitutions of palm oil (Han et al. 2012). According to Bahurmiz and Ng et al. (2007), there was no discernible impact of the dietary lipid source on the moisture, protein, or ash content of tilapia fillets after 20 weeks of the diet. However, tilapia fed the PFAD diet exhibited statistically lower fillet lipid content than fish fed the CPO or RBDPO diets when compared to control FOs. In comparison to SFO, the CPKO and CLO diets did not significantly differ in terms of whole-body lipid levels after 8 weeks of feeding hybrid tilapia, according to (Ng et al. 2001); however, fish fed the SFO diet had significantly more total muscle lipid than fish fed the CLO-based diets. However, fish fed the CPO and CPKO diets exhibited significantly higher bone ash than fish fed the SFO diet.

During an 8-week feeding trial, it was discovered that the amount of dietary palm oil had a significant impact on the lipid, moisture, ash, and crude protein contents of the fish's muscle, liver, and entire body, with the highest level being obtained at 6–8% in comparison to those fed a control diet (Ayisi et al. 2017). The total body's protein and moisture contents did not significantly alter across dietary regimens. The liver's lipid content increased more with increasing dietary PO than in the control group. However, there were no appreciable differences between the large yellow croaker (*Larimichthys crocea*) fed diets with graduated levels of PO and the control in terms of the moisture content of the liver, the moisture, and lipid contents of muscle (Li et al. 2019). Whole-body lipid deposition in fish fed diet 4F6P was significantly lower than in other dietary groups.

On the other hand, the dorsal lipid contents gradually decreased with increased palm oil levels but there was no significant difference in ventral muscle in red sea bream compared to FO (Komilus et al. 2008). Additionally, due to PO substitution, *Cirrhinus mrigala's* muscle proximate composition did not change dramatically (Singh et al. 2012). However, fish fed 25% PO had a much lower protein content than fish fed 100% PO than FO. In Japanese Catfish *Silurus asotus* Juveniles, there was no appreciable variation in the whole-body moisture, protein, lipid, and proximate ash composition between treatments as compared to the control (Asdari et al. 2014). Fish fed diet 4F6P deposited considerably less total body lipids contents than fish fed other diets. Another study reported that the red sea bream's dorsal lipid levels steadily reduced as the amount of palm oil increased, but there was no discernible variation in the ventral muscle (Komilus et al. 2008). The amounts of dietary palm oil had a substantial impact on the composition of the body's macrominerals, which are calcium (Ca), potassium (K), sodium (Na), phosphorus (P), and magnesium (Mg). Iron (Fe), zinc (Zn), manganese (Mn), and copper (Cu) had similar trends in whole-body micromineral composition when compared to controls in the African Catfish, *Heterobranchus longifilis* (Ble et al. 2018). Compared to crabs fed a diet of FO, those fed diets of PO and PO + VA showed a significant reduction in crude protein and increased total lipid content throughout the body (Huang et al. 2022). The different diets unaffected the moisture and ash content of the crabs. However, when fish were fed with increasing amounts of dietary palm oil compared to the control, the content of lipids whole body and muscles increased (Lim et al. 2001).

Following a 56-day feeding with groupers (*Epinephelus coioides*), noted that the whole-body crude protein content increased in dietary FO replacing level; however, it did not influence the whole-body moisture, crude lipid, and ash content as compared to PO group. Additionally, the incremental dietary PO inclusion levels did not affect the muscles' lipid, protein, or moisture contents. In contrast, the hepatic lipid and moisture contents tended to increase with increasing dietary PO inclusion levels. Hepatic moisture and lipid levels were considerably lower in diets with 75% or more PO substitution than in the control diet. Another study also reported that Africa catfish fed the CLO, CPO, CPKO and CLO + PFAD diets, CLO + SBC diet, and fish fed the RBDPO diet had the lowest quantities of alpha-tocopherol as compared to the highest concentrations in the muscle of fish fed the SFO diet (Ng et al. 2003). After 8 weeks of feeding, Nile tilapia (*Oreochromis niloticus*) fed on CPO displayed the most outstanding level of total carotenes compared to those in control (Wickramanayake et al. 2021). In response to rising dietary levels of alpha-tocopherol derived from RBDPO and CPO, alpha-tocopherol concentrations in muscle and liver tissues increased linearly. At all inclusion levels, African catfish, *Clarias gariepinus*, fed CPO-supplemented meals had approximately three- and five-times higher amounts of alpha-tocopherol in their muscle and liver tissues, respectively, than fish fed RBDPO-supplemented diets as compared to FO (Lim et al. 2001).

11.5.5 Effects on Biological Indices

Fish stocks have been identified using morphological features and biometrical traits, such as morphometric measurement and meristic count. These techniques continue to be the easiest and most accurate ways to identify different species (Turan 2004). In phylogenetics, the analysis of variations and differences in the morphometric and meristic traits of fish populations is crucial because it yields data for further research on the genetic improvement of stocks.

Compared to fish fed the FO diet, the GSI for both male and female tilapia exhibited greater values in fish fed the palm oil-based diets, particularly the CPO diet, than those offer the control diet (Bahurmiz and Ng 2007). Fish fed the CPKO and CLO + PFAD diets had considerably higher HSI scores than fish fed the SFO diet, whereas fish fed the SFO and CLO + SBC diets had significantly lower VSI scores than fish fed the CLO and CPO diet (Ng et al. 2003). The HSI and VSI values for each treatment did not differ. For the same reason, CY did not differ substantially differ between the control and the other two treatments in snakehead (*Channa striatus*, Bloch 1793) fingerlings (Aliyu-Paiko and Hashim 2012). A similar result was also observed in large yellow croaker (*Larimichthys crocea*) (Li et al. 2019) and in Japanese Catfish *Silurus asotus* Juveniles fed a palm oil diet (Asdari et al. 2014). Also, after 8 weeks of feeding, there was no difference between the different groups in the protease activity of the anterior, middle, and posterior intestines (AI, MI, and PI) compared to those fed FO in Nile tilapia. However, there was a trend of increasing lipase activity along with increasing PO levels, with 50% PO recording the highest amylase activity in AI, MI, and DI (Christain et al. 2018).

11.5.6 Effects on Lipid-Related Genes Expression

Crabs fed a PO diet had higher DGAT1 gene expression in the hepatopancreas than crabs fed a FO diet. In contrast, crabs fed diet PO + VA had lower levels of DGAT1 mRNA in the hepatopancreas than crabs fed diet PO. However, the mRNA levels of CPT1a, CPT1B, CAAT, and CPT2 in the hepatopancreas of crabs fed FO were the lowest, whereas the opposite was found in PO diet. Additionally, CPT1a, CPT1B, CAAT, and CPT2 gene expressions were higher in crabs given a PO + VA diet than in crabs on a PO diet alone (Huang et al. 2022). In grouper, the mRNA levels of the FAS, G6PD, LPL, PPARA, and D6FAD genes in the liver showed positive linear and/or quadratic responses, whereas the SCD, HSL, ATGL, FABP, SREBP-1C, and ELOVL5 genes displayed an opposite trend with increasing dietary PO inclusion levels, as compared to FO group. Another study also reported that, except LXR and ELOVL 5, the expression levels of PPAR-α, PPAR-β, ME, LPL, and G6PD genes increased as dietary PO inclusion levels increased. Expression levels of PPAR-α, ME, G6PD, LXR, and LPL were influenced significantly with dietary PO inclusion in *Oreochromis niloticus* as compared to those fed FO diet (Ayisi et al. 2018).

11.5.7 Effects on Antioxidant Capacity

When RO generation exceeds the available antioxidant system, oxidative stress occurs (Adly 2010). The expression of antioxidant enzymes is suppressed by oxidative stress (Wiernsperger 2003). The best natural source of carotenoids is present in crude palm oil (about 15 times more than carrots), which significantly protects cells and tissues from the detrimental effect of free radicals by acting as biological antioxidants. When a higher lipid diet is consumed, a buildup of free radicals is associated with degenerative diseases such as steatosis in fish species (Abasubong et al. 2017). Therefore, it is essential to administer a diet high in antioxidants that can hinder the occurrence of free radicals. Red palm oil is processed palm oil that has been deodorized and acidified and it retains 80% of the natural carotenoids, making it an excellent source of vitamin A. These organic antioxidants are thought to prevent cellular deterioration by acting as free radical buffers and protective barriers.

It has also been demonstrated that consuming PO helps to improve antioxidant status by raising levels of antioxidant enzymes (Ayeleso et al. 2014). However, the liver anti-oxidative enzyme activity in Japanese flounder fed experimental diets for 60 days reveals that the anti-oxidative enzyme activity of fish fed diets containing palm oil was lower than that of the control group. The differences between these two groups were insignificant, despite the control group having the most outstanding levels of SOD and CAT (Han et al. 2015). Compared to fish given FO, fish fed PO and LO was reduced in T-AOC content of the liver, but did not significantly differ from fish fed FO. However, fish fed LO showed significantly greater liver MDA levels than fish fed FO or PO, whereas fish fed PO had significantly lower values than the FO group in giant yellow croaker *Larimichthys crocea* (Mu et al. 2019). According to Li et al. (2019) research, fish fed diets containing 100% PO had significantly lower plasma levels of total antioxidant capacity (T-AOC) and catalase activity (CAT) than fish fed diets containing up to 66.7% PO in large yellow croaker. However, these differences were not statistically significant compared to the control (*Larimichthys crocea*). There were no appreciable variations in the CAT, SOD, or LYZ treatments. However, serum malondialdehyde (MDA) was significantly lower in fish fed 100% PO compared to all other groups, whereas total antioxidant capacity (TAC) was significantly higher in fish fed FO diet compared to all other groups. Nevertheless, Nile tilapia fed FO, 25% PO, and 50% PO exhibited considerably greater glutathione reductase (GR) levels than fish fed 75% and 100% PO (Christain et al. 2018). Another study shows that, fish fed a 10PO diet had considerably higher SOD and CAT activity than fish fed a FO diet, whereas Fish fed 2PO, 4PO, 6PO, and 8PO diets did not significantly differ in SOD and CAT activities in juvenile Chu's Croaker, *Nibea coibor* (Huang et al. 2016). The MDA concentration, SOD and GPx activity in the hepatopancreas of crabs given FO were considerably higher than those fed PO. However, compared to crabs fed PO alone, those given vitamin (VA addition) in PO dramatically boosted the activities of SOD and GPx and decreased the MDA content in the crabs' hepatopancreas. Different diets did not affect T-AOC in the hepatopancreas, whereas crabs fed PO displayed a lower value than those fed FO. Compared to crabs fed PO alone, VA added to the PO increased the T-AOC level in the crabs' hepatopancreas (Huang et al. 2022).

11.5.8 Effects on Inflammatory and Immune Response

Inflammation is crucial in the body's reaction to tissue damage and pathogen invasion. The process begins quickly and subsides when the infections are eliminated, restoring the tissue damage. Numerous different molecules act as mediators and controllers of immunological and inflammatory responses. Proteins, pro-inflammatory cytokines like tumor necrosis factor (TNF) and interleukin (L)-1 and -6, membrane phospholipid derivatives like diacylglycerol and ceramide, eicosanoids like prostaglandins (PG) and leukotrienes (LT), and other molecules like CAMP, inositol phosphates, and reactive oxygen species are among these molecules (Abasubong et al. 2022). The immune system primarily produces pro-inflammatory cytokines, but endothelial cells and fibroblasts can also produce them. On a biological level, TNF is a catalyst that starts a cascade of cytokine synthesis. The molecule is rapidly released in response to inflammatory and infectious stimuli and encourages the production of numerous other cytokines, such as IL-1 and IL-6, with many shared functions (Akira et al. 1990). In an animal model, iNOS, nitric oxide, cytokines (IL-4, IL-8, and TNF-), COX-1, COX-2, NF-kB, and prostaglandin E2 were evaluated as indicators of inflammation. TRF dramatically decreased the production of pro-inflammatory cytokines and inhibited the release of prostaglandin and nitric oxide, making it effective against inflammatory responses in a dose-dependent manner. TRF suppressed the expression of NF-kB and stopped the induction of iNOS and COX-2 at higher concentrations.

In the liver of the large yellow croaker *Larimichthys crocea*, dietary palm oils significantly reduced expressions of arginase I and interleukin 10, and elevated expressions of tumor necrosis factor, interleukin 1, toll-like receptor 22, and myeloid differentiation factor 88 (Mu et al. 2019). Large yellow croakers fed the 100% PO diet had the most significant levels of IFN, IL-1, and TNF mRNA expression compared to those fed other diets. Compared to the control, fish fed a diet containing 100% PO had the lowest mRNA levels of all dietary treatments in large yellow croakers (*Larimichthys crocea*), which exhibited a negative trend for IL-10 mRNA expression (Li et al. 2019). The mRNA level of the Keap1 gene was considerably higher in crabs fed the PO diet compared to crabs fed the FO diet, whereas crabs fed the PO + VA (palm oil with an addition of vitamin) diet had lower levels of Keap1 mRNA than crabs fed the PO diet. Compared to crabs fed the FO diet, crabs on the PO diet had lower levels of LZM and proPO gene expression. However, in the hepatopancreas of crabs fed the PO diet compared to those on the FO diet, there was a significantly greater gene expression level of ADAM17, LITAF, IL-16, MyD88, Toll2, and Relish, while MyD88, Toll2, and Relish gene expression was reduced in crabs fed a PO + VA diet compared to those on a PO diet. (Huang et al. 2022).

11.6 Conclusion

In conclusion, our research shows that palm oil is a better option than other vegetable and fish oil in terms of availability, affordability, and sustainability. Furthermore, it can be concluded that palm oil can partially or entirely replace fish oil in aquafeeds without harming growth, feed utilization, body and fatty acid composition, antioxidant, and immunological response. Due to the abundance of palm oil in developing nations compared to the scarcity and high cost of fish oil, we advise using palm oil instead of fish oil to reduce the cost of feeding fish species that might be sustainable.

References

Abasubong KP, Li XF, Zhang DD, Jia ET, Xiang-Yang Y, Xu C, Liu WB (2017) Dietary supplementation of xylooligosaccharides benefits the growth performance and lipid metabolism of common carp (*Cyprinus carpio*) fed high-fat diets. Aquac Nutr 24:1416–1424. https://doi.org/10.1111/anu.12678

Abasubong KP, Li XF, Adjoumani JJY, Jiang GZ, Desouky HE, Liu WB (2022) Effects of dietary xylooligosaccharide prebiotic supplementation on growth, antioxidant and intestinal immune-related genes expression in common carp *Cyprinus carpio* fed a high-fat diet. J Anim Physiol Anim Nutr 106(2):403–418. https://doi.org/10.1111/jpn.13669

Abbasi A, Oujifard A, Torfi Mozanzadeh M, Habibi H, Nafisi Bahabadi M (2020) Dietary simultaneous replacement of fish meal and fish oil with blends of plant proteins and vegetable oils in yellowfin seabream (*Acanthopagrus latus*) fry: growth, digestive enzymes, antioxidant status and skin mucosal immunity. Aquac Nutr 26:1131–1142. https://doi.org/10.1111/anu.13070

Abdullah N, Sulaiman F (2013) The oil palm wastes in Malaysia. Intech

Adly A (2010) Oxidative stress and disease: an updated review. J Immunol Res 3:129–145. https://doi.org/10.3923/rji.2010.129.145

Ahmad W, Stone D, Schuller KA (2013) Dietary fish oil replacement with palm or poultry oil increases fillet oxidative stability and decreases liver glutathione peroxidase activity in barramundi (*Lates calcarifer*). Physiol Biochem 39:1631–1640. https://doi.org/10.1007/s10695-013-9815-539

Akira S, Hirano T, Taga T, Kishimoto T (1990) Biology of multifunctional cytokines: IL6 and related molecules (IL1 and TNF). FASEB J 4:2860–2867

Akpanabiatu MI, Ekpa OD, Mauro A, Rizzo R (2001) Nutrient composition of Nigerian palm kernel from the dura and tenera varieties of the oil palm (*Elaeis guineensis*). Food Chem 72: 173–177

Aliyu-Paiko M, Hashim R (2012) Effects of substituting dietary fish oil with crude palm oil and palm fatty acid distillate on growth, muscle fatty acid composition and the activities of hepatic lipogenic enzymes in snakehead (*Channa striatus*, Bloch 1793) fingerling. Aquac Res 43:767–776. https://doi.org/10.1111/j.1365-2109.2011.02888.x

Alvarez A, Fontanillas R, Hernández-Contreras A, Hernández MD (2020) Partial replacement of fish oil with vegetal oils in commercial diets: the effect on the quality of gilthead seabream (*Sparus aurata*). Anim Feed Sci Technol 265:114504. https://doi.org/10.1016/j.anifeedsci.2020.114504

Asdari R, Biswas A, Yamamoto S, Araki H, Kawashima K, Hashim R, Takii K (2014) Effect of dietary palm oil and medium chain triglycerides on growth and fatty acid profiles of Japanese catfish *Silurus asotus* juveniles. Aquac Sci 62(1):45–54

Ayeleso A, Brooks N, Oguntibeju O (2014) Modulation of antioxidant status in streptozotocin-induced diabetic male wistar rats following intake of red palm oil and/or rooibos. Asian Pac J Trop Med 7:536–544. https://doi.org/10.1016/S1995-7645(14)60090-0

Ayisi CL, Zhao J, Rupia EJ (2017) Growth performance, feed utilization, body and fatty acid composition of Nile tilapia (*Oreochromis niloticus*) fed diets containing elevated levels of palm oil. Aquac Fish 2:67–77. https://doi.org/10.1016/j.aaf.2017.02.001

Ayisi CL, Zhao JL, Hua XM, Apraku A (2018) Replacing fish oil with palm oil: effects on mRNA expression of fatty acid transport genes and signalling factors related to lipid metabolism in Nile tilapia (*Oreochromis niloticus*). Aquac Nutr 24:1822–1833. https://doi.org/10.1111/anu.12821

Ayisi CL, Zhao J, Yame C, Apraku A, Debra G (2019) Effects of replacing fish oil with palm oil in diets of Nile tilapia (*Oreochromis niloticus*) on muscle biochemical composition, enzyme activities, and mRNA expression of growth-related genes. Fish Aquatic Sci 22:25. https://doi.org/10.1186/s41240-019-0139-y

Bahurmiz OM, Ng W (2007) Effects of dietary palm oil source on growth, tissue fatty acid composition and nutrient digestibility of red hybrid tilapia, *Oreochromis sp.*, raised from stocking to marketable size. Aquaculture 262:382–392

Balbuena-Pecino S, Riera-Heredia N, Gasch-Navalón E, Sánchez-Moya A, Fontanillas R, Gutiérrez J, Navarro I, Capilla E (2021) Musculoskeletal growth modulation in gilthead sea bream juveniles reared at high water temperature and fed with palm and rapeseed oils-based diets. Animals 11:260. https://doi.org/10.3390/ani11020260

Baryeh EA (2001) Effects of palm oil processing parameters on yield. J Food Eng 48:1–6

Bassim HH, Abdul LA, Ng AH (2003) Removal of residual oil from palm oil mill effluent using solvent extraction method. Jurnal Teknologi 38:33–42

Bell JG, Henderson RJ, Tocher DR, Mcghee F, Dick JR, Porter A, Smullen RP, Sargent JR (2002) Substituting fish oil with crude palm oil in the diet of Atlantic salmon (*Salmo salar*) affects

muscle fatty acid composition and hepatic fatty acid metabolism. J Nutr 132:222–230. https://doi.org/10.1093/jn/132.2.222
Benadé SAJ (2003) A place for palm fruit oil to eliminatevitamin A deficiency. Asia Pac J Clin Nutr 12:369–372
Benedito-Palos L, Navarro JC, Sitjà-Bobadilla A, Gordon Bell J, Kaushik S, Pérez-Sánchez J (2008) High levels of vegetable oils in plant protein-rich diets fed to gilthead sea bream (*Sparus aurata* L.): growth performance, muscle fatty acid profiles and histological alterations of target tissues. Br J Nutr 100:992–1003. https://doi.org/10.1017/S0007114508966071
Berger KG (2007) Trans-free fats with the products of the oil palm—a selective review. Czech J Food Sci 25:174–181. https://doi.org/10.17221/688-CJFS
Ble CM, Etchian OA, Otchoumou AK, Yapi JN, Yao LA (2018) Effects of dietary palm oil on the whole-body mineral composition of African catfish, *Heterobranchus longifilis* (Teleostei, Clariidae). Palm oil, pp 171–181
Carter C, Finley W, Fry J, Jackson D, Willis L (2007) Palm oil markets and future supply. Eur J Lipid Sci Technol 109:307–314. https://doi.org/10.1002/ejlt.200600256
Christain LA, Zhao J, Wu JW, Loor JJ (2018) Replacement of fish oil with palm oil: effects on growth performance, innate immune response, antioxidant capacity and disease resistance in Nile tilapia (*Oreochromis niloticus*). PLoS One 13:e0196100. https://doi.org/10.1371/journal.pone.0196100
Corley RHV, Tinker PB (2003) The products of the oil palm and their extraction. In: Corley RHV, Tinker PB (eds) Theoil palm, 4th edn. Blackwell Science, Oxford, pp 445–466
Das S, Nesaretnam K, Das DK (2007) Tocotrienols in cardioprotection. Vitam Horm 75:285–299. https://doi.org/10.1016/S0083-6729(06)75011-7
de Souza Alves LF, Rocha JDM, dos Santos Cardoso M, de Freitas JMA, Feiden A, Boscolo WR (2021) Palm oil in diets for Nile tilapia (*Oreochromis niloticus*) post-larvae. Res Soc Dev 10:1–10. https://doi.org/10.33448/rsd-v10i14.22099
Edem DO, Eka OU, Umoh IB (2002) Feeding of red palm oil-supplemented diets to rats may impact positively on vitamin A status. Int J Food Sci Nutr 53:285–291. https://doi.org/10.1080/09637480220138115
FAO (2018) The state of world fisheries and aquaculture 2018—meeting the sustainable development goals. Rome. Licence: CCBY-NC-SA 3.0 IGO
Fattore E, Fanelli R (2013) Palm oil and palmitic acid: a review on cardiovascular effects and carcinogenicity. Int J Food Sci Nutr 64:648–659. https://doi.org/10.3109/09637486.2013.768213
Fonseca-Madrigal J, Karalazos V, Campbell PJ, Bell JG, Tocher DR (2015) Influence of dietary palm oil on growth, tissue fatty acid compositions, and fatty acid metabolism in liver and intestine in rainbow trout (*Oncorhynchus mykiss*). Aquac Nutr 11:241–250. https://doi.org/10.1111/j.1365-2095.2005.00346.x
Foran JA, Carpenter DO, Hamilton MC, Knuth BA, Schwager SJ (2005) Risk-based consumption advice for farmed Atlantic and wild Pacific Salmon contaminated with dioxins and dioxin-like compounds. Environ Health Perspect 113:552–556
Foster R, Williamson C, Lunn J (2009) Briefing paper: culinary oils and their health effects. Nutr Bull 34:4–47
Fountoulaki E, Vasilaki A, Hurtado R, Grigorakis K, Karacostas I, Nengas I, Rigos G, Kotzamanis Y, Venou B, Alexis MN (2009) Fish oil substitution by vegetable oils in commercial diets for gilthead sea bream (*Sparus aurata* L.); effects on growth performance, flesh quality and fillet fatty acid profile. Aquaculture 289:317–332. https://doi.org/10.1016/j.aquaculture.2009.01.023
Fukada H, Kitagima R, Shinagawa J, Morino H, Masumoto T (2020) Effects of complete replacement of fish oil with plant oil mixtures and algal meal on growth performance and fatty acid composition in juvenile yellowtail *Seriola quinqueradiata*. Fish Sci 86:107–118
Gudid SN, Lim LS, Yong A, Yanuhar U, Shapawi R (2020) Growth performance and organoleptic quality of hybrid grouper (*Epinephelus fuscogutattus* ♀ × *Epinephelus lanceolatus* ♂) fed palm-

oil based diets at grow-out stage. Sains Malaysiana 49:1567–1576. https://doi.org/10.17576/jsm-2020-4907-09

Gunstone FD (2011) Vegetable oils in food technology: composition,properties and uses, 2nd edn. Blackwell Publishing, West Sussex, pp 25–133

Guo H, Chen C, Yan X, Li Y, Wang S (2021) Effects of different dietary oil sources on growth performance, antioxidant capacity and lipid deposition of juvenile golden *pompano Trachinotus ovatus*. Aquaculture 530:735923. https://doi.org/10.1016/j.aquaculture.2020.735923

Han YZ, Ren TJ, Jiang ZQ, Jiang BQ, Gao J, Koshio S, Komilus CF (2012) Effects of palm oil blended with oxidized fish oil on growth performances, hematology, and several immune parameters in juvenile Japanese sea bass, *Lateolabrax japonicas*. Fish Physiol Biochem 38: 1785–1794. https://doi.org/10.1007/s10695-012-9675-4

Han YZ, Jiang ZQ, Ren TJ, Koshio S, Gao J, Komilus CF, Jiang BQ (2015) Effect of dietary fish oil replacement with palm oil on growth performance, hematology and liver anti-oxidative enzymes of juvenile Japanese flounder *Paralichthys olivaceus* (Temminck & Schlegel, 1846). J Appl Ichthyol 31:518–524. https://doi.org/10.1111/jai.12776

Hodar AR, Vasava RJ, Mahavadiya DR, Joshi NH (2020) Fish meal and fish oil replacement for aqua feed formulation by using alternative sources: a review. J Exp Zool India 23(1):13–21

Hof K, West CE, Weststrate JA, Hautvast J (2000) Dietary factors that affect the bioavailability of carotenoids. J Nutr 130:503–506. https://doi.org/10.1093/jn/130.3.503

Huang Y, Wen X, Li S, Li W (2016) Effects of dietary fish oil replacement with palm oil on the growth, feed utilization, biochemical composition, and antioxidant status of Juvenile Chu's Croaker, *Nibea coibor*. J World Aquac Soc 47(6)

Huang Q, Wang X, Liu J, Wang H, Miao Y, Zhang C, Zhang M, Qin C, Qin JG, Chen LQ (2022) Effect of vitamin A supplementation on growth performance,lipid deposition, antioxidant ability, and immunity in Juvenile Chinese Mitten Crab *Eriocheir sinensis* fed diet with fish oil totally replaced by palm oil. Aquac Nutr 2022:3746245. https://doi.org/10.1155/2022/3746245

Komilus CF, Shichi N, Koshio S, Ishikawa M, Makita C (2008) Influences of palm oil blended with fish oil on growth performances and lipid profiles of Red Sea bream *Pagrus major*. Aquac Sci 56:317–326

Koushki M, Nahidi M, Cheraghali F (2015) Physico-chemical properties, fatty acid profile and nutrition in palm oil. J Paramed Sci 6:117–134

Kushairi A, Ong-Abdullah M, Nambiappan B, Hishamuddin E, Kadir A (2019) Oil palm economic performance in Malaysia and R&D progress in 2018. J Oil Palm Res 31:165–194

Li X, Ji R, Cui K, Chen Q, Chen Q, Fang W, Mai K, Zhang Y, Xu W, Ai Q (2019) High percentage of dietary palm oil suppressed growth and antioxidant capacity and induced the inflammation by activation of TLR NF κB signaling pathway in large yellow croaker (*Larimichthys crocea*). Fish Shellfish Immunol 87:600–608. https://doi.org/10.1016/j.fsi.2019.01.055

Lim PK, Boey PL, Ng WK (2001) Dietary palm oil level affects growth performance, protein retention and tissue vitamin E concentration of African catfish, *Clarias gariepinus*. Aquaculture 202:101–112. https://doi.org/10.1016/s0044-8486(01)00563-4

Lupiañez-Perez I, Uttumchandani SK, Morilla-Herrera JC, Martin-Santos FJ, Fernandez-Gallego MC, Navarro-Moya FJ, Lupiañez-Perez Y, Contreras-Fernandez E, Morales-Asencio JM (2015) Topical olive oil is not inferior to hyperoxygenated fatty aids to prevent pressure ulcers in high-risk immobilised patients in home care. Results of a multicentre randomised triple-blind controlled non-inferiority trial. PLos One 10:e0122238. https://doi.org/10.1371/journal.pone.0122238

Ma CY, Xu ZH, Lv H (2019) Low n-6/ n-3 PUFA ratio improves inflammation and myocardial ischemic reperfusion injury. Biochem Cell Biol 97:621–629. https://doi.org/10.1139/bcb-2018-0342

Mba OI, Dumont M-J, Ngadi M (2015) Palm oil: processing, characterization and utilization in the food industry—a review. Food Biosci 10:26–41. https://doi.org/10.1016/j.fbio.2015.01.003

Mock TS, Francis DS, Jago MK, Glencross BD, Smullen RP, Keast R, Turchini GM (2019) Altered levels of shorter vs long-chain omega-3 fatty acids in commercial diets for market-sized Atlantic

salmon reared in seawater—effects on fatty acid composition, metabolism and product quality. Aquaculture 499:167–177
Mozaffarian D, Rimm EB (2006) Fish intake, contaminants, and human health: evaluating the risks and the benefits. JAMA 296:1885–1899. https://doi.org/10.1001/jama.296.15.1885
Mu H, Wei C, Zhang Y, Zhou H, Pan Y, Chen J, Zhang W, Mai K (2019) Impacts of replacement of dietary fish oil by vegetable oils on growth performance, anti-oxidative capacity, and inflammatory response in large yellow croaker *Larimichthys crocea*. Fish Physiol Biochem 46:231–245. https://doi.org/10.1007/s10695-019-00712-8
Nasopoulou C, Zabetakis I (2012) Benefits of fish oil replacement by plant originated oils in compounded fish feeds. A review. LWT Food Sci Technol 47:217–224. https://doi.org/10.1016/j.lwt.2012.01.018
Ng WK, Lim PK, Sidek H (2001) The influence of a dietary lipid source on growth, muscle fatty acid composition and erythrocyte osmotic fragility of hybrid tilapia. Fish Physiol Biochem 25: 301–310. https://doi.org/10.1023/A:1023271901111
Ng WK, Lim PK, Boey PL (2003) Dietary lipid and palm oil source affects growth, fatty acid composition and muscle a-tocopherol concentration of African catfish, *Clarias gariepinus*. Aquaculture 215:229–243
Ng WK, Yan W, Ketchimenin P, Yuen KH (2004) Replacement of dietary fish oil with palm fatty acid distillate elevates tocopherol and tocotrienol concentrations and increases oxidative stability in the muscle of African catfish, *Clarias gariepinus*. Aquaculture 233(1–4):423–437. https://doi.org/10.1016/j.aquaculture.2003.10.013
Ng WK, Tocher DR, Bell JG (2007) The use of palm oil in aquaculture feeds for salmonid species. Eur J Lipid Sci Technol 109:394–399
Norhuda I, Omar A (2009) Mass transfer of palm kernel oil under supercritical conditions. Proc World Acad Sci Eng Technol 49:169–172
O'Brien RD (2010) Fats and oils: formulating and processing for applications, 3rd edn. CRC Press, Boca Raton
Obibuzor JU, Okogbenin EA, Abigor RD (2012) Oil recovery from palm fruits and palm kernel. In: Lai O-M, Tan C-P, Akoh CC (eds) Palm oil: production, processing, characterization and uses. AOCS Press, Urbana, pp 299–328
Oil World (2013) Oil world annual 2013. http://www.oilworld.biz/app.php. Released June 201
Ping B, May CY (2000) Valuable phytonutrients in commercial red palm olein. Palm Oil Deve 32: 20–25
Poku K (2002) Small-scale palm oil processing in Africa. FAO Agricultural Services Bulletin, #148. Food and Agriculture Organization of the United Nations, Rome
Ravichandran S, Kumaravel K, Florence EP (2011) Nutritive composition of some edible fin fishes. Int J Zool Res 7:241–251. https://doi.org/10.3923/ijzr.2011.241.251
Rice R (2009) Nutritional value of fish oils. In: Rossell B (ed) Fish oils. Blackwell, Chichester, pp 131–154
Riera-Heredia N, Sanchez-Moya A, Balbuena-Pecino S, Fontanillas R, Gutierrez J, Capilla E (2020) The combination of palm and rapeseed oils emerges as a good dietary alternative for optimal growth and balanced lipid accumulation in juvenile gilthead sea bream reared at an elevated temperature. Aquaculture 526:735396. https://doi.org/10.1016/j.aquaculture.2020.735396
Röbbelen G (1990) Mutation breeding for quality improvement—a case study for oilseed crops. Mutat Breed Rev 6:1–44
Sambanthamurthi R, Sundram K, Tan YA (2000) Chemistry and biochemistry of palm oil. Prog Lipid Res 39:507–558. https://doi.org/10.1016/s0163-7827(00)00015-1
Schroeder MT, Becker EM, Skibsted LH (2006) Molecular mechanism of antioxidant synergism of tocotrienols and carotenoids in palm oil. Agric Food Chem 54:3445–3453. https://doi.org/10.1021/jf053141z

Singh SK, Rather MA, Mandal SC, Das P, Dar SA (2012) Effects of dietary fish oil substitution with palm oil on growth, survival, and muscle proximate composition of *Cirrhinus mrigala* (Hamilton, 1822). Isr J Aquac 809:1–8

Subsinghe R, Soto D, Jia J (2009) Global aquaculture and its role in sustainable development. Rev Aquac 1:2–9. https://doi.org/10.1111/j.1753-5131.2008.01002.x

Sun Y, Neelakantan N, Wu Y, Lote-Oke R, Pan A, Dam RV (2015) Palm oil consumption increases LDL cholesterol compared with vegetable oils low in saturated fat in a meta-analysis of clinical trials. J Nutr 145:1549–1558. https://doi.org/10.3945/jn.115.210575

Sundram K, Sambanthamurthi R, Tan YA (2003) Palm fruit chemistry and nutrition. Asia Pac J Clin Nutr 12:355–362

Tan CP, Man YBC (2000) Differential scanning calorimetric analysis of edible oils: comparison of thermal properties and chemical composition. J Am Oil Chem Soc 77:143–155

Tavares-Dias M, Moraes FR (2006) Hematological parameters for the Brycon orbignyanus Valenciennes, 1850 (Osteichthyes: Characidae) intensively bred. Hidrobiologica 16:271–274

Torstensen BE, Bell JG, Rosenlund G, Henderson RJ, Graff IE, Tocher DR, Lie O, Sargent JR (2005) Tailoring of Atlantic salmon (*Salmo salar* L.) flesh lipid composition and sensory quality by replacing fish oil with a vegetable oil blend. Agric Food Chem 53:10166–10178. https://doi.org/10.1021/jf051308i

Tseng Y, Lin YH (2020) Effects of dietary supplementation with coconut oil on the growth, fatty acid profiles and some lipid metabolism relative gene expressions of orange-spotted grouper *Epinephelus coioides*. Aquac Nutr 26:201–210. https://doi.org/10.1111/anu.12981

Turan C (2004) Genetic and morphologic structure of Liza Abu (Heckel, 1843) populations from the Rivers Orontes, Euphrates and Tigris. Turk J Vet Anim Sci 28:729–734

Turchini GM, Torstensen BE, Ng WK (2009) Fish oil replacement in finfish nutrition. Rev Aquacult 1:10–57

Turchini GM, Francis DS, Senadheera SPSD, Thanuthong T, Silva SSD (2011) Fish oil replacement with different vegetable oils in Murray cod: evidence of an "omega-3 sparing effect" by other dietary fatty acids. Aquaculture 315:250–259. https://doi.org/10.1016/j.aquaculture.2011.02.016

Tyagi VK, Vasishtha AK (1996) Changes in the characteristics and composition of oils during deep-fat frying. J Am Oil Chem Soc 73:499–506. https://doi.org/10.1007/bf02523926

Vincent CJ, Shamsudin R, Baharuddin AS (2014) Pre-treatment of oil palm fruits: a review. J Food Eng 143:123–131. https://doi.org/10.1016/j.jfoodeng.2014.06.022

Wahid MB, Abdullah SNA, Henson IE (2005) Oil palm—achievements and potential. Plant Prod Sci 8:288–297. https://doi.org/10.1626/pps.8.288

Wickramanayake D, Kalutharage NK, Cumaranatunga P (2021) Muscle pigmentation of Nile tilapia (*Oreochromis niloticus*) fed on crude palm oil incorporated fish feed. Sri Lanka J Fish Aquat Sci 26:111–120. https://doi.org/10.4038/sljas.v26i2.7591

Wiernsperger NF (2003) Oxidative stress as a therapeutic target in diabetes: revisiting the controversy. Diabetes Metab 29:579–585

Wu SJ, Ng LT (2007) Antioxidant and antihepatoma activities of palm oil extract. J Food Lipids 14:122–137

Wu S-J, Liu P-L, Ng L-T (2008) Tocotrienol-rich fraction of palm oil exhibits anti-inflammatory property by suppressing the expression of inflammatory mediators in human monocytic cells. Mol Nutr Food Res 53:309. https://doi.org/10.1002/mnfr.200990004

Zou Y, Jiang Y, Yang T, Hu P, Xu X (2012) Minor constituents of palm oil: characterization, processing, and application. In: Lai O-M, Tan C-P, Akoh CC (eds) Palm oil: production, processing, characterization and uses. AOCS Press, Urbana, pp 471–524

Chapter 12
A Dynamic Study of the influence of *Jatropha curcas* on Growth and Haematological Indices in Finfish

Kenneth Prudence Abasubong, Ndakalimwe Naftal Gabriel, Jean-Jacques Yao Adjoumani, Aniefiokmkpong Okokon Okon, Mfon T. Udo, Abia Alice Etim, and Hesham E. Desouky

Abstract *Jatropha curcas* is a multipurpose tree that has the potential to be a biodiesel alternative. Although the jatropha plant is grown worldwide, it is most commonly found in Central and South America, Africa, and South Asia. The Jatropha plant produces various valuable products, the most notable of which is the oil-producing seed. Its components can also be used to produce human food, animal feed, fertiliser, fuel, and traditional medicine. The seed cake of Jatropha curcas is a low-value byproduct of biodiesel production. The seed cake is high in protein, but it also contains trypsin inhibitors, phytic acid, lectin, and saponin, as well as phorbol esters, a poisonous substance. Before the seed cake can be used as aquafeed, various detoxification techniques must be used. This chapter discussed the chemical composition of this plant, antinutrient components, the detoxification process, and its applications in aquafeed. The Jatropha plant can produce goods for various purposes other than serving as a dietary alternative to fishmeal, which should be investigated and improved. Finally, we believe that the use of Jatropha in

K. P. Abasubong (✉) · J.-J. Y. Adjoumani
Key Laboratory of Aquatic Nutrition and Feed Science of Jiangsu Province, College of Animal Science and Technology, Nanjing Agricultural University, Nanjing, China

N. N. Gabriel
Department of Fisheries and Ocean Sciences, Faculty of Agriculture, Engineering and Natural Science, Sam Nujoma Campus, University of Namibia, Henties Bay, Namibia

A. O. Okon · A. A. Etim
Department of Animal and Environmental Biology, University of Uyo, Uyo, Akwa Ibom State, Nigeria

M. T. Udo
Department of Fisheries and Environmental Management, University of Uyo, Uyo, Akwa Ibom State, Nigeria

H. E. Desouky
Department of Animal, Poultry and Fish Production, Faculty of Agriculture, Damanhour University, Damanhour, Beheria, Egypt

© The Author(s), under exclusive license to Springer Nature Singapore Pte Ltd. 2023
N. N. Gabriel et al. (eds.), *Emerging Sustainable Aquaculture Innovations in Africa*, Sustainable Agriculture and Food Security,
https://doi.org/10.1007/978-981-19-7451-9_12

aquafeeds should be encouraged, and more research into its effects on non-specific immunity and the expression of genes involved in growth, stress, and apoptosis in aquatic species should be conducted.

Keywords Aquaculture, *Jatropha curcas* · Protein isolate · Functional properties · Anti-nutritional factors

12.1 Introduction

As we near the middle of the twenty-first century, the supply of high-quality, nutrient-rich food confronts vast challenges due to the growing human population; by 2050, there will be 9.7 billion people on the earth, needing a 25–70% increase in food production (Hunter et al. 2017). In addition, competing interests exist for agriculturally based input commodities, and the basis of natural resources is depleting (Benton et al. 2018). Although the livestock and food industries are increasing production to meet demand, this poses serious problems such as overgrazing, water scarcity, and the loss of natural biodiversity (Benton et al. 2018; Rivera-Ferre et al. 2016; Michalk et al. 2019). It is now acknowledged that raising aquatic species for food (also known as aquaculture) would contribute significantly more to the world's budget for animal-derived protein. According to annual growth rates over the past three decades, aquaculture has been the fastest-growing food production sector, with annualised growth rates of 10% in the 1990s and 5.8% yearly between 2000 and 2016 (FAO 2018).

Aquaculture is now one of the world's fastest-growing agriculture sectors, thanks to recent advancements in its growth and development (FAO 2018). Due to the nutritious value of fish, demand has rapidly increased without a matching increase in output (Gogoi et al. 2015), resulting in a supply deficit. Farmers are urged to wake up to prevent the impending inadequate protein intake due to this severe supply shortage in a growing world population. In addition, it has been shown that fish feed costs between 60 and 70 percent of the overall recurring production costs (Tacon and Jackson 1985; Tacon 1994), essentially preventing fish producers from making a profit. This is a result of the limited availability of conventional fish feed and the high cost of the components due to its competition with people and businesses.

The lack of ingredients like fish meal, fish oil, and soybean meal is the main factor raising the price of aquafeed. The contribution of those substances to sustainable aqua-feed production may also be impacted by increased human demand for the nutrients they provide. Therefore, there is grave concern regarding the long-term availability of these feed ingredients for aqua-feed production (Cruz-Saurez et al. 2007; Cho 2010; Dedeke et al. 2013). Hence, finding a different protein source is crucial if we develop affordable feed ingredients for small- and medium-sized fish farmers based on sustainable and renewable feed resources (Agbebi et al. 2009; Barnes et al. 2012). It is also necessary to consider whether the selected feed ingredients conflict with concerns for human food security.

One of the most researched plants protein sources is soybean meal (SBM), which is a good component for aquafeed production (Kaushik et al. 1995). However, soybean meal prices have risen because of competition with human food and rising demand in other feed industries (FAO 2006). Also, Ray et al. (2013) reported that the yield trends of most crops, like rice, soybean, groundnut, etc., are insufficient to meet the human requirement in the coming years. Hence, exploring an alternative, less expensive, non-edible ingredient is imperative to satisfy the aquaculture requirement. Various studies have used different plants and their products, such as extracts, oils, and powders, as feed supplements in other animal species (Roy et al. 2014; Abd El-Hack et al. 2016). The global oil industry is now attempting to utilise non-edible seeds like rubber seeds, neem seeds, *pongamia, karanja, mahua, Jatropha* etc., for biodiesel production as there is debate on utilizing edible seeds for the same (Butler 2006; Meher et al. 2006).

A promising candidate for this industry is *Jatropha curcas*, a drought-resistant tropical shrub Jatropha (*Jatropha curcas*) is one seed that may have the potential for both nutritional and medicinal uses. Utilising non-conventional feedstuffs, such as jatropha seed meal, would help decrease the cost of feeds with a subsequent reduction in the cost of production. Jatropha belongs to the *Euphorbiaceae* family (Saetae and Suntornsuk 2010; Barros et al. 2015) and is cultivated primarily for biofuel production. The meal is a by-product of biofuel processing, with each ton of Jatropha's seed producing about 200–300 L of biofuel and 700–800 kg of the meal (Brodjonegoro et al. 2005). In addition, Jatropha is being sold in aqueous extracts or tincture forms for various health applications. The use of raw JM in animal nutrition has problems with anti-nutritional factors, including lectin, tannin, saponin, phytate, phorbol esters and trypsin inhibitors (Makkar and Becker 1999). These components can be removed or negated by either physical or chemical methods (Belewu and Sam 2010). Therefore, in this chapter, we reviewed the use of Jatropha in aquafeeds, considering its anti-nutritional factors, detoxification, and uses. Also, its dynamic study on growth and haematological indices in finfish were discussed.

12.2 *Jatropha* as a Plant

Jatropha is a gregarious shrub with a height of approximately 1.8 m that is a common weed of field crops and a member of the *Euphorbiaceae* family. It is typically grown in West African rainforests with high rainfall. Jatropha is well-known for its therapeutic uses, including as a purgative and laxative. It is a little perennial tree that can grow for another 40–50 years, depending on the soil and habitat (Foidl et al. 1996; Openshaw 2000). The plant begins flowering in about 6–30 months and takes 4–5 years or longer to reach the complete fruit-bearing stage (Islam et al. 2010a, b). Jatropha has robust branches, smooth, gray-colored bark, and thick, soft pale green leaves. Typically, seeds produce one tap root with four lateral roots, while cuts do not produce tap roots (Islam et al. 2010a, b). Jatropha seeds are dark in colour and weigh 50–75 g per 100 (Islam 2011). Although it can grow at higher altitudes and withstand moderate frost, it is mostly found at altitudes between 0 and 500 m, where average yearly temperatures are at least 20 °C. Extreme settings are places where it cannot grow. Jatropha is prompted to flower and produces fruit when the weather is more relaxed and it is raining.

Jatropha may be grown as a fuel crop in more than 80 countries globally, with 17 Asian nations. In regions with 250 to over 1200 mm of annual rainfall, Jatropha can be planted on farms as a cash crop or as a hedge to guard fields (Katwal and Soni 2003). It may quickly grow on soil with appropriate aeration and drainage systems but cannot grow in locations with harsh conditions (Islam et al. 2010a). Additionally, it may thrive on degraded fields and is well suited to marginal soils. Additionally, it may thrive on degraded fields and is well suited to marginal soils. Although it can grow at higher altitudes and withstand moderate frost, it is mostly found at altitudes between 0 and 500 m, where average yearly temperatures are at least 20 °C. Like the cassava plant, jatrophas are perennial shrubs or trees that can withstand drought and serve various purposes (Elbehri et al. 2013). The leaves of the deciduous jatropha tree fall off during the dry season. The lateral roots stop soil erosion, and the taproot holds the plant in the ground, securing the ground against landslides. The trunk has a smooth, grey bark that, when cut, leaks liquid, sticky latex.

The smooth leaves are 10–15 cm long and wide, 4–6 lobed, and often pale green (Raheman 2012). About 38% of the husks and 62% of the seeds make up the dry jatropha fruit. The black seeds resemble castor seeds in form (Raheman 2012) as shown in Fig. 12.1. They are composed of 60–70% kernels and 30–40% Testa (shells). Oil makes up about 44–62% of the kernels (King et al. 2009).

12.2.1 Anti-nutritional Factors in the Jatropha Plant

Anti-nutrients are compounds that interfere with the digestion of food and negatively impact animal health and productivity, either directly or by the metabolic products they produce in living systems (Makkar 1993). Animal consumption of plants is typically constrained by the many toxins they create, including alkaloids, terpenoids, tannins, saponins, cyanogenic, glycosides, and poisonous amino acids (Cheeke 1998). Total phenols in jatropha curcas meal vary from 0.2 to 0.4%, whereas tannins are present in insignificant levels at 0.02–0.04%. According to (Makkar et al. 1998), it is impossible to identify condensed tannins in jatropha kernel meal, and the stem bark's tannin content is shallow (outer dark bark: tannins 0.7% and condensed tannins 0.2%; inner green bark: tannins 3.1% and condensed tannins 1.7%; with tannins expressed as tannic acid equivalent and condensed tannins as leucocyanidin equivalent; (Makkar et al. 2008). The non-haemolytic saponin concentration in JM from various regions ranged from 1.8 to 3.4%. The main poisonous component of Jatropha curcas has been discovered as phorbol esters (phorbol-12-myristate 13-acetate) (Makkar et al. 1997; Makkar and Becker 1997, 2010). Phorbol esters are bioactive derivatives of diterpenes that have a variety of cell-related actions. The main anti-nutrient in Jatropha seed/seed meal is trypsin inhibitors (Goel et al. 2007).

Fig. 12.1 Jatropha plant parts: (**a**) male flower, (**b**) female flower, (**c**) mature fruits, (**d**) seeds, (**e**) Green leaves, (**f**) inflorescence, (**g**) Mature tree

Another antinutritional component of Jatropha is phytic acid, which has been shown to have detrimental effects on growth, feed intake, feed conversion ratio, and thyroid function, as seen, for instance, in Atlantic and Chinook salmon (Denstadli et al. 2006).

12.2.2 Jatropha Detoxification

Heat labile and stable heat chemicals are two different categories of anti-nutritional factors. Heat labile proteins rapidly inactivated by heat include antinutritional factors such as lectins, protease, and amylase inhibitors. Heat-resistant substances include phenols, tannins, and phytic acids. Compounds that are heat stable often withstand heat processing without being damaged. Antinutritional agents that limit specific enzyme secretion, such as protease and lipase inhibitors, are typically responsible for greater pancreatic enzyme secretion. This may affect how lipids, carbohydrates, and proteins are digested. Heat-stable anti-nutrients are eliminated through ingredient processing techniques, including solvent extraction.

Since raw Jatropha seeds or oil revealed distinct toxicities in several animal species, its use in animal diets is restricted due to anti-nutritional and toxic components. However, before employing JM as a source of nutrients for animal feeds, its antinutritive and harmful components must be reduced (Annongu et al. 2010; Agboola and Adenuga 2015). Following heat treatment, the non-toxic genotype protein or meal isolates could provide excellent protein-rich additions to the diet of animals (Makkar et al. 1999). Thermal degradation, germination, immersion in distilled water, extraction of methanol, lye treatment, hot water treatment, and fermentation can reduce amounts of anti-nutritional components to safe levels (Akande et al. 2006). After heat treatment, which removes components such as trypsin inhibitors and lectins that are anti-nutritional and can also reduce phorbol ester levels by 97.9%, the non-toxic JM has good nutritional value. Various treatments, including a combination of chemical, physical, and biological approaches to detoxify JM as animal feed, were reported in a study by Sumiati et al. (2007). The treatments used in this experiment were: (a) heat treatment using autoclave at 121 °C for 30 min; (b) addition of NaOH at 4%, followed by autoclaving at 121 °C during 30 min; (c) fermentation with Rhizopus oligosporous. The results showed that these treatments decreased the curcin and lectin effects and increased protein utilization efficiency and retention of the meal's phosphorus, calcium and metabolisable energy values. Fermentation using Rhizopus oligosporous was the best method to detoxify the meal and increase the nutritive value for poultry. However, when JM is used above 10% in the diet, it could cause higher bird mortality (Agboola and Adenuga 2015).

Although simple processing methods such as soaking and fermentation appear cost-effective (Kajihausa et al. 2014; Solomon et al. 2017; Okomoda et al. 2020); they are ineffective against thermal-labile antinutrients (Kumar 2008). Also, the cost implication and inability to reuse chemicals after detoxification hampered the acceptability of chemical extraction as a commercially viable method of feed detoxification (Aderibigbe et al. 1997). Though using heat treatments such as toasting and hydrothermal processing is successful, these techniques are critiqued for the additional expense of processing and the potential for denaturing vital nutrients when used for an extended period (Alatise et al. 2014; Tiamiyu et al. 2015; Okomoda et al. 2016). Solid-state fermentation has been proven to be a unique technique for detoxifying plant products, such as castor bean with tannin and phytate (Madeira et al. 2011), soybean bran (Wolski et al. 2009), Jatropha seed cake (Belewu and Sam 2010; Joshi et al. 2011), and sesame oil cake (Singh and Satyanarayana 2008). It might be due to the use of microorganisms in converting harmful or antinutritional substances in the substrate into less hazardous ones. A successful outcome was reported from the Pseudomonas aeruginosa PseA-based fermentation of Jatropha seed cake (Joshi et al. 2011).

12.2.3 *The Potential Benefits of* Jatropha curcas

Since the beginning of time, medicinal plants have been utilised both as a medicine and a source of cures for illnesses. An exceptional contribution to human health has been made by plant-derived medications, which have also served as a source for the creation of modern medications, drug compounds, and novel prescriptions (Jain and Tripathi 1991). Additionally, various active complex chemicals found in medicinal plants provide a plentiful supply of energetic substances utilised in the food industry, cosmetics, and medicine (Ahmed et al. 2016). The plant's broad therapeutic potential is demonstrated by the bioactive compound's many segments, which include the highest concentration of phytochemical substances, including tannins, phytosterol, glycosides, phenolic compounds, flavonoids, sapogenins, and steroids. (Agbogidi and Eruotor 2012). Additionally, phytochemicals comprise a variety of primary and secondary substances, including total sugars, amino acids, proteins, and phenolic substances, including terpenoids and alkaloids (Phull et al. 2020). Bioactive and phytochemicals in medicinal plants have distinct physiological effects on the human body (Chehregani and Malayeri 2007).

All plant components, including the leaves, seeds, and bark, are prepared for use in veterinary medicine and traditional medicine (Duke 1988; Asuk et al. 2015). Animals' hearts benefitted from the methanol extract of jatropha leaves. It is possible to stop bleeding from wounds by applying the sap emanating from the stem of Jatropha. According to Thomas et al. (2008), the roots of the jatropha plant are used as an antidote for snakebites. The plant's latex contains alkaloids such as jatrophine, curcain, and jatropham, which are crucial anti-cancerous agents. Numerous skin conditions have been successfully treated using jatropha oil (Marroquin et al. 1997). Jatropha kernel oil is potentially used in cosmetics due to its 36% linoleic acid (C18: 2) content. Regardless of the solvents used, this plant has a higher concentration of phytochemicals in its leaves and a lower concentration in its roots. *J. curcas* has abundant flavonoids and polyphenols in its parts (leaf, stem, bark, and shell), with the leaf showing the most substantial concentrations. These phytochemicals have anti-oxidative properties and protect against allergies, platelet aggregation, inflammation, hepatic toxicity, microbes, ulcers, viruses, and tumours (Gutierrez-Orozco and Failla 2013; Syed et al. 2013). There is potential for certain *J. curcas* diterpenoids to be used as antibacterial, antiviral, anti-inflammatory, and antihypertensive medications. These activities and substances may also have hallucinogenic, antioxidant, and sweetening effects (Kumari et al. 2003). The meal has a crude protein level of 58–60% and an actual protein content of 53–55% when processed in a cottage industry, retaining 11% of the meal's oil.

Due to its non-edible nature and recycling ability, jatropha oil seems to have much potential as a raw resource for industrial uses. Jatropha oil has drawn industrialists and academicians to investigate it as a material for the synthesis of alkyd resins due to its cost-competitiveness compared to other oils such as soya, rapeseed, etc. (Satheesh Kumar et al. 2010). Owing to the sociological, economic, and environmental benefits, polymers made from renewable resources, mainly plant oils, have received much attention lately (Lu and Wool 2008). Sunflower/palm oils, tallow (animal fat), and jatropha oil are comparable. It has fatty acid and is used as a base for soap manufacturing, among other things. Both primary and small industrial companies have employed jatropha oil to produce soap for decades. For instance, a significant industry uses it in India (Hindustan Lever). Additionally, the clear oil has been utilised as an insecticide, polish, varnish, candle fuel, and

Table 12.1 Uses of different parts of *J. curcas* L

Jatropha part	Uses	References
Leaves	For medicinal uses	Orwa et al. (2009)
	Anti-inflammatory substance	Warra (2012)
	Animal feed	Musa et al. (2018, 2021)
Fruits hulls	Combustibles	Brittaine (2010)
	Green manure	Orwa et al. (2009)
	Biogas production	Achten et al. (2008); Ghosh et al. (2007)
Latex	Wound healing	Orwa et al. (2009)
	Medicinal uses	Nahar and Ozores-Hampton (2011)
Seeds		
Seed oil	Soap production	Warra (2012)
	Fuel production	Lele (2007)
	Insecticide production	Srinophakun et al. (2011); Achten et al. (2008)
Seed cake	Fertilizer production	Achten et al. (2008); Ghosh et al. (2007); Patolia et al. (2007)
	Biogas production	Staubmann et al. (1997); Achten et al. (2008); Ghosh et al. (2007); Patolia et al. (2007)
	Animal feed production	Musa et al. (2018, 2021)
	Fodder (from non-toxic varieties)	Gaur et al. (2011)
Seed shell	Combustibles like fruit hulls	Brittaine (2010)

lubricant. Jatropha oil is less competitive than soybean and rapeseed oils despite seed oils being utilized to make biodiesel on a larger scale. Additionally, it is worthwhile looking into the idea of using jatropha oil to create alkyd resin because it has a high concentration of monounsaturated oleic and polyunsaturated linoleic acids, which indicate a semi-drying ability (Odetoye et al. 2010).

Jatropha's protein can be derived from the leaves and press cake (Lestari et al. 2011). The Jatropha seed cake primarily consists of proteins. Various proteins have been manufactured commercially for use in food and other products, including soy protein, gelatin, and casein. However, the poisonous curcin and phorbol esters are found in the jatropha seed (Lestari et al. 2010). Additionally, the seed cake contains these chemicals, which restricts the use of jatropha seed cake for food and feed applications without additional detoxification. Technical applications of protein from Jatropha press cake include emulsifier, coating, bioplastic, foaming agent, and adhesive (Lestari et al. 2011) (Table 12.1).

12.3 *Jatropha curcas* in Aquaculture Practices

Aquafeed is a critical factor in the expansion and development of aquaculture production. It represents a sizable portion (30–75%) of the average fish farm's overall operational costs (Rumsey et al. 1993; El-Sayed 2002). Fish meal has traditionally been the primary source of protein in aquafeeds for various reasons, including its high protein content, abundance of essential amino acids, excellent nutritional and energy digestibility, lack of antinutrients, and availability of vital fatty acids, energy, and minerals. Most freshwater and marine fishes find it highly appetizing and digestible (Watanabe et al. 1997; Glencross et al. 2004). Therefore, a prospective ingredient must have a few qualities to be a feasible replacement, such as widespread availability and a reasonable price. Additionally, it must be simple to transport and store. Plant protein sources should be considered for aquafeeds because they are readily accessible and economically priced. A range of plant protein components might make suitable replacements for fish meals as a source of protein in fish diets.

12.3.1 Chemical Composition of J. curcas *Leaves*

Jatropha leaves might be used as a source of protein. Additionally, amino acids from leaf proteins may be used to create functionalized bulk compounds. The chemical composition of the Jatropha leaf is shown in Table 12.2. According to Lestari et al. (2011), protein and acid-insoluble lignin made up most of the Jatropha leaf. In leaves, there were soluble sugar and polysaccharide carbohydrates. About 65% weight-for-weight of the polysaccharide was converted to glucose after severe acid

Table 12.2 Chemical composition of Jatropha leaf (Khalil et al. 2003)

Component	Compositions (% weight dry basis)
Fat	8.2
Crude protein	20.6
Carbohydrate	
Soluble sugar	15.3
Polysaccharide	10.2
Arabinose	0.6
Xylose	1.0
Mannose	0.6
Galactose	1.5
Glucose	7.1
Pectin	3.9
Lignin	
Acid insoluble lignin	23.5
Acid soluble lignin	2.8
Ash	12.0

hydrolysis. Ash, soluble sugar and lignin were all in significant concentrations in the jatropha leaf. This suggests that extracting and purifying the protein from Jatropha leaves should include acid washing to eliminate lignin that isn't soluble in acid and dialysis to get rid of salts.

12.3.2 Jatropha curcas *Meal (JCM) in Aquafeed*

Utilising non-traditional feedstuffs, like jatropha seed meal, could lower the price of fish feeds and production costs. Each ton of jatropha seed produces roughly 200–300 L of biofuel and 700–800 kg of meal as a byproduct of refining the biofuel (Brodjonegoro et al. 2005). Due to the high crude protein (CP) content of Jatropha curcas meal (JCM), which is produced following oil extraction, it has been suggested that JCM could be used to formulate animal feed (Makkar and Becker 2010; Makkar et al. 1998). However, compared to other plant protein meal sources, Jatropha meal tends to have a significant amount of crude protein, lipids, and ash content than CSM, RSM, SBM, and RPCM. As indicated in Table 12.3, the amino acid profile of the Jatropha meal seems similar to that of FM. Compared to soybean meal, jatropha kernel meal has higher concentrations of all essential amino acids (apart from lysine) (Kumar et al. 2010). Consequently, it is anticipated to be an excellent feed ingredient in the future and will likely replace fish and soybean meals.

The kernel meal recovered after oil extraction is a fantastic source of nutrients and comprises 58–62% crude protein (Makkar et al. 2008). However, their application in fish feed is constrained by the high concentrations of antinutrients such as trypsin inhibitor, lectin, and phytate (Makkar et al. 2008) and the critical poisonous component, phorbol esters (PEs) (Makkar and Becker 1997). As a result, modifications in the haematological parameters of fish after feeding them JCK can gauge how the antinutrients affect the fish's state of health (Musa et al. 2018; Okomoda et al. 2020). Similarly, it has been suggested that the high quantities of antinutrients in fish diets contribute to histological abnormalities in the liver and intestine (Dharmani et al. 2009; Kumar et al. 2019). Therefore, the feed elements must be detoxified before including in the fish diet. Jatropha kernel meal can be detoxified by deactivating lectin and trypsin inhibitors by heat treatment and extracting PEs using organic solvents. However, other methods include soaking (Okomoda et al. 2021), toasting (Musa et al. 2018, 2021) and fermentation (Shamna et al. 2014) as seen in Table 12.4.

12.3.3 Jatropha Oil in Aquafeed

Fish oil (FO) is the primary lipid source used in formulated diets for aquaculture. It contains high amounts of n-3 polyunsaturated fatty acids (PUFAs), such as eicosapentaenoic acid (EPA) and docosahexaenoic acid (DHA), which promote

Table 12.3 Typical composition of commonly used aquaculture feed ingredients

	JKM	SBM	CSM	RSM	RPCM	FM
Crude protein	665	441	449	378	665	645
Crude lipid	11.4	15	5	38	85.6	78
Crude ash	82	63	66	68	39	213
Essential amino acids composition (g kg^{1})						
Arginine	69.7	32.1	46.5	22.7	49.7	43.6
Histidine	21.7	11.6	11.1	10.1	15.4	14.4
Iso leucine	26.7	20.3	12.5	14.9	25.7	27.9
Leucine	46.7	35	24	27.2	52.9	52.2
Lysine	23.3	28.2	17.1	22	18.9	49.9
Phenylalanine	30.4	23.9	23	16.4	36.2	29.1
Methionine	10.6	5.3	5.7	7	20.2	20.6
Threonine	22	17.9	13.1	16.6	24.7	30.3
Valine	31.6	21	17.6	19.1	35	33.5
Non-essential amino acids composition (g kg^{1})						
Alanine	29.4	19.6	15.7	16.7	38.5	39.7
Asparginine	68.7	50.3	36.6	26	59	62
Cystine	2.3	6.2	6.4	7.6	13.7	10.1
Glycine	31.5	19.3	16.3	18.8	28	45
Glutamine	112.1	85.9	85.3	69.5	118.3	94.8
Proline	32.2	21.6	14.1	22.4	21.9	28.3
Serine	30.6	23.1	17.7	16.4	32.5	32.9
Tyrosine	18.8	16	11.3	11.1	32.4	25.1

JKM Jatropha kernel meal, *SBM* Soybean meal, *CSM* Cottonseed meal, *RSM* Rapseed meal, *RPCM* Rice protein meal, *FM* Fish meal
Adopted from Harter et al. (2011); Abasubong et al. (2018); Cai et al. (2018)

survival, health, and make balanced diets palatable and attractive (Pike and Jackson 2010; Teves and Ragaza 2016). The extraction and use of plant lipids as a substitute for FO in the diets of many fish species is well documented as it has been found to provide adequate fish growth and achieve commercial size within a reasonable time (Sutili et al. 2017; Turchini et al. 2010). Table 12.5 compares the fatty acid composition of *Jatropha curcas* oil with the fatty acid composition of other common vegetable oils. Results from these research efforts suggest that *Jatropha curcas* oil could be a valuable feedstock for biodiesel production, with a dramatic reduction in costs of production. Polyunsaturated fatty acids (PUFA) like linoleic acid (18:2n-6) and alpha-linolenic acid (18:3n-3) can be found in *Jatropha curcas*, which is also a good source of both saturated and unsaturated fatty acids, making it a reliable candidate for replacement of fish oil.

Table 12.4 Effect of processing methods on proximate compositions and anti-nutritional compositions of Jatropha curcas seed (adopted from Michael et al. (2019))

Nutrient (%)	Raw	Boiled	Toasted	Soaked	Fermented
Dry matter	93.50	94.13	94.80	93.88	93.50
Protein	37.68	28.33	30.46	29.65	31.46
Lipid	42.36	12.35	6.75	12.96	13.55
Ash	3.27	4.66	7.25	4.71	4.84
Fibre	3.40	2.86	6.13	3.02	2.16
NFE	6.79	45.93	44.21	43.54	41.49
Anti-nutrients (g/100 g dry weight basis)					
Tannins	0.151	0.036	0.011	0.038	0.042
Phytic acids	0.094	0.029	0.008	0.030	0.032
Saponins	0.092	0.046	0.013	0.048	0.056
Oxalates	0.067	0.045	0.013	0.050	0.055
Terpenoids	0.022	0.016	0.006	0.019	0.020
Trypsin inhibitor	0.425	0.196	0.052	0.231	0.285
Glycosides	0.061	0.026	0.013	0.030	0.033
Flavonoids	0.101	0.061	0.022	0.066	0.068
Alkaloids	0.070	0.026	0.015	0.028	0.032

Table 12.5 Fatty acid composition of plant oil

Fatty acid	GNO	SFO	JCO	SBO	CSO
Oleic (18:1)	58.68	21.1	44.7	23.4	17.2
Linoleic 18:2	21.77	66.2	32.8	53.2	55.0
Palmitic 16:0	8.23	–	14.2	11.0	24.4
Stearic 18:0	2.46	4.5	7.0	4.0	2.2
Palmitoliec 16:1	0.11	–	0.7	–	0.4
Linolenic 18:3	0.34	–	0.2	7.8	0.3
Arachidic 20:0	1.83	0.3	0.2	–	–
Myristic 14:0	0.12	–	0.1	0.1	0.8
Saturated	16.81	11.3	21.6	15.1	27
Monounsaturated	58.79	21.1	45.4	23.4	18
Polyunsaturated	22.11	66.2	33	61.0	55

GNO groundnut oil, *SFO* sunflower oil, *JCO* Jatropha oil's, *SBO* soybean oil, *CSO* cottonseed oil

12.4 A Dynamic Study of Dietary Inclusion of *Jatropha curcas* in Aquafeed on Growth and Haematological Indices in Finfish

12.4.1 Substitution of Soybean Meal with Fermented Jatropha Kernel Meal: Effect on Growth Performance, Body Composition, and Metabolic Enzyme Activity of **Labeo rohita**

Phulia et al., (2017) developed four iso-nitrogenous (336 g kg^{1}) and iso-energetic (20 MJ kg^{1}) diets that contained 0, 100, 200, and 300 g kg^{1} FJKM in replacement of 0%, 33.3%, 66.7%, and 100% soybean meal protein, respectively in *Labeo rohita* fingerlings. These diets were designated control, T1, T2, and T3, respectively. From their findings, it can be deduced that the T2 and T3 groups performed better than the other groups in terms of weight gain (percent WG), specific growth rate (SGR), protein efficiency ratio (PER), protease, aspartate aminotransferase (AST), and alanine aminotransferase (ALT) activities, and PER, couple with a reduced feed conversion ratio. At the same time, there were no appreciable differences in the hepatosomatic index (HSI), intestinal somatic index (ISI), amylase, lactate dehydrogenase (LDH), malate dehydrogenase (MDH), superoxide dismutase (SOD), and catalase activity between the various dietary groups. When the fish's entire body composition was examined after the feeding trial, it was found that the control group had a considerably higher ether extract and a smaller amount of crude protein than the groups fed FJKM. They concluded that rohu fingerlings might use FJKM effectively without compromising growth performance, food utilization, or metabolic response.

12.4.2 Dietary implications of toasted Jatropha curcas kernel on the growth, hematology, and organ histology of **Clarias gariepinus** *fingerlings*

Musa et al. (2021) developed a diet using JCK that was nutritionally assessed after being toasted for various amounts of time (0, 10, 20, and 30 min). This was divided into four batches for the intended treatments. The control group was the initial batch (i.e., raw JCK without processing). The three other batches underwent 10, 20, and 30 min of toasting. Their findings imply that prolonged toasting increased the nutritional properties of the JCK since they showed more significant weight gain, specific growth rate, feed conversion efficiency, and survival in the fish-fed diet containing toasted JCK than those in control. This study also observed that dietary inclusion of JCK toasted beyond 20 min tends to decrease the growth performance of the fish significantly.

Contrary to this trend, protein accumulation in the carcass was not affected by the inclusions of JCK processed for a prolonged time. The protein content of the fish fed the toasted JCK was also significantly higher than those fed the raw *Jatropha*. However, the antinutrients continuously decreased with prolonged processing. The growth, carcass analysis, and haematology of the fish groups fed toasted JCK at varying duration also did better than those fed raw JCK. Notably, the performance tends to reduce for those fed JCK toasted beyond 20 min. The estimated cost of producing 1 kg of the fish is substantially reduced by feeding the processed JCK than raw JCK. Histological examination of the intestine and liver tissues revealed less histopathological degeneration for fish fed processed JCK compared to the control. It was concluded that the processing of JCK by toasting should not exceed 20 min to improve the nutritional composition of the feed ingredients and their dietary utilisation by fish.

12.4.3 Effect of Replacing Different Levels of Dietary Fishmeal with J. curcas *Kernel Meal*

Krome et al. (2014) created four diets by substituting JKM for fishmeal in various degrees: 0% (Control), 50% (J50), 75% (J75), and 100% (J100). JKM and blood meal were used in place of fishmeal in a fifth diet to replace 70% and 20% of the fishmeal to reduce the amount of crystalline lysine. According to their findings, fish fed the control diet gained much more body mass than fish given any other treatments. However, the specific growth rate (SGR) and feed conversion ratio (FCR) did not change substantially between the control, J50, and J75 diets. Fish fed the control diet had a lower body protein content than fish fed the JKM-based diets, but their body fat and energy contents were higher. It was also possible to see an adaptation in the fish fed diets J50, J75, and J100, which had worse FCR values for the majority of the first third of the trial but equal (or, in the case of J75, noticeably better) FCR values during the last 2 weeks. The authors added that despite significantly slower growth, JKM should still be investigated further in the hunt for substitute plant feedstuffs for tilapia diets because the growth observed in 75% replacement of fishmeal was highly encouraging.

The dietary inclusion of socked Jatropha curcas kernel (JCK) and its impact on *Clarias gariepinus* were studied by Okomoda et al. (2021). Three JCK treatments (i.e., soaking for 24, 48, and 72 h) and a control group were evaluated for 56 days. As opposed to the control JCK, the results demonstrated that soaking significantly enhanced proximate composition and decreased anti-nutrient. Along with the growth improvement, it was also reported that the dietary administration of soaked JCK increased haematological variables and carcass protein. Fish fed on diets containing soaked JCK (i.e., for 72 h) showed less evidence of histopathological degeneration than fish raised on diets containing raw JCK, according to histological analysis of the gut and liver tissues. The goblet cells in the intestine of the *C. gariepinus* fed raw

JCK were depleted, and the epithelial lining tend to shed off. however, in the treatment group, the epithelial lining appeared unaltered and the goblet cell was enhanced. The amount of necrosis in the liver of *C. gariepinus* fed raw JCK was significant, whereas the number of necrotic cells appeared to decrease in the fish fed soaked JCK. The authors concluded that soaking was consequently determined to be a considerably simpler way of nutritionally enhancing JCK for administration to *C. gariepinus*.

Musa et al. (2018) examined the nutritional value of hydrothermally processed *J. curcas* kernel meal (JCK) using *C. gariepinus*, an African catfish. The JCK's nutritional properties improved as the process went on (0, 30, 60, and 90 min). After that, four isonitrogenous (35% CP) and isocaloric (315 kcal g^{1}) diets were created and fed to *C. gariepinus* fingerlings for 56 days. The processed JCK used in these diets was at a 29% concentration. In comparison to the control diet, the processed JCK performed better. Using the second-order polynomial regression analysis, the ideal processing time that resulted in the most significant weight gain was 62 min. The blood parameters of the fish significantly improved after the processed JCK meal was added to their diet as opposed to when they were just given raw JCK. Similarly, adding the processed JCK lowered the cost of producing feed and fish. The nutritional profile of JCK and its dietary consumption by African catfish *C. gariepinus* fingerlings were shown to be enhanced by hydrothermal processing.

12.4.4 Dietary Inclusion of Detoxified J. curcas *Kernel Meal: Effects on Growth Performance and Metabolic Efficiency in Common Carp,* Cyprinus carpio *L.*

According to Kumar et al. (2010), common carp were fed isonitrogenous diets (38% crude protein) for 6 weeks, including a control diet containing fish meal (FM) protein-based protein and two other diets that substituted 75% of FM protein with detoxified Jatropha kernel meal (DJKM, Jatropha group) and soybean meal (SBM, Soybean group). Body mass gain, metabolic growth rate, protein efficiency ratio, protein productive value, energy retention, the effectiveness of metabolised energy for growth, and energy retention efficiency were determined after the experiment. For the Control and Jatropha groups, these parameters were high and statistically comparable, while for the Soybean group, they were significantly lower. A contrary pattern was seen for the energy expenditure per g protein kept in fish bod, heat released, gross energy uptake, metabolised energy intake, energy expenditure per g protein fed and apparently unmetabolized energy did not differ significantly from one another. Finally, the authors concluded that common carp–fed plant protein (DJKM and SBM) and FM protein–based diets exhibited equal average metabolic rates.

12.4.5 *Heamato-immunological and Physiological Responses of* Labeo rohita *Fingerlings to Dietary Fermented* J. curcas *Protein Concentrate*

Shamna et al. (2014) employed solid-state fermentation (SSF) to detoxify JPC, and a 45-day feeding trial was done to examine how feeding fermented JPC (FJPC) influenced the growth, haemato-immunological responses, and physiological responses of rohu fingerlings. Seven different iso-nitrogenous meals, including the control diet (without JPC or FJPC), J5 (5% JPC), J10 (10% JPC), J20 (20% JPC), FJ5 (5% FJPC), FJ10 (10% FJPC), and FJ20 (20% FJPC), were prepared and fed twice daily. The control and FJ fed groups showed a general, linear, and quadratic pattern in the weight gain and specific growth rate values. Additionally, there was a significant difference in feed efficiency, with the control group recording a higher value comparable to FJ fed groups and JPC fed groups recording the lowest value. All JPC fed groups and the 5% FJPC group had significantly lower amounts of red blood cells (RBC) and hemoglobin than the control and other FJPC groups, according to the results of the hematopathological tests. The greatest blood glucose levels of any group were found in the JPC fed groups at 10% and 20%. Similar to serum total protein and albumin, RBC and hemoglobin behaved similarly. The J20 group had the lowest globulin value, while the FJ10 group had the highest value, significantly greater than the other groups. J10 and J20 had the highest superoxide dismutase (SOD) activity in the muscle compared to other groups. J20 exhibited higher SOD activity in the liver. The outcome suggests that solid-state fermentation is the best approach for purifying protein concentrate made from Jatropha cake before feeding it to rohu. According to the authors, FJPC can be consumed by rohu at a rate of 20% without negatively affecting their hemato-immunological or physiological response.

12.4.6 *Dietary Inclusion of Detoxified* J. curcas *Kernel Meal: Effects on Growth Performance and Metabolic Efficiency in Common Carp,* Cyprinus carpio *L.*

According to Kumar et al. (2010), common carp were fed isonitrogenous diets (38% crude protein) for 6 weeks, including a control diet containing fish meal (FM) protein-based protein and two other diets that substituted 75% of FM protein with detoxified Jatropha kernel meal (DJKM, Jatropha group) and soybean meal (SBM, Soybean group). Body mass gain, metabolic growth rate, protein efficiency ratio, protein productive value, energy retention, the effectiveness of metabolised energy for growth, and energy retention efficiency were determined after the experiment. For the Control and Jatropha groups, these parameters were high and statistically comparable, while for the Soybean group, they were significantly lower. A contrary pattern was seen for the energy expenditure per g protein kept in fish bod, the heat released, gross energy uptake, metabolised energy intake, energy expenditure per g protein fed and apparently unmetabolized energy did not differ significantly from one another. Finally, the authors concluded that common carp–fed plant protein (DJKM and SBM) and FM protein–based diets exhibited equal average metabolic rates.

12.4.6.1 Growth Performance and Haematological Indices of African Catfish (*C. Gariepinus* Burchell 1822) Fed Graded Levels of Processed *Jatropha curcas* Leaf Meals

Four practical diets were created at various levels, representing T1, T2, T3, and T4 correspondingly, at inclusion levels of 0%, 1.5%, 3.0%, and 4.5%, and at substitution levels of SBM of 3.5%, 7.0%, and 10.5%. The manufactured diet (Coppens), which also functioned as the control, was the fifth treatment group (T5). The outcomes demonstrated that the treatment diets increased the performance of African catfish. When *J. curcas* leaf meal inclusion levels reached a particular threshold, the response variables rose and were statistically different for practically all of the parameters assessed. The haematological indicators revealed a considerable improvement in the performance of the catfish fed the treatment diets, suggesting that JLM had positive impacts on *C. gariepinus*. As a result, the authors concluded that, *J. curcas* leaf meal may be a reliable supply of protein components in aquaculture diets, which may assist reduce production costs.

12.5 Conclusions and Perspectives

Feed is the essential component of the aquaculture production system, and demand for aquatic organism feed is expected to nearly triple by the end of the decade due to a significant increase in population. Because of this expansion, more protein sources than fishmeal or soymeal must be used. Products derived from the Jatropha plant may be the best option for meeting a significant portion of the protein requirements of the growing feed market. Its use in aquaculture nutrition has been accepted due to its excellent amino and fatty acid composition, which is comparable to fishmeal. Regardless, the research discussed in this chapter broadens the range of feed ingredients available to the feed industry. It also demonstrates how food and energy security can be effectively integrated and establishes links between the bioenergy and feed industries. It is clear from the preceding discussions that the Jatropha plant can produce goods for purposes other than serving as a dietary alternative to fishmeal, which needs to be explored and improved. Finally, we believe that the use of Jatropha in aquafeeds should be encouraged and that more research into its effects on non-specific immunity and the expression of genes involved in growth, stress, and apoptosis in aquatic species should be conducted. Using raw Jatropha kernel meal in aqua feed, on the other hand, may cause intestinal inflammation due to antinutritional factors, which may be associated with growth retardation. As a result, JKM may be used to replace up to 50% of the protein in fishmeal without affecting shrimp development or nutrient uptake. If the replacement levels are exceeded, the nutrient profile of the feeds must be carefully reviewed to ensure that the intended production levels are met, and fish and shrimp health is maintained. Regardless of the detoxifying method, high JKM inclusion (>50% fishmeal protein replacement) may have a negative impact on growth and dramatically reduce protein, fat, and energy digestibility. The majority of these effects, however, were observed in *C. gariepinus* rather than other species, such as common carp.

References

Abasubong KP, Liu WB, Adjoumani Y, Xia SL, Xu C, Li XF (2018) Xylooligosaccharides benefits the growth, digestive functions and TOR signaling in *Megalobrama amblycephala* fed diets with fish meal replaced by rice protein concentrate. Aquaculture 500:417–428

Abd El-Hack ME, Alagawany M, Farag MR, Tiwari R, Karthik K, Dhama K, Zorriehzahra J, Adel M (2016) Beneficial impacts of thymol essential oil on health and production of animals, fish and poultry: a review. J Essent Oil Res 28:1–18

Achten WMJ, Verchot L, Franken YJ, Mathijs E, Singh VP, Aerts R, Muys B (2008) Jatropha bio-diesel production and use. Biomass Bioenergy 32:1063–1084

Aderibigbe AO, Johnson COLE, Makkar HPS, Becker KA, Foidl N (1997) Chemical composition and effect of heat on organic matter- and nitrogen-degradability and some antinutritional components of jatropha meal. Anim Feed Sci Technol 67:223–243

Agbebi OT, Otubusin SO, Ogunleye FO (2009) Effect of different levels of substitution of fish meal with blood meal in pelleted feeds on catfish Clarias gariepinus (Burchell, 1822) culture in net cages. Eur J Sci Res 31:6–10

Agbogidi OM, Eruotor PG (2012) Morphological changes due to spent engine oil contamination and its heavy metal components of Jatropha curcas Linn seedlings. In: Planetary Scientific Research Center conference proceedings, vol. 21

Agboola AFA, Adenuga AA (2015) Performance and organ histopathology of growing Japanese quails (*coturnix coturnix japonica*) fed heat treated jatropha seed cake substituted for soyabean meal. Trop Anim Health Prod 18:1–8

Ahmed M, Phull AR, Bibi G, Mazhar K, Ur-Rehman T, Zia M, Mirza B (2016) Antioxidant, anticancer and antibacterial potential of Zakhm-e-hayat rhizomes crude extract and fractions. Pak J Pharm Sci 29:895–902

Akande TO, Odunsi AA, Adedeji OS (2006) Toxicity and nutritive assessment of Castor (*Ricinus cummunis*) oil and processed cake in rat diet. Asian J Anim Sci 5:330–339

Alatise SP, Adedokun MA, Adelodun OB, Ajiboye GE (2014) Effects of boiled Jatropha Kernel Meal as a substitute for soyabeans meal in diet of African mud catfish (*Clarias gariepinus*) fingerlings. J Fish Aquat Sci 9:446–454

Annongu AA, Belewu MA, Joseph JK (2010) Potentials of jatropha seeds as substitute protein in nutrition of poultry. Anim Sci J 4:1–4

Asuk AA, Agiang MA, Dasofunjo K, Willie AJ (2015) The biomedical significance of the phytochemical, proximate and mineral compositions of the leaf, stem bark and root of Jatropha curcas. Asian Pac J Trop Biomed 5:650–657

Barnes ME, Brown ML, Rosentrater KA, Sewell JR (2012) An initial investigation replacing fish meal with a commercial fermented soybean meal product in the diets of juvenile rainbow trout. Open J Anim Sci 2:234–243

Barros CR, Rodrigues MAM, Nunes FM, Kasuya MCM, Daluz JMR, Alves A, Ferreira LMM, Pinheiro VA, Mourao JL (2015) The effect of Jatropha curcas seed meal on growth performance and internal organs development and lesions in broiler chickens. Braz J Poultry Sci 17:1–6

Belewu MA, Sam R (2010) Solid state fermentation of Jatropha curcas kernel cake: proximate composition and antinutritional components. J Yeast Fungal Res 1:44–46

Benton T, Bailey R, Froggatt A, King R, Lee B, Wellesley L (2018) Designing sustainable land use in a 1.5° world: the complexities of projecting multiple ecosystem services from land. Curr Opin Environ Sustain 31:88–95

Brittaine R (2010) Jatropha: a smallholder bioenergy crop. In: FAO, Food and Agriculture Organization of the United Nations. The potential for pro-poor development, vol 8. Integrated Crop Management, Rome

Brodjonegoro TP, Reksowardjojo IK, Tatang D, Soerawidjaj H (2005) Jarak Pagar Sang Primadona. Departemen Teknik Kimia, InstitutPertanian Bogor

Butler RA (2006) Why is oil palm replacing tropical rainforests? Why are biofuels fueling deforestation? http://news.mongabay.com/2006/0425-oilpalm.html

Cai W-C, Jiang G-Z, Li X-F (2018) Effects of complete fish meal replacement by rice protein concentrate with or without lysine supplement on growth performance, muscle development and flesh quality of blunt snout bream (Megalobrama amblycephala). Aquac Nutr 24:481–491. https://doi.org/10.1111/anu.12581

Cheeke PR (1998) Natural toxicants in feeds, forages, and poisonous plants. Interstate Publishers

Chehregani A, Malayeri BE (2007) Removal of heavy metals by native accumulator plants. Int J Agric Biol 9:462–465

Cho SH (2010) Effect of fishmeal substitution with various animal and/or plant protein sources in the diet of the abalone Haliotis discus hannaiIno. Aquac Res 41:e587–e593

Cruz-Saurez LE, Nieto-Lopez M, Guajardo-Barbosa C, Tapia-Salazar M, Scholz U, Ricqui-Marie D (2007) Replacement of fishmeal with poultry by-product meal in practical diets for Litopenaeus vannamei and digestibility of the tested ingredients and diets. Aquaculture 272: 466–476

Dedeke GA, Owa SO, Olurin KB, Akinfe AO, Awotedu OO (2013) Partial replacement of fish meal by earthworm meal (*Libyodrilus violaceus*) in diets for African catfish, Clarias gariepinus. Int J Fish Aquat 9:229–233

Denstadli V, Skrede A, Krogdahl A, Sahlstrøm S, Storebakken T (2006) Feed intake, growth, feed conversion, digestibility, enzyme activities and intestinal structure in Atlantic salmon (*Salmo salar* L.) fed graded levels of phytic acid. Aquaculture 256:365–376. https://doi.org/10.1016/j.aquaculture.2006.02.021

Dharmani P, Srivastava V, Kissoon-Singh V, Chadee K (2009) Role of intestinal mucins in innate host defense mechanisms against pathogens. Innate Immun 1:123–135

Duke JA (1988) CRC handbook of medicinal herbs. Handbook of medicinal herbs, vol. 5, p 74

Elbehri A, Segerstedt A, Liu P (2013) A global assessment of sustainability biofuels and sustainability challenge: issues, trends and policies for biofuels and related feedstocks. FAO, Rome

El-Sayed AFM (2002) Alternative dietary protein sources for farmed tilapia, Oreochromis spp. Aquaculture 179:146–168

FAO (2006) The state of world fisheries and aquaculture. Food and Agriculture Organization of the United Nations, Rome, pp 18–21

FAO (2018) The state of world fisheries and aquaculture 2018—meeting the sustainable development goals. Rome. Licence: CC BY-NC-SA 3.0 IGO

Foidl N, Foidl G, Sanchez M, Mittelbach M, Hackel S (1996) Jatropha curcas L. as a source for the production of biofuel in Nicaragua. Bioresour Technol 58:77–82

Gaur S, Viswanathan B, Seemamahannop R, Kapila S, Book NL (2011) Development and evaluation of an efficient process for the detoxification of Jatropha oil and meal. http://precedings.nature.com/documents/6118/version/1. Accessed Nov 22
Ghosh AD, Chaudhary R, Reddy MP, Rao SN, Chikara J, Pandya JB (2007) Prospects for Jatropha methyl ester (biodiesel) in India. Int J Environ Stud 64:659–674
Glencross B, Evans D, Hawkins W, Jones B (2004) Evaluation of dietary inclusion of yellow lupin (*Lupinus luteus*) kernel meal on the growth, feed utilizations and tissue histology of rainbow trout, *Oncorhynchus mykiss*. Aquaculture 235:411–422
Goel G, Makkar HPS, Francis G, Becker K (2007) Phorbol esters: structure, biological activity, and toxicity in animals. Int J Toxicol 26:279–288
Gogoi B, Kachari A, Dutta R, Darshan A. and Narayan D. D (2015) Fishery based livelihood approaches and management of fishery resources in Assam, India, Int J Fish Aquat Stud, 2: 327-330
Gutierrez-Orozco F, Failla ML (2013) Biological activities and bioavailability of mangosteen xanthones: a critical review of the current evidence. Nutrients 5:3163–3183
Harter T, Buhrke F, Kumar V, Focken U, Makkar HPS (2011) Substitution of fish meal by Jatropha curcas kernel meal: effects on growth performance and body composition of white leg shrimp (*Litopenaeus vannamei*). Aquac Nutr 17:542–548
Hunter MC, Smith RG, Schipanski ME, Atwood LW, Mortensen DA (2017) Agriculture in 2050: recalibrating targets for sustainable intensification. Bioscience 67:386–391
Islam AKMA (2011) Improvement of biodiesel production through genetic studies of Jatropha curcas. Ph.D. thesis, Department of Chemical and Process Engineering, Universiti Kebangsaan Malaysia, Bangi, 254p
Islam A, Yaakob Z, Anuar N, Osman M (2010a) Propagation potentials of genotypes and different physiological ages of stem cuttings in *Jatropha curcas* L. J Agric Sci 1916–9752(2):75–82
Islam AKMA, Anuar N, Yaakob Z, Osman M (2010b) Improving plant growth and yield of Jatropha (*Jatropha curcas* L) through apical bud pinching. Int J Fruit Sci 10:281–293
Jain DC, Tripathi AK (1991) Insect feeding-deterrent activity of some saponin glycosides. Phytother Res 5(3):139–141. https://doi.org/10.1002/ptr.2650050311
Joshi C, Mathur P, Khare SK (2011) Degradation of phorbol esters by Pseudomonas aeruginosa PseA during solid-state fermentation of deoiled *Jatropha curcas* seed cake. Bioresour Technol 102:4815–4819
Kajihausa OE, Fasasi RA, Atolagbe YM (2014) Effect of different soaking time and boiling on the proximate composition and functional properties of sprouted sesame seed flour. Niger Food J 32:8–15
Katwal RPS, Soni PL (2003) Biofuels: an opportunity for socioeconomic development and cleaner environment. Indian For 129:939–949
Kaushik SJ, Cravedi JP, Lalles JP, Sumpter J, Fauconneau B, Laroche M (1995) Partial or total replacement of fishmeal by soybean protein on growth, protein utilization, potential estrogenic or antigenic effects, cholesterolemia and flesh quality in rainbow trout, Oncorhynchus mykiss. Aquaculture 133:257–274
Khalil HPS, Aprilia NA, Bhat AH, Jawaid M, Paridah MT, Rudi D (2003) A Jatropha biomass as renewable materials for biocomposites and its applications. Renew Sust Energ Rev 22:667–685. https://doi.org/10.1016/j.rser.2012.12.036
King AJ, He W, Cuevas JA, Freudenberger M, Ramiaramanana D, Graham IA (2009) Potential of Jatropha curcas as a source of renewable oil and animal feed. J Exp Bot 60:2897–2905
Krome C, Jauncey K, Fedderke S, Focken U (2014) Effect of replacing different levels of dietary fishmeal with Jatropha curcas kernel meal on the development of Nile tilapia *Oreochromis niloticus* (Linnaeus, 1758). J Appl Ichthyol 30:1–6. https://doi.org/10.1111/jai.12414
Kumar V (2008) Detoxification of Jatropha curcas seed meal and its utilization as a protein source in fish diet. Comp Biochem Physiol Part A Mol Integr Physiol 151:13–14

Kumar V, Makkar H, Becker K (2010) Dietary inclusion of detoxified Jatropha curcas kernel meal: effects on growth performance and metabolic efficiency in common carp, *Cyprinus carpio* L. Fish Physiol Biochem 36:1159–1170

Kumar V, Makkar HPS, Romano N, Becker K (2019) Utilization of a by-product from the Jatropha biodiesel industry as a fish meal replacer in common carp *Cyprinus carpio* L. diets. J Appl Aquac 31:1–20

Kumari GNK, Aravind S, Balachandran J, Ganesh MR, Ravikumar K (2003) Antifeedant neo-clerodanes from *Teucrium tomentosum Heyne* (Labiatae). Phytochemistry 64:1119–1123

Lele S (2007) Development of the Jatropha cultivation and bio-fuel production system. [Internet]. http://www.svlele.com/jatropha_plant.htm

Lestari D, Mulder J, Sanders PM (2010) Improving Jatropha curcas seed protein recovery by using counter current multistage extraction. Biochem Eng J 50:16–23

Lestari D, Mulder J, Sanders PM (2011) Jatropha seed protein functional properties for technical applications. Biochem Eng J 53:297–304

Lu J, Wool RP (2008) Additive toughening effects on new bio-based thermosetting resins from plant oils. Compos Sci Technol 68:1025–1033

Madeira JV, Macedo JA, Macedo GA (2011) Detoxification of castor bean residues and the simultaneous production of tannase and phytase by solid-state fermentation using Paecilomyces variotii. Bioresour Technol 102:7343–7348

Makkar HPS (1993) Antinutritional factors in foods for livestock. In: Gill M, Owen E, Pollot GE, Lawrence TLJ (eds) Animal production in developing countries. Occasional publication no. 16. BSAP, pp 69–85

Makkar HPS, Becker K (1997) Nutrients and antiquality factors in different morphological parts of the Moringa oleifera tree. J Agric Sci 128:311–322

Makkar HPS, Becker K (1999) Nutritional studies on rats and fish (carp Cyprinus carpio) fed diets containing unheated and heated Jatropha curcas meal of a non-toxic provenance. Plant Foods Hum Nutr 53:183–190

Makkar H, Becker K (2010) Jatropha curcas, a promising crop for the generation of biodiesel and value-added coproducts. Eur J Lipid Sci Technol 111:773–787

Makkar HPS, Becker K, Sporer F, Wink M (1997) Studies on nutritive potential and toxic constituents of different provenances of Jatropha curcas. J Agric Food Chem 45:3152–3157

Makkar H, Aderibigbe AO, Becker K (1998) Comparative evaluation of non-toxic and toxic varieties of Jatropha curcas for chemical composition, digestibility, protein degradability and toxic factors. Food Chem 62:207–215

Makkar H, Becker K, Nitis I, Shin M (1999) Plant toxins and detoxification methods to improve feed quality of tropical seeds. Asian Australas J Anim Sci 12:467–480

Makkar HPS, Martinez-Herrera J, Becker K (2008) Variations in seed number per fruit, seed physical parameters and contents of oil, protein and phorbol ester in toxic and non-toxic genotypes of Jatropha curcas. Plant Sci J 3:260–265

Marroquin E, Blanco J, Granados S, Caceres A, Morales C (1997) Clinical trial of *Jatropha curcas* sap in the treatment of common warts. Fitoterapia 68:160–162

Meher L, Kulkarni M, Dalai A, Naik S (2006) Transesterification of karanja (*Pongamia pinnata*) oil by solid catalysts. Eur J Lipid Sci Technol 108:389–397

Michael KG, Sogbesan OA, Onyia LU, Shallangwa SM (2019) Nutritional evaluation of processed Jatropha curcas seed meals. DRJAFS 7:131–136

Michalk DL, Kemp DR, Badgery WB, Wu J, Zhang Y, Thomassin PJ (2019) Sustainability and future food security—a global perspective for livestock production. Land Degrad Dev 30:561–573

Musa SO, Tiamiyu LO, Solomon SG, Ayuba VO, Okomoda VT (2018) Nutritional value of hydrothermally processed Jatropha curcas kernel and its effect on growth and hematological parameters of *Clarias gariepinus* fingerlings (Burchell, 1822). Aquac Rep 10:32–38

Musa SO, Okomoda VT, Tiamiyu LO, Solomon SG, Abol-Munafi AB (2021) Dietary implications of toasted Jatropha curcas kernel on the growth, haematology, and organ histology of *Clarias*

gariepinus fingerlings. Trop Anim Health Prod 53:232. https://doi.org/10.1007/s11250-021-02678-3
Nahar K, Ozores-Hampton M (2011) Jatropha: an alternative substitute to fossil fuel. (IFAS publication number HS1193). University of Florida, Institute of Food and Agricultural Sciences, Gainesville
Odetoye TE, Ogunniyi DS, Olatunji GA (2010) Preparation and evaluation of Jatropha curcas Linneaus seed oil alkyd resins. Ind Crop Prod 32:225–230
Okomoda VT, Tiamiyu LO, Uma SG (2016) Effects of hydrothermal processing on nutritional value of *Canavalia ensiformis* and its utilization by *Clarias gariepinus* (Burchell, 1822) fingerlings. Aquac Rep 3:214–219
Okomoda VT, Musa SO, Tiamiyu LO, Solomon SG, Abol-Munafi AB (2020) Fermentation of hydrothermal processed Jatropha curcas Kernel: effects on the performance of *Clarias gariepinus* (Burchell, 1822) fingerlings. Aquac Rep 18:100428
Okomoda VT, Musa SO, Tiamiyu LO, Solomon SG, Alamanjo CC, Abol-Munafi AB (2021) Dietary implications of detoxified Jatropha curcas Kernel for *Clarias gariepinus* fingerlings. Vet Sci 8:152
Openshaw K (2000) A review of *Jatropha curcas*: an oil plant of unfulfilled promise. Biomass Bioenergy 19:1–15
Orwa C, Mutua A, Kindt R, Jamnadass R, Anthony S (2009) Agroforestree database: a tree reference and selection guide version 4.0. http://www.worldagroforestry.org/sites/treedbs/treedatabases.asp
Patolia JS Ghosh A, Chikara J, Chaudharry DR, Parmar DR, Bhuva HM (2007) Response of Jatropha curcas L. grown on wasteland to N and P fertilization. Paper presented at the FACT seminar on Jatropha curcas L. agronomy and genetics, Wageningen. Article no.34
Phulia V, Sardar P, Sahu NP, Fawole FJ, Shamna N, Gupta S (2017) Substitution of soybean meal with fermented Jatropha kernel meal: effect on growth performance, body composition, and metabolic enzyme activity of Labeo rohita. Fish Physiol Biochem. https://doi.org/10.1007/s10695-017-0447-z
Phull AR, Abbas Q, Ali A, Zia M, Haq IU, Kim SJ (2020) Antioxidant, cytotoxic and antimicrobial activities of green synthesized silver nanoparticles from crude extract of Bergenia ciliate. Future J Pharm Sci 2:31–36
Pike IH, Jackson A (2010) Fish oil: production and use now and in the future. Lipid Technol 22:59–61. https://doi.org/10.1002/lite.201000003
Raheman H (2012) Chapter 14. Jatropha. In: Chittaranjan K, Joshi CP, Shonnard DR (eds) Handbook of bioenergy crop plants. CRC Press, Boca Raton
Ray DK, Mueller ND, West PC, Foley JA (2013) Yield trends are insufficient to double global crop production by 2050. PLoS One 8:e66428
Rivera-Ferre MG, López-i-Gelats F, Howden M, Smith P, Morton JF, Herrero M (2016) Re-framing the climate change debate in the livestock sector: mitigation and adaptation options. Wiley Interdiscip Rev Clim Chang 7:869–892
Roy T, Banerjee G, Dan SK, Ghosh P, Ray AK (2014) Improvement of nutritive value of sesame oilseed meal in formulated diets for rohu, *Labeo rohita* (Hamilton), fingerlings after fermentation with two phytase-producing bacterial strains isolated from fish gut. Aquacult Int 22:633–652
Rumsey GL, Hughes SG, Winfree RA (1993) Chemical and nutritional evaluation of soy protein preparations as primary nitrogen sources of rainbow trout Ž. *Oncorhynchus mykiss*. Anim Feed Sci Technol 40:135–151
Saetae D, Suntornsuk W (2010) Antifungal activities of ethanolic extract from Jatropha curcas seed cake. J Microbiol Biotechnol 20:319–324
Satheesh Kumar MN, Yaakob Z, Maimunah S, Abdullah SRS (2010) Synthesis of alkyd resin from non-edible Jatropha seed oil. J Polym Environ 18:539–544

Shamna N, Sardar P, Sahu NP, Pal AK, Jain KK, Phulia V (2014) Nutritional evaluation of fermented jatropha concentrate in *Labeo rohita* fingerlings. Aquac Nutr 21:33–42. https://doi.org/10.1111/anu.12138

Singh B, Satyanarayana T (2008) Phytase production by a thermophilic mould *Sporotrichum* thermophile in solid state fermentation and its potential applications. Bioresour Technol 99: 2824–2830

Solomon SG, Okomoda VT, Onah RE (2017) Nutritional profile of soaked *Cajanus cajan* (L.) Mill sp. and its utilization as partial replacement for soybean meal in the diet of *Clarias gariepinus* (Burchell, 1822) fingerlings. J Appl Ichthyol 33:450–457

Srinophakun P, Saimaneerat A, Sooksathan I, Visarathanon N, Malaipan S, Charernsom K, Chongrattanameteekul W (2011) Integrated research on Jatropha curcas plantation management. World Renewable Energy Congruences, Linkoping

Staubmann R, Foidl G, Foidl N, Gübitz GM, Lafferty RM, Arbizu VMV, Steiner W (1997) Biogas production from Jatropha curcas press-cake. Appl Biochem Biotechnol 63–65:457–467

Sumiati A, Sudarman LN, Hidayah I, Santoso WB (2007) Toxicity of Jatropha curcas L. meal toxins on broilers. Proceeding of seminar AINI (Indonesian Association of Nutrition and Feed science) VI, July 26–27, 2007, pp 195–201

Sutili FJ, Gatlin DM, Heinzmann BM, Baldisserotto B (2017) Plant essential oils as fish diet additives: benefits on fish health and stability in feed. Rev Aquac 10:716–726

Syed DN, Chamcheu JC, Adhami VM, Mukhtar HR (2013) Pomegranate extracts and cancer prevention: molecular and cellular activities. Anti Cancer Agents Med Chem 3:1149–1161

Tacon AGJ (1994) Feed ingredient for crustacean's natural foods and processed feed stuffs. FAO Fish Circ 866:1–67

Tacon AGJ, Jackson A (1985) Utilizaiton of conventional and nonconventional protein sources in practical feed sp. In: Mackie CAM, Bell JG (eds) Nutrition and feeding in fish. Academic, London, pp 119–145

Teves JFC, Ragaza JA (2016) The quest for indigenous aquafeed ingredients: a review. Rev Aquac 8:154–171

Thomas R, Sah NK, Sharma PB (2008) Therapeutic biology of Jatropha curcas: a mini. Curr Pharm Biotechnol 9:315–324

Tiamiyu LO, Okomoda VTN, Agbo AO (2015) Nutritional suitability of Leucaena leaf meal in the diets of *Clarias gariepinus*. J Fish Sci 9(1):351–355

Turchini GM, Torstensen BE, Ng WK (2010) Fish oil replacement in finfish nutrition. Rev Aquac 1: 10–57

Warra AA (2012) Cosmetic potentials of physic nut (Jatropha curcas Linn.) seed oil: a review. Department of Biochemistry, Kebbi State University of Science and Technology, American J Sci Ind Res. http://www.scihub.org/AJSIR. issn:2153-649X, https://doi.org/10.5251/ajsir.2012.3.6.358.366

Watanabe T, Veraakunpiriya V, Watanabe K, Kiron V, Satoh S (1997) Feeding of rainbow trout with non-fish meal diets. Fish Sci 63:258–266

Wolski E, Menusi E, Remonatto D, Vardanega R, Arbter F, Rigo E, Ninow J, Mazutti MA, Luccio M, Oliveira DD (2009) Partial characterization of lipases produced by a newly isolated *Penicillium sp.* in solid state and submerged fermentation: a comparative study. LWT Food Sci Technol 42:1557–1560

Part II
Water Quality Management

Chapter 13
Applications of Aquatic Plants in the Remediation of Aquaculture Wastewater: An Opportunity for African Aquaculture

Anna Alfeus and Ndakalimwe Naftal Gabriel

Abstract Aquaculture has proven to enhance food production to meet the growing population's food security demand. The sustainability of aquaculture farming requires environmental sustainability, particularly the disposal of wastewater produced during aquaculture farming. The large volume of wastewater exchanged during production poses a challenge to safe disposal. Wastewater from aquaculture contains high concentrations of nitrogen, chemical oxygen demand, and phosphorus, mainly from uneaten feeds. The nutrients contaminate water bodies and threaten the life of aquatic organisms in the water by boosting the growth of toxic algae. The treatment of wastewater from aquaculture before disposal is a necessity. Currently, small-scale farmers discard untreated wastewater into ponds that do not treat wastewater because of the inability to afford treatment facilities. Commercial aquaculture farming uses conventional methods that create secondary pollution of increased carbon footprint resulting from high energy consumption. Plants have proven to be efficient in removing nitrogen and phosphorus and improving the water quality produced in aquaculture. Therefore, this chapter has looked at studies using plants to remove contaminants in aquaculture wastewater, and as prospects for African aquaculture farmers.

Keywords Aquaculture · Wastewater · Nitrogen · Phosphorus · Phytoremediation

A. Alfeus (✉)
Department of Public Health, School of Nursing and Public Health, Faculty of Health Science and Veterinary Medicine, Oshakati Campus, University of Namibia, Oshakati, Namibia
e-mail: aalfeus@unam.na

N. N. Gabriel
Department of Fisheries and Ocean Sciences, Faculty of Agriculture, Engineering and Natural Science, Sam Nujoma Campus, University of Namibia, Henties Bay, Namibia

© The Author(s), under exclusive license to Springer Nature Singapore Pte Ltd. 2023

N. N. Gabriel et al. (eds.), *Emerging Sustainable Aquaculture Innovations in Africa*, Sustainable Agriculture and Food Security,
https://doi.org/10.1007/978-981-19-7451-9_13

13.1 Introduction

The global population continues to expand, with the current equivalence of 74 million births added to the world population every day until 2027, placing a high demand on food production to feed the growing population (FAO 2018). Responding to the population demands, agriculture supply, and global requirements in energy supply continue to grow, leading to the increase in waste products that will deteriorate the environmental quality if not correctly managed (Tian and Lin 2018). In the case of agricultural supplies, fish consumption has also increased, leading to fish production through aquaculture. The state of world fisheries and aquaculture has indicated that the production of fish worldwide has grown tremendously, contributing to food security and world economic growth with an estimated value of US$ 119 billion in 2010 (FAO 2012). By 2011 the world fisheries production stood at 154 million tonnes, with 63.6 million tonnes mainly coming from inland and marine aquaculture (FAO 2012). About 131 million tonnes of fish produced were for food consumption, with Asia accounting for the consumption of about two-thirds of total fish production (89.08 million tonnes). In comparison, Africa is the least consumer of fish, with 9.4 million tonnes (FAO 2012). Aquaculture fish farming is also increasing due to the increased usage of fish models in research and development activities (Johansen et al. 2006).

Fish farming requires a high volume of water during production, resulting in a large volume of wastewater discharged into the environment (Nogueira et al. 2018). The regular exchange of water is required to maintain the health and welfare of the fish by providing freshwater with feeds and removing wastewater (Johansen et al. 2006). The wastewater is usually discharged into water streams or pre-treated through sedimentation tanks. Sedimentation tanks aid in removing suspended materials, but not dissolved particles posing a risk to the receiving water bodies. The use of sedimentation tanks applies to small-scale and rural farmers who cannot afford advanced wastewater treatment facilities (Hendra et al. 2017). The inability to afford advanced treatment equipment leaves no explicit provision for communal aquaculture farmers to treat wastewater before discharging it into the environment; hence, the possibility of discharging untreated wastewater into the water bodies is unattended. Discharging untreated aquaculture wastewater has a detrimental effect on the water bodies and poses a severe threat to natural habitats and human health (Mustafa and Hayder 2021). The detrimental effects are mainly due to the high loading of suspended solids and dissolved nutrients from the accumulation of by-products, e.g., fish excretions and uneaten feed (Benedito et al. 2013). Wastewater from fish farming has a high concentration of nitrogen and phosphorus, which lead to the eutrophication of aquatic bodies where this wastewater is disposed (Evans et al. 2019). For these concerns, effective wastewater treatment before discharging into the environment is required (Mustafa and Hayder 2021). Developed countries such as Australia, China, and Denmark have enacted aquaculture legislation stipulating standards on ammonia, oxidised nitrogen, phosphorus, and suspended sediments and issuance of a discharge permit or license to the aquaculture facilities before discharging wastewater in the water bodies (FAO 2021). In addition, the Namibian Aquaculture Policy of 2001 stipulated that no person shall discharge wastewater generated by aquaculture facilities that may harm human or environmental health without treatment (FAO 2022). The Namibian legislation implies that aquaculture farmers should determine wastewater quality and then decide to discharge based on the results. Large-scale or commercial aquaculture facilities have used conventional treatment methods in treating wastewater, such as ion exchange, adsorption, reverse osmosis, chemical precipitation, and electrochemical treatment to remove organic and inorganic contaminants (Mustafa and Hayder 2021). However, these methods require high energy consumption and maintenance costs, as well as release high carbon emissions, and excess sludge discharge that would still contain toxic contaminants. The challenges associated with current waste water treatment methods indicate that there is a need to explore alternative methods of wastewater that are affordable, efficient, and easy to implement for rural and commercial fish farmers.

13.2 Phytoremediation as a Remediator for Aquaculture Wastewater

The phytoremediation technique employs the application of plants for wastewater remediation. Phytoremediation is efficient in improving ecological water quality (Hendra et al. 2017), removal of metals (Fawzy et al. 2012), xenobiotics (Del Buono et al. 2020) and herbicides (Mimmo et al. 2015), as shown in Table 13.1. Plants aid in removing physical, biological, and chemical contaminants in wastewater. Evidence of about 30 aquatic plants from the different levels of the aquatic environment exist in phytoremediation. These include the free-floating plants (*Pistia stratiotes, Salvinia molesta, Lemna spp., Azolla pinnata, Landoltia punctata, Spirodela polyrhiza, Marsilea mutica, Eichhornia crassipes,* and *Riccia fluitans),* submerged *(Hygrophilla corymbosa, Najas marina, Ruppia maritima, Hydrilla verticillata, Egeria densa, Vallisneria americana* and *Myriophyllum aquaticum*), and emergent plants (*Distichlis spicata, Cyperus spp., Imperata cylindrical, Iris virginica, Nuphar lutea, Justicia americana, Diodia virginiana, Nymphaea spp., Typha spp., Phragmites autralis and Hydrochloa caroliniensis*). The combination of free-floating, sub-emerged and emergent plants have been promising in the natural or constructed wetland (Jeke et al. 2015). A constructed wetland for phytoremediation purposes is an artificial system that simulates a natural ecosystem with various emergent, submerged, and floating aquatic species (Del Buono et al. 2020). In the constructed wetlands, the contaminants are physically removed and eventually degraded by plants or microbes or subjected to sedimentation (Shelef et al. 2013). For example, halophytes are salt phytoremediators or bio-indicators of water quality. A study by Shelef et al. (2013) found that *B. indica*, a halophytic annual, accumulates sodium to up to 10% of its dry weight. In addition, the study also demonstrated that *B. indica*,

Table 13.1 Phytoremediation efficiency of potential plants used in wastewater treatment from various sources

Types of wastewater	Types of plant	Function	References
Polluted river (domestic wastewater)	Water Hyacinth (*Eichhornia crassipes*)	Highly efficient in removing COD (68.21%), total nitrogen TN (89.4%), and ammonium nitrogen NH^{+}_{a}–N from a polluted river	Lu et al. (2018)
Polluted river (domestic wastewater)	Water lettuce (*Pistia stratiotes*)	Highly efficient in removing COD (68.21%) and total phosphorus (93.6%) from a polluted river	Lu et al. (2018)
Polluted Nile river (Industrial effluent, agricultural and domestic waste)	*Ceratophyllaceae demersum*	Absorb heavy metals (Pb, Cd, Cu, Zn)	Fawzy et al. (2012)
Contaminated soil and water	Maize, Sorghum, rice, cereal	High ability to absorb heavy xenobiotics (Naphthalic Anhydride, Flurazole, Fenclorim, Fenchlorazole ethyl)	Del Buono et al. (2020)
Contaminated water with pesticides (Agricultural waste)	*Italian ryegrass (Lolium multiflorum L.)*	Ability to remove about 30–40% herbicide terbuthylazine (TBA) in an aqueous solution	Mimmo et al. (2015)
Industrial wastewater	*C. cuprina*	Able to tolerate a mixture of heavy metal (Al, As, Cd, Cu, Cr, Fe, Mn, Ni, Pb, Sn, Zn) and hydrocarbons contamination (THC, PHE, PYR, LAS) from industrial wastewater	Guittonny-Philippe et al. (2015)
Industrial wastewater	*Alisma. lanceolatum*	Proliferate in the root-shoot ratio in a mixture of heavy metals (Al, As, Cd, Cu, Cr, Fe, Mn, Ni, Pb, Sn, and Zn) and hydrocarbons contamination (THC, PHE, PYR, LAS). Heavy metal caused an increase in leaf senescent in the plant	Guittonny-Philippe et al. (2015)
Industrial wastewater	*Iris pseudacorus*	The interaction of heavy metals (Al, As, Cd, Cu, Cr, Fe, Mn, Ni, Pb, Sn, and Zn) and hydrocarbons (THC, PHE, PYR, LAS) mixtures lead to the following: (1) an increase of R/S caused by the interaction between organic pollutants and metals; (2) an increase of the leaf senescent process mainly caused by metals; and (3) inhibition of aerial elongation mainly caused by organic pollutants	Guittonny-Philippe et al. (2015)
Aquaculture wastewater	*Centella asiatica*	Efficient in removing 98% of ammoniacal nitrogen (NH_3-N), 90% of total suspended solids, and 64% of phosphate	Nizam et al. (2020)

(continued)

Table 13.1 (continued)

Types of wastewater	Types of plant	Function	References
Aquaculture wastewater	*Ipomoea aquatica*	Efficient in removing 73% of ammoniacal nitrogen (NH_3-N) and total suspended solid and 50% of phosphate	Nizam et al. (2020)
Aquaculture wastewater	*Eichhornia crassipes*	Efficiently removing 74% of ammoniacal nitrogen (NH_3-N), 96% of total suspended solids, and 98% of phosphate	Nizam et al. (2020)
Aquaculture wastewater	*Pistia stratiotes*	Efficiently removing 78% of ammoniacal nitrogen (NH_3-N), 98% of total suspended solids, and 89% of phosphate	Nizam et al. (2020)
Aquaculture wastewater	*Salvinia molesta*	Efficiently removing 63.9% of ammoniacal nitrogen (NH_3-N), 89.3% of total suspended solids, and 88.6% of phosphate	Nizam et al. (2020)

reduced the concentration of H_2O_2, a marker for plant stress, in successive treatment stages, which indicates the improvement of the water quality (Shelef et al. 2013).

13.2.1 Mechanisms of Actions During Phytoremediation

There are five plant-based technologies of phytoremediation, with each having a different mechanism for remediating polluted water bodies:

Phytofiltration—This process involves the use of plant roots (rhizofiltration) or seedlings (blastofiltration) to absorb contaminants from aqueous mediums (Sarma 2011).

Phytoextraction—This process involves the ability of the plant to absorb contaminants from the wastewater through its root system (Mimmo et al. 2015). The contaminant subsequently translocates to the shoots for harvesting; hence, the process allows the removal of the contaminant (Sarma 2011). Since the harvested shoots contain toxic chemicals, farmers can use the tissues for non-food purposes such as energy production or incineration, followed by ash disposal in a landfill (Shelef et al. 2013). In some circumstances, especially in the case of metals that may have a commercial value, plant tissues can be processed to recover the metal as a salt after the phytoextraction and harvesting. The recovery technology of the metal salt is known as phytomining. Harvesting the plant is essential because it prevents the recontamination and recycling of contaminants in the water environment through decaying plant tissues.

Phytostabilisation—Plants reduce the mobility of the pollutants in the soil by binding them to the soil particles via complexation or precipitation. Consequently,

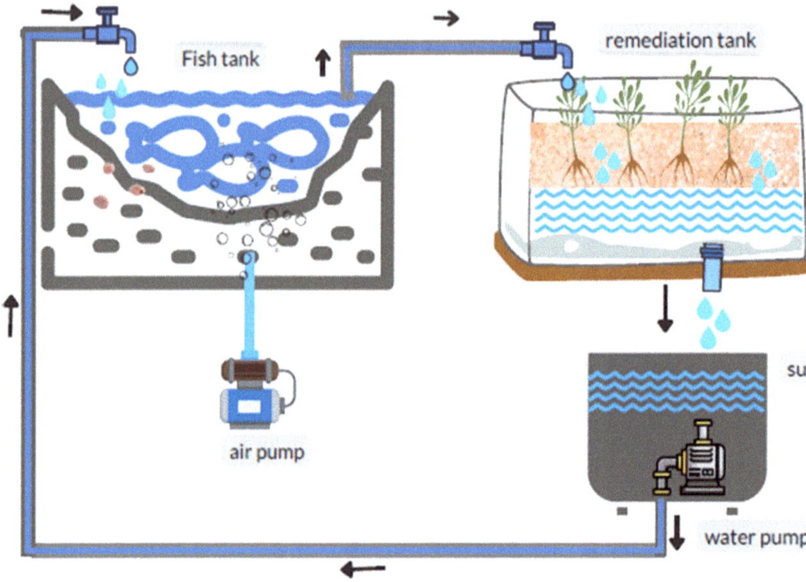

Fig. 13.1 Schematic diagram of a recirculation aquaculture system aided by phytoremediation in treating wastewater

this action prevents the leaching and runoff of the pollutant into the environment (Sarma 2011). Rhizostabilisation is the dominant phytoremediation process for removing trace elements from the water environment (Jeke et al. 2015). Rhizostabilisation happens because the translocation of trace elements from the roots to the shoots (above-ground biomass) does not occur in wetland plants. Thus, above-ground biomass harvesting becomes an ineffective strategy for removing trace elements (Jeke et al. 2015).

Phytovolatilization—The plant extract and volatilize the contaminants, releasing them into the atmosphere (Sarma 2011).

Phytodegradation—Refer to species capable of enzymatically transforming organic pollutants into no-more toxic derivatives (Fig. 13.1).

13.3 Factors to Consider in the Selection of Plants for the Phytoremediation Process

Plant selection is a vital phytoremediation management criterion (Sarma 2011). The selection of the plant influences the fruitfulness of the phytoremediation strategy. Native indigenous plant species are usually a priority for phytoremediation due to their excellent capacity to adapt to native climatic conditions and seasonal cycles (Sarma 2011). Some essential criteria in selecting plant species include:

- The level of tolerance with regard to contaminants known in the fish farm wastewater
- The efficiency in the accumulation, translocation, and uptake of contaminants
- High growth rate and biomass yield
- Tolerance to waterlogging and extreme drought conditions
- Availability and habitant preference, e.g., submerged, floating plant, or emerging plant
- Tolerance to high PH and salinity
- Root characteristics, depth of root zone

13.4 Success Stories of Plants Used in Wastewater Treatment

13.4.1 Pistia stratiotes

P. stratiotes are common plants used in wastewater treatment from agricultural processes (Mustafa and Hayder 2021). The wide application of these aquatic plants is due to their availability, resilience in a toxic environment, bioaccumulation potential, invasive mechanisms, and biomass potentials (Mustafa and Hayder 2021). *Pistia stratiotes* are also known for treating polluted rivers with domestic wastewater. The plant exhibits COD and nutrients removal properties from Shanghai, China.

Pistia stratiotes have shown 61.70% efficiency in the removal of COD concentrations. The COD concentration was reduced in the first four days of the experiment to less than 30 mg/L from the initial concentration of 60 mg/L at the beginning of the experiment (Lu et al. 2018). The experiment indicates that *P. stratiotes* improve water quality because COD is the chemical dissolved oxygen required to break down organic matters that lead to eutrophication in water bodies (Lu et al. 2018). Therefore the removal of COD preserves the aquatic inhabitants from ecological degradation and increases the biological oxygen demand reducing the algal growth and consequently reducing organic matters (Lu et al. 2018). The phytoremediation process used in the COD removal was phytofiltration. In the same experiment using *P. stratiotes* in the domestic wastewater from a polluted river, the TN (Total Nitrogen) concentration from the *P. stratiotes* ponds reduced from the initial concentration (Day 1) of 17.25–4.01 mg/L on day 20 of the experiment (Lu et al. 2018). The experiment showed a TN removal efficiency of 77% after 20 days of treatment. The removal of total nitrogen took place through the phytodegradation process. *P. stratiotes* showed 93% efficiency in removing ammonia nitrogen (NH_4^+-N), causing a steady decline in NH_4^+-N from 13.68 mg/L on day 1 to 0.9 mg/L on day 20, respectively (Lu et al. 2018). Contrastingly, *P. stratiotes* showed no uptake of nitrate nitrogen (NO_3^--N); therefore, the concentration of NO_3^--N increased from the initial concentration (Day 1) of 0.155–5.05 mg/L to day 11 of the experiment

(Lu et al. 2018). Again, *P. stratiotes* exhibited 88% efficiency in removing total phosphorus in the water resulting in a decrease in the TP concentration from an initial concentration of 1.70 mg/L to 0.2 mg/L after 20 days of treatment (Lu et al. 2018).

13.4.2 Spirodela Polyrhiza *and* Salvinia Molesta

These macrophytes *(Spirodela polyrhiza* and *Salvinia molesta*) have been proven to have efficient phytoremediation properties in treating water from the fish farm (Hendra et al. 2017). The evidence came from an in-vivo study for 14 days at 25 ± 1 °C under fluorescent tubes (1000 lux) with a 24 h-photoperiod. The study determined the impact of macrophytes on nitrate (NO_3–N), phosphate (PO_4^{3-}), ammonia (NH_3–N), chemical dissolved oxygen (COD), turbidity, MLVSS, (a procedure that tested the impact on the fixed and volatile solids) and pH (Hendra et al. 2017). In addition, the study evaluated the biomass of the macrophytes as a result of the uptake of nitrogen, phosphorus, and ammonia (Hendra et al. 2017).

Nitrate, ammonia, and phosphates are crucial nutrients the plant takes and requires for its growth. The *S. molesta* and *S. polyrhiza* recorded no nitrate intake on day 14 because the nitrate levels in wastewater were 45 mg/L and 25 mg/L, respectively (Hendra et al. 2017). The concentration kept increasing because nitrate concentration was zero at the inception of the experiment (Hendra et al. 2017). The occurrence of nitrate in the fish water system was due to the nitrification process. Nitrification is a microbial process where ammonia is oxidised to nitrite and nitrate. Ammonia-Oxidising Bacteria (AOB) and Ammonia-Oxidising Archaea (AOA) oxidise ammonia to nitrite and produce a nitrate (Hendra et al. 2017). The macrophytes' no uptake of nitrate was due to the plant's preference to take up ammonia instead of nitrate. The study showed that both S. *polyrhiza* and *S. molesta* were efficient in phosphate uptake, removing 16.05 mg/L phosphate on day 14 (Hendra et al. 2017). The achieved high efficiency was because the plant takes up phosphate by absorption through its roots, leaves, and shoots. The plants uptake phosphate and convert it to orthophosphates, which serve the metabolic activities (ATP) for the plant during growth and building other plant structural components (Hendra et al. 2017). *S. molesta* and *S. polyrhiza* macrophytes took up all the ammonia concentration in the wastewater by days 8 and 10, respectively. The significant drop in ammonia concentration is due to the direct consumption in the nitrification process that runs concurrently with the water treatment process.

13.4.2.1 Water Quality After Phytoremediation

The phytoremediation process affects the quality of fish farm wastewater. The parameters used to check for the water quality are chemical oxygen demand (COD), mixed liquor volatile suspended solids (MLVSS), turbidity, and pH (Hendra et al. 2017). COD determines the waste water's effect on the environment once discharged (Hendra et al. 2017). Therefore, COD measures the oxygen required to oxidise soluble and particulate organic matter in the water (Hendra et al. 2017). It is an important water quality parameter as it provides an index to assess the effect of discharged wastewater on the receiving environment (Hendra et al. 2017). By the end of the experiment (Day 14), the COD level for *S. molesta and S. polyrhiza* decreased to 75 mg/L and 30 mg/L, respectively. The significant reduction of COD during the treatment was due to the filtration of suspended solids and the increased absorption of dissolved nutrients in the roots (Hendra et al. 2017). *S. molesta and S. polyrhiza* had a similar trend in pH value, and pH fluctuations were minimum for both plants, ranging between 7.62 and 7.77 (Hendra et al. 2017). Phytoremediation using *S. molesta* and *S. polyrhiza* plants improved wastewater's turbidity after 14 days of the study period. The turbidity reading for *S. molesta* decreased gradually from 298 NTU on day 0 to 54 NTU on the last day of the experiment. The same goes for *S. polyrhiza;* the turbidity decreased from 137 NTU to 5 NTU on day 14 (Hendra et al. 2017). The study also showed that both *S. molesta* and *S. polyrhiza* reduced the concentration of total suspended solids (TSS) to 40 mg/L and 23 mg/L, respectively, at the end of the experiment.

13.4.2.2 Effect of Phytoremediation on Biomass

Phytoremediation increases the fresh weight of *S. molesta* and *S. polyrhiza* (Hendra et al. 2017). The new weight of *S. molesta* increased to 142.43 g, achieving an 85% increase in weight (Hendra et al. 2017). On the other hand, the new weight for *S. polyrhiza* rose to 141.62 g, achieving an 84% increase in weight (Hendra et al. 2017). The sufficient nutrients available in the fish farm wastewater to support the growth of macrophytes is attributed to the positive increment of biomass (Hendra et al. 2017). The nutrients came from inorganic dissolved nutrients and mineralisation of the organic suspended solids, originating from uneaten feed and fish excretion (Hendra et al. 2017). Aquaculture farmers can produce valuable by-products from the biomass, such as fertilisers, biofuel, and fish feed which can ultimately generate side income (Hendra et al. 2017).

13.4.3 Myriophyllum Elatinoides *and* Eichhornia Crassipes

A similar study compared the uptake of two forms of nitrogen namely nitrogen ammonia ($NH^{+}{}_{4}$), nitrate ($NO^{-}{}_{3}$) and phosphorus ($PO^{3-}{}_{4}$) by free-floating species, namely *M. elatinoides*, *E. crassipes*, and *A. philoxeroides* in an aquatic environment consisting of different level of nitrogen ammonia (10, 20, 50, 100, 200, 400, and 600 mg/L), nitrate (1, 5, 10, 20, 30, 50, and 100 mg/L) and phosphorus (1, 5, 10, 20, 30, 50, and 100 mg/L) concentrations in a constructed wetland (Li et al. 2021). The seedlings of *M. elatinoides*, *E. crassipes*, and *A. philoxeroides* were allowed to grow for 20 days; then, they were washed with deionised water and cultivated in calcium sulfate solution for 1 day to cause starvation, which maximised the uptake of N and P by plants during the experiments (Li et al. 2021). The initial weighting of the seedlings took place, and 10 g of each seedling stayed in a 1 L flask consisting of 800 mL of nutrients at different concentrations (Li et al. 2021). The study showed that *M. elatinoides* and *E. crassipes* were more favourable to the uptake of nitrogen and phosphorus than *A. philoxeroides*. The results of this study show that the uptake of NH_4^+ was higher than the uptake of NO_3^- by the two species, with the maximum uptake rate of NH_4^+ detected at 500 mg/L in *M. elatinoides* and 400 mg/L in *E. crassipes* (Li et al. 2021). The maximum dry weight for *M. elatinoides* and E. *crassipes* were 14.1 ± 1.0 mg/g and 13.6 ± 2.4 mg/g per hour, respectively (Li et al. 2021). The results show that *M. elatinoides* adapted better to wastewater with high NH_4^+ than E. *crassipes*. The result further demonstrated higher efficiency for *M. elatinoides* and *E. crassipes* in the uptake of NH_4^+ and that both species could tolerate high NH_4^+ concentration in the water environment (up to 600 mg/L) (Li et al. 2021).

Regarding the uptake of NO_3^-, the results for *M. elatinoides* and *E. crassipes* were 4.1 ± 0.2 and 4.3 ± 0.3 mg/g dry weight. The results implied that *M. elatinoides* and *E. crassipes* adapt very well and could efficiently remove NO_3^- in highly contaminated NO_3^- concentration water environments (up to 50 mg/L) (Li et al. 2021). It's worth noting that the results show that the uptake for NH_4^+ for all the species was three times higher than NO_3^-, suggesting that two species favoured the uptake of NH^4_+ more than NO_3^-, although *E. crassipes* had the highest preference for nitrate than any of the other species (Li et al. 2021).

With regards to the uptake of phosphorus (PO^3_4), the uptake rate increased rapidly with increasing concentration, although it decreased at the maximum concentration (100 mg/L) (Li et al. 2021). At the maximum concentration of exposure to phosphorus (100 mg/L), phosphorus uptake was 4.5 and 3.6 mg/g dry weight per hour for *M. elatinoides* and *E. crassipes*, respectively (Li et al. 2021). The results of this study indicate that *M. elatinoides* and *E. crassipes* could efficiently absorb more phosphorus from high P-concentration wastewater, and their ability did not deteriorate with increasing phosphorus concentrations up to 80 mg/L (Li et al. 2021).

A different study in Shanghai, China, tested the phytoremediation efficiency of *E. crassipes and M. spicatum* in a polluted river with domestic waste. Both plants showed efficiency in removing COD in wastewater with 68.21% and 62.55%, from the initial concentrations of 66 mg/L and 72 mg/L, respectively (Lu et al. 2018). *Eichhornia crassipes* was 5% more efficient in COD removal than *M. spicatum* because of *its* rich root system. These plants use phyto-filtration to remove the COD through the roots. The root system also provides a suitable environment for microorganisms to survive (Lu et al. 2018). Once these plants have removed COD, aerobic microorganisms degrade organic matter and nutrients into inorganic compounds, which the plants then utilise through phytodegradation (Lu et al. 2018). Therefore, these plants play two roles: COD degradation and nitrogen removal and fixation.

Eichhornia crassipes and M. spicatum reduced the total nitrogen (TN) concentration from the initial concentration (Day 1) of 16.57 mg/L and

16.85 mg L^{-1} to 2.2 mg/L and 3.89 mg/L on day 20 of the experiment (Lu et al. 2018). Therefore, *E. crassipes and M. spicatum* exhibited a TN removal efficiency of 87% and 77%, respectively, after 20 days of treatment (Lu et al. 2018). The phytoremediation process of nitrogen happens through three processes which are mainly: plant uptake, nitrification/denitrification, and volatilisation. Similarly, *E. crassipes and M. spicatum* showed 96% and 93% efficiency in removing ammonia nitrogen ($NH^{4}{}_{+}$-N), respectively. The initial concentration of $NH^{4}{}_{+}$-N concentrations of 12.45 mg/L and 11.8 mg/L reduced steadily to 0.53 mg/L and 0.82 mg/L on day 20, respectively (Lu et al. 2018). *E. crassipes and M. spicatum* showed no uptake of nitrate nitrogen *(NO_3^--N)*. Particularly for *E. crassipes,* the NO_3^--N concentration increased up to day 11 of the experiment, while the NO_3^--N concentration remained the same during exposure to *M. spicatum* throughout the entire process, indicating that the nitrification-denitrification process was negligible with *M. spicatum* (Lu et al. 2018). Plants usually take up total nitrogen and ammonium nitrogen, which they need during growth. The denitrification and volatilisation process is vital for the removal of nitrate nitrogen. With regards to the removal of total phosphorus, the *E. crassipes and M. spicatum* showed 84% and 80.55% efficiency resulting in a reduction of TP from the initial concentration of 1.89 mg/L and 1.80 mg/L to 0.30 mg/L and 0.35 mg/L, respectively, after 20 days of treatment (Lu et al. 2018).

13.5 Limitation of Phytoremediation as a Wastewater Treatment Strategy

Phytoremediation has several limitations that require further intensive research on plants and their mechanisms. Phytoremediation is generally a slow process compared with conventional treatment options. Plants yield low biomass and have a reduced root system that does not efficiently support phytoremediation. Most likely, phytoremediation does not prevent the leaching of contaminants into underground water tables (Sarma 2011). Environmental conditions also determine the efficiency of phytoremediation as the survival and growth of plants are adversely affected by extreme conditions, toxicity, and general conditions of the water bodies. In phytoremediation technology, multiple metal-contaminated waters require specific metal-accumulating plant species and therefore require extensive research before the application (Sarma 2011). The phytoremediation strategies in a site contaminated with mixed heavy metals require a selection of different plant species that conform to one another. For example, the cadmium/zinc model hyperaccumulator *Thlaspi caerulescens* is sensitive toward copper (Cu) toxicity, which becomes a problem in the remediation of Cd/Zn from soils in the presence of Cu (Sarma 2011). Despite some limitations, there is a global acknowledgement of phytoremediation technology as a better environmental sustainability strategy. Various research laboratories are currently engaged in further research activities to overcome the limitations.

13.6 Conclusion and Prospects of Phytoremediation as Wastewater Treatment in African Aquaculture

This chapter outlines that fish consumption has increased tremendously due to population growth and the quest to ensure food security. Fish aquaculture activities will grow to provide for the increasing population. Africa has the world's highest birth rate and contributes tremendously to world population growth. Therefore, there is a need to intensify aquaculture activities in Africa as one of the fastest ways to ensure food security and income generation. The sustainability of fish aquaculture on the African continent is questionable unless there is an improvement in current wastewater disposal practices. The challenges associated with aquaculture farming on the African continent are due to the inability to afford conventional treatment methods of aquaculture wastewater. The phytoremediation technique employs plants for wastewater remediation that African farmers can use. This treatment method is affordable, efficient, and easy to implement. Evidence of *P. stratiotes*, *Sp. polyrhiza*, *S. molesta, E. crassipes and M. spicatum* towards water quality improvement and removal of nitrogen and phosphorus substrates in wastewater appear in this chapter. Despite that, there is a need to conduct studies on native species and their phytoremediation capacities from the African context.

References

Benedito E, Figueroa L, Takeda AM, Manetta GI (2013) The influence of fish cage culture on δ13C and δ15N of filter-feeding Bivalvia (*Mollusca*). Braz J Biol 73(4):743–746. https://doi.org/10.1590/S1519-69842013000400009

Del Buono D, Terzano R, Panfili I, Bartucca ML (2020) Phytoremediation and detoxification of xenobiotics in plants: herbicide-safeners as a tool to improve plant efficiency in the remediation of polluted environments. A mini-review. Int J Phytoremediation 22(8):789–803. https://doi.org/10.1080/15226514.2019.1710817

Evans AE, Mateo-Sagasta J, Qadir M, Boelee E, Ippolito A (2019) Agricultural water pollution: key knowledge gaps and research needs. Curr Opin Environ Sustain 36:20–27. https://doi.org/10.1016/j.cosust.2018.10.003

FAO (2012) The state of world fisheries and aquaculture. https://www.fao.org/documents/card/en/c/I9540EN/

FAO (2018) OECD-FAO agricultural outlook 2018–2027. https://doi.org/10.1787/agr_outlook-2018-en

FAO (2021) National aquaculture legislation overview. https://www.fao.org/fishery/en/nalo/search

FAO (2022) National aquaculture legislation overview—Namibia. In: Fisheries and aquaculture. https://www.fao.org/fishery/en/legalframework/na/en

Fawzy MA, Badr NES, El-Khatib A, Abo-El-Kassem A (2012) Heavy metal biomonitoring and phytoremediation potentialities of aquatic macrophytes in River Nile. Environ Monit Assess 184(3):1753–1771. https://doi.org/10.1007/s10661-011-2076-9

Guittonny-Philippe A, Petit ME, Masotti V, Monnier Y, Malleret L, Coulomb B, Laffont-Schwob I (2015) Selection of wild macrophytes for use in constructed wetlands for phytoremediation of contaminant mixtures. J Environ Manage 147:108–123. https://doi.org/10.1016/j.jenvman.2014.09.009

Hendra R, Masdeatresa L, Ramli M, Rossani RB, Ayu G, Kristina M (2017) Phytoremediation capabilities of Spirodela polyrhiza and Salvinia molesta in fish farm wastewater: a preliminary study. OP Conf Ser: Mater Sci Eng 206(1):012084. https://doi.org/10.1088/1757-899X/206/1/012084

Jeke NN, Zvomuya F, Cicek N, Ross L, Badiou P (2015) Biomass, nutrient, and trace element accumulation and partitioning in Cattail (*Typha latifolia L.)* during wetland phytoremediation of municipal biosolids. J Environ Qual 44(5):1541–1549. https://doi.org/10.2134/jeq2015.02.0064

Johansen R, Needham JR, Colquhoun DJ, Poppe TT, Smith AJ (2006) Guidelines for health and welfare monitoring of fish used in research. Lab Anim 40(4):323–340. https://doi.org/10.1258/002367706778476451

Li X, Li Y, Li Y, Wu J (2021) The phytoremediation of water with high concentrations of nitrogen and phosphorus contamination by three selected wetland plants. J Water Proc Eng 40:101828. https://doi.org/10.1016/j.jwpe.2020.101828

Lu B, Xu Z, Li J, Chai X (2018) Removal of water nutrients by different aquatic plant species: an alternative way to remediate polluted rural rivers. Ecol Eng 110:18–26

Mimmo T, Bartucca ML, Del Buono D, Cesco S (2015) Italian ryegrass for the phytoremediation of solutions polluted with terbuthylazine. Chemosphere 119:31–36. https://doi.org/10.1016/j.chemosphere.2014.04.114

Mustafa HM, Hayder G (2021) Recent studies on applications of aquatic weed plants in phytoremediation of wastewater: a review article. Ain Shams Eng J 12(1):355–365. https://doi.org/10.1016/j.asej.2020.05.009

Nizam NUM, Hanafiah MM, Noor IM, Karim HIA (2020) Efficiency of five selected aquatic plants in phytoremediation of aquaculture wastewater. Appl Sci 10(8):2712. https://doi.org/10.3390/APP10082712

Nogueira SMS, Junior JS, Maia HD, Saboya JPS, Farias WRL (2018) Use of Spirulina platensis in treatment of fish farming wastewater. Rev Cienc Agron 49(4):599–606. https://doi.org/10.5935/1806-6690.20180068

Sarma H (2011) Metal hyperaccumulation in plants: a review focusing on phytoremediation technology. J Environ Sci Technol 4(2):118–138. https://doi.org/10.3923/jest.2011.118.138

Shelef O, Gross A, Rachmilevitch S (2013) Role of plants in a constructed wetland: current and new perspectives. Water 5(2):405–419. https://doi.org/10.3390/w5020405

Tian P, Lin B (2018) Regional technology gap in energy utilization in China's light industry sector: non-parametric meta-frontier and sequential DEA methods. J Clean Prod 178:880–889. https://doi.org/10.1016/j.jclepro.2018.01.017

Chapter 14
African Aquaculture: Enhancement of Water Quality for Sustainable Freshwater Finfish Culture

E. Omoregie

Abstract Though Africa's contribution to global aquaculture production is still insignificant, aquaculture in Africa has come a long way since it was first introduced over 50 years ago. Commercial finfish aquaculture in Africa is on the increase, with Egypt, Nigeria and South Africa being important producers. The attributes of Africa include under-utilized water and land resources, available and inexpensive labour, high demand for fish and a climate that favours a year-round growing period. However, the optimal use of these resources has frequently been curtailed by poor infrastructure and a lack of production inputs. The potential for expansion is nevertheless considerable but requires several enabling factors that include: a positive perception of aquaculture, sound policies at the national level, strong public institutions, availability of nutrient inputs, conducive investment policies to attract increased private-sector participation, and access to credit for commercial-scale enterprises. In addition to these is enhancing water quality within the rearing systems for improved production. Water quality within the aquaculture rearing system includes all physical, chemical, and biological factors that influence the beneficial use of water for fish cultivation. Any characteristic of water that affects the survival, reproduction, growth, production, or management of fish in any way is of critical importance to the sustainability of growing aquaculture in Africa. This review article, therefore, highlights the various water quality parameters and management of the most important parameters for sustainable aquaculture production on the African continent. The review focuses on best practices in improving pond water quality, drawing on global experiences and research findings from the African continent in improving water quality for sustainable aquaculture in meeting local demand for protein intake per capita.

E. Omoregie (✉)
Department of Natural and Applied Sciences, Namibia University of Science and Technology, Windhoek, Namibia
e-mail: eomoregie@nust.na

© The Author(s), under exclusive license to Springer Nature Singapore Pte Ltd. 2023

N. N. Gabriel et al. (eds.), *Emerging Sustainable Aquaculture Innovations in Africa*, Sustainable Agriculture and Food Security,
https://doi.org/10.1007/978-981-19-7451-9_14

Keywords Africa · Aquaculture · Fish farming · Finfish production · Sustainability · Water quality

14.1 Introduction

14.1.1 Current Status of Aquaculture in Africa

Global aquaculture (both inland and marine environments, excluding aquatic plants) has risen significantly over the past two decades to approximately 85.33 million tonnes in 2019, from an annual average of 14.9 million tonnes between 1986 and 1985 as reported by FAO (2021). Globally, in 2019, inland aquaculture produced mostly farmed finfish (51.3 million tonnes, or 62.5% of the world's total), mainly in freshwater, compared with 57.7% in 2000 (FAO 2021). The rapid growth in global aquaculture production as reported by Bostock et al. (2010) has been driven by a variety of factors, including pre-existing aquaculture practices, population and economic growth, relaxed regulatory framework and expanding export opportunities. While global aquaculture production continued to be dominated by China and other Asian countries, the contribution of aquaculture to global fish production reached 48.0% in 2019, up from 6.5% in 1980 (FAO 2021). Unfortunately, Africa's contribution to global aquaculture production is still insignificant. It is however worth noting that production in the continent has increased several folds within the three decades. In 2019, production from the African region was at 2.40 million tonnes, up from 0.11 million tonnes in 1995 (Fig. 14.1) and accounted for 17.9% of

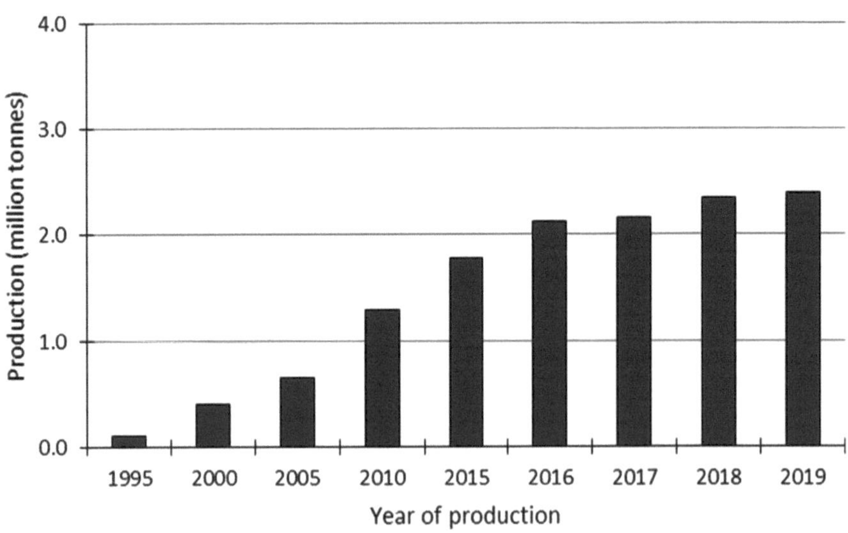

Fig. 14.1 Aquaculture production in Africa (1995 to 2019) (FAO 2020, 2021)

Table 14.1 Top 10 aquaculture producers in Africa in 2018 (Source: Adeleke et al. 2021)

No.	Country	Production (metric tonnes)	Regional share (%)	Global share (%)
1	Egypt	1,561,457	71.10	1.90
2	Nigeria	291,233	13.26	0.35
3	Uganda	103,737	4.72	0.13
4	Ghana	76,630	3.49	0.09
5	Zambia	24,300	1.11	0.03
6	Tunisia	21,756	0.99	0.03
7	Kenya	15,124	0.69	0.02
8	Malawi	9014	0.41	0.01
9	Madagascar	7421	0.34	0.01
10	South Africa	6181	0.28	0.01

total fish production in Africa (FAO 2021). Between 1995 and 2019, the region recorded a compounded annual growth of approximately 15.6% (Halwart 2020).

There is a considerable impetus for the development of aquaculture in sub-Saharan Africa (Machena and Moehl 2000). Aquaculture production in Africa is dominated by finfish in inland environments, with a production of 1.89 million tonnes in 2018, with very insignificant production of other aquatic organisms (FAO 2020). As reported by FAO (2021), Egypt and Nigeria are the only two African countries in the top ten global aquaculture producers. In 2019 production from Egypt was 1.64 million tonnes up from 0.92 million tonnes in 2010, while that from Nigeria was 0.29 million tonnes, up from 0.22 million tonnes in 2010.

In addition to Egypt and Nigeria, other key African producers are Uganda, Ghana, Tunisia, Kenya, Zambia, Madagascar, Malawi, and South Africa. Table 14.1 shows the top 10 aquaculture producers in Africa with their respective regional and global shares. These countries experienced significant growth within the past decade due to numerous factors such as capacity building in critical subject areas, embracing good governance, research and development, access to credit facilities and mainly due to the promotion of private sector-led aquaculture development (Satia 2017). Private sector-led initiatives gave rise to investments in sound management, emerging production systems, the formulation and utilization of aquafeeds and the emergence of dynamic and robust producer associations and service providers (Satia 2011; Adeleke et al. 2021). As documented by Maulu et al. (2021), aquaculture's relevance in the food production sector in Africa will depend on its ability to grow sustainably.

14.1.2 Freshwater Finfish Aquaculture Production Systems in Africa

Freshwater finfish aquaculture production systems in Africa range from small-scale to medium-scale. While small-scale systems are mainly extensive with minimal inputs, large-scale is intensive with profit being the main objective.

Small-scale to medium-scale systems, mainly carried out in rural settings and operated at household or community levels utilize extensive pond systems and are integrated to varying degrees with other agricultural enterprises. The main driving force is household or community food security. The level of intensity indicates that these systems will rely primarily on on-farm inputs including organic fertilizers and simple supplemental feeds. As reported by Jamu and Ayinla (2003) earthen ponds are the dominant production system in small to medium-scale systems in Africa. These systems generally require minimum or no capital investment and are not mechanized, with minimal paid labour in several African countries.

Large-scale systems could also be classified as commercial systems where profit is the main motive. Large-scale systems in African aquaculture production have been referred to as those having a water surface area of five hectares or more or producing more than five metric tonnes annually. These systems tend to be capital intensive, relying on wage labour, external energy sources and mechanization. There are commercial farms using ponds, cages, raceway, and recirculating systems; however, ponds are the principal production unit (Machena and Moehl 2001). Main large-scale aquaculture production systems on the African continent are in Egypt, Nigeria, and South Africa.

The use of cages in natural and artificial lakes for aquaculture production has gained increasing use in several African countries. Musinguzi et al. (2019) noted that cage aquaculture is expanding on African natural and artificial inland waters and has the potential to close the fish supply deficit in the region and provide other social benefits such as employment and income. The report by Musinguzi et al. (2019) revealed that the number of cage production systems in Africa was 263 installations in 2019, with more than 20,000 cages between them. These were divided among eight countries: Ghana having 36.1% of the installations, Uganda 17.9%, Kenya 16.4%, Tanzania 13.3%, Rwanda 8%, Zimbabwe 3.8%, Zambia 3% and Malawi 1.5%. The rise in cage culture has been attributed to the improvement of technology for cage culture in reservoirs and water bodies not suitable for conventional fisheries and the availability of technical support and high-quality inputs like fish feed or fry (Eng and Tech 2002).

14.1.3 Major Freshwater Finfish Cultured Species in Africa

Production of several species of tilapias has dominated aquaculture production on the African continent, the main reason being that aquaculture research and development on the continent have concentrated on these species (Jamu and Ayinla 2003). Other indigenous fish species with high local demand have also contributed to higher aquaculture production on the continent. For example, clariids such as the African catfish (*Clarias gariepinus*) have overtaken tilapia as major culture species in Nigeria (FAO 1999, 2022a), and the common carp (*Cyprius carpio*) production in Egypt is in decline in preference to the indigenous Nile tilapia (*Oreochromis niloticus*) (Brummett 2000). Currently, the production of the Nile tilapia from Egypt is more than 200,000 tonnes per year (FAO 2022b). This market demand trend dictating the choice of indigenous fish species for culture will likely continue in the future and direct aquaculture expansion towards fish production for niche markets. Almost half (43.6%) of African aquaculture production consists of Nile tilapia (Kausar and Salim 2017), followed by the African catfish (11.9%) and common carp (10.5%) (Tumwesigye et al. 2022).

14.2 Water Quality in Aquaculture Production System

In all aquaculture production systems, be it earthen ponds, raceways or recirculatory rearing environments, water quality depends on the physical, chemical, and biological parameters that influence the beneficial use of water that leads to anticipated fish growth. Interactions between these various parameters, either within the rearing environment or external sources, are vital to enhancing the growth of the fish being reared. It is therefore of paramount importance that African aquaculture producers are familiar with the role of these parameters and how to ensure optimal water quality within the production system.

Increasing aquaculture production within the rearing systems involves overcoming a series of limiting factors within the systems. In several African countries, emphasis has shifted to improving water quality and waste management. Assuming some minimum initial set of environmental conditions (such as proper water temperature, low dissolved oxygen, salinity, ammonia, and pH), the limitations on productivity progressively shift from providing more food to providing more oxygen and removal of growth-limiting waste products (Tucker and Hargreaves 2012).

Ibrahim and Naggar (2010), Bhatnagar and Devi (2013), Adebola et al. (2015) and Adeleke et al. (2021) have all highlighted the importance of water quality parameters in aquaculture production in Africa. Of these parameters, Ibrahim and Naggar (2010) noted that temperature, dissolved oxygen, carbon dioxide, ammonia, pH, and salinity are paramount, as uncontrolled fluctuations in these parameters lead to low production. Rutaisire et al. (2017) noted that apart from production cost and fish management practices, aquaculture production in several developing countries is highly dependent on the water quality of the rearing systems. For this reason, improved knowledge in the management and maintenance of enhanced water quality in the rearing systems will lead to improved freshwater fish production on the African continent.

14.2.1 Temperature

Suitable water temperatures for maximum growth for fish species cultured in Africa range between 25 and 32 °C. Temperature, as noted by Boyd and Lichtkoppler (1982), has a pronounced effect on chemical and biological processes within the fish-rearing environment. During colder months (when water temperatures are below 20 °C), the growth of the cultured fish is reduced due to lower metabolic activities and a reduction in food consumption (Abdel-Tawwab and Wafeek 2017). Water temperature could also affect metabolic activity, kinetics, and oxidative stress in fish (Kammer et al. 2011), thereby affecting energy metabolism and many other processes, hence unfavourable water temperature is detrimental to increased aquaculture production.

When the Nile tilapia which has an optimal temperature for growing between 25 and 28 °C (El-Sayed 2006) was exposed to cadmium under different temperature regime, Abdel-Tawwab and Wafeek (2017) observed that unfavourable water temperature combined with the energetic cost associated with the cadmium exposure resulted in altered haematological responses in the fish, ultimately leading to reduced growth in the fish (Table 14.2). In addition, the metal uptake rate in fish can increase with increasing exposure temperature (Bervoets et al. 2009). Finally, temperature itself may become a stressor, especially near the thermal tolerance limits, in which case mixture exposure principles such as antagonism and synergism may be applicable (Heugens et al. 2003).

As most aquaculture production in Africa is from earthen ponds, control of water temperature is almost non-existence as the reduced growth during colder months is compensated for by the faster growth rate during favourable months of warmer water. In the more commercial production in the recirculatory system in some African countries such as Egypt, Nigeria and South Africa, the use of electrical heaters to maintain a uniform temperature all year round is gaining acceptance despite the associated cost.

14.2.2 Carbon Dioxide

The primary sources of carbon dioxide in the aquaculture-rearing environment are derived from respiration by phytoplankton and aquatic animals, including the fish being cultured. Another primary source is the biochemical degradation of organic matter within the pond sediments. Carbon dioxide is not particularly toxic to fish, but fish generally avoid carbon dioxide concentrations above 5 mg/L (Boyd 2020), and uncontrolled level within the pond system is a limiting factors to higher production (Boyd et al. 2020). Contractions above 20 mg/l can stress the cultured fish if they are exposed for several hours, while higher levels can have a respiratory and physiological effect, eventually leading to death. Generally, the overall effect of higher

Table 14.2 Changes in red blood corpuscles (RBCs), haematocrit (Ht), and haemoglobin (Hb) in Nile tilapia exposed to waterborne Cd concentrations at different water temperatures for 8 weeks (Source: Abdel-Tawwab and Wafeek 2017)

Water temperature (°C)	Cd conc. (mg/L)	RBCs ($\times10^6/\mu L$)	Ht (%)	Hb (g/L)
		Individual treatment means[a]		
20	0.0	1.252^{c}	12.63^{c}	44.2^{c}
24		1.601^{a}	15.12+	$56.2^{a,b}$
28		1.612^{a}	15.54^{a}	58.3^{a}
32		1.513^{b}	13.85^{b}	50.3_{b}
20	0.5	0.936^{e}	9.24^{e}	28.3^{e}
24		1.004^{d}	11.77^{d}	31.8^{d}
28		1.008^{d}	11.87^{d}	32.5^{d}
32		$0.987^{d,e}$	9.28^{e}	$30.0^{d,e}$
Pooled SLM		0.057	0.524	2.35
		Means of main effects		
Water temp.				
20		1.094	10.94	36.3
24		1.303	13.45	44.0
28		1.310	13.71	45.4
32		1.250	11.57	40.2
	Cd conc.			
	0.0	1.495	14.29	52.3
	0.5	0.984	10.54	30.7
Two-way ANOVA		*P* value		
Water temperature		0.0001	0.0001	0.0001
Cd concentration		0.0001	0.0001	0.0001
Temperature × Cd conc.		0.0001	0.0001	0.0001

[a]Treatments means represent the average values of three aquaria per treatment. Duncan multiple range test was conducted for individual means only if there was a significant interaction (ANOVA: $P < 0.05$). Means followed by the same letter are not significantly different

[b–e]Means followed by the same letter are not significantly different ($P > 0.05$)

levels of carbon dioxide concentration in water is the reduction of respiratory efficiency and the tolerance of cultured fish to low dissolved-oxygen concentrations.

Carbon dioxide concentrations in aquaculture ponds typically are 5–10 mg/L in the morning hours but can exceed 20 mg/L in ponds with significant feed inputs. Carbon dioxide concentrations in fishponds are usually highest when dissolved-oxygen concentrations are lowest (Hargreaves and Brunson 1996; Makori et al. 2017) due to the relationship between the production of carbon dioxide during respiration and its day-time consumption during photosynthetic activities within the pond water. There is a diurnal cycle of carbon dioxide within the pond water, with increased levels during the night and decreased levels during the daytime (Fig. 14.2).

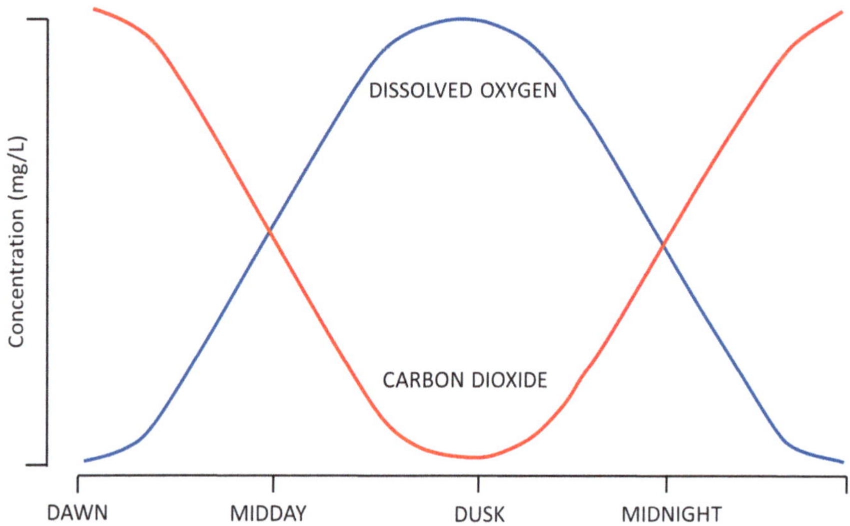

Fig. 14.2 Diurnal variations of carbon dioxide and dissolved oxygen levels in a fish pond (Source: Hargreaves and Brunson 1996)

The relationship between reduced tilapia production in Africa and carbon dioxide levels in the rearing environment has been reported in some countries. In a study by Makori et al. (2017), the growth of the Nile tilapia, *Oreochromis niloticus* in earthen ponds in Kenya, low pH values were observed in these ponds because of elevated carbon dioxide levels; this subsequently led to low tilapia yield in these ponds.

14.2.3 Dissolved Oxygen

In Africa, dissolved oxygen is probably the most critical limiting factor within the rearing environment for aquaculture species production due to higher water temperatures all year round. Even though the atmosphere is a vast reservoir of oxygen, the solubility of oxygen in pond water is highly dependent on other factors, such as temperature, phytoplankton concentrations, excess organic wastes, and stocking density. Though oxygen will diffuse into the water from the atmosphere, its rate of diffusion is relatively prolonged. Photosynthesis by phytoplankton is the primary source of dissolved oxygen for cultured species. Due to photosynthetic activities within the water, dissolved oxygen concentrations in production systems undergo a diurnal pattern over a 24-hr period with the highest concentrations usually being in the daytime and the lowest concentrations at night (Fig. 14.2).

Dissolved oxygen can rapidly be lost from the rearing water, the main reason being respiratory activities of the biota (including the fish being cultured) and biodegradation of organic materials. For enhanced aquaculture production, more

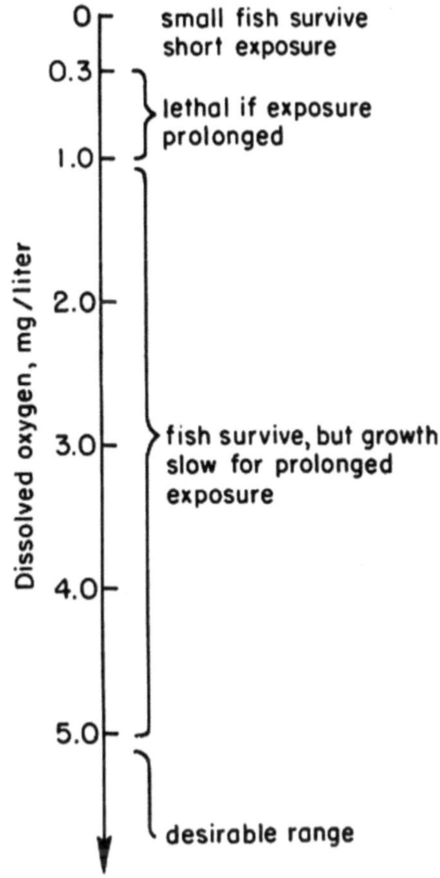

Fig. 14.3 Effects of dissolved oxygen levels on pond cultured fish species (Source: Boyd and Lichtkoppler 1979)

oxygen must enter the water than being utilized for respiratory activities and biodegradation. Cultured species require adequate levels of dissolved oxygen for survival and growth and the minimum levels for survival will depend on the length of exposure. Consistence pond water of ranges above 5 mg/l is preferable for most species, while ranges below 5 mg/l over considerable period are considered not adequation for good production (Fig. 14.3). A fish may survive a given minimum level for 1 day or so; however, when exposure is for several days, it will die. Low levels of dissolved oxygen also predispose the culture species to become more susceptible to diseases which will eventually lower production.

It is well known that tilapia can tolerate hypoxic and even anoxic conditions for short periods and are thus better suited than other species to hyper eutectic conditions that may exist in static water aquaculture systems (Lim et al. 2006). This is one of the most important contributing factors to why the successful production of pond tilapias has been sustained in several African countries. Studies have shown that the incipient oxygen requirements for the Nile tilapia (*Oreochromis* niloticus) are between 1.39 mg/l and 2.92 mg/L (Tsadik and Kutty 1987). These authors also reported that the food conversion ratio (FCR) for the Nile tilapia was inversely proportional to the dissolved oxygen level (1.45 at higher dissolved oxygen levels and 6.75 at lower dissolved oxygen levels).

14.2.4 Ammonia

Ammonia, which is a colourless, pungent gas reaches cultured fish production systems as a product of the biochemical metabolism of animals (including fish being culture) and biochemical bacterial degradation of organic materials. The un-ionized component of this gas is extremely toxic to the cultured fish at levels (above 3.0 mg/l); fortunately, concentrations in the rearing system are not too high to affect fish growth. The pH and temperature of the water regulate the production of un-ionized in the rearing system.

Ammonia blocks oxygen transfer from the fish gills to the blood and can cause immediate and long-term gill damage (Joel and Amajuoyi 2010). Studies have also revealed that ammonia chronic un-ionized ammonia exposure may affect pond fish in several ways, for example, gill hyperplasia, muscle depolarization, hyperexcitability, convulsions and finally, death (Ip et al. 2001).

Ip et al. (2004) noted that in the tropics, air-breathing fish species, including the African catfish, can tolerate toxic levels of ammonia when stranded in puddles of water. Such environmental ammonia tolerance is usually associated with a high tolerance of ammonia at the cellular and subcellular levels (Saha and Ratha 1998). The African lungfish *Protopterus aethiopicus* was observed by Loong et al. (2007) to defend itself against ammonia toxicity when confronted with high concentrations (30 or 100 mmol/l) of environmental ammonia, as the *Protopterus aethiopicus* could decrease its skin permeability to ammonia when exposed to high levels of environmental ammonia.

14.2.5 pH

The pH, which measures how acidic or alkaline water is, depends on several factors interacting within the production system; most importantly is the level of carbon dioxide. The optimum pH range for most aquatic organisms is 6.5–8.5, and the acid and alkaline death points are around pH 4 and pH 11, respectively (Boyd 2020) (Fig. 14.4). During periods of active photosynthesis (daytime), carbon dioxide is removed from the water by phytoplankton and other aquatic plants, thereby increasing the water alkaline levels, hence pH is highest at dusk and lowest at dawn. Fish and other aquatic animals avoid high carbon dioxide concentrations.

Wokoma and Marioghae (1996) reported that the median lethal time (LT_{50}) for the tilapia, *Tilapia guineesnsis* increased with pH from 1.2 h at pH 2.0 to 62 h at pH 3.0. the critical median pH was 3.3 (Fig. 14.5).

Fig. 14.4 Effect of pH on pond cultured fish species (Source: Boyd and Lichtkoppler 1979)

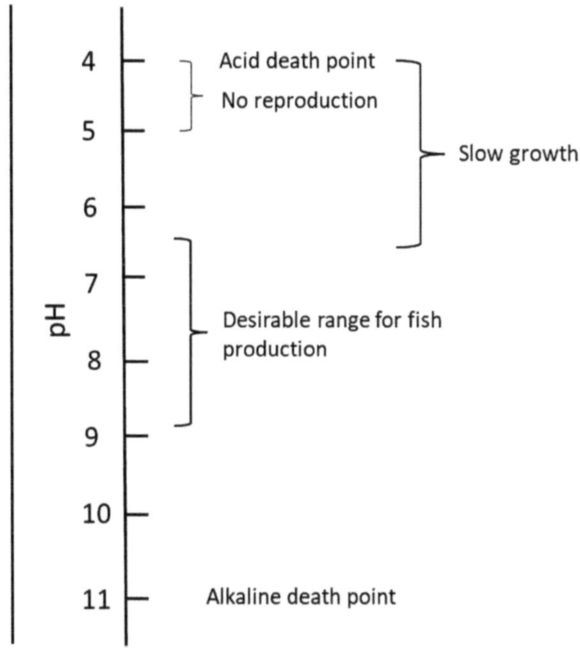

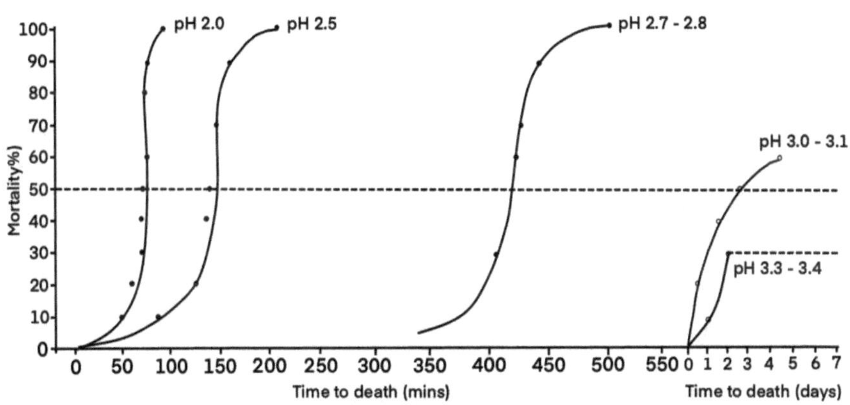

Fig. 14.5 Time to death of *Tilapia guineensis* juveniles in experimental tanks with various pH levels (Source Wokoma and Marioghae 1996)

Uzoka et al. (2015) observed that the optimum pH range for the best growth of the African catfish, *Clarias gariepinus* is between 6 and 7, while at values below 5 and above 8, survival rates were grossly affected (Fig. 14.6).

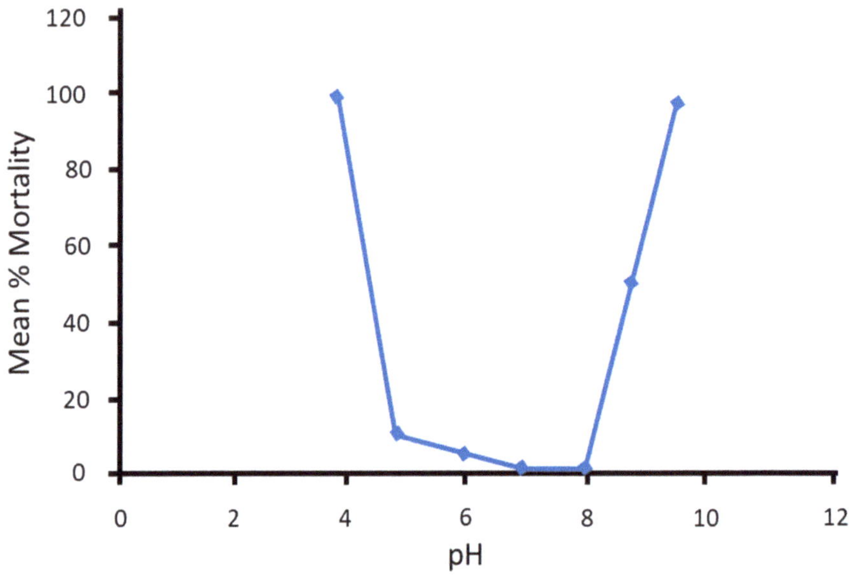

Fig. 14.6 Mortality of the African catfish, *Clarias gariepinus* reared at varying pH values at 6.0 mg/l of dissolved oxygen and 26.5 °C temperature. (Source: Uzoka et al. 2015)

14.2.6 Salinity

Salinity, the total concentration of all dissolved ions in water, is essential for thriving freshwater fish culture as the osmotic pressure of water increases with increasing salinity. Most aquaculture species have a relatively wide range of salinity tolerance; however, changes outside the optimal range lead to stress, and, if extreme enough, death could result (Ridha 2008; Qiang et al. 2013; Boyd 2020). Research suggests that a shift in salinity from the iso-osmotic point is associated with a reduction in fish growth and feed utilization, likely due to an increase in the energy required for osmoregulation (Sardella and Brauner 2008).

14.3 Water Quality Management in Africa Freshwater Fish Culture Systems

The maintenance of good water quality within the rearing system is a prerequisite for the successful production of cultured fish to meet the protein requirements of the ever-rising population on the African continent. Continuous monitoring of water quality parameters should be of high priority so that conditions that can negatively affect the growth of cultured fish be avoided for the sustainability of the system. Monitoring of a single parameter does not usually tell much, but monitoring several parameters put together can serve as indicators of dynamic processes occurring in the pond.

An intensive culture system requires intensive fish feeds to be provided. This result in nitrogenous compounds and other organic matter remains building up as wastes in the water leading to reduced dissolved oxygen (Hoang et al. 2020), eutrophication (Cao et al. 2016; Wu et al. 2020), algal bloom (Gobler et al. 2012; Sin and Lee 2020) and microbe growth including pathogenic bacteria (Liu et al. 2020). Additionally, high ammonia concentrations induce oxidative stress, immunosuppression, and even tissue damage in fish (Wang et al. 2020). High nitrite levels lead to inhibitory effects on the immune system (Guo et al. 2020).

Gondwe et al. (2011) demonstrated that establishing cage culture in the lake was a significant source of nutrients in the lake's epilimnion. Estimates from aquaculture production records indicate that 71% to 88% of nutrients added through the feed to fish cages in Lake Malawi are lost in the surrounding environment from fish cages.

Most of the water quality problems explained above can be solved with adequate water exchange, though this is not practicable with a cage culture system. However, water has always and will continue to be challenged in several African countries, hence the need for proper water quality management.

14.3.1 Maintenance of Dissolved Oxygen

In aquaculture systems, problems with inadequate dissolved oxygen for cultured fish are the consequences of eutrophication arising from unconsumed fish feeds and faecal droppings. The appearance of phytoplankton bloom indicates eutrophication; in the fertilized system, fertilization should be halted. In addition to maintaining the proper fish stocking density and avoidance of overfeeding (as decomposing faeces and wasted feed both lead to oxygen depletion), there are several methods to maintain appreciable dissolved oxygen in rearing systems, however, the best practicable and effective method is the use of mechanical devices such as tractor powered wheel aerators as reported by Boyd et al. (2018). The agitation and circulation of water caused by these mechanical devices increase the diffusion of atmospheric oxygen into the pond water.

14.3.2 Maintenance of Adequate pH RANGE

Pond water with high levels of alkalinity and low hardness would usually have above range pH value during eutrophication for an appreciable growth rate of cultured fish. Boyd and Lichtkoppler (1979) recommended the application of ammonium fertilizers to lower the pH of pond water. The ammonium ion in the applied fertilizer is nitrified to nitrate with the release of hydrogen ions, eventually lowering the pond's pH. On the other hand, in pond water with extremely low pH levels, agricultural limestone or other liming materials often are applied to neutralize bottom soil acidity and maintain an adequate pH within the pond water (Han et al. 2014). However, requirements for using modified lime on acid-sulphate lands or pyritic, an aquaculture regime, are found to be inappropriate and unreliable (Boyd 2017). Fitrani et al. (2020) observed that hydrated lime (Ca $(OH)_2$) and burnt lime (CaO) administered in acid-sulphate-containing soil and water raised pond pH from as low as 2.69 to desirable levels of 7.4–8.6. Fitrani et al. (2020) revealed that soil characteristics, type, and dosage of lime.

material are crucial elements to be considered in improving the pond bottom soil with acid sulphate content. Results from this study have demonstrated that every liming material used in different dosages will affect both soil pH and water pH significantly, which will reduce the percentage of organic carbon and enhance the alkalinity at varying degrees.

14.3.3 Best Practices for Fertilizer Applications

Both inorganic and organic fertilizers have often been applied in semi-intensive aquaculture systems to improve the primary production of the ponds and subsequently improve fish growth (Das et al. 2005). Inorganic fertilizers used in fishponds are the same for crops. Boyd and Lichtkoppler (1979) noted that primary nutrients in inorganic fertilizers are usually present as relatively simple compounds (nitrogen, phosphorus, and potassium) dissolved to give nitrate, ammonium, phosphate or potassium ions. However, due to the rising cost of inorganic fertilizers, especially in several African countries, greater attention has shifted to using organic fertilizers (animal manuals), as reported by Bwala and Omoregie (2009) in aquaculture production.

Various organic manures of animal origins have been tried with pond tilapia production on the African continent with good results (Naiel et al. 2022). In their research to investigate the effects of various organic fertilizers with or without adsorbents on the productivity, antioxidant status and immune responses of the Nile tilapia raised in cement ponds, these authors noted that it is possible to infer that the use of fish sludge in the presence of sawdust showed a preferable effect on performance, survival (Table 14.3), antioxidant and immune status of exposed fish (Table 14.4) without altering the biochemical parameters (Table 14.5) followed by fish sludge plus sugar beet pulp compared to the other treatments. This revealed the potential properties of fish sludge that enable its application as an organic fertilizer in fishponds. The utilization of an effective adsorbent such as sawdust or sugar beet pulp is recommended to purify water from impurities; however, sawdust was somewhat more effective than sugar beet pulp.

Bwala and Omoregie (2009) reported improved tilapia (*Oreochromis niloticus*) yield in ponds fertilised with the appropriate level of pig manure as the nutrients in the manure stimulated primary productivity in the pond leading to improved water quality (Table 14.6). In addition to stimulating primary productivity, fish production

Table 14.3 Growth performance, feed efficiency and survival rate of the Nile tilapia cultured in ponds fertilised with several types of organic wastes for 56 days (Source: Naiel et al. 2022)

	Experimental groups					
Parameters	CNT	CD	FS	FS + SD	FS + SBP	*P* value
IW(g)	51.96 ± 0.22	52.23 ± 0.19	52.46 ± 0.15	52.21 ± 0.17	52.13 ± 0.17	0.607
FW (g)	80.9 ± 0.25^{c}	81.5 ± 0.40^{c}	103.4 ± 0.75^{a}	104.7 ± 1.69^{a}	99.7 ± 0.20^{b}	<0.001
WG (g)	28.96 ± 0.25^{c}	29.29 ± 0.33^{c}	50.90 ± $0.81^{a,b}$	52.45 ± 1.70^{a}	47.59 ± 0.34^{b}	<0.001
SGR (%)	0.79 ± 0.74^{c}	0.80 ± 0.67^{c}	1.21 ± $0.15^{a,b}$	1.24 ± 0.30^{a}	1.16 ± 0.83^{b}	<0.001
FI (g)	56.13 ± 0.18	55.86 ± 0.14	55.31 ± 0.16	55.74 ± 0.19	55.75 ± 0.17	0.115
FCR (g/g)	1.94 ± 0.12^{a}	1.91 ± 0.20^{a}	1.09 ± $0.21^{b,c}$	1.07 ± 0.13^{c}	1.17 ± 0.02^{b}	<0.001
PER (g/g)	1.72 ± 0.16^{c}	1.75 ± 0.18^{c}	3.07 ± $0.52^{a,b}$	3.14 ± 0.19^{a}	2.85 ± 0.24^{b}	<0.001
SR (%)	100	100	100	100	100	0.191

Values within the same row having different superscripts are significantly different ($P < 0.05$)
Data were presented as the mean ± standard error.
CNT: control group with no fertilization; *CD*: a fertilized group with cow dung; *FS*: a fertilized group with fish sludge; *FS + SD*: a fertilized group with fish sludge combined with sawdust; *FS + SBP*: a fertilized group with fish sludge combined with sugar beet pulp; *IW*: initial weight (g); *FW*: final weight (g); *WG*: weight gain (g); *SGR*: specific growth rate (%/d)2; *FI*: feed intake (g); *FCR*: feed conversion ratio (g/g); *PER*: protein efficiency ratio (g/g); *SR*: survival rate (%).
[a–c]The significance value of $P < 0.05$ provided in the row immediately below the Table

using manure may be similar to or even more significant than production using inorganic fertilisers, as the fish can also feed directly on the manure.

In an investigation by Elnady et al. (2016) on the impact of fish farm management on the physicochemical properties of water and sediments in earthen ponds in Egypt, the annual average dissolved oxygen concentrations were slightly higher in the fertiliser fish farm compared to the unfertilised farm, this they attributed to the presence of higher phytoplankton density induced by organic fertilization and accompanied by the higher photosynthetic rate of oxygen production.

14.3.4 Phytoplankton Management

Phytoplankton plays a significant role in stabilizing the pond ecosystem, minimizing the fluctuations of water quality and serving as the primary source of energy flow within the pond; for this reason, the monitoring and management of the phytoplankton population in aquatic production is very vital for improved fish production on the African continent. A healthy phytoplankton population in the pond enriches the

Table 14.4 Serum biochemical parameters of Nile tilapia reared in fertilized ponds with several organic wastes (Source: Naiel et al. 2022)

Parameters	Experimental groups					*P* value
	CNT	CD	FS	FS + SD	FS + SBP	
Serum protein constituents						
TP (g/dL)	5.64 ± 0.16	6.01 ± 0.13	5.65 ± 0.23	5.79 ± 0.17	6.15 ± 0.14	0.095
ALB (g/dL)	3.44 ± 0.07[b]	3.72 ± 0.10[a,b]	3.95 ± 0.08[a]	3.81 ± 0.21[a,b]	4.31 ± 0.44[b]	<0.001
GLOB(g/dL)	2.20 ± 0.14	2.27 ± 0.15	1.69 ± 0.24	1.99 ± 0.26	1.84 ± 0.23	0.113
ALB: GLOB	1.59 ± 0.23	1.67 ± 0.13	2.42 ± 0.25	2.08 ± 0.32	2.58 ± 0.49	0.019
Serum hepatic and renal indicators						
ALT (U/L)	92.01 ± 1.61[b]	102.30 ± 1.55[a]	95.83 ± 1.18[a,b]	97.48 ± 0.71[a,b]	98.87 ± 0.51[a,b]	0.006
AST (U/L)	70.98 ± 0.64	66.20 ± 1.95	66.71 ± 0.56	66.75 ± 1.19	68.08 ± 0.72	0.159
Urea(mg/dL)	1.31 ± 0.11[b]	1.44 ± 0.78[b]	2.07 ± 0.19[a]	1.29 ± 0.48[b]	1.46 ± 0.43[b]	0.011
Creatinine (g/dL)	0.004 ± 0.11	0.004 ± 0.21	0.005 ± 0.23	0.006 ± 0.03	0.006 ± 0.14	0.107

Values within the same row having different superscripts are significantly different ($P < 0.05$). Data were presented as the mean ± standard error

CNT: control group with no fertilization; *CD*: a fertilized group with cow dung; *FS*: a fertilized group with fish sludge; *FS + SD*: a fertilized group with fish sludge combined with sawdust; *FS + SBP*: a fertilized group with fish sludge combined with sugar beet pulp; *TP*: total protein; *ALB*: albumin; *GLOB*: globulin; *ALB/GLOB*: albumin: globulin; ratio; *ALT*: Alanine Aminotransferase; *AST*: Aspartate transaminase

[a,b]The significance value of $P < 0.05$ provided in the row immediately below the Table

system with oxygen through photosynthesis and lowers the levels of carbon dioxide, ammonia, nitrite, and hydrogen sulphide. Using ammonia as a nitrogen source for growth can reduce unionised ammonia, which can be toxic to aquatic animals at relatively low concentrations. In ponds where supplemental feeding is limited, as in several African countries, phytoplankton form an abundant base of the food web, as they are the leading primary producers and serve as an essential food source for other organisms. In a study by Degefu et al. 2011 on fish cage farming in the Rift Valley and North Shoa reservoirs in Ethiopia, they noted the significance of phytoplankton in improving fish production. Notwithstanding the beneficial aspects of phytoplankton in aquaculture ponds, it is commonly accepted that most water quality problems in aquaculture ponds result from the unmanaged growth of phytoplankton communities (Smith 1991).

Dawah and Gomaah (2005) and El-Otify (2015) highlighted the significance of fertilization with inorganic and organic fertilisers in managing a healthy phytoplankton population to improve pond water quality in Egyptian aquaculture, which has subsequently led to Egypt becoming the top producer of farmed fish in Africa.

Table 14.5 Antioxidant and immunity activities of Nile tilapia reared in fertilized ponds with several organic wastes (Source: Naiel et al. 2022)

Parameters	Experimental groups					*P* value
	CNT	CD	FS	FS + SD	FS + SBP	
Oxidative stress assay						
GSH (nmol/L)	2.83 ± 0.22[c]	5.06 ± 0.18[b]	5.80 ± 0.36[a,b]	6.32 ± 0.20[a]	5.62 ± 0.41[a,b]	<0.001
CAT (U/L)	100.2 ± 0.97[b]	108.3 ± 0.21[b]	122.8 ± 0.87[a]	124.7 ± 0.81[a]	125.2 ± 0.45[a]	<0.001
MDA (IU/ml)	13.98 ± 0.13[a,b]	14.40 ± 0.35[a]	12.93 ± 0.19[b]	10.39 ± 0.24[c]	9.88 ± 0.32[c]	<0.001
TAC (ng/ml)	0.13 ± 0.58[d]	0.14 ± 0.70[d]	0.26 ± 0.22[c]	0.35 ± 0.85[b]	0.41 ± 0.67[a]	<0.001
Immunity parameters						
ACH50(U/ml)	450.4 ± 0.66[d]	569.4 ± 0.16[c]	699.5 ± 0.10[b]	750.1 ± 0.43[a,b]	803.8 ± 0.21[a]	<0.001
Lysozyme (μg/ml)	19.36 ± 0.26[c]	23.17 ± 1.02[b]	30.47 ± 0.85[a]	30.73 ± 0.39[a]	30.87 ± 0.72[a]	<0.001
NBT (mg/ml)	0.32 ± 0.33[b]	0.82 ± 0.83[a]	0.90 ± 0.69[a]	0.89 ± 0.36[a]	1.02 ± 0.31[a]	0.001

Values within the same row having different superscripts are significantly different ($P < 0.05$). Data were presented as the mean ± standard error

CNT: control group with no fertilization; *CD*: a fertilized group with cow dung; *FS*: a fertilized group with fish sludge; *FS + SD*: a fertilized group with fish sludge combined with sawdust; *FS + SBP*: a fertilized group with fish sludge combined with sugar beet pulp; *GSH*: glutathione reductase; *CAT*: catalase; *MDA*: malonaldehyde; *TAC*: total antioxidant activity; *ACH50*: total complement activity; *NBT*: nitro blue tetrazolium

[a–c]The significance value of $P < 0.05$ provided in the row immediately below the Table

Table 14.6 Mean values (±)* of water quality parameters in various experimental tanks during period of investigation (Source: Bwala and Omoregie)

Parameters	Treatment				*P* – value
	LCPD	MCPD	HCPD	Control	
DO (mg/l) - day	7.84 ± 0.38	8.92 ± 0.44	7.77 ± 0.56	7.77 ± 0.47	<0.01
DO (mg/l) - Night	5.28 ± 0.95	6.91 ± 1.03	6.82 ± 0.14	6.80 ± 1.08	<0.01
FCD (mg/l) - day	0.07 ± 0.02	0.10 ± 0.03	0.15 ± 0.034	0.05 ± 0.02	<0.01
FCD (mg/l) - Night	1.04 ± 0.02	1.00 ± 0.07	0.98 ± 0.02	1.00 ± 0.01	<0.001
TA (mg/l)	74.51 ± 2.30	70.92 ± 2.74	70.15 ± 2.81	63.63 ± 2.82	<0.01
pH (mg/l)	9.20 ± 0.10	9.50 ± 0.10	9.59 ± 0.11	8.99 ± 0.16	<0.05
Phosphate (mg/l)	0.03 ± 0.01	0.05 ± 0.01	0.05 ± 0.01	0.03 ± 0.01	<0.01
Nitrate (mg/l)	5.96 ± 1.29	8.17 ± 1.25	9.34 ± 1.47	1.51 ± 0.14	<0.01
Ammonia (mg/l)	0.29 ± 0.10	0.45 ± 0.12	0.55 ± 0.13	0.18 ± 0.06	<0.05
Temp (°C) - day	26.10 ± 0.37	26.28 ± 0.34	26.33 ± 0.35	26.56 ± 0.34	<0.001
Temp (°C) – Night	26.13 ± 0.48	25.25 ± 0.48	26.13 ± 1.18	26.25 ± 0.96	<0.001

*Values with different superscripts in a row are significantly different ($P < 0.05$)

DO: Dissolved oxygen; *FCD*: Free carbon dioxide; *TA*: Total alkalinity; *LCPD*: Low concentration of pig dung; *MCPD*: Medium concentration of pig dung; *HCPD*: High concentration of pig dung; Control (No-manure)

Otieno et al. (2021) observed improved growth of the African catfish when reared in phytoplankton enriched pond fertilized with both inorganic and organic fertilizers compared to unfertilized ponds, which was low in phytoplankton population.

14.3.5 Best Practices to Reduce Aquaculture Waste for Improved Water Quality

The growth in aquaculture production in Africa has led to the increased use of fish feed applied to the culture system. Unconsumed feeds eventually lead to poor water quality. In addition to unconsumed feeds, Turcios and Papenbrock (2014) observed that undigested feed ingredients, which are passed as faecal droppings by cultured fishes, also significantly lead to poor water quality. Similarly, a high volume of wastes in the rearing pond, especially toxic inorganic nitrogenous substances (NH_4^+ and NO_2^-), form part of the significant water quality problems in intensive African aquaculture systems as reported by Akinwole et al. (2016). For these reasons and others, the control and management of this waste play a significant role in improving water quality. Feed and feeding systems can effectively reduce wastes resulting from the fish feed through proper management of the inputs into the culture system.

To reduce waste arising from unconsumed fish feeds in the ponds, Westers (1995) recommended the following:

- That the species and fish size-specific potential performance of any diet to be supplied must be known,
- There should be knowledge of the biomass of the fish in the system,
- Adequate information on the health and physiological status of the fish must be available,
- Uniformity in the size of fish is very important for them to accept the same size of pellet,
- The feed should be sieved to remove dust and broken pellets before being fed, and.
- The feed must be fed effectively to ensure little or no waste results from the uneaten feed.

The use of grains that are low in phytate is also encouraged in fish feed formulation; this is to reduce the amount of phosphorus released into the water through unconsumed feed or fish metabolic waste. Hardy (2010) reported that the majority of the phosphorus in plant protein cannot be utilized by fish, which are monogastric animals. Orisasona and Ajani (2015) observed improved growth rate and mineral utilization in the African catfish, *Clarias gariepinus* fed phytase-supplemented toasted lima bean. These authors attributed the recorded improved performance to better water quality parameters in the culture medium as phosphorous in the diets was utilized by the fish, thereby reducing excessive eutrophication in the rearing system.

Table 14.7 Haematological parameters of *Clarias gariepinus* juveniles reared in alum and *Moringa oleifera* seed powder treated fish tank water (Source: Akinwole et al. 2016)

Parameters	Before	Control	Alum treated water	Moringa treated water
PCV (%)	35 ± 0.00	25.67 ± 5.03[a]	17.00 ± 1.73[b]	27.00 ± 1.73[a]
Hb (g/100 ml)	11.6 ± 0.00	8.37 ± 1.60[a]	5.37 ± 0.12[b]	8.53 ± 0.15[a]
RBC (10^3/mm^3)	3.21 ± 0.00	2.18 ± 1.04[a]	1.14 ± 0.01[b]	2.58 ± 0.55[a]
WBC (mm^3)	14,000 ± 0.00	12,933.33 ± 3010.54[a]	20,300 ± 259.81[b]	14,950.00 ± 3377.50[a]
Platelet (mm^3)	220,000 ± 0.00	168,333.33 ± 62,947.0[a]	266,666.67 ± 37,527.77[a]	177,666.67 ± 89,645.60[a]
Lymphocytes (%)	70 ± 0.00	64.67 ± 5.86[a]	48.67 ± 2.31[b]	60.00 ± 5.57[a]
Heterophils (%)	23 ± 0.00	27.33 ± 6.66[a]	44.00 ± 1.73[b]	34.33 ± 4.16[c]
Monocytes (%)	3 ± 0.00	3.67 ± 0.58[a]	3.67 ± 0.58[a]	3.33 ± 1.53[a]
Eosinophils (%)	4 ± 0.00	4.00 ± 1.00[a]	2.67 ± 1.15[a]	2.67 ± 1.53[a]
Basophils (%)	0 ± 0.00	0.33 ± 0.58[a]	1.00 ± 0.00[b]	0.00 ± 0.00[c]

Note: Values are expressed as mean ± SD. The values with different superscripts are significantly different ($P < 0.05$)

The settleable waste solids in the pond can be removed when accumulated through properly placed drains at the bottom of the cultured tank, while the suspended solids are more difficult to remove. The usual method for removing suspended solid wastes is by flocculation by adding coagulant or flocculation aids. Numerous substances have been used as coagulants in solid waste removal from water, including synthetic and natural materials such as aluminium sulphate (alum), ferric chloride, ferrous sulphate, and lime (Ebeling et al. 2004). One major drawback is the adverse impacts of these substances on the physiological effects of cultured species. Using agro-based materials as coagulants in fish tanks is receiving promising results (Raghuwanshi et al. 2002; Akinwole et al. 2016). One of such is *Moringa oleifera*. In an investigation on the haematological responses of the African catfish, *Clarias gariepinus*, Akinwole et al. (2016) reported that the fish cultured in tanks which had *Moringa oleifera* as a coagulant for the removal of solid waste from the tanks, did not exhibit signs of haematological impairment and were healthier than their counterparts in tanks with alum and tanks without any form of coagulant (Table 14.7).

References

Abdel-Tawwab M, Wafeek M (2017) Fluctuations in water temperature affected waterborne cadmium toxicity: Hematology, anaerobic glucose pathway, and oxidative stress status of Nile tilapia, *Oreochromis niloticus* (L.). Aquaculture 477:106–111. https://doi.org/10.1016/j.aquaculture.2017.05.007

Adebola OA, Adeniyi AA, Oluseun AB (2015) Effects of water exchange on water quality parameters, nutrient utilization and growth of African catfish (*Clarias gariepinus*). Int J Livestock Prod 6(5):57–60

Adeleke B, Robertson-Andersson D, Moodley G, Taylor S (2021) Aquaculture in Africa: a comparative review of egypt, nigeria, and uganda vis-a-vis south africa. Rev Fish Sc Aquat 29(2):167–197

Akinwole AO, Dauda AB, Ololade AO (2016) Haematological response of *Clarias gariepinus* juveniles reared in treated wastewater after waste solids removal using alum or *Moringa oleifera* seed powder. Int J Acarol 6(11):1–8

Bervoets L, van Campenhout K, Reynders H, Knapen D, Covaci A, Blust R (2009) Bioaccumulation of micropollutants and biomarker responses in caged carp (*Cyprinus carpio*). Ecotoxicol Environ Safety 72(3):720–728

Bhatnagar A, Devi P (2013) Water quality guidelines for the management of pond fish culture. Int J Environ Sc 3(6):1980–2009

Bostock J, McAndrew B, Richards R, Jauncey K, Telfer T, Lorenzen K, Little D, Ross L, Handisyde N, Gatward I, Corner R (2010) Aquaculture: global status and trends. Philos Trans R Soc B Biol Sci 365(1554):2897–2912

Boyd CE (2017) Use of agricultural limestone and lime in aquaculture. CAB Rev 12(15):1–10. https://doi.org/10.1079/PAVSNNR201712015

Boyd CE (2020) Carbon dioxide, pH, and alkalinity. In: Water quality. Springer, Cham. https://doi.org/10.1007/978-3-030-23335-8_9

Boyd CE Lichtkoppler F (1979) Water Quality Management in Pond Fish Culture. Research and Development Series No. 22, Project AD/DSANG0039, Auburn, Alabama

Boyd CE, Lichtkoppler F (1982) Water quality management in pond fish culture. International center for aquaculture, agriculture experiment station, 4th edn, Auburn, USA, p 30

Boyd CE, Torrans EL, Tucker CS (2018) Dissolved oxygen and aeration in ictalurid catfish aquaculture. J World Aquacult Soc 49:7–70

Boyd CE, D'Abramo LR, Glencross BD et al (2020) Achieving sustainable aquaculture: Historical and current perspectives and future needs and challenges. J World Aquacult Soc 51:578–633. https://doi.org/10.1111/jwas.12714

Brummett RE (2000) Indigenous species for African aquaculture development. In: Nielsen J, Bert TM (eds) Ecological and genetic effects of aquaculture on the environment, and their solutions. Kluwer Scientific, Dordrecht

Bwala RL, Omoregie E (2009) Organic enrichment of fish ponds: application of pig dung vs. tilapia yield. Pak J Nutr 8(9):1373–1379

Cao W, Wang Y, Sun L, Jiang J, Zhang Y (2016) Removal of nitrogenous compounds from polluted river water by floating constructed wetlands using rice straw and ceramsite as substrates under low-temperature conditions. Ecol Eng 88:77–81

Das PC, Ayyappan S, Jena J (2005) Comparative changes in water quality and role of pond soil after application of different levels of organic and inorganic inputs. Aquac Res 36:785–798

Dawah AM, Gomaah SA (2005) Phytoplankton dynamics in earthen ponds stocked with African catfish (*Clarias gariepinus*) feeding with different diets. Egypt J Phycol 6(1):1–15

Degefu F, Mengistu S, Schagerl M (2011) Influence of fish cage farming on water quality and plankton in fish ponds: a case study in the Rift Valley and North Shoa reservoirs, Ethiopia. Aquaculture 316(1–4):129–135

Ebeling JM, Ogden SR, Sibrelli PL, Rishel KL (2004) Application of chemical coagulation aids for the removal of suspended solids (TSS) and phosphorus from the micro screen effluent discharge of an intensive recirculating aquaculture system. North Am J Aquat 66:198–207. https://doi.org/10.1577/A03-056.1

Elnady AM, Shaker IM, Abdel Wahed RK, Soliman MAM (2016) Impact of fish farm management on physico-chemical properties of water and sediments in earthen ponds. Egypt J Aquat 6(2): 1–20

El-Otify AM (2015) Evaluation of the physicochemical and chlorophyll-a conditions of a subtropical aquaculture in Lake Nasser area, Egypt. Beni-Suef Univ J Basic Appl Sci 4(4):327–337

El-Sayed AFM (2006) Tilapia culture. CABI Publishing, CABI International, Wallingford, Oxfordshire

Eng CT, Tech E (2002) History of cage culture. In: Woo PTK, Bruno DW, Lim LHS (eds) Disease and disorders of finfish in cage culture. CABI Publishing, Oxon

FAO (1999) Fishery Statistics: Aquaculture production. FAO Fisheries Series No. 58. FAO, Rome, p 178

FAO (2020) The State of World Fisheries and Aquaculture 2020. Sustainability in action. Rome. https://doi.org/10.4060/ca9229en

FAO (2021) FAO Yearbook. Fishery and Aquaculture Statistics 2019. Rome/Roma. https://doi.org/10.4060/cb7874t

FAO (2022a) *Clarias gariepinus*. Cultured Aquatic Species Information Programme. Text by Pouomogne, V. Fisheries and Aquaculture Division [online]. Rome. [Cited Tuesday, March 8th 2022]. https://www.fao.org/fishery/en/culturedspecies/clarias_gariepinus/en

FAO (2022b) Oreochromis niloticus. Cultured Aquatic Species Information Programme. Text by Rakocy, J. E.. Fisheries and Aquaculture Division [online]. Rome. Updated 2006-05-19 [Cited Tuesday, March 8th 2022]. https://www.fao.org/fishery/en/culturedspecies/oreochromis_niloticus/en

Fitrani M, Wudtisin I, Kaewnern M (2020) The impacts of the single-use of different lime materials on the pond bottom soil with acid sulfate content. Aquaculture 527:735471

Gobler CJ, Burson A, Koch F, Tang Y, Mulholland MR (2012) The role of nitrogenous nutrients in the occurrence of harmful algal blooms caused by *Cochlodinium polykrikoides* in New York estuaries (USA). Harmful Algae 17:64–74

Gondwe MJS, Guildford SJ, Hecky RE (2011) Physical–chemical measurements in the water column along a transect through a tilapia cage fish farm in Lake Malawi, Africa. J Great Lakes Res 37(1):102–113. https://doi.org/10.1016/j.jglr.2010.10.001

Guo K, Ruan G, Fan W, Fang L, Wang Q, Luo M, Yi T (2020) The effect of nitrite and sulfide on the antioxidant capacity and microbial composition of the intestines of red swamp crayfish, *Procambarus clarkii*. Fish Shellfish Immunol 96:290–296

Halwart M (2020) Fish farming high on the global food system agenda in 2020. FAO Aquat Newslett No 61:ii–iii

Han Y, Boyd CE, Viriyatum R (2014) A bicarbonate titration method for lime requirement to neutralize exchangeable acidity of pond bottom soils. Aquaculture 434:282–287

Hardy RW (2010) Utilization of plant proteins in fish diets: effects of global demand and supplies of fishmeal. Aquacult Res 41(5):770–776

Hargreaves JA, Brunson M (1996) Carbon dioxide in fish ponds. Starkville, Mississippi: Southern Regional Aquaculture Center (SRAC) Publication No. 468. pp 1–6

Heugens EH, Jager T, Creyghton R, Kraak MH, Hendriks AJ, van Straalen NM, Admiraal W (2003) Temperature-dependent effects of cadmium on Daphnia magna: accumulation versus sensitivity. Environ Sci Technol 37(10):2145–2151

Hoang MN, Nguyen PN, Bossier P (2020) Water quality, animal performance, nutrient budgets and microbial community in the biofloc-based polyculture system of white shrimp, *Litopenaeus vannamei* and gray mullet, *Mugil cephalus*. Aquaculture 515:734610

Ibrahim N, Naggar GE (2010) Water quality, fish production and economics of nile tilapia, *Oreochromis niloticus*, and African Catfish, *Clarias gariepinus*, Monoculture and Polycultures. J World Aquacult Soc 41(4):574–582

Ip YK, Chew SF, Randall DJ (2001) Ammonia toxicity, tolerance, and excretion. Fish Physiol 20: 109–148

Ip YK, Chew SF, Randall DJ (2004) Five tropical air-breathing fishes, six different strategies to defend against ammonia toxicity on land. Physiol Biochem Zoo 77(5):768–782

Jamu DM, Ayinla OA (2003) Potential for the development of aquaculture in Africa. NAGA, World Fish Center Quarterly, 26(3): 9–13

Joel O, Amajuoyi C.S (2010) Determination of the concentration of ammonia that could have lethal effect on fish pond. ARPN J Eng Appl Sci, pp 1–4

Kammer AR, Orczewska JI, O'Brien KM (2011) Oxidative stress is transient and tissue specific during cold acclimation of three spine stickleback. J Exp Biol 214:1248–1256

Kausar R, Salim M (2017) Effect of water temperature on the growth performance and feed conversion ratio of *Labeo rohita*. Pak Vet J 26:105–108

Lim CE et al (2006) Feeding practices. The Hawthorn Press, Stroud, pp 547–559

Liu L, Hall G, Champagne P (2020) The role of algae in the removal and inactivation of pathogenic indicator organisms in wastewater stabilization pond systems. Algal Res 46:101777. https://doi.org/10.1016/j.algal.2019.101777

Loong AM, Tan JYL, Wong WP, Chew SF, Ip YK (2007) Defense against environmental ammonia toxicity in the African lungfish, *Protopterus aethiopicus*: bimodal breathing, skin ammonia permeability and urea synthesis. Aquat Toxicol 85(1):76–86

Machena C, Moehl J (2000) African Aquaculture: A Regional Summary with Emphasis on Sub-Saharan Africa. In Proceedings of the Technical Proceedings of the Conference on Aquaculture in the Third Millennium, Bangkok, Thailand, 20–25 February 2000; NACA: Bangkok, Thailand; FAO: Rome, Italy, 2001; pp 341–355

Machena C, Moehl J (2001) Sub-Saharan African aquaculture: regional summary. In R.P. Subasinghe, P. Bueno, M.J. Phillips, C. Hough, S.E. McGladdery and J.R. Arthur, eds. Aquaculture in the Third Millennium. Technical Proceedings of the Conference on Aquaculture in the Third Millennium, Bangkok, Thailand, 20–25 February 2000. pp 341–355. NACA, Bangkok and FAO, Rome

Makori AJ, Abuom PO, Kapiyo R, Anyona DN, Dida GO (2017) Effects of water physico-chemical parameters on tilapia (*Oreochromis niloticus*) growth in earthen ponds in Teso North Sub-County, Busia County. Fish Aquat Sci 20(1):1–10

Maulu S, Hasimuna OJ, Haambiya LH, Monde C, Musuka CG, Makorwa TH, Munganga BP, Phiri KJ, Nsekanabo JD (2021) Climate change effects on aquaculture production: sustainability implications, mitigation, and adaptations. Front Sustain Food Syst 5:609097. https://doi.org/10.3389/fsufs.2021.609097

Musinguzi L, Lugya J, Rwezawula P, Kamya A, Nuwahereza C, Halafo J, Kamondo S, Njaya F, Aura C, Shoko AP, Osinde R, Natugonza V, Ogutu-Ohwayo R (2019) The extent of cage aquaculture, adherence to best practices and reflections for sustainable aquaculture on African inland waters. J Great Lakes Res 45(6):1340–1347

Naiel MA, Gewida AG, Merwad ARM, Abdel-Hamid EA, Negm SS, Alagawany M, Farag MR (2022) The effects of various organic fertilizers with or without adsorbents on the productivity, antioxidant status and immune responses of Nile tilapia raised in cement ponds. Aquaculture 548:737593

Orisasona O, Ajani EK (2015) The growth and mineral utilization of *Clarias gariepinus* fingerlings fed phytase-supplemented toasted lima bean (*Phaseolus lunatus*) diets. J Aquat Res Dev 6(9):1

Otieno PA, Owiti DO, Onyango PO (2021) Growth rate of African catfish (*Clarias gariepinus*) and plankton diversity in ponds under organic and inorganic fertilization. Afr J Food Agricult Nutr Dev 21(2):17545–17559

Qiang J, Wang H, Kpundeh MD, He J, Xu P (2013) Effect of water temperature, salinity, and their interaction on growth, plasma osmolality, and gill Na^+, K^+-ATPase activity in juvenile GIFT tilapia *Oreochromis niloticus* (L.). J Thermal Biol 38(6):331–338

Raghuwanshi PK, Meindloi MJ, Sharma AD, Malviya HS, Chaudhiri S (2002) Improving filtration quality using agrobased materials as coagulation aid. Water Qual Res Can 37(4):745–756

Ridha MT (2008) Preliminary observation on salinity tolerance of three sizes of the GIFT and non-improved strains of the Nile tilapia *Oreochromis niloticus*. Eur J Sci Res 24(3):373–377

Rutaisire J, Kasozi N, Nandi S, Sundaray JK (2017) A review of Uganda and Indias freshwater aquaculture: key practices and experience from each country. J Ecol Nat Environ 9(2):15–29. https://doi.org/10.5897/JENE2016.0615

Saha N, Ratha BK (1998) Ureogenesis in Indian air-breathing teleosts: adaptation to environmental constraints. Comp Biochem Phsyiol 120A:195–208

Sardella BA, Brauner CJ (2008) The effect of elevated salinity on 'California' Mozambique tilapia (*Oreochromis mossambicus* × *O. urolepis hornorum*) metabolism. Comp Biochem Physiol C148:430–436

Satia BP (2011) Regional review on status and trends in aquaculture development in sub-Saharan Africa - 2010/Revue régionale sur la situation et les tendances dans l'aquaculture en afrique subsaharienne - 2010. FAO Fisheries and Aquaculture Circular,I,III,IV,V,1-7,9-23,25-33,35-41,43-45,47-51,53-59,61-67,69-117,119-137,139-161,163-191. https://ukzn.idm.oclc.org/login?url=https://search.proquest.com/docview/1315322106?accountid=158225

Satia PB (2017) Regional review on status and trends in aquaculture development in sub-saharan africa - 2010/Revue régionale sur la situation et les tendances dans l'aquaculture en afrique subsaharienne - 2010. FAO Fisheries and Aquaculture Circular, I, III, IV, V, 1-7, 9-23, 25-33, 35-41, 43-45, 47-51, 53-59, 61-67, 69-117, 119-137,139-161,163 -191. https://ukzn.idm.oclc.org/login?url=https://search.proquest.com/docview/1315322106?accountid=158225.

Sin Y, Lee H (2020) Changes in hydrology, water quality, and algal blooms in a freshwater system impounded with engineered structures in a temperate monsoon river estuary. J Hydrol Regional Stud 32:100744

Smith DW (1991) Mechanistic simulation modelling of phytoplankton-oxygen dynamics in aquaculture ponds. In: Brune D, Tomasso J (eds) Aquaculture and water quality. The World Aquaculture Society, Baton Rouge, LA, pp 436–459

Tsadik G, Kutty MN (1987) Influence of ambient oxygen on feeding and growth of tilapia, Oreochromis niloticus ARAC/87/WP/10.United Nation Development Programme. Food and Agriculture Organization of the United Nations, Nigerian Institute for Oceanography and Marine Research Project RAF/87/009

Tucker CS, Hargreaves JA (2012) Freshwater ponds. In: Tidwell J (ed) Aquaculture production methods. Wiley-Blackwell Publishing, Ames, IA, pp 191–244

Tumwesigye Z, Tumwesigye W, Opio F, Kemigabo C, Mujuni B (2022) The effect of water quality on aquaculture productivity in Ibanda District, Uganda. Aquat J 2:23–36. https://doi.org/10.3390/aquacj2010003

Turcios AE, Papenbrock J (2014) Sustainable treatment of aquaculture effluents—what can we learn from the past for the future? Sustainability 6(2):836–856

Uzoka CN, Anyanwu JC, Uche CC, Ibe CC, Uzoma A (2015) Effect of pH on the growth performance and survival rate of *Clarias gariepinus* fry. Int J Res Biosci 4(3):14–20

Wang L, Sun Y, Xu B, Sagada G, Chen K, Xiao J, Zhang J, Shao Q (2020) Effects of berberine supplementation in high starch diet on growth performance, antioxidative status, immune parameters and ammonia stress response of fingerling black sea bream (*Acanthopagrus schlegelii*). Aquaculture 527:735473

Westers H (1995) Feed and feeding strategies to reduce aquaculture waste. In: Timmons MB (ed) Aquacultural engineering and waste Management. NRAES-90. Ithaca, NY, Northeast Regional Agricultural Engineering Service, pp 365–376

Wokoma K, Marioghae IE (1996) Survival of *Tilapia guineensis* under conditions of low dissolved oxygen and low pH. In The Third International Symposium on Tilapia in Aquaculture, ICLARM Conference Proceedings Vol. 41, No. 575, pp 442–448

Wu Z, Zou R, Jiang Q, Elser JJ, Zhao L, Ye R, Liu Y (2020) What maintains seasonal nitrogen limitation in hyper-eutrophic Lake Dianchi? Insights from stoichiometric three-dimensional numerical modelling. Aquat Sc 82(4):1–12

Chapter 15
Nutrient Budget of Cage Fish Culture in a Lacustrine Environment: Towards Model Development for the Sustainable Development of Nile Tilapia (*Oreochromis niloticus*) Culture

Safina Musa, Christopher Mulanda Aura, Tumi Tomasson, Ólafur Sigurgeirsson, and Helgi Thorarensen

Abstract Carried out fundamentally in an open system, cage culture-derived nutrients can exacerbate the quality of the lacustrine environment. Information on nutrient loading from African inland waters is scarce, yet sustainable development of fish cage culture depends on it. This chapter reviews siting of fish cages, nutritional content, digestibility of fish feeds, and nutrient load in wastes of Nile tilapia in African inland waters. In addition, this chapter proposes a theoretical model for nutrient (nitrogen N and phosphorus P) budget in a Nile tilapia cage aquaculture farm to calculate the amount (kg) of N and P produced and released to the environment for each ton of fish produced basing on best and worst-case scenarios. The review shows that majority of the cages are sited nearshore and/or in shallow areas that could exacerbate environmental challenges. Poor digestibility of fish feeds, particularly P, raises concern due to the risk of eutrophication. The majority of the feeds used in African inland waters for cage fish culture recorded N deficiency in relation to P that could lead to poor retention, hence high nutrient loading into the

S. Musa (✉)
Kenya Marine and Fisheries Research Institute, Kisii, Kenya

C. M. Aura
Kenya Marine and Fisheries Research Institute, Kisumu, Kenya

T. Tomasson
Marine and Freshwater Research Institute, Hafnarfjordur, Iceland

Ó. Sigurgeirsson
Hólar University College, Sauðárkrókur, Iceland

H. Thorarensen
Hólar University College, Sauðárkrókur, Iceland

Faculty of Biosciences, Fisheries and Economics, UiT The Arctic University of Norway, Tromsø, Norway

© The Author(s), under exclusive license to Springer Nature Singapore Pte Ltd. 2023

N. N. Gabriel et al. (eds.), *Emerging Sustainable Aquaculture Innovations in Africa*, Sustainable Agriculture and Food Security,
https://doi.org/10.1007/978-981-19-7451-9_15

environment. The theoretical model shows that about 46% of N and 39% of P from feed input are released into the environment for each tonne of tilapia produced. However, when the feed loss is high but at the same time the nutrient retention in fish is inefficient, 91% of N and 89% of P from feed input are discharged into the environment. Sensitivity analysis shows that nutrient loading from cage culture is very sensitive to feed loss, FCR and nutrient retention. The paper concludes with recommendations that need to be considered to minimise nutrient loading and its impact on the environment.

Keywords Nile tilapia · Cage culture · Digestibility, Nitrogen, Phosphorus · Nutrient loads

15.1 Introduction

Globally, wild fish stocks are at their production limit at a time of rapid human population growth, urbanisation and income increase have sent demand for fish protein skyrocketing (Akintola et al. 2013; FAO 2016; Anderson et al. 2017). The dwindling catches have increased the interest in cage culture as an alternative source of fish (Aura et al. 2017; Musinguzi et al. 2019; Hamilton et al. 2020; Musa et al. 2021a), and aquaculture will necessarily play a central role in bridging the widening gap between fish demand and its supply (FAO 2018; Obiero et al. 2019; FAO 2020).

Cage fish culture is an old practice and dates to the late 1800 in Southeast Asia (Bao-Tong 1994) but has recently expanded throughout the world due to its benefits. As compared to pond fish culture, cages can be stocked at higher densities hence high production per unit volume of water; many types of existing water bodies can be used, hence reducing pressure on land, a relatively low initial investment is required in an existing body of water, ease of harvesting of fish, less manpower is required and high return on investment (De Silva and Phillips 2007; EL-Sayed 2006). For a long time in Africa, cage fish culture has been reported to be still in its infancy (Bostock et al. 2010; Asmah et al. 2016; Aura et al. 2018). However, by 2010, the cage fish culture industry in Africa was reported to be emerging at a faster rate than any other region (Bueno et al. 2015). The rapid expansion of cage fish farming on African inland waters has been reported in Lake Victoria in Kenya (Aura et al. 2018), Lake Victoria in Uganda (Blow and Leonard 2007), Lake Volta in Ghana (Asmah et al. 2016), Lake Kariba in Zimbabwe (Berg et al. 1996), Lake Malawi in Malawi (Blow and Leonard 2007), with Lake Victoria recording the highest number of cage aquaculture installations by the year 2019 (Table 15.1). In sub-Saharan Africa, the production of aquaculture fish has increased more than sixteen-fold since 1995 (FAO 2018), driven primarily by the expansion of tilapia cage aquaculture (Satia 2011).

While cage aquaculture is expanding in sub-Saharan Africa, such systems may have negative environmental consequences. Contrary to pond fish farming, which depends on fertilisers with high N and P contents to promote biological productivity, cage systems are seldom fertilised. Yet, N and P are essential elements for

Table 15.1 Estimated number of cages on African inland water bodies by 2019, adopted from Musinguzi et al. (2019)

Country	Water body	Estimated total number of cages
Kenya	Lake Victoria	12,086
Ghana	Lake Volta	3817
Ghana	River Volta	3184
Zambia	Lake Kariba	254
Rwanda	Lake Kivu	208
Rwanda	Lake Muhazi	199
Uganda	River Nile	135
Malawi	Lake Malawi	53
Uganda	Lake Albert	
Uganda	Lake Kyoga	102
Uganda	Kazinga channel	10
Uganda	Lake George	10
Uganda	Lake Kawi	3
Tanzania	Lake Kumba	40
Uganda	Lake Mugogo	
Uganda	Lake Pallisa	4
Tanzania	Lake Tanganyika	
Uganda	Reservoir	10
	Total	20,114

organismal development (Ackefors and Enell 1994; Von Sperling and Chernicharo 2005). Consequently, fish feeds for cages have higher N and P content (Musa et al. 2021b). Cage aquaculture raises concerns about water quality deterioration due to solid wastes (Ngupula et al. 2012; Aura et al. 2018) and soluble wastes, especially nitrogen and phosphorus compounds. Over time, this may cause eutrophication (Aura et al. 2018), algal blooms and changes in zooplankton community structure (Braaten 2007; Ngupula and Kayanda 2010; Villnas et al. 2011; Kashindye et al. 2015; Egessa et al. 2018). Therefore, the rapid expansion of cage fish culture in most African inland lakes, such as Lake Victoria, systems already under severe environmental stress (Hecky et al. 2010), is highly questionable.

With the burgeoning industry coupled with little regulation, the use of more inputs, mainly fish feed, is likely to skyrocket (Henriksson et al. 2018; Musa et al. 2021b), synonymous with increased waste generation. Moreover, the high densities of fish in cages would translate to the high production of wastes from unused feeds and faeces. This could be detrimental to the lake's ecosystem health, threatening the future sustainability of capture fisheries even more and preventing the development of a sustainable blue economy.

Sustainable cage fish culture and the development of a sustainable blue economy will depend on understanding the nutrient loads of cage farms in freshwater aquaculture since every ecosystem has a maximum assimilative capacity, which is determined by the maximum acceptable environmental impacts (Samuel-Fitwia et al. 2012). Furthermore, reducing the environmental footprint of cage culture operations requires estimating the amount of waste associated with such systems and their management. Yet, the fate and quantitative contribution of the new N and P sources emanating from feed wastage in cage fish culture in African inland waters is scarce. Understanding the nutrient budget of cage fish farms is useful in lacustrine development, management, and policy formulation. This chapter reviews factors affecting nutrient loads and their impacts, quantify nutrient loadings from cage fish culture in African inland waters from reported literature and hypothesised nutrient budget and carries out sensitivity analysis on the hypothesised model to explore and better understand the effects of uncertainties on nutrient loadings in the production of Nile tilapia to guide cage culture investments.

15.2 Factors Affecting Nutrient Loads and their Impacts on Inland Waters

15.2.1 Siting of Cages

Cage systems, if not correctly cited, can cause eutrophication, habitat degradation, and cause conflicts with other users (Beveridge 1984). These scenarios are highly likely to occur in African inland waters due to the burgeoning industry and because most cage fish farms in African inland waters use backyard fish feeds with low water stability (Musa et al. 2021b), which can worsen environmental challenges from such systems (Beveridge 1984). The majority of the fish cages (>70%) in African inland waters are sited nearest to the shoreline (Table 15.2), contrary to best practices that require cages to be placed within the 200 m distance from the shoreline of the lakes. Furthermore, almost all cages in African inland lakes are in shallow waters (4–8 m) (Musinguzi et al. 2019) despite recommendations that cages should be placed in deeper waters (>10 m) (Kamadi 2018). Nearshore and shallow areas have low flushing rates, resulting in high nutrient loading and increased phytoplankton

Table 15.2 Estimated distance (range and mean) between the shoreline and cages (Musinguzi et al. 2019)

Water Body	Distance of cages from shoreline (m)	
	Range	Mean
Lake Kariba	220.2–1759.8	894.4
Lake Kivu	5–120.1	41.3
Lake Kumba	N/A	66.7
Lake Malawi	N/A	1100
Lake Muhazi	48.23–150	82.6
Lake Tanganyika	141.99–142.0	141.99
Lake Victoria	21–665	211.6
Lake Volta	0–860	191.7
River Nile	13.4–621	178.5
River Volta	0–321	30.2

biomass from excess feeds. Most inland lakes, such as Lake Victoria, are already choking on excessive nutrients from industrial and agricultural wastes. Therefore, inappropriate siting of cages could exacerbate environmental challenges. Moreover, a regulatory framework for cage aquaculture for most African inland lakes is inadequate. Therefore, the burgeoning industry may pose a threat to ecosystem health.

The majority, if not all, of the African inland lakes, have not been mapped for suitable sites for cage culture, hindering sustainable development of the industry. However, preliminary delineation of suitable sites for cage farms in the Kenyan part of Lake Victoria has been undertaken, with approximately 9% of the total area delineated as most suitable for fish cages (Fig. 15.1) (Aura et al. 2021). The findings could be a model for other African inland lakes where tilapia cage culture already occurs or may occur in the future.

15.2.2 Nutritional Content and Digestibility of the Feeds

Just like other cultured species, nutrition is essential, not only for the growth of tilapia but for the environmental sustainability of cage systems (Musa et al. 2021b). Kong et al. (2020) reaffirm that fish feed quality is a critical factor in determining the environmental impact of aquaculture. Most of the studies carried out on fish feeds in Africa (Table 15.1) have shown that the dietary protein content for feeds follows the recommended levels (25–35%) for Nile tilapia larger than 10 g (Balarin and Haller 1982; Tacon 1987; El-Sayed and Teshima 1991; Khattab et al. 2000). However, backyard feed in Africa seems to record higher fibre content, hence inferior to extruded feed (Table 15.1). Fibre content above 8–12% is undesirable in fish feed because it reduces digestibility (De Silva and Anderson 1995; Leal et al. 2010); hence would translate to high nutrient loading into the environment. A high level of fibre has also been reported to reduce dietary protein utilisation in several species (Leary and Lovell 1975; Fontainhas-Fernandes et al. 1999). The low digestibility of backyard feed could also be attributed to high ash content, which is in line with Kitagima and Fracalossi (2011), who reported low dry matter digestibility for fish and shrimp offal meals with high ash contents. Similar results have also been observed in rainbow trout (*Oncorhynchus mykiss*) (Bureau et al. 1999) and hybrid tilapia (*O. niloticus* × *Oreochromis aureus*) (Zhou and Yue 2012). Overall, the high digestibility of nutrients in extruded feed could have been enhanced by extrusion cooking (Cheng and Hardy 2003; Barrows et al. 2007; Gaylord et al. 2008), thereby making commercial feed superior to backyard feed.

Most of the fish feeds in Africa have higher P content (above 1%) (Table 15.3) despite recommendations that P content for tilapia feeds should be less than 0.7% (KEBS 2015). Hence, apart from losses due to unavailability, the excess P in fish feeds cannot be metabolically utilised by fish and will ultimately be released into the environment (Roy and Lall 2004; Kong et al. 2020). This can increase the pollution potential from fish feeds. Fish feeds are the significant production cost for

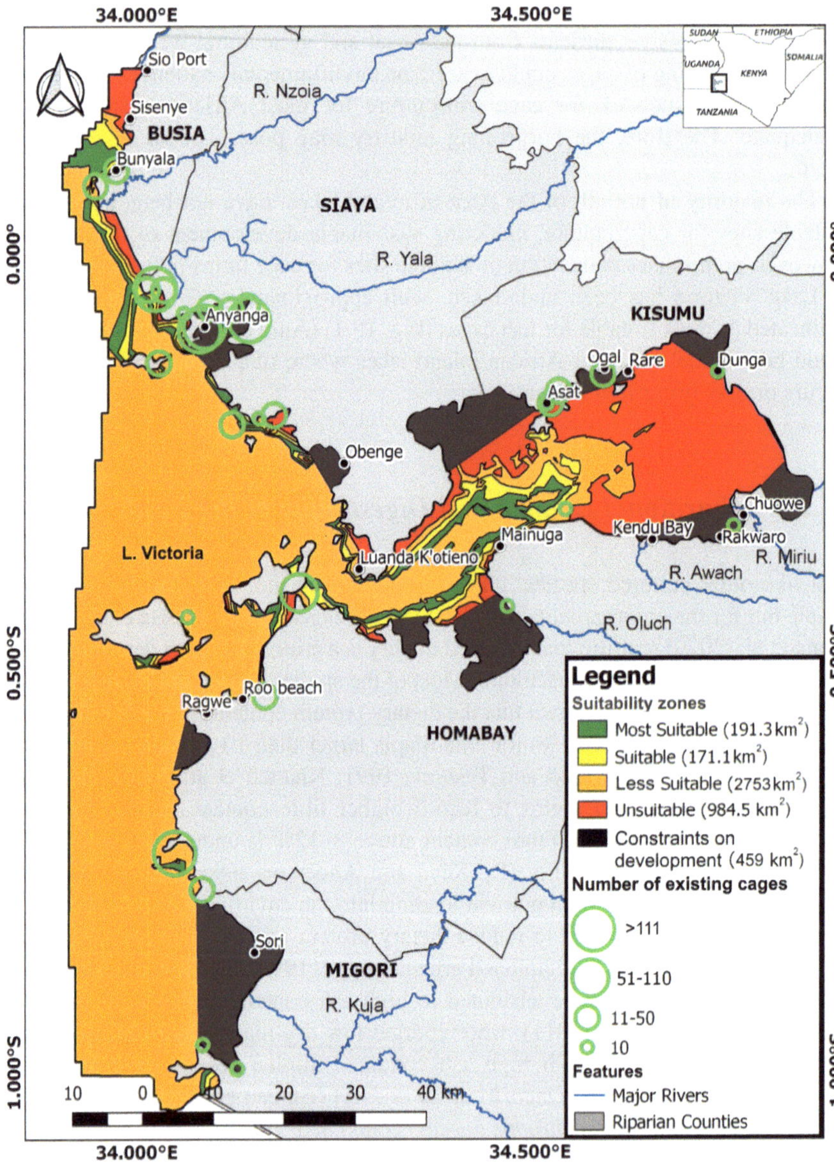

Fig. 15.1 Map of Lake Victoria, Kenya, showing potential suitability for cage fish culture. (Aura et al. 2021)

aquaculture (Naylor et al. 2000; FAO 2020) and commonly account for over 60–70% of the cost of producing tilapia (Bolivar et al. 2006; Elnady et al. 2010; Musa et al. 2021a). Due to the high costs of fish feeds, many efforts are being diverted to replacing the expensive animal protein with plant protein ingredients.

Table 15.3 Nutritional content (g kg^{-1}) for pelleted and extruded feed used for Nile tilapia cage culture in African inland waters

Nutrients (g/kg)	Musa et al. (2021a, b)	Musa et al. (2021a, b)	Neto and Ostrensky (2015)	Gondwe et al. (2011)	Karikari (2016)
Total dry matter	948	947.8	902.3	845	915.5
Digestible dry matter	680.7	560.3	608.5	–	–
Total organic matter	800.2	804.4	806.8	–	–
Digestible organic matter	605.2	577.3	578.9	–	–
Crude protein	301	282	276.7	359.4	350
Digestible protein	277.3	245	236.8	–	–
Crude fibre (g/kg)	42.1	168.2	42.8	–	–
Ash	92.4	130.4		–	77
Total phosphorus	10	11.5 ± 1.0	14.5	8.7	14
Digestible phosphorus	5.87	3.2 ± 0.6	6.5	–	

Plant ingredients have been reported to increase the digestibility of protein fraction of plant ingredients (Pezzato et al. 2002; Neto and Ostrensky 2015). However, plant ingredients have been associated with higher P loss due to the low digestibility of P. According to Ravindran et al. (1994), Up to 80% of the total P content in plant ingredients is reported to be in phytate. Most monogastric aquatic animals lack endogenous enzymes for phytate hydrolysis (Cao et al. 2007). The low digestible P content in fish feeds in Africa, particularly in backyard feed, could be due to the high inclusion of plant ingredients in the diets (Musa et al. 2021b), raising concern due to the risk of eutrophication, especially in freshwater lakes such as Lake Victoria that has been reported to be highly eutrophic (Ochumba and Kibaara 1989; Lung'ayia 2000; Kling and Mugidde 2001).

15.3 Nutrient Load in Wastes in African Inland Waters

The amount of waste produced in cage fish farming depends on several factors, including feed quality, feed processing method and feed loss. Extrusion processing of fish feeds has been reported to produce quality pellets and improve faecal size and durability in water, hence reducing pollution in effluents (Welker et al. 2018). Notably, extruded feeds have been reported to have high water stability compared to pelleted feeds, hence fewer nutrients leaching from the feeds (Musa et al. 2021b).

Table 15.4 Reported types of fish feed, FCR and nutrient loading in cage fish farming in African inland waters

Reference	Type of feed	FCR	Total amount of nutrient involved (kg)		Nutrient recovered in fish (kg)		Net amount of waste output (kg)	
			N	P	N	P	N	P
Musa et al. (2021a, b)	Commercial feed	1.6	76.8	16	27.2	8.5	49.6	7.5
Musa et al. (2021a, b)	Backyard feed	2.8	126	30.8	21	7.8	105	23
Karikari (2016)	Commercial feed A	2	123.4	26.9	29.9	4.1	93.5	22.8
Karikari (2016)	Commercial feed B	1.7	105.4	22.95	29.83	4.41	75.6	18.6
Gondwe et al. (2011)	Commercial feed	2.7	155.3	23.5	50.6	8.1	104.7	15.4
Neto and Ostrensky (2013)	Commercial feed	1.35	69.23	19.86	24.23	5.56	45	14.3

This reduces the pollution potential from the aquaculture system. Table 15.4 shows the feed types and N and P budgets from available literature on tilapia cage culture in African inland waters. The N and P loading varied considerably with higher FCR (>2), giving the highest N (>100 kg/ton) and P (>23 kg/ton) loadings. Notably, the environmental loading of P and N per kg of tilapia produced seems to be more than twice as high when backyard feed is used compared to extruded feed (Table 15.4).

Mass balance analysis for cage fish culture has been carried out for a long time in temperate environments, and it has shown that about 31% N and 31% of P added through fish feeds were removed as fish biomass, and about 69% of N and 69% of P were discharged into the environment (Gowen and Bradbury 1987; Holby and Hall 1991; Hall et al. 1992). For the few mass balance models for tilapia in Africa, >30% of N added through fish feeds have been reported to be removed by fish at harvest. However, less than 25% of P added through fish feeds were removed by fish at harvest (Table 15.4). The assimilation of N from feed by fish in the tropical region was comparable to the temperate region, while the assimilation of P was much poorer than in temperate studies. The poorer assimilation of P in the tropical region herein could be because the majority of the fish feeds reported N deficiency compared to P, as indicated by lower N:P ratios in feed as compared to fish. The lowest N:P ratio in feeds in the tropical region confirms that P in fish feeds could be more than required for growth. Research in temperate and tropical countries concur that fish feeds are the primary source of added N and P from fish cage culture in a lacustrine environment (Gondwe et al. 2011; Neto & Ostrensky 2013; Karikari 2016; Musa et al. 2021b). Hence, the addition of N deficient fish feeds in African inland waters will not only reduce the growth rate of caged tilapia but will lead to poor retention and high nutrient loading into the environment. In most freshwater lakes such as Lake Victoria, phytoplanktons are limited by N rather than P (Guildford and Hecky 2000; Gikuma-Njuru and Hecky 2005; Mwamburi et al. 2020), favouring heterocystous N-fixing cyanobacteria. Loss of N deficient fish feed from cage farms could exacerbate this effect.

The environmental losses of nitrogen and phosphorus from cages in tropical countries proved to be threefold more significant than those reported in the literature for laboratory experiments and pond culture (Fernandes et al. 2007; Boyd et al. 2008; Azevedo et al. 2011). This could have been associated with culture systems, and it could also be because most of these studies did not estimate feed loss. It could also indicate that fish cage culture may have higher inputs of nutrients to the environment than pond fish farming, which could become a bone of contention for the industry.

15.4 Theoretical Mass Balance Model

In this section, we will use a theoretical mass balance model to estimate the levels of N and P discharged from cage fish farms producing a tonne of tilapia. The hypothetical model uses average values from published literature on the different components to formulate the model using various assumptions on feed loss, FCR, N and P content of feed and fish. The nitrogen content of farmed tilapia is 3% (on a wet weight basis) (Neto and Ostrensky 2013). The phosphorus content of tilapia is 0.85% (Musa et al. 2021a, b). The current cage culture of tilapia utilising commercial feeds limits feeding loss to 5% (Musa et al. 2021b). For juveniles > 10 g, 25–30% crude protein level is recommended (Balarin and Haller 1982; Tacon 1987; El-Sayed and Teshima 1991; Khattab et al. 2000). Phosphorus content in tilapia feeds have been reported to be between 1–1.6 (Neto and Ostrensky 2013, Musa et al. 2021b). Previous studies on Nile tilapia have reported FCR of 1.4–4.4 (El-Sayed 1998; Al-Hafedh 1999; Liti et al. 2005, 2006; Kubiriza et al. 2017; Musa et al. 2021b). In the hypothetical model, a total input of 64 kg and 16 kg for N and P, respectively, is required to produce a tonne of Nile tilapia (Fig. 15.2). With FCR of 1.4, a total of 26 kg (46.42%) N and 5.5 kg (46.88%) P is released into the environment for every tonne of Nile tilapia produced in cages. A total of 30 kg (53.57%) N and 8.5 kg (60.71%) P were retained by harvested fish. According to Boyd and Queiroz (2001), 61.9–77.2% of nitrogen from feed inputs is loaded into the environment, while phosphorus loads account for 43.8–89.4% of feed inputs. The low TN and TP loadings recorded in the hypothetical model (Fig. 15.2) were based on moderate values for FCR and feed loss in tilapia culture. However, higher FCR of >3 have been recorded for tilapia (Gondwe et al. 2011; Kubiriza et al. 2017); hence the nutrient loadings, in reality, may be higher than those recorded in the hypothetical model.

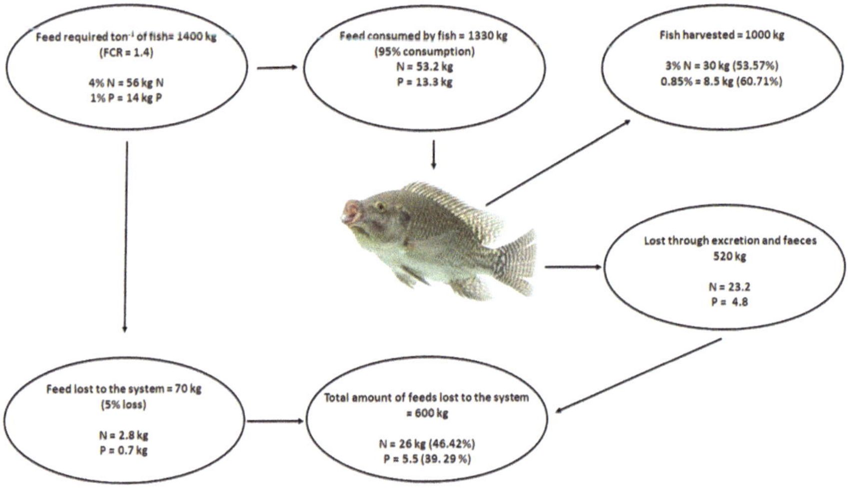

Fig. 15.2 Theoretical model for nutrient mass budget for a conjectured production of one ton of Nile tilapia in cages in a lacustrine environment

15.4.1 Sensitivity Analysis of the Model

Many factors can affect the loading rates of nutrients in a lacustrine environment; hence the nutrient loads reported in African inland waters in Table 15.4 above and in the theoretical model (Fig. 15.2) may vary with different factors. Musa et al. (2021b) reported a feeding loss of up to 25% for cage fish farms in Lake Victoria, Kenya. However, higher feed loss exceeding 30% has been reported under aquaculture elsewhere (Thorpe et al. 1990), with a corresponding increase in FCR values. Wu (1995) recorded a feeding loss of up to 40% when fish were fed on trash fish. Sometimes higher N and P have been reported in fish feeds (8% N reported by Hall et al. 1992 and 2.14% P reported by Foy and Rosell 1991) and lower in fish muscle.

In a scenario where cage farms use fish feeds with higher feed loss (e.g. 20%) and, in essence, higher FCR (e.g. 4), leaving other factors constant, the farm would discharge about 5 times the amount of N and 6 times the amount of P in the environment compared to the theoretical model (Fig. 15.3a). In the second scenario, where the feed loss is high, but at the same time the nutrient retention in fish is inefficient, the cage farms would discharge about 91% of N and 89% of P in the environment (Fig. 15.3b). This is in line with the studies of Handy and Poxton (1993), who showed that when the feed wastage is high and the N retention rate is lower, greater than 90% of the supplied N is lost to the system. The model indicates that nutrient loading from the cage culture of Nile tilapia is very sensitive to feed loss and, in essence, the FCR of the diet. Nutrient retention is the next factor that affects nutrient loading in a lacustrine environment. In aquaculture feed cost accounts to upto 70% of the production costs (Watanabe 2002; El-Sayed 2006; Cheng et al. 2010; Khalil et al. 2019; Allam et al. 2020). The values have been reported to be

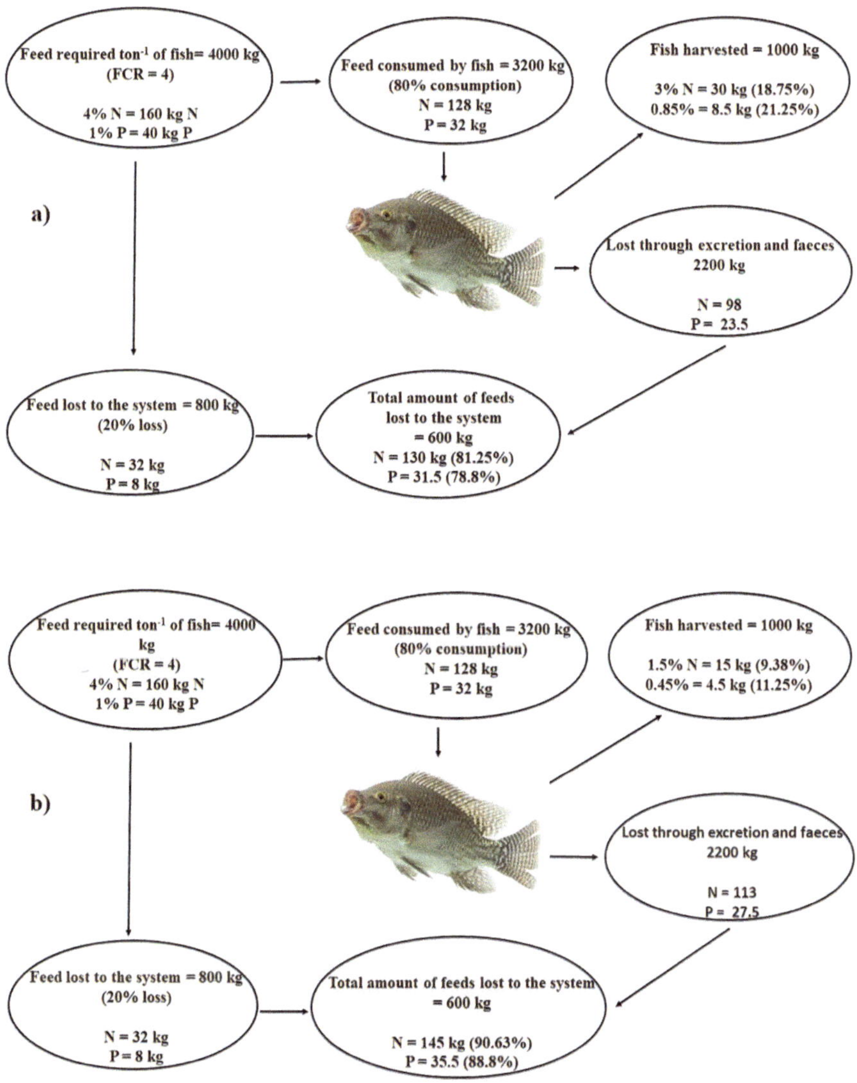

Fig. 15.3 Mass budget for a conjectured production of one ton of Nile tilapia in cages in a lacustrine environment for two different pollution scenarios: (**a**) when the rate of feed loss is high hence higher FCR and (**b**) when the rate of feed loss is high, FCR is high with poor N assimilation and retention

even higher (>70%) in cage culture (Musa et al. 2021b). The need to minimize feed losses cannot be overemphasized, not only for environmental sustainability in fish cage culture but for economic production issues (Talbot and Hole 1994; Musa et al. 2021b).

15.5 Conclusion and Recommendations

Feed quality is a key factor in determining the impact of aquaculture on the environment. The nutrient loads in African inland waters are higher than desirable due to the low digestibility of feeds translating to higher FCRs. The low N content in relation to P and high fibre contents of fish feeds result in a higher nutrient discharge into the environment. In addition, the use of backyard fish feeds for fish cage culture seems inferior to commercial feeds not only due to high fibre content but primarily due to low water stability that could cause a disproportionate increase in total P and N output loading from cage fish farming. The use of commercial fish feed is highly recommended for cage fish culture in African inland waters. We recommend the zonation of suitable sites for cage fish farming in all African inland lakes to ensure proper water circulation and, in essence, good water quality. Good water quality will ensure a high appetite for fish, resulting in the increased digestive function of the intestine and increased digestibility of nutrients in the intestines, translating to low FCRs. In addition, using best practices in feeding regimes will go a long way in reducing FCR and, in essence, the cost of production. There is a need to enhance the N content of fish feeds to reduce P discharge into the environment and limit the proliferation of nitrogen-fixing cyanobacterial species.

Furthermore, there is a need to incorporate phytase in plant-based fish feeds to enhance the bioavailability of P and reduce the nutrient discharge into the environment. The environmental sustainability of the cage culture industry is very sensitive to feed loss. Hence, feeding management practices, particularly those that reduce feed loss, is a crucial point in reducing the input of these nutrients in the aquatic environment. For example, using water-stable pellets through extrusion would be one way of reducing feed loss to the environment. We recommend fast-tracking of regulations for inland waters to control locations of new entrances and relocation of existing cages to appropriate locations. Furthermore, mapping suitable sites for cage fish culture in African inland waters coupled with best management practices is imperative so that aquaculture remains within the carrying capacity of inland water bodies for the environmental sustainability of the industry.

References

Ackefors H, Enell M (1994) The release of nutrients and organic matter from aquaculture systems in Nordic countries. J Appl Ichthyol 10:225–241

Akintola SL, Brown A, Bakare A et al (2013) Effects of hot smoking and sun drying processes on nutritional composition of giant tiger shrimp (*Penaeus monodon*, fabricius, 1798). Polish J Food Nutr Sci 63(4):227–237. https://doi.org/10.2478/v10222-012-0093-1

Al-Hafedh Y (1999) Effects of dietary protein on growth and body composition of Nile tilapia, *Oreochromis niloticus* L. Aquac Res 30:385–393

Allam BW, Khalil HS, Mansour AT et al (2020) Impact of substitution of fish meal by high protein distillers dried grains on growth performance, plasma protein and economic benefit of striped catfish (*Pangasianodon hypophthalmus*). Aquaculture. https://doi.org/10.1016/j.aquaculture.2019.734792

Anderson JL, Asche F, Garlock T et al (2017) Aquaculture: its role in the future of food. In: Frontiers of economics and globalization, vol 17. Emerald Publishing Limited, Bradford, pp 159–173

Asmah R, Karikari A, Falconer L (2016) Cage aquaculture in Lake Volta, Ghana. Guidelines for a sustainable future. Te Leverhulme Trust. Royal Society, Stirling. University of Stirling

Aura MC, Musa S, Yongo JE (2017) Integration of mapping and socio-economic status of cage culture: Towards balancing lake-use and culture fisheries in Lake Victoria, Kenya. Aquac Res 49(1):532–545. https://doi.org/10.1111/are.13484

Aura MC, Nyamweya C, Njiru JM et al (2018) Exploring the demarcation requirements of fish breeding and nursery sites to balance the exploitation, management and conservation needs of Lake Victoria ecosystem. Fish Manag Ecol 26:451–459

Aura CM, Musa S, Nyamweya CS, Ogari Z, Njiru JM, Hamilton SE, May L (2021) A GIS-based approach for delineating suitable areas for cage fish culture in a lake. Lakes Reserv Sci Policy Manag Sustain Use 26(2):e12357

Azevedo PA, Podemski CL, Hesslein RH et al (2011) Estimation of waste outputs by a rainbow trout cage farm using a nutritional approach and monitoring of water quality. Aquaculture 311: 175–186

Balarin JD, Haller RD (1982) The intensive culture of tilapia in tanks, raceways and cages. In: Muir JF, Roberts RJ (eds) Recent advances in aquaculture. Croom Helm, London, pp 265–356

Bao-Tong H (1994) Cage culture development and its role in aquaculture in China. Aquac Res 25(3):305–310

Barrows FT, Stone DAJ, Hardy RW (2007) The effects of extrusion conditions on the nutritional value of soybean meal for rainbow trout (*Oncorhynchus mykiss*). Aquaculture 265:244–252

Berg H, Michelsen P, Troell M et al (1996) Managing aquaculture for sustainability in tropical Lake Kariba, Zimbabwe. Ecol Econ 18(2):141–159. https://doi.org/10.1016/0921-8009(96)00018-3

Beveridge MCM (1984) Cage and pen fish farming. Carrying capacity models and environmental impact. FAO Fish Tech Pap (255):131 p

Blow P, Leonard S (2007) A review of cage aquaculture: sub-Saharan Africa. In Halwart M, Soto D, Arthur JR (Eds). Cage aquaculture – Regional reviews and global overview, pp. 188–207. FAO Fisheries Technical Paper. No. 498. Rome, FAO; pp 192–206

Bolivar RB, Jimenez EBJ, Brown CL (2006) Alternate day feeding strategy for Nile tilapia grow out in the Philippines: marginal cost-revenue analysis. N Am J Aquac 68:192–197

Bostock J, McAndrew B, Richards R, Jauncey K, Telfer T, Lorenzen K, Little D, Ross L, Handisyde N, Gatward I (2010) Aquaculture: global status and trends. Philos Trans R Soc Lond Ser B Biol Sci 365(1554):2897–2912. https://doi.org/10.1098/rstb.2010.0170

Boyd CE, Lim C, Queiroz J, Salie K, de Wet L (2008) Best management practices for responsible aquaculture. Report, 24 pp

Boyd CE, Queiroz JF (2001) Nitrogen, phosphorus loads vary by system. The advocate 3pp. https://www.researchgate.net/profile/Claude-Boyd/publication/313108117_Nitrogen_and_phosphorus_loads_by_system_USEPA_should_consider_system_variables_in_setting_new_effluent_rules/links/58ab610792851cf0e3ca4a15/Nitrogenand-phosphorus-loads-by-system-USEPA-should-consider-system-variables-in-setting-new-effluent-rules.pdf

Braaten R (2007) Cage aquaculture and environmental impacts. In: Bergheim A (ed) Aquacultural engineering and environment, vol 661. Kerala, Research Signpost, pp 49–91

Bueno GW, Ostrensky A, Canzi C, de Matos FT, Roubach R (2015) Implementation of aquaculture parks in federal government waters in Brazil. Rev Aquat 7(1):1–12. https://doi.org/10.1111/raq.12045

Bureau DP, Harris AM, Cho CY (1999) Apparent digestibility of rendered animal protein ingredients for rainbow trout (*Oncorhynchus mykiss*). Aquaculture 180:345–358

Cao L, Wang W, Yang C et al (2007) Application of microbial phytase in fish feed. Enzym Microb Technol 40:497–507

Cheng ZJ, Hardy RW (2003) Effects of extrusion processing of feed ingredients on apparent digestibility coefficients of nutrients for rainbow trout (*Oncorhynchus mykiss*). Aquac Nutr 9: 77–83
Cheng Z, Ai Q, Mai K et al (2010) Effects of dietary canola meal on growth performance, digeston and metabolism of Japanese seabass, *Lateolabrax japonicus*. Aquaculture 305:102–108. https://doi.org/10.1016/j.Aquaculture2010.03.031
De Silva SS, Anderson TA (1995) Fish nutrition in aquaculture. Chapman & Hall Aquaculture Series, London, 319 pp
De Silva SS, Phillips MJ (2007). A review of cage aquaculture: Asia (excluding China). In Halwart M, Soto D, Arthur JR (eds). Cage aquaculture-Regional review and and global overview, pp 18–84. FAO Fisheries Technical Paper No. 498. Rome, FAO; p 241
Egessa R, Pabire GW, Ocaya H (2018) Benthic macroinvertebrate community structure in Napoleon Gulf, Lake Victoria: effects of cage aquaculture in eutrophic lake. Environ Monit Assess 190:112
Elnady MA, Alkobaby AI, Salem MA, Abdel-Salam M, Asran BM (2010) Effect of fertilization and low quality feed on water quality Dynamics and growth performance of Nile tilapia (*Oreochromis niloticus*). J Am Sci 6:1044–1054
El-Sayed AFM (1998) Total replacement of fishmeal with animal protein sources in Nile tilapia *Oreochromis nilotcus* (L.) feeds. Aquac Res 29:275–280. https://doi.org/10.1046/j.1365-2109.1998.00199.x
El-Sayed AFM (2006) Tilapia culture. CABI Publishing, Wallingford, GB
El-Sayed AFM, Teshima S (1991) Tilapia nutrition in aquaculture. Rev Aquat Sci 5:247–265
Fernandes M, Lauer P, Cheshire A (2007) Preliminary model of nitrogen loads from southern bluefin tuna aquaculture. Mar Pollut Bull 54:1321–1332
Fontainhas-Fernandes A, Gomes E, Reis-Henriques MA (1999) Replacement of fish meal by plant proteins in the diet of Nile tilapia: digestibility and growth performance. Aquac Int 7:57–67
Food and Agricultural Organization of the United Nations (FAO) (2016) The State of the World Fisheries and Aquaculture. http://www.fao.org/3/i5555e/i5555e.pdf
Food and Agricultural Organization of the United Nations (FAO) (2018) The State of the World Fisheries and Aquaculture. http://www.fao.org/3/i9540en/I9540EN.pdf
Food and Agricultural Organization of the United Nations (FAO) (2020) The state of the world fisheries and aquaculture. Sustainability in action. Food and Agricultural Organization of the United Nations (FAO), Rome. https://doi.org/10.4060/ca9229en
Foy RH, Rosell R (1991) Loadings of nitrogen and phosphorus from a Northern Ireland fish farm. Aquaculture 96:17–30
Gaylord TG, Barrows FT, Rawles SD (2008) Apparent digestibility of gross nutrients from feedstuffs in extruded feeds for rainbow trout (*Oncorhynchus mykiss*). J World Aquac Soc 39: 827–834
Gikuma-Njuru P, Hecky RE (2005) Nutrient concentrations in Nyanza Gulf, Lake Victoria Kenya: Light limits algal demand and abundance. Hydrobiologia 534:131–140
Gondwe M, Guildford S, Hecky R (2011) Physico-chemical measurements in the water column along a transect through a tilapia cage fish farm in Lake Malawi, Africa. J Great Lakes Res 37: 102–113
Gowen RJ, Bradbury NB (1987) The ecological impact of salmonid farming in coastal waters: a review. Oceanogr Mar Biol Annu Rev 25:563–575
Guildford SJ, Hecky RE (2000) Total nitrogen, total phosphorus and nutrient limitation in lakes and oceans: is there a common relationship? Limnol Oceanogr 45:1213–1223
Hall POJ, Holby O, Kollberg S, Samuelsson MO (1992) Chemical fluxes and mass balances in a marine fish cage farm. IV. Nitrogen. Mar Ecol Prog Ser 89:81–91
Hamilton SE, Gallo SM, Krach N et al (2020) The use of unmanned aircraft systems and high-resolution satellite imagery to monitor tilapia fish cage aquaculture expansion in Lake Victoria, Kenya. Bull Mar Sci 96(1):71–93

Handy RD, Poxton MG (1993) Nitrogen pollution in mariculture: toxicity and excretion of nitrogenous compounds by marine fish. Rev Fish Biol Fish 3:205–241
Hecky RE, Mugidde R, Ramlal PS (2010) Multiple stressors cause rapid ecosystem change in Lake Victoria. Freshw Biol 55(1):19–42
Henriksson PJG, Belton B, Murshed-e-Jahan K (2018) Measuring the potential for sustainable intensifcation of aquaculture in Bangladesh using life cycle assessment. Proc Natl Acad Sci. https://doi.org/10.1073/pnas.1716530115
Holby O, Hall POJ (1991) Chemical fluxes and mass balances in a marine fish cage farm. II. Phosphorus. Mar Ecol Prog Ser 70:263–272
Kamadi G (2018) Floating Fish Farms Become a Threat to Lake Victoria. Business Today
Karikari AY (2016) Assessment of Environmental Impacts of Cage Aquaculture on Lake Volta of Ghana. PhD thesis, Department of Fisheries and Watershed Management, Ghana
Kashindye BB, Nsinda P, Kayanda R et al (2015) Environmental impacts of cage culture in Lake Victoria: the case of Shirati Bay - Sota, Tanzania. SpringerPlus, Cham. https://doi.org/10.1186/s40064-015-1241-y
KEBS (2015) Compounded Tilapia feeds-Specifications. KS 2289-1:2016 ICS65.120
Khalil HS, Mansour AT, Goda AMA et al (2019) Effect of selenium yeast supplementation on growth performance, feed utilization, lipid profile, liver and intestine histological changes, and economic benefit in meagre, *Argyrosomus regius*, fingerlings. Aquac Nutr 501:135–143. https://doi.org/10.1016/j.aquaculture.2018.11.018
Khattab Y, Ahmad M, Shalaby A et al (2000) Response of Nile tilapia (*Oreochromis niloticus* L.) from different locations to different dietary protein levels. Egypt J Aquat Biol Fish 4:295–311
Kitagima RE, Fracalossi DM (2011) Digestibility of alternative protein-rich feedstuffs for channel catfish, Ictalurus punctatus. J World Aquac Soc 42:306–312
Kling HJ, Mugiddc R (2001) Hecky RE (2001) Recent changes in the phytoplankton community of Lake Victoria in response to eutrophication. In: Munawar M, Hecky RE (eds) Great lakes of the world: food webs. Health and Integrity, Backhuys, Leiden, pp 47–66
Kong W, Huang S, Yang Z et al (2020) Fish feed quality is a key factor in impacting aquaculture water environment: evidence from incubator experiments. Sci Rep 10:187. https://doi.org/10.1038/s41598-019-57063-w
Kubiriza GK, Akol AM, Arnason J, Snorrason S, Tómasson T, Thorarensen H (2017) Practical feeds for juvenile Nile tilapia (*Oreochromis nilotcus*) prepared by replacing *Rastrineobola argentea* fishmeal with freshwater shrimp (*Caridina nilotca*) and mung bean (Vigna radiata) meals. Aquac Nutr 00:1–8
Leal ALG, de Castro PF, de Lima JPVE et al (2010) Use of shrimp protein hydrolysate in Nile tilapia (*Oreochromis niloticus*, L.) feeds. Aquac Int 18:635–646. https://doi.org/10.1007/s10499-009-9284-0
Leary DF, Lovell RT (1975) Value of fiber in production-type diets for channel catfish. Am Fish Soc. https://doi.org/10.1577/1548
Liti D, Cherop L, Munguti J, Chhorn L (2005) Growth and economic performance of Nile tilapia (Oreochromis niloticus L.) fed on two formulated diets and two locally available feeds in fertilized ponds. Aquac Res 36:746–752
Liti DM, Waidbacher H, Straif M, Mbaluka RK, Munguti JM, Kyenze MM (2006) Effects of partial and complete replacement of freshwater shrimp meal (*Caridina niloticus* Roux) with a mixture of plant protein sources on growth performance of Nile tilapia (*Oreochromis niloticus* L.) in fertilized ponds. Aquac Res 37:477–483. https://doi.org/10.1111/j.1365-2109.2006.01450.x
Lung'ayia HBO, M'harzi A, Tackx M (2000) Phytoplankton community structure and environment in the Kenyan waters of Lake Victoria. Freshw Biol 43: 529–543
Musa S, Aura CM, Okechi J (2021a) Economic analysis of tilapia cage culture in Lake Victoria using different cage volumes. J Appl Aquac. https://doi.org/10.1080/10454438.2021.1884632
Musa S, Aura CM, Tomasson T, Sigurgeirsson O, Thorarensen H (2021b) A comparative study of the effects of pelleted and extruded feed on growth, financial revenue and nutrient loading of Nile tilapia (*Oreochromis niloticus* L.) cage culture in a lacustrine environment. J Appl Aquac. https://doi.org/10.1080/10454438.2021.2011528

Musinguzi L, Lugya J, Rwezaula P et al (2019) The extent of cage aquaculture, adherence to best practices and reflections for sustainable aquaculture on African inland waters. J Great Lakes Res. https://doi.org/10.1016/j.jglr.2019.09.011
Mwamburi J, Basweti G, Owili M, Babu J, Wawiye P (2020) Spatio-temporal trends of nutrients and physico-chemical parameters on lake ecosystem and fisheries prior to onset of cage farming and re-opening of the Mbita passage in the Nyanza Gulf of Lake Victoria. Lakes Reserv Res Manag Sustain Use 25:292–313. https://doi.org/10.1111/lre.12329
Naylor RL, Goldburg RJ, Primavera JH, Kautsky N, Beveridge MCM, Clay J, Troell M (2000) Effect of aquaculture on world fish supplies. Nature 405:1017–1024. https://doi.org/10.1038/35016500
Neto RM, Ostrensky A (2013) Nutrient load estimation in the waste of Nile tilapia Oreochromis niloticus (L.) reared in cages in tropical climate conditions. Aquac Res 46(6):1309–3322. https://doi.org/10.1111/are.12280
Neto RM, Ostrensky A (2015) Evaluation of commercial feeds intended for the Brazilian production of Nile tilapia (*Oreochromis niloticus* L.): nutritional and environmental implications. Aquac Nutr 21(3):311–320. https://doi.org/10.1111/anu.12154
Ngupula GW, Kayanda R (2010) Benthic macrofauna community composition, abundance and distribution in the Tanzanian and Ugandan inshore and offshore waters of Lake Victoria. Afr J Aquat Sci 35(2):185–192
Ngupula GW, Ezekiel CN, Kimirei IA et al (2012) Physical and chemical characteristics of the Tanzanian inshore and offshore waters of Lake Victoria in 2005–2008. Afr J Aquat Sci 37(3): 339–345
Obiero KO, Meulenbroek P, Drexler S et al (2019) The contribution of fish to food and nutrition security in Eastern Africa: emerging trends and future outlooks. Sustainability 11:1636. https://doi.org/10.3390/su11061636
Ochumba PBO, Kibaara DI (1989) Observations on blue-green algal blooms in the open waters of Lake Victoria, Kenya. Afr J Ecol 27(1):23–34. https://doi.org/10.1111/j.1365-2028.1989.tb00925.x
Pezzato LE, Miranda ECD, Barros MM (2002) Apparent digestibility of feedstuffs by Nile tilapia (Oreochromis niloticus). Braz J Anim Sci 31:1595–1604
Ravindran V, Ravindran G, Sivalogan S (1994) Total and phytate phosphorus contents of various foods and feedstuffs of plant origin. Food Chem 50:133–136
Roy PK, Lall P (2004) Urinary phosphorus excretion in haddock, *Melanogrammus aeglefinus* (L.) and Atlantic salmon, *Salmo salar* (L.). Aquaculture 233:369–382
Samuel-Fitwia B, Wuertza S, Schroederb JP et al (2012) Sustainability assessment tools to support aquaculture development. J Clean Prod 32:183–192
Satia BP (2011) Regional review on status and trends in aquaculture development in SubSaharan Africa – 2010. FAO Fisheries and Aquaculture Circular 1061/4. ISSN 2070-6065
Tacon ADJ (1987) The nutrition and feeding of farmed fish and shrimp - a training manual. 2. Nutrient sources and composition. GCP/RLA/075/ITA, Field Document 5/E. FAO, Rome, Italy, p 129
Talbot C, Hole R (1994) Fish diets and the control of eutrophication resulting from aquaculture. J Appl Ichthyol 10:258–270
Thorpe JE, Talbot C, Miles MS, Rawlings C, Keay DS (1990) Food consumption in 24 hours by Atlantic salmon (*Salmo salar* L.) in a sea cage. Aquaculture 90:41–47
Villnas A, Perus J, Bonsdorff E (2011) Structural and functional shifts in zoobenthos induced by organic enrichment - Implications for community recovery potential. J Sea Res 65:8–18
Von Sperling M, Chernicharo CAL (2005) Biological wastewater treatment in warm climate regions. IWA Publishing, London

Watanabe T (2002) Strategies for further development of aquatic feeds. Fish Sci 68:242–252. https://doi.org/10.1046/j.1444-2906.2002.00418.x

Welker TL, Overturf K, Snyder S (2018) Effects of feed processing method (extrusion and expansion-compression pelleting) on water quality and growth of rainbow trout in a commercial setting. J Appl Aquac. https://doi.org/10.1080/10454438.2018.1433095

Wu RSS (1995) The environmental impact of marine fish culture: towards a sustainable future. Mar Pollut Bull 31:159–166

Zhou QC, Yue YR (2012) Apparent digestibility coefficients of selected feed ingredients for juvenile hybrid tilapia, *Oreochromis niloticus* × *Oreochromis aureus*. Aquac Res 43:806–814

Part III
Aquaculture Development and Innovations in Africa

Chapter 16
Aquaponics as a Sustainable Food Production System with Promising Development Perspectives in Morocco

Maryam El Bakali and Mustapha Aba

Abstract Moroccan water and land resources are under increased stress, which could have a negative impact on agricultural output, therefore, raising questions about food security. Due to the effects of climate fluctuations on Morocco's semi-arid and arid climate, as well as water stress brought on by the depletion of natural water resources, innovative agricultural techniques must be sustainably developed to ensure food security through agricultural food production. For these reasons, the aquaponics system in Morocco has the potential to significantly contribute to the environmental, social, and economic sustainability of the nation while conserving and rationalising water, a resource that is essential for the sectors of agriculture as well as aquaculture, which happen to be growth drivers of major economic importance in the country. As a matter of fact, aquaponics, which has gained popularity and credibility across the globe, functions by combining aquaculture and hydroponics in a recirculating system, promoting water reuse and nutrient recycling. In this chapter, alternative sustainable agricultural and aquaculture food production methods are presented, along with a theoretical overview of aquaponics and a discussion of its perspectives in Morocco based on the result of the first ever Moroccan study on small-scale aquaponics production systems. The intention is to incorporate these systems into Morocco's extensive agricultural sector to reap its socioeconomic and environmental advantages.

Keywords Aquaculture · Agriculture · Aquaponics · Water · Food · Sustainability · Morocco

M. El Bakali (✉)
BV2MAP, FPL, Adelmalek Essaadi University, Tetouan, Morocco

M. Aba
Aquaculture Scientific Expert, Fish Nutrition, Region of Rabat, Morocco

© The Author(s), under exclusive license to Springer Nature Singapore Pte Ltd. 2023
N. N. Gabriel et al. (eds.), *Emerging Sustainable Aquaculture Innovations in Africa*, Sustainable Agriculture and Food Security,
https://doi.org/10.1007/978-981-19-7451-9_16

16.1 Introduction

Food security has emerged as a critical development issue in the twenty-first century facing the world's growing population, with the intensification of global food production as one of the most critical challenges to achieve it (Frόna et al. 2019). Food insecurity can drastically affect diet quality, potentially leading to undernutrition and obesity. In fact, ensuring access to a healthy diet is a prerequisite for achieving the sustainable development goals (SDG) target of eradicating all forms of malnutrition (FAO 2020). To attain this goal and ensure food security, it is essential to recognise the reliance of food production on the availability of resources, such as land, freshwater and nutrients (Conijn et al. 2018).

The most crucial factor in this regard is the amount of water. Although water is a renewable resource, non-renewable stocks are depleting, considering that 70% of all freshwater used by humans goes into agriculture (FAO 2020), and given the looming water crisis, particularly in the North African region, including Morocco, which has one of the world's poorest freshwater resources, which are primarily underground (Hamed et al. 2018). Morocco is a semi-arid Mediterranean country with irregular and scarce rainfall, making surface water and groundwater resources critical for socioeconomic development (Schilling et al. 2012). In a country where agriculture is an important economic sector and a heavy consumer of water, the most severe impact would most likely occur during water shortages, with serious consequences for rural livelihoods, economics, and food security (Corner et al. 2020). Accordingly, innovative solutions aiming to increase food production are required. Such solutions should strive to achieve less water consumption without further compromising the environment to ensure greater food security for the population. In fact, the increased demand for food and the scarcity of water makes it necessary to develop a sustainable system, primarily as the agricultural sector reflects its dependence on climatic conditions, particularly rainfall (Harbouze et al. 2019). According to the FAO (2016), to achieve food security objectives while considering the threat of climate change, the transformation and adaptation of agricultural systems that demand significant water resources, especially in semi-arid areas, will be required. For these reasons, the search for innovative forms of production that consume less water has become a mainly debated issue due to the need for food security and the depletion of natural water resources in Morocco. In that respect, the aquaponic production system is a technique that has successfully been used in many countries (Goddek et al. 2019a; b). In African countries, aquaponics systems are relatively new. The low adoption of this new technique may be related to the low penetration of innovative fish production systems such as recirculating aquaculture systems, which are an integral part of aquaponic systems (Obirikorang et al. 2021). Egypt, South Africa, and Kenya are the countries that appear to have relatively widely adopted this technology in Africa.

Morocco, like all countries around the world, faces numerous challenges in terms of food security and agricultural productivity, primarily the need to increase food production and availability as well as access to food (Toumi 2016). Despite all the advantages of aquaponics, such as low water consumption, reduced environmental impacts, and the production of two sources of income in a single system, its use in Morocco is still in its early stages (El Bakali 2022a, b). More research is needed to provide additional information to enable the implementation of this system in Moroccan conditions. In this context, this work aims to present an alternative form of sustainable food production using aquaponics and discuss its prospects in Morocco.

16.1.1 Aquaculture in Morocco

Morocco has a favourable geographical position due to its 3500 km of coastline spread across two seafronts and its 200 nautical mile Exclusive Economic Zone in the Atlantic. These assets, combined with a world-class upwelling zone, make the Moroccan coast one of the most fish-rich areas, with an annual production potential exceeding 1.5 million tonnes of fish (Doukkali and Kamili 2018). According to the Department of Maritime Fisheries (2019), Morocco's maritime fisheries sector produced nearly 1.46 million tonnes and was valued at nearly $1.2 billion. Morocco has implemented a strategy within the framework of the "Halieutis" plan, which is set to run until 2020, but the authorities have set goals for a second phase (2020–2030). The strategy comprises three major axes: resource sustainability, performance, and sector competitiveness (Saad & Maria 2017).

Aquaculture is defined by the FAO (2020) as the activity of rearing aquatic organisms and is one of the world's fastest-growing production modalities. Its prospects for growth continue to soar as a result of its enormous potential, as it aims to meet the growing demand for fish, despite the current stagnation of extractive fishing. Statistical data show that aquaculture has begun to contribute to more than half of the world's fish supply, highlighting its importance both locally and globally. Recognising the state of global aquaculture production acceleration, Morocco has chosen to position itself in the aquaculture sector to diversify its economy, make aquaculture a growth driver for the fisheries sector, contribute to food security and become more integrated into the international seafood trade.

In Morocco, aquaculture activity is institutionally governed by two Departments of the Ministry of Agriculture: The Marine Fisheries Department (acronym: DPM) manages marine aquaculture through the National Aquaculture Development Agency (acronym: ANDA), and the High Commission for Water, Forests, and the Fight against Desertification manage freshwater aquaculture (acronym: HCEFLCD).

16.1.2 Marine Aquaculture

Marine Aquaculture is one of the 16 big projects of Halieutis strategy, and it is positioned at the level of the axis of durability as a priority sector, leading to the establishment of a driver of growth and job creation for the fisheries sector. Oyster farming in the lagoon of Oualidia introduced the marine aquaculture sector to Morocco in the 1950s, and it has been known as a significant development by the launch of many other projects (Kaddioui et al. 2018), with 290 new projects in 2021. Figure 16.1 shows the most essential stages in the development of Moroccan marine aquaculture.

16.1.3 Freshwater Aquaculture

Freshwater aquaculture is an older sector introduced by rainbow trout farming in 1924 in Morocco. The HCEFLCD has launched an ambitious plan from 2015 to 2024 to develop and promote aquaculture in Morocco, to reach 50,000 tonnes of fish by 2024, which includes 20,000 tonnes produced by the private sector and 30,000 tonnes through restocking (DPM 2019). The said strategic plan has outlined among its general objectives making fish farming one of the engines of socioeconomic development in rural and mountainous areas and establishing a profitable and sustainable fish farming sector in each region of the Kingdom, which creates value while respecting the environment. Moreover, it strives to position freshwater fish as an essential source of animal protein supply in rural areas. According to the Directorate of Water and Forests of the Ministry of Agriculture, the species of Moroccan freshwater aquaculture are classified into three main groups of species and their dates of introduction in Morocco are shown in Table 16.1 (Mouslih (1987), Azeroual (2003) and Aba et al. (2014).

16.2 Agriculture in Morocco

Morocco's agricultural sector, the mainstay of the country's food security, is highly vulnerable to climatic hazards, particularly drought and scarcity of water resources (Bouchaou et al. 2011). In 2017, the agricultural and fisheries sector represented 13.6% of Morocco's GDP. Moroccan economic growth is thus closely linked to that of the agricultural sector. Indeed, the substantial variations in the added value of the agricultural sector, which demonstrate the dependence of this sector on climatic conditions, and rainfall, are reflected in the GDP growth (Harbouze et al. 2019).

The Moroccan state is aware of the current constraints and future challenges facing agriculture and has developed a long-term strategy to address them (Belahsen et al. 2016). This strategy, called the "Green Morocco Plan" (PMV), extends from 2008 to 2020 and carries out the ambition to make agriculture a real engine of growth and socio-economic development for the country (ADA 2021). It stands on two main pillars: the first one aims to develop modern, efficient agriculture that meets the requirements of the market by relying on the promotion of private investment and the establishment of an aggregation model. The second pillar intends to evolve

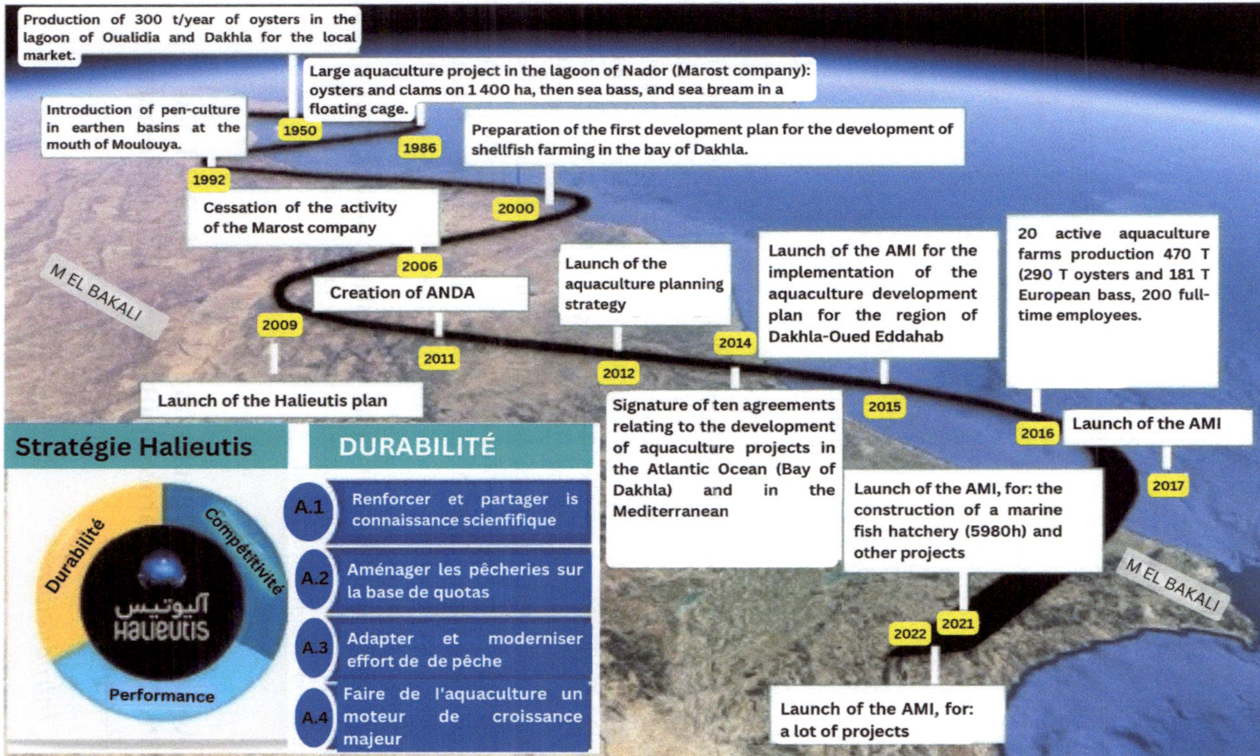

Fig. 16.1 Most essential stages in the development of Moroccan marine aquaculture

Table 16.1 Species of Moroccan freshwater aquaculture

Native species	Brown trout (*Salmo trutta*) Blue barbel Common barbel (*Barbus barbus*)
Migratory species	Allis shad (*Alosa alosa*) Eel (*Anguilla anguilla*) Muge cephale (*Mugil cephalus*)
Introduced species	Rainbow trout (*Oncorhynchus mykiss*) (1925) Pike (*Esox lucius*)) (1938) Black-bass (*Micropterus salmoides*) (Beginning of the last century) Silver carp (*Hypophthalmichthys molitrix*) (1983) Grass carp (*Ctenopharyngodon idella*) (1983) Common carp (*Cyprinus carpio)* (1924) Nile tilapia (*Oreochromis niloticus*) (2004) Gambusie (Gambusia affinis) (1929) Tanche (*Tinca tinca*) (1934) Pikeperch (*Sander lucioperca*) (1939) Rotengle (*Scardinius erythrophthalmus*) (1935) Red-footed Crayfish (*Astacus astacus*) (1914) American crayfish (*Orconectes limosus)* (1937)

the structure of Moroccan agriculture by supporting small farmers in securing and improving their income, with the aim of reducing rural poverty and consolidating the socio-economic fabric of the poorest territories. 12 years after the implementation of this plan, Morocco has launched a new strategy under the name of " Generation Green 2020-2030" that places the human element at the heart of its concerns. According to the Moroccan Ministry of Agriculture, the sustainable development of Moroccan agriculture has gained new momentum since the launch of this new strategy. Strongly linked to the human element, this foundation aims to consolidate the achievements of the Green Morocco Plan while making a qualitative and technological leap through specific actions on agricultural sectors, distribution chains, quality, and innovation, as well as in terms of preserving natural resources and strengthening the resilience of the sector. In this context, aquaponics, which incorporates aquaculture and hydroponics, can play an essential role in the sustainable production of agricultural food.

16.3 Aquaponics, an Opportunity for Sustainable Food Production in Morocco with Promising Development Perspectives

16.3.1 Introduction

Aquaponics, which combines the Greek words "hydro" (water) and "ponos" (labour), is a method of growing plants in various types of chemically inert

Table 16.2 Aquaponics: approaches, production scales, system designs

Aquaponics	
Level of production intensity (Foucard et al. 2019)	Production scales (Foucard et al. 2019)
Low-Tech • Usually lacking specific equipment dedicated to biological and mechanical filtration. • Clay beads and other culture media which may be sufficient in adequate quantity to filter the suspended solids which will then enrich the medium after microbial degradation. • The density of fish farming is generally very low ($\leq$10 kg / m^3).	Small scale A small fish tank associated with a small surface of vegetable culture on gravel or NFT (nutritive technical film). Goal: Self-production or recreational use
Middle-Tech • Mechanical filtration system of the decanting cone type and/or filtration foams or even a ball or sand filter. • A specific compartment dedicated to biological filtration. • The density rarely exceeds 20 kg of fish per cubic meter of water.	Middle scale A fish tank associated with a plant culture surface on gravel or NFT (nutritive technical film). Goal: "Demonstrative" structures (urban environment, on the roofs of buildings or on land of local communities in urban areas
High-Tech • a biological filtration system • a very efficient mechanical filter (of the drum filter type) coupled or not with passive filtration. • the aeration of the water by mixing (when the density of fish farming is low: $\leq$50 kg/m^3). • and/or oxygenation of the water by supplying liquid oxygen (when the density of fish culture is high, $\geq$50 kg / m^3 up to a bearable biological limit specific to each species of fish).	Commercial aquaponics *Goal*: • commercial production, • integration of a level of technicality allowing the production up to a few tons of fish per year for large production areas.
Approaches (Foucard et al. 2019)	System designs
Fish farming approach: Fish production *Role of aquaponics:* • Treatment of solid and dissolved water discharges from existing fish farming facilities through systems combining filtration elements (simple and inexpensive). • Effective means to reduce the rate of nitrogen and phosphorus molecules present in the water before discharge into the water course.	Coupled Aquaponics Systems consist of one connected water layer like the UVI system (Rakocy et al. 2006). Fish is usually a secondary aquaponics product
Mixed approach: Plant and fish production *Role of aquaponics:* • Establishment of a balance between the fish and plant compartments. • Decrease of water consumption and production of plants on a large scale with the only help of fish effluents.	
Plant-based approach: Plant production *Role of aquaponics:* • Optimisation of the use of water and reduction	Decoupled Aquaponics Systems Consists of separated aquaculture and hydroponic systems with a controlled connection

(continued)

Table 16.2 (continued)

Aquaponics	
Level of production intensity (Foucard et al. 2019)	Production scales (Foucard et al. 2019)
of the use of N-P-K nutrient solutions, which have a significant environmental impact. • Feeding the plants with a nutrient solution (organo-mineral) as a main or a complementary intake to a conventional hydroponic nutrient solution.	(Goddek et al. 2015). Fish is usually a secondary aquaponics product

substrates, such as sand, gravel, or liquid (water), to which nutrients are added, but no soil is used (Savvas 2003; Douglas 1975). This is done within a closed recirculating system (Thorarinsdottir 2015, Rakocy et al. 2006).

The concept of aquaponics, using fish waste to fertilise plants, has been utilised for thousands of years with applications in early Asian and South American civilisations (Somerville et al. 2014). According to Watten and Busch, it was not until the 1990s that academic research on aquaponics was incorporated into contemporary food production systems. Aquaponics is now considered a new and emerging industry with a relevant place in the broader, global agricultural production context of technology integrating fish culture with the aquatic plant (Knaus and Palm 2017a, 2017b). Given the water crisis currently affecting the whole world in general and Morocco with its arid and semi-arid climate, Moroccan agriculture must adopt new cultivation systems which use water rationally to minimise the impacts of its depletion as well as the discharge of aquaculture effluents, both for aquaculture and hydroponics via the aquaponics technique. Organic farming systems combining both techniques were fostered to meet the abovementioned needs (Pollard et al. 2017) but not yet in Morocco. Aquaponics is now considered one of the "blue growth" approaches. A climate-resilient system that focuses on improving productivity and performance because it offers opportunities for innovation and for production in environments where agriculture would not be traditionally possible (FAO 2017a).

16.3.2 The Symbiotic System of Aquaponics

The symbiotic biological principle in aquaponics stems from the fact that the nutrients needed for plant growth and development are very similar to the waste produced by fish (Espinosa-Moya et al. 2018). The nitrogen needed for plant growth is derived from the proteins consumed by fish, which retain 20–30% of the ingested dietary nitrogen, while 70–80% is released into the water as waste (Schreier et al. 2010). The reliance on the bacterial ecosystem is a characteristic of aquaponics (Kasozi et al. 2021). The nitrification process is carried out by two major groups of nitrifying bacteria (Somerville et al. 2014; Zou et al. 2016; Daims et al. 2015), ammonia-oxidizing bacteria (AOB) and nitric-oxidizing bacteria (NOB). They metabolise ammonia in the following order: AOoxidises ammonium ($NH4+$), producing nitrite ($NO2-$), and the NOB further oxidise the nitrite to produce nitrate ($NO3-$). In aquaponics, the most common AOB is *Nitrosomonas*, and the most common NOB is *Nitrobacter*. In conclusion, the aquaponics ecosystem is entirely dependent on bacteria. Ammonia concentrations in the water will kill the fish if the bacteria are not present or are not working correctly. To keep ammonia levels near zero, it is critical to maintain and manage a healthy bacterial colony in the system at all times (Somerville et al. 2014).

In aquaponics, the filtration system is the critical component for the balance of this technique since it is where the conversion of nitrogenous compounds in aquaponics is the process of nitrification. This process involves the chemical element nitrogen (N), which is essential for all life forms, including plants.

The presence of nitrifying bacteria in aquaponics attached to the biological filtration system is mandatory. These microorganisms, represented by Nitrosomonas and Nitrobacter, are responsible for the natural process of nitrification from the waste generated by aquatic organisms from fish feed and for the conversion of ammonia ($NH3$) to nitrite ($NO2-$) and nitrite to nitrate ($NO3-$), thus transforming toxic substances produced by fish into nutrients assimilable by plants (Schmautz et al. 2017). By consuming these nutrients, plants, together with bacteria, play an essential role in the biological filtration of the water, ensuring its proper condition for normal fish development (Kasozi et al. 2021).

Figure 16.2 shows the summary of the process of the symbiosis principle in the aquaponics system.

16.3.3 Types of Aquaponics Systems

A typical aquaponics system includes a fish tank for aquaculture, a biofilter for nitrification, and a culture bed for hydroponics (Love et al. 2015). Aquaponics systems are classified into three types based on the type of culture bed used (Engle 2015; Delaide et al. 2017): nutrient film technique (NFT), ebb-and-flow (EAF), and deep-water culture (DWC), also known as RAFT beds.

16.3.3.1 Nutrient Film Technique (NFT)

The Nutrient Film Technique (NFT) is a soilless hydroponics technique in which a continuous shallow stream of water carrying all essential plant nutrients flows down a channel or gully, where it meets plant roots before making its way to a nutrient reservoir and is then recirculated, minimising pump usage (Al-Tawaha et al. 2018). NFT systems are however only suitable only for smaller vegetation, such as lettuce, spinach or other leafy greens and herbs, because channels can become clogged by

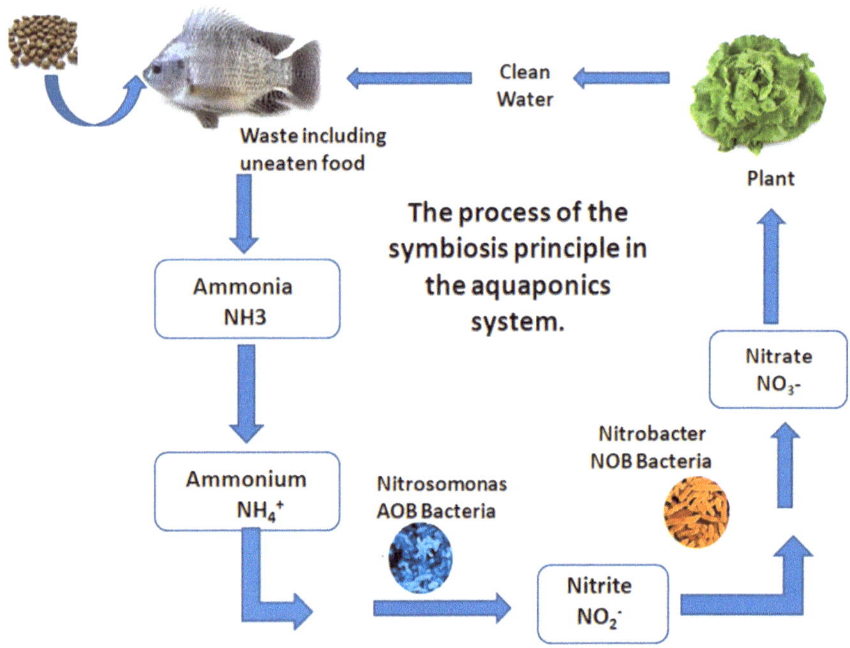

Fig. 16.2 The summary of the process of the symbiosis principle in the aquaponics system

plants with more extensive root structures or by unfiltered aquaculture wastes (Silva et al. 2015).

16.3.3.2 Floating Raft (Deep Water Culture)

Deep Water Culture (DWC) is a hydroponic technique that continuously supplies nutrient-rich water to the plants' roots, keeping them constantly submerged in water and oxygen (Forchino et al. 2017). The DWC system has the advantage of being highly oxygenated, using less fertiliser, and having low maintenance costs and monitoring time (Domingues et al. 2012; Wongkiew et al. 2017). Because it allows plants to absorb nutrients directly from the water, DWC is commonly used in aquaponics.

16.3.3.3 Media BED TEChnique

Media-filled bed units are the most common design for small-scale aquaponics. This method is highly recommended for most developing countries, as these designs are space-efficient, have a low initial cost, and are suitable for beginners due to their simplicity. The medium in media bed units is used to support the roots of the plants, and the same medium also serves as a filter, both mechanical and biological (Somerville et al. 2014).

16.3.4 Aquaponics: Approaches, Production Scales, System Designs

The following table presents an overview of the various approaches and system designs, as well as production scales that characterize aquaponics.

16.4 Aquaponics and the Sustainable Development Goals

The United Nations defined the Sustainable Development Goals (SDGs), a global agenda adopted in September 2015, with 17 goals to be achieved by 2030. These objectives include actions to eradicate poverty, promote prosperity and well-being for all, protect the environment and natural resources, and combat climate change. Aquaponics can directly contribute to the achievement of the SDGs, specifically SDGs 1, end poverty, SDGs 2, zero hunger and sustainable agriculture, which address the need to disseminate actions that promote food security; SDG 6, which aims to ensure the availability and sustainable management of water, SDG 8 for growth and employment, and SDG 12 which addresses responsible consumption and aims to ensure sustainable production and consumption patterns.SDG 13 for climate change resilience and water stewardship, as well as SDG 14 for marine resource conservation and sustainable use, are all highly relevant to aquaponics development (FAO 2017b).

16.5 Benefits of Aquaponics

A proper discussion regarding the sustainable development of the aquaponics technique requires the inclusion of three inseparable aspects: social, economic, and environmental issues.

16.5.1 Economic Benefits

Aquaponics has enormous potential as a sustainable solution, as it has shown promising results for the development of food production while also providing new opportunities for entrepreneurship and business creation (El-Essawy et al.

2019). Several studies (Goda et al. 2015; Sunny et al. 2019) have concluded that the revenues obtained can essentially cover the costs of aquaponics production. Other authors (Quagrainie et al. 2017; Greenfeld et al. 2018; Rizal et al. 2018) claim that the larger the aquaponics system, the more profitable it is, which appears to be true for many large-scale commercial systems.

16.5.2 Social Benefits

Aquaponics has a significant impact on several social dimensions, including health, well-being, and education (Hart Emily et al. 2013). It was also shown to facilitate community cohesion, another potential social dimension (Konig et al. 2016). Other potential social impacts of aquaponics include (1) improved community food security with a relatively inexpensive source of protein, (2) inspiration in design and personal conception of aquaponics farms, (3) income generation, and (4) job creation with better working conditions (Specht et al. 2014).

16.5.3 Environmental Benefits

To reduce the negative environmental impacts of agriculture, it is preferable to use more efficient methods to reduce waste disposal and recycle nutrients, significantly save energy, and reduce gas emissions within the system (Beddington 2011). Agriculture and aquaculture production currently occupies a large area across the mainland and aquatic environments, where it has a significant negative impact, causing soil erosion, soil and groundwater pollution from pesticides, fertilisers, and animal waste, as well as the production of greenhouse gases (Goudie and Heather 2013). The combination of crop production and aquaculture within aquaponics systems reduces the environmental impact significantly. Moreover, aquaponics can also help to reduce freshwater depletion by encouraging sustainable farming and food production practices (Greenlee 2009). Aquaponics has the potential to be an essential component of the "blue and green" water paradigm. Furthermore, it is possible to incorporate it into the local water cycle using treated grey water and rainwater instead of freshwater (Vadiee and Martin 2012).

6. The New Perspectives of Aquaponics in Morocco

Aquaponics systems are good candidates to respond to the challenges posed by Morocco's population growth, climate fluctuations the country often faces as well as limited access to water resources for agricultural activities. It is also a valuable tool to help design new models of the Moroccan agricultural system. One example is the case of the aquaculture industry. Like other human activities, its problems concern the scientific community in many ways, principally for its large waste discharges into the environment along with its accelerative growth rate (Martins et al. 2010).

Table 16.3 Water quality parameters of the aquaponics system tested in Morocco

		Experimental days					
		0	7	15	22	28	35
	Inlet	0.84 ± 0.05	0.99± 0.02	0.99 ± 0.06	0.96 ± 0.02	0.93 ± 0.04	0.97 ± 0.02
NH_3	Outlet	0.62 ± 0.08	0.82 ± 0.11	0.83 ± 0.02	0.76 ± 0.01	0.72 ± 0.13	0.85 ± 0.01
	% reduction	26.05	17.27	16.16	20.82	22.51	12.37
	Inlet	0.050 ± 0.004	0.061 ± 0.001	0.062 ± 0.005	0.070 ± 0.005	0.068 ± 0.002	0.067 ± 0.001
NO_{2-}	Oulet	0.042 ± 0.004	0.052 ± 0.001	0.054 ± 0.008	0.063 ± 0.005	0.060 ± 0.005	0.060 ± 0.001
	% reduction	16	12.90	14.76	10.01	11.76	10.45
	Inlet	48.92 ± 0.19	56.02 ± 0.22	60.98 ± 0.18	76.62 ± 0.32	79.99 ± ± 0.53	89.02 ± 0.45
NO_{3-}	Outlet	40.02 ± 0.15	45.22 ± 0.10	52.22 ± 0.08	66.92 ± ± 0.15	69.09 ± 0.21	78.12 ± 0.45
	% reduction	18.19	19.27	14.61	12.65	13.62	12.24

Thanks to the results obtained in this field, aquaponics has demonstrated sustainability benefits which will allow Morocco to develop economically viable aquaponic systems capable of cultivating species at variable densities, even with an unfavourable climatic regime and limited water availability.

Aquaponics is currently being tested and promoted in several countries across five continents, where the technology has improved and adapted to various conditions such as climate, cultivated species, and production costs, among others (Goddek et al. 2019a; b).

Except for one study on a small-scale aquaponics production system to produce a combined crop of carp and plants, experimental systems and commercial aquaponics farms have never been tested in Morocco, and research on aquaponics systems has so far been entirely theoretical and restricted to small-scales (El Bakali, 2022a, b). In this experiment, a DWC aquaponics system was installed and effluents from a Silver carp (*Hypophthalmichthys molitrix*) tank were redirected to plants (lettuce, pepper, mint). As mentioned above, bacteria transform in this process fish waste into nutrients that plants can absorb. The fish tank is then refilled with purified water. Each plant's height was measured once a week together with dissolved oxygen, pH, water temperature, NO3−, NO2−, and NH3 concentrations.

Fish growth was assessed using body weight and total length. The study reached encouraging results, particularly the evaluation of nitrogen removal efficiency and its effect on fish and plant growth rates (Table 16.3). The growth rates of fish and plants were remarkable, with no pathological abnormalities observed in fish. During the experiment, the mean growth of Silver carp had significantly improved ($P < 0.05$).

The average final length was 18.25 ± 1.89 cm, and the average weight was 85.06 ± 20.10 g. Plants grew quickly despite the absence of pesticides or fertiliser (the height was between 2.11 cm and 4.05 cm). Additionally, the water quality was excellent in terms of water temperature (19–22 °C), pH (6–7.3). This study found that using an aquaponics system had a significant impact on nitrogen reduction ($NO2-$ (12.6%), $NH3$ (19.04%), and $NO3-$ (15.1%). (Table 16.3).

Several reviews on the subject have been conducted, two of which have been published, to establish a database that can be used when establishing aquaponics and integrated aquaculture projects. One of them (El Bakali and Aba (2021) discussed using aquaculture phosphorus waste in integrated aquaculture. These discharges are pollutants that contribute to the eutrophication of aquatic environments, but they also contain macro-elements required for fish feeding and fertilisers for soil fertilisation. Therefore, exploitation of these effluents is required to ensure the aquaculture sector's environmental sustainability in the context of integrated aquaculture with agriculture. The other (Aba & El Bakali 2020) investigates the advantages of integrating aquaculture with irrigation in water resource rationalisation. Indeed, the water scarcity threatening agriculture in Morocco, as well as the desire to increase productivity while considering the environmental impacts of this production sector, necessitates the development and adoption of a more sustainable agricultural model based on ecological and socioeconomic considerations. Integrating aquaculture with irrigation is an excellent way to reduce nutrient discharge and convert aquaculture wastes into valuable agricultural products. Using aquaculture effluents for irrigation would be an unprecedented step forward in Morocco, ensuring food security and establishing a resilient foundation to the challenges posed by climate change.

16.6 Conclusion

Aquaponics is a sustainable food production technology that, despite its usage for several years in other countries, is not widely known in Morocco. Aquaponics exhibits the prospect for the sustainable development of food production in Morocco, as it can serve as an essential component of sustainable rural infrastructure, in line with current public policies, particularly when taking into account the implemented strategies for the sustainable development of the agricultural sector in Morocco, the climate variations that country is experiencing, and the scarcity of water resources. Within the framework of implementing this new technique in Morocco, it would be prudent to inventory the potentialities of each region, conduct pilot studies, and ensure the training of agricultural personnel. One of the main advantages of this type of innovative technology is that it can be adapted on a small or large scale while taking up minimal space, resulting in a significant positive socioeconomic impact at the local level with no negative environmental consequences.

The use of aquaponics as an agroecological alternative is an approach that aims to strengthen the resilience of Morocco's farming sector, as farmers are the first victims of climate fluctuations by providing a sustainable and inclusive response to nutritional issues and a better rationalisation of water resource use. Furthermore, aquaponics as an agroecological alternative paves the way for establishing the sustainable triad, which includes social, environmental, and economic aspects.

References

Aba M, Belghyti D, Benabid M (2014) The main species of freshwater fish aquaculture interest in Morocco, current status and prospects. Int J Fish Aquat Stud 2(1):216–218

Agence de Développement Agricole (ADA) (2021) Plan Maroc Vert (PMV). ADA, Rabat. Available at http://www.ada.gov.ma/PlanMarocVert.php (Accessed 03 July 2021)

Al-Tawaha AR, Al-Karaki G, Sirajuddin SN, Makhadmeh I, Wahab PEM, Youssef RA, Al Sultan W, Massadeh A (2018) Effect of water flow rate on quantity and quality of lettuce (Lactuca sativa L.) in nutrient film technique (NFT) under hydroponics conditions. Bulg J Agric Sci 24:793–800

Azeroual A (2003) Monographie des poissons des eaux continentales du Maroc: Systématique, Distribution et Ecologie. Université Mohammed V Agdal. Faculté Des Sciences Rabat; p 164

Beddington SJ (2011) The future of food and farming. Int J Agric Manag 1(2):2–6

Belahsen S, Khellaf A, Belahsen M (2016), Evaluation de la stratégie agricole du Maroc (Plan Maroc Vert): Une analyse en équilibre général dynamique, in Dossiers de Recherches en Economie et Gestion, No. 5 (June), pp 13–46

Belghazi S, Sarraf M (2017) Littoral, Le Coût de la Dégradation de l'Environnement au Maroc, environment and natural resources global Practice discussion Paper #5. Groupe de la Banque Mondiale, Janvier, p 104

Bouchaou L, Tagma T, Boutaleb S, Hssaisoune M, El Morjani ZEA (2011) Climate change and its impacts on groundwater resources in Morocco: the case of the souss- massa basin. climate change effect on groundwater resource. A Glob Synth Find Recomm; pp 129–144

Conijn JG, Bindraban PS, Schröder JJ, Jongschaap REE (2018) Can our global food system meet food demand within planetary boundaries? Agric Ecosyst Environ 251:244–256

Corner R, Fersoy H, Crespi V (eds) (2020) Integrated agri-aquaculture in desert and arid lands: Learning from case studies from Algeria, Egypt and Oman. Fisheries and Aquaculture Circular No. 1195. Cairo, FAO. https://doi.org/10.4060/ca8610en

Daims H, Lebedeva EV, Pjevac P, Han P, Herbold C, Albertsen M, Jehmlich N, Palatinszky M, Vierheilig J, Bulaev A, Kirkegaard RH, von Bergen M, Rattei T, Bendinger B, Nielsen PH, Wagner M (2015) Complete nitrification by Nitrospira bacteria. Nature 528:555–559

Delaide B, Delhaye G, Dermience M, Gott J, Soyeurt H, Jijakli MH (2017) Plant and fish production performance, nutrient mass balances, energy and water use of the PAFF Box, a small-scale aquaponic system. J Aquac Eng Fish Res 78:130–139

Domingues DS, Takahashi HW, Camara CAP, Nixdorf SL (2012) Automated system developed to control pH and concentration of nutrient solution evaluated in hydroponic lettuce production Comput. Electron Agric 84:53–61. https://doi.org/10.1016/j.compag.2012.02.006

Douglas JS (1975) Hydroponics, 5th edn. Bombay, Oxford, pp 1–3

Doukkali M, Kamili A (2018) Système Marocain de Production Halieutique et sa dépendance du Reste du Monde/ Moroccan Fishing Production System and its dependence on the rest of the World. RP-18/07

El Bakali M (2022a) Aquaponics systems for reuse water in continental fish farms: preliminary study of the feasibility of its introduction in Morocco. Paper presented at the Aquaculture Canada and WAS North America 2022, St Johns, Newfoundland, Canada, August 15–18, 2022

El Bakali M (2022b) Aquaponics systems for reuse water in continental fish farms: preliminary study of the feasibility of its introduction in Morocco. Paper presented at the aquaculture Africa 2021, Alexandria, Egypt, March 25–28, 2022
El Bakali M, Aba M (2021) Phosphorus waste production in fish farming a potential for reuse in integrated aquaculture agriculture. Int J Environ Agric Res 7:5–13
El-Essawy H, Nasr P, Sewilam H (2019) Aquaponics: a sustainable alternative to conventional agriculture in Egypt – a pilot scale investigation. Environ Sci Pollut Res 26:15872–15883. https://doi.org/10.1007/s11356-019-04970-0
Engle CR (2015) Economics of aquaponics South. Reg Aquac Cent; pp 1–4
Espinosa-Moya A, Álvarez-gonzález A, Albertos-alpuche P (2018) Growth and development of herbaceous plants in aquaponic systems. Acta Univ Multidisp Sci J 28:1–8
FAO (2016) The state of food and agriculture: Climate change, agriculture and food security. Author, Rome. ISBN 978-92-5-109374-0
FAO (2017a) The future of food and agriculture - trends and challenges, Rome, p 180
FAO (2017b) Food and agriculture. In: Driving action across the 2030 agenda for sustainable development, Rome, p 40
FAO (2020) The State of World Fisheries and Aquaculture 2020. Sustainability in action. Rome
Forchino AA, Lourguioui H, Brigolin D, Pastres R (2017) Aquaponics and sustainability: The comparison of two different aquaponic techniques using the Life Cycle Assessment (LCA). Aquac Eng 77:80–88
Foucard Pierre, Tocqueville Aurélien, Baroiller Jean-François, Gaumé Matthieu, Labbé Laurent, Lejolivet Catherine. 2019. Aquaponie : Associer aquaculture et production végétale. Versailles : Ed. Quae, 209 p. (Savoir faire) ISBN 978-2-7592-2964-2
Fróna D, Szenderák J, Harangi-Rákos M (2019) The challenge of feeding the world. Sustainability 11:5816
Goda AMAS, Essa MA, Hassaan MS, Sharawy Z (2015) Bio economic features for aquaponic systems in egypt. Turk J Fish Aquat Sci 15:525–532
Goddek S, Delaide B, Mankasingh U, Ragnarsdottir K, Jijakli H, Thorarinsdottir R (2015) Challenges of sustainable and commercial aquaponics. Sustainability 7:4199–4224. https://doi.org/10.3390/su7044199
Goddek S, Joyce A, Kotzen B, Dos-Santos M (2019a) Aquaponics and global food challenges. In: Goddek S, Joyce A, Kotzen B, Burnell GM (eds) AQUAPONICS Food Production Systems, 1st edn. Springer, Cham, pp 3–17. https://doi.org/10.1007/978-3-030-15943-6_1
Goddek S, Joyce A, Kotzen B, Dos-Santos M (2019b) Aquaponics and global food challenges. In: Aquaponics food production systems. Springer, Cham, pp 3–17
Goudie AS, Heather V (2013) The earth transformed: an introduction to human impacts on the environment. John Wiley & Sons, New York
Greenfeld A, Becker N, McIlwain J, Fotedar R, Bornman JF (2018) Economically viable aquaponics? Identifying the gap between potential and current uncertainties. Rev Aquac 11: 848–862
Greenlee LF (2009) Reverse osmosis desalination: water sources, technology, and today's challenges. Water Res 43(9):2317–2348
Hamed Y, Hadji R, Redhaounia B et al (2018) Climate impact on surface and groundwater in North Africa: a global synthesis of findings and recommendations. Euro-Mediterr J Environ Integr 3: 25. https://doi.org/10.1007/s41207-018-0067-8
Harbouze R, Pellissier JP, Rolland WK (2019) Rapport de synthèse sur l'agriculture au Maroc. [Rapport de recherche] CIHEAM-IAMM. pp 104. ffhal-02137637f
Hart Emily R, James B, Webb AJ, Danylchuk A (2013) Implementation of aquaponics in education: an assessment of challenges and solutions. Sci Educ Int 24(4):460–480
Kaddioui A, Idhalla M, Kassila J, El Mdari M, Belhsen O, Errhif A (2018) Aquaculture in morocco: growth performance of *crassostrea gigas* in two lagoons on the Atlantic shore Int. J Adv Res 6(11):243–254

Kasozi N, Abraham B, Kaiser H et al (2021) The complex microbiome in aquaponics: significance of the bacterial ecosystem. Ann Microbiol 71:1. https://doi.org/10.1186/s13213-020-01613-5
Knaus U, Palm HW (2017a) Effects of fish biology on ebb and flow aquaponical cultured herbs in northern Germany (Mecklenburg Western Pomerania). Aquaculture 466:51–63. https://doi.org/10.1016/j.aquaculture.2016.09.025
Knaus U, Palm HW (2017b) Effects of the fish species choice on vegetables in aquaponics under spring-summer conditions in northern Germany (Mecklenburg Western Pomerania). Aquaculture 473:62–73. https://doi.org/10.1016/j.aquaculture.2017.01.020
Konig B, Junge R, Bittsanszky A, Villarroel M, Komives T (2016) On the sustainability of aquaponics. Ecocycles 2:26–32
Love DC, Fry JP, Li X, Hill ES, Genello J, Semmens K, Thompson RE (2015) Commercial aquaponics production and profitability: findings from an international survey. Aquaculture 435:67–74
Martins C, Eding E, Verdegem M, Heinsbroek L, Schneider O, Blancheton J, D'orbcastel ER, Verreth J (2010) New developments in recirculating aquaculture systems in Europe: a perspective on environmental sustainability. Aquac Eng 43:83–93
Mustapha ABA, El Bakali M (2020) The benefits of the integration of aquaculture and irrigation for an efficient use of blue water in order to strengthen food safety in Morocco. IOSR J Agric Vet Sci (IOSRJAVS) 13(12):01–09
Rapport d'activité du Département de la Pêche Maritime (2019). Ministère de l'Agriculture, de la'Pêche Maritime,du Développement Rural et des Eaux et ForêtsDépartement de la Pêche Maritime, p 82
Mouslih M (1987) Introduction de poissons et d'ecrevisses au Maroc. Hydrobiol Trop 20(1):65–72
Obirikorang KA, Sekey W, Gyampoh BA, Ashiagbor G, Asante W (2021) Aquaponics for improved food security in africa: a review. Front Sustain Food Syst:5. https://doi.org/10.3389/fsufs.2021.705549
Pollard G, Ward JD, Koth B (2017) Aquaponics in urban agriculture: social acceptance. Horticulturae 3(2):39
Quagrainie KK, Flores RMV, Kim HJ, McClain V (2017) Economic analysis of aquaponics and hydroponics production in the U.S. Midwest. J Appl Aquac 30:1–14
Rakocy JE, Masser MP, Losordo TM (2006) Recirculating aquaculture tank production systems: Aquaponics- integrating fish and plant culture. Southern Regional Aquaculture Center Publication 454:16
Rapport d'activité du Département de la Pêche Maritime (2019). Ministère de l'Agriculture, de la Pêche Maritime, du Développement Rural et des Eaux et Forêts Département de la Pêche Maritime. p 82
Rizal A, Dhahiyat Y, Zahidah AY, Handaka AA, Sahidin A (2018) The economic and social benefits of an aquaponic system for the integrated production of fish and water plants. IOP Conf Series: Earth Environ Sci 137:012098. https://doi.org/10.1088/1755-1315/137/1/012098
Savvas D (2003) Hydroponics: A modern technology supporting the application of integrated crop management in greenhouse. Food Agric Environ 1:80–86
Schilling J, Freier KP, Hertig E, Scheffran J (2012) Climate change, vulnerability and adaptation in North Africa with focus on morocco. Agric Ecosyst Environ 156:12–26
Schmautz Z, Graber A, Jaenicke S, Goesmann A, Junge R, Smits THM (2017) Microbial diversity in different compartments of an aquaponics system. Arch Microbiol 199:613–620
Schreier HJ, Mirzoyan N, Saito K (2010) Microbial diversity of biological filters in recirculating aquaculture systems. Curr Opin Biotechnol 21:318–325
Silva L, Eucario GL, Escalante E, Fitzsimmons KM, Lozano DV (2015) Evaluation of biomass yield and water treatment in two aquaponic systems using the dynamic root floating technique (DRF). Sustainability 7:15384–15399
Somerville C, Cohen M, Pantanella E, Stankus A, Lovatelli A (2014) Small-scale aquaponic food production: Integrated fish and plant farming. FAO Fish Aquac Tech Pap; p 589

Specht K, Siebert R, Hartmann I, Freisinger UB, Sawicka M, Werner A, Thomaier S, Henckel D, Walk H, Dierich A (2014) Urban agriculture of the future: an overview of sustainability aspects of food production in and on buildings. Agric Hum Values 31:33–51

Sunny AR, Islam MM, Rahman M, Miah MY, Mostafiz M, Islam N, Hossain MZ, Chowdhury MA, Islam MA, Keus HJ (2019) Cost effective aquaponics for food security and income of farming households in coastal Bangladesh. Egypt J Aquat Res 45:89–97

Thorarinsdottir RI (2015) Aquaponics guidelines, Haskolaprent, Iceland

Toumi L (2016) Sustainable food security in Morocco: challenges & opportunities. AGROFOR Int J 1(1):30–40

Vadiee A, Martin V (2012) Energy management in horticultural applications through the closed greenhouse concept, state of the art. Renew Sustain Energy Rev 16:5087–5100

Watten BJ, Busch RL (1984) Tropical production of tilapia (*Sarotherodon aurea*) and tomatoes (*Lycopersicon esculentum*) in a small-scale recirculating water system. Aquaculture 41(3): 271–283

Wongkiew S, Hu Z, Chandran K, Lee JW, Khanal SK (2017) Aquaponic systems for sustainable resource recovery: linking nitrogen transformations to microbial communities. Aquac Eng 76: 9–19

Zou Y, Hu Z, Zhang J, Xie H, Guimbaud C, Fang Y (2016) Effects of pH on nitrogen transformations in media-based aquaponics. Bioresour Technol 210:81–87

Chapter 17
Enhancing Food Production Employing Integrated Aquaculture in Namibia. Fish Integration with Poultry

Medusalem Jairus

Abstract The global human population is increasing, putting pressure on several resources that are key to sufficient food production. Current agricultural practices are not efficient in food security for the projected world population; hence new food production technologies such as aquaculture integration must be practised. Aquaculture integration has the potential to increase food productivity and come to the rescue of Africa's fish food security crisis. Fish-poultry farming is a sustainable integrated farming system that involves raising birds such as chicken, duck, geese, and fish simultaneously. In this type of integration, poultry excreta are used as fish feed since it contains nutrients that are needed for fish pond fertilisation, which increases the pond's productivity. It has been found that there is a more efficient use of resources when integrating aquaculture with poultry compared to farming with fish alone, with the costs related to fish culture processes reduced by about 70%. However, this farming system has not gained so much recognition in Africa. Therefore, this chapter highlighted how food production could be enhanced using integrated aquaculture, with specific reference to fish integration with poultry farming in the Namibian context.

Keywords Aquaculture · Integration · Sustainability · Poultry · Food production

17.1 Introduction

Food security is one of the most vital and fundamental to human existence and survival. The global population is rising, and existing agricultural practices cannot guarantee food security in the near future. An approximation has been made that food production will be required to double by 2030 to sustain the anticipated human global population (Zajdband 2011). Thus, alternative food production techniques

M. Jairus (✉)
Department of Fisheries and Ocean Sciences, Sam Nujoma Campus, University of Namibia, Henties Bay, Namibia

© The Author(s), under exclusive license to Springer Nature Singapore Pte Ltd. 2023

N. N. Gabriel et al. (eds.), *Emerging Sustainable Aquaculture Innovations in Africa*, Sustainable Agriculture and Food Security,
https://doi.org/10.1007/978-981-19-7451-9_17

should be considered to avail sufficient food for human consumption. While considering other possibilities for food production maximisation, it should be noted that such techniques are sustainable and environmentally friendly. Traditional farming systems are proven capable of producing food in an environmentally sound manner (Herrero et al. 2010), and these may include some commonly practised farming systems in the aquaculture sector.

Aquaculture is one of the fastest sectors and means of food production globally. In 2014, aquaculture is said to have bypassed capture fisheries to become the major source of fish food for human consumption. Moreover, in 2016, global aquaculture production was estimated at 110.2 million metric tonnes (Tran et al. 2020). Aquaculture and capture fisheries have played a significant role in contributing to global food security (Center for Food Security, CFS 2014). However, due to the pressure imposed on wild fisheries using anthropogenic effects, such as illegal, unreported, and unregulated (IUU) fishing and the use of fish meal as feed in aquaculture (Choi et al. 2020), food security in this sector is expected to be reduced. Thus, meeting the increasing demand for fish in the future will continue to depend on the capacity to further expand aquaculture production sustainably (Tran et al. 2020). Aquaculture integration has the potential to increase food productivity and come to the rescue of Africa's fish food security crisis since Asia accounts for most of the aquaculture food production globally (FAO 2017).

Aquaculture integration is the farming of fish with either animal or crop husbandry. Integrated culture is not a new farming practice, but it also exists naturally. The natural ecosystem is a great example of integrated culturing where several plants and animals live together in the same area of land (Reddy and Kishori 2018). Integrated fish farming is a type of farming practice commonly practised in East and Southeast Asian countries, and it is one of the powerful and stable sustainable technologies (Gebru 2021). This farming system has not gained so much recognition in Africa. However, some progress on integrated aquaculture systems has been reported in a few African countries, such as vegetable fish farming in Ghana and Malawi (Gebru 2021). There are different aquaculture integration practices, and fish integration with poultry is one of them. Hence this chapter highlights how food production could be maximised through integrated aquaculture, with reference to fish integration with poultry farming.

17.2 Fish-Poultry Integration System

Fish-poultry farming is an integrated farming system that involves raising birds such as chicken, duck, geese, and fish concurrently. The waste or excreta from poultry serves as feed for the fishes in the fertilised pond (Adeyemi et al. 2022). Fish-poultry farming is still an understudied area in the field of land-use practice. However, this farming system is progressively becoming tolerable and popular among farmers (Adeyemi et al. 2022). The setup of a fish-cum-poultry farming system depends on the farmer's choice. It may also depend on the availability of materials to build a poultry house.

It is recommended that the poultry house is constructed over or adjacent to the fish pond to ensure maximum utilisation of poultry excreta (Gebru 2021). Raising chicken over the fish pond maximises land use, and the poultry house is always hygienic. The chicken house is built so that chicken excreta fall directly into the fish pond. Poultry manure is known to contain more nutrients than other livestock wastes. Based on Sana (2011), it naturally contains less moisture, fibre and compounds such as fish pond fertilisers. Much of the nutrient-constituting feedstuff supplied to poultry is discharged as urinary or faecal waste. The nutrients can then be utilised as pond fertiliser to stimulate the formation of natural nutritional organisms like phytoplankton and detritus (Sana 2011). The tropics, such as in Namibia, where average temperatures persist over 25 °C, are perfect for farming with fish using poultry excreta as a nutrient; however, this practice is also feasible in subtropical and lower-temperature (>20 °C) environments in appropriate seasons of the year (Sana 2011).

The proportion of nitrogen and phosphorus discharge, predominantly in the utmost existing forms (liquified inorganic nitrogen, dissolvable volatile phosphorus), has been employed as an indicator of faecal quality for fertilisation of fish pools (Little and Satapornvanit 1996). The feed constituents fed to poultry can affect the consequent manure value and emission of nutrients for fishpond fertilisation. For instance, manure attained from foraging Muscovy ducks fed different levels of a rice cellulose supplement (100, 75 and 50% of ad libitum) had different emission characteristics (Little and Satapornvanit 1996). Therefore, to avoid over-fertilisation of the fish pond, it is essential to understand what poultry integrated with fish consumes.

17.3 Significances of Fish-Poultry Integration

As a farmer, one always looks forward to maximising their gains by minimising farming inputs. Uddin et al. (1998), claimed that the integration of aquaculture with poultry results in more efficient use of resources than farming with fish alone. The costs related to fish culture processes are lessened by about 70% (Uddin et al. 1998) when integrated with chickens since fish farming uses chicken waste and excess chicken feed as food and fertiliser for the fish pond. A comparative study by Shoko et al. (2019), found out that, gross fish yield, net fish yield and net annual yields attained from fish-poultry integration were significantly higher than the yields from the non-integrated system. Additionally, their (Shoko et al. 2019) partial enterprise budget analysis indicated that fish-poultry integration was more lucrative than the non-integrated system.

The integration of poultry-fish agriculture gives chances to the families with a lack of resources with little monetary investments and resolves the matters of women empowerment and living security at the gross root level (Gangwar et al. 2013). The practice of integrating poultry and fish can give prospects for living standards and food security to the families of Namibian rural areas too. The implementation of combined poultry-fish agrobusiness in various arrangements such as intensive broiler farming, backyard poultry agrobusiness, etc. leads to the protection of natural resources and the creation of supplementary revenue or employment opportunities, particularly for the youths and female labourers in the communities (Gangwar et al. 2013). Some studies have indicated that traditional aquaculture production systems are wasteful and unprofitable, unlike integration systems (Olapade et al. 2017). The productivity of any aquatic body is generally linked to the quality and quantity of plankton available, which are crucial to fish production as they serve as fish food. Thus, poultry excreta increase pond biological productivity, resulting in increased fish production (Gebru 2021).

Fish-poultry integrated systems could be an excellent remedial action to use fishmeal as a feed component in aquaculture production. Fish meal is in demand not only for fish feed production but also for poultry and livestock feed production (Ngugi et al. 2017). Based on Ayoola (2010), aquaculture feeds usually contain a more significant percentage of fishmeal than other animal diets. Thus, calls for sustainable aquaculture have been made, where aquaculture can grow without putting pressure on wild fish stocks (Choi et al. 2020). It has thus been introduced when fish nutritionists and scientists look for alternative ingredients to replace fishmeal completely or partially (Ayoola 2010). Fish-poultry farming would then come in by fully replacing synthesised aquaculture feed, including fishmeal incorporated feed, with poultry excreta as feed or as a fish pond fertilisation agent.

17.4 Constraints in Aquaculture Integration

The integrated poultry-fish aspect of farming is still very new compared to other farming methods, such as mixed farming or rotational farming, which have been in existence for over a hundred years ago (Abiona et al. 2011). As a result of this, there is a necessity for more subject matter specialists in this area of farming to contribute speedy dissemination of information to practising and intending farmers in the coming years. Furthermore, the extent to which integrated fish farming could maximise farmers' revenues is inhibited by problems observed during farming operations. In a study by Abiona et al. (2011), most respondents identified inadequate finance as a significant problem, with 91.2% recorded for integrated fish farmers and 82.7 for nonintegrated fish farmers.

In the Namibian farming context, the case is very similar to Abiona et al. (2011)'s study; there are little to no funds to get this type of farming blooming, especially in rural areas. More farmers are involved in poultry farming, which is mostly domestication than they are involved in fish farming or both. However, to increase food production, especially in rural areas of Namibia, farmers should consider making use of available organic materials to construct poultry houses over fish ponds. Fish ponds could be in the form of earthen ponds, which are only burrowed into the ground and not constructed with concrete since the cost of concrete and labour would be high. There is a general view that well-off farmers with good farming skills and enough investment tend to intensify their farming systems, while the poorer farmers tend to move in the direction of diversification (Phong 2010). Thus, the poorer farmers need financial support, for instance, from the government, to diversify their farming on a larger scale. There is a necessity for discrete government financial support in the form of subsidies for the sustainable advancement of combined poultry-fish agriculture in African rural areas.

Water is one input that must be there for successful poultry-fish integrated farming. Global water coverage is estimated to be approximately 71%, but only 3% is freshwater (Bhandari 2003), and freshwater is essential for this type of farming. Almost one-fifth of the world's population lives in areas of physical water scarcity, and 500 million people are approaching this state (Nashima et al. 2013). Water scarcity is one of the constraints in poultry-fish integration farming in areas where rainfall is seasonal or dry areas such as most parts of Namibia. Smallholder farmers may be willing to get involved in such innovative and sustainable farming practices, yet they are faced with such challenges. This challenge may as well be tackled in different ways, and rainwater harvesting is one of them.

Rainwater harvesting is a method of collecting rainwater from natural or man-made surfaces to be stored and used for productive purposes such as human and livestock consumption, irrigation, and household tasks (Baker et al. 2007). Rainwater harvesting for agricultural purposes has gained some recognition recently (Eseoghene 2019), although less has been discussed it being used in aquaculture. Harvested rainwater is used mainly in the domestic, agricultural, and industrial sectors (Rahman et al. 2019). Thus, it can be a perfect solution for farmers willing to integrate poultry with fish to maximise their returns. Additionally, rainwater is said to involve less to no costs in harvesting, and it is also safe for agricultural purposes (Nashima et al. 2013).

17.5 Controversies around Aquaculture Integration

Although aquaculture integration, regarding poultry-fish integration, is promising in food security, it has been looked at with different opinions globally. Public health alarms have been raised about this specific integration on several occasions. The risks of direct pathogen transfer to humans in fishponds fertilised with manures, whether consumers, producers, or intermediaries, have been most evaluated (Little and Satapornvanit 1996). There have also been implicit connections between integrated livestock-fish systems and influenza pandemics (Maclean 1993). This distressing concept has therefore led to general commentaries and debates on the desirability and effects of integrated farming. As per Little and Satapornvanit (1996), the decisive eutrophication of water, leading to blooms of lethal blue-green algae, has also been pointed out as a problem. Although the possibility of intoxicating fish and mammals from poultry-waste fertilised water exists, their controlled use in fish ponds decreases the likelihood of contamination to other water bodies (Little and Satapornvanit 1996). Gabriel et al. (2007) have pointed out Cyanobacterial blooms to be undesirable in aquatic ponds because they are relatively poor aquatic food bases. In addition, such blooms are poor oxygenators of pond waters, with some species producing odorous metabolites, giving the cultured fish species an undesirable flavour (Gabriel et al. 2007).

17.6 Conclusion and Recommendations

Gebru (2021) recommended that the most suitable fish species for fish-poultry integration are those that can filter feed on phytoplankton and zooplankton from the water. Species including silver carp (*Hypophthalmichthys molitrix*), common carp (*Cyprinus carpio*), grass carp (*Ctenopharyngodon idella*) and tilapia (*Oreochromis spp.*) have been pointed out. It is also recommended that the poultry house be inside and raised over the pond (Fig. 17.1) or beside the pond since it allows poultry manure to fall directly into the pond thereby allowing the poultry house to be clean (Gabriel et al. 2007). Several studies have recommended chickens as the birds suitable for fish-poultry integration compared to other birds, including ducks and geese. In most cases, layer chickens have been identified to be suitable; however, broilers can also be utilised in such integrative practices. Olapade et al. (2017) have recommended that to maximise farm profits in aquaculture integration, a triple integration system must be chosen. They suggested a fish, rice cum poultry

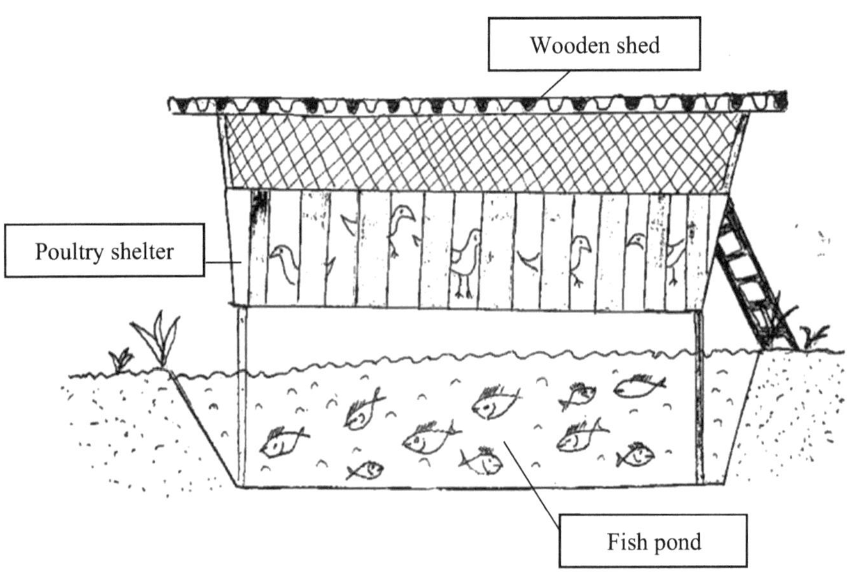

Fig. 17.1 The poultry-fish integration setup

system, which simply involves the raising of birds, culturing of fish (*Clarias gariepinus*) and alternatively the cultivation of rice. In Namibia, this type of integration would be appropriate in the Zambezi and Kavango regions because they are adjacent to rivers with plenty of water for rice cultivation.

Integrated aquaculture systems have not gained so much attention in the African agricultural sectors, yet it has so much potential for food security. This type of farming, about fish-poultry integration, has been found to reduce the farm's production costs. Some studies have indicated that traditional aquaculture production systems are wasteful and unprofitable, unlike integration systems. Poultry excreta increase pond biological productivity, resulting in increased fish production. The tropics, such as in Namibia, where average temperatures remain above 25 °C, are perfect for culturing fish with poultry concurrently. Nevertheless, various constraints exist in this farming practice, including short of funds and the water scarcity problem. On top of that, fish-poultry integration has also been linked to controversies, such as public health anxieties, including the risk of direct pathogen transfer to humans in fishponds fertilised with manures. However, the controlled use of chicken manure and proper pond management is key to the success of fish-poultry integration.

References

Abiona BG, Fakoya EO, Alegbeleye WO, Fapojuwo EO, Adeogun SO, Idowu AA, Aromolaran AK (2011) Constraints to integrated and non-integrated fish farming activities in Ogun State, Nigeria. J Agric Sci 3(4):233

Adeyemi FM, Ojo OO, Badejo AA, Oyedara OO, Olaitan JO, Adetunji CO, Akinde SB (2022) Integrated poultry-fish farming system encourages multidrug-resistant gram-negative bacteria dissemination in pond environment and fishes. Aquaculture 548:737558

Ayoola A (2010) Replacement of Fishmeal with Alternative Protein Sources in Aquaculture Diets. Master of Science thesis, North Calorina State University

Baker SW, Opperman GL, Summers EA (2007) Rainwater harvesting in informal settlements of Windhoek, Namibia. BSc Thesis, Worcester Polytechnic Institute, United States

Bhandari BB (2003) "What is happening to our Freshwater Resources? Institute for Global Strategies. Environmental Education project". Tokyo

Centre for Food Security, High Level Panel (CFS, H) (2014) Sustainable Fisheries and Aquaculture for Food Security and Nutrition: A Report by the High-Level Panel of Experts on Food Security and Nutrition of the Committee on World Food Security. Rome

Choi DG, He M, Fang H, Wang XL, Li XQ, Leng XJ (2020) Replacement of fish meal with two fermented soybean meals in diets for rainbow trout (*Oncorhynchus mykiss*). Aquac Nutr 26(1): 37–46

Eseoghene O (2019) Assessment of rainwater harvesting potential and appropriate technologies in Abuja, Nigeria, Doctoral dissertation, PAUSTI, JKUAT

FAO (2017) Fishery and Aquaculture Statistics Food Balance Sheets. FAO yearbook/annuaire/anuario 2015. Rome, FAO; p 403

Gabriel UU, Akinrotimi OA, Bekibele DO, Anyanwu PE, Onunkwo DN (2007) Economic benefit and ecological efficiency of integrated fish farming in Nigeria. Sci Res Ess 2(8):302–308

Gangwar LS, Saran S, Kumar S (2013) Integrated poultry-fish farming systems for sustainable rural livelihood security in Kumaon Hills of Uttarakhand. Agric Econ Res Rev 26(347-2016-17106): 181–8

Gebru T (2021) Integrated Aquaculture with Special Reference to Fish Integration with Animal Husbandry to Enhance Production and Productivity. J Agric Aquac 3(2):306

Herrero M, Thornton PK, Notenbaert AM, Wood S, Msangi S, Freeman HA, Bossio D, Dixon J, Peters M, van de Steeg J, Lynam J, Parthasarathy Rao P, Mcmillan S, Gerard B, McDermott J, Serand C, Rosegrant M (2010) Smart investments in sustainable food production: revisiting mixed crop-livestock systems. Science 327:822–825. https://doi.org/10.1126/science.1183725

Little D, Satapornvanit K (1996, September) Poultry and fish production-a framework for their integration in Asia. In: Proceedings of the second FAO electronic conference on tropical feeds. Available at http://www.fao.org/ag/aga/agap/FRG/abstract/little2.txt

Maclean JL (1993) Developing-Country Aquaculture and Harmful Algal Blooms. In Pullin, RSV, Rosenthal H, Maclean JL, 1993 Environment and Aquaculture in Developing countries. ICLARM Conf. Proc; vol. 31. pp 252–284

Nashima FP, Hipondoka M, Iiyambo I, Hambia J (2013) The potential of rainwater harvesting: a case of the city of Windhoek, Namibia. J Water Res Ocean Sci 2(6):170–174

Ngugi CC, Oyoo-Okoth E, Manyala JO, Fitzsimmons K, Kimotho A (2017) Characterization of the nutritional quality of amaranth leaf protein concentrates and suitability of fish meal replacement in Nile tilapia feeds. Aquac Rep 5:62–69

Olapade OJ, Bangura H, Tholley JB, Momoh RR (2017) Economic differential of integrated fish, rice cum piggery and fish, rice cum poultry production systems. Afri J Food Agric Nutr Dev 17(3):12325–12342

Phong LT (2010) Dynamics of sustainability in Integrated Agriculture-Aquaculture systems in the Mekong Delta. PhD Thesis, Wageningen University, Wageningen, The Netherlands

Rahman MM, Rahman MA, Haque MM, Rahman A (2019) Sustainable water uses in construction. In: Sustainable construction technologies. Butterworth-Heinemann, Oxord, pp 211–235

Reddy PR, Kishori B (2018) Integrated rice and aquaculture farming. In: Aquaculture-plants and invertebrates. Intech Open, London

Sana SS (2011) An integrated project of fishery and poultry. Math Comput Model 54(1–2):35–49

Shoko AP, Limbu SM, Lamtane HA, Kishe-Machumu MA, Sekadende B, Ulotu EE, Mgay YD (2019) The role of fish-poultry integration on fish growth performance, yields and economic benefits among smallholder farmers in sub-Saharan Africa, Tanzania. Afri J Aquat Sci 44(1): 15–24

Tran N, Le Cao Q, Shikuku KM, Phan TP, Banks LK (2020) Profitability and perceived resilience benefits of integrated shrimp-tilapia-seaweed aquaculture in North Central Coast, Vietnam. Marit Policy 120:104153

Uddin MS, Das GB, Hossain A, Rahman MA, Mazid MA, Gupta MV (1998) Integrated poultry-fish farming: a way to increase productivity benefits. CRC Press, Boca Raton, FL

Zajdband AD (2011) Integrated agri-aquaculture systems. In: Genetics, biofuels and local farming systems. Dordrecht, Springer, pp 87–127. (in press)

Chapter 18
Fishing for Answers: Should Afrotropical Farmers use Cages or Ponds for Grow-Out of Nile Tilapia?

Safina Musa

Abstract Despite the scarcity of economic and environmental feasibility studies on aquaculture production systems, they are critical in determining which farming system to invest in. The system you select will determine the likelihood of your investment's success. This study looks at the aquaculture production systems used in Africa, as well as their output rates, cultivated species, economic viability, and nutrient loadings. The challenges and constraints to expanding aquaculture in Africa are highlighted, along with key considerations. According to the findings, the most common freshwater aquaculture culture system in Africa is an earthen pond-based semi-intensive method. Cage systems, on the other hand, are becoming more common in freshwater lakes. Pond farmers would earn more money if they produced fingerlings. However, the farm's overall productivity and profitability appear to increase as grow-out ponds are integrated with other farming systems, such as poultry. Despite the high initial investment, cage systems are preferred in Africa for grow-out tilapia aquaculture. However, due to the high nutrient loading of cage systems, they may be less advantageous than pond systems. The unprofitability of African grow-out ponds appears to be a managerial problem rather than a systemic one. Grow-out pond systems can perform better with proper management.

Keywords Aquaculture · Aquaculture-integration · Cage systems · Earthen ponds · Aquaculture economics

18.1 Introduction

In Africa, the fisheries sector plays various roles in supplying food, income, employment, and livelihood support services (De Graaf and Garibaldi 2014). According to AUC-NEPAD (2014), 10.4 million tonnes of fish are produced in Africa, where fish is the primary source of animal protein for more than 30% of the population

---

S. Musa (✉)
Kenya Marine and Fisheries Research Institute, Kisii, Kenya

© The Author(s), under exclusive license to Springer Nature Singapore Pte Ltd. 2023
N. N. Gabriel et al. (eds.), *Emerging Sustainable Aquaculture Innovations in Africa*, Sustainable Agriculture and Food Security,
https://doi.org/10.1007/978-981-19-7451-9_18

(AUC-NEPAD 2014). According to De Graaf and Garibaldi (2014), 12.3 million people rely on the fisheries sector for their livelihood directly or indirectly, and the industry contributes 1.2% of the GDP (AUC-NEPAD 2014). Landings from wild capture fisheries have been dwindling worldwide while aquaculture surges (FAO 2022a, b). African nations are taking a closer look at the prospects given by aquaculture because of the decline in capture fisheries resources, overfishing in inland waters, rising population growth rates, and increased demand for fish.

Aquaculture has received and continues to receive enormous support from the national, county, and several non-governmental organisations throughout Africa, which see it as the new frontier for development. As a result, with a growth rate of 11.4%, aquaculture production in Africa was the fastest growing (FAO 2016). However, when the assistance is removed, most of these farms' operations cease. For example, under the Fish Farming Enterprise Productivity Programme (FFEPP), the Kenyan government assisted fish farmers in building ponds, lowering input costs, and providing agricultural inputs from 2009 to 2012. Thanks to the FFEPP, major milestones in Kenya's aquaculture sector had been achieved by the program's conclusion in 2012. More specifically, as more farmers joined the industry, Kenya's aquaculture output increased from 4000 to 20,000 metric tonnes, making Kenya the continent's fourth-largest producer of aquaculture (SDF 2016). However, by 2015, there had been a severe reduction in productivity: according to the KNBS (2015, 2018), tilapia pond production had dropped by 37%, and there were significantly fewer operating fish farms nationwide (SDF 2016). The majority of farmers gave up on maintaining their ponds in favour of other farming endeavours, leaving the nation littered with ponds. Pond fish farming appears to be the principal cultural system in the majority of African nations, similar to Kenya, with aquaculture still receiving substantial subsidies. The sustainability of pond fish farming in Africa depends on a number of important aspects, including high-quality seed and feed, effective management techniques, and system productivity. Low pond productivity, however, continues to be the primary obstacle to the development of aquaculture in the majority of African nations (Kubiriza et al. 2018; Mulokozi et al. 2021; Musa et al. 2022a). As a result, the sector is characterised by the constant emigration of old pond farmers and the influx of new/suspicious farmers, as reported in Ghana (Afram 2021), Uganda (Kubiriza et al. 2018), and Kenya (Musa et al. 2022a). As fish farming begins to take root in Africa, several questions will need to be addressed, among them: Can aquaculture gain impetus without subsidy in sub-Saharan Africa? Is pond farming economically sustainable for African countries?

The ability of aquaculture to remain lucrative and competitive over time is a prerequisite for its economic sustainability. Support for new fish farms may help aquaculture in Africa flourish, but if the enterprise is not viable or promotes ethical business conduct, it is of little use (Guillen et al. 2019). According to Hishamunda et al. (2014), aquaculture can only be sustained by subsidies if it is economically viable. It is vital to assess the viability of the culture systems for African entrepreneurs to assist them in evaluating and making an informed decision with their investment because the aquaculture sector is projected to contribute to food security and the reduction of poverty in the continent. However, there is a dearth of data on the economic performance of various African fish culture systems. Fish farming is therefore viewed as a marginal and risky industry in Africa which makes it extremely difficult for existing fish farmers to obtain loans from financial institutions and insurance for their investment (Pillay and Kutty 2005; Aura et al. 2018). Furthermore, the absence of performance measures discourages new recruits from joining the industry. Additionally, choosing the best production system is a crucial first step in starting or growing an aquaculture business. Thus, the current analysis emphasises the profitability of aquaculture production systems for Nile tilapia culture, aquaculture production systems in Africa, species grown, and nutrient loading of frequently used aquaculture production systems.

18.2 Aquaculture Production Systems in Africa

Africa primarily uses extensive, semi-intensive, and intensive aquaculture production techniques. Depending on the species being raised and the accessibility of land and water, these systems use concrete, earthen, and liner-lined ponds, tanks, raceways, and cages (Fig. 18.1). However, semi-intensive earthen ponds are the primary method of production for freshwater aquaculture in Africa, including Egypt (El-Gayar 2003; Kleih et al. 2013), Kenya (Musa et al. 2012b), Uganda (Isyagi et al. 2009), Tanzania (Mulokozi et al. 2021), and Nigeria (Anetekhai 2010).

18.2.1 Extensive Systems

These systems are characterised by low input, low-density stocking, no artificial feeds, and a poor yield per unit area. The fish rely only on naturally occurring food sources in the culture water. Typically, the stocked fish are allowed to reach the receiving water's natural carrying capacity. In Egypt, extensive systems have been used for many years, primarily in the form of net enclosures. According to Shaalan et al. (2018), some regions of Egypt still engage in substantial extensive aquaculture, with outputs of 0.25 to 0.75 tons per year (Shaheen et al. 2013; Soliman and Yacout 2016). The technique is mostly used in Kenya's dams and water reservoirs, with yields of 500–1500 kg/ha/year (Ngugi et al. 2007). In Nigeria, extensive systems are used, primarily for subsistence, in reservoirs and undrainable ponds (Daramola et al. 2017; Okwodu 2016). In Tanzania, the majority of pond fish farming is done extensively, mainly for subsistence (Mulokozi et al. 2021). Large stagnant ponds are used for massive fish farming in Uganda, with yield hardly topping 0.2 kg/m^3 (Shoko et al. 2011).

Earthen ponds
Source: Author

Liner ponds
Source: Author

Above ground/backyard ponds
Source: Author

Tanks
Source: Author

Concrete ponds
Source: Author

LVHD cages
Source: Author

Raceway
Source: Online

Recirculating aquaculture
Source: Online

Fig. 18.1 Culture systems in Africa. Note: LVHD (low volume high density)

18.2.2 Semi-Intensive Systems

Over 90% of African aquaculture systems use semi-intensive production methods (FAO 1999; FAO 2008; Mucai et al. 2011). To increase natural yield, the systems are fertilized with animal excrement such as that of cattle, sheep, and poultry, among others. In addition to natural foods, low-protein feed (10–30%) is available (Soliman and Yacout 2016). The pond's production cycle lasts between 5 and 6 months when the best management techniques are used (Anetekhai 2010). Most of these systems are used to cultivate low-value species such as catfish and tilapia.

More than 70% of aquaculture production in Kenya (Musa et al. 2012b) and Uganda (Kubiriza et al. 2018) is produced using semi-intensive methods. The output from semi-intensive ponds, under competent management, is between 1–2 tons/ha/year in both Kenya and Uganda (Brummett 1999). In Tanzania, semi-intensive ponds account for more than 50% of aquaculture production with a yield of 1.5 tons/ha/year under best management practices (Mulokozi 2021). The entire aquaculture production in Egypt is 73% semi-intensive pond culture systems, with fish yields ranging from 5 to 20 tons/ha/year (Shaheen et al. 2013; GAFRD 2014). Nigeria's production is predicted to be more than 10,000 kg/ha/year (Iruo et al. 2018).

18.2.3 Intensive Systems

Raceways, recirculating aquaculture systems (RAS), and cages are some of the intensive aquaculture systems used in Africa. According to research (Aubin et al. 2006; Colt et al. 2008), intensive systems are effective at using both land and water. The requirement for complete diets with crude protein values >30%, which is expensive and out of the price range for the majority of farmers, is a significant disadvantage of intensive systems. Additionally, because it raises operating expenses, the high energy need is a significant bottleneck for systems like RAS (Aubin et al. 2006; Colt et al. 2008). Intensive systems, like RAS, have a low adoption rate because of the initial financial investment. However, it has been noted that due to economic factors, semi-intensive systems are being replaced by intensive systems in African nations like Egypt (FAO 2020). The growth of intensive aquaculture in Egypt, according to GAFRD (2014), caused a 50% decrease in fish production from semi-intensive systems in 2012 compared to 2011. In Egypt, intensive methods have been reported to produce yields of between 100 and 150 tons per hectare per year (Shaheen et al. 2013). According to FAO (2016), the production from raceways in Kenya ranges from 10,000 to 8000 kg per year, whereas the production from RAS is 200 tonnes (SDF 2016).

Inland waters in Africa have seen a faster uptake of cage aquaculture, including Lake Victoria in Kenya (Aura et al. 2018), Lake Victoria in Uganda (Blow and Leonard 2007), the Lake Volta in Ghana (Asmah et al. 2016), the Lake Kariba in

Zimbabwe (Berg et al. 1996), and the Lake Malawi in Malawi (Blow and Leonard 2007). Production from cages has been estimated to range from 5 to 35 kg of fish per m^3 in Lake Victoria, Uganda (Mbowa et al. 2016), 50 kg per m^3 in Lake Victoria, Kenya (Musa et al. 2021b), 42 kg per m^3 in Lake Malawi (Gondwe et al. 2011), and 20 to 40 kg per m^3 in Lake Volta, Ghana's (Karikari 2016).

18.2.4 Integrated Agriculture and Aquaculture Systems (IAA)

The primary goals of integrating aquaculture into larger farming systems are to increase food production, protect the environment, provide food security, and diversify sources of income. In IAA, fish can be combined with poultry (Fig. 18.2), pigs, rabbits, sheep, goats, or cattle in a design that enables the use of waste products from one system as inputs into another. The systems' ability to create synergy amongst several businesses makes them unique (Edwards 1998; Rakocy et al. 2003). The systems are effective at utilising both land and water, making them perfect for rural locations where a lack of fresh water is a problem. However, the technique is not commonly used in Africa, and in the few instances that have been reported, it is primarily used for subsistence (Jamu 2001). Additionally, the approach has demonstrated improvements in farm productivity and profitability in the few cases reported in Africa (Dey et al. 2010; Shoko et al. 2011; Mulokozi et al. 2021).

Fig. 18.2 Integrated aquaculture system (Source: Author)

According to Shaalan et al. (2018), aquaponics and aquaculture-based rice farming are the most popular integrated aquaculture practices in Egypt, where 34,537 tons of fish have been produced annually (GAFRD 2014). Although not frequently used by farmers who mostly use farm animal manure for pond fertilisation, aquaculture operations are linked with crop or livestock production in Kenya (Ogello et al. 2013; Ogello and Opiyo 2011). IAA recorded production of roughly 200 kg/ha/year in Kenya (Van Dam et al. 2006). Notably, the adoption of IAA has led to a 2–26% increase in agricultural production and a 22–70% increase in total farm food production in Kenya. With integration, fish production in Malawi increased from 900 to 1500 kg/ha/year, and IAA's ecological footprint decreased nearly 42 times that of conventional farms (Brummett 1999). The most prevalent IAA system in Tanzania is the integration of tilapia and vegetables, with an estimated 3.2 tons/ha/year of production (Mulokozi et al. 2021). Fish raised in Tanzania under IAA have displayed faster growth rates than fish raised in conventional farms (Mulokozi et al. 2021). In addition, the IAA system generated greater economic benefits than a non-integrated one (Mulokozi et al. 2021). According to reports, IAA is still in its infancy in Uganda (MAAIF 2012). However, IAA has reported yields of up to 3.7 tons per hectare every year (MAAIF 2012; Maseruka 2004).

18.3 Cultured Fish Species in Africa

The Nile tilapia and African catfish dominate the aquaculture sector in Africa (Fig. 18.3). The Nile tilapia is the most widely cultivated freshwater fish in Africa, except for Nigeria, where catfish account for over 80% of aquaculture production

Nile tilapia African catfish

Fig. 18.3 Main cultured species in Africa

(Anetekhai 2010). This is because they are hardy, widely accepted, grow quickly, tolerate crowded conditions, are highly disease resistant, and feed primarily on very low trophic levels (Siddik et al. 2014; Amin et al. 2019; Mahmoud et al. 2021). Although in small amounts, other species, including carps and rainbow trout, are also cultured in Africa.

18.4 Profitability of Aquaculture Production Systems for Nile Tilapia Culture

The economic viability of an aquaculture operation is essential for its success. High-profit margins should be the goal because aquaculture has been viewed as a marginal investment, making it necessary for the farms to satisfy their debt obligations. Nile tilapia grow-out systems using pond and cage systems have shown positive returns above variable costs in both Kenya (Musa et al. 2021b) and Uganda (Kubiriza et al. 2018) (Table 18.1). Both ponds and cages are lucrative for tilapia growth in Kenya and Uganda, and probably across all of Africa, according to positive returns above variable expenses. According to studies conducted in Kenya, the total fixed production cost per kg of Nile tilapia produced in cages is \$0.2 (Musa et al. 2021b), while the cost per kg of Nile tilapia produced in ponds is \$0.8. (Unpublished data, KMFRI, Kenya). In light of this, grow-out pond farmers will report a negative return over total costs, whereas cage farmers will report a positive return. This shows that running pond systems for grow-out is not financially viable over the long term in Kenya and Uganda, and probably in all of Africa. As a result, likely, grow-out pond

Table 18.1 Productivity of grow-out ponds and cages in Uganda and Kenya (data for ponds and cages in Uganda is derived from Kubiriza et al. (2018); while for cages in Kenya is derived from Musa et al. (2021a, b) while for ponds is from unpublished data from aquaculture farms in Kenya)

Parameter	Pond (Uganda)	pond (Kenya)	HVLD cage (Uganda)	HVLD cage (Kenya)
Volume of common facilities (m^3)	1000	450	22.5	8
Cost/m^3	1.46	1.29	35.6	20.3
Body mass of stocked Nile tilapia (kg)	0.002	0.005	0.008	0.015
Stocked biomass (kg/m^3)	0.005	0.015	0.75	1.9
Survival (%)	60	80	72	91
Biomass harvested per cubic metre (kg)	0.63	0.7	26.9	51.2
Production duration (months)	9 to 14	8 to 12	6 to 8	6 to 8
Production cycles per year	1	1	2	2
Average farm gate price (USD)	2.3	3	2.3	3
Gross profit above variable costs (USD)	107.1	36.1	725.8	806.5
Profit margin per kg of fish above variable costs (USD)	0.17	0.18	1.2	1.97

fish growers in Kenya, Uganda, and perhaps throughout Africa are losing money, but they continue to operate. The persistence of the grow-out pond farmers is unclear. Two theories have been put out, though. The first is that farmers do not keep good records and are therefore unaware that their operations are not earning them profits. Second, pond farmers can survive thanks to subsidies from the government and other organizations.

Investment costs for cages appear to be higher than those for ponds in both Kenya and Uganda and likely throughout all of Africa (Table 18.1). This might prevent it from being adopted, especially by smallholder farmers. However, low volume high density (LVHD) cages are superior to ponds for growing tilapia because they offer more significant profit margins per kilogram of fish produced in Uganda and Kenya, respectively (Table 18.1).

Similar research on the financial viability of ponds for the production of fingerlings has been undertaken in Kenya and Uganda. In Uganda, fingerling production has been claimed to provide money per cubic meter (USD) of ponds that is approximately 177 times greater than for grow-out of tilapia (Kubiriza et al. 2018). Similarly, in Kenya, producing fingerlings generates about 150 times more money per cubic meter (USD) of the pond than grow-out tilapia (Unpublished data, KMFRI, Kenya). The results show that ponds are more profitable for producing tilapia fingerlings in Kenya and Uganda than grow-out tilapia, and probably throughout Africa. Which brings up the crucial question Why does producing fingerlings in ponds pay off better than grow-out of Nile tilapia? Why are cages more profitable for the grow-out of Nile tilapia than ponds?

According to Table 18.1, the size of fish in cages is around three times that of fish in ponds. This would imply that fish in cages would grow to market weight more quickly than fish in ponds. Additionally, when fed a nutritionally balanced diet, Nile tilapia appears to take roughly 12 months to reach table size (500 g) in pond systems. The fish would require 6 to 9 months in cages to reach the same weight (Kubiriza et al. 2018; Musa et al. 2021b). According to this, cage farmers—unlike pond farmers—can have two production cycles each year. In Uganda, it has been estimated that 3500 fingerlings/m^3 are generated every 21 days when ponds are used for Nile tilapia spawning (Kubiriza et al. 2018). According to Musa et al. (2012a), each female tilapia in Kenya has a fecundity rate of about 1050 eggs per 30 days, which translates to roughly 4000 fingerlings/m^3 every 30 days.

On the other hand, after a year, pond farmers stocking roughly 4 fish/m^3 would only get less than 2.5 kg/m^3. Pond farmers who produce fingerlings would make over USD 180/m^3/month in contrast to those who produce table-size fish and only make less than USD 10/m^3 after more than 10 months, based on the lowest price of fingerlings in the Lake Victoria basin of 0.05 USD and the highest farm-gate price of tilapia of 3.57 USD (Ngugi et al. 2017). Therefore, the current analysis shows that pond systems are better for producing fingerlings than table-sized fish in Uganda and Kenya, as well as likely throughout the rest of Africa. Even the production of fingerlings would have produced poor results if the issue of low productivity in ponds was related to the system. Considering all of these aspects, low pond profitability can be more of a management problem than a facility one.

18.5 Nutrient Loading of Commonly Utilized Aquaculture Production Systems

Wastes in effluents from aquaculture systems are often produced by uneaten food and fish waste. Deterioration of the quality of the water and bottom sediment can result from these (Musa et al. 2022b). Nutrient enrichment and eutrophication of the lacustrine environment are predicted to take place as a result of the aquaculture sector's fast expansion in Africa, notably the expanding cage culture sector. Because of the high temperatures, it is anticipated that receiving waters in the tropics may react to pollution, particularly oxygen depletion, more quickly (Beveridge and Phillips 1993; Gowen and Rosenthal 1993; Berg et al. 1996). However, little is known about the nutrient loadings from the diverse culture systems in Africa and the tropics in general. A comparison of nutrient loadings from different culture systems would be helpful for guiding aquaculture investments to ensure the sustainability of the sector.

According to nutrient loading tests conducted in ponds and cages in Africa, cages appear to have more nutrient loading than ponds (Table 18.2). Unless the water quality deteriorates, farmers typically do not exchange pond water very often. In this sense, pond bottoms could act as sinks for organic debris and nutrients. On the other hand, cages operating in open systems may release more nutrients into the environment. This may suggest that cages have a larger potential for environmental pollution than fish ponds if they are not managed appropriately. Fish ponds may have a high retention capability for P and N, limiting the eutrophication of downstream aquatic ecosystems. More so in most freshwater lakes like Lake Victoria, which are already choked by large nutrient loads from industrial and agricultural wastes (Hecky et al. 2010), discharge of P and N from fish cages into the lacustrine ecosystem will cause industry strife. This would disfavour cage culture compared to pond fish farming.

Table 18.2 Nutrient loads from pond and cage systems in Africa

System	FCR	N load (kg N/tonne)	P load (kg P/tonne)	Source
Pond	1.6	53.2	8.5	Boyd et al. (2008)
Cages	2.8	105	23	Musa et al. (2022a, b)
Cages	2	93.5	22.8	Karikari (2016)
Cages	2.7	104.7	15.4	Gondwe et al. (2011)
Cages	1.4	45	14.3	Neto and Ostrensky (2013)

18.6 Challenges/Constraints in Aquaculture Development in Africa

Fish consumption will primarily come from culture fisheries due to the decrease in capture fisheries and the explosive growth in demand for fish. One cannot overstate the importance of having effective production systems to close the gap between the rising demand for fish and the available supply. However, a variety of unrelated circumstances may have an impact on aquaculture production systems' prospects, reducing the output of even the most effective systems. Generally speaking, the limitations in Africa appear to be nation-specific (Table 18.3). However, challenges like low pond productivity, high feed costs, low fish prices, and insufficient aquaculture policies appear to be present in Kenya, Tanzania, Uganda, Egypt, and Nigeria (Table 18.3), as well as likely across all of Africa. More than 60% of

Table 18.3 Constraints in Aquaculture and fish farming in Africa (Rutaisire et al. 2009; Munguti et al. 2014; Igoche et al. 2019; Kaleem and Sabi 2021; Mulokozi et al. 2021)

Challenges/constraints in fish farming in Africa				
Kenya	Tanzania	Uganda	Egypt	Nigeria
Poor infrastructure	Limited extension services	Availability of fish feeds	Weak control	Inadequate infrastructure
Lack of quality fish feeds	Poor adoption of BMPs	High cost of feeds	Lack of reliable marine hatchery	Inadequate supply of fish feed
Poor quality seeds	Inadequate funds	Low price of fish	Pressure on natural fry	Irregular electricity supply
High cost of fish feeds	Poor hatchery facilities	Poor extension services	Food supply problems	Poor finance
Poor adoption of BMPs	Poor market/price	Inadequate aquaculture policy	Lack of planning and control	High cost of feed
Low price of fish	Limited funding	Subsistence approach	Frequent pollution and eutrophication risks	Land acquisition
Post harvest losses	Irregular electricity supply	Poor pond productivity	Reduced market	High price of input
Lack of comprehensive aquaculture policy	Poor infrastructure	Poor adoption of BMPs	Limited availability of sites	Disease and poaching
Poor extension services	Post harvest losses	Post harvest losses	Chronic pollution hazard	Poor extension services
Poor pond productivity	Poor pond productivity	Inadequate infrastructure	High prices	Poor market/price
Subsistence approach	Inadequate aquaculture policy	Poor pond pruductivity	Poor hatchery facilities	cannibalism

Note: *BMP*: best management practice

aquaculture production costs are related to fish feeding (Watanabe 2002; El-Sayed 2006; Cheng et al. 2010; Khalil et al. 2019; Allam et al. 2020). In cage culture, the figures have been reported to be much higher (>70%) (Musa et al. 2021b). Therefore, a marginal return on investment would result from the high price of fish feeds in African nations. The primary fish species raised in African nations is tilapia, which is also a low-value and hence relatively inexpensive fish species. Thus, high fish feed costs, low fish prices, and competition from low-cost imported fish would further cut into aquaculture profitability. Inadequate aquaculture policies also result in an unfavourable economic environment in Africa for this type of industry.

18.7 Conclusion and Recommendation

For successful aquaculture, appropriate production systems are vital. In Africa, the pond system is the most common culture system. However, in Kenya and Uganda, and probably, the whole of Africa, ponds seem to have higher productivity for tilapia fingerling production while cages seem to be more efficient for grow-out of tilapia. Furthermore, most grow-out pond fish farmers are making losses and they may not even be aware of it. However, IAA in all cases reported in Africa has proved to be more profitable than the typical unitary pond farming, yet very few farmers have embraced this approach. Hence, IAA could be the "lost coin" for present and future sustainable aquaculture development in Africa. Investment costs for LDHV cages seem higher than ponds, but the returns appear to be more lucrative than ponds. However, nutrient loading from cages seems to be higher than pond systems. In order for small-scale farmers to maximise returns on investment, there is a need to prioritise the development of ponds for fingerling production in Africa as opposed to the current grow-out production. However, low productivity from grow-out pond seems to be more of a management issue than a system issue. The suggestion is to prioritise ponds for fingerling production and cages for the grow-out of Nile tilapia in Africa. Furthermore, nutrient management from cages is paramount for the sustainability of the sector. In addition, there is a need to develop and adopt sound aquaculture policies and strategic framework in African countries to create enabling business environment. In particular, specific policies targeting IAA is highly recommended for African countries.

References

Afram F, Agbo NW, Adjei-Boateng D, Egna H (2021) Effects of feeding strategies on growth performance and economic returns on the production of Nile Tilapia (Oreochromis niloticus) in Fertilized Ponds. Aquac Stud 21(2):63–73

Allam BW, Khalil HS, Mansour AT, Srour TM, Omar EA, Nour AA (2020) Impact of substitution of fish meal by high protein distillers dried grains on growth performance, plasma protein and

economic benefit of striped catfish (*Pangasianodon hypophthalmus*). Aquaculture. https://doi.org/10.1016/j.aquaculture.2019.734792
Amin A, El Asely AM, Abd El-Naby AS, Samir F (2019) Growth performance, intestinal histomorphology and growth-related gene expression in response to dietary Ziziphus mauritiana in Nile tilapia (*Oreochromis niloticus*). Aquaculture 512:734301
Anetekhai AM (2010) Catfish aquaculture industry assessment in Nigeria. Afr J Biotechnol 9(1): 73–76
Asmah R, Karikari A, Falconer L (2016) Cage aquaculture in Lake Volta, Ghana. Guidelines for a sustainable future. Te Leverhulme Trust. Royal Society, Stirling. University of Stirling
Aubin JE, Papatryphon HM, Van der Werf G, Petit J, Morvan YM (2006) Characterisation of the environmental impact of a turbot (Scophthalmus maximus) recirculating production system using Life Cycle Assessment. Aquaculture 261(4):1259–1268
AUC-NEPAD (2014) Policy framework and reform strategy for fisheries and aquaculture in Africa: creating a conducive and enabling environment for the fish sector to create equitable, social and economic development in Africa. http://hdl.handle.net/20.500.11822/26707
Aura MC, Musa S, Yongo E et al (2018) Integration of mapping and socio-economic status of cage culture: towards balancing lake-use and culture fisheries in Lake Victoria, Kenya. Aquac Res 49(1):532–545. https://doi.org/10.1111/are.13484
Berg H, Michelsen P, Troell M et al (1996) Managing aquaculture for sustainability in tropical Lake Kariba, Zimbabwe. Ecol Econ 18(2):141–159. https://doi.org/10.1016/0921-8009(96)00018-3
Beveridge MCM, Phillips MJ (1993) Environmental impact of tropical inland aquaculture. In: Pullin RSV, Rosenthal H, Maclean JL (eds) Environment and aquaculture in developing countries. Rome, FAO, pp 136–213. https://hdl.handle.net/20.500.12348/2954
Blow P, Leonard S (2007) A review of cage aquaculture: sub-Saharan Africa. In M. Halwart, D. Soto and J.R. Arthur (Eds). Cage aquaculture – Regional reviews and global overview, pp. 188–207. FAO Fisheries Technical Paper. No. 498. Rome, FAO; pp 192–206
Boyd CE, Lim C, Queiroz J, Salie K, de Wet L (2008) Best management practices for responsible aquaculture. Report; p 24
Brummett RE (1999) Integrated Aquaculture in Sub-saharan Africa. Environ Dev Sustain 1:315–321. https://doi.org/10.1023/A:1010087108029
Cheng Z, Ai Q, Mai K et al (2010) Effects of dietary canola meal on growth performance, digeston and metabolism of Japanese seabass, Lateolabrax japonicus. Aquaculture 305:102–108. https://doi.org/10.1016/j.Aquaculture2010.03.031
Colt J, Summerfelt S, Pfeiffer T, Fivelstad S, Rust M (2008) Energy and resource consumption of land-based Atlantic salmon smolt hatcheries in the Pacific Northwest (USA). Aquaculture 280(1–4):94–108
Daramola JA, Osofero SA, Kester CT, Gbadamosi OK (2017) Overview of status of aquaculture in Nigeria with reference to Ekiti state. J Agric Sci 2(3):447–452
De Graaf GJ, Garibaldi L (2014) The Value of African Fisheries; Vol FIPS/C1093, FAO: Rome, Italy; p 67. Available online: http://www.fao.org/documents/card/es/c/d155e4db-78eb-4228-8c8c7aae5fc5cb8e/ (Accessed on 29 January 2019)
Dey MM, Paraguas FJ, Kambewa P, Pemsl DE (2010) The impact of integrated aquaculture–agriculture on small-scale farms in Southern Malawi. J Agric Econ 41:67–79
Edwards P (1998) A systems approach for the promotion of integrated aquaculture. Aquac Econ Manag 2(1):1–12. https://doi.org/10.1080/13657309809380209
El-Gayar OF (2003) Aquaculture in Egypt and issues for sustainable development. Aquac Econ Manag 7(1–2):137–154. https://doi.org/10.1080/13657300309380336
El-Sayed AFM (2006) Tilapia culture. CABI Publishing, Wallingford, GB
FAO (1999) Lao PDR guidelines for broodstock and hatchery management. Food and Agriculture Organization of the United Nations, Rome
FAO (2008) Fishery and aquaculture statistics 2006. Food and Agriculture Organization of the United Nations, Rome

FAO (2016) The State of World Fisheries and Aquaculture 2016. Contributing to food security and nutrition for all. Rome, FAO, p 200
FAO (2020) Fishery and aquaculture statistics. Global production by production source 1950–2018 (FishstatJ). Retrieved from FAO Fisheries and Aquaculture Department [online] website: www.fao.org/fishery/statistics/software/fishstatj/en
FAO (2022a) The state of world fisheries and aquaculture: towards blue transformation. FAO, Rome, p 266
FAO (2022b) The State of the world's fisheries and aquaculture 2022: Towards blue transformation. Food and Agricultural Organization of the United Nations, Rome
GAFRD (2014) General authority for fish resources development. In: Fish statistics year book. Ministry of Agriculture and Land Reclamation, Cairo
Gondwe M, Guildford S, Hecky R (2011) Physico-chemical measurements in the water column along a transect through a tilapia cage fish farm in Lake Malawi. Afr J Great Lakes Res 37:102–113
Gowen RJ, Rosenthal H (1993) The environmental consequences of intensive coastal aquaculture in developed countries: what lessons can be learnt. In: ICLARM Conference Proceedings 31, pp 102–115
Guillen J, Asche F, Carvalho N et al (2019) Aquaculture subsidies in the European Union: Evolution, impact and future potential for growth. Mar Policy 104:19–28
Hecky RE, Mugidde R, Ramlal PS (2010) Multiple stressors cause rapid ecosystem change in Lake Victoria. Freshw Biol 55(1):19–42
Hishamunda N, Ridler N, Martone E (2014) Policy and governance in aquaculture: lessons learnedvand way forward. FAO Fisheries and Aquaculture Technical Paper No. 577. Rome, FAO. 68 pp. (also available at www.fao.org/3/a-i3156e.pdf)
Igoche LE, Makwin F, Akpenseun TT, Kaye J, Oyedapo FA (2019) Assessment of fish farming in plateau state, north Central Nigeria. Asian J Fish Aquat Res 4:1–10. https://doi.org/10.9734/ajfar/2019/v4i130047
Iruo FA, Onyeneke RU, Eze CC, Uwadoka C, Igberi CO (2018) Economics of smallholder fish farming to poverty alleviation in the Niger Delta Region of Nigeria. Turk J Fish Aquat 19 (4):313–329. https://doi.org/10.4194/1303-2712-v19_4_06
Isyagi NA, Veverica KL, Asiimwe R, Daniels WH (2009) Manual for the commercial pond production of the African catfish in Uganda. Kampala, 222. https://www.researchgate.net/profile/Nelly_Isyagi/publication/267969523_Manual_for_the_Commercial_Pond_Production_of_the_African_Catfish_in_Uganda/links/56209b4008aed8dd19404b1b.pdf
Jamu D (2001) Tilapia culture in Africa: opportunities and challenges. In Subasinghe S, Tarlochan S (eds.). Tilapia: production, marketing and technological developments. Proceedings of the Tilapia International Technical and Trade Conference on Tilapia, Kuala Lumpur, Malaysia; pp 105–112
Kaleem O, Sabi ABS (2021) Overview of aquaculture systems in Egypt and Nigeria, prospects, potentials, and constraints. Aquac Fish 6:535–547
Karikari AY (2016) Assessment of Environmental Impacts of Cage Aquaculture on Lake Volta of Ghana. PhD thesis, Department of Fisheries and Watershed Management, Ghana
Khalil HS, Mansour AT, Goda AMA, Omar EA (2019) Effect of selenium yeast supplementation on growth performance, feed utilization, lipid profile, liver and intestine histological changes, and economic benefit in meagre, Argyrosomus regius, fingerlings. Aquac Nutr 501:135–143. https://doi.org/10.1016/j.aquaculture.2018.11.018
Kleih U, Linton J, Marr A, Mactaggart M, Naziri D, Orchard JE (2013) Financial services for small and medium-scale aquaculture and fisheries producers. Mar Policy 37:106–114. https://doi.org/10.1016/j.marpol.2012.04.006
KNBS (2015) Kenya Bureau of National Statistics - Economic survey 2015. Nairobi, Kenya
KNBS (2018) Kenya Bureau of National Statistics - Economic survey 2018, Nairobi, Kenya

Kubiriza G, Sserwambala SP, Ssebisubi M, Sigurgeirsson O, Tomasson T, Thorarensen H (2018) Harnessing the comparative production economics of ponds and cages for improved aquaculture sector in Uganda. Paper presented at International Institute of Fisheries Economics & Trade
MAAIF (2012) Department of Fisheries Resource Annual Report 2010/2011. Ministry of Agriculture Animal Industry and Fisheries
Mahmoud HK, Reda FM, Alagawany M, Farag MR (2021) The stress of abamectin toxicity reduced water quality, growth performance, immunity and antioxidant capacity of *Oreochromis niloticus* fish: modulatory role of *Simmondsia chinensis* extract as a dietary supplement. Aquaculture 534:736247
Maseruka J. Lack of Funds Affects Fish Farmers' Progress in Uganda. Published by The New Vision, 21st July 2004
Mbowa S, Odokonyero T, Munyaho AT. 2016. Floating fishcage farming a solution to Uganda's declining fishery stocks. Economic Policy Research Centre Policy Brief. https://innodev.org/sites/default/files/66%20Floating%20Fish%20Cage%20Farming%20a%20Solution%20to%20Uganda%E2%80%99s%20declining%20fishery%20stocks.pdf(66)
Mucai M, Wangila BC, Norman N (2011) Factors determining structure and development of fish farming among small scale operators in Western Kenya. In: Samaki News: Aquaculture Development in Kenya towards Food Security, Poverty Alleviation and Wealth Creation; Vol. 7, No. 1; pp 30–45
Mulokozi D (2021) Integrated Agriculture and Aquaculture Systems (IAA) for Enhanced Food Production and Income Diversification in Tanzania. Doctoral dissertation, Department of Physical Geography, Stockholm University
Mulokozi DP, Berg H, Tamatamah R, Lundh T, Onyango P (2021) Assessment of pond and integrated aquaculture (IAA) systems in six districts of Tanzania. J Agric Rural Dev Trop Subtrop 122(1):115–126
Munguti JM, Kim J, Ogello EO (2014) An overview of Kenyan aquaculture: current status, challenges, and opportunities for future development. Fish Aquat Sci 17(1):1–11
Musa S, Orina PS, Aura CM, Kundu R, Ogello EO, Munguti JM (2012a) The effects of dietary levels of protein and greenhouse on growth, behaviour and fecundity of Nile tilapia (*Oreochromis niloticus* L) Broodstock. Int J Sci Res:2319–7064
Musa S, Aura CM, Owiti G, Nyonje B, Orina P, Charo-karisa H (2012b) Fish farming enterprise productivity program (FFEPP) as an impetus to *Oreochromis niloticus* (L.) farming in Western Kenya: Lessons to learn. Afr J Agric Res 7(8):1324–1330
Musa S, Aura CM, Okechi J (2021a) Economic analysis of tilapia cage culture in Lake Victoria using different cage volumes. J Appl Aquac. https://doi.org/10.1080/10454438.2021.1884632
Musa S, Aura CM, Tomasson T, Sigurgeirsson O, Thorarensen H (2021b) A comparative study of the effects of pelleted and extruded feed on growth, financial revenue and nutrient loading of Nile tilapia (*Oreochromis niloticus L.*) cage culture in a lacustrine environment. J Appl Aquac. https://doi.org/10.1080/10454438.2021.2011528
Musa S, Alando P, Lewo R, Akidiva A (2022a) Synopsis of aquaculture in Kenya: Some gamechangers for the industry. https://africanfoodfellowship.org/synopsis-of-aquaculture-in-kenya-some-gamechangers-for-the-industry.html. Retrieved on 8/7/22
Musa S, Aura CM, Tomasson T, Sigurgeirsson O, Thorarensen H (2022b) Impact of Nile tilapia Cage Culture on Water and Bottom Sediment Quality: The ability of a Eutrophic Lake to Absorb and Dilute Perturbations. Accepted under Lakes & Reservoirs: Research & Management
Neto RM, Ostrensky A (2013) Nutrient load estimation in the waste of Nile tilapia *Oreochromis niloticus* (L.) reared in cages in tropical climate conditions. Aquac Res 46(6):1309–1322
Ngugi CC, Bowman JR Omolo BO (2007) A new guide to fish farming in kenya. aquaculture collaborative research support program, Naitobi, KE
Ngugi CC, Nyandat B, Manyala JO, Wagude B (2017) Social and economic performance of tilapia farming in Kenya. In Cai J, Quagrainie KK, Hishamunda N, eds. Social and economic performance of tilapia farming in Africa, pp. 91–111. FAO Fisheries and Aquaculture Circular No. 1130. Rome, Italy

Ogello EO, Opiyo MA (2011) A review of the African catfish production in Kenya: Opportunities and challenges. Aquaculture development in Kenya towards food security, poverty alleviation and wealth creation. Samaki news: Vol. VII. No. 1
Ogello EO, Mlingi F, Nyonje B, Charo-Karisa H, Munguti J (2013) Can integrated livestockfish culture be a solution to East Africa's food insecurity? A review. Afr J Food Agric Nutr Dev. 13: 8058–8076. http://www.bioline.org.br/pdf?nd13066
Okwodu NE (2016) Aquaculture for sustainable development in Nigeria. World Sci News 2(47): 151–163
Pillay TVR, Kutty MN (2005) Aquaculture: principles and practices, 2nd edn. Blackwell Publishing Ltd., Oxord. ISBN: ISBN-10: 1-4951-0532-1; ISBN-13-978-1-4051-0532-3
Rakocy J, Shultz RC, Bailey DS, Thoman ES. 2003. Aquaponic production of tilapia and basil: comparing a batch and staggered cropping system. In South Pacific Soilless Culture Conference-SPSCC 648. pp 63–69. https://uvi.edu/files/documents/Research_and_Public_Service/AES/Aquaculture/Tilapia_and_Basil.pdf
Rutaisire J, Charo-Karisa H, Shoko AP, Nyandat B (2009) Aquaculture for increased fish production in East Africa. Afr J Trop Hydrobiol 12:74–77
SDF (2016) Kenya Fish Farming Enterprise Productivity Capacity Assessment and Gap Analysis Report. Authored by Simon Macharia and Anthony Kimani. Ministry of Agriculture, Livestock and Fisheries, Republic of Kenya. Nairobi, Kenya
Shaalan M, El-Mahdy M, Saleh M, El-Matbouli M (2018) Aquaculture in Egypt: Insights on the current trends and future perspectives for sustainable development. Rev Fish Sci Aquac 26(1): 99–110. https://doi.org/10.1080/23308249.2017.1358696
Shaheen A, Seisay M, Nouala S (2013) An industry assessment of tilapia farming in Egypt (p. 1). African Union, International Bureau for Animal Resources (AU-IBAR)
Shoko AP, Getabu A, Mwayuli G, Mgaya YD (2011) Growth performance, yields and economic benefits of Nile Tilapia oreochromis niloticus and kales brassica oleracea cultured under vegetable-fish culture integration. Tanz J Sci 37:37–48
Siddik MAB, Nahar A, Ahamed F, Hossain M (2014) Over-wintering growth performance of mixed-sex and mono-sex Nile tilapia *Oreochromis niloticus* in the northeastern Bangladesh. Croat J Fish 72(2):70–76
Soliman NF, Yacout DMM (2016) Aquaculture in Egypt: Status, constraints and potentials. Aquac Int 24(5):1201–1227. https://doi.org/10.1007/s10499-016-9989-9
Van Dam AA, Kaggwa RC, Kipkemboi J (2006) Integrated pond aquaculture in Lake Victoria wetlands. In: Halwart M, van Dam AA (eds) Integrated irrigation and aquaculture in West Africa: concepts, practices and potential. Rome, FAO, p 181
Watanabe T (2002) Strategies for further development of aquatic feeds. Fish Sci 68:242–252. https://doi.org/10.1046/j.1444-2906.2002.00418.x

Chapter 19
Aquaculture Development Perspectives in Sierra Leone: The Challenges of Critical Inputs and Political Will

Julius Olufemi Olapade and Annmarie Bangura

Abstract This chapter discussed the challenges facing the aquaculture sector in Sierra Leone and the contributions that governance has made to its growth. Freshwater resources in Sierra Leone support aquaculture and the farming of aquatic organisms, mainly fish. Various aquaculture grant projects and interventions funded by USAID, the European Union, CORAF/WECARD, AfDB, and a variety of other international donor partners, including WorldFish, have recently benefited Sierra Leone. FAO has been an essential partner in aquaculture development since the end of the civil war, offering technical cooperation programs and implementing aquaculture projects throughout the country, particularly the TCP/SIL/3104 project. Njala University's Department of Aquaculture and Fisheries Management pioneered the integration of agriculture and aquaculture with assistance from CORAF/WECARD, a Multi-Donor Trust Fund (MDTF). Furthermore, since 2007, the university has trained people in fisheries and aquaculture. It has since produced a large number of accomplished professionals who are currently contributing significantly to Sierra Leone's aquaculture revival efforts. The species of culture that are of interest are *Clarias* spp. and *Oreochromis niloticus*. Sierra Leone's efforts to institutionalise fish farming, whose contribution to the nation's socioeconomic life is nonexistent, are still hampered by several factors. The nation's aquaculture infrastructure is hindered by a supply of genetically unsound fish seeds, the majority of which are obtained from the wild, a scarcity of high-quality, affordable fish feed, a lack of technical and technological know-how, albeit in moderation, and poor aquaculture governance. To ensure the long-term sustainability of the aquaculture sector, the governance of modern aquaculture businesses is thought to need to balance ecological and human factors. Poor governance is a source of resource misallocation, an indicator of industry stagnation, and an indicator of irreversible environmental damage.

J. O. Olapade (✉) · A. Bangura
Department of Aquaculture & Fisheries Management, School of Natural Resources Management, Njala University, Njala PMB Freetown, Sierra Leone
e-mail: ojulius@njala.edu.sl

© The Author(s), under exclusive license to Springer Nature Singapore Pte Ltd. 2023
N. N. Gabriel et al. (eds.), *Emerging Sustainable Aquaculture Innovations in Africa*, Sustainable Agriculture and Food Security,
https://doi.org/10.1007/978-981-19-7451-9_19

Keywords Aquaculture infrastructure · Fish fingerlings · Feed · Poor governance · Development partners

19.1 Introduction

Sierra Leone is endowed with suitable land and good waters comprising freshwater, brackish and marine, where fish species can be cultured. Its shoreline is approximately 560 km long, consisting of estuaries of three large river networks (the Scarcies, Sierra Leone and Sherbro rivers) and four coastal islands. The country's inland water resources consist of rivers, lakes, IVSs and floodplains that support a large number of aquatic organisms (Turner et al. 2000). Sierra Leone's lowland is made up of 690,000 ha of Inland Valley Swamps (IVSs), and 145,000 ha of large, saucer-shaped basins (bolilands). The lowland is interspersed with 130,000 ha of riverine grasslands and 200,000 ha of mangrove swamps. The country's ecosystem supports agricultural production and meets the resource needs of the local communities, especially through hunting, fishing, and foraging (Scoones 1991; Adams 1993). Fish is the number one source of animal protein in Sierra Leone and the cheapest, but it mostly comes from the marine fisheries sector, pressuring the resource.

Despite Sierra Leone's enormous resources endowment, food insecurity, a visible dimension of poverty and destitution, is chronically rife. Food security, as defined by FAO, is a condition when all people, always, have physical and economic access to sufficient, safe and nutritious food to meet their dietary needs and food preferences for an active and healthy life. As in many other third-world nations, chronic hunger is widespread in Sierra Leone. The majority of her, over 6.3 million people, are faced with hunger and malnutrition, and according to the 2021 Global Hunger Index, Sierra Leone ranks 106th out of 116 countries; at a score of 31.3 on GHI, the country is classified as having severe hunger problems.

Notwithstanding the recent increase in food production, malnutrition is still rife, especially among children below the age of five, while households find it challenging to meet their daily nutritional needs. Poverty remains disproportionately rural, with 78% of the poor living in rural areas. As a result, many people are food insecure and suffer from malnutrition, are more vulnerable to shocks, need assistance and are unable to contribute to the national economy. It has been reported by FAO (2003a; b) that malnutrition in Sub-Saharan Africa is on the rise in both absolute and relative terms. FAO (2003a, b) reported that more than one-third (34%) of the population of SSA is undernourished. This figure which is an increase of nine million since the 1996 world food summit, most times comes with dire and irreversible consequences on the physical, social and economic development of the affected people. In 1990 alone, 2.4 million people were affected by malnutrition in Africa. According to the 1996 human development report, 22.5 million African children are malnourished; it is believed that this figure could have increased since then. Malnutrition remains an important contributor to infant morbidity and mortality in Sierra Leone. It is a major impediment to the manpower and economic development of the country. It is estimated that between 15,000 and 20,000 African women die each year (41–45 every day) due to severe iron deficiency anaemia. Vitamin A deficiency in children is common across the whole continent, contributing to the deaths of more than half a million African children annually (UNICEF 2004). Fish, a source of "rich food for poor people", is critical for improving Africa's food deficit and nutritional issues. According to FAO (2003a; b), fish provides 22% of the protein intake in SSA. In West African countries, for instance, where fish has been a central element in local economies for many centuries, the proportion of dietary protein that comes from fish is exceptionally high – 47% in Senegal, 62% in the Gambia and 63% in Sierra Leone and Ghana respectively.

The global decline in landing from the capture fisheries has created a huge supply gap, making it difficult to sufficiently meet the dietary protein needs of the poor people of Africa. Sierra Leone's annual landings from the marine fisheries are put at about 200,000 metric tonnes, a far cry from the pre-war values. This decline is a pointer to the fact that fish stocks have approached or even exceeded the point of maximum sustainable yield. This is a clarion call for the development and intensification of aquaculture, a sector of the economy with the potential to redress the fish demand-supply deficit, especially in response to the shrinking but economically and socially essential capture fisheries in terms of its contribution to households` food and nutrition security. According to FAO statistics for 2008, aquaculture, the rational rearing of aquatic organisms of economic benefits to man, is a fast-growing industry worldwide; it supplies almost half of all fish consumed globally. Aquaculture has a very high prospect of bridging the wide gap between fish supply and demand. The rationale behind aquaculture development is to make available good quality fresh fish that will provide affordable fish proteins to the poor and the fast-growing population. This will also reduce the pressure on captured marine environments. It is expected that an increase in production will greatly complement current efforts aimed at achieving the United Nations Millennium Development Goals (MDGs), especially the eradication of extreme poverty and hunger, reduction in child mortality, improvement of maternal health, prevention of diseases, promotion of gender equity and women empowerment. Bamba (2004) observed that aquaculture development in Sierra Leone needs refocussing using new approaches in order to make it relevant in terms of foreign exchange earnings, poverty alleviation and security of food and nutrition.

The country's aquaculture infrastructure suffers from the lack of good quality fish seed, lack of good quality fish feed and the lack of technical and technological expertise, howbeit sparingly, and defective aquaculture governance. It is believed that the governance of modern aquaculture business would need to reconcile ecological and human aspects to assure sustainable development of the industry over time. Bad governance is a precipitator of misallocation of resources, a precursor to stagnation of the sector and irreversible environmental damage. This paper explores the challenges of the Sierra Leone aquaculture industry and the roles of governance in its development (Fig. 19.1 and Table 19.1).

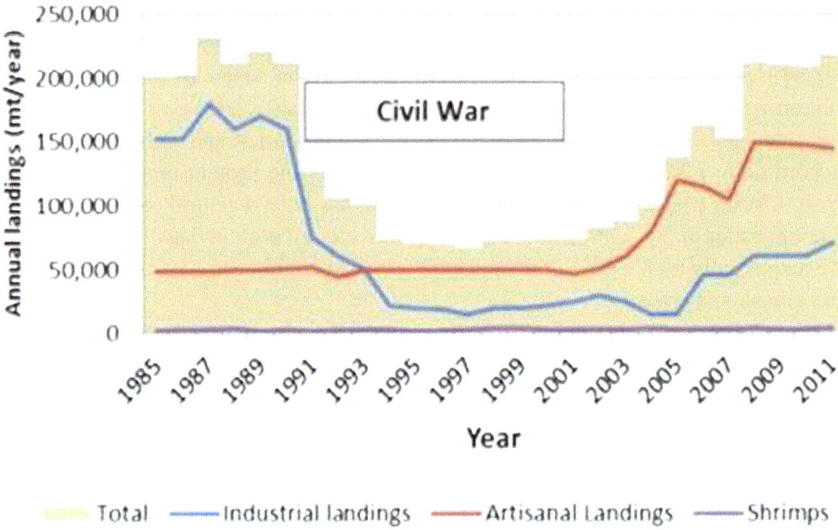

Fig. 19.1 Annual Fish landing Marine fisheries in Sierra Leone (Source: Hecht et al. 2012)

19.2 Tracing the Dynamics of Sierra Leone Aquaculture Development

It suffices to point out that aquaculture in Sierra Leone has made some gains since its inception in early 1970. Unfortunately, the pace of its development is slow and challenging. The enormous potential of fish culture in the country is yet to be fully commercialised, as it is still largely practised at the subsistence level and as a backyard activity. Its potential for food security, employment and household income generation remains adequately exploited. The aquaculture sector, due to its underperformance has not been able to contribute to reducing the pressure on captured marine environments and make available good quality fresh fish to the poor and fast-growing rural population of Sierra Leone. The government of Sierra Leone, through the Ministry of Fisheries and Marine Resources, implemented measures and put in place policies to promote inland fisheries and aquaculture development to make fish sufficiently available for the rural population, especially for those in the coastal villages.

Fish cultures in Sierra Leone are localised in the south (Bo, Moyamba and Pujehun), the north (Tonkolili and Bombali) and the east (Kailahun, Kenema and Kono). The reasons for establishing fish culture facilities, including earthen ponds, cannot be divorced from the existence of suitable IVs, good topography and clean all-year-round water, which favours the culture of tilapia by smallholder farmers. Integration of fish with other agricultural endeavour is not alien to Sierra Leone but recent. In early 1970, farmers received tilapia fingerling supply from Cote d'Ivoire to pioneer the culture of fish in earthen ponds, which was the prevalent system of fish culture in Sierra Leone.

Table 19.1 Fish production, import, export and the per capita availability of fish in Sierra Leone (Source: (COFREPECHE 2013)

Sector 2000	2001	2002	2003	2004	2005	2006	2007	2008	2009
Aquaculture 30	30	30	30	30	30	30	30	40	40
Inland fisheries 14,000	14,000	14,000	14,000	14,000	14,000	14,000	14,000	14,000	14,000
Marine fisheries 60,730	61,147	66,556	79,865	110,173	130,110	133,081	129,610	189,582	186,000
Fish export 6708	6197	7634	6330	5537	5961	5608	5619	5562	6128
Fish Import 2787	3433	2362	2603	1836	1781	1412	2733	1644	2288
Per capita Availability (kg/capital/year) 16.8	16.6	17.1	19.7	26.5	27.8	27.3	26.1	35.15	33.4

The promotion of tilapia culture *Oreochromis niloticus* in earthen ponds was an essential component in the Bo-Pujehun GTZ programme in the 1980s, and this acted as a trigger in the dissemination of fish culture technology in the Southern Province, primarily in Bo and Pujehun districts. Fish integrated into rice paddy was demonstrated to farmers in the Bo district as part of the Bo-Pujehun project. The culture of wild-sourced *Clarias gariepinus* and *Heterobranchus sp* in earthen ponds has also been promoted by research institutions and local and international Non-Governmental organisations. The 2005 Sierra Leone aquaculture baseline survey revealed the existence of 1127 fishponds nationwide. Only about half of these ponds (657) were active, while the remaining 40% have been abandoned.

In 2009 however, Dabo et al. (2009) reported that there were 2593 fishponds in 12 districts including the western area. According to Dabo et al. (2009), 83% of the ponds were located in Tonkolili district. The figures posted by Dabo et al. (2009) were not significantly different from the 2087 fishponds recorded by WorldFish in a recent aquaculture assessment for Tonkolili and Bombali districts alone. A significant proportion of these ponds (98.6%) is located in the Tonkolili district. Individuals/families owned about 84% of the ponds, with men holding 80%, while the remaining 4% of ponds belonged to women. The freshwater fishpond culture of Nile tilapia (*Oreochromis niloticus*) was initiated at Makali in 1977 by the Ministry of Fisheries and Marine Resources together with Catholic Relief Services, USAID, and the American Peace Corps (FAO 1992). Farmers owned 1–4 fishponds, with surface areas ranging from 100 to 500 m^2/pond. The yield from these ponds was put at 1.5 to 2.5 tonnes/ha/year, 50 percent of the maximum output attainable under the prevailing conditions during the initial stages of experimentation. The productivity of the ponds was probably limited by the lack of critical inputs such as the improved strain of fish and nutritional fish feed; the knowledge and technical capacity of the support beneficiaries then were at their lowest, thus the observed low performance. Rice bran, cassava peels, household left, and termites were the local feeds dispensed to fish in ponds by farmers regardless of the feeding habit and feed requirements of the fish under culture. Farmers in the districts often applied chicken and goat manure to boost the primary productivity of the ponds.

Available information on aquaculture production in Sierra Leone is provided by Dabo et al. (2009) Table 19.2. Aquaculture production figures are mere estimates because there is no detailed information on several ponds actively under culture. Fish farming accounts for only about 40 tonnes per annum, a small percentage of annual fish production (Agricultural Sector Master Plan Study, 1992). This production figure contradicted the 30 tonnes per annum posited by FAO in its statistical bulletin of 2001. The production figure put forward by FAO is composed of Nile tilapia (*Oreochromis niloticus*) valued at US$ 45,000, based on a cost of US$ 1.5/kg.

The mangroves, rivers, estuaries and intertidal zones of Sierra Leone were exploited freely by locals for crustaceans, especially oysters, which were in abundance (Olapade and Bangura 2019). An attempt was, however, made to domesticate oysters through culture practices. The first effort to culture mangrove and mud oysters in Sierra Leone was through a research trial conducted in 1964 in Bonthe. Unfortunately, the research trial failed due to improper site selection, which led to

Table 19.2 Results of the Aquaculture baseline survey of 2009 ((Dabo et al. 2009)

District	No. of Ponds	Average size ponds	Percentage active ponds (%)	No. of active ponds	Pond areas in production	Production (t/yr)
Bo	277	304	52	143	4.35	6.53
Bombali	28	479	36	10	0.49	0.73
Bonthe	3	325	66.7	2	0.07	0.11
Kailahun	20	330	70	14	0.47	0.70
Kambia	12	195	0	0	0.00	0.00
Kenema	5	384	40	2	0.08	0.12
Koinadugu	7	763	100	7	0.53	0.80
Kono	25	347	8	2	0.07	0.11
Moyamba	4	233	0	0	0.00	0.00
Port Loko	12	560	58	7	0.38	0.58
Pujehun	11	196	90.9	10	0.19	0.28
Tonkolili	2164	344	73	1590	54.76	82.13
Western Area	25	295	52	13	0.39	0.58

the total abandonment of the research effort. In 1973, a 10-year oyster culture research project was implemented jointly by the Government of Sierra Leone (GoSL) and the International Development Research Centre (IDRC) of Canada (Sankoh et al. 2018) as a sequel to the 1964 effort. The chosen culture species for the IDRC project was *Crassostrea Tulipa*, which was raised using rafts, trays and sticks. The success recorded after the trials indicated the suitability of the environment and the feasibility of year-round production. Oyster culture using raft showed promise, as the growth of 1 cm per month was recorded, with the possibility of obtaining market-size oysters in a 7-month cycle (Olapade and Bangura 2019). However, oyster culture in Sierra Leone could not be commercialised because wild oysters were abundant, and women efficiently harvest and sell them at lower prices in the market (Sankoh et al. 2018).

The culture of shrimp in Sierra Leone has not been vigorously pursued. Still, in the late 1980s, a feasibility study for shrimp culture was undertaken by the Sierra Fishing Company for the commercial production of shrimps in the country (Sankoh et al. 2018). Interest in promoting the mariculture of fin fishes and crustaceans in Sierra Leone is of late growing, with foreign investors reaching out to the Ministry of Fisheries and Marine Resources on the feasibility of marine aquaculture of fin fish and crustaceans.

In recent years, especially since early 2000, Sierra Leone has witnessed significant growth in aquaculture from projects implemented by organisations like FAO, CORAF/ WECARD, WorldFish/ USAID, European Union, World Bank and African Development Bank (AfDB), to name but few. FAO, 2001 has been partnering with GoSL to promote agriculture and aquaculture in Sierra Leone. The FAOTCP/ SIL/2904 project has contributed to the construction and rehabilitation of ponds, training of farmers, purchasing equipment (fish and animal feed production

Plate 19.1 Farmers` pond stocked with improved Nile tilapia by FAO

machines) and supporting the integration of fish with crops and animals for livelihood enhancement (Plate 19.1).

The Department of Aquaculture and Fisheries Management, Njala University, with funding provided by CORAF/WECARD on behalf of the Multi-Donor Trust Fund (MDTF), promoted the sustainable integration of rice with fish and piggery in Sierra Leone. The Poverty Eradication and Grassroots Empowerment through Sustainable Integrated Aquaculture Development: Fish cum rice and Piggery production (LFA/06/CF/CW/2011-14/) for the first time, raised awareness on the benefit of integrating agriculture with aquaculture for maximum resource utilisation and improved profits. Seawright Mining Company supported the Department of Aquaculture and Fisheries Management, Njala University, with the installation of Recirculation Aquaculture Facilities for research and training; these facilities are the first of their kind in the country (Plate 19.2). In 2016, the United States Agency for International Development (USAID)-funded the Feed the Future Sierra Leone Agriculture Project to develop rice and fish farming systems to optimise production and improve food availability, nutrition, and income of farmers. The project focusing on Tonkolili District was implemented by WorldFish (WorldFish 2016). The implementation outcomes were astounding as beneficiaries were trained to undertake fish farming as a business. Njala University is currently implementing the ENABLE Njala project, a sub-component of the Sierra Leone agribusiness and rice value chain project (SLARiS) funded by AfDB (SLARiS – 21,001,550,400,116/ P-SL-A00–019). The ENABLE project supports the commercialisation of aquaculture as one of its critical components. It is worth mentioning that some of the students who graduated from Njala University and IMBO – FBC have taken to self-employment in commercial aquaculture. The future of aquaculture in Sierra Leone looks promising, especially with the emergence of private aquaculture farms scattered all over the country.

Plate 19.2 Recirculation Aquaculture facilities at Njala University

19.3 Critical Challenge to Aquaculture Development in Sierra Leone

Aquaculture is the only viable alternative for filling the fish demand gaps created by declining capture fisheries in Sierra Leone. It has many prospects not only in alleviating undernutrition and poverty but as a source of foreign exchange for the country. In the face of the dwindling performance of the capture fisheries, Aquaculture has become a viable and sustainable alternative for meeting the increasing fish demand of the people. Sierra Leone's rural economy, which is based on subsistence cropping and extensive livestock grazing, favours the development of aquaculture, which essentially is also an agricultural activity. The operation of aquaculture on a small-scale, low-cost, utilising family labour or at a high cost under intensive operation provides opportunities for the poor and the rich to improve their living standards apart from providing employment opportunities. Despite the enormous opportunities and potential aquaculture avails in the country, the sector is still confronted with serious growth setbacks. The growth of the industry will depend upon its ability to compete and meet related challenges of availability of seed, feed, and credit, as well as ensuring an investment climate conducive to the commercialisation of aquaculture investment. A significant obstacle to aquaculture development is over-reliance on marine waters, rivers, lakes, floodplains and IVSs for fish supply. Sierra Leone does not lack sector-specific policies and regulations as was the case in some other African countries. Still, there appears to be a lack of implementation and monitoring to ensure the effective adoption of enacted policies and regulations. Public and market infrastructure, which are among the significant drivers of aquaculture, are poorly developed in the country. The government and the competent ministry, saddled with the management of the fisheries and aquaculture in the country, appears to be paying lip service to aquaculture, thus further crippling its development. Positive and pro-active political will to drive aquaculture growth seems to be lacking in principle. The development of aquaculture policies and strategies has always been the time lapse between policy formulation, policy adoption and the formulation of concerted action plans, so that strategy may no longer apply to rapidly changing circumstances. Inadequate or misdirected government funding is a critical inhibitor to the growth of the fledgling aquaculture sector. The discouraging poor performance of donor-supported aquaculture projects, which were anchored on a high-cost extension approach, could not be sustained by the government owing to a lack of funds; the system also failed to transfer a strange concept of animal husbandry to the beneficiary rural farmers.

The factors bulleted below are considered top constraints hampering aquaculture development in Sierra Leone.

- Poorly coordinated aquaculture development policies and strategies.
- Few fish farming traditions in the country.
- Inappropriate technologies and approaches and poor technical know-how of a significant proportion of the farmers.
- Lack of improved fast-growing fish seeds (fingerlings).
- Unavailability of high-quality but least-cost feed.
- Prohibitive transport costs and poor transport infrastructure.
- The existence of many non-functional government stations.
- Weak extension services hamper the effective coordination of research efforts.
- The weak feedback loop between researchers and end users of research outcomes.
- Inadequate information management systems (Plate 19.3).

Plate 19.3 Sinking fish feed production training for Njala University interns at MFMR Makali

19.4 Strategies for Sustainable Development of Aquaculture in Sierra Leone

The dwindling growth of aquaculture in Sierra Leone since its inception could be linked to the development strategies put forward in the 1980s, which promoted culture systems that are at variance with the traditional farming experiences of the rural farmers. Strategies that do not encourage production efficiencies and intensities to produce more fish using less land, water and financial resources will not auger well for the future of aquaculture in the country. In order, therefore, for aquaculture to be sustainable, there is a need to put in place appropriate strategies that appropriate the uptake of new technologies and takes care of the effects of climate change, environmental risks, biosecurity, and fish health concerns. Strategies that will not only enhance productivity but open up markets for fish sales (Ragasa et al. 2022). The African Union's aquaculture action plan for Africa, 2016–2025 (AU-IBAR 2019a), which has spelt out the vision for Africa's aquaculture sector, needs to be promoted and supported for the industry to contribute to improved fish supplies meaningfully and generate economic growth, wealth, and better nutrition. In turn, African member states need to continue improving or creating the necessary enabling policies and environments that would support private sector development and growth. This will strengthen aquaculture value chains and attract more investment. There is the need to encourage external investments as a springboard for growth, notably for establishing large integrated fish farms and feed mills. Having realised what aquaculture can generate, government support has generally increased. This has given the private sector the confidence to bring in emerging technologies, farm new species and apply best management practices (BMP).

Careful zoning, proper selection of sites suitable for aquaculture and improvement in the efficient use of resources, including energy and pond aeration, can aid aquaculture growth (Clough et al. 2020). The deployment of RASs and aquaponics in cities and areas with unfavourable temperatures for aquaculture will, according to Obirikorang et al. (2021) enable small-scale and medium-scale farmers to intensify and increase pond productivity. It is also imperative for research institutions in the country, especially the university, to embark on research on the genetic enhancement of aquaculture species to allow for faster growth and more efficient use of feed is needed. For meaningful production gains to occur, emphasis should be placed on developing better-performing strains through genetic enhancement. In addition, the development and application of improved broodstock and hatchery management techniques are required to avoid inbreeding, interspecific hybridisation, and contamination of improved strains through introgression from feral species.

19.5 Conclusion

The objective of modern commercial fish farming, besides playing a role in ensuring food security, is to produce fish for sale and earn profits from the farmer. Sierra Leone aquaculture no doubt has passed through phases of growth and the signs are obvious that the sector can contribute significantly to critical issues of the national economy, especially contributing to the government agenda of food security and zero hunger. The full potential of aquaculture as a job-creating venture for growing the rural economy and capacitating youths and women can only be realised if the associated drivers of the sector are appropriately addressed. Production must be well planned from the onset as an essential step in the farming investment. There is an urgent need to develop and promote aquaculture technologies that increase the intensification of production, coupled with the development of robust marketing strategies that allow farmers to respond better to changing consumer demands. Markets are the indispensable driver of aquaculture development, adaptation and innovation. The need to develop the markets and the aquaculture value chains is indispensable for the sustainability of the sector. There is also the need for alignment of government policies and regulations to favour aquaculture practices in the country. The competent authorities, saddled with the responsibility for the development of the sector need to devote more resources to policy research on the facilitation and promotion of aquaculture. The Ministry of Fisheries and Marine Resources (MFMR) must affect control, monitoring and evaluation of the sector's activities through robust extension services cum outreaches to ensure conformity with enshrined rules and regulations.

References

Adams WM (1993) Indigenous use of wetlands and sustainable development in West Africa. Geogr Jour 59:209–218

AU-IBAR (2019a) Communiqué - Establishment of the Southern African Regional Platform for Non-State Actors in Fisheries and Aquaculture [online]. Nairobi, AU-IBAR. https://www.au-ibar.org/en/node/223 (Accessed 01 May 2022)

Bamba V (2004) Report of the mission on sustainable aquaculture development in Sierra Leone. FAO Consultancy Report

Clough S, Mamo J, Hoevenaars K, Bardocz T, Petersen P, Rosendorf P, Atiye T, Gukelberger E, Guya E, Hoinkis J (2020) Innovative technologies to promote sustainable recirculating aquaculture in easternafrica: a case study of a Nile Tilapia (*Oreochromis niloticus*) Hatchery in Kisumu, Kenya. Integr Environ Assess Manag. 6(16):934–941. https://doi.org/10.1002/ieam.4295

COFREPECHE (2013) A comprehensive aquaculture baseline study: Sierra Leone. Final Technical Report. Project ref. N° WA-1.2-B1. Strengthening fisheries management in ACP countries. Downloaded from http://acpfish2-eu.org/uploads/projects/id309/WA-1.2-B1%20FTR.pdf

Dabo KK, Sei S, Mamie JC, Kamara S, Mansaray M, Bundu A, Kamara PM (2009) Report on an inventory of existing fish ponds by the Ministry of Fisheries and Marine Resources aquaculture program. Sierra Leone: MFMR

FAO (1992) Agricultural Sector Review/Programme – Sierra Leone, Vol. 1. Unpublished
FAO (2003a) Agricultural sector review and formulation of agricultural development strategy. TCP/SIL/2904 (A)
FAO (2003b) The State of Food Insecurity in the World (SOFI 2003). Rome: Food and Agriculture Organization, 36. Retrieved June 20, 2022 from Fish&FoodSecurity in Africa.pdf (iclarm.net)
Hecht T, Abban K, Elago P, Kaunda E, Peacock N (2012) Sierra Leone aquaculture needs assessment, NEPAD NPCA Working group on aquaculture
Obirikorang KA, Sekey W, Gyampoh BA, Ashiagbor G, Asante W (2021) Aquaponics for improved food security in Africa: a review. Front Sustain Food Syst:5. https://doi.org/10.3389/fsufs.2021.705549
Olapade OJ, Bangura H (2019) The fishery and culture potential of the mangrove oyster (crassostrea tulipa - larmerk 1819) in selected coastal communities of sierra leone. World Jour Fish and Mar Sci 11(4):35–40. https://doi.org/10.5829/idosi.wjfms.2019.35.40
Ragasa C, Charo-Karisa H, Rurangwa E, Tran N, Shikuku KM (2022) Sustainable aquaculture development in sub-Saharan Africa. Nature Food (3): 92–94. Accessed 29 April, 2022 from www.nature.com/natfood
Sankoh S, Teoh SJ, Phillips MJ, Siriwardena SN (2018) Sierra Leone aquaculture assessment with special emphasis on Tonkolili and Bombali districts. Penang, Malaysia: WorldFish. Program Report: 2018-04
Scoones I (1991) Wetlands in dry lands: Key resources for agricultural and pastoral production in Africa. Ambio 20:366–371
Turner RK, van den Bergh JCJM, Soderqvist T, Barendregt A, van der Straaten J, Maltby E, van Ierland EC (2000) Ecological-economic analysis of wetlands: scientific integration for management and policy. Ecol Econ 35(1):7–23, Elsevier
UNICEF (2004) The State of the World's Children 2004. Online at http://www.unicef.org/sowc04/ United States Department of Agriculture. 2002. National Nutrient Database for Standard Reference, Release 15. Washington, DC: USDA
WorldFish (2016) Feed the Future Sierra Leone Agriculture Project. Penang, Malaysia. Factsheet: 2016–08. Downloaded from https://www.worldfishcenter.org/publication/feed-future-sierra-leone-agriculture-project (Accessed May 1, 2022)

Chapter 20
The Namibian Mariculture: Productivity, Challenges and Opportunities

Victoria Ndinelago Erasmus, Stephanus Shifafure Hamutenya, Oliver Numwa, and Elizabeth Petrus

Abstract Mariculture has grown rapidly worldwide; however, in Namibia, it remains relatively limited. Globally, mariculture has contributed immensely to food security and improved livelihoods, thus, these benefits can also be significant in Namibia if more effort is made to increase productivity and penetrate more international markets. In Namibia, mariculture is a lucrative industry, albeit of low-quantity production. In this chapter, we narrated the milestones leading up to the current mariculture status in Namibia, evaluated the current state of mariculture off Namibia, investigated the possible impacts of climate change on mariculture and analysed challenges in this subsector. There are major environmental and economic challenges associated with the mariculture of individual farms and the Namibian mariculture subsector at large, which require collective efforts to be addressed. We provide, for the first time, annual mariculture productivity from 2008 to 2019, which shows a declining trend that negatively impacts employment opportunities and economic gain. The most important part of this chapter is the identified opportunities that can advance this sector, in the quest to contribute to food security and economic growth.

Keywords Mariculture · Productivity · Challenges · Opportunities · Namibia

V. N. Erasmus (✉)
Fisheries Observer Agency, Walvis Bay, Namibia

Nova Research Consultancy, Swakopmund, Namibia

S. S. Hamutenya
Ministry of Fisheries and Marine Resources, Aquaculture, Kamutjonga Research, and Training Centre, Mahango, Namibia

O. Numwa
Independent Researcher, Windhoek, Namibia

E. Petrus
Ministry of Fisheries and Marine Resources Mariculture, Lüderitz, Namibia

© The Author(s), under exclusive license to Springer Nature Singapore Pte Ltd. 2023
N. N. Gabriel et al. (eds.), *Emerging Sustainable Aquaculture Innovations in Africa*, Sustainable Agriculture and Food Security,
https://doi.org/10.1007/978-981-19-7451-9_20

20.1 Introduction

20.1.1 Aquaculture in Namibia

The growing human population coupled with an already existing nutritional challenge comes with an intense demand for food, a global pressing matter. Food produced/harvested from the ocean represents an important part of the solution to this dilemma; however, the current production levels are too low to meet these demands. For this reason, food production should be increased to ensure adequate food security for present and future generations. In addition to wild-captured fish, some food is produced through aquaculture to meet food demands for human consumption, reduce harvest pressures on land food production systems, combat nutritional challenges and contribute to economic growth (FAO 2020; Naylor et al. 2021). Globally, the aquaculture sector has grown exponentially over the past years, contributing immensely to food security (Ahmed et al. 2019). It was estimated that in 2018, aquaculture contributed 46% to the total seafood world production (FAO 2020). Countries such as China (Crona et al. 2020; Garlock et al. 2020), followed by India, Indonesia, Vietnam, Bangladesh, Egypt, Norway, Chile, Myanmar and Thailand (FAO 2018) are leading in aquaculture food production. Many initiatives regarding the aquaculture sector, such as the Aquaculture Stewardship Council (ASC), a leading standard for responsibly farmed seafood, have been developed to support this sector.

In other African countries, aquaculture is also making slow progress. Namibia has thrived in marine fisheries management and governance (Sumaila et al. 2004; Paterson et al. 2013). However, the same cannot be said about Namibia's aquaculture subsector, both the marine water and freshwater aquaculture collectively. Despite Namibia's extensive investment in infrastructure, Research, and development (R&D), training and capacity development, aquaculture production has remained relatively low (FAO 2020). For a lengthy period now, aquaculture has been deemed important to Namibia, as it is specifically addressed as a development priority in all five National Development Plans (NDPs) and Government's Vision 2030 and in the Harambee Prosperity Plan (HPP) document, wherein it is envisaged that by the year 2030, aquaculture will have grown to become a thriving industry (GoN 2012, GoN 2004). The fifth National Development Plan (NPD5), covering the period 2017–2022, indicates that aquaculture promotion is the desired outcome, and this will be attained by the promotion of investments in mariculture. Many sequential steps have been taken to get the Namibian aquaculture subsector to where it is now, starting with establishing the Aquaculture Policy in 2001 (MFMR 2001). Namibia then passed the Aquaculture Act 18 of 2002 in 2002 to regulate and control aquaculture activities, provide for the sustainable development of aquaculture resources and to provide for related matters. This step made Namibia one of the first Southern African Development Community (SADC) the Member States to translate the sector's policy into a legislative framework. The Ministry established the Aquaculture Directorate in 2003 with the mission of developing aquaculture responsibly and sustainably to achieve socioeconomic benefits for all Namibians, while also ensuring environmental sustainability. The aquaculture (Licensing) Regulations were gazetted as per government notice 246 of 2003, made in terms of the Aquaculture Act 18 of 2002, section 43. In 2004, the first Aquaculture Strategic Plan (MFMR 2004) was developed, the second strategic plan was developed in 2009, and the third strategic plan in 2017 ended in 2022. The marine aquaculture master plan, created in 2012, serves as a roadmap for the economic and social environment necessary for the industry's expansion. In 2020, a pilot project was implemented in three SADC Member States with existing National Aquaculture Strategies, namely, Botswana, Malawi and Namibia (SADC 2020).

Despite these developments, aquaculture remains an under-researched field in Namibia. Most studies concerning aquaculture in Namibia have been centred around fish feed (Gabriel et al. 2019), anaesthesia use in aquaculture (Gabriel et al. 2020), the contribution of aquaculture to food security (Villasante et al. 2015) and aquaculture Policy and Institutional Capacity (Britz 2006). Studies on mariculture are even more limited. The studies by Mapfumo (2009) on the history and development of shellfish cultivation in Walvis Bay and an emerging shellfish farming industry in Namibia (Murta and Kibria 2017) in Namibia are the most relevant to this discussion. Mariculture or marine aquaculture is a branch (subsector) of aquaculture in which aquatic species are raised within the marine environment. Looking at mariculture in the African context, in Nigeria, it is described as non-existent, while in Egypt, mariculture is still emerging and not as well developed as freshwater aquaculture. The South African mariculture industry is described as the most developed in Africa (Adeleke et al. 2021). This chapter evaluates the current state of mariculture in Namibia, including productivity, investigates the possible impacts of climate change on mariculture and analyse challenges and opportunities in the mariculture subsector in Namibia.

20.1.2 Milestones in the Namibian mariculture

Mariculture takes place along the Namibian coast, part of the nutrient-rich Benguela Current Ecosystem located between 17°S and 29°S, sharing borders with Angola and South Africa. Mariculture in Namibia is a very intimate subsector that is commercially exploited. Although the mariculture farms are privately owned, they receive support from the Ministry of Fisheries and Marine Resources (MFMR) through a routine water quality monitoring programme which provides timely information to producers about the occurrence of any pollution or natural phenomenon which may have a harmful or detrimental effect on the aquatic environment or any aquaculture product. The programme includes monitoring Harmful Algal Blooms (HABs) (MFMR 2018). Additionally, the Namibian Mariculture Association (NMA) coordinates mariculture farmers. In 2012, Namibia was listed among the top eight leading African countries in mariculture production, contributing 0.2% to Africa's mariculture production (Mmochi 2016). When our interest is in maximising economic growth, increasing the employment rate and improving food security, all sectors are going through microscopic viewing to identify gaps that need to be bridged to achieve the above. The maritime industry has many of these gaps; when closed, there is potential for maximum economic and livelihood security gain.

20.2 Mariculture Productivity in Namibia

Globally, most species farmed under mariculture are seaweed, molluscs, crustaceans and marine finfishes; however, off Namibia, only bivalve shellfish and molluscs are cultured. No marine finfishes are cultured in the Namibian marine waters yet. Currently, mariculture off Namibia is dominated by oysters (mostly Pacific oyster *Crassostrea gigas*, and to a lesser extent the European oyster *Ostrea edulis*), muscles (*Mytilus galloprovincialis*) and South African or perlemoen abalone *Haliotis midae* (Fig. 20.1a–c). Mariculture is dominated by oyster production in Walvis Bay, Swakopmund and Lüderitz (Pacific oyster and European oyster).

20.2.1 European Oysters

European oysters *Ostrea edulis* are endemic to the western European coast and south to Morocco and the Mediterranean but were translocated to Namibia in 1990 (Bromley et al. 2016). European oysters are not farmed for commercial purposes in Namibia but instead at a very minimum scale, mainly for research purposes. They are slow growing compared to the Pacific oysters (Fig. 20.1a). They are found among the Pacific oysters in a very minimum quantity of about 10 individuals out of 10,000 of Pacific oysters. European oysters are slow growers, and there is a limited market for them; hence more attention is on the Pacific oysters.

20.2.2 Pacific Oyster

The Pacific oyster, *Crassostrea gigas*, is the most common oyster species farmed worldwide, accounting for more than 98% of total oyster production. (Petton et al. 2021). In particular, in Namibia, the Pacific oyster is the main oyster farmed in Namibia (Murta and Kibria 2017) and would reach production of more than 1000 tons. Marine aquaculture in Namibia is majorly dependent on molluscan shellfish because these species are described as best suited to the physical–chemical features of the northern Benguela Ecosystem.

Fig. 20.1 Species (**a**) European oyster *Ostrea edulis*, farmed through mariculture in Namibia (picture credit: Elizabeth Petrus, August 2022). (**b**) Pacific oyster *Crassostrea gigas* farmed through mariculture in Namibia (picture credit: Elizabeth Petrus, August 2022). (**c**) Abalone *Haliotis midae* farmed through mariculture in Namibia (picture credit: Elizabeth Petrus, August 2022)

20.2.3 South African Abalone

South African or perlemoen abalones *Haliotis midae* are not endemic to Namibia; they were introduced in early 2000s (Faul and Coetzer 2020) and are now being farmed in Namibia, specifically in Lüderitz (Murta and Kibria 2017). Abalone spat production is mainly done in hatcheries using flow-through land-based systems (Murta and Kibria 2017). Abalones are slow-growing species that require 3–5 years to reach market size (Iitembu 2005).

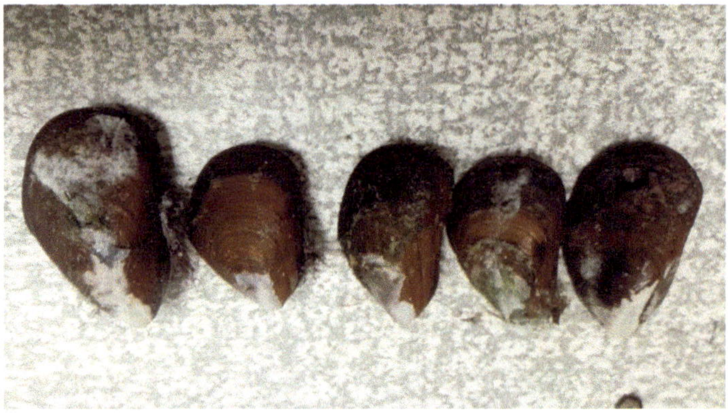

Fig. 20.2 Mediterranean mussel, *Mytilus galloprovincialis* farmed through mariculture in Namibia (picture credit: Stephanus Shifafure Hamutenya, August 2022)

20.2.4 Mussels

Mussel farming in Namibia was based on two mussel species, the indigenous black mussel, *Choromytilus meridionalis* and the exotic Mediterranean mussel, *Mytilus galloprovincialis* (Murta and Kibria 2017). Mussels accumulate and depurate toxins more rapidly than other species (Rourke et al. 2021). Because of the frequent occurrence of toxins in the mussel flesh, this affected the mussel industry as they would test positive for the presence of toxins, and harvesting from the harvested would be put on hold until they are safe for consumption again. Currently, there is no mussel farming being practised in Namibia (Fig. 20.2).

20.2.5 Other Organisms

The red seaweed (*Gracillaria verrucosa*) has also been cultured off Namibia (Critchley et al. 1991; Iitembu 2005; Britz 2006). Although there have been mentions of seaweed culturing off Namibia (Britz 2006; Mapfumo 2009; Chiripanhura and Teweldemedhin 2016), no records for seaweed were given in the recent MFMR 2019 and 2020 reports. This is mainly because the use and consumption of red seaweed in Namibia are limited. There is a new company in Namibia working on a pilot project to farm Giant kelp, *Macrocystis pyrifera*. Kelp is currently being grown at their control site offshore. This is to determine whether the kelp will survive in Namibia because it is a foreign species that is being introduced for the first time into Namibian waters. So far, it appears to be well-adopted and rapidly expanding.

20.3 Mariculture Farming Systems in Namibia

Pond, cage, raceway, longlines and recirculation systems are the five primary aquaculture techniques. Oysters off Namibia are cultured in open waters on longlines and in shallow inshore flow-through systems in baskets/bags (Murta and Kibria 2017; MFMR 2018) (see Fig. 20.3).

Oyster farming in Namibia started in the 1980s; it is the most established and productive species farmed through mariculture in Namibia (Britz 2006; Murta and Kibria 2017). The main advantage of farming oysters is the fact that no feed is required; these animals enjoy an unlimited supply of nutrients from the marine waters. In freshwater aquaculture, especially in Namibia, feed is a major limiting factor. Although oysters generally take a prolonged period (even up to 18 months or longer) to grow to market size (±60 g), the Namibian-grown oysters, in particular, Pacific oysters are reported to grow faster (8–10 months) mostly due to readily available nutrients in the Benguela Current Ecosystem (Britz 2006; Mapfumo 2009). Pacific oysters would take about 2 years to reach market size elsewhere in the world, while in Namibia they would take 6–8 months to reach market size, of course, benefit from the nutrient-rich and cold Benguela current upwelling system. Although literature (Mapfumo 2009) indicates that the Pacific oysters thrive in temperatures between 14 and 27 °C, personal observations have shown that 20–27 °C is too high for oysters, it can cause mortality (Elizabeth Petrus-per. observation) A key achievement in the Namibian mariculture is the local production of oyster spats (in Lüderitz and Swakopmund) (Murta and Kibria 2017), although too small to sustain all the farms. Previously (in the 1990s and early 2000s), all oyster spats were sourced from overseas, mainly from Chile (Mapfumo 2009).

The farming of abalone in Namibia is mainly through onshore-based flow through a tank culture system and ranching that is based in Lüderitz. The naturally

Fig. 20.3 Buoyance on oyster bags suspended on ropes and embedded in water. Pictures were taken around mariculture farms in Lüderitz, Namibia, in March 2022. (Picture credit: Saima Kapia)

occurring seaweed known as kelp along the coastline of Namibia is used as feed for the adult abalone, juvenile feeds on the benthic microflora such as diatoms that are abundantly distributed in the seawater in the Lüderitz area.

20.3.1 Productivity Trends in Namibian Mariculture

The number of mariculture farms has an impact on production. Between 2018 and 2021, Namibia had nine operational mariculture farms each year. The number of farms has remained constant, although fluctuations were observed in productivity. Looking at the production trends of five species; Pacific oysters, European oysters, abalones, blue mussels and Mediterranean mussels in Namibia from 2008 to 2019, there is a gradual decline in production (Fig. 20.4). Annual mariculture production (oysters, mussels and abalone) averaged 411 tons from 2008 up to 2019, with the highest production in 2008 of 569.6 tons and the lowest production of 188.31 tons recorded in 2019 (Fig. 20.4). Based on data not presented here, mariculture production in 2002 was reported to be 600 tons and worth about N$6 million.

In 2004, there were 120 tons of seaweed produced and 132 tons in 2008 (Chiripanhura and Teweldemedhin 2016), but there seems to be limited progress with these seaweed species at the moment. In addition to earnings, mariculture employs a small fraction of people. The latest (2022) MFMR unpublished data records indicate that in 2018 about 185 people were employed in this industry; however, this number declined to 168 in 2020 and further reduced to 159 in 2021. The unemployment rate (which in 2018 was estimated at 33.4% in Namibia based on Trading Economics 2019) can be reduced if production is increased in the mariculture sector. The numbers of employees in this sector between 2018 and 2021 represent a minute fraction of the Namibian population, which was 2,632,885 as of 2022, based on Worldometers (https://www.worldometers.info/world-population/namibia-population/). A decline in production has domino effects on employment numbers and economic contributions. An increase in productivity might also boost local consumption of seafood (Erasmus et al. 2021).

20.4 Market and Economic Contribution of Mariculture to Namibia

The market for Namibian mariculture products is narrow; the main export markets are in South Africa (Murta and Kibria 2017) and Asian countries, mainly Hong Kong, China and Japan, with some emerging new markets in Russia (MFMR 2018). Few products are bought locally by restaurants (Chiripanhura and Teweldemedhin 2016). In 2004, it was estimated that 70% of the oyster production was destined for South Africa Market (Iitembu 2005). The most significant financial advantage was

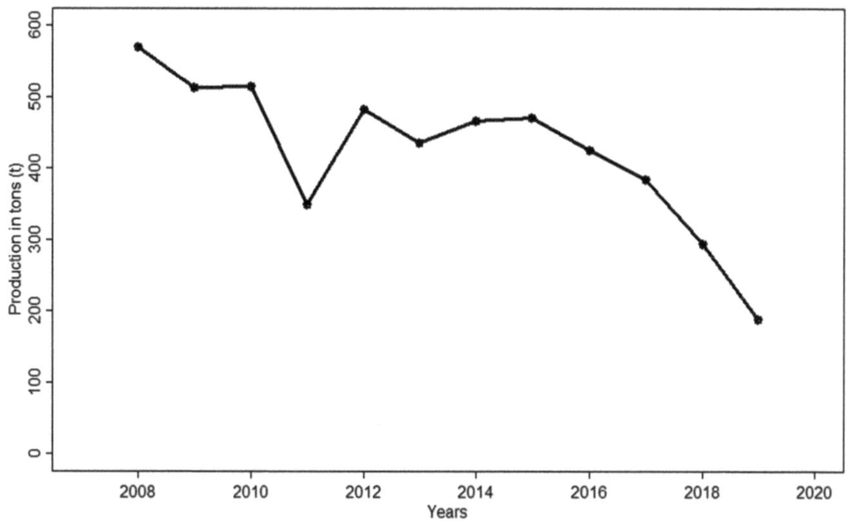

Fig. 20.4 Total production of mariculture products from Pacific oysters, European flat oysters, abalones, blue mussels and Mediterranean mussels between 2008 and 2019 off Namibia. (Data source: MFMR Unpublished data)

realised in 2016 and the lowest in 2018 when examining the final market size amounts without spats (Fig. 20.5).

20.5 Challenges Associated with Namibian Mariculture

Despite the impressive economic benefits of mariculture (Fig. 20.4), this sector is handicapped by various challenges ranging from environmental variabilities to a lack of funds and infrastructure.

20.5.1 Environmental Impacts

The influence of climate change on aquaculture has already been identified (Froehlich et al. 2018). The Namibian waters constantly experience the proliferation of harmful algae blooms (HABs), which are biotoxin-producing algae (van der Lingen et al. 2016; Murta and Kibria 2017). HABs cause mortality in fish and shellfish because they cause the environment to be anoxic by attaching to the gills. Shellfish feed on phytoplankton; some of these phytoplankton species produce toxins, which are then accumulated in the flesh of the shellfish. These accumulated toxins are not toxic to the organisms, and they are harmful to humans when they consume contaminated shellfish. The mariculture grow-out areas are monitored by

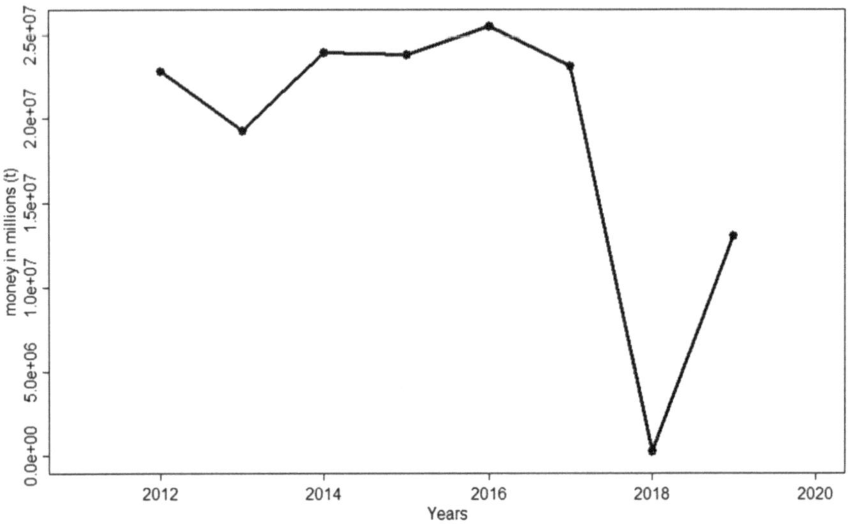

Fig. 20.5 Total production of mariculture products from Pacific oysters, European oysters, abalones, blue mussels and Mediterranean mussels between 2012 and 2019 off Namibia (Data source: MFMR Unpublished data)

the Mariculture Division under the program of water quality and disease control. The division's main focus is on water analysis for phytoplankton with the aim of monitoring the occurrence of toxin-producing species. If the presence of the toxin-producing species exceeds the set limit, flesh samples of the organisms are then sent to the Namibia Standard Institute (NSI) for analysis of the presence of the toxin associated with whatever species is present. If the species test positive for the toxins, then another retest will be conducted. Should the retest fail again, the farm will temporarily stop selling its products to the public for about 2 weeks until a negative result. The closure of the farm is to allow the organisms to self-depurate any accumulated toxins.

Other types of HABs are oxygen-depleting algae that die after the bloom, leading to decomposition, which uses up oxygen, causing an anoxic condition. This leads to fish 'walkout'. HABs can lead to measures such as closing production areas, which is detrimental to this sensitive business. Algae blooms in Namibia have been a significant constraint for years (Mapfumo 2009; Murta and Kibria 2017), still with no solution to help farmers to cope with these natural disasters. The impact of HABs on mariculture is a global concern (Brown et al. 2019).

In some areas, especially in the central region of the Namibian coast, sulphate reduction by anoxic bacteria is the source of 'sulphur eruptions' typified by a 'rotten egg' odour. This can result in mass mortalities of fish and other marine organisms, caused by these organisms being trapped against the coast by these toxic and often anoxic waters. This phenomenon only affects a limited part of the shelf, particularly the coastal waters around Walvis Bay. Higher incidences of 'sulphur eruptions' are linked to interannual scale periods of decreased upwelling intensity in the central Benguela ecosystem (Emeis et al. 2004; Monteiro et al. 2006).

Environmental variables such as sea surface temperature (SST) rise (caused by the intrusion of Angolan warm water, e.g. Benguela Niños) are thought to trigger algae blooms and sulphur eruption. Mariculture farmers who had not established themselves could not break even due to the sulphur eruption (Chiripanhura and Teweldemedhin 2016). Extreme occasional strong wind affects mariculture operations by, for instance, damaging farm structures. Sea level rise reduces processing capacity, displacement of shore-based processing plants, safety at sea issues and other impacts on infrastructure. Rough weather, extreme events and unfavourable weather conditions can damage infrastructures at the mariculture farms and processing facilities. There has been an increasing concern over ocean acidification, which is harmful, especially to organisms with shellfish, i.e. oysters (Kroeker et al. 2013).

20.5.2 Contaminants

Heavy metal contamination, mainly cadmium, in the water may cause accumulation in the shellfish. Because shellfish are filter feeders, they also filter contaminants into their bodies. For this reason, muscles, especially *Mytilus* spp., are used as biological indicators of pollution in water bodies (Azizi et al. 2018). Other heavy metals such as mercury, zinc, lead and arsenic, tested by NSI, are regularly conducted because they are a requirement before export. To export mariculture products, the concentrations of these heavy metals should be below 3.0 mg/kg for most countries such as South Africa and China. In 2014, the farmers exported mariculture products to Hong Kong without evaluating the presence of cadmium, while in Hong Kong, these products were evaluated for various contaminants, and they tested positive for cadmium. The entire consignment was sent back to Namibia, leading to irrecoverable economic and reputational losses and damages suffered by the producers.

20.5.3 Other Marine Organisms and Microbial Diseases

Other marine organisms might interfere with mariculture farming. In particular, jellyfish washout gets stuck on the oyster bags, a major concern. Mussels that grow on the oyster bags are also a significant concern; this leads to the oyster bags becoming heavy. Heavy oyster bags and ropes can break to the point of no repair.

In terms of pathogens, generally, the most prevalent disease, Pacific Oyster Mortality Syndrome (POMS), has become panzootic and represents a threat to the oyster industry (Petton et al. 2021). However, no reports of this pathogen in Namibia have been observed elsewhere. Pathogens such as *vibrio* spp., *salmonella* spp. and *cholera* spp. affect the consumers, thus, farms close temporarily when their products test positive for these pathogens. The data on major disease outbreak from microbial attacks, e.g. *Escherichia coli* on Namibian mariculture farms is insufficient to make any conclusion. However, when they occur, these diseases are described as chronic problems in this industry (Brown et al. 2019).

20.5.4 Lack of Funds and Infrastructure

The lack of specialised technical knowledge, logistical infrastructure and difficulties in access to credit and markets were listed as hindrances in the mariculture subsector (Villasante et al. 2015). Namibia only exports these goods to a small number of nations suggesting that market access is a constraint on this industry. Additionally, since running an oyster farm and the logistics involved are pretty expensive, a farmer needs to have access to a boat for regular maintenance, which should be done every 2 weeks. The production costs are intensified because oysters must be transported live or chilled and are transported mainly by flight to ensure freshness. Because of the risky nature of this business, financial institutions are primarily sceptical about loaning new entrants' funds to start mariculture businesses. Access to technology has also been previously listed as a constraint (Britz 2006). For instance, abalone production farm requires a lot of funds to set up, and requires a lengthy period of time (about 8 years) before income can be generate income, this could be a contributing factor there are few abalone farmers in Namibia and hardly any new entrants in the recent years.

20.5.5 Market

New entrant farmers are struggling to penetrate the market. The expansion and sustainability of Namibia's oysters and other mariculture products are hampered by their limited access to other export markets, such as those in the EU, the United States, Russia and other Asian markets with stricter import regulations (Murta and Kibria 2017).

20.6 Drawbacks of Mariculture

Although we are advocating for the growth of the mariculture subsector, we need to be cognisant of the possible impacts of this activity on the marine environment and its organisms. The operations might generate waste (e.g. oyster bags and ropes used to suspend bags) that might detach and settle at the sea bottom, thereby causing plastic pollution (Fig. 20.5). Plastic pollution is a critical problem globally (Galgani et al. 2021; Horton 2022). Furthermore, dead oyster shells might accumulate and be

Fig. 20.6 Oyster bags and ropes from mariculture production. Pictures were taken around mariculture farms in Lüderitz, Namibia, in March 2022. (Picture credit: Saima Kapia)

a nuisance (Fig. 20.6). Oyster shells are also sharp and potentially dangerous for those near the beach or processing plants. However, these by-products can be recycled to ensure that they contribute to the circular economy.

Depending on the farming system used, wastewater from mariculture activities in Namibia is pumped back into the ocean, which might change the chemistry of the water in the vicinity. Additionally, nutrients, particularly those from the feeding and cage systems, tend to accumulate around bags. Moreover, farm escapees might alter species composition, which would disrupt food chains and food webs. This, in turn, can change the biodiversity's genetic diversity pool. Mariculture has few adverse side effects beyond those already mentioned.

20.7 Opportunities in Mariculture

20.7.1 Culturing Marine Finfishes

Marine finfishes such as silver kob (*Argyrosomus inodorus*), although not currently farmed have the potential to be farmed through mariculture based on extensive research on these species (Tjipute 2011). The potential for finfish mariculture off Namibia was also identified by (Akegbejo-Samsons 2022). Many African countries involved in mariculture are culturing finfish such as flat-head grey mullet (*Mugil cephalus*) and European *sea bass* (*Dicentrarchus labrax*) in Egypt (Adeleke et al. 2021). Since finfish are not currently a part of Namibian mariculture, there is an urgent need to diversify this industry's focus in order to make it more commercially viable and boost food production. There is a need for a rigorous search for potentially cultivable candidate species to supplement what is currently cultured. The Namibian waters are home to diverse species, and some might make suitable cultivable species. When productivity is increased, the employment rate and food security status will improve.

20.7.2 Capacity Building

Mariculture might be new to Namibia, but some countries have been practising this for decades. Developed countries such as China are leading players in aquaculture support and capacitate developing countries to improve their mariculture fish farms. There will be less reliance on outside expertise once the farmers and aspiring farmers are capacitated. Additionally, Namibia can strengthen regional cooperation with South Africa, which shares borders and marine species with Namibia and has thriving mariculture, and we can tap into their expertise.

20.7.3 Promotion of Both Small- and Large-Scale Mariculture

Looking at the profit made from the current production, this industry has the potential to contribute significantly to economic growth if practised on a large scale. Beginning with a high output of oyster spats. More players need to get on board to set up more mariculture farms, both small-scale and large-scale farms. The public should be engaged to get more information on how to participate in mariculture. Production quantity from mariculture is insignificant; specifically, in 2012, Namibian mariculture made up the least of the top eight leading countries in Africa; however, new analyses are needed to evaluate the current position in this regard. Additionally, mariculture can be developed as an artisanal program for coastal-based communities. When productivity becomes more significant, we do not see market opportunities as bottlenecks. Namibian seafood products such as hake are already in demand in many European countries.

20.7.4 Resilience to Climate Change

Globally, climate change has received significant attention (Gíslason et al. 2020), and Namibian waters are not exempted (Junker et al. 2017). Namibia needs to invest in rigorous research to identify species that are less sensitive to HABs outbreaks so that the economic losses during algae blooms are limited. It is common knowledge that species respond differently to changes in environmental parameters. Furthermore, they have varying optimal temperatures or oxygen tolerance, for example. If these species are unavailable, the current ones can be genetically modified to be resilient to these recurring challenges.

20.7.5 Technology

The application of technology in various fields and sectors has changed the approach and accelerated its development. This can also be true for mariculture in Namibia. Farmer and aspiring farmers can employ the use of electronic monitory systems (EMS) that can be deployed/launched to farm locations to aid the monitoring of the growth of the oysters and other farmed species. This would lessen the capital and labour invested in boats that do physical inspections on these farms. Devices that detect changes in the water chemistry can be installed on structures to alert the farmers. Additionally, if finfishes are cultured in this manner, Fish Aggregating Devices (FADs) can be installed to attract forage fishes to the farmed fish in cages, making feeding more accessible and less costly. The use of technology in mariculture can boost production.

20.7.6 Financial Investment for Start-ups

One of the critical issues facing potential mariculture farmers is a lack of start-up capital. The government and external investors can increase financial investment in the farmers and aspiring farmers to redress this problem.

20.8 Conclusion

Although there are major persistent challenges in the mariculture subsector in Namibia, Namibia's efforts to develop aquaculture have paid off, economically, for mariculture and not much for freshwater aquaculture. It is evident that mariculture farms (especially for mussels) close to Walvis Bay station experience diverse threats and stress from physical and biochemical factors, leading to the accumulation of metals in their body and shells. The narrated opportunities have the potential to improve and grow the mariculture sector in Namibia. Other countries with similar coastal characteristics, such as Angola and South Africa, can capitalise on the discussed opportunities to benefit their mariculture industry. Mariculture has an enormous potential to address social problems such as food insecurity and unemployment and, at the same time, remove pressure from wild capture fisheries. These benefits are directly proportional to an increase in production. The main strength of mariculture is that it is not limited by water, space and feed. Arid maritime countries such as Namibia can take advantage of the limitless water supply from the ocean. Therefore, it is anticipated that aspiring mariculturists would be able to realise the potential in mariculture as discussed in this chapter and that this sector will expand in the future, moving forward.

References

Adeleke B, Robertson-Andersson D, Moodley G, Taylor S (2021) Aquaculture in Africa: A comparative review of Egypt, Nigeria, and Uganda Vis-À-Vis South Africa. Rev Fisheries Sci Aquat 29(2):167–197. https://doi.org/10.1080/23308249.2020.1795615

Ahmed N, Thompson S, Glaser M (2019) Global aquaculture productivity, environmental sustainability, and climate change adaptability. Environ Manag 63:159–172

Akegbejo-Samsons Y (2022) Aquaculture and fisheries production in Africa: highlighting potentials and benefits for food security. In: Mupambwa HA, Nciizah AD, Nyambo P, Muchara B, Gabriel NN (eds) Food security for African smallholder farmers. Springer Nature Singapore Pte Ltd, Gateway East, Singapore

Azizi G, Akodad M, Baghour M, Layachi M, Moumen A (2018) The use of Mytilus spp. mussels as bioindicators of heavy metal pollution in the coastal environment. A review. J Mater Environ Sci 9(4):1170–1181

Britz PJ (2006) A Review of Aquaculture Policy and Institutional Capacity in the BCLME Region with Recommended Regional Policy Options. Report BCLME project LMR/MC/03/01. Development of Responsible Aquaculture Policy for the BCLME Region

Bromley C, McGonigle C, Ashton EC, Roberts D (2016) Bad moves: Pros and cons of moving oysters – a case study of global translocations of *Ostrea edulis* Linnaeus, 1758 (Mollusca)

Brown AR, Lilley M, Shutler J, Lowe C, Artioli Y, Torres R, Berdalet E, Tyler CR (2019) Assessing risks and mitigating impacts of harmful algal blooms on mariculture and marine fisheries. Rev Aquac:1–26

Chiripanhura B, Teweldemedhin M (2016) An analysis of the fishing industry in Namibia: the structure, performance, challenges, and prospects for growth and diversification. www.agrodep.org/sites/default/files/AGRODEPWP0021

Critchley KW, Rotmann G, Molloy FJ (1991) The Namibian seaweed industry: present and potential. Bioresour Technol 38:137–143

Crona B, Wassénius W, Troell M, Barclay K, Mallory T, Fabinyi M, Zhang W et al (2020) China at a crossroads: an analysis of China's changing seafood production and consumption. One Earth 3:32–44

Emeis KC, Brüchert V, Currie B, Endler R, Ferdelman T, Kiessling A, Leipe T, Noli-Peard K, Struck U, Vogt T (2004) Shallow gas in shelf sediments of the Namibian coastal upwelling ecosystem. Cont Shelf Res 24:627–642

Erasmus VN, Kadhila T, Thyberg KL, Kamara K, D'Almaida G (2021) Public perceptions and factors affecting domestic marine fish consumption in Namibia, southwestern Africa. Reg Stud Mar Sci 47:101921

Faul A, Coetzer W (2020) Development and operations of proposed abalone and mussel mariculture activities and seaweed collection at Lüderitz: Environmental Assessment Scoping Report

Food and Agricultural Organisation (FAO) (2018) The state of world fisheries and aquaculture: meeting the sustainable development goals. Food and Agriculture Organization of the United Nations, Rome

Food and Agricultural Organisation (FAO) (2020). The State of World Fisheries and Aquaculture 2020. Sustainability in action. Rome. https://doi.org/10.4060/ca9229en

Froehlich HE, Gentry RR, Halpern BS (2018) Global change in marine aquaculture production potential under climate change. Nat Ecol Evol 2:1745–1750

Gabriel NN, Wilhelm M, Habte-Tsion H-M, Chimwamurombe P, Omoregie E, Iipinge, LN, Shimooshili K (2019) Effect of dietary Aloe vera polysaccharides supplementation on growth performance, feed utilization, hemato-biochemical parameters, and survival at low pH in African catfish (*Clarias gariepinus*) fingerlings

Gabriel NN, Erasmus VN, Namwoonde A (2020) Effects of different fish sizes, temperatures, and concentration levels of sodium bicarbonate on anaesthesia in Mozambique tilapia (*Oreochromis mossambicus*). Aquaculture. https://doi.org/10.1016/j.aquaculture.2020.735716

Galgani F, Brien AS, Weis J, Ioakeimidis C, Schuyler Q, Makarenko I, Griffiths H, Bondareff J, Vethaak D, Deidun A, Sobral P, Topouzelis K, Vlahos P, Lana F, Hassellov M, Gerigny O, Arsonina B, Ambulkar A, Azzaro M, Bebianno MJ (2021) Are litter, plastic and microplastic quantities increasing in the ocean? Microplast Nanoplast 1:2

Garlock T, Asche F, Anderson J, Bjørndal T, Kumar G, Lorenzen K, Ropicki A et al (2020) A global blue revolution: aquaculture growth across regions, species, and countries. Rev Fisheries Sci Aquat 28:107–116

Gíslason D, Helyar SJ, Óskarsson GJ, Ólafsdóttir G, Slotte A, Jansen T, Jacobsen JA, Ólafsson K, Skirnisdottir S, Dahle G, Siegstad H, Joensen H, Curti KL, Grégoire F, Masse J, Sveinsson S, Daníelsdóttir AK, Pampoulie C (2020) The genetic composition of feeding aggregations of the Atlantic mackerel (Scomber scombrus) in the central North Atlantic: a microsatellite loci approach. ICES J Marine Sci 77:604–612

Government of Namibia (GoN) (2004) Vision 2030. National Planning Commission, Windhoek. Accessed from http://www.gov.na/vision-2030

Government of Namibia (GoN) (2012) Namibia's Fourth National Development Plan: NDP 4 2012/13 to 2016/17. National Planning Commission, Windhoek

Horton AA (2022) Plastic pollution: when do we know enough? J Hazard Mater 422

Iitembu JA (2005) Analysis of Marine Aquaculture Developments in Namibia: Environmental, Economic and Legislative considerations. Master of Science in International Fisheries Management Norwegian College of Fishery Science, University of Tromsø, N-9037, Tromsø, Norway

Junker T, Mohrholz V, Siegfried L, van der Plas A (2017) Seasonal to interannual 176 variability of water mass characteristics and currents on the Namibian shelf. J Mar Syst 165:36–46

Kroeker KJ et al (2013) Impacts of ocean acidification on marine organisms: quantifying sensitivities and interaction with warming. Glob Chang Biol 19(6):1884–1896

Mapfumo B (2009) History and development of shellfish cultivation in Walvis Bay, Namibia. EC FP7 Project, SARNISSA

Ministry of Fisheries and Marine Resources (MFMR) (2001) Towards Responsible Development of Aquaculture: Namibia's Aquaculture Policy. Ministry of Fisheries and Marine Resources

Ministry of Fisheries and Marine Resources (MFMR) (2004) Namibia's Aquaculture Strategic Plan. Ministry of Fisheries and Marine Resources

Ministry of Fisheries and Marine Resources (MFMR) (2018) Ministry of Fisheries and Marine Resources Annual Report 2017/2018. (Unpublished Report). Ministry of Fisheries and Marine Resources, The Republic of Namibia, Windhoek

Ministry of Fisheries Marine Resources (MFMR) (2019) Ministry of Fisheries and Marine Resources. Statistics. Unpublished Landing Data. Ministry of Fisheries and Marine Resources, The Republic of Namibia, Windhoek

Ministry of Fisheries Marine Resources (MFMR) Mariculture data. (Unpublished data). Ministry of Fisheries and Marine Resources, The Republic of Namibia, Windhoek

Mmochi A (2016) Assessment of food security from marine resources. Regional State of the Coast Report

Monteiro PMS, van der Plas A, Mohrholz V, Mabille E, Pascall A, Joubert W (2006) Variability of natural hypoxia and methane production in a coastal upwelling system: oceanic physics or shelf biology? Geophys Res Lett 33:L16614. https://doi.org/10.1029/2006GL026234

Murta G, Kibria G (2017) An emerging shellfish farming industry in Namibia. Global Aquaculture Advocate. https://www.aquaculturealliance.org/advocate/emerging-shellfish-farming-industry-namibia/?headlessPrint=AAAAAPIA9c8r7gs82oWZBA

Naylor RL, Hardy RW, Buschmann AH, Bush SR, Cao L, Klinger DH, Troell M (2021) A 20-year retrospective review of global aquaculture. Nature 591:551–563. https://doi.org/10.1038/s41586-021-03308-6

Paterson B, Kirchner C, Ommer RE (2013) A short history of the Namibian hake fishery, a social-ecological analysis. Ecol Soc 18(4):66

Petton B, Destoumieux-Garzón D, Pernet F, Toulza E, de Lorgeril J, Degremont L, Mitta G (2021) The Pacific oyster mortality syndrome, a polymicrobial and multifactorial disease: state of knowledge and future directions. Front Immunol. Frontiers. In press. https://doi.org/10.3389/fimmu.2021.630343. hal-03128446

Rourke WA, Justason A, Martin JL, Murphy CJ (2021) Shellfish toxin uptake and depuration in multiple Atlantic Canadian molluscan species: application to selection of sentinel species in monitoring programs. Toxins (Basel). 13(2):168. https://doi.org/10.3390/toxins13020168. PMID: 33671640; PMCID: PMC7926447

SADC (2020) Annual Report 2020/2021. https://www.sadc.int/news-events/news/sadc-pilot-projects-align-regional-and-national-aquaculture-frameworks-region/

Sumaila UR, Boyer D, Skogen MD, Steinshamn SI (2004) Namibia's fisheries: introduction and overview. In: Sumaila UR, Steinshamn SI, Skog M, Boyer DC (eds) Ecological, economic and social aspects of Namibian fisheries. Eburon, Netherlands, pp 1–9

Tjipute M (2011) Feasibility study for mass production of the silver kob, Argyrosomus inodorus, in Namibia. United Nations University – Fisheries Training Programme, Reykjavík

Trading Economics (2019) Namibia unemployment rate viewed 04 2020, from https://tradingeconomics.com/namibia/unemployment-rate

Van der Lingen CD, Hutchings L, Pitcher GC, Lamont T (2016) Climate change, dinoflagellate blooms 1045 and sardine in the southern Benguela current large marine ecosystem. Environ Dev 17:230–243. https://doi.org/10.1016/j.envdev.2015.09.004

Villasante S, Rodríguez SR, Molares Y, Martínez M, Remiro J, García-Díez C, Lahoz C, Omar I, Bechardas M, Elago P, Ekandjo M (2015) Are provisioning ecosystem services from rural aquaculture contributing to reduce hunger in Africa? Ecosyst Serv 16:365–377. https://doi.org/10.1016/j.ecoser.2015.07.003

Chapter 21
Climate SMART Best Practices in Aquaculture and Fisheries with Specific Emphasis on Sierra Leone

Olapade O. Julius

Abstract In Sierra Leone, just like in any other developing nation, the effects of climate change are perspicuous, affecting food security, social services, social cohesion, and human displacement and migration. Solar radiation received by the earth and human activities such as bush burning, charcoal burning, deforestation, intensive use of land for agriculture and other biotic activities has been implicated in causing the incrcasc in global warming. The precarious and vulnerable conditions of many fishing and coastal communities due to climate events are glaringly evident, leading to poverty and underdevelopment. Climate change, a variation in weather pattern distribution and or average weather conditions over some time, is impacting the infrastructural base and socio-economic sectors of the country, leading to increase deforestation and a decline in agricultural productivity. Climate change has become a subject of intense public debate, especially by researchers and policymakers, and has put the government of Sierra Leone on the decision-making edge. The fisheries and aquaculture sector of the country shares in the adverse outcomes of climate incidences. The industry is regarded as high risk in the context of climate change as they are easily vulnerable to changes in environmental variables that further compound the socio-economic woes of the fishing communities, and communities that depend heavily on fish and ancillary activities for food security and income generation. This chapter reviewed the literature on the impact of climate change on the fisheries and aquaculture sector with specific emphasis on Sierra Leone to understand climate SMART best practices in the all-important sector that contribute significantly to the nation's Gross Domestic Product.

Keywords Fisheries · Aquaculture · Coastal communities · Climate events · Vulnerable · Sierra Leone

---

O. O. Julius (✉)
Department of Aquaculture & Fisheries Management, School of Natural Resources Management, Njala University, Freetown, Sierra Leone
e-mail: ojulius@njala.edu.sl

© The Author(s), under exclusive license to Springer Nature Singapore Pte Ltd. 2023

N. N. Gabriel et al. (eds.), *Emerging Sustainable Aquaculture Innovations in Africa*, Sustainable Agriculture and Food Security,
https://doi.org/10.1007/978-981-19-7451-9_21

21.1 Introduction

The role and contributions of the fisheries and aquaculture in terms of food supply, security and income generation globally have been discussed severally by researchers. About 43.5 million people are believed to work in the fisheries and aquaculture sector, many of whom come from third-world countries. In reality, it is thought that the fisheries and aquaculture sector support close to 200 million livelihoods when the processing, marketing, distribution and supply industries are added up. More than 1.5 billion people from the third-world nation benefit from aquatic foods, which supply 20 per cent or more per capita animal protein intake. According to FAO (2008), marine products are the most widely traded foodstuff globally and contribute to export earnings of Asian and most third-world countries. The small island state mainly depends on the fisheries and aquaculture sectors for about 50 per cent of animal protein needs. Whatever affects this sector, no doubt, can affect the livelihood of those who depend on it.

Climate change is one environmental factor creating severe concern for the management and productivity of the fisheries and aquaculture sectors. According to FAO (2008), climate change will pressure livelihoods and food supplies. Its effects would be felt across ecosystems, societies and economic sectors of countries, including the fisheries and aquaculture subsector. Food quality, mainly from fishing and aquaculture, is critical as a developmental issue. Compared to mainstream agriculture, the fisheries and aquaculture sectors has peculiar interactions and needs concerning climate change. Aquaculture is known to complement supply and has links with the capture fisheries, a unique subsector closely linked with global ecosystem processes. It has become glaring that changes in fishing practices, aquaculture operations, location of landing, farming and processing facilities will be influenced by changes in habitat, species composition and distribution.

The pronounced influence of climate change on the fisheries and aquaculture in Sierra Leone is worrisome, affecting the livelihoods and the food security of the people who depend on the sector (Benjamin 2015). Climate change means that many dry areas are going to get drier, wet areas are going to get wetter, and these are current realities in Sierra Leone. It is, however, important to mention that climate change will be more significant over land than over sea because land retains heat more than water. Benjamin (2015) noted increasing evidence that Sierra Leone will be particularly hit by vertical rises and falls in air currents. The author opined that the country might be caught between the devil of droughts and the deep blue seas of floods—a 'great tragedy' (Benjamin 2015). The Intergovernmental Panel on Climate Change (IPCC) elevated the threats of climate change to human society and the ecosystem as a top priority. Therefore, it is essential to focus on the effects of climate change on fisheries and aquaculture, a crucial economic sector in the country, and its pronounced impact on the coastal and riparian communities in Sierra Leone (Benjamin 2015). One interesting thing to note is that most artisanal fishers and coastal dwellers lack adequate knowledge of Climate Smart Practices and sustainable environmental practices. This has further increased their vulnerability and risks to fisheries and the environment. The impact of climate change on fisheries and aquaculture sector and the exposure of the people makes it urgently imperative for practical education on earth system science; the human and behavioural aspects of climate change, and the broad societal action to smart energy choices at the household level (Gardner and Stern 2008). Education should cover food production, nutrition security, and economic growth and development. This paper aims to provide relevant information on climate change adaptive strategies that will guide practical fisheries and aquaculture production in Sierra Leone. The information in this paper will provide practical starting points to actors involved in the fishing and aquaculture sector of Sierra Leone in the face of climate change events.

21.2 Causes of Climate Change

Simply put, climate change is a variation in weather pattern distribution or average weather conditions over an extended period. The observed changes may be caused by so many factors, including biotic processes, the type of solar radiation by the earth and human activities that results in global warming (Carbon posting or emissions). Human activities are notoriously implicated in the warming of the globe (IPCC 2007; National Research Council 2010). Deforestation, increasing population pressure, intensive agricultural land use, overgrazing, bush burning, extraction of fuel wood and other biotic resources are believed to contribute to an increase in average global temperature. This elevated temperature, according to Benjamin (2015), is caused primarily by increases in greenhouse gases such as carbon dioxide (CO_2). According to Cunningham and Cunningham (2004) and Osborn (2010), climate change occurs when temperature increases, especially by 0.2 °C, with differences in rising in precipitation and rise in the ocean level. CO2 is the pre-eminent greenhouse gas responsible for global warming. Other gases that have been reported in studies by researchers include methane and nitrous oxide. These gases come from fossil fuels, landfills and agriculture, and industrial processes.

21.3 Climate Change Impact on Fisheries and Aquaculture

Climate change affects fisheries and the aquaculture sector in diverse ways, discussed under two categories – effects on the ecosystem and human livelihood sustenance. Climate change affects the four dimensions of food security as presented here:

1. Availability—alteration of habitats affects the stock composition and species distribution, consequently influencing aquatic food supply.

2. Stability—this will be influenced by factors such as changes in productivity of the ecosystem, seasonal and increased supply variability, and risks.
3. Access—availability and access to aquatic foods will be influenced by livelihood patterns, catching or farming opportunities.
4. Utilisation—there will be a change in the type of aquatic products readily accessed and the way they are used by people. Meaning communities will start to utilise species that were not traditionally preferred.

21.4 Climate Change and the Aquatic Ecosystem

Greenhouse gas (GHG) accumulation in the atmosphere and water is a physical phenomenon that influences changes in the physical properties of water, especially water temperature and acidification of water bodies; it also affects ocean currents and rising sea levels. The ecological functions in the aquatic systems, their frequency and intensity, are affected by climatic events (Cochrane et al. 2009). Climate change and its associated events have far-reaching effects, both direct and indirect on fisheries and aquaculture. There is a reduction in the productivity of most tropical and subtropical aquatic ecosystems. The impact of the changes on the physiological and behavioural processes of fish and their prey has been variously reported. Evidence abounds for the modification of the distribution of marine species by global warming. There are changes in the size and productivity of the habitats of warm water species that are being moved towards the pole.

21.4.1 Specific Impact of Climate Change on the Ecosystem

- Displacement of tropical fish species towards the pole, and the shrinking in the size and productivity of their habitats.
- Reduction in the productivity of both tropical and subtropical aquatic ecosystem.
- Elevated temperature with both positive and negative effect on the fisheries and aquaculture systems.
- Effects on seasonality of certain biological processes like the food webs which in turn affect fish production negatively. There is also increased spread of vector-borne disease, a result of alien species invasion.
- Differential warming between land and ocean, and between polar and tropical regions affect freshwater and marine resources stability.

  – Other consequences of this warming are:

    Floods.
    Drought.
    Storms.
    Change in climate pattern – El Nino.

Plate 21.1 Coastal erosion effect in Sierra Leone (Source: https://www.google.com.sl/search)

- A rise in sea level, glacier melting, ocean acidification and changes in precipitation.
- Ground water and river flows effect on coral reefs, wetlands, rivers, lakes and estuaries.
- Uncertain supply of freshwater (Plate 21.1).

21.5 Climate Impact on Livelihoods and Food Security

The world's aquatic ecosystem benefits many people globally as a critical component of the global food production system ensuring food security and economic prosperity. The fisheries and aquaculture sectors are particularly important in any nation's development, playing a significant role in food security and enhanced livelihood of billions of people in developing countries. FAO (2009a; b) reported the precarious and vulnerable states of many fishing and coastal communities worldwide. This sad situation results from fishery resources overexploitation, habitat degradation, poverty and underdevelopment of the rural coastal communities. The effect of climate change, according to FAO (2009a, b), is becoming pronounced in fishing and coastal communities. Climate events threaten inland fisheries and fish farming worldwide, causing adverse effects on the food supply and livelihoods of the poor population. The fisher folks in the coastal communities in Sierra Leone depend on the overfished fishery resources and inhabit areas deficient in basic social amenities and infrastructure. The vulnerability of the fisheries and aquaculture sectors to climate change is profound and affects the communities that depend on them. This vulnerability, however, depends on the potential impact (sensitivity and exposure) and adaptive capacity of the sectors. Ecological (semi-arid and coastal locations) and social (significant dependence on fish for protein, low adaptive capacity, weak economies and low human development) factors, according to WorldFish Center (2007) have made the African fisheries sector more vulnerable.

21.5.1 People, Communities and Vulnerability

Vulnerability to climate change by people and communities, according to the Intergovernmental Panel on Climate Change (2001), vulnerability to change depend to a greater extent on the degree of exposure, the sensitivity of a system to such changes and the adaptive capacity of the system. The most vulnerable to climate change are the developing nations, which are primarily limited in terms of resources to adapt: socially, technologically, and financially. Climate change is anticipated to have far-reaching effects on developing countries sustainable development, including their ability to attain the United Nations Millennium Development Goals by 2015 (UN 2007). Many developing countries' governments have given adaptation action a high, even urgent, priority. Vulnerability in fisheries and aquaculture rests on certain factors, such as identification of exposure of concern, scale and phase for adaptation planning, and the availability of data for planning. Allison et al. (2009) described the vulnerability of national economies to climate from the perspective of the potential impact on the country fisheries, while Bell et al. (2011) focused on the vulnerability of species, food webs and ecosystems and explored the issues related to tunas, their food web, coral reefs, mangroves, freshwater habitats and fisheries activities in the tropical Pacific islands.

Cinner et al. (2012), to understand the links between the human and aquatic system and coral reef-dependent fishing communities' vulnerability to climate change, build upon the IPCC model. Impacts of climate change to be experienced by fisheries and aquaculture-dependent economies, coastal and riparian communities are shifts away from traditional fishing grounds or changes in available fish species. Direct risks due to sea level rise, stronger sea surges and changes in the frequency, distribution or intensity of tropical storms may happen to fishers, farmers and coastal communities. Other risks to be experienced are those of human diseases related to increased air and water temperature. Climate change will also impact food security, social services, social cohesion, and human displacement and migration. The vulnerability of the fishing and coastal communities is perspicuous, with almost palpable poverty and underdevelopment. These communities do not have easy access to capital and lack the skills to sustainably exploit available fish stocks and other natural resources and improve the degraded ecosystems. As noted in this paper, the vulnerability of the fisheries, aquaculture and fishing communities depend significantly on the uncertain ability of individuals or systems to anticipate these changes and adapt, not just their exposure and sensitivity to change. De Silva and

Soto (2009) noted that the high population densities of the tropics, where the bulk of the world's aquaculture production is situated, make it more vulnerable.

21.6 Climate Impact on Fisheries and Aquaculture

The impact of climate change is not felt only by the diverse ecosystems but by societies, economies, livelihoods and food supplies (FAO 2008). According to WorldFish Centre (2007), ecological and social factors have made West and Central African countries the most vulnerable. The degree of vulnerability of the fisheries and aquaculture sector is dependent on either the severity or extremity of the climate elements. The solar heat energy absorbed by the aquatic habitats makes the fisheries sector particularly vulnerable. Climate change influences the physical and chemical variables of water bodies, particularly water temperature. It affects the physiological functions of fish which are cold blooded, water supplies and the populations, the normal resiliency and productivity of the aquatic ecosystems, livelihood and food security (Plate 21.2).

21.6.1 Impact on Fish Physiology and Population

The physiological and biochemical processes of most freshwater and marine fish species are dictated by the prevailing ambient water temperature. Smith (1989) observed that the breathing rates, feed consumption, enzyme activities, oxygen

Plate 21.2 Flooding of the Njala University fish farm as a result of weather variability

Table 21.1 Temperature tolerance of selected cultured species from a different ecology Modified from Ficke et al. (2007)

Climate/temperature guild/ species		Incipient lethal temperature (°C)	
Tropical	Lower	Higher	Optimal range
Redbelly tilapia (*Tilapia zilli*)	7	42	28.8–31.4
Guinean tilapia (*Tilapia guineensis*)	14	34	18–32
Warm water subtropical			
European eel (*Anguilla anguilla*)	0	39	21–23
Channel catfish (*Ictalurus punctatus*)	0	40	20–25
Temperate polar			
Arctic charr (*Salvelinus alpinus*)	0	19.7	6–15
Rain bow trout (*Oncorhynchus mykiss*)	0	27	9–14
Atlantic salmon (*Salmo salar*)	−0.5	25	13–17

consumption and feed metabolism are altered by abnormally high temperature and this, according to him, affects fish growth. An increase in fish population is influenced by how fast the fish grow and reach maturity size, the fecundity and recruitment into the exploitable phase. The number of fish available for harvesting based on the sustainable yield principle is a function of the population size. There is, however, a decline in the quantity and quality of freshwater and marine fish population because of the pressure exerted on it through overfishing and pollution. The recruitment phase (larvae, fry and fingerlings) is heavily affected by predation, competition and water quality, thus limiting survival to few that thrive in the adult phase. A decrease in fish population is exacerbated by the increase in water temperature, with a limiting effect on oxygen transport, a situation that could significantly impact aquaculture and result in changes in the distribution and abundance of both marine and freshwater species (FAO 2008) (Table 21.1).

21.6.2 *Impacts on Water Flow*

Climate change is causing a general increase in precipitation worldwide, and Africa is the most prone. One of the events of climate change is the flooding of rivers, lakes and reservoirs with some effects that may be severe, as often witnessed in Sierra Leone and elsewhere. It is therefore becoming increasingly necessary for countries to be well prepared to handle the devastating effects of climate change, especially flooding that has become a yearly event. The coastal zones in Africa are the most vulnerable to the severe impacts of coastal erosion, flooding and storm surges. Social wellbeing, livelihood security, water resources and critical economic sectors like tourism, agriculture and fishing are the most affected. Negative repercussions of climate change on the livelihood of the coastal communities reduced fishing productivity, ecosystem degradation and low farming outputs. Effects of climate change are not all together negative; it is good to know that inundation of adjacent land areas

Plate 21.3 Inundation of fishponds in Kenema caused by weather variability

because of increased rainfall and flooding is beneficial to fisheries. Flooding expands the littoral zones and increases the diversity of the ecotones for fish feeding, breeding and rearing of the juveniles (Plate 21.3).

21.6.3 Impact on Water Quality and Fish Distribution

Climate change influences water temperature, which shares an inverse relationship with oxygen. The solubility of oxygen in water by extreme temperature and the favour survival and multiplication of parasites and bacteria. The cumulative effects of this high temperature, according to Halls (2009), are the negative effect on fish survival, natural food availability, growth and reproductive success of wild fish population and farmed fish species. The capacity of the different water bodies to sustainably produce fish is impaired by climate change. African lakes, as reported by Anonymous (2009), are expected to experience a decrease in annual rainfall and temperature due to the atmospheric temperature on the continent that is higher than the global average. Changes in temperature and precipitation are most likely to affect the wetlands and shallow rivers. Consequently, primary productivity will be lowered, and aquatic organism distribution will be influenced because of the effect of temperature on lake and reservoirs stratification; limited or no seasonal turn over; greater deoxygenation of the bottom layers. Studies have shown that temperature is key in determining the stability of the ocean water. Temperature more than other factors like salinity and depth exerts greater influence on water stability. The result of the variation of water temperature in the different parts of the Atlantic (Ocean) is the variation in the water density, with concomitant effect on distribution of organisms and fishing. The risk associated with abnormally high temperature is the displacement of stenothermal and eurythermal species to unfavourable habitats that impair survival, growth and reproduction (Table 21.2).

21.7 Climate-Smart Approaches in Fisheries and Aquaculture

Climate SMART approaches are specific, measurable, achievable, realistic, and timely coping strategies in vulnerability to climate events. Climate-smart measures for fisheries and aquaculture are not different from that of other sectors. The strategy must consider cross-cutting themes of development and environment. For climate-smart to be useful for development, there are important issues to be resolved as outlined here.

1. It must respond to the growing daily demand for aquatic food; address specific issues of food and livelihoods across the entire supply, value, and benefit chains.
2. Be able to deploy effectively new technologies and also embrace market and socially driven changes within and around the sector.
3. It should identify specific gaps in capacity, efficiency, and system resilience for the sector, particularly those which may increase under climate stress, and identify particular action to be taken for these gaps.
4. Prescribe appropriate options for better policy and management integration within and across the sector, in terms of understanding the function and flows of goods and services from the aquatic systems as well as defining efficient use of these resources.
5. The strategies should connect well with related development objectives, such as hunger eradication, poverty alleviation, resource protection and rehabilitation, nutritional safety and health, personal and community empowerment, self-determination and vulnerability reduction.
6. Must connect with approaches that are recognisable and actionable by policy agents to work effectively with practitioners and beneficiaries at all levels – based on clear evidence of functionality and effectiveness.

21.7.1 Climate SMART Best Practices in the Fisheries of Sierra Leone

More than half (56%) of trapped green or biological carbon captured globally is captured by marine living organisms – this is called blue carbon. Thus, a crucial mitigating approach is to maintain and improve the ability of forests and oceans to absorb and bury carbon-carbon sinking. Three pathways recognised for engaging in mitigation are as follows:

Table 21.2 Ways in which climate change may directly affect production from fisheries and aquaculture

Drivers	Biophysical effects	Implications for fisheries and aquaculture
Increase in frequency and/or intensity of storms	Large waves and storm surges. Inland flooding from intense precipitation. Salinity changes. Introduction of disease or predators into aquaculture facilities during flooding episodes	Loss of aquaculture stock and damage to or loss of aquaculture facilities and fishing gear. Impacts on wild fish recruitment and stocks. Higher direct risk to fishers; capital costs needed to design cage moorings, pond walls, jetties, etc. that can withstand storms; and insurance costs
Drought	Lower water quality and availability for aquaculture. Salinity changes	Loss of wild and cultured stock. Increased production costs. Loss of opportunity as production is limited
	Changes in lake water levels and river flows	Reduced wild fish stocks, intensified competition for fishing areas and more migration by fisher folks
Changes in sea surface temperature	More frequent harmful algal blooms; Less dissolved oxygen; Increased incidence of disease and parasites; Altered local ecosystems with changes in competitors, predators and invasive species, and changes in plankton composition	For aquaculture, changes in infrastructure and operating costs from worsened infestations of fouling organisms, pests, nuisance species and/or predators. For capture fisheries, impacts on the abundance and species composition of fish stocks
	Longer growing seasons; Lower natural mortality in winter; Enhanced metabolic and growth rates	Potential for increased production and profit, especially for aquaculture
	Enhanced primary productivity	Potential benefits for aquaculture and fisheries but perhaps offset by changed species composition
	Changes in timing and success of migrations, spawning and peak abundance, as well as in sex ratios	Aquaculture opportunities both lost and gained. Potential species loss and altered species composition for capture fisheries
	Damage to coral reefs that serve as breeding habitats and may help protect the shore from wave action (the exposure to which may rise along with sea levels).	Reduced recruitment of fishery species. Worsened wave damage to infrastructure or flooding from storm surges.
El Niño-Southern oscillation	Changed location and timing of ocean currents and upwelling alters nutrient supply in surface waters and, consequently, primary productivity	Changes in the distribution and productivity of open sea fisheries
	Changed ocean temperature and bleached coral	Reduced productivity of reef fisheries
	Altered rainfall patterns bring flood and drought	See impacts for precipitation trends, drought and flooding above

(continued)

Table 21.2 (continued)

Drivers	Biophysical effects	Implications for fisheries and aquaculture
Rising sea level	Loss of land	Reduced area available for aquaculture. Loss of freshwater fisheries
	Changes to estuary systems	Shifts in species abundance, distribution and composition of fish stocks and aquaculture seed
	Salt-water infusion into groundwater	Damage to freshwater capture fisheries. Reduced freshwater availability for aquaculture and a shift to brackish water spaces
	Loss of coastal ecosystems such as mangrove forests	Reduced recruitment and stock for capture fisheries and seed for aquaculture. Worsened exposure to waves and storm surge and risk that inland aquaculture and fisheries become inundated
Higher inland water temperatures		Reductions in fish stocks
	Raised metabolic rates increase feeding rates and growth if water quality, dissolved oxygen levels, and food supply are adequate, otherwise possibly reducing feeding and growth. Potential for enhanced primary productivity	Possibly enhanced fish stocks for capture fisheries or else reduced growth where the food supply does not increase sufficiently in line with temperature. Possible benefits for aquaculture, especially intensive and semi-intensive pond systems
	Shift in the location and size of the potential range for a given species	Aquaculture opportunities both lost and gained. Potential loss of species and alteration of species composition for capture fisheries
	Reduced water quality, especially in terms of dissolved oxygen; Changes in the range and abundance of pathogens, predators and competitors; Invasive species introduced	Altered stocks and species composition in capture fisheries; For aquaculture, altered culture species and possibly worsened losses to disease (and so higher operating costs) and possibly higher capital costs for aeration equipment or deeper ponds
	Changes in timing and success of migrations, spawning and peak abundance	Potential loss of species or shift in composition for capture fisheries; Impacts on seed availability for aquaculture
Changes in precipitation and water availability	Changes in fish migration and recruitment patterns and so in recruitment success	Altered abundance and composition of wild stock. Impacts on seed availability for aquaculture
	Lower water availability for aquaculture. Lower water quality causing more disease. Increased competition with other water users Altered and reduced freshwater supplies with greater risk of drought	Higher costs of maintaining pond water levels and from stock loss. Reduced production capacity. Conflict with other water users. Change of culture species

(continued)

Table 21.2 (continued)

Drivers	Biophysical effects	Implications for fisheries and aquaculture
	Changes in lake and river levels and the overall extent and movement patterns of surface water	Altered distribution, composition and abundance of fish stocks. Fishers forced to migrate more and expend more effort

Excerpted from WorldFish Policy Brief (http://pubs.iclarm.net/resource_centre/ClimateChange2.pdf)

1. Improve knowledge of water–climate interactions and how aquatic ecosystems function at various levels to take up and sequester CO_2.
2. Prevent the further loss and degradation of coastal and other aquatic ecosystems and catalyse their recovery. It is essential to determine how much CO_2 the aquatic ecosystems can offset in a year (3–7% or 7200Tg CO_2).
3. Define how these 'Blue Carbon' sinks could be further managed and, in some cases, further extended.

21.7.1.1 Local Win–Win Approaches

There are win–win approaches that could sequester GHG, enhance adaption and contribute to food security, rural livelihoods, poverty reduction and environmental services. Specific interventions include but are not limited to the following.

- Invest in aquaculture of algae and seaweeds.
- Invest in microalgae production for biofuels.
- Stop forest burning.
- Avoid cutting down riparian forests especially mangrove trees.
- Engage awareness education on the impact of climate.
- Plant more trees.
- Stop sand mining and dredging.
- Invest in alternative energy options.
- Provision of alternative income-generating opportunities for coastal dwellers.

21.8 Gender Perspectives in Climate Smart Agriculture

Gender should be considered in climate smart agriculture, especially from resource access competition, risk vulnerability, livelihood shift, distribution and processing in which women take the leading role. It is certain that with variations in rainfall patterns and higher temperatures, most farmers will have to shift what they produce and how they produce it. The contribution of women to fisheries and aquaculture is often undervalued or misinterpreted, with their related dependence and vulnerability due mainly to inadequate gender awareness and involvement (FAO 2009a, b). To achieve the desired transformative changes in agriculture and food security, there is a need to tackle gender issues by recognising it as a critical component in climate-smart agricultural practices. The actions stated below will go a long way to integrate gender into CSA in Sierra Leone and elsewhere.

1. **Invest** in 'action research' initiatives that test new farming practices and value-added activities with women and men. We need to learn together what works best and how to support all those producing food in different environments in a wide range of farming systems.
2. **Catalyse** and support strategic and structured partner engagement efforts with local governments, private sector and civil society organisations working closely with women, as well as men and other food system actors.
3. **Strengthen** the capacity of these partners in gender-disaggregated data collection and analysis and forward-looking and inclusive, evidence-based local adaptation planning efforts.
4. **Test** innovative communication strategies, together with private and public sector partners in many countries, to reach more women and youth with much-needed information on exciting new options and opportunities in agriculture.

21.9 How to Respond to Climate Change Impact

- Awareness-raising through the synthesis of observations on the mechanisms behind climate change and its potential impact on fisheries, aquaculture and aquatic ecosystems; the development of relevant guidelines ensuring that climate change impact assessment covers aquatic ecosystems and fisheries and aquaculture adequately.
- Knowledge improvements through a better understanding of risks—who and what is affected – and the role and implications of vulnerability (different areas, regions, and scales); harmonisation of indicators databases; strengthening and/or creating working groups to access impacts and consequences; and development of guidelines.
- Implementation of activities through targeting ongoing planning and development processes, lobbying regional fisheries and other organisations and non-governmental organisations (NGOs) regarding guidelines, capacity building, and encouraging relevant organisations to include climate change in their action plans and to identify leaders and key players.

21.9.1 Strategies for Climate Change Adaptation

- Awareness raising through targeted communication strategies, synthesising current knowledge, and identifying and targeting community leaders and movers.

- Knowledge improvements through identifying benefits of well-managed fisheries and aquaculture systems; training in key themes, use of ecosystem approaches, pilot projects, monitoring and impact assessments; identification and targeting of vulnerable communities and enhancement of systems for monitoring and assessing risk from natural hazards.
- Implementation of activities such as dissemination of key messages, convening multilevel meetings, capacity building and empowerment of policymakers; promotion of diversified livelihoods for vulnerable communities, insurance schemes, disaster relief funds and the integration of fisheries and aquaculture into the climate change mitigation and adaptation strategies of other sectors.
- Identification of resources and partners to ensure financing is available for fisheries and aquaculture adaptation strategies; development of resource mobilisation teams and strategies; entering strategic partnerships and exploring the possibilities for funding at the community level.

21.9.2 Climate Change Mitigation and Policy Actions

- Awareness raising through the development and dissemination of key policy messages, development of best practices brochures and integration action in ongoing mitigation processes.
- Knowledge improvement through workshops and specific technical reviews and case studies; better understanding and use of the potential of aquatic environments (and aquatic food production systems).
- Implementation of activities such as testing approaches to emission reduction; the role of certification and labelling in marketing products; technical guidelines; linking fleet decommissioning and efficiency improvements with carbon markets; mainstreaming mitigation into policies; development of national frameworks and setting emission reduction targets for the sector.
- Identify resources and partners to ensure short-term to long-term financing through various donors from the private sector, national governments, and multilateral and bilateral agencies.

21.10 Conclusion

There is no gainsaying that the fisheries and aquaculture sector of Sierra Leone is a significant revenue generation sector that contributes to the national gross domestic product (GDP). It is also important to mention that the fisheries and aquaculture sector plays a significant role in world food security, providing nutritious food and contributing to economic growth, development, income and livelihood of millions of people, especially in Africa. The sector contributes to the livelihood of the fishing and fish farming-dependent inhabitants of the coastal and riparian communities.

Unfortunately, the sector is being impacted by climate change, making the fishing and coastal communities more vulnerable. Climate change influences the rise in sea temperatures and migration of fish stocks from equatorial latitudes towards the colder waters; it also affects the sizes of fish, migratory patterns and mortality rates of wild fish stocks. The challenges confronting the fisheries and aquaculture sector demean its sustainability and productivity. The influences of climate change on the fishing and coastal communities of Sierra Leone are becoming alarming. Annual flooding and coastal erosion have become an issue of grave concern that renders the fisheries sector and coastal communities at high risk and vulnerability. The resilience, sustainability and productivity of this sector would depend on the appropriation of appropriate management strategies. The use of climate SMART approaches has been proposed to enhance the sustainable production of the fisheries sector and to make the fisher folks and coastal communities more resilient to the vagaries of climate change. This paper espouses important climate SMART practices that would help enhance the capacity of the fisher folks to deal with climate events.

References

Allison EH, Beveridge MCM, van Brakel M (2009) Climate change, small-scale fisheries and smallholder aquaculture. In: Culberg M (ed) Fish, trade and development. Stockholm, Royal Swedish Academy of Agriculture and Forestry, pp 73–87. (in press)

Anonymous (2009) Fisheries and aquaculture in a changing climate. FAO, ICES, ISDR and Others. http://siteresources.worldbank.org/EXTARD/Resources/336681-1224775570533/MultiagencyPolicyBriefCOP15.pdf

Bell JD, Johnson JE, Hobday AJ (eds) (2011) Vulnerability of tropical Pacific fisheries and aquaculture to climate change. Noumea, Secretariat of the Pacific Community, p 925. http://www.spc.int/cces/climate-book/spc-publications-onclimate-change/

Benjamin G (2015) Effects of climate change in sierra leone. Concord Times Newspaper, Published February 2015. Retrieved from http://slconcordtimes.com

Cinner J, McClanahan TR, Graham NAJ, Daw TM, Maina J, Stead SM, Wamukota A, Brown K, Bodin O (2012) Vulnerability of coastal communities to key impacts of climate change on coral reef fisheries. Glob Environ Chang 22(1):12–20

Cochrane K, De Young C, Soto D, Bahri T (2009) Climate change implications for fisheries and aquaculture: overview of current scientific knowledge. Fisheries and Aquaculture Technical Paper No. 530. Rome, FAO. 212 p. ftp://ftp.fao.org/docrep/fao/012/i0994e/i0994e.pdf)

Cunningham WP, Cunningham MA (2004) Principles of environmental science, inquiry and applications, 2nd edn. McGraw-Hill Publishing Co. Ltd. Inc., Oxord, p 303

De Silva SS, Soto D (2009) Climate change and aquaculture: potential impacts, adaptation and mitigation. In K Cochrane, C De Young, D Soto, T Bahri (eds). Climate change implications for fisheries and aquaculture. Overview of current scientific knowledge. *FAO Fisheries and Aquaculture Technical Paper*. No. 530. Rome. FAO. pp 151–212

FAO (2008) Report of the FAO expert workshop on climate change implications for fisheries and aquaculture, Rome, April 7–9, 2008. FAO Fisheries Report No. 870, Food and Agriculture Organization of the United Nations, Rome, Italy, pp 1–32

FAO (2009a) Fisheries and aquaculture: Multiple risks from climate change. Food and Agriculture Organization. http://www.fao.org/news/story/en/item/38060/icode/

FAO (2009b) Strategic Framework 2010–2019 (available at www.fao.org/about/19185-1-0.pdf)

Ficke AD, Myrick CA, Hansen LJ (2007) Potential impacts of global change on freshwater fisheries. Rev Fish Biol Fisheries 17:581–613

Gardner GT, Stern PC (2008) The short list: the most effective actions u.s. households can take to curb climate change. Taylor and Francis Group, Philadelphia. http://www.environmentmagazine.org/Archives/Back%20Issues/SeptemberOctober%202008/gardner-stern-full.html

Halls AS (2009) Addressing fisheries in the climate change and adaptation initiative. Fish Res Dev Melkong Region 15:1. http://archive.iwlearn.net/mrcmekong.org/Catch-Culture/vol15_1May09/Fisheries-Climate-Change.htm

Intergovernmental Panel on Climate Change (IPCC) (2001) Climate change 2001: impacts, adaptation, and vulnerability. IPCC third Assessment Report. http://www.grida.no/publications/other/ipcc_tar/)

IPCC (2007) Climate change: impacts, adaptation and vulnerability. In: Parry ML, OF Canziani, Palutikof JP, van der Linden PJ, Hanson CE (eds) Contribution of Working Group II to the Fourth Assessment Report of the Intergovernmental Panel on Climate Change. Cambridge University Press, Cambridge, UK, p 976. http://www.ipcc.ch/pdf/assessment-report/ar4/wg2/ar4_wg2_full_report.pdf

National Research Council (2010) Advancing the science of climate change. America's climate choices: Panel on advancing the science of climate change. The National Academies Press, Washington, DC

Osborn L (2010) History of changes in the earth's temperature. http://www.currentresults.com/Environment-Facts/changes-in-earth-temperature.php

Smith RR (1989) Nutritional energetic. In: Halver JE (ed) Fish nutrition, 2nd edn. Academic Press, New York, pp 2–31

UN (2007) The Millenium Development Goals Report, United Nations. New York. http://www.un.org/ millenniumgoals/pdf/mdg2007.pdf

WorldFish Center (2007) Fisheries and aquaculture can provide solutions to cope with climate change. Fisheries and aquaculture can provide solutions to cope with climate change. Issues Brief 1701, WorldFish Center, Penang, Malaysia, pp 1–4

Chapter 22
The Potential of Small-Scale Freshwater Aquaculture for Household Nutritional Security and Malnutrition Alleviation in Namibia

Rebekka Ndatolewe Gabriel, Ndakalimwe Naftal Gabriel, and Ottilie Nameya Shikesho

Abstract Malnutrition is a widespread problem, especially in sub-Saharan Africa, of which Namibia is part. This chapter aims to discourse on small-scale freshwater aquaculture, its contribution to improving food security at the household level and its potential to relieve the malnutrition burden in Namibia. Fish is an excellent source of nutrients essential for human health and is part of the solution to building solid food systems and maintainable quality diets. Although it is still in its infancy, Namibia's aquaculture industry has the potential to grow. In the same vein, small-scale freshwater aquaculture has the potential to improve food security and thus reduce malnutrition prevalence, particularly in rural Namibia, where the majority of the poor live. However, there is a need to differentiate small scale from commercial farming to ease the regulatory problems on farmers potentially farming for household consumption. The government still has a long way to go to fully exploit the potential of small-scale aquaculture. Among others, there is a need for aquaculture promotion, education, technical knowledge and support, financial support, policy reviews and intersectoral collaborations with sister sectors such as agriculture.

Keywords Aquaculture · Namibia · Malnutrition · Freshwater · Nutrition

---

R. N. Gabriel (✉)
Faculty of Health Sciences and Veterinary Medicine, Department of Community and Mental Health Nursing Science, University of Namibia, Windhoek, Namibia
e-mail: rgabriel@unam.na

N. N. Gabriel
Department of Fisheries and Ocean Sciences, Faculty of Agriculture, Engineering, and Natural Science, Sam Nujoma Campus, University of Namibia, Henties Bay, Namibia

O. N. Shikesho
Faculty of Health Sciences and Veterinary Medicine, University of Namibia, Oshakati, Namibia

© The Author(s), under exclusive license to Springer Nature Singapore Pte Ltd. 2023

N. N. Gabriel et al. (eds.), *Emerging Sustainable Aquaculture Innovations in Africa*, Sustainable Agriculture and Food Security,
https://doi.org/10.1007/978-981-19-7451-9_22

22.1 Introduction

By 2020, roughly 768 million people worldwide were estimated to be undernourished. Of those, more than half (418 million) live in Asia and more than one-third (282 million) in Africa (FAO et al. 2021). This loosely means that one in five people was facing hunger in Africa in 2020. Malnutrition has been linked to approximately 45 percent of childhood deaths globally (Ndivelao et al. 2016; Onyango et al. 2018). Defined by the World Food Programme (WFP) as 'a state in which the physical function of an individual is impaired to the point where he or she can no longer maintain adequate bodily performance process such as growth, pregnancy, lactation, physical work and resisting and recovering from disease' (Bain et al. 2013), malnutrition is an ill much too common in many limited resources countries, including sub-Saharan Africa, where some of the highest rates have been reported (Akombi et al. 2017). Malnutrition includes both undernourishment/undernutrition and over nourishment/overnutrition. Of those, undernourishment is the most common form of malnutrition experienced. The Food and Agriculture Organization of the United Nations (FAO) defines undernourishment as the inability of an individual to acquire enough food to meet the daily minimum dietary energy requirements over a year (FAO et al. 2021). The World Health Organization (WHO) recommends 0.66 g/kg body weight/day protein intake, a recommendation numerous developing countries fall short of (Schönfeldt and Hall 2012). Coincidentally, poverty has been nominated as one of the major contributing factors to malnutrition (Adeyeye et al. 2017). Some major poverty influences in Africa have been attributed to economic depressions, bad governance, unemployment, war, environmental factors such as drought/ famine, climate change, and population growth (Otekunrin et al. 2019) (Fig. 22.1).

Namibia is not exempted from elevated malnutrition rates. In fact, Namibia has continued to report elevated malnutrition rates since it gained its independence in 1990 (Henghono, R N, Nghitanwa E M 2019; Bauleth et al. 2020). Thirty years later,

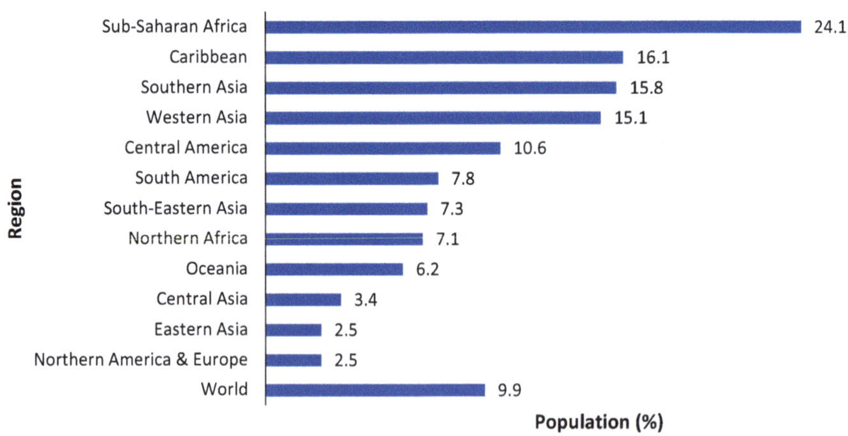

Fig. 22.1 Prevalence of undernourishment by Region, 2020, Source:(Statistica 2021)

not much has changed as the country was ranked 19th on the Global Hunger Index (GHI) in 2019 (Otekunrin et al. 2019, 2020a, b). According to WHO's global nutrition report, Namibia has made no progress towers lowering childhood wasting with 7.1% of children under 5 years still wasted and has achieved small progress towards lowering childhood stunting with 22.7% of children under 5 years still stunted (WHO 2021). Albeit the saddening statistics, there is hope. Generally, hunger indicates a lack of food security in any country. The United Nations General Assembly (UN-GA) and Sustainable Development Goal (SDG) two makes it a priority to end hunger and malnutrition by the year 2030 (Thilsted et al. 2016; Otekunrin et al. 2019). This prompts governments to implement measures towards becoming more self-sustainable in terms of achieving food security. Some measures that could be a possible solution to malnutrition and a step closer to attaining food security are backyard gardening and small-scale fish farming/aquaculture. It is estimated that more than 200 million people in Africa depend on fish consumption for high-quality yet low costing protein (Obiero et al. 2019). Despite this, compared to the rest of the world, African aquaculture production has remained insignificant on a global scale (Jamu and Ayinla 2003).

Many Africans depend on rainfall, they generally depend on inland fisheries, dams, rivers, lakes and other freshwater ecosystems for constant food supply and income (Nasr-Allah et al. 2020; Simmance et al. 2021). This is also the case in Asia and Latin American fields (Nasr-Allah et al. 2020). There is limited information on the potential of fish consumption to overcome the ill of malnutrition which is detrimental to overall health (Herman-Roloff et al. 2011; Roy et al. 2020). Moreover, the critical role that fish consumption play towards good nutrition, in particular in poor households, has vaguely been recognised and sometimes ignored altogether to date (Thilsted et al. 2016). Moreover, small-scale fisheries remain undocumented and overlooked in fisheries and food system development, limiting the assessment of household fisheries contribution to the quality of household diets (Lynch et al. 2016; Funge-Smith and Bennett 2019). This chapter will focus on the importance of small-scale aquaculture in alleviating malnutrition and promoting food security in Namibia.

22.2 Climate Change and its Influences on Food Production in Namibia

Climate change has been among the most significant pressures on food production and health the world has faced in recent years. The concentration of greenhouse gases has been increasing at exhilarating rates since the 1700s due to human activities transforming the composition of the global atmosphere (Mohanty 2021). It is projected that climate change will worsen the dry conditions experienced in Namibia, coupled with soil erosion and flood, when it eventually rains (Reid et al. 2008). Being the driest country in the Saharan desert, Namibia is and has been experiencing evidence of climate change prolonged, and drought conditions have been recorded in the country over the past recent years. This is terrible news, especially such that over half the population of the country depend on subsistence farming. This renders the country vulnerable to climate change. There is increased pressure on land resources to upsurge food production and better the livelihood of those living in absurd poverty, especially in rural areas (Taapopi et al. 2018). This translates to the need for initiatives to improve food availability while taking pressure off the land.

22.3 Important Inland Aquaculture Fish Species

Marine and freshwater aquaculture are the two types of aquaculture sectors in Namibia, with the latter having the most species variety. Private fish farmers, who raise highly valuable species, dominate the marine aquaculture industry. Freshwater aquaculture, on the other hand, involves communities, and this is the sector in which the government has committed a significant amount of money to empower communities to create their food, income and jobs. Although it has been primarily agreed that aquaculture increases access to food, there are deliberations on whether it has been able to mitigate the reduction in dietary diversity and micronutrient intake as it focuses on a few selected species (Belton et al. 2014; Bogard et al. 2015). Deliberations that in no way dispute that generally, fish provide more protein and macronutrients than other animal protein sources.

Three spotted tilapia (*Oreochromis andersonii),* tilapia Mozambicus (*Oreochromis mossambicus)*, red tilapia (hybrid tilapia), redbreast (*Tilapia rendalli*), African catfish (*Clarias gariepinus*), and common carp (*Cyprinus carpio*) dominate Namibian freshwater farming. After carps, Tilapia is the second farmed fish in the world and is expected to take over from carps in the near future (Eknath and Hulata 2009; Menaga and Fitzsimmons 2017; Mtaki et al. 2021). Several attribute this fish variety popular in aquaculture. These include ease to breed in captivity, having a short production cycle because of fast growth rate, acceptability of artificial feeds after yolk-sac absorption, and marketability and stable market prices (Wang and Lu 2016; Prabu et al. 2019; Abaho et al. 2021). Apart from the latter, the foremost crucially can be a determining factor when selecting species for small-scale aquaculture. Tilapias are also considered hardy fish that can tolerate varying degrees of physical and chemical environmental factors, making them suitable for farmers with limited technical knowledge (Kapinga et al. 2019).

Carps, which is the most important farmed aquatic animal, comes from the Cyprinidae family. They are the longest farmed fish, dating back as far as 2500 years (Miao and Wang 2020). Grass carps translate plant proteins into animal proteins by direct digestion and absorption of plant material. In addition, they are well known for their delicious and nutrient-dense meat, extensive adaptability to a large range of environmental conditions, and wide temperature tolerance and are one of the inexpensive fish in the aquaculture (Lu et al. 2020). Catfish is the most common cultured fish in Africa and is considered a traditional fish in the northern Namibia (Haimene 2018; Amponsah et al. 2021). This fish is very hardy, can feed on a wide variety of feeds, grows rapidly, and has a high survival rate in poorly oxygenated water as well as high market demand (Dauda et al. 2018; Tesfahun 2018; Abdul Kari et al. 2021). Aside from the latter, these characteristics are essential in small-scale aquaculture, where farmers may struggle to abide by the high cost of feed and maintain good water quality regularly. Overall, the most important aquaculture species pose specific characteristics that make them suitable for small-scale farming.

22.4 Nutritional Value of Fish and Importance of Fish Consumption

Alleviating malnutrition by 2030 will require a significant change not only in everyday diets but also through the consumption of nutrient-rich food inclusive for people in poor and middle-income countries. When focusing on the nutritional value of food supplies, it is agreed that fish is a major nutrient-dense animal source of food for a substantial percentage of the nutritionally susceptible people. Fish delivers a healthier food source overshadowing other terrestrial animals consumed as meat products (Bene et al. 2016; Xie et al. 2021). However, even with so many benefits, some people remain uneducated about the importance of fish consumption. Fish is composed of 18–20% protein and provides high biological value easily digestible protein that is essential for body growth and development, maintenance and repair of tissues, and for construction of essential enzymes and hormones (Tacon et al. 2020; Maulu et al. 2021). The lack of high-quality protein has been linked to stunting in children (Kwasek et al. 2020). Fish also contain less fat than red meat (Tacon et al. 2020) (Table 22.1).

The main health benefits of fish are attributed to their high content of n-3 long-chain polyunsaturated fatty acids (FAs) (n-3 LC-PUFA). These are linked to numerous health benefits, including positive cardiovascular health, improved nervous system and increased metabolism. They are also associated with decreased preterm birth, lower risk of infant low birth weight, improved visual health in infants, enablement of early neurodevelopment in children, prevention of dementia and cognitive decline and a decreased risk for developing age-related macular degeneration, particularly eicosapentaenoic (EPA) and docosahexaenoic acid (DHA) when

Table 22.1 WHO n-3 LC-PUFA recommended intakes, Source: (Maulu et al. 2021)

World Health Organization	Age	AI (Adequate Intake; per day)
Eicosapentaenoic + Docosahexaenoic acid	2–4 years	
	4–6 years	150–200 mg
	6–10 years	200–250 mg
	Adults	200–250 mg

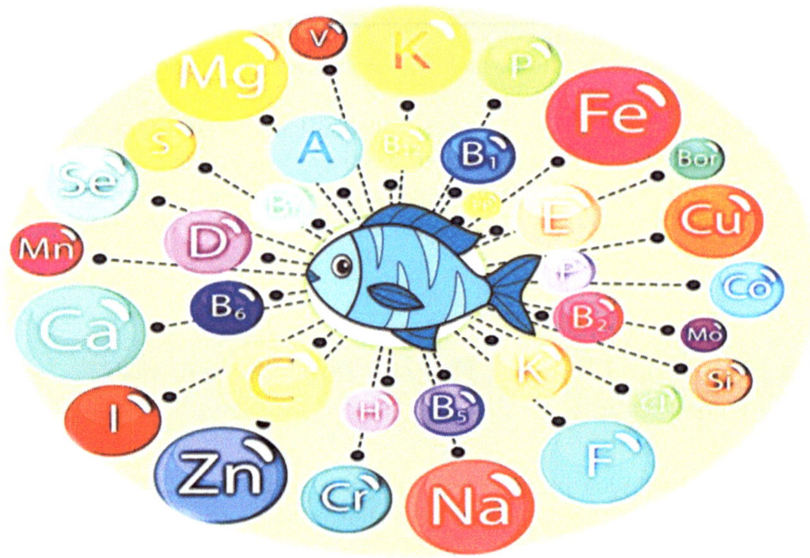

Fig. 22.2 Fish is a source of vital vitamins and minerals for human growth, Source: (Maulu et al. 2021)

consumed in sufficient amount (Monroig et al. 2018; Muhlhausler et al. 2018; Cave et al. 2020). In addition, fish is rich in most essential amino acids particularly methionine, lysine, taurine, which are limited in other kinds of muscle food (Calder 2018). The compounds found in fish are often not readily available in other diets (crops and animals), despite their massive physical benefits and cognitive development to both adults and children (Bene et al. 2016).

It is agreed that the nutritional value of fish depends on the diet to a higher degree (Sobczak et al. 2020); however, the nutritional value of fish, especially for human optimum growth, cannot be denied. Fish is an important source of vitamins A, D, and some vitamins from group B. Vitamin A is essential for numerous physiological processes, including maintenance of surface tissues, healthy immune system, good vision, bone development and reproduction, among many others (Gilbert 2013; Maulu et al. 2021). The vitamin A in fish is more readily available in the body than in plant food (Maulu et al. 2021). Deficiency of vitamin A results in an increased risk of severe infection, this makes the deficiency worse as infection increases the body's demand for vitamin A (Chea et al. 2021). Children are especially at risk if they are malnourished (Chea et al. 2021). Certain fish species are rich in vitamin A, particularly those eaten whole with the head and viscera (Kwasek et al. 2020) (Fig. 22.2).

The vitamin D in humans is mainly acquired from the sun as many foods do not contain enough vitamin D for human growth and development (Balami et al. 2019). Vitamin D stored in the fish liver is essential for bone growth as well as for the prevention of rickets, low bone-mineral density, osteoporosis and other calcium

Table 22.2 Some essential minerals found in fish muscles, Source, (Pal et al. 2018)

Element	Average value (mg/100 g)
Sodium (Na)	72
Potassium(K)	278
Calcium (Ca)	79
Magnesium (Mg)	38
Phosphorus (P)	190

metabolism disorders, including malnutrition (Reddy et al. 2010; Mishra 2019). It is necessary for thyroid function and regulates blood pressure (de la Guía-Galipienso et al. 2021; Pardabaevna 2022) (Table 22.2).

Fish contains numerous high bioavailability minerals that are important for the human body. These include: iron, calcium, zinc, phosphorus, selenium fluorine, and iodine (Maulu et al. 2021). An excellent source of these are small fish that are eaten whole, including heads and bones. Iron is critical in the formation of haemoglobin, which is responsible for oxygen transportation in the body (Kwasek et al. 2020; Maulu et al. 2021). Iron deficiency may lead to impaired brain function and anaemia (Balami et al. 2019; Maulu et al. 2021). It also result in poor learning abilities and poor cognitive development in infants and children (Balami et al. 2019). In pregnancy, iron deficiency has been linked to maternal mortality, increased risk of sepsis and low birth weight (Abbaspour et al. 2014). In large doses, selenium is toxic to the human (Balami et al. 2019). It is an essential antioxidant trace element that is essential for the normal function of the thyroid (Mojadadi et al. 2021). Regrettably, selenium deficiency is far too common globally and often requires supplementation (Gorini et al. 2021). Calcium plays a role in various metabolic processes and is responsible for bone density, normal functioning of tissues and the nervous system (Balami et al. 2019; Mishra 2019; Maulu et al. 2021). Given the abundance of nutrients that fish provide, it can be agreed that they provide more than just protein to our diets and are crucial for human health.

22.5 The Role of Small-Scale Aquaculture in Increasing Food Security and Alleviating Malnutrition in Namibia

Sub-Saharan Africa has the highest malnutrition prevalence in the world. Undernourishment, a significant health problem, has been increasing over recent years (Onyango et al. 2019). With malnutrition rates this high, it is projected that poor diet and insufficient food consumption are directly and indirectly responsible for more than half of children's deaths in sub-Saharan Africa (Drammeh et al. 2019). This is a strong indicator of the lack of food security in this region. Moreover, it was estimated that the number of food insecure individuals in the same region has increased to about 17 million people by 2021(Drammeh et al. 2019). For decades, continuing food insecurity, malnutrition and hunger have continuously been

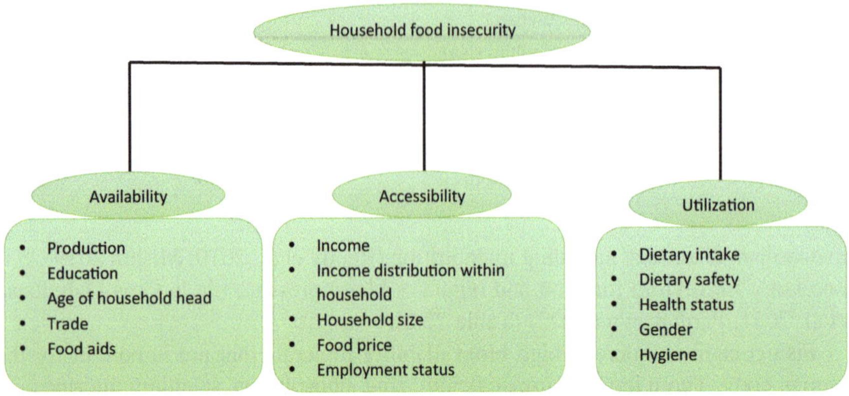

Fig. 22.3 Conceptual model of household food insecurity, Source: (WFP)

discussed as a global issue exacerbated by lack of access and poor redistribution at household level (Drammeh et al. 2019).

Although Namibia has one of the highest GDPs in Africa, it also suffers from major income disparities. More than 80% of Namibia's population live in rural areas and are dependent of subsistence farming as a source of food. However, climate change rendered the country prone to prolonged flooding and recurrent droughts amongst others. Floods and recurrent drought meant that subsistence farmers were left vulnerable to hunger as conditions made it impossible to produce food for themselves. Household food insecurity has been termed a prominent risk factor of malnutrition. Similarly, it jeopardizes dietary intake. Food security was termed to exist by the World Food Programme (WFP) when 'all people, at all times, have physical and economic access to sufficient, safe and nutritious food to meet their dietary needs and food preferences for an active and healthy life' (Crush et al. 2019). Even though there has been a debate on how best to measure food security, there is no doubt that Namibia as a sub-Saharan country has a long way to go as far as food security is concerned. In the rise of the COVID-19 pandemic, like other numerous countries, Namibia has suffered major food access disruptions in forms of supply chains, lockdowns and increases in food prices, a situation which has further worsened the already existing food insecurity (Fig. 22.3).

Various studies have reported that, similar to many other African countries, Namibia has a high prevalence of stunted and underweight/undernourished population, specifically in children under 5 years (Akombi et al. 2017; Drammeh et al. 2019; UNICEF 2020). This has placed pressure on the government to implement solutions that will not only yield fast results but are also cost-effective and sustainable to increase food production and end hunger in the country. Historically, home food procurement has been how people secure food for household consumption (Niles et al. 2021). This included but was not limited to hunting, gardening, fishing, foraging and livestock. Over the years, some of these activities have received significant interest and have picked up more than others. To date, numerous countries have embraced backyard and community gardens as part of the efforts to increase food security (Dorado et al. 2018; Nkrumah 2018; Fehr and Moseley 2019). However, the same cannot be said for small-scale aquaculture.

Small-scale aquaculture is defined as 'low-production medium-scale aquaculture, based on increasing natural water productivity, polycultures, and using alternative feed prepared with local or waste supplies' (Villasante et al. 2015). Millions of people look up to fish as a source of income and food. In the same vein, it was found that people in rural areas depend on fishing for improved access to food (Villasante et al. 2015). In the wake of global food shortages, aquaculture can foster the bridge to seal the gap in food insecurity. Small-scale aquaculture practised at the household level may be the answer to food supply chains and accessibility issues. This is specifically significant in females comprising households as researchers have found that women's catch is mainly aimed at family consumption, unlike men's catch which is usually aimed at market sales (Lauria et al. 2018).

Contrary to studies found that Namibians do not consume fish regularly (Erasmus et al. 2021), others have found that, since engagement in fish farming, fish consumption increased in rural households as well as fish consumption frequency (Villasante et al. 2015). Seeing that most of Namibia's population lives inland in rural areas, the introduction of subsistence small-scale rural aquaculture may see an upsurge in food availability which will subsequently curb malnutrition (Hlophe-Ginindza and Mpandeli 2020; Arthur et al. 2022). This was supported by a study that constructed a village computable general equilibrium (CGE) model to examine whether aquaculture improves local livelihoods in the Zambezi region, Namibia. This study found that not only did aquaculture improve households' income, but it also increased fish availability and consumption, which in turn meant a reduction in malnutrition cases (Gronau et al. 2020). Recommendations to increase small-scale fish farming might include increasing up farming and agricultural activities plus encouraging interministerial and stakeholders' collaboration.

22.6 The Potential of Small-Scale Aquaculture Development in Namibia

Despite being highly recommended as a source of food and income at a household level and is the fastest growing food-producing factor worldwide, aquaculture has seen a slow take-off in Namibia. Aquaculture in Namibia can be traced back to the 1800s, but it only took off in the 1990s in Namibia (Iitembu et al. 2022). To date, the country contributes a minor fraction to global aquaculture production. The Ministry of Fish and Marine Resources (MFMR), in conjunction with the Namibian government, donors and international agencies, made great efforts to develop the aquaculture sector in Namibia. This was due to aquaculture being identified as a high-priority area of development. The main legal framework that guided the administration of aquaculture in the country is the aquaculture act, which was,

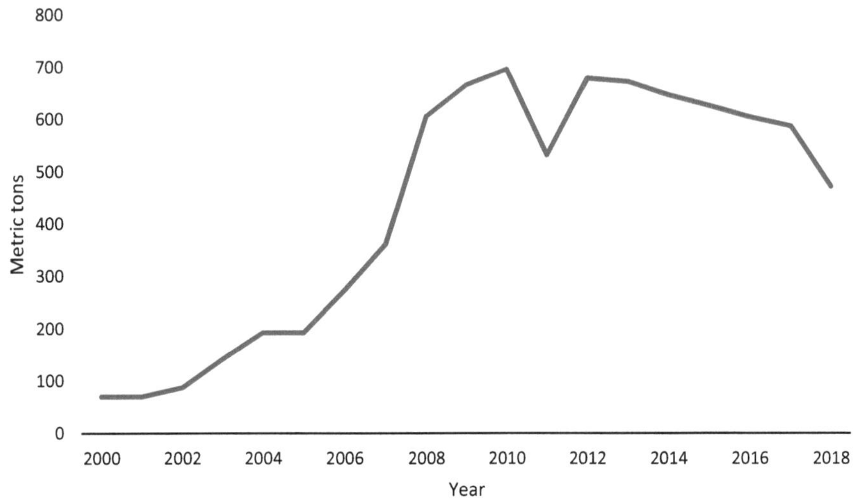

Fig. 22.4 Aquaculture production in Namibia, 2000–2018, Source: (World Bank)

however, only adopted in 2002 (Moyo and Rapatsa 2021). Despite the slow take-off, aquaculture has a promising future in the country that has the potential to contribute significantly towards attaining self-reliance and food security.

Namibia has a western coastline on the Atlantic Ocean. The Namibian coastal waters are some of the richest fishing grounds in the world (Tall and Failler 2015). However, the country has no notable natural freshwater bodies that would be excellent for large-scale/ commercial fish farming. There also are no big lakes known on an international level. The country has significant rivers that form borders with neighbouring countries such as Angola, Zimbabwe, Zambia, Botswana, and South Africa, where little fishing for local markets takes place. They are comprised mainly of Tilapia, catfish, and tiger fish. However, the country enjoys permanent water bodies in dams and sinkhole lakes. It also has non-perennial rivers that mostly flow during the rainy season. Marine aquaculture in the country is, however, trivial and limited to the waters of the Benguela ecosystem. Traditionally, subsistence small-scale freshwater aquaculture is not a norm in the country; thus, current activities are government and donor-led (Iitembu et al. 2022) (Fig. 22.4).

Notwithstanding the framework in place to support aquaculture development in the country, the development of rural small-scale aquaculture may suffer a setback as there is no distinction between community-based and commercial farming. This generates regulatory problems which cannot be easily met by potential small-scale fish farmers willing to farm fish for household consumption.

22.7 Conclusion and Recommendations

The aquaculture industry has a promising future in Namibia, especially with support from the ministry of fisheries and development partners. Moreover, small-scale aquaculture can increase food security and improve the quality of diets in Namibian households, thereby reducing the prevalence of malnutrition, especially in rural areas where poverty is far too common. Because fish is far more consumed than other animal proteins in many countries, this sector can also be an alternative in increasing protein supply to meet the demand of the growing population. However, for small-scale aquaculture to take off, we recommend the following be implemented:

- Invest more energy in aquaculture production education.
- Consolidation through fish farming development policies.
- Promotion of aquaculture production at the household level.
- Financial support for prospective farmers.
- Technical knowledge and support to prospect farmers.
- Intersectoral collaboration and engagement of stakeholders.

References

Abaho I, Masembe C, Akoll P, Jones CLW (2021) The use of plant extracts to control tilapia reproduction: Current status and future perspectives. J World Aquac Soc:593–619. https://doi.org/10.1111/jwas.12863

Abbaspour N, Hurrell R, Kelishadi R (2014) Review on iron and its importance for human health. J Res Med Sci 19:164–174

Abdul Kari Z, Kabir MA, Abdul Razab MKA et al (2021) A replacement of plant protein sources as an alternative of fish meal ingredient for African catfish, Clarias gariepinus: a review. J Trop Resour Sustain Sci 8:47–59. https://doi.org/10.47253/jtrss.v8i1.164

Adeyeye SAO, Adebayo-Oyetoro AO, Tiamiyu HK (2017) Poverty and malnutrition in Africa: a conceptual analysis. Nutr Food Sci 47:754–764. https://doi.org/10.1108/NFS-02-2017-0027

Akombi BJ, Agho EK, Merom D et al (2017) Child malnutrition in sub-Saharan Africa: a meta-analysis of demographic and health surveys (2006-2016). PLoS One 12:35–63

Amponsah SK, Agodzo S, Agbeko E, Osei EA (2021) Impact of tank geometry on production of African Catfish (Clarias gariepinus). Afr J Agric Res 17:165–172. https://doi.org/10.5897/ajar2020.15239

Arthur RI, Skerritt DJ, Schuhbauer A et al (2022) Small-scale fisheries and local food systems: Transformations, threats and opportunities. Fish Fish 23:109–124. https://doi.org/10.1111/faf.12602

Bain LE, Awah PK, Geraldine N et al (2013) Malnutrition in Sub - Saharan Africa: burden, causes and prospects. Pan Afr Med J 15:1–9. https://doi.org/10.11604/pamj.2013.15.120.2535

Balami S, Sharma A, Karn R (2019) Significance of nutritional value of fish for human health. Malaysian J Halal Res 2:32–34. https://doi.org/10.2478/mjhr-2019-0012

Bauleth MF, Mitonga HK, Pinehas LN (2020) Factors associated with the nutritional status of children under-five years of age with diarrhoea in Ohangwena Region, Namibia. Int J Healthc 6: 23. https://doi.org/10.5430/ijh.v6n2p23

Belton B, van Asseldonk IJM, Thilsted SH (2014) Faltering fisheries and ascendant aquaculture: Implications for food and nutrition security in Bangladesh. Food Policy 44:77–87. https://doi.org/10.1016/j.foodpol.2013.11.003
Bene C, Arthur R, Norbury H et al (2016) Contribution of fisheries and aquaculture to global food security. World Dev. https://doi.org/10.1016/j.worlddev.2015.11.007
Bogard JR, Thilsted SH, Marks GC et al (2015) Nutrient composition of important fish species in Bangladesh and potential contribution to recommended nutrient intakes. J Food Compos Anal 42:120–133. https://doi.org/10.1016/j.jfca.2015.03.002
Calder PC (2018) Metabolism of polyunsaturated fatty acids by cells of the immune system. Elsevier Inc., Amsterdam
Cave C, Hein N, Smith LM et al (2020) Omega-3 long-chain polyunsaturated fatty acids intake by ethnicity, income, and education level in the United States: NHANES 2003–2014. Nutrients 12: 1–13. https://doi.org/10.3390/nu12072045
Chea EP, Lopez MJ, Milstein H (2021) Vitamin A. StatPearls Publishing, Treasure Island, FL
Crush J, Nickanor N, Kazembe L (2019) Informal food deserts and household food insecurity in Windhoek, Namibia. Sustain 11:1–15. https://doi.org/10.3390/su11010037
Dauda AB, Natrah I, Karim M et al (2018) African catfish aquaculture in Malaysia and Nigeria: status, trends and prospects. Fish Aquac J 09:1–5. https://doi.org/10.4172/2150-3508.1000237
de la Guía-Galipienso F, Martínez-Ferran M, Vallecillo N et al (2021) Vitamin D and cardiovascular health. Clin Nutr 40:2946–2957. https://doi.org/10.1016/j.clnu.2020.12.025
Dorado JB, Viajar R V, Azaña GP, et al (2018) Diversity and change in food wellbeing. Divers chang food wellbeing; pp 225–242. https://doi.org/10.3920/978-90-8686-864-3
Drammeh W, Hamid NA, Rohana AJ (2019) Determinants of household food insecurity and its association with child malnutrition in Sub-Saharan Africa: a review of the literature. Curr Res Nutr Food Sci 7:610–623. https://doi.org/10.12944/CRNFSJ.7.3.02
Eknath AE, Hulata G (2009) Use and exchange of genetic resources of Nile tilapia (Oreochromis niloticus). Rev Aquac 1:197–213. https://doi.org/10.1111/j.1753-5131.2009.01017.x
Erasmus VN, Kadhila T, Thyberg K et al (2021) Public perceptions and factors affecting domestic marine fish consumption in Namibia, southwestern Africa. Reg Stud Mar Sci 47:101921. https://doi.org/10.1016/j.rsma.2021.101921
FAO, IFAD, UNICEF, et al (2021) The State of Food Security and Nutrition in the World 2021. Transforming food systems for food security, improved nutrition and affordable healthy diets for all. Rome
Fehr R, Moseley WG (2019) Gardening matters. Afr Geogr Rev 38:67–80. https://doi.org/10.1080/19376812.2017.1286247
Funge-Smith S, Bennett A (2019) A fresh look at inland fisheries and their role in food security and livelihoods. Fish Fish 20:1176–1195. https://doi.org/10.1111/faf.12403
Gilbert C (2013) What is vitamin A and why do we need it? Community Eye Health J 26(84):65
Gorini F, Sabatino L, Pingitore A, Vassalle C (2021) Selenium: an element of life essential for thyroid function. Molecules 26:1–14. https://doi.org/10.3390/molecules26237084
Gronau S, Winter E, Grote U (2020) Aquaculture, fish resources and rural livelihoods: a village CGE analysis from Namibia's Zambezi Region. Environ Dev Sustain 22:615–642. https://doi.org/10.1007/s10668-018-0212-1
Haimene EP (2018) Assessing the socio-economic impact of aquaculture on small scale fish farmers – a case study of Ohangwena and Oshikoto regions in Namibia
Henghono RN, Nghitanwa EM, NHN (2019) Factors associated with malnutrition among children under the age of five years in Katutura Health Centre, Windhoek, Khomas region. Int J Med Sci Heal Res 3:21–31
Herman-Roloff A, Llewellyn E, Obiero W et al (2011) Implementing voluntary medical male circumcision for HIV prevention in Nyanza Province, Kenya: lessons learned during the first year. PLoS One 6:4–8. https://doi.org/10.1371/journal.pone.0018299
Hlophe-Ginindza SN, Mpandeli NS (2020) The role of small-scale farmers in ensuring food security in Africa. in: food security in Africa. IntechOpen, London, p 13

Iitembu JA, Gabriel NN, Tjipute M et al (2022) The governance of aquaculture in Namibia as a vehicle for food security and economic growth. In: Food security for African smallholder farmers. Springer, Singapore, pp 391–403

Jamu DM, Ayinla OA (2003) Potential for the development of Aquaculture in Africa. NAGA, WorldFish Cent Q 26:9–13

Kapinga IB, Limbu SM, Madalla NA et al (2019) Dietary Aspilia mossambicensis and Azadirachta indica supplementation alter gonadal characteristics and histology of juvenile Nile tilapia (Oreochromis niloticus). Aquac Res 50:573–580. https://doi.org/10.1111/are.13931

Kwasek K, Thorne-Lyman AL, Phillips M (2020) Can human nutrition be improved through better fish feeding practices? a review paper. Crit Rev Food Sci Nutr 60:3822–3835. https://doi.org/10.1080/10408398.2019.1708698

Lauria V, Das I, Hazra S et al (2018) Importance of fisheries for food security across three climate change vulnerable deltas. Sci Total Environ 640–641:1566–1577. https://doi.org/10.1016/j.scitotenv.2018.06.011

Lu X, Chen HM, Qian XQ, Gui JF (2020) Transcriptome analysis of grass carp (Ctenopharyngodon idella) between fast- and slow-growing fish. Comp Biochem Physiol D Genomics Proteomics 35:100688. https://doi.org/10.1016/j.cbd.2020.100688

Lynch AJ, Cooke SJ, Deines AM et al (2016) The social, economic, and environmental importance of inland fish and fisheries. Environ Rev 24:115–121. https://doi.org/10.1139/er-2015-0064

Maulu S, Nawanzi K, Abdel-Tawwab M, Khalil HS (2021) Fish nutritional value as an approach to children's nutrition. Front Nutr 8. https://doi.org/10.3389/fnut.2021.780844

Menaga M, Fitzsimmons K (2017) Growth of the tilapia industry in India. World Aquac 48:49–52

Miao W, Wang W (2020) Trends of aquaculture production and trade: carp, tilapia, and shrimp. Aisan Fish Sci 45: HS-10-HS-16

Mishra SP (2019) Significance of fish nutrients for human health. Int J Fish Aquat Res 2:32–34

Mohanty A (2021) Impacts of climate change on human health and agriculture in recent years. In: TENSYMP 2021–2021 IEEE Region 10 Symposium. IEEE

Mojadadi A, Au A, Salah W et al (2021) Role for selenium in metabolic homeostasis and human reproduction. Nutrients 13:3256

Monroig O, Tocher DR, Castro LFC (2018) Polyunsaturated fatty acid biosynthesis and metabolism in fish. In: Polyunsaturated fatty acid metabolism. Elsevier Inc., Amsterdam, pp 31–49

Moyo NAG, Rapatsa MM (2021) A review of the factors affecting tilapia aquaculture production in Southern Africa. Aquaculture 535. https://doi.org/10.1016/j.aquaculture.2021.736386

Mtaki K, Limbu SM, Mmochi AJ, Mtolera MSP (2021) Hybrids production as a potential method to control prolific breeding in tilapia and adaptation to aquaculture climate-induced drought. Aquac Fish 0–5. https://doi.org/10.1016/j.aaf.2021.04.005

Muhlhausler BS, Collins CT, Gould JF et al (2018) Polyunsaturated fatty acids: metabolism and nutritional requirements in pregnancy and infancy. In: Polyunsaturated fatty acid metabolism. Elsevier Inc., Amsterdam, pp 111–134

Nasr-Allah A, Gasparatos A, Karanja A, et al (2020) Employment generation in the Egyptian aquaculture value chain: implications for meeting the Sustainable Development Goals (SDGs). ScienceDirect 520

Ndivelao P, Tjipepa T, Lubchak V (2016) Childhood Malnutrition in Namibia. Top Issues Clin Theor Med 2:21–22. http://essuir.sumdu.edu.ua/handle/123456789/47882

Niles MT, Wirkkala KB, Belarmino EH, Bertmann F (2021) Home food procurement impacts food security and diet quality during COVID-19. BMC Public Health 21:1–15. https://doi.org/10.1186/s12889-021-10960-0

Nkrumah B (2018) Edible backyards: Climate change and urban food (in)security in Africa. Agric Food Secur 7:1–5. https://doi.org/10.1186/s40066-018-0196-y

Obiero K, Meulenbroek P, Drexler S et al (2019) The contribution of fish to food and nutrition security in Eastern Africa: emerging trends and future outlooks. Sustain 11:1–15. https://doi.org/10.3390/su11061636

Onyango AW, Jean-Baptiste J, Samburu B, Mahlangu TLM (2019) Regional overview on the double burden of malnutrition and examples of program and policy responses: African region. Ann Nutr Metab 75:127–130. https://doi.org/10.1159/000503671
Onyango WA, Jean-Baptisteb J, Samburuc B, Mahlangu TLM (2018) Food and nutrition handbook. World food programme
Otekunrin OA, Otekunrin OA, Fasina FO, Omotayo AO (2020a) Assessing the zero hunger target readiness in Africa in the face of COVID-19 pandemic. J Sustain Agric 35:213–227. https://doi.org/10.20961/carakatani.v35i2.41503
Otekunrin OA, Otekunrin OA, Momoh S, Ayinde IA (2019) How far has Africa gone in achieving the zero hunger target? Evidence from Nigeria. Glob Food Sec 22:1–12. https://doi.org/10.1016/j.gfs.2019.08.001
Otekunrin OA, Otekunrin OA, Sawicka B, Ayinde IA (2020b) Three decades of fighting against hunger in Africa: progress, challenges and opportunities. World Nutr 11:86–111. https://doi.org/10.26596/wn.202011386-111
Pal J, Shukla B, Maurya AK et al (2018) A review on role of fish in human nutrition with special emphasis to essential fatty acid. Int J Fisheries Aquat Sci 6:427–430
Pardabaevna IG (2022) What is vitamin D deficiency dangerous and how to diagnose it. Peerian J 2: 1–24
Prabu E, Rajagopalsamy CBT, Ahilan B et al (2019) Tilapia – an excellent candidate species for world aquaculture: a review. Annu Res Rev Biol 31:1–14. https://doi.org/10.9734/arrb/2019/v31i330052
Reddy M, Laughon K, Sun L et al (2010) Prepregnancy risk factors for antepartum stillbirth in the United States. Natl Inst Heal 42:115–125. https://doi.org/10.1086/498510.Parasitic
Reid H, Sahlén L, Stage J, Macgregor J (2008) Climate change impacts on Namibia's natural resources and economy. Clim Policy 8:452–466. https://doi.org/10.1080/14693062.2008.9685709
Roy A, Aftabuddin M, Bayen S et al (2020) Changing dimensions of 'Fish for All' from 'food and livelihood' to 'nutritional security'. Int J Fish Aquat Stud 8:320–324. https://doi.org/10.22271/fish.2020.v8.i5d.2340
Schönfeldt HC, Hall NG (2012) Dietary protein quality and malnutrition in Africa. Br J Nutr 108. https://doi.org/10.1017/S0007114512002553
Simmance FA, Kanyumba L, Cohen P, et al (2021) Sustaining and improving the contribution small-scale fisheries make to healthy and sustainable food systems in Malawi In partnership with i Authors Citation Creative Commons License. World Fish Press
Sobczak M, Panicz R, Eljasik P et al (2020) Quality improvement of common carp (Cyprinus carpio L.) meat fortified with n-3 PUFA. Food Chem Toxicol 139:111261. https://doi.org/10.1016/j.fct.2020.111261
Statistica (2021) Share of undernourished people worldwide in 2020, by region. https://www.statista.com/statistics/273291/number-of-people-with-malnutrition-worldwide/
Taapopi M, Kamwi JM, Siyambango N (2018) Perception of farmers on conservation agriculture for climate change adaptation in Namibia. Environ Nat Resour Res 8:33. https://doi.org/10.5539/enrr.v8n3p33
Tacon AGJ, Lemos D, Metian M (2020) Fish for health: improved nutritional quality of cultured fish for human consumption. Rev Fish Sci Aquac 28:449–458. https://doi.org/10.1080/23308249.2020.1762163
Tall A, Failler P (2015) Fisheries and Aquaculture industry in Namibia Fisheries and Aquaculture industry in Namibia. In: The Ministerial Conference on Fisheries Cooperation among African States Bordering the Atlantic Ocean (ATFALCO). p 45
Tesfahun A (2018) Feeding biology of the African catfish Clarias gariepinus (Burchell) in some of Ethiopian Lakes: A review Feeding biology of the African catfish Clarias gariepinus (Burchell) in some of Ethiopian Lakes: a review Agumassie Tesfahun. Int J Fauna Biol Stud 5:19–23

Thilsted SH, Thorne-Lyman A, Webb P et al (2016) Sustaining healthy diets: the role of capture fisheries and aquaculture for improving nutrition in the post-2015 era. Food Policy 61:126–131. https://doi.org/10.1016/j.foodpol.2016.02.005
UNICEF (2020) Levels and trends in child malnutrition: Report 2020
Villasante S, Rivero Rodríguez S, Molares Y et al (2015) Are provisioning ecosystem services from rural aquaculture contributing to reduce hunger in Africa? Ecosyst Serv 16:365–377. https://doi.org/10.1016/j.ecoser.2015.07.003
Wang M, Lu M (2016) Tilapia polyculture: a global review. Aquac Res 47:2363–2374. https://doi.org/10.1111/are.12708
WHO (2021) Global nutrition report; the state of global nutrition. UK Development Initiatives, Bristol
Xie D, Chen C, Dong Y et al (2021) Regulation of long-chain polyunsaturated fatty acid biosynthesis in teleost fish. Prog Lipid Res:82. https://doi.org/10.1016/j.plipres.2021.101095

Chapter 23
The Southern Mullet (*Chelon richardsonii*) as a Potential Candidate Species for Aquaculture in the Southern African Region

Veronica Kapula, Wilhelm Haihambo, Festus Nashima, and Johannes Iitembu

Abstract This study investigated the potential of the southern mullet (*Chelon richardsonii*) as an aquaculture candidate. The southern mullet lives in marine, brackish, and freshwater environments. It is a low-trophic level species with a diet primarily comprised of detritus and plankton. The species is also a target species of a small-scale fishery off Namibia. The fish's biology makes it an ideal aquaculture candidate that can contribute to food security. This species has the possibility to be cultured with other fish species and feed on leftover feed as well as wastes acting. Moreover, it can be cultured in single-culture conditions. The culturing of this species will reduce pressure on wild stocks in both Namibia and South Africa, in which the latter is reported to be regionally overexploited. However, more biological studies will be needed to identify a specific method that can be used to culture the southern mullet optimally. Economic feasibility studies will also be required to address issues related to mass production, markets, and profitability.

Keywords Aquaculture · Food Security · Low Trophic · Southern Mullet · Sustainability

23.1 Introduction

Global fish production was predicted to exceed 179 million tonnes in 2018, with a total first-sale value of USD 401 billion, with aquaculture accounting for 82 million tonnes for USD 250 billion (FAO 2020). Aquaculture was responsible for 46% of overall production and 52% of fish for human consumption (FAO 2020). China

V. Kapula (✉) · W. Haihambo · F. Nashima · J. Iitembu
Department of Fisheries and Ocean Sciences, Sam Nujoma Campus, University of Namibia, Henties Bay, Namibia
e-mail: vkapula@unam.na

© The Author(s), under exclusive license to Springer Nature Singapore Pte Ltd. 2023

N. N. Gabriel et al. (eds.), *Emerging Sustainable Aquaculture Innovations in Africa*, Sustainable Agriculture and Food Security,
https://doi.org/10.1007/978-981-19-7451-9_23

continued as the major fish producer in 2018, accounting for 35% globally (FAO 2020). A substantial share of output in 2018 came from Asia (34%), excluding China, followed by the Americas (14%), Europe (10%), Africa (7%), and Oceania (1%) (FAO 2020). Captured fisheries have mainly remained steady since the late 1980s, with annual harvests ranging between 86 million and 93 million tonnes (FAO 2020). Captured fisheries are thought to have reached a plateau, and no further expansion is envisaged (Maani 2017). The aquaculture industry serves as a vital source of nutrition in some of the world's fastest developing countries and will be critical in meeting future global fish demand (Kamalii et al. 2022). In 2001–2018, global aquaculture production of farmed aquatic animals increased at a rate of 5.3% per year on average (FAO 2020). Aquaculture has been a promising industry, with a faster growth rate than any other food-producing industry in the world (Subasinghe et al. 2009; Pandey & Kumar 2021).

Aquaculture contributed between 16 and 18% to the total fish production in Africa (FAO 2020). Many African countries are far below their targets (Golden et al. 2016; FAO 2020). Africa only contributes around 2.7%, with Egypt being the major producer and Nigeria significantly increasing its aquaculture production to become Africa's second-largest producer (FAO 2020). However, this cannot be said for Southern African countries, whose production remains significantly low (El-Sayed 2013). Southern Africa can potentially increase aquaculture production (Brummett et al. 2008).

Low-trophic level fish species are considered more environmentally friendly to farm than high-trophic level fish species (Pauly et al. 2001). This is because they have a low demand for animal protein (Tacon et al. 2011). In contrast to carnivorous fish species, which rely heavily on fish meal and oils, low-trophic level fish species may be given a diet rich in plant-based proteins. Fish meal has recently been the dominant protein ingredient in fish feed, considered a golden standard protein source (Daniel 2018; Hodar et al. 2020). However, its production from wild-caught fish has reached a plateau over the years, making it difficult to obtain, very expensive, and unsustainable (Naylor et al. 2009; Nunes et al. 2014; Egerton et al. 2020). Fish meals and oils have received much attention because they are mainly derived from wild-caught fish (Naylor et al. 2009; Cao et al. 2013; Jones et al. 2015). Wild-caught fish could be used for direct human consumption, but the supply to the fish meal industry is more preferred given its demand and profits, which dampens efforts to increase direct human consumption (Delgado 2003; Naylor et al. 2009). As a result, using fishmeal and oil in aquafeeds has raised concerns about the environmental sustainability of farming carnivorous fish species such as salmon (Naylor et al. 2009; Ytrestøyl et al. 2015). In reality, humans consume more fish than the fishmeal industry; this has been demonstrated by many researchers (Byelashov and Griffin 2014). However, the fishmeal industry does contribute to pressure on wild-caught fish (Naylor et al. 2000, 2009). Reduced reliance on wild-caught fish in aquafeed is widely acknowledged as a critical long-term strategy for aquaculture growth (Rust et al. 2011). Research has indicated that fish feed can be supplemented with plant-derived protein, reducing the need for fish meals and oils (Rust et al. 2011). This has been primarily achievable in low-trophic level fish species, which are better equipped to digest plant proteins than high-trophic level fish species (Turchini et al. 2019).

Concerns about the environment have prompted widespread calls to refocus fish farming on low trophic level species fed non-fish natural diets. In addition, Olsen (2011) believes that one of the solutions to sustainable aquaculture is to introduce lower trophic level fish species that do not require fish meal in their diet and can entirely rely on proteins derived from alternative sources. Reports from higher institutions such as the World Resources Institute, World Wildlife Fund, and Asia Pacific Fisheries Commission acknowledge this and advocate for aquaculture production and sustainability goals to be met by farming fish low in trophic level (Waite et al. 2014). The 2019 Californian Ocean Resiliency Act (SB-69) of the United States requires producers to focus on low-trophic level fish species (BigeLow et al. 2020). Africa needs to expand on this and introduce new aquaculture candidate species that feed at a low-trophic level to promote security while utilising resources in a sustainable way.

Mullets are fish species from the Mugilidae family distributed worldwide that feed at a low trophic level (Whitfield 2016). They are distinguished by their tolerance to a wide variety of salinities and temperatures (Whitfield 2016). A distinctive mullet, the Southern mullet (*Chelon richardsonii,* previously *Liza richardsonii*) (Durand and Borsa 2015) is found in the southern African region (Whitfield 2016). It is an important fish species that have a significant contribution to the socioeconomic of small-scale fishers in Namibia and South Africa. However, Horton (2018) and Horton et al. (2019) reported the species exhibiting signs of overexploitation in South Africa. No population studies are available from Angola and Namibia; thus, this study refers to reports from South Africa. The Sothern mullet is commercially important (de Villiers 1976; Horton 2018; Horton et al. 2019). Due to its tolerance to various salinities, it could be a valuable species in brackish and freshwater aquaculture (Bok 1983). The biology and economic value of the southern mullet make it an excellent aquaculture fish species that can be introduced into the southern African region to promote sustainable aquaculture, which will contribute to food security. This chapter discusses the biology, ecology, reproductive traits, and aquaculture prospects of the southern mullet in the southern African region.

23.2 Geographical Distributions

Southern mullets are distributed along coastal waters and estuaries from Lobito, Angola to KwaZulu-Natal, South Africa (DAFF 2014). The juveniles and adults are common in Eastern and Western Cape estuaries; however, this species is usually more abundant in the nearshore marine environment (Bennett 1989). The distribution of this species along coastal waters might be attributed to the high natural productivity of the Benguela system that happens near shore (Fig. 23.1).

Fig. 23.1 The red solid line shows the geographical distribution of the southern mullet (*Chelon richardsonii*) as described by Branch (2017) (map adapted from Google maps)

23.2.1 Biological and Feeding Ecology of Southern Mullet

Southern mullet (*Chelon richardsonii*) is a fish species from the Mugilidae family (Whitfield 2016). It can be identified with a silvery sheen that is usually darker above and white below, with gill covers that have a blotch and an elongated and pointed snout (Branch 2017). It is euryhaline species that can tolerate a wide range of salinities (Branch et al. 1985; Branch 2017; Whitfield 1996, 2016). It can also tolerate a wide range of temperatures (Whitfield 2016) recorded within its distribution area, from slightly below 9 °C to slightly above 20 °C. The southern mullet reaches a maximum length of 400 mm (Branch 2017). It is marine-estuarine dependent, reproducing in the marine environment, and the hatched fry migrate toward the shore where they spend their juvenile phase before moving into estuaries as adult fish (Branch 2017; Whitfield 2016; Whitfield 2019).

Mugilids are characterised by a 'cardiac' stomach and a long alimentary canal for the digestion of diatoms and detrital material (Marais 1980). However, all species have distinctive feeding patterns that minimise interspecific competition. Generally, mullets are oligophagous, having a diet dominated by benthic floc, detritus, meiofauna, microphytobenthos, and smaller epifauna (Whitfield 2016). Large quantities of inorganic particles are found ingested within most mullet's food items. Blaber and Whitfield (1977), Masson and Marais (1975), and Whitfield (1988) showed that primary dietary items ingested by juvenile and adult mugilids in local estuaries are particulate organic debris, pennate diatoms, unicellular and filamentous algae, flagellates, macrophytic plant material, blue-green algae, ostracods, foraminiferans, and small invertebrates, e.g., gastropods and harpacticoid copepods. In addition to food, the estuarine population of mullets ingest a significant amount of silt and fine sand compared to the environment population that feeds on planktons (De Villiers 1987; Marais 1980; Romer and McLachlan 1986). Mullets obtain their food mostly in shallow waters that are associated with high organic content (Whitfield 2019).

Southern mullets travel in schools and mainly feed on phytoplankton, fine algae, benthic diatoms, detritus of bottom sediments, and other marine invertebrates (Branch 2017). The estuarine populations of *C. richardsonii* appear to reach physiological conditions more than marine populations because they do not lose significant energy to reproduction compared to the marine population (De Decker and Bennett 1985). Southern mullets larger than 20 mm SL feed on a regular mullet diet, while postlarval less than 20 mm SL ingests copepods and macruran larvae (Whitfield 1985) predominantly. An early study by Marais (1980) indicates that *C. richardsonii* found in Swartkops estuary feed mainly during the day and rarely at night.

23.2.2 The Reproductive Characteristics of Southern Mullet

Mullets are documented to spawn and reproduce in several temperatures (Abraham et al. 1966; Van der Horst and Erasmus 1981). Southern mullet matures at 180 mm SL (de Villiers 1987). However, Branch (2017) reported different results that this species attains sexual maturity at 230 mm. This difference in results could be from different populations. Southern mullets found in Algoa Bay are reported to have a noticeable gonadal development that happens between September and April and spawns during spring and summer, while in the Swartkops estuary, they are reported to be summer spawners. In addition, Van der Horst and Erasmus (1978) reported *Liza dumerili,* a closely related species, to spawn during the summer period in the Swartkops estuary. According to Lasiak (1983) and van der Horst and Erasmus (1981), *C. richardsonii* found in the Eastern Cape waters spawn often close inshore between September and March. Lamberth and Whitfield (2013) reported spawning during early and late summer peaks. It appears that *C. richardsonii* spawns during summer; however, Bennett (1989) and Whitfield and Kok (1992) reported continuous recruitment into Western Cape estuaries that takes place all year. This species has a greater sexual development that takes place between September and March with spawning taking place inshore (Lasiak 1983). It lays eggs in the marine environment, and hatched fry migrates nearshore, where they develop into the next stage (Cambray and Sok 1989).

23.2.3 Environmental Preferences of Southern Mullet

The southern mullets are found in marine, brackish, and freshwater environments (Branch 2017).

Most mugilids occupy predominantly estuarine nursery areas; however, the juvenile *C. richardsonii* inhabit both the marine and estuary environment (Beckley 1984; Romer and McLachlan 1986; Wallace et al. 1984). Estuarine juvenile mullets prefer water less than 1 m to capture zooplankton from the benthos found near the bottom during the day. At this juvenile stage, the number of sand grains increases microbenthic foods associated with sand grains become overwhelmingly dominant. Estuaries have excessive nutrient concentration and low oxygen levels; thus, southern mullets are adapted to a low oxygen environment.

23.3 Mullet Fishery

The southern mullet is the main target species of the inshore net fishery on the west coast of Namibia and the east coast of South Africa. Small-scale fishers sell this fish in coastal towns and inland towns. The southern mullet is managed under a combination of gear restrictions, total allowable effort (TAE), and closed areas in South Africa. In Namibia, it is managed through an input control scheme. There is no documentation of the exact amount that is specific to the southern mullet; however, half of the 1500 tonnes (t) per annum allocated to the net fisheries in South Africa are estimated to be the southern mullet species (Horton 2018). In Namibia, there are 10 individuals permitted to catch mullets, who have reported catching a combined amount of 10 tonnes per month and approximately 120 tonnes per annum (W. de Klerk, personal communication, 18 July 2022).

23.4 The Aquaculture Potential of Southern Mullet

Flathead grey mullet (*Mugil cephalus*) has been well studied and understood in cultured conditions. It is an essential species in aquaculture that is reared in both single and polyculture (Mires 1969; Katz et al. 2002; Lupatsch et al. 2003; Israel et al. 2017). Grey mullets can be used as cleaner fish feeding on waste particles from other fish ponds and cages (Katz et al. 2002; Lupatsch et al. 2003). This method of culture is used to maximise production. Southern mullet is closely related to *M. cephalus* (Durand and Borsa 2015), inhibiting the same environment in southern Africa. Southern mullet has not been introduced into aquaculture; however, it has as potential to be cultured, which will contribute to food security in the southern African region. An early study has successfully artificially hatched eggs of *C. richardsonii* collected from the wild (Cambray and Sok 1989).

Furthermore, mature females have also been collected from the wild and artificially spawned in captivity (Bok and Jongbloed 1987). The larvae development of *C. Richardsonii* is similar to that of *M. Cephalus* (Brownell 1979; Cambray and Sok 1989). This shows that the southern mullet can be cultured in captivity. However, more research is necessary, with special emphasis on developing suitable feeds for fry. Bok (1989) reported many mortalities in newly hatched fry. The study highlighted a challenge in supplying suitable feed for the newly hatched fry. The diet was changed to live feed rotifer, *Brachionus plicatilis*, and fewer mortalities were recorded. This has also been reported in *M. cephalus*, which had experienced a similar challenge. Watanabe et al. (1983) fed *M. cephalus* fry with *B. plicatilis* and *Artemia nauplii* which improved the survival of the fry. The growth rate of *C. richardsonii* reported by Bok (1989) was similar to that of *M. cephalus* reported by Kuo et al. (1973). With advancements in technology and better methods of culturing aquatic animals, *C. richardsonii* can be cultured in captivity from broodstock to the next generation.

23.4.1 Economic and Market Characterisation of Southern Mullet

The mullets are sold at a price starting from N$ 10 per/kg in Namibia. Their price is highly variable; it depends on the amounts caught in that season (W. de Klerk, personal communication, 18 July 2022). They are sold as frozen or salted and dried into a form called bokkoms (Branch 2017; W. de Klerk, personal communication, 18 July 2022). The market for mullets can only be expanded if this species is introduced in aquaculture and farmed to complement captured stocks. The southern mullet has the potential to be farmed as it has an established market in both Namibia and South Africa. However, further studies are required to examine this species' economic feasibility. The market is very crucial in aquaculture.

23.5 Conclusions

Southern mullet feed at a low trophic level with a diet primarily comprised of detritus. This makes it a potential candidate that can contribute to food security while also addressing the issue of trophic levels in aquaculture. It has the potential to be cultured with other fish species to feed on their wastes and act as biological control. Moreover, it has the potential to be cultured successfully in single-culture conditions in both intensive and extensive systems. With the awareness that the stock of *C. richardsonii* has been overexploited in South Africa, culturing this species will reduce pressure on wild stocks while maintaining stable consumption levels. However, more studies are recommended to identify a specific method that can be used to farm the southern mullet to maximise production and profits. Economic feasibility studies on tor mass production of this species are recommended.

Fishers in Namibia claim that the catches have drastically decreased over the years. Unlike in South Africa, it is difficult to determine the cause of the decline in the wild population; however, concerning the over-exploitation reported in South Africa, it could be the same happening in Namibia. Population studies are recommended to provide specific information on possible causes of the decline of catches in Namibia, which can be used to assist in managing the stock.

References

Abraham M, Blanc N, Yashouv A (1966) Oogenesis in five species of grey mullets (Teleostei, Mugilidae) from natural and landlocked habitats. Isr J Zool 15:155–172

Beckley LE (1984) The ichthyofauna of the Sundays Estuary, South Africa, with particular reference to the juvenile marine component. Estuaries 7:248–258

Bennett BA (1989) A comparison of the fish communities in nearby permanently open, seasonally open, and normally closed estuaries in the southwestern Cape, South Africa. S Afr J Mar Sci 8: 43–55

BigeLow F, Friedman L, Freeman C (2020) California Legislature

Blaber SJM, Whitfield AK (1977) The feeding ecology of juvenile mullet (Mugilidae) in south-east African estuaries. Biol J Linn Soc 9:277–284

Bok A (1983) The demography, breeding biology and management of two mullet species (Pisces: Mugilidae) in the Eastern Cape. South Africa

Bok AH (1989) Rearing of artificially spawned southern mullet. Afr J Wildlife Res 19:31–34

Bok AH, Jongbloed H (1987) A preliminary study on the induced spawning of the southern mullet, *Liza richardsonii*. S Afr J Wildl Res 17:82–85

Branch G (2017) Two oceans: a guide to the marine life of southern Africa. Penguin Random House South Africa, Cape Town

Branch GM, Bally R, Bennett BA, De Decker HP, Fromme GAW, Heÿl CW, Willis JP (1985) Synopsis of the impact of artificially opening the mouth of the Bot River Estuary: implications for management. Trans R Soc S Afr 45:465–483

Brownell CL (1979) Stages in the early development of 40 marine fish species with pelagic eggs from the Cape of Good Hope

Brummett RE, Lazard J, Moehl J (2008) African aquaculture: realizing the potential. Food Policy 33:371–385
Byelashov OA, Griffin ME (2014) Fish in, fish out: perception of sustainability and contribution to public health. Fisheries 39:531–535
Cambray JA, Sok AH (1989) Early development of artificially spawned southern mullet, *Liza richardsonii* (Smith, 1846). Afr Zool 24:193–198
Cao L, Diana JS, Keoleian GA (2013) Role of life cycle assessment in sustainable aquaculture. Rev Aquac 5:61–71
DAFF (2014) Status of the South African Marine Fishery Resources, 2014. Technical report, DAFF
Daniel N (2018) A review on replacing fish meal in aquafeeds using plant protein sources. Int J Fish Aquat Sci 6:164–179
de Villiers G (1976) Exploitation of harders along southern African shores. The South African Shipping News and Fishing Industry Review May, pp 57–61
De Villiers G (1987) Harvesting harders *Liza richardsonii* in the Benguela upwelling region. S. Afr J Mar Sci 5:851–862
Delgado CL (2003) Fish to 2020: Supply and demand in changing global markets. WorldFish
Durand JD, Borsa P (2015) Mitochondrial phylogeny of grey mullets (Acanthopterygii: Mugilidae) suggests high proportion of cryptic species. C R Biol 338:266–277
Egerton S, Wan A, Murphy K, Collins F, Ahern G, Sugrue I, Stanton C (2020) Replacing fishmeal with plant protein in Atlantic salmon (*Salmo salar*) diets by supplementation with fish protein hydrolysate. Sci Rep 10:1–16
El-Sayed A (2013) Tilapia feed management practices in sub-Saharan Afric
FAO (2020) The State of World Fisheries and Aquaculture (SOFIA) - Meeting the Sustainable Development Goals, Fao, Rome, Italy
Golden CD, Allison EH, Cheung WW, Dey MM, Halpern BS, McCauley DJ, Myers SS (2016) Nutrition: Fall in fish catch threatens human health. Nature 534:317–320
Hodar AR, Vasava RJ, Mahavadiya DR, Joshi NH (2020) Fish meal and fish oil replacement for aqua feed formulation by using alternative sources: a review. J Exp Zool India 23:13–21
Horton M (2018) Age, Growth and per-recruit assessment of the Saldanha and Langebaan stock of *Chelon richardsonii* (Master's thesis, University of Cape Town)
Horton M, Parker D, Winker H, Lamberth SJ, Hutchings K, Kerwath SE (2019) Age, growth and per-recruit stock assessment of southern mullet *Chelon richardsonii* in Saldanha Bay and Langebaan Lagoon, South Africa. Afr J Mar Sci 41:313–324
Israel A, Guttman L, Shpige M, Neori A (2017) Development of polyculture and integrated multi-trophic aquaculture (IMTA) in Israel: a review. Isr J Aquac 69:20874
Jones AC, Mead A, Kaiser MJ, Austen MC, Adrian AW, Auchterlonie NA, Sutherland WJ (2015) Prioritization of knowledge needs for sustainable aquaculture: a national and global perspective. Fish Fish 16:668–683
Kamalii A, Wino AJ, Meenatchi S, Athithan S, Antony C, Ahilan B (2022) Effects of black soldier fly larvae on fish nutrition. Biol Res Today 4:140–142
Katz T, Herut B, Genin A, Angel DL (2002) Grey mullets ameliorate organically enriched sediments below a fish farm in the oligotrophic Gulf of Aqaba (Red Sea). Mar Ecol Prog Ser 234:205–214
Kuo CM, Shehadeh ZH, Milisen KK (1973) A preliminary report on the development, growth, and survival of laboratory-reared larvae of the grey mullet, *Mugil cephalus* L. J Fish Biol 5:459–470
Lasiak TA (1983) Aspects of the reproductive biology of the southern mullet, *Liza richardsonii*, from Algoa Bay, South Africa. Afr Zool 18:89–95
Lupatsch I, Katz T, Angel DL (2003) Removal of fish farm effluents by grey mullets: a nutritional approach. Aquat Liv Res 34:1367–1377
Maani K (2017) Dynamics of worldwide fisheries decline. In: World scientific book chapters. World Scientific, Singapore, pp 127–145

Marais JFK (1980) Aspects of food intake, food selection, and alimentary canal morphology of *Mugil cephalus* (Linnaeus, 1958), *Liza tricuspidens* (Smith, 1935), *L. richardsonii* (Smith, 1846), and *L. dumerili* (Steindachner, 1869). J Exp Mar Biol Ecol 44:193–209
Mires D (1969) Mixed culture of Tilapia with carp and gray mullet in Ein Hamifratz fishponds. Bamidgeh 21:24–32
Naylor RL, Goldburg RJ, Primavera JH, Kautsky N, Beveridge MCM, Clay J, Troell M (2000) Effect of aquaculture on world fish supplies. Nature 405:1017–1024
Naylor RL, Hardy RW, Bureau DP, Chiu A, Elliott M, Farrell AP, Nichols PD (2009) Feeding aquaculture in an era of finite resources. Proc Natl Acad Sci 106:15103–15110
Nunes AJ, Sá MV, Browdy CL, Vazquez-Anon M (2014) Practical supplementation of shrimp and fish feeds with crystalline amino acids. Aquaculture 431:20–27
Olsen Y (2011) Resources for fish feed in future mariculture. Aquac Environ Interact 1:187–200
Pandey PK, Kumar VS (2021) Biofilm in aquaculture production. In: Advances in fisheries biotechnology. Springer, Singapore, pp 401–422
Pauly D, Tyedmers P, Froese R, Liu LY (2001) Fishing down and farming up the food web. Conservation 2:1–25
Romer GS, McLachlan A (1986) Mullet grazing on surf diatom accumulations. J Fish Biol 28:93–104
Rust M, Barrows FT, Hardy RW, Lazur AM, Naughten K, Silverstein JT (2011) The future of aquafeeds NOAA/USDA alternative feeds initiative
Subasinghe R, Soto D, Jia J (2009) Global aquaculture and its role in sustainable development. Rev Aquac 1:2–9
Tacon AG, Hasan MR, Metian M 2011 Demand and supply of feed ingredients for farmed fish and crustaceans: trends and prospects. FAO Fisheries and Aquaculture Technical Paper (564), I
Turchini GM, Trushenski JT, Glencross BD (2019) Thoughts for the future of aquaculture nutrition: realigning perspectives to reflect contemporary issues related to judicious use of marine resources in aquafeeds. N Am J Aquac 81:13–39
Van Der Horst G, Erasmus T (1978) The breeding cycle of male *Liza dumerili* (Teleostei: Mugilidae) in the mouth of the Swartkops estuary. Afr Zool 13:259–273
Van der Horst G, Erasmus T (1981) Spawning time and spawning grounds of mullet with special reference to *Liza dumerili* (Steindachner, 1869). S Afr J Sci 77:73–78
Waite R, Beveridge M, Brummett R, Castine S, Chaiyawannakarn N, Kaushik S, Phillips M (2014) Improving productivity and environmental performance of aquaculture. WorldFish
Wallace JH, Kok HM, Beckley LE, Bennett B, Blaber SJM, Whitfield AK (1984) South African estuaries and their importance to fishes. S Afr J Sci 80:203
Watanabe T, Kitajima C, Fujita S (1983) Nutritional values of live organisms used in Japan for mass propagation of fish. Rev Aqua 34:115–143
Whitfield AK (1985) The role of zooplankton in the feeding ecology of fish fry from some southern African estuaries. Afr Zool 20:166–171
Whitfield AK (1988) The fish community of the Swartvlei estuary and the influence of food availability on resource utilization. Estuaries 11:160–170
Whitfield AK (1996) A review of factors influencing fish utilization of South African estuaries. Trans R Soc S Afr 51:115–137
Whitfield AK (2016) Ecological role of Mugilidae in the coastal zone. Biology, Ecology, and Culture of Grey Mullets (*Mugilidae*); pp 324–348
Whitfield AK (2019) Fishes of Southern African estuaries: From species to systems. Afr J Aquac Sci. 45(1-2):229–230
Whitfield AK, Kok HM (1992) Recruitment of juvenile marine fishes into permanently open and seasonally open estuarine systems on the southern coast of South Africa
Ytrestøyl T, Aas TS, Åsgård T (2015) Utilization of feed resources in the production of Atlantic salmon (*Salmo salar*) in Norway. Aquaculture 448:365–374

Part IV
Aquaculture Animal Welfare

Chapter 24
Some Significant Parasites in Aquaculture and Their Potential Impact on the Development of Aquaculture in Africa

A. M. Amakali, A. Halajian, M. R. Wilhelm, M. Tjipute, and W. J. Luus-Powell

Abstract Many African countries have experienced significant growth in aquaculture development in the last two decades. This growth may have been brought about by the realisation of aquaculture as a viable vehicle for development, the understanding of the biology of indigenous species with good traits for culture, the adoption of new farming technology and the adoption of enabling legislative frameworks by governments that encourage the development of this sector. The development of aquaculture in Africa was initially established to provide additional protein sources of food to cater for the growing population, improve food security, provide employment and generates income (to reduce poverty). The potential for further growth is vast as the continent has many positive attributes. Various diseases, including parasitic infections, however, pose threats to the development of the aquaculture sector as the disease can lead to mortality, reduce growth and reproduction rates and fitness of the culture fish stock and render the infected fish not marketable. Some fish diseases are zoonotic (can be transferred from animals to

---

A. M. Amakali (✉)
Department of Fisheries and Ocean Sciences, Sam Nujoma Marine and Coastal Resources Research Centre (SANUMARC), University of Namibia, Henties Bay, Namibia

National Marine Information and Research Centre (NatMIRC), Ministry of Fisheries and Marine Resources, Swakopmund, Namibia
e-mail: Annette.Amakali@mfmr.gov.na

A. Halajian
Research Administration and Development, University of Limpopo, Sovenga, South Africa

M. R. Wilhelm · M. Tjipute
Department of Fisheries and Ocean Sciences, Sam Nujoma Marine and Coastal Resources Research Centre (SANUMARC), University of Namibia, Henties Bay, Namibia

W. J. Luus-Powell
DSI-NRF SARChI Chair (Ecosystem Health), Department of Biodiversity, University of Limpopo, Sovenga, South Africa

© The Author(s), under exclusive license to Springer Nature Singapore Pte Ltd. 2023
N. N. Gabriel et al. (eds.), *Emerging Sustainable Aquaculture Innovations in Africa*, Sustainable Agriculture and Food Security,
https://doi.org/10.1007/978-981-19-7451-9_24

humans). For this reason, various studies globally (including histopathology, Health Assessment Index (HAI) and molecular work) have addressed parasites of cultured fishes and how they affect and/or influence the productivity of aquaculture organisms. Many of such studies aimed to understand the behaviour and life cycles of these parasites and determine the nature of pathology to the fish host. This would help in finding ways to prevent and control parasite epidemics, when necessary, in aquaculture set-ups and improve the productivity of this sector. This chapter discusses the importance of studying parasites and their effects in an aquaculture set-up.

Keywords Aquaculture · Mariculture · Fish · Fish health · Fish diseases · Fish parasites

24.1 Introduction

A parasite is an organism that lives in or on another larger organism of a different species, referred to as host species, upon which it depends for food and/or shelter (Rohde and Rohde 2005). Parasites are often small, short-lived and commonly hidden within organisms during their parasitic phase. Their effects on their hosts may be evident and profound or subtler (Rohde and Rohde 2005). Typically, they attract attention only when they cause pathology and disease (effects on host behaviour, decreased fish growth, reduced host total body weight, decreased fecundity and increased mortality) or somehow degrade biological products; thus, production, yields and economic benefits consequently increase healthcare costs (Marcogliese 2002; Stewart 2005; Hutson et al. 2011; Iwanowicz 2011; Khalil et al. 2014). For example, Merella et al. (2009) reported an outbreak of *Sciaenacotyle panceri* Sonsino, 1891, on cage-reared meagre (*Argyrosomus regius* Asso, 1801) from the western Mediterranean Sea after the fish started showing non-specific disease signs such as lethargy, emaciation, gill anaemia and mortality.

It is important to distinguish between ectoparasites and endoparasites in finfish, defined by which organs of the fish they infest or infect, external or internal organs, respectively (Poulin 2004). The main differences between ecto- and endoparasites are four-fold: Firstly, ectoparasites have direct life cycles including only one fish host and infest fish via free-swimming infective larvae (Poulin 2004). Unlike endoparasites, ectoparasites do not need different hosts to complete their life-cycle, so it is easier to multiply within a short period of time on the host (Poulin 2004; Reed et al. 2009; Whittington and Kearn 2011). Endoparasites living mostly in the gastrointestinal tract, on the other hand, have complex life cycles involving at least two host species. They are acquired by fish hosts via ingestion and could be prevented by controlling fish feed (Poulin 2004).

Secondly, the species richness of ectoparasites per host is typically greater than that of endoparasites. Gill parasites, especially, attach to the host as a result of the gaseous exchange between water and the gills. As the water passes through the gills during this gaseous exchange process, the gills accumulate most free-living parasite species in the water column. Gills hence accommodate more parasite species compared to all other host organs (e.g. Amakali 2019). Fish hosts with a broad diet, for instance *Clarias* spp. Scopoli, 1777, which feed on a wide variety of food items including detritus, fishes, zooplankton, macrophytes, insects, phytoplankton and gastropods, however, may have greater endoparasites species richness than ectoparasites.

Thirdly, endoparasites often occur at much higher abundances than ectoparasites (Poulin 2004), as they are acquired from a daily diet of the fish host and are not exposed to external environmental changes. Endoparasites are also affected by changes in the immune response of fish (Aydoğdu et al. 2015), which plays an important protective role for the fish host (Rubio-Godoy 2007). Some immune responses are activated when the parasites are in abundance. Some parasites, cestodes for instance, have less tolerance to these immune responses compered to others such as digenean trematodes. This depends on the mode of feeding associated with the parasites (Rubio-Godoy 2007; Aydoğdu et al. 2015).

Lastly, there is an effect of the external environment on the parasite, where the ectoparasites are subjected to water quality variations that influence their well-being (Poulin 2004). Monogeneans and copepods living on the external surfaces of fishes are exposed to water currents and changes in their physical and chemical environment that make robust attachment structures and copulation organs necessary. When fish die due to parasitic infections, deaths can often be associated with changes in parasite densities and community composition (Iwanowicz 2011). Frequently, the damage associated with these dead fish is relative to the rate of parasite infestation, i.e. the state of the fish being invaded by parasites (Bruno et al. 2013). A lightly infected fish will show few or no symptoms, while a heavily infected fish may become physiologically harmed and die (Iwanowicz 2011; Mumba 2014).

Parasites generally do not kill their hosts, but some severely stress the affected fish to the point of biological and economical concern (Bruno et al. 2013). High intensities of ectoparasites cause excess mucus secretion, loose scales, dermis injuries such as haemorrhages, open sores, ulcers exposing connective and muscle tissues, inflict reproductive damage (Deaton 2009) or osmotic problems affecting respiratory functions (Bruno et al. 2013). Consequently, damaged skin and gills make the fish host more susceptible to secondary infections, possibly from viruses, bacteria or other microorganisms that may also contribute to mortalities (Rohde and Rohde 2005). Martins et al. (2015) and Kotob et al. (2017) reviewed the impacts of different secondary infections, also called co-infections, on fish species.

Parasites use the nutrition from the host they invade. However, the severity of diseases and the resulting mortality is usually greater in cultured fish than in wild fish (Scholz 1999; Ternengo et al. 2010; Labella et al. 2011). In the wild, fish can get enough nutrition for their own needs and the needs of the parasites. Sufficient intake of readily and naturally available nutrients also satisfies the pathogens and hence decreases fish stress while simultaneously increasing the fish resistance to disease (Bruno et al. 2013). In farmed fish, however, natural feeds are not always readily available. In addition, feed is neither usually increased nor altered with the presence of demanding pathogens or parasites in the fish (Scholz 1999). This may lead to an increased number of parasites that cause stress to the fish, giving rise to diseases and further leading to pathological changes, a decrease in fitness and a reduction of the market value of the fish (Scholz 1999).

Aquaculture, both freshwater and marine, has been increasing in many African countries as a means to provide food to cater to the growing populations to generate foreign investment and earnings and also increase the rate of employment, and hence reduce poverty (e.g. Tjipute 2011). Despite this increased effort, the contribution from Africa to the world's aquaculture is still insignificant (from a mere 0.4% in 1996 (FAO 2016) to approximately 2.7% in 2019 (Halwart 2020)). This growth is, however, expected to increase.

Various diseases, including parasitic infections, pose a threat to the development of the aquaculture sector as it leads to loss of biological fitness (reduced growth, reproduction and survival rates) and reduced product marketability (poor quality, unattractive and undesired size). Diseases can also negatively impact the people who depend on aquaculture for a basic income (Mumba 2014). In addition, diseases emanating from aquaculture can be transferred to wild fishes and cause ecological damage (Thieltges et al. 2020).

Parasites that infect fish species are ubiquitous, primarily surviving in a dynamic equilibrium with their host(s) and they are often overlooked, but any changes in the environment, both anthropogenic and natural, can alter the parasite-host equilibrium and cause disease or mortality in fish (Iwanowicz 2011; Justine et al. 2012). Fish parasite infections arise from poor aquaculture management, high-density conditions and increased fish stress. It has been established that the interaction among these pathogens, hosts and their environment results in the development of fish diseases (Labella et al. 2011). In addition to the biological, economical and economic losses caused by parasites, some of the parasites are zoonotic. This means that they can be transmitted to humans through the consumption of infected fish that is either undercooked or consumed raw (Mumba 2014). Millions of people globally are infected by parasites, and many more are at risk of infection.

The economic loss experienced due to parasite infection is usually in the event of an intense parasite occurrence in an aquaculture set-up when the cost of production is increased because of the investment loss in dead fish, the cost of treatment incurred and decreased growth during convalescence that leads to loss of income. Mortality often occurs when there is a change in parasite density and community composition and when a stage is reached when a heavily infected fish become physiologically impaired and die. Labella et al. (2011) highlighted that to apply measures to control parasites and diseases limiting the production of cultured fish, studies involving factors of pathogenic organisms and aspects of the parasite life cycle and a better understanding of environmental conditions affecting fish cultures are a prerequisite.

The intensification of aquaculture and the introduction of new aquaculture species into environments create situations where parasite burdens increase exponentially in high-density cultures (Woo and Leatherland 2006) and emerging infectious diseases (EID). EID can be defined as previously unknown diseases, or the spread of an existing disease into a new host or geographic area (Krkošek 2010). EID causes much ecological damage, especially in some aquaculture systems such as cage systems where the barriers are weak or non-existent.

Disease management mechanisms in Africa are not well developed, and there exists a porous and, in some instances, not harmonised biosecurity system. In many instances, fish health is not prioritised until extreme impacts are observed, so the opportunity to manage and control parasites and diseases at the source is missed. Most farmers react to large outbreaks rather than preventing or managing infections, most likely because of insufficient information on the ecology of pathogenic parasites, their prevention and control (Iwanowicz 2011). The diseases and specific identity of the parasites infecting cultured fish are rarely known, and very few parasite species, classified only to their genera, are recorded (Woo and Gregory 2014). This chapter is a summary of some of the known ecto- and endoparasites affecting marine and freshwater fish species to identify and bridge the knowledge gaps.

24.2 Potential Aquaculture Parasites

24.2.1 Monogenea

Monogeneans arc a group of ectoparasite flatworms (phylum Platyhelminthes) found in freshwater, brackish and marine habitats. They are associated with a one-host life cycle, shed their eggs straight into the water column, and after which hatching, the free-swimming larvae infect a new host directly and are highly host-specific (Paperna 1980; Stewart 2005; Amakali 2019). Some are viviparous such as *Gyrodactylus salaris* Malmberg, 1957, and give birth to individuals almost the same size as the adult, with another embryo ready to be born. Monogeneans have caused worldwide chaos in intensive culture facilities primarily due to their ability to reproduce rapidly (Stewart 2005). Monogeneans are also organ-specific. This characteristic has led to interesting models for evolutionary research into host–parasite relations with specific haptoral make-up suitable for the organ they inhabit. They are commonly found on the fish skin, fins and gills and feed on epidermal cells, mucus or blood. In heavily infected fish, this leads to emaciation, lethargy and anaemia. Gill epithelial hyperplasia, excess mucous production and mechanical damage to the gills causing respiratory difficulties in fish have been reported because of monogenean flukes in captivity (Stewart 2005). There are, however, some studies that have found monogeneans in the internal organs of the fish with specialised organs for attachments. This includes dactylogyrid monogeneans such as *Enterogyrus* Paperna, 1963, documented from the stomach of freshwater fish by Bayoumy and El-Monem (2012). Luus-Powell et al. (2020) also reported other species of *Enterogyrus* from the stomachs of cichlid hosts documented from Africa, including two new species of *Enterogyrus* found in the stomach of the Mozambique tilapia, *Oreochromis mossambicus* in South Africa. A monogenean parasite from the species of the *Amphibdella* Chatin, 1874, represented the most interesting monogenean parasitic adaptation, parasitising the blood system of electric rays from the family

Torpedinidae (Luus-Powell et al. 2020). In addition, Amakali et al. (2022) found and described monogenean *Calceostoma* sp. in the stomach of marine fish.

Monogeneans have been reported to cause severe fish mortalities in hatcheries all over Africa. *Diplectanum oliveri* Williams, 1989, a monogenean gill parasite of marine fish both *Argyrosomus japonicus* (dusky kob) and silver kob, *A. inodorus* (Griffiths & Heemstra 1995) is currently regarded in South Africa as the most persistent ectoparasite associated with the culture of both *Argyrosomus* species, causing pathological tissue changes in the areas associated with attachment and feeding, which can result in stock losses (Joubert 2012). Diplectanids have been reported several times in marine aquaculture from Africa and worldwide (e.g. Amakali et al. 2022), increasing mortality in sciaenid. Cultured fish (e.g. in tanks) are usually held in more crowded environmental conditions than fish in the natural environment. This promotes infestation and makes it easier for monogeneans to find a host fish in capture aquaculture (Hecht and Endermann 1998). Additionally, captive environments may have stressful effects on cultured fish, which may stem from aggressive behaviour by the tank mates, poor or insufficient nutrition, handling injury and poor water quality (e.g. Hecht and Endermann 1998; Stewart 2005; O'Rourke and Rosenbaum 2015; Mogorosi 2019). This may consequently weaken the immune system of the fish and how it responds to and fight the present parasites, thereby allowing for the rapid proliferation of parasites.

Risk assessment of parasitic helminths on cage- or pond-cultured Nile tilapia in Uganda and Kenya revealed that monogeneans (*Cichlidogyrus tilapiae* Paperna, 1960 and *C. sclerosus* Paperna & Thurston, 1969) are high-risk parasites, particularly in pond-raised fish (O'Rourke and Rosenbaum 2015). *Cichlidogyrus* and *Gyrodactylus* have also been reported to infect tilapia in several fish farms in the

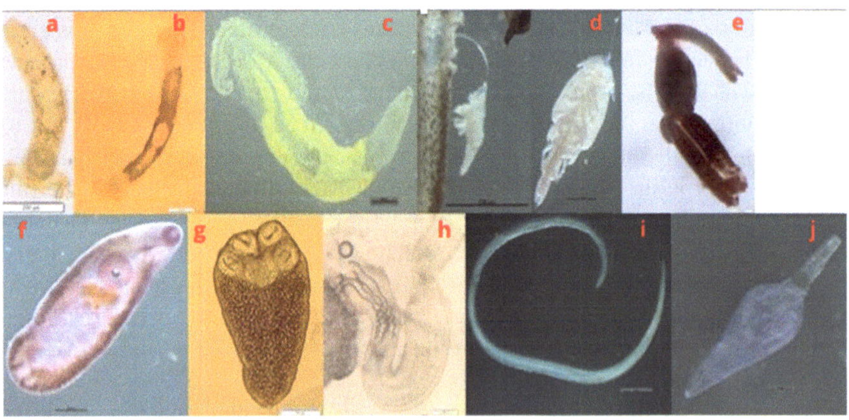

Fig. 24.1 Some marine parasites infecting fishes from Africa, ectoparasitic monogeneans: *Diplactunum* sp. (**a**), *Calceostoma* sp. (**b**), *Sciaenocotyle* sp. (**c**), Copepods Caligus sp. (**d**) and Brachiella sp. (**e**). Endoparasitic digenean trematode Helicometrina sp. (**f**), cestode tetraphyllidean plerocercoids (metacestodes) (**g**) and Callitetrarhynchus sp. larvae (**h**), nematode Anisakis sp. larvae (**i**) and acanthocephalan hook worm Corynosoma sp. (**j**)

eastern region of Saudi Arabia. Infected fish suffered from respiration difficulties due to the damage to gills, haemorrhage, fin rot and increased mucus secretion.

Diseases and damages caused by monogeneans in aquaculture set-ups have resulted in the need for trials to be conducted to assess the effects of anthelmintics on the flukes. Although fish farming contributes more than 10% of fish produced worldwide, no anthelmintics have been developed to precisely control or treat monogenean flukes in aquaculture (Stewart 2005; Mo 2020; Norbury et al. 2022). Monogeneans are challenging to eliminate, as most treatments are not 100% effective, merely reducing parasite numbers. The natural life cycle allows for the recovery of parasite numbers in days. Furthermore, some treatments that may be effective on the parasite may be harmful to the host or the environment and thus cannot be used. For this reason, it is imperative to identify a chemical/treatment that is safe to use on the host and can effectively eliminate the monogeneans to control disease outbreaks in culture environments.

Stewart (2005) studied the effect of praziquantel (10, 20 and 40 mg/l), hydrogen peroxide (30 mg/l), copper sulphate (0.2 mg/l), formalin (100 and 200 mg/l) and freshwater and observed that praziquantel (40 mg/l) and freshwater were significantly effective at eradication of *Calceostoma* sp. Freshwater successfully eradicated 100% of the parasites after an hour and praziquantel after 6 h of exposure to the treatment. Norbury et al. (2022) also reviewed and reported on PZQ's current use in aquaculture and discussed its effectiveness against various flatworm parasites of fish and issues that may arise after administration.

According to Mo (2020), *Gyrodactylus salaris*, a freshwater monogenean, is sensitive to changes in the chemical composition of the water. It is sensitive to the most used chemicals for bath treatment of farmed salmon parr and salmon eggs (e.g. high salinity salt water, formaldehyde and compounds containing chlorine and

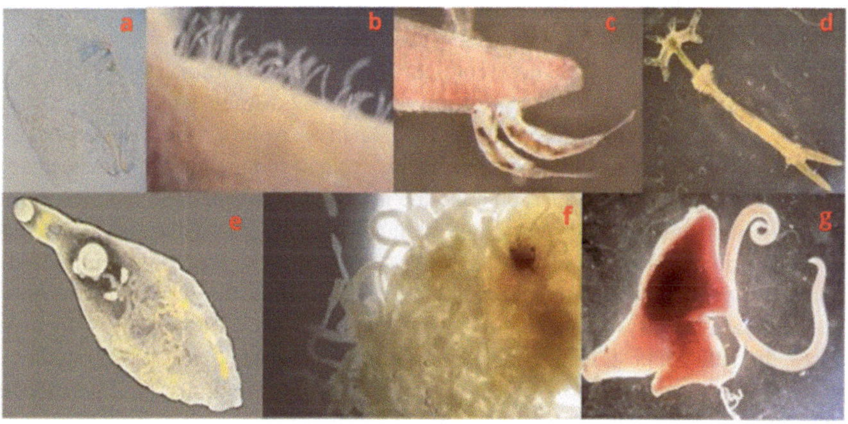

Fig. 24.2 Some freshwater parasites infecting fishes from Africa: gyrodactylus sp. (**a, b**), copepodid larvae (**c**) and copepod Lernaea sp. (**d**), digenean trematode (**e**), adult cestode (**f**) and nematode larvae (**g**)

iodine). In addition, *G. salaris* is sensitive to slightly acidic solutions of aluminium sulphate ([Al_2 $(SO_4)_3$]; AlS). AlS is less toxic to fish than *G. salaris* in moderately acidified waters. Furthermore, disinfecting fish eggs from infected farms (iodine-containing compounds have been used) was reported to be another way of eradicating the *G. salaris* parasite that may have contaminated the eggs.

24.2.2 Digenea

The digenean trematodes are flatworms (phylum Platyhelminthes) and represent the largest group of parasites and comprise approximately 18,000 families (Bannai 2017). They have been reported and described throughout a broad geographical range from multiple fish hosts across broad taxonomic ranks. Adult-stage digeneans usually have a dorso-ventrally flattened, oval body with a smooth, spiny or corrugated surface, a sucker around the antero-ventral mouth, and an additional ventral sucker or acetabulum. Both suckers are used for attachment and locomotion. The digestive system consists of a pharynx connected to the mouth opening, a short oesophagus and two blind intestinal caeca. Most trematodes are hermaphrodite, containing both male organs (testes, ducts and copulatory system) and female organs (ovary, vitelline glands, ducts and uterus). Some also contain a specialised copulatory organ which is used for differential diagnosis. Eggs are evacuated to the genital opening and are usually oval and operculated.

The general life cycle of digenean trematodes involves multiple hosts (which make them heteroxenous), and they usually require (with some exceptions) a mollusc as their first host (e.g. Amakali 2019). The development of rediae and cercariae takes place in the snails and crustaceans. Small fish serve as the second intermediate host, and adult trematodes develop in big fish, piscivorous birds and mammals that feed on infected small fish, serving as definitive or final hosts. Digeneans are common in wild fish, where infections are usually asymptomatic, while unless the intermediate host, commonly aquatic snails, or fish, is present, they are uncommon in cultured fish (Norbury et al. 2022). Adult parasites in fish are usually found in the intestine, though some, such as Aporocotylids (blood flukes) reside in the cardiovascular system. In the life cycle of blood digeneans, the cercaria emerges from the intermediate invertebrate host and penetrates and matures in the definitive fish host, and the resulting adult releases eggs into the fish's vascular system (Bullard and Overstreet 2002). These eggs may be sequestered in the gill, heart, kidney, liver, spleen, pancreas or other organs, where they cause inflammation and decrease the physiological and mechanical efficiency of these organs. In some cases, they kill the host. In addition to internal digeneans, Mele et al. (2022) studied a digenean trematode *Didymodiclinus marginati* from the gills of *Epinephelus marginatus*.

Adult trematodes, infecting the digestive tract of fishes, are considered harmless, even when their numbers are high. Extraintestinal trematode infections, on the other hand, are potentially pathogenic. Pathological data on blood flukes (sanguinicolids which can cause considerable damage to the gills and impair respiration) are relevant to African fish. Adult worms and trapped eggs can physically obstruct the passage of blood, causing clotting and subsequent necrosis, while escape of miracidia through the gill epithelium causes blood loss and may lead to anaemia (Hecht and Endermann 1998). The proliferation of the arterial endothelium was reported in common carp infected with *Sanguinicola inermis* Plehn, 1905. The *S. inermis* hosts experience loss of blood that causes a pale colour of the gills and a decline in packed cell volumes and oxyhaemoglobin levels. Heavy infection compromises the host's ability to withstand stressful conditions, for example, heavily infected cultured carp suffocated during transportation (Hecht and Endermann 1998). In chronic infections, adult worms scatter and become stranded in the heart, kidneys and caudal vessels. Dispersed eggs become encapsulated and may also become surrounded by a focal granuloma.

Treatment of fishes debilitated by digenean parasites is difficult, and only the combination of stock destruction and facility disinfection is a realistic option for managing cases in freshwater systems. However, because this is usually not possible in marine systems, early detection and identification of the parasite, careful site selection and construction of culture facilities, and elimination of infected hosts (definitive or intermediate) are important (Bullard and Overstreet 2002).

24.2.3 Cestoda

Cestodes or tapeworms (phylum Platyhelminthes) infect fish in adult and larval forms. They are known worldwide for fish of the families Cyprinidae, Poecilidae, Cichlidae and Centrarchidae. Records of African hosts, all from southern Africa, include the common carp, *Labeobarbus kimberleyensis* Gilchrist and Thompson, 1913, *Enteromius trimaculatus* Peters, 1852 and *Oreochromis mossambicus* Peters, 1852 (Paperna 1996). The most important tapeworms in Africa that infect fish in the adult form is the Asian tapeworm *Bothriocephalus acheilognathi* Yamaguti, 1934 (Paperna 1996). Infections with *Ligula* Bloch, 1782 plerocercoids in the body cavity and by encysted cyclophyllidean cysticercoids are widespread in Central and Southern African fish. *Ligula* infections are very common in *Enteromius* spp. and in the open water cyprinid *Rastrineobola (Engraulicypris) argenteus* Pellegrin, 1904 of Lake Victoria. It also occurs occasionally in cichlids (*Haplochromis* spp. from Lake Victoria, and *Oreochromis* spp. from Israel).

Cyclophyllidean cysticercoids are common in viscera of siluriformes, *Clarias* and *Bagrus* spp., and in cichlids; they have also been reported from *Enteromius* spp. Infections have been reported in the Sudan, in Lake Victoria and the lesser Rift Valley lakes, in Lake Kariba, Zambia, the Niger and in Ghana (Paperna 1996). In recent years, there have been several reports of the non-native *Atractolytocestus* in Africa (Scholz et al. 2015). Although seems it should not be considered a serious pathogen of cultured common carp (Gjurčević et al. 2012) but quick movements of this cestode and potential spillovers, like recent reports in a native fish in

South Africa (Dos Santos and Avenant-Oldewage 2022), are alarming and need more attention and investigations.

Amakali (2019) reported cysts of *Callitetrarhynchus* sp. larvae as well as unidentified tetraphyllidean plerocercoids (metacestodes) from the stomach of marine fish silver kob from Namibia. Larval *Callitetrarhynchus* sp. has been recorded from other fish hosts such as the red grouper (*Epinephelus morio* Valenciennes, 1828, Pisces: Sarranidae) and hake (*Merluccius gayi peruanus* Ginsburg 1954).

24.2.4 Nematoda

Adult and larval nematodes (roundworms) potentially infect all fresh and brackish water fish, with heavier infections occurring in fish occupying higher positions in the food chain, e.g. predatory fish. Nematodes are very distinctive in shape, with a solid cuticle. Because of their resistant cuticle, these worms last longer than flatworms in post-mortem conditions. Most adult forms are large enough to be visible to the naked eye. Khalil (1971) reports 40 species of adult nematodes, representatives of nine families of fish in Africa. The majority occurs in the alimentary system, and only a few enter tissues or inner cavities. The most common nematodes in an aquaculture set-up are *Contracaecum* spp. (in freshwater aquaculture) and *Anisakis* spp. (in Mariculture) both from the family Anisakidae.

The life cycle of nematodes involves crustaceans as transport or first intermediate hosts, fish and cephalopods as secondary intermediate or paratenic hosts and cetaceans, pinnipeds and fish-eating birds as final or definitive hosts (Molina-García and Sanz 2002; Fuentes et al. 2022). Their occurrence can cause a deterioration of fish quality and can be of great concern to human health if ingested in raw or undercooked fish. *Anisakis simplex* parasite species, for example, cause human anisakiasis, a food-borne disease, through the consumption of raw, salted, marinated, undercooked, previously not frozen or conveniently treated fish (Fuentes et al. 2022). Food-borne parasitic infections have been identified as one of the most significant public health problems (Khalil et al. 2014). In addition, inhalation of nematode antigens could also put handlers at risk of developing asthma (Fuentes et al. 2022). Larval nematodes occur either encysted in tissues or free in body cavities, most often in the abdominal or pericardial cavity. Larvae of *Contracaecum* Railliet and Henry, 1912 tend to escape from their cysts and crawl out of their host body after death. Larvae usually emerge from isolated cysts if incubated in 0.9% saline solution at 37 °C. Anisakid larvae are variable in size, often very large and thick, up to 60 mm long and 3 mm in diameter, with characteristic outgrowths (appendices) of either the anterior end of the intestine or the posterior end of the oesophagus (the ventriculum) or both: in members of *Contracaecum* appendices are formed (in opposite directions) from both the ventriculum and the intestine.

24.2.5 *Class Hexanauplia, Sub-class Copepoda*

Copepods are a group of crustaceans (phylum Arthropoda, subphylum Crustacea). Their life cycle involves a series of nauplius and copepodid stages (Hogans and Trudeau 1989). The time it takes to complete the life cycle depends on water temperature. High temperatures reduce the time it takes to complete the life cycle when compared to low temperatures. Copepods have been reported on cultured and wild fish (Johnson et al. 2004). Some species could be a vector for viruses, bacteria and protozoans and are responsible for most disease outbreaks in cultured systems, having the potential to affect growth, fecundity, the market value of fish products and the survival of their host (Johnson et al. 2004). They are also intermediate hosts for important fish parasites, including tapeworms and nematodes and parasites that infect humans and can serve as vectors of serious human diseases like cholera. The most severe crustacean parasite that may become problematic under intensive aquaculture conditions in Africa is *Lernaea cyprinacea* Linnaeus, 1758, found anchored to the fish's skin *L. cyprinacea*. Infection with this parasite has been associated with reduced host weight, growth and fecundity (Welicky et al. 2017). Other copepods may also attach to gill filaments and cause epithelial hyperplasia and may be indirectly responsible for fish kills (Piasecki et al. 2004).

Members of the family Caligidae and Lernanthropidae are the most reported parasite species on marine fish (Johnson et al. 2004; Rameshkumar et al. 2014). These species are often referred to as sea lice. Caligid copepods generally have direct life cycles consisting of two free-living planktonic nauplius stages, one free-swimming infectious copepodid stage, and four to six attached chalimus stages, one or two pre-adult stages, and one adult stage (Johnson and Albright 1991). Notable exceptions include *Caligus punctatus* punctatus Shiino, 1955 and *C. elongatus* Nordmann, 1832, in which the pre-adult stage is reported not to occur (Kim 1993). With the development of various treatments and management strategies to reduce sea lice infection levels, mortality caused by sea lice has been significantly reduced. Economic losses due to sea lice are primarily from the costs of treatment, the costs of the management strategies, the costs associated with reduced growth rates that are a direct result of infection and/or treatment and the costs of carcass downgrading at harvest (Johnson et al. 2004). The other collected copepod families, such as Lernaeopodidae, Pennellidae, Siphonostomatoida and Tetraodontidae, are also known marine fish parasites (Rameshkumar et al. 2014).

Parasitic copepods feed on host mucous, tissues, and blood and their attachment can become secondarily infected by bacteria and fungi and increase susceptibility to primary diseases. The relationship of the number of parasitic copepods to the severity of the disease is dependent on the size and age of the fish, the general state of health of the fish, the species of copepod and the developmental stages present. The infection rate can become severe and prolonged under poor water quality or crowded conditions (Hecht and Endermann 1998). Copepod parasitic infections are predominantly fatal to early juvenile fish. Infection by parasitic copepods of the mouth has been documented and reported to impair mouth breeding in *Oreochromis* species.

24.2.6 Acanthocephala

Acanthocephala is a phylum closely associated with the Cestoda phylum (Amin 2013). They are an integral component of the parasite fauna of pinnipeds. Acanthocephala is readily recognised by their evaginable thorny anterior proboscis crowned with several rows of recurved hooks that serve as an attachment organ and 'drills' firmly into the walls of the intestines and stomach of the host. In the encased larval stage, in tissues, the spiny proboscis is retracted (Amakali et al. 2022). The attachment with the proboscis causes damage and changes to the tissues exposing the tissues to other secondary infections and increasing the host's susceptibility to diseases and infection (Silva et al. 2014). The number and arrangement of the hooks on the proboscis are the main criteria for the differentiation of species. A wider range of anatomical details determines higher taxa (Kabata 1985). Acanthocephalans lack a mouth and digestive tract. They absorb their nutrients directly through their body surface. Adult acanthocephalans usually live in the lumen of the digestive tract only, but sometimes they bore through the walls of the digestive tract and come to lie in the abdominal cavity (Hayunga 1991). The worms are sac-like, containing lemnisci connected to the proboscis and genital organs opening posteriorly. The sexes are separate, and the male opening is within a membranous bursa. An alimentary canal is absent.

All acanthocephalans develop via one or more intermediate hosts (heteroxenous). Adult acanthocephalans are all gut parasites. Eggs are laid into the intestinal lumen and evacuated with faeces. The first intermediate hosts of piscine acanthocephala are amphipods, isopods, copepods or ostracods. The first larvae, the acanthella (acanthor), hatch from eggs after being swallowed by a suitable invertebrate host. Some species will develop to the adult stage when their larvae in the invertebrate host are ingested by the definitive vertebrate host (Paperna 1996). Fishes can also serve as intermediate hosts, harbouring a second larval stage (the acanthor or cystacanth). Definitive hosts of such acanthocephalans are either predatory fish or piscivorous birds. Pathogenic effects of acanthocephalans are due to the attachment of the adult parasite in the digestive tract and the encapsulation of larval stages in the tissues. In low to moderate infections, pathological effects are localised around the attachment of the adult worm. The extent of damage is proportional to the depth of penetration of the proboscis. It is negligible when parasites are attached to the epithelial mucosa only and becomes extreme, with extensive granuloma and subsequent fibrosis, when the worm's proboscis is anchored in the muscle layer or entirely perforates the intestinal wall (Kabata 1985; Paperna 1996). The depth of penetration of some species may vary in different host fishes. Extensive inflammation, peritonitis due to gut perforation and systemic clinical changes (anurhersia), will occur only in massive infections, most often in farmed fish. Information on infection among fish in

Africa on acanthocephalan is minimal. Halajian et al. (2018) documented a checklist of acanthocephalan parasites in South Africa.

24.3 Control and Treatment of Parasites

Human activities have been shown to be vital in spreading pathogenic diseases in farmed fish. There are several control measures for several diseases that affect aquaculture important species. The most important approach in controlling most diseases is the preventative measures that include good husbandry practices (good water quality, appropriate stocking densities, good feeding regime, removal of predisposing factors and stressors) and vaccination against any possible disease.

There are several considerations before treatment of any type of fish disease can be undertaken:

- Whether the disease is treatable, and the prognosis for successful treatment.
- Feasibility of treating the fish where they are being kept, considering the costs, the effect of handling (stress) and the prognosis of successful treatment.
- The prescribed concentration of the active ingredient of the treatment solution.
- Established regulations related to the type of medications approved, the appropriate withdrawal periods after vaccination before harvesting the fish for human consumption.

Registrations of parasite treatments and chemicals depend on individual countries, and farmers must check what is registered and then use the products according to the labels. There are very few (if any) registered treatments for fish parasites in Africa. In fact, there is no registered treatment for aquaculture fish parasites in South Africa. Generally, the most practicable preventative method of controlling digenean infection in farmed fish is eliminating the vector snail/intermediate hosts. Available measures include the use of chemical molluscicides, environmental manipulation and use of molluscophagous fish. The environmental limits imposed on snail survival in fish farm systems can also involve regular weed control, especially in earth ponds, performed manually or with herbicides (Paperna 1980) that destroy snail populations. Experience with commercial fish farms is still insufficient. One still needs professional advice on the best environmental and stock-friendly herbicide and the best ways to use it.

Likewise, the most common way to avoid nematode infestation is by treating pondwater with an organophosphate to kill all intermediate copepod hosts (Hecht and Endermann 1998). Prevention of larval nematode infection by keeping away piscivorous birds is impractical not only in fishing areas in natural habitats or man-made impoundments but even in fish ponds. In fish ponds, preventive treatments of *Contracaecum* by eliminating copepods may be of some value if suitably timed soon after contamination. The anthelmintic praziquantel (PZQ) was reported to effectively treat a range of flatworm parasites in various fish species and has potential for broader application than its current use in the global aquaculture industry. Norbury et al. (2022) evaluated routes of PZQ administration, along with issues related to palatability, pharmacokinetics and toxicity in fish, and discussed PZQ's effects on non-target species, environmental impacts, and the development of drug-resistance. Although PZQ has been an obvious control measure for platyhelminth parasites in aquaculture, application of PZQ for the treatment of fish for human consumption is only registered for use in several jurisdictions worldwide, for only certain parasites under specific conditions.

The encouraging prospects of aquaculture growth in Africa have not been paralleled with targeted aquatic animal and plant health management and biosecurity measures designed to prevent and control the outbreak of diseases. These aquatic animal and plant health management and biosecurity measures are critical requirements for the sustainable development of the aquaculture industry (Lee and O'Bryen 2003; Delabbio et al. 2005; Eissa et al. 2016). Several African countries have actively adopted and developed aquatic animal, plant health and biosecurity strategies and are signatories to organisations tasked with animal health, such as the World Organization for Animal Health (OIE), while other countries are making strides to apply those measures (FAO 2018). The developed aquatic animal and plant health and biosecurity strategies are using the application of the Progressive Management Plan (PMP) for improving Aquaculture Biosecurity (AB) which is comprised of four progressive stages, is risk-based, proactive and collaborative, and being country-specific (FAO 2007).

24.4 Summary and Discussion

The growth and development of aquaculture (both fresh water and marine) in Africa are still slow compared to other parts of the world, so research into fish diseases and parasites is not a high priority. However, the lessons learnt in the operating aquaculture set-ups should point to the understanding of how imperatively essential it is to build the research and diagnostic capacity in Africa to deal with fish disease problems. A majority of fish losses in African aquaculture are associated with non-infectious causes and can readily be avoided by appropriate husbandry and management techniques (Hecht and Endermann 1998). Chemical therapy of fish is expensive and requires expertise to properly administer and use. There is, therefore, a need to find and investigate alternative treatment technologies and more environmentally friendly forms of treatment. Proper site selection and design of rearing structures can reduce the number of infectious stages that are transported to and/or retained within the rearing environment, as well as ensure that fish stocks remain healthy and thereby more resistant to infection (Johnson et al. 2004). Factors such as water depth, tidal range, patterns of water circulation, flow rate, temperature and salinity have been suggested as important factors concerning parasite infestation.

Control of parasite infestation and infection in culture systems can be done accordingly depending on whether the parasites have direct life cycles or there are intermediate hosts involved. A good management strategy involves keeping intermediate and definitive hosts separate. Early detection and identification of endoparasites could be essential for eliminating susceptible intermediate hosts from the area of fish in tanks, pens, ponds or raceways. Monitoring several fish from each group to assess all parasites and diseases is advised. Infected fishes such as brood stock or fingerlings should not be transported to other facilities. Regular inspection for infestations and infections in each facility could help reduce or end the spread of disease from the culture facility to the facility by fish movements. However, such an application would probably be impractical and cost-prohibitive for marine pens or cages. Moreover, the biodiversity of endemic fauna inhabiting sites below and near containments should be preserved and protected (Johnson et al. 2004). Modifying husbandry practices can be a very effective method to reduce the magnitude of infection by ectoparasites, especially copepods. Using husbandry practices to control ectoparasite abundance requires a good knowledge of parasite biology (e.g. growth rates, duration of survival of infectious stages off-host) and host range (Johnson et al. 2004). As with other infectious diseases, management activities (e.g. stocking density and water quality management) that reduce stress and maintain optimal fish health are likely to reduce the impact of ectoparasites, particularly copepods. In pond culture, overcrowding and poor water quality have been cited as factors responsible for developing ectoparasitic diseases (Hecht and Endermann 1998; Johnson et al. 2004; Stewart 2005; O'Rourke and Rosenbaum 2015; Mogorosi 2019).

Year-class separation is also a very effective technique that has been successfully used, significantly reducing the infection rate of newly introduced juveniles. Following sites prior to restocking can reduce subsequent infection rates, providing that the fallow period is long enough to ensure that all infectious stages have died due to a lack of hosts (Johnson et al. 2004). The effectiveness of these husbandry techniques depends on the absence of wild hosts and/or other infected sites within transport distance for the infectious stages. Frequent cleaning of nets or other techniques that improve water flow through the rearing habitat may result in lower rates of infection, due to improved fish health and removal of infectious stages off-site. Net fouling has been demonstrated to result in the retention of high numbers of naupliar and copepodid stages within net pens. Increased flushing rates of a land-based grow-out facility reduce the level of infection.

24.5 Conclusion and Recommendations

Disease outbreaks and subsequent mortalities caused by parasites in aquaculture set-ups are now rare due to the development of various effective treatments. However, significant economic losses still occur due to reduced feed conversion and growth, indirect mortality, loss of product value and treatment costs. Although it is well understood that parasites have a significant impact on aquaculture, there are relatively few recent published reports of disease and/or disease treatments. Careful site selection and good husbandry practices are a prerequisite to a healthy and parasite-free aquaculture set-up and to prevent parasite outbreaks. The risk of alien and invasive fish and introduction of new parasites (Tavakol et al. 2017) or spillover of already introduced parasites (Dos Santos and Avenant-Oldewage 2022) from them must be considered as potential risks to the aquaculture industry in the continent.

It is of great value that more checklists of different parasites are documented in different African regions to make a baseline of existing parasites in each region to, at a later stage, analyse which parasites can potentially cause economic loss and which cannot. Furthermore, determining which parasite species cannot cause economic loss in insignificant numbers, but if spillover or increase in prevalence and intensity occurs, then, potentially, they can cause economic loss in aquaculture set-ups.

Lastly, there are very few (if any) registered treatments for parasites in Africa. This, therefore, highlights the gap in registering some products in Africa for use in fish culture in future.

References

Amakali AM (2019) Ecto- and endo-parasites of silver kob (Argyrosomus inodorus) from northern Namibia (21° 24°S) (MSc dissertation, University of Namibia)

Amakali AM, Halajian A, Wilhelm MR, Tjipute M, Heckmann R, Luus-Powell W (2022) Selected parasites of silver kob (*Argyrosomus inodorus*) (Actinopterygii: Sciaenidae) from northern Namibia. S Afr J Sci 118(1/2). https://doi.org/10.17159/sajs.2022/9139

Amin OM (2013) Classification of the Acanthocephala. Folia Parasitol 60(4):273–305

Aydoğdu A, Emre N, Emre Y (2015) Prevalence and intensity of parasitic helminths of thicklip grey mullet *Chelon labrosus* in hosts in Beymelek Lagoon Lake in Antalya, Turkey, according to season, host size, age, and sex of the host. Turk J Zool 39(4):643–651

Bannai MA (2017) The Parasites *Monascus* sp. (Fellodistomidae) and *Helicometrina nimia* (Linton, 1910) (Opecoelidae) Digenea of *Pampus argenteus* and Greasy Grouper *Epinephelus tauvina* (Forsskål, 1775) (Teleostei: Serranidae) Fishes, Arabian Gulf, New Host and New Geographical Records. Int J Mar Sci 7(10):88–95

Bayoumy EM, El-Monem SA (2012) Functional adaptation of branchial and stomach dactylogyrid monogenean: Cichlidogyrus and Enterogyrus isolated from Oreochromis niloticus. In Proceedings of the 5th Global Fisheries and Aquaculture Research Conference, Faculty of Agriculture, Cairo University, Giza, Egypt, 1-3 October 2012 (pp. 353–60). Massive Conferences and Trade Fairs

Bruno DW, Noguera PA, Poppe TT (2013) A colour atlas of salmonid diseases, vol 91. Springer, Aberdeen

Bullard SA, Overstreet RM (2002) Potential pathological effects of blood flukes (Digenea: Sanguinicolidae) on pen-reared marine fishes

Deaton R (2009) Effects of a parasitic nematode on male mate choice in a live bearing fish with a coercive mating system (western mosquitofish, *Gambusia affinis*). Behav Process 80:1–6

Delabbio J, Johnson G, Murphy B, Hallerman E, Woart A, Mcmullin S (2005) Fish disease and biosecurity: attitudes, beliefs, and perceptions of managers and owners of commercial finfish recirculating facilities in the United States and Canada. J Aquat Anim Health 17:153–159

Dos Santos QM, Avenant-Oldewage A (2022) Smallmouth yellowfish, Labeobarbus aeneus (Teleostei: Cyprinidae), as a potential new definitive host of the invasive parasite *Atractolytocestus huronensis* (Cestoda: Caryophyllidea) from common carp: example of recent spillover in South Africa. Aquat Invasions 17(2):259–276

Eissa AE, Moustafa M, Abumhara A, Hosni M (2016) Future prospects of biosecurity strategies in Egyptian fish farms. J Fish Aquat Sci 11(2):100–107

FAO (2007) Aquaculture development. 2. Health management for the responsible movement of live aquatic animals. FAO Technical Guidelines for Responsible Fisheries. No. 5, Suppl. 2. Rome, FAO

FAO (2016) The State of World Fisheries and Aquaculture (SOFIA). Food and Agriculture Organization, Rome, p 190

FAO (2018) Development of a Regional Aquatic Biosecurity Strategy for the Southern African Development Community (SADC) FAO Fisheries and Aquaculture Circular No. C1149. Rome. p 344

Fuentes MV, Madrid E, Cuesta C et al (2022) Anisakid nematodes and potential risk of human anisakiasis through the consumption of hake, Merluccius spp, sold fresh in Spanish supermarkets. Pathogens 11(6):622

Gjurčević E, Beck A, Drašner K, Stanin D, Kužir S (2012) Pathogenicity of Atractolytocestus huronensis (Cestoda) for cultured common carp (Cyprinus carpio L.). Veterinarski arhiv 82 (3):273–282

Griffiths MH, Heemstra PC (1995) A contribution to the taxonomy of the marine fish genus Argyrosomus (Perciformes: Sciaenidae), with description of two new species from southern Africa. Ichthyol Bull JLB Smith Inst Ichthyol 65:1–40

Halajian A, Smales LR, Tavakol S, Smit NJ, Luus-Powell WJ (2018) Checklist of acanthocephalan parasites of South Africa. ZooKeys (789):1. https://doi.org/10.3897/zookeys.789.27710

Halwart M (2020) Fish farming high on the global food system agenda in 2020. FAO Aquac Newslett 61:II–III

Hayunga EG (1991) Morphological adaptations of intestinal helminths. J Parasitol 77(6):865–873

Hecht T, Endermann F (1998) The impact of parasites, infections and diseases on the development of aquaculture in sub-Saharan Africa. J Appl Ichthyol 14(3–4):213–221

Hogans WE, Trudeau DJ (1989) Preliminary studies on the biology of sea lice, *Caligus elongatus*, *Caligus curtus* and *Lepeophtheirus salmonis* (Copepoda: Caligoida) parasitic on cage-cultured salmonids in the lower Bay of Fundy. Can Tech Report Fish Aquat Sci No. 1715

Hutson KS, Catalano SR, Whittington ID (2011) Metazoan parasite survey of selected macro-inshore fish of southeastern Australia, including species of commercial importance. James Cook University. Douglas, Australia. No. 2007/225

Iwanowicz DD (2011) Overview on the effects of parasites on fish health. In Proceedings of the Third Bilateral Conference between Russia and the United States. Bridging America and Russia with Shared Perspectives on Aquatic Animal Health; pp 176–184

Johnson SC, Albright LJ (1991) The developmental stages of *Lepeophtheirus salmonis* (Krøyer, 1837) (Copepoda: Caligidae). Can J Zool 69(4):929–950

Johnson SC, Bravo S, Nagasawa K, Kabata Z, Hwang J, Ho J, Shih CT (2004) A review of the impact of parasitic copepods on marine aquaculture. Zool Stud 43(2):229–243

Joubert CJH (2012) The potential of commercial Praziquantel formulations as " off label" treatments for *Diplectanum oliveri* (Monogenea) infecting cultured *Argyrosomus* species in the South African marine finfish aquaculture industry (Doctoral dissertation, University of the Western Cape)

Justine JL, Briand MJ, Bray RA (2012) A quick and simple method, usable in the field, for collecting parasites in suitable condition for both morphological and molecular studies. Parasitol Res 111(1): 341–351

Kabata Z (1985) Parasites and diseases of fish cultured in the tropics. Taylor & Francis Ltd., Milton Park

Khalil LF (1971) Checklist of the helminth parasites of African freshwater fishes. Commonwealth Agrcultural Bureau (CAB) Press, St Albans

Khalil MI, El-Shahawy IS, Abdelkader HS (2014) Studies on some fish parasites of public health importance in the southern area of Saudi Arabia. Rev Bras Parasitol Vet 23(4):435–442

Kim IH (1993) Developmental stages of Caligus punctatus Shiino, 1955 (Copepoda: Caligidae). Pathogens of wild and farmed fish: sea lice; pp 16–29
Kotob MH, Menanteau-Ledouble S, Kumar G, Abdelzaher M, El-Matbouli M (2017) The impact of co-infections on fish: a review. Vet Res 47(1):98
Krkošek M (2010) Host density thresholds and disease control for fisheries and aquaculture. Aquac Environ Interact 1:21–32
Labella A, Berbel C, Manchado M, Castro D, Borrego JJ (2011) *Photobacterium damselae* subsp. damselae, an emerging pathogen affecting new cultured marine fish species in southern Spain. In: Recent advances in fish farms. Institution of Technology, Malaga
Lee CS, O'Bryen JP (2003) Biosecurity in aquaculture production systems: exclusion of pathogens and other desirables. World Aquaculture Society, Baton Rouge
Luus-Powell WJ, Madanire-Moyo GN, Matla MM, Přikrylová I (2020) Monogenean parasites from the stomach of *Oreochromis mossambicus* from South Africa: two new species of *Enterogyrus* (Dactylogyridae: Ancyrocephalinae). Parasitol Res 119(5):1505–1514
Marcogliese DJ (2002) Food webs and the transmission of parasites to marine fish. Parasitology 124(7):83–99
Martins ML, Cardoso L, Marchiori N, Benites de Pádua S (2015) Protozoan infections in farmed fish from Brazil: diagnosis and pathogenesis. Rev Bras Parasitol Vet 24(1):1–20
Mele S, De Benedetto G, Giannetto A et al. (2022) Morphological and molecular study of *Didymodiclinus marginati* n. sp. (Trematoda: Didymozoidae) gill parasite of *Epinephelus marginatus* from the central and western Mediterranean Sea. Parasi pp 1–31
Merella P, Cherchi S, Garippa G, Fioravanti ML, Gustinelli A, Salati F (2009) Outbreak of Sciaenacotyle panceri (Monogenea) on cage-reared meagre Argyrosomus regius (Osteichthyes) from the western Mediterranean Sea. Dis Aquat Org 86(2):169–173
Mo TA (2020) Gyrodactylosis (*Gyrodactylus salaris*). In: Climate change and infectious fish diseases. CABI, Wallingford, p 404
Mogorosi LK (2019) A general disease and parasite survey of commercially important fishes of the Free State (Doctoral dissertation, University of the Free State)
Molina-García AD, Sanz PD (2002) *Anisakis simplex* larva killed by high-hydrostatic-pressure processing. J Food Prot 65(2):383–388
Mumba V (2014) Occurrence and Distribution of Fish Parasites of Potential threat to the Aquaculture Sector along the Kavango River. MSc thesis, University of Namibia
Norbury LJ, Shirakashi S, Power C, Nowak BF, Bott NJ (2022) Praziquantel use in aquaculture–Current status and emerging issues. Int J Parasitol Drugs Drug Resist 18:87–102
O'Rourke DP, Rosenbaum MD (2015) Biology and diseases of amphibians. In: Laboratory animal medicine. Academic Press, Cambridge, pp 931–965
Paperna I (1980) Parasites, infections and diseases of freshwater fishes in Africa. CIFA Technical paper; p 7
Paperna I (1996) Parasites, infections and diseases of fishes in Africa - An update CIFA Technical Paper. No.31. Rome, FAO. p 220
Paperna I, Thurston JP (1969) Monogenetic trematodes collected from cichlid fish in Uganda; including the description of five new species of Cichlidogyrus. Revue de Zoologie et de Botanique africaines 79(1/2):15–33
Piasecki W, Goodwin AE, Eiras JC, Nowak BF (2004) Importance of Copepoda in freshwater aquaculture. Zool Stud 43(2):193–205
Poulin R (2004) Macro ecological patterns of species richness in parasite assemblages. Basic Appl Ecol 5(5):423–434
Rameshkumar G, Ravichandran S, Maran V (2014) Occurrence of parasitic copepods in Carangid fishes from Parangipettai, Southeast coast of India. J Parasit Dis 38(3):317–323
Reed P, Francis-Floyd R, Klinger R, Petty D (2009) Monogenean parasites of fish. Fisheries and aquatic sciences. University of Florida UF, IFAS Extension. FA28, USA 4; pp 1–4
Rohde K, Rohde PP (2005) The ecological niches of parasites. In: Marine Parasitology. Clayton, Csiro Publishing, pp 286–293

Rubio-Godoy M (2007) Fish host-monogenean parasite interactions, with special reference to Polyopisthocotylea. In: Advances in the Immunobiology of Parasitic Diseases. Trivandrum, Research Signpost, pp 91–109
Scholz T (1999) Parasites in cultured and feral fish. Vet Parasitol 84(3–4):317–335
Scholz T, Tavakol S, Halajian A, Luus-Powell WJ (2015) The invasive fish tapeworm *Atractolytocestus huronensis* (Cestoda), a parasite of carp, colonises Africa. Parasitol Res 114(9):3521–3524
Silva RZ, Pereira J, Cousin JCB (2014) Histological patterns of the intestinal attachment of *Corynosoma australe* (Acanthocephala: Polymorphidae) in *Arctocephalus australis* (Mammalia: Pinnipedia). J Parasit Dis 38(4):410–416
Stewart KA (2005) Embryonation and efficacy of treatments on monogenean gill flukes infecting silver kob (*Argyrosomus inodorus*), Doctoral dissertation, University of Cape Town, Cape Town
Tavakol S, Halajian A, Smit WJ, Hoffman A, Luus-Powell WJ (2017) Guppies (Poecilia reticulata) introducing an alien parasite, Camallanus cotti (Nematoda: Camallanidae) to Africa, the first report. Parasitol Res 116(12):3441–3445
Ternengo S, Agostini S, Quilichini Y, Euzet L, Marchand B (2010) Intensive infestations of *Sciaenacotyle pancerii* (Monogenea, Microcotylidae) on *Argyrosomus regius* (Asso) under fish-farming conditions. J Fish Dis 33(1):89–92
Thieltges DW, Bouwmeester MM, Goedknegt AM, Poulin R (2020) Collateral diseases: aquaculture impact on wildlife infections – A review. J Appl Ecol 58:435–464
Tjipute M (2011) Feasibility study for mass production of the Silver kob, *Argyrosomus inodorus*, in Namibia. United Nations University - Fisheries Training Programme
Welicky RL, De Swardt J, Gerber R, Netherlands EC, Smit NJ (2017) Drought-associated absence of alien invasive anchorworm, *Lernaea cyprinacea* (Copepoda: Lernaeidae), is related to changes in fish health. Int J Parasitol Parasites Wildlife 6(3):430–438
Whittington ID, Kearn GC (2011) Hatching strategies in monogenean (Platyhelminth) parasites that facilitate host infection. Integr Comp Biol 51(1):91–99
Woo PT, Gregory DWB (eds) (2014) Diseases and disorders of finfish in cage culture. Centre for Agriculture and Bioscience International, Wallingford
Woo PT, Leatherland JF (eds) (2006) Fish diseases and disorders, volume 1: protozoan and metazoan infections, 2nd edn. CAB International, London

Chapter 25
Interactions Between Pre-harvest, Post-harvest Handling and Welfare of Fish for Sustainability in the Aquaculture Sector

O. C. Ojelade, F. O. A. George, I. Abdulraheem, and A. O. Akinde

Abstract Fish and other aquatic products are nutrient-dense and a relatively accessible source of animal protein that transcends various social and cultural norms. The demand for fish has been steadily rising and now significantly outweighs the supply due to the world's acceptance of fish and its products. However, because of their biological makeup and the presence of autolytic enzymes, fish are highly perishable and require careful welfare handling techniques to prevent spoilage. Furthermore, the presence of enzymes and microbes speeds up the rate of fish product spoilage, increases post-harvest waste and lowers the quality of fish products, which could result in foodborne illness if consumed. However, to make fish available for consumption, several processes must be carried out, including feed withdrawal (fasting), air exposure, crowding within the equipment, handling, sorting and loading. The quality and nutritional value of fish products are ultimately determined by these pre- and post-harvest procedures. It is interesting to note that pre- and post-harvest practices are emerging welfare concerns in fish farming that have a significant impact on the productivity of these aquatic products, their shelf life and fish sustainability in the aquaculture industry. The texture and colour of the flesh, an increase in lactic acid production and a decrease in muscular pH are all signs of compromised welfare and the beginning of spoilage during pre- and post-harvest handling activities of fish. This hastens the onset of rigor mortis and spoilage, which lowers the market value and acceptability of these fish products. Beyond pre-harvest and post-harvest, fish slaughtering procedures must be welfare-friendly and stress-free to maintain the texture, colour and appearance of the fish. It is interesting to note that the majority of fish slaughtering techniques have reportedly been found to be inhumane, which has a negative impact on the quality of fish products. Therefore, humane treatment and slaughter of fish products during pre- and post-harvest activities contribute significantly to increasing fish productivity, enhancing

O. C. Ojelade (✉) · F. O. A. George · I. Abdulraheem · A. O. Akinde
Department of Aquaculture and Fisheries Management, Federal University of Agriculture, Abeokuta, Ogun State, Nigeria
e-mail: ojeladeoc@funaab.edu.ng

© The Author(s), under exclusive license to Springer Nature Singapore Pte Ltd. 2023

N. N. Gabriel et al. (eds.), *Emerging Sustainable Aquaculture Innovations in Africa*, Sustainable Agriculture and Food Security,
https://doi.org/10.1007/978-981-19-7451-9_25

livelihood opportunities for fish farmers, boosting return on investment, reducing societal malnutrition and achieving fish sustainability along with higher foreign exchange earnings.

Keywords Deterioration · Humane · Handling · Sector · Shelf life · Texture

25.1 Introduction

Fish and other aquatic products constitute an essential component of man's diet. Its consumption cuts across several religious and socio-cultural beliefs, and it is relatively cheaper than other animal sources of protein (Omoare et al. 2013). Rasco et al. (2015) posited that fish provides the most promising animal nutritious source of protein and is also regarded as the most traded food commodity with numerous economic benefits to several people in the world (FAO 2018). Fish and its products supply 19% of animal protein intake to Africans; it also provides several micronutrients and essential fatty acids with long-chain polyunsaturated fatty acids, which cannot be easily gotten from similar food commodities (Bene et al. 2015). Fish and its products further provide a reliable source of income to millions of fish farmers and a means of livelihood for many fish handlers and marketers (World Bank 2017). However, despite the economic, social, and nutritional benefits of fish to society, there is a great concern about the sustainability of the Aquaculture sector in bridging the ever-widening gap between fish demand and the dwindling supply from the capture fisheries (Fig. 25.1).

Interestingly, there is a continuous global increase in the human population (Fig. 25.2a) which translates to an increase in the demand for fish and its products

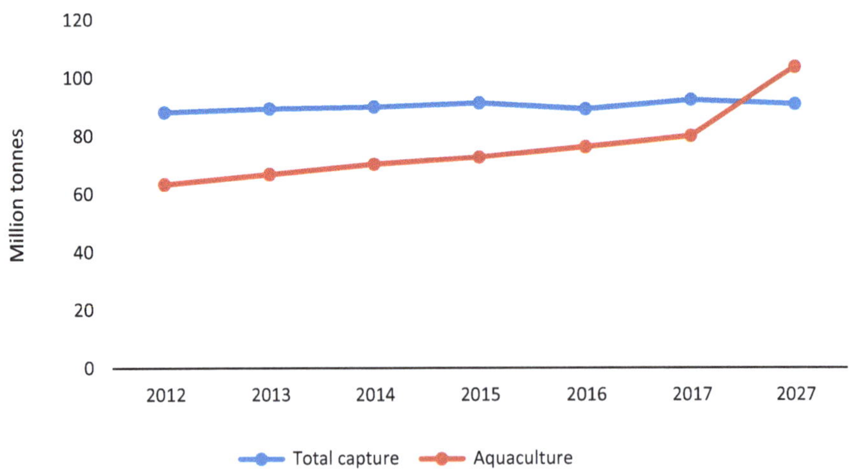

Fig. 25.1 Total fish supply from capture fisheries and aquaculture sector. Source: Food and Agricultural Organization (2020)

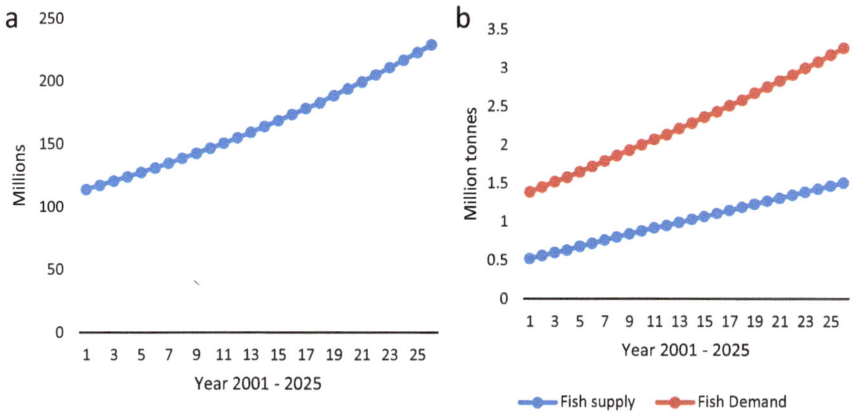

Fig. 25.2 The projected human population in millions (**a**) and global fish demand and supply in million tonnes between 2001 and 2025 (**b**) (Amosu et al. 2017)

that largely outweighs the total supply from the various fisheries sectors (Fig. 25.2b). In addition, the Food and Agriculture Organization (2010) reported that 85% of the world's capture fish stocks are either fully exploited, overfished or have collapsed. Moreover, Ayinla (2012) stated that most capture fisheries are approaching their biological limit, while the global production from the aquaculture sector has quadrupled over the last 20 years. Thus, the Aquaculture sector is considered a viable alternative to meeting the nation's need for self-sufficiency in fish production (Jerimoth et al. 2017). The sector can potentially increase the total domestic fish production for the populace to meet the ever-rising demand for fish products (Harvey 2004; FAO of the United Nations 2006, 2020; OECD/FAO 2017).

The intensive production of fish and other aquatic products in a controlled environment in the Aquaculture sector gives a favourable opportunity to carefully ascertain positive welfare for these cultured fishes for optimum production rate (Håstein 2004; Thant 2019; Martos-Sitcha et al. 2020). Fish species held in a confined environment could be given freedom from stress, discomfort, injury and other associated non-humane handling procedures for higher productivity (Lines and Spence 2012; Daskalova 2019). Ashley (2007) proposed the need to improve the wellbeing and health status of aquatic animals without compromising their welfare to boost the production and survival rate of these cultured fish species under controlled conditions. In addition, the application of welfare-friendly acts in the Aquaculture sector was asserted by Martos-Sitcha et al. (2020) to enhance fish productivity and improve the economic return on investment for the Aquaculturists toward fish food security in the sector.

However, the growing public interest in improving the welfare of fish in the Aquaculture sector stems from both ethical (welfare) and production (fish products) perspectives (Daskalova 2019; Ojelade et al. 2022). Conte (2004) stressed the need to understand the implication of improving fish welfare in the Aquaculture industry. Fish cultured in a stress-free environment will be less susceptible to disease outbreaks which will directly reduce the cost of fish maintenance practices with a reasonable survival rate for a higher return on investment (Toni et al. 2018). The relevance of good welfare in the Aquaculture sector is necessitated to increase fish output from this sector, curb malnutrition in the society, end poverty among the fisher farmers, and ascertain the quality of fish products sold to the consumers (Ashley 2007; Martos-sitcha et al. 2020; Ojelade et al. 2021). Interestingly, Brown et al. (2010) and Rasco et al. (2015) opined that maintaining positive welfare in fish farming alleviates the stressors imposed on these aquatic animals in captivity and exposes them to the freedoms of animal welfare.

Unfortunately, fish are a highly perishable food commodity that spoils soon after death which makes them prone to high post-harvest losses (Akinola et al. 2006). Yalch et al. (2020) stated that a more significant percentage of perishable foods, including fish and its products, is lost or wasted along the fish supply chain. In addition, Getu et al. (2015) categorised losses along the fish supply chain into physical, nutritional and economical to the fish stakeholders. However, over ten million tonnes of fish are lost to post-harvest wastage per year (FAO 2010); it is noteworthy to state that the volume of post-harvest wastage in the fisheries sector serves as a stumbling block to the achievement of fish sustainability. Kabahenda et al. (2009) stated that uncontrolled fish post-harvest wastage directly reduces fish supply, increases the cost of the available fish products and alters the consumers' access to nutritious fish foods.

However, many reported losses in the Aquaculture sector mainly occur during fish handling, transportation and storage activities (OIE 2008; Yalch et al. 2020). Wall (2001) corroborates the need to develop appropriate ethical fish handling, harvesting, transportation, preservation, processing and storage guidelines to boost the relevance of Aquaculture in increasing fish production. However, several welfare concerns are raised about pre-slaughtering and slaughtering procedures within the Aquaculture sector (Southgate and Wall 2001). Thus, it is essential to note that effective fish handling methods will delay fish spoilage keep the quality of fish flesh and other aquatic products and contribute positively to animal protein supply in developing countries (FAO 2010; Rasco et al. 2015).

25.1.1 Fish Spoilage

Fish spoilage is a complicated process of deterioration in the quality of fish flesh caused by bacteria, enzymes and chemical constituents of the fish (Lines and Spence 2012). Immediately fish is harvested from water; death tends to occur at any point in time, depending on the species, temperature, size, lipid content, handling method and available storage facilities (Poli et al. 2002; Ohshima 2005). Moreover, several postmortem changes occur in fish after death which could render the fish products unfit for human consumption. Thant (2019) reported that changes in fish quality are caused mainly by sensory, autolytic, bacteria and hydrolysis activities. These changes alter the odour, appearance, taste, texture and quality of the fish and, in most cases, render the fish products unfit for human consumption and thus classified as post-harvest losses in the fisheries sector. However, Rasco et al. (2015) stressed the need for the application of welfare-friendly procedures to these fish products during handling procedures as strategies for delaying the process of spoilage, deterioration and means of curbing fish post-harvest losses.

25.1.1.1 Fish Post-harvest Losses

Fish losses can be described as a decrease in the quality and quantity of edible fish products that, if permitted to manoeuvre the supply chain, could affect the utility derived by the final consumer. These losses along the supply chain could occur during fish harvest, post-harvest and transportation activities. Moreover, Getu et al. (2015) categorised these losses into nutritional, physical, quality and economic losses. It could lead to post-harvest wastage, a reduction in the prices of these fish products and a low-profit margin for the fish farmer. On the other hand, this post-harvest wastage reduces the quality and nutritional value of fish products (Kabahenda et al. 2009), which gets to the consumers and serves as a threat to curbing malnutrition in society. Thus, the welfare of these aquatic animals should be enforced at all aquaculture production levels. Ensuring stress-free and welfare-friendly harvesting and handling methods would curb the amount of post-harvest wastage of fish (Southgate and Wall 2001).

25.1.1.2 Factors Affecting Fish Spoilage

Temperature plays a significant role in the spoilage rate of fish species; most of the microflora responsible for spoilage in fish multiply rapidly with an increase in the ambient temperature. In the tropics, fish deteriorates rapidly within a few hours after harvesting if not subjected to appropriate preservation techniques (Thant 2019). Valtysdottir et al. (2010) reported that the spoilage rate in fish is directly caused by the enzymatic activities, microbial growth of the fish and lipid oxidation which could alter its nutritional and physical attributes. However, these microbial changes dictate the quality of the fish flesh, colour, appearance and ultimate acceptability of these fish products by the consumers. Thus, it becomes imperative to elongate the period for which the fish products remain safe and fit for human consumption (shelf life) while maintaining their quality until it gets to the hand of the final consumer (Wall 2001). Although fish is generally wholesome and safe, its quality could be contaminated through inappropriate handling methods. Thant (2019) stated that the quality of fish products is directly dependent on the ambient temperature, relative humidity of the air, hygiene of the handlers and technical know-how. Moreover, fish could be further contaminated through exposure to chemicals and other hazards during post-harvest handling, which accelerates the spoilage rate of these fish species (Kabahenda et al. 2009). Improper handling of fish products might cause physical damage such as injuries and loss of fins and other external appendages; this will expedite enzymatic activities and make the fish susceptible to rapid deterioration. Physiologically, a compromise in the welfare of live fish species increases the level of glucose and cortisol in the blood; this results in a rapid decrease in the energy reserve of the fish and an increase in lactic acid production (Poli et al. 2002; Rasco et al. 2015). Thus, it is essential to reiterate the adoption of good welfare by all fish handlers; this is necessitated because most fish consumers have recently indicated their concerns and interest in the slaughtering methods applied in the post-harvest sector.

25.1.2 The Concepts of Fish Welfare

Conte (2004), Broom (2014), Brown (2014) and Sneddon et al. (2018) gave various definitions that described the concept of animal welfare. The definitions of poor welfare can be summarised as the exposure of animals and fish species to stressors which exceeds the coping capacity of the animals. Good welfare could be described as the provision of the most fundamental needs of physical well-being (adequate food, comfortable rearing environments, quality and quantity of water), and the ability to express species-specific behaviours in the presence of conspecifics.

OIE (2008) and EFSA (2009) opined that fish species are sentient beings that can feel pain and distress. Thus, the sentience nature of fish could be regarded as the first prerequisite that calls for the application of good welfare in the Aquaculture sector. Subjecting these fish species to compromised welfare or handling procedures could lead to an alteration in their behaviour, stress-related physiology and ultimately death. Håstein (2004) defined the welfare of fish as the measurable traits in the objective condition of the fish (function-based), subjective experience of the fish (function-based) and the ability of the aquatic animal to live a natural life within its aquatic ecosystem (nature-based). Kristiansen and Juell (2002) further described the welfare of farmed fish as the extent to which a fish can adapt to its rearing conditions and find the same rewards. Thus, the 'five freedoms' approach attempts to summarise the welfare of the cultured fishes in the aquaculture production system and post-harvest sector (Webster 2001; Ashley 2007). The United Kingdom Farm Animal Welfare Council (FAWC 2012) proposed these 'five freedoms' as follows:

1. **Freedom from Hunger and Thirst**: Aquatic animals in a confined rearing environment should have equal and optimum access to quality and quantity diets and water to maintain health and perform all basic life activities. In addition, this freedom from hunger and thirst should be enjoyed by fish during harvesting and transportation until the point of slaughtering and death. Consequently, feed withdrawal before harvesting should be kept to the barest minimum, while live transportation of fish in containers and bowls without water, which is commonly practised by fish farmers (Plate 25.1), is a procedure that compromises the welfare of these fish species.

Plate 25.1 Fish exposure during post-harvest activities before transportation Source: Field Survey, 2022

2. **Freedom from Discomfort:** Cultured fishes should be reared in a suitable living environment, free from discomfort or aches. At harvesting, the use of inappropriate gear due to its availability and cost-effectiveness is highly discouraged to prevent exposure of the harvested fish to unnecessary discomfort (Sneddon et al. 2018). Transportation bowls and containers should not be too small for the size of fish being transported while over-stocking the fish in such small bowls during transportation puts these fish in a stressful condition and a form of discomfort that they should be free from.
3. **Freedom from Pain, Injury or Disease**: Aquatic lives kept in a captive culture environment should not be made to suffer from pain, wounds or disease. However, rapid diagnosis and treatment of fish species can be employed when a disease outbreak occurs (Chandroo et al. 2004). Over-crowding and over-stocking of fish in gears and transportation bowls during harvesting and transportation should be strictly avoided to make these aquatic animals free from pain and injury. These post-harvest procedures pose a form of pain to these fishes. Moreover, Martos-Sitcha et al. (2020) reported an increase in the stress level of fish species during transportation which could increase aggressive acts, injury and susceptibility to disease outbreaks.
4. **Freedom to Express Normal Behaviour**: Different facilities should be provided for aquatic lives to ascertain their ability to express their natural behaviour. A good rearing space equipped with adequate facilities and other conspecifics should be made available to encourage the display of their natural behaviours and eliminate stress or discomfort (Ojelade et al. 2022). On the other hand, during transportation, the provision of convenient and spacious transportation containers

filled with water will make the live fish feel at home and express normal behaviour.
5. **Freedom from Fear and Distress**: All living conditions for cultured fishes should not expose them to mental suffering or stress. Pre-harvest, harvest and post-harvest activities should not impose any form of fear on these aquatic lives. Sudden and prolonged air exposure during harvesting and transportation activities could expose the fishes to fear and distress, which might alter the behaviour and physiology of the fishes and, subsequently, the quality of the flesh of the fishes (Poli et al. 2005).

Thus, fish are considered animals that could feel pain and any other form of discomfort in their environment. Certainly, a compromise in the welfare of fish represents the most significant factor affecting fish sustainability. Therefore, aquaculturists and other fish handlers should give these aquatic animals the listed five freedoms while handling the fish, during harvesting, transportation and slaughtering to maintain good welfare, increase productivity and deliver quality fish products to the consumers.

25.1.3 Fish Harvesting

The harvesting of fish encompasses a series of activities or processes necessitated to remove cultured fishes from water with the use of several harvesting equipment and fishing gears. Poli et al. (2005) categorised the harvesting procedure as a traumatic period for fish species, affected mainly by its duration, intensity and struggle during harvesting. The fish being harvested swim continuously within the gear in an attempt to escape, which increases the production of glucose and other stress hormones in fish. However, fish harvesting is a compulsory procedure since all fin and shellfish cultured in a confined environment are ultimately removed from their rearing facilities for human consumption, either as food or for other purposes. Consequently, harvesting requires adequate technical know-how to aid the survival of the fish species, maintain their quality for the consumers and reduce the quantity of fish lost to the post-harvest sector. Unfortunately, Gustavsson et al. (2011) reported that about 35% of fish landings from the different fisheries sectors are lost to post-harvest wastage. Thus, it is essential to adhere to welfare-friendly acts during the handling, harvesting and slaughtering.

25.2 Fish Post-Harvest Activities

During harvesting, fish species are subjected to various activities such as feed withdrawal (fasting), air exposure, crowding within the gear, handling, sorting, loading, offloading, storage and transportation (EFSA 2009). These activities directly dictate the survival rate of live fish for marketing, the quality of the fish products and the final economic value derived from these fish products. Thus, it is essential to review the application of welfare procedures to these activities to increase the nutritional and socio-economic benefits derived from these sustainable aquatic products.

25.2.1 Feed Withdrawal

Fish species often have several hours of starvation or fasting before handling, harvesting or transportation procedures. This fasting is necessary to empty the fish's gut before harvesting, to reduce the activities of the bacteria in the gastrointestinal tracts and to minimise the build-up of metabolic wastes and ammonia and subsequent spoilage rate (Lines and Spence 2012) during these handling and transportation procedures. However, this entire process and period of starvation should be kept to the barest minimum to prevent a compromise in the welfare of the fish species (Ashley 2007). Lemieux et al. (2004) reported the consequence of prolonged starvation on fish growth, muscle protein and fat composition, while Martinez et al. (2003) asserted that prolonged starvation could lead to reduced nutrition, changes in metabolic activity and increased aggression. Fishes should not be starved for more than 72 h in an attempt to empty their gut content before harvesting or transportation activities (Poli et al. 2005; Robb 2008). Webster (2001) categorically stated that excessive period of feed withdrawal from fish species causes an infringement of the principles of the five freedoms of animal welfare. Moreover, feed withdrawal during harvesting poses welfare threats that could lead to weight loss, aggressiveness, cannibalism and physical injuries that lower fish quality, acceptability and risk of mass mortality (Southgate and Wall 2001). Thus, starving (feed withdrawal) of fish should be done only when there is a full assurance that harvesting will take place soonest in order not to impose continuously and repeated suffering on these aquatic animals.

25.2.2 Air Exposure

Fish and other aquatic animals are poikilothermic, and thus their body temperature is dependent on the ambient temperature. During harvesting, the water level in the rearing facilities is reduced, and fishes are exposed to air temperature, which might be prolonged due to unnecessary delay in the harvesting procedure (Plate 25.2); this has an excellent welfare implication for these animals since they are no more in their natural aquatic environment. Thus, immediately after the water level in the rearing ponds is lowered, live fish meant for transportation should be transferred to containers filled with water to prevent undue air exposure. HSA (2005) reported that all harvesting processes should be rapidly and humanely done without further stressing

Plate 25.2 Cultured fishes exposed to atmospheric air in a concrete tank prior to harvesting (Ogunsina 2017)

the fish to prevent prolonged suffering or discomfort to fish species. Poli et al. (2005) opined that exposure of fish to asphyxia is not humane since it poses a deleterious effect on the flesh, quality and shelf life of the fish. Consequently, the period of exposing fish to air during handling should be greatly reduced to limit the risk posed to the welfare and health of this aquatic fauna.

25.2.3 Crowding Within the Gear

Prolonged exposure of fishes to crowding within the harvesting equipment has several welfare implications for the fish. This unnecessary delay and exposure to poor holding conditions within harvesting gears are caused mainly by inadequate preparation by the aquaculturists and fish handlers for the harvesting process. Lines and Spence (2012) categorised fish crowding as a principal act that imperils the welfare of cultured fishes. Crowding within gear results in many fish species competing for limited dissolved oxygen within the given space, thus making breathing difficult for the fish (Plate 25.3). Brown et al. (2010) asserted that prolonged crowding of fish within gear could lead to an inflation of swim bladders in some fish species. However, an undue extended period of crowding within the gear is a dangerous post-harvest activity that makes the aquatic animals susceptible to disease, and this might lead to asphyxiation, suffocation, stress, physical damage, bruises, injuries and damage to the flesh and fins of the fish (Poli et al. 2005). All of these affect the physical and economical value of the fish products and the satisfaction derived by the consumers.

Plate 25.3 Crowding of harvested fish within the harvesting equipment. Source: Personal Survey, 2022

25.2.4 Handling

All harvested fish should be handled on clean surfaces and with clean hands and materials to prevent increased bacteria load on the flesh and skin of these aquatic animals. Any form of unhygienic handling (Plate 25.4) could reduce the shelf life of the fish and accelerate the rate of fish spoilage. Moreover, Thant (2019) noted the relevance of the hygienic handling of Aquaculture fishes during post-harvest activities. Thus, humane handling of fish requires continuous contact with uncontaminated surfaces and hands to delay the spoilage rate of these aquatic animals. Furthermore, fish species should be cleaned of all attached mud and dirt before applying either high- or low-temperature preservation techniques.

25.2.5 Sorting

Fish sorting during harvesting should be done rapidly to prevent additional stress on the aquatic animals. They should be sorted into species and sizes before subjecting the fish to low- and high-preservation techniques or even sold live to the marketers (Plate 25.5). Fish physically injured, with bruises and bleeding, should be rapidly removed from the harvested fish. Any delay in these activities could lead to quality deterioration and subsequent spoilage rate, causing an increase in post-harvest wastage.

Plate 25.4 A grubby cargo area of pick-up trucks used for live fish transportation. Source: Personal Survey 2022

Plate 25.5 Sorting of live fish into sizes prior to transportation

25.2.6 Loading and Off-Loading

The welfare of harvested fish should not also be compromised during loading and off-loading activities before and after the transportation procedures. Fishes have

Plate 25.6 Loading of live fish cultured in earthen ponds prior to transportation. Source: Personal survey 2022

been earlier stressed during feed withdrawal and other harvesting procedures, so it is very important to minimize the level of stress at this stage of post-harvest activities (Plate 25.6). Their welfare should be prioritized, and they should be kept in water during transportation to gain some level of energy before off-loading activities.

25.2.7 Transportation

Fishes should be transported as fast as possible to relieve the fish from the stress of confinement in bowls and other transport containers. It is essential to state that every form of delay in the transportation process could increase the level of mortality in the fish being transported. Transportation of live fish should be done with water in their transportation containers or bowls. These transportation facilities should be welfare-friendly, and they should permit water quality monitoring and an avenue to replace the water during long periods of transportation when necessary. These are ways of improving the welfare of fish and eliminating the stress that could increase mortality during fish transportation. Transportation of live fish in bowls and containers without water should be discouraged among fish handlers, this method imposes stress on the fish, and their welfare is highly compromised.

Interestingly, all pre-harvest, harvest and post-harvest activities in the Aquaculture sector can be controlled and the entire process pre-determined. Controlling the time, conditions of harvest, harvesting types of equipment and use of well-trained handlers will go a long way in ascertaining the welfare, quality of the fish flesh and invariably the consumers' acceptability, economic and market value and the return on investment to the aquaculturists.

25.3 Fish Slaughtering

Fish slaughtering is usually in three stages, and it involves pre-harvest activities which have been dealt with, the stunning and eventual killing of the fish. Stunning of fish involves activities that render the fish unconscious within the period of slaughtering or killing. Moreover, stunning fish can be achieved through immediate and gradual loss of sensibility (Rasco et al. 2015). The latter method is not welfare-friendly as the fish are exposed to slow and continuous prolonged torture until death. Fish are sentient animals that have the cognitive ability to feel pain and discomfort, which necessitates the importance of ascertaining the welfare of these fish species. Thus, their slaughtering should be humane and stress-free. At slaughter, maintaining the welfare of fish is necessary through the application of humane slaughtering procedures, which entails that fish should be carefully handled and rapidly stunned to initiate an immediate loss of sensibility before bleeding (Southgate and Wall 2001; Van de Vis et al. 2003). Interestingly, the most practised and available slaughtering methods used by fish handlers do not meet these requirements of immediate insensibility.

Although the commonly available methods of killing fish were chosen due to their ease of application and cost-effectiveness, they include asphyxiation in air or ice, depriving fishes of oxygen in a covered container, cutting live and removal of gills without stunning (evisceration), use of complex objects on the head, use of salts in a covered container and being processed alive are non-humane crude methods of fish slaughtering (Robb and Kestin 2002; Robb et al. 2000; Ogbonna et al. 2017). These listed slaughtering procedures impose immense suffering on these aquatic animals since the methods do not involve immediate loss of sensibility. Specific rules and guidelines to uphold the welfare of this aquatic fauna, such as the appropriate humane slaughtering methods, should be adopted by all fish handlers (Southgate and Wall 2001; Wall 2001; Poli et al. 2005; HSA 2005). Fish at slaughter should be stunned, and the blood drained almost immediately to improve their welfare and the quality of the fish products for the consumer. Ideally, fish should be kept in water until death; however, when this is not affordable, fishes should not be exposed to air for more than 15 s to curb aversive behaviour in these aquatic animals (HSA 2005). The use of percussive (automated flow-through system) and electrical (electrified water) stunning methods makes the fish lose its sensibility almost immediately, which is the best way to safeguard the welfare of these aquatic animals and improve their flesh quality (Kristiansen and Juell 2002). Lines and Spence (2012) stated that the quality and taste of fish flesh reduce with increased stress during pre-harvest, harvest and post-harvest activities, which often affects consumer acceptability of the products. Thus, necessary equipment for large-scale and effective stunning fish should be made available to the fish handlers in the local and regional marketing arenas.

25.4 Conclusion and Recommendation

Providing a welfare-friendly procedure in rearing, harvesting and post-harvest activities should be adopted by all because it is a two-edged sword that improves the quality of the fish while also increasing the economic benefits derived by aquaculturists. Harvesting techniques should be free of stress, with no delays, overcrowding within the gear, or asphyxiation. Aquaculturists should embrace modern harvesting techniques while slaughtering methods should render the fish insensible before stunning and bleeding. To immediately put the central nervous system to sleep, stunning should be performed quickly. In the Aquaculture sector, innovations such as an automated killing machine incorporating welfare-friendly practices to cause the fish to die before regaining consciousness from stunning are recommended. Fish handlers at the pre-harvest, harvest and post-harvest levels must be trained and retrained to fulfil their responsibilities as fish caregivers. Continuous research should identify welfare-friendly handling and slaughtering methods for cultured fish.

References

Akinola OA, Akinyemi AA, Bolaji O (2006) Evaluation of traditional and solar fish drying systems towards enhancing fish storage and preservation in Nigeria (Abeokuta Local Governments as case study). J Fish Int 1:44–49

Amosu A, Hammed M, Adeniyi T, Adeyemi A (2017) Possible aquaculture development in Nigeria: evidence for commercial prospects. J Agric Sci Technol 7:21–32

Ashley P (2007) Fish welfare: current issues in aquaculture. Appl Anim Behav Sci 104:199–235

Ayinla OA (2012) Aquaculture Development and Appropriate Enterprise Combination in the BRACED States. In the High level meeting of experts and the meeting of BRACED States Commissioners for Agriculture. Songhai Farms, Port -Harcourt. Oct 31 –Nov. 2, 2012. pp 1–41

Bene C, Barange M, Subasinghe R, Pinstrup-Andersen P, Merino G, Hemre GI, Williams M (2015) Feeding 9 billion by 2050 – putting fish back on the menu. Food Security 7:261–274

Broom DM (2014) Sentience and animal welfare. Published by CABI, Wallingford, p 71. https://doi.org/10.1079/9781780644035.0001

Brown C (2014) Fish intelligence, sentience and ethics. Anim Cognition 18:1–17

Brown JA, Watson J, Bourhill A, Wall A (2010) Physiological Welfare of commercially reared cod and effects of crowding for harvesting. Aquaculture 298:315–324

Chandroo KP, Yue S, Moccia RD (2004) An evaluation of current perspectives on consciousness and pain in fishes. Fish Fish 5:281–295

Conte FS (2004) Stress and the welfare of cultured fish. Appl Anim Behav Sci 86(3–4):20523

Daskalova A (2019) Farmed fish welfare: stress, post-mortem muscle metabolism, and stress-related meat quality changes. Int Aquat Res 11:113–124

EFSA (2009) General approach to fish welfare and to the concept of sentience in fish. Scientific opinion of the panel on animal health and Welfare. EFSA J 954:1–27

FAO (2010) Report of the FAO expert consultation on trade in fisheries and aquaculture services. FAO Fisheries and Aquaculture Report FIAM/1230 (En), p 26

FAO (2018) The State of World Fisheries and Aquaculture 2018 - Meeting the sustainable development goals. Rome, p 61. Licence: CC BY-NC-SA 3.0 IGO

FAO (2020) The state of World Fisheries and Aquaculture (SOFIA): sustainability in action. Food and Agriculture Oganization, Rome

Farm Animal Welfare Council (2012). Five freedoms of Animal Welfare by the farm Animal welfare Committee; p 141

Food and Agriculture Organization of the United Nations (2006) Nearly half of all fish eaten today is farmed, not caught. FAO Newsroom. www.fao.org/newsroom/en/news/2006/1000383/index.446html. Accessed 20 Aug 2008

Getu A, Misganaw K, Bazezew M (2015) Post-harvesting and major related problems of fish production. Fish Aquac J 6:154

Gustavsson J, Cederberg C, Sonesson U, Otterdijk R, Meybeck A (2011) Global food losses and food waste. FAO, Rome, pp 16–17

Harvey DJ (2004) U.S. Seafood market shifts to aquaculture. U.S. Department of Agriculture Economic Research Service, AmberWaves, April. www.ers.usda.gov/AmberWaves/april04/Findings/USSeafood.htm

Håstein T (2004) Animal welfare issues relating to aquaculture. In Proceedings of the Global Conference on Animal Welfare: an OIE Initiative Paris, France: World Organization for Animal Health, pp 212–20

HSA (2005) Humane harvesting of salmon and trout: Guidance notes No. 5. Humane Slaughter Association, Wheathamstead

Jerimoth E, Irabor K, Ebuka A (2017) A review of aquaculture production in Nigeria: problems and prospects. J Northeast Agric Univ Engl Ed 2017(30):11–15

Kabahenda MK, Omony P, Hüsken SMC (2009) Post-harvest handling of low-value fish products and threats to nutritional quality: a review of practices in the Lake Victoria region. Regional Programme Fisheries and HIV/AIDS in Africa: Investing in Sustainable Solutions. The WorldFish Center. Project Report 1975

Kristiansen TS, Juell JE (2002) How can we document the Welfare of farmed fish? In Proceedings of the "Aquaculture Europe 2002: Sea Farming Today and Tomorrow". Special Publication 32: 285–286

Lemieux H, Dutil JD, Guderley H, Larocque R (2004) Growth, starvation and enzyme activity in white muscle of Atlantic cod: at what point do muscle metabolic capacities change? Mar Freshw Behav Physiol 37:287–294

Lines JA, Spence J (2012) Safeguarding the Welfare of farmed fish at harvest. Fish Physiol Biochem 38:153–162

Martinez M, Guderley H, Dutil JD, Winger PD, He P, Walsh SJ (2003) Condition, prolonged swimming performance and muscle metabolic capacities of cod *Gadus morhua*. J Exp Biol 206: 503–511

Martos-Sitcha JA, Mancera JM, Prunet P, Magnoni LJ (2020) Editorial: welfare and stressors in fish: challenges facing aquaculture. Front Physiol 11:162

OECD/FAO (2017) OECD-FAO agricultural outlook 2017–2026. OECD Publishing, Paris

Ogbonna CC, Omoyinmi GAK, Omoare AM (2017) Utilisation of low cost technology: a catalyst for reducing post harvest fish losses in Lagos State, Nigeria. Int J Voc Tech Educ Res 3(2):9–21

Ogunsina O (2017) harvesting catfish in a concrete pond/youtube.com

Ohshima T (2005) Lipid oxidation and quality deterioration of seafood, in Advanced topics for fisheries and marine science. 2005, WIDE Project School Internet Working Group

OIE (2008) Welfare of fish in aquaculture; https://www.oie.int/doc/ged/D4917.PDF

Ojelade O, Iyasere O, Durosaro S, Oyebanji F, Abdulraheem I, Akinde A (2021) The implication of being in isolation or not on the welfare of African catfish (*Clarias gariepinus*). Recent Adva Animal Welfare Sci 8:78–79

Ojelade O, Iyasere O, Durosaro S, Abdulraheem I, Akinde A (2022) Social isolation impairs feed intake, growth and behavioural patterns of catfish under culture conditions. Animal 16:100521

Omoare AM, Fakoya EO, Abiona BG, Oyediran WO (2013) Fish Marketing: A Panacea towards sustainable agriculture in Ogun State, Nigeria. World Academy of Science, Engineering and Technology (WASET) Conference held at Holiday Inn London – Wembley, London, UK, from July 9–10, 2013. pp 439–444

Poli BM., Zampacavallo G, Iurzan F, de Francesco M, Parisi G, Mosconi G (2002) Biochemical stress indicators changes in sea bass as influenced by the slaughter method. In Proceeding of the "Aquaculture Europe 2002: Sea Farming Today and Tomorrow". Special Publication n. 32, pp. 429–430

Poli BM, Parisi G, Scappini F, Zampacavallo G (2005) Fish welfare and quality as affected by pre-slaughter and slaughter management. Aquac Int 13:29–49

Rasco B, Down K, Ovissipour M (2015) Humane harvesting initiative: the influence of harvest and post-harvest handling practices on fish welfare and product quality. J Aquac Res Dev 6:303

Robb DHF (2008) Welfare of fish at harvest. In: Branson EJ (ed) Fish welfare. Blackwell Publishing, London, pp 217–242

Robb DFH, Kestin SC (2002) Methods used to kill fish: field observations and literature reviewed. Anim Welf 11:269–282

Robb DHF, Wotton SB, McKinstry JL, Sørensen NK, Kestin SC (2000) Commercial slaughter methods used on Atlantic salmon: determination of the onset of brain failure by electroencephalography. Vet Rec 147:298–303. to 2020

Sneddon LU, Lopez-Luna J, Wolfenden DCC, Leach MC, Valentim AM, Steenbergen PJ, Bardine N, Currie AD, Broom DM, Brown C (2018) Fish sentience denial: muddying the waters. Anim Sentience 3:11–18

Southgate P, Wall T (2001) Welfare of farmed fish at slaughter. In Pract 23:277–284

Thant N (2019) Improvement of post-harvest handling of aquaculture fish in Myanmar. United Nations University Fisheries Training Programme, Iceland final project. http://www.unuftp.is/static/fellows/document/Nyo18prf.pdf

Toni M, Manciocco A, Angiulli E, Alleva E, Cioni C, Malavasi S (2018) Review: assessing fish welfare in research and aquaculture, with a focus on European directives. Animal 13:161–170. https://doi.org/10.1017/S1751731118000940

Valtysdottir K, Margeirsson B, Arason S, Lauzon H, Martinsdóttir E (2010) Guidelines for precooling of fresh fish during processing and choice of packaging with respect to temperature control in cold chains. Matis, Reykjavik

Van de Vis H, Kestin S, Robb D (2003) Is humane slaughter of fish possible for industry? Aquac Res 34:211–220

Wall AJ (2001) Ethical considerations in the handling and slaughter of farmed fish. In: Kestin SC, Warriss PD (eds) Farmed fish quality. Fishing News Books, Blackwell Science, Oxford, pp 108–115

Webster AJF (2001) Farm animal welfare: the five freedoms and the free market. Vet J 161:229–237

World Bank (2017) The Sunken Billions Revisited Progress and Challenges in Global Marine Fisheries. Washington, DC: World Bank. Environment and Sustainable Development series. https://doi.org/10.1596/978-1-4648-0919-4. License: Creative Commons Attribution CC BY 3.0 IGO

Yalch T, Lofthouse J, Nordhagen S (2020) Creating alliances and fostering innovations to reduce post-harvest food loss: Experiences from GAIN's Postharvest Loss Alliances for Nutrition. Global Alliance for Improved Nutrition Working Paper #9. Geneva, Switzerland, 2020. https://doi.org/10.36072/wp.9

Chapter 26
Alternative Fish Anaesthetics: Perspective on their Application in African Aquaculture and Fisheries Research

Wilhelm Haihambo, Ndakalimwe Naftal Gabriel, Kenneth Prudence Abasubong, and Rebekka N. Gabriel

Abstract This chapter reviewed herbal agents and nonchemical methods of anaesthetizing fish in aquaculture, as well as the prospects for their application in African aquaculture and fisheries operations and research. For intensive aquaculture, more handling and transportation are required. These activities may cause stress and physical harm to the fish, putting their well-being at risk. Anaesthetics are frequently used to immobilize fish during handling and transport, reducing stress, and the risk of physical injury. Anaesthesia can be either synthetic or natural. Nonchemical methods of anaesthetizing fish are also available. Synthetic anaesthetics (i.e. phenoxyethanol, benzocaine, tricaine methanesulfonate, MS-222, and quinaldine) are deemed unsustainable due to their high cost, unavailability in most African countries, and negative effects on the physiology of farmed fish and the environment. As a result, several herbal extracts example essential oils from *Eugenia aromatica*, *Aniba rosaeodora*, *Cinnamomum camphora*, and *Lippia alba* have been reported to induce anaesthesia in fish. The same was reported for nonchemical agents (such as carbon dioxide, sodium bicarbonate, electroanaesthesia, and lower temperatures). Because these alternative anaesthetics are less expensive and readily available, they may be preferable to synthetic anaesthetics in African aquaculture and fisheries research. More research is needed, however, to optimize different alternative anaesthetics in aquaculture, so that fish welfare is protected during operation and research.

W. Haihambo (✉) · N. N. Gabriel
Department of Fisheries and Ocean Sciences, Sam Nujoma Campus, University of Namibia, Henties Bay, Namibia

K. P. Abasubong
Key Laboratory of Aquatic Nutrition and Feed Science of Jiangsu Province, College of Animal Science and Technology, Nanjing Agricultural University, Nanjing, China

R. N. Gabriel
Faculty of Health Sciences and Veterinary Medicine, University of Namibia, Windhoek, Namibia

© The Author(s), under exclusive license to Springer Nature Singapore Pte Ltd. 2023
N. N. Gabriel et al. (eds.), *Emerging Sustainable Aquaculture Innovations in Africa*, Sustainable Agriculture and Food Security,
https://doi.org/10.1007/978-981-19-7451-9_26

Keywords Anaesthetics · Aquaculture · Herbal extracts · Essential oils · Nonchemical anaesthetics

26.1 Introduction

The human population is rapidly increasing, and there is an increase in demand for animal protein to feed the growing human population (Gjedrem et al. 2012). Fish contributes significantly to the total animal protein consumed by humans worldwide. As a result, the demand for fish protein is increasing. Captured fisheries have reached their peak, and no increase in production is expected due to the overfishing of fish species (Maani 2017). Meanwhile, aquaculture has grown rapidly over the years, filling the void left by the fish protein demand (Subasinghe et al. 2009).

Aquaculture's rapid expansion has been largely attributed to increased finfish intensification and seaweed production (Kumar and Engle 2016). Intensive farming is associated with handling and transporting activities that can lead to stress (Rehman et al. 2017). Stress negatively impacts fish's immune systems, making them vulnerable to diseases (Tacchi et al. 2015). Stress is harmful to animal welfare and production and should be avoided during operations (Kibenge 2019). Fish welfare is a critical issue for the aquaculture industry because it influences production and public perception (Ashley 2007). Research into the handling and transportation of live fish for increased commercial viability is critical for protecting the welfare of farmed fish and improving production (Bodur et al. 2018). However, there are challenges between welfare and production in several areas, including handling and transportation, which appear to be associated with lower individual fish welfare when not practised ethically (Ashley 2007). In recent years, such practices have received a great deal of attention and debate.

Anaesthetics are used to reduce stress and the risk of physical injury, thereby aiding in the preservation of animal welfare during handling and transportation (Zahl et al. 2012). Anaesthesia is a recommended tool to be used during fish handling, transportation operations, and fisheries research (Hoseini et al. 2019). Anaesthesia can be defined as the biological condition in which sensation, responsiveness, and voluntary neuromotor control are lost through the application of a chemical or nonchemical agent (Summerfelt 1990). Anaesthesia reduces the stress and likelihood of physical injuries during stressful events. Reduced stress and physical injuries are a steppingstone to preserve the welfare of fish during stressful events. During anaesthesia, fish feel less pain and become more relaxed. As a result, anaesthesia can be used to safely handle, transport, and work on fish (Martins et al. 2019).

Several synthetic agents are used in aquaculture and fisheries research to anaesthetize fish. 2-phenoxyethanol, benzocaine, tricaine methanesulfonate (MS-222), and quinaldine are examples of synthetic agents commonly used to aanesthetize fish (Martins et al. 2019; Ross and Ross 2009). The United States (U. S) Food and Drug Administration (FDA) has only approved MS-222 for use in fish for human consumption (Huang et al. 2010; Topic Popovic et al. 2012). This is a similar approach taken by countries such as Spain, Italy, the United Kingdom, and

Norway. Other synthetic agents are only approved to be used for research purposes. Synthetic agents are prohibited due to safety concerns, while natural agents are more developed and are expected to have a bright future (Coyle et al. 2004). Synthetic anaesthetics have been reported to have adverse impacts on the physiology of the fish, the user, and the environment (Coyle et al. 2004). As a result, synthetic anaesthetics are termed unsustainable. Alternative methods of anaesthetizing fish, such as the use of herbal products and nonchemical methods have been studied and documented.

Several studies and reports on the efficacy of herbal products have been conducted. Several herbal products have been investigated with the aim to replace unsustainable synthetic anaesthetics. As a result, herbal products have been studied and discovered to possess anaesthetic properties in different fish species. This chapter reviewed herbal agents and nonchemical methods of anaesthetizing fish in aquaculture, as well as the prospects for their application in African aquaculture and fisheries operations and research.

26.2 Herbal Extracts as Anaesthetics in Aquaculture

Herbal extracts are gaining popularity among researchers as potential anaesthetics for fish. This is because commonly used anaesthetics such as tricaine methanesulphonate (MS-222) (Skår et al. 2017), 2-phenoxyethanol (Ghanawi et al. 2013), and etomidate (Readman et al. 2017) are either prohibitively expensive, unavailable, particularly in Africa, or have been linked to adverse side effects in fish such as stress and haemorrhagic disorders (Gressler et al. 2014). Essential oils and their constituents (such as carvone, myrcene, linalool, menthol, cineole, and eugenol) are herbal extracts that have been extensively researched as anaesthetics (Hoseini et al. 2019). These substances have been shown to have not only hypnotic or sedative effects on fish but can also be toxic (Purbosari et al. 2019). *Eugenia aromatic* clove oil is an effective herbal anaesthetic for fish (Purbosari et al. 2019). Clove oil is rarely used as an anaesthetic due to its low therapeutic index. The reason for this is that even slight changes in dosage have the potential to kill or prevent fish from recovering (Kamble et al. 2014).

The investigation of herbal extracts as potential anaesthetics in aquaculture was broadened to include other herbs. For example, essential oil extracts of rosewood (*Aniba rosaeodora*) and camphor (*Cinnamomum camphora*) at 300 lL1 were reported to have effectively anaesthetized goldfish (*Carassius auratus*) without any adverse effects. *Lippia alba* essential oils at 200–300 mg/L anaesthetized tambaqui (*Colossoma macropomum*) in less than 4 min. *Lippia alba* chemotypes (citral and linalool) were able to cause anaesthesia in silver catfish (*Rhamdia quelen*) without affecting their physiological functions (de Freitas et al. 2018). Thymol and carvacrol caused sedation at 25 mg/L and anaesthesia at 50–-100 mg/L in the same fish (Bianchini et al. 2017). *Aloysia triphylla, Ocimum americanum*, and *L. alba* have also been shown to be effective anaesthetics in Nile tilapia (*Oreochromis niloticus*) (Teixeira et al. 2017; Rucinque et al. 2021), citronellal, linalool, and myrcene in common carp (*Cyprinus carpio*) (Mirghaed et al. 2016; Yousefi et al. 2018), *A. triphylla in* catfish (*Lophiosilurus alexandri*) (Becker et al. 2017), *Eugenia cayrophyllata* in African catfish, (*Clarias gariepinus)* (Adeshina et al. 2016), and *Eucalyptus globulus)* and *Origanum vulgare* in silver kob (*Argyrosomus inodorus*) (Gabriel et al. 2022). This finding provides a solid foundation for African aquaculture researchers and farmers to build on as they explore the use of herbal extracts as anaesthetics in fish farming and fish management. Herbal extracts, in particular, are a better option for African aquaculture because they are effective, have few side effects, are widely available, cost less money, and may act as immune boosters, antioxidants, and anti-stress agents, and antimicrobial agents (Hoseini et al. 2019).

Furthermore, *Aloysia triphylla* (40–50 mg/L), *Lippia sidoides* (20–50 mg/L), and *Mentha piperita* (40–90 mg/L) induced anaesthesia in *C. macropomum*. However, at higher doses, these essential oils may cause severe damage to the fish, including gill fibrosis and necrosis, hypertrophy and hyperplasia of the lamellar epithelium, lamellar fusion, and chloride cell proliferation (Brandão et al. 2021). Similarly, Bianchini et al. (2017) discovered higher mortality when silver catfish were exposed to monoterpenoid (carvacrol). This is a clear indication that these products in aquaculture need to be optimized to ensure they are not harmful to the fish. Moreover, it appears that the anaesthetic mechanism of essential oils and their constituents is reasonably well understood. According to Manayi et al. (2016), essential oils induce anaesthesia due to their lipophilic nature, which allows them to easily penetrate cell membranes and influence brain functions by interacting with the gamma-aminobutyric acid receptor, GABA (inhibitory neurotransmitter) (Zahl et al. 2012; Manayi et al. 2016). In other words, essential oils may influence the swimming behaviour and state of consciousness of fish by increasing the activity of the GABA receptor, as demonstrated in *R. quelen* after exposure to carvacrol and thymol (Bianchini et al. 2017). However, more research is needed to determine how different essential oils and their chemotypes induce anaesthesia in various fish species.

26.3 Nonchemical Methods

26.3.1 Carbon Dioxide

Carbon dioxide gas (CO_2) is potentially alternative nonchemical method of anaesthetizing fish in aquaculture and research. It was first described by Fish (1943) as a potential anaesthetic for fish. Carbon dioxide can be delivered in two ways, the first method involves directly blowing carbon dioxide gas in water and the second method is dissolving sodium bicarbonate ($NaCO_3$) in water. The advantage of carbon dioxide is that it does not leave any residues in the flesh of the fish after exposure and has no secondary effects on the handler and the environment (Gilderhus and Marking 1987). Furthermore, carbon dioxide method is cheap to administer compared to chemical anaesthetics that are generally expensive (Fish 1943). However, the method of using CO_2 has some shortcomings such as the reduced efficiency to induce deep anaesthesia observed by Gilderhus and Marking (1987) and the acute and transient experience of hyperactivity in fish possibly caused by the acidification of water. Gilderhus and Marking (1987) also observed the recovery time of fish exposed to CO_2 to be long. Unbuffered CO_2 is reported to cause an increase in the stress indicators such as blood adrenaline and cortisol concentrations (Iwama et al. 1989). A range of 200 to 500 mg CO_2 concentration is recommended for anaesthetizing salmonids (at pH 6–9 and 12 °C) (Gilderhus and Marking 1987).

Sodium bicarbonate ($NaCO_3$) releases carbon dioxide (CO_2) gas in the water column which suffocates fish and make them temporarily unconscious (Gelwicks et al. 1998; Peake 1998; Opiyo et al. 2013). Sodium bicarbonate has been reported to be effective at inducing anaesthesia in various fish species such as *Oreochromis spp.* (Charo-Karisa et al. 2013; Opiyo et al. 2013; Avillanosa and Caipang 2019; Gabriel et al. 2020; Hasimuna et al. 2021; Haihambo and Gabriel 2022; Siavwapa et al. 2022), *Cyprinus carpio* (Altun et al. 2009; Bahrekazemi 2018), *Clarias gariepinus* (Githukia et al. 2016), *Liza parsia* (Sonawane and Kulkarni 2001), *Hippocampus kuda* (Pawar et al. 2013), ornamental fish (Caipang et al. 2021), *Rutilus kutum* (Babaiinezhad and Bahrekazemi 2019), and nonsalmonid fishes (Peake 1998). A recent report by Peake (1998) reported that sodium bicarbonate is more effective when combined with acetic acid (CH_3COOH). This is because, sodium bicarbonate alters the pH of water which continues to stress fish after exposure, but when combined acetic acid, it neutralizes the pH. The effectiveness of the combined method is not compromised, and it remains effective. Haihambo and Gabriel (2022) have exposed the combination of sodium bicarbonate and acetic acid to *Oreochromis andersonii* fingerlings and reported induction and recovery time within 3 min, respectively, at all concentrations used.

Carbon dioxide has a potential to be used as an anaesthetic in fish; however, best methods to administer this gas are deemed necessary in both freshwater and marine fish (Iwama et al. 1989). There are limited studies that have reported CO_2 as a possible fish anaesthetic tool. Further studies are recommended to determine other possible impacts these methods may have on fish before it can fully be advertised for large scale operations.

26.3.2 Electroanaesthesia

Electroanaesthesia is a method commonly used to immobilize and capture fish for research and broodstock purposes (Cowx and Lamarque 1990; Reynolds 1996). This method uses electricity to produce a shock that temporarily paralyses fish, making it easy to work with them. There are three types of electric currents that are utilized to immobilize fish, and these are alternating current (AC), direct current (DC), and pulsating forms of AC and DC. These methods have different mechanisms of action.

Direct current is reported to possibly cause anodotaxis, electronarcosis, and electrotetany. Alternating current is only reported to cause electronarcosis. The main advantages of electroanaesthesia are that it does not leave any resides in the flesh of the fish, it is environmentally friendly, it produces a rapid induction of anaesthesia and recovery, and has a low operating cost (Ross and Ross 2009).

This method has reduced long-term effects if the method is used appropriately. It causes minor physiological impacts in fish such as those observed in *Labeo rohita* (Chakraborty et al. 2022). Electroanaesthesia has been concluded by (Reid et al. 2022) to be as effective at inducing anaesthesia as synthetic anaesthetics such as MS-222 and thus can be used as an alternative method. However, wild fish exposed to electroanaesthesia seem to be more susceptible to predators (Schreck et al. 1976). Electroanaesthesia induces immediate elevation in plasma corticoid and lactate concentrations. This has been reported in study that exposed rainbow trout to electroanaesthesia (Madden and Houston 1976). Plasma glucose levels and cardiovascular rates were also reported to increase after exposure to electroanaesthesia. The effectiveness of electroanaesthesia depends on several factors such as the water conductivity, temperature, fish size, and species. In the past, alternating current was mostly used over direct current. It was later found that alternating current has an adverse damage to the fish compared to the direct current (Madden and Houston 1976; Ross and Ross 1984).

26.3.3 Hypothermia

Hypothermic anaesthesia uses a cooling effect to sedate fish (Erikson et al. 2006). This is because when temperatures are higher than 10 °C, hypothermic anaesthesia is less effective. However, deep induction cannot be achieved using this method of anaesthesia, unless coupled with a chemical anaesthetic (Mittal and Whitear 1978). Hypothermic anaesthesia induces light sedation characterized by an absence of motion, reduced power of exertion, and diminished nerve sensitivity (Hovda and Linley 2000). It can be achieved when temperature is changed to near 0 °C by immersing fish in crushed ice or ice water (Summerfelt & Smith 1990). This is only applicable for transporting fish but not for invasive activities such as surgery due to its inability to induce deep anaesthesia. Hypothermia provides an alternative method when chemical anaesthetics are not desirable. It has reduced impacts on the fish, the handler as well as the environment and it is relatively cheap.

26.4 Conclusion and Perspectives

Synthetic anaesthetics are being phased out in favour of more sustainable alternatives. This is to achieve the goal of preserving the welfare of the animal during operations while maintaining the aspect of sustainability and achieving maximum production. Herbal anaesthetics are inexpensive and simple to use, but they are just as effective as synthetic anaesthetics. They may be very suitable in African aquaculture and other developing countries. Nonchemical methods are also available and can be used in conjunction with other anaesthetics to achieve deep induction. However, more research on fish species using these methods is recommended in order to determine specific species safe limits. Furthermore, there have been few studies that looked at the combination of nonchemical methods such as hypothermia and carbon dioxide with herbal products. There are recommendations in the literature to combine these nonchemical methods with synthetic agents that are not sustainable. As a result, research in this field is advised. Most essential oil mechanisms of action are not fully understood, and more research is needed to address this issue. Analgesic essential oils, such as clove oil, are used in human dentistry. It is recommended that essential oils be studied for their analgesic properties, which are critical in blocking pain in fish during invasive activities.

References

Adeshina I, Jenyo-Oni A, Emikpe B (2016) Use of *Eugenia cayrophyllata* oil as anaesthetic in farm raised african catfish *Clarias gariepinus* juveniles. Egypt J Exp Biol (Zool) 12:71–76

Altun T, Bilgil R, Danabaş D (2009) Effects of sodium bicarbonate on anaesthesia of common carp (*Cyprinus carpio* L., 1758) juveniles. Turk J Fish Aquat Sci 9(1):29–31

Ashley PJ (2007) Fish welfare: Current issues in aquaculture. Appl Anim Behav Sci 104:199–235. https://doi.org/10.1016/j.applanim.2006.09.001

Avillanosa AL, Caipang CMA (2019) Use of sodium bicarbonate as an inexpensive general anesthetic for juvenile red tilapia hybrids. Int Aquat Res 11:287–294

Babaiinezhad L, Bahrekazemi M (2019) Effects of three anesthetics of clove extract, sodium bicarbonate, and lidocaine on blood parameters and cortisol level in male and female broodstocks of Caspian kutum (*Rutilus kutum*). Aquat Biol 7:260–270

Bahrekazemi M (2018) Anaesthetic effects of sodium bicarbonate, 2-phenoxy ethanol, clove extract and thyme extract on hematological indices and cortisol amount in common carp (*Cyprinus carpio*). Util Cultivation Aquat 7:19–27

Becker AG, Luz RK, Mattioli CC, Nakayama CL, Silva WDS, Leme FDOP, Baldisserotto B (2017) Can the essential oil of Aloysia triphylla have anesthetic effect and improve the physiological parameters of the carnivorous freshwater catfish *Lophiosilurus alexandri* after transport? Aquaculture. 481:184–190

Bianchini AE, Garlet QI, Da Cunha JA, Bandeira G, Brusque ICM, Salbego J, Heinzmann BM, Baldisserotto B (2017) Monoterpenoids (thymol, carvacrol and S-(+)-linalool) with anesthetic activity in silver catfish (*Rhamdia quelen*): evaluation of acetylcholinesterase and GABAergic activity. Braz J Med Biol Res 50:e6346

Bodur T, Afonso JM, Montero D, Navarro A (2018) Assessment of effective dose of new herbal anesthetics in two marine aquaculture species: Dicentrarchus labrax and Argyrosomus regius. Aquaculture 482:78–82

Brandão FR, Farias CFS, de Melo Souza DC, de Oliveira MIB, de Matos LV, Majolo C, Chagas EC (2021) Anesthetic potential of the essential oils of *Aloysia triphylla*, *Lippia sidoides* and *Mentha piperita* for *Colossoma macropomum*. Aquaculture 534:736275

Caipang CMA, Deocampo JE, Pakingking RV, Suharman I, Fenol JT, Onayan FB (2021) Utilization of sodium bicarbonate as anesthetic during routine husbandry activities in ornamental fish. In IOP Conference Series: Earth and Environmental Science 1:012001. IOP Publishing

Chakraborty N, De A, Ghosh SK, De TK (2022) On the investigation of electroanaesthesia in *Labeo rohita* under DC and PDC electric field. J Fish 10:101208. https://doi.org/10.17017/j.fish.359

Charo-Karisa H, Ogello E, Opiyo M (2013) Effectiveness of Sodium Bicarbonate as an Anaesthetic for different sizes of Nile tilapia (*Oreochromis niloticus* L., 1758) Juveniles. Int J Aquat Sci. 4: 14–22

Cowx IG, Lamarque P (1990) Fishing with electricity: applications in freshwater fisheries management. Wiley, Hoboken

Coyle SD, Durborow RM, Tidwell JH (2004) Anesthetics in aquaculture, vol 3900. Southern Regional Aquaculture Center, Texas

de Freitas SC, Baldissera MD, Bianchini AE, da Silva EG, Mourão RHV, da Silva LVF, Baldisserotto B (2018) Citral and linalool chemotypes of *Lippia alba* essential oil as anesthetics for fish: a detailed physiological analysis of side effects during anesthetic recovery in silver catfish (*Rhamdia quelen*). Fish Physiol Biochem 44:21–34

Erikson U, Hultmann L, Erik Steen J (2006) Live chilling of Atlantic salmon (*Salmo salar*) combined with mild carbon dioxide anaesthesia: I. Establishing a method for large-scale processing of farmed fish. Aquaculture. 252:183–198. https://doi.org/10.1016/j.aquaculture.2005.05.013

Fish FF (1943) The anaesthesia of fish by high carbon-dioxide concentrations. Trans Am Fish Soc 72:25–29. https://doi.org/10.1577/1548-8659(1942)72[25:TAOFBH]2.0.CO;2

Gabriel NN, Erasmus VN, Namwoonde A (2020) Effects of different fish sizes, temperatures, and concentration levels of sodium bicarbonate on anaesthesia in Mozambique tilapia (*Oreochromis mossambicus*). Aquaculture. 529:735716

Gabriel NN, Chikwililwa C, Liswaniso GM, Louw S, Namwoonde A (2022) The effects of eucalyptus *Eucalyptus globulus* and oregano *Origanum vulgare* essential oils on anaesthesia response in a Namibian marine species, silver kob *Argyrosomus inodorus*. Afr J Mar Sci 44: 205–213

Gelwicks KR, Zafft DJ, Bobbitt JP (1998) Efficacy of carbonic acid as an anesthetic for rainbow trout. N Am J Fish Manag 18:432–438

Ghanawi J, Monzer S, Saoud IP (2013) Anaesthetic efficacy of clove oil, benzocaine, 2-phenoxyethanol and tricaine methanesulfonate in juvenile marbled spinefoot (*Siganus rivulatus*). Aquac Res 44:359–366

Gilderhus PA, Marking LL (1987) Comparative efficacy of 16 anesthetic chemicals on rainbow trout. N Am J Fish Manag 7:288–292. https://doi.org/10.1577/1548-8659(1987)7<288:CEOACO>2.0.CO;2

Githukia CM, Kembenya EM, Opiyo MA (2016) Anaesthetic effects of sodium bicarbonate at different concentrations on African catfish (*Clarias gariepinus*) juveniles. J Aquac Eng Fish Res 2:151–158

Gjedrem T, Robinson N, Rye M (2012) The importance of selective breeding in aquaculture to meet future demands for animal protein: a review. Aquaculture. 350–353:117–129. https://doi.org/10.1016/j.aquaculture.2012.04.008

Gressler LT, Riffel APK, Parodi TV, Saccol EMH, Koakoski G, da Costa ST, Llesuy SF (2014) Silver catfish *Rhamdia quelen* immersion anaesthesia with essential oil of *Aloysia triphylla* (L'Hérit) Britton or tricaine methanesulfonate: effect on stress response and antioxidant status. Aquac Res 45:1061–1072

Haihambo W, Gabriel NN (2022) Sodium bicarbonate and acetic acid: an effective anaesthetic for three spotted Tilapia, *Oreochromis andersonii* fingerlings. J Appl Anim Res 1:1–11

Hasimuna OJ, Monde C, Bbole I, Maulu S, Chibesa M (2021) The efficacy of sodium bicarbonate as an anaesthetic agent in *Oreochromis macrochir* juveniles. Sci Afr 11:e00668

Hoseini SM, Taheri Mirghaed A, Yousefi M (2019) Application of herbal anaesthetics in aquaculture. Rev Aquac 11:550–564

Hovda J, Linley TJ (2000) The potential application of hypothermia for anesthesia in adult pacific salmon. N Am J Aquac 62:67–72. https://doi.org/10.1577/1548-8454(2000)062<0067:TPAOHF>2.0.CO;2

Huang WC, Hsieh YS, Chen IH, Wang CH, Chang HW, Yang CC, Ku TH, Yeh SR, Chuang YJ (2010) Combined use of MS-222 (Tricaine) and isoflurane extends anesthesia time and minimizes cardiac rhythm side effects in adult zebrafish. Zebrafish 7:297–304. https://doi.org/10.1089/zeb.2010.0653

Iwama GK, McGeer JC, Pawluk MP (1989) The effects of five fish anaesthetics on acid–base balance, hematocrit, blood gases, cortisol, and adrenaline in rainbow trout. Can J Zool 67:2065–2073. https://doi.org/10.1139/z89-294

Kamble AD, Saini VP, Ojha ML (2014) The efficacy of clove oil as anesthetic in common carp (*Cyprinus carpio*) and its potential metabolism reducing capacity. Int J Fauna Biol 1:1–6

Kibenge FS (2019) Emerging viruses in aquaculture. Curr Opin Virol 34:97–103

Kumar G, Engle CR (2016) Technological advances that led to growth of shrimp, salmon, and tilapia farming. Rev Fish Sc Aquac 24(x):136–152. https://doi.org/10.1080/23308249.2015.1112357

Maani K (2017) Dynamics of worldwide fisheries decline. In: World scientific book chapters. Singapore, World Scientific Publishing Co. Pte. Ltd., pp 127–145. https://ideas.repec.org/h/wsi/wschap/9789814619745_0011.html

Madden JA, Houston AH (1976) Use of electroanaesthesia with freshwater teleosts: Some physiological consequences in the rainbow trout, *Salmo gairdneri* Richardson. J Fish Biol 9:457–462. https://doi.org/10.1111/j.1095-8649.1976.tb04694.x

Manayi A, Nabavi SM, Daglia M, Jafari S (2016) Natural terpenoids as a promising source for modulation of GABAergic system and treatment of neurological diseases. Pharmacol Rep 68: 671–679

Martins T, Valentim A, Pereira N, Antunes LM (2019) Anaesthetics and analgesics used in adult fish for research: a review. Lab Anim 53:325–341. https://doi.org/10.1177/0023677218815199

Mirghaed AT, Ghelichpour M, Hoseini SM (2016) Myrcene and linalool as new anesthetic and sedative agents in common carp, *Cyprinus carpio*-Comparison with eugenol. Aquaculture. 464: 165–170

Mittal AK, Whitear M (1978) A note on cold anaesthesia of poikilotherms. J Fish Biol 13:519–520

Opiyo MA, Ogello EO, Charo-Karisa H (2013) Effectiveness of sodium bicarbonate as an anaesthetic for different sizes of Nile tilapia (*Oreochromis niloticus* L., 1758) Juveniles. Int J Aquat Sci 4:14–22

Pawar HB, Ingole BS, Sreepada RA (2013) Efficacy of sodium bicarbonate as anaesthetic for yellow seahorse, *Hippocampus kuda* (Bleeker, 1852)

Peake S (1998) Sodium bicarbonate and clove oil as potential anesthetics for nonsalmonid fishes. N Am J Fish Manag 18:919–924

Purbosari N, Warsiki E, Syamsu K, Santoso J (2019) Natural versus synthetic anesthetic for transport of live fish: a review. Aquac Fish 4:129–133

Readman GD, Owen SF, Knowles TG, Murrell JC (2017) Species specific anaesthetics for fish anaesthesia and euthanasia. Sci Rep 7:7102

Rehman S, Gora A, Ahmad I, Rasool S (2017) Stress in aquaculture hatcheries: source, impact and mitigation. J Curr Microbiol 6:3030–3045. https://doi.org/10.20546/ijcmas.2017.610.357

Reid CH, Raby GD, Faust MD, Cooke SJ, Vandergoot CS (2022) Cardiac activity in walleye (*Sander vitreus*) during exposure to and recovery from chemical anaesthesia, electroanaesthesia and electrostunning. J Fish Biol 101:115–127. https://doi.org/10.1111/jfb.15077

Reynolds JB (1996) Electrofishing. In: Murphy BR, Willis DW (eds) Fisheries techniques, 2nd edn. American Fisheries Society, Bethesda, MD, pp 221–253

Ross LG, Ross B (1984) Anaesthetic and sedative techniques for fish. Anaesthetic and Sedative Techniques for Fish. https://www.cabdirect.org/cabdirect/abstract/19852254885

Ross LG, Ross B (2009) Anaesthetic and sedative techniques for aquatic animals. John Wiley & Sons, Hoboken

Rucinque DS, Ferreira PF, Leme PRP, Lapa-Guimaraes J, Viegas EMM (2021) *Ocimum americanum* and *Lippia alba* essential oils as anaesthetics for Nile tilapia: Induction, recovery of apparent unconsciousness and sensory analysis of fillets. Aquaculture 531:735902

Schreck CB, Whaley RA, Bass ML, Maughan OE, Solazzi M (1976) Physiological responses of rainbow trout (Salmo gairdneri) to electroshock. J Fish Res 33:76–84

Siavwapa S, Hasimuna OJ, Maulu S, Monde C (2022) A comparative analysis of the anaesthetic effect of sodium bicarbonate (NaHCO3) on male and female three-spotted tilapia (*Oreochromis andersonii*). J Appl Anim Res 50:269–274

Skår MW, Haugland GT, Powell MD, Wergeland HI, Samuelsen OB (2017) Development of anaesthetic protocols for lumpfish (*Cyclopterus lumpus* L.): Effect of anaesthetic concentrations, sea water temperature and body weight. PLoS. One. 12:e0179344

Sonawane UD, Kulkarni GN (2001) Anaesthetic effects of clove oil and sodium bicarbonate on the fry of *Liza parsia*. Iranian J Fish Sci. 3:49–62

Subasinghe R, Soto D, Jia J (2009) Global aquaculture and its role in sustainable development. Rev Aquac 1:2–9. https://doi.org/10.1111/j.1753-5131.2008.01002.x

Summerfelt RC (1990) Anesthesia, surgery, and related techniques. Methods for fish biology

Summerfelt RC, Smith LS (1990) Anesthaesia, surgery, and related techniques. In: Schreck CB, Moyle PB (eds) Methods for fish biology

Tacchi L, Lowrey L, Musharrafieh R, Crossey K, Larragoite ET, Salinas I (2015) Effects of transportation stress and addition of salt to transport water on the skin mucosal homeostasis of rainbow trout (*Oncorhynchus mykiss*). Aquaculture. 435:120–127

Teixeira RR, de Souza RC, Sena AC, Baldisserotto B, Heinzmann BM, Couto RD, Copatti CE (2017) Essential oil of *Aloysia triphylla* in Nile tilapia: anaesthesia, stress parameters and sensory evaluation of fillets. Aquac Res 48:3383–3392

Topic Popovic N, Strunjak-Perovic I, Coz-Rakovac R, Barisic J, Jadan M, Persin Berakovic A, Sauerborn Klobucar R (2012) Tricaine methane-sulfonate (MS-222) application in fish anaesthesia. J Appl Ichthyol 28:553–564. https://doi.org/10.1111/j.1439-0426.2012.01950.x

Yousefi M, Hoseinifar SH, Ghelichpour M, Hoseini SM (2018) Anesthetic efficacy and biochemical effects of citronellal and linalool in common carp (*Cyprinus carpio* Linnaeus, 1758) juveniles. Aquaculture. 493:107–112

Zahl IH, Samuelsen O, Kiessling A (2012) Anaesthesia of farmed fish: Implications for welfare. Fish Physiol Biochem 38:201–218. https://doi.org/10.1007/s10695-011-9565-1

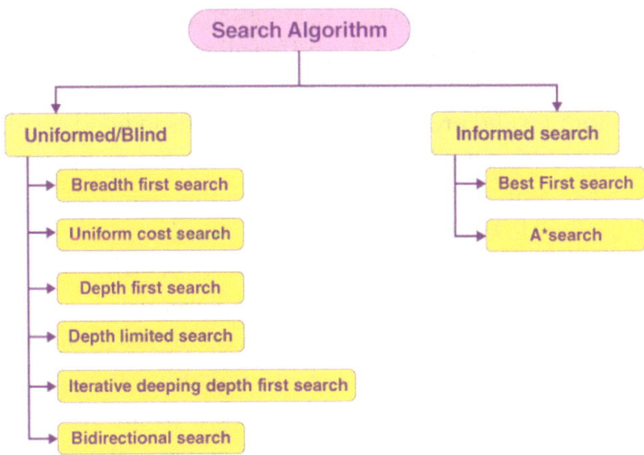

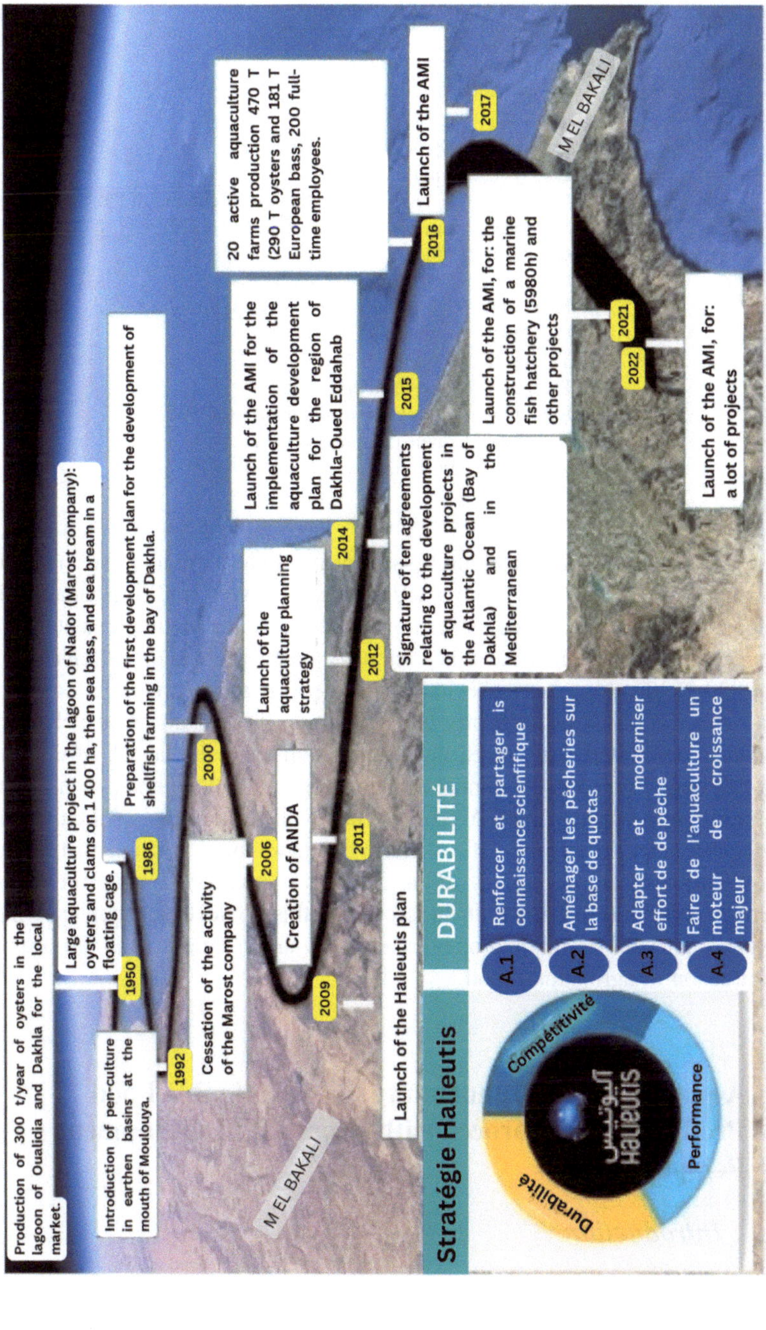

MIX
Papier aus verantwortungsvollen Quellen
Paper from responsible sources
FSC® C105338

If you have any concerns about our products,
you can contact us on
ProductSafety@springernature.com

In case Publisher is established outside the EU,
the EU authorized representative is:
Springer Nature Customer Service Center GmbH
Europaplatz 3, 69115 Heidelberg, Germany

Printed by Libri Plureos GmbH
in Hamburg, Germany